OLD FASHIONED RECIPE BOOK

→ AN ENCYCLOPEDIA OF COUNTRY LIVING ←

Carla. A good picture taker and a happy thought make a portrait . . .

OLD FASHIONED RECIPE BOOK

→ AN ENCYCLOPEDIA OF COUNTRY LIVING ←

CARLA EMERY

Illustrated by Cindy Davis

BANTAM BOOKS · TORONTO · NEW YORK · LONDON

OLD FASHIONED RECIPE BOOK

A Bantam Book / published by arrangement with Carla Emery.

PRINTING HISTORY

Carla Emery's edition / March 1974

2nd printing	....March 1974	5th printing	.......May 1974
3rd printing	......April 1974	6th printing	....January 1975
4th printing	.......May 1974	7th printing	.....March 1977

Bantam edition / November 1977

ISBN 0–553–01068–9

Published simultaneously in the United States and Canada

Bantam Books are published by Bantam Books, Inc. Its trade-
mark, consisting of the words "Bantam Books" and the por-
trayal of a bantam, is registered in the United States Patent
Office and in other countries. Marca Registrada, Bantam
Books, Inc., 666 Fifth Avenue, New York, New York 10019.

PRINTED IN THE UNITED STATES OF AMERICA

0 9 8 7 6 5 4 3 2 1

HOW IT ALL BEGAN

Back in 1969, Grandma Emery gave us a subscription to the magazine *Organic Gardening* and sent two years worth of back issues to boot. It got me to thinking about how it seemed so many city people were wanting to move to the country and all the things they needed to know. Besides we needed the money and I thought if I wrote a book and sold it I could help us get moved from our three acres of land to the bigger farm we dreamed of. I'd never finished writing anything longer than a poem before but that didn't dampen my enthusiasm. I put together a Table of Contents—pretty much the one you see in this book—listing everything I thought "Back to the Earthers" would need to know (whether I myself knew it or not). I thought a little and decided I could write it

in about two or at the most three months. Since it takes two months to place an ad anyway, I wrote one that described all the great offerings of my book-to-be and put it in the classified columns of three different magazines. I offered my book-to-be for $3.50 per copy. Two months later the ads came out, hundreds of people answered and I hadn't yet written the final sheet of any one page of the book. I was beginning to discover that writing a book wasn't all the way I had imagined it. But I cashed all those checks instead of returning the people's money as I probably should have. That Table of Contents and those cashed checks were to become a heavy burden I bore for the next four years. It came very near being a horrible disaster.

THANK YOU FOR MAKING
THIS BOOK HAPPEN

There were so many over such a long period of time I know I'm not going to include everyone. Please forgive me if you should be here and you aren't.

God. Read the Butters section of the Sweets chapter.

The Subscribers. People who bought into a dream, usually not knowing at first it was a dream and not a real book that they were buying and yet very few scolded me and many, many of them wrote me specially time and again to offer encouragement, recipes, congratulations when it was over. And they told their friends about the book so that more and more orders came in.

Everyone Who Worked To Help Make It Happen. Some on the promise of a book when we got done. Some on the promise of money when we made some.

(And they really had to wait a long while because we lost money on the first 875 books. They were sold at $3.50 each which was less than what it cost to make them.) Some because they thought it was fun and some as an act of mercy.

Every Merchant Who Helped Make It Happen by in effect giving me a loan. I borrowed money by not paying bills. I owed everybody in town, the grocery, the drugstore, the department store, the hardware. Down in Lewiston I owed even more horrendous sums of money to the paper wholesaler and office-supply store.

The People Who Loaned Me Money Outright. May God Bless Them.

The People Who Prayed for Me and my Family. May God Bless Them.

THE MAKING OF A BOOK

The 1st edition of this book came out in four issues. The approximate dates are in the Chronology. The paper was fibertint which at that time cost $1.02 a ream (that's 500 sheets) and was the same stuff small Churches printed their Sunday bulletins on. It was the cheapest paper of all which is why I used it, even though it bleached and faded something awful when exposed to light and tore easily and wasn't much to look at. I started using colored paper from the very start because white paper doesn't mimeograph well on both sides—the printing will show through. But people liked the colored paper for its cheeriness and because it helped organize the book a little bit. In that first edition I was always short of money. It seemed like I never turned out to have enough of any one color of paper and then I'd finish up with some other color I was long on. So the 1st edition ended up kind of rainbow style. Then came the big paper crisis and they stopped making fibertint completely so the very last of the 1st edition was printed on a cheap paper kind of like children's colored construction paper.

Then there was the problem of how to bind it. I punched the paper with three holes. At first by hand with a little paper puncher, one hole at a time, then with a little three-hole puncher, then we found out you could order the paper prepunched for a little extra money and with a sigh of relief that problem was solved. At first we bound the books with metal rings that you could open and slip through the holes and then snap shut. We used all sizes. We didn't know how to buy them wholesale and just went around to all the stores in Lewiston and Moscow and bought them out of rings, anything from a half inch to two and a half inches in diameter. Later we had to replace the rings of all the people who had started out with ones smaller than two inches because the book just couldn't be squeezed in there. I never dreamed in the beginning how big this book was going to turn out to be.

I got so many complaints on how the covers tore when the rings went through I bought more paper of a tougher quality and had it printed up the street at the Kendrick *Gazette* since my mimeograph machine couldn't handle the heavier material. But I got some complaints then that the new covers stained badly (and they did!). So they weren't very suitable for a recipe book. So by the 3rd edition we were trying a new cover type called a "plastisheen," with which the Kendrick edition is still covered, which is supposed to be proof against catsup and what not.

We also discovered another and better kind of mimeograph paper called Mustang. It went through the machine with not so much skipping of sheets (when they stick together so the inside ones don't get printed). Or general jamming up in the machine (which is awful and inky paper goes every which way and it takes you five minutes at least to get going again). We wanted to have as many colors as possible so that almost every chapter could have its own color. We've ended up using about half Carlton and half Mustang. The Mustang is a little heavier paper, a little brighter colored, and a little harder to see through.

Then the metal ring supply went into a crisis. We had them bought up as far away as Los Angeles and Chicago. There wouldn't be another shipment from Japan for six months and then the price was going to go way up on them. In the meantime people were ordering books. We had to find something else. We tried glue binding our own. They were ugly and awful. We tried using leather, not right for mass production. We tried three-ring binder notebooks—too expensive. We tried plastic-coated wire twisted into sort of a nice bow-type thing. It *worked*. The bookstores thought those wire rings were too strange but ordinary people liked them generally. We put out tens of thousands more books using those homemade wire rings. We could get them in all sorts of colors. Lots of times at fairs I was able to offer people a choice of blue or black or orange or some other color rings. Orange was the general favorite!

But the bookstores continued to complain about the rings. It made the books hard to package and mail because they were sort of bulky on the ring side and not nicely square and flat. And there were still individuals who complained about them too and told me they wanted my book to be like other books. We researched binding processes for about a year with no luck finding anything we could afford. Finally we heard about a Velo-Bind machine. It wasn't unmanageably expensive, though not cheap either. We bought. The Velo-Binder punched 12 little holes on the side to be bound and then put through 12 plastic strips that were sealed front and back to a plastic strip. The binding wasn't as sturdy as the ring style but it looked way "slicker" and the bookstores got quiet and happy. Individual people now complained about the Velo-bound books though so we tried in our advertising to give them a full choice of the hardbound (which nobody ever complained about!), the three-ring punched with wire rings, the book enclosed in a school-type three-ring binder notebook or the Velo-bind style.

The 1st edition had chapter headings and some other pictures drawn by Virginia Boegli, a high school friend of mine from Montana. She quit drawing for the book and moved to Denver. Mary Hanks, a friend from up the road here in Idaho, an entomologist who catches grasshoppers for his chickens with a butterfly net, did a lot of the photos for the book. Then Phil Scofield, a thorough professional, staff photographer with the *Daily Idahonian* in Moscow, came along and took more pictures for us.

I met Cindy Davis one day as I was handing out brochures at a booth in Coeur d'Alene, Idaho. It was a strange coincidence that we were both at that place at that time. I hadn't been out selling books like that for a year and a half. I did the Food Fair because Nancy, who was supposed to do it, got sick at the last minute. I was supposed to do TV and radio shows in Spokane that day. I skipped them and did the fair instead which really upset the TV and radio people and Julaine, who worked hard to get me the appointments. But it just seemed like I was supposed to do that fair. Cindy lives on a homestead in northern Idaho. She comes to town every two weeks. She came to town and saw a poster in the health-food store advertising the Food Fair and decided to have a look at it. I knew Cindy by her drawings. I think she is the finest artist doing homestead-type drawings in this country. I had admired her pictures in *Cloudburst I* and *Out of the Molasses Jug*. She illustrated *Cloudburst II*. I had never dreamed she lived not much more than up the road from me. We were so excited to meet each other.

Cindy came to the School of Country Living to see me the next Monday. We talked about her doing pictures for this book. We talked about a *fully* illustrated version, which is no small job on a book this size, for the Kendrick mimeographed version and for the Bantam version which was being planned too since I had sold paperback reprint rights to them. I told Cindy what I'd pay her to do the pictures. Cindy sat and looked at me. She started to cry. "Oh, Carla," she said. "That's enough to buy the piece of land we've been dreaming of!" And then she sat and thought a minute more. "And next year we can go ahead and have our baby!" She jumped up and ran over and we hugged each other tearfully. I was so happy, too. Because this book had needed illustrating so badly, and I knew it, but I never had anybody to do it before. And it was so beautiful and appropriate and right that she and her husband would use their illustrating money to buy a piece of land and have a baby. They are exactly the kind of people this book is for and all about.

Then Toni Burbank came from Bantam. She is my editor there and a person who really campaigned to get them to want this book and come through with the money for it. I was really paranoid about it at first. Looking back I can see Toni and I were each scared of the other and each coming on so big and tough and being wretched inside. I was afraid she would really be trying to change the book—to slick it up and make it something I couldn't feel was mine. But it didn't turn out that way at all. Every single change in the Bantam edition she asked my permission on, and if I said no, then it didn't get changed. She turned out to be, in fact, a wonderful help. We went over the whole book together, page by page, paragraph by paragraph. We reordered some things to organize it a little more sensibly, fixed all the typos, and I wrote lots of new material. I felt so good in fact about the work we did for the Bantam edition that we used that same version to be the mimeographed 7th Kendrick edition.

So the contents have changed with the editions, too. I trust it is getting better as well as bigger all the time and that the copy you are reading is going to be useful, enjoyable, comprehensive and reliable for you.

My prayer is that this book will be a good thing in your life.

CONTENTS

Our farm—seen from across Potlatch River Canyon. What you're looking at is Brady Gulch with the highway to Troy winding down it. Moscow is about 27 miles up that road (Troy is about 12). Kendrick is about half a mile on down. The big flattish field is our hay and grain field. The house sets in that timbered hollow just about in the middle of the picture.

Here are all the Emerys except Gradma Neoma and Grandpa Pat. They came to live by us later, and baby Jacob who came along later too. From left to right it's me, Sara in my arms, Dolly in her plaid winter coat, and Daddy Mike holding Luke, the family monkey whose pants are always on the slip, and big brother Dan. Oh, the picture is also missing middle girl-child Rebecca. You'll meet her in some of the other pictures.

I'd like you to meet Diann Groseclose and Darlene Nye (left to right):
Diann was chief mimeographer and Darlene the stencil typer back before the electronic
stencil maker and they, more than any other people, worked to get this book happening.
They are standing in front of where we still make the Kendrick edition, and as I
write these words I'm sitting at a typewriter right inside that right front window.

The Kendrick edition is put together one page at a time, one chapter at a time.
Round and round the table they go—feet aching, backs aching. About half are
Kendrick and Juliaetta neighbors, half are visitors from far away, all come to
try their hands at book making. There are 2,000 sheets in each of those
stacks and one trip clear around that table puts just one chapter together.

MAMA'S MAMA

Here is a poem that was shown me by a dear old
lady named Maude Dougharty. She didn't know
who wrote it.

Mama's Mama, on a winter's day,
Milked the cows and fed them hay,
Slopped the hogs, saddled the mule,
And got the children off to school,
Did a washing, mopped the floors,
Washing the windows and did some chores,
Cooked a dish of home-dried fruit,
Pressed her husband's Sunday suit,
Swept the parlor, made the bed,
Baked a dozen loaves of bread,
Split some wood and lugged it in,
Enough to fill the kitchen bin,
Cleaned the lamps and put in oil,
Stewed some apples she thought might spoil,
Churned the butter, baked a cake,
Then exclaimed: "For Mercy's Sake,
The calves have got out of the pen!"
Went out and chased them in again,
Gathered the eggs and locked the stable,
Returned to the house and set the table,
Cooked a supper that was delicious,
And afterwards washed all the dishes,
Fed the cat, sprinkled the clothes,
Mended a basket full of hose,
Then opened the organ and began to play,
"When You Come To The End Of A Perfect Day."

ODDMENTS

MISCELLANEOUS RECIPES

I've never tried any of these recipes. I'm not sure if anybody should. If you try one let me know what happened.

Turkey Stuffing—Combine 3 eggs, 1 teaspoon salt and pepper, 1 green pepper, cut up, 1 cup celery, cut up, 2½ cups popcorn, washed, and 3 cups uncooked rice, washed. Mix well. Stuff turkey, loosely. Put in the oven at 350°. Bake until popcorn pops and blows the hind end off the turkey.

7th edition, May 28, 1976. Somebody let me know. "Dear Carla Emery, I have tried your recipe published in the *Government Lands Digest*—the turkey stuffing. But it was a flop the rice was dry and still hard and not even one corn popped. I had to throw out the whole stuffing. What went wrong? My husband was MAD."

Stone Soup—A poor man's specialty. Start with one large, smooth, clean, round stone. Add ½ teaspoon salt and ample water. Boil 2 hours. In the meantime ask around at the neighbors for possible other ingredients. At the end of 2 hours add any vegetables or meat (check the mousetrap) that you have been able to lay hands on. Cook 2 more hours. Remove the stone (save it for the next batch) and eat the soup.

Elephant Stew—You'll need 1 medium-sized elephant, 2 rabbits (optional) and salt and pepper. Cut the elephant into small bite-sized pieces. Add enough brown gravy to cover. Cook over kerosene fire about 4 weeks at 465°. This will serve 3,800 people. If more are expected the 2 rabbits may be added. But do this only in emergency. Most people do not like hare in their stew.

Mouse Pie—Ingredients:

1 cup macaroni	1 medium-sized can
5 fat field mice	tomatoes
Butter	Salt and pepper
½ medium-sized onion, thinly sliced	1 cup cracker crumbs

Boil macaroni 10 minutes. While it is cooking, fry the field mice long enough to fry out some of the excess fat. Grease a casserole with some of this fat and put a layer of macaroni in it. Add onions, then tomatoes, salt and pepper well. Add field mice and cover with remaining macaroni. Sprinkle top with cracker crumbs, seasoned with salt, pepper and butter. Bake at 375° about 20 minutes—or until mice are well done. *Note:* If in cold weather and rain it is difficult to find field mice, a good substitute is about 10 "little pig" sausages. Ruth Thoreland, Yakima, Washington, gave me this one!

Musgoes—One day I was at a place and the lady invited me in for dinner with her family explaining that they were having Musgoes. I had to ask, "What are Musgoes?" She answered, "I just go to the refrigerator and point saying 'This musgo, that musgo!'" Courtesy of John Ramem, Jamestown, North Dakota.

Recipe from a Texas Newspaper (Of Course!)

1 whole camel, medium sized
1 whole lamb, large sized
20 whole chickens, medium sized
110 gallons water
5 tablespoons black pepper
Salt to taste
12 kilos rice
2 kilos pine nuts
2 kilos almonds
1 kilo pistachio nuts
60 eggs

Skin, trim and clean the camel, lamb and chickens and boil until tender (be sure your pot is big enough). Cook rice until fluffy. Fry nuts until brown and mix with the rice. Hard boil the eggs and peel them. Then stuff the chickens with eggs and rice. Stuff the lamb with 5 of the chickens and some rice. Stuff the camel with the lamb and more rice. Broil in a large tray and place the camel on top. Place remaining stuffed chickens around the camel. Decorate rice with boiled eggs and nuts.

P.S. This recipe is great if you're tired of the same old turkey or ham for a holiday dinner. It's guaranteed to excite ohs and ahs from your guests and it's so delicious that you won't have to worry about leftovers.

The following three recipes were written by first graders from the Cloverdale Grade School at Hebo, Oregon.

Cookies With Chocolate Chips—Put eggs and powder in dough, then you stir it with a thing you use for stirring. Put the chocolate chips in. Turn oven on to 10°. Cook for about an hour and a half. By Troy.

Potato Chip Recipe—Peel some (about 5) potatoes. Then slice them. Put them in a big kettle. Put boiling water in it. Put it on a big plate, with paper on it so it won't burn the plate. Then you eat them. By Brittany.

Macaroni and Cheese—You set the table. Then you wait for your dad to come home. Then you start eating the macaroni and cheese. By Latina.

Northern Beaten Biscuits—(Yukon Recipe) Mix 1 cup lard with 4 quarts flour until you have got the lard consumed in the flour. Add 1 tablespoon salt and enough cold water to make a stiff dough. Knead into round shapes. Place on a stump and beat 1,500 times with the flat of an ax. Bake in a mud oven.

Pennsylvania Dutch Scripture Cake—Here's one you read the verses and bake the cake both! Behold there was a cake baken. 1 Kings 9:16.—½ cup butter (Judges 5:25)—2 cups flour (1 Kings 4:22)—½ teaspoon salt (Leviticus 2:13)—1 cup figs (1 Samuel 30:12)—1½ cups sugar (Jeremiah 6:20)—2 teaspoons baking powder (Luke 13:21)—½ cup water (Genesis 24:11)—1 cup raisins (1 Samuel 30:12)—3 eggs (Isaiah 10:14)—cinnamon, mace, cloves (1 Kings 10:10)—1 tablespoon honey (Proverbs 24:13)—½ cup almonds (Genesis 43:11). Blend butter, sugar, spices and salt. Beat egg yolks and add. Sift in baking powder and flour, then add the water and honey. Put fruits and nuts through food chopper and flour well. Follow Solomon's advice for making good boys—1st clause of Proverbs 23:14. Fold in stiffly beaten egg whites. Bake for 1 hour in 375° oven.

Scripture Cake (this one works)—(Try it on a cooking friend leaving out the explanations in parentheses and see if she can figure it out!)

Matthew 10:42—1 cup (water)
Jeremiah 6:20—1 cup (sugar)
1 Samuel 25:18—1 cup (raisins)
Matthew 25:4—1 teaspoon (oil)
2 Chronicles 9:9—1½ teaspoons (spices)
Psalms 35:23 (stir)
Isaiah 38:21 (boil)
Luke 16:24 (cool)

Then add:

1 Kings 4:22—2 cups (flour)
1 Corinthians 5:8—1 teaspoon (leavening)
Luke 14:34—¼ teaspoon (salt)
Genesis 43:11—½ cup (nuts)
Isaiah 2:4 (beat)
Leviticus 26:26 (bake)
Luke 15:23 (eat)

IF YOU'VE CONSIDERED MOVING TO THE COUNTRY

Yes! Get out of town. Get as far into the country as you can get. Get as far away from neighbors as you can. Go where the majority is sky and earth and the animals and plants that are of it. They are nearer the Truth than you, and you'll learn and benefit by association with them. You'll be going to Reality. You'll be giving yourself a chance to escape the lures of human mythology, of all of our delusions and foolishness. They breed in big cities, they flourish there far from Nature. Cement and smog and skyscrapers are hothouse environments for them, but they are as unreal as the house of perpetual feasting where so many pilgrims were separated from their progress.

Every tool of the mass media reenforces these tragic human illusions that lead people to waste their lives pursuing "contentment" or "adventure" or "success" where they can only find disappointment. So get rid of your radio, television, record player. Buy a piano or guitar and learn to make your own music. Better yet in silence discover that there are soft, though wordless, messages coming to you from all the living things you share the land with, and even the mighty maternal arm of the mountains is meant to be thrown around and cherish your being—for you come from dust and you will return to dust and the mountain is made of it, too.

Read your news because you can control that input a little better and read only as much as necessary. Have your round-table discussions on your knees with the whole family holding hands and God in it too. Find someplace where it is quiet enough to perceive that God's love and advice travel through airwaves as surely as do radio and television. Get far enough away from everybody else so you're forced by circumstances to discover what being a family really means and in the process you'll discover what being a woman means, too. Cut yourself rudely off from the opinion makers and give yourself a chance to find out what you really want and need. Try to raise food and try to raise children and I guarantee you and your

husband will learn together genuine humility and the ability to pray.

But don't move to the country in search of a notion of a freedom that pictures you lying on the grass all of a fine summer's day chewing on a succession of hay straws. True freedom doesn't mean a vacuum.

And in the kind of freedom I'm talking about you work 12-hour days in the summer. Finding freedom is a strange kind of paradox, anyway. Like the spiritual truths that you can actually get by giving, and conquer by simply loving and having faith. And yet it is true that you can get more by giving than any other way. And you can conquer anything by love and by faith. And as for freedom, you get freedom by giving yourself into a kind of bondage in a promise to serve. You give yourself to a man, yourself, and your future life to be possessed by him, and you win a freedom in so doing. You have children by him, and then you must work harder than ever serving them selflessly day and night for all the years they need you. And you win still more freedom. You give yourself to God and say Lord, not my will but Thine always be done, and then all things are truly possible and you are truly free—in this life and forever after. And yet the freedom is all by bowing your head and saying I will serve, faithfully and not asking any reward but that I should only have done as well as it was possible for me to do. And then the blessings come. It is the same with the land you have. And give yourself to the plants to nurture them. You will be there to plow and spread manure. To pull the weeds that threaten to stifle them and to give them precious water to drink when they would die or could not thrive without it. For the animals, you promise to love them, feed them, doctor them, forgive them the aggravations they cause you. And in return, by the manufacture of their flesh they will sustain you and your family. The animals and plants you are possessed by give you still more of that *real* freedom.

I love this life and I recommend it but now let me do a little debunking. The rewards are largely the spiritual cultivation that work and austerity bestow. The easy way to do things is to do one thing and do it well. But if you commit yourself to this kind of life you're committing yourself to trying to do a hundred incompatible and competitive things and like as not your first year 75 of them will fizzle. It happens to me constantly. I've never yet grown a three-pound tomato. I have a friend who grows big ones, but I'm happy to get them store size.

Furthermore the goats never give as much milk as the references say they will nor do the hens lay as faithfully. My garden doesn't produce like anybody's magazine article, and it doesn't look like any of the photographs. I'll add, however, that it feeds us. At least some of the orchard crop usually gets attacked by some combination of animals and disease. This year the robins took most of the cherries, the fungus got into the pears and an early frost prevented the apricots and peaches. (The apple, raspberry, plum and blackberry crops were fine.) The bees don't make as much honey as they are supposed to. Everything that eats requires more feed than you expect and by fall you can toboggan from the house to the barn across all that manure. Nobody dares step onto the front porch barefoot, and I wouldn't even suggest having a picnic in the yard.

But if I don't let the chickens roam in my organic garden, armies of insects come to take their place. Thousands of grasshoppers and potato bugs and

tomato worms—long green monsters with horns and big mouths—all kinds of hungry, creeping, crawling, leaping things.

And nothing that is supposed to stay confined does. We are constantly having to put some variety of animal or other back in its appointed place. They go over, under, through, or—failing that—the children leave gates and cage doors wide open. In the mechanical realm any machine that we want urgently and can manage to get started will break down later, usually after a half a day. The routine vehicles are regularly subject to gas shortage, flat tires, ruined spark plugs, extinct batteries, burnt-out generators or worse. It is obvious to me that my Amish ancestors are quite right that these contrivances are not approved by Providence.

We often have sick animals that require first aid and in the spring the kitchen doubles as a veterinary hospital. Nevertheless we invariably lose some of the crop of baby animals. The milk goats frequently get horrible gashes on their teats from trying to jump barbed wire fences. Cows and goats occasionally eat nails or wire and would die of lingering indigestion if we didn't feed them a magnet. Some baby chicks always smother, or drown, or get trampled by a galloping old hen, or run over by the car, or squeezed by the baby. Baby pigs catch cold and goslings are the worst of all for taking a fatal chill. Baby calves and goats are sometimes taken by diarrhea or more serious diseases. I will add that this does not apply to kittens and puppies. They all live to grow up and reproduce themselves in cheerful abundance providing they have no market value.

And last but not least, this ideal of rural living turns out to be pathetically dependent on city money. And Mike has to drive 28 miles each way and be away in town all day to make it. The land was so expensive. And so is everything else. The constant mechanical repairs and gas to commute to work average about $150 a month. A spring supply of garden seed can easily be $30 to $50. All the animal and plant categories require store props that add expense—buckets, medicine, machinery and housing. Fencing is very expensive.

And the job that pays for the farm also means that Mike is away every day, and long days because of commuting and overtime. So with all these things that require so much time and effort (and that's where you save money is by doing it yourself) the woman is Johnny-on-the-spot when the bull goes through the fence or the pigs suddenly appear in the garden or the pickup gets a flat tire or the house catches on fire. The small homestead is a famous woman killer so be reminded of all the realities and relax—you can't do everything. The thing to do is survive!

Take a leaf from our revered Colonial great-grandmothers who grew their own wool and flax, spun the thread, wove the cloth, and grew all their own food and drink. They washed those precious homespun clothes never more than once a month (some preferred only every two or three months). They drank out of a single vessel which circulated from hand to hand around the table and ate two or three to a bowl which helped save on dishwashing. They specialized in one pot meals—mainly stew. When cold weather came the children were sewn into their winter underwear and wore it until spring when everybody had a bath. So just admit you can't be an old fashioned girl and continue doing as much of everything else as you used to and decide what you're going to neglect. Or better yet just go ahead and neglect it because deciding takes time.

People are always asking me how I manage to get so much done. My husband asks me how I manage to keep track of it all. The honest truth is I don't. I don't really get that much done, and Lord knows I don't keep track of it all. But for what it's worth here are some habits I have that might help explain whatever accomplishment is left to explain.

1. Don't discuss the obvious.
2. Don't own a television or radio. Read no worldly magazines and only the front and back pages of a newspaper.
3. Quit a job when you're losing efficiency.
4. Go to bed when you're tired.
5. Eat less salt and less sugar, and use less heat.
6. Keep records of things to do, things to buy.
7. Then get somebody else to do as much of that as possible.
8. Don't drink coffee, tea, colas, alcohol, smoke cigarettes, chew snooze or use drugs. Stay at home.
9. Sing a lot.
10. Pray a lot.

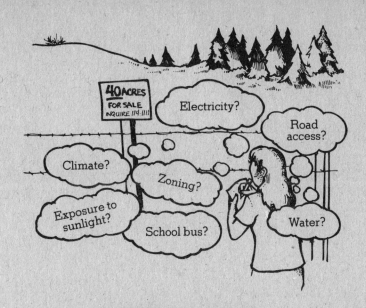

GETTING THE LAND

You can't live the life this book loves without land, at least enough of it for a garden and some animals—a hen house, rabbit pens, goat or cow quarters (preferably ample pasture and a barn). So you need land and that isn't easy. Land is expensive if it's good for gardening or pasture, which is what you want. The turnover is slow so you may have to wait quite a while for a piece located where you want it. The demand is high so you may have to be ready to leap when the chance does come along. Prices are high, higher all the time. Down payments required are big—cash really talks in land deals, or property that you own already and can trade with. Interest will be a heavy additional load.

You are probably going to have to think way, way ahead to get your piece of land. You'll probably have to make lots of sacrifices and work two jobs to boot. But you can do it if you really want to. Think where you want your land to be. Can you get a job near there? Would some kind of special training make it possible for you to earn a living there? Well, jobs in really rural areas are hard to find. Openings go first to local people and they should. The rural jobs are often highly specialized such as logging or farm equipment operating (which means you have to be a skilled mechanic too). If you are city bred you don't know anything about these things and the potential employers know that even better than you. Furthermore the small rural industries around here are closing down because of the antipollution laws so competition for jobs is getting more and more keen.

You'll have to learn your way around, learn where to ask and whom to ask for. You may have to pick a spot near a university or medium-sized town. The transition period will bring real hardships of body and soul. Mike and I have both spent time in New York, and I'm sure it's the same agony in reverse when the city kid tries to make it in the country. But please remember that the country people are as much a part of the new environment you're going to as the rabbits and trees you admire so much. They are afraid you're going to come and turn their beloved area into just what you are running away from. If you call them "red-necks" and refer to the courage of their convictions as "prejudices," you're casting a dark shadow over your whole endeavor to start with that's going to make it harder and less fulfilling. Their customs may be very different from yours. Their values may be different. But not necessarily bad. So try to be open-minded and to return the neighborliness that they are going to show you, or if they don't, be patient and trusting until they size you up. Be prepared to prove your worth if necessary. They are protecting a precious thing—a human social environment full of old wholesome values.

Once you know where you want to live and you have commenced earning a living there, you can always shop around for land. Avoid real estate agents if you can. The ideal contract is one made directly between you and the owner. (But have your own lawyer read it over before you sign it.) The owner also prefers to deal directly with you rather than through a real estate agent because then the down payment all goes to him. Without a realtor in the picture you almost certainly can make the deal for a lot less cash down. Realtors get huge fees and insist upon them the day the contract is signed—meaning that their fee is paid out of the down payment. On a $30,000 deal, for example, the real estate company typically may get $3,000 cash. The realtor with whom you personally have been dealing may get $1,000 of that. So the down payment is $5,000 or more if the owner says he wants at least $2,000 down for himself. In most of the real estate deals I've been involved in, if a realtor was there the majority of the down payment asked was because of the real estate fee.

So lots of owners are quite willing to carry the contract for you and to deal directly with you. Then all you need to get moving is money enough for a down payment to suit the owner. It's best if you have this saved up. The bank probably won't loan you any money unless you're terribly prosperous already, in which case you don't need my advice anyway. It's against the law to borrow money to put down on an FHA deal. Even with prime credit it's impossible to get more than about $1,500 from a loan company and what you pay back in interest is so great you'd be way ahead saving your money or getting it someplace where you don't pay a lot of interest. So be humble if you must borrow—borrow from your folks or friends rather than from interest-charging banks or loan companies. But consider this. If you have to borrow money to make the down payment, for the first couple years you'll be paying every month:

1. On the farm contracts.
2. For the money borrowed to make the down payment.
3. For housing if the land is unimproved (a trailer? to build?).
4. To stock the land—seeds, animals, fences.
5. Property taxes (higher in urbanized areas or near them).

That is a heavy burden.

A willing owner would probably have his own lawyer draw up a contract since he has dealt in land before and knows a lawyer. He'll split the fee with you (about $75 each) and will choose a bank to hold the contract in escrow until you have paid the last dime on it—30 years later or whatever. Then you'll get your deed from the bank. You send your payments to the bank. They record them and then pay the money to the owner:

It is typical on these contracts that if you are over ten days late with a payment, the owner can send you a certified letter of warning and then take back his farm, complete with your down payment and improvements. That is a very hot seat to have to sit in for umpteen years, but there really isn't any other way but to pay cash outright. Be sure, however, that your contract stipulates that you can pay it off faster if you want to. That way if you should strike it rich, you can get out from under the thing quicker. This is a good deal for owners, some of whom make a habit of selling their land at impossible terms to people that they figure can't make it. Then they can take it back and sell it to somebody else.

So be tough minded in your dealings. You're going to have to live with this a long time. Double-check everything the owner or real estate agent tells you with your neighbors, ASCS* and any other relevant source. Especially double-check what he says about *water*. And if you are told there is an "assignable lease" check that because it's very possibly not true. Insist on seeing everything in person and look hard. Then come back and look again. And again. You'll see more each time.

But maybe you can't find anything but real estate agents, and you want to save the 10% you can save by finding an owner. Well, ask around the stores, gas stations, neighbors. Watch the advertisements. Put in an ad of your own describing how many acres you want, with or without buildings, what type land, and how much you can put down—such as: "Wanted to buy. 15 or more acres suitable for garden or pasture in Scrumptious School District. Buildings not necessary. Have $2,000 to put down . . . telephone number." And give it lots of time. Let it run all year if need be.

If you find an owner, don't talk numbers in a hurry. If possible, get three good prospects before you make a deal. These will give you perspective on what is available and how much it costs. Get ready an offer—don't make it for everything you have in cash or the most you think you could pay unless the owner is taking sealed bids. Make it for the smallest amount down and the smallest total price that you think has a chance. You'll need the rest of that money to get started on the place. The owner may say no. If so, say you've got to work on it and come back with somewhat better terms to offer him—such as a high monthly payment. Watch those interest points closely. They are going to really cost you. Calculate how much each interest point will cost you in cash.

Your deal will either be for a regular monthly payment for a stated number of years, such as $92 a

---

*ASCS stands for Agriculture Stabilization and Conservation Service which is government and free advice. Check at your county courthouse to find them.

month for nine years; or a payment plus interest payable on a certain date annually (or semiannually), such as $1,000 a year plus interest payable November 1. On a $30,000 contract with $5,000 paid down that would mean a payment of about $2,800 the first year, a little less (very little) each succeeding year as there is less principal to pay interest on. Large "farm" type parcels are often handled on the payment plus interest basis. The November payment assumes you have just sold your crop and have your year's cash in.

WHERE SHOULD I HUNT FOR LAND?

1. As far away from a big city as possible. Near the cities land prices are high, taxes are high. You've got to go hundreds of miles from any major metropolitan area to find land at its true agricultural value.

2. Don't go where everybody else is going. Certain very scenic and well-publicized areas like the Hamilton area south of Missoula, Montana, and the Clearwater Valley in Idaho, parts of Colorado, Oregon and northern Idaho in the Coeur d'Alene region are getting so many immigrants it's creating great problems of sewage disposal, pressure on the school system and whole valley bottoms of fertile land getting covered with homes. (Better to put your house on the untillable hillside.) Land in that sort of too-fast growing area is already expensive and going up. If there are signs advertising real estate services and land for sale and you can see new homes left and right—don't buy there. Find a valley that is emptier. Don't put a creek, timber and the view of a snow-capped mountain range on your list of necessities. That isn't fair to Mother Earth. Consider the Plains States—Kansas or Nebraska. Consider the more arid areas like eastern Montana. Consider the real cold places like Wyoming and the Dakotas and northern Minnesota where less hardy folk refuse to go.

3. Don't wait for a land promoter to shove a deal under your nose. Be prepared to work personally at getting your piece of land.

When you do get a certain piece of land to consider buying, worry first about a water supply (see the Water section of this chapter). And are there access rights or might you be surrounded by people who might padlock their gates? Do you realize that it could easily cost $3,000 or more to bring in either electricity or a phone? That the school bus may not be willing or able to come there to get your children? That the county zoning board might consider it illegal for you to build your home unless you are capable of meeting every detail of the building code? Don't give up—just be forewarned. These are things to look for.

Frank Ryset is the teacher of self-defense in land buying at our School of Country Living. Each week this past summer he was for two days a bookstore owner, one day a teacher and three days or so a real estate agent. He's an honest man and sincere. He dictated to me the following advice on your land buying:

"Land can be cheap and available, but if there is no road to get to it, or if the road is only good for four months out of the year, your land value is only worth one-third the value of land that you can drive to year-round. Water is another problem. For $3,000 you could buy land. But it might cost $6,000-$8,000 to drill a well, to pipe water in, or put in an aqueduct to bring water to you. Water to irrigate land and produce the crops you want to raise to live on becomes almost as important as the land and the productivity of the land which you will buy. Sure maybe today you don't have any desire or at least any need to have a school bus coming by your door. But many of us ten years later will have acquired one or two young ones who are going to need basic education and school attendance is also a requirement of most state laws. If you have to board your children out for schooling—what's life? That's nine months of separation.

PRODUCTIVITY OF THE LAND. "If you're not a farmer there are many different ways you can tell whether land is fertile or not. Pay attention to the vegetation you see . . . like how high is the sagebrush? If the sagebrush were only up to his boot tops my dad didn't think it was worth plowing, but if it was up to the horse's belly he thought more than likely we could make that land produce. How deep is the grass, how lush are the trees? Have the berry bushes borne fruit? The person who is selling maybe hasn't really taken as good care of the land as you intend to. So you are going to be able to increase the production. Soil testings are available from commercial organizations or county agents or you can use a kit of your own. They will tell you in technical terminology that land's productivity.

ZONING. "Most zoning has already been imposed by a governmental body. You find this land you like and it looks like it will produce. Now you go to the county zoning board to find out more. In that area are there any acreage limitations? We mean how many acres per living unit is the requirement of the county. Maybe they won't let you buy less than five acres, for example. Five acres per family. Is there a land use requirement? This is imposed by county health boards stating that only one sewage system can be put on, for example, a five-acre parcel, depending on the percolation or absorption rate of the land. Timber utilization is another fast approaching zoning restriction. Under these regulations you would not be able to fell trees on your property without permission of the zoning officer of the county. In the West some of our counties are zoned and some are not. Or sometimes part of a county is restricted while another portion is still clear of this type of ordinance. When buying in a 'subdivision' or in a prelaid out area be sure you check for covenants imposed upon the land by former owners. A former owner of the property, the one who sold to the subdividers who in turn are selling to you, can put covenants upon the future owners to restrict what they will build. There have been covenants where only one family could occupy a building, or only one house be built per ten acres, or even that you can't have a pig on the property." I kid you not . . . Frank once bought one that was like that. We've got a covenant on the School of Country Living property that we can't tear down any building. Even if we wanted to replace it with a $500,000 structure, tearing down a building would still mean that we had broken a contract and could mean foreclosure. So we are very careful not to do that.

And then Frank continued: "Read the fine print of any contract and have your own lawyer. It'll only cost $50 or so. And never sign a contract that contains a balloon payment clause. That's an old and rotten trick on the buyer. An example of the balloon payment is if a fellow bought an apartment house for $62,000, with payments of just over $500 a month before taxes on principal and interest. He knew it was a good deal, but it never worried him until after eight years he went to his lawyer to ask what the 'balloon payment' was that the contract said was coming due in two years. His lawyer then explained that the balloon payment meant the entire rest of the principal and interest became due and payable on that date, two years from then. He lost the apartment house and everything he had invested in it because most of his payments had been going for interest and taxes and the bank wouldn't loan him any money to make the payment.

"Another friend of mine didn't worry about getting title insurance for the property he had just bought. It was a piece of land in the center of a block. He had his own private driveway, no one else came in and out of there. He lived on it for three years. Then one morning his neighbor had built a fence across his driveway. He went to the sheriff, to the county—the driveway was really just an easement, entirely at the discretion of the other owner. It took a long court battle and almost as much in legal fees as he had paid for the house to secure a permanent open easement to his property."

Frank isn't the only one who knows horror stories of land buying. So don't not buy—but buy very carefully and in as informed a way as you can.

OF LAND AND MONEY

Since I finished revising the land buying section I've already got more revising to do. Tom Mundrick of Los Angeles, California, wrote me some really good questions—good enough for everybody to hear the answers.

Lots of people write me questions. Some of the questions I get are really hard. I'm still looking for a recipe for persimmon root beer one lady asked me for. Some are easy like how do you make ricotta cheese, or what do you do about an iron frying pan that has started to stick. (They weren't easy for me but they were for some friends of mine who helped me!) Some questions are easy and yet they're hard because they're so broad. But usually the broad ones are so important that I try anyway. That's the way Tom's questions are.

He asked, "How much land do you need for a few cows, hogs, chickens, ducks, etc.?" To pasture a cow and grow a garden, if you have all good soil and there is plenty of water to irrigate all of it, you can manage with two acres. Three, four or five would be better. Five acres of good irrigable ground is hard to find. You're more likely to find vacant wooded areas, or steep areas, or shallow soils. And so much depends on the skill of the gardener—a half acre would do for some people.

Then Tom asked me, "Is there a certain type of soil necessary for growing produce as opposed to field crops?" The answer is you need good soil whether for field crops or produce. And then consider that some produce likes clay, some sand. But you can grow almost any plant in almost any soil if you have enriched it with enough manure and other organic material and get on enough water in the growing season. Manure adds humus to sandy soils—that by themselves have the problem of draining too fast—and changes them so they can hold water (and nutrients) longer. Manure loosens up a clayey soil, whose big problem is that it won't drain good enough, and thus makes it possible for crops, especially root crops, to do better in there. Good soil comes from manure—or sawdust—or straw—or household table scraps—anything that was once alive.

You can grow forage crops where you can't grow produce. That means, in effect, you could live on a diet largely based on milk and meat (which your animals manufacture from the grass they eat) where you can't grow enough vegetable-type foods to keep you going—cold climate places. Cheat grass which grows on rocky hillsides (useless for vegetable gardening) is a forage crop. There are much better ones. But cows can eat cheat grass in the spring and get fat. (Goats get abscesses from it though.)

Loam is your best soil. "Loam" means a soil that is neither real clayey nor real sandy. It's sort of in-between and has lots of organic material in it. A good rule of thumb is that if you are looking at a deep soil (2 or 3 feet) that has a real good crop of something—even grass or weeds—and if it's dry on top within a couple days after a rain, that's what you want. The dryness means the soil drains enough to dry out so it isn't a swamp (which you couldn't till) and yet it holds nutrients. That luxuriant weed patch or grass growing there proves that the nutrients are abundant.

Ground under timber presents special problems. Under pine trees those falling pine needles have made the ground very acid, and you can't garden there unless that is corrected. The trees mean not enough sunlight is going to come through to grow anything very well. And forcing your plants to compete with timber for water and nutrients is giving them heavy competition because those are plants too—big, strong ones. So you would have to clear a place for the garden and clearing timber isn't easy. And then you would have to haul in a bunch of stuff to neutralize the soil—or wait a long time.

Tom asked me if I could give an approximate cost for land, animals, seed and housing. That's another impossible question but so important that I have to try anyway. Land prices are going up. But that's not as bad as it sounds because so are all other prices and land is one place you can put your money that seems to be inflation proof. Land does not depreciate (become less in value with time) the way cars, trailer houses and boats do. Land becomes worth more with time. And it is still one of the biggest bargains around if you shop in the right place. Timbered land in Idaho is about $900 an acre now. Oregon prime land is between $1,500 and $2,000 an acre in small lots. Land is generally cheaper per acre in big hunks than in little ones. I'd say to get started find about three to five acres of good, tillable rainy-place or irrigable land and expect to pay $1,500 an acre or so for it. (On the edge of town it's twice that or more, depending on the town. In a very remote area or in an agriculturally poor area it might be one-third that, or less.)

If there's no house you'll need another $3,000 or so for a cheap used trailer house. Or build your own. Don't cover up a fifth of your land with a big expen-sive sprawling house and another big hunk with lawn that's mostly there to look at. Keep your house small and use that land like a real farmer. Have a big garden and animals to mow the grass where you have grass.

As for animals, an average goat will cost you $50. An average small cow will be around $350, a large one around $400-$450. Your first year's supply of seed and tree starts will be at least $100. Tool cost depends completely on how many of what you get. Whether it's a spade or a tractor. When you set out to grow your own food there's no way you're going to have all the money you could spend, because there's no end to the things you probably would like to buy. You just have to do what you can with what you have.

Tom asked me if there was any special feed or type of pasture necessary for the animals. The feed question is really complex. I've tackled that under each animal in this book. I do urge people to learn to raise as much of their own animal feed as possible—not to get it from the store—not even to get the components for it from the store. The old-timers raised food for their livestock as well as their kitchen, and so can you. Animals raised on homegrown feed typically gain weight a little slower—give somewhat fewer eggs and somewhat less milk. The value you gain in self-sufficiency, reduction in cost and the healthiness of your product more than outweighs that.

THE HOMESTEADERS

I recently got a letter from some friends who are squatting on national forest land in Alaska. They live there year-round in a tipi and there in the tipi their first baby was born last winter. That's a hard way to live, and though I'm all for getting out on the land, I don't know as I'd recommend that particular style. It's best to own your own piece of earth if you can. That way you can feel like you're building something permanent that nobody can chase you off of and that can stand for your children to inherit. And their children from them. Then you can plant things like sugar maples that take a long time to mature and feel like you and your descendants will get the sweets of the labor.

Che Che Gammon wrote this description for you of how she and her husband are living.

"We live in our 20-foot tipi in Alaska. Last year our baby was born here. I was really worried about having enough heat and food. But we seemed to make the best of the situation.

"First, we built an 'ozan' type roof for the 'inner roof' of the tipi out of scrap canvas. By connecting it to the liner inside the tipi, we were able to keep more heat in. The next problem was the floor. We had to make the floor stay warm, even though it was freezing all the time. We used a chain saw and made sawdust by cutting up biscuits of wood. After laying down about 6 inches of sawdust, we decided that would be enough. Then more scraps of canvas were used to cover the floor. Then we laid down deer hides I stretched and scraped all over the tipi for more warmth.

"The next problem was the biggest one by far. What to use for heat. We used an open fire for a while, but I knew that the diapers I'd be washing by hand would be really sooty if I dried them in that manner. So this was not the answer. Next we tried a small airtight stove. After cooking on it for a while and trying to bake one loaf of bread at a time in my Dutch oven, we decided again this really wouldn't be ideal. So we found an old wood stove and patched her up and we were happy to find this solved our problem of heat and cooking and also the drying of clothes.

"When we had picked this site for our tipi, the creek was of great concern. We were lucky enough to pick one that didn't freeze up in winter, or didn't run dry in summer. It is fed by an underground stream. It isn't too far from our tipi, so we pack the water in with big buckets and I have a huge water boiler on the stove for hot water anytime we need it. Also if it rains a lot, like it does here, a rain barrel is the answer. We take our baths in two galvanized buckets (the same ones I wash in).

"During the winter, the tipi was real dark inside. The 'ozan' we put up was working, but we never thought about the light problem. A couple of kerosene lamps were acquired and some candles were made. It was not the best light, but you could see a lot better.

"Though our problems seemed to be getting smaller, there were still many things to consider, one of which was food. One thing that really helped us out, was during the summer we went fishing for salmon and I canned it up. I also picked a lot of 'goose tongue' and canned that. With all the different kinds of berries growing wild, I soon discovered the trick of making jams and canning berries. We also grew a garden of considerable size of root crops and other vegetables. (Seaweed makes a good fertilizer!) During the winter there was deer we hunted to eat and soon different kinds of fowl. We are also very lucky where we live to have crab. Everything seems to be plentiful here. Especially love."

I'm not a bit worried about Che Che, her husband and their son. They're obviously going to be fine and they've a lot to teach the rest of us.

There are as many styles of homesteading as there are homesteaders. Are many people really leaving the city for the country? Yes. The population statistics people in Washington, D.C., are amazed. For the last 80 years the story was always the same. Country kids leaving the country, going to the city, cities getting bigger. But in the last three years this trend has not only stopped but reversed itself in a dramatic way. Several million people have moved to the country in the last few years. Is there room for them? Yes. Eighty years ago there were three times as many people living in rural America as there are today. Small towns were bigger and there were countless villages that today are vanished from the land completely. I see no harm in people living there again. In new villages rising up. I do hate though to see people go to the small towns and make them cities, or flood into scenic resort areas or areas where promoters have been promoting hard. They are needed most where the towns once were but now aren't, and where the promoters haven't already promoted.

There's a lot of confusion over the word "homesteading." Some people still think it means to qualify to be given land by the government by living on it, building a house on it and so on. That used to be true but land that you can get that way is now almost impossible to find. Now the word "homesteading" is used to mean just getting to live on the land a fairly simple style of life. And when people who were raised in cities try to do it I believe it's every bit as much of a challenge for them as crossing the plains was for our pioneer ancestors. People are going all kinds of places to do their homesteading. To Alaska. Or Canada. To the mountains of Appalachia or the western United States. To Maine. No matter where you do it, if you can be someplace where you can raise a garden and have some animals like chickens and goats or cows you're well on your way. If it's true what they say about the climate getting colder I guess you won't want to homestead in cold parts of Canada or northern Alaska.

For the past 40 or 80 or so years school districts across America have been in a mood of consolidation. The statistics favored it as people were leaving the land. School consolidation hastened their departure and made unlikely their return. I want to see the country schools come back as parents and children return to the country. I hope and trust that school administrators will be able to see how totally the population trend has changed. That they will remember how many great American Presidents, writers, thinkers, and scientists came out of those one-room country schoolhouses. That when perplexed by the economics of it, they'll remember that in the old days the schools were built, maintained and repaired by parents of the students and the teacher was usually the wife of a nearby farmer, glad to work at a very reasonable wage to have the job.

Somebody is going to ask—where were you raised, Carla? Where did you go to school? I was raised on a farm in Montana. I rode horseback to a one-room country school.

Who are these people who are moving to the country? Are they young? Old? They are some of everybody. I've been reading their wonderful letters for five years now, trying to answer their questions, trying to help. They are young, just graduated, just married, just beginning. They are in the middle years, making the massive change, starting all over. They are elderly, just retiring, feeling free for the first time and determined to use that freedom to live as they always dreamed. Are they hippies? Squares? They are some of everybody. Hippies, yes. Living in communes. Living alone. Trying the most adventurous and newfangled notions in country living—and the most traditional. They are John Birch Society members trying to be ready for a time they fear the economy will collapse. Latter-Day Saints preparing for a time of trials, Christians getting ready for the Last Days. They are anybody who is discovering he loves the earth and his fellow earth citizens—the plants and animals—and he is called and drawn by an irresistible love call, in his body and mind to come, come and fellowship with them and make his life with them.

The following letter is from Edith Brown of Vaughn, Washington.

"Chauncey and I moved from Seattle last Valentine's Day to our 40 acres that we bought for taxes 40 years ago. I had always vowed I would never live on a farm as I felt four years of homestead living in my early years were more than enough. When we came to look at our property a year and a half ago, the apple trees in the old, old orchard were in full bloom and were a sight to behold. We observed that folks were preparing to move to the property across the road from our place and that our dead-end road would begin to have some life. I changed my mind.

"Last summer, Chauncey raised a tremendous garden and we can hardly believe all the improvements made in the past year. We bought a used mobile home, an old truck, new tractor, rototiller and other equipment from sale of stock in our machine shop in Seattle so we have enjoyed a very busy, but happy year. We have put 35 of our 40 acres in trust for our six children and hope to develop the wooded acres with Christmas trees. If all goes well for my sister and her husband, they will move out on an acre beside us next spring."

These letter excerpts show that the routes back to the land are as individual as the people taking them. The only important thing they all had in common that I can see was being married and a big mutual determination to go live a rural life.

Barbara Ingram and her husband made the move to the northern Idaho forestland after eight childless years of marriage. She conceived their first year on the land. I get a lot of these "Hooray, Carla, we're on the land at last" letters and at least three others besides Barbara have mentioned that after despairing of being able to conceive, their first year in the wilderness also brought their first baby.

"On leaving the city. If you are moving to an established place there is not near the problem. If you are moving to an undeveloped piece of ground in a new place there are three things you must have. Groceries. Six months' to a year's supply. Hand tools, all you can accumulate. And all the junk you can haul. Too many people give it all away, get out here

and find they could have used it or traded it for something they could use.

"We came to our five undeveloped acres 2½ years ago. We brought with us an 8 x 35-foot trailer ready to fall apart and loaded to capacity with stuff and groceries. And $20 and high hopes. You can make it with no money if you can make your land payment and have stuff to work with. But you can't make it without food until you get started. The first year bang! I got pregnant which was impossible. We had been married 9 years. This year I broke my arm. Fun and games. Two months ago we bought a generator. So now we have electricity for such things as a washing machine. But for two years we have lived with no plumbing, no electricity and no gas. We have a spring 300 feet from the house. We hauled water in buckets until Bob started hauling it in barrels with the jeep.

"With lots of faith things happen. With a band saw we built a large room on the trailer, chicken house, goat shed, rabbit hutches and some fences. Our room on our trailer cost $120 and it's 12 x 35 feet. We tore down an old barn for materials. Bob got a job at a shake mill but the first year there was no job to be had. Thank goodness for the groceries.

"We brought with us a pair of peacocks. Now we have 25 hens laying 60 dozen eggs a month. A nanny and billy goat. Rabbits everywhere. (What we don't eat, we sell.) Whites Wabbit Wanch in Coeur d'Alene and the Lewiston Co-op will pay 45¢ a pound, live weight, for rabbits 4½ to 5 pounds. The cheapest way to raise them is on hay and oats. You get just as fast a weight gain as with pellets. But use New Zealand rabbits, at 6 months they are as big as a common rabbit at a year and a half. Our latest addition is one jersey cow named Julie.

"We have survived the worst flood in 70 years, the worst drought in 40 years, the worst plague of yellow jackets in the history of the area, the worst forest fire season since 1907, the deepest snow in 10 years—7 feet (last winter)! I had to have Clay Caesarean section and no help when I came home. This year I got my first broken bone and must do it all with one hand. But we've made it and things are looking up more all the time. It takes guts, hard work and a big faith that the Lord will help you over the humps. But it can be done by middle-aged people with no money. We are stronger, healthier and feel younger, even if we do go to bed after a 16-hour day, year-round, dead tired. It's a good tired!"

Barbara and her husband planned and prepared carefully for their move. Marion Earnhart and hers left it in God's hands:

"Dear Carla, I grabbed up your book on a last-second shopping trip before leaving Seattle, Washington. God had led us to sell or give away everything we had and take only what would fit in our V.W. Bug. After traveling through Oregon, Idaho, Wyoming, Colorado, back through Wyoming and Montana, we were on our way to Canada when we ran out of food, money and things to sell. We spent the night in a little city park praying every minute. The next day my husband got a job that kept us going until we found a ranch job that included a place to live.

"I am now in the middle of nowhere, on a ranch, trying to figure out how they get those great big cows in those little tiny packages I'm used to buying. Amazing!!! Actually I spend most of my time chasing down the flies in my kitchen and trying to keep my husband's stomach half-way full.

"I really love your book. (You forgot to tell me taffy takes 4 hours.) It saves me asking my husband a lot of dumb questions. What I really love best is your notes on how you get through your days.

"It makes me feel better to know I'm not the only one that prays to get through the day. Most people seem to pray for such big things and I seem to spend my days praying for food, clothes and patience (I have a nasty mouth). It is so hard to pray for tomorrows when todays are so long. Right now, I'm praying for a ride into town to catch up on my wash. I guess I'll just be happy that my taffy came out eatable for today, and try something else tomorrow.

"Thank you for your book, and God bless you and your family. With love from a fellow Christian farm wife and fan."

Of course, working on somebody else's farm is a good education but it shouldn't end there. What you want in time is that place of your own. Linda Lanigan, now living with her husband on their own farm near Council, Idaho, wrote me about the long serious road of apprenticeship they took to get there. And incidentally, if any of you readers need help or would be willing to accept apprentice farmers on your farm—hardworking, intelligent, honest people willing to work for nothing or very little more just for the opportunity to learn—write me and I'll match you with such a worker. Tell me what kind of farm you have, how many workers you need, and when and for how long. I'll be grateful for the opportunity you are offering them and so will they.

So Linda and Wal Lanigan went slowly and carefully, accepted a hard apprenticeship on other people's farms, and here's how they turned out:

"We are both from large cities, east coast and west coast. We left seven years ago and first went to Oklahoma where a buddy of my husband's from Vietnam had a job for us on a large dry-land wheat farm where they also fed out a couple hundred steers a year. We learned a lot, mainly that we didn't want to stay there, but that we definitely wanted to farm and live in the country! Next was Colorado, more experience but Colorado is more of a resort state (and was too expensive). So we came to Idaho, first to King

Hill. There we worked for a large rancher, we had our own place back up in a beautiful canyon. My husband learned a lot about flood irrigation and all about calves. The man ran about 3,000 head of cows and calves. Then we moved to Indian Valley, Idaho, and more ranch work.

"Anyway, after five years of hard-earned experience and below poverty wages we felt like we were ready to work our own place. We spent about a year looking for just the right place, it had to be perfect, including the fact that whoever sold us the place would have to help us finance it. After working that many years for farmers and ranchers averaging about 50¢ an hour there wasn't much chance of saving a down payment. We did manage to collect most of the things necessary to a small homestead, a couple of milk cows and goats, chickens, rabbits, horses and all the things I needed for my part. A good tiller for my garden that I paid for by custom tilling, a large canning pressure cooker and a good butter churn, etc.

"We went to FHA and they were willing to finance us because of our experience and we found our place and the people that own it have helped us with a personal loan. So in about two months we take possession of the place. We got a really good deal on the place and only 5%-6% interest on the land and personal loans. But still we will be doing everything we can in order to make payments. My husband has a full-time job working for the county, he operates the grader, plowing snow in winter and fixing roads during the summer. The hours are fairly flexible and when they are steady it's only during the summer. I will be driving the school bus, there are only six children going to school from our valley and it's only 27 miles to school so I will have plenty of time. So we have two salaries plus the sale of steers, plus my husband's shoeing and breaking and training a few horses each summer."

I've gotten another letter from Linda since this one. They are moved in on their new farm and things are going real good for them.

Isaiah E. Nucleus wrote me a little about homesteading in Arizona:

"Here in southern Arizona there are some very special demands if you are ever to get anything to grow. Hopefully, we have a good crop of melons in the making here, but it has been unusually difficult to grow here in the Southwest this year. This is a part of the nation where so many people have been drawn because of climate, to come back to the land only to find that a long period of sunshine doesn't necessarily prove a boon to growing. The special problems here of soil and basically man-applied waterings have caused many of my neighbors to quit in disgust. The lessons are hard learnt. I watched helplessly this year while a visiting group of hungry Mexican beetles devoured a half-acre of beans in a few days then departed, at least they didn't eat my melons too. I find it embarrassing not to be able to order a copy of your fantastic book, but I'm writing this letter on a borrowed typewriter and raising two girls, 8 and 9, on a farm never seems to leave much excess other than love and happiness."

Isaiah is hanging in there but he's right—it isn't all easy and there are some that do give up or don't like it. Alaska is one of the toughest places. The pipeline building has caused such an influx there that housing is practically nonexistent and prices are higher than ever. The Alaska Homestead Act is no longer in existence, so if you want a place you've got to buy it.

The homestead problem I hear about most often from wives newly moved from city to country is loneliness—*desperate* loneliness. The problem husbands most dread and most often encounter is joblessness and general money shortage. If you give up it will probably be because of one of these two—or both. Darlene LaDow wrote me this letter: "Two and a half years ago, my husband and I decided to give up a comfortable suburban life (home and job) and move to Orcas Island, Eastsound, Washington, in the Straits of San Juan de Fuca. Island living had a lot of pros and cons. Our four children loved and feared the place (aged 12-13-14-15). We were terribly lonely. Meaningful work escaped us. We decided to leave after only 6 months."

The U.S. Census Department says the biggest growth areas are the upper Great Lakes of Michigan, Wisconsin and Minnesota, the Rocky Mountains, the southern Appalachia coalfields and the Ozark-Ouachita areas. All good places—but there are others, too.

One friend of mine is homesteading in Mexico. She wrote me such a useful and interesting letter about it that I'm going to print it here in case some of you could profit by her information.

"About homesteading in Mexico. There's one problem and it is acquiring land. It is a little hard for a 'gringo' to buy land in Mexico, unless a relative or good friend is a Mexican citizen. My husband's father was born here in a Mormon colony so he's a citizen of both countries and this farm is in his name. You can become a citizen (quickly) but I think it costs a little (at least $1,000).

"We are located 100 miles (roadwise) southeast of Douglas, Arizona, and as far as the road goes—it takes about 4 to 6 hours to get here, depending on the condition of the road (they grade it every once in a while when the rains wash parts of it away) and how fast you drive. Taxes are no problem here. I think our taxes for the farm are about $10 or $20 a year. You can do just about anything you want on your property. When my sister's little boy died last year, they buried him on the farm here. The Mexican officials didn't like it very much when they found out but wrote us out a permit to have a family cemetery here. It is easier in the long run to buy equipment and so forth here in Mexico (if they have it) because you can't bring a lot of items across the border unless you fork over the money. Schools are a problem if your kids don't know Spanish. Some of our boys have picked up quite a bit working with the help. We would have to provide transportation if we wanted to send them to San Miguel schools. Actually we teach our own here. I think they would rather us send them to school in San Miguel (8 miles away), but they haven't given us any trouble so far.

"The soil here is very good. We had a sample taken and all it lacked was a little iron. The pigweed will grow as high as 8 to 10 feet with a trunk of 3 to 4 inches diameter. We are on the Bavispe River and the land all along the river for miles is rich silt. Lumber is cheaper here but very rough. Adobes are the cheapest way to build, also good insulation, but they crumble and wash away after a few years. We have rigged up a big oven for burning the adobes and can do 3,000 at a time. It takes 36 hours of heat. They come out a nice rust color brick. Each adobe weighs about 40 pounds. They are about 12 x 15 inches and 4 inches thick. Wages are cheap; the standard wage for men is 30 pesos a day which is $2.40. You can probably get a maid for about $1 a day. The temperature doesn't go much under 15°-20° in the winter. Snow is very rare. It gets a little hot in the summer, but we have rain in June, July and August and it cools down. The last frost is usually in April—sometimes one in May. The first frost in the fall is usually in November, sometimes the end of October. Some crops can be grown year-round such as the cole vegetables. You can sell your crops and most of what you grow for more than farmers in the United States get for theirs.

"We have cows, chickens, pigs, and have just started raising geese. (They roost on our porch every night—ick—we have to get some fencing to keep them in the orchard.) We have about 30 big peach trees that are producing lots of peaches. We have also started an apple orchard and vineyard, also a few pear, plum, pecan, cherry, orange, lemon and grapefruit trees. I hope they all do well here.

"Coming back to citizenship. Some of our children have been born here—so we can put deeds, etc., in their name if we have to. My father-in-law is 75 years old but still does a full day's work."

A SURVEY OF HOMESTEAD POSSIBILITIES

(Assuming You Have No Electricity, Gas or Running Water)

If you're living in a tent first you need sleeping cover, clothes, food, water, dishes. A place to build your fire and plenty of fuel for all stages of it. Then a worktable—like a plank between two stumps. Anything that can be cooked in frying pans, kettles or reflector ovens can be managed with a campfire. But stick to the simple ingredients and simple procedures because you didn't bring your kitchen. If you have to do all your cooking over an open fire you especially need one or two cast-iron frying pans, a Dutch oven, a coffeepot and big pan to heat dish and washing water in.

If you have to haul water to your site get as much per trip as you can by using the biggest containers you can find. In addition, rig all your buildings with good metal gutters set up to drain into prepared containers. Keep a separate cistern for this rainwater which you can collect whenever feasible and use it for washing. If the rainwater is dirty just strain it through several thicknesses of cloth. Use biodegradable soaps and then you can take your used wash water and pour it on your garden plants.

If you have a baby where you are cooking over an open fire, nurse it if you possibly can. If you can't sometimes you may have to use your own body as a bottle warmer when you are caught without a fire. Put the bottle inside your clothes between your breasts if they are ample enough for the job or inside your belt tight against your body. That will at least take the chill off the milk if you are warm-blooded. Fix a bottle and take it to bed with you to keep it warm if you expect a night feeding when the fire will be out. Use the tight cap and put the nipple on only when you're ready to feed to prevent leakage. SMA formula keeps sweet a lot better than regular milk under these conditions. If you've never nursed a baby and want more information (mother's milk is the healthiest!) write La Leche League International, 9616 Minneapolis Avenue, Franklin Park, Illinois 60131, which will send free pamphlets to answer your questions—and Karen Pryor's book *Nursing Your Baby* which you can mail-order from La Leche League for $1.75 or from Pocket Books, Department 59, 1 West 39th Street, New York, New York 10018.

Honest I do believe in nursing your own baby if you can. And most mothers have a tendency to give up too easy and the same for doctors and nurses, who are supposed to be helping you. Breast milk is the perfect formula, perfect temperature, perfect amount if all is well, and provides natural immunities to certain diseases. It helps space babies, it's convenient—and a lovely experience. I've had a number of letters taking me to task for apparently not always nursing my

babies. I started all five on the breast. The first weaned herself. I had to go away for 24 hours (should have taken her but I didn't realize). When I came back she had already gotten used to a bottle and refused the breast. I was broken-hearted. The second I nursed for 7 months. I was under great stress at the time and during the latter months couldn't make enough milk. That was Danny. He wouldn't take a bottle or a pacifier. He never did once. I had to nurse him. I finally got him onto a cup but by then damage was done to my right breast. He had strained so hard so much trying to get out milk that just wasn't there, that I developed a chronic abscess that returned with each of my three subsequent lactations. Nursing on that side was sheer agony. And yet I hung in for at least the first six weeks to make sure I had the baby safely started before I put it on the bottle. Danny's growth was stunted by his shortage of milk as an infant, and I'm lying here writing this with my right breast swathed in bandages after having had a tumor removed that probably developed off that old abscess. I wish I had known more about bottles and formulas that second lactation. Most mothering seems to be learned by experience in an atmosphere of crisis.

If you are eating out of the grocery store except for some wild foraging like daily fish catches, when fall comes and days get shorter and shorter and colder and colder what has been wonderful will become more and more miserable. Summer is manageable just about anywhere. It's the other three seasons, especially winter, that you want to really *prepare for*. You have to prepare to keep warm and to keep fed. These great wild food forage types would have pretty lean pickings outdoors in February.

MEAT—Without electricity to run a deep freeze you can't keep meat frozen except if you live where there is a really bad winter. Anywhere else your outside temperature will be freezing sometimes but then you'll get off-season thaws, too. So you'll have to either rent a locker in a nearby town, which doesn't cost much, or you'll have to can most of your meat after butchering. You can "corn" any meat by an old-time type recipe and have it keep, but the concentration of salt and nitrites and nitrates in the corned meat is so high that I don't think you'd want to live on that exclusively. You can also dry the meat in small strips—jerky. But again it isn't as tasty or chewable as canned meat. You may can any type of meat. Just bone it out first. Directions in detail for all this is later on in the book. For variety, you can make mincemeat at the beginning of the cool season and it will keep during the winter months in an outdoor place. Depending on the coolness of your climate, November or later should be killing time for the big animals like cow or elk. The cold weather will refrigerate the meat enough to keep it while you're getting it canned up. Small animals such as chickens and rabbits are good summer meat because you can kill them the morning of any day you plan to eat them.

VEGETABLES—You may can them or keep them in a root cellar. Cabbage and cucumbers pickle very well. But you can only stand so much pickled stuff in your diet. And a root cellar isn't right for *all* vegetables. Onions will go bad in it. They need to be braided or bunched or dried and put in an onion-type bag and hung someplace airy and dry. Squash and pumpkins need dry air too and not to be piled up. If they are touching one another they go bad faster. I keep squash, pumpkins and onions in the attic or in our bedroom, the squash and pumpkins spread out on the floor and the onions boxed or hung up.

Some sources recommend leaving root vegetables in the ground all winter. It never has worked for me. When I needed them the garden was always either so mucky I would sink to my neck or else frozen so solid that the prospect of a carrot was hopeless without a blowtorch. For special information on ways to keep each particular kind of vegetable check in the Vegetables chapter. You can dry vegetables too, and if you do it right they turn out delicious.

FRUIT is the easiest and most versatile type of food in its primitive preserving possibilities. You can store apples as long as you manage to keep them cold but not frozen. That requires a real weather sense, but the results are worth the trouble because crisp fresh apples are such a treat when all the other food is secondhand out of jars and so on. Lots on keeping apples in the Sweets chapter. You may also can whole fruit or fruit sauces, which means mashed fruit, or fruit butters which are sweetened, mashed, cooked down fruit, or jams and jellies which are fruit flavored sugar, but I'd go easy on that. You can preserve fruit by spicing and brandying which is in Sours, but you can't eat very much of it like that. You can dry fruit and it is just delicious, keeps well and is easy to do in the first place for most kinds of fruit. More detailed directions for all this stuff are later on. Apples and plums are the most trouble-free fruits to raise. Apricots and berries next. It takes about seven years to get a standard apple tree really going. But a well-established orchard bears loads of fruit for years and years even with no attention at all.

MILK will really be important to you because it will be a "fresh" food in the off-season. But the natural season for milk is spring and summer so if you want winter milk you've got to plan carefully ahead and breed goats in June for November kidding or breed cows in January for October freshening. You should have plenty of extras, too, because your cow or goat could get mastitis or have twins (or quadruplets in the case of a goat) or get run over. In fact, if you have only one animal something like that is almost certain to happen. And you've got to have plenty of good winter feed for the milk producers. You can easily make cheese from cow's or goat's milk and butter from cow's milk. (Butter from goat's milk is not so easy.) Your hard cheese will keep fine. It may mold on the outside but the inside is OK. Butter can be preserved in saltwater if you have extra. Without refrigeration you may be concerned about milk souring. You need a big milk supply so that you won't need to store milk. You can feed the extra milk to pigs or chickens. You can figure one sow per cow or several little pigs. If you want to make cheese you can still feed the leftover whey to them. There is lots of food value still in the whey. But remember if you are going to feed milk to chickens, it must be soured first. The real old-timers maintained their chickens on soured milk rather than the grain or chicken feed we give them nowadays. But they were very careful not to give them sweet milk since they believed it would cause indigestion and throw off the egg production.

EGGS—Without electric lights and special heat, hens won't lay much in wintertime. (Ducks will though—the Khaki Campbell breed.) But from very early spring on through fall they should lay well for you, and you can store extra eggs in water glass for winter use. (See the Dairy chapter.) That's what I do. They store fine under water glass raw in the shell. Only problem is the price of water glass keeps going up. The chickens will keep laying longer if they are confined to a chicken house or barn and don't get their feet chilled. And remember that in very cold weather, when everything is frozen, you should take them (as well as the rabbits) *warm* water twice a day or at least once so they can have a drink. The way I like to get more chickens is just let the hens set that want to and go ahead and raise a family. The hens can do a much better job of raising chickens than I can. That way you don't need special feed for the chicks.

GRAIN, BEANS—It's not easy to raise grain the old fashioned way. But it sure does store easy. And then all you need is a grinder and a stove to make bread. Store grains in mouseproof containers. Mice will gnaw through paper or cloth. Not that I'm against sharing with a mouse in principle. But when one dies in the grain sack, it makes you feel funny about eating the flour afterwards.

CAMPFIRE COOKING—There are whole books written on this subject from how to start a fire and where to start it on through—there's a real art to it and nine-tenths of it is practice. The easiest way is to import a wood cook stove, set it up in your camp and use *that*. Gather wood on dry days and store it under shelter for wet ones. You can do this in a semipermanent camp. If you're living on the trail do this: Lay a little mound of really flammable dry stuff in an open place, on dirt or sand if you can, and away from dry brush or grass. (Please don't start a forest fire!) Like very loosely wadded toilet paper or the wrappers off tin cans or one of my book brochures crumpled up. Paper doesn't burn good flat. You've got to get air in there. Or dry grass. Now make a tipi of very slender dry sticks over that and then bigger and bigger ones that you can add later. Use three matches bunched together to start the fire. To fry try to have time enough to let a good roaring blaze burn down to coals. When desperate though you can fry on a flame. Have a circle of big flat-topped rocks around the outside of your fire circle. They will help hold the heat. To stew just make a place for your kettle down in there among the rocks. Don't use pans with handles that will burn.

BAKING—A reflector oven, or Dutch oven in a hole (see Cast-Iron Cookware section, later in this chapter) or build a mud oven. If you have clay soil it's a natural. Start by building a strong, dome-shaped frame of willow branches and sticks about 2 feet wide by 3 feet long. Cover your branch canopy with a layer of mud 6 inches to 1 foot thick. Leave a large square opening at one end to be your oven door and at the top opposite end insert a large tin can that is open at both ends and that will be your chimney. After the mud is completely dry build a fire inside and burn out all your wooden framework. Cool and scrape the insides clean. To bake in your mud oven, first build a fire inside it and heat the mud to red hot. Then rake out the fire and put in your sourdough bread, or bannocks, or stew or roast. Close the door with a slab of flat rock and it should bake wonderfully.

READING—If you are expecting to do some really primitive living you need lots of other help besides this book. Get a subscription to the *Mother Earth News* by sending $10 for one year ($12 in Canada) to P.O. Box 70, Hendersonville, North Carolina 28739. The magazine comes out six times a year and has been getting better ever since it started. There is really detailed information in every issue and they are very conscious of these kinds of problems. You can also write them for *Mother's Bookshelf*, a catalog of do-it-yourself, survival and self-sufficient-type books.

Countryside is a wonderfully clean-cut and thoroughly sensible homesteaders' magazine. They print letters from people and have experts to answer your questions in the pages of the magazine. I highly recommend it. Especially good on goats, poultry, rabbits and such. Subscription rates are one year for $9, two for $16, three for $23 ($1 a year higher if you live in Canada). Write to Jerry Belanger, Route 1, Box 239, Waterloo, Wisconsin 53594. Jerry also has a homestead supply mail-order business called the General Store.

John Shuttleworth, the creative genius and hard driver behind the *Mother Earth News*, Jerry Belanger, who is the creative genius and hard driver behind *Countryside* and I, whoever I am and whatever I am, are all the same age—36 as of this writing. That's a curious thing. The other big important magazine in the homestead field is *Organic Gardening* put out by Rodale Press. You can find your first copy of that at any health-food store. A one-year subscription is $7.85 from 33 East Minor Street, Emmaus, Pennsylvania 18049.

If I had to name categories, I'd say read *Organic Gardening* for your garden, *Countryside* for your animals and the *Mother Earth News* for homemade housing, alternative energy and such kinds of thing.

Organic Gardening was there way, way the first. It has maybe 300 plus employees in their publishing house and all and a nice new brick building at Emmaus, Pennsylvania with a big parking lot. *Mother Earth News* has about 60 employees headquartered in the basement of a defunct hosiery factory in Hendersonville, North Carolina, another small town. Jerry has seven people upstairs and downstairs in a little shop on Main Street in Waterloo, Wisconsin. He started out ten years ago with eight pages every other month.

There are lots of other little magazines, one for each topic, and I'll mention them as I come to them—like the *American Bee Journal*, *Chinchilla World* and the *American Pigeon Journal*.

Here are some good catalogs for homesteaders:

Herter's, Inc.
Route 1
Waseca, Minnesota 56093
Send $1 for their 629-page catalog. Mostly hunting and fishing supplies.

Cumberland General Store
Route 3, Box 479
Crossville, Tennessee 38555
Send $3 for their 250-page *Wish and Want Book*.

Nasco
901 Janesville Avenue
Fort Atkinson, Wisconsin 53538
Three *big* catalogs: *Agricultural Sciences, Arts and Crafts, Farm and Ranch Catalog*.

Maid of Scandinavia Company
3244 Raleigh Avenue
Minneapolis, Minnesota 55416
Free color wish book—kitchen supplies.

Garden Way Publishing Co.
Charlotte, Vermont 05445
Book catalog and homestead supply catalog too.

Sears, Roebuck & Co.
Doesn't mail catalogs any more—too expensive. But you can pick one up at a Sears store when they are in.

Montgomery Ward & Co.
To get on their catalog list you must make a minimum number of orders over a 6-month period.

HOW TO PINCH A PENNY

Don't buy land until you've landed a steady job within reasonable commuting distance, or otherwise have income you're sure of. Less than 40 miles is what I used to say, but since the price and availability of gas has become a problem, I'd say 20 or less now. Don't buy anything new if you can help it. Write what you need on a list and then watch and wait. You probably don't need all that anyway. Never buy on impulse. Buy only what's on your list. If you see something you like, go home and think about it. If it was really that good, you can put it on next month's list. Attend auctions, yard sales, go to secondhand stores. If you can't find a bargain, wait.

Buy out of season, that's fall for animals. Because everybody is trying to buy them in the spring when the grass is bursting out all over, but people don't want the expense and bother of feeding and caring for them through winter. It's winter, too, for gardening and farming equipment. In the summer hunt for stoves and heaters and your winter fuel supply. Learn to scavenge junkyards.

Buy your vehicles used and learn enough mechanics to keep them running. Shop auto junkyards for used parts when you have breakdowns. Possibly $200 should do it for a pickup and $150 for a car. Then don't risk that precious heap with cross-country adventure. Stay home.

You don't need an automatic washer unless you have many children. You can wash by hand. You don't need a dryer at all—a clothesline will do in summer with a clothesrack standing near the stove or lines in the basement for winter. Learn to patch. You don't need new sheets. Learn to sleep between patched ones or between blankets. Stop washing so much and using bleach and machine drying and all your clothes will last longer. You don't need a freezer. You could can it all. Advertise for used jars. You don't need an electric stove or oil heater if you have dead trees on the place and wood burners are cheaper to get or make (out of an oil drum). You don't have to have a telephone. Use postcards.

Buy your rototiller used in the dead of winter when prices are down. Or cheaper yet, spade your garden to break up the clods, then rake. Then hoe to keep the weeds down. Don't buy a snowthrower. Stay home when it's that bad or take the time to tunnel by hand. Don't buy buildings—build them and buy your material used. Scout around and you'll find where to get used 2 x 4's, used cement blocks, used tin sheets for roofing and siding and used bricks. You can mix and lay your own cement, or tear down somebody's unwanted old building in return for the materials.

Get animals that can forage and reproduce themselves like Chinese white geese, goats and Banty chickens. Don't buy purebred, registered stuff. It isn't worth the extra price in your situation. Learn to live off what you can raise and to raise what you want to live off. Plan ahead for several cash crops (in case one or two fail) because you can't make it without cash. A good job is the most reliable "cash crop." Buy cheap and sell dear. But don't take handouts. You'd be destroying the very heart of what you're trying to accomplish. There's certainly something you're willing to do or can do that nobody else around is willing to do or can do and that's your marketable asset that you can put up for sale. If it turns out to be mopping floors or ironing for people—fine. I spent a good bit of my life first doing housework for people, later ironing for them. It's a lot more prideful than being on welfare and better for your God-given soul.

It's getting harder all the time to be poor but honorable though. And I think this country needs to do some hard rethinking about the value of appearances. I drive around and see suburbs that are supposed to be the ultimate in quality living. But what I really see is a lot of expensive houses covering the earth that the people only spend a little time in. And I see nonstop manicured lawns, front and back. What is a lawn? It's grass that no animal is going to eat occupying ground where no vegetable, berry or fruit is going to grow. I drive around looking for a garden and only occasionally do I see one—and invariably it's in the backyard as if using the ground to grow food instead of that cosmetic grass is almost a shameful thing. I've heard there are city laws that sometimes say you *have* to have a lawn or say you can't keep rabbits or chickens on your land. I think that is wrong. I think it's making people slaves to an unreal standard of appearance that says everybody has got to look rich. It is as far away from the realities as possible, denying the fact that we live by God's gifts of food born from the plants that grow in ground, nurtured by manure, by food from animals that have given birth so they will make milk to feed their babies—and ours, and who give their extra males to be our meat nurturing us as we have nurtured them.

You don't need a chain saw right now. There's bound to be somebody around that has one already and will make wood with you on halves for the help. You don't need a power mower. You're not in the suburbs. Get a hand mower or picket a goat in the yard or just let it grow. You don't need to paint the inside of the house. Wash the walls. There are lots of women who would accept even living in a tent to get started living in the country. I spent a summer in one once and it's a very happy memory. With the money saved (that would have been rent) by the tent living, I was able to buy a very small trailer to live in by the time really cold weather came.

Once somebody would have given you a start in Banty chickens and a couple kid goats to raise if you made friends and were sincere. Now so many people are trying to get started with them that they've become scarce and expensive. Rabbits are still easy to come by though. Neighbors will give you starts of horseradish, strawberries, raspberries, Egyptian onions and lots of other perennials if you'll let them know ahead of time in early spring and late fall when they are digging the excessive growth out of their gardens. If they don't give it away they'll be throwing it away and they'd just as soon give it away. Baby rabbits shouldn't cost more than a dollar each. You only need two. They are as prolific as the tradition says. Baby pigs are fairly cheap, too. Feed the farm animals your leftovers and get out and scrounge for them too. Offer to take away neighbor families' garbage and they may save it for you if they don't have animals of their own. You may have to do without dogs and cats so you won't have to feed them. Help somebody with his haying in return for some hay. He'll be happy to save on the cash outlay.

The theme song of all this is—take what somebody else doesn't want and with a little extra effort make it work. And do the job yourself.

If you are making a change from the city to the country bring all the city money with you that you can. Jobs are easier to find in the city and wages are much higher. But buy in the country because prices for goods and labor if you are paying for it are cheaper there. Prices for scarce goods are often cheaper right in my little country grocery store in Kendrick than they are in bigger Moscow or Lewiston, 27 miles away. You wouldn't expect it to be that way but for some reason it is. That's assuming you're buying in the regular places the local people patronize and not those that depend on tourist trade which are invariably expensive.

To become a homesteader is to become a curious combination of poor and rich. You'll be poor in loose cash but richer than you ever were before because you'll have a piece of earth that is *yours*. You probably look destitute. This isn't hard for young couples but for older couples trying to make the change it isn't easy to move from an urban middle class to a rural lower class along with all the rest of the culture shock involved. It hurts to look poor and know everybody else is thinking that.

I remember once on a trip to buy goats when I was pregnant, accompanied by three little ones, and had accidentally donned one of my boots and one of Mike's, which of course didn't in the least match, and was generally dressed for animals rather than people. We stopped at a little restaurant along the highway to eat. A wonderfully neat and scrubbed and uptight-looking couple with two little uptight-looking children were at the table next to us and the husband kept looking at us. When I went up to pay my bill the restaurant man told me that that man, who had already left with his family, had paid it for us. I was embarrassed and furious. I wanted to run after him and explain that although I might look poor it was for that reason that I wasn't really poor. That he had his big new car and the next month's rent on his apartment in town but we had 115 acres and a growing flock of goats and money enough to buy an occasional meal along the road too. And happy healthy children who knew how to clamber up a mountain just like the goats, yell like hooligans, and how to put a seed under the dirt just like you're saying a prayer, and on and on and on like that. But he was already gone.

The restaurant man wouldn't accept my money or take it in case he ever came back and my boots indeed didn't match. There was nothing to do but go on down the road and get the new goats.

WHEN IT GETS VERY COLD

You, me, and everybody else could get along with a lot less heat if we had to. When you heat with wood the fire goes out in the stove or fireplace after you go to bed. I was raised that way and I live that way. There are ways to keep warm and in this section I'm passing on all the ones that I can think of. The only risk you run with having the heat off at night is your water freezing. If you leave it running a little it won't do that either because running water doesn't freeze up.

BATHING UNDER PRIMITIVE CONDITIONS—Use your clothes boiler for baths. Or a big galvanized tin tub. That's what my mother used. Once a week in winter is enough. My father used to say that more winter bathing than that was unhealthy for the skin. Be that as it may, in winter when you're heating with one wood stove in a tent or cabin the children do run a risk of colds every time you give them a bath. To miminize the risk don't bathe children at all under those conditions if they have any sign of a cold, even if it goes on and on. The dirt won't harm them really (and here I know I'm taking on the entire national force of public health nurses!), but a chill almost certainly will worsen their cold. Instead just spot wash them when and where needed—face, hands and privates. When you're ready to bathe them, heat the kitchen, heat the water, and then run them through the tub one at a time with a good scrubbing and no lingering. You can rinse them with a tea kettle or pitcher just as they are ready to step out of the tub. Then into a thick dry towel for a brisk drying off and back into warm clothes pronto.

SICKNESS—Winter is also sickness time for children. Have a copy of Doctor Spock and a flashlight or something on hand to read it by. Crises always happen in the middle of the night, usually Saturday night (unless you have a Seventh-Day Adventist doctor in which case it would be Friday night). And make sure the children have all their D.P.T. shots as soon as possible. Whooping cough is very much around masquerading as a cold that hangs on and on in children who have not been immunized against it. Even very small babies can get it. If they do, there is nothing doctors can give you to help. The disease takes at least two months to run its course (and usually until spring), and you're fighting for the baby's life every night of that. Only faithful, careful, tireless nursing can pull the infant through, and maybe not even that. You must get up with the child every time he coughs, which will be about every 15 minutes all night long and every time he naps, during this illness. Don't worry about him getting thin. It's the lesser evil since solid food and rich liquids like milk and milk soups—more than a few sips—are quite likely to be thrown up and cause choking when they mix with the very heavy phlegm that marks this disease. Noncaffeinated soda pop like 7-Up will be easiest on his stomach. Exposure to draft or chilling will immediately worsen whooping cough or set back any improvement.

MMM—By a year old get the child immunized against 10-day measles, German measles and mumps. You can get all three in one shot. That's much easier than struggling through both kinds of measles which children almost certainly will get sooner or later if you don't have them immunized against it.

Croup will show up sooner or later. Spock has very good directions for dealing with it. For at least three nights after a definite croup have the child sleep near enough so you will be sure to wake up if he gets in trouble again. It can return unexpectedly in the wee small hours. If its return is a possibility, be prepared before you go to bed. Leave pans of water on the stove and a good fire going so there will be steam to hold the child's head over. Keep him dry and warm.

CLOTHING—A friend of mine wears homemade quilted britches for cold mornings out. She cuts them out of an old blanket of flannel, a little larger than for regular sewing. Then she puts the patches on the separated pieces until they are covered like a quilt. Then sews up her seams and adds a draw string for a belt. Keep children in plenty of dry clothes. Long underwear is a good idea. Long heavy panty hose for girls if they are wearing dresses. Get quick at clothes changing or learn to do it in bed.

CHANGING BABIES—To keep from having to change (and chill) the babies so often use two or three cloth diapers at once rather than just one. Be sure and wash them only in a very mild soap and rinse well. These extra diapers are also good insurance against them having wet outer clothes and are espe-

cially needed at night. If your baby is still soaking through into his clothes and bedding at night you'll just have to train yourself to wake up and change him as often as necessary to keep him warm and dry. Stake out a warm spot near the stove and set it up for your diaper changing area. Have everything ready so you can work very fast. A big thick rug near the heat stove will do. You can lay the baby there, kneel by him and do the job.

SLEEPING—Be sure and keep the small children's feet covered. "Zoot suits" make it easy. These woolly "blanket sleepers," as Montgomery Ward's calls them, are the best thing I know. They cover a child from neck to toe. I buy the heaviest weight I can get. For extra cold weather give them socks, pants and a T-shirt inside the zoot suit. If it's colder than that at night, or if you have a child who doesn't stay under his covers, put two or even three zoot suits on him at bedtime (or daytime), one right on top of another. If you have the hairless variety or a child that's very prone to head colds or earaches, rig up a nightcap. You can use a sweat shirt with a hood or a soft bonnet that ties under the chin, but not too tight.

Bed wetting is a real problem. Housebreak in the spring and if you haven't won out by fall go back to diapers for the rest of the winter. If they're too big for diapers but still wetting the bed cover the mattress with plastic and dry the bedding every day (no use trying to wash it every day). When the child wakes up and cries because his sleeping clothes and bed are wet just help him out of the wet clothes, into something dry (be prepared) and bed him back down with his head at the other end of the bed or pull off the wet sheets and put him between some blankets and don't make yourself or the child miserable over it. It happens more to mothers than they'll admit. Most of them I think.

Mike wears long underwear to bed when it gets awfully cold and so do I. We use sheet blankets for everybody. Montgomery Ward's has them. Have plenty of bedding and let the little ones sleep two by two or more. They help keep each other warm as well as cheerful. In cold weather you can easily fit six children into a double bed because they instinctively make themselves small and cuddle up. In summer they'll spread out and need more bed space. Being miserably cold a lot of the day is manageable if you can sleep snugly warm at night. If you have a big thick rug on the floor by the heat stove the children will naturally go there to dress in the morning and fall asleep at night. Use lots of heavy, thick blankets and quilts on the bed.

HOT WATER—Keep a kettle on the stove and you can warm bottles whenever you need them by just setting them in the hot water. They'll be ready very quickly. An infant can stand a lot of cold if he's kept warmly wrapped and is accustomed to it and gets warm milk in his tummy. But don't feed him cold milk, and keep him out of drafts. You can train yourself to wake up and put more fuel in the stove when needed.

When making hot water for any purpose—baths, dishes, clothes washing, shampoos—boil water in your usual container. Then pour hot water until your working pan is partly full and add cold from the cold supply until you have the combined temperature just right. That way you can make the most of your pan space and not use up all your hot water at once, get just the temperature you want.

THE FIRE BUILDER in cold weather is every morning's hero. It's usually the mother. See the Wood Cook Stove section for more on this.

CLEAR TO THE LAST RESORT—If you're still building your house consider insulating the roof and walls. If you're cold and don't have heavy thermal drapes that can completely cover your windows hang blankets over them (heavy army type). Wave your hand slowly around the suspicious areas like around the sides of your windows and above and below your doors to find out where the cold drafts are coming in, and then plug those holes by tacking or taping newspaper or plastic over windows and add an insulating lining to the door. Storm windows on the outside of windows really help insulate. If you don't have the regular glass kind improvise by nailing a layer of heavy clear plastic over the outside of all windows. Tack it down all the way around the edges with cardboard or thin wood strips. We do this every fall and take it off every spring. With the plastic storm windows on the outside and curtains on the inside not much heat is lost. If you don't have an enclosed porch storm doors also really help hold in your heat. Make sure the storm doors have good springs so they will stay tightly shut. If you haven't a door to the pantry or closets hang a blanket or plastic curtain over the openings.

You don't need but one door in wintertime. Seal off the others and you'll save heat. A Billings, Montana, lady (where it really gets cold) wrote me a great "dire emergency" method for sealing doors and windows that let cold in around the edges. She said to tear cloth strips, wring them out in water and poke in those drafty cracks. As they freeze they will expand and make a perfect seal. Frances E. Render is her name and she says she has used this trick "on the north side during temperatures of 30°-40° below with a strong wind and it worked great!" It helps to have a porch-type enclosure outside with one operating door. Seal off as many infrequently used rooms as you can for the duration of the cold weather. Keep the bedroom doors shut so you don't have to heat these rooms during the daytime. Close off the bathroom and only heat it when needed. You can put a little electric heater in there if you have electricity and turn it on only when someone will be in there awhile.

If you did all these things and your fire is burning fine, by now you ought to be feeling warmer. If getting firewood is a problem have you considered burning newspapers? You can roll them up tightly and make your own sort of presto log. (You can make a sort of blanket out of them too for the bed.) Check your damper to make sure it's closed and you aren't losing heat up the chimney. If your heat stove is in the kitchen, a nice wide high doorway (about twice or more the usual width) with no door, of course, will help heat circulate into an adjoining room where you want it—like your living room.

STILL COLD? How about the Eskimo technique for keeping warm. Wear lots of clothes always, eat rich food and take a dog to bed—a nice furry variety. If you're still cold, take two dogs to bed, or three . . . If you're still cold—get married! If that doesn't do it I give up!

OF WASHING

DISHES—I don't buy metal scratch pads. The soap in them is too strong and the metal causes fine grooves in my pans that eggs and such delicate things will stick in. I can do the tough jobs with a combination of soaking, a spatula and my fingernails. I don't dry dishes. I rinse them in very hot water—use a ladle to get them out. Then stack on the drain rack and let them dry themselves. Except for the ironware. It needs a special drying to prevent rusting.

CLOTHES—I wear old clothes—pants and tops. I'm not really proud of it. I wish I could wear dresses. I used to wear bib overalls. They're even less attractive but handier. I can bring back three dozen eggs in my pockets from a foray into the hayloft or carry a batch of baby chicks home in those many deep pockets. Whatever the outfit, it's important that I can drop to my knees for a spurt of weeding in the garden without worrying about either my knees or my clothes. They are cool in summer and cover me in all the right places I need to be covered for climbing over fences or into fruit trees or under the house. I don't think it makes good sense to buy clothes that have to be sent to a cleaner. I often do think what fun it would be to have old fashioned long cotton gowns to wear and I do wear long dresses to Church and for any other excuse to dress up.

AND DIRT—The modern philosophy seems to be that you wear a garment part of one day and then put it in the wash. It wasn't so in the good old days. Clothes were washed when they were dirty, really dirty. The frequent machine washing takes a toll on our clothes, especially the automatic dryer. That's where all that "lint" comes from—you have that much less clothes, towels, and bedding. My mother wanted day clothes to be carefully folded and laid out to wear again the next day. She wanted night clothes folded and put under the pillow for wearing again the next night—until wash day. Aprons covered dresses and were only whisked away as company knocked on the door. There were Sabbath clothes which were not allowed to get dirty and everyday ones which were not expected to be clean.

WASHING BY HAND—If you're washing diapers by hand use diaper liners or some kind of water absorbent paper to keep the glob of glop from really getting into the cloth. And do it every morning first thing after breakfast so you'll have it done and out of the way. To wash dishes or clothes, heat the water first and have lots, if possible, so you can change frequently. In the old days "washing" clothes meant boiling them—which is also a technique for agitation when you think about it. You can boil dirty dish towels with a little lye as a matter of routine. When the wash water gets dirty use the rinse water for wash water and get new rinse water.

Otherwise soap and washboard with lots of water as hot as your hands can stand it and then the elbow grease does it or use a plunger in the bathtub. A rubber toilet-type plunger is actually easier on the clothes and still gets them clean. Rinse in at least two waters to get as much of the soap out as you can. Then wring out the water by twisting each piece to squeeze it out. Then hang up to dry. For drying, a clothesline made of rope or wire stretched high between two points is handiest. You can just throw the clothes over on a calm summer day. But if the wind is blowing or the sun not hot or if you are trying to dry indoors you had better use clothespins so you can hang the clothes out with as few doublings as possible. If you're using clothespins to hang clothes out in the dead of winter dipping them in saltwater first will keep them from freezing to the clothes. Or dry indoors on a clothesline or on fold-up racks.

FLAT IRONS—The old fashioned irons were meant to be heated on the top of your range or else kept heated by hot coals put into a hollow chamber inside the iron. To iron with flat irons you need two or more so one can be heating while you are ironing with the other. But as far as I'm concerned the best way to handle the ironing problem is to keep everybody in the kind of clothes that don't require ironing—Levis and sweat shirts and the long underwear!

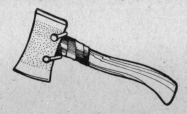

FIREWOOD
(And Posts)

February is an awful time to be out scouting for wood. The wood is best gotten during the fine dry days of midsummer and early fall, cut, and stored under shelter inside a shed or at least under a tarp. If you have two buildings close together you can roof over the gap with tin sheets or something cheap, put a back on it and have a very adequate woodshed.

HOW TO FALL A TREE—This is dangerous if you aren't experienced so go cautiously. Find the one you want. Standing *dead* tamarack, red fir, or black pine are the best in this part of the country. White and yellow pine are fairly good. Cedar's good for a hot quick fire to set off harder woods but it doesn't last. Bull pine, white fir or any spruce are not very good firewood but will do if you can't find anything else. It's ideal to find a snag (dead tree) that still has bark and branches on it. The bark and branches show that it hasn't been dead too long and hasn't had time to rot. Or a blow-down with bark and branches will be all right if it's not too wet. Use green wood (live wood) only if you have cut it and let it age at least six months to dry out good.

To cut it down you just have to use a chain saw. You can do it with an ax, but if your tree is big enough to bother cutting down at all that would be a pretty big struggle. A 12-inch chain saw is cheaper, lighter and easier to handle than a 16-inch one, but it won't cut as big a tree. In general, a chain saw can handle a tree with a diameter almost twice the length of its blade, though if you really know what you're doing you can stretch that. You've got to oil it all the time you're sawing by a squirt attachment. You get a round file which is the same size as the teeth on your saw and file them sharp between sawings. The rakers on the chain also have to be filed down regularly. Different wood conditions require different heights for the rakers. Sawing frozen wood is different, too. You need a manual or somebody who knows what they're doing to help you get started with a chain saw. Hang onto your chain saw warranty. They break down a lot, especially the cheaper brands. The big ones are used by sawyers who are falling trees on a professional scale. Small ones have only recently come on the market and are hard to find in used outlets. The chain saw runs by a gasoline motor. Once in a while you can get a new one on sale for as low as $125. The lighter saws are cheaper and won't wear you out near as bad.

Decide which way you want the tree to fall. You'll have to take into consideration which way it's leaning already. I don't know any way to make a tree fall uphill from a decided lean. If possible, you want to knock it down toward the road so you won't have to haul the pieces so far to your pickup or truck. Try not to fall it uphill because it might bounce back downhill when it hits and hurt somebody. Make a V-shaped cut on that side of the tree (the side where you want it to fall) sawing up toward the center of the tree from the

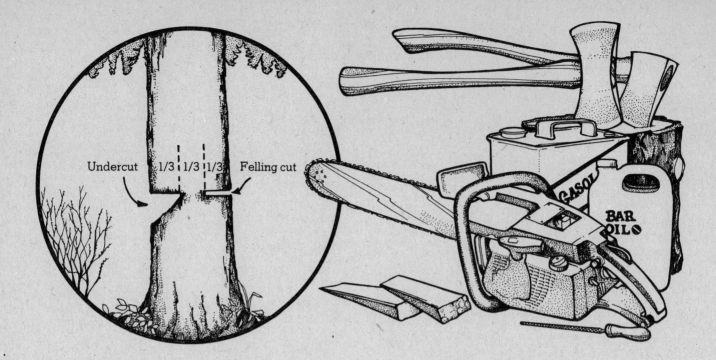

Undercut 1/3 | 1/3 | 1/3 Felling cut

ground angle and down toward the center of the tree from the sky direction. The V-shaped wedge should have its point one-third of the way into the tree. That's important. The wedge should have about a 30° angle. Take the wedge of wood out.

Now saw from the opposite side of the tree with your cut on a line to meet the point of the "V." Go slowly the last few inches and when things start to creak and clatter get the heck out of there. The tree should be starting to topple over toward the "V."

You'll be about one-third of the way in from the other side when it starts to go. On trees over a couple feet in diameter you should use a wedge. Hammer the wedge in by using the saw after you get the cut deep enough to take it. As you saw deeper, hammer the wedge in deeper. When you get one-third of the way in, take the saw out and keep hammering the wedge in until the tree falls. Usually the fellows here use a regular "falling" plastic wedge. You can buy them at a saw shop.

Once the tree is on the ground you can finish wherever you want to. If you have a big logging truck you can load the whole log up and take it home, or you can saw it up on the spot and take chunks home to split. Know how long a piece your stove takes (a little shorter than the length of the firebox). That's how long your segments should be. Before the wood is stove-ready the segments have to be split with an ax, double-bladed or single. Save a couple of blocks of really good hard wood with wide diameter to be chopping blocks. Indispensable for woodmaking and for slaughtering poultry, too.

TO CHOP WOOD—Everybody's got their own way of chopping. A friend of ours only lifts the ax to shoulder height, then brings it down with a big grunt and the wood splits. Another friend raises it straight over his head. Mike holds the ax strong in his left hand, loose in his right hand, and then brings it down kind of pulling with the left hand and pushing with the

right hand. The best stroke for me uses both hands on the ax as if you were holding a baseball bat. Only farther apart. If you're right-handed start the ax out back of your right shoulder behind your head with your back arched backwards just a trifle (or you can alternate shoulders with every swing) and then bring it forward and down moving your shoulder and chest forward at the same time. Maybe taking such an interest in ax technique is unwomanly—I don't have to chop wood now much thank heavens—there's plenty else. But I was my father's only child and I chopped it aplenty for my mother (as well as hauled water by the bucketful up the creek bank to keep the porch tank full).

Strive for accuracy before you strive for force—at least enough so you don't hit your foot. Once you're sure you can put the blade onto the wood, you want to give it all the power you can. Use a good big ax, a heavy one, because you can get a lot more force with it. Wear the heaviest boots you have in case you miss and be forewarned of the possibility that chips can fly up into an eye or the ax blade can hit a knot and be deflected so don't let children stand near when you're chopping. My little boy got an ax blade in his forehead from an ardent backswing when he got too close up behind another boy who was chopping. No more harm done now than a little scar but it's a lesson. If you want to be really safe wear ski goggles, a hard hat and steel-toed boots!

Try to hit your block of wood right in the center. Mike says you don't want the ax absolutely perpendicular to the stump when it strikes. I aim to get it square on. If your wood doesn't split from the center you can try taking slabs off the edge awhile before you tackle the heart. If you can get your ax in but not out the other side pull it out and try again, striking in the same place again and again. Look for a natural crack to strike into. There usually is one in old wood. If you're still finding it hard, use wedges and a wood splitting maul or sledgehammer instead of the ax.

KNOTS—With tamarack or red fir you won't have too much trouble with knots. With cedar they're impossible. A "knot" is where a branch grew out of the trunk. That branch extends like a holding pin all the way through the trunk to the center. It prevents the trunk from splitting naturally. You can split away from the knot and just throw the knot away unless it's small enough to burn itself. But big cedar knots are too huge for anything but a bonfire. Cedar blocks make dandy furniture though so if you see a knot in the block you could just reserve it for a stool or something.

KINDLING—Some of the wood has to be resplit very fine for starting fires. Those little sticks are called "kindling." My father always insisted on a very neatly arranged stack of wood on the porch where I carried it from my chopping station in the yard by the woodpile. It was arranged by graduated sizes with the real small kindling on the left end and getting bigger as it moved to the right. That way my mother could easily find whatever size sticks she wanted. You need real dry wood for kindling. Wood on the green side burns OK in a big fire but it makes terrible kindling because it is so damp. To make kindling out of it you have to split it into small kindling-size sticks and then dry them out some place like in your warming ovens and *then* it will work to start a fire.

Kindling is made with a hatchet because those little sticks won't stand up by themselves. You have to hold them up with your left hand and chop up with your right hand using the short-handled hatchet. The thing with using a hatchet is not to cut your fingers off. Either learn unbelievably good aim or learn to let go just before the hatchet blade strikes so the fingers are out of harm's way. I keep the hatchet back of the wood range, hanging on the wall by its neck—a nail on each side. *High* out of reach of the children. That's where the other wood stove implements are kept too.

The wood supply on my parents' porch was enough for a week. I use both a porch and a kitchen woodbox near the stove. It has to be filled once a day in cold weather. It's 2½ feet wide, 4 feet long, 3 feet high, and bottomless so I can pick it up and sweep up the sawdust come spring. I toss all the paper-type garbage in it in wintertime for starting fires.

If you are using coal it has to be stored where it won't get wet. It requires more shelter than wood. To bring the coal to the stove from its storage place in your woodshed, or a corner of the garage or cellar, the coal scuttle is traditional. Any bucket will do, though. You usually only need a bucket at a time in the kitchen if you're using wood mostly. The coal is to get a hotter fire than wood will give you and a longer lasting one—you would put in the coal the last thing before going to bed. Tamarack holds a fire about as well though.

MAKING FENCE POSTS ("splitting rails")—A "wedge" is a piece of metal shaped like an ax blade, flat on top, like a single-bladed ax head with no handle. Wedges are sharpened a little bit, but not too sharp, because they tend to get stuck if they're too sharp. You need at least two wedges to make fence posts. Cedar is the popular wood to make them out of because it is wonderfully easy to split. Cedar is a nice wood anyway. It has a good smell and a pretty appearance.

Pick a point on the side of the pole and up toward the "top." Try to make that point a natural crack if there is one. There usually is in old wood. Tap the wedge in. Then drive it in with a sledgehammer as far as it will go. Take a second wedge and start driving it in where your pole still isn't split apart farther down the line. That will loosen up the first wedge and put it at the farthest point of the split from the second wedge (you're working your way from the top down) and keep going this way until you've finished splitting it.

Another way to get fence posts is to start by falling the tree—like long, straight pines. Regular posts you want to be about 3 or 4 inches across so that's what the diameter of your tree should be, because kinds other than cedar don't split well. After falling them you cut them across to be the length you want. For uprights that's how high you want your fence to be plus how deep you want it to go in the ground. Corner posts need to be really husky—so more than 4 inches diameter is good to use there. The poles to lay lengthwise can be longer.

Now you want to skin your pole. You smooth off all the knots and then strip away the bark. A flat-headed shovel is a good bark stripper. Hardwood doesn't need a preservative treatment but softwood does. That's to keep bugs from lunching on it till your fence collapses in a heap of dust. So soak those poles for two months in a vat of used motor oil and then they'll last longer than you will. If you haven't got that kind of time, soak them in a mixture of pentachlorophenol and oil for a couple of days. If you have neither the time nor the money, use red fir, cedar or black pine because they are the most rot resistant. You'd get 15 years out of an untreated cedar post around here—less in a more southern or wetter climate. And it also depends on soil acidities and that gets complex.

OF WOOD COOK STOVES

I remember the wood stove we had when I was a little girl. It was our only heat and a grateful presence on winter days. Mother raised bread behind the stovepipe. The spring chickens first lived in a box on the floor back of the stove before they graduated to the bathtub. Hot water came from a tank attached to the right-hand side of it with a circulating pipe rigged up to pass near the firebox and heat it. I started out cold mornings sitting on top of the stove. As it got warmer I scooched away from the firebox. Then I leaned on it. When it got hot enough so I couldn't lean on it anymore I was thawed out enough to function anyway. I never could understand how my mother managed to get up in that icy house leaving my father and me in our warm beds and make the fire. Now I understand better. Necessity is the progenitor of toughness. I mean when you have to you can.

Now I have both an electric stove and two old fashioned wood ranges in my kitchen. I use my younger Montag Duchess white-enameled stove in winter as a cupboard and the top as a work area. In summer it moves to the backyard under a canopy to be my canning stove. The electric stove I like to bake in, and it's a blessing on hot summer days because I can cook a meal without heating up the kitchen too much. But I prefer the wood stove for frying, stewing, such delicate businesses as making cottage cheese and cream cheese, and for its friendly and practical warmth on cold days since it heats the kitchen area. My working wood cook stove is a big black box with "Monarch" on it in nine places, warming ovens on top and lots of metal fancywork. It's a good stove too.

The old-style wood and coal range is a large iron box which may or may not be on legs. In either case it should be placed well enough out from the wall not to be a fire hazard and set on an asbestos sheet underneath to protect your wooden floor. When you are first setting up a wood cook stove it's important to get it level. Put a frying pan on top with a few drops of water in it for an indicator. The drops of water should go to the center of the pan. The firebox is on the left. At the bottom of the burning area is a movable grate—an iron grill with interlocking fingers which is opened by a special handle to let ashes fall down into the ash pan, a trap which occupies the lowest level under the firebox. You can keep the grate shaker

hung up near the stove along with the scraper, poker, pot holders, hatchet and lid lifter. The poker is just a long metal stick with a spiral handle used to move chunks of wood away from the sides of the firebox, or to do whatever poking you need to in the fire without burning your hand.

On very cold mornings, if there is no other heat, I let the children build the fire. It keeps them occupied while the house is warming up. Otherwise, they just stand around the cold stove and complain. The basics are—you burn a match to the heat enough to light kindling to light bigger hunks of wood that will burn with enough heat to kindle coal.

Besides fuel fires need air. The range is connected with the chimney vent by means of the stovepipe. There is a damper in the pipe and probably another at the front of the grate and another at the back or side of the firebox. Technically the ones that are above the fire are "dampers," the ones in front of it are "drafts." A new fire needs lots of air. The two lower dampers are probably shifted by metal handles to open or close air holes into the firebox. The stovepipe damper is a plate just the diameter of the pipe with an outside handle. It may be adjusted to obstruct the pipe and slow (dampen) the fire by limiting the airflow (draft). The "flue" is the hole inside the chimney or stovepipe through which your draft flows. If you let your fire get big and roaring a little bit be-

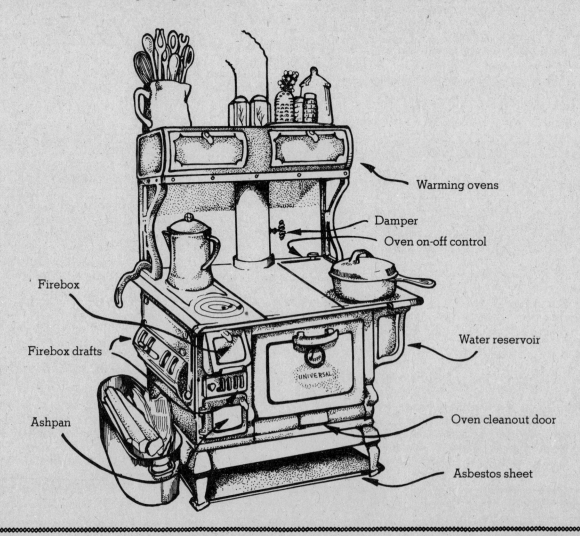

Warming ovens

Damper

Oven on-off control

Firebox

Water reservoir

Firebox drafts

Ashpan

Oven cleanout door

Asbestos sheet

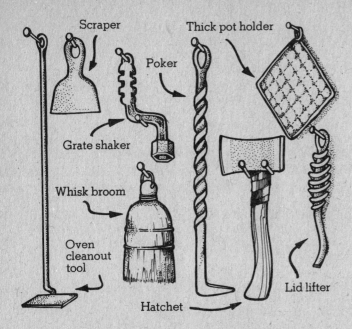

Scraper

Thick pot holder

Poker

Grate shaker

Whisk broom

Oven cleanout tool

Hatchet

Lid lifter

fore you damp down, it will help burn up and blow out the cinders in the stove and stovepipe that can't be so easily reached any other way.

TO BUILD A FIRE

1. Clean out the ashes. Shake the grate with the shaker to get all the old cold ashes down into the ash pan. Take it out and empty it onto the garden or into the lye barrel or garbage. If you are using coal, be thrifty and pick out any half-burned chunks. Having all those old ashes out helps the new fire get air. Besides if you don't empty your ash pan now it will be overflowing by noon with ashes and hot cinders. You'll *have* to empty it and the tray will be very unwieldy to carry anywhere.

2. Separate sheets of newspaper. Wad them up and put into the firebox. Or use any discarded papers or paper containers. Add some of your finest kindling on top, then bigger chunks of wood. One stick of wood never burns well alone. (There's some profound philosophy there if I ever get time to ponder it—a sermon even.) Light the paper with a match as near the bottom as you can. Fire travels up. Have all the dampers wide open.

As the fire gets going, keep it supplied with fuel of the appropriate size for the stage it's at. As it gets going good you can gradually cut back on the draft. You will waste fuel and have a hard time heating your stove and oven if you let all your hot air go directly up the chimney, which is what it will do with all the dampers left open.

So when your fire is going really well, cut back the draft, meaning turn that damper in the stovepipe, until it starts smoking. Then turn it back enough so you have no smoke. If the chimney damper is shut too tight, you'll have smoke all over the place. If it's open too wide, the fire will roar and consume like crazy—but it won't make the room warm. Close the damper at the back or to the side of the firebox, shut or almost shut. Adjust your front one to the point that the fire's health seems to require. The hotter your fire

the more dampening it can stand. If your fire is too slow, give it more air.

If your fire still isn't burning well, try loosening up the pile of fuel. Not only does the fire in general need air, but at first every individual stick needs an air supply. I carefully arrange them log cabin or tipi style to assure this. Once it gets going you needn't be so particular.

Softwoods, such as pine and cedar, have a coarse fiber that burns quickly. Pine is very pitchy. They are good kindling. You can tell a pitchy wood in the fire because it does a lot of noisy popping. For a long-term steady fire, especially for oven baking, hardwood or coal are nicest. Bituminous coal doesn't make as hot a fire as anthracite and it's smokier.

WOOD COOK STOVE REPAIR—Assuming you don't lose a lid lifter, or worse yet one of your stovetop lids, the first problem likely to happen to you is that the stove liner—the firebrick material which lines the inside of the firebox and protects the metal—will first crack and then gradually crumble away. This takes *years*.

I didn't used to know how you could replace these worn-out firebox parts but Kate Casper of Milton-Freewater, Oregon, wrote and told me. Kate and her husband live on a small ranch in the foothills of the Blue Mountains. The Malleable Iron Range Company, Beaver Dam, Wisconsin 53916, has firebrick linings, hard-coal firebox and standard firebox parts for Monarch ranges. Write Malleable: Attention "Repair Sales." They also sell things like lid lifters and cranks and cleaning rods to go with their stoves.

Barbara Ingram who started life on five Idaho acres three years ago and has survived fire, floods and broken bones also told me there is a way to re-line any stove that has a firebrick-type liner. It's called refractory cement. You buy a can of it and a small putty knife. Apply a very thin layer to the part to be replaced. Let it dry hard. Then apply another real thin coat. Keep it up until the area is built up to match the rest. It will resist temperatures up to 8,500° and is the stuff they use in blast furnaces. One of the biggest refractory cement companies in the whole country is in Troy, Idaho, 12 miles up the road from where I live. As for tools for a wood stove try Atlantic Stove Works. *Mother Earth* has the address for them. They make wood stoves, etc.

Katya Morrison, of Mount Airy, Maryland, a beautiful Christian who lives in the bottom of a barn with her family and has 10 goats and 40 chickens, shared her experience with us. "After using our wood stove awhile, the lining of the firebox cracked. We tried fine clay but that didn't work. However plain cement made with just sand has lasted beautifully and is easy to do."

Home Service Appliance, 1101 E. Sherman Avenue, Coeur d'Alene, Idaho 83814, is able to order new grates, brick liners and so on for wood cook stoves. I don't know where they get them from. Pati Sandstrom of Olympia, Washington, wrote me another of those beautiful letters that keep my courage up and keep me trying even though I don't have time to answer her properly. And she sent us all good advice on getting replacement parts for wood stoves: "My 73-year-old bachelor uncle told us that most wood cook stoves and heaters have a small metal plate on the back with a serial number and the name and address of the company. Some of the companies are still in business. Why not write and see? Also you might take the information to a hardware store and see if they have or can get the parts. My uncle has gotten parts for his heater this way. We plan on getting parts for our Ashley heater and rebuilding it this summer. The only address I can give you at this time is the Ashley Auto Heater Company, 1604-17th Avenue S.W., P.O. Box 730, Sheffield, Alabama 35660. I'd suggest using the P.O. Box number instead of the street address."

Marily (what a pretty name!) Sturman of Port Orchard, Washington, wrote me too. "You ask for information on where to buy parts for a woodburner stove—well—here it comes: Washington Stove Works, Everett, Washington 98201. They carry all parts for all their WSW stoves. We have a 1905 one and they have all replacement parts to be ordered through a local dealer here in Port Orchard. I imagine many parts would fit other makes."

Now that's really putting our heads together!

When the time comes that you need another wood cook stove or wood heater or if you're looking for your first one, it's probably going to cost you some money and effort. For a wood heater one way is to find a barrel (not one that has ever held insecticides because it would put out deadly fumes when heated) and buy a Barrel Stove kit that includes a 6-inch pipe collar, legs and a door. Countryside carries them for $49.50 (Countryside General Store, 130 E. Madison Street, Waterloo, Wisconsin 53594). You can buy heater-type wood stoves from $280 on up from Countryside or Sears. But you can buy cheapie heaters from $22 on up from the Cumberland General Store. Send $3 to Cumberland General Store, Route 3, Box 479, Crossville, Tennessee 38555, for their catalog. It's well done, fascinating and contains a lot of rare items and real bargains I've never seen elsewhere. They are slow on delivery—but so is everybody else. A wood cook stove will cost you about $250. There are shortages. You'll probably have to order and then wait to get a new one.·

Fisher stoves can also be ordered right from the manufacturer. Factory and delivery location is 2103-196th S.W., Lynwood, Washington 98036.

THE TOP OF THE STOVE—The oven of a wood stove is hard to work with but the top more than makes up for it. Cooking on top of a wood stove the heat is more even and potentially milder than with an electric or gas stove. You will be delighted with your fried eggs because the texture of eggs cooked alone or in mixtures is directly affected by the temperature at which they are cooked. Cooked below the boiling point of water the egg white is firm but tender and the egg yolk is tender and like a salve. Eggs cooked at too high a temperature are first tough, then leathery, then crispy. Fry your eggs in a little butter in a cast-iron pan on the right-hand side of the wood range.

It's basic to know that the different parts of the stove top have different temperatures. The hottest area is usually just to the right of the firebox. (If the draft isn't good the hottest may be right over the firebox.) You can adjust your cooking temperature just by moving the pan to a suitable place on the stove top. Start it boiling over the hot part, then settle it down to the rate you like by moving it over some distance to the right. The far right is the traditional place for making cottage cheese and keeping dishes warm when a meal is waiting for the eaters.

This kind of stove is hard on perishable pot handles—wooden or plastic ones. The stove top is hot all around the pan as well as under it and a wooden handle such as on a coffeepot may even catch fire. The traditional handles are metal and you pick them up with a pot holder. You can make a pot holder by folding an old washrag in half and then folding it in half again and sewing down all around the edges. Or you can sew down enough layers of cotton rags to get a manageable thickness and then attach a loop to hang it up by. It can be round or square, about 7 inches across is nice. Crocheted ones burn you through the holes unless they have an extra cloth filling or you use them several at a time stacked like pancakes. Keep the pot holders hanging on nails handy to your stove. You'll be using them a lot.

For stirring on top of a wood stove you need long-handled wooden spoons. You can use a clean stick if you haven't wooden spoons. Wood doesn't conduct heat. The long handle helps you keep your arm away from the heat. Any metal spoon will quickly heat up and burn your fingers. Then you'll drop it in the pot.

The old fashioned flat irons, griddles, waffle pans and other "hot air" pans including the *kugelhupf* (apple dumpling pan) are meant to be put right on the hot range top. (If you want to use these pans on an electric burner put a metal pie pan over the burner—otherwise they'll get too hot in one spot.)

Potato Lefse is a Scandinavian dish traditionally baked right on top of a wood range although you can use a pancake griddle. Boil 5 large, peeled potatoes, then mash them and add ⅓ cup cream, 3 tablespoons butter and 1 teaspoon salt. Beat until the mixture is fluffy. After it has cooled add enough flour to roll out thinly, as for pie crust, or even thinner, using your rolling pin. Start with walnut-sized balls. Roll out to tortilla-sized pancakes. Use the center panel of the stove top or you can bake on a grill or in a heavy skillet. Clean and oil it and then bake there, turning as often as you need to keep from scorching.

Wheat Lefse—Mix ½ teaspoon salt with 3 cups whole wheat flour. Add ¼ cup oil and 1 cup water, mix and knead. Roll dough thin like for Potato Lefse. If your dough is sticky, add a little more flour. Cook like the Potato Lefse. You can eat plain, or buttered, or like pancakes, or like tacos with a filling rolled up inside (keep them hot) like mashed dry beans, green onion and tomato.

THE OVEN—The oven of a good wood range is beside the firebox and is heated by hot air circulating from the firebox over, down the far side and under the oven. If your oven is not heating or is heating unevenly the problem may be accumulated soot in those areas. My mother taught me to clean them out once a week. You can lift off the top of the range to clean the top area and sides. The bottom is reached through a little door under the oven. There is a special tool for cleaning there called a "stove scraper." You can buy a stove scraper from the Wood Stove Company, Route 1, Box 28, Troy, Idaho 83871. That's just 12 miles up the road from where I live. I know the fellows who make them. They sell each rake for $2.50 plus the shipping charges. May they prosper! But if you can't afford to subsidize a struggling young company, you can order them cheaper from Hunt and Mottlet Company, P.O. Drawer 1876, Tacoma, Washington 98401. Price $.90 Item Zemer #7 length 30".

Ovens vary between stoves and with the kind of fuel you are using and the weather. You'll have to get to know your individual oven and fuel. Throw away your former standards for baking. Just be grateful if it isn't raw and isn't burnt. Disregard suggested cooking times. Your oven may be faster or slower or both. Keep an eye on what's happening in there. If the oven doesn't have a builtin thermometer by all means go out and buy one of those little portable oven thermometers that you can hang or set inside. That way you'll never have to bother with the famous flour or paper tests. The problem isn't finding out the temperature—it's controlling it!

If your oven is too cool stoke up the fire with more fuel. If the oven is too hot leave the door open a crack and ease up on feeding the fire. If one side is obviously getting more heat than the others the oven is hotter there and you will need to move your baking pan a time or two during the baking to rotate that hottest side. If you have several pans in the oven rotate them all to take turns in the hot spot. If the top is browning too fast cover it with greased or wetted brown paper. You can put a whole pie into a paper bag. Old fashioned cast-iron frying pans, Dutch ovens, and gem (iron muffin) pans are helpful since the cast iron absorbs heat and distributes it evenly throughout the surface of the pan.

ON WOOD—OR THE LACK THEREOF—Burning wood seems easy and natural to me. But I live in a timber-producing area, have timber here on the farm and a sawmill and wood products plant both just down the road. Correspondents tell me that in the East, wood is very scarce and very high priced, that wood stoves are hard to come by and that insurance companies won't insure a home that is heated with wood. The latter doesn't bother me particularly. I've never been sold on the notion of insurance. I see in the cities that the tallest, fanciest skyscrapers seem to be built by the insurance companies. I like the idea of people doing their own deciding about how they're going to provide against problems, disasters, and old age and being allowed to allocate their money according to that personal decision instead of being forced to do it in a particular (and incidentally very expensive) way. Anyway, if you haven't got dead trees around then a wood cook stove isn't necessarily right for you.

CAST-IRON COOKWARE

My favorite pans are my cast-iron ones. They are indestructible. They don't even get lost, because they are too heavy for the kids to lug away. I have a smallish iron fry pan and a big one and then a big Dutch oven for stewing, roasting, boiling spuds and so on. If you are campfire cooking, iron cookware will really help because it evens out the heat and holds it good. You can buy cast-iron muffin pans called "gem pans." If you have a gem muffin pan and not the recipe you can use any muffin recipe in it but here's one that is guaranteed to work.

Gems—First grease your iron gem pan and put it in a hot oven (400° or thereabout). Now sift together 1 cup flour and 2 teaspoons baking powder or just mix them good if you don't have a sifter. In another bowl break an egg, beat it, add 1 teaspoon sugar, a pinch of salt and 1 tablespoon melted butter or cooking oil. Now add the flour alternately with ½ cup milk. You could double or triple this recipe if you need to. By now your gem pans should be smoking hot. Pour the batter into the individual cups. Bake. They will need only about 10 minutes to get done.

BRAND-NEW IRON COOKWARE has a factory applied preseasoning coating. So first wash your pan good with soap to get that off. Now you want to give it its first seasoning.

Frank Womac Jr. of Pomeroy, Washington, made me the gift of a beautiful cast-iron frying pan. He had carefully seasoned it already for me. This is the letter he sent along. It's the best description I've ever seen of how to coat an iron pan:

"If your cast-iron cooking utensils do not look like this, they have not been properly seasoned. Fifty years ago all cast iron came with instructions for this coating.

"This fry pan has one coat outside and three inside. I have six coats on my own that have been there over thirty years and only had to touch up the bottom a few times.

"This coating has roughly the characteristics of Teflon only it can be repaired if damaged. Will not rust and only care needed is wash with soap and water, rinse and dry (not necessary).

"Very little grease is required to cook and it is practically stick free.

"When coating wears thin on bottom (gets hazy) or some idiot uses a scraper to clean it, or coating burned off by overheating, just recoat as per instructions. If coating badly burned on bottom just use soap

Waffle iron

Gem pan

Skillets

Dutch oven

Griddle

and water and real coarse steel wool and scrub entire coating from bottom then recoat.

"Baked beans, stews, roasts, etc. can be left in Dutch ovens treated this way without worrying about rust or metallic taste as there is no exposed metal. Outdoor cooking doesn't hurt it.

"Never overheat cast iron—300° to 350° is plenty hot to cook anything. Higher heat only burns the coating off and soon warps the bottom.

"So here's how to coat your pan: Wash, rinse and dry. Then rub generous coating of *suet* over entire utensil (inside and out). Suet is available at any meat market, usually without charge, if you don't have your own. Place in 425° oven for 15 minutes. Apply second coat inside and return to oven for another 15 minutes. Apply third coat inside (just smear it on real heavy and don't worry about it as it will smooth out by itself). If more coats are wanted just repeat the procedure. After applying final coat bake for 2 more hours, turn off oven and leave pan in oven to cool gradually.

"Do not put lid on Dutch oven while treating it as it will seal and you will need a crowbar to pry it open. That's all there is to it. No rust and no wiping and oiling. Actual time to put on these three coats was about 2 minutes.

"Oh, I forgot to mention that the first coat may be spotty and have bare spots. Don't worry, just apply second and third coats and it will turn out like this.

"Also, if you insist, you can use a plastic chore girl to clean it without much damage.

"Just to satisfy yourself, take this pan and wash it in hot soap and water and rinse. Do not wipe dry and see the results.

"Anyway I hope you have more enjoyable frying with lots and lots less work."

CARE OF YOUR PAN—Never use a metal scratcher pad on it since that will scratch sharp places in the surface that food will stick in. Your pan will get blacker with use and that's what it's supposed to do. Mine are all coal black. Never cook food high in acid content in a cast-iron (or aluminum) pan. The acid will work on the pan and your dish will pick up more iron content than will taste good. Don't store food in your pan unless it's well seasoned. It's for *cooking* in.

THE BASIC DUTCH OVEN is made of heavy iron and comes in basic sizes from 8 to 16 inches across and 4 to 6 inches deep. They make them in aluminum too, but I wouldn't have one of the things. My Dutch oven is my very favorite kettle. If I had to give up every pan or pot in the house the one I'd keep is that one. It has a tight-fitting heavy lid that holds in the steam when that's what I want. The heavy iron heats evenly so I'm safer from scorching in that kettle than any other. I can make it do for a frying pan in a pinch. I can cook a moist good roast in it with ¼ cup of water because it holds the steam so well. It's ideal for cooking on a campfire. You can put it right in the coals of an open fire or use a bean hole. You can use it to bake a roast or boil a stew or to bake bread and biscuits or boil potatoes, or fry fish.

Some Dutch ovens have three short legs making them like a tripod. That's good for camping use, but I'd vastly prefer the flat bottomed kind in the kitchen. They always have tight-fitting lids which are slightly domed in the center. The lid has a handle and sometimes the outer rim is turned up (flanged) for the purpose of holding hot coals when you're having cookouts. But that flanging isn't essential. The pot itself has a bail (handle).

Dry your Dutch oven after every washing. Grease it if you want. I don't follow the school of thought that says you shouldn't wash an iron pan. That's sort of unreal. But I never use a metal scratcher on them. If you are having trouble with an iron pan rusting, grease it after every washing. My Dutch oven must be at least 40 years old though and it hasn't rusted yet.

DUTCH OVEN IN A HOLE—Dig a hole about twice as deep and wide as your kettle, or bigger. Build a fire in it and let it burn until there are plenty of red hot coals. Scrape a depression or remove some coals. Set the oven down in the hole and cover it over with the removed coals. Then cover oven, coals and all, with the dirt dug out to make your pit. The dirt cover should end up being at least 4 inches thick. If you aren't very confident of your bed of coals you could build another fire on top of the dirt. Wait 4 to 8 hours and your beans or roasted meat or stew should be just fine. This is best I think for one of those huge Dutch ovens when you're planning on serving twenty or more people. For forty people use two or three Dutch ovens in the same hole (make it bigger).

ROASTING IN A DUTCH OVEN—I often put the frozen roast into the Dutch oven. Especially if it's some wild meat that we got into the freezer in the nick of time. Such meat will be trying to spoil the evening of the day I thaw it, but if I thaw and cook at once it's safe. I add a little water, seasonings, and chopped onion or any other vegetables just meant for flavor. (Vegetables meant for eating wait until the last hour to go in.) Add the lid and cook as long as it takes. Depends on the size of the roast. I start the oven at 400° and then finish at 350° or lower if I have the time. The slower I can cook it the better I like the results.

A good cook would preheat the Dutch oven, then grease it and sear the roast (that means fry it all over the outside) to brown it before adding the water and the lid and cooking it. I'm usually in too much of a rush. After the roast is done, while Daddy Mike is carving it, I toss a handful of flour into the good brown juices left in the pan and churn it like crazy with the eggbeater to get ahead of the lumps. Then add salt and put it on the table for gravy. Baked potatoes are a natural with a Dutch oven dinner. We have them with a choice of gravy, butter or homemade cream cheese whipped (just like dairy sour cream).

DEEP-FAT FRYING IN A DUTCH OVEN—The Dutch oven is good for this—better than any other container you have. The only problem is it ties up your Dutch oven so maybe you'll want to invest in two if you love deep-fat fried food. My husband does. I fill the kettle half full of home rendered lard, heat it to where it is just starting to smoke and commence to fry. Homemade French fries are good. Don't add the fries until they promptly float. Stand by on the ready to fish out the ones that are done or else they will just proceed to burn. Burned stuff will taint your whole kettle of grease. French fry just before the meal and take the food out onto a towel to soak up the extra grease. French fried bland vegetables are good—like summer squash, peeled and sliced ½ inch thick, or green tomatoes. Dip the vegetables in beaten egg (add a little milk to stretch it), then in flour, then in egg again, then in flour. Onion rings are good, too. Peel and slice the biggest onions you have. Then break the rings into groups of about three, dip into the batter and fry. Green pepper rings are also good. If you didn't burn anything you can just keep the grease in the oven in the refrigerator between uses, clarifying it by cooking some potato in it and straining occasionally when it gets dark. You can serve leftover French fried food by warming it up to sizzling again in the oven (not the Dutch oven).

BAKING IN A DUTCH OVEN—To make bread in the rough. Grease oven. Preheat. Set raised and ready loaf into the oven. Or pour in your cornbread or cake batter. Make sure the Dutch oven is level. Cover. Set oven into bean hole prepared as above. Cover with coals and dirt and leave 3 hours. The preheating is very important to all Dutch oven baking. Or you can bake with a few coals under and a lot over right by the fire and on top of the ground. But be careful it burns easily on the bottom. Or you can bake in your Dutch oven in the stove oven.

HOTCAKES—Fry on the oiled, heated bottom of the oven or on the upside-down lid if you have that shape of lid. OK in a pinch but I'd rather use a frying pan or griddle.

BISCUITS, PIES, CORN BREAD AND THE LIKE—Preheat oven and lid. Grease oven. For biscuits put them in the bottom as the pan is sitting in the coals. You don't need to cut them out—just break off chunks of fairly firm dough. Turn them over when browned and then set the lid on the oven. Put the coals on the lid. It will take about 10 minutes and you learn by experience just how many coals are needed. Cook pies in a pie pan inside the oven. To make corn bread just grease your oven and pour in the batter. You don't need to preheat.

You can mail-order Dutch ovens from Morgan Brothers. These are the real good old-time iron ones. But if you have a chance to buy other than mail order, I'd do it just for your own satisfaction. For camping I'd recommend one with legs. For home use one with a flat bottom. Morgan Brothers in Lewiston, Idaho, sells a 3¾-quart oven for $5.47 on up to a 12-quart size for $15.90. Ask for a lid too. Morgan Brothers has other ironware too like old-style long griddles and skillets and a Dutch oven-type thing only it has a long handle and no bail called a chicken fryer. And they carry an old-time crane for holding a Dutch oven over a fireplace on an outdoor fire. You can write them for details if you're interested.

HOW TO BUY AT AUCTION

A "real" auction is when a householder offers his household goods and/or machinery for sale by auction on his property. You may have to drive many miles, but if you are interested in obtaining working "antiques" at a reasonable price this is one of the best ways.

The price you pay at an auction is affected by the wealth of the town where the auction is held, the number of buyers present and the popularity of the item being sold. In our area the worst time to go to an auction is in September in a wheat farming community. The wheat farmers are the most prosperous single economic class in the area. In September they have just gotten paid for their crop, and they live far enough from easy shopping to be willing to pay a "new" price for a used item.

The best time to be at the auction is either right at the beginning or near the end. The crowd is thinnest then and competitive bidding least lively. Your natural enemy will be the antique dealer. But you and he may not always see eye to eye on what is of value. A wheelbarrow in good condition for $1.50 might be a real buy to you and considered of no value to him. To avoid making a bad buy try to get to the auction early enough to carefully examine all the merchandise spread out for people to look at. Note what you want

person who is recording each sale by price and name or number of person buying—and ask for your total, telling him your name or number. He will add it up and you'll pay him on the spot. If you drove a pickup to the sale it will be easier for you to get the stuff home. Just go around and gather up the things you bought and take them. If you didn't drive a pickup maybe you could buy one there. Sometimes an auction is a good place to get a bargain vehicle if your bank account can handle the cash transaction.

Don't get into a contest with somebody who is bidding unreasonably high. It isn't worth it. Such a person is probably a novice at auctions and has made up his mind to be brave and *buy* that particular item no matter what the cost. He is playing to win and not by common sense and he'll get the item of course. Keep in touch with used market prices on the kind of items you shop for and then you'll know when it's a bargain and when it isn't.

WATER

7th edition, May 27, 1976. You *have* to have some. To drink. To wash your face. To water your animals. And your plants. But most of us don't need near as much as we've gotten used to thinking we do. And a few of us need more—like people who aren't watering their plants enough for full production. But actually that's a point of contention around here. Vegetables and fruits like watermelon and cantaloupe grown without irrigation are considered to be higher quality than those grown with it and can fetch a higher price. But pasture and hay sure will do more with water on it. An unirrigated hay field around here will produce two cuttings a year. With irrigation, lots of dry hot weather and diligence you could get five . . . and that's in northern Idaho. But household water use is something else.

I once lived in Wyoming in a tiny community where every person trucked in their water in big tanks from 30 miles away or so . . . every drop of it. And then I once lived on the banks of the Wind River outside Thermopolis, Wyoming, in a tent and I had a whole river full of running water right outside my front door but none in a faucet. If it would have stayed summer forever I might never have left. Somebody researched the question and discovered that when water has to be carried from a well people use an average of 8 gallons a day. If you give them a pump attached to their kitchen sink they'll use more—up to 10 gallons per person per day. If you give them running hot water in the kitchen, they'll use 20 gallons a day. And if you put in a complete pressurized plumbing system they'll use 30 gallons a day.

Did you know that every time you take a bath in a bathtub you use from 8-20 gallons of water, 3 to 5 more every time you flush a toilet and 1 or 2 gallons every time you use the bathroom washbasin? It has amazed me in my travels that it seems like the dryer the spot you go to the more water they are using. In dry southern California where they bring their water in from so far, water seems abundant in a way that amazes me. Of course, in Idaho all our water is pumped up a hill from a tiny spring and then it flows

to bid on and decide what the top price you would pay for it is. That way you can make sure you're present when something you want comes up, and you will know if the antique chamber pot has holes in the bottom or not and won't get swept away in the excitement of the contest and pay more than the object really is worth to you. The best auction attitude is that you would like to have it but you could live without it if need be.

When bidding you have to catch the auctioneer's eye or that of his assistant on the platform. Once you get in your first bid or two the auctioneer will be watching for your bid and will understand how you are signaling and will even wait for you to think awhile if things are going slowly. But the first time nod your head, or wave your arms or yell, if necessary, to get his eye so he'll know you are "in." Make sure you're not bidding against your spouse. I've seen that happen several times. Make sure you're not bidding accidentally. My husband once bought a cake by scratching his head!

Hang back as long as possible before opening a bid. Then leave it as low as possible. I recommend bidding a quarter on anything for an opener. I've gotten many an interesting and useful item for a quarter that way. If there are several items of a kind and the auctioneer announces that he is selling them to the highest bidder, he to take as many as he wants—stop bidding. Almost certainly the winning bidder will not want all the items. After he has won the bid and named how many of the items he wants, the bidding will be reopened on the remaining items. If he overbid the item and no one wants the rest at his price, and he probably did, the auctioneer will then reauction the remainder arriving at a lower sale price—and still lower until they are finally all sold.

Payment is made by check or cash. Anytime you want to leave the sale go up to the auction clerk—the into the house by an unpressurized gravity system from a cistern up the hill so all that pressure startles me and seems wasteful. I'm not prepared for all the water that comes shooting out the faucet. Running hot water is such a luxury. I used to live without it and when I had it again counted it one of the grandest things in life. One thing about a limited family system—if we use too much water we run out. We have to wait for the cistern to fill up again. If we use too much hot water we run out of that too. So we've learned to be careful, especially in summer when the flow is lowest and we need it most for irrigating the garden.

If you don't have a spring on your place you can consider drilling a well. First you must find a competent drilling contractor unless you want to try digging one by hand. Chances are the latter won't work. To find the drilling contractor use the Yellow Pages and newspaper ads. Inquire into the money side of it in advance. Try to find somebody a neighbor will recommend. You can get additional information on how to shop for a water well and a free pamphlet, "When You Need A Water Well" by writing National Water Well Association, Dept. NUFM, 88 East Broad Street, Columbus, Ohio 43215. They will also provide you with a listing of well-drilling contractors in your area.

If you try that old fashioned thing called "dowsing" the results may surprise you. It really does work. Over on the School of Country Living property we dowsed all over the place and located an iron pipe that somebody else had placed in there that actually runs a continual stream of good water. It was a literal Godsend since it was just where we needed irrigation water for our garden. We traced it underground by dowsing way up the hill and finally came to a point where the pipe stuck out of the ground in midair, dry as a bone. It's a mystery I'm not going to take a chance of messing up by trying to understand it more—there is that pipe, dry at one end and water coming out the other. Maybe there's a crack in the middle and an underground stream entered.

If you start asking around you will probably hear of somebody to come dowse your place. He'll find you a good place to dig for a well. Or you can try it yourself. Some people can and some can't and nobody knows why or why not. We use an unwound coat hanger. Mike can and I've never tried. He's better at climbing up and down mountains and around in the brush than me, anyway. He's a one-man water department and clambers down the mountain every time I turn the faucet and no water comes out—to see what went wrong this time. The trouble with self-sufficiency is you also have to be able to be self-sufficient for upkeep and repair and there tends to be a lot of it with any system. If you want to try it for yourself, unwind two metal coat hangers to make straight wires out of them. Take the end of one in each hand and hold them somewhat loosely pointed straight out in front of you, parallel to each other. Walk around. If they want to cross and make an X you have dowsed yourself some water flowing underground. Of course I know people whose rods swing out instead of in. Anyway they'll do *something*.

The metal rods seem to work better than the traditional forked twig. Some people hold it from shoulder level, others at waist level. To start walk very slowly over a known vein of water or buried water pipe. Talk to yourself and to the rod while you're doing it—not because the rod understands but because it will help you concentrate. If you are experimenting with pipes bringing water to your house it will help you to have water running in the pipe. A forked twig, unlike the wires that either turn in or out will pull down. Mark the spot on the ground where you got the reaction. You may think just then you'll remember but sometimes it's hard to find again. Now walk back toward the spot from another direction and mark where you get the reaction again. Working like this at the School property we discovered a round shaped wet area that would be the perfect spot to dig a well . . . or maybe there was once a well there that has been covered on top. Right now we don't need a well so it doesn't matter because we found thirteen springs on the school grounds.

A spring is a place where water literally comes out of the ground. It is a real blessing. If you've got a spring you can improve it by digging it out so the water doesn't just seep up in a mud hole, but so you've got it tiled around where the water comes out and/or sink a pipe in there to catch that and bring it to a stock watering tank or down to your house (put the buildings down hill from the spring and you've got a perfect water system set up). Bury your pipe over three feet deep or whatever the neighbors tell you the frost line is in that area so it won't freeze in winter. For summer usage only bring it down in cheap plastic pipe. Springs can be very deceiving. For one thing they tend to be seasonal. They may run wonderful in the rainy season and dry up completely in the dry times when you need them most. They may be good in a cycle of good years and dry up in a cycle of dry years. They have a tendency to move and come out someplace else where you may or may not be able to rediscover them. Generally the bigger the water flow the safer you are. The flow can be measured if you'll take a bucket of known quantity and a watch to the spring and count how many gallons you get in a minute. You're safest with a flow that will equal 100 to 150 gallons a day.

River water has the problem of often being polluted. Irrigating out of it isn't as simple as it used to be. You have to get permission from your state government first.

FARM MACHINERY

(Including Horses)

The basic farm machine is something to pull other things with . . . like a team of horses or a tractor. And then comes the thing you pull, a machine that makes farming easier like a plow or disc or springtooth. A horse can outpull a little Ford tractor, especially in cold and deep snow kind of weather when the tractor won't even move. A horse can pull 16-foot logs. But remember to stop and rest two or three times on a 200- or 300-foot pull. Pat the animal and let her know you appreciate her when she's given you a good hard pull. That really makes a difference in the quality of future performance you'll get from her. Horses aren't nearly the dumb animals many people think. And they've got feelings too. Practice is important for them too, just as it is for you if you're trying to play the piano. So getting out there every day and hitching them up and using them helps them to stay at their best (keeps you in practice for your role too). When you are first training them to pull load them real light, then gradually increase the load. You want to take good care of your draft horse and that will help her give you the most she can. Horses can eat all kinds of hay that even cows can't, like timothy hay but don't give them moldy hay. Moldy hay gives them a sickness called "a heavy horse." There is an old saying that if you want to have a good pulling horse always leave one pull in him. That means quit working him while he is still pulling. And on a terrible hot 105° day bring him in at noon with you and give him a two-hour break in the shade, which break will also help you.

What kind of load can a team handle? They could pull a ton for a short distance but couldn't keep it up. They could pull 300 pounds easy for all day. The state of your horses' feet is important. Don't buy an animal with badly split hooves, and bring in the horseshoer regularly. He is called a farrier and around here there are a couple that run continuous advertisements in the newspapers. Horseshoes are vital if your animal is going to be walking on pavement or gravel a lot which is hard on hooves, which nature didn't design for such hard surfaces. But even working on dirt on your farm the hooves can stand some trimming. To get yourself started with draft horses you need a team

(take someone with you who knows draft horses). It will cost you from $1,500 to $5,000. Then you need harness and hopefully you can buy a set from the same person who sells you the horses because harness is hard to find. Better have him show you how to harness them and hitch them up before you bring them home because you may have a hard time figuring it out for yourself later on. If the wooden parts—called hames—seem dry you can oil them with tongue oil or neat's-foot oil. Put it on hot and rub it in good. Same for the leather.

Draft horse breeding is a good field for you to make money in now because the supply is so short and interest in them is really reviving. But keeping a big draft horse stud is not all fun and games. They are so big and any male is a potentially mean animal. We have neighbors that keep a stud. They take beautiful care of their horses but one day he simply up and bit a big chunk out of the lady's face. That was an Arabian stud. A draft horse stud could be twice the weight and if he is somewhere near where a mare in heat is he could be very hard to handle no matter how nice his disposition. You can artificially inseminate horses, cows or goats. Ask around for a man in the AI trade in your area. Or ask the nearest vet, he'll know for sure. A month or a month and a half before a draft mare foals (has a baby) you can still have her working but then it's time to let her quit. And then a month after she foals you can get her back into harness. It will help keep her in shape to be working soon again.

I urge anyone interested in draft horses or mules to have a subscription to the *Draft Horse Journal* which comes out four times yearly and is the *best* in its field. $6.00 for one year ($6.50 for Canada). Write *Draft Horse Journal*, Route 3, Waverly, Iowa 50677.

Some kind of machinery is important if you are farming over an acre. To spade even an acre by hand is asking a lot of yourself. You can handle up to two or even three acres with a rototiller and maybe ask a neighbor to come in and plow it once in the spring for you. If you're going to cultivate more than that you need a horse or a tractor of your own.

TRACTORS come in all sizes (as do horses). You need one small enough that you can afford it and big enough to do your work. This is assuming horses are not for you. There are some companies coming in now with lines of machinery especially for truck farms, orchards, vineyards or homesteads. There are some with the engine in the rear and then you can see exactly what you're doing with the tillage equipment in front and those are pretty handy. Before you buy your first tractor you have to decide what you want to use it for. You don't want it either underpowered or overpowered. Underpower won't get your job done and wears out your tractor sooner. If you overpower (buy too big a tractor) you're wasting money and gas, and you're inefficient. There's a distinction between diesel and gas engines. A diesel 50 horse is real powerful. Fifty horse in gas really isn't that big. Get a hold of a farm equipment dealer like John Deere or Allis Chalmers and talk to your neighbors. Not to buy right off but to start educating yourself about the choices. Look around for some used equipment if you have mechanical skills. There are some small air-cooled models that are reasonable for a real small farm. Sears and so on also put out small riding tractors like a riding lawnmower that are fine for orchards and little jobs. You don't want a farm-size tractor on 10 acres or less. Your smallish tractor will cost between $700 and $2,000.

Then you need your farm implements. Horse-drawn equipment is hard to find but it can be done. You may have to do some renovating. Implements, like tractors, come in all sizes. A plow can have one blade or a whole row of them. Each blade is called a "bottom." So a five-bottom plow has five cutting blades. Each implement has a specific action on the soil and you have to decide what combination you want.

PLOW—This is to break the soil, loosen it and turn it over. If you are cultivating virgin ground this is appropriate and most people plow first no matter what they do later. The plow actually turns the soil over to a given depth, usually 4 to 6 inches. You can set it to plow the exact depth you want. But a plow is not always the best thing. If you have very shallow topsoil then a plow is not a good tool for you because you don't want to bury it. The plow is appropriate in soils where you have humus that extends below the plowing depth. All over northern Minnesota the topsoil is kind of thin. There lots of farmers come through instead with a chisel plow in the spring. That's a tool that sends 7 or 14 fingers down in there to open up the soil. The chisel plow breaks up hard pan and helps the water to soak in and roots to be able to grow down and get trace minerals and yet you don't disturb the surface. Your precious topsoil is a nice organic material with worms and compost and energy and you want more rather than less of it. But most people don't have topsoil that thin.

ROTOTILLER—Most gardeners around here plow and then come through and rototill it and rototill several times more through the summer as needed to keep the weeds down. The rototiller is a tool you walk behind. A rototiller can play the same role as a disc and springtooth and spiketooth harrow, only it can't plow. Except if you have a rear-tined self-propelled rototiller you can supposedly make it plow too—that's why the Troy-Built people say they're so special. And indeed Troy-Built is the best rototiller on the market (and the most expensive) but it really doesn't plow nearly so good as a tractor pulling a plow. You haven't a chance trying to plow with a regular rototiller. Those little front tined ones won't cut unplowed earth at all. There are umpteen models of rototillers.

DISC—A disc helps break up the big chunks turned up by the plow.

SPRINGTOOTH—Comes in all types and sizes but basically it breaks up the little chunks into even finer chunks and smooths the soil surface which gets ready for seeding. To plant a seed and get it to grow good, your seed bed has to be fine, well broken down particles of earth. With too large clods, air gets in there and your soil dries out. Then you've got little dry seeds lying there between big chunks of earth. How many times you pull the springtooth over the same field depends on your soil and how easy it is to break up.

SEEDER—Big grain fields are easiest planted with a seeder. Most small gardens are seeded by hand unless you're seeding more than an acre and then you can get that little rolling seeder on one wheel like Countryside carries. But a drill means a big machine for seeding grains, grasses and hay. Although if you haven't got a drill or can't borrow one you can broadcast seed them.

There is new equipment hitting the market every year. Stuff is being imported from overseas that we've never seen before. India is manufacturing horse-drawn farm equipment. Most of the new machinery is for large-scale farming but there's some for small and labor intensive-type farming (like orchards and truck gardens).

YOUR LAND IS A SPIRITUAL RESPONSIBILITY

I believe we should live morally and spiritually as if Jesus were coming in the next five minutes, but economically and ecologically we should live as if He won't be here for 5,000 years more. I think it's a crime against that precious heritage God promised Abraham and the rest not to cherish and try to preserve this earth—His splendid creation. If it is going to come into destruction this should be no doing of any *Christian* hands. So please brothers and sisters let us struggle to preserve in health, beauty and usefulness this planet that God has given us and our descendants to be our home until that last day when we shall indeed be raised to be with Him. Let us be able to report our stewardship proudly.

Tom Fox is one of those guys who can do anything—build it, repair it, figure out a way. That's country living brains. Here he is putting the finishing touches on a gate.

Mike is chopping kindling for our wood cook stove. He loves to "make" wood every step of the way, from getting the dead timber sawed up in the woods right down to chopping the kindling. Mike loves to build a fire and keep it going and then late at night he'll sit there by the friendly warmth with his feet up or playing the guitar and singing to himself.

At the School of Country Living, Dick Isaacson and Stephen Kendle and Jerry Bayer are riding the stoneboat (a cart with no wheels that just drags along on the ground) behind Barney and Babe, our Belgian team. They're going to get a load of rocks from the river bottom to build the foundation of a primitive log cabin.

The older children are good chore-doers.
This is freckle-nosed Danny peering over a
load of kindling that Daddy chopped. The
children love to build forts and railroads
out of that kindling across my kitchen floor.

Imogene's root cellar is the best made
one I know. Can you figure out how the double
doors are? The outside one is standing open.
The wall is about 18 inches from outer door to
inner door (which you can't see). Up top you
can see the screened openings that ventilate
the top area above the roof of the cellar.

Imogene cans hundreds of quarts
of fruits and vegetables for storage
inside her root cellar every year.

FOOD PRESERVATION

HOW TO PRESERVE A HUSBAND

Be careful in your selection; do not choose too young and take only such as have been reared in a good moral atmosphere.

Some insist on keeping them in a pickle, while others put them in hot water. This only makes them sour, hard and sometimes bitter. Even poor varieties may be made sweet and good by garnishing them with patience, well sweetened with smiles and flavored with kisses to taste. Keep warm in a steady fire of domestic devotion and serve with peaches and cream.

When thus preserved, they will keep for years.

PRESERVED CHILDREN

Take one large field,
Half a dozen children,
Two or three small dogs,
A pinch of brook and some pebbles.
Mix the children and dogs together;
Sprinkle the field with flowers;
Spread over all the sky of deep blue and bake in the sun.
When brown, set away to cool in the bathtub.

365 INDEPENDENCE DAYS
(An Introduction to Food Preservation)

A person has to choose what they're going to struggle for. Life is always a struggle whether you're struggling for anything worthwhile or not, so it might as well be for something worthwhile. Independence days are worth struggling for. They're good for me, good for the country and a good life for the children to be growing up in. I think being married to a good man, raising children and raising food are the most important worldly things there are. And the most rewarding.

The best food product is the one you can grow or make yourself starting with as natural ingredients as possible. The results may not look the best, and they may not taste the best, but they really are the best because that's the way we were meant to get our food and that's what we were meant to eat. That's what I believe and I think when it comes to believing you just have to believe whatever you believe and let it go at that without any more fuss. My ideal woman is milking a cow or goats, gardening and caring for her children herself as well as preparing meals (and washing dishes). She hasn't got time for fancy cake decorating and vegetable dishes with eight ingredients. And my ideal woman wants to use as few store ingredients and as few store gadgets as possible. She's looking for from-scratch recipes or else not looking at all.

There are a certain few basics to cooking in any food category. A person needs a recipe maybe to guide them through the first few times before striking off on their own to do recipeless cooking. But women in this country nowadays have themselves in a state of slavery to recipes that are unreasonable, inappropriate and expensive. They are running to the store way too often to get the strange ingredients that turn up in their recipes. It has them trying to cook Japanese, Indian, Greek or whatnot food out of an American garden, which just won't grow the special foods of another climate zone. And worst of all it keeps them ignorant about the wonderful magic at the heart of a household—the magic that turns turnips and cream and apples and meat into food and you can say to your family here's what we worked so hard to get and isn't it good! You can't cook happily, freely, independently, until you can throw away your recipe books and just make good things out of what the Lord is giving you.

That's the way Great-grandmother did it. She looked in the larder, the cellar and then took a walk through the garden to see what she had. And then she made menus for the next couple days. When she had eggs and milk aplenty, a little honey and some stale bread, the family had a bread pudding. In May she served rhubarb with it, in June strawberries, in July raspberries, in August blackberries and in September peaches—because that's the way they grew.

To have 365 days of independent eating you've got to learn to eat what you can grow and you've got to learn to grow what you want to eat. At first it will be hard but stick to it. If you don't like what you have, eat it anyway and use the energy of your distaste to figure how to get what you'll like better. If your only meat is elk, eat elk until you can raise something else. If you miss bacon get four little pigs. In six months they'll be 200 pounders and you'll have a year's supply of bacon plus a sow to breed and keep the bacon coming. If you're still living in the city and you don't have anything but dreams, try for fun buying only what you imagine you could grow—in a natural unprocessed state—like whole grains and see if you can learn to live off it.

When lettuce is in season have a salad every day—you can't preserve it. If you miss it in the off-season contrive a way to raise winter lettuce in the house. If you miss sweets learn beekeeping. If you have barley and corn make your bread, pancakes and pie crust out of barley flour, cornmeal crust and a bear meat filling. If you have some tough old hens past their laying prime, three extra male goats and a hundred rabbits then learn good ways to cook tough old hens, goat meat and rabbit.

Keep plugging away at it. All spring I try to plant something every day—from late February when the early peas and spinach and garlic can go in on up to midsummer when the main potato crop and the late beans and lettuce go in. Then I switch over and make my rule to try to get something put away for the winter every single day. That lasts until the pumpkins and sunflowers and late squash and green tomatoes are in. Then comes the struggle to get the most out of the stored food—all winter long. It has to be checked regularly and anything added to the menu that's on the verge of spoiling, wilting or otherwise soon becoming useless. Or it can be preserved a new way. If a squash gets a soft spot I can cut it out, cook, mash, can or freeze the rest for a supper vegetable, pie, or to be added to the bread dough.

You have to ration. You have all the good food you can eat right at arm's reach and no money to pay . . . until you run out. You're likely to have either no elk at all or a lot of it (an elk is meatwise about as much as a whole cow). Rotate when you have a variety. If you have elk, beef, and some odds and ends of chicken, trout and ham, eat elk on A night, beef on B night, and alternately chicken, trout, and ham on C night. Garden crops have a tendency to either fail completely or else overwhelm with abundance. Fruit comes by the barrel but only for a short period of time unless you can preserve it.

If you haven't previously raised your own food I would guess it takes more food to keep your family going than you realize. Do you know how many

cows, goats, chickens, sheep, etc., you need for one year's supply of milk and meat? How many bushels of grain (how many acres of it)? How many heads of cabbage, sacks of potatoes? You can find out to a certain extent by keeping records and next by experience. It takes a *lot*. Because people doing hard outdoor work have bigger appetites. Because you have animals to feed too. Because you have to allow for loss by crop failure or spoilage in storage. Pumpkins and fruit you have to figure from harvest to harvest—a full 12 months. Greens you store from fall to spring because you'll have them fresh from dandelion greens in the spring to your last cutting of Swiss chard or mustard greens in the fall. Meat is a crop that you can harvest in the winter but not the summer except for very small animals like poultry and goats. Milk is year-round—providing you have more than one animal milking and stagger the time they come fresh. You have to have enough winter feed in storage for them. A hungry cow won't just loyally grow lean. She'll either go way down on the milk or she'll go through the fence and range onto the neighbors. (She is also likely to leave in search of a bull when she needs one—fences hold only contented cows.)

So plan ahead. If you didn't breed your milker x months ago, she won't be milking when you want her to. If you butcher thirty chickens in June and have chicken every Sunday you'll have no more after Christmas until next summer. And did you save layers? They won't lay in the winter but they will make up for it in May. Did you preserve eggs in water glass or by freezing during the period when the hens lay like crazy—from May to October (or sooner)? Because you won't see another egg until spring. I'll confess honestly I never manage to do it all right. But we keep struggling toward the ideal.

Here are a few specific ideas that may help you. There are more in the other chapters.

FRUITS, BERRIES, NUTS—It takes a few years to get production going unless you inherit them. In the meantime you can compensate by scavenging for wild fruit and berries. Find out where they are and when. The general rule is to freeze berries and can fruit but you may also can berries if need be. You'll want a good supply of canning jars. Figure on at least 80 quarts of fruit for a couple and 40 more for each child and that's a desperate minimum. That's only a quart a week per person during the nine months when fruit is out of season. Then you need rhubarb, strawberries, raspberries, cherries and early apples to carry you until the big fruits are ripe again.

VEGETABLES—What varieties you can raise depends on your elevation, the part of the country you live in, your rainfall or water supply and so on. Your first garden is almost certain to have some failures. You'll have to get to understand its peculiarities. But I'm sure you can raise something that first year and a person can survive on onions, turnips and potatoes, if need be. Replant as soon as you're sure a crop isn't making it. You can plant potatoes, beans and onion sets clear up to July 15. Just keep them well watered. An acre in garden is a minimum for me. If you have only a little room and it's your first garden I recommend Swiss chard (no spinach), bush beans, bush peas, squash and tomatoes if you've the climate for them, onions from sets and leaf lettuce.

DAIRY—There can't be too much milk. If your family doesn't need it all, you can raise calves, pigs and chickens on it, feed the dog and cat and make butter and cheese. I separate the cream out for buttermaking, refrigerate whole milk for cooking and table use and separate out the curds from the rest for cheese. The animals get the whey. My recipes use real cream and butter in them because hopefully you are milking and have these. You'll need a barn and hay supply for winter, stanchions, buckets and maybe a separator to help get the cream if it's goats you have. You can store surplus butter in the freezer.

STARCHES—Plant kidney beans for your homemade chili—an agreeable way to use up some goat burger. Have a grainfield if you can. My ideal is a field of wheat and rye mixed because that's what they did in the old days—raised it together, harvested it together and baked it together. And a big patch of field corn for cornmeal. Not the same as sweet corn. But hand harvesting grains is hard and inefficient. So plant a big potato patch. That's starch, too.

MEAT—This family of seven (and very often extras) can use two big calves, four pigs, maybe half an elk and 50 or more chickens a year. The pigs supply cooking grease as well which can be canned or stored in the deep freeze.

PRESERVING NOTEBOOK—Now that you've got the idea I can help you find a way for your personal family to sort its way through all this. Keep a notebook. Put in the notebook when you butchered what and about how many pounds of meat you put into the deep freeze. Put in there how many chickens you had and how many eggs you got, and how many goats you were milking and how much milk you got, and how many seed packets of what you planted or how many pounds of potatoes and then in the fall write down how many bushels of spuds you had to go into storage. That makes it possible to learn from experience. If you've the time and the patience you can put down more detail even than that and you'll find it helpful. Write down the total amount you're spending every week on food and where you're spending it. Compare that to the number of mouths you're feeding. See if you can bring it down by using more homegrown ingredients. Note how much you preserved of what and when you ran out. Note even what recipes you used in your food preserving and if you added to or subtracted from the basic recipe and refer back to that the next year to see if you want to do it again or if you want to change. I don't do that. I'm always too busy but a very organized friend named Lin Shoemaker in Pullman, Washington, up the road from here does just this and she really recommends the system.

You'll get used to planning ahead for an entire year—from garden to garden, from slaughter to slaughter in order to prevent feast-and-famine. Then in the long winter evenings when you're planning for next summer, adjust where needed. Not enough eggs? Save more hens from the chopping block this year. Couldn't eat all those pickles? You won't need so much garden space for cucumbers next year.

SPECIFIC HOW-TO-DO-IT FOOD PRESERVING PROCEDURES—This chapter will introduce you to the methods. Look under each specific vegetable in the Vegetables chapter for canning, freezing, drying, or root cellar storage procedures. You'll also find out how to make vegetable juices in that chapter. Fruits and berries and how to preserve them are in the Sweets chapter as well as here. Real sweet foods like jams and jellies and fruit butters are in the Sweets chapter, too. Pickles and sauerkraut, relishes and some pickled vegetables are in the Sours chapter. For a great big, conservative and encyclopedic book on food preserving try *Putting Food By*, by Ruth Hertzberg, Beatrice Vaughan and Janet Greene. The book comes from Vermont where generations of careful housewives have perfected their food preserving art. Order from Garden Way, Charlotte, Vermont 05445.

HOMESTEAD MENUS THROUGH THE YEAR

Here are some menus. I didn't create them specifically for this book. When I remembered to I wrote them down after we ate. I'm really proud of the way we eat because the table usually is set mostly with the fruit of our own labor and God's mercy. It isn't "gourmet" cooking and it isn't "health food" cooking either. But I think that if we raise it ourselves without adding poisons, have plenty of it and plenty of different kinds of food, that's surely the most natural and a plenty healthy way to eat.

In the menus that follow "dried fruit" means fruit dried in our frontyard. "Mayonnaise" means homemade. "Butter" means from our own churn and "bread" means from our oven. "Bacon" or "ham" means home-cured and "sauerkraut" means out of our crock as does "pickles." "Root beer" and "ginger ale" are homemade, too. We always have milk and usually tea on the table whether I wrote it down or not. We gather camomile, wild strawberry leaves, wild and tame mint and rose hips here on the farm and dry them for tea. Camomile is my favorite. The home gathered tea is even better than what you can buy at the store.

SNACKS for company, for husband or children famished between meals, for the afternoon tea break, or a bedtime family treat are legal here. Lots of old-time farm families have a regular midmorning and midafternoon mini-meal for the working men when they are putting in long summer days. We take something like a gallon of cold tea and sandwiches out to the field and the work stops for a few minutes. I don't fight snacks as long as the food is homegrown and home prepared. I do blacklist store cookies, potato chips, pop and candy.

Fresh, canned or frozen fruit	Homemade popsicles
	Homemade crackers
Dried fruit	Jerky
Pickles	Bread, with butter or
Popcorn	honey

Leftovers like sliced, cold roast or cold boiled potatoes are good with some salt or butter. Mike doesn't like to eat leftovers, except potatoes and meat, so if somebody doesn't snack them up the chickens or pigs get them—except for bread which metamorphoses into bread pudding or dishes that I can serve for lunch when it's woman and children.

Thanksgiving 1972

Gander stuffed with Sage Dressing (the one that bit Danny twice)

Sliced Tomatoes (last of the fresh ones. They were picked green just before frost and stored to ripen gradually)

Cooked Pumpkin mashed with Butter

Boiled Green Beans with Onion and Bacon

Boiled Potatoes, Giblet Gravy

Sweet Crock Pickles, Bread, Cheese

Brandied Peaches (we buried them in September and dug them up for Thanksgiving)

Root Beer

Thanksgiving 1973

Roast Goose stuffed with Sauerkraut

Giblet Gravy

Mashed Potatoes

Baked Acorn Squash halves (a dab of butter and honey cooked in the heart)

Boiled Swiss Chard

Brandied Peaches

Mincemeat Pie

Christmas Dinner

Turkey and Dressing and Peach Catsup

Potatoes and Giblet Gravy

Boiled Green Beans

Carrot and Dried Fruit Salad (grated carrot tossed with chopped dried fruit and mayonnaise)

Bread, Butter

Pumpkin Pie

BREAKFASTS
(If your chickens aren't laying leave out the eggs)

Cornmeal Mush
Bread, Butter, Honey
Soft-Boiled Eggs

Toasted Sourdough Bread
Pork Chops
Applesauce
Scrambled Eggs

Homemade Grape Nuts (recipe in Grains chapter) with Cream
Sliced Fresh Peaches
Poached Eggs

Cornmeal Mush
Home Canned Fruit
Elk Sausage (use ⅓ pork meat)
Fried Eggs

Leftover Boiled Potatoes (sliced and fried)
Elk Sausage
Home Canned Tomato Juice
Fried Eggs

French Toast (bread sliced and dipped in an egg-milk mixture and fried)
Honey, Butter
Bacon
Wild Plums

Summer Breakfast
(cooked outdoors)

Pancakes (baked on the top of a wood stove)
Goat's Butter, Honey
Stewed Wild Apples
Home-Cured Bacon

LUNCHES

May Lunch

Scrambled Eggs
Leftover Boiled Potatoes (fried with sautéed chopped green [Egyptian] onions)
Asparagus Spears

Fried Leftover Cornmeal Mush with Butter and Molasses or Honey
Blackberries
Bacon
Bread, Butter

Hamburger
Sliced Fried Leftover Boiled Potatoes
Tomato Catsup (homemade)
Bread, Butter, Jelly

Leftover Stew Warmed Up (extended with some fresh vegetables)
Bread, Butter, Wild Plum Sauce
Mint Tea with Honey

A Special Lunch

Cold Leftover Steak (sliced in strips)
Fried Potatoes and Onions
Hard-Boiled Eggs
Canned Applesauce
Bread, Butter
Iced Wild Strawberry Leaf Tea

Ground Leftover Ham and Pickles on Bread
Cottage Cheese (we eat it with milk and honey except Mike who prefers it with salt and pepper)

Sandwiches of Herb Bread and Sliced Cold Venison Roast
Canned Juice
Pickles

SPRING AND SUMMER SUPPERS

Potatoes
Bread
Creamed Onions
Dandelion Greens
   Stewed
Raw Fresh Asparagus

Dandelion Greens and
   Bacon Bits
Roast Ham and Gravy
Potatoes
Stewed Rhubarb
Radishes

Lettuce Salad (leaf let-
   tuce)
Radishes
Potatoes
Fried Meat and Milk
   Gravy
Strawberries on Leftover
   Bread with Cream

Leftover Sliced Cold
   Roast
Bread and Apple Pud-
   ding (crumbled bread
   crust baked with milk,
   sliced cored apples,
   beaten egg, honey,
   cinnamon)
Warmed-up Leftover
   Gravy Extended with
   Milk (to go on the
   meat)
Boiled Swiss Chard

Chicken Stew (old layer
   with carrots, potatoes,
   onions, turnips) and
   Dumplings
Blackberry-Apple Bread
   Pudding (berries, ap-
   ples, milk, bread
   crust, honey, baked
   and served with
   cream)
Iced Camomile Tea

Picnic

Fried Chicken
Potato Salad
Leaf Lettuce Salad
Raspberries in Whipped
   Cream
Ginger Ale

*When You're Hot
And Tired*

Potato Salad (made ear-
   lier and chilled)
Barbecued Meat (hus-
   band cook it)
Tossed Green Salad
   (children make it)
Raspberry Ice (made
   ahead)
Corn-on-the-Cob
Sliced Fresh Fruit
Roast Mustard Greens
Potatoes
Half-Cured Pickles
Carrot Sticks
Boiled Peas
Boiled New Potatoes
Fried Chicken and
   Gravy
Bread, Butter

WINTER SUPPERS

Boiled Sliced Turnips
Roast and Gravy
Baked Potatoes
Pickles
Bread, Butter
Junket Pudding

Elk Roast and Gravy
Sage Dressing
Baked Squash
Spinach
Mashed Potatoes
Mincemeat Cookies

Pork Chops
Gravy
Boiled Peas
Yeast Biscuits
Boiled Potatoes

Steak and Gravy
Mashed Potatoes
Cole Slaw (Homemade
   Dressing)
Cream-Style Corn

Crumb Bread, Cherry
   Jelly
Canned Apricots
Stew with Meat, To-
   matoes, Carrots,
   Cabbage
Raw Turnip Slices
   dipped in Herbed
   Sour Cream

Leftover Sliced Cold
   Roast
Bread and Apple Pud-
   ding (crumbled bread
   crusts baked with
   milk, cored sliced ap-
   ples, eggs, honey and
   cinnamon)
Mashed Boiled Turnips

A SYSTEM FOR MENU PLANNING

My mother taught me the following basics of
menu planning. I've heard of other systems but this is
the one I grew up with. It has served me well enough
that I'll pass it on. To me if something *works* then it
was obviously made in Heaven. This worked for me
and my mother and for all I know for Great-
grandmother, too. But it's sort of like Infinite Good-
ness. I'm always striving after it and often falling
short. Still if you're striving after a *good* thing usually
even your failure will be a sort of success.

BREAKFAST—Include a fruit or fruit product, a
meat, a starch, eggs and a beverage.

A "fruit" could be a glass of fruit juice, or sliced
orange sections (cut orange on the equator, then get
about four sections out of each hemisphere and eat
with fingers), a grapefruit half, half cantaloupe or
muskmelon, stewed or canned fruit, fresh sliced fruit
on cereal or in pancakes, berry syrup hot for breakfast bread or preserved fruit on bread.

A "meat" could be bacon, link sausage, patty
sausage, ham slices, breakfast steak, pork chops or
fried trout.

A "starch" could be leftover boiled potatoes, fried
in butter maybe with a little chopped green onion or
green pepper added (sauté first), or grated and fried
(that makes hash browns). Use leftover mashed
potatoes mixed with egg and milk (chopped onion optional) to make patties and fry in a little butter for

potato pancakes. Or have homemade bread, plain or toasted, or biscuits, pancakes, waffles, crêpes or corn bread. Or any hot cereal. Or a cold one like homemade grape nuts. Or leftover rice warmed with hot milk and honey.

"Eggs" can be an ingredient in the breakfast bread, or fried slowly over low heat in butter, or boiled, poached, scrambled, souffléd or in an eggnog (1 egg or 2, about 1½ cups milk, a little honey, a few drops of vanilla or a little berry syrup for flavoring beaten with your egg beater).

LUNCH varies so much depending on who is eating. If you are feeding a man who works near enough home to eat lunch with you then you may even want to reverse the lunch and supper menus. If your man can't get home for lunch, make lunch time for using up leftovers for you and the toddlers or the cat. That's what I do. Mike takes a packed lunch to work. It usually consists of two leftover sliced meat sandwiches on homemade bread and some variety of extras such as hard-boiled eggs, pickles, a ripe tomato or carrot sticks. In the winter he takes Postum (made with milk) in his thermos or soup and tea, and in the summer cold tea or root beer or ginger ale. On weekends we often grind leftover meat to make sandwich spreads. Then we have sandwiches, milk and fruit.

SUPPER—Your menu should include a meat, a starch and two vegetables. One of the vegetables should be raw. One should be green. The other should be a yellow, red or white vegetable. For a special dinner have three vegetables, one green, one otherwise, and one raw and add something sweet and something sour to the menu.

A "meat" can be any kind of meat prepared any way.

A "starch" usually means boiled, baked, or mashed potatoes, bread, dumplings or noodles in my meals. In Taiwan it would mean rice.

A "green vegetable" could be peas, beans, Brussels sprouts, broccoli, cabbage, collards, spinach, lettuce or any of the many other leafy greens, green onions, green peppers and so forth.

A "yellow, red or white vegetable" could be carrots, turnips, squash, sweet potatoes, cauliflower, parsnips, pumpkin, corn, radishes, beets, tomato, eggplant and the like.

Something "sour" could be anything out of the Sours chapter—a pickle or catsup usually.

Something "sweet" to me usually means fruit or a pudding sweetened with honey.

The "beverage" in summer is homemade root beer or ginger ale, cold water, iced tea and milk for the small children. In winter it's tea or honey and lemon with hot water, or a mulled beverage, or eggnog or milk lassie made with hot milk.

FOOD PRESERVATION

We share this wonderful world with myriad invisible but ravenous little critters who love to eat exactly the same things we do. The food preservation game is to get a move ahead of them and of "enzymes," which are chemicals contained in the food itself that can cause undesirable changes. Salt, sugar, alcohol, sodium benzoate, sulfurous acid and sodium metabisulfate are "chemical" preservatives that, in effect, poison or make the food yuk to the beasties. Drying makes it impossible for them to live in there. Freezing puts them all to sleep. Canning kills every last one in the food and seals it up tight so that more can't get in. Cellar storage takes advantage of natural defenses that certain foods have to keep from spoiling.

There are one or two optimum methods of keeping any single type of food. In my opinion tomatoes, large fruits, syrups, fruit butters and juices are all best kept canned. Cucumbers and cabbage are best pickled (preserved in salt). Green beans are good either canned or frozen. Corn, greens, peas, baby turnips, baby carrots, extra bread, meat and hides waiting to be tanned are in my freezer. Berries are better frozen than canned. Fruit, except berries, is also very good dried. Apples are good made into sauce or butter and canned. Or you can dry apple rings. Or freeze slices in syrup for pie making. Onions, potatoes, winter squash, big turnips and big carrots will keep in the root cellar best.

OF JARS, LIDS—Get ready for your food preserving ahead of time because when the harvest is on you'll be frantic. If you plan to can get your jars, lids and screw bands ahead of time. Preferably buy them by the case a year ahead because the stores sometimes run out at the peak of the season. Save all the bottles and glass containers that come into your life. Quart and pint mayonnaise type jars may be used for canning. There are three lid sizes: "regular," "63" (which is small) and "widemouthed" (which is big).

Many of the jars for commercial products can use one of them. The glass isn't quite as heavy as in regular canning jars, but if you are careful that the food you put into the jars is hot or has hot water or juice poured over it before you put it in the hot canner it won't break.

Any gallon jar (glass or plastic) is good for many things—holding milk, pickling, anything you need a "crock" for. Small jars can hold dried herbs and spices, dried jerky, dried fruits, crackers, or pickled and special dainties that don't require absolute sealing. Paraffin covered jellies can go there too. Baby food jars can be used with the original lid for open kettle canning of high acid foods. Tighten the lids when you take them out of the canner. Save your lids to match up after you empty the jar. (Except for "pop" bottles, used for home bottled beverages, for which you'll have to buy new lids.) Widemouthed jars can also be used for table glasses, or to hold seeds, crayons, Scrabble letters and other odd things. In the summer the children need jars with holes punched in the lid for grasshoppers, spiders and so on.

Reusing the original twist-on type lid as well as

the jar in canning is a riskier business, but there are people who do it. They say the lids can be used over and over as long as the enamel doesn't become damaged.

If you want to experiment with recycling store lids in your canning do it with fruits and jellies. Tighten the lid when you are ready to seal after the heat period. If you should want to use this type of lid in the pressure canner remember not to tighten the lid before pressuring. Just get it on enough so it won't fall off and then quickly and thoroughly get the lids tightened down after you have let the canner pressure down. Chicken and fish are hard on lids so use brand-new lids with them if you possibly can.

CANS are worth saving too. (Of course not very many bottles and cans come into this household because we make so much of our own food. Maybe in other styles of life you would simply be buried under them.) You can use them for "glasses" to hold beverages. The 46-ounce juice cans are good lard holders and you can just fit a baggie over the top to make a fairly tight cover before putting it away in the freezer. One-gallon cans are good lard containers, too, and good grain holders to feed the chickens. Punch a couple little holes in the bottom of your small cans and you can start plants in them indoors. Cans make the healthiest plant pots I know except for those peat pots which aren't as sturdy and aren't reusable and you have to buy them in the first place. Or put the right size baggie inside to line the can and you can fill it with liquid or food, tie or wire shut the baggie at the top and use it for a freezer container.

PLASTIC BREAD SACKS, PICKLE JARS, PLASTIC BUCKETS—Jeannie Travis, from Kell, Illinois, is a real saver like me. This is what she wrote me. "Mom tells me she got new plastic bread sacks at the day old bakery. They were supposed to be 100 for $1 but there were more like 200. They should be about right for

your family freezing. If you know someone who works in a restaurant or school they can save bread bags for you. I get the big pickle jars free at a restaurant and also the large plastic buckets. When available at other places those plastic buckets are 50 cents each." Thank you Jeannie for the ideas!

AND TOYS—There are three places in my kitchen where children are especially welcome. One is their box that holds toys, coloring books and so on. The second is the special drawer where I keep my lid collection which doubles as a toy assortment. They think of their own games and the possibilities are practically infinite. Toddlers love the clunky bright metals, especially the doughnut shaped canning screw tops. Bigger children make up matching games. The woodbox is their other favorite kitchen toy box. All kinds of forts, houses, barns, highways, railroads and towers go up on my kitchen floor. They all end up in the stove, of course, but then the children are very willing to haul me in more wood.

CANNING SUPPLIES

JARS—How many will you need? If you put up 100 quarts of green beans your family could eat 2 quarts a week all year-round. The same for corn or fruit. So you can figure by what you think you'll need. Whether your garden will produce that much or even more is another question and probably will vary with the year.

WHAT TYPE OF JARS?—The widemouthed jars are good for large whole fruits, such as peaches and pears, and for canning meat and pickles. The "63" jars (small size) are hard to fill, especially for hot pack canning. Very liquid items like juices or small fruits such as cherries, berries and apricots go into them best. The size jar you want also depends on how much your family can eat up at a meal. For my size family it works out best to put up butters, jams, jellies and taco sauce in half pints to minimize spoilage before the food gets used up. All fruits go into quarts and the most popular ones into half gallon jars because they go fast. Catsup and vegetables work out best in pint jars, except string beans and tomatoes which are in quarts.

GETTING JARS—The cheapest way is to have everybody saving their mayonnaise, Sanka and so on kinds of jars for you. If you are in a rush put a wanted-to-buy ad out for used jars. But check the rims carefully before you put down your money. Do this by running your finger over the top of the rim and checking for nicks. Even the tiniest nick makes a jar unusable for canning. A nicked jar rim won't seal right. You can also buy canning jars new at big grocery outlets.

I'm really enthusiastic about the imported French old-style canning jars with glass lids. You buy jar, lid, rubber ring and bail. They just came on the market in the last year or so and are still fairly hard to find. The rubber rings are very thick so they can be used over and over many times. They're too thick for old fashioned American jars so you need the French jars to go with the French rings. They are not cheap but

Canning funnel

Screw bands

Lids

on the other hand you don't throw any part away so it's all there again for the next year. They are shipped from France in cases of more than a dozen. Sizes range from ½ liter (1 pint, 1 oz.) to 3 liters (12¾ cups), and prices from about $1.40 to $3.50 each retail. (Case prices are lower.) You can buy extra rings, since when canning meat and low acid vegetables you might want to play it really safe and use new rings, but use old rings on all the other stuff. Extra rings from Red Apple Culinary, 605 W. First St., Spokane, Washington 99204, are 13¢ each for the two smaller sizes and 15¢ for the largest size. The French jars won't fit in your conventional racks so you'll need a special jar lifter. That's called "Mac's Canning Aid" and you can mail-order one. Send $2 to Keith Mac-Donald, Rt. 2, Box 69, Colville, Washington 99114. Another source for imported glass canning jars is Manca Import-Export Company, 1990 Alaskan Way, Seattle, Washington 98101.

LIDS—One dozen brand-new metal jar lids sell for around 35¢. When you have your own jars and screw bands and grow your own food, the lids are virtually the only expense in canning. Used lids don't seal right. The old-time sealing rubbers (as compared to our current metal lid with sealing compound around the rim) and glass jar lids and porcelain lined screw caps are not obtainable now. If you have a few in your basement (I do) they are antiques. At least that's what I used to think until a lady wrote to say, "Porcelain lids (called 'Zinc') and rubbers are available. My local Shoprite has them occasionally." And then I discovered the French jars, too.

Sealing lids of not so many years back may have had more adhesive than they currently do because it seems like open kettle canning didn't have so many failures then. If you open kettle can, really press down on that lid to try to get it to seal. My favorite canning method is water bath because I've had considerable bad luck with open kettle canning—with the stuff going moldy on me. But I have friends who have better luck so maybe they know something I don't. Any jar lid that has that funny plasticy rim around the inside edge can be used for hot pack canning—safest to use with jellies and pickles. Heat softens the stuff

and it makes a very decent seal. Catsup bottles mostly have it and they can be reused for your homemade catsup.

SCREW BANDS can be used over and over like the jars. You can stretch your materials by removing screw bands after the jars are sealed and cooled, wash them and use them again for the next set of jars to go into the canner. But my personal preference is to have enough screw bands to leave them on just because I don't want to bother taking them off during the busy canning time. I'm also afraid of disturbing the seal. If you wonder if a jar is the right size for canning test it with a screw band. If one of the three sizes will fit, it's OK. If a screw band is rusty, bent or has the top edge pried up it won't work right and might as well be thrown away.

FUNNEL—A widemouthed canning funnel is hard to find these days. My mother used one. I finally got a 1920 glass one at an auction. If you don't have one you'll wish you did because you'll be always burning your fingers. They are especially necessary for hot pack canning.

THE FOOD—Keep it clean. Above all make sure you don't let any dirt into the jar or food mixture because the most difficult bacteria to kill are those that live in the soil. The food to be canned should not have bruise spots or decay (although the children or I have let lots of little ones through and it never did any harm) and should be as freshly gathered as possible. If you can manage two hours from garden to jar you'll be a wonder and have the best tasting canned food possible (more important for vegetables than for fruits). When peeling large fruits for canning you can prevent discoloration by keeping them in a brine (2 teaspoons salt per quart of water) and drain off the brine when you're ready to pack or precook the fruit. Or you can just work fast which is what I do.

BOOKS—To can really happily you need more information than I can give you here. For total canning coverage written for you by experts (which I'm not):

Ball Blue Book, Dept. PK-6, Box 2005, Muncie, Indiana 47302. $2.00.

Ball Brothers also has a pamphlet, "Some Aspects of Food Preservation" which is very educational on the basics of you versus the beasties. 5¢ plus postage.

Kerr Home Canning Book—Kerr Glass Mfg. Corp., Dept. 125, Sand Springs, Oklahoma 74063. $1.00.

From the U.S. Department of Agriculture you can get two good booklets—"Home Canning of Fruits and Vegetables" and "Home Canning of Meat and Poultry." Call up your county extension agent to get copies or else send 15¢ for each one to the Superintendent of Documents, U.S. Government Printing Office, Washington, D.C. 20402. There is also "Making Pickles and Relishes at Home" (G-92—15¢), "How to Make Jellies, Jam and Preserves at Home" (G-56—30¢).

Freezing and Canning Cookbook—put out by the *Farm Journal*, Doubleday and Co., Garden City, New York, a big hardcover, is good, though I like the Ball and Kerr books better.

HOW TO STORE CANNED FOOD—You have to store it someplace where it can't possibly freeze. Freezing would break your jars as the water expands. By leaving at least ½ inch head space in the jar you protect it to a certain extent but not all the way. That's why canned food is usually stored together with root vegetables in your root cellar if you have one. If not it needs a cool, dark place so if you have a basement that would be a good place. The coolness helps hold down enzyme and microbe activity in stored food, and the dark helps protect color. If you live in an earthquake-prone area, canned food arranged on shelves is very vulnerable to the slightest tremor. In that kind of area store canning jars in boxes flat on the floor with cardboard strips as cushions between the jars. When you run out of floor space use strongly attached shelving with edging strips to prevent the jars from falling off.

HOW LONG WILL CANNED FOOD KEEP?—No matter whether you use brand-new jars or scavenged jars and no matter how carefully you can the food, home-canned food doesn't last forever. The best way to proceed is to plan so you eat up during the winter everything you canned the fall before. It will keep nine months for sure. That way you can eat from your garden in the summer and from your garden via the jars during the winter. If you manage right you'll polish off the last jarful as the new garden is starting to produce. Meat is a food you can harvest year-round and if you can plan on eating canned meat within six months I'd feel better about it. But sometimes you may not plan right or something happens and it doesn't get all eaten up. OK. Low acid vegetables like corn, beets, green beans I would open up the jars and give them to the pigs rather than keep them another winter. Or put them at the front of the shelf and make it a point to use up as soon as possible. High acid things like fruit and tomato juice you can let go into a second year. It doesn't improve them to sit forever though. What will happen as the years go by is gradually one by one the lids will lose their seal and the contents of a high acid jar would turn moldy. If you were *really* hungry you could take off the moldy part and eat the rest but it's unappetizing.

GETTING READY TO CAN

1. Run your finger around the rim of each jar to check for nicks. A nicked rim can't be depended on to seal properly.

2. Wash jars *clean* in hot soapy water. If you can't get it clear clean don't use it to can in. Get a headstart on this part of it by getting them thoroughly clean after you take the food out so they'll be all ready for the new year's coming and all you need to do is get the dust thoroughly off.

3. Give them a scalding rinse and turn upside down to drain on a clean folded cloth.

4. You get your lids ready by letting them spend a little time in boiling water. The lid company says to pour boiling water over the lids and then let them set in that water without further heating until you are ready to use. Certain neighbor ladies and volume

canners I know insist that the lids don't seal properly without a good boiling and that you can get better results with modern lids if you boil a little extra. I don't know who is right. When I have canned I'll confess I boiled my lids. I didn't get 100 percent sealing either, but then again it wasn't bad. We had canned fruit all winter from those boiled lids. So this is another place where you're going to have to experiment and make up your own mind just how *you* are going to do it.

5. Now you fill the jars. You can either *cold pack* or *hot pack*. Hot pack is safer to use with low acid foods because you have extra heating time involved. Cold pack is easier because you don't have to handle hot food. *To cold pack* you simply pour or put the fruit, tomatoes, sauerkraut, pickles, whatever into your jar. Then you can pour over either a lukewarm or hot liquid. The only potential problem at this time is that if the temperature of your food and your jar differ drastically your jar may crack. That's because glass expands with heat and contracts with cold and so if you poured something hot into a cold jar the inside might expand enough to crack the outside and blooey, food all over your table and no jar.

To hot pack you precook the food to be canned in a kettle on the stove, preheat your jars like in your oven enough so they won't crack when filled, and then fill the jars with hot food through a wide-mouthed funnel.

HIGH ACID AND LOW ACID FOODS

High Acid:	Low Acid:
Fruits	All other vegetables
Tomatoes	Low acid varieties of
Ripe pimentos	tomatoes
Rhubarb	Meat, poultry, fish
Sauerkraut	

Understanding the terms "high acid" and "low acid" is vital if you want to stay alive. Different foods naturally contain varying amounts of acid and the acid strength plays an important role in food preservation. As the acid strength increases, the temperature or time needed to kill the beasties decreases. High acid foods can be processed by cooking from 10 to 25 minutes (different times for different foods). Low acid foods such as beans and corn need as much as 5 hours of constant hard boiling to destroy spores (the most resistant seed form) of the beasties. If you goof and your high acid food spoils, and you get mold on the top, throw it out to the pigs or chickens. But unless all the spores of the bacillus botulinus are destroyed in canned vegetables (low acid foods), the remaining spores will grow and develop an invisible powerful poison toxin. You can open the jar and it will look and smell fine. That's why it is recommended that all low acid home-canned foods be boiled 15 minutes before serving or tasting—because the poisonous toxin is destroyed by boiling. And that's why *only* the pressure canner method is recommended for canning low acid foods, because it's safe enough, and the open kettle and water bath methods aren't. There's too much risk of your kettle dropping below the boiling point, even briefly.

CANNING TIMETABLES

These are the "generally accepted" figures. Note that the farm wife type canners I know water bath can vegetables and meats for longer than the times given here rather than the officially published times which are not as long. Many of them water bath can fruits less than the recommended times. One neighbor lady I know cans all her fruit by just letting it boil on the stove the given amount of time, then pours it into a jar, tightens the lid and puts it away. I've tried that and most of it molded. You can experiment with high acid foods but not with low acid ones. That neighbor uses the "open kettle" system for canning the fruit that most people "hot water bath" can.

This table is for an altitude of 1,000 feet or less. For each 1,000 feet more that you live above sea level you should add 1 minute to the processing time if the time called for is 20 minutes or less. Add 2 minutes for each 1,000 feet if the processing time called for is more than 20 minutes. The pressure cooker times are set for sea level. For each 2,000 feet that you live above sea level increase the pressure by 1 pound. You have to process longer for larger-sized jars because it takes them longer to heat. For processing half-gallon jars of high acid food add 10 minutes to water bath time, 5 minutes to pressure cooker time. To process half-gallon jars of low acid foods increase time 20 percent over the time for quarts. If you are processing in half-pint jars or smaller use same time as for pints.

HIGH ACID FOODS

How to Prepare	Boiling Water Bath Minutes Pints	Quarts	Pressure Cooker Minutes	Pounds	How to Prepare	Boiling Water Bath Minutes Pints	Quarts	Pressure Cooker Minutes	Pounds
Apples Pack hot, cover with hot liquid.	20	25	10	5	**Peaches** Peel, pack, add liquid.	20	25	10	5
Applesauce—hot pack.	20	25	10	5	**Pears** Peel, pack, add liquid.	25	30	10	5
Apricots Wash, halve, take out pits. Pack in jars. Add liquid.	20	25	10	5	**Pineapple** Peel, slice, take out eyes and core, hot pack, add liquid.	30	30	15	5
Berries (except strawberries and cranberries) Wash, stem, pack, add liquid.	15	20	8	5	**Plums** Pack, add liquid.	20	25	10	5
Cherries Can with pits, pack, cover with liquid.	20	20	10	5	**Preserves** Follow recipe, hot pack, process at 180° (simmering rather than "boiling").	20	20	—	—
Cranberries Wash, stem, boil 3 minutes in heavy syrup, pack.	10	10	—	—	**Rhubarb** Cut in chunks. Precook or bake. Hot pack, add liquid if needed.	10	10	5	5
Currants Wash, stem, pack, add liquid.	20	20	10	5	**Strawberries** Stem, hot pack, cover with hot juice.	15	15	—	—
Dried Fruits Soak overnight in cold water. Boil 10 minutes in same water, pack.	15	15	—	—	**Tomatoes** (high acid type) Scald, dip in cold water, peel, core, quarter, pack.	35	45	10	5
Figs Cook 2 minutes, make syrup, cook 5 minutes in syrup, pack.	20	30	10	5	**Tomatoes** (low acid type) Scald, peel, core, quarter, pack.	45	55	15	5
Fruit Juices Make your juice, pour into jars.	10	10	—	—	**Tomato juice** Follow recipe, hot pack.	10	10	—	—
Grapes Wash, stem, pack, add liquid.	20	20	8	5					
Nuts Pack, oven process at 225° for 45 minutes.	—	—	—	—					

LOW ACID FOODS

Always boil canned low acid vegetables and meats in a pan without a lid for at least 15 minutes before tasting or using! Pressure cooker canning recommended.

VEGETABLES		Boiling Water Bath Pts. & Qts.	Pressure Cooker Minutes Pts.	Qts.	Lbs.
Asparagus	Hot pack, add liquid	3½ hrs.	25	30	10
Beans, green & yellow	Snap, hot pack	3½ hrs.	20	25	10
Beans, lima	Shell, hot pack loosely	5 hrs.	40	50	10
Beets	Wash, boil, skin, hot pack	3½ hrs.	30	40	10
Broccoli	Hot pack	3½ hrs.	25	40	10
Brussels sprouts	Hot pack	3½ hrs.	45	55	10
Cabbage	Hot pack	4 hrs.	45	55	10
Carrots	Hot pack	3½ hrs.	25	30	10
Cauliflower	Hot pack	4 hrs.	25	40	10
Corn	Cut off cob, hot pack loosely	5 hrs.	55	85	10
Greens	Wash, hot pack loosely	4 hrs.	70	90	10
Hominy	Hot pack loosely	5 hrs.	60	70	10
Mushrooms	Hot pack loosely	4 hrs.	30	35	10
Okra	Hot pack	3½ hrs.	25	40	10
Onions	Hot pack	3½ hrs.	40	40	10
Parsnips	Peel, chunk, hot pack	3½ hrs.	20	25	10
Peas	Shell, hot pack	3½ hrs.	40	40	10
Peppers, green	Cut out seed pod, hot pack	3½ hrs.	35	35	10
Peppers, pimento	Bake or boil, peel, remove seeds	40 min.	10	10	5
Potatoes, white	Peel or scrape, hot pack	4 hrs.	40	40	10
Pumpkin	Peel, chunk, precook, hot pack	4 hrs.	60	80	10
Rutabagas	Peel, slice or cube, hot pack	3½ hrs.	35	35	10
Squash, summer	Cut in equal-sized pieces, hot pack	3½ hrs.	25	30	10
Squash, winter	Peel, chunk, precook until tender, hot pack	4 hrs.	60	80	10
Sweet potatoes	Precook 20 minutes, peel, hot pack	4 hrs.	65	95	10
Turnips	Peel, chunk, hot pack	3½ hrs.	20	25	10
MEATS	Pack raw or precooked, salt 1 teaspoon per quart unless presalted in recipe (sausage, ham). Do not add liquids to meat packed raw. Pack loosely	5 hrs.	75	90	10
FISH	Pack raw without liquid. Use only fresh, firm fish	6 hrs.	100	100	10

PICKLES

These are the USDA recommendations from "Making Pickles and Relishes at Home," Home and Garden Bulletin No. 92.

		Boiling Water Bath Minutes
Bread-and-Butter	qt.	10
Bread-and-Butter	pt.	5
Chutney	pt.	5
Cross-Cut Slices	pt.	5
Dill Green Beans	pt.	5
Sweet Gherkins	pt.	5
Piccalilli	pt.	5
Pepper-Onion Relish	pt.	5
Corn Relish	pt.	15
Watermelon Pickles	pt.	5
Peach Pickles	qt. or pt.	20
Pear Pickles	qt. or pt.	20
Fermented Whole Dills	qt.	15
Unfermented Whole Dills (fresh pack kind)	qt.	20
Sauerkraut	qt.	15

OPEN KETTLE METHOD

You don't even need a canning kettle to do it this way. It is very quick and appropriate for putting up small amounts but you risk mold. The "open kettle" method is a hot pack method—a hot pack that has no water bath time at all. The boiling before filling the jars is all the killing treatment the germs will get. That's why it is important to use this method only with the safest high acid foods. I would not even use it for "preserves and pickles" that involve low acid vegetables. Here I differ from the experts. I'm afraid you might run into a recipe that calls itself a "pickle" but actually isn't acid enough to be safe.

Open kettle canning is excellent for fruit preserves, marmalades, jams, jellies and very salty and vinegary pickles and relishes. It is good for high acid fruits and tomato products. The important thing is that the food should have cooked the required amount of time and that jar, lids and food all reach the boiling point.

PROCEDURE:

1. The food is boiling in a kettle on the stove and has cooked the required amount of time.

2. The screw bands and sealing lids are boiling in water in another pan.

3. Your jars have been washed clean in hot soapy water, scalded and drained.

4. Now combine! Use a big metal ladle and a widemouthed metal funnel sitting in the top of your jar to help you. Fill and seal one jar at a time before going on to the next, letting the food in your kettle boil merrily away while it waits its turn. Remember to leave at least ½ inch space between your packed food or liquid and the top of the jar.

5. Have ready a clean dish towel to wipe the jar rim and screwing side. Seeds or pulp might interfere with a good seal.

6. As quickly as possible after having filled the jar so as to retain your heat until safely sealed, lay the boiled lid, sticky side down, next to the jar rim. Then put the doughnut shaped screw band on top of that and screw it as tight as you can. Now grab up your dish towel and use it to get hold of that hot metal and tighten some more, really strain.

7. Now let jars cool standing upright, not touching, on cloth or paper or some more or less insulating surface so you don't risk glass breakage from having a hot jar on a cold surface.

8. Some experts recommend waiting until the jar is cold to test the seal but that worries me. Some jars, most in fact, seal very soon after filling, almost immediately. But some seal a little later on. The "seal" takes place when airflow between the jar and the outside is cut off. The air inside the jar is contracting because it is cooling and so you have a vacuum effect inside the jar which pulls the lid downward and reinforces the seal. You can tell whether the jar is sealed or not by looking at the lid. If it is sealed the lid is curved downward toward the center because the vacuum inside is pulling it inward. If it is not sealed it is straight across the top. If it is sealed you can tap it with a fork or spoon and it will make a clear ringing sound because of the tension on it. The only exception to this would be if you got the jar too full and food is touching the lid. Then it wouldn't make the canner's famous and beloved "ping." If the lid is not sealed the sound is lower pitched and not musical or prolonged. After you've heard the difference a few times you'll never mistake it. You can feel the seal, too, the downward curve to the center of the lid.

If your jars didn't seal within 10 minutes at the most, I'd advise you to take the food out and start over. Or just put the jar that didn't seal in the refrigerator with a mental note to yourself to use it up like you would any other refrigerator food within a reasonable period of time.

HOT WATER BATH CANNING

Women tend to have strong preferences for their own canning methods and if you could get an open kettle canner, a hot water bath canner and a pressure cooker canner in the same room together it would make for a lively discussion.

Canning in a pressure canner is great for vegetables because it is safer and saves so much *time* and as soon as I've got the money (sell enough of these books) I'm going out and buy me one. (I have a friend who advertised in the newspaper and got a used one for $10.) But a pressure canner is a pure nuisance to can fruit in because fruit requires only about 8 minutes or less of actual canning and the cooker drives you frantic waiting for the thing to either heat up or cool down so you can get on with the next batch. So for canning fruits, if my experience is any help, I'd say use the hot water bath method.

When the fruit is ripe in our orchard I can from morning to night using two big enamel water bath canners. It keeps me moving because as soon as I have the eight jars that each canner will hold loaded with fruit and juice it is time to take out the last batch and load in the new ones. That's because of the handling involved in getting the fruit ready—like washing, picking out the leaves and pulling out the stems for cherries.

I read in a book you're supposed to also prick each cherry with a sterilized needle. Didn't say why. But I put up over a hundred quarts of cherries every June and though they tend to contain an occasional stem, leaf, or worse, because I put the children to work packing for me, they are really very attractive looking and fine tasting though I've never put a needle to one yet. So take what you read in books with a grain of salt. Including this one because although I really tried hard I still had to get a few pieces of it out of the public library.

MATERIALS: You need a "canning kettle." They come in 4- or 6-quart sizes and aren't expensive. The kettle is enamel and equipped with a jar-holding rack which is very useful. Hardware stores have them. A *do-it-yourself canner* is any container large enough to hold jars covered with boiling water. You can make a *big* canner out of an old fashioned copper washtub. Put it on two burners at once. It will hold 16 quarts at a time. The jars should be covered with ½ inch of water while they are canning, or so I've always thought. If you have trouble with your water boiling down keep an extra pan of water boiling on your stove and add boiling water to the canner out of that. The problem is getting your jars out of the water. You won't have a rack because they don't make them that big. For proper sealing the jars must be removed from the water while hot. The beginning of the cooling causes a vacuum to develop inside the jar which sucks the lid down tight. You can often hear the pleasant "ping" pop sound as it seals. For rackless canning there is a "grip tight jar lifter" that you can order from Kerr Glass Mfg., Dept. 124, Sand Springs, Oklahoma 74065 for $1.25.

SUGAR—Sugar is said to help hold color and flavor but I know people who don't use any at all when they can or who use *much less* than the directions say. Their fruit cans safely without spoilage and that is the important thing. Or you can use honey. I even know a family that has developed a no-sugar, no-water method of canning!

PROCEDURE:

1. Fill the kettle two-thirds with water and put it on to boil. You need a *very* big hot burner or a very hot stove top to can with this method.

2. Put a pan that will hold about a gallon of water on to boil to make your canning liquid.

3. Fill your clean jars with the fresh cut high acid food—whole fruit, or cooked tomatoes or whatever. Remember to leave ½ inch head space at least.

4. Boil your lids and screw bands.

5. Make your canning liquid (to pour over fruit) by adding sugar, honey, or a combination. Or add nothing to the hot water.

6. Pour the liquid over the fruit in the jars. (If you are canning juice or tomatoes or something else that doesn't need liquid added skip this step.) Wipe the top of your jar clean.

7. Put a lid and screw band on the jar and screw firmly down.

8. Load your jars into your rack. Then, holding the rack by the two handles, lower it into your canning kettle. Adjust the water level so that it is at least ½ inch above the tops of the lids. Work fast enough so that your jars are still quite hot from the hot liquid being poured in, otherwise they may crack when they hit the boiling water. (Commercial jars, like mayonnaise jars, crack easier than regular canning jars.)

9. When the water in the kettle returns to a cheerful boil (don't confuse the bubbles of air escaping from the inside of the jars for a boil), start timing and boil it the recommended processing time being very careful that it never drops below a boil in which case you would have to start your timing all over again.

10. When you put your rack in I hope you remembered to leave the handles standing straight up out of the water to remove it with. Using pot holders or gloves, carefully lift that rack of jars out and set on the floor or a table. This is a dangerous time. Have the children out of the way of scalding hot drips. Don't wear shoes with slippery soles. Have strong arms. Although the directions say not to, I tighten the lids as much as I can the minute I can get my hands on them. Then set aside to seal on a surface warm enough that they won't crack by the temperature contrast. Test for seal.

Here's a lady who *really* had lots of experience hot water bath canning fruit and who wrote us a wonderfully detailed description of her system. She is Florence Ward of Quilcene, Washington. "I have canned for over 50 years. When we lived on a dairy ranch for 17 years, I used to can around 600 quarts of fruit and meats each year. Pickles too. We had five children—all married long since. Fruit, such as

peaches and apricots, cherries and pears—I've canned thousands of quarts of them.

"They do not have to have boiling liquid poured in the jar. My jars are always thoroughly washed after using the contents and the lids put on to keep out dust and the like, over the winter. I wash each jar before using it again, in soapy water and rinse thoroughly. I scald peaches, dump into cold water, peel and place in jars. I pour warm syrup over the fruit in the jar as soon as I fill it. That way the fruit will not turn dark. When I have seven jars filled, which is what my canner holds, I wipe the top of each jar carefully, screw on the lids which have been boiled. I never boil the rings. I set them in lukewarm water in the canner which has a wire rack in the bottom. Turn my electric stove to one turn below high. When the water gets near the boiling point I turn on high—let boil about 3 to 5 minutes, lift the canner from the burner to the cold trash burner, which is beside the electric range and take the lid off of the canner. I have the water bath just to the bottom of the screw threads on the jar. I have a jar lifter and after wiping all the water off the lids with a dry cloth, just dab with the clean cloth till it absorbs all the moisture on top of jar lids. Lift each one out and put in a cardboard box or wooden pear lug—on the floor beside the trash burner. Lay a dish towel or newspaper on top of the jars to keep cold drafts from hitting the jars. When one pear lug is full of jars, I take the paper off and set another pear lug on top, ready for more jars from the canner.

"The canning books usually call for cooking the fruit about 20 minutes. I don't know how one would have anything but mush. Three to five minutes of boiling time is plenty. The fruit is fresher tasting and firmer, yet cooked. I seldom have a jar that doesn't seal. I can't help but think some of failing to seal is caused by people covering the jars with water. I have never done that. It absolutely is not necessary. Neither do the jars have to be hot, nor the syrup hot. It takes a little longer to get them to boil. I always have just warm (lukewarm) water in the canner. By the time I have seven more ready for the canner, the others are ready, or just about ready to take off. I use the regular dark blue enamel canner, with lid to fit. We raise a large garden and I still can—but do even more freezing. Freeze vegetables, fruits such as strawberries, huckleberries, blackberries, logans, blueberries, melon cubes, raspberries, rhubarb, apples, cascades, and of course all meats." Florence, it makes me hungry just to read your letter!

Part of Florence's argument is over the "raw or cold pack" method of filling the jars to be processed versus the "hot pack" method. Except she goes one step beyond, because "raw or cold pack" means you fill the jar with unheated or raw food and then add boiling liquid and put into your hot water bath canner. Florence doesn't even add hot liquid. She adds it lukewarm. (Note also that Florence puts jars full of lukewarm liquid into a canner full of lukewarm water. Lukewarm jars put into boiling water would crack.) From the points of view of food preservation it really doesn't matter as long as you process it the proper length of time—or long enough. "Hot pack" means you got the food to be canned boiling or precooked open-kettle style and then loaded your jars with the hot food and then went ahead and processed it the right amount of time in your hot water bath canner, which certainly does give you an extra margin of safety. It can have another advantage too. Some foods cook down a lot in the first stage and your available jars can be made to go a lot farther if foods like apples and rhubarb are hot packed.

PRESSURE COOKER CANNING

This is the only method recommended for canning low acid foods. That means any *meats, poultry, fish and vegetables*—except most tomatoes (yellow tomatoes are a low acid variety). Even using this method these *low acid foods should be boiled 15 minutes in an uncovered pan before tasting or using.*

Except sometimes for green beans I freeze all my low acid foods rather than can them. Lots of other people do can them, however. My mother did. You need a pressure canner to do it by this recommended method. (My mother canned them in a water bath using the very long processing times.) The price of pressure canners at my local hardware store is about $48. I like the taste and convenience of frozen meat and vegetables. Frozen vegetables taste "fresher" than canned ones except for green beans which only keep well in the freezer for a few months and after that are better canned. And you have to keep your mind on a pressure cooker. They can be very dangerous.

Sandra Oddo of Hurley, New York, is a real pressure cooker fan. Since I've never used one I'll pass on what she says about it. "A year ago I got a pressure canner from Sears for $24 (can 4 quarts, hold 8) and now I wouldn't be without it. It's too small for mass canning, but perfect for what's left of the lentil soup after we've had a ham—canned soup heats faster than frozen, too—and for food deliberately mass cooked so there will be leftovers for pressure canning

which saves later work. It saves enormously on fuel. Would you believe that 45 minutes turns a 3-year-old rooster into a tender stew?" Sounds great to me. Also makes me realize that one reason I love my big heavy Dutch oven with the heavy iron lid so much is because it functions to a certain extent like a pressure cooker. It saves heat and it's a great tenderizer.

And here's Maureen Darby of Leslie, Arkansas, with more pressure canning enthusiasm and experience to share: "Pressure canning is an excellent way of preserving food. The cost of the canner is easily offset by the fact that it requires far less fuel to operate than it would to can in boiling water—even if one is cutting wood to stoke the fire. The amount of time and energy expended to cut the wood and haul it in is that much more than with a pressure canner. I canned for the first time this summer and even canned fruit under pressure. I did have to watch it closely but it was better than waiting for the amount of time necessary to boil the quantity of water needed to cover the jars. We don't own a freezer. The initial cost and the cost of the electricity to run them make them impractical—besides the constant worry of power shortage. As long as the jar lids are available I intend to continue pressure canning our food. Also hope to do more drying."

PROCEDURE:

1. Put wire basket in.

2. Put 2 quarts of boiling water in and set on low heat.

3. Put filled jars with tops screwed on into canner on the wire basket. (Setting jars directly on canner bottom will break them.)

4. Put lid on pressure cooker and screw on until it is tightly closed.

5. Check petcock valves with a toothpick if you haven't used the cooker lately.

6. Turn up the heat. Listen for the steam—when you hear it start timing. Listen to that loud steaming noise 8 minutes. This is air leaving the jars and canner.

7. Close the petcock. (Screw the screw down into the knob on the lid.) More modern pressure cookers do this automatically.

8. Watch for the pressure gauge to reach 10 pounds.

9. Adjust your heat source so the gauge stays at 10 pounds. If higher, turn heat down. If under, turn heat up. More than 10 pounds may crack the jars. Turn the gauge so you can keep an eye on it as you do your other work in the kitchen. Process for the recommended amount of time—*pressure cooker time.*

10. When the jars have been processed, take the pressure cooker off the heat and let it cool. Wait until the pressure gauge has gone down to zero, then wait at least 2 minutes more before opening the petcock. Let the pressure go down of its own accord. Don't try to rush it.

11. Open the petcock valve slowly. Let the canner cool a little more.

12. When you can hear and see no more steam open the lid.

13. Take your jars out. If you leave them in the canner they may not seal. Tighten the lids. Cool and check for sealing.

CANNING MEAT

My mother canned a lot of meat when I was a little girl, and one of my most pleasant childhood memories is of the taste of her canned venison stew. You may can any kind of meat. Chicken and rabbit may be canned on the bone but all the bigger meats, of course, are cut away from the bone before canning. You may can with or without liquid. I liked my mother's way of doing it—she canned with liquid and a few vegetables thrown in for taste. It made a quick and easy meal that was always good and nourishing. Canning is a good way to handle tough cuts because they get cooked 5 hours in the process and are never tough when it's over. Don't try to can any meat that has turned dark or smells like it's starting to spoil. If you are canning sheep be careful to take off the thin outer layer of skin which has a strong flavor (mutton is a hard meat to work with and make palatable anyway).

A way to keep from wasting the bones is to boil them up for a soup stock and can that. Soup is a great thing to have on hand for general cooking purposes. Season your meat or soup stock before canning it, using salt, a few vegetables and onion, celery leaves, bay leaf, or what you like, put your lid firmly on the jar and process 105 minutes at 10 pounds in your pressure canner or 5 hours in a water bath.

OF CORPORATIONS, HOSPITALS, SCHOOL AND THE 7TH EDITION

May 18, 1976. Somebody wrote and suggested that when I add material for new editions of this book I give the date so there it is. I've been writing on this book six years now. I don't have a baby any more. Sara just had her third birthday and Luke is 4. Becca is ready for the first grade next fall and Dolly will be 12 in a few weeks. Danny is a dignified young man of 8. This 7th edition has been a long time coming, longer than any of the others. This year it seems like I've done everything *but* write. And the year before that. Last summer was the first attempt at a School of Country Living . . . well, here's the story as told in the *Newsletter* I send out in spring and fall (free) to people who have mail-ordered a copy of this book from me here at Kendrick, Idaho.

I'm back at the old typewriter table in my living room. Luke is singing and talking to himself on a chair next to me and playing with the stapler that he already broke so I guess he might as well keep it. Dolly is in the kitchen making pancakes for little Sara. It's Sunday. Dolly was sick to her stomach this morning and had an earache last night so I stayed home with her and the two little ones today while Daddy Mike took Danny and Becca to Church. We've been listening to gospel records all morning and I have a beautiful feeling of peace of mind. Next thing I should try to tell you all that happened since you last heard from me in September.

Last summer's session of the School of Country Living really ended with a whimper, not a bang. I ran totally out of money. Had to let go all the teachers who were on salary (I had been paying room, board and $2.10 an hour based on a 40-hour week) and that really upset both teachers and students. I had about 35 students whom I gave room, board and $10 a week to be there. When I announced the School would have to close Labor Day it was a real moment of heartache and desolation for all of us. I was $10,000 overdrawn on our own books and had $85,000 more in debts. It was a hairsbreadth from foreclosure on the 386-acre School farm most of that fall. I went out on the road to try to raise money to pay off the debts from the School and to talk about next summer's school—which at the time seemed as mad as the March hare to more logically equipped individuals. But I just couldn't give up. I figured I could either slink off with my tail between my legs and go bankrupt and say "I'm whipped" or I could say "I'm hurting from a whole lot of experience with something I never had any experience with, and experience is something if you're willing you can look at and learn from." So I looked at it hard and tried to understand what I had done wrong and decided to do a lot of things different from what I had done before but *not* to give up.

I went back on the road with all five children and me living in the van and going from town to town all around the whole United States. Julaine was setting up appointments for me from Los Angeles and we kept in close touch on the telephone. Darlene, Diann, Ivy, Kay and the crew back at the Living Room Mimeographer in Kendrick were standing by to make and mail the books they hoped I'd create orders for. Mike was lonesome at home taking care of the big zoo of domesticated animals we had developed for the School and the stock cows that were to eat the grass crop. I didn't get on any big national shows because I wasn't that important but Julaine could generally get TV, radio shows and newspaper interviews for me in the smaller towns where big star types didn't bother to go. So I'd do like five cities a week. Work all day. Typical day would be maybe two TV shows, two radio shows and a newspaper interview. I'd get done about four o'clock and then in the evening drive a few hundred miles to the next town with laundromat and grocery store stops as needed. We were so desperate for money to pay bills that I had run up over everybody's dead body trying to make my School go that I just couldn't ask them for money back in Idaho. So I literally peddled my way. When I had a live show I'd suggest that folks could meet me at the public library or a downtown park or some such and I'd show them my books for sale and pictures of the school and pass out my free brochures. When I got low on both gas and cash and no live show I'd set out with a couple books and knock on bookstore doors or pass out brochures to whoever was around until somebody bought one. I traded books for gas in gas stations, sold one to a stranger whom we asked for directions and got a bath when somebody invited us home. Many a morning I washed my hair in the sink of a TV station bathroom before the show. The plumbing plugged up in the van and all through the Midwest we stunk worse than a load of upset skunks and practically died of asphyxiation from the fumes until we finally completely quit using the thing and it composted naturally and was done. I was grubbier and tireder as every day went on. "Sparkle, Shirley!" I'd remind myself as the lights came on. And in true show business style I'd sparkle through the show as best I could and then drag back to the parking lot.

In New York City we got to do the "To Tell the Truth" show and that was a good respite. They fed us and bought us a room in a fine hotel. The children bounced on the beds and played in the bathtub and drove the hotel staff crazy. There was only one other show to do in New York because nobody else had wanted me. That was a sort of blessing. This trip was much busier than the one before had been.

But now the poor old van was getting sick. And without Mike, who had always changed my tires and oil and fixed engines for me, I was helpless. I barely made it through the Holland Tunnel and the engine died in the intersection of 6th Avenue and something-or-other street right in downtown Manhattan. I gave my next to last dollar to some fellows to push it out of the intersection to the curb. Somebody stuck their head in the window and said "What are you going to do?" "I'm going to sleep," I answered. He appeared to be dumbfounded. I was too tired to care. It was the middle of the night and I'd been fighting that engine all afternoon. It had taken me three jump starts with long waits between to get that far and I had a show to do the next day. I crawled in the back and went to sleep.

In Grand Rapids, Michigan, with 2½ weeks to go before my 3½-month tour would be over, after doing two live TV shows in the morning and a taped radio interview, and while having lunch at the press club with two reporters I collapsed with some strange heart action—"brady rate of 50." An ambulance took me to Butterworth Hospital. They thought I was maybe having a heart attack but I wasn't. The doctors recommended I quit the tour and have someone come out to drive me home. I left the hospital and drove that evening to Chicago, ignoring their advice. Two days later I had another ambulance ride and it was about 44 days before I got out of the hospital to stay after that one. I wasn't really sick and yet I really was. It was "physical and emotional exhaustion." I found out that you can get so tired that nothing works right. So weary that your heart can't beat straight and your legs can scarcely hold you up. So discouraged that the light hurts your eyes and noises hurt your ears and anything is too much. Battle fatigue. I didn't want to bother people by making a big to-do but I was quietly convinced I was going to die. I made my peace with my Lord and waited for Him to take me

home. The only impediment to a quiet departure seemed to be that I was leaving all those debts. Home in Kendrick things were even worse since I wasn't able to be chief salesperson any more. People were working without pay. Checks were bouncing. I told Julaine to put paperback reprint rights on the book up for auction. That one thing I was determined to take care of before I died. I waited, it seemed to me barely hanging on, for another day and yet another night while the bids were gathered, feeling a trifle dishonest because we hadn't told them they were buying a dying authoress. The bidding was slow and grueling but the ante gradually rose. One outfit that we had expected to bid high, that had offered me $40,000 cash last summer when the School was in such trouble and I turned them down with tears pouring down my cheeks because I needed it so bad, dropped out and didn't bid at all. An unexpected source, Avon, came in with a vigorous bid of $110,000. But Bantam's Charles Bloch, their West Coast agent, who had wanted this book ever since he first saw me on TV got Bantam to offer me $115,000 cash advance and the thing was done. Lying on my back in a hospital bed I scrawled my name onto the contract. I got well the next day. I got well so fast it was embarrassing.

If I hadn't been feeling sick and desperate, unable to go out and fight any other way, I'm sure I would never have signed the Bantam contract. I think I was meant to do so. I think somehow the *Old Fashioned Recipe Book* is meant to get into as many hands and into as many homes as possible and I'm not supposed to get in the way of that. Bantam has to sell a lot of copies just to get their advance back. And Bantam gave me a very unusual deal. That's what makes it bearable for me. They don't have an exclusive right to the book. I can keep on printing my own Kendrick version and selling it to you. I can print as many, sell as many, at whatever price I want. I can change the material continuing to do the new editions that keep bettering, I trust, this book. When they can, if they want to, they'll catch up to what the Kendrick version is doing.

So I went home from the hospital and I had a big decision to make. Should I take what was left of the money after paying debts and live a quiet peaceful life with my family and forget all the past struggles and troubles? Or should I take the extra Bantam money and try for another session of the School of Country Living? A part of me really wanted to drop out and most of the time I was sick I was saying very firmly that this was it. I was quitting. But there was another voice in me that said to get back to work. That there were things to be accomplished and the responsibility was mine to do them and almost with a heavy heart and a sense of despair at first at plunging back into the maelstrom I said "yes." I didn't try to resist. As soon as the urge to go back to work really became an issue in my heart I simply said "yes" and settled it. I've been working very hard ever since.

FREEZING

THE FREEZER—For this kind of job the small space on top of a refrigerator isn't adequate. Freezers can be upright or chest type. The chest type gives you more room for your money because you can pack it practically solid without everything falling out every time you open the door. We have the biggest chest type there is. Cost about $250. (Still isn't paid for—Ward's charge card.) Some big families I know use two chest freezers. But I think one can do it for most families if you stagger the input. Vegetables and berries go in season. If you can your fruit that saves room. Wait to butcher until the weather is quite cold and there is room growing in the freezer from the vegetables getting eaten up. I defrost once a year. Early spring is the ideal time when the freezer is naturally at its emptiest before the new produce comes on in the garden.

When you are setting up your freezer put the cord and plug in a place as protected as possible from little gremlins. All they have to do is pull that plug to bring on a terrible disaster in the freezer. Consider putting it on a back porch. That will save you electricity in the winter. At least have it in a relatively cool part of the house. You can refuse that $50 worth of extra gadgets and a repair contract. You won't need any of it.

CONTAINERS—Plastic freezing bags and boxes are sold in grocery outlets. I don't use them. I think the plastic baggies with wire ties for the necks are the best bargain. I bag all the vegetables. Each bag holds the amount we would use at one meal. That isn't always the same, though. As the year wears on it takes larger portions of the frozen food to satisfy our hunger. Even when it still looks and tastes good it seems to be losing some food value and you have to eat more to get your hunger satisfied. Since the baggies aren't too sturdy, especially when holding peas and beans, I pack the smaller bags into a large plastic baggie for final disposition.

Chickens can go into big baggies. Be sure and squeeze as much air out as possible before you tie up any bag for freezing. Other meats are wrapped with butcher paper and fastened with *freezer tape* which your butcher can tell you how to get if your grocer can't. Plain baggies don't work well for foods containing free liquid. In that case I line a tin can or odd-sized jar that can't be used for canning or one with a chipped rim with a baggie (the baggie also makes air

space in the bottom of the jar that prevents the jar breaking when the frozen liquid expands), pour in the liquid and tie it at the top. Freeze it in the upright position and once frozen it can go any which way. You can also freeze using regular canning materials, in which case you have the additional protection of the canning seal. Just pour the food in your jar, put on the lid and screw the band down tightly. That is probably the best freezer container because it's an airtight, leakproof, moisture-proof, odorproof container, but I'm too short on jars to do much. When canning in good jars don't use the baggie but be sure and leave an inch of space at the top to allow for expansion during freezing.

The freezer protects your food because at that low temperature the beasties can't grow. Other things happen though. If your container isn't well closed the food will, over months, dehydrate. If your vegetables aren't blanched or your large fruits packed in a syrup, the action of enzymes inside them will cause undesirable changes in color, flavor and food value. Over the months the frozen vegetables and fruits do slowly lose some quality and food value. There is a big difference in the green beans for some reason.

Meat does wonderfully well in the freezer, even over long periods, and in my experience generally keeps much longer than the authorities say it will, as does everything else. But there is still a big difference between peas, corn or beans that have been in the freezer two weeks and those that have been in there seven months.

COOKING FROZEN FOODS—Because when you freeze foods you don't kill the beasties, just put them to sleep, it is important to thaw and cook the food in as fast a sequence as you can. Foods that have been frozen, especially vegetables, are subject to very fast deterioration once thawing has set in. In the case of vegetables I peel off the baggie and put the frozen hunk directly into a little boiling water. I serve as soon as it is thawed and hot. I drain the cooking liquid into the gravy or the pig bucket. Put a big glob of homemade butter on the vegetable and serve.

Frozen roasts and roasting meats, like ribs, I put into the oven still frozen. Frying meat I thaw in the refrigerator the morning I plan to use it. It takes several hours to thaw a jar of frozen stuff like stew (quart). I put it in a pan of warm water. Gradually raise the water to simmering. As the contents of the jar start to liquefy I can raise the temperature of the water. But I can't rush it or I'll crack the jar. When I thaw out a stew I usually add some fresh vegetables out of the root cellar or garden to make it taste better.

When the string beans are in really bad shape I can make them most palatable by putting the ice hunk directly into a frying pan with a little bacon grease or a smear of oil and stirring them as they thaw, adding a little previously fried onion chunks or green spring onions out of the garden (the multipliers are ready by March).

There is more information about freezing in the *Freezing and Canning Cookbook* listed under Canning and in Ann Seranne's *The Complete Book of Home Preserving* put out by Doubleday and Company, Garden City, New York. I see she has also written books called *The Home Freezer* and *The Complete Book of Freezer Cookery* which sound promising. But there is no substitute for your own experience.

WHAT TO FREEZE—The important point here is that freezing is most suitable for young, tender vegetables. For example, when I thin the carrots I wait until I have some "baby" size, finger size you can say. I pull those out and freeze them for my freezer supply. That way I don't have to throw away any plants. I come back and get more later if the garden needs more thinning or my freezer needs them. Big carrots don't freeze well. They are better kept in the ground or in the root cellar. Those baby carrots can then be frozen whole. The same goes for the baby beets. Beans for freezing should be no more than half grown, the long slender stage before they have gotten fat and tough with the beans inside too well developed. Full-grown vegetables are better off canned or in the root cellar.

HOW TO FREEZE—The most important things here are speed and temperature control. Get vegetables from the garden to the kitchen as rapidly as possible. Then get them from the kitchen counter into your blanching pot. Then immediately after the blanching is completed put the vegetable into an ice bath or cool in a colander under a stream of running cool water until you have their temperature down as low as possible. Now quickly package and freeze. This is even more important for corn than for any other vegetable because corn loses taste quality and nutrition exceptionally fast. It's worth the trouble though because frozen cream-style corn is *so* good!

The reasoning is this: The blanching destroys a lot of the bacteria and enzymes (blanching times for all vegetables are given in the Vegetables chapter). The immediate chilling hastens freezing and reduces as much as possible that period of neutral temperature during which the bacteria would quickly rebuild their numbers. The thicker the vegetable (beets and whole carrots as compared to peas for example) the harder it is to cool, so you should have it cooled as much as possible before packaging. Some vitamin enthusiasts might object to all that sloshing around in water but if the water doesn't get it the bacteria will and I personally think you're ahead with the water. The exception is if you're only working with a small amount. You can package it in small packages hot and the freezer will cool it.

But not everyone agrees that it is necessary to blanch before freezing. Ione Thompson of Colusa, California, wrote me about this: "We do not care to blanch many of our vegetables we freeze as they lose flavor and crispness. With peas and beans (also all fish) we clean and put into plastic cartons and cover with water. When frozen, take from carton and put in baggie and return to freezer. On corn and asparagus, wrap tightly in foil and then put in baggies or freezer paper and freeze." So there's another way to do it.

MATERIALS: A deep kettle on the stove full of boiling water. A colander and/or big sieve (to hold your vegetable to be frozen) that can be immersed in the kettle without having the rim or handles go under water. Two buckets or double sinks full of ice and water. Then for example, do peas like this:

1. Put shelled peas in the colander and sink colander, peas and all, in the boiling water.

2. Leave it there just long enough for the water to return to a boil and the peas to change color—that is "blanching."

3. Lift out the colander full of peas and let it drip a moment. Immerse in ice water number one. Stir with your fingers to help it cool.

4. In a minute or two move it to ice water number two.

5. When the peas are thoroughly chilled, drain, package and put the packages in the freezer.

You'll have the absolute best tasting peas, corn or whatever using this system. If you want to freeze vegetable slices such as broccoli, cut them before the above processing. However, the corn is the exception. You could freeze it right on the cob but that is a big waste of freezer space. Instead blanch and then put your corn, still on the cob, through ice waters one and two. After it comes out of "two," hold the cob upright on a wooden cutting board and with a sharp knife cut the kernels away close to the cob. When you have a good-sized pile, bag it up and put the bags of cream-style corn in the freezer. ("Cream-style" corn means loose kernels cut off the cob—no real cream involved.)

It really helps to have more than one person working at this freezing game, especially with corn. Since corn cobs don't fit nicely into colanders a system is to tie a batch of ears in a dish towel and suspend it on the end of a stick for blanching and ice waters one and two. Then you can untie and let them out for cutting off the cob. Or sometimes for larger vegetables and corn I put them directly into the kettle of water. When it boils up I fish the corn out using two potato mashers, one in each hand. I fish out smaller vegetables with a sieve, then hold them under the sink faucet to cool. I blanch greens by stuffing as many as I can into a pot of boiling water and don't try to cool them at all—just bag up, burning my fingers all the while, and freeze.

Melons, lettuce, onions, cucumbers, radishes and whole tomatoes can't be successfully frozen. To freeze berries I just wash them, bag them up and put them in the freezer. Fruits, except rhubarb, are not scalded but packing them in a syrup keeps apples, peaches, plums and apricots in better shape than if they are exposed to air. A sugarless syrup that will do the job is a mixture of ¼ teaspoon citric acid to 1 quart water or ¼ teaspoon ascorbic acid to each 1 cup syrup. You can buy the acid at any grocery store under a trade name. Apples are a special case. All they need is to be immersed in boiling water for 1½ to 2 minutes to prevent their browning.

The Vegetables chapter includes freezing directions wherever appropriate. Here are freezing directions for fruits.

Item	Preparations	How to Pack
Apples	Wash, peel, core, slice, scald, drain, chill	Cover with syrup
Apricots	Wash, halve, pit	Cover with syrup
Berries— Black, Blue, Raspberries, Cherries (sour and sweet)	Wash, chill, pit	Mix with sugar or honey
Currants	Sort, wash, drain, stem, crush	Cover with syrup
Peaches	Wash, peel, pit, halve or slice	Cover with syrup
Pears	Wash, peel, core, halve or slice	Cover with syrup
Pineapple	Wash, peel, core, slice or dice	Cover with syrup
Plums, Prunes	Wash, pit, slice	Mix with sugar or honey
Rhubarb	Wash, trim, cut into 1-inch pieces, blanch	Precook and hot pack
Strawberries	Wash in ice water, stem, slice or leave whole	Mix with sugar or honey

When putting food in your freezer—if it is a chest type—make sure you don't get the vegetables all on the very bottom. I try to make up and down columnar areas so I always have something of everything on top. The meat takes up a lot of room so it goes on one whole side and the vegetables and fruits on the other. When I only have a little of something—like packages of butter, or cream cheese, or bread—it goes into the baskets on top so it doesn't get lost down among the rest. I like to package in plastic bags because it saves freezer space.

When you have a freezer there is always the nightmarish possibility of the power going off. The fuller your freezer is, the longer it can hold out without electricity. If your freezer is outdoors and the temperature there is below zero anyway—fine. If you know where you can buy dry ice, twenty-five pounds of it would hold a ten-cubic-foot freezer for at least two days. Don't open the lid if you can help it, in order to keep the cold air in.

If your food does suffer some thawing you can cook up fruits and refreeze or can. Or if fruits didn't clear thaw out but still had ice crystals in them they can just be refrozen. If vegetables get even a little thawed out they are really going downhill fast. When it has happened to me I just threw them out to the chickens. When my meat has thawed just partly I've refrozen it and used it up fairly soon thereafter. I don't know if that's according to the rules but it looked fine and smelled fine and I gave it a good cooking to make sure. Meat that thawed and didn't look fine and smell fine I gave to the animals. Our electricity has never been off long enough to matter. What invariably happened to me is that some child pulls the plug and it takes me a day to find out though I try to have an unconscious habit of glancing at that light that indicates the freezer is on as I go by. This seems to be a spring phenomenon so I haven't yet had to set up a special time for cleaning out my freezer. When the spring thaw comes I just say "Praise the Lord" and very quickly finish emptying the freezer. Then wash it clean, plug it back in, put back in what I dare, and threaten the children with horrible vague happenings if they ever do that again.

Since the first edition of this book came out several people have written to tell me that you can buy a special attachment for a plug that makes it childproof. It sounds like a great thing.

And I wanted to mention to you too the wonderful jams, jellies, spreads and pie fillings you can make and freeze. They have a more fresh fruit flavor, you don't have to slave over the stove so much, there are more vitamins and you can put them in the freezer in almost anything. Look in the Sweets chapter for specific recipes. "Sweets" to me means fruit and that's where I put all the fruit kinds of things.

OF FOOD PRESERVATION AND EXPERTS

If I had to name fast some basic principle of living I'd say it's knowing when to be reverent and when to be irreverent. Here's a time to be irreverent. Since I wrote that section on freezing, I have met and talked to a very nice new neighbor who lives entirely on raw food. He has done this for many years and he told me a lot of things I didn't know before. I'm really just like everybody else—inclined to believe what I read. I have read for years that you can't freeze melons— accepted that and never tried it myself. But here's a man who because of his special needs did try and discovered that the expert who said that was wrong.

Here's how he does it. He cuts out 1-inch chunks of the melon heart. He uses various varieties of melon like casaba and honeydew. He doesn't use any rind. If the melon itself hasn't given him enough juice for packaging by the dicing process he mashes a little extra to give him juice to pour over. He packages in plastic baggies just like I do. He told me he also freezes grapes and they freeze very well. This was a new one on me too. He said he takes the grapes off the stem, washes them and bags them up just like that in the plastic bags. He said that they were practically like fresh when thawed. I have another friend who has no freezer whose family lives off their own produce. She cans quarts and quarts of whole grapes, strawberries and raspberries every year, which is also something the experts advise against. The literature on drying food that the government will send you if you request it gives the impression that berries don't dry very well, but there's an old man who lives near here who dries lots of berries just like his mother did before him when they wintered mostly on dried food. His dried berries cook up after soaking in water and make fine pies. I think the moral to all this is if you really have a need try it anyway just in case the experts might be wrong—including me who is no expert anyway, unless it be at writing down what my wise friends tell me.

Water bath versus pressure canning is a topic where many ladies of long kitchen experience challenge the experts, who now say that it is dangerous to water bath can vegetables. I faithfully quoted the most respected official sources in my discussion of canning, yet are they really right? It would be awful to be responsible for anybody poisoning themselves and I didn't want to take a chance of that—neither does anybody else who writes a book. That's why you always read such conservative statements in print. But to be totally honest with you only a few people in this land of home gardeners and canners own pressure canners. The others can their vegetables the old fashioned way of water bath canning. They use the old standard times. For example, one lady I asked particularly about this said she boils all vegetables 3½ hours and meats 5 hours. She has been feeding her family out of those home canning jars for a good 40 years and nobody in the family got sick yet of botulism poisoning. She cans on a wood cook stove, commences counting the 3½ hours after the water with the jars in it comes to a good rolling boil. I can on a wood stove too. It's quite an experience to keep that fire roaring all the time on those hot summer days. One smart lady I know has her wood canning stove in the basement. That helps a lot though you can't watch it as closely.

As long as you are canning high acid foods like fruits you can try any system because the worst you risk is losing your food to mold. Here are two letters I've received. I'll let each speak for itself. Note though that extension agent types say oven canning is bad because "foods are not processed at proper temperatures and jars may explode."

"I do a lot of canning by the oven process and have had good results. The oven temperature is set at 250° and time controlled. I use a good many salvaged glass jars and lids. I get new twist off lids whenever I can find them. I use the oven to pasteurize juice, using 200° or less, and if used lids, I dip in paraffin wax for a safe long-time seal. Some juices I put up in 1971 and 1973 I used in 1975 and some wild plum juice put up in 1971 made a very good plum jelly in 1975. I do figs in the oven at 250° for 1½ hours. Never tighten a lid on a jar in oven process. Do the tightening when it has completed the cooking time. There is not much information available on oven processes but I find it easier because the kitchen doesn't get so hot and I can get more jars done at once." That's from T. D. Sommerville from Plymouth, North Carolina. I'll bet T. D. Sommerville knows how to survive on an empty pocketbook better than most of the rest of us.

Judy Smith of Silverdale, Washington, wrote me: "I believe about botulism and pressure canning. We've had several cases of botulism around here— one old couple (in their 70's) didn't make it—their 'luck' ran out, as they had been canning hot water bath corn, beans, etc. Boiling water bath is not safe for meat, low acid vegetables, no matter how long you boil. Some people have *luck* for a long time—then whammo. To me $48 (I've seen them on sale for $40) is cheap at twice the price for a pressure canner."

The usual canning references also say that cauliflower, broccoli, cabbage and Brussels sprouts "change color" and "get strong" when they are canned. Well, all vegetables change color in one way or another when they are cooked, and I can give you the word of experience that they do not change to any undesirable taste when they are canned though, of course, they aren't as nice as raw. So ignore the words of the experts and if you can't freeze (they taste better frozen), go ahead and can them.

PICKLED BEETS—Here's a place where I feel *more* cautious than the experts. I've seen newspaper reports of botulism from canned pickled beets. Now some standard canning directions have said to simply bring pickled beets to a boil and then hot pack them. They assume that the increased acid content removes any botulism danger. Since I know for sure of an instance when that didn't work, I would suggest that if you are going to can pickled beets you give them the full recommended canning time for unpickled beets. Also if anybody sees a news report of botulism that gives information as to what food was involved I would really appreciate your sending it to me so I can continue trying to understand this problem.

ABOUT BOTULISM

May 18, 1976. I'm writing an insert to bring this chapter up to date for the 7th edition. Some people did write to me and here's what I learned. A lady doctor from Rochester, Minnesota, wrote me that she recently saw a lady with botulism who had canned some mushrooms. She just tasted one and spat it out. She said commercial firms occasionally have problems with canned mushrooms, too. I found out also that last year there were 20 reported incidents of botulism involving 30 persons and resulting in 7 deaths in the United States. That is an increase reflecting the rising number of people starting to grow gardens and can for the first time. There were two botulism incidents last year concerned with home-canned tomatoes. This may reflect the development of lower acid varieties of tomatoes. You can protect yourself by mixing citric acid with your tomatoes before canning, ¼ teaspoon citric acid per pint and ½ teaspoon per quart. You can get citric acid at drugstores.

CAUTION!
Boil low acid
foods 15 minutes
uncovered
before tasting

Botulism poisoning is caused by a bacteria that is practically everywhere in the soil and so you'd better assume it's present on your garden food. The bacteria dies easily enough but it's the "seed" form of it called spores that is so hardy. The spores can resist a *lot* of boiling, but they can't resist heating under pressure which is why the pressure canning is recommended. Under ordinary circumstances you could drink a whole glass of them and it probably wouldn't hurt you. Acid and sugar inactivate them and that's why high acid foods, sweet preserves and pickled foods aren't supposed to be a danger. The only circumstances under which they can hurt you is a combination of *no air*, low acid and low sugar content. In other words the dangerous jar is the one that was *sealed* and had contents that were low in acid (any vegetable or meat except tomatoes) and low in sugar (not a preserve) and in which not enough heat had been applied in processing to kill every last spore. Then the spores can grow and under those circumstances can produce a poison that is one of the strongest known. It is said that 16 ounces of botulism toxin would be enough to kill the entire world's population.

What are the symptoms? At first nausea and vomiting, later blurred vision, dry throat and difficulty in swallowing. Then comes progressive weakness that can paralyze the respiratory tract as well as the limbs. The poison does that because it affects the nervous system, breaking down communication between motor nerves and the muscles. The symptoms ordinarily appear within 18 to 36 hours of poisoning but have been known to take as long as eight days to become evident.

The spores are very hard to kill by boiling but the toxin *is* destroyed by boiling. That's why the rule that all canned low acid vegetables or meats be boiled 15 minutes before tasting or using. You are supposed to boil with the lid off because the toxin vaporizes into the air and if you kept the lid on it wouldn't be able to escape. You should take this precaution even if the food looks fine because botulism toxin has no smell,

taste or visible sign that anything is wrong in the jar. The botulism cases that I know about involved pickled beets, tomatoes (for which pressure canning has not in the past been recommended), beans, cabbage, carrots and peppers which had been water bath canned. It has also happened in some cases where the food was pressure canned.

FRESH VEGETABLE STORAGE

Planning for fresh vegetable storage starts with planning your garden. Beets, late cabbage, carrots, celery, parsnips, potatoes, sweet potatoes, salsify and turnips can be stored without canning, freezing or drying—in a root cellar-type situation. So can late fall apples, onions and big winter squash. So if you want to make it easier on the food preserver in the family or reduce dependence on electricity or availability of jar lids think in terms of fresh vegetable storage. In that case you would plant a larger portion of your garden to these kinds of foods.

This old fashioned way of food preserving is going to require a real adjustment in your attitude if you're used to thinking of preserved foods as a near absolute—that you put your cans or jars on the shelf, your packages in the freezer and forget about them until needed. It isn't so with storage of fresh vegetables and fruits, nor is it so with dried, salted, sugared, spiced and alcoholed foods. These items require upkeep—regular, faithful attention all the while you have them. They need to be checked at least once a week for signs of problems. For example, green tomatoes and apples that have begun to spoil need to be checked almost every day or two.

Be ready to make a switch from this method of preserving to another if it looks like you're going to lose some food, salvage what is possible and can, dry, pickle, freeze or eat it. You also want to remove spoiling vegetables or fruits because the rot spreads to others if you let it go.

Crock pickles need to be checked for excessive mold on top. If it happens, pour off the brine, boil it, add another cup of vinegar and an extra handful of salt, then pour it back onto the pickles.

Dried fruits and vegetables need to be checked for signs of mold. If you have mold, heat in your oven, then repackage. Grains and grain products like flour need to be checked for insect infestation. The cure is to heat the food in the oven at 150° for 20 minutes with the oven door slightly ajar to prevent overheating—don't have the amount too large to be heated all the way through for at least 15 minutes of that time. If you get bugs in your home-dried fruits put them in a small cheesecloth bag and dip into boiling water for 6 seconds. Dry again and then store in something bug proof.

When you check your green tomatoes remove any that are spoiling and take out the ones that have turned red for kitchen use. Jams and jellies may develop surface mold which can merely be removed and that jar brought to the kitchen for current consumption. You'll be in a race with decay all winter long just as you were in a race to preserve nature's abundance from your garden and orchard all summer long.

If the apples start going, make a lot of pies or applesauce or freeze apple slices in syrup for pies. If a squash or pumpkin has developed a soft spot cut that spot out for the animals and cook up the rest to use, can or freeze.

My cellar is my favorite room in the house next to the kitchen. (Well, in wintertime I love also that big bed in our bedroom with all the thick quilts on it that I hate to rise out of on cold mornings.) The walls are lined with shelves on which the canned goods rest plus all our typical needs. I try to shop only once a month and keep things bought ahead as much as I can so when we need something I can head for the cellar rather than the store.

On the floor are the pickle crocks, jugs of vinegar, cooking oil, honey and so on. On a wooden platform on the floor are cans of oatmeal, flour and garbage cans of wheat. The deep freeze is in another part of the basement. But not everything can be kept in the cellar. It doesn't have a dirt floor. That's bad for vegetables. In fall it's too damp and in winter it's too hot once we have the wood furnace going.

If you want to find out if your basement is damp, test for condensation by placing a small mirror against the wall. Should droplets or fog appear on the mirror after a few hours, it means that condensation is the cause of dampness. Ventilation fans might help but aren't worth it. Pumpkins, squash, and onions need a *very* dry place. They need to be stored in a dry but not cold room. They must *never* freeze. That ruins them completely. It's best if they don't touch each other in storage. Don't bruise them in the harvesting process.

Dried beans, peas, soybeans and the like can be stored in airtight cans in your cellar. Potatoes, late cabbage, cauliflower and Chinese cabbage like cool

and moderately moist conditions so a root cellar is OK. Carrots, endive, grapes, beets, parsnips, salsify, rutabagas, turnips, late celery, kohlrabi and winter radishes need to be quite cool—32°-40° and storage under moist sand is best for them. *Don't wash them* before storing. Just leave the garden dirt on, it helps them keep. Parsnips and salsify are often left in the ground over the winter with a mulch over them. For detailed instructions check under each vegetable's name in the Vegetable chapter, or for fruits in the Sweets chapter.

Some people say you should leave most of the root vegetables in the garden over winter. I've tried it and despaired. Every time I want something out of the garden the ground is either frozen so solid I can't dig it up or so wet and muddy that it's all I can accomplish to pull myself back out of the garden soil much less bring an armload of vegetables with me. If the ground freezes down far enough to freeze your vegetables they get soft and are no good anyway.

For additional information on root cellar storage I recommended Farmers' Bulletin No. 1939, USDA, "Home Storage of Vegetables and Fruits," available free from your County Extension Agent or the Office of Information, U.S. Department of Agriculture, Washington, D.C. 20025. But the bulletin that *really* has the best information is 879, put out by the USDA in August 1917. You can get a copy from Homestead General Store, Box 1112, Woodstock, Georgia 30188.

LONG TERM STORAGE CONTAINERS—The plastic cans sold with or without handles as you prefer and with airtight lids by Perma-Pak Company are reasonably priced and useful for holding grains, beans, flour, honey; for curing meat; making sausage; hauling produce and milk; curing pickles, sauerkraut, and holding brandied fruit. This company has a lot of bargains in freeze-dried foods and will send a price list free on request. (Perma-Pak, 40 East 2430 South, Salt Lake City, Utah 84115.)

Big plastic garbage cans can be used for anything where a "wooden barrel" is called for such as tanning. Can in a big enamel or stainless-steel kettle (enamel is cheaper but it doesn't last as long because the enamel will chip).

Crocks are romantic but a 20-gallon crock cost $28 here at Morgan Brothers the last time I looked. They do carry them from 1½ to 30 gallons. (Morgan Brothers, 1305 Main St., Lewiston, Idaho 83501.)

If you are interested in storing large quantities of food for a very long time (like years) make some Mormon friends. They have really made a complete study of this and have lots of practice too. I am blessed with a Mormon mother-in-law who is a dear and precious mother to me and has guided me to a lot of learning. They'd rather be called "Latter-Day Saints" but I wasn't sure if you would know what that means.

When you have made your major weekly inspection, sorting out what's bad and should be fed to the pigs and chickens (which is *good* for them) and set aside what needs to be cooked up next week for the family, then stop a moment, admire your shelves cov-

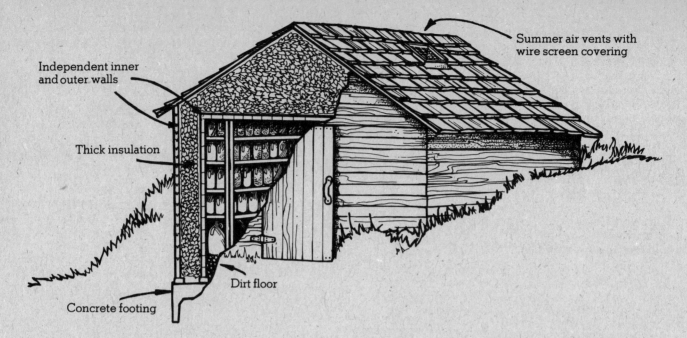

Summer air vents with wire screen covering

Independent inner and outer walls

Thick insulation

Concrete footing

Dirt floor

ered with home canned food, your deep freeze full of vegetables and meat, the boxes of apples in the garage, the crocks of pickles and boxes of root vegetables covering your cellar floor and the cabbage waiting in trenches outside in the garden. Feel good about what your family accomplished and secure about the future and give thanks to your Good Lord for it.

BUILDING A ROOT CELLAR

The cellar of mine that I mentioned before is not a proper root cellar. It is adjacent to the furnace room and has a concrete floor, and so it is not suitable for storing root vegetables or foods requiring cool air. It *is* great for storing your year-round supplies of home canned goods, general supplies and dried foods which is what I use it for. The little three-acre farm we had before this one had an ideal root cellar exactly like what I'm going to describe to you. They are very common around here. We don't have one here yet and are getting along as best we can for the time being with other methods, using the attic for some things and one of our outbuildings for others.

A proper root cellar can be a little building sitting by itself or adjacent to another building or it can be a real dirt cellar under an outbuilding. It should be near the house because you will be going there a lot in very cold weather and you don't want a long hike. The floor should be *dirt* because root vegetables keep much better on a natural ground floor than they do on boards or concrete. The floor should be dug out to *at least* a foot below natural ground level (more is better) so that you actually step down into your root cellar. It is dug down to put it below the level to which the ground generally freezes in winter. The walls are double and wooden and can enclose a storage cellar space as large or small as you like. The walls are best set on a concrete footing. If you have the concrete footing go down a couple feet on the very outside, it prevents rodents digging under. There are no windows but the roof has summer air vents with a wire

covering to keep out rodents. There should be two of these ceiling vents at least. They should be square, about 12 inches by 12 inches. After the freezing weather comes you stuff them up. Most people keep their canned goods in the root cellar, too, which uses the wall space from floor to ceiling with wooden shelves for holding jars. The vegetables go on the floor. A root cellar could be as small as 6 by 6 feet inside dimensions but more is nicer, especially if you have a large family. It will be mighty full in the fall but have lots of room in the spring.

There is a space of 2 feet between the inner and outer walls all the way around which is filled with a good insulation like wood chips or sawdust (free around here since we are a land of sawmills). There can be a layer of plastic in between the wood and insulation. If the outside boards are done tongue and groove—that makes it even better insulated. It's important in your construction also to have the outer and inner walls as independent as possible because anywhere they connect will draw frost into your root cellar. You have to connect them around the door but you don't have to anywhere else so *don't.* What you are building is a house inside a house with insulation in between the walls. The roof consists of a flat layer of boards (the inside house), 3 feet more of insulation and then a gently sloped roof above that (the outside house) with a considerable overhanging eave. (That makes possible a good depth of insulation across the entire inside area of the cellar, except where your air vents go through in summer. They reach up through the insulation to the free air above.) The roof does not need to shed snow—snow is itself a good insulation. The door area should also be insulated by making two doors, one for the outside wall and one for the inside, and you can add hanging blankets inside the door area for additional insulation.

Bill Rogers lives in Wheatland, Wyoming, which is on a high mountain plateau and is one of the coldest places in these United States. He's always thinking of ways to help me and his ideas on root cellar building are going to help you, too!

"Your description of the double house, insulated, is great but let's come back to the real ranch and mountain vegetable cellar. Most of us in the mountains have caves. We dig them in the mountainsides and it is extremely laborious although not so laborious as you might think, going into rocky mountainsides—usually not blasting. Often your caves amount to no more than a slice into the hillside, walled up and roofed over. My own is inadequately insulated but it became much more usable and dependable when I built a toolshed in front of the door—keeping it always sheltered and shaded. It never freezes, so I am inclined to believe I could not better my cave if I did insulate expensively.

"Some people in more level country shore up a huge mound of earth covering a specially constructed storehouse. An entrance way with a dead air space 3"–4" thick between the inner and outer doors is really necessary in the way of insulating. This type of construction is necessary where the water table is high at any time of the year. Where the water table is relatively low throughout the year, some people excavate a cellar and have done so since the days of the first pioneers. Two doors are necessary—one on the surface and one at the bottom of the steps. Ventilators are necessary for all types of vegetable cellars. Much more care is necessary in vegetable storing than most people realize. I lost my potatoes last winter due to the lack of air circulation through them. Cabbages keep fresh in bushel baskets, however! One of our garden problems is that in our short growing season everything ripens with a rush and you cannot use it—unless you can put the surplus in storage. Frost comes and everything will be lost unless you can move wheelbarrow loads into storage."

TO STORE YOUR ROOT VEGETABLES inside all you have to do is put them into cardboard or wooden boxes and stack the boxes on top of each other to be used as needed. Don't use any plastic. It promotes mold. Or you could put them in a pile in a corner with dirt thrown over them or use a permanent wooden bin. Potatoes stored in a wooden box in this kind of a root cellar will still be all right the following June except for having lots of sprouts. Incidentally don't eat potato sprouts. They aren't good for you. Just snap them off.

If you don't and can't have such a root cellar your safest alternative is a hole in the ground. Make a trench longer than wide so it isn't such a struggle to get it covered with dirt. It doesn't matter if the ground is damp when you dig it. Line the hole, bottom and sides, with cardboard from boxes. Put your vegetables in loosely—not in bags. Put your carrots in one area, potatoes in another and so on. Mark on the outside with stakes so you know where to dig for what. Now cover the vegetables over with more cardboard. Cover the cardboard with at least one foot of dirt. It helps to have a ventilating pipe at the center. When it rains you can cover it. When it turns bitterly cold you can remove the pipe and fill the hole in with dirt. But in the meantime it aids air circulation.

Don't dig the root vegetables that you plan to store until the last moment. That is after the first light frosts when you have signs that you are going to have a *hard* frost. Here it means sometime in October. Then dig them and transfer to storage in one operation. Don't wash the vegetables. When you go to get vegetables out of storage in the ground get fifty pounds of potatoes at a time and equivalent amounts of other vegetables to hold you for a good while. That way you don't have to be digging out there any more than necessary. For directions on how to cellar store apples see the Sweets chapter.

I think the biggest single principle of cellar-type storage is that you should put away more than you would expect to need in order to allow for losses during storage. The thing that makes storage of this type reasonable is owning a pig or chickens which will recycle all the food that doesn't keep into bacon and eggs. By late March seven-eighths of your winter squash will either have been brought up to the kitchen for cooking—or it will have spoiled or be near enough spoiled so that you have fed it to the animals. In other words, if you let all of the squash set on the shelves all winter long in whatever condition it was (and that would hasten spoilage of the remainder) only seven-eighths of it or less would make it to March. The moral to this is that the way to go about this kind of storage is to put away far more than you expect to use and keep garbage-eating kinds of animals. If you do end up with good food left over you can share it with your neighbors (or the animals).

So we get little pigs in the spring and feed them all summer on the leavings from canning and freezing. Come fall we butcher the spring pigs which are just the right size for that and get more little pigs. We feed them on the food in storage that isn't making it—the green tomatoes that rotted instead of ripening, the apples that went bad prematurely, the spoiled pumpkins. About the time that source of food is really slowing down it is early spring and still cold enough for butchering if you pick the right day and the pigs are big and ready. We never need to buy them so much as a cupful of feed and feed them no grain at any time in their lives—milk and vegetables is it. So I take the pig's bucket with me to the cellar every few days to check the food in storage. A big pig gets nearly five gallons a day of this food, extra milk and table scraps. (There is no way I know to feed a pig more than it can eat.) If I fed it ten gallons it would manage to eat all that too, but five is more than enough even for a big pig.

DRYING

Drying is a basic and delicious way to preserve. It's easy, cheap and everybody loves the results. Research on drying and dehydrators is going forward at a marvelous speed and results are better all the time. Recent problems with canning lids, shortages of jars and threats to public power have really impressed on me the importance of knowing how and being equipped to dry. And friends have fed me their home-dried foods that eliminated my last shred of prejudice against dried vegetables. They were delicious!

Dried foods require less space and weigh less than foods preserved in any other manner. They are preserved because of the very low moisture content. Most microscopic beasties won't grow in a low moisture environment. The beasties aren't dead—just waiting.

See the Sweets chapter for detailed directions on how to dry each individual fruit and how to make fruit "leather," which is a dried fruit pulp. Drying details for individual vegetables are under the special entries in the Vegetables chapter. For beans and peas, look near the end of Vegetables under Beans. How to dry herbs is in the introduction to the Herbs chapter. For how to dry coconut and peanuts see the Nuts section of Vegetables. For dried meats and fish, look in the Meats chapter under Jerky, Ham and Fish.

I'm an amateur when it comes to drying vegetables. That's the trouble with trying to write an encyclopedia. Sooner or later you arrive at a place where you don't know what you're talking about. Well, I'm trying to learn. Anyway, when it comes to drying vegetables I think you'd be better off reading other books too. The wife of Granville Beitzel who lives at Palouse, Washington, and is a very dynamic and generous lady who really knows her drying shared the following list and comments about it.

Extension Bulletin #2313, revised May 1974, "Home Drying of Fruits and Vegetables," extension bulletin #8671, May 1974, "Construction of a Fruit or Vegetable Drying Cabinet." These two small bulletins are available free from the Extension Service, College of Agriculture, W.S.U., Pullman, Washington 99163.

Dry It—You'll Like It by Gen MacManiman (published 1973, 64 pages) sells for $3.75 plus 60¢ postage and handling and you can buy it direct from us here in Kendrick, Idaho 83537. How to dry foods, includes many recipes, also detailed plans for building your own dryer. It's a fun drying book!

Home Food Dehydration, The Hows, What, and Whys . . . $4.95 by Emma Wheeler (published in July 1974, 160 pages). Very complete. Until now there has been only scattered information on dehydrating foods at home. This book attempts to put all the pertinent facts under one cover. Write: Wheeler Enterprises, 7855 South 114th, Seattle, Washington 98178.

I've found some good drying books too. A favorite of mine is a reprint of a government bulletin, "Drying Fruits and Vegetables in the Home with Recipes for Cooking," Farmers' Bulletin 841, United States Department of Agriculture, June 1917. You can get a copy by writing Homestead General Store, Box 1112, Woodstock, Georgia 30188.

And then there's *Home Food Dehydrating: Eco-nomical "do-it-yourself" methods for preserving, storing and cooking.* Actually the largest part of this 151-page book is recipes using dried foods. You can order a copy by writing Horizon Publishers, P.O. Box 490, 55 East 300 South, Bountiful, Utah 84010.

You can dry either by sunshine or in the oven. I prefer sunshine drying. I'm not just a nature nut. Taste is good and there is no risk of burning or a scorching. If you are drying early in the season before the flies and wasps are about you can simply put the food out on trays. Your climate matters a lot though. Easy in Arizona. Hard in Seattle. To dry outside you have to have a climate where the air is reasonably dry and the sun hot. If it rains all the time you're out of luck. Do your first work early in the morning of a day that promises to be dry and hot. Take the trays in at night to avoid dew and set them out again the next sunny morning until the drying is done. Fruits will be sticky when done, not "crispy" like vegetables. Once the bugs are on you must dry indoors in the oven (where you risk burning and your quantity is limited) or else put the food inside a bug-proof dryer.

STRINGING IT UP TO DRY—My neighbor Ethel Groseclose does lots of apple slices this way every summer. She peels and cores and then slices the apples to get doughnut shaped pieces. Then she threads them on a strong string (not too close together) and hangs it all up either in the sun or indoors to get dry. This system works well for green beans too, if you have the patience.

TRAYS AND RACKS—You can make portable things to dry food on by making square (more or less) frames of soft lumber. Across the top staple or thumbtack a single thickness of curtain netting or some other strong but very porous cloth. If you make your frame at least a couple inches smaller than the inside of your oven you can also use these trays for oven drying. If you have a problem with the cloth sagging reinforce it underneath with string stretched from side to side. That 1917 drying bulletin I told you about suggests drying on "sheets of paper" or "old pieces of muslin held down with stones." Insects are the biggest threat to purely open air drying. Wasps will eat up your whole crop—they love fruit. And a fly now can mean a maggot later in some types of food. That is the real advantage of drying inside the house like in a sunny window spot or up in your attic which is probably sufficiently warm, dry and bug free. You can arrange a stack with 3 to 4 inches between each tray over your wood cook stove or heater and dry food that way too.

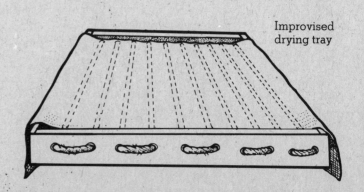

Improvised drying tray

SCREENED-IN OUTDOOR SUN DRYER—Or you can build a screened sun dryer to use outside in the direct sunlight. To do this most easily start with something wooden on four legs with a vaguely boxlike structure. Like an unused rabbit hutch. I have a neighbor who did this. He replaced the top and bottom of the hutch with screen. He hinged the top and just like that they had a wonderful dryer in which to put the food trays. You can even fix it so that more than one level of drying trays can be loaded in at once. Mike made me an outdoor dryer out of an old wooden table. Same procedure, screen on the top and screen on the bottom. The top was hinged to lift up and the food trays went inside. I have to confess the nice dryer made out of a table ended up becoming a rabbit hutch for Becca's two Christmas bunnies. Life has strange quirks and turns and I have a patient, loving and beloved husband.

OVEN DRYING—If you have an oven and you can buy a portable oven thermometer and set it inside there you have a drier. The only problem with oven driers is it often is hard to get a steady heat at a *low* enough temperature. The ideal drying temperature is 95° to 110°. Up to 150° is manageable but not desirable. Over 150° is potentially disastrous. Air circulation is also a problem in the oven if you have a tight fitting door. You want air around the food to absorb moisture from it and carry it away. So prop the oven door open at least a half inch. Gas ovens need to be propped open 8 inches or more. If you can't find an oven thermometer you can feel your way to a certain extent. The food should feel cooler than the air in the oven. If it feels warmer to you, you either need less heat or the door open wider. Don't make your trays solid wall to wall or the air can't circulate properly and the food nearest the heat will scorch and that farthest from it won't dry. Every couple hours or so swap tray positions around in the oven and stir the food on the tray itself to try to get the chance at drying more evenly distributed and places where wetness is hiding exposed to the heat. Oven drying is *much* quicker than attic, string, or outside drying. Vegetables may be done in as little as 5 to 12 hours. Fruits in 6 hours or so. But oven drying, unlike sun drying, means you have to be on hand and keep an eye on what's going on. A few vegetables have individual drying requirements that are a little different from the general rule.

There are plans for making an electrical dehydrator in *Dry It—You'll Like It* or you can get a set free by writing the County Extension Agent, Home Economics, P.O. Box 1107, County Courthouse, Pendleton, Oregon 97801, and asking for Extension Circular 855, "How to Build a Portable Electric Food Dehydrator" put out by the Extension Service, Oregon State University. It requires a little wiring know-how as well as carpentry to build your own.

If you would like a dehydrator but don't know how or want to make one then you're going to be wanting to buy one. Quite a number of dehydrator makers are getting going around the country. Here are some I know about. Gen MacManiman, author of *Dry It—You'll Like It* makes and sells what she calls her "Living Foods Dehydrator" for $124.95. Address is P.O. Box 546, Fall City, Washington 98024. The Wheelers (remember their book *Home Food Dehydration*) also have a dehydrator for sale. I don't know the price. Write Wheeler Enterprises, Inc., 7855 South 114th, Seattle, Washington 98178. Jay and Shirley Bills, authors of *Home Food Dehydrating* market their Mountain Valley Dehydrator, a $139.50 model and a larger $169.50 model. They have had special sales in the past for mail-order customers offering them for less, $126.50 and $149.50. Writing books about food drying and selling dryers seem to just naturally go together! And then there's United Vito-Way, P.O. Box 2216, 826 S. Broadway, Everett, Washington 98203 that sells all sizes dryers, an Equi-Flow Dehydrator, 5-tray style for $99.95, a 10-tray model for $139.95, a Dri-Rite dehydrator (metal) for $199.95, and a 20-tray floor model Equi-Flow Dehydrator for $229.95. If you ask around at your local co-op market or health food store you may well discover someone up the road from you is making them too and at a real bargain.

WHICH FOODS DRY BEST—Apples, apricots, cherries and coconut are the easiest fruits to dry. Dates, figs, guava, nectarines, peaches, pears and plums dry well, too, but not whole. Avocado, blackberries, bananas, breadfruit, dewberries, loganberries and grapes are not so easy to dry. It can be done though. For blueberries, dry out of doors two sunny days in a row, then in the oven at low heat until they are rubbery and look like raisins.

All the rule books say to start with only the best produce but actually if *fruit* is too ripe or bruised you can still dry it. Wash it, cut out the worst of it and make the fruit into a leather. Being squishy won't harm the leather a bit. Look in the Sweets chapter for detailed directions on making fruit leathers.

Vegetables that are easy to dry are mature kidney, lima, mongo, pinto, red, black and soy beans; green lentils; chili peppers; herbs like parsley; celery tops; mature sugar, cow, chick, pigeon or other peas; sweet corn; sweet potatoes and onions. Vegetables that are hard to dry are asparagus, beets, broccoli, carrots, celery, greens of any sort, green snap beans, okra, peppers, pimentos, pumpkin, squash and tomatoes. Drying doesn't work at all with lettuce, melons, cucumbers and radishes.

TO BLANCH OR NOT TO BLANCH—*Vegetables* to be dried are generally first cut up unless they are already small like peas, then blanched a varying amount of time. *Fruits* are not blanched. But some old-time home dryers disagree with the government-type drying experts. I've got a letter from a lady called Crystal Glenn (which is a beautiful name) of Aspen, Colorado, who has lived on a farm most of her 52 years, made soap, bread, butter, cottage cheese, raised chickens and dried foods. And she says that she has never steamed her fruit before drying it although this is recommended nor has she pasteurized her vegetables. She says, "I've never had anything spoil or get wormy." Crystal also had some real good advice on drying surfaces. Don't use screen to dry food on because it contains zinc and cadmium and can be harmful. She recommends synthetic materials or string wound back and forth several ways or porous cloth or nylon net. Crystal isn't the only one who objects to being told she has to blanch. Catherine Humes, a West Coast expert on natural dyes for wool, spinning and black sheep, wrote me that the only food she ever steams before drying is potatoes so they won't turn black. Farmers' Bulletin 841 put out by the USDA in 1917 agrees: "Blanching of vegetables is considered desirable by some housekeepers, but it is not strictly essential to successful drying."

TO PASTEURIZE OR NOT—Some experts say you're supposed to heat your dried foods up once before sealing to "pasteurize." Just about everybody disagrees with this one.

TO POTASSIUM METABISULFITE OR NOT—Other experts says you should treat light fruits by soaking 15 minutes in a solution of 1 tablespoon potassium metabisulfite in 4¼ cups cold water before drying to prevent darkening, "loss of nutrients" and "to repel insects." I've dried a lot of fruit and never yet used it and so have a lot of other people. But maybe I'm wrong. If I am dozens of people will write and tell me so and I'll be sorry I stuck my neck out.

TO SULFUR OR NOT TO SULFUR—I never have met anybody who pasteurized or potassium metabisulfited, just read about it. I have met blanchers and I have met sulfurers. I've also met them what don't and them what don't consciously won't and them what do say it's the thing to do and both sides dry food and it stores and they eat it and they're alive so I really don't have the answers for you except that it's easier not to and I don't and everything seems to be fine and I don't give a hoot or a howl what color things are. Sulfuring is supposed to help preserve texture, flavor, and color, repel insects, prevent loss of vitamins, mold, slow the aging process (in people or food?) and aid in reconstituting dried food. If it truly does all that I can see why it's worth the trouble.

Sulfur fumes are injurious and you should do your sulfuring outside and avoid breathing the fumes. That isn't necessarily bad either. So's lye dangerous and I didn't tell you not to make hominy, pretzels and olives. See I'm trying to be very calm and reasonable about all this. Sulfur is a yellow colored, naturally occurring earth substance, not a factory produced chemical. Burning sulfur in the basement I am told will help keep away bugs and mold. If you use it right I'm told sulfur vanishes from the heat of drying and cooking. But here's a subjective piece of evidence. All your store-bought dried fruit except the organic kind is sulfured and when you taste home dried unsulfured fruit I bet you can immediately tell the difference. I can. The unsulfured tastes much better to me. It digests better for me too. (I have an internal, automatic early warning system for preservatives.) Well, I tried hard but I ended up just coming right out and saying it. Incidentally, that 1917 Farmers' Bulletin doesn't say one word in its 29 pages of small print about sulfur—doesn't have the word in there just like the people who wrote it had never heard of the practice.

Forgive me if you are a sulfur believer. If you are undecided and want to try sulfuring for yourself here's how: Buy a sulfur source like a sulfur candle or plain sulfur from a hardware store or sulfur strips from winemaking stores or plain sulfur in powdered form. Garden suppliers and drugstores sometimes carry sulfur, too. Sometimes it is called "sublimed sulfur" or "flowers of sulfur." The most convenient setup is to have your fruit spread out a single layer deep on drying racks in a dryer that you have moved outside. You need 2 teaspoons of sulfur, plain, for each pound of fruit you are treating. Not everybody agrees on that amount though. I know a lady who uses 1 heaping teaspoon sulfur for a large dryer full of racks and that's enough for her. The more sulfur you have the longer you can let it burn but people don't agree on that either—how long it should burn. Some say 1 hour for sliced fruit and 2 hours for quartered fruit. Some say 30 minutes for anything. Anyway you set your sulfur in a low can in a corner of your dryer on a hot pad or sulfur strips on a foil pan on a hot pad and light it. After it has finished burning let the fruit stand in the fumes another half hour. Then bring your dryer back in the house and finish the drying process.

STEP BY STEP DRYING DIRECTIONS

1. Gather your vegetables in the garden. Avoid overripe ones. You can make fruit leather out of over-ripe fruits but you're better off to raise chickens on the overripe vegetables. Get started on the drying as soon after harvest as possible. Early in the morning is a good time to harvest. Then you've got all that first day to get them started drying.

2. Wash off the dirt if there is any. Scrub if necessary. Dry off.

3. Do the necessary shelling, peeling, slicing or what not. Slice about ¼ inch thick (a little thicker for peaches, tomatoes and zucchini). An important rule of drying is that smaller pieces give you faster drying and that fast drying is important. If you slice peaches rather than merely halve and pit them it takes more time at the beginning but it saves time and struggle later on. Same goes for your other foods, especially vegetables. Because vegetables are low in acid and spoil easier, they need to be cut thinner than fruits to dry quickly before any microscopic beasties can move in. On the other hand you've got a point of diminishing return on the thin slicing. Carrots, zucchini, pumpkin, sweet potatoes, squash and turnips thinly sliced and dried turn into wonderful snack chips—good plain, good with a dip. But if you slice too thin, some foods like tomatoes and zucchini tend to stick to the tray. But then again almost everything sticks to some degree or other and that cures itself as they continue drying.

4. The next step is blanching. For vegetables only. This is the step Crystal Glenn and Catherine Humes leave out. Many people do blanch though, especially if the vegetables are old, or have been gathered too long or were grown under very dry conditions. They are done steaming when a piece from the center feels heated clear through when you press it and is wilted, tender but not completely cooked. If you don't have a steamer, a sieve put in the pan,

hanging over the boiling water, will do or a bag with the food in it suspended over the edge of the pan. The important thing is to keep the food out of the boiling water below so that you are actually *steaming* it and not *boiling* it. Keep a lid on up above so your steam isn't getting away.

5. Now you spread your vegetables or fruit on the drying trays, one layer only in thickness. Except for leafy stuff like parsley or herbs which can be loosely mounded a couple inches deep.

6. Now set the trays out in the sun or in your attic or in your sun dryers or in your oven or in your electric dehydrator. Dry at a low temperature for better flavor and color, and no risk of burning. Don't "cook" the food instead of drying it.

7. Turn big hunk kinds of food two or three times a day at least to speed drying and prevent sticking and stir finer kinds of food.

HOW DRY SHOULD YOU DRY IT? If you intend to use it pretty soon, say within the next few weeks, keep it on the chewy side. Don't dry to brittle hard. You never dry fruits to brittle hard, anyway. Fruits are done when they're leathery and tough. But when you are drying for long-term storage you want to get your vegetables as hard and even brittle as possible before you stop. Not all the food will be equally dry when you're ready to stop. You could separate out moister feeling pieces for quick consumption. If you put them in storage with the others they may mold.

PACKAGING FOR STORAGE—Package your dried food up right away before it can start to reabsorb moisture from the air which it will. Put it in airtight containers like heavy plastic bags. Inside those put in one-meal-sized containers like baggies. If you protect from light, air and dampness it will keep a year easy, even more. The texts say it won't keep more than six months but mine has. Homemade teas will keep even several years though you have to use more.

Store containers in a cool, dry, dark place. If you store your vegetables separately you can experiment with soup making, trying more or less of various ones (less of the stronger ones). Dried chopped vegetables are nice to use in homemade soups, like bouillon cubes, as flavorings. Once you know the combination you like you can combine and store in one container for a soup mixture, chowder, stew or broth. Dried cabbage and chard when ground fine in a seed mill make a powder that is nutritious and good added to anything from soup to salad.

TO EAT IT—Dried foods make great snacking. Just eat as is. Especially fruits but you'll find that well-dried vegetables like corn (dried moist and chewy, not hard) are delicious too. You can use your dried fruit anywhere it calls for "raisins" or "currants" or any other dried fruit. Or you can cook dried fruits with water and serve them stewed. Just cover with cold water and soak. Soaking ½ to 2 hours will do, up to 6 hours of soaking may make it even more tender. Cook the food in the same water in which it soaked to save food value. But greens, cabbage, tomatoes, soup mixtures and powdered dried vegetables are cooked without soaking. Drop them into enough water to cover and cook until tender. Dried tomatoes, okra, peppers, string beans and corn are good in your soup mixture or in casseroles or as flavorings. Drying vegetables kills a lot of their flavor so add something like basil, garlic or onion. Corn is good cooked with butter or creamed.

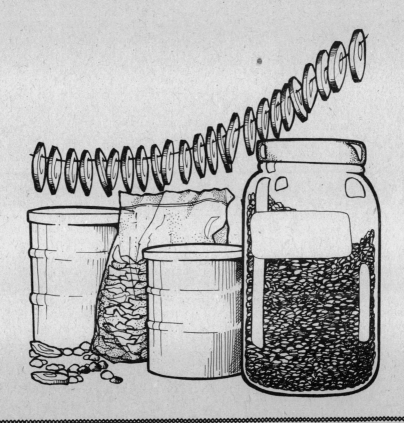

SUGARING, SALTING, ALCOHOLING, LARDING

Sugar, salt and alcohol were the original "chemical" preservatives. At sugar concentrations of 50 to 60 percent its preserving action begins to work. Above 70 percent nothing grows. A 5-percent salt solution reduces bacterial activity, 10 percent stops most of it, and 15 percent stops anything. Wines and foods containing over 14 percent alcohol by volume are self-preserving, by the effect of the alcohol. Wines and foods with a weaker concentration of alcohol can become sour and vinegary.

Because 15 percent salt and 70 percent sugar don't appeal to human taste, the former brine and the latter syrup were diluted in old days before use. That was before canning and freezing were common and these methods of food preservation were really important. Pickles were removed from the brine for a day and soaked in several changes of clear water. Syrups were diluted to taste with water.

My favorite food "preserved in sugar" is pure honey which will keep almost literally forever. You can make any jam into a self-preserving recipe by altering the amount of sugar used to be the required 70 percent. Then even if a bit of mold grows on the top it hasn't ruined the whole batch. Scrape off the mold and use what's underneath. But it's better healthwise to dry fruit or make fruit leather or can fruit for a winter sweet because those all are naturally sweet enough without adding sugar. Recipes and more information about making sweet preserves are in the Sweets chapter of this book.

Most recipe books way, way oversalt in my opinion. But on the other hand there is a time and a place for salt and pickling is one. The best guide to salt intake is nature. Salting tends to become a habit, and a very bad one, as does sugaring food. Just use common sense. A person who does little physical labor and spends the summer in an air-conditioned office doesn't need much salt in his food. However, if you spend your summer days working hard out in the sun and in the evening come home to a hot house you need as much salt as you hunger for and plenty of water or diluted, unsweetened fruit juice to help you with all that perspiring. The secret is—don't let salting become merely habit because needs vary according to the time of year and your activity.

Salting is a method of food preservation well worth considering. Carrots, beets and turnips keep well salted. They also do well in a root cellar. String beans and corn are two good vegetables that you can't store in your root cellar plain but they salt well. Peas and onions do *not* salt well but viewing food preservation from a very primitive "survival" angle that's all right because peas dry very well and onions also store well dried and put away on a shelf where they won't freeze. Peppers, cauliflower and asparagus salt well but need to go into a brine rather than be put down in dry salt. Any salted vegetable must be freshened by soaking overnight in several changes of water, then promptly cooked. A vegetable that has been preserved in salt will spoil amazingly fast once the salt is out, so you must be very prompt getting it from your brine crock through the freshening waters and then cooked and to the table.

Here is your basic procedure to dry salt vegetables: Any root vegetable would be peeled and sliced or chunked. Corn should be cut off the cob. String beans snapped into sections. Use a glass, crockery or wood container to store the food in—nothing made of metal. You'll need about 1 pound of salt for every 4 pounds of vegetables. Put a layer of salt on the bottom of your container, then a layer of vegetable, then salt, and so on until it is full. You can add more at later dates as your crop in the garden gets ready for harvest. When you have as much vegetable in there as you want (don't go clear up to the brim), pour over a final layer of salt. Lay a plate on top weighted down with a boiled stone or a jar full of water or some such. Lay a cloth over the whole thing to keep flies from dying in it. Let rest two weeks changing the cloth weekly. What will happen is the salt will draw the natural juices out of the vegetables and create a brine. Now you can either continue with the plate or remove the plate lid arrangement and seal with paraffin. When you need food you can take some out and replace either the plate or repair the paraffin seal. Either way you *must* keep your vegetables out of contact with the air. You can make sure that the water level is always higher than the vegetables by adding more water as it evaporates. Or use the paraffin. The peppers, cauliflower and asparagus that I mentioned that you don't dry salt you pack in a strong brine. Pack whole vegetables in your crock or whatever and pour over a brine of 3½ pounds salt per gallon water. The rest of it is the same. You can salt down in canning jars too. Pack the green beans down in jars between layers of salt and then close up the jars.

Sauerkraut making and crock pickles—which are salted down in a weak enough brine that you get a limited fermentation that we like—and many other kinds of vinegar-salt recipes are in the Sours chapter. Foods preserved in alcohol I call "brandied" and that is covered in Sours too. Brandied food should be kept cool and airtight. Burying deep in the ground works well. The trouble with preserving food by brandying is among other things that it will give you a hangover. I'd hate to have to get drunk to eat.

Another traditional method of food preservation that I've heard mentioned a lot is "larding." I've never tried it and I'm not sure I really understand how it works. Here's a letter from August Bartelle, now of San Diego, California, who remembers about it. "After slaughtering a hog, the fat was rendered into lard. Those cuts of the hog that were not cured for smoking or made into sausage, like the shoulder, were fried. While still hot these slices of pork steak were preserved through the winter by larding. In a large crock, layer on layer of the fried steaks was covered with hot lard. This meat was then used through the winter by scraping the lard off each layer, the amount necessary for a meal removed and reheated. The used lard was reused in pies or other baking or cooking and ultimately for soap." It all sounds so easy. I wish that someone else who has tried this would write me.

GRAINS

OF BOOK WRITING, AND MY CHILDHOOD AND GRAIN GROWING

For you this is near the beginning of my book. For me, as I write, it is near the end. I started with the back of the book. I didn't know how to write when I started and wanted to do my learning in some dark corner where it would be as unnoticeable as possible. So I did Definitions and Measures first. Then Home Industries and Herbs. Then I wrote Sours and the the first part of Meats except the Introduction. Then I wrote the first and last sections of Dairy and all the Oddments. Then I did the rest. It's been a long journey. Four years in time. Three babies have been born since I started, making a total of five children, four of them preschoolers. I've been through some hard and deep periods of adjustment with my children, my husband, my friends and neighbors, and with God. And all along I struggled to bring this book to life as if it were kind of a baby, too—a child born part brain, part spirit, part paper and ink.

I wrote it always under pressure. Not just the pressure of other responsibilities and the never completely resolved question of whether I even had the right to take so much of myself from my housework and my husband and the children to do something like this. Not just money pressure as I took every spare cent of ours over all those years for my electric typewriter, mimeograph machine, advertising, paper and so on. Not just pressure of knowing I was a little fish in a big ocean where big fishes eat little fishes—big companies with research staffs that discover what books the public wants and order them written, printed, advertised, sold, and then on to the next book. And knowing at this stage that the idea that was such a good idea four years ago has already been done and redone in the four years since while I mopped floors and comforted children and listened to my husband's troubles and wondered if I was ever going to finish it at all.

The real pressure was simply that I couldn't stop. Maybe it's like having a compulsion. I swore off time and time again. Promised my husband, myself, God, that I was through. And kept going back. In the end I felt like God wanted me to finish and helped me find a way to write that didn't really harm my family. But it made me slow and I'm finishing this book now in the knowledge that when I advertise "Candles, Sausage Making, Cheese" I'm not offering something completely new any more. But I have faith that this book is a better one. Maybe because it did all come about so slowly and because I was living it even when I couldn't be writing it. And because it isn't just a textbook written by a staff in a library. There's a lot of my soul in this book. When I sit down to the typewriter now I feel like I'm starting to write another letter to an old friend who will really understand. That's kind of like the way I feel when I pray.

I also kept going back because a certain group of people wouldn't hear of me stopping. They were the people who answered my first little ad when I figured I could get my book written in a couple of months. That was in 1971. I sent them those first three chapters I wrote and bad as they now seem to me those people, who paid $3.50 each for the book I proposed to write, from then till now just wouldn't let me quit. They besieged me with the most loving and beautiful letters insisting that my book was needed and that I could write and declaring that they were willing to wait, however long it took, but I must not give up. So when I write, I am writing to them. People whose letters I often had no time to answer or took two years to do it. But I figured if I put the time instead into writing the book they would prefer that anyway. In this book when I say a "friend" gave the recipe to me it is sometimes a neighbor down the road, but it is sometimes also a neighbor across the nation, or even in Turkey, France, or Haiti. Those first chapters traveled so far.

Here I am at the typewriter with a little girl in a red polka dot maxidress sitting in my lap. She's three and her name is Rebecca. We all call her Becca. She's been fighting with Luke, who, though just two, has the approach of a professional football player and she needs comfort. Danny, five, is sitting in the big overstuffed chair pretending something and Sara, seven months, is crawling around on the floor looking for something she hasn't tasted or touched before. Dolly is at school. Mike is at work and I'm going to tell you all I knew, know, and could find out about grains.

In a way it's an easy subject for me. Before my father went into the sheep and cattle business, he was a wheat rancher in the hard wheat area around Clyde Park, Montana. That's the same wheat that is now sold as "organic" because the farmers raise it without fertilizer or pesticides (or irrigation). We would get 15 bushels to the acre on a terrible stand and 80 to 100 on a fabulously good one. Usually it was around 40. We suffered losses from grasshoppers and from hail, from drought, and from cloudbursts that beat down the stalks so the combine couldn't get to the heads to thresh them. But in good years, like right after World War II when the price was up and the yields were good, my father made as much as $10,000 a year.

It was all done on a big-scale commercial basis. During the busy seasons of tilling and planting the tractors went night and day, with big headlights on them at night. We had our own underground gas tanks and gas pumps for the tractors to fill up at. In combining season the big combines went round and round the fields catching up the golden waves of grain in their great revolving paddles. I sat high up in the combine's hopper and played with the wheat flowing into it in a steady orange stream. The wheat came out of a spout from the complex threshing machinery below. The driver drove the combine and I sat up there in that hopper watching first my feet get covered with wheat, then my knees and finally my arms.

Or I would crawl up on top of the grain and amuse myself with all the fascinating bugs that come along with the grain. Grasshoppers in all sizes and colors—yellow legs, orange legs, blue legs, green legs, and all sorts of combinations. Dear little ladybugs, red with black spots, and ugly old green ones that we called stinkbugs because there was such an awful odor to them. When the hopper was heaping full of grain it would be unloaded into the back of a waiting truck. About three hopperfuls would fill our truck. Then it would be on the way to the granary in Clyde Park. Another truck would wait at the field to get filled with the hopperfuls of grain from the combine.

Daddy Harshbarger wasn't always so highly organized and mechanically oriented. When he met my mother he was farming in western Washington with a team of horses, very much the way his father, a dairy farmer, had lived outside Xenia, Ohio. Daddy's mother was a Dunker and his father a Quaker. He had lots of Brethren and Amish relatives and all four denominations are peopled by honest, hardworking and conservative Pennsylvania Dutch and Germans. Change isn't easy for them. But the first year Daddy was married to Mama (who had been working as a schoolteacher when he met her), changes came whether he was ready or not. Potato bugs got all the potato plants. A drought got the alfalfa. I don't know what all else happened but by summer's end Daddy had gone broke and lost his farm.

They auctioned off the team of horses and other farm effects, bought a little Model something or other, and went to California Grapes-of-Wrath style. I was born January 18, 1939, in Los Angeles, while my father spent day after day going from door to door in search of a job—any job. He finally did get one as a butler and chauffeur to the movie star Dorothy Lamour. Really! My mother got to come along as cook, I was boarded out. Daddy had some great stories of those days. He loved to tell a story. But he wasn't really in his heart a butler-type or a California-type though he would do anything he had to do to make an honest living.

I think about it now and I bet Dorothy was proud of her butler. He wasn't awfully tall but he stood up so straight he seemed taller than he was. Coal black hair, very white skin when he wasn't in the sun a lot, a big nose like butlers are supposed to have, and stern, blue eyes when he wanted to look at you like that. He also loved to speed. And when Dorothy would tap him on the shoulder from her stylish seat in the rear and say: "Faster, Carl, faster . . ." those eyes would twinkle and he happily went faster. Daddy got older and he got two laugh wrinkles for every worry wrinkle. That's how he was.

Well, it took Carl five years of butlering in California, logging in Oregon and defense work at a shipyard in Washington to finally work his way back to another farm. *This* time he mechanized all the way and there were five postwar years of big crops and good prices. The annual fall wheat check would come in and Daddy would buy the latest model of Mercury and my mother would mutter darkly as he went faster and faster. He always passed everything on the road. It scared Mother and me both to death to drive with him though he was a brilliant driver. We weren't made of the same stuff as Dorothy, I guess. But speeding and all Daddy was still a solid Quaker gentleman in his heart and the way he treated his family.

So that kind of wheat ranching I understand well. But as for the notion of raising just enough for your own family's needs, sowing and threshing by hand, I'm a beginner too.

TO PLANT any kind of grain you have to get your seed. You can hold back part of your crop from year to year for seed. Just keep it dry and it will keep very easily just like dried peas or beans. If you can see weed seeds in the grain, a way to get rid of them before planting is to stretch wire mesh across the bottom of a wooden box. Shake your grain in it and the weed seeds will sift out because weed seeds are usually smaller than your grain. Weed seeds are good pig and chicken feed.

If for some reason you are using old grain for seed, and maybe you aren't too sure about it, you can test to see if it can still grow by putting some of the seed in a cotton flannel cloth between two dinner plates or between moist blotting papers. Keep it moist constantly and at a moderate temperature. If not very many of the seeds sprout, it means you'll have to plant the seed that much thicker to get a reasonable stand on your ground.

The regular seed catalogs like Burpee and Gurneys don't carry wheat. It would be expensive to ship heavy grain seed so far away. If you live in a farming area you should be able to ask around and find a "seedsman" who wholesales grain, hay and field crop seeds in general to farmers. He'll happily sell you some, too, even though you don't need a whole truckload. It will be relatively cheap, too. If for some reason you must mail-order your grain seed, the first year anyway, you can buy things like barley, buckwheat, rye (spring or winter) and wheat from Earl May Seed and Nursery Company, Elm Street, Shenandoah, Iowa 51601. Or Robson Quality Seeds, Inc., Hall, New York 14463. Or R. H. Shumway Seedsman, 628 Cedar Street, Rockford, Illinois 61101. Or Wyatt Quarles Seeds Company, P.O. Box 2131, Raleigh, North Carolina 27601.

Here is the amount to buy: 96 to 110 pounds of barley are planted per acre for an expected yield of one to one and a half tons per acre. Fifty-six to sixty pounds of buckwheat are planted per acre. Sixty-four to one hundred pounds of oats are planted per acre for an expected yield of one and a half to two tons of grain. Seventy to eighty pounds of rye are planted per acre. Ninety pounds of wheat are planted per acre for an expected yield of 60 to 70 bushels per acre. About one-fourth bushel of corn seed per acre is needed. These amounts are for a mechanical-type seeding operation. If you are broadcast seeding you had better use more because you will lose a lot of your seed to birds or failure to get underground.

Commercial grain farmers seed their fields using a "drill" pulled by a tractor. The drill lets the seed fall into a little trench it makes in the soil in just the right amount and makes about a ten-foot swath of rows about three inches apart everywhere it is pulled. Before the drilling the ground is well tilled to be loose for the seeding operation. If you aren't going to drill there are several types of hand seeders available. One is a machine that you wear. It has a canvas bag of grain seed on a frame. At the bottom is a fan fastened to a crank. As you walk through the field you turn the crank which turns the fan and blows the seed out in front of you. My local seedsman carries them. The address is Brucke and Company, Seedsman, Kendrick, Idaho 83537. To broadcast the seed completely by hand, reaching in a bag that you carry, is the worst way although old-time pictures make it the most romantic. It's hard to get it even and it's hard to get the ground covered when you have anything more than ten square feet to work on.

After any type of broadcast seeding you need to come back and try to get the seed covered with an inch or so of dirt. That isn't easy either. But if the seed lays on top the birds will come and fill their tummies and unless you have the luck of a wet spring the germination rate won't be so good. If you have a tractor go over the ground pulling a spiketooth harrow after your broadcast seeding. That's a good way to handle field corn, too. For just an acre or so of grain and when you don't have a tractor, use your rototiller to prepare the ground, then broadcast seed and then come along with a hand tool and cover it up as fast as you can. *Note:* You don't weed a grainfield. There's no place to stand that wouldn't mash the good guys.

This last spring we planted fifty acres to a combination of peas and oats. Mixed the pea and oat seed and planted it together. We were raising the mixture of winter feed for the cows and chickens. Well there was a terrible drought and most of it never germinated. In August we were having to feed hay to keep our cows alive because there was no grass. It didn't rain one drop all summer. The price of hay shot up from the normal $45 a ton to $80 a ton or more. When the rains finally came in the fall that field up there finally turned green. The seed didn't die. It just waited. But December is no time to make hay. You have to get your grain planted before the good spring rains have stopped coming and hope that there will be enough summer rains to finish the job.

Rye and wheat don't have to be planted in the

spring. You can plant "winter" varieties in the fall. They will start to grow then die back in winter but they don't kill off completely unless you have terribly cold weather with no snow cover. Snow insulates the ground and prevents it from freezing. Last winter in December there was no snow cover and a prolonged spell of below freezing weather—like ten or more below. A lot of farmers around here lost their winter wheat crop and a lot of waterlines froze up that ordinarily would be buried deep enough to be all right (including ours). In ordinary years when the winter wheat makes it through all right it does better than the spring wheat because the next spring it has a head start and takes off with the first warmth, just like my February peas.

CUTTING THE GRAIN is done on big stands by combines. Present day combines are huge space-age machines that cost maybe $40,000 new. (A brand-new caterpillar tractor costs $80,000.) They are quite a sight rolling down the highways around here usually four or so in a line with flag vehicles in front and behind as they travel from one farmer's fields to another. The combines are generally owned by a combining company that harvests a farmer's grain in return for a percentage of his crop, like one-third. They are not so different from the kind I rode in as a little girl—just much, much bigger. And the cabs are very sophisticated. Like a little house atop the rest of it with air conditioning. The combines cut and thresh the grain from the stalks and separate the threshed grain and pour the final product into their hopper all in a flash from something like a 16- or 18-foot swath and they move fast too. (It was only an 8-foot swath when I was a little girl.)

Since the combine operation is a combined cutting and threshing one the grain has to be dead ripe. It won't thresh good unless it is. How many times I went with my father to the field and watched as he snapped the head of a stalk of wheat and rubbed it apart between his fingers to get a look at the kernels and see how hard they were. He wanted grain so hard that it couldn't be dented with the fingernail and that shattered out of the husk relatively easily. If you are harvesting by hand though you don't want such dead ripe grain. There is so much more handling to do you will lose your grain off the heads by shattering. You want to reap it after the grain has stopped being milky and before it shatters.

A *scythe* with a *grain cradle* is the ideal tool for cutting grain by hand. You can mail-order a scythe from Montgomery Ward's garden catalog, but I don't know where you'd find a grain cradle. If anybody does I wish you'd write me so I could buy one and put it in the book for other people to get one too. A "cradle" is an attachment of fingerlike wooden rods that fits on a scythe. It makes it much easier to lay the grain evenly in a swath the old-timers tell me. I've seen them in our local museum and I can see how much it would help. Somebody that works with wood should start making them again because I'm positive you could sell enough to make it worthwhile. Same with hand operated butter churns.

You can cut grains and grasses for hay with a sickle as well as a scythe. Lightweight sickles are at

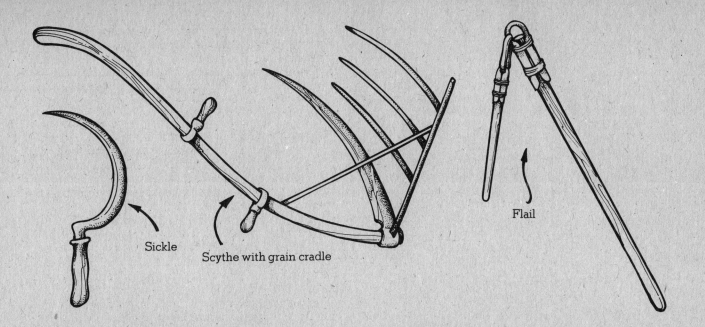

Sickle

Scythe with grain cradle

Flail

most hardware stores. The sickle is best for short, rough or patchy growth. It has a short handle and a short blade and would break your back to use it for very long. A scythe has a handle about six feet long and a long gently curved blade. It is used in a swinging motion. If fitted with a cradle it would catch the grain as it falls so that it can be tossed into one heap for making a sheaf. The sickle-bar tractor mowers used to cut hay aren't suitable for grain because they run over it shelling out some of your grain. For a really beautiful description of how to use a scythe by somebody who has done a lot of it read the article called "Grow Wheat in Your Garden" in *Organic Gardening* magazine, January, 1972.

After the grain is hand reaped it is *shocked* by setting up in sheaves to cure. We shock our cornstalks (and everybody else's who will let us) every year and store the shocks in the barn for part of the winter feed supply for the cows. We yank the plants out of the ground after the corn has been harvested and they have had a while more to stand there and get dry. We gather them into bundles as big as we can work with and tie it around the middle with twine. Then they are loaded into the back of the pickup. When we get a pickup load we drive it to the barn and unload there. We lean them upright around the walls of the haymow. To feed we just toss a bundle to the cows.

For winter pig feed we plant three acres of field corn. It is broadcast seeded by hand, then covered by a tractor pulling a spiketooth harrow. The corn is let dry right on the cob on the plant and the whole thing is dried, pulled up, bundled and then stored. To make silage, which is a feed pigs like very much, you chop this corn, mix with some water and stock grade molasses and let ferment in a *dark*, confined area.

THRESHING is the process of separating the grain from the straw and chaff. Wheat and rye have no adherent husk. Oats and barley do and require an additional step to get the husks off the grain after the grain is off the straw. A combine threshes. Lacking the use of a combine, carry the sheaves to the threshing floor. This should be a wood, hard dirt or even

cement floor—one that won't be harmed by the pounding and that won't lose the grain into cracks. A *flail* is for beating the grain off the "ear." It is a wooden handle at the end of which a stouter and shorter stick is hung (as with a leather thong) so as to swing freely.

You can make one out of a broom handle or similar stick, with about a foot cut off. Take the cutoff piece and attach it to one end of the longer stick with wire or a thong. You beat the grain with the loose end. A wide flat flail would work better than the round broom stick end though. Or use a plastic baseball bat.

As often as necessary gather up the straw with a pitchfork to keep it centered until the grain is beaten out. Remove the straw with a pitchfork when the flailing is done. The heavier grain and chaff will be on the floor. Shovel up the grain, sweep up what remains after the shoveling.

Now you want to winnow. The easiest way is to pour the grain from a high place in a light breeze to a container below—as much as 20 feet. The breeze will carry the lighter straw and chaff away. Or use a fan. Sack the grain. You can buy new gunnysacks at a feed-and-seed store or make your own. Be sure not to use an old sack that has held commercial seed grain. The grain may have been treated with mercury.

STORING YOUR GRAIN—To store grain shift it out of paper or cloth containers into plastic or metal cans with tight lids. For large amounts you can use big garbage cans. If you don't the mice will find it. Despite the fact that I have a large and expert mouse catcher on patrol (a gray cat called Smokey) my cellar is afflicted with mice. Those things can climb straight up a wooden or concrete wall to get on a shelf. They'll gnaw a hole in the corner of anything gnawable until the contents spill out. The grain stored in the barn we have in burlap bags. The barn has mice too, but there is so much grain out there it does no harm to share a little and the animals don't mind. We do keep the grain in a room which helps keep the bigger animals out. Once I had a cat that I refused to feed and kept her on an exclusive diet of mouse. She did succeed in absolutely exterminating a mouse population in both house and barn and thrived on it. But after the mice were all gone she wasn't interested in my handouts and moved on to the birds and baby chicks. She wiped out $30 worth of young chickens the following spring so I finally took her to the pound and got another cat. This one catches mice for fun rather than hunger and she isn't nearly as efficient.

If you have mice you'll know it because they invariably leave their little dark calling cards mixed in with whatever they are eating.

If you have an insect problem there will be kernels with insect holes and insect-chewed kernels, along with the adult insects, alive or dead. Before storing be sure your wheat is free of seeds and chaff. For small quantities you can use 5-gallon cans with airtight lids. They are available both in metal and plastic (Perma-Pak).

The turkey red (dark hard) winter wheat, dark hard spring wheat, and Marquis wheats store best. Don't wash or freeze your wheat before storage. Have it as dry as possible. Insects can't reproduce in the grain when the moisture content is below 10 percent. If you are storing in cans and fear insects may be a problem, you can either: A—put a tablespoon of crushed dry ice on the bottom of the can, pour in the wheat, wait 30 minutes and put the lid on or: B—spread the wheat ¾ inch or less deep in a tray and heat at 150° for 20 minutes, then pour in and put the lid on. (Heated wheat won't germinate for seed.) Metal cans will eventually get rust holes (like in years), but they will last longer if you avoid setting them directly on cement or dirt floors. Lay down wooden planks or set them on wooden shelves.

If you have in storage 40 pounds for each child in your family and 300 pounds for each adult that should be plenty for your year's supply until the next harvest. If you have wheat left over don't worry. It will keep indefinitely as long as the moisture content is under 10 percent and the storage location relatively cool.

GRINDING IT—Grain should be well hardened and dry for grinding. And you don't want to make it all into flour at once because your homemade flour is

not degerminated and won't keep like store flour does unless you freeze it. It is best to grind within a week of when you plan to use the flour. If you are survival minded and/or like the health and taste of home-ground flour you will want to have your own grain in storage whether you can raise it or not.

The cheapest way to get whole grains for home grinding is by going to a grain elevator and buying grain there just like the farmers do to feed their stock. There's nothing wrong with it for human consumption. It will have some dust and weed seeds and a few husks in it. As you need it, winnow it or wash it, pick out the remaining husks by hand, grind, cook and eat. You can buy it from health food stores and organic type outlets but it will cost a whole lot more. If you have a Latter-Day Saint (Mormon) friend or will call their Church listed in your directory, they can also help you buy wheat in quantity for long-term storage because all Mormons are supposed to have a year's supply of food in storage at all times including whole grain, powdered milk and honey.

If you just want to experiment with grinding, popcorn is the most commonly available—make it into cornmeal.

The organic grain is raised on fields without chemical fertilizers or pesticides. Most hard red wheat is "organic" because that's the way it is raised. That's Montana wheat. The soft wheat types raised in northern Idaho and eastern Washington are raised on ground treated yearly with a lot of chemical fertilizer, either laid down with farm equipment or by airplanes flying over the field. And then chemical weed killers and bug killers are either put on by tractor pulled spray equipment or more usually sprayed on the field by airplane. Most of the soft wheat crop is exported.

You can mail-order wheat and rye berries (that means the whole grain), soybeans for grinding, rolled oats and many unusual grains and seeds like millet and chia from Walnut Acres, R.D. 1, Penns Creek, Pennsylvania 17862 or Arrowhead Mills, P.O. Box 866, Hereford, Texas 79045. Or El Molino Mills, 3060 West Valley Blvd., Alhambra, California 91803. How much? One family I know uses 4 bushels of wheat, 1 bushel of oats and 2 bushels of shelled corn a year.

From the subjective point of view, "lazy" and very busy people would probably prefer to use an electric grinder. It is hard work with the hand grinders to get it fine enough so as to not have chunks in it. They really produce a "fine meal" rather than a "flour." In order to get a flour grind you have to crank very hard and often the hand flour grinders will not grind it fine enough without grinding it several times through, although their advertising says these problems have been overcome so perhaps that is a thing of the past. If you do have a problem grinder you can try putting the grain through, sifting out the "grits" and putting through again, and so on until you are satisfied with your flour.

Some grinders are equipped with a flour bag for the outlet. After the grinding is done the bag can be removed from the outlet. "Stone grinding" means that the grain is reduced to flour texture by rubbing against a stone surface in a manner similar to the old-style waterpowered gristmills. But stone wheel mills, whether electric or hand, cannot be used for soybeans because the oil from the beans will damage the stone. They will produce a fine flour though whether electric or hand models. In most commercial mills today the flour is made by crushing the grain between a series of rollers much like a wringer washing machine. Almost all the grinders are adjustable for "fine" or "coarse" grinding. "Grits" are made by cracking grain on one of the coarser settings and then removing the "fines" by sifting. The coarser grits are cooked in water or milk, being then a type of hot cereal. The finest setting mills out a "cake" flour.

These grinders can be used for all the grains including rye, wheat, corn, rice, barley, oats, as well as soybeans, chestnuts, peanuts, lentils and dried peas for a variety of flours. Just make sure your food is dry and shelled before you put it through. There is usually a large screw clamp to provide firm attachment to a bench or table while you are grinding. But Mill and Mix sets on a tabletop. The expensive electric models can put out as much of 100 pounds of flour per hour and can run around the clock if you need them to. They are just like kitchen appliances. You plug it in, pour your grain in the hopper and it grinds your baking flour. The hand models work as long as you have the strength and will to turn the crank. Hand grinders come in various sizes but an average output would be 4 pounds of flour per hour. A hand grinder fitted with stones is available from All-Grain Company, P.O. Box 115, Tremonton, Utah for $49.50. They can also fit a Corona Hand Mill with stones for $39.50. A household 8-inch stone burr mill made by Meadows Mill Company is available from Walnut Acres, R.D. 1, Penns Creek, Pennsylvania 17862.

Perma-Pak, 40 East 2430 South, Salt Lake City, Utah 84115, carries a selection of eight grinders ranging from a $10.95 hand grinder, adjustable for coarse or fine grinding to a $249.95 very sophisticated electric model. Health food stores sometimes have grinders for sale. Or you can get information directly from manufacturers. Lee Engineering Company, 2021 West Wisconsin Avenue, Milwaukee, Wisconsin 53201, sells electric models, ranging from $95 to $170 or you can inquire about Corona Hand Mills from Smithfield Implement Company, 97 North Main Street, Smithfield, Utah 84335. The Little Gem Mill stone grinds electrically. You can mail-order one for $139.95 from Ed and Lucille McInerney, 4028 N. Maple St., Spokane, Washington 99205. Or you can use a blender.

The most interesting (but also most expensive!) grinder of all is the Mill and Mix. It is sold privately through distributorships sort of like Shaklee (the "Basic H") and Tupperware. The salesman will demonstrate for you or your group and it's really a worthwhile lecture on home grinding and bread making—for free. The distributors I know are local—Verda Bigsby of Lacrosse, Washington 99143 (that's her full address) and Ed Larson, 909 E. 6th, Moscow, Idaho 83843. I'm sure if you wrote them they'd be glad to put you in touch with a Mill and Mix representative in your area. Mill and Mix has only one model which is a combination grinder and bread mixer. It can either be electric

or manual as you choose. You can buy either the Mill or the Mix separately. Together they cost about $358.

One or two quarts of grain at a time is about right for a small family. To make life easier with a hand grinder, just save the coarse particles for cracked wheat cereal. After grinding your own grain to make flour, you can sift bran from a *hard* wheat flour to get a relatively light flour for piecrust or light muffins.

COOKING WITH HOME-GROUND FLOUR is well and thoroughly covered in two inexpensive paperbacks available from the Perma-Pak mentioned earlier. A lot of bookstores are carrying them now, too. *Make a Treat with Wheat* is a collection of excellent recipes using stone-ground whole wheat flour, cracked wheat and whole wheat. It is written by Hazel Richards, copyrighted by Hazel Richards and distributed by Hazel Richards, 2857 Hermosa Way, Salt Lake City, Utah 84117. She sounds like somebody I ought to meet. The other book is *Wheat for Man* by Rosenvall, Miller, and Flack put out by Bookcraft, Salt Lake City, Utah. More good recipes in it.

The home-ground flour has a higher lipid (oil) content and will deteriorate faster because of this. It is not degerminated or bleached and requires special care in storage. It can quickly become "oxidized"—a rancid-type (not poisonous) flavor. I've used plenty of rancid flavored flour, but fresh is so much nicer! Also, weevils and other insects may quickly infest it. So keep the flour in a cool place if you will be using it within a week. If you plan to keep it longer than that refrigerate or freeze it. Flour will absorb odor and dampness, too, so use an airtight container if possible. For a small quantity a glass jar—for large quantities the 5-gallon metal or plastic cans that you can buy with fitted lids.

GRINDING FOR ANIMAL FEED—Many farms in the past were equipped with larger burr or hammer or roller mills to grind grain for the chickens and livestock. It is more nourishing for them when ground some beforehand. In some cases you can adjust these grinders to make baking flour, too. Roller mills will dehull oats into groats for table use.

CEREAL

Throw away your notions about cereal and start over. I'm talking about the cereal you make yourself. You can get two kinds of cereal from your home grinder, one on the coarse grind and one on the fine. If you have more settings you can get more kinds. Or you can "grind" in a blender. Or you can cook the whole grain for still another variety. I think cereals are nicest cooked in a double boiler, a steamer or baked in the oven. Cooking in a double boiler is the safest method. Cooking in a pressure cooker is the shortest.

You can make the cereal in any recipe thicker by adding more grain or thinner by using less. You can cook it in milk instead of water or in part milk and part water or in all water or a fruit sauce. You can add raisins or dried, fresh or canned fruit at any stage, or nuts or any sweetening or yogurt. Salt isn't necessary. In general about four parts liquid to one of cereal is appropriate for coarsely ground cereals from the whole grain. Rolled cereals take two parts liquid to one of cereal. A "gruel" means a very thin cereal. A "mush" is a medium one and a "porridge" means a very thick one.

Basic cooking procedure—The general rule is the larger your particles the longer they will take to soften and the more water they will absorb. For cereals ground as fine as cornmeal or finer, the basic cooking procedure is to add the cereal slowly to rapidly boiling water, stirring at the same time. Stir continuously in the case of fine particled cereal until it has set, not at all afterward if possible. Cook until done. Watch carefully so it doesn't scorch, or cook in a double boiler. Really fine grained, flour-type cereals should be first mixed with cold liquid to keep them from lumping, or made gravy style. Coarse grains like whole grains or cracked ones would take quite a while to cook, but you can speed that up by precooking them for 2 or 3 minutes in boiling water and then letting soak in that liquid for several hours or better yet overnight. Then they will cook up faster than they would have otherwise.

I am corrected—I used to pitch in this section for slow cooking of cereals. Great-grandmother was absolutely convinced that an insufficiently cooked grain didn't taste good and was a "mechanical irritant to the digestive system." Times have really changed and Great-grandmother and I have both been learning. In those days mechanical irritants to the digestive system were abundant apparently. Recent headlines on the nutrition scene, however, are that having some dietary fiber in your food every day not only protects you from constipation but from cancer and so the avoidance of mechanical irritation gets put in perspective. Dried fruits, nuts, seeds, whole grains and cereal are where the fibers and bulk and mechanical irritants come from and now they are good guys. So I'll quit worrying about whether the cereal is done enough.

How to have homemade cereal for breakfast (without getting up earlier than you want to)—Cook the day before and refrigerate overnight. If you cooked it in a double boiler, it can be warmed up in the same container. Or start it very late in the evening and let cook all night at a low temperature. If you plan to warm up cracked wheat, oatmeal or such coarse grain preparations use an extra half cup of water when you make them the night before. It also helps if you heat the milk or cream to be used on warmed-up cereal. I like cereal for lunch with the children, too.

Letters from cereal lovers—Wendy Neidhardt of Fox, Arkansas, wrote me: "I put stone-ground cornmeal or ground wheat berries in boiling water (adding slowly so as not to disturb boiling) and cook for no longer than 15 minutes. I sometimes add instant powdered milk at the end of the cooking process, stir, and let sit for a minute to increase the protein content." Maureen Darby of Leslie, Arkansas, wrote me too: "I recommend pressure cooking for grains. I think it cooks them better and conserves more food value . . . because they don't need such long cooking. We eat cracked grain or oats or cornmeal every morning for

breakfast. I believe it would lose much of its food value if overcooked. I cook our cornmeal and rolled oats about 10 minutes, just in a pot on the stove. The cracked grain gets about 15 minutes cooking time." I've been told that grains ground really fine like a flour can be boiled as little as 5 minutes. Some people recommend that this fine cereal be poured into a pan with cold water, then constantly stirred until the gruel comes to a boil. Then continue stirring until it is finished cooking, thick, and smooth.

BASIC GRAIN RECIPES

Grain and Vegetables—If you have leftover whole or cracked grain, any kind that isn't mushy but still can be separated into the individual grains, you can make this dish. Peel and chop 1 onion, 1 celery stalk and 1 green pepper or carrot for every cup of grain you're going to use. Brown the onion in a little oil until soft. Then stir in your grain and continue cooking until it is warmed through. Add a pinch of salt, 2 cups boiling water, the chopped vegetables, cover and simmer until the vegetables are finished cooking. Season with a pinch of thyme and of basil and a slice of garlic.

Egg Foo Young with Leftover Cooked Grain—Cut up onions and either celery, carrots, peppers or some other vegetable or combination you prefer. Fry the vegetables in some oil until they are looking done enough. Add precooked grain and stir it into a mixture with the vegetables. Season with salt and soy sauce. Add 2 eggs and stir together until cooked.

Grain Soup—Use 1 cup grain to 4 cups water. Simmer an hour or so with a little salt and whatever else you want to add—vegetable, meat. This is a good place to hide leftovers for a nourishing and tasty recycling.

BARLEY

Until the sixteenth century barley was the chief bread plant of Europe. Today wheat is preferred to barley by home grain growers because the outer husks of barley are tough and adhere closely to the kernel so it doesn't thresh easily like wheat, buckwheat and rye. (Neither do oats and rice.) Barley is fine animal feed. It is also used to make malt. Best adapted to the north temperate zone, barley requires less moisture for growth than any of the other cereal plants. Get the ground ready, if possible, in the preceding fall for seeding spring barley. Seed winter barley in the early autumn at 1½ to 3½ pounds per 1,000 square feet. It is mature when the straw is yellow and heads droop. (Cut before it is dead ripe.) Make medium-sized shocks that are loose enough to have air circulating. Sheaves that were exposed to dew or rain will have weathered kernels.

Because of the husk, barley is "pearled" for people eating. Animals can eat it straight, if necessary. But they'll get much more food value out of it if you put the barley through a chopper for a coarse chop. A pearling machine is equipped with wire brushes that take the hull off the barley so don't raise

barley for your own consumption unless you feel sure you have access to a pearling machine or have figured out a do-it-yourself system. Unless you're going to put barley, husk and all, through a grinder, which is what one lady I know does. I don't know how they did it in Europe in the Middle Ages when "black barley bread was a staff of peasant life." "Black" referred to the fact that it was parched. It tastes better parched although I've tried it both ways and parching isn't absolutely necessary. To parch simply toast the flour in your oven in a flat pan until it is darkened.

Barley breads can be made to leaven by adding some wheat flour or by using baking powder. A plain loaf of all barley bread can be made by simply substituting barley flour for white flour in a bread recipe. The loaf is small, heavy and very moist like an unleavened or sourdough bread. If unparched it will have a slightly bitter taste. Barley breads are crumbly when warm. Let them cool before slicing and you'll have better luck. You can buy barley flour at health food stores.

Baked Barley—Soak 6 tablespoons of your pearled barley in cold water overnight. In the morning pour off the water and put the barley in a baking dish. Pour 7 cups of boiling water over it. Add salt, if desired, and bake in a moderate oven (325°) about 2½ hours, or until the barley is completely soft and all the water is absorbed. When it is about half done, add about 4 tablespoons sugar or a pour of honey mixed with grated lemon peel. You can eat it warm with cream or serve it cold molded in cups with cream on the side. You can also make it nice by stirring in raisins before you serve it. Get the raisins ready by pouring boiling water over them and letting them stand until they soften before stirring them in.

Barley Pudding—Wash ½ cup pearled barley. Presoak for an hour to partially soften. Combine barley, 4 cups milk, ⅓ cup honey, ½ teaspoon salt, ½ teaspoon cinnamon and 1 tablespoon shortening. Pour into a buttered baking dish. Bake at about 300° for 3 hours. Stir it three times during the first hour to keep the barley from settling in the pudding.

Malt means a grain, generally barley, that has been softened by steeping in water and then allowed to sprout. At this stage it is called "green malt." The green malt is commercially dried in a kiln and sometimes roasted like coffee. The sprouting develops the enzyme "diastase," which is capable of converting to sugar the starch of the malt and also that of the raw grain mixed with it. Because of this, malt has been important in brewing.

You can make a simplified homemade malt. Sprout your barley, then "crack" the green malt by going over it with a rolling pin. Then toast or roast it to obtain the desired effect—pale, medium, dark or very dark. "Malt extract" is a syrup containing malt flavoring. "Malted milk" is evaporated milk combined with extracts of malted barley and wheat.

Barley Whole Wheat Bread—This does rise, stays wonderfully moist and is delicious! Dissolve 1 heaping tablespoon dry yeast in 1 cup warm water. Combine 2 tablespoons corn oil, 1 tablespoon salt and 2½ cups warm water. Add the yeast mixture. Add 2 cups barley flour and enough whole wheat flour to make a dough. Knead until done. Divide into two loaves and put into greased loaf pans. Let rise until doubled in bulk. Bake at 425° for 20 minutes, then at 275° for 40 minutes.

Barley Water—This is a traditional beverage for invalids. Soak 1 tablespoon pearl barley overnight in 3 cups water. In the morning simmer slowly, stirring frequently, until the barley is very soft and your liquid is reduced to 1 cup. Strain. Add salt to taste.

Barley Muffins—I recommend these! Sift together 2½ cups barley flour, 2 teaspoons baking powder and a dash of salt. Beat 2 eggs slightly. Combine eggs, ¼ cup rich cream and ¼ cup honey with dry ingredients and mix well. Pour batter into muffin tins (makes a big dozen) and bake at 400° for 25 minutes.

Steamed Barley Brown Bread—Sift 2 cups cornmeal, 1 cup barley flour, 2 teaspoons baking powder, ½ teaspoon soda and 1 teaspoon salt. Combine 1 cup molasses and 2 cups cold water and then stir into flour mixture. Put into 3 pint cans and steam for 4 hours.

Potato and Barley Drop Cookies—Put ingredients together in the order given: 1 egg lightly beaten, 1 cup mashed potatoes, ½ cup melted fat, ¾ cup corn syrup or molasses, 1⅓ cups (level) barley flour, 2 level teaspoons baking powder, ½ teaspoon salt and ½ teaspoon vanilla. Beat egg, potato and fat to a cream, mix in corn syrup or molasses, then add sifted dry ingredients. A half cupful of nut meats or dried fruit may be added. Drop by spoonfuls on well-greased cookie sheet and bake in moderate oven.

Barley Cereal—Sprinkle ¾ cup barley into 3 cups boiling water. Add ½ teaspoon salt. Simmer until tender (1½ hours, maybe). Drain. Add butter and honey or cream and honey.

Barley Pastry—Sift 2 level cups barley flour, ¼ level teaspoon baking powder and ½ teaspoon salt; cut in 6 tablespoons shortening. Add very cold water to make a soft dough. Mix well and press into pie plate with the hands. Patting it into shape gives more satisfactory results than rolling. Have pastry ¼ inch thick. This is enough for two crusts.

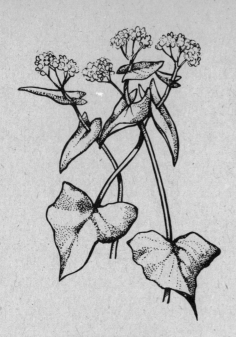

BUCKWHEAT

Buckwheat is not a true cereal since it is not a member of the grass family, but it is classed here as such because of the use made of its seed. It's actually a relative of rhubarb and is believed to have originated in Asia. Here it grows especially well in colder areas from Pennsylvania north into Canada. It is cut just before killing frost and threshes easily. A 30-bushel per acre yield is considered large. Spring-planted buckwheat can be ripe and ready for harvest in June. Or buckwheat can be seeded with rye in July. After harvest the rye continues to grow, producing grain or a crop for plowing under the next spring. (Crimson clover can be used that way too.) Buckwheat is also useful if you have bees because of the long season, its beautiful white flowers and nice tasting honey.

You can order seed from Farmer Seed and Nursery, Faribault, Minnesota 55021. Plant 3 to 4 pecks per acre. The grain matures in 60 days. Another type of buckwheat is grown for fodder so you want to make sure you have the right one. Food buckwheat is a bushlike plant that grows about 3 feet high. The leaves are heart shaped. Buckwheat is adapted to poor soils and moist, cool climates. Dry, hot weather affects it adversely.

When the grain is completely developed in its hull, has turned dark brown and you have had one or two frosts (makes it thresh easier) you can combine or cut. A scythe and cradle or sickle will work. If your weather is dry, shock in the field until threshing time. The grain must be absolutely bone dry when you cut it and when you thresh it. Thresh by laying the grain on a wooden floor and flail until the seeds are beaten from the stalks. Separate from the chaff by pouring from a high place into a container below in a moderate breeze. Then grind your flour as needed.

Molasses is used in buckwheat recipes to improve the color of the product since without it the breads are a blah gray color. If you can't grow it, you can buy buckwheat flour at health food stores.

Buckwheat Pancakes—Dissolve 1 teaspoon dry yeast in a little warm water. Add 1 teaspoon sugar, enough lukewarm water to measure 4 cups, 1 teaspoon salt and enough buckwheat flour to make a thin batter (about 3¼ cups). Let it work overnight. In the morning add 2 tablespoons molasses. Make dollar-sized pancakes. Heat and shine your griddle. All buckwheat pancakes tend to be doughy—the addition of even just a trace of wheat flour helps counteract that.

Sourdough Buckwheat Pancakes—Save a cup of the above batter. Make the recipe using the cup of starter instead of yeast. Let rest overnight. Add ½ teaspoon soda in the morning before cooking the pancakes. Any kind of buckwheat griddle cake makes a fine quick lunch.

Buckwheat Pancakes with Cornmeal—Pour 2 cups boiling water over ½ cup cornmeal. When it has cooled to lukewarm add 2 teaspoons dry yeast, then 1 tablespoon molasses, ½ teaspoon salt and 2 cups buckwheat flour. Let it rest overnight. In the morning dissolve ½ teaspoon soda in ⅓ cup hot milk and mix well with batter. This also can be made into a sourdough recipe by simply holding back some of the batter to use in place of the yeast in future recipes.

Quick Buckwheat Cakes—Take as much or little of your buckwheat flour as you think you'll need and add enough sour cream to make a pancake batter that's on the thick side. About 1 cup liquid to 1½ cups flour is right. Stir in a couple tablespoons bacon grease, if you have it. Shine your griddle and drop batter by tablespoonfuls. Good with butter and honey, sour cream—or what have you.

Yeast Buckwheat Buttermilk Cakes—The evening before you want them, dissolve 1 teaspoon dry yeast in 1 cup lukewarm water. Add 1 cup buttermilk, 1½ cups buckwheat flour, 3 tablespoons whole wheat flour, ½ teaspoon salt and mix well. Let work overnight. Bake the next day on a griddle.

Sourdough Buckwheat Cakes—Keep a cup of the above batter for starter. Substitute your cup of starter for the 1 cup water and yeast in the yeast buckwheat cakes recipe. If you keep your starter in a cool place, such as a refrigerator, and use it (holding out a cup of the new mix for the next starter) every couple days you'll have the traditional sourdough buckwheat cakes for breakfast.

Kasha is "green" buckwheat. It should be dry roasted first under a low flame for about 15 minutes until it turns a nice brown color. You can substitute kasha where you'd use rice.

What I wrote in the above paragraph is what I've learned but not anything I know from personal experience. I've cooked with kasha but never made it. A reader wrote me for advice about getting kasha from buckwheat. I didn't know what to tell him. Maybe you can answer his questions, and we'll add your answer to the next edition of this book. Tom Harvey of Rockport, Washington, asked: "We are growing about an acre of buckwheat this year and can't seem to find anyone locally who knows the procedure for threshing out kasha. To harvest buckwheat groats in our area (where frosts are late and soggy) we understand that we need to windrow the grain first to allow it to dry. Do you know or know of someone who knows the methods and machinery necessary for obtaining kasha?"

Kasha, Egg and Onion—To 1 cup kasha add 1 tablespoon butter or oil, stir, and let melt and coat the grains. Add 1 beaten egg and stir constantly over high heat until the egg is dry. Add 2 cups boiling water (otherwise it spits like crazy). Add some chopped onions that have been sautéed in butter. Put the lid on and lower the heat. Let simmer on low, low heat for 20 minutes. When done dish into bowls and eat.

Kasha Pirogen—Make a basic pie dough except add 3 or 4 eggs so that the dough is more elastic than a regular pie dough. Roll it out to piecrust thickness. Cut into squares (2 inches or more). Take a square in the palm of the left hand, take a spoonful of cooked kasha and place in the center of the square. Moisten the edges of the square and fold the square over, using a slight pressure on the edges to seal. When you have a batch of squares filled drop them into boiling water. Leave in 2 or 3 minutes and they're done. Eat immediately or fry in butter until crisp and brown. Jeanie Karp taught me all this about kasha. She used to live in the Bronx. Now she is my neighbor down the road.

Buckwheat Mush—Place 2 cups water and a pinch salt in a saucepan and bring to a brisk boil. Keep at the boiling point and add 1 cup buckwheat flour. Believe it or not, do not mix the buckwheat flour into the water. Just leave it there and let boil for 5 minutes. Now make a hole in the center of the flour with a wooden spoon and boil again for 10 minutes. Pour off half the water and set aside. Now mix well the buckwheat flour and remaining water. Add 2 tablespoons hot melted butter. Cover and cook over low heat 5 more minutes. If it seems too dry to you, pour in some more of the extra water you poured off before and mix it in. For an extra tasty touch fry 3 slices of cut-up bacon until brown and crisp and pour over the buckwheat mush before serving.

The only other way to make buckwheat mush is to mix your buckwheat flour with *cold* water first, 1 cup flour to 1 cup cold water. Then gradually stir into 4 cups boiling water in the top of a double boiler. Then cover and simmer for 15 minutes.

Fried Buckwheat Mush—Cut it up after it has gotten cold and set, fry in a little oil and serve with butter and syrup, same as cornmeal mush.

Buckwheat Roll—Sift together 3 cups buckwheat flour and 1 teaspoon salt. Combine with 1½ cups boiling water or enough boiling water to make a manageable, workable dough. You've got to make this recipe quickly while the dough is still hot otherwise it won't handle well. Lay the dough on a floured table or breadboard and roll out about ¼ inch thick. Sprinkle on something sweet like honey or jelly, or ¼ cup sugar and ¼ rendered fatback cracklings if you want the genuine Slovenian touch. Roll it up like a jelly roll and lay in a greased baking pan. Bake at 350° for 1 hour.

Buckwheat Noodles—Combine 2 eggs, ⅓ cup powdered milk, 1 teaspoon salt and enough buckwheat flour for a stiff dough (it will take about a cup). Roll out on a surface covered with wheat flour. Cut in ¼-inch strips. Dry for 30 minutes. Drop into boiling water gradually so boiling doesn't stop. Add 1 tablespoon powdered sage to water for seasoning. Cook until done, drain and serve with butter.

CORN

Buttered corn on the cob seems more like a vegetable and that's the chapter you'll find it in. Corn ground into cornmeal and used to make bread is in this Grains chapter. So are cornmeal dishes, hominy, tamales and popcorn. Corn as a vegetable is the same corn you usually can, freeze or use fresh as the vegetable dish on your table. It's generally a "sweet" corn variety. Corn for feeding animals and making cornmeal and hominy is generally "field" corn. Field corn varieties like Dent or Flint are a little tougher than sweet corn but they produce way more per acre. Popcorn is still another variety—the one, of course, that pops the best. It's on the tough side unless you pop it. It isn't all that simple either though because there is still "green corn," a Victorian favorite variety of sweet corn that has green kernels. And "white corn," a Southern favorite, which has white kernels and is especially valued for the white cornmeal you can make from it. It isn't quite as nourishing as yellow corn. There is Indian corn, too, which has all different colors of kernels. People dry it to make pretty flower arrangements or heap them in a basket in the middle of the dining room table. You can make cornmeal out of it, too. You can feed it to your animals and it becomes milk, meat and eggs.

So you start by deciding what kind of corn to grow and ordering your seed. Hopefully after your

first year you will have learned how to save your own. It's exactly the same as for making cornmeal only you don't grind up the kernels, you plant them next spring. Order the kind of corn you want. You want them all? Well, the problem there is they all cross-fertilize. Unless you can plant them at least 50 feet apart, you'll end up with some curious mixtures next year—popcorn that won't pop and sweet corn on the tough side. Popcorn actually makes great corn-meal. Field corn is the highest producer and you can have field corn on the cob if you want, too, though it won't be as tender and sweet as sweet corn on the cob. If you are planning on saving your own seed, don't buy hybrids because you can't save that seed anyway and have it work out right. Field corn is not even listed in a lot of garden catalogs. You'd have to use the wholesaler's catalog like Ball's *Blue Book* or get it from a seedsman doing business with farmers. You can plant the popcorn they sell in stores for popping or buy it through seed catalogs. You'll need to buy 10 to 12 bushels of seed for every acre you plan to plant in corn. Corn is a good crop to be ambitious about. It is food for every man and beast on the place—really high-quality feed. It's a bread, it's a vegetable, it's entertainment. The cobs are fuel to burn and the stalks are as good as hay for winter feeding.

Now that you've decided what kinds of corn to plant, you have maturity dates to consider. You can get a 65-day corn, a 75, an 85, a 100 and everything in between. As a general rule the longer the corn takes to mature, the bigger the ear and the more ears you get. If you live up high or up north you want a quick maturing corn. If you have a nice long season you can plant corn of several maturing dates. The advantage is that is you don't have 5 acres of corn all ripen within three days. It doesn't matter so much for making cornmeal or stock feed because you can leave it there. But if you want sweet table corn or to can and freeze a bunch of it or to sell it at a truck garden stand you could get frantic trying to get it taken care of while still in the few days of perfect taste and tenderness. Another way to do is to plant all quick maturing corn but plant in succession, say every two weeks until midsummer. How much corn to plant? If you're not afraid of work I'd say you can handle up to 5 acres without fancy machinery. Try to keep children and birds out of your newly planted field. They'll eat the seed.

When do you plant corn? It's a grass like wheat and rye and oats but by far the tenderest one. Corn won't come up until the temperature down there where the seed is lying is up to at least 60°. It takes even more warmth than that for a good germination rate. You can get something called a "soil thermometer" and stick it in the ground to find out what the temperature is down there. Corn needs lots of heat to grow too. If you have cool, rainy, cloudy weather, day after day, week after week, your corn will scarcely grow no matter what kind you planted. It wants long hot days of full sunshine and then it will grow so fast and so high you'll be amazed. This heat loving tendency to some extent wipes out your best laid plans of succession planting and planting seeds

with varying maturity dates because with a cool June none of it will grow very fast and then once the sunshine gets going good the late ones all seem to be hurrying to catch up.

Weeding corn is the next problem and here, too, it is different from the other grasses and grains in this chapter. With the others you do your weeding before you plant. You accomplish that by giving the ground a real good tilling as early as you can possibly get in there, trying to kill every weed seed that has turned into a little green aboveground plant. Then you wait two weeks, or however long it takes, for that field to look greenish again. That's another bunch of weed seeds in there that have now germinated. You go in there and cultivate again to kill all those weed plants. If you get started early enough you can give it still another treatment, otherwise go ahead and plant your grain. Then it's on its own as far as competing with the weeds goes. Some grains like buckwheat are such fast growers that they are weedlike themselves and can race to maturity safely ahead of the competition. A good fall cultivation also helps keep your grainfield clear of weeds. But with corn you have to weed.

And that points up another difference between corn and the other grains. With those you broadcasted seeds and then raked the seed to try to get it covered or maybe you planted just before a rain and the rain beat the seed further into the ground and splashed a nice wet mud cover over it. But corn is planted in rows no matter how big the field. You don't have to bend over placing each seed by hand though. For big professional cornfields there are big tractor-pulled planters for all the different types of grains. For a smaller-sized patch there is a seeder wheel that you walk along pushing down the row and it plants for you. Space your corn rows to allow for the method of seeding you're going to use. If you plan to rototill out the weeds make the rows rototiller width plus a little. Tractor cultivators designed specially for corn can be adjusted to fit row widths of from 36 to 42 inches. If you are going to hoe you can plant as close as 20 inches row to row. Go through that corn at least twice between seeding time and maturity getting out the weeds.

Why are weeds such a threat to corn? Well, corn is what you call a "heavy feeder." Remember how Squanto the Indian told the Pilgrims to put a fish in there with the corn seed? Corn is a grain high in nourishment. It pulls that nourishment not only out of the sunshine but also out of the soil. This is something to keep in mind. Before you plant corn, manure the corn patch generously or somehow get some good humus-type material in there for the corn plants to work with. Avoid planting your corn in the same part of the garden or your land year after year. That's called "continuous corn." The only way you can get away with it is to really pour the fertilizer and eventually the insecticides into the land because corn insects will move in there and gradually build strength year after year. The best plant for leaving in the ground the kind of food corn needs is some kind of alfalfa or clover. So if you are ready to recycle a hay field corn is a great succession crop. A perfect crop rotation is vegetable, wheat, clover, corn and around again. If this is a big field that you don't want to grow vegetables in then a good rotation is alfalfa or clover for a couple years, a year of corn, then a year of wheat or another noncorn grain.

Corn has a lot of troubles with plant diseases and insects but ninety percent of the damage is generally done in hybrid cornfields. So your first line of defense against corn insects and diseases is to plant nonhybrid seed. It always says on the packet of seed, in the catalog or wherever you are shopping whether it's hybrid or not so you won't have any trouble there. The next defense is to rotate your corn year after year into different parts of your land. That way when the corn-eating beasties hatch out and look around for corn you can at least make them work a little to find it. Another line of defense is succession planting, because generally one crop will get it the worst and somehow the others will get through pretty good. A matter of the fine timing of beastie life cycles I guess. You can hand pick borers and earworms on a reasonable-sized patch of corn, but that's about impossible if you have more than an acre or so of it.

To harvest corn for canning, freezing, selling on the ear, or quick table use you've got to move fast. To harvest for cornmeal making and feeding the animals and making hominy you have lots of time. That makes it easier to handle a big acreage. Let your corn dry in the field until after the first heavy frost (unless your weather is too wet for field drying). Corn for cornmeal doesn't have to be picked at once when ripe. It can be left on standing stalks in the field for weeks, or even months, without heavy loss. Or you can cut the plants and put them in big bunches, called shocks, weeks before you pull the ears off the stalks and husk them. Then gather the ears. Store them unhusked in gunnysacks in a dry shed or room. If you are having trouble drying your corn, peel back the husk to the butt of the corn and tie together bunches of husks. Then hang the corn bunches up for about a month.

If you live in commercial corn-growing areas you can help harvest fields you never planted by getting permission to glean the left-behind ears after the cornpicking machine is finished. If a farmer has used a corn sheller to harvest his fields there won't be enough left to bother. A cornpicker is kinder to the gleaner. Best places to hunt are at the ends of rows on the ground and the places where the cornpicker first entered the field.

When the corn is really dry you can shell all the ears at once or you can shell them a few at a time on winter evenings. The pioneers shelled corn by firelight, scraping the cobs on the iron edge of the wooden shovel or some other firm metal edge such as the handle of the long-handled frying pan. Another system is to set the edge of a knife blade in a piece of wood and scrape on the back of the blade. You can buy a "hand corn sheller" for $2.50 from Countryside General Store. It's a round metal ring that slips over the cob to shell it. Or you can merely put pressure with your thumbs on the dry kernels and they will pop

right out. Too much of that though and you end up with blistered fingers! You don't have to shell corn to feed to the larger animals. Serve horses, mules, ponies, goats and pigs their corn, cob and all. The horses will eat the whole cobs.

Incidentally the corncobs make nice children's playthings—building logs and such. When added to a fireplace fire they make a bright light. They can be used for smoking hams and bacon if you're short on apple and other hard woods as you probably are. And the husks can be used to make husk filled mattresses (see Home Industries).

To store the dried kernels put into tightly lidded containers. This corn can be ground for cornmeal, or treated for hominy and grits. It will be all yellow cornmeal. The drier your shelled corn is the more safely it will store. If you are drying it artifically remember the grain dries first where a stream of air enters the grain and last where the air leaves. Keep stirring it. A high temperature speeds up the drying but may damage the grain. You can't use grain dried above 110° for seed—it won't germinate very well. At higher temperatures kernels start to crack. It's OK for animal feed though even when dried at 180° to 200°.

When the corn kernels are really hard and dry you can put them through your grinder. First use the coarse setting. Then put it back through on a fine one. Then set as you would regular cornmeal. Home-ground cornmeal is a little coarser than commercial cornmeal. You can rig up a sifting apparatus of screen with a wooden frame. The large particles that don't pass through the screen can be reground until you're content with them. Or you could grind corn in a mortar. It's easier than you think. The American Indians used a mortar made of a hollowed block of wood with a heavy block of wood for a pestle. Stone works much better. It is best to make the cornmeal approximately a week's worth at a time. The store-bought cornmeal is degerminated to improve its keeping quality. Yours isn't. It's therefore better food for you and any other form of life. Keep it in the refrigerator, if you have one, and use within a reasonable period of time. Warmth is what's hard on your cornmeal. That and the fact that it will absorb odors.

If you have cows or goats don't abandon the corn patch after gathering the corn. Let the cornstalks dry in the field for a while, then come along with a corn knife and cut them at the base. A corn knife has a straight blade, about 1½ feet long, kept very sharp. If you don't have a corn knife use a sickle or whatever you can muster. Cut off about three stalks at a time with the corn knife and lay them down. Cut three more and so on. When you have a bundle of 15 or 20 stalks, tie them with string or something. If your corn needs more drying, or if you have no indoor storage space, lean several bundles together upright at the top to form a shock. The leaves will shed and will keep as well as hay. Cows and goats prefer them to hay. To store the cornstalks other than in shocks haul them into your barn and pile anyway you please—like logs is OK. Or just let cows or pigs go in the cornfield and graze.

EATING CORN AND WATER

You could be in terrible shape for money and make it if you had some dried corn. Your shoes might get holes. You could stuff cornhusks in the bottoms. Shell off the corn and burn the cobs for warmth. And eat the corn with water if you don't have anything else. The exact recipe you make depends on how much water you add. If you add just a little water to your cornmeal you make a kind of corn bread. If you add somewhat more you've got cornmeal mush. More than that and you've got a cornmeal gruel. For variety you could make hominy from wood ashes, lye and corn but if you've truly got a food shortage don't do that because you lose some food value. If you have some fat of any sort you have shortening to add to your bread. Some dried fruit, honey or maple syrup gives you an Indian pudding. Add beans and you've got succotash. Add meat and you have a stew. You can tell I'm a corn lover!

Cornmeal and Water Bread—It's called "pone" or "flatbread" or "hoecakes," or "johnnycakes." You just mix cornmeal with water and bake it by an open fire or in an oven. It takes some work to eat it because it isn't flabby soft. The best way to make cornmeal and water bread is to heat 1½ cups water to boiling for every 2 cups of cornmeal you plan to use. Combine the cornmeal and boiling water, stirring constantly. If you want to add salt, mix it with your cornmeal beforehand. You can stir in your shortening while you're mixing, 3 tablespoons per 2 cups cornmeal—if you have it and want to use it. Let stand covered until it cools down enough to work with. Now form into your shape for cooking. Lay your dozen or so hoecakes on a greased pan to bake. Takes a little over half an hour in a 350° oven. There's a specially shaped iron baking pan they sell that you can bake these in, or you can bake them in a greased iron frying pan. A corn dodger means salted cornmeal and water dough wrapped in wet cornhusks, pressed into a flat form and baked in the hot coals and ashes. No matter which way you make your corn and water bread you can eat it enjoyably with some butter or hot gravy poured over.

Cornmeal Gruel—You can make this with as little as 2 tablespoons of cornmeal. Mix your cornmeal with enough cold water to have it all nicely wet. Boil at least 2 cups of water. Pour your cornmeal-water mixture into the boiling water. Boil an hour or so, stirring once in a while. Add a little salt and hot milk if you have it and like the taste.

CORNMEAL MUSH

The amount of time you cook a cereal depends on the size of the pieces it is ground into. With store cereals it depends how much it has been precooked. For you it depends on how much you have precooked or presoaked it, too. The easiest way to make cornmeal mush is to mix your cornmeal with enough cold water to thoroughly moisten it, then add to boiling water a bit at a time, stirring constantly. Or if you have a very quick arm you could just sprinkle the cornmeal, stirring constantly, into rapidly boiling wa-

ter. If you don't get it well mixed very fast it has a tendency to lump. Salt to taste. It will cook in half the time over direct heat but you'll have to be careful to prevent scorching or sticking. If you have time cook in a double boiler.

Figure 30 minutes over direct heat, or 1 hour in the double boiler. The exact amount of time will be unique for your particular cornmeal. You may find you want to cook it as much as 3 or 4 hours. You can hurry your cornmeal some by soaking it overnight. Same applies to grits and hominy. Cook them in the same water in which they were soaked. About 3 cups water should be right for each ½ cup cornmeal. That would include the cold water you use to moisten it. Don't be afraid to make lots of cornmeal mush because there are good uses for the leftovers.

Fried Mush—If you are going to make fried mush just be sure and get your leftover cornmeal mush poured into another pan before it gets cold. Preferably pour while hot into a pan or mold which has been rinsed in cold water and smooth the surface of the cornmeal. Try to use a pan of such size that the mush will be about 2 inches in depth. Let cool until firm. When you are ready to fry your mush (for breakfast the next morning maybe or for lunch the next day) turn the cornmeal out of the mold or cut ¾-inch slices and lift them out. Optional, roll in flour until dry. Or roll in flour and then in beaten egg, or egg and then crumbs, or flour and then egg and then crumbs! Fry in some butter over a medium to hot heat, turning once, just long enough to heat through and put a nice brown crust on the outside. Serve with syrup and butter. If you are frying in some other oil, heat it quite a lot before dropping the mush in.

Spoon Fried Mush—Mrs. Owa Malone of Portland, Oregon, wrote me a beautiful letter full of her good recipes and questions about recipes in this book that she didn't understand or couldn't make work. I really am glad when someone writes to tell me a recipe is bad. It's usually a typographical error and that way we can fix it in the next edition. Anyway, Mrs. Malone also wrote: "I wanted to share with you *my* Missouri mother's way of making fried mush. She cooked it same as any mush but instead of chilling and molding it and slicing for frying, she just dropped large spoonfuls of the fresh mush into hot fat and fried until brown and crisp. It will sputter and pop a bit—but soon settles down—and makes such a nice fluffy patty as compared to the cold sliced kind."

Fried Mush and Bacon—Fry your bacon until done and remove from pan, putting it someplace where to keep warm. Dip your cold cornmeal mush slices into flour, egg and crumbs. Fry in the hot bacon fat until brown and crisp on both sides. Drain on absorbent paper or cloth and serve with the bacon.

Fried Mush with Bacon Scraps—Break up your leftover bacon and add it to the leftover corn mush before pouring it into a pan to set.

Greaseless Leftover Mush—Slice the set mush into slices 1 inch thick, then make cubes about 1 inch square. Put the cubes into serving dishes and pour over them hot rich milk or cream. Cover the dishes

---

and let stand in a warm place until the cornmeal is heated through, then serve. Or slice the cold cornmeal mush thin, brush each slice with thick sweet cream and brown in a medium oven until heated through.

CORN PUDDINGS
(Indian Puddings)

Molasses Pudding—Heat 2 cups milk in the top of a double boiler. Pour ¼ cup cornmeal into ½ cup cold milk and stir until mixed. Then add the cornmeal-cold milk mixture gradually to the hot milk, stirring constantly. Cook 15 minutes more, stirring occasionally. Add 2 tablespoons butter and ½ cup molasses. If you like spices add cinnamon and ginger to taste. Add 1½ cups more milk. Pour into baking dish and bake in a slow (250°) oven about 3 hours.

Plain Pudding from Leftover Corn Bread—Crumble enough leftover corn bread to measure 1 cup. Add 2 cups milk and 2 egg yolks. Gently fold in 2 beaten egg whites. Bake slowly in a dish set in a pan of hot water for about 1 hour. Optional—sweeten with molasses or sugar, or add currants or raisins. More puddings made with leftover corn bread at the end of this chapter.

CORNMEAL BREADS

These aren't made of just cornmeal and water. They have more ingredients and they are even better tasting and more nourishing for you.

Cornmeal Waffles—Pour 1½ cups boiling water over 1 cup cornmeal. Add ¼ cup melted butter. Stir in 1½ cups buttermilk. Separate 2 eggs and stir in the yolks. Sift 1 cup flour with 1½ teaspoons baking powder, ¼ teaspoon baking soda and ½ teaspoon salt. Blend dry ingredients with cornmeal mixture. Beat the 2 egg whites you have waiting and fold into batter. Bake in your waffle iron until crisp and brown. Very light.

Cornmeal and Home-ground Wheat Flour Corn Bread—Combine 1 cup cornmeal, 1 cup home-ground wheat flour, ½ teaspoon salt and ½ tablespoon baking powder in a bowl. In another bowl stir together 1 egg, ½ cup honey and 1 cup milk. Then pour the liquid ingredients into the dry ones and stir it up together. Add ¼ cup melted butter—or lard if that's the best you can do. Stir a moment more but don't overstir because you don't want to stir your bubbles out. Pour into a greased 8-inch square baking pan, or whatever you have that will work, and bake in a 375° oven for about 30 minutes.

Corn Gems—Maybe you've seen old-time cast-iron gem pans in the cast-iron department of your favorite hardware store and maybe you've wondered what you're supposed to bake in those peculiar shaped spaces. Here is a real old-time corn gem recipe. It's the same as the cornmeal and home-ground wheat flour recipe just above only you use 2 eggs instead of 1 and use 2 teaspoons baking powder instead of a teaspoon and a half. Preheat your gem pans,

grease them and pour in your corn gem batter. They will take about 15 minutes to bake in a 400° oven. You can make oatmeal and whole wheat gems, too.

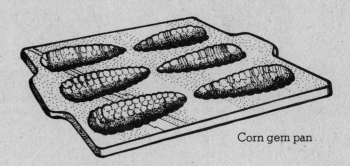

Corn gem pan

Southern Spoon Bread—Here's a recipe sent to me by Mrs. Donald E. Woodliff of Petersburg, Tennessee, who likes to grind her own cornmeal. She says, "One of our favorite recipes is this one for Southern Spoon Bread. Scald 2 cups milk. Add ½ cup cornmeal. Cook together until thick. Add 1 teaspoon salt, ½ teaspoon baking powder, 2 tablespoons sugar and 2 tablespoons melted butter. Beat the yolks of 3 separated eggs and add to cornmeal mixture. Let it cool a few minutes while you are beating the 3 egg whites to soft peaks and then fold the beaten egg whites into your batter. Pour into a well-buttered 1½-quart casserole, bake at 375° for 30 to 45 minutes, or until golden brown and puffed like a soufflé. I hope you will try it and find it a refreshing substitute for either a bread or vegetable."

Real Southern Hush Puppies with White Cornmeal—Mrs. Phil R. Cahoon of Citrus Heights, California, sent me this recipe. "I have served it hundreds—if not thousands—of times to everyone's delight. They all admit hearing about it, but never having tried them—Hush Puppies! Hush puppies are a bread all true Southerners eat with fish. To eat a roll or any other kind of bread would ruin the whole meal. First you fry a big mess of fish. (A 'mess' means enough to feed everyone that's there and any more that may show up.) Fry fish dipped in cornmeal in deep fat. Drain on a brown grocery bag. (Save your paper towels.) Hush puppies are always, I must repeat, *always* fried in the fish grease, behind the fish, otherwise you would just have fried corn bread. Make as many as you have people, but the recipe should serve 5 or 6 people. Combine 2 cups white cornmeal, ½ cup flour, ½ teaspoon salt, ½ teaspoon soda, ½ teaspoon baking powder, 1 cup chopped onion and 1 egg in a bowl. Add enough buttermilk to make a batter, not too thin! Drop by tablespoonfuls in the hot fish grease. The hush puppies will be a golden brown when done. Turn as needed to brown evenly."

No-Fish Hush Puppies—Mrs. Edna Chavez of Cypress, California, has her own ideas about hush puppies. She wrote me about a goof in one of my cracker recipes and sent me this one while she was at it. "Some people think you must have fish with hush puppies, but I make them for after-school snacks: 1 cup cornmeal, 1 cup flour, dash of salt, ½ teaspoon soda, 1 egg. Add as much chopped onion as you like.

We like lots. Mix all together with enough milk to make a very stiff dough. Drop by teaspoonfuls into hot oil. Fry on one side, turn to brown the other side, then drain. They taste a lot like onion rings. We love them."

HOMINY

The Yellow Dent corn is good for hominy. It's the old standard field corn. When dried it has the "dent" in the top. Also good are the Flint corn, Indian and the other hard corns. These are all grown usually for stock feed, silage, ground meal and so on, and are different from the sweet corn you usually grow in the garden. You need dried corn to start with. It has to be really dry before you can comfortably shell it. Leave on the plant longer than you would other corn, but, in our case, we would pick in the fall—before the rainy season starts. Then hang up, still in the husk, or put the ears in a gunnysack and store in a shed or some such. Here we would think of making hominy about October. Husk and shell the corn. As with popcorn push on the kernels with your thumb and it will just pop off the cob.

You are ready to use a hominy recipe once you have your corn dried and shelled. You can choose a soda or a lye method. Lye cuts the outside husk well but you really have to do a lot of rinsing. Incidentally, you can make a sort of hominy from shelled wheat using these same recipes. No matter which recipe you decide to use, read the first one for general orientation since it has a lot of hints I don't repeat afterwards.

Boiled Soda Method Hominy—Use 3 rounded tablespoons baking soda per 1 gallon water. Make enough of it to cover your corn kernels, at least 2 inches over. Remember each grain will puff up to three or four times the dried size so allow for expansion. About 2 quarts corn will be all right. Use a 5-gallon granite canner. You can't use aluminum. Boil it heavily about 2 hours—until you can feel the hulls slip off when you pick it up in your fingers. While boiling keep it covered—add more water if needed. (Optional, let soak overnight before commencing to boil.)

This is the ticklish thing. The hulls are too coarse to eat and have to come off, but when the hulls slip there is nothing to protect the corn and it needs fresh water so get the soda water off before the hulls come off or the soda will leach out all the good stuff in the corn. Put on fresh water. Now it increases in volume. Change the water at least one more time, more if you like. When the corn has doubled in bulk wash it very hard in a continuous flow of water in a dishpan or colander, rubbing it with your hands to let the fine stuff out. (Beware of clogging the sink with hulls.) Don't worry about the black spot at the bottom of the kernel—it shows the end of the germ.

Put on in fresh water and cook again. You could add salt and sweetening at this time although some people don't add this until serving time. Salt to taste; use maybe 2 heaping tablespoons sugar or honey for sweetening. Cook until you can chew the kernels. It will be done after about 4 hours of boiling. Cool. Drain it. Package and freeze if you want. To prepare

the hominy for a meal thaw it in water. Drain the water off. Put milk on it. Bring to a boil. If there is soda left in the hominy the milk will curdle so add 3 to 4 tablespoons evaporated milk and 2 tablespoons butter.

Unboiled Soda Method Hominy—In a crock or a large good-quality plastic can put corn to soak in soda water. Use 4 level tablespoons baking soda per gallon water. Keep in a cool place and covered. Test every day to see if the hulls are ready to come off. Figure on over a week though. When the hulls are loosened wash them away under plenty of running water. This hominy can be stored in a solution of a cup of pickling salt per gallon water until wanted. Then rinse and soak in fresh water with several changes.

Wood Ashes Hominy—Fill a large granite kettle half full of hardwood ashes. Nearly fill with hot water and boil 10 minutes. Drain off the water and put it into the granite kettle (not aluminum). This is your lye solution. Pour in your corn. Use one-fourth as much corn as you have solution. Boil until the hulls loosen. Then skim the corn out of the lye water and rinse, preferably in a colander under running water, until the hulls are off.

Hominy Grits—Dry the hominy. Put it through a grinder set for coarse grind. Finish drying and store for use. To cook add boiling water and salt to taste and cook until done. Homemade grits may take as long as 4 hours to cook properly. Use about three and a half or four parts water to one of grits. You can hasten the cooking time by soaking them overnight beforehand. (Cook them in the water in which you soaked them.) Grits may be eaten with a dab of butter, or pour into a rectangular dish—like a buttered bread pan. When firm, cut into slices and brown slowly in hot fat or butter. You can make leftover cooked grits into croquettes by combining 3 cups cooked grits with 2 eggs and seasoning. Then form into flat round cakes. Dip into beaten egg, then into bread crumbs, again into egg and fry in hot lard or butter until brown. If short of eggs, use 1 egg and a little milk.

Boughten Lye Hominy—Dissolve 4 tablespoons of lye in 2 gallons of cold water. (One level tablespoon lye equals ½ ounce.) Keep your spoon dry! Add 2 quarts of corn and boil a half hour. Take off the heat and let the corn soak in the solution about another 20 minutes. Skim out the corn and commence rinsing and working to get the hulls off. When the hulls are all off (and the dark kernel tips removed if you want), cover the hominy with fresh water and bring to a boil. Then change water and bring to a boil again and so on at least four times. Then cook in a final water until the hominy is *tender*.

Plain Buttered Hominy—Rinse and soak overnight in fresh water 1 cup or more of your homemade hominy. Next day boil it in a covered pan covered with water until all the water has evaporated. Stop before it burns! Now stir in a little butter and serve. This is a South American native dish and they must know something because that's where corn and hominy come from.

Hominy Bacon and Eggs—Mrs. H. J. Clough of

82

Long Beach, California, is a hominy lover and sent me this recipe: Boil several cups of hominy until tender. Fry 4 slices of bacon per person. Drain bacon fat off. Add the drained hominy. Cook in the pan where the bacon fried until well warmed and then add an egg and milk mixture just as if you were going to scramble eggs by themselves. Stir constantly until the egg part of the mixture is cooked. Serve with toast for a breakfast or a salad for a quick dinner.

TAMALES

A proper tamale has three layers. Outside is the cornhusk. Just inside that comes an "envelope" of cornmeal. To make your envelope mix 4 cups yellow cornmeal, 1 teaspoon salt, 2½ cups stock (leftover from cooking the meat part of the filling) and ¼ pound of fat (lard is fine for the fat). Beat this thoroughly to make it light. Your meat mixture is then arranged so it will be inside the cornmeal layers. Another way to do it is to mix the cornmeal with the meat mixture from the start. Below are several possible meat fillings to use and an example of the meat filling-cornmeal combination. The meats are interchangeable. You could read "chicken" or "veal" for beef.

The cornhusks that hold the tamale filling are wrapped around it while it is cooking. The soft inner husks of green corn are best to use, but you can also use tougher husks. Trim away top and bottom ends of the husk. Leave them about 6 inches long and rinse in boiling water. If you have to use very tough husks soaking in cold water for a few hours will help. Then wipe dry before using.

To tie up your tamales you can use husk ties or string or you can just stack them in your steamer for cooking and hope they stay together. It's safer to tie. To make husk ties tear some husks into strips.

To make the tamales spread on two or more husks your cornmeal envelope mixture. Put filling in the middle of that. Roll up. Fold both ends of the husking down like you would a Christmas package wrapping paper. Now tie. If you are using a meat-cornmeal combination just lay on the husks as much filling as they will contain and then wrap. When you

are using a cornmeal envelope it helps to shape the meat into rolls the size of your little finger before you put them on the cornmeal paste envelope.

Cooking the tamales is done by steaming or boiling. If you have a steamer or can rig up one by making a rack in the top part of your canning kettle, stack the tamales in it and cook until well done. If you are going to boil them, put a kitchen lid in the bottom of a deep kettle. Cover that with extra husks. Stack the tamales on top of that. Add boiling stock that you cooked the meat in. You may add a few dried red peppers if you want the tamales extra hot. Cover tightly and cook until well done.

Meat Filling—Boil a pound of meat with 1 onion, 2 garlic cloves and a couple bay leaves. When the meat is tender, save the stock for making the envelope and cooking it. Dice the meat and sauté the cubes in a bit of oil. For "hot" tamales add chili powder. For regular tamales add some mashed garlic or just salt and paprika. You could sometimes add a few olives or raisins to each portion of meat as you put it into the tamale. Or green pepper, chopped onion and celery, tomatoes, cream-style corn or whatever else you have. If you are rushed you can just shred or chop or grind the meat instead of sautéing it.

Meat-Cornmeal Combination—Boil a chicken until tender. Cool and remove all the bones. Save the broth. Add any or all of the following ingredients or anything else that you have and sounds good to you. A half pound of seeded raisins, minced, ½ cup stoned olives, a fresh red pepper, chopped fine, 6 hard-boiled eggs, chopped (if you decide on the eggs mix them in after the cornmeal). Make a paste with 2 cups yellow cornmeal moistened with the reserved hot chicken stock. Season to taste with salt and onion juice. Add enough water so you can cook it in a double boiler, stirring, about 15 minutes. Then combine the meat mixture.

POPCORN

You can get your popcorn seed start by ordering *popcorn* (not regular corn) from a seed catalog or by planting the popcorn sold in stores for popping. But don't plant your popcorn by sweet corn or field corn. It will cross-pollinate and then your popcorn won't pop so well and your sweet corn may be on the tough side. The varieties should be planted at least 50 or 60 feet apart.

It is important to dry the popcorn right after it is grown. Leave it on the plant until after the first hard freeze. Then pick it. Instead of pulling the husks off, just strip them back to the butt end of the cob. Tie the husks of a bunch of cobs together with string and hang the bunch up to dry in a basement or similar cool, dry place where air can circulate around it. Let the popcorn hang for a month. Then you can take it down and hull it off with your fingers. Push on the kernels with your thumb and they will just pop right off the cob. If you have chaff, pour the corn from one pan to another to get rid of it. Or you can leave the cobs on the plant until dry and then pick and shell—*if* your weather stays dry.

(a) spread cornmeal mixture on husks

(c) roll up

(b) place small roll of meat mixture at edge of cornmeal

(d) tie with string or husk ties

After the popcorn kernels are shelled off, store in clean half-gallon (or whatever size is handy) jars with lids. Store in a cool dry place. It will keep for a long time in dry storage. However, if it is stored awfully long, it may become too dry to pop. A *real* tight lid on your jar helps with that.

Popcorn pops better if it has been aged for a year so get a year ahead on your supply. That's doubly a good thing because I'd like to think that you have a supply of seed corn (which your popcorn potentially is) on hand. Popcorn pops better chilled so let it spend some time in the refrigerator or in a jar outdoors in the cold before you pop it. Dutch ovens are good popcorn poppers. So is an iron frying pan if it has a lid.

To pop—Allow ½ cup of the dry corn for every quart of popped corn that you want. Melt about 1 tablespoon cooking oil in your Dutch oven or some other heavy pan with a tight-fitting lid. When the oil is hot, add the popcorn, cover and cook over medium heat. Shake the pan on top of the heat constantly until you don't hear much more popping and then you take it off the heat to prevent burning in the bottom of the pan. To butter the popcorn just melt some butter in another pan, pour it over the popcorn and stir to mix. Sprinkle with salt if you like. The butter already provides some salt though.

Popcorn flour—You can grind unpopped popcorn and use same as any other cornmeal.

Popcorn Cake—This is something different and fun for a child's birthday party. Ingredients: 7 cups of unsalted popcorn—free of unpopped kernels, 1 cup butter or margarine, 1 large package of marshmallows. Heat marshmallows and butter in a double boiler until melted. Pour this warm mixture over the popcorn and mix gently until the popcorn is well coated. Press this mixture into a greased angel food cake pan. When cooled (may be placed in refrigerator if in a hurry) remove from pan onto a plate. If it sticks run a little hot water over the outside of the pan. Slice with a serrated knife when ready to serve. Not really health food but I serve something besides homemade bread and carrot sticks on birthdays. It's only once a year.

Popcorn Balls—A friend wrote to tell me she wished I had a recipe for popcorn balls in this book. I had thought you probably all had one already. Generally I get requests for recipes that are hard to find. But sometimes the requests are for things like popcorn balls and spaghetti sauce that seem easy to me. To make popcorn balls you melt about 3 tablespoons butter in a heavy saucepan, add 3 cups brown sugar and ¾ cup water. Mix it all up until the sugar is dissolved. Boil until it reaches 238° on your candy thermometer. Have ready 3 quarts freshly popped corn. Pour the syrup over the corn. Dip your hands into enough flour to coat them and form the popcorn balls. Then cool the balls on a greased cookie sheet. For a nice optional touch you can premix a cup of shelled peanuts with your freshly popped popcorn before pouring over the syrup.

Cracker Jacks—Violet Stewart sent me this one: "Start with 8 or 9 cups of popped corn. Put into a dishpan with enough room to move it around easily.

In a separate pan combine 2 cups packed brown sugar, 1 stick of margarine or butter, 1 teaspoon salt, ¾ cup of white syrup or light sorghum and 1 teaspoon vanilla. Cook together at a full rolling boil for 5 minutes. Just to be sure, if it spins a thread, it is ready. Add ½ teaspoon soda. (Hold pan over dishpan of corn before adding soda so if it runs over it will fall on the corn.) Stir a moment. Pour over popped corn. Stir till all is coated well. Put in a roaster in 200° oven for 1 hour. Look now and then—some ovens are hotter. Stir occasionally so it will not get in one mass. Store in a covered container. It keeps well."

MILLET

7th Edition, June 2, 1976. There didn't used to be a millet section but I've been learning interesting things about it and heard from a friend who does grow it so I'm adding a new section here. Millet is unusual because of being the only alkaline grain. It's supposed to be good for people with acidosis or bad breath! You could see it growing in the Red River Valley of North Dakota . . . or all over northern China. It has a bland flavor compared to other grains. And is a little weird because when cooked in water a sort of okra-like gooey stuff will rise to the surface. Birds are crazy about it which can be a real problem at harvest time. Most of the American millet production is for sale as a birdseed component. Here in Idaho there are beautiful fields of golden yellow rape, which is another ingredient in the commercial birdseed mixture.

Millet seems really worth considering for people food. It is the basic starch food in many countries of the world, full of good living and growing energy. Good in drought areas because it can go dormant when the rains stop and then start growing again when it rains and show no harmful effects for the delay. Good for places with poor soil because millet doesn't care. Good for weedy ground because millet, like buckwheat, grows fast and thick and can outcompete the weeds. That's what I'm told and it sounds good enough to look into. Harvest like the other

small-headed grains. If birds are getting too much of the crop it is possible to cut off the heads a day or two before they are ripe and the birds move in, and then finish ripening and drying them where you can keep off the birds.

To cook with millet first brown it in a frying pan with a very little oil, then go ahead and use in your recipe. That makes it more flavorful.

Millet Cereal—Combine 1 cup millet, 1 teaspoon salt and 3 cups water. Bring to a boil, then turn down the heat and cook slowly about 30 minutes, or until soft—maybe a little sooner or later. Serve with butter, dried fruit, sweetening or milk or a combination.

Millet Soup—Cook millet with onions, celery, carrots and potatoes until everything is tender and the broth is tasty. Season and serve.

Millet Casserole—Bake millet with cheese, broccoli, sesame seeds and enough liquid to keep it moist.

OATS

Oats do best in cool, moist climates. They are easy to grow. You plant in spring as soon as the ground is ready to cultivate and get ready for seed. Oats used to be important because they were the main grain fed to workhorses. Now the usual farmload puller eats gasoline instead of oats and everybody's worrying about Arab politics instead of the weather. Thirty-seven bushels per acre is a fine yield. Oats do better drilled (machine seeded) than broadcasted. They can be covered 1 to 1½ inches or even up to 2 or 3 inches where there is a problem of dryness. Oats need more moisture than the other grains. The ground should be well prepared the fall before seeding. Seed at the rate of 8 to 10 pecks per acre. If you broadcast use more. Seed as early in the spring as possible since oats grow best before warm, dry weather sets in. Oats are harvested when half the leaves are green and the grain is in the dough stage—to avoid loss from premature shelling. Sheave, then set up the sheaves in long narrow shocks running north and south. As soon as the grain is cured haul the sheaves carefully to your threshing area and thresh promptly to avoid further losses. Now you've got a bunch of fine horse feed.

To prepare oats for food the husk must be thoroughly removed. Here's the reason it isn't smart for you to expect to grow your own oats for oatmeal. Husking oats is a lot harder process than with wheat. First the grain must be kiln dried to loosen the husks, then put through a special milling process. One commercial method of hulling oats is to use two millstones with enough space between them to grind off the hulls without grinding the "groats," which means hulled ready-to-cook-and-eat oats. These groats can be used in soups the same as barley or can be made into a porridge. If you did manage to grind off the husks at home you'd still have one more step to go through—winnowing out the hulls in the wind or before a fan. But I don't know of any machine sold for the purpose of hulling oats at home. There are sources where you can buy roller mills that could

make you rolled oats or wheat or rye flakes but in the case of oats I don't think they would do you any good without the hulling process.

So you can raise oats for hay, or pasture, or winter stock food. We let the animals feed on them in the field while they're still green. Then we mow and bale what's left for winter food for them. So all we need to do is bale in the summer and unbale in the winter and the animals get bulk and grain without any attempt at sheaving, drying, milling or rolling. Chickens can't digest whole oats very well. They would prefer wheat or any ground grain. They'll get some good out of them though.

You can buy hulled oat groats from health food stores or mail-order outlets specializing in whole grains like Sioux Millers at Whiting, Iowa 51063. Or you can buy the ones sold for animal feeds. You can grind oat groats in a regular grinder—the same kind you'd use for wheat. Oats, like barley, don't leaven so you can't make a good bread out of oat flour alone, unless it's a very thin tortilla-like bread—an oatcake. But you can add oat flour to any other bread recipe as a part of the mixture. Oats originated in Scotland where they were the staff of life in the form of your choice of oatcakes or porridge. I wonder how the Scots got their oat husks off.

Here are some oat recipes:

Oatcakes—They ground their groats in old Scotland to make this out of oat flour. But you can make it with rolled oats, too, to get a notion of it. Mix the ground or rolled oats with enough water to make a dough. Knead and knead and knead as you would bread. Then roll out as thin as you can. Cut into squares. Fry on an iron plate or griddle or in a pan that is just shined with oil. The reason you make them with water is that made with cream they get crumbly. Serve warm with butter and honey or as you like.

Porridge—If you are making it out of home-ground groats you first grind, then cook with water and maybe a pinch of salt. The coarser you grind the longer it will need to cook. Use about four parts water to one part grain for coarse oatmeal and give it plenty of time to cook—cooking continuously and slowly in a double boiler or steamer. Add some cream just before serving. It's nice also if you stir in fruit.

Groat Cereal—Put oat groats, salt and water in a casserole. Use two parts water to one part groats. This is unground and not rolled but it is hulled oats. Plan on cooking it a long, long time. (Put it on the night before you want it for breakfast.)

Rolled Oat Cereal—Use 1 part rolled oats to 2½ parts water. Cook in a double boiler with a tight lid. Allow about an hour. This is for real rolled oats that haven't been given one of those precooking treatments. Good with raisins or chopped apples added about 20 minutes before you take it off the heat.

Oat Flour—You can make it by putting groats or rolled oats through a grain mill or twice through a regular food grinder.

Oat Flour Apricot Fritters—Sift together ½ cup oat flour, ½ cup rice flour (health food stores carry it) and 1 teaspoon baking powder. Add 1 teaspoon honey, a pinch of salt, 1 egg, ¼ cup milk and 1 cup stewed apricots. Drop mixture by tablespoonfuls into hot deep fat. Fry until a golden brown. Drain. You can roll in powdered sugar for a fancy touch. Doesn't make but a dozen.

GRANOLAS

When I was a little girl I used to like a bowl of raw rolled oats with milk and honey for breakfast in the summertime. Then somebody came along and invented granola which is even better. You'll be shopping at your health food store (or grocery store) for some of these ingredients. Pretty hard to have almonds, coconuts and carob growing in your yard unless you live in California.

Pruneola—I got this recipe from Sunray Orchards of Myrtle Creek, Oregon 97457, which mail-order wonderful organic prunes in case you can't raise your own. Pit and snip into small pieces 1 pound prunes. Set aside. Combine 1 pound rolled oats (not the quick-cook kind), 1 cup shredded coconut, 1 cup chopped unblanched almonds, 1 cup hulled sunflower seeds, 1 cup wheat germ and ½ cup sesame seeds in a large bowl. In a small pan mix ½ cup honey with ½ cup vegetable oil and heat to just under a boil. Stir the liquid into the rolled oats mixture and mix well. Spread about one-third to one-half of the mixture in a thin layer in a large shallow pan. Bake in a 325° oven for 25 minutes, stirring occasionally. Repeat with remaining mixture or use two or three pans. When all the mixture has been baked, stir in the small pieces of prunes. Break mixture into small pieces, if necessary. Let cool completely. Store in a tightly-covered container or in plastic bags. Makes about 3 pounds pruneola.

Granola—Mix together 1 cup rolled oats, 1 cup rolled whole wheat, ½ cup grated dried coconut, ⅓ cup wheat germ, ½ cup chopped nuts (almonds, cashews or peanuts), ½ cup hulled sunflower seeds

and 7 teaspoons sesame seeds, if you can get them. Now heat in a pan same as for Pruneola 5 tablespoons honey, 5 teaspoons vegetable oil and 1 teaspoon vanilla. Mix with dry ingredients. Bake as with Pruneola. Then add ¼ cup seedless raisins, or any chopped dried fruit like prunes, dates, currants or apricots. Be sure to add the fruit while the granola is still warm. Store.

Uncooked Granola—Here are proportions for any amount. Make your recipe one-half cereal, and have at least half of that half be rolled oats and the rest some kind of other rolled cereal like wheat flakes or rye flakes. Then add one-fourth dried fruit or some kind of fruit if you're going to eat it right away, and one-fourth nuts or seeds and sweetening and extras like maybe powdered milk or wheat germ. I can guarantee you it will be good to eat. You can eat this make-your-own granola anytime after you've given it a good shaking up to mix all ingredients together like in a big grocery bag. Helps if you use brown sugar for the sweetening rather than molasses or honey and that way you don't have anything wet and sticky in there! You can make a cold breakfast cereal out of it by pouring over cold milk and eating as is. You can make a hot cereal for a winter's morning by cooking a short time in a little water.

Granola recipes are fun to make and so good to eat and so healthy! Here are two more for you to enjoy. Store any granola in an airtight container. It will keep several weeks. Best stored in plastic bags or jars in the refrigerator, or in the freezer.

Easy Granola—Served with milk. Start by getting out 6 cups rolled oats, 2 cups grated or preshredded coconut, 2 cups nuts (any kind—almonds, cashews, walnuts—only chop them up somewhat), ⅔ cup sesame seeds or sunflower seeds, ⅔ cup bran flakes and ⅔ cup wheat germ. Take each of the preceding ingredients by itself and roast in a 300° oven until lightly toasted. Now combine. Pour over and stir in ½ cup oil and ½ cup honey (or molasses or sorghum or maple syrup). When you have it stirred together really thoroughly, roast in the oven again at 250° until golden brown. Now stir in 2 cups chopped dried fruit—any kind or a mixture.

Sun Dried Granola—In your big bread bowl put *first* 5 cups oatmeal *then* (right on top) pour over (premix these!) ½ cup honey, ½ cup hot water, ½ cup oil and 2 teaspoons vanilla. Now add 1 cup sunflower seeds, 1 cup sesame seeds, 1 cup flaxseeds, 1 cup grated coconut, ¾ cup chopped nuts and ¾ cup chopped dried fruit. Mix up good. Spread thinly to dry. Give it two days at least.

Other Ways to Use Granola—Add a cup or two to your bread or cake (you'll have to add more liquid too), or to poultry stuffing, cabbage roll stuffing or apple stuffing. Eat it plain as a snack or use as an ice cream topping. Serve stirred into yogurt instead of with milk. Or use it as a topping on cooked fruit. Or make candy out of it by mixing with peanut butter, honey and powdered milk and rolling into little individual balls. Or start with an egg and 2 tablespoons of milk, add enough granola to make a batter and fry in a greased skillet for pancakes (top with yogurt).

RYE

Rye grass thrives in cool climates and poor soils. It is the cereal grain least injured by disease and insects. It is even hardier than wheat. The kernel resembles the wheat grain and is processed in the same way. This makes it a real possibility for your homestead growing situation. Plant the same time as you would for wheat (see on ahead in the Wheat section). Plant 1½ bushels per acre. Your rye will ripen about a week before wheat would. In old-time England the rye and wheat seeds were often planted premixed, then the two grains were reaped, threshed, ground and baked together. The result was called "maslin" bread. I was really interested when I read that because I almost always add at least a handful of rye flour to my wheat bread. It does good things for the taste. Rye straw was also useful in the old days. They made hats, matting and so on from it. Rye will thresh out just as easily as wheat with no problem hull like you have with oats. The big drawback of rye, as compared to wheat, is its lower gluten content. That means that rye breads are heavy and harder to get done clear through compared to wheat flour breads. Foodwise rye is not quite as good as wheat but by no means poor. The high plains of Eastern Colorado are a famous rye growing area of the United States.

Rye makes good sprouts. (See Sprouts in the Vegetables chapter.) With a roller machine you can "flake" it for a rolled oats kind of thing. With a grinder you can make grits for cereal or flour for bread.

Rye doesn't absorb moisture like wheat flour so cut down on liquids when you are substituting in recipes or else use correspondingly more rye flour. Anything you're going to knead with rye flour in it will tend to be sticky. Sourdough rye bread is an excellent moist, good keeping bread—recipe in Sourdough section. Caraway, anise and orange peel are good flavors in rye baking. So are spices, brown sugar and molasses.

Rye Fruit Bread—Cut up dried prunes, discarding the seeds, or any other kind of home-dried fruit until you have ½ cup. Sprinkle a little flour over them so that they won't stick together. Sift together 2½ cups rye flour, 1 scant teaspoon salt, 2 teaspoons baking power and ½ teaspoon soda. Combine ¼ cup molasses, 1½ cups water and 2 tablespoons cooking oil or melted lard. (If you use melted lard have your water warm.) Combine with dry ingredients, add the fruit and mix well. Pour into a greased loaf pan. Bake about an hour in a 350° oven.

Here follow some excellent recipes from the Mary Mills Service, Fisher Flour Mills Company, 3235 16th Avenue S.W., Seattle, Washington 98134. You can get more by writing to them. The gentleman who gave me permission to use them in this book stated to me very specifically that I could only do so if I used the brand name of his product in each recipe so I am cooperating accordingly. But frankly, these recipes will work with your home-ground rye flour too, although the gentleman stressed that he couldn't guarantee anything but Fisher's in them.

All Rye Snack Bread—1 loaf 4 x 8 x 2½ inches. Preheat oven to 350°. Besides 2½ cups Fisher's rye flour (sifted) you'll need: 1 teaspoon salt, 2 teaspoons baking powder, ½ cup sliced pressed figs, ½ teaspoon soda, 1½ cups lukewarm water, ¼ cup molasses and 2 tablespoons oil or melted shortening. Sift Fisher's rye flour with salt and baking powder. Add figs and stir enough to coat the fruit with flour. Put soda in a 2-cup measure or larger, add lukewarm water and molasses, stir until it foams a little, then dump all at once into the center of flour mixture. Pour oil on top and stir until smooth. Grease the loaf pan well, bottom only, and smooth in the dough well up on sides of pan. Bake at 350° for 55 minutes. Cut sides of loaf away from pan immediately on taking from the oven. Cool on rack before storing. The youngsters "just love it" with peanut butter for after-school sandwiches.

Seeded Rye Bread—Add ¼ teaspoon each caraway and anise seeds to the above recipe and omit the figs. Or use ½ teaspoon of either of the seeds.

Raisin Rye Bread—Use ½ cup moist seeded or seedless raisins instead of the figs.

Buttermilk Rye Bread—Substitute buttermilk for the 1½ cups water in the recipe and increase soda to 1 teaspoon. Omit baking powder.

Rye Scones (wheatless, eggless, milkless)—Makes 8 wedges. Use a pancake griddle, if possible, or a heavy frying pan. Do not grease. Sprinkle with ½ cup Fisher's rye flour and heat until flour begins to color slightly (medium heat is best). Besides ¾ cup sifted Fisher's rye flour you'll need: ¼ to ½ teaspoon salt and 1 cup mashed Irish potatoes. The wetness of the potato may make more or less flour necessary. For flavor it is better to steam the potatoes in their jackets, but leftover mashed potatoes (without milk, if for a milkless diet) are satisfactory. Sift the salt with the flour, add to the potato and work well with fingers. Sprinkle Fisher's rye flour on a board or paper towel. Pat out the mixture into a 9-inch round, crimp the edges like a pie, cut in 8 or 9 pie-shaped wedges, lift to hot griddle and cook 5 minutes on each side. Eat hot with whatever the doctor allows in the way of "spreads." For the family, butter and syrup are nice.

Rye Pastry—One two-crust 9-inch pie. Preheat oven to 450°. Besides 2 cups Fisher's rye flour you'll need: 1 teaspoon salt, ⅔ cup shortening and 3 to 4 tablespoons water. Sift and measure rye flour. Sift again with salt. Cut half of shortening into dry ingredients until the consistency of cornmeal. Cut in remaining shortening to lumps the size of a pea. Sprinkle water over dry ingredients, tossing dampened particles aside. Use only enough water to hold particles together. Knead until smooth. Roll out about ⅛ inch thick. For baked pie shell, fit in pan and bake at 450° for 10 to 12 minutes.

Rye Quick Bread (wheatless)—Makes one 1½-pound loaf. Preheat oven to 325°. Besides 2½ cups unsifted Fisher's rye flour, you'll need: ¾ tablespoon salt, 1 tablespoon baking powder, 1 tablespoon sugar, 1 egg, well beaten, 1½ cups milk, 2 tablespoons melted butter or salad oil and 1 tablespoon caraway seeds or grated orange peel, if desired. Combine dry ingredients. Beat egg with milk; add melted butter or salad oil and combine with dry ingredients. Stir in caraway seeds or orange peel. Bake in well-greased loaf pan at 325° for 1 hour. Let stand in pan for 15 minutes before turning out onto a rack.

Rye Griddle Cakes—2½ cups Fisher's rye flour, ½ teaspoon salt, 1 teaspoon soda, 1 egg, beaten, 1¾ cups sour milk or buttermilk, 1 tablespoon melted butter and ¼ cup honey. Spoon flour from sack lightly. Measure and mix with salt and soda. Beat egg, add milk, butter and honey and beat gradually into dry ingredients until smooth. Bake on lightly greased griddle, turning but once. Variations: If wheat is allowed in diet, Fisher's Blend Flour may be used in place of part of the rye flour. Also, sweet milk may be used in place of the sour or buttermilk, but the product is not as tender. If using sweet milk, omit the soda and add 4 teaspoons baking powder.

Rye Flour Cake—7 tablespoons butter or margarine, 1 cup granulated sugar, 2½ cups Fisher's rye flour, ½ teaspoon salt, ½ teaspoon cinnamon, ½ teaspoon ginger, ¾ teaspoon nutmeg, 2½ teaspoons baking powder, 1 cup milk or orange juice and 1 teaspoon vanilla. Cream the shortening and add sugar gradually, beating well. Sift together dry ingredients three times. Add to first mixture, alternating with the liquid. Add vanilla and beat well. (If you use orange juice omit vanilla.) Pour into two well-greased, wax paper lined, 8-inch layer pans. Bake at 375° for 35 to 40 minutes.

Rye Flour Porridge—Mix 1 cup Fisher's rye flour, 1 teaspoon salt and 1 cup cold water into a smooth paste. Stir the mixture into 4 cups boiling water in the top of a double boiler. Cook about 20 minutes, stirring once in a while. Serve with molasses and butter.

Rye-Wheat Cereal—Here are some other good rye recipes. Esther R. McMenamin, Kennewick, Washington, makes a cereal from coarse ground rye and wheat, mixed together, one part rye to two parts of wheat. Cook (add a pinch salt) in two parts water to each one of cereal for about an hour. Serve with milk or cream and sweetening.

Steamed Rye—You can serve rye as your starchy item the same way you would rice. (You can substitute whole wheat in this recipe if you want.) Wash 2 cups raw (unroasted) whole rye and then soak in 4 cups water or soup stock for 3 hours. Now add 1 teaspoon salt and simmer until the grain is tender and all water is absorbed. You may have to add more water, stock, tomato juice, or soy sauce to get it done.

Flaked Rye—Looks like rolled oats. You can buy at a health food store. To use it as a breakfast cereal, boil 2 cups water and a pinch of salt. Slowly stir in 1 cup flaked rye. Reduce heat to simmer and cover pan tightly. Cook until all water is absorbed. Eat with honey and cream. Good!

TRITICALE

A new grain, produced by crossing wheat and rye. It's supposed to have the high yield of wheat and the disease and drought resistance of rye. It makes better bread than rye, but not as good as wheat, has protein content comparable to soy, produces more per acre I'm told than either wheat or rye. How's that for hybrid vigor!

WHEAT

Wheat is a good grain for you to plant. You can manage a crop of it in your backyard if you can keep people and dogs from trampling the tender stalks. You can harvest and store and grind all without expensive or inconvenient machinery. It is good food for both man and beast and away and above the handiest flour for making breads because of the combination of good food value and good baking quality—the gluten that makes the bread have air bubbles in it! There are different kinds of wheat to choose from. Spring wheats are planted in the spring and harvested in the summer. Winter wheats are planted in September and harvested next July or August. Winter wheat is generally a higher producer than spring wheat, but there is a slightly higher risk factor involved because a torrential downpour shortly after seeding could wash out your seed, or an extra freezing cold winter, with no snow cover to keep the plants snugly warm underneath (in their opinion), would kill out your whole crop. But if you did lose the winter wheat crop there would still be a chance to plant another time with spring wheat. Winter wheat that is planted in September with enough moisture comes up within a week and looks like a newly planted lawn, green and lovely. You could let the cows go in there and graze but don't overdo it. The wheat needs to gather some energy to winter on. The cold weather will come and the wheat seems to turn brown and die. Remember it is a grass. Next spring it will magically reappear and continue growing up and up, from two to four feet high depending on how much moisture it gets and how much fertility was in the soil. Wheat, like corn, needs a soil with plenty of nutrients in it to do well.

Get ready for your wheat crop by laying manure or some other fertilizer on the field and tilling it in if possible. Till as much as you can before and after your grain crop to keep weeds from getting a hold in the field. You won't be able to cultivate or weed once your wheat is planted. You won't be able to water either so you can only plant wheat where you will get adequate rainfall unless you are planting such a small patch that you can water by sprinkling from outside the patch because you *cannot* go walking through there. Every step of man or beast in your wheat field wipes out that much more of your crop. The stalks are tall and very fragile and once downed don't get up again. A severe hailstorm with big heavy stones or a torrential downpour that beats everything into the ground can also ruin your wheat crop. Most full-time wheat farmers carry hail insurance against such a possibility because a certain percentage of the years you're almost certain to lose some or most of your crop when the hailstones happen to fall on your fields.

So the kind of wheat you plant depends on what time of the year you are planting it. It also depends on what part of the country you are planting in. Different types are better suited to special season lengths and amounts of rainfall and soil types. It's all somewhat complicated and you really would do best to ask at your local granary (which buys grain from farmers) or feed store or seed store, or any grain growing farmer in your area what types are generally raised around you. Any of them are *food.*

Hard red winter wheat keeps better than any other kind and because of the high gluten content makes the best bread (rises higher and easier). Soft red winter wheat contains slightly less gluten and is used commercially as a pastry flour—makes good piecrusts. It has a trifle less protein. Durum wheat is the highest in protein content and can stretch the farthest when cooked. So that's the kind that gets made into spaghetti and macaroni and noodles. Soft white wheat is considered the most inferior type but it makes manageable noodles and buns and huge quantities are raised in this eastern Washington-Idaho area for export to the Far East. All the wheats are very hardy; the hard reds are the hardiest of all. Wheat can stand a cold winter, a short summer and a relatively dry climate. But a moisture shortage will cause a smaller harvest. You start by buying your seed from a seedsman but then you can save your own seed for the next plantings.

So first you have your ground ready, tilled and retilled to kill all the weeds you can, and richly fertilized with manure or by having grown a legume or green manure crop in there previously. You can even grow alfalfa or red clover together with winter wheat. The hay crop will not really take off until after you harvest the wheat. You can either plow it under in the fall for green manure or you can harvest it as a hay crop the following summer. You plant your wheat seed broadcast style by hand or using a little portable broadcasting machine that straps onto you unless you have a big enough field to make drilling worthwhile. (A drill is a big machine pulled by a tractor specially for seeding grain.) Plant around 90 pounds per acre and expect a return of from 45 to 90 bushels per acre. That interprets to mean that on a fraction of an acre you could grow enough wheat to be a year's supply for your family and your animals.

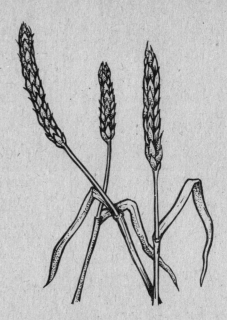

Once your wheat is seeded it helps if you rake it under or roll it down like you would grass seed. Or if you plant in the very early spring, rains and freezing and thawing will do the job of covering it for you. Then there is nothing left to do but struggle all spring to keep people and animals out of your wheat field.

Harvest time comes. The wheat has grown tall and headed out with a big "bushy" top full of those wonderful grain seeds. First it all was green and then it started turning yellow all over and getting dry looking. For a huge field you could pay someone with a combine to come in and harvest it for you. That would be the easiest way to do it. Or you can harvest by hand the old-time way. First the wheat kernels are in a "dough" stage. You can shell them out in your hand but when you bite one it is soft. Wait until the whole grain head is brittle and the grain of wheat is so hard you can't dent it with your thumbnail. You are ready to reap. The grain must be completely dry when it is cut. Wait even for the dew to go off and for a hot sunny day. But if you leave it too long the heads will shatter and spill the grain onto the ground.

Cut the wheat with a scythe, bundle it and put it in shocks to cure. Then thresh, winnow and store for grinding as needed. Ideally the grain should dry for a month or more before threshing because threshed grain that is not totally dry will heat up enough when stored in a pile to destroy its capacity for germination (not its food value). Commercially the grain is threshed in the field by the combine and then dried in storage by forcing warm air through the pile. It dries first where the air enters the pile and last where it leaves it. You can accomplish drying with small quantities by stirring the grain regularly. Those long lovely yellow stalks are called straw. They make wonderful bedding for your goats or rabbits or nesting box stuff for your chickens. They are good in the garden as mulch.

Don't grind your wheat until you want to use it. It loses food value and taste when ground and lying around. If you grind it only very coarsely you have "cracked wheat." Bulgur is wheat that you have boiled, then dried, then cracked. You can use bulgur in any recipe that calls for cracked wheat or cracked wheat in any recipe that calls for bulgur. And there's couscous. I didn't know about that until my friend Cindy from Ludlow, Vermont, wrote me this letter: "When visiting Algeria in October of '74 I picked up one of the ultimate treats of the world. Couscous is a coarsely ground wheat accompanied by a bowl of lamb or chicken stew." And then she sent me some couscous recipes which I'll print a little later here. So there's bulgur and there's cracked wheat and there's couscous, all more or less interchangeable. But did you ever try cooking whole wheat? I just love it. And so does Greta Forbish who lives in Portland, Oregon, and wrote me a long letter about the good old days:

"Both my parents were frugal by nature and felt it was a sin to waste a single ounce of nature's sustenance. Mother said that when I was still a toddler in 1914, they lived on $200 a year which included taxes, food, clothing, fuel, and incidentals while Papa was studying to become a lawyer. Good Heavens, I find it difficult to get by with $200 a month! The taxes on their property, which Papa still maintains, have risen from $12 to $412 and we can expect another leap this year. And this is what is now termed a 'depressed area' though in my youth it was a respectable lower middle-class district and it was quite safe for a lone teenager to walk eight blocks to the library after dark, or for a group of giggling girls to attend the local movie theater and thrill to Hoot Gibson or Clara Bow and come back without being molested. (Local movie theater is now showing X-rated films—'Girls on Parade,' 'Maisie's Bedroom,' 'The Men in Her Life,' etc. And here I am still dreaming of John Gilbert and Norma Shearer.)

"There was another thing that my mother did during my early years and that is to cook whole wheat. Papa bought this in five-pound sacks from a local hay, grain and feed store. Mother sorted it over each night and removed the spears and other residue and soaked it to skim off the chaff. After we got our gas range she cooked it overnight in a double boiler with plenty of salted water and by morning it had swelled to double its bulk and could be eaten with enthusiasm with sugar and cream, although I always preferred a dollop of butter and a sprinkle of brown sugar. I used this with my older children (now 42 and 40) and they loved it. As far as I know you can't buy whole wheat except through a health food outlet and the price puts you in the gourmet food category—and I recently read a recipe that put it practically on the wild rice stratum!"

Actually though you can still buy wheat from your local "hay, grain and feed" store, clean it up a little the way Greta's mother did, and cook it all night for a cereal breakfast the next morning. It's called "frumenty."

Frumenty—Takes a good while to cook anyway except in a pressure cooker (30 minutes or so). On the top of the stove in a double boiler plan on simmering at least 4 to 6 hours. Or soak 24 hours in water enough to cover, then put the wet wheat in a covered oven dish, cover with water and let cook in a slow oven for 12 hours. Or you can presoak the whole wheat in water (2⅔ cups water per 1½ cups whole wheat berries) for 8 to 10 hours. Then bring the wheat and soaking water to a boil with 1 teaspoon salt. Boil gently until tender and the kernels break open. Figure on about an hour. Before serving your cooked wheat you can mix with milk and dried fruit, stir up, cook together a few moments and set out to eat. Or serve plain like Greta's mother did with cream or butter or sweetening added at the table.

Cracked Wheat Cereal—Simmer ½ cup cracked wheat or your wheat grits left over from grinding, which you sifted out of your wheat flour, in 2½ cups water until tender. How long it will take depends on how big your chunks are—from 1 to 3 hours. Add salt to taste while cooking. Serve hot with a slosh of rich, thick cream, some fresh blackberries or whatever you like with your cereal.

Graham Mush—This is the quickest wheat cereal you can make. Grind your wheat fine as for baking flour. For every cup of flour add 1 cup cold water and ½ teaspoon salt. Mix into a smooth paste. Then stir the mixture into 4 cups boiling water in the top of a double boiler. Cook until it tastes done and is of a nice cereal consistency. It will take maybe 20 minutes. Good with any dried fruit cooked in with it and served with milk or butter and sweetening. Or cook in all or part milk. Or in applesauce or any other fruit sauce. Cook in a couple cups blackberries that have been stewed and put through a sieve to get out the seeds.

Fried Wheat Mush—Leftover cracked wheat breakfast cereal or graham porridge can be poured into a bread pan to get cold and set up, then sliced and fried to be a hot mush. Serve with butter and syrup.

Whole Wheat Casserole—Here's something else you can do with the whole grain besides eat it for a cereal. Rinse off 1 cup whole wheat (in a strainer). Bring 3 cups tomato juice to a boil and then pour in the wheat. Simmer 3 hours, or until the wheat is tender. (You'll have to add more liquid while it's cooking.) Now add 1 chopped onion, 2 minced cloves garlic, 1 cup chopped celery, ¼ cup soy sauce, 1 teaspoon salt and a bay leaf. Basil or oregano is good too! Let simmer more until the flavors are soaked in. Now cover with grated cheese and bake in the oven, uncovered, until the cheese is bubbly.

Traveler's Bread—Geraldine Strusek of Carmel Valley, California, wrote me a beautiful letter about her Minnesota childhood. "There in that big old kitchen was love, food, and a secure kind of feeling that comes over you as you enter its warm kingdom." My mother's kitchen was like that too! Geraldine said to grind 2 cups of northern wheat. Then add dried fruit (figs, dates, raisins, prunes) and nuts, crushed fine. Stir to be quite stiff with cold water as briskly as you can (to get air bubbles in it). If you got it too sticky add more wheat flour until you can cut it in cakes from a roll ½ inch thick. Bake.

Cracked Wheat Bread—You make cracked wheat by putting wheat through on the coarsest grind. Pat Brunton, Maple Valley, Washington, sent me this one. Bring to a boil and simmer until tender: 1 cup cracked wheat, 2 tablespoons salt, 4 tablespoons shortening, 2 cups water. Dissolve 3 tablespoons yeast in 1 cup warm water. Put above in large bowl and add: 8 tablespoons molasses, 1 can evaporated milk (13 ounces), 5 cups flour.

Mix, add another 5 (more or less) cups flour. Flour your hands. Knead dough (sort of push it together!) till dough sticks in a ball. Grease ball and let rise till doubled in bulk. Knead again, put in 6 loaf pans and let rise. Bake at 350°—about 40 minutes. "While it is baking have a nap—the smell of homebaked bread eliminates dusting, scrubbing and all those stupid things."

Puffed Wheat—In your heavy iron frying pan or Dutch oven heat 1 tablespoon oil to very hot. Now add ½ cup whole wheat, put on the lid and turn off the heat. The wheat will pop just like popcorn, and it's good with milk and a sweetening for a breakfast cereal or you can serve buttered to eat plain like you do popcorn.

Couscous—Spread 2 cups couscous on a baking sheet. Sprinkle with water and lightly mix to moisten all grains. Place couscous in a colander lined with a paper towel or use a special couscous cooker. Cover and steam 20 minutes. Stir couscous. Steam 20 minutes more. Stir in a little butter and place on platter. Meanwhile place 1 cup chopped carrots and 1 cup chopped turnip in pan under colander. Cook until almost tender. Drain. Add salt and pour 3 cups homemade vegetable broth all over. Add 1 cup peas, 2 cups cooked garbanzo beans and 1 cup cooked chicken. Heat until boiling. Pour stew over couscous on platter. Cindy Roundy's recipe. She first wrote me because she wanted to know how to make her own snowshoes!

THE HISTORY OF LEAVENING THE WAY I FIGURE IT
(In Four Parts in Roughly Historical Order)

To "leaven" means to lighten bread and make it rise with air bubbles. Bread is leavened to make it light and porous. Unleavened bread won't cook through unless it is rolled as flat and thin as a tortilla. When it is leavened by chemical reaction, the carbon dioxide as it is made in the middle of the dough causes it to "rise." Breads can be unleavened, leavened with air beaten into eggs (or just air beaten into the batter), leavened with baking powder, or soda and sour milk or buttermilk, or with commercial yeast cultures, or by the wild yeasts that are always in the air and on containers (sourdough and salt rising breads).

The people who raised wheat soon discovered wild yeasts (or the yeasts discovered them since it's a mutual help thing). The transition from accidental "proofing" to the deliberate cultivation of a goodly growth from wild yeast and the addition of it to the bread dough was quick and happened at least as far back as ancient Egypt. And that's what all the old-time recipes for "starter," "railroad," "everlasting," and "potato" yeasts are. You can't make yeast. Only God can make a tree and only God can make yeast. But they're all around unless you live in the Klondike in February. If you put out something tempting to eat like a bowl of lukewarm potato water you're bound to have a fine supply soon—the exact length of time depends on how far north you live, the season and how antiseptic your environment is.

You can leaven bread containing wheat flour because of the phenomenon of "gluten" that stretches to make a bubble when carbon dioxide gas is released inside the bread, thus lightening or "leavening" the loaf. For centuries the staple peasant bread of Europe was "black barley bread" which was a bread made of parched barley flour. They couldn't leaven that any way. The Scotsmen who discovered oats growing in their hills and learned to make flour from them ate oatcakes—a sort of tortilla—for their staple and you can't leaven that. If you rush wheat flour and don't add yeast or baking powder you can make an unleavened bread of it. If you let wild yeasts get a bare start in the loaf by leaving it set overnight (if you live in a southerly happy-yeast habitat like California) you'll get a little homemade yeast-type leavening that they call "proofing" bread. Unleavened breads are moist, close grained, some-

times rather crumbly, but equally as nourishing as leavened ones. (Maybe more so because I don't like baking powder residues.)

As the yeasties live and work like any other critter their residence soon gets befouled with waste products. So if left on and on in the same pot (and fed regularly) they produce a floating layer of grain alcohol (which the Klondikers drank and immortalized with the name "hooch," but I don't recommend the stuff) as well as carbon dioxide bubbles. So the painstaking pioneer ladies, trying to reduce the sourness (because this was really what we know now as sourdough starter) made it fresh for every bread making.

The Klondike gold rush brought to prominence another way of doing it. You can't catch wild yeasts in the Klondike in February. So they kept a culture going in the famous sourdough pot and it got really *sour*. But from that came the first "baking powder." Refined soda was coming on the market and the bread makers discovered that a pinch of soda added to a cup of sourdough (acid) made bubbles practically instantly in the batter. So instead of messing around with real sourdough breads they started living on pancakes which they leavened by combining their soda with their homemade acid.

Well, soda can combine with any acid and do the same thing so recipe books soon had breads and cakes leavened with soda and vinegar, soda and lemon juice, soda and molasses (yes, it contains acid too) as well as soda and sourdough. Then cream of tartar came on the market, and there were recipes combining soda and cream of tartar to get the same reaction. Some housewives premixed it themselves in the right proportions and combined it with cornstarch to help keep their powder dry until they wanted the acid and base to react. That's the homemade baking powder you've heard about. Finally some started selling these mixes and those were the first commercial baking powders. Since then they've found different and stronger dry acids to use in place of cream of tartar, which are your "double" and "triple" acting baking powders.

UNLEAVENED BREAD

That probably makes you think of a Jewish Passover bread. It looks like a cracker. Any flat cracker could be an unleavened bread. So are tortillas and *chapattis* and any other primitive bread. It's flat and thin so it can cook through. I'll tell you a story. Once I was going to give a bread making lesson to some very nice girls. When we got to the leavening part of it we discovered there was no yeast in the kitchen and no baking powder to be found, no soda or sour cream either. So I said, oh well, we'll do without it. I made a huge batch, about 12 loaves, of wonderful stuff. The bread had lots of applesauce and raisins and canned peaches and peach juice. It would have been as yummy as a fruitcake if it would have baked. It didn't. After the first hour it was still raw clear through, dense and moist and not in a good way. Like dough. I blithely told them to just bake it another hour. The second hour didn't help much. It got a thick tough crust on it and the inside was still like dough. I felt doubly like an idiot because I had marched into the enterprise acting like such a know-it-all. My mother's oft-repeated admonition rang in my ears—"Pride goeth before a fall." So I can tell you for a fact that even though modern times have put bubbles in bread to an indefensible extreme it is also true that bread with no bubbles at all should be

thin and flat like a tortilla. If you want to read the best book in the world about making tortillas look for a copy of *The Tortilla Book* by Diana Kennedy, published by Harper and Row, 10 East 53rd Street, New York, N.Y. 10022.

Tortillas are an unleavened bread that can be made out of all kinds of flours. It's the shape of the end product rather than the ingredients that makes a tortilla a tortilla. You can make hominy by my directions and dry it. Then if you grind that in a mortar or run it through a food chopper several times to make a flour and moisten that flour to make a soft dough you have *masa*. The *masa* is patted out thin or shaped in a press to make cakes about 5 inches in diameter. They are baked on a lightly greased griddle, turning frequently, until they are thoroughly cooked.

Mike once had a job in a town 8 miles from the Mexican border (Bisbee, Arizona). We used to cross the border and go a few miles more to eat supper at a real Mexican restaurant (not the tourist kind right on the border). In that little town there was a tiny shop with a tortilla press. There a jolly fat baker in a big apron, just like the ones in children's books, turned out neat piles of tortillas all day long.

You can make a tortilla out of cornmeal by stirring 1 cup boiling water into 1 cup cornmeal. Then add salt and a couple teaspoons bacon grease and mix. Pat into thin cakes and bake on a griddle the same as for *masa*. If you make it out of flour you get another sort of tortilla. If you make it partly out of flour and partly out of mashed potatoes you'd have *lefse*, a Scandinavian dish. Or a Jewish unleavened potato pancake.

Hazel wrote me this description of how to make *Flour Tortillas*. I couldn't say it better so I'm just going to quote her: "Sift together 2 cups flour and 1 teaspoon salt. Cut in 1 tablespoon shortening and add just enough cold water to make a stiff dough. It will take about ⅔ cup water. Knead on floured board. (I don't know how to tell you how long.) When ready make small balls and put aside about 8 to 10. With hands slightly moist dip them in the flour. Now work the balls into flat round disks. Either roll out, or as I do turn the dough and stretch it, until you have a tortilla with no holes about the size of a bread-and-butter plate and about ⅛ inch thick. I cook mine on a lightly greased griddle—that flat kind (*do not fry*). Cook on both sides. A little scorch won't hurt. Just don't burn holes. As they come off the griddle place between two towels or a folded towel. This will soften the tortillas so you can roll them when you get to the filling."

For the filling part you make them into a sandwich sort of thing. If you eat the store kind they are awful. If you fill them with some grated cheese or some homemade cottage cheese, some garden leaf lettuce, chunks of garden ripened tomato, homemade taco sauce and some homemade refried beans (see Vegetables) you have a wonderful meal that is not only food for the body but entertainment for the whole family. Taco night at the Emery house is Daddy Mike's night to cook. It happens when he wants to give me an evening off and becomes both a rite of love and great fun for all. I love standing back and letting Daddy slave over the hot stove. The children slice tomatoes, grate cheese and shred lettuce. Grated turnip is wonderful with tacos, too, and so is radish, especially the long white kind. We try to find something new to put in the tacos every time we eat them just for the fun of it and they generally taste better than ever.

Chapattis are a traditional bread from India. Combine 2 cups ground wheat flour, 2 tablespoons oil or melted fat of some sort, ¾ cup water and ½ teaspoon salt. Knead same as for tortillas; make little balls the size of a golf ball. Let rest about 1½ hours. Roll out flat and thin. Cook on griddle. Don't oil the griddle—oil each side of the *chapatti.*

An Easier Tortilla Recipe—Merry Collins who lives in Kennewick, Washington, wrote specially to tell me about an easier way to make tortillas than the first one written. So now in the 7th edition I am able to add it here. This recipe is easier because "all the ingredients are warm and liquid. My friend Mary Rivera is its originator and it took her quite a while to arrive at it as she makes tortillas in the same fashion you make bread. She has a rolling pin that was her mother's. It was made by soaking an unpainted broom handle in water for several days until it swelled and cutting it to approximately 12 inches. Here's *Lupe's tortilla de herina.* Mix together 3 cups flour, 1 tablespoon baking powder, 1 teaspoon salt, 3 tablespoons vegetable oil and 1 cup very hot water. Form a large dough ball. Let rest for a few minutes. Form small dough balls. Mary grabs as much as she can pull off in her left palm. It is just the right amount. Then the glob of dough is made round by pulling the edges in but keeping it against the left palm. It makes the top nice and smooth. Then the balls are rolled out, round, and put on an ungreased preheated griddle (cast iron) at a medium heat. After bubbles begin forming turn and cook on the other side. We store them in a crockery pot with a lid or in a plastic bowl. They should be stacked inside a clean dish towel. It took me quite a while to be able to get these tortillas rolled out round. I used to get teased about my tortillas that looked like states they were so misshapen."

LEAVENING WITH AIR

Sponge cakes and popovers are leavened simply with air beaten in. The problem in these batters is to get and keep in as much air as possible. The egg whites and egg yolks are usually beaten separately and all the ingredients mixed well. Then the egg white is gently folded in to keep from driving out the air which has been whipped into the eggs. The more air you have in the batter the larger volume of batter there will be and the finer texture. Air leavened batters should be baked or cooked at a relatively low temperature for as long as it takes.

When the egg whites are beaten, air is trapped in them and the eggs become fluffy and white. Then the eggs containing the air are mixed with the flour and other ingredients and put into the oven to bake. Air expands when heated and this makes the cake "rise." When you cut the cake you can see the holes made in it by the expanding air bubbles.

I prefer air leavened types among the quick breads because I'm not crazy about chemicals and the taste of baking powder. Popover batters should be thoroughly beaten at least several minutes with your eggbeater or blender. Then pour immediately into your baking container, preferably a preheated one to reduce the baking time and help keep the air bubbles. Use a hot oven to start with until your batter has risen all it will from the expansion of the air bubbles as they heat, then reduce the temperature to prevent burning. Preheat and grease a muffin pan, 8 custard cups or a regular popover pan. Heat the oven to 450° because you want to get those right into a hot oven.

Popovers—Mix 1¼ cups flour, ¼ teaspoon salt, 1 teaspoon sugar, 1 cup milk, and 2 well-beaten egg yolks. Beat the batter thoroughly and then fill the popover spaces about half full of batter. Bake at the hot temperature 20 minutes, then turn the oven down and let continue baking until the popovers suit you. Some people like them dry inside and prick the popovers and then leave them in 20 minutes more. Good for breakfast.

Crepes Suzettes—When I recently was nine months pregnant and avoiding salt and had given up baking powder and soda as an aid to health these were a delicious mainstay. They are bland alone but spread them fresh and hot with sour cream, apple butter, or what you like, roll them up and eat or just fork up like a pancake and I'm sure you'll like them. Ingredients: 4 or more eggs, separated, 1½ cups milk, 1 cup flour. Mix flour, milk and egg yolks. Beat whites stiff and fold in. Grease a round frying pan enough to make it shine and heat it medium hot. Pour a ladle full of the batter in and if the pan is not level, keep turning the pan until the batter is making a round pancake covering the bottom. When the bottom is done turn and cook on the other side. Serve immediately. It is important to cook these as slowly and gently as possible for maximum tenderness and tastiness. The more eggs you use in them the nicer they are.

ABOUT BAKING POWDER

Baking powder is basically a mixture of cream of tartar, soda and cornstarch. You can make your own. All you need is a scale to weigh ounces (or grams). "Double-acting" baking powder is a mixture that pro-

duces gas bubbles during mixing and again during baking. "Single-acting" baking powder is the kind containing cream of tartar and just leavens once. If you are making your own baking powder and using it, remember to mix and bake immediately for the best result.

To substitute your own baking powder for recipe baking powder (they usually intend the double-acting) just double the amount. Use 2 teaspoons of your single-acting baking powder for each teaspoon of double-acting baking powder called for. In any old-time recipe that calls for "saleratus" use baking powder. There is still another baking powder available on the commercial market besides the soda-cream of tartar one (Royal) and the double-acting (Calumet, Clabber Girl, Davis). This type is about one-fourth less strong in effect than the double-acting and is called a "phosphate" baking powder. Rumford and Dr. Price are brand names of this type.

Katya Morrison wrote me from Mount Airy, Maryland, about the brand called Royal. She said: "I know how you feel about baking powder—however, there is one type of baking powder called Royal—a baking powder which contains cream of tartar, tartaric acid (the acid of grapes), bicarbonate of soda and starch. From what I understand it is the best there is but I have a hard time finding it. It works well with no bitterness." That aftertaste bitterness sure is one of the problems with baking powder so if this one doesn't have it I'm glad you told me, Katya. God bless you, too.

Mrs. Essemen's Baking Powder Recipe—Measure out 12.34 ounces (350 grams) of cream of tartar, 5.30 ounces (150 grams) bicarbonate of soda and 3.53 ounces (100 grams) of cornstarch. You don't actually have to be all that precise, especially with the cornstarch—if you can manage a rounded off ounce that's near enough. Sift them together ten times and then spread out to dry if there is any dampness in your batch. You could use flour instead of cornstarch if you want and the exact amount isn't awfully important. Using this single-acting baking powder recipe remember it is important to get your cake or whatever into the oven as soon as it is mixed. When using this baking powder increase the amount the recipe calls

for. If it calls for 1 teaspoon of baking powder use between 1½ and 2 teaspoons of yours.

The general proportion of cream of tartar to soda in homemade baking powder is 2 to 1. If you want to make a huge quantity use 1 pound cream of tartar and a half pound soda. Usually, a little extra cream of tartar is included to make sure all the soda is acted on.

A gentleman from Metairie, Louisiana, made a batch of Mrs. Essemen's baking powder. It worked fine for him but he calculated that the cost was more than five times that of the same amount of store baking powder. He wrote to ask me what was the use of that expensive formula. I don't have a good answer to that one. Quite often making things yourself will be more expensive than buying them when you include all the general investments you have to make. And invariably it is more work and trouble than grabbing a box or bottle off the supermarket shelf. Maybe the recipe is here to give you an option or to help you understand better what is in the store box of baking powder. I've never made it myself but I'm proud of Mrs. Essemen for knowing how and I wanted to share that know-how with all of you.

Baking Powder Substitute—For each teaspoon of double-acting baking powder called for (or each 2 teaspoons single-acting baking powder) use ¼ teaspoon baking soda plus ½ cup sour milk or buttermilk. Let the ½ cup sour milk or buttermilk replace a half cup of sweet milk or other fluid called for in your recipe.

Soda when dissolved with an acid—sour milk, buttermilk, vinegar, molasses, lemon juice—releases a gas which leavens bread. The proper proportion is ½ teaspoon baking soda per cup sour milk, buttermilk or molasses. Molasses varies in acidity and ½ teaspoon soda will be right for between ½ and 1 cup molasses. Use 1 cup to be safe. A half teaspoon of soda is the right amount to combine with 1 tablespoon of vinegar or 1 tablespoon of lemon juice. In this case your recipe should contain at least 1 cup of sweet milk, too. Never dissolve soda directly in the sour milk, buttermilk, vinegar or molasses since that would release the gas too soon and your dough will be less light. Always sift the soda with the flour. One-half teaspoon baking soda equals 2 teaspoons baking powder in leavening property. Don't use soda without an equivalent amount of acid in your recipe.

Soda means baking soda or "bicarbonate of soda," $NaHCO_3$. Whether you use baking powder or soda plus an acid the reaction that occurs involves the action of an acid on sodium hydrogen carbonate (your soda) which releases the gas carbon dioxide to leaven the batch. When sour milk is used the acid that reacts with the soda is lactic acid, $HC_3H_5O_3$.

The "phosphate" baking powders are made with calcium phosphate, $CaH_4(PO_4)_2$, or sodium dihydrogen phosphate, NaH_2PO_4, as the acid part. Double-acting baking powder uses sodium aluminum sulfate, $NaAl(SO_4)_2$, as the acidic component. The base in each case is soda. The best baking powders are considered to be ones in which the acid is only moderately soluble. If the acid dissolves too easily, the carbon dioxide gas will be released before rather than during the baking. The heat of the baking causes the completion of the chemical reaction in these baking powders.

Cream of tartar baking powder consists of soda (sodium hydrogen carbonate, $NaHCO_3$), cream of tartar, which is potassium hydrogen tartrate, $KHC_4H_4O_6$, and starch (cornstarch or flour). The starch is added to keep water vapor in the air from causing the powder to form a solid cake. Also, to prevent a premature reaction between the components.

Cream of tartar is found in grape juice. If you make your own you may notice floating crystals of crude tartar, also called argol. The crude tartar is less soluble in alcoholic fluid than in water and so is deposited when wine is made from grape juice at a greater rate. The argols that form when wine is made are about 90 percent cream of tartar. Soda reacts with cream of tartar much more slowly than it does with molasses, sour milk and lemon juice—hence its use in baking powder.

In grape juice that has been home canned several months you get big chips of argol on the bottom of the jar. You could pulverize that to make cream of tartar.

Here's a table for quick reference on all those figures:

ONE TEASPOON DOUBLE-ACTING BAKING POWDER EQUALS

1½ teaspoons phosphate baking powder
2 teaspoons homemade baking powder (or single-acting baking powder)
½ teaspoon soda plus 1 cup sour milk
½ teaspoon soda plus 1 cup sour buttermilk
½ teaspoon soda plus 1 tablespoon vinegar plus 1 cup sweet milk
½ teaspoon soda plus 1 tablespoon lemon juice plus 1 cup sweet milk
½ teaspoon soda plus ½ to 1 cup molasses (use 1 cup when in doubt)
½ teaspoon soda plus ½ teaspoon cream of tartar

BAKING POWDER RATIO TO FLOUR

1 teaspoon baking powder per cup flour for cakes in which eggs are used.
2 teaspoons baking powder per cup flour for biscuits, muffins and waffles.
¾ tablespoon baking powder per cup flour for buckwheat and whole grain flours and meals when eggs are not used.

TIPS ON USING A SODA LEAVENED BATTER

1. Add the soda or the dry mixture containing your soda last.
2. Avoid mixing the batter much after the soda has been added. Overmixing will knock out the gas that you need to raise your dough.
3. Get your batter to pan or oven as quickly as possible to preserve the leavened effect.
4. Be advised that lots of people believe soda isn't really very good for you or your digestive tract and they could be right.

QUICK BREADS

"Quick" breads are breads leavened with baking powder, baking soda or air beaten into eggs or the batter. That's quick compared to yeast breads where you wait a couple of hours for the yeast to work.

Prune Rye Bread—This is a favorite of mine. It makes two small loaves. It is very heavy and moist. It keeps well and my children love it as much as a "sweet." First put your dried prunes on to cook, enough to make 1 cup when cooked enough to be able to cut out the pits. Sift together 6 tablespoons baking powder, 2 cups rye flour, 3 cups wheat flour, ½ teaspoon salt and ½ cup honey. Add 1 egg, 1¾ cups milk and mix it well. When your batter is mixed add 1 cup chopped cooked, pitted, dried prunes and stir just enough to distribute them. Pour into 2 (6 x 3-inch) greased loaf pans or one (11 x 3 x 3-inch) and bake at about 350° for about an hour. After baking when the bread has cooled enough, wrap it in foil, a cloth, or plastic for a tender crust.

Soft Gingerbread—Combine 6 cups flour, 3 cups molasses, 1 cup rich cream, 1 cup butter, melted, 2 eggs, beaten, and 2½ teaspoons ginger (you might want more ginger). Bake at 350° to 375° for 45 minutes. This makes a *lot* of gingerbread.

Jeanie Johns's Cake Leavened with Soda and Vinegar—Mix in a pan: 1½ cups flour, 1 cup sugar, 3 tablespoons cocoa, 1 teaspoon baking soda, and ½ teaspoon salt. Melt 6 tablespoons shortening and stir in. Add: 1 tablespoon vinegar, 1 cup cold water, and 1 teaspoon vanilla. Make holes in the cake and stir. Bake immediately in a preheated 350° oven for 25 to 30 minutes.

Grape Nuts—Ingredients: 3½ cups sifted whole wheat flour, 1 teaspoon soda, ½ cup brown sugar, 2 cups sweet milk and 2 tablespoons vinegar, ¾ teaspoon salt.

Mix flour, soda, sugar and salt. Add sour milk and beat until smooth. Spread dough ¼ inch thick on a greased cookie sheet. Bake in a 375° oven about 15 minutes. When cool, grind in food chopper. Don't dry it completely or you'll get flour. Let it finish drying

RIPE BANANAS MARKED DOWN

---

after grinding. Before serving, mix in anything else you would like, nuts or fruit. You can bag and tie with wire in family-sized portions. Handy for an instant breakfast.

Banana Nut Bread—Ingredients: ⅔ cup peanut oil, 2½ cups unbleached flour, 1¼ cups honey, 6 large ripe bananas, mashed, 1¼ teaspoons baking powder, 1 teaspoon soda, and ¼ teaspoon sea salt.

Mix 2 minutes. Add ⅔ cup (goat's) milk, 2 eggs, and beat. Lastly add ⅔ cup sunflower seeds (roasted). Makes 2 loaves. Bake at 350° oven until done—can check with a toothpick but usually 35 to 45 minutes will do.

SQUAW BREAD

7th edition, June 8, 1976. A friend wrote to ask if I could help her find a "squaw bread" recipe. I didn't know one but printed her request in my *Newsletter* and did I ever get squaw bread recipes! Here are a few of the most interesting ones.

Kiowa Squaw Bread—George Lawrence wrote me from Denver, Colorado, that for the past few years he has belonged to a YMCA group there which was studying the life of the American Indian. George says to use biscuit dough with very little shortening. Flavoring is optional. Roll out, cut into squares and make a few indentations with a knife in the squares. Drop into boiling fat and remove when golden brown.

Osage Indian Squaw Bread—Nancy Clough from Long Beach, California, sent me this Oklahoma recipe. She said: "Indian influence is strong in the State of Oklahoma. The seal is of the five Indian nations—Cherokees, Creeks, Choctaws, Chickasaws and Seminoles. They made up the old Oklahoma Territory. The Osage Indians are also well represented. Mix together 2 cups flour, 1 teaspoon salt, 2 teaspoons baking powder, 1 tablespoon melted lard and 1½ cups cold water until you get a dough. Roll dough out thin. Cut into squares. Punch holes in squares with knife. Drop them into hot fat. Turn over when golden brown and have both sides well done."

Yavapai Squaw Bread—Marion Stick from Phoenix, Arizona, is of Pima Indian descent. They have wonderful fried bread, too. But the Pima Indians ate lunch together with the Yavapai Indians in the Superstition Mountains and she was so enthused about that Yavapai Squaw Bread she got the recipe and sent it to me too! This is a modern version of the original squaw bread: Combine 2 cups flour, 1 teaspoon salt, 2 teaspoons baking powder, ½ cup powdered milk and 1 tablespoon sugar in a bowl. Gradually add enough warm water (about 1 cup) to make a soft dough. Divide dough in half and flour lightly. Pat a small amount into a 6- or 8-inch circle (very thin). Fry quickly in hot oil (275°) about 2½ or 3 inches deep. Drain on absorbent paper. While warm, dust with powdered sugar. It's delicious! (Note dough that is overhandled will tend to make a tough bread.)

Dough Bod Squaw Bread—Russell Shorten of Colfax, Washington, wrote me: "One day I was making

what I call 'dough bods' and an old Indian friend came by and said his mother used to make them and called it squaw bread. She cooked hers over an outdoor fire. You simply take bread dough at the stage you usually make it into a loaf (about enough to make a good sized bun), flatten it with your hands and fry it in a skillet of good hot grease. We eat it hot with butter and jelly. My friend said his mother filled a washtub with it and the older it got the better it tasted."

It sounds to me like the original squaw bread probably was an unleavened bread because it is always rolled flat and thin. That would make sense because baking powder wasn't always around.

HOMEMADE READY MIXES

The store mixes are pretty terrible stuff. But the basic notion of combining your dry ingredients ahead of time for maybe seven to ten bakings isn't so bad if you're a baking powder cook. It won't work with yeast. That's why homemade mixes are here in the baking powder section. If you do make your own mixes they will be at least a third cheaper than the ones you buy in the store and have no preservatives in there. The University of Missouri Extension Division has out a booklet (Circular 846, "Missouri Mix for Home Baking") with 20 pages of recipes for everything from applesauce spice cake to pizza based on their basic mix recipe. The other drawback to mixes, besides the fact they depend on baking powder, is that you aren't using freshly ground flour. Whole grain cornmeal or wheat flour ground at home loses quality almost literally every hour it waits between the grinding and the baking. If you've never eaten food made from freshly ground grain you've never realized how flat and insipid the flour you're used to really tastes. So there are the pros and cons of mixes. You can make your own mix recipe by combining dry ingredients of your favorite recipe, quadrupling and using as needed, leaving out the ingredients you've already got in.

Missouri Mix—Combine ⅓ cup baking powder, 1 cup plus 2 tablespoons powdered milk, 4 teaspoons salt and 9 cups flour. Blend thoroughly by sifting together. Cut 1½ cups lard into flour mixture. Store in refrigerator and use within a month. This mix makes biscuits by adding ½ cup water to 2 cups mix.

Homemade Biscuit, Dumpling, Shortcake, Waffle, Muffin, Coffee Cake, Etc. Mix—If you have to do a lot of baking and you're really desperate for time, make this dry mix. To use add enough milk to make a soft dough and proceed. You should store it in the refrigerator where it will keep at least a month. Your basic proportions are for every cup flour, 1 teaspoon baking powder, ½ teaspoon salt and 3 tablespoons shortening cut in. Thus for 10 cups of flour, sifted and measured, add 10 teaspoons baking powder and 5 teaspoons salt. Then mix and sift again. Cut in 1⅞ cups shortening (⅞ cup would be 1 cup minus 2 tablespoons) until the mixture has a fine even crumb. Keep in a closed container.

STEAMED PUDDINGS

"Pudding" to Great-grandmother meant a hot, moist, spiced and sweetened kind of bread.

She had a regular "steamer" and they are again becoming available at hardware stores that carry cooking utensils. But if you don't have one and your recipe says to "steam" it—don't despair. Check the directions below for exactly the type of steaming you want to do. When finished lift the can or mold out of the kettle and remove its cover, if any. Cool. Loosen the pudding around the edges with a knife.

TO STEAM A PUDDING—Pour into a well-greased (use butter) 2-quart mold, bowl or casserole (or 2 1-pound coffee cans, steaming each in a separate kettle). You can cover with aluminum foil, covering as tightly as you can. The general rule is to steam until the pudding springs back when touched lightly in the center. To serve try offering the pudding hot, cut into slices, and with a sauce. To reheat in the mold, cover and steam 30 minutes, or wrap in aluminum foil, if not in the mold. When steaming puddings don't open the steamer and let air in on the pudding except when necessary to replenish the water.

STEAMING IN A PRESSURE COOKER—Place a filled 1-quart mold on a rack in the bottom of a 4-quart pressure cooker (for a larger mold you would need a larger pressure cooker). Add 5 cups water. Steam 20 minutes without pressure. Close vent. Steam 50 minutes at 10 pounds pressure. This is equivalent to about 4 hours of steaming.

STEAMED IN A CAN—Pour your batter into as many greased 1-pint cans (16-ounce size) or a little bigger as you need. Fill them half full. Cover with lids, heavy paper or cloth tied on with string, or leave uncovered. (I leave them uncovered and haven't had soggy bread yet!) Choose a big enough pan that has a lid. On the bottom of the pan fit a smaller pan upside down and set your cans of batter on top of it. Pour in water to almost halfway up around the cans. Put cover on and boil the water slowly until time is up. (If you haven't pans the right size use crumpled foil, a rack, canning jar lids, or whatever you can devise to keep the cans from resting directly on the bottom of the pan.)

STEAMED IN A MOLD—Maid of Scandinavia (3245 Raleigh Avenue, Minneapolis, Minnesota 55416) carries old fashioned pudding molds for steaming in a larger pan. They are fluted with a center cone and have lock-on lids. Grease mold, pour half full of batter for a soda mix, fuller for unleavened. Proceed as for steaming in a can. Nice but not necessary.

A DO-IT-YOURSELF MOLD can always be arranged by greasing a basin, filling it half to two-thirds full and covering with a greased paper, then a cloth tied around the edges—or even just a cloth. You can put the basin in a pan, fill with water to halfway up the basin and boil.

Before starting to mix the pudding have your ingredients ready, your pans greased, or your bag floured, and the water boiling in the pan. These old-time puddings are soda leavened and that means you want them to start firming as soon as possible after the soda hits the acid. Renew the water as it boils away. The longer you steam the puddings, the lighter they will be.

STEAM IN A BAG—Cook it in a bag in a colander or perforated steamer over boiling water with the lid on. Check recipe for whether or not to flour bag.

HOW TO "BOIL" BREADS AND PUDDINGS—When it says in your old-time recipe book "boil the pudding three hours and a half" or "boil the bread three hours and then bake it ten minutes" it means to boil in a pudding bag. The pudding bag was and is a cloth bag in which to pour a pudding or bread batter. It is buttered and floured before the pudding is poured in. Then tie securely with string and put into the kettle and boil until done.

For a "pudding bag" use a white cotton of tight weave such as a diaper. Wring bag out in hot water, then rub well with flour to get it in all the spaces. Take some boiling water and slop it around on it until you have a kind of paste all over. Don't fill it over half full. Have your water boiling. All boiled puddings must be put into boiling water, it mustn't stop boiling all the time it's in there, and the pudding must always be covered with the water. Put a small plate or saucer under the pudding bag if there is a possibility of it sticking to the bottom of the pan. When you want to serve the pudding hot, as soon as it comes out of the boiling water dip it into a pan of cold water and the cloth shouldn't stick to it. A boiled pudding is best when sent directly to the table.

Helen's Carrot Pudding—Sift together:

1 cup flour	½ teaspoon allspice
1 teaspoon soda	¼ teaspoon cloves
½ teaspoon cinnamon	¼ teaspoon salt

Grate until you have 1 cup grated raw potato (no peel) and 1 cup grated raw carrot (no peel). Combine grated vegetables and sifted dry ingredients. Add ½ cup melted shortening, 1 cup sugar, 1 cup raisins and ½ cup chopped nuts, if desired. Mix well and put in a greased pan and steam 3½ hours. Serve with a sauce. Here is a hard sauce that's good on it.

In a pan combine:

½ cup sugar	⅛ teaspoon nutmeg
1 tablespoon cornstarch	1 cup boiling water
⅛ teaspoon salt	

Cook until thickened. Then add 2 tablespoons butter and 1½ tablespoons lemon juice (juice of half a lemon). The pudding and sauce are good hot or cold. You can keep the sauce in a jar in the refrigerator and use as needed. Good on any of these boiled or steamed puddings. These puddings require a sauce over them to serve, usually.

BOILED IN A BAG!

These recipes are really old-timers. Boiling in a bag originated with the Colonial pot. There was one big iron pot hung in the fireplace. The menu was stew most days. To make a side dish or "pudding" or "bread" (depending on how firm it turned out) the batter was poured into a floured cloth, tied up and hung over the edge of the pot to boil in with the stew. You can do it too. They even made custards this way—"batter puddings"—but they are too broken up for our modern tastes. You can tie a pudding bag with a strip of cloth or a wire around the "neck."

Very Plain Pudding—1 cup molasses, 1 cup water, 1 teaspoon soda, 1 teaspoon salt. Thicken with flour to make a batter like that for a cupcake, pour into pudding bag.

Indian Pudding—Warm 1 cup molasses and 1 cup milk and stir well together. Beat 2 eggs and stir gradually into the molasses-milk mixture. Add ½ pound beef suet, chopped fine (the butcher will fix some for you), 1¾–2 cups cornmeal, ½ teaspoon *each* cinnamon and nutmeg and a little grated lemon peel. Mix well. Dip your cloth into boiling water, shake, flour, pour in the mixture and tie up leaving room for the pudding to swell. Boil 3 hours. Serve hot with rich cream or a pudding sauce.

Apple Dumplings Boiled in a Bag— Combine 2 cups sweet milk with 1 tablespoon vinegar, ½ teaspoon soda and 1 teaspoon salt. Melt ½ cup butter and mix all together. Add enough flour to make dough a little stiffer than a biscuit dough. Divide the dough into 6 to 8 portions. Peel and core that number of apples. Roll out each section of the dough. Set an apple in the center of each one. Fill the apple center with brown sugar. (Optional, a sprinkle of cinnamon.) Then wrap the dough around the apple and pinch the edges together tightly.

Take a cloth (man's handkerchief is just right) and set the dumplings in the center of it. Bring up all four corners and tie them. Use a deep kettle. Have the water boiling with ½ teaspoon salt in it. Put the dumplings into the boiling water and keep them covered with water throughout the cooking period (weight them with a plate on top, if necessary). Boil 40 minutes. Take out, remove from handkerchief. Serve as is with cream or a colorful sauce or bake 10 minutes at 450° on a cookie sheet with just a sprinkle of sugar on top of each one to brown. Cut into quarters or whatever size pieces you prefer to serve. You can do the same thing with peaches.

SAUCES FOR PUDDINGS

Brandy Sauce—Combine 1 well-beaten egg, ½ cup butter and 1 cup sugar. Add 2 tablespoons boiling water. Put your mixture into the top of a double boiler and stir until the sauce boils. To prevent sugaring keep covered when you can't stir it and when stirring, keep the sides stirred down into the mixture to prevent crystals from forming there. Then add 1½ teaspoons brandy (or more). This is the thing for the fancy, fruitcake type puddings and for the whole wheat pudding in the next section. To warm up add rich cream and mix well.

Hard Sauce—Cream 3 tablespoons butter with ¼ cup powdered sugar and dash of salt. Stir in 1 teaspoon grated lemon peel and 1 teaspoon lemon juice. Add ¾ cup more powdered sugar alternately with 1 tablespoon cream. Beat sauce until fluffy. Good on fruit puddings.

Lemon Sauce—Good on molasses puddings. Combine ½ cup sugar, 1 tablespoon cornstarch, a dash of salt and 1 cup water over heat, stirring constantly until thickening takes place and sauce boils for 1 minute. Stir in 1 teaspoon grated lemon peel, the juice of ½ lemon and 1 tablespoon butter.

Orange Sauce—Good on carrot pudding. Mix ⅓ cup sugar, 1½ tablespoons cornstarch, ¼ teaspoon salt, 1 cup orange juice, ½ cup water, ½ teaspoon grated lemon peel and 1 teaspoon lemon juice in a pan. Heat, stirring constantly, until thickening takes place and sauce boils 1 minute. Serve hot.

BOSTON BROWN BREADS

Whole Wheat Pudding is either a very tender, nice Boston Brown Bread or a firm pudding to be served with a sauce as you prefer. Take 2 cups whole wheat flour, ½ teaspoon soda, ½ teaspoon salt and mix together good. Stir in 1 cup milk and ½ cup molasses, then add 1 cup chopped dates. Mix and pour into 3 buttered pint cans. Steam 2½ hours. Optionally substitute a cup of ripe strawberries or blackberries or the berries you like or raisins for those chopped dates. I like it *better* that way. Or use chopped dried figs or chopped apple. You can serve with whipped cream.

Plain Boston Brown Bread—This is my favorite. Beat 1 egg slightly. Combine it with ½ cup sugar and ½ cup molasses. Add 1 teaspoon salt and ½ teaspoon soda to 1 cup sour milk (or else 1 cup sweet milk with a tablespoon of vinegar added). Combine with egg mixture. Mix in 2¾ cups whole wheat flour. Butter 3 pint cans and divide the batter among them. Steam 1 hour. Then bake in a preheated 400° oven for 25 minutes. The neighbor children love this hot from the oven, sliced and buttered.

Mrs. Essemen's Boston Brown Bread—Sift together 1 cup cornmeal, 1 cup rye meal, 1 cup whole wheat flour (or graham) and ½ teaspoon salt. Add ¾ cup molasses, 1 cup sour milk (you can sour sweet milk with vinegar if need be, 1 tablespoon will do it if you let it set a bit before using) and ½ teaspoon soda. (Optional, ½ cup raisins.) Mix and pour into washed and scalded vegetable cans. Use cans that are smooth, not ridged, on the inside. For me this recipe makes 4 13-ounce cans. Be sure to grease the cans well before putting your bread dough in. Fill the cans approximately half full to allow for expansion during steaming. Steam for 3 hours.

Christmas Plum Pudding—Before there was a fruitcake, there was plum pudding at Christmastime. The ingredients are very similar, but you don't need to "age" it. This one can be boiled in a bag, steamed in a bag or steamed in a mold. Soak overnight 1½ pounds seedless raisins, ½ cup chopped almonds, 2 ounces finely chopped candied citron, 2 cups finely chopped sour apples in 1 cup of good brandy. Then add 1½ cups bread crumbs (on the dry side, toast them if necessary), 1 cup finely chopped beef suet, ½ cup sugar, 1 cup molasses, 3 eggs, ¼ cup flour, 1 teaspoon *each* cinnamon and salt and ½ teaspoon *each* allspice and cloves. Grate the rind of a lemon and add. Mix well and pour into your buttered mold or dip a bag into boiling water, then flour it and pour the mixture into that. Steam 4 to 8 hours, the more the better. Serve with a brandy sauce (hard sauces which firm up when cool and become like frosting are traditional with this).

To really add a festive touch to the Christmas plum pudding (or any of the pudding recipes), soak sugar cubes in brandy or rum for about 5 minutes. Place the soaked sugar cubes around the plate in which the pudding has been placed, light the sugar cubes and serve flaming to your Christmas guests or just to your family. This will really make the children's eyes light up. The flame doesn't last too long, and it is easily blown out if you wish to do so.

FRUITCAKES

Fruitcakes can be almost an everyday affair or they can be a really high culinary art. I make a special bread at Christmastime which has pitted canned cherries and apricots and raisins and applesauce in it. Very popular with the children. I can't give you a recipe for it because like all my other breads I just put it together and it's never quite the same. If I had nuts I'd put some of those in too but I have no nut trees on this place. Here is a recipe I do have though for an everyday sort of fruitcake.

Everyday Fruitcake—You can let the children have all they want of this. Mix 4½ cups whole wheat flour, 2½ cups rye flour, 2 teaspoons salt and ½ cup oil. Add "fruits"—1 cup raisins, ½ cup roasted sunflower seeds, ½ cup roasted pecans, almonds or a mixture of nuts (but not peanuts) and ½ cup dried fruit, cooked enough to chop—prunes or apricots are good. Add enough water to make a dough (about 2⅔ cups). Knead and then make a loaf. One big loaf is better than two small ones.

Put into a loaf pan and let rest overnight. Brush the top with water, then bake at 275° for 1½ hours. When cooled to lukewarm wrap tightly in foil or plastic wrap and let season a couple days at least for the crust to soften and for the flavor to improve before eating.

Fruitcake that *isn't* for every day—the kind you serve at Christmas, Thanksgiving and Easter, or maybe just Christmas and Thanksgiving—can really be fun because something you do so seldom you can really put yourself out on. Here follows I think a really fabulous collection of very extra special twice-a-year kind of fruitcake recipes most of which were sent to me by readers to be included in this collection. If you have dried your grapes to make raisins and the same for your currants, and candied your own lemon peel, orange peel, citron and cherries, and shelled the nuts from your little nut tree, then you're ready to be rewarded with old fashioned fruitcake or plum pudding. But my guess is that you, like me, will end up visiting the grocery store for at least a few of these semiannual ingredients.

Some hints on making fruitcakes in general: To *chop suet*, sprinkle the suet liberally with flour while you are chopping it. That way it won't stick to the knife. And separate your seeded raisins and sticky candied fruit in a bowl of flour, rubbing until you have them all separate and each coated with flour before adding to your batter. When first baked the cake may have a hard dry crust. During the aging period the fruits and crust become moist, the flavors blend and it "seasons." There's a real art to this aging of fruitcakes. And a number of different ways to accomplish the same end.

Aging a cake two or three months—A well made old fashioned fruitcake should keep for two or three months easily. You need an airtight fruitcake type pan to store it in. You can buy them at hardware stores or in cooking utensil departments, if you don't have any around the house. Keep the can with the cake in it in a cool place to prevent mold. A cool basement or cellar would do. So would the refrigerator. To help them keep or to send through the mail soak the outside of the cake with a brandy bath. There are several different ways to do this.

You can paint it on with a pastry brush. Give it two or three brushings. If you do get mold anyway don't worry. Mold doesn't hurt a fruitcake. Just trim it

off. For sooner use just wrap the fruitcake tightly in foil or plastic. To make fruitcake last a very long time, you need to do more than this. They can be aged as long as three years, but a year is a sensible amount. That way you can plan on baking your fruitcakes after the Christmas rush is over for the *next* Christmas. To make them last that long you have to soak them with plenty of rum or brandy or some kind of strong alcoholic beverage. This prevents molding. *Then* you wrap them in cheesecloth or some such cloth that has been soaked in the alcoholic beverage. Overwrap in either plastic or foil and put in an airtight tin in a cool place—or buried in powdered sugar in an airtight tin and kept in a cool place. For real long storage it helps to poke the cakes with a skewer sort of thing and pour a little brandy or rum into the holes.

If you're not that confident and you'd like to keep an eye on what's happening start out by soaking cheesecloths in brandy and wrap each cake with about four lengths of cheesecloth. Then overwrap tightly with foil or plastic, put in a tin can and store in a cool place. Then every two weeks unwrap to see what's happening (and probably nibble). Resoak the cheesecloth, wrap it up and pack again. This system is good for six weeks easily.

To decorate cakes for serving you wait until after the storing time is up and you are ready to serve them. Doesn't matter if it has been two weeks or three years. Make a glaze by combining ½ cup light corn syrup with 2 tablespoons water in a pan. Bring to a full boil and then let cool off a little. Brush the surface crumbs off your unwrapped fruitcake. Brush the cake with glaze. Then lay candied cherry halves, citron and/or walnut halves on the cake for garnish and brush again with the glaze.

To make a gift of fruitcake wrap each one in plastic. Tie with a ribbon and decorate to suit yourself. Put in a box and gift wrap the box if you're going to deliver it in person. To mail you'd better send it in something really strong. I've gotten enough mashed fruitcakes delivered to have resolved that metal is the only way.

Mrs. F. W. Ferrell's Jam Cake—This is a special holiday cake. Mrs. Ferrell always makes two of these in early November—the first is cut on Thanksgiving and the second saved for Christmas. Ingredients:

½ pound butter
3 cups sugar
7 eggs, separated
1 teaspoon soda
1 cup buttermilk
1 cup chopped pecans
Vanilla
4 cups flour (more or less)
1 cup wild plum jam (preferably homemade)

1 cup dewberry jam (may substitute strawberry or blackberry)
1 teaspoon baking powder
About ½ teaspoon *each* cinnamon, nutmeg and cloves
2 packages seedless raisins (chopped)

Cream butter and sugar gradually. Beat for 5 minutes. Beat egg yolks until light and lemon colored. Beat egg whites separately until stiff and dry. Add yolks to butter-sugar mixture, then fold in egg whites. Dissolve soda in the buttermilk. Roll chopped nuts and raisins in flour. Add milk, jams, vanilla and nuts to the batter. Lastly add sifted dry ingredients. Beat thoroughly and place in lined cake pans. Bake in slow oven (300°). Cover with oiled paper during last part of the baking. (Makes 5 layers.) Fill and frost with caramel icing. *Note:* Dough should not be too thick.

Caramel Icing for Jam Cake—Ingredients: 6½ cups sugar, 2 cups milk, ½ cup butter, 1 teaspoon vanilla, 1 cup chopped pecans.

Put 5 cups sugar, milk and butter into a pan and bring to a boil. When boiling, add remaining 1½ cups sugar which has been slowly melted in another iron skillet. Cook until a soft ball forms when mixture is dropped into cold water. Add vanilla and pecans. Beat well. Cover each layer, top and sides generously with icing. Decorate tops and sides of cake with whole pecan halves. This cake ripens like a fruitcake. To serve, slice thinly since it is sweet as any confection and very filling. It keeps for months. If the icing dries out cover the cake with a slightly moist cheesecloth for a day or so.

Mrs. Neeley's White Fruitcake—Ingredients:

2 pounds white raisins
½ pound light colored citron
½ pound candied cherries
½ pound candied pineapple
1 small fresh coconut, grated
1 pound blanched almonds, chopped
4 cups flour
2 cups sugar

1 cup butter and Crisco (or mixed white shortening)
1 cup coconut milk (scant and add water if nut has not sufficient milk)
2 teaspoons baking powder
1 teaspoon vanilla
1 teaspoon lemon extract
8 egg whites

Sprinkle fruit and nuts with 1 cup of the flour and set aside. Cream sugar and shortening. Add coconut milk and flour sifted with baking powder, alternately to creamed mixture. Add flavorings, floured fruits and nuts. Mix well. Last add stiffly beaten egg whites carefully and lightly. Bake 1½ hours at 250° in a round tube pan 10 inches across and 4½ inches deep. Decorate with cherry halves and citron slices. This keeps well.

Old Fashioned Fruitcake—Put 6½ pounds of fruit and 1 pound of nuts into a bowl and pour 1 cup of dark rum over it all. Stir, cover and let rest overnight. For fruit use any combination you like of typical fruitcake stuff such as candied cherries, candied pineapple, citron, candied orange and lemon peel and raisins. The golden and muscat raisins end up tasting better I think than the regular ones. Currants are OK, too. So are dates and figs and dried chopped apricots and chopped pitted prunes and all sorts of home-dried fruits. For nuts you can use walnuts, pecans, Brazil nuts, almonds, filberts, a combination or whatever other nut you like except peanuts.

Cream together 1 pound butter and 1 pound brown sugar. Add 12 egg yolks (save the whites). Now add 4 cups flour, 1 teaspoon *each* salt, ground allspice and nutmeg and 2 teaspoons *each* cinnamon, mace and cloves. Stir in the fruits and nuts, too. Whip the 12 egg whites stiff and fold in. Bake in four 9½ x 4¾-inch loaf pans or 12 x 5 x 3-inch pans that have been oiled and, if possible, lined with parchment paper and then lightly oiled again.

It helps if you brush the tops of the cakes with milk. It takes a long time to bake these and you should use about a 250° oven. Figure 3½ hours for the large loaf pans, 2½ to 3 hours for the smaller ones. The toothpick test works. Let cool about 15 minutes before you try to peel the paper off.

Molasses Fruitcake—Combine 3 cups dark raisins or 3 cups chopped dates or pitted prunes, 3 cups golden raisins or 3 cups dried apricots, that have been chopped, and 2 (16-ounce) packages of mixed candied fruit or some equivalent and stir in some brandy or rum (or apple juice if you want to avoid the alcohol). Let soak overnight. Now cream together 3 cups butter and 2½ cups sugar, beat in a total of 12 eggs, then 1 tablespoon real vanilla extract, then a 12-ounce bottle of molasses, or the equivalent. Now add 1 tablespoon *each* grated orange and lemon peel. Sift together 7 cups flour, 2 teaspoons soda, 2 teaspoons salt, 2 tablespoons *each* ground cinnamon and nutmeg and 1 tablespoon ground cloves. Add 4½ cups chopped walnuts. Combine with egg-molasses mixture. Bake about 2 hours at 300° in floured 9 x 5 x 3-inch loaf pans that are lined with foil or else greased and lined with parchment paper which has been oiled on top too. Use the toothpick test. Cool completely before removing foil if you use that.

OF BREAD

I feel inadequate to really tell you how to make bread, which is paradoxical because it's probably the one thing I can do best. I could show you up to a point. The problem is I never use a recipe these days. I've included in this book the recipes I learned to make bread from. They are the basic ones from the *Fleischmann's Treasury of Yeast Baking* book that you can get free by writing the yeast company. They've been passing out the same book for umpteen years now because I got my first copy many, many years ago and recently sent for another one because the old one was in shreds. They had rewritten a little, but the recipes were basically the same. Frankly I prefer my older version, but it doesn't matter now because like I said I never use a recipe.

I make bread once every ten days or so— whenever we get near to running out. I mix my liquid in a 5-gallon bucket. I bring up flour from the basement in another bucket and combine in my liquid bucket until I have it dry enough to turn out in the middle of my big round kitchen table which is covered (over the tablecloth) with a heavy sheet of clear plastic. I finish adding flour there and knead the dough. Let it rise right there in the middle of the table. Punch down and commence putting in pans. My children love bread making day. They all get into the act. We make lots of rolls because it's something they can and like to do. So we make big rolls and little rolls, odd looking rolls and worse looking rolls. My only absolute demand is that their hands be washed before they help me. For them it's like modeling clay day. For me it's a race to get as much of the dough into proper loaf shapes and loaf pans before they have the whole five gallons made into a mountain of rolls. I like loaf bread better because there's a smaller percentage of crust and it keeps better and serves better.

When we bake, we keep about five loaves at a time in the oven. The first get rushed in before they are really done rising. The last ones may have had to be punched down in the pan to let rise again before they finally get a turn in the oven. The children go in the living room and wait for the cry of "hot bread." Then they all come running and the first couple of pans of bread go down the hatch on the spot. My children can eat a loaf of bread just for a snack between them all and I like it too, so I have to figure on at least one loaf of bread consumed per day and more likely three. I use the bread in other things, too, and that helps make it go. I make puddings and desserts, and stuff the roast chicken with bread plus seasoning mixtures.

So bread making here is on such a massive scale and usually so chaotic with all my helpers that we aren't too picky about the results. With all those pans in the oven at once I have a problem with poor circulation of heat and they tend to burn on the bottom. If that happens, I just slice off the whole bottom of the loaf and put it in the pig bucket. And my helpers haven't really reached a stage of high artistic perfection with their roll and loaf mixtures. But it seems to all get eaten up at an appallingly fast rate, and before I know it it's time to make bread again. I bag up the bread and keep the extra loaves in the freezer, pulling out just one or two ahead of time to thaw. The frozen bread isn't as nice as fresh bread. And fresh bread isn't as nice as hot bread just out of the oven, but it's still our staff of life.

In this household you can eat bread anytime. The children usually have it with their breakfast and at intervals all day long. Some people don't believe in letting the children eat between meals, but my bread is so healthy I don't worry about it. They eat at meals too, and even if they didn't I wouldn't mind since what they were full of was my bread. When we go visiting I usually take a loaf of bread as a hostess gift and when someone comes to visit I usually send a loaf home with them. If I'm tired or sick or didn't get home from shopping until six at night I don't have to worry—there's always bread. Even the rabbits like my bread and so does the cat.

One time when I made bread it was in April when the eggs and milk were really flowing. (The honey too—it's truly the land flowing with milk and honey when you have happy bees and happy cows and goats.) And just for fun I kept track of my ingredients. So here's the recipe if you want it. It turned out yellow and somewhat like a Jewish Challah bread—from all the eggs in it. I warmed a gallon of skim milk from the refrigerator on the stove and then combined it with 1¼ gallons whole milk which was still warm being fresh from the cow. I poured in a half gallon of thick cream that might have become butter but I decided would be the shortening component in the bread instead. (Adding cream is just as good as adding butter or oil for that matter.) Then 1 cup honey, which I'd gathered from a hive just two days before, and three dozen eggs. No kidding the hens were laying about three dozen a day and still are. Then 4 tablespoons dry yeast. I stirred that up, then began adding flour. Eventually about 40 to 45 pounds of flour went into it—I'm not sure just how much.

After it got to be too much for the bucket we poured it on top of the kitchen table and worked there. The kids spilled a big batch of flour on the floor. Luke fell off the table. We ran out of flour in the middle of the job and had to make more. The dough overflowed the bucket and then practically overflowed the table while we were struggling to produce more flour to sober the mixture up (down?) somewhat. Dolly and Danny rolled out thin tortillas of the fresh dough and fried them for our lunch, which was delicious, but then they splashed some grease on themselves and both cried a bit. We started at 9:30 A.M. and got the last loaf out of the oven about 3:30 that afternoon. There were 12 loaves of bread and about 12 pans of rolls made in all. Well those are the ingredients, crises, and general statistics from one day's bread making at the Emery house.

7th edition, June 8, 1976. I received this letter from a beautiful lady, Mary W. Lutzke of Sylvania, Ohio. I wrote back to her to ask if she would share it and she said yes. "Dear Carla, I've just been reading the *Mother Earth News* Interview in #33 and was especially interested in your acceptance of God's will. Two children of my four are retarded and to me the hardest prayer to say is 'Thy will be done' and mean it; but, once said, it is the happiest. Thought you'd like to read one of my poems called

"BREAD

"When times get tough
And pressures seem intolerably high,
I get a yen to give the yeast a try
And taste and smell the ancient real bread stuff.

"Is it the punch and knead that mends my soul?
The elemental peasant hidden deep?
Or fragrant smells of childhood long asleep?
The shiny growing life within my bowl?

"Oh, blessed time of trial turn on your heat
For I am yeast—swell, bubble, double, rise!
As I pass on to younger nose and eyes
The magic, healing nuances of wheat."

THE SCIENCE AND ART OF YEAST BREAD MAKING

So you see homemade bread is something that I not only preach but practice. Yet I can't give you any more exact recipe for my five-gallon-type, meal-in-a-couple-slices bread. But I'll get as close to that as I can. I've had enough experience to know though that you can't just start out and do it like me. I used to think that anybody could do it and whenever I got my hands on an innocent young girl or boy I'd leave them alone in the kitchen and say: "Make bread." They'd say OK, where's the recipe? I'd say, "I'm not giving you any specific recipe. I want you to learn to make it without a recipe like I do. Just be brave." I'll admit the results were without exception pretty awful. And yet maybe they were pretty good considering. The most common problem these young people ran into was that they would add too much flour. They didn't know from experience when to stop and they would knead in flour until the dough got so hard that they just couldn't knead any more and that's too much!

Maybe there is some kind of happy medium. I started out baking bread from recipes and gradually over the years learned so much about bread making that I know intuitively what will go with what. So maybe if you've never made much bread before, if you follow these recipes I'll give you—and also read and soak in everything I'm going to tell you about "intuitive" bread making—maybe you too can gradually work your way off the rigid recipe and get used to experimenting. Every time you bake bread you'll know more about making bread. If you make it once a week for a year, at the end of the year you'll be a *good* bread maker. I guarantee it. I wish you could have seen my first three loaves. They were just awful. There was no way to eat them. I threw them out. They were small and hard as a rock. I hadn't managed to make the bread rise and then I overbaked it.

If you're an absolute beginner read this section to get your bearings, but then turn on a few pages to use some of the recipes for your first few tries. That will give you your bearings on the amounts involved. Then someday when you feel brave and very knowledgeable about the art of yeast bread making turn back here and see if you can make it from scratch like I do. Your basic procedure for from-scratch bread making is to start with a liquid, then add some form of yeast. A sweetening for the yeasties to feed on is not necessary but improves the bread's speed of rising and general taste. Then some shortening, salt if you want, other things in the fruit and vegetable kingdoms, and finally your flours.

LIQUID—The more liquid you start out with the more bread you'll end up with. Your basic choice is milk, water or fruit juice. Water bread has a wheaty flavor and a lovely crust. It keeps better than milk bread. If you make the bread with milk it has more food value and delicious flavor when fresh. Milk also gives it a fine texture. Using syrup, molasses or honey for your sweeteners will help make a moist bread that stays soft and edible longer than it would otherwise. Like I said above make sure your liquids are warm. Many people scald unpasteurized milk to destroy an enzyme that supposedly makes bread gummy. I gave up doing that years ago when I got rushed for time and couldn't seem to see the difference anyway. But maybe to somebody somewhere it would make a difference. To "scald" means to heat until bubbles form around the rim of the pan. Not to actually boil. Then you have the problem of getting it cooled down so you can proceed with the bread making. I used to solve that by plopping my butter, which was right out of the refrigerator, into the middle of the scalded milk. That way the butter melted and milk cooled and it pretty much came out right to have the yeast added.

YEAST can be sourdough (homemade) or store-bought Fleischmann's or Red Star. My favorite way to buy it is in the big quart cans that they sell at Warehouse Food. I buy them ahead. When I need to open one I just cut off the top with the can opener. It keeps fine. If you don't make bread so often you can buy those little foil packages of Fleischmann's yeast (if there's another brand I never heard of it). One package is the equivalent of one tablespoon of yeast in any recipe. When I was younger yeast was sold in moist foil-wrapped cakes. Those are pretty well off the market now, replaced by the "dry" yeast. When we used the yeast cakes, we had to crumble them into the warm liquid. With the dry yeast you just pour it in and stir it up. Yeast is a living organism. So don't pour real hot water in on top of it or you'll kill it. If it is too cold it won't do any work for you either. A temperature on the warmish side of lukewarm is best—110°-115°, they say.

It is important to have your bread liquid the right temperature when you add it to the yeast or the yeast to it—not just the liquid you dissolve the yeast in but all of it. Because if you throw a lot of cold milk or water you chill down the whole dough. You can warm a liquid very quickly and easily. It takes a long time for a dough to warm up once you've got the flour in.

A working yeast consumes some variety of sugar in order to manufacture its by-product—carbon dioxide bubbles. It's main product, of course, is more yeast and that's why the action may start slowly and then get faster. The more yeast you start out with, the faster it will do the rising. But given time enough even a little yeast can do the job. However, if you take too long a time wild yeasts will start working in there, and you may have a sourdough taste when you didn't plan on it. By too long I mean hours and hours.

SWEETENING is not absolutely necessary. Yeast could, if necessary, find food in the other ingredients. But it encourages the yeast and seems to make the bread more appealing to would-be eaters if there is some sweetness added. It can be any sort of sugar—white, brown, powdered, confectioners', candy dissolved in water or fruit juice left over from canned fruits that were canned with sugar (which is what I often use). Or it can be honey, maple syrup or molasses. The former being what I often add when my bees are doing well. Molasses in a brown bread recipe makes the crust softer and helps keep it moist as does honey or syrup. If you have something like raisins or any fruit in the bread it carries in quite a bit of sweetening on its own.

SHORTENING if you're doing it yourself would be lard or butter. Either one should be melted before adding. I don't go real heavy on the shortening, but if I try to do completely without the bread is too crumbly. If I have cooking oil I may pour a slurp of that in for my shortening. Bacon grease would work too.

SALT is invariably found in bread recipes. But I never use any in my bread. When the bread is spread with butter there's enough salt that way and I've never observed that it was needed. I can make perfectly delicious breads without salt.

OTHER THINGS—I've reached the point in my bread making where I don't make a bread without some "other things." A whole wheat bread is improved so much by the addition of a quite large part of fruit, vegetable or both. My bread is always whole wheat, so when I get ready to make bread I start out by a thorough search of the refrigerator and cupboards to see what I have—like cereals, or rice, or corn bread or crusts but especially things like plenty of eggs as we have in spring, or mashed potatoes, or cooked squash or pumpkin, or canned fruit like apricots or peaches. In egg season I can make a rich delicious bread resembling the famous Jewish Challah by putting in a dozen eggs. In winter I usually bake a dozen squash before bread time. I bake them whole. It's easier than trying to cut them. After baking they are easy to open. I take out the seeds and scoop out the rest for the bread. For special occasions I use a lot of fruit. I pit canned cherries and use them with apricots or whatever fruit I have lots of. Raisins and nuts, if you have them, will be a welcome addition to the bread too. Leftover vegetables are fine. It helps to mash things like carrots or cabbage before you put them in. My bread is never quite the same. I've turned out some batches that were so heavenly that I've been wishing ever since I could do it again.

I remember particularly one Christmas bread I made that was just loaded with applesauce. I think it also had some apple plum butter in it. We had Mike's boss and family for dinner. The boss told his wife to get that "recipe." I couldn't tell her how. I wished I knew myself. Sometimes we play guessing games on guests. What do you suppose is in the bread? They're unlikely to come up with such ingredients as the scrapings of a jar of peanut butter and half a box of tapioca. But I go very easy with ingredients like peanut butter and tomatoes. And I've never added meat although I suppose a person could if it were ground.

FLOUR—No matter how tough a strain of yeast you have, the only dough it can make rise is one with wheat flour in it. And the only part of the dough it can raise is the wheat flour part. You couldn't make barley flour or pea flour rise if you used a whole quart of yeast. White flour rises easier than brown flour. A mixture of brown flour and rolled oats and rye won't rise near as well as straight brown flour (which is made from wheat and the oats and rye aren't). Wheat flour has this "gluten" stuff in it that is like bubble gum I guess. When air gets blown into it it makes a bubble and holds it.

So to get a leavened bread (one that has "risen") you should have at least half your flour be wheat flour. But for the other half you can use all kinds of things. I've put leftover cooked cereals of all sorts into my bread, leftover puddings, dry cereals of all sorts that I figured weren't going to get eaten before they got stale, tapioca base, cornmeal, oatmeal, farina, every sort of flour you can think of and it usually turns out fine. My favorite flavor is a dollop of rye flour in the bread. Just a little adds a really nice taste. Breads that include barley flour or some such that won't leaven don't rise so high or easily but, on the other hand, they have a close-grained moist quality that keeps much longer than regular bread.

MATERIALS FOR BREAD MAKING are so simple. All you need is something to mix it in. For me that's a bucket. For you it could be any sort of bowl or pan. If you are working in an old fashioned kitchen substitute potato masher when you see "blender" in a recipe. And substitute eggbeater or big mixing spoon and some elbow grease for "electric mixer." A clock helps but it isn't necessary. You do need something to make it in and an oven to cook it. If things are grim, large size (46-ounce) juice cans with one end neatly removed can be used to make do for baking bread as can large coffee cans. If you have pie tins or Pyrex

oven-type plates you can make dough into large rolls and bake it that way. Or you can make rolls and bake in a loaf pan. It is nicest if you can bake in a regular bread-type loaf pan. Any size or shape is fine—big or small. Any material if you don't have a choice. If you have a choice I'll tell you my favorite is glass loaf pans, such as Pyrex, because you can see how the bottom crust is doing and get it out of there before it burns on the bottom. I'm not enthused about those coated metals like Teflon, and I can't bear anything enameled because I turn around twice and it's chipped and rusting.

While I'm on the subject I'll add that cast iron is my favorite for roasting and frying on top of the stove and stainless pots with copper bottoms are the absolute best for cooking, especially dealing with fruits, if you can afford them. They are practically eternal so it's a good investment. Aluminum is to be shunned. It tends to dent, the handles scorch, and it gets odd-looking with age, especially the coffeepots. The shiny metal, which I suppose you could call steel in the bread pan line, will start to rust as it gets older which isn't nice. But I keep using the pans anyway. The pottery cooking ware is great although it shares with glass the possibility of breaking. But it's pretty tough.

Any oven will bake bread. If you can't get your oven hot you can make biscuit-shaped things and cook them in a frying pan on top of the stove, turning once. Really very tasty!

PROCEDURE—Basically I just combine my yeast and milk or water or juice. Then add sweetening and shortening. Then add my vegetables and fruit and eggs or whatever odd ingredients. Now I take a second look to see if I have enough. If not I add more liquid to make it up to the amount of bread I want to end up with. The volume of the final dough batch will be the same as your liquid plus less than half. With luck that doubled will be your amount of baked bread, but I usually don't get it all risen that high.

Now I start adding flour. I mix it in with one hand, scooping with the other. Anybody else would use a spoon but I'm the sort to just plunge right in there with my fist. I end up that way, anyway. The odd variety flours and other dry ingredients go in first. Then the basic whole wheat flour since I want at least fifty percent of that. You learn when the dough has just the right amount of flour by experience. The feel of the dough will tell you when you have enough. And the looks of it.

Then knead, let rise, and so on.

THE SPONGE METHOD—If you use a starter or homemade yeast it's better to use the sponge method. To do this combine your homemade yeast, the liquids and just enough flour to make a batter that will drop from a spoon. Let that work and rise overnight. In the morning stir in the remaining flour and proceed with your kneading and so on. Some recipe books give you a sponge method for regular breads. It's a way of doing it but I don't really see the point with regular breads.

Kneading and raising the dough are factors that will make quite a difference in how you feel about your results—how smooth the texture is, how it holds together and how porous it is. So don't skimp on them. Actually I love to knead bread. It sort of affects me like milking a cow does: very calm, very peaceful, accomplishing something worth doing and no way to rush about it.

I've seen some really long kneading times recommended—as much as an hour in some old-time recipe books. They must have had hired help to do it. And I've seen as many as four risings suggested in some recipes. Like everything else I do, for better or for worse I've discovered the easiest and briefest method. The kneading should be done until the bread itself tells you it's done. You'll learn by experience. When it stops getting holes in it and feels silky. But remember white bread will cooperate the best with this kneading process. Other flours are progressively stickier, and if you added enough flour so they wouldn't be sticky, your bread would turn out too hard and dry so you just have to learn to knead a sticky dough. Rye is bad that way and whole wheat is worse than white. If you dip your hands into the flour bucket regularly it helps.

For a good rising of your bread you need a really warm kitchen. Too hot to be comfortable ordinarily. In summer that's no problem. In winter when I know I'm going to make bread I get the wood stove going especially strong. For small batches of bread I know people who set it in the oven with a pilot light or in a crock with a light bulb to get the right temperature.

Enough of the prelude. Here follows the . . .

AND SO ON OF BREAD MAKING—First work the dough in your bowl, bucket or whatever until it loses part of its stickiness. You are working it all into one big ball sort of as if you were working with clay. If you rub your hands together you can make little snakes of the dough between your fingers and they will drop off. Flour the place where you're going to knead. Any smooth surface will do. Turn the dough out of your container into the middle of your floured kneading surface.

Knead by pulling the dough side farthest from you up and then pushing it into the top center of your ball. When you pull the dough up, your hands are fingers down as if you were playing the piano or

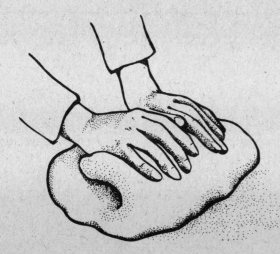

typewriting. You punch the pulled up dough into the center of your dough ball with the heels of your two palms. Give the whole ball of dough a quarter turn more or less, depending on how big it is to start with, then pull and punch again in the new place. Continue doing this as fast and continuously as you can. You'll really develop a rhythm for it after a while and it gets to be fun.

When you first begin the dough will be soft and sticky and without a smooth surface. The longer you knead the smoother the surface will be. It gradually loses much of the stickiness. If it doesn't, add more flour but beware of too much. Now for white bread when you get so you can knead on an unfloured dry board without immediately getting gummed up, the kneading may be considered done. When the surface of your dough ball breaks it means you haven't really gotten all the flour worked in yet and beware of adding more. With white flour you'll really notice when the magic moment arrives. It changes from a tough, undisciplined glob of something somewhat firmer than goop to a smooth, cooperative roundish mass. That's the time to quit and get it ready for a rising. If you are worried that you may have gotten too much flour in, there is nothing to be done about it now. You cannot add moisture after once creating your dough ball. Trying would make an awful unmanageable mess. That's experience talking. So be careful to start with less flour and gradually work up as you knead to the perfect combination.

THE FIRST RISING—I just leave mine in the middle of the table. I don't have to grease the top. There is so much dough there it just doesn't dry out. And also because I made such a moist dough anyway with all that stuff like squash and eggs and cherries in it. But for regular bread, especially a white bread, you must do a little more than this. Get ready a bowl that will hold twice the amount of dough you're looking at because you expect it to at least double. Lightly grease or oil that bowl and remove the ball to it. Lightly grease or oil the top of your dough ball. You can do that by putting it in the bowl, then sliding it over the upside down and the top that was on the bottom is now greased.

You grease the top because otherwise you may have a sort of crust before the bread ever sees the oven just from a drying out action. And that "crust" is hard to knead back in. Judge with your eye where the dough will be at on the bowl when it has doubled in amount. Cover with a clean cloth to keep specks and drafts from it and set it in a nice warm place. My dough has its own warmth because I used all that nice warm liquid and the kitchen is hot. Your smaller amount needs heat help from the outside because what heat it has it will tend to lose if your rising area is too cold. Eye the clock—on the average it would take an hour for the first rising. Of course, if you used a lot of nonwheat flour in the bread it may never get up to double. In that case have a notion in your head when to give up and go on to the next step of punching down.

TO PUNCH DOWN you observe that your dough is up as far as you are going to let it get and preferably not so far that it is sagging by itself. To test its readiness poke it with your fingers. If it springs back a little it can rise some more. If it collapses easily and stays down it's more than ready for punching. Shove your working fist into the middle of the puffed ball of dough and push down as far as you can go. Then with the same fist punch the rest of the dough over and into the middle. Turn the ball over, put your cloth back over it and let it rise again.

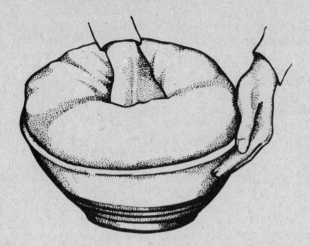

Now at this point comes a division in practice. I let it rest 15 minutes and during that time I'm getting the bread pans oiled and ready. Then I make my loaves, put them in the bread pans and set in a warm place to rise enough to be baked. If I'm in a tremendous rush for the first couple loaves (like if we are out of bread) I even let a couple loaves have the *first* rising in a bread pan and then bake which gives them a total first and last of only one rising. Using the system I'm going to describe you get two risings. Many, many people believe in a total of three—you let it rise, punch down, let it rise again, punch down, put in your bread pans, let rise and bake. I suppose the more you let it rise and then punch down, the finer grained the bread might be or something, but I've never had the time and it would tie up my kitchen table too long. Can't see any difference the times I let it have an extra rising either.

So after my bread has had its first rising I call the children and we start making rolls and loaves. There's more than one way to do either one. I use a bread knife to cut off what I figure is enough for a loaf from one side of the dough ball. I aim to get the bread pan just a little over half full so that when the bread doubles in amount it will just nicely rise over the top of the pan. I fold the cut edges of each loaf piece to the underside and pinch them together to make a seal, gently molding it at the same time into a vaguely rectangular shape. Then I lay it in the pan and press it down if it needs any more molding. If I goofed and haven't got enough dough, I cut off another piece and patch them together.

Virginia Boegli, who made the drawings for several editions of this book, has a much more sophisticated way of making loaves. She:

1. Flattens into a rectangle her piece of dough.
2. Stretches into a long strip by slapping dough on the table.

3. Folds into thirds, pressing out bubbles and sealing seams.
4. Folds up, starting on the long side. (The roll should be almost as long as your loaf pan.)
5. Pinches together ends and long seam.
6. Places in pan and greases the top.

I don't grease the top, never seem to think of it, but it is a good idea. Sometimes I butter the tops of white bread when it comes out of the oven. Just rub a hunk of butter over it. Makes a nice effect.

To make rolls I pull a handful of dough out of the dough ball and pinch the torn edges together at the bottom to seal. I pat it into shape and set in the oiled pan. Once in the pan, either loaves or rolls, set in a warm place until almost doubled in bulk. They can finish rising somewhat in the oven but can't do the whole thing since the heat will kill the yeasties.

BAKING—The oven should be about 350°. A white loaf cooks quicker than any other kind. Rolls are also pretty quick. Unleavened and sourdough breads take the longest. If it's a wood stove put a pie plate or some kind of lid above the bread to prevent burning the crust. Don't let the bread rise too long before baking it. You know you can have "fallen" bread the same as a cake. When the bubbles become big and visible and the whole affair looks spongy you are going to have a falling. Practice will help you know when the time to bake comes and when it is time to stop baking. When the crust is sort of golden brown and the loaf sounds hollow when you rap it with your knuckles (be quick as not to burn them!) or tap with your fingertips it should be done.

EATING—You are now in a class (upper) with the little red hen. Cut your homemade bread with a serrated (sort of a sawtooth) knife. Slice a half inch thick if it is white bread that rose good. Thinner otherwise. Spread it with room temperature (softened) butter or what you like. Never cut more than you can get eaten right away since white bread dries out very quickly and other kinds of bread dry out sooner or later. Keep the remainder of your loaf in a plastic bag. Bread will freeze and keep indefinitely so you can put the extra loaves in your freezer. Freeze immediately after baking and cooling for maximum freshness. Put in a plastic bag to retain moisture and soften the crust. If you wrap a loaf of bread that is fresh out of the oven in a dish towel while it is cooling you get a much nicer (softer) crust. Some bread types are hard to slice, crumbly and easily mashed when they are fresh out of the oven. They will be fine though after they have set over night and firmed up.

YEAST BREADS

The easiest bread to make is a basic white bread. I never use white flour now. But if you are just learning to make bread you might want to start with a recipe that uses 100 percent white flour or unbleached. It rises better and generally cooperates better. You can learn what you're doing with a white bread recipe and then move on to one that uses a heavier flour. Or you can just plunge in with any old recipe that takes your fancy. The enthusiasm will carry you over the difficulties. In case you want it, here follows the recipe I learned my first bread baking with.

Carla's White Bread—Scald 1 cup milk until there is a little rim of bubbles around the edge of the pan. Add 6 tablespoons sugar, 4 teaspoons salt and 6 tablespoons margarine or butter to the hot milk. (If the butter is fresh out of the refrigerator it will hasten the cooling process!) When the milk mixture has cooled to lukewarm you can proceed.

Into your big bread bowl (preferably a heavy crockery one) measure 3 cups of lukewarm water. Dissolve 2 packages yeast in the water. Add the milk mixture and about 5 cups of white flour. Mix until smooth. Keep adding flour until you have a kneadable dough. Flour your breadboard, turn the dough out onto it and commence kneading.

Allow the dough to continue to absorb flour and knead until it is smooth and elastic. You'll learn the feel of what you want. When it is ready, let it rest while you wash out the mixing bowl, dry, and then grease it inside very lightly. Put your dough into the greased bowl, turning it once to grease the top. Cover with a dish towel and leave in a warm place until it doubles in bulk (make a mental note of where it will have to get to be doubled in bulk).

When it has doubled, punch it down by sticking your fist into the middle of it. Then go get ready four bread pans. The conventional size is 9 x 5 x 3 inches but any vaguely approximate size will do. Cut the dough carefully into four sections. Take one section at a time and fold under to turn in the severed edges, seal and shape into a loaf. Put each loaf into a bread pan. Cover and allow to rise in your warm place again until doubled in bulk.

When doubled in bulk, bake in a preheated 400° oven about 30 minutes. You'll learn to tell by the color of your crust just when the golden moment comes. If the loaf sounds hollow when tapped, it's done. When done loosen the sides gently, if necessary, and turn out onto an oven grill to cool. Butter the top crust immediately for a softer crust.

Virginia's White Bread—Mix 2½ cups liquid, 3 tablespoons sugar, 1 tablespoon salt and 2 tablespoons shortening. Dissolve 2 envelopes (tablespoons) yeast in ¼ cup lukewarm water and add to other ingredients. Mix in with spoon, then by hand, 7 to 7¼ cups flour. Turn dough out on floured board and let rest a few minutes (about 10). Knead until smooth and elastic (8 to 10 minutes). Grease bread dough and put in a large bowl or pan such as a clean dishpan. Cover with a cloth and let raise in a warm place out of drafts until doubled in bulk.

You can test this by jabbing two fingers into the dough. If this causes the dough to slowly collapse it is ready to punch down. Punch and fold it into a firm ball and let rise again almost doubled in bulk. Divide into two pieces. Let dough rest on floured table 10 minutes. Shape into loaves. Put in pans. Grease. Let rise to just above top of loaf pans. Bake at 425° for 25 to 30 minutes. Turn out on racks to cool.

This dough may be used for sweet rolls, buns, cinnamon loaves, cheese or onion loaves by adding these ingredients when shaping the bread.

Grossmamma Baum's Basic Yeast Bread—Grossmamma lives in Seattle, Washington. She has used this basic recipe for more years than most of us have lived. "Each time I make bread it is a little bit different. Use the basic, toss in raw peanuts, sesame seed, sunflower seed, dried fruit. Use honey, molasses instead of sugar. Each time you have a new taste and texture. I won a blue ribbon at the Western Washington Fair last year, but if they asked me for the recipe I could only give them the basic recipe and say I put in a little of this and that."

(3 Loaves)	(4 Loaves)	(5 Loaves)
3 cups warm water	4 cups	5 cups
2 cakes yeast	2 cakes	2 cakes
½ cup sugar	¾ cup	1 cup
3 teaspoons salt	4 teaspoons	5 teaspoons
5 level tablespoons shortening	7 tablespoons	8 tablespoons
8 to 10 cups unsifted flour (usually much more)		

Dissolve yeast in warm water, add sugar, salt and shortening. Add flour until no more can be added. Dough should be elastic. Knead and place in warm place. Raise until double in size. Punch down and knead again—pinch into loaves. Let rise approximately 1 hour.

Bake at 350° for 40 minutes.

Wipe lightly over top of loaves with oil or shortening after removing from pans.

Whole Wheat Bread #1—Scald 2 cups milk and ¼ cup water. Add 2 teaspoons salt and ¼ cup honey (or molasses). Dissolve 2 tablespoons dry yeast in ½ cup warm water. When the milk mixture is lukewarm add it to the yeast mixture. Add 1 cup of rye flour and enough whole wheat flour to make a workable dough. Knead. Wash and grease bowl. Return dough to bowl and grease top. Let rise until doubled in bulk. Punch down and let rise again. Cut dough into two parts. Shape each into a loaf. Put loaves in greased pans and let rise until doubled in bulk. Bake at 375° for 35 to 40 minutes. Remove from pan. Butter top crust. Leave out the rye flour if you want.

Whole Wheat Bread #2—Scald ¾ cup milk until it

just gets bubbles around the rim. Add ⅓ cup butter, cut up to help it dissolve in the hot milk. When the butter is dissolved, add ¼ cup sugar, 1 tablespoon salt and ⅓ cup molasses. In your large bread mixing bowl dissolve 2 tablespoons dry yeast in 1½ cups lukewarm water. Add milk mixture, then 5 cups of whole wheat or graham flour (no need to sift). When that is well mixed add *white* flour enough to make a soft but kneadable dough.

Knead on floured board until it feels done (300 times maybe). Wash and grease your bowl. Return dough to it and let it rise until doubled in bulk. Punch down the dough. Grease 2 regular-size bread pans. Divide the dough in half and shape each half into a loaf. Put the loaves into the bread pans and let them rise again until doubled in bulk. Then bake at 400° about 30 minutes. Remove from pan to cool. You may need to slip a knife in at the side to loosen the loaf.

Rye Bread—The procedure is similar to the white and brown bread. Scald 1 cup milk. Add 1 tablespoon butter, then 3 tablespoons honey, 2 teaspoons salt and 1 tablespoon sugar. In your bread bowl dissolve 1 tablespoon yeast in ¾ cup warm water. Add the milk mixture. Then add 2½ cups rye flour. (If you want to add caraway seeds now's the time.) Mix well. Add enough *white* flour to make a soft but kneadable dough. Knead until done. Let rise, covered, in greased bowl until doubled in bulk. (It takes longer than the others to raise.) Punch down.

Cut the dough in half. Mold each half into a ball. Grease a cookie sheet and then sprinkle with cornmeal. Flatten the top of your ball a little and put the round loaves on the baking sheets (if you prefer an oval shape make that). Brush the loaves with 1 egg white beaten with 2 tablespoons of water. Let these loaves rise, then bake at 400° for 25 minutes.

Mrs. Arthur Johns's Oatmeal Bread—Soften 2 tablespoons yeast in ½ cup warm water and set aside. Combine 1½ cups boiling water, 1 cup oatmeal, ½ cup molasses, ⅓ cup shortening and 2 teaspoons salt. Cool to lukewarm. Add yeast. Stir in 2 cups white flour and 2 beaten eggs. Beat well. Add 4 cups more white flour (more or less) to make a soft dough. Grease top, cover tightly and refrigerate overnight. Shape into two loaves, let rise until doubled in bulk. Bake at 375° for 45 minutes.

French Bread—(For people who don't like to knead bread dough.) Combine 2½ cups warm water and 2 tablespoons dry yeast. Add 2 teaspoons salt and 1 tablespoon melted butter. Add flour to make a dough (about 7 cups—no need to sift). The dough will be on the sticky side. Turn out of your bowl long enough to wash and then grease it. Put the dough back into the bowl, grease the top of it and let rise, covered, until it has doubled in bulk. Flour your breadboard.

Divide the dough in half and roll out each half with your rolling pin into a rectangle about ¼ inch thick. Now roll up the dough as if you are making a jelly roll, beginning at a wide side. Make the roll as tight as possible and when all done seal the edges by pinching as tight as possible. Grease your cookie sheet and then sprinkle it with cornmeal. Put the

loaves of French bread on it, spread a dish towel across them and let rise until doubled in bulk. Bake at 450° for 30 minutes.

The Penn View Christian School Ladies' Mashed Potato Doughnuts—Put 1½ cups lukewarm potato water in a large bowl. Add 1 tablespoon dry yeast, dissolve and let rest 5 minutes. Add ⅔ cup sugar, 1½ teaspoons salt. Mash potatoes and measure 1 cup. With the mashed potato mix ⅔ cup shortening and 2 eggs. Beat together until well mixed and then add to yeast mixture. Add 7½ cups flour. Mix and pour onto floured board to knead. Knead until smooth. Cover and let rise 1½ hours. Punch down and let rise again for ½ hour.

Roll on floured surface until ¼ inch thick. Cut with doughnut cutter. Place on flat pan until doubled in bulk, or until the top is puffed up without wrinkles—about 45 minutes at 85°. Fry in hot fat (350°-375°). Put the top side of doughnut in fat first. Brown on both sides, 1 to 1½ minutes per side. Remove. Drain.

Coat with granulated sugar while hot if you like. Or sprinkle with confectioners' sugar when cold.

No-Fry Doughnuts—Just as if you were making bread combine 2 packages yeast, ¼ cup warm water, ½ cup scalded lukewarm milk, ½ cup sugar, 2 eggs, 1 teaspoon salt, ⅓ cup shortening, 1 teaspoon nutmeg, 4½ cups flour and ½ teaspoon cinnamon. Knead, cover and let rise for 50 to 60 minutes. Turn onto floured board and roll with a rolling pin until it is about ½ inch thick. Cut with a doughnut cutter and carefully lift with a spatula onto a greased cookie sheet. Brush with melted butter. Let rise until doubled in bulk. Bake at 425° for 8 to 10 minutes. Brush with more butter. Dust with cinnamon and sugar. From the kitchen of Cathy Frame.

Doris Gronewold's Own Original Recipe for Brown Bread—Scald 3½ cups (goat's) milk. Add ¼ cup shortening, 6½ tablespoons sugar, 2½ tablespoons salt to this and cool to lukewarm. Set aside 4 teaspoons coarse dry yeast dissolved in 1 cup of warm water. Then add 1 cup of wheat bran (which is finely ground). Add yeast. Then finish off with whole wheat flour—9 cups or so. Let rest 10 minutes, then knead for 10 minutes. Let this rise 2 hours. Punch down, let rise 1 hour again. Shape into four loaves. Let rise 1 hour. Bake in hot oven, 425°. This bread is very moist and a good moist keeper. Doris's children love it as toast, too, with jam and butter.

Yeast Rolls—In preparation: measure 6½ cups flour. Combine 2 cups warm water (110°-115°), 2 packages yeast and dissolve well. Now add ⅓ cup sugar, 1 tablespoon salt, 2 cups flour, 2 eggs and ⅓ cup shortening. Beat for 1 minute. Mix together well and let rest 20 minutes. Work in remaining flour (4½ cups approximately). Shape dough into a long roll on floured board. Cut half of recipe into 16 equal-sized pieces. Shape each into a ball. Lay the balls on a greased pan. Let rise, covered, for 45 minutes or longer. Bake at 375° for 30 minutes. Brush tops with melted butter and serve hot.

English Muffins—Dissolve 1 package dry yeast in 1½ cups warm water. Add 3 tablespoons sugar, ½ cup powdered milk, 1 teaspoon salt, 1 beaten egg and 3 tablespoons butter. When that is well mixed add about 4 cups flour. Let rise until doubled in bulk. Punch down. Shape into muffin shapes—flatten them enough. Oil a griddle and then scatter a little cornmeal on it. Fry them on the griddle like a pancake. Turn them over when one side is done to get the other side done. Serve warm. If you have trouble getting them done in the middle you can slice in half and fry those insides too to finish the job.

OF SOURDOUGH BREADS AND STARTERS

I hate to say it but there's a certain element of hoax potential in this sourdough business. You don't have to send away for a starter or get it from a friend and then struggle to keep it going. If you have a special interest in keeping a special starter going, OK. (Incidentally you can package it in baggies and freeze indefinitely.) But anybody who wants an *authentic* and *usable* starter and who lives in a normal (food around and air circulating) environment rather than a totally antiseptic one (an operating room) need only mix a cup of flour with a cup of water and leave it covered with a light cloth up to 5 days. If you have trouble getting it started, add some yogurt.

The time of year and the part of the country you live in will be a factor. A sourdough-carrying miner trekking to the Klondike in the dead of winter might do well to cherish his starter. On the other hand I have a friend in Georgia who gets not only wild yeast but wild mold in hers with no trouble at all. The more southerly, humid, and summerishly you are located the quicker the starter will go.

Starters will vary in sourness. The thickness will make a difference too. Too thin a sponge will tend to work real fast and burn itself out, while too thick a one works too slow. You will have to learn to kind of keep an eye on it and adjust as you go.

Wild yeasts are always in the air, in soil, and on containers. They cause a fermenting action like that of tame yeast. Acetic bacteria are always in the air, too. They take the alcohol produced by yeasts and break it down further to make vinegar. That's why your juice turns first to wine and then to vinegar. And that's why your sourdough batter needs to be used at least *twice* a week and replenished to keep it from becoming *too* sour. You don't need salt, sugar or store-bought yeast to make a starter. Flour and water (or leftover cereal or really any *food* and water) will do it.

Liquid yeast is a light color and looks foamy or effervescent when it is good. It has a sharp, biting flavor and an odor similar to very weak ammonia. If the liquid yeast has a sour odor or looks watery it isn't good. If in doubt you can test your liquid yeast by taking a small quantity, adding a little flour to it and setting it in a warm place. If fermentation begins within 15 or 20 minutes you have good yeast. With very active yeast, stir it down when it nears the top of your container. If you want you can strain your finished product and keep it in the refrigerator until wanted.

Sourdough starter can be started from commercial yeast but over a period of time it will probably contain a lot of wild yeasts too. You can buy sourdough starter or get some from a friend but the easiest way of all is to start your own. Sourdough bread is not as light as regular yeast bread but some people, including me, enjoy its slightly sour flavor and fine compact texture. Keep your starter in a warm spot. It takes 2 to 5 days to get the sour, bubbly effect that tells you it's ready to work for you. A glass jar is a fine container.

SOURDOUGH STARTERS FROM SCRATCH

1. *Glen Howerton's Sourdough Starter*—Mix a cup of flour with a cup of water. Leave it covered with a light cloth in a warm place. As soon as it starts to "boil," that is, ferment, it is ready to use in bread. The more you use it the better your bread will turn out. When you want more just add flour and water to get it as full as you want.

2. *Milk and Water Starter*—Mix a cup of unpasteurized milk with a cup of flour. If your milk is pasteurized let it stand 24 hours first. Leave covered with a light cloth in a warm place.

3. *Starter with Commercial Yeast*—Mix a cup of flour, a cup of water and a package of dry yeast.

4. *Hazel's Starter*—Use: 1 package dry yeast, 2½ cups warm water, 1 tablespoon sugar, 1 tablespoon salt, 2 cups sifted flour.

Dissolve yeast in ½ cup lukewarm water. Let stand 10 minutes. Stir, add remaining water, sugar, salt and flour. Mix well. Let stand in a covered bowl for 3 days at room temperature (78° to 80°). Container should be big enough to let starter rise to about 4 times its starting size. Stir down every day.

TO REPLACE STARTER AS IT IS USED add 1 cup lukewarm water, ½ cup flour and 1 teaspoon sugar. Cover and let stand until ready to use. If not used often enough to keep active divide into 1-cup portions and freeze in baggies.

Once your sourdough batter is really good from constant use, or if you started with number 3 above, keep your sourdough jar in the refrigerator if you don't plan to use it so often. The sourdough will eventually separate with a liquid on the top. When you want to use it just stir it up and go ahead. The sour smell is natural.

COOKING WITH A SOURDOUGH STARTER for leavening usually begins with a sponge made the night before. A typical sponge would be made by putting a cup of your starter in a bowl, mixing with 2 cups of warm water and 2½ cups of flour. Mix well and let rest in a warm place overnight. In the morning before you proceed with your recipe put a cup of your sponge back into your starter jar—it's this act that makes your starter get better with time and this is why you should use it at least twice a week. An alternative is to "feed" your starter with sweet or floury scraps. This is to give occupation to yeast and so prevent the starter from being taken over by acetic bacteria. Even if your batter has eggs, sugar and salt in it you can still put back 1 cup into your starter jar and *must* to keep your starter going. If you don't want to put any of your batter back just mix up a cup of flour with a cup of water and add that to the sourdough jar to replace what you borrowed.

If your starter does turn undesirable on you, seeming just too weak, throw it out and make a new one. Or try an old fashioned liquid yeast recipe for a change. The principle is the same except that the sourdough pot has a more colorful reputation than the liquid starter which housewives didn't try to keep going. They simply made it and then used it unless they made homemade cakes from dried yeast. If you're going on vacation or are tired of baking you can freeze your starter for long periods of time and have it wait for you.

HOMEMADE YEAST CAKES

If you're using homemade yeast you may find it is overactive in warm weather. These yeast cakes should keep five months or so.

Homemade Yeast Cakes from Your Liquid Yeast—Mix 2 cups lively liquid yeast, 1 tablespoon salt and 1 tablespoon wheat flour. Let the batter rise until light. Then stir in enough cornmeal to make a stiff dough. Let rise again. Roll very thin. Cut into 3-inch squares. Dry in the shade in clear, windy weather or in a warm (but not hot) oven. Turn often to prevent souring. When dry, tie in a bag and hang in a cool, dry place. To use soak in warm water, about 2 cups per 3-inch square of homemade yeast cake and when dissolved go ahead with your recipe. The 3-inch square will leaven 16 cups of flour. For less flour, use less yeast and less water.

Homemade Yeast Cakes Made from Hops and Store Yeast—You can buy hops at a health food store put up for "tea." Boil a handful of the hops in 4 cups water for 30 minutes. Then mix in ½ cup whole wheat flour and let cool to lukewarm. Now add 3 packages of dry yeast (or 1½ cups homemade liquid yeast). Let rise until very light. Thicken with cornmeal until stiff. Roll thin. Cut into 3-inch cakes. Dry as above.

Violet's Yeast Cakes—Take either dry or moist yeast cakes. Dissolve in warm water—never hot which would kill the beasties. Add a couple quarts more warm water and mix in dry cornmeal and a little flour. Get it as stiff as you can work it. Press out in a dry pan rinsed with cold water. Press down smooth with hands. Set to dry. Cut it before it is too dry. When it is dry wrap in paper and put away until you need yeast cakes and use as any store-bought dry yeast. It will last a year at least. If you put a cake in warm water for a few minutes and it does not bubble or look a little foamy it is just like any dry yeast that has lost its strength.

SOURDOUGH RECIPES

You can make all kinds of things with a sourdough starter. I've been really enthused about sourdough baking in the past so I can hardly wait to pass on to you quite a collection of recipes. I hope you have as good luck with them as I did. I really love all the basic sourdough breads. And I think there's no other bread as good as these for digestibility. They are all sour, moist and heavy and my children hate them except when spread with butter and toasted, especially under a broiler. So your family may find them too strange, too. But they can get used to them.

There are certain breads that improve with age and unleavened and sourdough breads are like that. So are fruit breads like banana, squash bread and fruitcake. If you put them in the freezer in a plastic bag they'll improve somewhat with age. They may seem milder after a week than they did immediately after baking. Sourdough breads don't need to be frozen though. They will keep moist for quite a while. Even if you don't have a plastic bag to store the loaf in or even a metal bread box don't worry if it's sourdough bread. Tomorrow just cut off the first slice and give it to the chickens for breakfast. The next slice will be moist and just right.

You can order a really good little book of sourdough recipes from Giulieri and Carlile, 9 Fawn Creek Court, Pleasant Hill, California 94523. I can't remember just how much it is but not much—like a couple dollars. It's a self-published book like mine (but mine is self-printed too).

To serve sourdough bread I trim off the crust if it's hard. Then I spread the slice with butter and leave it under the broiler long enough to melt the butter, warm the bread through and just start to toast the top. It's a great winter breakfast.

These recipes are appropriate for *my* starter which is the 1 cup flour–1 cup water kind. That's a very liquid starter and if you are using one that has proportionately more flour to the water you don't want to add as much other liquid when you make the recipe. My sourdough recipes are also adapted to a starter which is replenished almost every day meaning that it isn't awfully sour. It won't take the quantity of soda recommended in some people's sourdough recipes. Personally I vastly prefer the sour taste to a soda taste so I use a minimum of soda when trying out new recipes. You can usually safely cut the amount of soda they say in half.

Most sourdough bread recipes now circulating cheat by including packaged yeast in the recipe. I'm a purist and haven't given you any of that kind. I want *real* sourdough breads. When you are waiting for your dough bread to rise keep it in a very warm (but not hot) place and be patient. In my experience sourdough takes longer to start rising. It just sits there looking lifeless and helpless until you are ready to despair and then suddenly next time you look it's off and going. Then you can let it rise, punch down, let it rise again, punch down, shape into loaves or biscuits and let it rise again with no trouble at all. Or leave out one rising if you're rushed. The old-timers for whom bread and milk was a *meal*, usually supper (and sometimes breakfast too), took a lot of trouble with their bread. They usually let it rise three times altogether in order to get the lightest grain possible.

Sourdough Pancakes—The night before make sure that you're going to have enough starter for this. If necessary make more. By morning it will be ready enough. Mix 2 cups starter, 2 cups flour, 2 beaten eggs, 1 tablespoon sugar, ½ teaspoon salt, 2 tablespoons melted butter or oil and enough milk to make a good pourable batter (about 1½ cups depending on how thick your starter is). Lastly, add ½ teaspoon baking soda, mix well, then let it rest a few minutes. Heat your griddle or frying pan and shine it with oil before each panful of pancakes. Fry on medium heat. Make them dollar size for best results and be sure they are cooked through.

Incidentally, you can't make good pancakes in a big pan on a little burner. You need even heat and *heat* over the entire bottom of your pan. And sourdough pancakes are even sourer if underdone. If you have batter left over, you can refrigerate it a couple days, then add a pinch of soda, enough milk to make it the right consistency again and make more pancakes.

Sourdough Whole Wheat Pancakes—The night before combine 2½ cups whole wheat flour, 2 cups water and ½ cup starter. This makes a lot of pancakes. If you have a small family cut the recipe in half. In the morning add 2 beaten eggs, 2 tablespoons oil or melted butter, ½ teaspoon salt, 2 tablespoons honey and milk enough to make an easily pourable pancake batter (probably about 1 cup). Then add 1 teaspoon soda and mix well. Let it set a few minutes. Heat a griddle or frying pan moderately, shine it before each panful of cakes, make dollar-sized cakes and cook them through.

Sourdough Soda Bread—The night before mix together 1½ cups starter and 1½ cups warm water. Let work until morning. In the morning add ½ teaspoon soda and mix well. Then add ¼ cup melted butter, ½ cup sugar and 1 teaspoon salt. Add enough flour for a kneadable dough. Knead into shape, let rise, punch down and let rise a second time. Again punch down and shape into loaves. Put the loaves into your greased loaf pan, let rise again. Bake in a moderate oven.

Sourdough Whole Wheat Bread—This is a variety bread. It has quite a strong taste when first made, but mellows a little with time. Makes a good appetizer or sampler, unless you really love strong dark breads. The night before combine 4½ cups whole wheat flour, 1 cup starter and 3¾ cups lukewarm water. In the morning add 1 teaspoon soda, ½ cup oil, 2 teaspoons salt and enough more whole wheat flour to make a kneadable dough (about 5 cups). The dough tends to be sticky. This will make 2 loaves. Cut your kneaded dough into two parts. Make each into a loaf and put into a greased loaf pan. Let rise in pan until almost doubled in bulk or till it is a little above the top of the pan. Keep in a very warm place for the rising. (Maybe 2 hours.) Bake 20 minutes at 425°, then at least an hour longer at 375°.

Hazel's Sourdough Bread—Ingredients:

½ cup milk or water (I use skim milk)
1 cup starter (use Hazel's)
2 tablespoons sugar
2 or 3 cups sifted flour
2 tablespoons shortening

Scald milk, add sugar, shortening and stir. Cool mixture to lukewarm and add starter. Stir in flour (add enough flour to make a medium dough). Put onto floured board or flat surface, knead about 10 minutes of hard work. Put into greased bowl and brush top lightly with melted shortening or cooking oil. Cover with a cloth and let stand in a warm place (80° to 85°) with no draft on it, for about 1½ to 2 hours, or until doubled in bulk. Punch down with spread fingers and let rise again to double size (about half an hour). Punch down as before, let it rest about 10 minutes, then shape into loaves. Put loaves in small greased loaf pans. Let stand until doubled in bulk, takes about 1 hour. Bake about 30 to 40 minutes in a 400° oven. Just before putting bread in oven, put a pot of already boiling water in oven for 5 minutes. For a rich brown crust, brush with egg whites or milk—I use milk.

Sourdough Rye Bread—The night before combine 1 cup starter, 3¾ cups warm water, 2 cups rye flour and 2½ cups white flour. Let it set in a warm place. In the morning take ½ cup oil, 2 teaspoons salt, ½ teaspoon soda and add that to the sponge. Stir it up. Add 5½ cups rye flour and 1 cup white flour. Knead 5 minutes. The dough is softer and stickier than regular bread. Divide into loaves (depends on the size of your pan—I made 3) and place in oiled bread pans. Slit tops lengthwise down the middle. Put it in a very warm room and give it as much as 5 hours and try to get it up at least 50 percent. (It rises soon after it goes into the oven.) Brush tops with water. Bake in preheated 425° oven 20 minutes. Brush tops with water. Continue baking at 375° oven for 1¼ hours.

Sourdough French Bread—This bread is very crusty. It is good sliced, buttered and heated under the broiler. The night before make your sponge of 4½ cups flour (white or whole wheat mixed with it), 2 cups starter, 3 cups water and enough flour to make a kneadable dough.

Shape into your French loaf. This recipe makes 2 loaves. Put them side by side, seam side down, on a cookie sheet that has been sprinkled with cornmeal. Let rise until you get a decent expansion—maybe 3 hours. The loaves may tend to spread out rather than rise. In that case bake them before they start drooping over the edge of the cookie sheet! Bake at 425° oven for 20 minutes and then at 375° for 1 hour.

Sourdough French bread is sliced about an inch thick somewhat on the diagonal. It tastes best to me buttered and toasted briefly on the top side under the broiler.

Plain Brown Sourdough Bread—The night before you plan to bake, mix 4½ cups whole wheat flour, 1 cup starter and 3¾ cups lukewarm water. In the morning your sponge will be light and bubbly. Add to it ½ teaspoon soda, ½ cup oil, 2 teaspoons salt and enough flour to make a kneadable bread dough (about 5 cups, but the exact amount will vary with how thick your starter was). But be forewarned—the dough will stick to your hands more than usual kneaded bread. Knead about 5 minutes. Form into loaves. This recipe will make two 1-pound loaves. Oil your bread pans.

Let the bread rise in the pans until it is about a third larger. The exact amount of time needed will vary. Keep it in as pleasantly warm a place as you can. It will need 2 hours at least. Brush the tops with water when you are ready to bake. Bake 20 minutes in a preheated 425° oven and then at least an hour at 375°. I like this bread best hot from the oven buttered or wrapped in foil, plastic, or paper tightly for two days until the crust and center equalize their moisture. The same dough can be used for whole wheat muffins.

Sourdough Applesauce Cake—Mix 1 sourdough starter, 1 cup applesauce, 1½ cups white flour and ¼ cup milk. In a separate bowl cream ¼ cup lard, ½ cup white sugar and ½ cup brown sugar. Add 1 beaten egg, ½ teaspoon cinnamon, ¼ teaspoon cloves, ¼ teaspoon nutmeg, ¼ teaspoon allspice, a pinch of salt and 2 teaspoons soda. Combine this bowl with the contents of the other. Add a handful of dates, raisins, nuts or what you like. Bake 1 hour in a moderate oven. Let the cake cool in the pan and then turn it out upside down carefully because it is very fragile. It will be a moist, delicate treat. If you are a spice lover you can double all the spice amounts.

Sourdough Spiced Oatmeal Cookies—Cream 1 cup lard with 1½ cups brown sugar. Add 1½ cups sourdough starter and 3 cups rolled oats. Sift together 1½ cups flour, ½ teaspoon salt, 1 teaspoon soda, 1 teaspoon cinnamon and ½ teaspoon *each* cloves and allspice. Add dry ingredients to first bowl, mix well and chill in the refrigerator a couple of hours. Tear off pieces of dough and pat into cookie shapes or roll out on floured board and use your cookie cutter. Bake on greased cookie sheets 18 minutes at 400°. The exact time will be affected by how big and thick you make them.

Sourdough Cornmeal Cakes—Beat well together 4 cups flour, 2 cups cornmeal, ½ cup milk, ½ cup starter, 3 eggs and 2 teaspoons salt. Let rise overnight in a warm place. Bake on a griddle in the morning.

SALT RISING BREADS

Of all things I've tried to do in the old-time way, most have turned out fine. Vinegar, home-cured hams and salt rising breads are the only three I can think of that really gave me a hard time. In the case of vinegar, Mrs. Eggers made it so it can be done. In the case of hams I finally did get the information I needed. (Coaxed it out of a handsome custom cutter who probably would be unhappy with me if he knew it was for a book. I really pride myself on being an honest and forthright person, but I was desperate after three years of struggle and failure with the Ham Problem.)

Salt rising bread is merely a bread recipe with a self-enclosed starter. The problem is that they insist that the whole thing has to get going so *fast*. And I wonder just what the mystique of the salt really is, because salt actually inhibits bacterial growth. But I have heard that "salt rising" is a term that started out being "self rising" and it just got copied wrong way back when and maybe that is the explanation. My impression is that the wild yeasts and bacteria are the same for salt rising bread as for regular sourdough bread. The difference is that the sourdough maker gives his starter a *real* chance to get going. Then he holds back part of it for another day and makes bread with the rest. The salt rising bread maker makes a starter, then incorporates it in the bread and it is supposed to rise and be baked within 12 hours.

Some people think that salt rising bread is an attempt to catch a different microscopic organism from the sort you usually get in sourdough bread. Maybe so. But since my early struggles two people in the world have written me how to do it. One is J. O. Pettit, a gourmet hobby cook from Los Angeles. He says his recipes work for him about 3 out of 7 times. The other is a housewife, Janet Harestead of Eagle Point, Oregon. She says anyone can make it. Since J. O. can do it 3 out of 7 times and Janet can do it always, I'm letting *them* teach you how just as they told me in their letters.

Here is Mrs. Harestead's letter: "To make salt rising bread you *must* have raw milk, not pasteurized, and you *must* have fresh ground corn, not store-bought cornmeal because the bacteria have been sterilized out of packaged cornmeal. If you have a gas stove use the pilot light to keep your dough warm. If your stove is electric put it on a oven in a little covered quart crock. They are about $2 at the hardware with lids. From then on anyone can make it.

"Ingredients—4 cups raw milk, ½ cup coarse, white or yellow cornmeal, 1 tablespoon sugar, 5 tablespoons lard, ¾ teaspoon salt and 11 cups sifted flour.

"Scald 1 cup milk and pour over cornmeal. Let stand in a warm place to ferment. It takes about 24 hours. Heat 3 cups milk with sugar, lard and salt *only* until lukewarm. Stir in 3½ cups flour and then cornmeal mixture. Place bowl containing these ingredients in pan of lukewarm water for about 2 hours, or until bubbles work up from the bottom. Then stir in 5 cups of flour and knead in 2½ cups more. Place dough in three 5 x 10-inch pans.

"Let rise until doubled in bulk. Bake in moderate oven, for about 10 minutes. Then increase heat to moderately hot oven, gradually. Bake bread 45 to 60 minutes in all. Do not attempt to bake bread in cold damp weather, unless house is heated and you do not have drafts. Be sure to protect the starter from chill drafts.

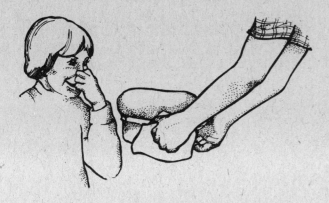

"If the starter turns to custard consistency your oven is too hot. It stinks very much and while baking it can drive some people out of the house. But it's all worth the bad smell and trouble, believe me. For I think it's the finest bread, especially toasted and served hot with fresh butter. My grandmother has baked it ever since who knows when. And it's a treat to receive a couple of loaves from her for Christmas or anytime. Please try this. The reward is worth the stink and trouble. (I used to bake other breads my husband called bricks run over by trucks.)"

Mr. Pettit, 63 years old, is an industrial psychologist by profession, and was born in Bisbee, Arizona. He says of salt rising bread: "The 'starter' can be extremely temperamental, and more often than not it refuses to start. For one thing it must have a higher temperature than for yeast—around 115° or 120°—and that temperature must be maintained for several hours, often 10 or 12. You have probably discovered

that there are two kinds of starters—one made with scalded milk, cornmeal, sugar and salt, and the other made with sliced raw potatoes, cornmeal, sugar and salt over which boiling water is poured. The raw potato formula 'starts' more easily than the other, but it generates an odor which I find most unpleasant, though it does not affect the finished product; the bread made with either formula looks, tastes, and smells the same, both having a mild and pleasantly cheeselike odor and flavor most esteemed by those of us who like this particular bread.

"Since holding a steady temperature around 120° is a must, I discovered not long ago that one of these electrically-heated quart containers for making yogurt at home works beautifully. Set the yogurt maker on a hot-pad (so it will not be sitting on a cold surface) and cover it with a tea towel to boost the temperature to as near 120° as possible. In the second stage, when the starter is mixed with flour and additional liquid for the first rising, set the bowl in an oven which is kept faintly warm by its pilot light. What people do who do not have gas ovens with pilots I do not know. A batch of salt rising bread can easily conk out on you at this stage if it is not kept warm enough, and I have even had it conk out for the same reason when in the baking pans for the final rising.

"Fresh stone-ground cornmeal, such as can be bought in so-called health stores, will work better than cornmeal bought in the supermarkets. I have never known the reason for the cornmeal in the starters, but I have a suspicion that the little critter responsible for the ferment frequently nests in it. I have almost never been able to get a starter to 'start' using regular 'store-bought'n' (supermarket) cornmeal. The packages state that the meal has been 'degerminated' to assure the consumer that the product will remain fresh. This is a lot of b.s., it has been degerminated because the manufacturer can make a fat profit out of the oil which can be extracted from the corn germ, what the consumer gets is a processed product with decreased food value! So the bugs in health food cornmeal are not processed to death, and starters will start from it. Sometimes, anyhow.

"The main trick is in keeping the starter and succeeding stages warm enough (around 120°) to maintain the beast responsible for the ferment in a happy frame of mind. No, I don't think the organism is the same one that forms starters for sourdough breads. That one is one of the lactobacilli. It and its relatives, as you probably already know, are responsible for the formation of lactic acid in sour milk, naturally fermented dill pickles, sauerkraut and such, which gives them their distinctively sharp tastes. They are easier to get started and considerably less temperamental than the one involved in salt rising bread. The latter is probably also an organic-acid-forming organism, but I suspect that its acid is more closely related to isovaleric (which is found in elderly cheese and comes close to smelling—pardon the expression—like unwashed feet) than to lactic acid. This, of course, is just a speculation on my part."

J. O.'s Salt Rising Bread #1—Starter: Put in a suitable jar (a 12-ounce jam or pickle jar is recommended) ¼ cup of yellow or white cornmeal (preferably fresh stone-ground, generally available in so-called health food stores), 1 teaspoon salt, 1 tablespoon sugar, ¼ teaspoon baking soda, 1 cup scalded milk.

Stir well, sit the jar in a pan of hot water and place in a very warm spot, such as an oven in which a pilot light is burning, or even better, in one of the relatively inexpensive quart-size electrically heated yogurt makers. Sit the yogurt maker on a pot holder so that it will not be in contact with a cold surface, and cover with a folded dish towel to help hold the temperature near 120°. Let stand overnight until well fermented and very bubbly. This can take anywhere from 8 to 14 hours, and generally 10 to 12. The starter should have a marked but not unpleasant odor, rather like that of a sharp Cheddar cheese. If it has not fermented at the end of 14 hours or so, throw it out and try again some other time!

After the starter is well fermented pour it into a mixing bowl and add:

1 cup warm water, 1 teaspoon salt, 1 tablespoon sugar, 2 tablespoons melted shortening or salad oil (Mazola, Wesson, etc.), 2 cups all-purpose flour.

Mix well, cover the top of the mixing bowl with plastic wrap and set the bowl in a pan of very hot water.

Place in the oven or other warm place to rise until very light and bubbly. This can take from 1 to 2 hours. When the batter has reached this stage sift in 3 cups all-purpose flour and mix well.

Turn out on a well-floured board and knead for 7 or 8 minutes, adding flour to the board as needed to prevent sticking. (Some of the cornmeal will work out of the dough as you knead it; this is normal.)

When smooth and elastic, shape into two loaves and place in well-greased small-sized bread pans (8½ x 4½ x 2½ inches). Cover pans with a dish towel and place in a warm place to raise until at least doubled in bulk. This can take as long as 2 hours. Bake in a preheated 350° oven for 40 minutes, or a little longer until golden brown. Turn out of pans to cool. The texture of this bread is finer and more compact than that of ordinary yeast breads, and it should be sliced a little thinner. Keeps well for 2 or 3 weeks if wrapped and refrigerated.

J. O.'s Salt Rising Bread #2—Starter: Peel and slice very thin into a 1 or 2 quart-sized glass casserole

1 medium-sized potato (preferably a Russet). To the sliced potato add:

1 tablespoon sugar, 1 teaspoon salt, 2 tablespoons yellow or white cornmeal (preferably fresh stone-ground obtainable from so-called health food stores), 2 cups boiling water.

Mix well, place the lid on the casserole and wrap the dish in a heavy terry cloth bath towel. Put in a warm place to ferment, such as an oven which has a pilot light burning. Let stand overnight until very bubbly. This can take from 8 to 14 hours, and very often 10 to 12. At this stage the starter will have an odor vaguely like that of sharp Cheddar cheese.

After fermenting, remove the potatoes from the casserole and pour the remaining liquid into a mixing bowl and add:

1 cup very warm milk, 1 teaspoon salt, 1 tablespoon sugar, ⅛ teaspoon baking soda, 3 tablespoons melted shortening or salad oil (Mazola, Wesson, etc.), 2 cups all-purpose flour.

Mix well until smooth, cover the top of the mixing bowl with plastic wrap and set the bowl in a pan of very hot water.

Place in oven or other warm place to rise until very light and bubbly. This can take 1 or 2 hours. When the batter has reached this stage sift into it 3½ cups all-purpose flour and mix well.

Turn out on a well-floured board and knead for 7 or 8 minutes, adding flour to the board as needed to prevent sticking. (Cornmeal will work out of the dough as it is kneaded; this is normal.) When the dough is smooth and elastic, shape into two loaves and place in well-greased small-sized bread pans (8½ x 4½ x 2½ inches). Cover pans with a dish towel and place in a warm place to rise until at least doubled in bulk. This can take 2 hours or so. Bake in a preheated 375° oven for 10 minutes; then reduce heat to 350° and bake for 30 to 35 minutes longer until golden brown. Turn out of pans to cool. The texture of this bread will be finer and more compact than that of ordinary yeast breads, and it should be sliced a little thinner. Makes an excellent toast having a mildly cheeselike flavor and odor. Keeps well for two or three weeks if wrapped in plastic and kept in the refrigerator. *Note:* If the starter has not fermented at the end of 12 or 14 hours, discard it and try again some other time.

CRACKERS

Cracker recipes at first I had trouble finding. But finally I got together a really nice selection. There is a hardtack recipe in the Definitions section near the end of this book. I think it's more a historical curiosity than a genuine edible at this point. Be sure to roll any cracker dough out to uniform thickness so it will brown evenly in the oven. My real favorites, though, are the ones where you make bread first and then slice and toast it to make your "cracker." That's zwieback which is delicious, healthy, and perfect for teething babies, and rye melba crackers. You can actually make this sort of cracker out of any homemade bread. Just slice, toast, and you have a "cracker." Cracker just means flat dry bread.

If your crackers are good and dry and you store them in an airtight container, they should keep as long as a month. If you are making crackers for storing use vegetable oil instead of butter in the recipe since butter crackers get stale faster. You can freeze crackers but in the freezer they may soak up a little dampness that will affect their crispness. There are some kinds of crackers that are best not stored—those that have a little dampness in them and taste better that way.

Home cracker making is a lost art I'd like to see revived. It's a lot healthier than feeding the children half food, half cookies. You can make it half food, half crackers. And on their crackers they can have good things like a slice of cheese with the Swedish crispbread or just serve them plain with milk. Zwieback is so good of itself you don't need butter or honey on it or *anything* with it.

Zwieback—Scald ½ cup milk. When lukewarm add 2 tablespoons yeast and dissolve. Then add ¼ cup sugar or half as much honey, ½ teaspoon salt, 3 eggs and then enough flour to make a workable dough. Make the dough more tender than for regular bread. That means use less flour. Let rise in bowl until light. Shape into oblong rolls about 2 inches in diameter and 4 inches long. Space about 2 inches apart in a buttered pan in parallel rows. If you're not familiar with zwieback buy a package at the store just to give you a notion where you're trying to get to. Your homemade zwieback will taste and look very much like the store product.

Let rise again. Rolls will more than double. Bake 20 minutes at 400°. Remove from oven when agreeably browned and cool. Then chill in refrigerator. When cold, cut carefully into crosswise slices ½ inch thick—like store bread slices. Brown evenly in the oven at 400° about 10 minutes. They need to be dry all the way through.

Melba Toast is made by slicing day-old bread very thin. Cut slices ¼ inch thick to toast. Melba toast when toasted should be very thin and crisp. The slices are put in a pan side by side and baked in the oven at 250°-325° for 15 to 18 minutes. The bread should be very fine grained so it will cut into thin even slices. Unleavened bread is most like this. Older bread that is thoroughly chilled will cut better than fresh bread. Ideally melba toast is delicately brown and totally dry.

Rye Melba Crackers—This recipe gives you results closest to the little packets in cellophane of rye melba crackers that you've seen in restaurants. Start by making sourdough rye bread from the recipe in the sourdough section. Or use any other sourdough rye bread recipe you prefer. If that seems all too much trouble use the recipe on page 116 called simply "rye crackers." It's a lot quicker and easier though the results aren't quite as fine. After your sourdough rye bread is made, chill it in the refrigerator the way you did for zwieback. Cut off the crust and discard. Cut the inside into very thin slices as near to ⅛ inch as you can manage. That is one reason besides taste that sourdough rye works so well for this because it is a very close grained bread and not full of air holes that would make your cracker crumbly. Spread on a cookie sheet in a single layer and bake at 250° until completely crisp and dry.

Herbed Rye Melba Crackers—Mix 1 teaspoon dried marjoram (or 2 tablespoons chopped fresh), 2 teaspoons lemon juice and ½ cup melted butter. Brush that over the toast and return to the oven for 10 minutes.

Quick Rye Crackers—Don't sift your rye flour. Combine 2 cups rye flour, ¾ cup unsifted white or unbleached flour, ½ cup wheat germ, ½ teaspoon salt, 1 teaspoon baking powder and 6 tablespoons butter or margarine. Cut the butter in with a pastry cutter or two knives until you have a mixture with particles about like cornmeal. Add ¾ cup milk and 1 slightly beaten egg.

Mix, roll out, cut into diamond shapes by making parallel lines one way diagonally and then the other. Put the crackers onto a cookie sheet, prick with a fork and bake at 325° until lightly browned. Takes about 30 minutes.

Crispbread is a Swedish yeast cracker. In a big bowl dissolve 2 tablespoons yeast in ½ cup warm water. In a separate saucepan melt 1 cup butter or margarine or the equivalent of your homemade butter. Then add 1½ cups milk to the butter and heat *only* until lukewarm. Combine with your yeast mixture. Now add about 2 teaspoons honey (don't bother to measure—it doesn't have to be exact), 1 teaspoon salt and 2 cups whole wheat flour. It's good too made with rye flour, all or any percentage. Stir it up, then add about 4 cups more unbleached or white flour. Knead your dough, then let rise for 30 minutes. Knead again. Divide your dough into sections. Roll out very thin. If you want to look authentic use a knobbed rolling pin. Cut into rectangles about 2½ by 4 inches. You can roll it out right on your baking sheet and cut it there and let it do its last rising there too which makes it all easier. Let rise 30 minutes again. Bake at 350° until light brown. Takes about 15 to 20 minutes. Your pieces will have sort of grown back together where you cut them. Break the pieces away from each other.

Yeast Crackers—This is a fine-tasting white cracker for people who don't like sweets. Not flaky, it is a very hard cracker. The night before make a "sponge" (or you can make it in the morning and set it in a warm place for 3 to 4 hours, or till risen) using 3 cups flour, 3 tablespoons margarine (cut into flour till very fine, or melted and added with water) and 1 teaspoon active dry yeast. Mix well, cover (but not tightly or the gas will blow the lid off!) and let sit overnight (or several hours). In the morning add to the sponge, 1 teaspoon salt and ¼ cup milk mixed with 1 tablespoon vinegar. Stir in as best you can, then add about 2 cups flour, working in with spoon then hands. More flour may be needed, enough to make a manageable dough. Divide in halves or fourths to make rolling easier. Roll and stretch dough thin. I prefer to use a Tupperware pastry sheet (a heavy plastic) and not too much flour on it near the edges, that way I can roll the dough and kind of stick it to the edges of the plastic to hold it taut and thin. The dough is very elastic (if using white flour) and is hard to keep stretched any other way. Prick thoroughly and if desired sprinkle with salt. Cut with a pastry wheel or pizza cutter or knife. Bake on cookie sheets at 325° for 20 to 30 minutes until lightly browned. Remove done crackers from sheet, and return the ones that aren't quite dry enough to the oven for another few minutes.

Cream Wafers—These are delicious, good hot or cold, and easy to make. Sift 1½ cups flour with ½ teaspoon salt. Gradually add heavy cream to make a dough. You'll need about ½ cup. Knead on a floured board until smooth and then roll as thin as possible. Prick with a fork and cut out with a cutter in whatever shapes you want. I prefer round. Arrange on a greased cookie sheet and bake at 400° about 10 minutes, or until just delicately browned.

Cream Graham Crackers—Combine 4 cups whole wheat flour, ½ teaspoon salt, ¼ cup sugar or half as much honey and as much cream as it takes to make a rollable dough. Roll thin, prick with a fork, and arrange on a greased cookie sheet. Bake at 350° until done.

Sour Cream Graham Crackers—Combine 1 cup sour cream, 1 tablespoon melted butter, a pinch of salt, ½ cup sugar, 1 teaspoon soda and mix all together well. Add enough graham flour to make a stiff dough that can be rolled. Roll out to about a ⅛-inch thickness. Cut into the shapes you prefer and bake at 325° for 30 minutes (or 400° for 10 minutes). I like these.

Cheese Crackers—This is a flaky (like piecrust), tasty cracker. Use any yellow cheese. You can grate a soft cheese on the big holes and then work in with your fingers into the flour and margarine as you would make a piecrust. A hard cheese should be grated as fine as possible. Rub 3 tablespoons margarine into ¾ cup flour. Work in ½ cup grated cheese (measured after grating) and a dash of salt. Blend 1 egg yolk with 1 tablespoon cold water and add. Work it into a soft dough. Roll out very thin and cut into rounds, or whatever shapes you prefer. Bake at 350° for 8 to 10 minutes (exactly how long depends on how thick your dough was).

Pretzels—Make a dough of 4 cups flour, 1 tablespoon butter, ½ teaspoon salt, 1 rounded teaspoon dry yeast and enough water to make a rollable dough. Let dough rest 20 minutes. Then roll out, cut into strips and let dry a couple minutes. Shape into pretzels pinching ends together. Let stand until they begin to rise. Make a solution of 1 level tablespoon lye in ½ gallon boiling water or 2 tablespoons in a gallon (don't use an aluminum pan). Put the pretzels in the boiling water. As soon as they come up to the top take them out. Drain, brush with beaten egg yolk and sprinkle with coarse salt or caraway seeds. Bake on an oiled baking sheet. Set oven as high as you can, 700° if possible—we did it at 500°—and bake 10 minutes (2½ minutes if you have 700°). Take out of oven, turn oven down to 400°, set them back in and leave in until they are bone dry. Drying time varies a lot according to how they are cut out and how thick they are. Break into desired lengths. Put into jar with tight lid and they'll keep. They aren't exactly like store pretzels but it surprised me that they were *anything* like them. Not something I'd bother with every day, though.

Cereal or Gruel Crackers—2 cups gruel (rice, grain, soups or vegetables mixed), 2 cups whole wheat flour (if more flour is required, use rye, buckwheat or barley flour, or corn or millet meal, up to 2 cups per loaf), 1 teaspoon salt or soy sauce and ¼ cup oil (optional). Add salt and oil to gruel. Add remaining ingredients and work until pliable. Leave slightly moist. Let set in warm place or use at once.

Brush cookie sheet with oil or garlic butter, and sprinkle with salt. Roll dough out to ⅛ inch thick. Cut into any shape. Place on greased cookie sheet. Bake at 425° for 10 minutes. May also be deep fried.

Rye Crackers—1 cup rye flour, 1 cup white flour, 1 teaspoon sugar, ½ teaspoon salt, ½ cup melted butter, cooled, and ½ cup milk.

Stir flours together, add sugar and salt and stir. Combine butter and milk and pour over dry ingredients, stirring with fork until all moistened. Gather dough into ball and knead until smooth. Pinch off pieces the size of marbles and roll very thin to 3 or 4 inches diameter. Prick with fork and put on lightly greased baking sheet.

Bake at 400° for 10 minutes, or until lightly browned. Makes 48 3-inch crackers. (You can add 1 teaspoon caraway seed to dough and sprinkle tops with coarse salt.)

Swedish Hardtack—2 cups yogurt, ½ cup honey, ½ cup oil, 6 cups rye flour (or half rye and half whole wheat), 3 tablespoons nutritional yeast and 1 teaspoon salt.

Blend yogurt, honey and oil. Stir in remaining ingredients. Dough should be stiff. Knead. Roll out very thin on floured board. Cut into any shape. Bake at 425° about 15 minutes until brown. Wafers should be crisp and tender.

Keep in tightly covered container. Recipe does not say to oil pans. Would probably scorch quick either way, so watch them carefully.

Swedish Crisp Biscuits—1¾ cups white flour, 2 cups coarse rye meal or flour, 1 tablespoon sugar, 1 teaspoon salt, ½ cup butter and 1 cup milk.

Sift flours into bowl and add sugar and salt. Divide butter into parts and dot over the flour. Rub in well with fingertips and add milk until you have a fairly stiff dough. Work well till smooth and glossy. When it comes away from the sides of the bowl, roll very thin, prick with fork and cut into oblongs about 4 x 2½ inches thick.

Bake on buttered tins at about 385° to nice golden brown. This is a delicious toast substitute.

These recipes were sent to me by Mrs. George Baker. She lives in the state of Arizona. I've mislaid your address so I can't write and thank you, Anna.

Wafers—The whole gamut of crackers really offers a variety. Here are some you don't cook. You dry them like a fruit leather. You'll have to get the ingredients from a health food store. Get a little each of alfalfa seed, barley, buckwheat, corn, flaxseed, lentils, millet, mung beans, oats, rice, rye, sesame, wheat and almonds. If you can't find them all don't worry—just leave out what you have to. Combine in equal amounts—like ¼ cup of each. Soak just like you were going to sprout them (direction in Vegetables chapter). If some of them go ahead and sprout don't worry, your crackers will still be fine. Put a cupful of the mixture at a time in your blender with just enough water so it will blend. Add ¼ cup presoaked raisins. You want this to be very well blended. Add ¼ cup chia seeds (preground) now if you have them. If not, you can do without. Spread ¼ inch thick and even over parchment or plastic and dry in the sun or in a dryer or in a very low oven. When dry enough take away the paper or plastic and continue drying on a screen turning as needed. Cut into pieces and store.

Apple Wafers—Use ½ cup the above mix with ½ cup chopped apples. Blend and dry like a fruit leather.

PASTAS

The pastas were originally manufactured only in Italy and exported to the United States. So in Victorian days spaghetti was quite a treat. Times have changed. I spent a year and a half living in Taipei, Taiwan, in a spaghetti-making district. The Taiwanese called it "mien." Now, I would run right downstairs (I lived on the top floor in an apartment) and out the front door and find out how they make the spaghetti. But my interest then wasn't spaghetti, it was learning to speak Chinese. I do remember though the miles of spaghetti hung out to dry. It was made in many strands, about ten feet long, and they hung it out to dry in the hot tropical sun between poles like telephone lines. When I looked out from my balcony the view was spaghetti and more spaghetti—in sunshiny weather. When it rained the spaghetti was all taken in and the streets were just narrow, dirty and sadly naked.

Spaghetti, macaroni, elbow macaroni and all such ilk are really the same dough recipe squeezed out into different shapes. "Macaroni" is a comparatively large hollow tube. "Spaghetti" is smaller in diameter. Even thinner pasta is called "vermicelli." "Noodles" are broad and flat. Noodles are the easiest to make at home. You don't need any special equipment.

The old-time way of making macaroni in Italy was to combine ground wheat with hot water in the proportion of two-thirds meal to one-third water. The dough was then thoroughly mixed, put into a shallow vat and kneaded and rolled some more by machinery. When well rolled it was forced by a powerful plunger through the perforated head of strong steel cylinders which were arranged above a fire so that the dough was partially cooked as it was forced from the holes in the long strings. Afterwards it hung over metal rods or on cloth covered frames to finish drying.

In Taiwan they were making spaghetti on a cottage industry level because the little huts the *mien* was appearing out of couldn't possibly have held sophisticated machinery. So there has to be a way to make the stuff at home. I like spaghetti and having been raised by a wheat rancher and living right now in the midst of a tremendous soft wheat producing area, do-it-yourself spaghetti making doesn't seem a bit unreal to me.

Homemade noodles or any other homemade pasta is so good once you've tried it you'll literally never buy the store stuff again. The store stuff is made of flour and water. Your homemade noodles to be really good are made of flour and eggs.

To make anything but a noodle at home requires special equipment or more ingenuity than I have. I mention Maid of Scandinavia a lot in this book and here I will again. If you don't have their catalog send for one to Maid of Scandinavia Co., 3245 Raleigh Avenue, Minneapolis, Minnesota 55416. I don't own stock in that or any other company. I'm suggesting it just because it's a wise book that may be a real eye-opener for you. It's loaded with the kind of things you *won't* be interested in—fancy perishables and expensive aids to conspicuous consumption kitchenwise. But it's a *big* catalog and it also has a lot of real things in it that will be good for you because it never occurred to you such things could exist or that you could make anything like that for yourself.

And that includes a "noodle cutter . . . roll the dough, push the cutter over it and you have nine long strips of noodles, all evenly cut . . . so easily and quickly" for $1.25. And an "Ateco Cookie and Noodle Maker . . . special plate included for extruding noodles" for $3.55, which sounds to me more like it would make spaghetti than noodles. And a "Spaetzle Machine . . . those tiny dumpling-like noodles called spaetzle are especially popular with people of German, Polish and Hungarian backgrounds. The dough is mixed . . . then extruded through the holes in the machine into boiling water. After they have been cooked, the spaetzle are used in soups, stews, or are even fried as hash browns. The machine . . . is a sturdy pan with perforated bottom, wooden handles and removable crank . . ." It costs $7.

I don't own any of this stuff. I've had fantasies that if Maid of Scandinavia knew I was giving them all this great advertising maybe they'd send me a noodle cutter for Christmas. But they don't even know I exist. Same for Morgan Brothers. Last time I was in there the younger man gave me a kind of hostile "here's that hippie-looking woman again with all the dangerous-to-breakables children who kills time in my store and never buys anything" look. The old man isn't that way. He loves his store and what's in it like you would a museum. To him it's a precious collection of wonderful things and he's just so glad to have a chance to talk about them if you're in the least interested. They don't know my book exists and I wouldn't know how to tell them. Maybe somebody else who has read it could but I can't. I'm too far into it.

Last time I was at the paper wholesalers they had a new stock boy—a young man really. He loaded up my order that the manager pointed out to him and as I was about to leave he called after me, "Hey, what are you going to do with all that paper?" I mumbled something about "Underground press. Underground anyway," and thought of the Internal Revenue. I know what they do about unreported income. That's not my problem anyway. What about unreported losses? I know that wasn't a very descriptive answer but what could I say?

People often come up to me in our small town here and beaming or otherwise say "I heard you're writing a book." I want to be kind but that opening leaves me speechless. If I was to answer, really answer, it would be like trying to tell someone why you are in love with someone who doesn't love you back. I suppose they just expect me to glow with success and modestly murmur, "Yes." But to "book" I'm more likely to associate "depression, guilt, stubbornness, dream, heart, cry, weary" and so on. At least to the kind of book you try to print and sell yourself. And this is.

Well, back to noodles.

My children love it when Mama decides to make noodles—that's almost as good as bread making day. It's an act they can all get in on. Noodle dough is basically a couple of eggs, a pinch of salt and all the

flour it will absorb to make a stiff dough. I've arrived at that recipe after considerable trying this and that. You can make noodles out of water rather than eggs if you have no eggs but then they will taste like store noodles—bland. Your taste buds really respond to the extra food when they're made with eggs. But if your chickens won't lay you can make noodles out of butter and flour and that will do.

You roll out the dough, cut into narrow strips, separate them and spread them out to dry. If you have sunshine that will do the job best. But in winter you can dry just on a tray. If it's too damp or you don't have time you can drop them in the pot damp and limp. I've done that and they cook up fine. The thing about wet noodles is they won't keep. If your noodles are really crisp and bone dry you can put them in a jar and they'll keep a month.

Some people knead their noodle dough but I don't. I make it so stiff it would be miserable to try to knead it. Then I roll it as thinly as possible, cut into sections, pile the sections one atop another—about four high—and slice off noodles. The thinner you can roll the dough, the quicker and easier the noodles will dry and the quicker they will cook. Ten minutes for "paper thin" dried noodles. I never can get them that thin. I wonder if a person could put dough through wringer washer machine rollers? Maid of Scandinavia advertises a "Noodle Chef" machine for $30.75 that "will roll your dough for you, and will dial to 8 thicknesses. Then the special cutters will cut the dough into strips for you . . . two rollers for thin and wide noodles." For that price the machine would have to cook supper for me too.

My noodles are rolled out on the top of my kitchen table which is made of wood and doubles as breadboard. Cut with butcher knife and dried either on the table or on trays in the sun or in my fruit dryer in the sun. My noodles are not very thin. And not very narrow. They take anywhere from 20 minutes to ½ hour to cook. Noodle meals here are famous for everybody standing around hungrily saying, "Mama, aren't the noodles done yet?" And then I fish out enough for everybody to try and we argue over how raw is still edible. But when they finally get done, unless the flour off them has thickened the stew to the point where the long cooking caused it to burn on the bottom, they are really good. A meal to remember. And cheap. And easy to warm up your leftovers the next day for another meal. Which will be delicious too.

If your dough is too moist you'll have trouble with noodles sticking together. If your noodles have too much loose flour on them you'll have trouble with the stew thickening. Practice makes perfect. If scorching is too great a risk you can cook the noodles separately in boiling salted water. Noodles are great with any stew like chicken or beef or even in a vegetable soup. You can cook egg noodles plain and serve them just buttered, or with cheese cut into bits and stirred in with them. You can make noodles out of white flour, unbleached flour, or whole wheat flour. I don't know why you couldn't make them out of rye or barley or rice flour too, though I've never tried that. Baking powder in noodles makes them flat. I don't see any point in it. To make lasagne noodles just cut them wide—1 inch.

Basic Noodle Recipe more than enough for one stew. Two eggs, a pinch of salt and all the flour it can absorb.

Leftover Yolks Noodles is really a special noodle. To ¼ cup egg yolks add 1 tablespoon rich cream and enough flour to make your stiff noodle dough.

Eggless Noodles—Just an eggshell of water with a pinch of salt and flour. A teaspoon of butter and some special seasoning helps. Like a pinch of pepper, or ginger or nutmeg.

Green Noodles—Cook a small batch of your garden spinach or other greens. Drain and put through a sieve. Drain again. Combine 3 eggs, ½ cup of the spinach, 2 tablespoons butter and enough flour.

Egg and Milk—Combine 1 beaten egg, ½ teaspoon salt, 2 tablespoons milk and about 1 cup flour.

Noodles are the basic. If you have time to try new things for fun here are some other ways to do with noodle dough.

Pfarvel—Make a ball of stiff noodle dough and grate it coarsely. Spread out the grated dough and let it dry. Then add to boiling soup and cook 10 minutes.

Noodle Puffs—Make your favorite noodle dough. Roll out and let lay until moderately dry. Fold the dough over into halves. With a floured thimble cut out puffs. Press the thimble firmly enough so the edges stick together. Fry the puffs in deep fat until golden brown and serve as soup crackers. Put them in the bowl and pour the soup over them.

Ravioli—Make your favorite noodle dough only use less flour so that your dough is just stiff enough to roll and hold its shape. Roll it very thin and let it dry on a cloth for about an hour. You can make the ravioli with either a cheese filling or a meat filling.

Cheese Filling: Blend together 1 pound ricotta, ⅓ cup grated Romano, ½ teaspoon fresh chopped parsley, 2 eggs and a dash of salt. This is the real Italian thing.

Meat Filling: Ground cooked beef or a mixture of ground cooked leftover meat and sausage. Half as much bread crumbs as ground beef, and egg, some grated onion, chopped fresh parsley and salt. (Optional: pepper, nutmeg to taste, grated rind of a lemon.)

Now, cut the dough into 3-inch squares. Place 1 teaspoon of filling into the middle of each square. Fold the square over to make a triangle. Press the edges well together to seal. Set down on a floured board and let dry an hour more. Then have ready boiling salted water. Drop the ravioli in, a few at a time, until they're all in. Cook for 20 minutes. Serve with a gravy or a topping of grated cheese.

Potato Noodles—Use the equivalent of about 4 large potatoes, cooked and mashed. Leftover mashed spuds are fine to start with. Mix in 1 egg and a pinch

of salt. Maybe a little nutmeg. Add enough flour to get a good noodle-type dough.

Gertrude Johnson from Lamont, Washington, wrote me to try adding about ¼ cup melted butter to the eggs, salt and flour when making egg noodles. She says it makes the dough easier to handle and such *tender* noodles.

USING LEFTOVER BREADS

Keep your crusts and leftover bread odds and ends like heels in a paper bag in a dry, warm place where they will dry. Never store in a plastic container because they will promptly mold there. Take out and grate as you need or grate ahead of time and store in a tightly-lidded jar. If you grate ahead of time, be sure to store separately rye, whole wheat, and cornmeal bread crumbs.

Toast—You can toast rye, French or almost any other nonsweet bread, buttered, under your broiler on a grill, cookie sheet or in a cake pan. The firmer the grain or the staler the bread, the more butter for good results. Put the slices about 9 inches away from the broiler. Watch carefully to prevent burning. The butter softens bread that is getting a little stale and revives its flavor.

Bread Crumbs—To make bread crumbs dry out your stale bread in a slow oven, then put it in a paper bag and crush into crumbs with a rolling pin. Or with the palm of your hand rub through a sieve or colander. Or put the bread in a clean bag, tie it at the top and rub with your hands a few minutes. Or grate on a grater. Put the crumbs in a jar, put the lid on tightly or keep them dry until needed.

Croustades—Cut stale bread in 2½-inch slices. Remove crusts. Spread lightly with butter on one side if you like, then cut across to make cubes. Bake at 325° for 15 to 20 minutes, or until a golden brown, stirring occasionally. Serve with soup.

Croutons—Cut stale bread in ½-inch slices and remove crusts. Spread it lightly with butter on one side if you like, then cut across to make cubes. Bake at 325° for 15-20 minutes, or until golden brown, stirring occasionally. Serve with soup.

Milk Toast—This has fallen out of favor since the popularization of the unmentionable bread which is too salty and generally poor for this dish. Make it with homemade bread. Most simply toast some thinly sliced bread, butter it on each side, lay in a bowl and pour scalded milk over it. For extra richness use cream or part cream.

French Toast—Combine 1 cup milk, 2 slightly beaten eggs and a pinch of salt, if your bread is homemade. Dip each slice of bread long enough to coat each side, but not to soak. Heat and shine your griddle and brown the toast. Serve immediately with syrup and butter.

Brewis—This is a breakfast dish made with a cup of very fine dried rye or brown bread crumbs. Heat 2 cups rich milk to boiling. Then beat into it quickly the crumbs. Serve at once with cream.

To Thicken Gravies—Bread crumbs toasted and rolled, ground or grated fine can be used to thicken meat gravies.

Underdone Bread—This can happen to anybody. It has to me plenty of times. If the bread is too underdone to enjoy, turn it into zwieback or melba toast: zwieback if it is coarse grained, melba if fine. Just chill the bread for easier cutting, then trim closely off the crust, cut into ½-inch slices for zwieback, ⅛ inch for melba. Make slices about 1½ inches wide and as wide as your loaf. Spread out on a cookie sheet. Bake in a preheated 350° oven for about 20 minutes, or until dry and crisp clear through. Then store in a dry place like a tightly-covered glass jar, or in a plastic bag in your freezer and serve as needed. Good to keep on hand for the children.

Close grained and unleavened breads if possible should be grated before they get rock hard, then dry the crumbs in the oven in order to prevent mold. If you let the loaf dry, it is rock hard and has to be grated to make crumbs unless you manage to saw off small enough hunks to put through your grinder.

Crumb Pancakes—Grate until you have as many crumbs as you want. (Obviously this is my recipe because it's one half guess and the other half golly.) Add 2 eggs if the bread was a relatively eggless one. Add milk until you have a pancake type batter. Add a dribble of honey or some other sweetener like molasses or brown sugar. Let rest a bit to give the larger crumb hunks and brown sugar time to soften. Mix. Pour out pancake-type dollop and cook on a griddle. Serve with butter and syrup or just the way you usually do your pancakes.

Economical Bread—Combine 2 cups crushed dry bread crumbs, 2 cups whole wheat flour, 3 teaspoons baking powder, 1 teaspoon salt (if it was homemade bread crumbs, otherwise none). To 2 cups milk add 1 tablespoon molasses and 1 beaten egg. Stir liquid into dry ingredients and bake in a greased bread pan at 350° about 50 minutes.

PUDDINGS WITH LEFTOVER BREAD

Bread Pudding—If you use store bread in this recipe, it won't be as good as if the bread were homemade. Reduce the salt a bit for store bread. Soak 1½ cups chunked, dried bread in 2 cups milk (if your bread is fresh toast it in the oven before using). Add 1 tablespoon sugar, 1 tablespoon melted butter, 2 lightly beaten eggs, a pinch of salt and 1 teaspoon vanilla. Put into a buttered dish and set dish in a pan of hot water (an ovenproof dish or pan). Bake at 325° about 30 minutes. Test by inserting knife. If the knife comes out clean your pudding is done. Serve hot or cold with rich cream, berries or a pudding sauce.

Whole Wheat Crumb Pudding—Moisten 2 cups fine whole wheat crumbs with ½ cup thin cream. Add a cup or more of finely chopped fresh figs, 3 tablespoons sugar and 1 cup milk. Pour the mixture into a mold and steam about 2½ hours. Serve hot with rich cream or orange or lemon sauce.

Rye Crumb Pudding—(OK for whole wheat crumbs, too.) These crumbs should be very dry. If necessary give them a special oven heating. Cool and mix 2 cups crumbs with 1 cup currant, wild plum, or other tart jam. Pour into a mold and chill until set. Serve with whipped cream.

Crumbs and Applesauce—Line a buttered baking dish with dried crumbs ½ inch thick. Add a layer of applesauce, dot with butter, then a layer of crumbs and so on. Use 1 cup of thick applesauce for each cup of crumbs and about 1 tablespoon of butter for each. When the dish is full have crumbs as the top layer. Pat down until firm. Bake at 325° for 45 minutes. Serve with whipped cream.

Crumbs and Sliced Apples—Do the same as above. Use 1 cup sliced apples per cup bread crumbs. Sprinkle each layer of apples with 1 teaspoon cinnamon, dot with 1 tablespoon butter and sprinkle with ⅓ cup brown sugar. When finished, add ½ cup water per 2 cups bread crumbs. Bake at 350° for 45 minutes. Serve hot with whipped cream.

Crumbs and Fruit—Make it with any kind of fruit!

USING LEFTOVER CORN BREAD

Sour Milk Corn Bread Pudding—Crumble 1 cup (more or less) of dried corn bread crumbs. Soak them in 2 cups sour milk for about a half hour. Add 1 beaten egg, ½ cup raisins, ½ teaspoon soda, ¼ teaspoon cinnamon, and bake at 325° until it begins to set. Then spread 4 tablespoons molasses over the top and bake until you have a firm crust formed.

Corn Bread Stuffing—Combine 4 cups crumbled corn bread with 4 cups crumbled white bread (or brown), 1 medium onion, chopped, 1 teaspoon sage or poultry dressing, salt and pepper to taste and the broth from your cooked giblets. Moisten with more broth or milk as needed. This is enough stuffing for a 10-pound turkey. If you are stuffing a chicken, cut the recipe in half.

This is a picture my father had taken in his later years when he was teaching school. I feel a kind of awe whenever I see his face now. The first word I'd think of in relation to him would be "character." Daddy was a man of principle. If you had put him to the test he would have laid down his life. Right was right and wrong was wrong. Loyalty to his God, his country, his wife and child, and the giving of an honest day's work for his daily bread. He was so strong, yet so gentle and loving. The only time I ever saw him weep as a child was when he discovered a kitten had crawled in by the fan belt and got killed when he started an engine.

I spent most of my childhood on a series of three ranches. The first at Clyde Park, Montana, where Daddy raised wheat. The second at Bracket Creek, about 15 miles away from Clyde Park, where he raised sheep and cows. This is a picture of that Bracket Creek ranch, the one where I really left my heart. We didn't have any real close neighbors and my best friend in the world was my horse.

Pierre Champeaux taught at the School of Country Living its first summer. He had lots of experience with poultry, rabbits, goats, and farming in general. Here he is driving a small tractor mowing hay.

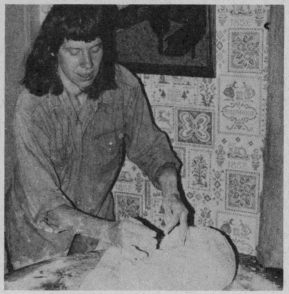

One day Mama Emery and the children
decided to make bread! We got all the liquid
ingredients stirred up in a bucket, then started
adding flour. As the batter got thick enough
to be dough we dumped it out onto the middle of
our kitchen table and kept adding flour. . .

A lot of kneading came next to get
the flour well mixed in and the texture smooth.
The picture on the wall was painted by Mike
when we were still waiting for him to get done
with college in New York—a wish picture. The
wallpaper is that "contact" kind and I love it.

Then the dough was left to rise
and it grew and grew. . .

Then came the fun part. We made loaves and rolls.
Part of that dough is now in the oven baking.
Dolly and Rebecca (left to right) are concentrating
hard on getting their rolls smooth and round.

VEGETABLES, NUTS AND SEEDS

THE GARDEN

If you really want to have a garden you can. I've heard from people who live in sunless rooms and have them filled with fragrant green stuff growing under special lights. I've read letters from and visited garden lovers in Nevada and New Mexico where the natural soil is actually poisonous to plant life or untillable in the most literal sense. They literally built their own soil bringing in sand, clay, organic material, mixing and matching and mulching until they had a mixture that would grow a garden. I've heard from a family that lives on a bare rock cliff and raises a wonderful yearly garden in 4 x 8-foot redwood boxes, 12-14 inches deep. I know Alaskans that do most of their gardening in greenhouses and desert dwellers that do part of it under light wooden slat roofs to keep out the extreme sun.

SEED—In temperate climates or worse, gardens begin in the winter when you're cold and housebound. Then you think about seeds. But before the seed came the plant. It's the same as saying which came first the chicken or the egg? One of the pleasures of wintertime—January, February—is reading seed catalogs, drawing maps of where you're going to plant what in your garden-to-be, ordering seeds off much-discussed lists. Garden seed and flower seed sellers are almost embarrassingly generous with their catalogs. You can easily get a dozen a year or more just by sending your name and address in and some outfits will keep you on their list year after year whether you buy or not. Lots of good picture cutting out and pasting for the little ones. But I'd really like to open your mind to the idea that seeds don't have to come from catalogs. A majority of the seed selling houses that you may deal with are brokers. They place orders for seeds all over the place and then re-sell them to you. Many of those seeds come from foreign countries like Australia and islands south of Florida. The whole act of letting something as important as your vegetable garden be totally dependent on a mail-order transaction is a real critical vulnerability if you're dreaming of self-sufficiency.

WHAT TO PLANT—Don't plant your garden from the pretty pages of seed catalogs. Every area has different conditions and half of what you order may not grow in *your* garden. Ask around for the great gardeners in town and go talk to *them* during the long winter months. They'll really enjoy helping you. They'll name you varieties that their long trial-and-error experience has proven to work in your area and they know the cheapest places to get the seed. I buy most of the seed (that I buy) in bulk from a local seedsman who sells mainly to farmers who are buying to plant field crops. Pea seed last year was something like 12 cents a pound. I order from catalogs only as a last resort.

If you haven't gardened before and you are trying to make up a basic list of what to grow, maybe it would help you to see a list of the vegetables we plant every year. We plant both leaf and head lettuce, bush beans, kidney beans, carrots, early and late corn, tomatoes, beans, Swiss chard, cabbage, radishes, green table squash and big winter squash, muskmelon, sometimes watermelon, too, pumpkins, eggplants, beets, sometimes sunflowers, green peppers, sometimes summer squash (zucchini), cucumbers, onion sets and sometimes onion seed, dill if we don't expect enough volunteers, turnips and potatoes. Asparagus is a perennial and doesn't need to be replanted. For the fruit orchard and berries, see the Sweets chapter.

LITTLE GARDEN—If your gardening space is limited plant the garden doubly carefully to make the most of what you have. A semishaded area unsuitable for tomatoes or root vegetables may successfully grow leafy vegetables like lettuce, chard, mustard or endive. Don't overplant things like herbs. Two parsley or chive plants can quite likely produce all you need unless your family is large. You can plant six rows of carrots, beets or onions in the same square footage that one row of squash would take because squash simply *will* spread out all over the place and the former ones don't. So limit or refuse summer squash, winter squash, cucumbers, watermelons, muskmelons, cantaloupes and corn because they are space hogs for what you get. French intensive gardening methods will give you even more vegetable productivity per square foot. Give preference to continuously bearing vegetables like chard compared to spinach. What I mean is with some vegetables like spinach and peas there is a brief period of productivity and then the plant is done for the whole summer. Others will keep making harvest for you until frost kills them—tomatoes, broccoli, kale, lima beans, squash of all sorts, eggplant, peppers, cucumbers, chard, Brussels sprouts. I wouldn't leave out peas though because they produce heavily while they are at it and then you can till up the ground they were in and plant something else. That's another way to get the most from your ground—plant another crop after one is harvested. Of course that works best with a long growing season. But in most places peas, lettuce, radishes, beets and carrots mature quickly enough that you can put in a second crop as soon as the first is harvested. You also get more productivity out of the garden if you stay on the ball with your harvesting. Broccoli, cucumbers, summer squash, beans and chard for example will stop producing if they aren't harvested. But if you keep them faithfully and regularly harvested then they keep producing.

FRENCH INTENSIVE METHOD is a way of gardening first used by French farmers centuries ago. It's good especially if you have only a very limited area to plant in. Like if you live in a trailer court like my mother-in-law did for a while in Los Angeles. Basically French intensive gardening is a three-step process.

First you dig deep to make your planting "bed." Each bed will be something like 4 feet wide by as long as is convenient before you need a walkway between—maybe 8 feet. Dig down something like 20-24 inches deep. A good way to organize your digging is to start on one side, going the long way, and dig a trench to the depth you need. Then dig another

one right beside it filling the one you just dig with the dirt you are taking out of the next (new) one and so on. After you have it all dug up, let rest a few days. Then break up clods and try to get the soil broken down to a fine texture. The deep digging helps plants sink deep, healthy roots and really get at the minerals they need.

Step two is your fertilizing process. The French farmers who started this had lots of manure. If you do, get ahead on this by covering the whole bed-to-be with 6 inches of good rotted compost or manure before you ever start your deep digging and then you will be spading in that compost as you go. After your deep digging is finished and the bed has sat and the clods are broken up, sprinkle a dusting of bone meal, an inch or more of well-rotted manure, and some wood ashes over the top and rake or cultivate this fertilizer into the top 3 to 6 inches. Then soak the resulting soil with a gentle spray. If you did it all right so far your French intensive garden bed is higher than the ground around it and this is as it is supposed to be.

Step three is your planting process and it is here that the most visible difference will be for you. Probably you're used to gardens planted in rows, a rototiller-width apart. That's fine if you have enough room to do it. But in the French intensive method you plant close, so close that the outer leaves of plants will touch as they approach mature size. So whether you are setting out transplants or planting from seed you are going to space way closer than you ever have before resulting in a solid mass of plants when they are grown—end to end and side to side in your raised garden bed. Now if you got it dug deep enough, and if you fertilized richly enough, if you keep it watered generously enough and keep it weeded carefully enough that little piece of earth will be able to support all those plants and well, too. See the reason for not making the bed too wide—you must be able to reach

in from outside all around to weed, or thin, or harvest as needed. Close spacing like this works best with leaf and root crops like lettuce, spinach, cabbage, beets, carrots and turnips. Big vegetables like corn and squash are going to take more room no matter how hard you try.

PERENNIALS—It's wonderful to be able to go out and harvest without ever having planted! Perennials are plants that come back all by themselves year after year. Rhubarb and asparagus, Jerusalem artichokes, fruit and nut trees, berry bushes, multiplier onions, garlic, many herbs are of this sort. It's important when planting them that you put them safely on the edge of your garden so that when you've hired somebody to come in and plow it is possible for him to do the job without tearing out your perennials!

CATALOGS—Here's a list of places you can write to get seed catalogs. But further on in the alphabetical listing by vegetable I'll give you directions for saving the seed for each particular vegetable. In some cases it's easy, in others it's hard. But most of the hardness is not having done it before. See the Sweets chapter for catalogs specializing in fruits and berries.

Order out of catalogs directed to your climate zone. That matter of days to maturity really can be important. Find out what the usual frost-free span is for where you live, that means the number of days from the last killing frost in spring to the first killing frost in fall. That is your growing season. That is how long your plants have to become mature and have some time left over for you to harvest. If you live in some place like Minnesota or Vermont you have way less days of growing season than if you live in North Carolina or Texas. The catalog entry on each vegetable generally tells days to maturity if you read carefully.

When you do order keep a record of what you ordered. The seeds may be a long time coming and in the meantime you can be having fun figuring out what you will plant where and when. Keep that record going all summer, which varieties you planted, what date you were able to start harvesting, whether the yield was good, how many feet of row you were able to plant with the seed you bought. You'll be so glad you did keep that record the next spring when you sit down to order again. Based on your summer's gardening experience, you may want to change some varieties and some quantities. Save the seed packets, too. Don't stick them up on wooden things at the end of each row because you will end up losing them to rain, kids, animals, wind or some such. And then you'll be sorry because the back of most seed packets contains a tremendous amount of information about growing the plant involved, from preparing the ground right through to harvest.

Gardener's marketplace
A fun free tearout and mail book of coupons. Write:
509 Westport Avenue
Norwalk, Connecticut 06851

Untreated seeds
Burgess Seed and Plant Company
P.O. Box 218
Galesburg, Michigan 49053

Vita-Green Farms
P.O. Box 878
Vista, California 92083

General catalogs
W. Atlee Burpee Co.
Warminster, Pennsylvania 18974,
or Clinton, Iowa 52732, or
Riverside, California 92502
Another good vegetable seed catalog.

Lakeland Nurseries
Hanover, Pennsylvania 17331
Some vegetables, fruits, flowers. Carries kiwi fruit and elderberries.

Jackson and Perkins
P.O. Box 217A
Medford, Oregon 97501

Mellinger's
North Lima, Ohio 44452
"1,000 horticultural items."

Henry Field Seed & Nursery Company
Shenandoah, Iowa 51601
Another good vegetable catalog.

Joseph Harris Company
Rochester, New York 14624
Vegetable seed catalog.

Seedway, Inc.
Hall, New York 14463
Glossy, colored vegetable catalog!

L. L. Olds Seed Company
P.O. Box 1069
Madison, Wisconsin 53701

Vegetable catalog.
Carries 11 varieties of potatoes but does not ship potatoes to California, Alaska, or Hawaii.

R. H. Shumway Seedsman
628 Cedar St.,
Rockford, Illinois 61101
Good *big* catalog.

Kelly Brothers
Dansville, New York 14437
A few vegetables and fruit, lots of flowers and trees.

George W. Park Seed Co.
Greenwood, South Carolina 29647
Nice catalog.

Professional magazines
Seedsmen's Digest
Single copy 50 cents, Subscription $5 a year. Write 1910 W. Olmos, San Antonio, Texas 78201. The agribusiness side of seed producing.

Seed World
One-year subscription, $5. Directed at somewhat smaller growers and more conscious of the vegetable seed trade. 434 S. Wabash Avenue, Chicago, Illinois 60605.

Varieties for southern states
H. G. Hastings Company
P.O. Box 4088
Atlanta, Georgia 30302

Wyatt-Quarles Seed Company
P.O. Box 2131
Raleigh, North Carolina 27602

California nurseries
Stribling's Nurseries
P.O. Box 793
Merced, California 95340
Warm climate varieties—figs, citrus, globe artichokes, olive trees.

California Nursery Company
Niles, California 94536
Warm-climate plants like globe artichokes, avocados, olive trees.

Cold climate
Stokes Seeds
P.O. Box 15
Buffalo, New York 14205
Has many Canadian customers and emphasizes varieties for Canadian Great Lakes area. Has large numbers of varieties (95 of tomatoes, 39 of onions).

Joseph Harris Company
Moreton Farm
Rochester, New York 14624
Emphasis on northeastern states.

J. W. Jung Seed Company
Randolph, Wisconsin 53956
Carries varieties for cold conditions.

Farmers Seed and Nursery Company
Faribault, Minnesota 55021
Another specializing in northern-adapted varieties. Good catalog.

Burgess Seed and Plant Company
Galesburg, Michigan 49053
Specializes in "Blizzard Belt" varieties including
Jerusalem artichokes.

Gurney Seed and Nursery Company
Yankton, South Dakota 57078
Good vegetable line. Good for northern gardeners.
I've ordered from them myself many years. Big (75-
page, 10½ x 13½-inch) catalog.

European
Breck's of Boston
200 Breck Building
Boston, Massachusetts 02210
Handles European varieties not commonly found
elsewhere.

THE BASICS OF
SAVING YOUR OWN SEED

It matters what plant you save seed from. You
want to be choosing a good heredity. So when you
buy the seed for plants that you're maybe going to
save seed from read the fine print. *Do not buy* "hybrid" varieties. Hybrids are famous for their vigor and
productivity but they also often don't breed true and
can throw back to ancestors having really bad
characteristics or sometimes they don't breed at all
which is even worse. So start with noncrossbred lines.
Your resulting garden plants won't always be as big
or colorful as the hybrid types, but I think it's a good
insurance for anybody to have plants you could save
seed from in case you couldn't buy it elsewhere—or
didn't want to. Vita-Green Farms, P.O. Box 878, Vista,
California 92083, used to specialize in seeds of this
type. Haven't heard from them lately so I don't know if
they are still at it or not.

You got your seed, it grew a plant, and you want
to know what to do now. Well, plants kind of fall into
seed saving categories. First come your annuals.
They flower and then every place a flower was they
make seed. They do this the same summer you plant
them. You'll see your radishes and spinach and multiplier onions do it first. When the plant is ready to
flower it stops putting energy into the food part you
would ordinarily grow it for and instead puts it into
stalk, flower and seeds. When saving seed from annuals you want one of the last to go to seed because
you want offspring that will make food as long as possible before it stops making food and starts making
seed. Well, I mean with leafy plants like lettuce and
spinach. Because peas and beans are something else.
I don't want to repeat myself a lot so I'm just going to
skim it here and then under each vegetable we'll do
more and that's repeating myself. Beats not saying it
at all. Would you believe sometimes I can't remember
what I've told you and what I haven't? So I say it
again just to make sure. Having written at this book
for seven years often I can't remember just what all is
in it or where. And somebody will ask me have you
got a recipe for oatmeal cookies and I truly don't
know. Have to look in the index like anybody else, assuming hopefully it's in the index as well as in the
book. Well, that's one problem—saying it too much.
The other one is not saying it at all.

For example, I wanted to do a really thorough
rewrite of this chapter some time before because I'd
learned so much more since I first wrote it and I knew
so much more about what people wanted and
needed to know from the letters they had written me
asking questions. So on one of my trips around the
country talking about country living (this is a 7th edition addition you're reading now) I wrote on vegetables in all my spare time, came back with pages and
pages of manuscript scribbly looking but honest and
ready to be typed up. After I got my scribbling done I
threw out the many wonderful letters and other such
source material that I used in writing it. Well, that
was the trip that got cut short when I got sick and
ended up spending something like 44 days in the
hospital, and when it was all over I couldn't find the
vegetables rewrite. That *really* hurt. It never did turn
up. Did you ever hear of that fellow in England, a
long time ago wrote a huge wonderful history of England in the days when England had more history
than anybody? He just had it all done and a new
housecleaner threw the whole thing in the fireplace
and burned it up. She didn't mean to do anything
bad. You remember what he did then? It had taken
him something like seven years to write the thing. He
sat down and wrote it all over again. It became a
very famous book and students studied it for
generations. That was a great man.

Here I am trying to rewrite vegetables after a
much smaller loss. I had that same sort of thing happen to me once before. Back in my college days, I decided to write a novel—a *great* novel, nothing halfway for me. I was about 24. Managed to spend a
whole summer in Canada writing, and more time
other places too until there was a pile of manuscript
about two inches high, very similar to your *Old
Fashioned Recipe Book* only mostly typed on only one
side. Raggedy emotional poetical stuff. But still my
life's work to date. I had it lined out to be an allegory
on five levels. I was going to be right up there with
Goethe and Dante. My mother had died when I was
20. She was an English teacher all her life, longed to
be a writer and would have been proud to think her
daughter was one. She did write part of a novel,
back in the days when the southern historical novel
was a big thing—everybody wanted to do a *Gone
with the Wind*—and sent it to a publisher and he
wrote back and said he liked it and then she wrapped
it up carefully in brown paper and string and never
touched it again. I think maybe because she was writing about her own very unhappy childhood as an alcoholic's daughter in Mobile, Alabama. When she
died they gave me the manuscript. I couldn't read it
then. The pain was too new and too great. But I set
out to write my own novel and hoped she would be
proud of me. I threw out everything I'd ever written
before, poems, short stories, because I didn't want to
be leaning on past accomplishments—I wanted to put
it all into this new manuscript. I worked a lot and a
long time and then it seemed right to let it rest awhile,
come back and look at it later.

About then there was an opportunity to go overseas to Taiwan because you know I was living a very
different life then and studying Chinese and I jumped
at the chance to go study right with people who were

born speaking it. I left all my books, most of them with my name written in them by my mother (she always gave me books for Christmases and birthdays) and my manuscript and hers and other such stuff in a house in Casper, Wyoming, and why there would be a whole other story. While I was gone a year and a half overseas my stuff got moved from the house into a man's garage. I didn't know whose or where, that's just what I heard. I came back and there's another whole story but to make it short a week before he had cleaned out that garage and burned or given away my stuff. Mother's manuscript and mine had been burned. I really thought I'd never write again.

I did though. But not for a while. First I had to fall in love. Love is an uprooting, healing powerful force. And I met Mike Emery and got uprooted, and healed and tossed emotionally and next thing you know I was writing poems. I never did go about writing the same as before though. I didn't hide away my stuff to meditate on it, perfect it, wait on it, dream of publishing it. I wrote poems and took them to a street corner in Greenwich Village (we lived in New York then) with lots of carbon copies and sold them a quarter each. Or just stood there and hoped somebody would stop and read the little booklets of poems I offered them. Sounds nuts, doesn't it? But it worked. Every reader taught me something by the expression on their face, by where they lingered and where they flipped pages. Every reader defined me to myself more earnestly as a writer and fired me up to go home and try again harder. And every reader fulfilled a rite of passage from my heart and mind to theirs that somehow was the meant destiny of every word I wrote and without which passage I was aborted and wretched.

So here you sit reading my *Old Fashioned Recipe Book*. Which is so far from perfect. And even some of it got lost forever. But there is *lots* left! Right? Pride goeth before a fall.

Hey, I was supposed to be telling you about saving seeds! OK. Root vegetables are generally biennials and that means they take two years to make seed. You could wait around and watch them all summer, like a carrot, for example, and it will never make a flower. The first year it makes a root and stores food in it. It's the *next* spring that things get exciting seedwise. That root vegetable now sends up a long stalk, way longer and taller than an annual could generally because it has all that stored food from a summer's growth in its root to draw on. The tall stalk flowers and then where each flower was, seeds will be.

Fruited plants make their seed inside the fruit. Like all the melons, tomatoes, green peppers, eggplant. First comes the flower, and then the fruit! In this case, you let the seed-bearing fruit get fully *ripe*. Then scoop out the seeds and let them dry. Like spread out on a newspaper.

Tubers are something else again. Here the plant sends up a stalk, flowers prettily above ground and then finishes the job underground making potatoes with eyes.

Flower seeds—You can save the seeds on almost any flower that has a flower head such as the zinnia. Go out in the fall when the flowers are dry. Remember the colors. Snip off with the scissors and dry flower heads. Store in a dry place for winter. In the spring break the head apart. The zinnia has about 100 seeds to a pod.

VOLUNTEERS—A garden that has been gardened for years tends to contain lots of volunteers. A "volunteer" is a plant that grew by its progenitors' efforts and not by yours. Potatoes, squash, dill and sunflowers often make up volunteers. The volunteer potatoes grow when you miss digging up some. The squash grows from the fruit you forgot to harvest. The dill and sunflower drop some seeds before you get there to harvest the seed heads. Volunteer spinach and radishes are common too. Whenever hardy plants get a chance to go to seed in your garden.

STORING SEEDS—Don't dry your seeds with artificial heat because you kill the tiny life stored within them and besides too dry can kill them. But protect them from dampness in storage because too much of that is bad for them, too. Get your seeds well dried and then store in glass or plastic sealed with freezer tape. Freezer tape because it won't let moisture through in either direction and that's just what you want. Store them under cool conditions and then they will last as long as their individual ability allows. What I mean is some seeds last better than others anyway. Squash, radish, turnip and lettuce seeds are very hardy anyway, whereas onion, spinach and corn seeds are easier lost.

WHEN TO PLANT—There are so many different vegetables and each one is a little different but here are some categories to get acquainted with. There are *frost-tender* vegetables and vegetables that can live through a light frost. It is very important that you don't plant frost-tender vegetables, either the seeds or by setting out started plants until after the last even light frost. "Frost" means when the temperature gets down around 32° or lower because that is freezing. You'll have to ask around to find out the average frost dates for your area and then give yourself some time to spare in addition to be safer. *Hardy* or *frost-hardy* vegetables can live through some degree or other of frost, just how much depending on the vegetable. Peas, beets and kale are in this class and so they can be planted as soon as you can get the ground ready in the spring or in midsummer for a late fall crop. *Semihardy* vegetables can survive a light frost but not a heavy one. In practice that means that seed will germinate at relatively low temperatures and can be planted 2 to 3 weeks before the expected last frost date.

Another category to get acquainted with is warm-season versus cool-season vegetables. Tomatoes, eggplant, green peppers, watermelon, cantaloupe and cucumbers are examples of warm-season crops. They are injured or killed by frost. Their seeds won't come to life in cold soil. They don't take off and grow well until your days are *hot*. Cool-season crops on the other hand are like lettuce, spinach, carrots, broccoli. You typically harvest their leaves, roots or stems rather than a seeded fruit like with the warm-season vegetables. Cool-season crops grow wonderfully in wet, chilly spring weather. If the weather turns hot they will "bolt" which means producing flowers and seeds instead of the leaves, roots, stems etc. that you want to harvest. So you want to plant cool-season vegetables to catch that part of your season and warm-season vegetables to catch the right part for them—the heat. For specific vegetable-by-vegetable information on when to plant before or after frost, general days to harvest and so on look in the alphabetically arranged section after this preliminary talk.

The best planting schedule for vegetables I've ever seen is by the USDA. Better than what you read on the seed packets. It will help you get an earlier start than you may now be doing on your garden. Anyone can reprint USDA material, so I am putting this in here for you (see following page).

INDOOR STARTING—The ones that have to be started in the house and then transplanted to the garden are eggplants, green peppers, tomatoes and cabbage. I think head lettuce is better off raised from seed in the garden, though I've seen recommendations to start it indoors. But this depends on your climate. Don't start baby plants in milk cartons. Eventually a poison works out of them that at about 6 weeks will start visibly harming your plants.

7th edition, January 20, 1977. This vegetable chapter is getting a thorough rewrite. And on the subject of plants started in milk cartons Mary Ann Shepherd of Del Mar, California, doesn't agree with me at all. She has experience to back her up too so I'll quote you what she says and then you can make up your own minds between what happened to me using milk cartons and how she seems to make it work: Says Mary Ann, "Milk cartons do grow plants—don't seem to harm seedlings. I use them as collars to blanch celery, put around my new lettuce seedings to discourage cutworms and start all sorts of cuttings (both flowers and vegetables) and seeds. For collars cut off tops and bottoms. For all else cut off tops (or open up) and use a tri-cornered beverage opener ('church key') to cut a drain hole on all four sides at the bottom (not in the bottom itself). When I go to transplant I slit the sides and bottom and plant the whole thing—the carton eventually disintegrates and you don't disturb the roots that way. My pine seedlings take about a year to germinate and grow to about 4 inches tall and they have lived happily in milk cartons for up to two years before I've transplanted them."

Don't start them in cardboard boxes—the bottoms get too soggy. Cans are best—any size. They have to have small holes punched in the bottom. Make your soil mixture in the fall before the ground gets too wet. One-third well-rotted compost and two-thirds dirt. Fill your cans with dirt *to the top.* Set the cans where there is plenty of sunshine at least part of the day such as on a windowsill. After the seeds get started, thin to no more than three in a small can, five in a big can. Water as needed. To set them out, dig a hole, shake the plants out of the can (easier if the soil is soaked ahead of time). Separate them keeping as much dirt on the roots as you can and try not to damage the roots. Set a plant in your hole, pack dirt in around it and give it a good soaking.

I set out cabbages, tomatoes, green peppers and eggplant every year. Plants I set out too early may be wiped out by cutworms or cold—always first set out a sampling, then wait a few days before setting out the rest. For dirtless roots, make a mud bath to plant them in. Cold, dirty work. If they have their own dirt, like in a peat pot where you plant it pot and all, give them a wet hole to sit in and plenty of good water for the next couple weeks. A hot, dry spell, even in May, can wipe out new unwatered sets because their root systems haven't had a chance to get normally established yet. Give them plenty of room to spread. Tomato plants get big. It's cheaper to start your own sets from seed than to buy them from a local nursery. Try not to mail-order. Start your own about 2 to 2½ months before you plan to set them out. I start in seed flats. For me that means a cardboard box with dirt in the bottom and then I transplant to tin cans.

I like those big tins the canned hams come in and gallon tins are great.

Make shelves across your sunniest windows. Don't have anything underneath that could be harmed by dripping water. You'll want to water them every other day, or whenever they look dry. Plants in peat pots dry out fast and have to be watered every day. Set them out, pot and all, or you'll be breaking off roots that have grown right into the pot side. Several light waterings beat one big flood, which has a tendency to go right through, leaving the plant still dry. Big containers of dirt are better than small ones. I use one plant to one soup can or peat pot once they are started in the seed flats. Or about six to a ham can.

The best time to set them out is the beginning of a cloudy, rainy spell. Cabbage sets are handy and can go out in the garden when you plant your green onions. But in my garden planting too early risks getting taken by cutworms. A little later is perfect. Tomato sets can go to the garden when you're positive the frosts and near frosts are over. Green pepper and eggplant sets should wait till the nights are not cold at all.

HOT FRAMES AND COLD FRAMES—This is more advanced than using a shelf or windowsill that gets lots of sunshine. You can find whole books on the subject and the information is really valuable if you live where winters are cold. A hot frame is a place to grow young plants dug down below ground level

EARLIEST DATES, AND RANGE OF DATES, FOR SAFE SPRING PLANTING OF VEGETABLES IN THE OPEN

Planting dates for localities in which average date of last freeze is—

Crop	Mar. 20	Mar. 30	Apr. 10	Apr. 20	Apr. 30	May 10
Asparagus¹	Feb. 1–Mar. 10	Feb. 15–Mar. 20	Mar. 10–Apr. 10	Mar. 15–Apr. 15	Mar. 20–Apr. 15	Mar. 10–Apr. 30
Beans, lima	Apr. 1–June 15	Apr. 1–June 20	Apr. 1–June 30	May 1–June 20	May 15–June 15	May 25–June 15
Beans, snap	Mar. 15–May 25	Apr. 1–June 1	Apr. 10–June 30	Apr. 25–June 30	Apr. 25–June 30	May 10–June 30
Beet	Feb. 15–May 15	Feb. 15–May 15	Mar. 10–June 15	Mar. 20–June 1	Apr. 1–June 15	Apr. 15–June 15
Broccoli, sprouting¹	Feb. 15–Mar. 15	Feb. 15–Mar. 15	Mar. 15–Apr. 15	Mar. 25–Apr. 20	Apr. 1–May 1	Apr. 15–June 1
Brussels sprouts¹	Feb. 15–Mar. 15	Feb. 15–Mar. 15	Mar. 15–Apr. 15	Mar. 25–Apr. 20	Apr. 1–May 1	Apr. 15–June 1
Cabbage¹	Feb. 1–Mar. 1	Feb. 15–Mar. 10	Mar. 1–20	Mar. 1–20	Apr. 1–May 1	Apr. 15–June 1
Cabbage, Chinese	(²)	(²)	Mar. 15–Apr. 15	Mar. 15–Apr. 15	Mar. 15–Apr. 15	Apr. 1–May 15
Carrot	Feb. 15–Mar. 20	Mar. 1–Apr. 10	Mar. 10–Apr. 20	Apr. 1–May 15	Apr. 10–June 1	Apr. 20–June 15
Cauliflower¹	Feb. 10–Mar. 10	Feb. 20–Mar. 20	Mar. 1–20	Mar. 15–Apr. 20	Apr. 10–May 10	Apr. 15–May 15
Celery and celeriac	Mar. 1–Apr. 1	Mar. 15–Apr. 15	Apr. 1–20	Apr. 10–May 1	Apr. 15–May 1	Apr. 20–June 15
Chard	Feb. 20–May 15	Mar. 15–May 25	Apr. 10–June 15	Apr. 15–June 15	Apr. 15–June 15	May 1–June 15
Chervil and chives	Feb. 10–Mar. 10	Feb. 15–Mar. 15	Mar. 10–Apr. 10	Mar. 10–Apr. 10	Mar. 20–Apr. 20	Apr. 1–May 1
Chicory, witloof	June 1–July 1	June 1–July 1	June 10–July 1	June 15–July 1	June 15–July 1	June 1–20
Collards¹	Feb. 15–May 1	Mar. 1–June 1	Mar. 1–June 1	Mar. 10–June 1	Apr. 1–June 1	Apr. 1–June 1
Cornsalad	Jan. 1–Mar. 15	Feb. 1–Apr. 1	Feb. 15–Mar. 15	Feb. 15–Apr. 1	Apr. 1–May 1	Apr. 1–June 1
Corn, sweet	Mar. 15–Mar. 15	Mar. 25–May 15	Apr. 10–June 1	Apr. 25–June 15	May 10–June 15	May 10–June 1
Cress, upland	Feb. 20–Mar. 15	Feb. 1–Apr. 1	Mar. 10–Apr. 1	Mar. 20–May 1	Apr. 10–May 10	Apr. 20–May 20
Cucumber	Apr. 1–May 1	Apr. 10–May 15	Apr. 20–June 1	May 1–June 15	May 15–June 15	May 20–June 15
Eggplant¹	Apr. 1–May 1	Apr. 15–May 15	May 1–June 1	May 10–June 1	May 15–June 10	May 20–June 15
Endive	Mar. 1–Apr. 1	Mar. 10–Apr. 10	Mar. 15–Apr. 15	Mar. 25–Apr. 15	Apr. 15–May 15	Apr. 15–May 15
Fennel, Florence	Mar. 1–Apr. 1	Mar. 10–Apr. 10	Mar. 15–Apr. 15	Mar. 25–Apr. 15	Apr. 15–May 15	Apr. 15–May 15
Garlic	Feb. 1–Mar. 1	Feb. 10–Mar. 10	Feb. 20–Mar. 20	Mar. 10–Apr. 1	Apr. 1–May 1	Apr. 1–May 1
Horseradish¹	Feb. 20–Mar. 10	Feb. 1–Apr. 1	Mar. 10–Apr. 10	Mar. 15–Apr. 15	Apr. 1–30	Apr. 15–May 15
Kale	Feb. 20–Mar. 10	Mar. 1–20	Mar. 10–Apr. 1	Mar. 20–Apr. 20	Apr. 1–20	Apr. 10–May 1
Kohlrabi	Feb. 10–Mar. 1	Mar. 1–Apr. 1	Mar. 10–Apr. 10	Mar. 20–May 1	Apr. 1–May 1	Apr. 10–May 15
Leek	Feb. 15–Mar. 15	Mar. 1–Apr. 1	Feb. 1–Apr. 1	Mar. 15–Apr. 15	Apr. 1–May 1	Apr. 1–May 1
Lettuce, head¹	Feb. 1–20	Feb. 1–20	Mar. 1–20	Mar. 15–Apr. 15	Apr. 1–May 1	Apr. 1–May 15
Lettuce, leaf	Apr. 1–May 1	Apr. 10–May 15	Feb. 15–May 15	Mar. 20–May 15	Apr. 1–May 15	Apr. 1–June 15
Muskmelon	Apr. 20–Apr. 20	Apr. 10–May 15	Apr. 20–June 1	May 1–June 15	May 15–June 15	May 20–June 15
Mustard	Feb. 20–Apr. 20	Mar. 10–Apr. 20	Mar. 10–Apr. 20	Mar. 20–May 1	Apr. 10–June 1	Apr. 20–May 1
Okra	Apr. 1–June 15	Apr. 10–June 15	Apr. 20–June 15	May 1–June 1	May 10–June 1	May 20–June 10
Onion¹	Feb. 10–Mar. 10	Feb. 15–Mar. 15	Mar. 1–Apr. 1	Mar. 15–Apr. 15	Apr. 1–May 1	Apr. 1–May 1
Onion, seed	Feb. 10–Mar. 10	Feb. 15–Mar. 15	Mar. 1–Apr. 1	Mar. 15–Apr. 15	Apr. 1–May 1	Apr. 1–May 1
Onion, sets	Feb. 1–Mar. 20	Feb. 20–Mar. 20	Mar. 10–Apr. 1	Mar. 15–Apr. 1	Apr. 1–May 1	Apr. 1–May 1
Parsley	Feb. 15–Mar. 15	Mar. 1–Apr. 1	Mar. 1–Apr. 1	Mar. 20–Apr. 20	Apr. 1–May 1	Apr. 1–May 1
Parsnip	Feb. 15–Mar. 15	Mar. 1–Apr. 1	Mar. 10–Apr. 10	Mar. 20–Apr. 20	Apr. 1–May 1	Apr. 15–June 1
Peas, garden	Jan. 1–Mar. 15	Feb. 1–Mar. 15	Feb. 20–Mar. 20	Mar. 1–Apr. 15	Mar. 20–May 1	Apr. 1–May 1
Peas, black-eye	Apr. 10–July 1	Apr. 15–July 1	May 1–July 1	May 10–June 15	May 10–June 15	May 10–June 15
Pepper¹	Apr. 10–June 1	Apr. 15–July 1	May 1–July 1	May 1–July 1	May 15–June 15	May 20–June 10
Potato	Feb. 10–Mar. 15	Feb. 20–Mar. 20	Mar. 10–Apr. 1	Mar. 15–Apr. 10	Mar. 15–May 1	Apr. 1–June 1
Radish	Jan. 1–May 1	Feb. 20–May 1	Mar. 1–May 1	Mar. 10–May 10	Mar. 20–May 10	Apr. 1–June 1
Rhubarb¹						Apr. 1–May 1
Rutabaga		Feb. 1–Mar. 1	Feb. 1–Apr. 1	Mar. 1–May 1	Mar. 20–May 20	Apr. 15–June 1
Salsify	Jan. 15–Mar. 1	Feb. 15–Mar. 1	Mar. 1–Mar. 15	Mar. 10–Apr. 15	Mar. 20–May 1	Apr. 15–May 15
Shallot	Feb. 15–Mar. 15	Feb. 15–Mar. 15	Feb. 15–Mar. 15	Mar. 1–Apr. 1	Mar. 1–May 1	Apr. 1–May 1
Sorrel	Feb. 10–Mar. 10	Feb. 20–Mar. 20	Mar. 1–Apr. 15	Mar. 10–Apr. 15	Mar. 10–May 15	Apr. 15–May 15
Soybean	Apr. 10–June 30	Apr. 20–June 30	May 1–June 30	May 10–June 20	May 15–June 20	May 25–June 10
Spinach	Jan. 15–Mar. 15	Feb. 1–Mar. 20	Feb. 15–Apr. 1	Feb. 15–Apr. 15	Mar. 20–Apr. 15	Mar. 25–June 10
Spinach, New Zealand	Apr. 1–May 15	Apr. 10–June 1	Apr. 20–June 1	May 1–June 15	May 1–June 15	May 10–June 15
Squash, summer	Apr. 1–May 15	Apr. 10–June 1	Apr. 20–June 15	May 10–June 15	May 10–June 15	May 10–June 15
Sweet potato	Apr. 10–June 1	Apr. 20–June 1	May 1–June 15	May 10–June 10	May 10–June 10	May 10–June 10
Tomato	Apr. 1–May 20	Apr. 10–June 1	May 1–July 1	May 5–June 10	May 10–June 15	May 15–June 10
Turnip	Feb. 10–Mar. 10	Feb. 20–May 1	Mar. 1–Apr. 1	Mar. 10–Apr. 1	Mar. 20–May 1	Apr. 1–June 1
Watermelon	Apr. 1–May 1	Apr. 10–May 15	Apr. 20–June 1	May 1–June 15	May 15–June 15	June 1–June 15

¹Plants.

²Generally fall-planted.

some, shielded on the sides with wooden walls and with a good-fitting glass lid in a frame that can be raised to get in and work with your plants but otherwise stays down to let in light and keep out cold. You can start frost-tender plants from seed in a hot frame same as you might in a tin can in your house. A cold frame or "hardening off" frame means you leave the lid up gradually more and more or transplant your tender young plants into a not-so-protected box where they will gradually get used to cold air and chilly nights before going out into the garden. Even in the garden you can protect plants from chill by putting the commercial product Hotkaps or a similar shelter over them.

Bill Rogers from Wyoming wrote me this about his hot frames: "I make them light and portable so that I can put them over vegetables not yet ripened in the fall. In the spring, I locate the hot frames near a rock or other shelter, exposed to maximum sunlight. Thus I obtain a month or six weeks additional on each end of the season and I have ripe tomatoes or cantaloupes or other vegetables which I could not have in our short growing season. The earth is over a heavy bed of manure for starting. And for both starting and finishing I make sure there is plenty of water.

"I use window sashes out of houses being wrecked; otherwise the cost of glass would run hot frames out of sight. I use scrap lumber for the frames but extend its life by painting—likewise the window frames and putty."

SOIL

There are shelves of wonderful books written on this subject, all by people infinitely smarter than I am so I sort of fear to tread here. But feeling like I got to say *something* here goes! Don't think of soil as something constant and unchanging and unchangeable. That just isn't so. Any soil, and especially a garden soil is in a process of constant change. Organic material is being taken out. That means material left over from something that was once alive—plant, animal, tree, seaweed, leaf, sawdust. Organic material is a natural fertilizer just like manure which is also natural or fertilizers which you buy in bags in stores which may or may not be natural in the fullest sense.

Plants can make food from sunshine in their green leaves and stems. They can also take it from organic-fertilizer kinds of materials in the ground. Wherever plants grow they are taking these materials from the ground. If it is a vegetable garden and you are carrying away their fruits and seeds then the organic material needs to be replenished every year to take the place of what you took away. Under natural circumstances the fruits spill onto the ground and rot as do the plant leaves and stems eventually and instead of being depleted the soil gets richer and richer as not only the original material returns but also the annual increment made by plants struggling to capture the energy of sunlight in their tissues. So to garden means automatically to fertilize—somehow—

every year to replace what you are carrying away. Otherwise your garden plants are going to be weaker and spindlier and your harvest smaller every year.

Compost is simply decayed organic material. Anything that was once alive makes good compost like leaves, coffee grounds, grass clippings, kitchen food scraps. But avoid meat and fat, which smell. In general you make a pile of the stuff, a bottomless wooden box works well, turn your pile with a pitchfork once a week to sort of stir it, keep it damp with a hose. Manure works the same way. Pile it up outside the barn and let it winter there. You really don't need to do anything else. In spring it will be ready to put on. Fresh organic material isn't ready for your plants to absorb. It can do more harm than good if you get in a hurry. Manure that isn't well rotted will kill your plants. Composting is in a nutshell techniques for hurrying up natural decomposition so you can get that organic material on your garden faster.

Green manure is another way of fertilizing your ground. It is more practical for a field or big garden than for a little one. It means growing a crop on that ground that is intended to be plowed back under to decompose and enrich the ground. That's all. Rye grass, barley, oats, clover and other legume-type crops are all good green manure. The green manure system will delay the rest of your garden though and you can't do it in the same spot you have perennials. Rye grass, buckwheat and alfalfa are probably the most popular green manure crops. Buckwheat develops so fast you can get a crop off it and then turn it under if your growing season is reasonably long.

Natural fertilizing basically means returning to the soil all the plant and animal residues that came from it originally. Don't plow your fertilizer in too deep. You want it in the *top* soil. Really work at your fertilizing. It's easily possible that with some effort to get more energy into your soil the garden area could produce five times as much food for your family as it is doing right now.

CULTIVATING has a triple usefulness. One is to break up the ground in the first place. You want to loosen the soil enough so you can plant seeds and pull weeds and so the plant roots can quickly and easily grow down and out to find the growing materials they need in the soil—food and water. It's technically possible to make a seed trench with a pickax, plant, and cover the seed by kicking the clods back over with your boot but you won't get much of a crop. Land that hasn't been cultivated before or not recently needs a good plowing to start with. You can get that plowing done in either the spring or the fall. If you plowed in the fall you'll have more work to do next spring. We spring tooth the ground in the spring, then till with the rototiller. Men usually love rototillers. They are too expensive to buy new for most people—like $222.95 or $289.95 in my Ward's catalog. So buy a used one if you can. Advertise in a wanted to buy column in your newspaper to track one down.

The second place where cultivating is really important is to work your fertilizer in. When you till under the leftover pea and bean vines and so on from the summer's garden you are really doing a green manure thing. When your compost pile is ready for the garden you want to till it in enough to sort of get it mixed up and stirred around with the dirt. When you put on manure same thing—you want to mix it up with the dirt. If you want to turn your whole garden into a wonderful compost pile that will grow great vegetables next summer start in the fall by spreading a layer of decayable stuff on the ground like grass, leaves, weeds, vegetable scraps. Now spread a 2-inch layer of manure on top of that. Now scatter lime or wood ashes saved from your wood cookstove on top of that. Now cover with straw. Add earthworms if you think maybe your garden could use more. It probably could. Water occasionally if the weather isn't doing the job. When you are ready to cultivate in the spring dig this all into the upper 4 or 5 inches of your ground.

The third important job cultivating does is fight weeds. There is only so much plant food in your garden. You worked really hard to get it there. If your garden has one weed for every vegetable plant then half your soil-type plant food is going to the weeds and half to your vegetable plants. That means your vegetable plants will be half as big and healthy and productive as they could be if there were no weeds. It isn't quite that simple but that's the general idea. You want to kill existing weeds and turn them into green manure. You want for sure to get rid of annual-type weeds before they have a chance to go to seed. If you let it happen you could have three generations of pigweed growing side by side happily in a single summer even in a shortish growing season.

WEEDING doesn't just happen while your crops are up. It's very important to get the ground tilled up really well in the spring before you plant your rows to get rid of the weeds that have already started, then at intervals as the weeds seem to be gaining again. Like every couple weeks during the growing season. Come through between your rows with a rototiller or a hoe. Weed by hand inside the row close between and beside the plants.

My objection to the rototiller is that, like all machines, it is not sufficiently discriminating. It can't go around a lovely volunteer that is in the middle of the row. It helps to have everything in straight long rows that are preplanned wide enough so you can go back and forth between with the rototiller. Our rototiller can be made shorter or longer in its bite and that's a help.

Once the crops are planted I do the close-in weeding, stooping over, or kneeling, or sitting with my bottom on some newspaper or piece of cardboard when the ground is damp. The best time to hand-weed is right after a rain when the ground is really damp. Then those long-rooted weeds come right up. They seem to relax their roots when the ground is wet and the soil gets soft. When it gets hot the roots really grab again. The machine weeding has to wait for drier ground so that the tiller forks won't gum up in mud. If you rototill clay soil while it is damp you really make a mess. Some people don't believe in weeding. I do, but sometimes I don't have time or strength to do a really good job. There is a definite difference in your crop if it doesn't have to compete with a lot of weeds for the available minerals, water and sunshine. Some crops can resist weeds better than others. Peas, corn and beans are pretty good that way. So is squash. Plants in a well-weeded row grow to several times the size they would without weeding.

Mulching doesn't discourage morning glory weed, of which I have lots. You don't know about morning glory? Happy innocence! I used to have nightmares about the stuff—seriously! A single morning glory plant (this is the wild weed type, not what you buy for the pretty flowers to climb your fence) a week old has a root 5 inches long. If you dig it up root and all and are careful not to leave it lying on dirt in the rain in which case it will reroot itself you can kill it. Otherwise when that same plant is six weeks old the root is 12 inches long and if you try to dig it out and fail to get all the root it will come back regrowing from what is left of the root. After ten weeks if you didn't get to it yet the root is 34 inches long, has buds on the lateral roots and you've lost the battle. By the end of the summer the roots will be 4 feet deep with side branches reaching 5 feet in every direction. After two summers the original plant will be a patch 17 feet wide with roots 19 feet deep. We finally found an answer to morning glory. You build a pig pen right on top of it and leave the pigs rooting happily there a few years. Then move the pigpen and lo! no morning glory and lots of good manure!

I once mulched my strawberries with hay. A lush stand of grass grew everywhere I had laid it. (From the seeds contained in it.) I'll never do that again. The grass was worse to get rid of than any of the other stuff I was trying to cover. We manure the ground in spring and fall and scatter leaves from town in the fall to build up the soil. The manure really makes a significant difference in the size of your crop and the workability of your soil.

BLACK PLASTIC has its fans. Here's what my Stites, Idaho, friend Barb Ingrams says about it:

"We don't have too big of a garden spot, but it

was big enough for my family. Glenn rototilled up the spot and then we laid black plastic over the whole thing. We both have backs that bother us, so this is done to eliminate a lot of weed pulling. Black has to be used so no sunlight can make weeds grow. For plants, cut holes about the size of the top of a 3-pound coffee can. For the rows of vegetables, take a board about the size of a 1 x 4 or 1 x 6 feet—depending on what the vegetable is—cut around the board on both sides and lift the strip out. Plant as usual. Instead of black plastic this year we are going to try newspapers. It would be planted in the same manner as for the plastic. In between the rows lay boards in the middle of them to make walking much easier and you don't pack the dirt down as bad. With the plastic the ground seems to hold the heat in better and also the water. For tomato plants the holes have to be quite a bit larger than for pepper or some other plants. We had a tomato plant grow over 4 feet and it was just a volunteer. With newspapers instead of picking up the papers at the end of the season just turn them under when you till. Saves a lot of time."

WATER

Vegetables in general need a lot of water. Most vegetables are about 85 to 90 percent water. Flowers can survive longer without water than vegetables, so can trees and bushes kinds of things. But some vegetables never recover from a drought and almost all of them will produce way more with abundant water than with a skimpy supply. A good way to decide where your garden should be and how large is to let your water supply provide the measure. Pick the sunniest spot available for a start because that's another thing your plants have to have—a minimum of six hours a day of sunshine. Hook up your water system in the middle of the sunny spot and see how much gets wet. Unless you live in an area with a dependable spring-to-fall long abundant rains, don't cultivate and plan to garden places that you can't get water to. For the area to be watered, if you are working with a limited water supply or if you can only afford to buy so much water to put on your garden figure that your garden needs about an inch of water a week, either from the sky or your system. Watering by trickle is most effective for the plants and you lose less by evaporation—that's like a porous hose or pipe with holes in it that lets out a slow steady flow of water for the ground.

It's good to give your garden a good soaking while you are at it rather than several light sprinkles. Light sprinkles encourage shallow root systems which don't do as good a job finding other needed food for the plant. Deep soakings encourage deep good root systems. An exception to this is newly planted seeds. If you want them to come up as fast as possible and to discourage birds and other poultry from digging them up and eating them try to water often enough to keep the soil continually moist, like morning and evening sprinkling every day until they are up.

Here we have heavy spring rains from February to June. Then it suddenly turns hot and there may not be another significant rainfall until the fall rains come.

All the early crops like carrots, green onions and peas do fine but for anything that matures later than June it has to be watered.

RAINBOW SPRINKLER—If you have good water pressure you can use a rainbow sprinkler—that's a contraption that you put on the end of the hose and it jerks back and forth spraying water over quite a large circle as it goes. It is adjustable to water in a full circle, half circle or quarter circle. You can set it up wherever you want it. Just pound the sharp pointed metal stake side into the ground wherever you want it to sprinkle.

SOAKER HOSE—We've never been blessed with enough water pressure to make one of those work, however, and so we use a soaker hose. This is a long hose with tiny holes along one side and the end capped so water is forced to spray up and out through the holes. It sprays up 3 to 5 feet through the holes (depending on your water pressure) and has a gentle soaking action that is good for young tender plants and older ones, too. We hook up two of them, one behind the other, to cover more territory and the whole thing is on the end of about 200 feet of hose so I can take the water wherever I want it in our big garden. If you try to make the water run uphill you lose water pressure correspondingly.

BUCKET—Another way to water is to carry the water in buckets and dump it on the plant. Don't laugh. I know a lady who has a magnificent orchard and garden and that's how she has always done it.

IRRIGATION—This means you have a way to bring a heavy flow of water by ditches into your garden. You then flood the garden with it, if you have lots, or else run it down little ditches alongside each row of plants. Mass flooding is really most appropriate for alfalfa fields.

The alfalfa field is watered a portion at a time by means of a system of ditches and dams. The ditches are just plain old "Vs" gouged in the dirt with a ditcher to carry the water where you want it to go. Where you want the water to stop and pour out of the ditch you plug the ditch with a dam of mud scooped up in your shovel from the ground beside. You have to spend all day out there either leaning on the shovel or digging with it to keep the water moving and thread the fine line between leaving the ground too dry and washing out the crop.

My father used to irrrigate this way. I recommend shorts, hip waders and a straw hat for an irrigating costume. The exact placement of the ditches is a fine art. The water has to flow downhill, of course, but you want it to flow slowly so it won't wash out your dams which means contouring the ditches appropriately to the slope of your land. Then they should be a reasonable distance from each other, say 15 to 20 feet for a hay field. Every field is different and the first summer will correct all your original estimates.

You need a top ditch to feed from your water source down to the field. This ditch has to divert the water from somewhere higher than the field so it can gravity flow down to it. That ditch feeds into one along the top side of your field from which all the contour ditches take off. You dam the top ditch wherever you want the water to flow into a contour ditch and cut out the side of the top ditch to let the water flow out into it. Start with the lower end and work your way back because you are weakening your ditch sides doing this. The top ditch is several feet deep. The contour ditches are less deep, like about 6 inches to a foot to facilitate overflow.

PIPES—Another way to water on a big scale—hay or truck gardening—is with a system of irrigation pipes. These are expensive. They can be either permanently installed or movable. You can buy movable irrigation pipe that isn't unreasonably heavy or pipe

that comes with built-in wheels. You buy heavy-duty sprinkers to go with it and a big pump to draw your water. This assumes you have a river or big pond or artesian well in your field to draw from.

Not all rivers are free water for irrigating. In some cases you have to pay annually for your water use and are allowed only as many cubic feet of water as you pay for, calculated by the inches of water and the time it flows. I've never known farmers to fight so bitterly for or over anything as water. I've personally known cases of near murder happen along ditch lines when a man down the line wasn't getting the water he was paying for and walked up the line to discover somebody else was diverting it onto his own ground.

ARTICHOKES TO WATERCRESS

From Garden to Kitchen

This chapter assumes that you are raising your own vegetables and literally does try to tell you in detail how to get them from the ground to your table. It's a huge subject. I'm giving it a very limited treatment, but maybe that can be seen as a blessing to you. This won't be at all technical. Everything that I'm going to say is something I think is important. What I didn't say I hope you don't need to know, anyway. There are great thick books on this subject. *How to Grow Vegetables and Fruits by the Organic Method,* edited by Rodale and Staff, and published by Rodale Books, Inc., is a good one.

I've tried especially to include hard-to-find recipes for things like chicory, kohlrabi and salsify that have become uncommon because they don't appear on supermarket shelves. Gardeners can and do raise them. I've also tried to include ample recipes for the homelier vegetables like cabbage, turnips and beets, which are often bypassed by gourmet cookbooks, but which must be an important part of the staff of life for northerly garden growers. I've told you how to save your own seed wherever possible and how to cope with each vegetable's peculiar problems.

For each vegetable I have included directions for canning, freezing, drying, storing—whichever are appropriate. For information on cantaloupe, watermelon, berries and fruits see the Sweets chapter.

ARTICHOKES—When can you eat a thistle? Once in an educated way I would have calmly replied, "Why when you eat a globe artichoke, of course!" Now, I'm not so sure. You see, globe artichokes do nicely in California but not in Idaho. The artichoke-growing center of the United States is just south of San Francisco on the Pacific Ocean where they grow mile on mile and every year there is an artichoke festival. But artichokes hate cold and are not growable under ordinary circumstances north of the line where zero temperatures happen. But I sure have seen artichoke hearts in glass jars in the grocery stores and in salads and boiled and served with melted butter to dip the

fleshy end of the leaf base in. So when the children and I were driving through California selling books I bought one in a grocery store. It looked good and we were used to eating out of grocery bags—one meal a day in a restaurant for hot vegetables, potatoes, and meat and the other two out of a grocery bag for economy's sake. So I bought an artichoke, carried it out to the car, sliced through it with a knife down to where I figured the tender, tasty artichoke heart was and took a bite. For a few moments after I thought maybe I was going to strangle. The thing resembled nothing I can think of so much as a fishhook pincushion cactus. It was full of sharp little needles and dry stuff that wanted to grab and choke. Well, when I had finally achieved spitting it out I threw the rest away and haven't been able to eat an artichoke heart since, even cooked. And you see that's all because I'm from Idaho and don't know any better.

To plant globe artichokes you can go either with seeds or with pieces off a going plant. But it's not an easy plant to raise (and not really very nutritious) so if you're just starting gardening I'd wait a year or so. It's a perennial and takes a lot of room so you need a

biggish garden for it. If it's seed you are planting, it won't bear fruit the first year unless you start it really early indoors. Six plants would be enough for an average-sized family. You can buy plants from California nurseries. Transplant plants from seeds or plants from nursery when they have three or four leaves apiece to rows 3 feet apart and 2 feet between each plant in the row. Or if you have access to some plants that are already going you can plant the side shoots that come from the base of the old plants. These are like sprouts and grow in the spring. You can cut and eat them like asparagus if you don't want to use them to start new plants. Your artichoke plant will live and bear pretty well for three or four years although the buds it produces may be smaller each year, unless you really load the manure on.

To save your own seed—You're better off not because it doesn't always breed true to form. Instead use the system of transplanting sprouts.

To harvest, get the buds before they flower. Harvest faithfully because if you keep taking the buds off so that no seed can form the plants will continue to produce until the end of the season. Make sure you pick before the buds have shown any sign of opening. Keep in the refrigerator if you must delay before using.

Artichokes are a sort of a large scaly head like the cone of a pine tree. What you eat is the flower bud before it opens. Cut off the stem close to the leaves, pull off the tough outer leaves and cut off the prickly tops with scissors. The edible portion is the thickened portion at the base of each scale and the core to which the leaflike scales are attached. When the artichoke is very young and tender the edible parts can be eaten raw as a salad. When it becomes hard as it does very quickly it must be cooked.

Boil with 2 tablespoons lemon juice until you can easily remove a leaf. After boiling drain upside down. Then the scales are pulled with the fingers from the cooked head and the thickened base of each scale is dipped in a sauce and eaten. I use melted butter served in a little individual container at each plate. I have a friend who says mayonnaise is the *only* thing.

The bottom or "heart" is the most delicate part of the artichoke. It can be cut up for a salad or stewed and served with a sauce.

Other sauces—French salad dressing on cold artichoke hearts. Hollandaise sauce or mayonnaise seasoned with lemon juice and mustard.

To fry, sauté hearts in butter until lightly browned. Season with salt and lemon juice. They go well with mushrooms (half sliced mushrooms, half sliced artichokes, season with salt and garlic powder and bake in a baking dish about 20 minutes) or in a salad.

To freeze or pickle the artichoke hearts, pull away the outer leaves until light yellow or white ones free of all green are reached. Then cut off the tops of the buds and trim to a cone. Wash in cold water. Scald 7 minutes and then freeze.

ASPARAGUS is a perennial that, once established may live and produce longer than you or I. It's the plant that literally shoots up overnight in my garden in the early spring, the second edible thing. (Multiplier onions are even earlier, radishes a shade later.)

To plant from seed—You can grow asparagus from seed even though people usually don't (they start with 1-, 2- or 3-year-old roots instead). Starting with seed is cheapest though and maybe time doesn't matter so much when you realize you are planting something that will last like an apple tree. The asparagus bed once started will produce every spring whether you do anything more to it or not. You may discover asparagus spears in an abandoned farmhouse yard in May just as if it expected folks home right away. Asparagus likes a winter cold enough to freeze the top 2 inches or so of ground and will do better than in a warmer climate. It does suffer from one disease called "rust," so when buying seeds or roots buy a rust-resistant variety like Mary Washington or Martha Washington. The big work with asparagus comes at the planting stage—you want to do it right and then you'll get long good returns.

Asparagus likes heavily fertilized soil and it will actually taste better to you if it gets the abundant soil nutrition it wants. Manure is best, compost second best. It being a perennial, be sure and plant it on the edge of your garden where it won't get plowed up. It will grow higher than your head but the stalks and leaves are delicately fernlike and beautiful once they get their little green berry things on them and won't shade your other plants. Asparagus needs less water than most other vegetables so you can put it on the edge of your waterable zone.

Spade or work the soil for your asparagus bed at least 15 inches deep and a foot wide. When you replace the dirt from your digging make it a rich mixture of dirt and manure or compost from the bottom up instead of just what you took out.

Plant your seeds in the early spring in the place where you intend to make your permanent asparagus bed.

You can figure 1 ounce of seed will produce about 75 plants. Plant about 1 to 1½ inches deep.

Toward the end of the first summer pick out your best plants and get rid of all the others so that you have only one plant about every 14 inches in your row and rows 1 foot apart if you will be weeding by hand or wider if by machine.

Protect young plants their first winter with a covering of 3 or 4 inches of loose manure or straw.

To plant from roots—Asparagus planted from seed produces a crop 1 to 3 years later than if you had planted roots. One-year-old roots may actually do better in the long run than 2- or 3-year-old roots.

Whether you're starting with seed or roots figure that 24 or 48 plants will generously supply your family. Plant the roots during the late fall or early spring. Same as with planting seed put those roots in to a bed that you really worked hard on getting the dirt loosened and mixing it up with lots of manure or compost. Set out your roots 14 inches (or thereabouts) apart and from 1 to 3 feet apart in rows as you prefer. Give the trench intended for roots enough dirt-manure mixture to make the bottom about 10 inches below ground level. Water lightly and then lay the roots in it with the top part up and the roots spread comfortably and natural looking. Now rake in over the roots about 3 inches of your good dirt-manure mixture and tamp it down. As the asparagus grows above the dirt level gradually add more of your mixture every couple weeks until by August you have the asparagus at ground level with the rest of the garden. Now you have healthy, well-fed roots, buried deeply away from the cold and other hazards and ready to produce forever! When you manure or compost the rest of your garden every year don't forget to get plenty on the asparagus too. It will produce that much better for you.

To harvest—Figure three years is the magic number. If you planted from seed cut no spears the first year and none the second spring. The third spring your plants are now three years old and you can take a limited cutting but keep it down to no more than two weeks. In the fourth year and from then on you can cut for a period of four to five weeks after they start growing spears but then stop cutting. You want to let the plants grow some—the leaves furnish food for the roots from sunshine and without them your asparagus plants would eventually die. A warning sign that you should stop cutting is when the stalks get skinny. Figure in general you can start cutting on four-year or older plants about mid-April and stop at the end of June, but sooner if like I said the stalks get skinny. On asparagus planted from roots the same schedule applies. Just be sure and re- member how many years old the roots were that you planted and apply the rule from there. Don't panic if you see skinny stalks even though you've been har- vesting absolutely according to the rule. Asparagus plants are generally male or female. Females grow nice plump stalks. Male plants have skinny ones. If you distinguish the two early in your bed's life, dig up the male ones and get rid of them, and replace with new ones hoping for girls, you'll have a more produc-

tive bed. But if you're going to dig out the boys do it while they're young or it can scarcely be done.

When you are harvesting asparagus there's no half way. You've got to take every spear or you'll have none. Because a spear that isn't cut grows into a tall, fern-leafy stem and no more spears at all from that plant that summer. A spear that is on the verge of outgrowing you will be getting tough and stringy. The best system is to cut off young shoots when about 4 or 5 inches above ground. You can actually cut them off a little below ground but it's safer for the plant if you don't and that below ground part has a tendency to be tough. If you stall and let the compact tip of the spear start to open you don't have a young, tender stalk anymore. Early morning is the best time to harvest since a hot day actually makes the stalks tougher and dryer. Make it a habit to get out to the asparagus bed every single day during your harvest- ing season, or every two at least.

To save seed—Seems kind of unreal when you consider the lifespan of asparagus, but some garden- ers suggest that you renew your bed every 15 or 20 years or maybe you'd like to give some to the neigh- bors. Asparagus makes seed every summer on the tip of its long stem in little berrylike fruits. Let them ma- ture, dry and store.

To prepare, wash and discard any tough bottom piece. Get rid of the scales that cling tightly to the lower half of the spear. Just lift the tip of each with a paring knife and pull it off. Or use a potato peeler if you're in a hurry. Get your asparagus from ground to table as fast as possible for best taste. If you aren't going to cook it right away, refrigerate it.

Raw—The tender new tips are good. Just snap off and eat. To boil, wash and remove any tough ends. Leave the spears long or cut into two lengths. But add the tender tops after the stalks have boiled for 10 or 15 minutes as they require less cooking. If you want to leave the stalks whole stand them on end in the water so the tips are out, then let down as soon as the bottoms begin to get tender. Boiled asparagus is good served just with a little butter, vinegar, salt and pepper. Or put a cream sauce sort of thing on spears cooked whole or cut into short pieces and serve on toast!

For salad, drain, chill, cut in pieces, arrange on lettuce leaves and serve with French dressing.

To fry, precook until half done. Use tender stalk tops for this. Tie stalks together, 5 ot 6 to a bundle. Dip in beaten egg, then into flour, deep fat fry.

For tough ends try this recipe:

Asparagus Soup—Cut about 1 pound asparagus into 1-inch pieces. Cook until tender with a little salt in 1 quart water. Make a white sauce by stirring 4 tablespoons flour into 4 tablespoons melted butter. Add to soup along with 1 beaten egg yolk and a dash rich cream.

To dry, use 3-inch tips only. Then split lengthwise.

To freeze, wash, remove scales and scald 2 to 4 minutes, depending on how large your stalks are. Chill, drain and pack.

To can, pack hot, cover with hot cooking liquid. Process in a pressure canner at 10 pounds pressure 25 minutes per pint container, 55 minutes per quart container.

BEANS—Which kind? There are green beans and yellow wax beans, bush beans and pole beans, European fava beans, scarlet runner beans that people grow for flowers, lima beans that make a great green vegetable, soybeans that you can make milk for the baby out of, umpteen kinds of beans for drying—pinto beans, kidney beans, white beans, black beans, and peas that act like beans—chick peas, and blackeyed peas—and maybe they really are beans but I don't think so. Books have been written about one kind of bean or another, especially the soybean and drying beans and they deserve that kind of coverage. There's one whole seed catalog just devoted to beans. I recommend it to all fellow bean lovers: Write the Vermont Bean Seed Company, Ways Lane, Manchester Center, Vermont 05255, for their seed catalog. They are bean and pea experts and welcome questions. But in the meantime I'm going to do the best I can to guide you wisely through this bean maze. Here are some advices for the beginner.

Beans do vary in the kind of soil they need, amount of fertilizer, growing season, hardness or easiness to grow, whether they bear awhile and stop or bear all summer, whether they make good eating as dried beans or not. So read the fine print. If you are a beginning gardener bush beans are the easiest, hardiest green type to grow, lima beans one of the hardest. Beans of all sorts are the legumes you read about. (A "legume" is a plant that has a seed that splits in half.) Peanuts are legumes and a sort of pea-bean when you look at it this way but I've got them in the Nuts and Seeds section later in this chapter. In general they are good food.

GREEN BEANS are also called "snap beans" and you really can and should snap them but that comes under preparation after harvest. Here I'm talking about BUSH green beans. Pole green beans are somewhat different and I'll tackle them later. Bush green beans are one of the easiest vegetables to grow. They will grow well even in poor soil. Their time from planting to picking can be around 60 days which makes them good in a short-season climate. They cannot live through frost but they can stand lots of heat if you keep them frequently watered.

To plant, put your first row in on the date of your supposed last frost. If you soak the seed overnight before planting it will speed it up by several days. Plant an inch deep and 2 to 4 inches apart. In 7 to 14 days your plants will be up. If you're short of garden space you can make your rows as little as a foot apart, but only if you're planning on weeding by hand and with a hoe. Otherwise make your rows about 2-3 feet apart. You can figure that a half pound of seed will plant a 50-foot row. If a killing frost takes your first planting just replant and keep planting another row or so every week or ten days through the spring. Seeds that are still not up through the ground during a frost will come up and thrive and mature ahead of the seed you planted to replace plants killed by frost.

If you live in a very wet climate cover your bean seed only shallowly rather than an inch or more because bean seed is liable to rotting and will survive better that way.

To harvest—Once they start, your bush green beans will bear for four to five weeks if you treat them right. They need regular watering and regular picking. If you don't keep them thoroughly picked they will stop producing. You can pick them at various stages and different people have different preferences. I like them best, especially for freezing, picked when they are still young enough that the beans inside the pods aren't completely filled out. Older beans will give you more bean but it won't be as tender. If you wait longer than that they start to be dried out and tough. Plan on picking beans at least every three days while they are on. That way you should be able to stay ahead of them. Pick into a big paper shopping bag or whatever you prefer. Early morning and after sunset are the times kindest to the picker and the beans come off just as fine. Bean vines aren't too husky and pull up or bruise easily so learn to handle them gently while picking. Bush green beans don't make the best dried beans so there isn't any point in drying seeds except in the case of saving your own seed. Can, freeze or start your drying the same day if possible, or at latest the next morning.

To prepare, pick and snap into about 1-inch lengths. Snap rather than cut. If you cut them you will cut some of the beans inside the pods and the pieces will fall out of the pod. Snap off both tips and throw the tips into your animal feed.

For Julienne-style beans, slice unsnapped beans lengthwise into slender strips.

Old Fashioned Beans—Add diced onion and bacon (or salt pork cut into small pieces) to your beans. Cook, covered, until the beans are done, adding water as necessary. This was a regular with my mother. If your meat and beans don't come out even in cooking time, try boiling the pork awhile first, then adding the beans.

To freeze green or wax beans, wash, snap, scald (boil 1 minute), chill, drain and pack. Use small "baby" beans, 3 inches long, for best results.

But here's a word from my own experience. Green beans don't keep as well in the freezer as any other vegetable I can think of. I don't know why that is but beans that have been in the freezer six months will be seriously losing their flavor. The best way to cope with that condition that I know of is to fry them with something flavorful like bacon grease or potatoes and onions. You can put the frozen hunk right into the frying pan, being careful not to burn any and cook from there. Or you may decide to can most of your green beans. In my experience that's the way they keep best, longest, tastiest.

To salt, see pages in the Food Preserving chapter.

To dry green beans you can use the pioneer method of stringing them that makes what they called "leather breeches beans." Start with tender green beans and a long needle threaded with a long strong thread. Sew the bean onto the string by pushing the needle right through the center of the bean. You'll have to keep pushing the beans down to the knot end as you work until the thread is loaded full with beans from knot end to needle. Now you hang up the string of beans to dry by one end in a warm place but out of sunlight. When they are completely dry you can store them in something else. The other way to dry them is to snap off the ends and snap into about 1-inch pieces, then spread on drying frames. If you sliced them they would dry quicker but you'd have bunches of little pieces. You do *not* have to steam them before drying.

To can, pack hot and cover with hot cooking liquid. In a pressure canner at 10 pounds pressure, process 30 minutes for pints, 40 minutes for quarts.

YELLOW WAX BEANS—The yellow bean varieties are basically grown and handled like green beans except they have a smooth, almost translucent shell and to me they don't taste as good and full of vitamins. They are easier to pick because the yellow is so obvious against the green leafy background.

POLE BEANS—Even if you decide to grow pole beans I'd advise you to put in a row or so of bush beans too because bush beans will be producing ten or so days before your pole beans. On the other hand pole beans have a longer harvest season than bush beans do once they get started and with care will keep making beans until frost finally kills the vines. Pole beans are more sensitive to cold than bush beans or drying beans and require a richer soil than any of the others except lima beans. Figure on planting your pole beans about two weeks later than you would the first row of bush beans. You don't have to stoop so much and hunt so hard to harvest pole beans but putting up the poles is a nuisance. You could let pole beans wander all over your ground but then they would cover other plants and grow all tangled up which would be even worse. You can let them grow in your corn row and use the corn stalks for poles but make sure you give the corn a head start.

To plant, remember they are going to get to be 6 or 8 feet high with lots of leaves so put them where they won't shade other vegetables and give them plenty of room. Kentucky Wonder is many people's favorite—that or Oregon Giants which really produce. Plant in hills 3 by 4 or 4 by 4 feet apart in the early summer. Have ready 6-foot "poles." There are lots of different ways you can arrange their poles. You could stand up a pole beside each "hill" of seed (they aren't really dirt mounds—I just mean that you plant four or five or six seeds in the same general area). Or you can arrange seeds and poles so that every three or four poles can be leaned together and tied at the top tipi style. Or you could use chicken wire instead of poles and plant them in a straight row to grow up the chicken wire . . . or a fence . . . or the corn like I said.

For the rest of it, just use the green bean directions.

FAVA BEANS—A cold climate bean that does well in Europe and is generally hard to grow in the United States. Also called "broad bean." It doesn't like hot weather but requires a long growing season.

Eating seeds that are not completely mature and are uncooked can make you sick. I'd suggest you not plant them until you're an accomplished gardener, have the right climate and are bored with all the usual vegetables.

LIMA BEANS are one of the hardest beans to grow successfully but the rewards make it worth the effort. There are pole limas or bush limas. It is not cold weather hardy and is slow growing, which makes the pole lima risky for colder climates. The bush lima grows faster than the pole lima but it still takes longer than a bush green bean or even a pole green bean to mature. You can't harvest from lima beans, bush or pole, near as long as you can from green beans—figure three to four weeks at the most, probably less. Lima beans have a harder time sprouting than other beans and you need to have their oil *really* loose and crumbly to help with that. Also soaking the seed overnight before planting will help, but don't more than half cover the seed with water or you're in trouble again. They don't like cold winds, are best when shelled green rather than dried. The pods are never eaten. They simply won't grow in poor soil; they need more fertilizing for a rich soil than any other kind of bean. The thing that makes lima beans worth it if you can grow them is that they are wonderfully tasty and wonderfully nutritious.

To plant in a row, make your rows 3 feet apart and the plants a foot to 20 inches apart in the row. Don't plant until the ground is thoroughly warm. Cover 1½ inches deep and place beans with the eye down. Pole limas should have only about three to four plants per hill. Lima seeds will take from 14 to 21 days just to sprout. Fordhook lima beans don't have as good a taste as the smaller ones but they're easier to grow and shell, and quicker. To shell, cut a strip off one side.

RUNNER BEANS, now sold as a flower, are climbers with lots of orange blossoms that bear from midsummer on to frost. They are pretty along any fence and if you're interested in the beans it saves you making poles. To eat green, choose very small ones and leave whole, otherwise slice finely. Cook in boiling salted water until soft and serve with butter. Older

pods can be saved and dried for eventual shelling and the big beans inside used like other dried beans. Runner beans have wonderful "Jack in the Beanstalk" type seeds, big and pretty colored. The children love to play with them.

SOYBEANS—This one is the vegetarian's favorite. You can make good meat substitutes with it. It's valuable beyond compare where dairy cows fall victim to insects and disease and babies are fed a milk made instead from soybeans. It makes a green bean as good tasting as lima beans and makes any grain eaten with it more nourishing because it contains an ingredient—lysine—missing from the grain. That means that a little bit of beans combined with brown rice or bread makes the brown rice or bread have something like 30 percent more protein value than it would without the soybeans. But I'm far from being expert on soybeans. Their greatest importance, even though they are good food for man or beast, is as a meat or milk substitute and obviously I'm not short that way. They are essential for those who can't or don't want to eat meat but I've been raised and lived all my life plentifully supplied with farm dairy products and meat. I'm going to do my best to tell you how to grow and use them anyway, with lots of help from good people with more experience than me who have written me but I'd suggest you do some reading beyond this book on the subject. Try *The Soybean Cookbook* by Dorothea Van Gunday Jones, published by Arco Books, 219 Park Avenue South, New York, New York 10003. Or the *Book of Tofu* by William Shurtleff and Akiko Aoyagi, published by Autumn Press, P.O. Box 469, Soquel, California 95073, the most recent and best on the subject.

To plant—The first problem with soybean growing is getting the right seed. Commercial farmers plant small seeded kinds intended for a large-scale operation, processing into oil and animal feed. Many of the so-called "edible" people varieties have other problems like a very long time to mature, or poor yields, or loss of seed before harvest by the pod shattering and spilling the soybeans on the ground even though they have a larger size and better flavor than the field soybean types. Until recently you couldn't try soybeans at all unless you had a growing season in the 80-or-more-day category and even then soybeans were a risky bet because cool or cloudy weather or an early frost could really reduce or wipe out your yield. For northern gardeners there is an exciting new soybean that will mature in only 45 days and that's no kidding. A Swede called Sven Holmberg experimented and worked 40 years to develop this variety that could be grown in places with short growing seasons. It is named the Fiskeby V Vegetable Bean and can be mail-ordered only from Thompson & Morgan Company, P.O. Box 24, Somerdale, New Jersey 08083. But the Fiskeby soybean isn't the perfect one for every garden—if you have longer, hotter summers then its yield will be poor, unless maybe you get it in at the very beginning of the growing season.

So if your climate is right for Fiskeby V Vegetable Bean plant that one. The next fastest maturing soybean takes at least 20 days more. Kanrich is an edible soybean that is very good for resisting field shattering,

takes 82 days to mature, but is on the small side. You can mail-order Kanrich seed from W. Atlee Burpee Company, Philadelphia, Pennsylvania 19132, or Nicholas Garden Nursery, Albany, Oregon 97321. You really have to have a good long, hot growing season for success with Kanrich though. Other edible soybean varieties you could try are Extra Early Green from Kitazawa Seed Company, 356 W. Taylor St., San Jose, California 95110, or Early Green Bush Soybean from Stokes Seeds, Inc., P.O. Box 548, Buffalo, New York 14240, or The Edible Soybean from The Natural Development Company, P.O. Box 215, Bainbridge, Pennsylvania 17502, or Giant Greenboy from Farmer Seed and Nursery, Faribault, Minnesota 55021.

Since there is such a difference in soybean varieties themselves I'll be safest advising you to plant them the way it says on the seed package. If it doesn't say, try rows 3 feet apart, with plants 6 inches apart. If your climate can handle it you'll get more yield by planting at two-week intervals, or less for as long as you dare. You need a halfway healthy and well nourished soil or your plants may not be strong. And in general don't plant until all danger of frost has passed.

To harvest, you can start picking when soybeans are green in the pod. That's the stage at which they resemble lima beans and you handle them cookingwise a similar way. They will be at that "green" stage for two or three weeks, probably in September, before they go on to become the dried stage. The Fiskeby V Vegetable Bean variety is more edible raw and on the raw side than the other soybean varieties. You can eat it raw from the garden, in salads where it will taste like peanuts, or stir-fried in a little oil alone or with other vegetables. Your other soybean varieties need more cooking, even to eat green. The next stage is when they dry in the pod. You want to harvest them as soon as they rattle in the pod because like I said before a big problem with soybeans is that the pods tend to shatter, if you don't get there promptly, and spill seed on the ground. So gather the pods and let them finish getting thoroughly dry in open containers, watching to make sure there is no mold on them. Once they are good and dry they will store nicely, even for several years, and you can use them in any dried soybean recipe. Just soak overnight before cooking.

To save your own seed, just use any of your dried soybeans.

To shell green soybeans—They are difficult to shell, but easier after having been cooked awhile right in the pods. So pick your beans for supper in the garden and then go ahead and boil the beans right in the pods. *Then* shell out and serve. Break pods crosswise and squeeze out beans.

To freeze green soybeans, boil in the pods about 5 minutes and then shell. You're going to have to let them cool some before you'll be able to shell. Then you can shell directly into the containers you're going to freeze them in. And freeze.

To eat fresh green soybeans, after cooking in the pod until tender, shell out, lightly salt, cool and serve as a snack; or serve buttered as part of a meal; or cool and add to salads; or cook with tomatoes, green onions and green peppers and serve.

To cook dried soybeans—The rules to success are thorough soaking in plenty of water beforehand (and then throw out the water and use new water for cooking) and long cooking or pressure cooking. There's a special reason why rather than the usual reluctance of dried beans to soften up. Soybeans contain something called "trypsin inhibitor" and what that amounts to is unless you destroy the "trypsin inhibitor" by *lots* of cooking the trypsin inhibitor in the soybeans will destroy the trypsin enzyme your very own pancreas makes that makes it possible for you to grow and digest protein. Well, every silver lining has a cloud seems like. But if you really, really cook the soybeans you eliminate the whole problem. And by soaking and pregrinding whole soybeans you reduce the cooking time needed. Ah, that all clouds were so easily eliminated. Figure the minimum for cooking whole soybeans is an overnight soak, using three times as much water as beans to start with, throwing out the soak water, plus cooking 4 to 6 hours regular or pressure cooking at 15 pounds for 20 to 30 minutes. To have some soybeans ready to cook on short notice you can go through the whole soaking process, then spread in a single layer on large cookie sheets and freeze, then store in containers in the freezer. The idea of spreading them out is to get them to freeze separately and they'll thaw and cook up quicker for you. When you want to cook your frozen beans you can then skip the soaking process and start them right out to cook. Presoaked and frozen beans won't take quite as long to cook.

Your soybeans are done cooking when very soft, so that you can easily mash a bean between your tongue and the roof of your mouth or between your fingers. When pressure cooking if you add 1½ teaspoons cooking oil per cup beans it will help prevent soybean seed hulls from stopping up the steam escape valve. If you pressure cook soybeans at less pressure than 15 pounds, like at 10, you should double the cooking time.

Cooked Dried Soybeans—In general, after you get them cooked stir in some flavoring and just a little more water and keep heated 10 minutes or so. Flavoring like per cup dried soybeans—2 tablespoons miso (read on), or a tablespoon or more of soy sauce; or 2 teaspoons lemon juice; or some butter; or chopped fried onion with miso and grated cheese stirred in; or some sweetening like molasses or honey along with a little miso or soy sauce; or chopped vegetables, like the kind you can eat raw, or cooked vegetables seasoned with a little salt or soy sauce and maybe garlic and what you like; or make a soup with your vegetables and soybeans by cooking on with extra water until the vegetables are done; or serve with yogurt; or do a refried bean thing like in Mexican cooking by drying out the extra moisture from your cooked beans on a baking sheet in the oven and then frying in oil, ½ cup at a time for 10 minutes or so. Serve crisp and golden brown and salted.

Soy Milk—Make sure you start with the "edible" people type soybean; otherwise your soy milk won't have the best flavor. Carefully clean the beans and

soak overnight. Two-and-a-half cups dried soybeans are the equivalent of 1 pound. Soak in 7 cups water per 1 pound soybeans. Now drain off soaking water and thoroughly wash three times in separate clean water, stirring briskly. That stirring and rinsing helps get out the beany taste. It also helps heat up your beans if you use hot water. While rinsing, keep the beans in a bowl with very hot tap water running slowly over them and fill your blender with boiling water to get it hot—for the next step.

Now you're going to blend up your beans with hot water. But first get ready your strainer. Do this by placing a large strainer over a deep kettle or bowl or pail. Inside the strainer lay unbleached muslin or nylon curtain material for a straining cloth—about 1 square yard or less, depending on your container size and how much soybean milk you're going to make. When your strainer is ready to go you can get back to the blending. Let's suppose you have a 1-quart blender—if not adjust for the smaller or larger size of your own blender. Put about 1½ cups of your soaked, hot soybeans into the blender. Add boiling water to fill the blender about two-thirds full. That will be about 2 cups of boiling water. Put the blender lid on. Cover that with a big folded towel and keep children away because steam pressure when you start to blend possibly could cause the lid to blow off. Run blender at low speed for 3 or 4 minutes, then at highest for about 5 more.

The next step is to drain off and separate your soy milk from the remains of the blended soybeans. As each portion of beans and hot water are finished in the blender, dump them into your straining setup. Gather up the edges of the strainer cloth after most of it has run through and put pressure on the soybean residue to get out as much more soy milk as you can. When you have blended and strained all your soybeans put the residue from the strainer cloth back into your blender together with 2 cups cold water. Blend. Drain and squeeze again. Now you have soybean milk. The exact amount of fluid in it is surprisingly flexible. For baby formula the pound of beans you started out with should be made up to about a gallon of milk. If you don't have that much you can simply add more water. But for cooking purposes and things like making white sauce a more concentrated soy milk works better. You can make a soy milk that totals out to a half gallon instead of a gallon, for each cup blend in a teaspoon of brown sugar, pinch salt, ¼ teaspoon vanilla, tablespoon oil (added gradually to mixture in blender) and Lo! it's *soy cream!* A more concentrated sort of soy milk is also the base for tofu making. But I'm getting ahead of myself. You're not done yet with your soy milk.

Now you are going to cook it to get rid of that antitrypsin agent that makes all the difference between an indigestible and a superdigestible and nourishing soy milk. You can do this in a deep kettle but you will have to watch it like a hawk to keep it from either scorching or boiling over and stir *continually* while it is boiling. Much the safest and easiest way is to rig up some sort of double boiler arrangement to heat the soy milk in. Make sure it spends at least 30 minutes at top heat. Now quickly chill and store under refrigeration if possible because it spoils easily just like real dairy products.

Soy Milk Baby Formula—Per gallon soy milk weigh out 100 grams of an edible oil like corn, soy, peanut or safflower and 300 grams of corn syrup. Place oil part in blender with as much hot soy extract (do this before you refrigerate) as will fit (blender three-quarters full) and blend. Added blended oil-soy milk mixture and corn syrup to rest of soy milk and bring to active boil again so that the oil and corn syrup will be sterilized too. Now cool and store. It will keep 3 to 5 days easily under refrigeration.

Other Flavorings and Fortifyings for Soy Milk—Per gallon add alone or in combination as you like 4 tablespoons oil blended in as in Soy Milk Baby Formula, ½ teaspoon salt, 4-6 tablespoons brown sugar, 1½-3 tablespoons vanilla, 1 tablespoon coconut flavoring.

Tofu—The Chinese pronounce it as if the "t" were a "d." So if you want to be really precise when shopping in the oriental food store, ask for "dofu." Or you can make it yourself. It's also called "bean curd" and is a staple in oriental cooking. Bean curd is 95 percent digestible compared to 68 percent for whole cooked soybeans and very healthy but that makes sense when you find out that all bean curd really is is the milk solids part precipitated out of soy milk—the soy exact equivalent for cottage cheese that you make from animal milk! Tofu itself is kind of bland tasting and you need recipes to use it. Those are coming up as soon as I tell you how to make it. To make cottage cheese you sour the milk to get your curds and whey to separate either by natural souring or by adding rennet or by adding lemon juice in the case of a whey cheese like ricotta. To make tofu you can sour the soy milk by adding lemon or lime juice, or cider vinegar or some unfamiliar sounding stuff like Epsom salts, calcium lactate or calcium carbonate. As in cheese making the exact amount of acid you add can really be quite flexible. So, in general, to make tofu start out by making soy milk by the recipe I already gave you. Now don't worry if you end up with it somewhat more concentrated than a gallon or even more dilute because you can make tofu anyway. In fact, I think it kind of helps if it's a little more concentrated than a gallon.

When your soy milk is done cooking and still hot, but not boiling, like about 180°, add whichever you're going to add. If it's a chemical-type thing dissolve that in a cup of soy milk separately and then stir gently into the rest. How much precipitant? Two or three tablespoons calcium lactate or calcium carbonate or ¼ cup lemon or lime juice or cider vinegar. Always stir in the same direction and pour in the precipitant mixture very slowly. It curdles quickly.

Now you pour it into something to set up, get firm, and get its shape. The Japanese pour the curd into large wooden frames with wire bottoms into which they sort of press it and that helps drain out the extra whey. You can do something like that too by building a square frame of wood, taking a husky wire mesh across the bottom, laying cheesecloth or some sort of straining cloth in the frame over the wire and

then pouring the curd into that making it spread out to an even thickness. You can put some gentle pressure on it to help the whey get out. But you don't have to use this system even though it's nice to be able to dump out the whole slab and cut into squares that look just like what the Japanese make. You get just as good tofu for eating purposes by draining the bean curd in a cloth laid inside any old strainer with a cloth over the top and a plate weighted on top to help press out the whey. That only takes a few minutes and either way it's ready.

To store your tofu, cut into squares like an inch on each side and keep the squares in cool water in your refrigerator until you get them used up. Change the water daily. Aging actually firms up your bean curd and makes it easy to handle if you don't overdo it. Or you can store your bean curd in whey saved from making it but that may contribute to its having a sourish taste if you used lemon juice or vinegar to make it.

Seasoning and cooking with tofu—You can mash it up and get something like cottage cheese, stir in salt to taste and some concentrated soy milk to moisten, and/or chopped chives, ½ cup per 2 cups soy cottage cheese, or chopped nuts, or serve with fresh fruit. Tofu is almost tasteless in its own right so the idea is to add flavor or use it in cooking and let it absorb flavor from whatever dish it's included in. But here I am really so ignorant let me step aside and let Melanie Kohler take over. She's another Hawaiian who has written me many a wonderful letter and sent me many a wonderful recipe which I *really* appreciate. She is also wonderfully patient because I observe with embarrassment that I received the letter I'm going to quote from more than three years ago and I have this sinking feeling I may never have even answered it. Well, Melanie, at last I'm getting your recipes into the book and I promise myself and you that I'm going to write *as soon as* I get done with this 7th edition rewrite! Here's Melanie talking.

"One of the simplest ways I fix tofu is just to cut it in cubes approximately 1 inch square, and put it in a bowl. It can be served just plain like that, or with shoyu (soy sauce) poured over, or a sauce made of a couple tablespoons soy sauce, a teaspoon or 2 of sugar, and some powdered garlic or ginger. Heat the sauce for a minute or 2, then pour over the tofu in the bowl and sprinkle some chopped

green onions or Chinese parsley (coriander or cilantro) on top and serve.

"Another easy way that I fix tofu when I have some unexpected guests is to slice in pieces about 3 inches square by ½ inch thick. I put these slices between some paper towels to absorb the excess water, then fry in some hot oil until golden brown (about ¼ inch of oil in a frying pan over medium-high heat), and remove the slices from the pan. Then, into the leftover hot oil still in the pan, I throw in a couple cloves of garlic and a piece of fresh ginger about the size of my thumb (use powdered garlic and ginger if you don't have fresh). Let the garlic and ginger brown slightly, then pour into the pan a mixture of ½ cup soy sauce, ½ cup sugar and 1½ or 2 cups of water. As you are bringing this mixture to a boil, place the slices of fried tofu back into the pan in the sauce, sprinkle some chopped green onion all over the top, put a cover on the pan, and let the whole thing simmer for a minute or 2. Serve immediately over hot steamed rice, and as the Hawaiians say, 'Ono!!!' (means delicious!).

"Here are some other tofu recipes that I've collected from various friends over the years:

"*Tofu Balls*—Mash, squeeze and drain 1 block of tofu. Combine 2 carrots (grated finely), ¼ cup chopped green onions, 1 cup chopped peanuts, 1 tablespoon sugar, 1½ teaspoons salt and 2 eggs with the mashed tofu. Form mixture into balls, roll in bread or cracker crumbs, and deep-fry until golden brown.

"*Tofu Casserole*—Cut tofu into cubes and fry lightly in a little oil. Place in a casserole dish and cover with tomato soup and sprinkle grated cheese on top. Bake at 350° until hot and bubbly. Cream of mushroom soup may be used instead of tomato, or plain brown gravy if you wish.

"*Tofu Loaf*—Mash and squeeze out as much water as possible from a block of tofu. Combine with the mashed tofu 1 carrot (grated finely), ½ cup soft whole wheat bread crumbs, 2 tablespoons mayonnaise, 1 onion (grated finely), 1 egg and ½ teaspoon salt. Mix well, pour into a greased pan, and bake at 375° for 45-60 minutes, or until lightly browned. Serve with catsup, brown gravy or as is. (This recipe is really ono too!)

"Tofu cubes may also be added to stir-fried vegetables for a quick entree. In that case add just before serving so the tofu doesn't get all mashed in the cooking. Or add tofu cubes to a plain soup broth to make it more nourishing. We really eat a lot of tofu in our house—I almost always have a block or two in our refrigerator, and it gets used fast!"

And, as soon as I get done with this 7th edition I'm not only going to send Melanie a letter—I'm going to send her a copy so she can see her recipes in print and know that I am truly grateful she took the trouble to sit down and write that all down and send it.

Miso is fermented soybeans, aged in wooden barrels for three years. It's dark colored and similar in flavor to bouillon. In fact you can use it any time a recipe calls for beef stock or bouillon cubes.

One kind is made from more or less straight soybeans, one kind from a soybean-barley mixture, one kind from a soybean-brown rice mixture, but really I don't know how to tell you to make it.

Soy Sauce—I used to wish I had a recipe for it and didn't. Finally somebody did send me one! It's those Hawaiians that really know their soy sauce. First somebody from Hawaii sent me a newspaper clipping that described a reporter's visit to a shoyu—that's soy sauce—factory there. It said a lot of your store soy sauce is chemically produced and takes only 24 hours to produce. But the real stuff is a fermented product like miso, almost a year in the making. Diamond Shoyu is made from a mixture of wheat and soybeans. The wheat is screened, roasted, crushed. Soybean meal is sprayed with hot water and then cooked for an hour in a pressure cooker. Then the crushed wheat and cooked soybean meal are mixed together, a special kind of mold is added and it is let set in a warm place for 4 days. Then it is left in a salt solution in special fermenting tanks for 10 to 12 months. Then the shoyu is filtered out from the solids, and sad to add in my opinion anyway monosodium glutamate and disodium 5-inosinate are added. But courage—Kathy Colin, who lives at Kailua, Hawaii, has sent her do-it-at-home recipe for us!

Kathy's Soy Sauce—Mix 10 cups soybeans, ½ cup molasses, ½ cup pure salt and 6 gallons water and cook until boiling. Lower heat and simmer 5 hours (should be about 5 gallons left). Strain. Pour into a 5-gallon glass jug. Seal airtight. Keep in a frequently sunlit spot like a window ledge or roof (and remember she lives in Hawaii!) for 1 year or more if it seems to need it and your patience is up to it. And, Kathy promises, "the resulting liquid will be a delectable light soy sauce."

To eat like salted peanuts—Not everybody that knows and loves soybeans lives in Hawaii. Lou Reed from Gillette, Wyoming, sent me this one. She says to soak your soybeans in water overnight. Drain on paper towel or a cloth until dry. Then put beans in a fine wire strainer that looks like a big tea strainer and cook in deep bacon grease until light brown. Add salt and onion salt. The onion salt is very important as it deadens the "soy" taste. Some other people I know toast the drained, soaked beans spread one layer thick over unoiled cookie tins or baking pans overnight and serve them still warm with a little oil and salt. I've heard also of soaking the beans in salt water before roasting and then you don't salt them afterward and of roasting them at about 250° for 2½ hours, shaking the pans every 15 to 30 minutes. Don't roast clear until dark brown. That's too much. They will still be slightly soft when you take them out of the oven and they get crunchy as they cool.

SHELL BEANS—If you like pinto beans and kidney beans, navy beans, dried lima beans, great northern beans, lentils, dried peas, chick peas, blackeyed peas, soybeans, dried, you're talking about what we can group as a category and call "shell beans." There are actually a bunch of peas in there too but so many similarities I am going to roll them up together rather than end up saying a lot of it twice. It's really easy to grow and dry your own beans for chili and soup and such. Eight to 12 quarts of kidney beans will make you a lot of chili. Your first problem is to choose the kind of beans to plant from so many possibilities. As usual it's smart to ask the neighborhood gardeners because the shell beans vary widely in the time required to mature and some of them work in one kind of climate but not in another. There are so many, like maybe about 75, different kinds I can't classify each one for you here and besides I don't know all the answers. But I can give you some starting information. Don't grow string beans for shell beans. The seeds dry too small and hard and they aren't as tasty as the others. In general large-seeded beans are easier to shell and will produce more per space than smaller-seeded beans. The common seed catalogs usually offer only the basic red kidney, pinto and marrow beans. For a shorter growing season than 90 or 100 days you need to look farther. Nichols Garden Nursery in Albany, Oregon, has a very good selection of shell beans.

Here are the best I know of arranged by length of growing season: *Dwarf Horticultural* (also called *Wrens Egg*) matures in 65 days. That's the quickest shell bean I know of. The beans are green-yellow spotted with red, large and easy to shell. *Black Valentine* matures in 70 days. Eat fresh or dried, black beans. *Pinto* beans take 90 days to maturity, can be used fresh or dried, have large spotted seeds and bear well. *Great Northern* beans also take 90 days to mature, have large white seeds, good for baking. *Navy* beans take 92 days, white bean, big yields. *Red Kidney* takes 95 days to maturity, bush-type bean, bright red, yield well, easy to shell, large seeds, great eating in soup or baked. *White Marrowfat* beans mature in 100 days, big white bean. The pods are inedible. *Lima* beans make fine shell beans. A friend wrote and recommended a kind called *Brown Dutch* from the Netherlands that don't shatter and she really likes.

To plant, choose your variety. Get ready the place to plant them. Soaking the beans for a few hours before planting will speed up germination. Most shell beans are bush-type beans. Plant around 4 inches apart with rows 18 to 20 inches apart. If the kind you choose happens to be a climber, then follow the directions on the package or for pole beans that I gave you earlier. Be sure and mark your shell bean rows in some way that will last because they will look just like your green bean plants. Water, weed and wait!

To harvest—Once your beans are grown you can dry them on the vine, or off of it in the shell, or out of the shell. Drying them in the shell seems to work best for most types. If you dried them on the vine you'd reduce or stop further production. Drying them in the shell is quicker too because you can later shell out of dried pods much easier than you can shell out of soft moist pods. Our summers are very hot and dry, perfect for drying fruits and vegetables except for the August hordes of wasps. But if you have lots of rain in summer or a rainy spell just when you are trying to dry the pods you can shell out the beans and finish drying them in your oven or dryer on trays. Trays made with some kind of material the air can get through work best.

The one place where you could goof is by not starting to dry them as soon as you pick them. If you leave them heaped up for very long, like in a bucket or in a pile—even in a very dry place—the lower layers will mold and get slimy and that is the end of the whole bucketful because those mold spores will be ahead of you. I use a sheet spread out on the ground in the full sun. I scatter them on it so that there aren't any on top of each other. In the evening I gather up the corners of the sheet to make a sack and haul it all in so they won't get damp again in the night dew, then put them out again the next morning. If the chickens are on the prowl, I put the beans on a flat roof to dry and get the job done before the chickens catch on. (They can fly really high if they want to. I've seen them fly up into the fruit trees, perch on a bough and eat apples or cherries all day.)

It really works better to dry right out in the sunshine than to try to dry indoors. It also helps avoid mold threat if you pick from the vines on a very dry day. Once your beans are dried you can shell directly into your storage containers (which can be virtually anything) or you can thresh them out onto a clean floor and get the kids to pick them up for you. I generally leave the shelling for later in the season after the rush is over because that is something that can be done later. Store your beans, shelled or unshelled, in sacks or jars or whatever in a cool, airy place.

After your beans or peas are dried, store them in airtight plastic, metal or glass containers. I use jars. I've left them all winter long in jars, both with and without lids, and they kept fine. The important thing is keeping the humidity down. If you live in the South you'll have a harder time keeping any dried food. If you are worried that bug eggs may be in with the seeds and you aren't planning to use them for seed you could store them in the freezer until needed. Or heat in the oven at 150° for 20 minutes with the door fixed slightly open to prevent overheating. Just don't put in too many at once to get heated clear through.

You are safest if the dried beans or peas are so hard and dry that they shatter when struck by a hammer. And then keep them in a bugproof container so mama bugs can't get in there to do their thing. If you do find little critters walking around, put the beans in a coarse sack or basket and dip into boiling water for just a minute or 2. Then hang up to drip dry. That should get rid of the insects and won't harm the general keeping qualities of the beans.

Flours—If you have your own flour grinder you can grind your own dried peas, lentils or soybeans to make a flour. The commercially produced pea and lentil flours are precooked so your homeground flours won't act exactly the same. These vegetable flours can be added to any bread-type recipe and are good that way. But don't substitute for wheat flour. Because soy flour browns so easily it is advisable to bake anything containing soy flour at a little lower temperature than you would otherwise.

Bean flour will provide more mileage foodwise out of your beans if that's what you happen to have a lot of one year. You can also just plain old cook and mash them and put them in the bread, soup and so on.

Cooking with dried beans and peas—Some store beans are partially precooked so make sure, whatever recipe you use, that the home-dried beans are actually done before you commence with the rest of it. In general they are soaked awhile and then cooked. If you cook them in the water in which they were soaked you save nourishment. Then they are combined with something like pork, molasses, tomatoes, onions or spices because tasted alone they are awfully bland foods.

The problem to be faced up to with dried beans is their gas manufacturing tendencies. My mother-in-law really pushes beans and is always telling me how much protein they have in them. Her son has iron control of his system and can deposit his total flatulence (gas) in the bathroom alone and behind the closed door in a maximum of three daily visits. I apparently come from another genetic line. My mother had this problem and so do I: When it hits me, that's it. I've been standing in Church singing a hymn and wanting to die with shame because everybody around me was wondering who had done the terrible thing and I was afraid they'd figure it out just from the look on my face. At least the hymn covered the sound effects but what about the rest of the time when I make sounds which to my embarrassed ears resem-

MOM, WHAT'S THAT YUKKY SMELL?

ble the backfire of our one-ton truck going down the mountainside to town with the muffler off?

And beans have a cumulative effect. One unfortunate week I served chili for supper. The next day Mike happened to lunch where they served him chili again. That evening I was sick in bed and asked my eight-year-old daughter, Dolly, to feed everybody something. It turned out she decided the best answer was to open another jar of chili. In the middle of the night Mike announced there was a distinct possibility he was going to die. He didn't, but we are careful about spacing our bean meals. That was the week when Mike was in a conference room with a group of executive types and even he was overcome by pressure to the point that the whole proceedings stopped while people wondered where it all was coming from.

Since the first issue of this book came out I've received in the mail a lot of helpful advice about how to keep beans from causing gas. J. O. Pettit, the salt rising bread expert, told me to keep a cruet of vinegar on the table and add a pour of vinegar to each serving of beans. Janet Kieffer wrote me that her Mexican cooking teacher said 1 teaspoon olive oil in a batch of beans helps take the gas out. Mrs. George Baker of Floresville, Texas, wrote me to put ¼ teaspoon ginger to 1 pound beans in cooking them.

That was up to the 7th edition. Now I have still more advice. Julia Reynolds from Galvin, Washington, says if I will try blanching and freezing the dried beans like I would string beans that will help the gas problems. Pansy Cietes from Spokane, Washington, says to combine each 1 cup dry beans with 1 level tablespoon Epsom salts and enough water to cover. Then bring to a full boil and boil 5 minutes (no more). Drain and rinse thoroughly, then soak as usual. (Rinsing is important she says as the salts will give the beans a slight bitter taste if not rinsed good.) Mrs. Evans of Rosalia, Washington, told me to cover the beans with cold water, add a teaspoon of soda and bring just to a boil. Then drain and rinse in clear water. Then cook in the regular way and she guarantees there will be no explosions! Abbie Pyne from Twin Falls, Idaho, says the *best* way to cook beans to prevent gas is to put 1 tablespoon castor oil to 1 cup dry beans when you put them on to cook. "When the castor oil is cooked it has no laxative effect and cuts the gas to almost none." Well, for sure it all proves that a lot of beautiful people read every word of this book!

Sauces for your beans—Because most dried beans are on the bland side a good tasty sauce can really improve them. Here are recipes for two basic sauces good with almost any dried bean:

Tomato Sauce—After the beans are cooked pour off the bean liquid. Per 3 cups bean liquid add 4 cups tomato juice, 2 tablespoons sugar or 1 tablespoon honey, 1 teaspoon salt, 1 tablespoon chopped onion and a pinch each of ground cloves, allspice, mace and cayenne. Catsup can be substituted for the tomato juice—1 cup catsup per 4 cups tomato juice.

Molasses Sauce—After the beans have been cooked pour off your bean water and for about 3 cups of bean water add 3 tablespoons of molasses, 1 tablespoon of vinegar, 1 teaspoon salt and ¾ teaspoon dry mustard.

A piece of salt pork, ham or bacon is good with beans. So after making your sauce (either one), add it to the beans along with some meat pieces. Use enough sauce to cover the beans. Then cover and bake about 5 hours in a moderate oven. You'll want to add water about once an hour.

BEAN RECIPES—Beans are truly international food. Here's a recipe sent to me by Peace Sullivan, a journalist who is working in Brazil but has bought a farm in Ireland with her husband, a UPI writer, for their future. Peace wrote that she was living in the middle of the jungle, with a huge avocado tree dripping with fruit outside the door, bananas and papayas and lots of beautiful jungle birds to sing to them. But she had very little luck with her vegetable garden. "The worst problem is the bugs, and a potent spray of garlic, onion and a very hot pepper seems to have no effect on them. I am enclosing a recipe for the Brazilian national dish, feijoada (pronounced feejoada). This dish was created by slaves as a way to use up the leftover parts of a pig that were given to them. The main thing to remember about feijoada is that you can vary it practically any way you want, as long as you keep the main ingredients—black beans and pork.

"*Black Bean Feijoada*—Soak 1 pound dried meat (carne seca, which is usually dried beef) overnight. Soak 3 cups black beans overnight. The next day drain the meat, cover with cold water, bring to a boil and boil 15 minutes. Drain and cool. Add 1 pound sausage, 1 smoked tongue, ¼ pound bacon and 1 pig's foot, cover with water, bring to a boil and simmer until meat is tender. In another pot, cook the beans until almost tender. It's nice to add a bay leaf to the beans. Then combine the contents of the two pots and simmer until meat is very tender and beans are soft enough to mash. Take out all the meat, put on a platter, and put the beans around it. Serve with rice, and an orange for each person. (The orange cuts the grease.) If you like you can make a sauce for the beans with a green onion, onion, fresh sausage, garlic and hot pepper. Or you can vary the feijoada by adding a pig's ears and tail, salt pork, some beef if you have it, or spare ribs, etc. Brazilians usually serve 'couve' along with the feijoada. The closest thing to couve in the U.S. is, I think, collards, but I think any dark green leafy vegetable would do. It's usually shredded and fried."

Garbanzo Cutlets—I'm trying to arrange these bean recipes in more or less alphabetical order. The garbanzo recipes are from Melanie Kohler of Haleiwa, Hawaii. "Run 3 cups cooked garbanzos through a grinder (or mash by hand). Combine the garbanzos with 1 cup mashed potatoes, ½ cup onion (chopped fine), ¼ cup chopped parsley, and salt to taste. Mix thoroughly and form into walnut-sized balls. Fry in deep hot oil and serve hot." Melanie is pretty much a vegetarian and she says garbanzo beans are a good source of protein.

Marinated Garbanzos—"One way my husband especially likes garbanzos is marinated in a sauce I make from cider vinegar, sugar, oil, salt, pepper. I don't know the exact proportions—I just mix things together until it tastes pretty good. Then I add the garbanzos (which have been soaked and cooked already) and an onion or two sliced in thin rings. Mix all together, cover and let sit in the refrigerator for at least a day before you plan to serve it."

Garbanzo Mock Roast—Melanie says garbanzos "may also be made into a roast very easily by combining the mashed beans with eggs, bread crumbs, oatmeal, chopped nuts, salt, sage, milk or whatever in any combination you wish. A roast of this kind is also very good cold. Slice and use like meatloaf for sandwiches."

To cook *kidney, navy* or *yellow eye* beans first sort and wash. Boil 2 minutes. Now take off heat and let soak an hour. Heat to boiling again and commence with your recipe.

Kidney Beans and Hamburger—Sauté a chopped onion in 2 tablespoons of butter until golden brown. Add 2 cups tomatoes, 1 pound hamburger, 2 cups kidney beans that have been cooked up, 1 teaspoon chili powder, and ½ teaspoon salt. Simmer an hour, adding water as necessary. You can make this in a big batch and freeze, or can for quick meals. To can it cook 5 hours water bath or 105 minutes pressure canner.

Lentils are red or green. You don't need to soak the red kind because they soften more easily. They can be used in recipes interchangeably though. They are good with corned beef.

Lentil Soup—Two cups lentils, 2 onions, 2 carrots, a turnip and 3 stalks of celery. Cut up the vegetables and combine in a pan. Add beef stock to cover, salt, pepper and a bay leaf and cook slowly 2 hours. Take out the bay leaf and put the soup through a sieve. Thicken with flour and serve.

Lentils and Cheese—Simmer a pound of lentils until soft. Strain or mash. Chop 1 onion and sauté in ¼ cup butter. Mix sautéed onion, butter and some grated American cheese with the lentils and season with salt and pepper to taste. Put all into a greased baking dish and then sprinkle more grated cheese and butter bits over the top. Bake until browned.

Honey Baked Lentils—Cook 1 pound lentils, drain and reserve fluid. Mix the cooked lentils with 1 teaspoon dry mustard, ½ teaspoon powdered ginger and 1 tablespoon soy sauce. Add ½ cup chopped onion and 1 cup of the lentil liquid. Pour mixture into a baking dish and pour ½ cup honey over the top. Cover and bake at 350° for 1 hour. Uncover dish for the last few minutes of baking to brown the top.

Lentil, Walnut and Rice Loaf—Sauté 1 onion (chopped) in 2 tablespoons oil or butter. Add ½ teaspoon salt and ⅛ teaspoon each thyme, garlic salt and celery salt. Add to onions 2 eggs, 2 cups lentil puree, 1 cup chopped walnuts and 1 cup cooked rice (brown or white). Pack mixture into a buttered loaf pan and bake at 350° for 45 minutes or until slightly browned on top.

Lentil and Walnut Loaf—Sauté ½ cup chopped onion in 2 tablespoons oil. Add 1 cup cooked, mashed lentils, ½ cup bread crumbs, ½ cup chopped walnuts, ¾ cup tomato sauce, 1½ tablespoons flour and ½ teaspoon salt. Pour into buttered casserole and sprinkle with 1 crushed bay leaf. Bake at 375° for about 45 minutes. Serve with brown gravy. This mixture may also be made into patties and fried.

Sour Cream Lima Beans—Start with 2 cups dried lima beans. Soak them in water at least several hours and then simmer until tender. Put the beans in a baking dish. Pour off your bean water. To 5 cups of the bean water add ¼ cup butter, 1 teaspoon salt, 1 teaspoon dry mustard, 3 teaspoons molasses, 1 cup sour cream and a small chopped sautéed onion. Cover and bake an hour.

Pork Sausage and Limas—Soak and then cook your lima beans. Pour off most of the liquid. Add some cooked pork sausage, tomato juice, salt, pepper (chili powder if you want) and serve.

Baked Beans—This recipe was sent me by Lillian Grimshaw of Cedar City, Utah. She grows pioneer pink eye beans and saves her own seed from year to year but she says it will work fine with white-type beans, too. "Pick over, wash and put 1 pint beans in cooking kettle. Cover with hot water and let soak overnight. Or bring to boil, turn off heat and let stand 1 hour, then turn on low heat and simmer until they are as tender as you want them. Remember adding cold water stops the cooking process so always add hot liquid unless you do not wish them to cook any more tender. We let ours cook to a mushy stage. Salt and tomato products toughen the skins so add after beans are cooked.

"In baking pan put 4 tablespoons brown sugar or molasses, ½ teaspoon dry mustard, 2 teaspoons salt, ½ teaspoon pepper. Mix together. Now rinse out all the catsup bottles you about used up or use 1 cup catsup. Put in ⅓ cup sweet pickle juice if you have it and all the potato water you drained from cooked potatoes and stored in the refrigerator. Use up any tomato juice or bottled tomatoes. Add any ham bones and bacon rinds you cut off and saved. Or put strips of bacon or a slice of ham on top. Bake for four hours more or less. Taste for salt. You may need to add more. Chopped onion may be added or a whole onion buried in the beans and then taken out. If you don't have potato water, peel a potato and cook with beans. Potato takes care of the discomfort some people get from eating beans. Good luck. Better reheated again and again."

Portuguese Bean Soup—They must have pink beans in Hawaii, too, because Melanie says she uses pink or red beans in this recipe. She says one of the easiest vegetarian dishes to fix is a good vegetable soup. "I just cook a cup or 2 of red or pink beans, then add whatever vegetables we happen to have growing in our garden—tomatoes, okra, peas, green beans, onions, celery, corn, etc. Simmer for a couple of hours, then add some macaroni about ½ hour before you're ready to eat. Serve with hot homemade bread (we especially like the cracked wheat bread that I make) and some fresh fruit salad, and you have

a meal that's out of this world! Oh, I forgot to add that you season the soup with some herbs from your garden—garlic, sweet basil, oregano and whatever else you want."

Fire Station Beans—George C. White, who has just retired after 44 years with a Fort Worth, Texas, area fire department sent me this recipe. He says this or some variation of this bean pot is cooked in almost all the fire stations in Texas. The recipe calls for pinto beans but he said "if you are a Yankee you just might have to use kidney beans. The pinto beans are soaked overnight and cooked slowly all day or until soft. Seasoning can be added in the form of bacon fat or if you do not have a hankering for the plain bean sort of beans add salt pork, ham hock, backbone, knuckles, pig tails or ears. Brown meat like ground beef with chopped onions, chopped or ground garlic, chopped celery and chopped bell pepper. Add to beans along with any or all other ingredients desired or available. Like brown sugar or molasses, mustard, oregano, mace, nutmeg, a few pods of whole chili, some cooked tomatoes, salt, pepper. Simmer for 30 minutes to an hour or until done. Serve with corn bread and fresh onions. This is a bean pot and not a chili."

Pinto Bean Bread—Marion Stick, from Phoenix, Arizona, sent me this Papago Indian recipe. "Start with 1 cup cooked pintos (chop small), add ½ cup shortening and ½ cup sugar, ½ teaspoon salt, 1 egg, and ¼ cup chopped nuts is optional. To 2 cups flour add 2 teaspoons baking powder, ½ teaspoon cinnamon, ¼ teaspoon nutmeg, ¼ teaspoon cloves. Sift over other ingredients, mix well, put in a greased loaf pan and bake 45 minutes at 350°."

Papago Pinto Beans—Combine 2½ cups of pinto beans, 7 cups water, 1 cup bacon or ham, 1 diced onion. Simmer all together for 2½ to 3 hours in an iron kettle being careful they do not scorch. Salt to taste after cooking. Serve as a vegetable.

"Fried" beans—Any kind of dried beans cooked by boiling and then served as a wet mixture of mashed and whole beans with some of the bean broth and seasonings.

"Refried" beans—Mashed cooked beans fried in oil with onions and seasonings (like garlic, tomato puree, red pepper) until the moisture has mostly evaporated but don't let them burn! Good with little cubes of Cheddar or jack-type cheese stirred in and let melt or melted over the top.

To can soybeans, lentils, garbanzos, kidney or pinto beans, put soaked beans in quart jars, using 3½ cups beans, hot water to 1 inch from the top and 1 teaspoon salt. Screw lids on, pressure cook with 2 quarts of water at 15 pounds pressure for 15 minutes. Let cool.

Saving your own seed is very easy and it's the same for the whole bean and pea family and the same as if you were drying them for the kinds you dry. Basically you leave the seeds in the pod on the plant until completely dry. (Soybeans are an exception to that because of their tendency to shatter.) Then shell and store. Store in as dry, but not hot, a place as you can. When shelling out get rid of small, strangely shaped, sick or otherwise weird ones. Just add them to the chicken feed. You'll find it interesting after a few generations of your home-grown seed to buy some store seed again and compare what you're raising with what they are. Lentil seeds should be stored in the pod rather than shelled out. For some reason they keep their germinating strength better when stored in the pod. But be sure they are absolutely dry before you store them.

For saving seed, those dried in the pod have a higher germination rate. Nature intended them to be dried in the shell, so, of course, it works better that way. Beans will cross-pollinate, so if you are growing more than one kind you'll get pure seed for sure by having them flower at different times or planting at some distance from each other. But bean crosses are not near the problem you have with say, squash and pumpkins, because beans are self-pollinated and though capable of crosses the odds are against it. And even if they do cross the result is sure to be edible, even if unfamiliar. For the very highest quality kind of seed collecting tag the plants that have most pleased you and leave that harvest alone while you are gathering the rest. Then specially harvest them for seed. Beans can be stored without much risk for up to three years and still have a good germination rate.

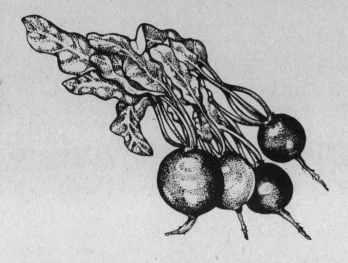

BEETS—The beet family includes sugar beets which are covered sort-of in the Sweets chapter under home-grown sugars, the problem being the processing of them for sugar isn't really practical on a family basis so far as I know. Mangel beets, also called wurzel or "stock beets," are animal rather than people food. They grow very large. You can use mangel beets plus carrots and the big varieties of winter squash to winter your goats on even if you can't grow hay. Cows will eat them too. Store mangel beets in a pit or root cellar. I read somewhere that feeding mangel beets to male goats makes them sterile. I don't believe it. Every goat owner I know around here feeds mangel beets to their goats. The various chards are actually a sort of beet, too, but they are covered under Greens later on in this vegetable chapter, as is beet greens. That leaves us with the common old garden beet which it seems like you either really

like or really don't like. If you really don't like—don't plant any.

To plant, first choose your kind of beet. They vary in maturing time from about 45 to 150 days, but mostly are on the quick side. They are easy to raise unless you have a heavy clay type soil which they don't like. They appreciate a cool climate and like any root vegetable they'll do much better if you have the soil well and deeply loosened so they can find and make space to grow in. They like manure and compost but unrotted manure will make them have lots of leaves and little root. For fresh eating, canning, freezing or drying, plant your beets as soon as the frost is out of the ground, and you can plant at intervals after that. For beets to be stored pit or root cellar style, later planting may be better. You can plant every two or three weeks until within a couple months of your first expected killing frost. Beets come in short, round-rooted varieties and long varieties. The long varieties are considered the best for pit storage but you've got to have the ground loosened deeper for them. Two ounces of seed in general will plant about 100 feet of row. Plant ½ inch deep, with seeds about an inch apart, and figure that they probably won't show above the ground for two or three weeks after that. If you carefully keep the soil moist while waiting for the seeds to germinate it will help speed them up to ten days or so.

To thin—Beet seed, unless you get the kind called Monogram, is different from the usual case because every "seed" really is a clump of seeds, as many as eight. So it really doesn't matter how carefully you space the seed planting—with beets you are going to be thinning. But thinning beets has a really good side. You can eat the thinnings. Eat like greens, root, leaves and all. When the small beet is about the size of a radish treat like chard or spinach, boil with bacon, add butter at serving time. You'll find them delicious! So using this gradual thin-and-eat policy, gradually thin your beets as they grow to an ultimate 3 or more inches apart. If you end up with a hole in your row you can transplant some thinnings to fill it up. Young beets transplant easily if you are gentle, set the beet plant in straight up and down in a hole deep enough to have room for all of it that way. Keep the whole transplanting process well watered. Water them for a good soaking before you take them out and again when settled in their new spot. The basic rule on thinning is simply that as soon as the plants begin to crowd each other, pull up every other one.

Beets have no tolerance for hot weather. That, other than poor, clay soil, is the only big problem you might have with them. If you live in a place as far north as Peace River, Alberta, Canada, like Marie Jeanne Cartier who wrote me a letter you don't have that problem though. She says back of their house you could walk through hill and dale practically up to the North Pole without passing a neighbor. Up there you don't have any heat problems with beets or turnips either. They never get tastless and woody like hot weather does to them elsewhere. A beet can grow and grow and will always remain tender. If you live in a hotter climate than Marie's, however, figure on digging and using your beets for sure before they get more than 3 inches in diameter. That's your best safeguard against bad beets. And a good argument for succession planting. I like beets best of all at the "baby" stage—that's around 1½ inches in diameter—for eating, freezing, canning or pickling.

To save your own seed—Beet pollen is wind carried and beet varieties will cross so your safeguard is to plant only one variety. They will also cross with Swiss chard. Beets are biennials like carrots and that means they store food in a root the first summer and then grow stalk, flower and seed from that root the second summer. You can pick out plants to save seed from and leave them in the row for two years until the process is finished if you won't be cultivating the ground but odds are they are in the middle of your garden and you need the rest of the row anyway. In that case leave them in the ground until late fall. Then dig carefully up, break off the leafy tops leaving about ½ inch of stem, and store in a special place buried under dirt deep enough so they won't freeze which depends on where you live and your ability to predict how cold it's going to get. In the spring, as early as you can, set the roots back out in a row with the tops just level with ground surface. They'll go ahead that second summer and make seed. When the seed is fully mature and dry cut off the seed clusters, take them indoors, rub it out by hand, give some extra drying and store.

To cook—No matter what else you're going to do with your beets start by giving them a good scrubbing with a brush and plenty of water to get the dirt off and cut off all but an inch of the tops. You can manage the tops like it says in the Greens part of this chapter. It's important not to cut off the tops lower down or peel the beets or remove any rootlets at this stage because that would make your beet bleed and you don't want that. Cover with boiling water and boil until the beets are slightly soft to touch. Takes 20 minutes to an hour, depending on your beet diameter, less for fresh beets, longer for stored beets. Now you drain, and slip the skins off, no peeling necessary. Cut off the root tails left and the stalk stub. Another way to precook beets is in the oven. That can take as long as 3 hours though. Try any precooked beet cut into slices and seasoned with salt, pepper, butter and a little vinegar or lemon juice.

Special Boiled Beets—Cook, peel and slice. Make a quick sauce by melting butter and stirring in chopped parsley, chives or other fine green onion, and garlic juice or finely chopped garlic. Now thicken sauce with a little flour and cook a few minutes. Add beets, a dash of vinegar, salt and pepper, and let it simmer as long as you can to soak up the flavor before serving—up to 30 minutes. Good with mashed potatoes.

Beet Soup—This is a famous and delicious way to eat beets. Here is a German recipe for the beet soup known in Europe as Borsch. But you can grow the ingredients in an American garden just as well. Cook 2 medium-sized diced potatoes, 1 cup shredded beets, 1 medium onion and 1 teaspoon salt until almost done. Keep soup on the thick side. Add 1 cup tomatoes or juice, ⅓ cup peas and some dill weed (if you don't have it you can do without it). Turn off heat. Carefully add a cup of light cream so it won't curdle from the tomatoes. Heat, do not boil, and serve.

Cold Beet Salad—Cook 1 pound beets until tender. Cool, peel and slice thinly. Combine 4 tablespoons vinegar, 4 tablespoons water, ½ teaspoon sugar, 2½ teaspoons caraway seeds, 1 small onion, chopped, 1 teaspoon ground cloves, 1 bay leaf, salt, pepper and 4 tablespoons oil. Pour over beets and let marinate several hours before serving.

To freeze, cut off tops, wash, scald and cook until tender. Peel, dice, chill and package.

To can, pack hot and cover with boiling water. Process 25 minutes for pints, 55 minutes for quarts in a pressure canner at 10 pounds.

Please be especially careful if you decide to can beets. They are a low acid vegetable and in my humble opinion more than the average subject to the botulism problem, especially in the pickled form which people seem to think turns them into a high acid vegetable.

To dry—By the time you boil them for 15 minutes or so to get the skins off, you have just as good as blanched them. Slice ⅛ inch thick and dry. They are delicious if you started with young tender beets. Real baby beets don't need any precooking. Just wash, peel, slice, and dry.

Pit or root cellar storage—Beets, like other root vegetables, are especially suitable for this kind of storage. And there are lots of variations on the exact way to do it. Start planning at planting time. Because if you have a long growing season beets for root cellar storage should be late planted beets. Otherwise they are going to be oversized, woody beets. Leave them in the ground as long as possible because they keep better there than anywhere. When you are ready to move them try to pick dry weather. Whack the green tops off with a knife. The basic principle of this storage is to keep them moist and as near freezing as possible but not ever let them actually freeze. If they are too warm in storage they'll sprout new tops and get woody inside. To bed in moist sand use a galvanized tub or wooden container. Make a layer of sand, a layer of beets, a layer of sand and so on. Jeanne told me about an old man in his 90s who stores his beets in a root cellar in a galvanized or plastic garbage can with an airtight lid. In the center he places a candle stub. Before closing the lid he lights the candle. The candle burns until all the oxygen is used up. He says that is what keeps the vegetables from softening. Each time he goes back for more beets (or turnips) he lights the candle again.

If you have a root cellar with a dirt floor you can put your beets in small piles along the wall. Don't store in large piles no matter what your system because they are more likely to heat and decay. Or you can store them in your basement or root cellar in wooden boxes. For outdoor pit-type storage make a bunch of small pits rather than one big one because once you open a pit it's better to get out all the vegetables in there at once. If you put a mixture of pit-storable root vegetables in each one that will be more convenient. Dig down as far as is not too big a struggle. Line the bottom with straw, leaves or some such. Pile up the vegetables on top. Cover the vegetables all over with more straw, leaves, etc. Put dirt over that. More for a colder winter. Make a tube of your bedding all the way to the top at one point and cover that with something like a shingle covered with a stone to be your ventilator.

BROCCOLI is a member of the cabbage family which includes Brussels sprouts, cabbage, kale and kohlrabi. Most of them, including broccoli, hate heat and don't do very well in my garden because of my hot summers. In most places you will end up buying plants and setting them out or setting out plants you grew yourself because your growing season won't be long enough to start it from seed. It likes well-manured ground, and beware of planting in the same place year after year. Roberta Van Slyke of Cortland, New York, wrote me that she plants her broccoli so as to mature in cooler weather and keeps it mulched with grass clippings or straw.

To plant, choose a variety suitable for your growing season. You can plant your seed in the house and it will take 3 to 10 days to germinate. Then figure five to seven weeks of growing indoors before the time for setting out. So you count backwards from your expected last frost to figure when you should plant the seed. If you were to start it too soon the plants might outgrow their containers or get potbound or spindly. And give them a hardening outdoors until all danger of frost is past. Greenbud is a variety that will mature 60 days from transplanting. Green Comet can mature in as little as 40 days from transplanting. Plant the seed ½ inch deep and an inch apart. Figure on 2½ to 3 feet apart when you transplant to the garden though because broccoli is a big plant—from 2 to 4 feet high. Make rows 3 feet apart. Broccoli needs some lime in the soil and may have trouble with insects or disease.

To harvest—The plant first produces a central cluster which may be as much as 8 inches across. Then come side sprouts. The general rule is that it is better to cut too early than too late. You can cut sprouts a week or two before they are actually mature. It will taste fine and be fine. Not all your plants will mature at the same time, which also spreads out the harvest. Just be sure to cut the sprout before any of the buds open into small yellow flowers, while they are still tightly closed. Cut with several inches of stem attached. The stem is good to eat as well as the leaves. After the central sprout is cut that makes the plant grow lots of side sprouts from where other leaves join the stem. None of those will get as big as the first one but together they can give you some good meals. You must stay on the ball with your harvesting. Broccoli that got away and flowered simply isn't food anymore and if you don't keep cutting regularly the plant will stop producing. If you do this your broccoli should keep producing until frost finally kills it.

To save your own seed—Cabbage, kale, Brussels sprouts, kohlrabi, broccoli and cauliflower are all insect pollinated and belong to the same family and will cross, so you can save seed only if you are growing only one of them or have them very widely separated—which isn't much of a guarantee the way

bugs can cover ground. All these plants are biennials, which means you have to wait for the second year of growth for them to produce seed. Store your chosen plants through the winter same as for beets. Seed stalks have a tendency to break and it will help if you tie them to some support. Pick seed stalks when mature, hang indoors to dry. Then remove seeds and store.

To cook—If bugs are a problem in your broccoli soak it for half an hour in 4 teaspoons salt to a gallon of cold water. If the stalks are big slice them lengthwise into pieces so that the flowerets are no more than 1½ inches across. Big broccoli stalks can be sliced at an angle and used like celery in salads, soups and Chinese stir-fry dishes. With garden fresh broccoli there should be no need to peel broccoli stems before cooking or to stand the sprouts in water. That's what you do for store broccoli that has been around long enough to start getting woody. The best basic treatment is to put the broccoli into a pan of cold water, bring to a boil, drain and rinse. Now finish cooking with fresh water. How long to cook depends on how big your spouts are so just keep testing for tenderness. Boiled broccoli is good with a cheese sauce or just buttered.

To freeze, use only young shoots with stems no more than 1 inch thick. Trim off outer leaves and anything woody. Wash. Debug in salt water. Wash again. Blanch stalks with 1½-inch heads for 3 minutes, smaller heads for 2 minutes. Chill, drain, pack.

To can, pack hot with cooking liquid and 1 teaspoon salt per quart. Process pints 30 minutes, quarts 35 in pressure canner at 10 pounds pressure.

BRUSSELS SPROUTS are in the cabbage, broccoli family. That means they are another not-easy-to-grow vegetable requiring long, cool summers, having some insect and disease problems, some special soil needs. Because I have hot summers I can't grow them successfully. Like broccoli you are probably going to plant your seed indoors, then transplant outside. The goal is little cabbage-type heads that can get as large as ping-pong balls—only don't let them get that large or they aren't as good. It's a funny-looking tall plant with a bunch of leaves at the top like a palm tree and wider at the bottom, tapering to the top, sprouts growing all around the sides of the stem. It requires a *long* growing season, about three months from transplanting to maturity.

To plant, seed should be ½ inch deep and 3 inches apart indoors figuring that it will grow indoors for four to six weeks before it is time to transplant. When you set outside after hardening off plant 3 feet apart. A little frost won't kill your sprout plants in the fall. It may even improve the crop.

To harvest—With a mild winter you can keep on picking sprouts until Christmas. Or move the plant to a cold frame and it will live and continue to produce. The plant will produce until it dies so long as you faithfully keep picking. Cut the sprouts from the main stem before they become tough or yellow. To harvest the sprout by hand just grab with two fingers and give a little twist. Pick lower sprouts first. Every time you pick a sprout break the leaf below it from the stalk which will make the plant form more leaves and more sprouts. You can get up to 100 sprouts per plant.

To save your own seed—Probably isn't worth the trouble. But read the directions under Broccoli because the same applies and that's what you do if you decide to try it.

To prepare—Soak in salt water same as for broccoli to debug and before canning. Remove all blemished leaves. Small sprouts will cook tender in 7 or 8 minutes. Don't cook until soft because that's overcooking and they lose texture, shape and vitamins. After boiling until tender drain and serve buttered, or with some sort of sauce, or a sprinkle of lemon juice or vinegar.

Sprouts and Chestnuts—For a delicacy, if you live in chestnut country, prepare about a pound of Brussels sprouts. Skin ½ pound chestnuts and boil separately until tender. Drain and mix the two together. Add a couple tablespoons butter, salt and pepper to taste. Serve hot.

To freeze, use dark green ones and not larger than 2 inches across. Cut off stems and remove wilted or tough leaves. Sort by size and debug. Blanch large heads 5 minutes, medium ones 4 minutes, small ones 3 minutes. Cool, drain, pack. They taste better frozen than canned.

To can, boil 3 minutes in water, pack hot with cooking liquid. Process pints 30 minutes and quarts 35 minutes in a pressure canner at 10 pounds.

CABBAGE—Gourmet cooks deplore the fact that this is the one member of the *Brassica* genus that is most commonly grown and loved by gardeners. They complain that it smells when cooked and isn't nearly as interesting as broccoli, Brussels sprouts, etc. I think there's a sound reason for the traditional emphasis on cabbage. It's the only one that stores easily and well through winter without any highly civilized props like a deepfreeze or canning jars. I think it's a little easier to grow than the others. Cabbage is a standard crop around here along with corn, peas, carrots, beets, turnips and potatoes. For really beautiful county fair heads, you can put some plants to grow inside special houses made of wooden frame with fine wire mesh nailed over the top and sides. That's to help with the bug problem cabbages have. An easier way to help bugproof cabbage heads is to scatter dillseed over so

it rests right between the cabbage leaves. Bugs don't like a house with dill in it. I found that out accidentally when I had dill growing in my cabbage row.

To plant—We have to start cabbages from seed in the house, then set them out in spring since the growing season here isn't long enough to raise them from seed in the garden. But maybe I'm working harder than I need to. I have a letter from Cathy Tate in Coulee City, Washington, who says she seeds cabbage, broccoli, kohlrabi, kale, cauliflower etc. right into the ground as early as she can, along with the early peas. She says they can take the cold and even a snow and has been doing it successfully for four years. A general rule on planting times that the old-timers held to was that for early spring cabbage in the South, you planted seeds in an outdoor bed and then transplanted to the garden before January 1; in the North you planted the seeds in a hotbed during February and set the plants in the open ground as early as the soil could be worked; for a late crop in the North you planted the seeds in a bed in the open ground in May or June and then transplanted to the garden in July. For early cabbages you want well-manured ground to hasten its growth. If you are planning to root cellar or pit store aim for late cabbage because early cabbage won't keep through the hot weather.

A little cabbage seed will go a *long* ways. An ounce may produce 1,500 to 3,000 plants. Plant where they will get full sunshine. If you do start from seed plant ½ inch deep and 3 inches apart and then transplant in your garden to a couple feet apart. They transplant best if you wait for a rain before setting out or soak your holes with water overnight before transplanting and give them a good soaking afterward too. If you are going through a period of dry, hot weather keep them generously watered or even give the plants some shade with boards or leaves. Cabbage is going to take up a lot of space for what you get if you have only limited garden space.

To harvest—There are cabbage varieties with all kinds of maturing dates and sizes from the Little League that makes a head about the size of a softball in 60 days to giant kinds that make 50-pound heads but take a long time doing it. When your cabbage head is ready cut its stalk just below the base of the cabbage. In ground that has been manured more than the plant can handle it may grow so fast that the head cracks open. If it does that harvest right away. It's fine to eat. Cabbage can stand quite severe frost but don't leave it out until the ground actually freezes. Decide how you're going to store it for winter before that happens. I used to think that you cut off the cabbage head and that was the end of the harvest. But it isn't so. If you cut off the head and leave the large lower leaves and root still healthy and growing, soon, many tiny little heads form, very sweet in flavor. Actually you can pick cabbage heads, the first or later ones at any size. Baby heads, boiled and buttered, are a real delicacy. The secret to getting more heads is to cut close to the head, leaving most of the stem. Keep on watering. About four more heads will grow, each the size of a baseball. Some people get more. The second crop of heads may be tougher and less tasty than the first big one, not so good for coleslaw but fine for boiling or pickling.

To save your own seed, turn back and read about broccoli seed for the whole story. If you decide to try it pick the firmest headed or your preferred plants, mark them, carefully store alive through winter, and set out the next spring. Support the seed stalks, pick seeds when mature, dry and store. The one real good thing about seed saved from the *Brassica* genus is that it has more longevity than almost any other seed group. So once you succeed in getting a batch it's easily good for five years.

To prepare, pull off the outer leaves. Cut out the stem including the central core which is bitter. Soak in salt water if need be to get out bugs. Store-bought cabbage is so lovely and pure because it is heavily sprayed with insecticides. I'd rather have the bugs. You can prepare cabbage by boiling. It cooks up way faster if you shred it first. Or it is good raw made into a salad generally called coleslaw. Caraway seed is good with boiled cabbage. Red cabbage is a different color but you can make it into sauerkraut or anything you can do with a regular cabbage. Here are a few special red cabbage recipes though to get you started if you're trying that kind.

Stewed Red Cabbage—Split cabbage and cut into thin slices. Soak in salt and water, then put in a pan with stock, if you have it, and a little butter blended with flour. Add pepper and salt to taste. Add ½ cup vinegar and some bacon. Stew until tender, remove bacon and serve.

Dutch Red Cabbage—Shred and boil until tender. Drain as dry as possible. Add 1 tablespoon olive oil, 1 tablespoon butter, 2 tablespoons vinegar, 1 onion, chopped finely, pepper and salt to taste. Simmer until all the liquid has evaporated. Eat hot or cold.

Fried Cabbage—Cook a shredded head of cabbage in 2 tablespoons hot bacon drippings in a large frying pan, covered, for 30 minutes, or until tender. Season with salt and pepper.

Here's a recipe that's a good way to use leftover roast.

Bubble and Squeak (English, I don't know what it means)—Sauté thin slices of leftover roast (any kind) gently in a little butter. Add lots of shredded raw cabbage. Season as you like—dill is nice and so is freshly ground pepper. Cover and cook until cabbage is barely tender. Transfer to a serving dish so the meat will be on top. Serve.

Cabbage Soup—Shred a small cabbage finely. Peel 3 apples and 1 onion and chop them. Put 6 cups of stock and ½ cup stewed tomatoes or tomato juice into a pan and add the vegetables. Cook gently for 30 minutes. Season to taste with salt, pepper, a drip of honey and the juice of 1 lemon.

Creamed Cabbage—Slice a half head of cabbage as for coleslaw and put in a deep hot frying pan. Add 2¼ cups water. Cover and simmer 10 minutes, or until tender. Pour off water and add ½ cup rich cream, 2 tablespoons butter and pepper and salt to taste. Add caraway seeds (optional).

Layered Cabbage Casserole—Cook ½ head of cabbage in hot boiling salted water. Drain and put in casserole alternating layers of cabbage, white sauce and grated cheese. Bake in a 350° oven about 10 minutes, more or less, until the cheese is well melted and then serve.

Grama's Cabbage—Cabbage doesn't have to be a plain dish. Try this one sent to me by Judy Burley from Surrey, B.C., Canada. She says it was her grandmother's recipe brought from Russia and suitable for a family feast. "Take 1 large head or 2 small heads of cabbage (preferably the curly leafed kind). Put in a pot with some boiling water to loosen leaves. Cover and set aside for 10 minutes. In a large bowl put 2 pounds of minced beef and 1 pound of minced pork. Add salt, pepper, garlic, onions (1 or 2), a couple of eggs, 2 or 3 handfuls of rice (not Minute Rice). Mix all together well. Now take the leaves off the cabbage carefully. Put a small handful of meat mix in a large leaf and roll up tightly. Put in the bottom of a large roaster-sized container until you've used up all the meat mixture. You will have cabbage left over. Now put a layer of cabbage leaves over the rolls, then add 2 cups tomato juice, another layer of leaves, 3 cups sauerkraut, another layer of leaves, cover this with either spareribs, pork steak or such. Add another 1½ cups of sauerkraut over this, salt and pepper, another 2 cups of tomato juice (I said a *large* roaster). Now cover tightly and bake in a 350° oven for 5 or 6 hours. By that time the smell will attract everybody for a long way around. We all love this. It is also great warmed up the next day."

Jeanie's Cabbage Rolls—Cook 1 cup brown rice. Steam 6 large cabbage leaves until tender. Sauté a chopped onion and a green pepper together in butter. When the onion is transparent, add 1 pound hamburger meat and ¼ cup water and fry. Combine cooked rice with hamburger. Stuff cabbage leaves with the mixture, fastening them together with toothpicks. Bake at 350° for 30 minutes. Serve with catsup.

Cabbage Bread—Arlene Jackson of Santee, California, sent me this recipe. She uses a package of hot roll mix to make it or bread dough. First she prepares the hot roll mix or her own bread dough. Then she crumbles 1 pound hamburger and browns it in a skillet. Drain off fat. In a separate skillet, brown 1 large diced onion in a little butter or shortening. Cut up 1 head cabbage, fine, as if for slaw, and add to onion mixture. Mix well and cover to steam or fry until cabbage is tender. Salt and pepper to taste. Stir hamburger into cabbage mixture. After dough has raised, knead, then roll out thin and cut into 4-inch squares. Fill with cabbage mixture and pinch dough shut. Place rolls in well-oiled pan in a 425° preheated oven. Bake 15 minutes or until brown. After removing from oven brush with oil and cover with a towel to keep warm until eaten. These may be frozen and reheated as needed. The rolls will be about 3-4 inches in size when baked.

Last and greatest is cabbage slaw, better known as coleslaw. There are infinite variations on the theme of raw shredded cabbage served with a sweet-sour cream dressing.

Viola's Coleslaw—About 2 cups chopped cabbage. Dress with 2 heaping tablespoons sour cream, 1 scant teaspoon vinegar, pinch of salt and pepper and a sprinkle of sugar (substitute a drip of honey if you can).

To freeze, use young small heads. Shred them as for slaw or cut into small wedges. Blanch wedges in boiling water for 3 minutes, leaves for 2 minutes, if you are using whole leaves, blanch shreds for 1½ minutes. Cool, drain and pack.

But I take all the blanching times on vegetables with more than a few grains of salt. I know from considerable experience it really doesn't matter that much. Don't worry about a half minute, or even a minute or 2. Times do matter very much with canning although I often let them run over because more time on canning does no real harm except maybe make the product a little softer. But never less.

Preserving cabbage—The traditional old time ways of preserving cabbage are by salting and fermenting, that's sauerkraut which is covered in the Sours chapter, and by pit or root cellar type storage which is after drying here in a minute. Once I wrote in this book that I had never heard of canning it. Well, Mrs. Helen Bish of Butler, Pennsylvania, read that and wrote to fill in my information gap. She has canned cabbage and says it turned out beautifully and here's her recipe.

Canned Cabbage—Cut cabbage as you would to cook. Cook in water until you can pack it in jars easily—a few minutes. Pack in jars. Put water that you cooked it in over the packed cabbage. Add 1 teaspoon salt to each jar. Can in a pressure cooker for 1 hour. When you use, pour water off and proceed with your recipe as you would with fresh cabbage. This is a good way to preserve early cabbage when it starts to burst. Mrs. Bish uses her canned cabbage to make corned beef and cabbage or potatoes and cabbage or fried cabbage.

To dry, use well-developed heads. Remove loose, bad outside leaves. Split the cabbage, get rid of the bitter core. Slice up the rest with a kraut cutter or some such arrangement and dry. The best way to use dried cabbage is to grind it up (like in a seed mill) and use the powder as an addition to anything from soup to salad. The flavor will be good and it will be nutritious. You can powder lots of other dried vegetables that way, and a variety mixed together makes a great instant vegetable broth.

Pit and cellar storage—There are many variations on this theme. This is how G. E. Marley from Hale, Missouri (which is not real cold) wrote me they do it: "You dig a pit about 2 or 2½ feet deep and line it with straw. Place the cabbage which has been pulled up roots and all in the pit with the roots up, cover with straw and shovel the dirt on top of the straw. Roll up a burlap sack or an old rug and leave it sticking out so you can get into the pit after the snow covers it and the dirt is frozen. This keeps the cabbage nice and crisp all winter long." He keeps apples, turnips and potatoes that way too. A shortcut and not as dependable version of Mr. Marley's system is to dig a trench in the garden, set the cabbage heads

in it exactly upside down with the root pointing straight up and cover with dirt completely. It's harder to find them though. A way to handle more cabbage heads is to enlarge the pit in diameter, making it a kind of circular affair. You can also stack the cabbages so that the root of each is covered by the head of another. Then cover with straw and dirt. Your pit will be safer if you dig a drainage ditch leading downhill and away from the circular trench to avoid the possibility of water settling in there and if you put the cabbages on a mound of dirt piled in the center of the pit to give them some extra drainage and protection that way. You can get out a few heads from time to time and cover the rest back up and they'll be all right. Slight freezing does not injure cabbage so you don't have to worry about them as much and cover as deeply as you do other pit-stored vegetables. A succession of heavy freezings and thawings though would certainly do them no good. You also can lay heads of cabbage in rows on shelves in a root cellar-type storage area, but if it has access to the house you'll smell cabbage all winter!

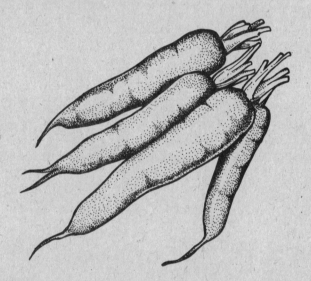

CARROTS I love. There are plenty of hard things in life. I'm not looking for them. Carrots are one of those easy-to-grow vegetables, productive in a limited space, quick to mature, disease and insect unscathed, happy colored, good tasting and nourishing, good easy winter keepers.

To plant, choose your variety. Most carrots take about two months to mature, a little longer for the long-rooted kinds. Chantenay, Nantes and Oxheart are good short-rooted carrots. Short-rooted carrots are the thing to grow if you have very rocky ground, or if the ground is shallowly cultivated or if your growing season is extra short. Imperator gets 9 inches long and Waltham Hicolor will grow a foot long. If your soil is not really well loosened by cultivating and also by having plenty of sand, peat moss or compost mixed in with it a long carrot just can't make it down through it and will end up having a weird stunted shape that is hard to cope with in the kitchen. Carrots prefer cool, wet weather to grow in. In the South that means spring and fall are better for them than midsummer. In southern gardens the short, quick-growing varieties do better than longer-rooted kinds.

Carrot seed is very small. An ounce will plant 150 feet of row. It is slow to germinate. If you soak in a little water overnight before planting it will speed up a little. Ideally you would plant the seed ½ inch deep and ½ inch apart in the place in the garden where you want it to grow—but carrot seed is so fine your fingers won't be able to make that happen exactly. So do the best you can and be encouraged with the thought that like with beets thinning is going to be something you can really turn to your advantage. Keep the place where you planted the seeds well watered and moist until they are up. We plant carrots mixed with a little radish seed because the carrots are so slow the weeds will get a start if we can't get out and cultivate. The radishes mark the row so we can get on with the hoeing and rototilling while the carrots are still working on waking up. You can make succession plantings of carrots as often as you like from the time the ground can be cultivated until it's too hot for carrots. It's a good idea to rotate them into different parts of your garden in successive years. To make your carrots grow quickly don't let the ground dry out.

To thin and harvest, start thinning when your carrots are 2 or 3 inches high. They will grow better if they aren't all smashed together. For the rest of their season keep thinning enough to leave growing room for the ones that are left. Don't do all the thinning at once but aim at having the carrots 2 or 3 inches apart by the time the season is at the end. Before you thin water the row well first and then pull your chosen carrots carefully so they don't break off at the top or in the middle. Figure on eating and freezing, canning, or drying the carrots you have thinned out. If you've never worked with any but store carrots before, these baby carrots are going to be a little unfamiliar at first. But you'll find that garden carrots fresh from the soil and baby carrots in particular taste better than you ever dreamed carrots could taste! Baby carrots are as tender as new potatoes. They don't need to be peeled. The big job with any stage of carrot, including the baby stage, is washing the dirt off. Cut off the green tops. Then carry them by the bucketful to the bathtub (at least that's where we do it), fill it with water and scrub the carrots under running water with a copper mesh pad (not a soapy pad, of course) or Tuffy plastic scrub pad or a scrub brush. Or sometimes we do the job out in the yard with a big tin tub and a hose. It takes a long time and a *lot* of tedious work to get all those carrots completely free of dirt. The rest is easy. Cook and eat. But you can't eat them all up right then. So we freeze them whole, unpeeled. Just bring to a boil, bag up and put in the freezer. Oh, I forgot to tell you, at thinning time I pull the *biggest* carrots and leave the rest to grow until I thin the biggest out again later for more freezing carrots. Thinning actually loosens the soil and helps the others grow.

To save your own seed—Carrots are a biennial like beets, a root vegetable that stores food the first summer and makes seed the second. That second year the carrot stalks are really a fine sight—4 feet high or more. In the process of making seed your root vegetables become inedible because they send all the food back up out of the root into the upper works and the root gets woody and blah. Carrots are cross-pollinated by insects so if you're going to raise seed only one variety should be growing at a time. They will also cross with wild carrots, the weed known as Queen Anne's lace, so keep all of those plants cut during flowering of the garden carrots. Choose your best plants and mark them. In the fall break or twist off the tops leaving only about an inch of green stem and then store the carrots buried under the ground deep enough so they won't freeze. Mark your spot. In the spring set them out in rows with the crown level with the ground and off they'll go again. The seeds don't all come at once and don't all ripen at once. First they come on the main stem and then on the branches. In either case wait until the greenish color disappears from the seeds and the branches they hang from. Then you can cut the stalks and give them some more air drying. Rub out the seed by hand and screen, sift or winnow out the sticks and stuff. A dozen carrot plants would probably give you enough seed for your family. Carrot seed kept dry and cool will stay healthy at least three years.

To cook your carrots remember that garden fresh carrots cook more quickly than store ones, smaller ones quicker than larger ones. They are tender when a sharp fork punches through with just a little pressure. Don't cook them mushy. You can eat them raw. Or in soups. But easiest just boiled and served with butter or creamed.

Carrot Salad is a good winter dish. Grate 3 or 4 carrots (depending on your family size and carrot size). Add any kind of fruit or fruits in combination. I like to use my home-dried fruit chopped into little bits. But apples, oranges, bananas, dates, raisins, pears, pineapple and coconut are all good with it. So is some grated turnip or cabbage. Toss it all together. Add mayonnaise mixed with a dribble of honey. Another sort of dressing for this carrot salad is to toss the grated carrot with salt and lemon juice before you add the other ingredients. It's good with nuts chopped in, too, or green onion.

Fresh Carrots in Lemon Butter—Peel 8 to 10 fresh carrots and leave whole if small or cut in lengthwise halves, if large. Put the carrots in a cooking pan with about 1 inch of boiling water and 1 teaspoon salt. Cover, bring to a boil again and cook until carrots are fork tender. Drain off water and leave carrots in pan. Add ½ teaspoon sugar or other sweetening, ¼ teaspoon ground nutmeg, 2 tablespoons butter or margarine and shake over low heat a few minutes. Sprinkle with 1 teaspoon fresh lemon juice.

Carrot Ring—Kay Arnold, who writes a wonderful cooking column for the *Monte Vista Journal* in Colorado, sent this recipe to me: "Set oven at 350°. Generously grease a 2-quart ring mold. Prepare your carrot pudding—beat 2 eggs into 2 cups milk. Add 1 tablespoon flour or ¼ cup fine bread crumbs, 1 teaspoon salt and 1 teaspoon sugar. Fold in 2 cups of finely grated carrots. Pour mixture into mold and bake 30 to 40 minutes or until firm. Invert onto serving dish and fill center with creamed peas to which chopped celery or lettuce or tiny pearl onions have been added. Garnish with fresh parsley and you have a vegetable dish to really serve with pride."

To freeze—Carrots for freezing should be the small ones between ½ and 1 inch in diameter. Bigger ones simply aren't good this way. Blanch the smaller of the small ones 3 minutes, larger ones 5 minutes. Cool before packaging. Freezer carrots are not nearly as tasty as fresh ones, even when you use baby carrots, but they have the enormous advantage of being handy for the pot, clean and ready to go and are fine in a soup or with some seasoning.

To can, use a pressure canner: 10 pounds pressure, 25 minutes for pints, 35 minutes for quarts.

To dry—You'll do best with young, tender carrots. Wash, peel, slice lengthwise into pieces about ⅛ inch thick, and dry.

Pit or root cellar storage—You can store carrots all winter in a galvanized or wooden tub or some such between layers of moist sand: layer of sand, layer of carrots, layer of sand and so on. Or you can store them in wooden boxes in a storage room in the basement if you have a cool one with a dirt floor or in a root cellar or under straw and dirt in pits the same as you would store beets. They are not ruined by slight freezing, being tougher that way than beets. This storage is not for your early crop of baby carrots.

The big carrots go into the root cellar in October. The tops are snapped off. It doesn't matter if the carrots accidentally get cut by the spade when you are digging them—they will still keep very well. I don't leave carrots in the ground. Once the whole crop froze on me. Last year it got so cold here it would not only have frozen anything in the garden but it actually froze 3 feet down and froze our water line which runs 800 feet uphill from a spring in the canyon bottom. The water stayed frozen from then (December 1) until spring and I did everything out of buckets of water hauled by my precious husband from the stock tanks or from 50-gallon drums which I hauled from town after the stock tank water was used up. That really gives a person some new angles on water. We are all accustomed to wasting water. If you are skeptical, uncouple the trap under your bathroom sink and replace it with a bucket. That way you have to empty all the water that flows through your sink by hand into your tub or toilet. You'll see what I mean fast. If that didn't convince you, do the same thing under your kitchen sink.

If you do have the climate to leave carrots in the ground they won't keep a second year. They start to get woody from the top down their second spring. The woody place is right where the outer layer meets the inner core—where they change color. You can still get some good though by starting your slicing from the tip. Discard the portion your knife can't pass through easily.

CAULIFLOWER—Cauliflower, broccoli, Brussels sprouts and cabbage are all members of the *Brassica* genus. Cauliflower is the hardest one of them all to grow. They look almost the same as little plants, only get different looking as they mature. In my climate everybody starts from seed in the house and sets out as early as possible after the last (always just a guess and hoping) hard frost.

The reason I have trouble growing these four is because, like celery and green pepper, they really prefer cool weather and it is hot here in the valley in the summertime. We can grow tomatoes, watermelon, cantaloupe and grapes much better. You may think that surprising about northern Idaho but if you study a really detailed climate map of the United States you'll find that there is a little finger of warmer country that goes up the Columbia River valley, then up the Clearwater River valley and finally up the Potlatch River valley to Kendrick where the valley ends. This probably is the warmest place for as far north as it is anywhere short of the west coast.

Out of the canyon, which is a steep 2,000 feet up, people can grow good broccoli and cabbage but not tomatoes.

A really honest and thorough introduction to cauliflower growing means warning you about all the things that can go wrong. Like I said cauliflower wants a cool, moist climate. Too much heat makes it head prematurely. It wants *lots* of heavy water, even irrigation, more if you have hot weather or a hot climate. It wants heavy mulching and if you don't mulch you have to be careful in your weeding because it has a very shallow root system. Commercial fertilizers will make it sick for sure and if you don't give it plenty of manure and compost it won't do well because it requires a richer ground than any other member of its family. You must have the soil deeply worked even though it is shallow rooted and watch carefully to make sure you don't let the ground dry out. It won't keep its flavor in storage as long as say a carrot though it sure does better than broccoli. It takes even more room in your garden than cabbage. It's a hard plant to grow in the southern United States though you can try to cope by planting the purplish curd (headed) long-season type or raise a quick-growing type by setting it out real early or plant it the late summer and try to get good cauliflower by late fall. But it isn't as hardy against frost as cabbage though once it starts to mature its head light frost won't hurt. It is subject to the same bunch of bugs and diseases as cabbage and if aphids get into the head they're next to impossible to get out again.

To plant—If that didn't completely discourage you here's how to grow it. Use the same basic rules as for cabbage with the exceptions I told you about above. Plant seed ½ inch deep, 3 inches apart if you're doing it outdoors. Raise for five to seven weeks before setting out. Then set out 20 inches or more apart. Figure 60 to 100 days to maturity (depending on your variety) from the time of transplanting.

To harvest—You can be really proud when you've got this far! You can either harvest your cauliflower plain or "blanched." That means to bring the leaves together over the head enough to shade it and tie them that way lightly. Don't do this until the head is fully developed though. Then leave it that way one to three weeks and that should result in the "curd" inside being nice and white. If you don't blanch it doesn't make your cauliflower any less edible. You can just pare off the yellowed outside if you don't like the look of it.

To save your own seed is also hard. Go back to broccoli and the same rules apply. Cauliflower seed will last five years or more once you've got it.

To cook, soak in salted water. Cut off the green leaves and cook just the curd part. Serve buttered or with a cheese sauce or as you like.

CELERIAC is a little known relative of celery. You almost never see it in grocery stores so if you grew it in your garden you'd really have a unique vegetable! It's common in Europe I'm told. It has other names like celery root, knob celery, and turnip-rooted celery. It is actually easier to grow than celery and good to eat in soups, as a vegetable and in salads. It doesn't need blanching like celery and has a taste like celery flavored with English walnuts. The part you eat is the enlarged root just above the ground which usually grows to a diameter of 4 inches or so. Don't eat the leaves. Celeriac isn't eaten raw like celery, only cooked. Once you've got it grown you can store right in the garden until you want to use it. Bring some dirt up on the sides and put a light mulch over to keep it from freezing. It's a dependable and good plant to grow. Rather than say everything twice, since you plant and care for celeriac exactly as you do celery I'm going to say it all just once under celery. You can use celeriac, like celery, before it is mature. Start using when they are 2 inches thick or so. If you don't want to store it in the place you grew it then dig up the roots as freezing weather is getting closer, cut off all but an inch of the tops and keep in a cool place. They will keep for months which is another great advantage of this underappreciated vegetable.

To prepare, scrub the root thoroughly. Scrape or pare. You can peel it after cooking if you want but it saves scrubbing if you do before. The necessary precooking can take a long time. A freshly dug whole root, say 3 inches thick, might take an hour and a half of boiling, lid on the pan, to really get done. If you peel it after cooking it's easier to do (you want to trim away those knoblike buds on the surface while you're at it). But if you want to speed up the cooking process peel first, then slice or cube it and maybe you can get it done in 20 minutes. Strangely enough, old celeriac will cook faster than fresh. The cooking water from celeriac makes a good soup base or addition to soup liquid. Now serve with melted butter or a tasty cheese sauce or white sauce. Add to flavor stews or soups.

To fry, cut precooked celeriac into slices ½ inch thick. Coat slices with flour on both sides, dip into slightly beaten egg whites, then dip into fine, dry bread crumbs. Cook in a buttered frying pan or in cooking oil over medium heat until lightly browned, first on one side, then the other. Sprinkle on a little salt and serve.

CELERY and celeriac aren't for just any garden or gardener. They are both difficult and demanding to grow even though celeriac is a little easier than celery. Celery probably originally grew in a swamp. It takes a very long time to mature, like about six months from planting the seed. It actually does better if transplanted once, or better yet twice so there's more work for you. It wants very rich soil, lots of manure, loves chicken manure. It doesn't like hot weather. In Florida it is planted in the fall for a winter crop. In the rest of the South it's a fall-planted crop maturing about Thanksgiving or Christmas. In areas with a cool summer you have a chance of growing it in summer if you start it indoors way ahead of time. My summers aren't cool so I can't grow it. For soil it wants a loose loamy one. Most of the commercial crop is grown on marsh or peat soils after they have been drained. It takes a lot of water and likes flood irrigation rather than having it sprinkled on. It may develop a disease called blight that will show by spots and holes on the leaves. I think celery is one vegetable that is actually better adapted to commercial growing on an intensive scale in an especially suitable part of the country than as a general garden vegetable. But if you want to try anyway here's the best set of directions I can supply you.

To plant, don't start with the store celery seed used for flavoring. It will grow but mainly grow more celery seed you can use for flavoring—it's a special variety of celery that doesn't make an edible stalk but quickly produces abundant seed. (On the other hand you might want that!) Plant seed for the variety you want first in the house or hotbed. Cover no more than ⅛ inch deep. You can merely press the seed into the soil. The seeds are very small and very slow to germinate. Water faithfully and don't let the bed dry out once if you can help it until the plants are up. Then ease off on the water lest you drown them. You can start a multitude of plants in a small box. When the second leaves appear transplant 1½ to 2 inches apart into larger boxes in which you will gradually harden them by exposure to open air and sunshine on warm days. When your outdoors is well past the last frost and dependably warm and the little celery plants are 5 or 6 inches high you can set them out in the garden. You can generally figure they'll spend 10 to 12 weeks indoors in their box before transplanting to the garden. Set the plants in the garden in rows 3 feet apart and 5 or 6 inches apart in the row. Keep the soil they are living in moist—remember they'd really prefer a swamp! Keep the weeds out. If you live in an area where you can plant the seed directly into the garden a light mulch over it will help get it up. After the plants come up you carefully remove the mulch. Fall celery is generally planted in a row in the garden and then transplanted when no more than 3 inches high.

To harvest—One help to the fact that celery takes so long to mature is that you can rob the plant of a stalk or leaf anytime through its growing period without ruining it. You can use harvesting as a way of thinning as soon as they get big enough to be worth the trouble. Half-grown celery is just as edible as full-grown. And in general garden fresh celery will taste better than any store celery. Cut plants at ground level and just leave the roots in the dirt to become compost. It used to be believed that all celery should be blanched before harvesting. That meant to gradually raise the dirt level around the sides or lay boards on each side or wrap brown paper around it the last ten days or so until it lost most of the green color. Blanching was supposed to make it grow a larger heart too. Now a lot of gardeners and growers don't blanch or only slightly. Blanching sure doesn't add any food value to the plant. It's a cosmetic measure and extra work.

To freeze, blanch 3 minutes, cool and package. But the results will be cooked.

To can, just add to your canned tomatoes, or meat stews or stock. There isn't much point in canning celery by itself. The only thing I know to make out of plain cooked celery is celery soup (just cooked celery with a white sauce made with cream to thicken the broth and an egg yolk beaten in with seasonings).

To root cellar or pit store, dig before hard frosts and store in boxes covered with dirt in your root cellar. Or leave in the ground, cover entire row with at least 6 inches of dirt and put a heavy mulch like straw over that. Or transplant to a cold frame in late fall, close side by side, or transplant to a box of damp earth in your root cellar. The idea is to keep as cool as possible without actually freezing.

CHARD is a beet with an undeveloped root and wonderful leaves. Look in the Greens section of this chapter for more on it.

CHICORY—See Chicory-Endive under Greens in this chapter and Chicory in the Herbs chapter for coffee making.

COLLARDS—See Greens.

CORN—Corn is one of my favorite vegetables. We grow a lot of it in our garden. Corn likes a hot summer and hot summers we have here. The hotter your weather the better your corn will thrive. Sometimes the first part of our summer is chronically wet, cloudy and cool. The corn will just seem to stand still as if it's never going to do anything. It will sprout reluctantly, grow a few inches, and then do nothing. Until the long hot days of sunshine in midsummer come and then it takes off as on signal and grows. It grows so fast you can practically see the difference from day to day, up and up and then straight on into making ears of corn and then suddenly you have it all there to be harvested because corn happens all at once when it does.

The original corn is what we now call field corn or Indian corn. It is native to the Americas and the one that is now grown for animal feed or making cornmeal or hominy. Sweet corn is what this section in Vegetables is all about and that is a variety of the original corn that has only been grown since about 1800. You can pick field corn and use it like sweet corn but it won't be as tender and delicious. You can dry, make cornmeal or hominy out of sweet corn. There is another big section on corn growing and using in this book in the Grains chapter because corn is not merely a vegetable like other vegetables. It is also a grain with all the basic importance that implies. So see the Grains chapter for field corn, grinding and hominy making, use as livestock feed, and popcorn. Recipes for cornmeal dishes like bread and pudding are in Grains too.

What variety to grow—Among the corns, even among just the sweet corns, there is a confusing abundance of kinds to choose from. Here's what I think about it. You have your choice of white, multicolored or yellow corn. Yellow corn is the usual kind; some people say it has more vitamins and minerals. I think it tastes the best. Green corn means sweet corn. You have your choice of hybrids or standard varieties. Hybrid corn varieties are famous for their husky productivity but you can't save the seed and get it to happen again. Because I believe you should be growing varieties you can save seed from, I'd recommend you grow standards.

Different corn varieties have different times to reach harvest. An "early" corn generally means about 60 to 65 days to maturity, but cold weather could make that longer. You plant early corn where your warm season is short, or you could make plantings of early corn every ten days or so from planting time on to midsummer. "Midseason" corn is 65 to 81 days to maturity and in general gives you a little bigger ear of corn than early corn does. "Late" corn takes 80 to 90 days to mature and usally is larger yet. Early corn can be planted closest. Figure on thinning to 6 inches for early corn, 8 inches for midseason corn, or 12 to 18 inches for late corn. Any of the three would be planted in early summer but early corn can be planted when soil temperature is around 55° to 70° whereas midseason and late corn need a warmer soil like 60° to 80°. That's a rough statement and what it interprets to is that early corn will cooperate and grow more readily in cool weather than midseason or late corn will.

So you're going to make a choice between successive plantings of early corn or planting more than one variety, an early one and then a midseason or late one. We usually do some of both. We plant some early corn in succession and then we plant also at least two varieties, an early one and a late one. Each planting will produce only one crop and that will tend to ripen all at once. If you are planting a lot of corn (and you will be if you are seriously depending on your garden to feed you and your animals) then a system to get fresh corn all through the late summer and stagger the food processing really matters.

The size of your garden also has to be a factor. Unfortunately, corn takes a lot of room for what you get. A typical stalk grows 5 or 6 feet tall and stalks are from 6 inches to a foot and a half apart, depending on your variety. You'll get two or three ears per stalk. That means to grow enough corn to fulfill all its wonderful possible uses you could easily plant 50 percent of your garden in corn. If your garden space is limited you might consider growing dwarf sweet corn. It can be crowded up (any of them can be grown closer than these directions say if you can get plenty of manure or compost into the soil and are desperate) more than any of the other varieties. But the ears are also somewhat dwarfed. If there is corn bacterial wilt disease in your area you will want to hunt for a variety that is resistant to it. Early yellow-grained corns are most susceptible.

To plant—Corn will grow on almost any kind of soil. The better nourished the soil, the better your harvest of corn. But for growing corn we don't use any special fancy fertilizers. We manure the whole garden every fall with what is collected from the barn, the chicken house, and the pig pen, so the corn area gets a feeding too. Plant where the corn will get *at least* six hours of good full sunlight a day and preferably more. Corn is one of the more frost-tender plants so don't plant until *all* danger of frost is over. That means you will be planting corn after most of your other garden vegetables, after the lettuce, peas, beans, beets, chard, turnips, cabbage and so on, but shortly before the most tender plants like cucumbers, muskmelons, watermelons and squash. Corn is always planted in

the garden from seed rather than started elsewhere and transplanted because transplants don't do well.

Plant the seeds about an inch deep in rows 2 or more feet apart. Not all your corn seed will germinate so it's customary, unless you're very short of seed, to plant a seed every 3 inches for early or midseason corn, every 4 to 6 inches for late corn and then thin if needed. Though I'll tell you honestly I'm always so grateful for every stalk that grows that I can't bear to thin at all and just try to give them extra good care and get a fine crop. If you want to plant Indian style in hills plant five or six seeds in hills 3 feet apart each way, and thin out to three to five stalks in a hill with the seed covered about 1½ inches deep. If you want to be *really* authentic put a rotten fish in each hill! Whether you plant in rows or hills, plant so that you have adjacent rows of corn that form a square-shaped corn area rather than one super long row of corn. There's an important reason why. Corn has to be pollinated to make corn. Corn pollen is carried by wind from the tassels on top to the silks of the ears and in a row of corn all by itself you risk that the pollen may all blow away. If the pollen all blew away no kernels would form. If you've seen ears of corn with grains missing the reason is probably that there wasn't thorough pollination. With several short rows of corn next to each other your chances of good pollination are best.

"Suckers," little mini-corn stalks, will sprout from the bases of your corn plants. Some books tell you to jerk those off but that's compulsive neatness and actually does more harm than good to the plant. Try hard at first to keep out the weeds between rows that would compete with your corn for nourishment and water, but get the most of your deep cultivating like rototilling done while the corn is still young and doesn't have a highly developed root system. Like come through with the tiller ten days after the corn is up and you can see where the rows are and again two weeks later. After that come through weeding by hand with a hoe. Hoe shallowly to protect the highly developed root system corn gets. Otherwise you may have easier weeding but if you disturb tender corn roots it will do more harm than good. When the hot days come and your corn is growing fast remember that although corn rejoices in heat you've also got to give it plenty to drink while the heat is on.

Corn bugs and pests—If you plant corn and then find something else ate most of it before you got there you won't be the first person it ever happened to. Against bacterial and fungus-type problems the best defense is well-nourished soil, plenty of sunshine, plenty of water. It also may help your troubles to faithfully harvest your corn a little on the early side and remove each stalk from the garden as fast as you have picked the last ear. You can shred the stalk for compost or dry and store it for winter fodder for your hay eaters. Corn earworms are a common problem no matter how carefully you attend to the rest of it. I've never had them for some reason, maybe because so many chickens roam in my corn patch, but lots of good gardeners do have them to fight. I wrote in an earlier edition of this book about some neighbors of mine that had heard of putting mineral oil on the corn ears to prevent earworm. It didn't work for some reason and they got very deformed ears of corn. Since then a number of people have sent advice. Mrs. Selkirk wrote me from Ennis, Montana, that "if anyone is having trouble keeping worms out of ears of corn—just take a tablespoon of mineral oil and put it in the center of the silks on each ear of corn as soon as there's enough silks, while it's still light and young." Another writer suggested to half fill an eye dropper with mineral oil and squirt it into the silk at the very tip of the ear as soon as the silk silts. Mrs. Grimshaw wrote me from Cedar City, Utah, that she has used the mineral oil for years. She says you can use any kind of oil but mineral oil has no taste. "We have a long snouted oil can that gets it right into the tip of the ear. When the silk shows good we take our oil can and a Jergens lotion bottle that has been cleaned and filled with mineral oil. One drop to each ear right down to the tip through the silk kills the larvae of the corn worm and really works!" From what I've learned from these dear readers I'd guess that my neighbor put the mineral oil on the corn too soon, before the silk was far enough developed.

To harvest—This is a rush job from start to finish. It will only be something like seven to ten days from the time that you can start eating a planting of corn until the last ears are in the last stage of maturity and must be harvested or else. Not all the ears get ripe at once. The ones nearest the top of the plant generally ripen first, lower ones later. What that means is you have to really watch your corn patch for the first ripe ears and then go through it every day or two while the harvest is on getting the ones that are ready. There is a day of absolute perfection in corn ripeness—you can actually start harvesting and eating several days before that and continue several days after that. But really underripe corn is tough and not very tasty, and if you wait too long you'll be mad at yourself for having let the golden moment pass you by.

To test the corn for readiness you watch the silk. A mature corn ear has dried silk. If you think the silk looks dried enough pull back a husk from the ear, puncture a kernel with your thumb nail. The juice that comes out is the corn "milk." Some people prefer to gather ears when the milk is still thin and sweet. Some wait until the milk is white and thicker and the kernels are fuller and more mature. That's up to you. Corn is starting to get dangerously near the overmature stage when the silk gets really dark brown or black. It feels nice and plump but it won't stay prime for more than a few more days. Perfect corn should practically squirt out milk when you dent it. Corn getting a little overripe will be moist but won't squirt. To get the ear off the stalk twist and snap it away with one hand while holding the stalk firmly with the other hand. Be careful not to damage the stalk itself because that will make it hard for the plant to finish up the other ears still in the making.

Once you have the ear separated from the stalk the rush is *really* on. All fruits and vegetables taste better when garden fresh but none is even in the same class with corn in the rate of deterioration from parent plant to table. This isn't just folklore. Sweet corn on the stalk is literally sweet. Fifty percent of its sugar becomes starch during a day's storage at 86°. At a lower storage temperature the sugar still turns into starch but not at quite such a fast rate. If you've never tasted anything but store corn on the cob this has never been an issue with you. Store corn has all long since turned to starch and in the absence of a choice it's good eating. But having gone to the trouble of growing your own sweet corn I want you to have the real thing. That means don't remove the husks after picking until your corn is actually being prepared for cooking or preserving because the act of unhusking alone hastens the change from sugar to starch. Keep the corn as cool as you can while it is waiting to be worked on. And keep the time span as short as possible from field to table.

So be careful with your corn. Don't go out in the morning and pick bushels of it unless you're sure you're going to be able to spend all day processing it because hanging around until the next day will mean a real taste loss for you. Getting from field to canning jar or deep freeze or drying tray ideally should take less than three hours. If you must store it keep the corn in its husk in the coldest part of your refrigerator short of freezing.

To save your own seed, don't save kernels from any hybrid corn because the corn plants that result, instead of being the variety that was the parent, will be an assortment of varieties, generally none of them much good. (That's true of any "hybrid" seed.) Any sweet corn varieties will cross and they will also cross with field corn or popcorn. This crossing takes place at the pollination stage when the wind carries pollen from the tassels (the male flower) to the silks (the females). Crossings even affect the kind of kernel and the taste of corn you get the same year it crosses! A stiff breeze can carry corn pollen a long ways. Commercial seed planters separate their corn plantings for seed by at least ¼ mile. For home use try to have separate varieties at least 200 feet apart, preferably with a building or tall trees in between them or plant varieties that are far enough apart in maturity dates that their flowering won't happen at the same time. If your corn crosses anyway it will still be edible.

Choose the best ears for your climate and mark them for saving. (If it's early corn you need, choose the earliest ears, etc.) Later you can pick the ears and bring them inside for drying when the husks are turning brown if you are anxious to turn the cows into the corn field or some such . . . or you can leave the seed ears on the plants for much longer. Frost won't hurt them. When you do bring the ears into the house strip back the husks and hang the cobs in a dry place. Don't shell out the corn from the ears until the kernels are completely hard and dry. Don't save from just one ear or plant for seed stock. That is inbreeding and it is almost sure to result in stunting and other bad qualities in your corn. Save the kernels from more than one ear and more than one plant and mix them before planting next year. Corn is one of the least hardy seed types for survivability in the seed. You really can't depend on it lasting well more than two years; planting it within one year would be better.

Corn on the cob—For the very best tasting corn of all put your water on the boil, go out to pick the corn, run all the way from the field to the kitchen, husk and cook the corn! Or for the super absolute don't boil the corn at all—roast the ear in a 375° oven for about 15 minutes. (Remove all but the inner layers of husks, take out the silk and tie the ends of the remaining husk together with string.) Never salt corn until after you are all done cooking because the salt tends to toughen it. You can roast corn on a grill over coals as well as in the oven. In that case shuck it first, lay the ears on the grill, turn them every so often until roasted on all sides. It will take about 10 minutes. No matter how you got your ears cooked, boiled, roasted, oven or grill, serve by rolling them in melted butter and eat joyously with your hands, one on each end of the cob. Make sure there is something like a napkin for people to wipe their hands and faces on afterwards.

Corn Cakes from Leftover Roasted or Boiled Corn—When you have leftover boiled or roasted ears, split the kernels lengthwise with a sharp knife, scrape the corn from the cobs, leaving the hulls on the cobs. For every 6 ears of corn combine 3 eggs, add salt and pepper to taste, form into small cakes and fry to a nice brown.

To freeze—Detailed directions for freezing corn are in the Freezing section of the Food Preservation chapter where I used it for an example.

Freezing whole roasting ears is sort of wasteful of your freezer space and not recommended by the experts but you can do it if you want to. Gather the ears. Trim excess silk with a scissors. Pack the whole, unhusked ears into plastic bags and put them in the freezer. There is no blanching. To cook these ears just let them thaw enough to get off the husk and silk. Then lay in fast boiling water. Let boil 5 minutes after the water returns to a boil. You can turn these into kernel corn by letting them thaw enough that you can cut the kernels off the cob.

"Whole-kernel corn is cut from the cob at about two-thirds the depth of the kernel and cream-style corn is cut from the cob at about the center of the kernel and the cob then scraped." I quoted that and it's unreal. When you are processing 200 ears of corn, you just grab the ear and whack down wherever the blade may land, don't scrape it afterwards, but move on to the next. Give the cobs to the pigs. Call it "cream-style" anyway. I freeze all my corn cut from the cob to prepare that way. I just warm it, drain the water (to the pigs or the gravy), add butter and serve. If there is leftover corn, which there seldom is, I can make fritters or soup with it or just warm up to serve again. If you do like me and freeze all your sweet corn home-style you'll want maybe sometimes to have a dish besides buttered corn. Here are some other good things to do with cream-style corn.

Corn Pudding—One quart corn off the cob, 2 cups milk, 2 eggs, 1 tablespoon butter, salt and pepper to taste. Bake in a pudding dish.

Corn Soup—Boil a beef soup bone in 1 gallon water with salt. Skim. Season. When meat is well done remove bone. Add corn from 12 ears. Just as corn is tender add 1 tablespoon butter. Tomatoes, too, if you like.

Cream of Corn Soup—Cut corn kernels from 3 ears of corn. Put the cobs into enough water to cover and cook 30 minutes. Strain and add the corn pulp to the boiling corn cob water and cook about 15 minutes. If you want to make this starting with frozen cream-style corn or leftover cooked corn use 2 cups of corn cut from the cob. Now add 2 cups of milk, a dash of salt and pepper, thicken with a little white sauce made from butter and flour and serve.

Corn Croquettes—Melt 4 tablespoons butter. Add 1 cup milk. Separate 2 eggs. Beat whites and yolks light. Add yolks to milk mixture, then whites. Add 1 quart cream-style corn, 1 cup flour and salt or pepper to taste. Fry one side and then the other in hot deep oil or lard. Drain and serve right away.

To can, cut the corn off the cob first, instead of last as you do when freezing. Pack in pints (quarts are not recommended). Pack hot. Process 1 hour and 25 minutes at 10 pounds of pressure.

To preserve by salting down, remove the husk and silk and cook the corn as if you were having it for supper. Cool and cut the kernels off the cobs as if you were going to freeze them. Put the cut-off corn into a crock. Pour over a salt brine made by using ½ cup pickling salt per gallon water. Be sure the corn is covered. Cover the crock with a cloth large enough to extend over the sides of the crock. On top of the cloth put a board cut to fit or a plate that will fit inside the sides of the crock right down on top of the corn. Weight the flat thing with a jar filled with water or a boiled rock or some such. Be sure that there is always enough brine to cover the corn. If the brine is evaporating, add more. If scum forms, remove it and wash the cloth.

To dry—There are three basic ways to dry corn: on the ear for making cornmeal or hominy, in the oven or sun (off corn cut off the cob while fresh, generally sweet corn) or by parching. The directions for the first way are in the Corn section of the Grains chapter.

To oven-dry corn you first harvest it as near the perfect stage as you can. Get off the husk and silk. Then either blanch by putting in boiling hot water and leaving there just long enough for the water to return to a boil or by steaming. An easy way to steam corn is to put the ears in a large kettle that has about an inch and a half of boiling water in the bottom. You stack the corn in there crisscrossed so the steam can get to it all, cover, and let steam 7 to 10 minutes. In either case cool the blanched corn enough so you can start cutting the kernels off. The blanching was to set the "milk" so you don't lose it. Cut the corn off the cob somewhere between half and three-fourths of the way to the cob. If you don't cut very close to the cob scrape part of the remaining corn on top of the corn kernels laid out on your drying trays. When you are really experienced at all this you'll be able to cut off kernels and roll the cob slightly so that rows of kernels fall onto your drying trays (enamel broiler trays or large cookie sheets or some such) with the cut side up. The rows of corn should be as close as possible together but don't have the corn more than one row thick up and down or it won't dry as quickly or be as nice.

Start at 250° for the first 15 minutes. Then continue at a lower temperature. An oven thermometer should give you a reading between 90° and 140°. Leave the oven door propped open. After the first 8 to 10 hours stir once in a while pushing the outside kernels to the center and the center ones to the outside since the outside kernels have a tendency to dry first. Be more careful to keep the heat down as you get nearer the end. Your finished dried corn is yellow—not brown, brittle and bone dry. Store in covered glass containers or bags in a cool, dry place.

As with so many of these processes though there's more than one "right" way. Bea Sorflaten wrote me from Santa Cruz, California, that she blanches her sweet corn, cuts it off the cob, and spreads it very lightly and evenly on pan, cookie sheet or cake pan. She puts it in the oven on lowest heat, for 1 day, 1 night and 1 day and it ends up a "delicious dark brown." To cook dried corn (1 cup will serve three or four people) first soak it overnight. Then simmer for 4 or 5 hours, being careful that the water does not boil away. When the corn is tender she drains off the water, covers the corn with milk, adds seasoning and serves.

To dry corn in the sun use only very young and tender corn and prepare at once after gathering. Blanch and cut off the cob same as for oven-dried. It will help if you can dry in the oven 10 or 15 minutes, then finish drying in the sun. You'll need dry, hot weather.

To parch—Sue Windover wrote me from Holland, Michigan, about her Ohio childhood . . . and about how to parch corn. "Mother was a devoted farm wife with a 2-acre garden, chickens, beef and hogs, who provided for her husband and two children. We belonged to the Dunkard Brethren Church in Bryan, Ohio, just a few miles from the Amish settlement in northern Indiana. The family has been on that particular farm for over 100 years. The rootedness feeling is very deep. Mother made soap, canned vegetables and fruits, and still stokes the wood furnace twice a day in the winter. Now, for a little practical advice. This is called 'parched corn.' During World War II, my great-aunt and uncle ran a small gas station in Bryan. They were unable to buy peanuts for their nut dispenser. So my aunt made parched corn to use instead. It was so popular, they continued to use the stuff even after peanuts were again available." Ruth Kellogg wrote me from Elk City, Idaho, about parched corn and other things too. She added that parched corn was a trail food to Indians and the trail blazers of the old West. This recipe is a combination of both their experience.

Take sweet corn after it is too hard to eat. The overripe ears are actually best. Let it ripen in the field. Then pull or pry the kernels off (don't cut, as you want the kernels intact) and put them in a hot oven in one layer on a cookie sheet, stirring until they are brown and crunchy. After they are baked you can add just enough oil so some salt will stick. Without the oil the parched corn will last forever (if you could keep people from eating it!). Sue takes the ears off the corn plant, pulls the husk back and hangs up to dry about 6 weeks or so before she shells the corn kernels from the ears, winnows and stores same as for popcorn. It is only at that stage that Sue parches her corn. She does it by heating about 2 tablespoons of lard in a covered heavy pot, then pours in a handful of corn, cooks over medium high heat, covered. She says it will sound just like popcorn popping. When the popping is completed she drains it on paper towels. "You now have a fine batch of parched corn. It looks like the inside part popped, expanded, inside the tough hide of the kernel. Sprinkle with salt and serve."

CUCUMBERS are talked about in the Sours chapter because they are so basic to pickling. But you can also eat them raw in salads and sandwiches and cooked in soups and vegetable dishes. They are not a really important food though as far as food value goes, just one that makes meals more interesting and pleasurable. Cucumbers are easy to grow if you have a warm summer and can avoid their insect and disease problems. Before World War II, especially in the South, people had simply given up trying to grow cucumbers because they suffered so from diseases. Then seed companies came out with disease resistant hybrids that solved most problems except the cucumber beetle. But hybrids are a problem in that you can't save your own seed. Another possible problem with cucumbers and all the vine crops like melons and squashes is that they are insect pollinated. That basically means bees and sometimes nowadays due to complicated pesticide problems there can be a real shortage of bees. A lack of bees would result in small or poorly shaped fruit or worse.

In a situation like that it's possible to hand pollinate your cucumbers and other vine crops. There are two kinds of blossoms, males and females. You can tell a male by its thin stem. The female generally has a tiny cucumber or pumpkin or such already formed. When the male blossom is so full of ripe pollen that some will dust off on your fingertip cut it off and carefully touch the sticky stigmas that you will find in the centers of the female blossoms with this pollen. That solves your problem.

Cucumbers are one of the most cold-sensitive plants you are likely to try in your garden. They can't be planted or transplanted into the garden until the weather is truly warm, later than the corn, same time as you would plant watermelon. A frost would be the end for them. They want a warm summer and lots of sunshine. They, like the other vine plants, take a lot of room unless you give the vines something to climb up. But generally they are allowed to just run over the ground. They want a well-manured, well-tilled ground, and plenty of water all through their growing season.

To plant—It's possible to transplant cucumbers but a little risky because they don't do well if their root system is disturbed. So if you start them inside do so by one of the systems that let you set them out in the garden in the same block of dirt that was growing them inside, like little peat pots. Or you can plant them in the garden under paper Hotkaps which gives you a little extra safety as the weather is warming up. We just plant from seed though, around June 1, which is when we can start to trust the weather to be warm and stay warm. Cucumbers are only 55 to 65 days to maturity so a late start still gives you time for a good crop if you have a halfway decently long growing season. Most people plant them in hills, 4 feet apart each way. We set aside a big section of the garden for these vine-type crops that are planted in hills instead of rows—the cucumbers, watermelons, muskmelons and summer and winter squashes. If you do want to plant cucumbers in rows instead of hills make the rows about 7 feet apart and thin the plants to 12 to 18 inches apart in the row. Plant the seed about an inch deep. In hills, thin to about four plants per hill if you have well-composted or -manured soil, less if you don't. But don't thin until the plants are at least 3 weeks old because they have a high fatality rate and you may end up with too few.

Weeding in your cucumber patch can be done thoroughly and with a rototiller all the while the little plants are at home on cucumber hill, but when they start "running" as it's called with long leafy stems going every which way covering the ground that's the end of the cultivating. By then it isn't a problem generally. If you do see an enemy taking hold on or near the hill itself which is where their roots are doing the majority of their feeding you can pluck it out by hand. But cucumber roots are tender so be careful you don't hurt the good guys.

In a very hot climate like on the Mississippi Gulf Coast you may do better with an early spring planting and a late summer one. If your climate is warm enough you can plant cucumbers in the open ground as early as February or March.

Watering—Cucumbers need plenty to drink, especially after they start making cucumbers. A cucumber is 95 percent water and it has to come from somewhere. Figure on a minimum weekly deep watering. You don't have to water every piece of ground the running vine is covering. If you're short of water concentrate it near the hill where the primary roots are. Once the cucumber vines start bearing fruit, as long as you keep watering, they will keep bearing cucumbers until the frost kills them. A few vines can produce a lot of cucumbers before the summer is over. But if you let your vines dry out badly the cucumbers will get a bitter taste so bad you can't eat them and even the very little ones that experienced

such drought will grow up with that bitter taste. So if they do dry out badly it's a good idea to pick all the cucumbers off, water the plant well and let it start from scratch again.

Beetles and diseases—Cucumber beetles do their damage while the plant is young, before it starts to run. Commercial farmers generally have more trouble with them than home gardeners. It doesn't take a whole lot of cucumber plants to give your family a good supply. If you live in cucumber beetle country (they attack the lower part of the stem and the underside of the leaves) you can protect the little plants by covering them with frames over which fly screen or mosquito netting has been stretched. Like a wooden box-type frame set into the dirt or a wire frame with the edges of the netting held down by covering with dirt. When the plants have grown big enough to hold their own you can store away the whole rigging for use next year. It helps control diseases if you destroy the old vines and cucumbers by burning at the end of each year and don't plant cucumbers in the same place in your garden any two years in a row. If you've never grown cucumbers before, the best way to find out what problems you are facing is simply to plant some and see what happens.

To save your own seed—The cucumber is a fruited plant that makes its seed inside the fruit. That's like all the melons, tomatoes, green peppers, and eggplant, pumpkin, squash and so on. The "fruit" in this case is the cucumber itself. Cucumbers are cross-pollinated with the pollen being carried from one flower to another by insects. That means any one cucumber variety will easily cross with another. There are many kinds of cucumbers sold, little yellow-colored "lemon" cucumbers, long crooked ones from the Orient, and so on. I'd recommend to avoid crosses you pick one good basic green, pickling type cucumber and plant just that, or separate varieties by preferably ¼ mile or at least 100 feet with some natural barrier like a house in between.

A lot of cucumbers are hybrids because of the better disease resistance hybrids have. But you will have to start with a standard, "open-pollinated" variety if you're going to save your own seed. A lot of gardeners seem to think that all the vine crops will cross but that isn't so. Cucumbers will *not* cross with watermelon, muskmelon, pumpkin or squash, but only with other cucumber varieties. Choose your best-looking cucumber fruits from your best-looking vines; really pay attention to *health*. The cucumbers intended for seed must be left to ripen on the vine. Mark them with a stake or some kind of tag so that somebody doesn't come along and accidentally pick them off. After being green your cucumbers for seed will turn yellow and then brown. The skin will become hard, almost like a gourd. And it is finally ready for harvesting for seed saving purposes. You can store the hard brown fruits for as long as several weeks in a cool place without them spoiling at this stage so you can wait until all your seed has finished getting ready and then process it all at once.

To get the seed itself cut the cucumber fruits in half, trying not to damage any more seeds than necessary as you do it. This same basic procedure from here on is what you do to harvest seed from any of the seeded-fruit-type vegetables. Spoon out the seed together with the surrounding pulp into a non-metal container like glass or crockery. Let rest at room temperature, stirring twice a day. This step is a kind of fermentation. After two to four days the jellylike pulp which was clinging around the seeds will change into a thin liquid that lets them go. You're ready for the next step when most of the seeds are at the dish's bottom and the liquid above is pretty much clear. Don't worry about the seeds that are still floating. They are doing that because they are hollow, no good, and wouldn't grow anyway. And don't get in a rush and skip this fermentation procedure because it actually acts to destroy possible seed-borne disease, very important with cucumbers.

Finish the seeds by filling your container with cool water, letting the good seeds settle to the bottom and pouring off what's left. Do that several times. Now spread the seeds out, no more than one layer deep, to dry like in a sunny window. *Not* by artificial heat like an oven or heat lamp because that could hurt or kill them. Figure on at least two days for them to dry and then you can store. Incidentally, when storing any seeds be sure and label what year they are, what variety and how you selected them. It's a long time until next spring or the spring after that and you're liable to forget these things. Store any seeds under cold, dry conditions and don't panic if they freeze. If the seed is *dry*, freezing not only won't hurt, it may even improve the crop. Your cucumber seeds are one of the long-lived sorts. They should keep their ability to germinate for five years easy, maybe more.

To harvest, keep picking to keep your vines producing. Pick while they're green and small for the best taste. Pick according to the size cucumber your recipe calls for. In general from 3 to 9 inches long is about right. You can actually pickle or eat any size but cucumbers that are getting yellow and seedy are not near as tasty. All you have to do once the cucumbers are big enough to suit you is gently pluck them off the vine and carry into the house. Store extras in the refrigerator while you're figuring out what to do with them. Really young, tender cucumbers can be used peel and all. The peel is actually the most nourishing part of the cucumber. On store cucumbers I'd say peel 'em because they are all waxed and wax is not the most nourishing part!

Here are some raw cucumber recipes.

Boats—If allowed to grow cucumbers will get very large, like 10 inches long. Such a huge fat cucumber makes a fine child's boat for the bathtub. Cut in half lengthwise, scoop out the seeds and there's your boat. You can feed the other oversized, yellowed or imperfect cucumbers to the chickens and pigs. When feeding them to chickens, break open first. If they aren't hungry enough to stoop to cucumbers those cucumbers still will make fine compost.

Sandwiches—In summer we eat lots of cucumber sandwiches. That consists of fresh cucumbers, peeled and sliced across. The bread is homemade of course. Spread it with mayonnaise, then with the sliced cucumbers and another slice of bread. Everyone loves

them. I like mine with slices of fresh garden tomato added too. And it makes a quick lunch at a time of year when cucumbers are abundant and time is not.

Instant Pickles are another tremendous favorite of mine and the family. I usually feel like I'm making oh so much and then discover that by the time the meal is on the table they are already two-thirds gone from little snitchers and big ones (my husband loves this too). I just peel and slice several cucumbers as for sandwiches. Put them in a bowl with salt, vinegar and water. Now you are going to ask: "How much of each?" Sigh. I never measure, just taste my way to success so I don't know. It adds up to just barely enough liquid to cover. About half vinegar and half cold water. Maybe ½ teaspoon salt. It is a salty dish. The salt pulls the bitterness out of the cucumbers. It needs to be made at least 15 minutes ahead of the meal to let the salt work. The longer you make it ahead the less salt you use. It won't keep, gets too strong.

Wendy Czebotar wrote me from Kennewick, Washington, that she makes a sort of Instant Pickle thing by slicing the cucumbers across in very thin slices, layering with salt in between from the salt shaker, and setting in the refrigerator for an hour. Then she takes them out, squeezes out all the excess water to make the cukes limp. She adds chopped onion, vinegar, oil, salt and pepper and calls it Instant Salad!

Sour Cream Cucumbers—Peel 3 cucumbers. Mix with ½ teaspoon salt. While the cucumbers are being worked on by the salt, peel and slice 3 small-to-medium onions and add. Make a dressing by beating 1 cup sour cream, 1½ tablespoons vinegar and 2 tablespoons sugar or equivalent of honey together. Pour dressing over and serve.

Yogurt Cucumbers—Jan Franco wrote me from Hamden, Connecticut, to suggest that cucumbers are also great in yogurt with a bit of dill weed and salt. She just slices them up and tosses them in the yogurt, no need to soak with salt. She's right.

Cooked Cucumbers and Tomatoes—Peel 2 cucumbers. Chop them up and combine with 4 chopped tomatoes. Season with salt, pepper and a few dill seeds. Sauté in a little margarine. Add a bit of lemon juice or vinegar and serve.

Fried Cucumbers—Edna Andrews wrote me from Ravensdale, Washington, with this recipe—a new idea to me. She said, "I slice the cucumbers and take these thin slices and salt, pepper and flour them. I put a thin amount of butter in skillet and I fry them. They are almost like fried green tomatoes but taste somewhat different."

To freeze—I've been told that if you wrap individual servings of sliced cucumbers in foil and freeze them they make a delicious dish that winter served unwrapped, unthawed, in individual dishes, with heavy cream mixed with a little dollop of lemon juice poured over them.

To dry—I used to think the only way to preserve cucumbers was by pickling. As on many other points my readers have been educating me. Jeanne Weston from Durango, Colorado, wrote me a lot of advice about home-drying foods including the information that you can *dry* cucumbers. She has done it. She says they make good salad flavorings. She cuts them thin and dries until brittle, stores until needed. Then she breaks up the dried cucumber into small pieces and scatters them over her winter salad.

DANDELIONS—Although I've read about a cultivated type of dandelion that makes better greens than the wild kind, I don't remember seeing it in any catalog and I sure haven't grown them on purpose. But dandelions are a vegetable most of us grow whether we intend to or not so we might as well get some good out of them. For some ideas read the Greens section of this Vegetables chapter, which although it doesn't mention Dandelions in particular should be helpful since most of them are handled similarly. (By me, anyway.) And for sure look under D in the Herbs and Flavorings chapter for lots more information (the dandelion jelly is a favorite with readers!).

EGGPLANT—This isn't one of the most nourishing vegetables but for me it's such an adventure to grow and to eat that I generally try anyway. Eggplant is actually a tropical perennial that we grow like an annual. It comes in all kinds of shapes and colors. The big purple ones that you see in supermarkets are there because that's what housewives expect and buy so that's what commercial growers raise. But there's a tender-skinned white variety that's good too, yellow and even striped ones and ones that have small fruits instead of big ones, and the ones that have long cucumber-shaped fruits instead of the usual-shaped ones. A "regular" eggplant plant will produce two to six fruits that will each weigh from 1 to 5 pounds depending on your climate, soil, care and the plant itself. The plant grows about 2 feet tall and should be about 3 feet apart in your garden so you can see it is one that takes up space. If you have a small garden it wouldn't be one of the most practical vegetables for you to raise for food value and productivity relative to the room it takes. And it's also one of the harder ones to raise unless you live in a southern state and even there you're always in danger of disease or bugs getting it.

To plant—In most climates you must buy plants at setting-out time which is when the soil is really warm, not only because a late frost will kill them, but also because, like corn, they won't do anything in cold soil but stand there and be weak and vulnerable to bugs and disease. Or you can start them yourself indoors eight to ten weeks before you figure setting out time would be. Plant ¼ inch deep and about ½ inch apart in virgin soil that hasn't been used to grow eggplant, peppers or tomatoes, to avoid bacterial wilt. When you do get ready to plant your eggplants or seeds in the garden follow the same rule about having them in a new place. If you do get the disease in your garden, pull out and burn affected plants. There isn't any other cure for it. If you have a hot summer your eggplants will love it but they need lots of water which they like better laid on irrigation style than sprayed on. They hate cold winds and love a really rich soil to put them where you got plenty of manure or compost into the soil.

To harvest—The eggplants usually ripen only one fruit at a time and that automatically spreads out your harvest. If you have plenty of eggplants you can start harvesting as soon as the fruits are as big as a large egg and they are shiny but at that stage I feel like a cradle robber and would rather wait. They grow slowly for quite a while until they reach the size determined by their variety. But for sure get them before they get too mature because the younger ones are more tender and have smaller seeds.

To save your own seed—The eggplant is a fruited plant like the cucumber. So the same basic procedure applies. It won't cross except with other eggplant varieties so choose one and stick with it. Leave the eggplants destined to make seed on the bush as long as possible until the eggplant itself turns brown and gather only just before frost. Then proceed by cucumber directions.

To cook, you can peel or not peel. Some people do and some don't. I don't. Your homegrown, freshly harvested ones will have a more tender peel that you could get off with a potato peeler if you want to. White ones generally are eaten skins and all. Some people salt slices of the eggplant before cooking, no matter what the recipe. Some people skip that. My mother salted it. I do. I've really no better reason than that. If you want to salt what you do is leave your eggplant peeled or unpeeled, sliced, sprinkled with salt between the slices, stacked and weighted down for about 30 minutes. (The only exception being if you're going to split it down the middle, scoop out the insides, and bake stuffed halves.) Then you pour off the liquid which seeps out, rinse the slices and proceed.

Mary Debonis sent me two eggplant recipes that she was given by an Italian friend. Here they are:

Eggplant Casserole—Fry 1 cup chopped onion and 1 chopped green pepper in 2 tablespoons olive oil for about 10 minutes. Boil 1 cubed eggplant until tender and drain. Put eggplant in casserole, then 1 cup of uncooked rice. Then add onion and peppers. Dissolve 1 bouillon cube in 1 cup of boiling water, pour over casserole and bake for 1 hour at 350°. Serve hot. Season as desired.

Italian-Style Eggplant—Slice an eggplant, dip into 2 beaten eggs, then into ½ cup flour. Fry in ½ cup of oil until brown, turning once. Now put in layers in a casserole, alternating with grated Italian cheese (1 cup in all) and Italian Gravy—a tomato sauce, the recipe for which is under Tomato. Salt and pepper as desired. Bake 20 minutes at 350° and serve. I'll probably never taste this one myself because I'll never have the time to make it but it sure sounds good.

Armenian Stew—This recipe and the following eggplant recipes were sent to me by Kay Arnold who writes a cooking column for the Monte Vista, Colorado, *Journal*. She is an eggplant salter too. This recipe takes ½ cup olive oil, 1 cut-up eggplant, 2 chopped onions, 3 cut-up carrots, 4 stems of celery, with tops, 1 green pepper, seeded and cut up, ⅓ pound green beans, 4 tomatoes, ½ cup catsup, 1 cup water, 2 teaspoons salt, ¼ teaspoon pepper, 1½ teaspoons sugar, 1½ teaspoons dry basil, 3 or 4 cups cut-up zucchinis. Heat the olive oil in a large pot and add onions and eggplant. Sauté. Cut up the vegetables interestingly (celery diagonally, carrots with a waffler, green pepper in triangles, etc.) all about the same size, and add. Add rest of ingredients except the zucchini and cook another 20 minutes. Serve with brown rice or noodles and garnish with fresh parsley and Parmesan cheese. Yum! And then Kay thanks Suzanne Gosar who gave *her* the recipe.

Moussaka—This is an eggplant casserole. Peel and cut the eggplant in strips from top to bottom. Blanch the strips in boiling water a minute or 2 and then line a greased baking dish with them from the center out, wheel-spoke style. Fill with diced eggplant, browned meat and onions, tomatoes, milk, eggs, bread crumbs and seasoning. Bake, covered, until well done and let stand 5 minutes before turning out upside down into a serving dish. Now don't ask me how much of which! Kay didn't tell me either but I know you're going to have to make it thick and that it will be good!

Fried Eggplant—First dip the sliced eggplant into an egg and milk mixture, and then into fine homemade bread crumbs. Then fry in oil, first on one side, then the other.

To dry, peel and slice ⅛ to ¼ inch thick. Dip immediately in a solution of 6 tablespoons vinegar to 1 gallon water and let rest for 25 minutes, then steam for 5 to 10 minutes, or until tender when tested with a fork. Dry. They are done when leathery to brittle.

To freeze, peel and slice or dice. Dunk into 3 teaspoons lemon juice per quart water to protect the color. Scald 4 minutes, dip again into the lemon-juice solution and freeze.

FENNEL is the plant bearing anise seed. The bulb can be used when it gets about 2 inches across.

To cook, peel and slice the bulb and as much of the stalk as is tender. Cook in boiling salted water until tender-crisp. Drain. Sprinkle with salt, pepper and butter.

GREENS—There are such basic similarities between the raw greens and cooked greens, and so little point in raising very many different kinds that I've gathered them all together here and tried to categorize them as much as possible to help you get a perspective on which are best for what. So the first section in this Greens department is what I call the five lettuces and that to me means the greens to eat raw. Next is a section on *salad dressings* and there you'll find how to make mayonnaise which again is a little strange because you just *don't* put mayonnaise on a tossed salad unless it has seafood, or chicken, or meat, or eggs or some such in it generally. But where would *you* put mayonnaise?

Then I've got a section on greens that grow in hot weather and the South which covers *collards* and *New Zealand spinach* in a serious way and some less common greens in a glancing kind of way. Then comes a section about greens that grow in winter and that's one where I've got *kale* and *endive* (*chicory*). Then comes greens to eat cooked which is really a matter of opinion. Some people will eat anything and everything raw and some greens that at one stage or in small amounts you could eat raw at maturity or in quantity you'd want to have cooked. Well, I put the root vegetable greens family—that's *beet greens*, and *turnip greens* and *chard* in that category. There too are *mustard greens* and *spinach*.

Finally comes a section on saving your own greens seeds which divides into annuals (spinach, lettuce) and biennials (beets, turnips, chard, kale, collards, Chinese cabbage) and a section on how to preserve greens by freezing, drying (no kidding, some people do it), canning. Wild greens like dandelions and poke salet aren't in this chapter at all. Look for them in the Herbs chapter.

THE FIVE LETTUCES—When you go to read your seed catalog you're liable to be overwhelmed with all the different kinds of lettuce they offer. But there's a way of dividing them up and making sense of it all and figuring out what's best for you and your garden.

1. *Crisphead lettuces*—The one everyone knows is iceberg lettuce with the big, firm head that you buy in the store and eat in the restaurant. It dominates the commercial lettuce market despite the fact that it has less color and less taste and less vitamin-mineral kinds of things than any other kind of lettuce because pure and simply it keeps the best, transports the best, and sells the best. For growing in your home garden these head lettuces are the hardest to grow and really least rewarding because of their lower food value. Head lettuce takes twice as long to mature as leaf lettuce. The inside leaves of a head lettuce are blanched because the sun couldn't get at them. That's the reason for the milder taste and less food value. The fact that head lettuce stores and ships the best isn't very important to the home gardener because he can grow other lettuces instead of eating stored head lettuce. Hot weather, especially hot nights, is the worst thing for head lettuce. Instead of making a head it will tend to go to seed under those circumstances, making first a long stalk up and getting a bitter taste in the pro-

cess. Fulton, Great Lakes and Imperial are varieties of crisphead lettuce.

2. *Butterhead lettuces* are sort of in between head lettuce and pure leaf lettuce. They make a head but not a tight, blanched sort like crisphead lettuce. It's a loose, leafy head-shaped affair. That gives them some of the best of both worlds. I don't even try to grow a crisphead lettuce in my garden but every year I do grow some butterhead-type lettuce as well as leaf lettuce. Those are my two favorites in salads and in my experience the two easiest to grow. Boston and Bibb lettuce are butterhead types. Any lettuce described in the seed catalog as making a "loose head" or some such probably is too. The butterhead lettuces have that wonderful garden fresh flavor, don't take much longer than leaf lettuce before you can harvest them, are green leafed and healthy. White Boston and Big Boston are some other good butterheads. But the butterheads are similar to the crispheads in that they can't stand hot weather. You will have more wonderful lettuce than you can eat for a brief period, then when the weather turns hot there's the end of it.

3. *Cos* is the fancy word for romaine, which comes in a lot of varieties like Paris White, Valmaine and Parris Island. It will tolerate more heat than head lettuce but not as much as leaf lettuce. It is not as easy to grow as leaf lettuce and takes way longer. Leaf lettuce matures in 40 to 45 days. Romaine needs 70 to 85 days to be ready. It is often planted in late summer or fall in warm-climate places to try to avoid the heat. Plant ½ inch deep and ½ inch apart if you're going to transplant. Thin or transplant to 8 inches apart. Romaine, like any other lettuce, shouldn't be crowded. Lettuce will stand up better under heat if it is well thinned and air can get in there and circulate. Where any kind of lettuce is crowded, the leaves may start to rot in heat, then bugs move in by the millions. Romaine varieties do best in the Pacific Coast climate.

4. *Loose-leaf lettuces*—These are the easiest to grow, the hardiest in hot weather, the most nourishing. Once you're used to leaf lettuce, iceberg lettuce is almost too bland to bear. Leaf lettuce has at first experience a stronger taste but you can soon get used to it and learn to love it. Leaf lettuce is ready way before the others, in 40 to 45 days, whereas head lettuce takes 80 to 95 days and needs all of it cool. There are many different varieties of loose-leaf lettuce: Simpson, Grand Rapids and Salad Bowl—Chicken lettuce is the all-time favorite of my chicken population. They take some of all my lettuces, but they really keep it trimmed down. Makes a good decoy.

Leaf lettuce or any of the other noncrisphead lettuces are very perishable once harvested from the garden and they don't last in the garden very long. The answer to that is succession planting about every two weeks. With some extra effort you can have lettuce every month of the year if you live in the South, and fresh lettuce for about eight months of the year if you live in a climate like the Midwest, by seeding early in cold frames (and in open ground, hoping for the best) and by moving the season's last lettuce, root and all, to a cold frame in the fall, close together, where they will last a good bit more. In real hot weather there are some loose-leaf lettuces that have been developed that are hardier than any of the other types and with extra protection can do well. (See the section on hot weather greens growing.)

If you don't overcrowd your lettuce you won't have trouble with diseases or bugs worse than some walking around on it that you can rinse off.

5. *Stem lettuce* is the most uncommon kind and I don't think really worth the bother unless you're making a lettuce collection. It comes under names like celtuce and asparagus lettuce, is mainly stem rather than leaf, and so you eat lettuce-type stems.

To grow lettuce—It likes deeply worked, crumbly soil that you have manured or composted the fall before. It needs water so if the rains don't rain you'll have to provide plenty another way. If watering isn't by natural rain, irrigation-type watering will be better for your lettuces than water sprinkled on. But sprinkling works if that's what you've got. You can plant lettuce in the garden or start it indoors and transplant. I'm just too lazy to start it indoors and transplant when with just a little more patience you can get it to grow outdoors.

To harvest lettuce—The nicest time to harvest in hot summer is early in the morning before either you or the plants get hot. Then you wash your lettuce and put it in the refrigerator until you use it. When you are thinning lettuces the thinnings are good to eat after you have cut off the root so it will help your salad supply to thin in stages, as the plants need more room, and as you need more lettuce! When thinning be sure and pull the plant up root and all because if you leave the root in there it will try to grow again and pull nourishment from the other plants. If you are cutting lettuce leaves away fairly early in the plants' life and they don't need thinning keep watering and you'll find they'll keep growing more leaves for a while. This is especially true of leaf lettuces. Some of the special hot-weather varieties will let you keep harvesting for a surprising length of time. To use your lettuce like that pick off outside leaves or cut the whole top of the plant off so you leave about the bottom third and it will take off and grow again, for a while anyway.

Salad making—In season we have salad every day. I send the children out to the garden to cut lettuce and pull a few green onions. My mother taught me to tear the lettuce with my fingers for the salad rather than cut it. So I tear it into pieces after washing and patting dry inside a fuzzy towel. (Not all the way dry, of course, but near enough.) Then I add the young green onions, chopped fine, and radishes, sliced thin, and dressing. Or grated peeled turnip. Some grated cabbage or carrot, too, or beets if I feel like it and have the vegetables. I use the part of the grater that makes long thin slivers.

The thing with lettuce is what you add to it. And you can add so many different things. Different kinds of lettuce make a great beginning. Then chunks of garden tomato or grated green peppers from the garden. For salad dressing I usually make a mixture of two-thirds salad oil, one-third vinegar, then add salt and garlic salt. For fancier dressings I add a little lemon juice, pepper or a pinch of dry mustard. If you add any kind of seafood, pour on some lemon juice and use a mayonnaise dressing.

When people come up to me and say "I hear you're writing a cookbook" I scarcely know what to answer because what I really am is a noncook. My own personal style of cooking is to cook foods as simply and quickly as possible. My great aim is just somehow to keep the six other mouths in this family so busy chewing that they can't complain. It's plain old fashioned cooking. Lots of everything but nothing fancy. I've never made a pie in my life. Someday I'm going to. I'd really like to if I could just get around to it. I have made maybe a thousand loaves of bread, I've no idea how many. That's the staff of life here, that and plain meat and gravy, potatoes, cooked vegetables and the salad in season.

HOMEMADE SALAD DRESSINGS

I make all my own salad dressings. The store ones really give me indigestion. Mine don't taste nearly as exotic to me but Mike claims they are much better. I am not too much on variety in the salad dressing department. It's usually a vinegar and oil dressing, or wilted lettuce dressing or homemade mayonnaise. Herbwise, though I'm liable to throw in anything and that really flavors them up. Herbs don't give me indigestion—it's the spices like pepper and red pepper and cinnamon and so on that do and I avoid them. But you don't have to. Mike just adds them at the table out of the shaker.

For dressings for potato salad see Potatoes in this chapter. For coleslaw dressing see Cabbage.

Two-Quarts Salad Dressing—One tablespoon salt, ½ teaspoon garlic powder, 1 tablespoon dry onion (or fresh), ½ teaspoon pepper, 1 tablespoon dried parsley, ½ tablespoon dry mustard, dash of red pepper, 1 tablespoon chopped capers and ½ teaspoon celery salt. Mix together 1 quart buttermilk and 1 quart mayonnaise, use wire whip or spoon, do not use a blender. Add the above seasonings. Stir to mix well. For a variation add 3 or 4 ounces blue cheese and 1 tablespoon lemon juice to 1 cup of dressing. Keep in refrigerator.

If you want to eat greens other than lettuce raw I'd recommend a wilted lettuce dressing because they are mostly on the strong side. I use lettuce for green salads and cook the greens.

Wilted Lettuce Dressing with raw greens—Use about a pound of greens. Wash and pat dry. Fry about 4 slices bacon. (You can use lard if you don't have bacon.) Take the bacon out and all the grease but about 2 tablespoons. Add 3 tablespoons vinegar and 2 tablespoons sour cream. Blend 1 teaspoon flour with an egg (not in a blender) and stir into pan mixture. Add ½ teaspoon salt and a tablespoon sugar or equivalent in honey. When the salad dressing is thickened and is boiling hot pour it over your greens. Add crumbled bacon, toss a moment to mix and serve immediately. This dressing has to be poured hot on the lettuce or it doesn't taste right. Serve immediately. You can enrich with mustard and onion salt. This is also good on leaf lettuce (as opposed to head).

French Dressing—This is our quick and easy favorite dressing on fresh garden lettuce. Wash about 1 quart of lettuce and pat dry inside a towel. Tear into pieces. Mix ¼ cup oil, 1 tablespoon vinegar, about 1 tablespoon lemon juice, ⅓ teaspoon salt and ½ teaspoon garlic salt. Toss with lettuce and serve.

Herb Dressing—If you are an herb gardener make some of this up in a jar and serve on green salads as you need it. Mix 1 teaspoon each chopped-up parsley, chives, tarragon and chervil and 2 cups sour cream. Add 2 tablespoons brown sugar, ¼ cup vinegar, ½ cup oil, a grind of pepper, dash of salt and 1 teaspoon dry mustard. Mix well.

Sour Cream Dressing—Without the above herbs you can still make a nice dressing by mixing 1 cup sour cream, 2 tablespoons lemon juice, 2 tablespoons vinegar, ½ teaspoon dry mustard, a grind of pepper and ½ teaspoon salt.

Homemade Mayonnaise—I've never really understood just what makes a person decide to send me a particular recipe but I can sure tell you for a fact they come in bunches. I've gotten more letters with ideas for preventing gas from dried beans, remedies for what to do when a wasp stings you, recipes for zucchini breads and zucchini pickles than anything else. But coming in a close second are the number of recipes I've been sent for how to make homemade mayonnaise! It proves for sure making homemade mayonnaise is no ways a lost art and not that hard. I've tried to choose the best of them to share with you here and to just use one of the ones that seemed basically the same recipe.

Mayonnaise is an "emulsion" and that means the protein of the egg is forming a thin stable film around tiny globules of the oil and keeping them suspended in the liquid. (And you can be sure I found that sentence in somebody else's book!) Homemade mayonnaise doesn't keep a long time like store mayonnaise because it doesn't have all the preservative glop in it and doesn't taste exactly like the store mayonnaise. Homegrown eggs tend to make better mayonnaise than store eggs. The big secret of mayonnaise making is to add the oil part very slowly, here's where a blender really helps. If you have to beat it by hand a two-person operation is best so that you can add the oil very slowly, like even a drop at a time, beating thoroughly after each addition. The more slowly you add the oil, the thicker and whiter your mayonnaise will be. You can make red mayonnaise by using vinegar that has stood on sliced boiled beets or you can make green mayonnaise by adding some mashed cooked spinach or boiled mashed green peas. If you let homemade mayonnaise wait too long before being used it may curdle. If this happens you can restore it by starting all over with an egg yolk. Add a little oil drop by drop again to the new egg yolk, then once started add your curdled dressing. P.S. Don't use a room temperature egg—it needs to be cold.

Mayonnaise at Half the Cost—Colleen Wilson wrote me from Lebanon, Oregon, with this recipe. "Combine 4 tablespoons cornstarch and 1 cup hot water. Cook until clear, stirring constantly. Combine 1 egg or 3 egg yolks, 1 teaspoon mustard, 1½ teaspoons salt, 2 tablespoons sugar, 3 tablespoons vinegar, 1 cup oil. Use a blender or beat by hand and combine ingredients with cooked cornstarch mixture until smooth. Cover and refrigerate. The first time I made it, it was OK. But the second time and so on, it's turned out great. I use 1 egg. (I would hate to waste three egg whites.) I also use mustard from a jar. I've kept it refrigerated for two months and it was still good!"

No-Sugar Mayonnaise—This one is from Nancy Haskell of Carlisle, Pennsylvania. She first saw a copy of this book in her library. I get lots of letters from people who started out with a library copy (generally to tell me they want a copy of their own) and with her letter she told me how she makes mayonnaise. "My family has given up sugar completely, so now many of the things which we used to buy in stores we must make ourselves. One of those is mayonnaise. This comes out white and thick just like commercial mayonnaise. The only difference is that it is slightly more tart, but that tartness is not discernible in most of the ways I use mayonnaise. A blender is a necessity, however, to get the good results. The ingredients you'll need are: 1 egg, ¾ teaspoon salt, ¼ teaspoon paprika, ¼ teaspoon dry mustard, 1 cup vegetable oil, 1 tablespoon vinegar, 1 tablespoon lemon juice. Combine egg, spices, vinegar, lemon juice and a start of the oil in the blender. Remove the small part of your blender lid and slowly pour in the rest of the oil while the blender is going continuously as you pour. This makes only slightly more than a cup so I find that I have to make mayonnaise frequently. But with this recipe it is so easy that I don't mind at all."

Herb-Flavored Mayonnaise—Mrs. Paul Kraft sent me this one from West Plains, Missouri. It's amazing how many places this book has traveled and made me friends! Even to countries overseas in Africa, Asia, South America and Europe. And *lots* of them to Canada. Every place that people are trying to figure out how to do things for themselves. "I realize not everyone has a blender but for those who do here is a fantastic blender mayonnaise recipe—Put in blender 1 egg, 4 tablespoons sugar, 4 tablespoons vinegar, 1 teaspoon dry mustard. Optional 1 teaspoon onion salt or 1 teaspoon garlic salt or 1 teaspoon garlic powder.

Blend until well mixed. Then slowly and in a steady stream add (while blender is still blending) ¾ cup oil. Blend until thick. Takes about 3 or 4 minutes. It will thicken more after standing. We love the garlic."

SALAD DRESSINGS MADE FROM MAYONNAISE— Making your own mayonnaise is just the beginning of good things. Then comes homemade Tartar Sauce for your fishwiches and Thousand Island Dressing for salads.

You know, back when I was reading books instead of writing books I used to wonder so much about the people that wrote them—what they were like, what things were like when they were writing. I'm sitting here in a not-very-clean orange bathrobe. It's one of three things left in the house that I can still get into because I'm nine plus months pregnant, running overdue as usual. I'm sitting on the side of my bed in moccasins typing at a little desk my mother bought me to study at when I was in high school and wow does that ever seem a long time ago. The big front drawer of it is missing, probably some kid or other dragged it away to play with and lost it years ago but the top still works fine to hold the typewriter. Dolly, Danny and Becca are all in school now (February 7, 1977). Luke and Sara are tumbling all around me playing their games now on top of the bed, now under the covers, now under the bed! Their noises are happy noises and that's what matters. Mike is out working. This is the year of our tenth anniversary and it's the best yet. That sounds like a glib phrase. It's more than that. The fact is our first years together were awful, just awful in any category you want to name. It took us years to learn how to live the love that got us married in the first place and then seemed to simply get buried forever under the debris of everyday living and its problems. We toughed out all those years mainly because both of us really wanted to stay married on the principle of it if nothing else and because children have a right to both their parents and because we never gave up at the same time and because deep down inside we loved each other even when all we could find or feel was hate. Over years and years there were so many times I stood in the door and pleaded, "Please don't go." And there were times when I broke windows and cried and stormed and said I couldn't take it anymore and he could just go (but never, never at the same moment he was saying he wanted to). That's in case you think I'm a saint and never did anything wrong, or crazy, or never had a problem that lasted more than five minutes. But aging has its blessings and so does every crisis and every suffering. And slowly we learned about each other and learned to accept each other for what we were and not to keep a head full of bad stuff about what he or she wasn't and what happened last week, last month or last year. Forgiveness is one of the basics that love is nourished by. If one of you has to forgive the other for the more spectacular sins, the other may have to forgive you for being dull and self-righteous. Life is a long time to try to live together and if you think your boat is never going to rock that's unreal. You're going to go through all kinds of horrible real-life nightmares and you're going to survive them and come out better for them and look back and see how in a way they were blessings.

Thousand Island Dressing—Combine 1 cup mayonnaise, ¼ cup catsup or chili sauce or some tomato stuff, 2 teaspoons parsley, 1 tablespoon finely chopped onion, a cut-up hard-boiled egg, 2 tablespoons cut-up fine green pepper (if you have it), ½ teaspoon sweet basil or dill. If you don't have all that don't worry, make it with what you have. Taste to see if it needs more salt or pepper, or anything.

Tartar Sauce is a variation of mayonnaise. The simplest way is to add ¼ cup chopped pickles and 1 tablespoon capers to 1 cup of mayonnaise. Or use only 1 tablespoon chopped pickle and add, in addition, 1 teaspoon onion juice and a dash of dry mustard. Or to your cup of homemade mayonnaise add 1 teaspoon *each* chopped green onion, green olives, parsley and pickles, and 1 tablespoon tarragon vinegar.

GREENS THAT GROW IN HOT WEATHER AND THE SOUTH—Most of the greens, either the lettuces or the ones we generally eat cooked, don't like hot weather so if you have hot summers or a southerly climate in general you have a special problem. Not an insurmountable one though. It's just a case of knowing which ones to grow.

Hot-weather lettuce—The advantage of being very far south is that you can grow lettuce in the winter months. You can plant in late summer so that the days and nights will be cool by the time it gets big enough to be serious and that gives you a good chance with even a heading kind of lettuce. Or you can grow in very early spring. For hot-weather growing the strongest are the loose-leaf varieties and special varieties of them have been developed that are better yet. Slobolt is a famous hot-weather variety; Oak Leaf and Salad Bowl are two others. Any lettuce seed is harder to sprout in hot weather. You can help by covering the newly planted seed with burlap or with wet sawdust and keep it wet until the seed has sprouted. Later you can give the lettuce a sun shelter by stretching burlap on upright sticks over the row like a light roof. A way to get ahead of hot weather in the spring is to plant your lettuce row the fall before after frost. It will lie dormant all winter and then come up first thing in the spring.

New Zealand spinach—Regular spinach is famous for not tolerating hot weather. New Zealand spinach is not really related to spinach at all but when cooked tastes similar enough and feeds you similar enough so it's a fine substitute. Real spinach, since it prefers cool weather, is grown in southern states, if at all, in the winter or late spring or fall depending on just what the climate is like. New Zealand spinach actually loves hot weather so that's one for your summer season. It originally came from New Zealand and Australia and is a lot easier to grow than the familiar spinach. It also produces way better. Spinach is a one-harvest plant. Then it goes to seed, but you can cut leaves off your New Zealand spinach for weeks, same as with chard or kale. No bug or disease bothers it. The only thing New Zealand spinach can't take is frost and it is slow germinating but you can speed that up by soaking the seeds for two or three days before you plant them. The New Zealand spinach plants grow much larger than regular spinach. Plant in rows maybe 3 feet apart, with the plants a foot or more apart. New Zealand spinach requires 40 to 55 days to maturity. I got a real fan letter on New Zealand spinach from Jeannie Williams of Yoncalla, Oregon. She gets her seed from Burpee and says it "can be picked over and over all summer, right up to a really hard freeze. The leaves slightly resemble ivy. My sister just whacks off the new growth, stems and all but my sister-in-law picks each leaf separately." I'll add that you can eat it stems and all just like the other greens.

Collards are a traditional southern food and the reason why is because they do well there. They take 75-85 days to reach maturity but once there, and even before you can be whittling leaves off them to eat. Collards need longer cooking that most of the other greens and you'll do better starting with young and tender leaves anyway. They are generally cooked by boiling with some good hickory smoked bacon or salt pork. The juices left in the saucepan are called "pot likker" and should be sopped up with hot corn bread. I've got at least a partial credential for talking about them because my mother was born and raised in Alabama. She left when about 20, first for a job in a bank in New York City, and then to take a teaching job at a practically brand-new whistle-stop-type town in Montana. That's where she met my father who had migrated that way from his birthplace in Xenia, Ohio. So I know about okra and collards and corn breads!

Collards are a member of that cabbage-Brussels sprouts-broccoli-kale family, the only one that really gets along in the South. They are like a tall growing kale, about 1 to 4 feet high depending on how they like your growing conditions, with smooth leaves. Sort of a cabbage that never forms a head. They are generally easier to grow and freer of disease problems than any other member of that cabbage family. You can grow them someplace besides the South and actually they get better flavored after a frost. In the South they plant collards in late summer for eating during the fall and winter, or start them indoors early to be set out as soon as the ground can be worked in spring. You plant the seed ½ inch deep and an inch apart if starting indoors, then set out to 18 to 24 inches apart. If you live in the North and want to try collards plant them early in the spring.

GREENS THAT GROW IN WINTER—Harold Okubo wrote me from West Jordan, Utah, about his experience with winter greens: "We have always tried to produce most of our food at home. I have an advantage over most people as I'm a commercial truck farmer (Japanese origin). There are ways to have some green leaf crops most of the winter. Like spinach—if you drill a patch about August 15 in this area by September 30 it will be large enough and it will be good all winter. We even dig it up from under the snow all winter. You can plant leaf and head lettuce in the fall of the year and let the young seedlings winter over. The lettuce will be ready to eat by April or May. If you put a plastic tent over some it will be earlier yet." I really appreciate a letter like that from somebody who obviously knows so much.

Kale is similar to collards in that it is another member of the cabbage family that you harvest leaf by leaf. I put it in this section because it handles cold so well that in a climate like our Midwest you can leave it out in the garden all winter and depend on it for greens. Kale is 60 to 70 days to maturity and can live through frosts. You can plant it indoors ½ inch deep and an inch apart and transplant to the garden 6 to 12 inches apart or start it in the garden and thin there. When cold weather comes along you'll find kale, the frilly, headless cabbage, the hardiest vegetable you've ever raised. It will grow right through winter unless your winters are very fierce. If frost does succeed in cutting it back, as soon as things warm up a little it will sprout new leaves. A good thick mulch will protect it from freezing to death in the worst weather. But it is as uncomfortable in summer as it is comfortable in cold weather. It has more vitamins than any of the other garden greens. You can harvest leaves as you need them—more will keep growing. When you thin you can eat your thinnings.

To cook kale, pick the large outside leaves and let the little center ones grow. That will give you the most use out of your plant. Kale leaves are too coarse for salad greens unless you use just the small young tender ones. Wash carefully and discard the hard pieces of stalk. Kale is good cooked like cabbage with pork. Or cook in salted water until tender. Then drain and chop fine. Then return to the pan with butter, salt and pepper to taste. Mix and melt the butter. Serve hot on buttered toast pieces. You can figure that 3 cups of raw kale from the garden will cook down to a cup of kale for the table. If you are using kale leaves in other recipes you may need to give them a special parboiling beforehand. They are not only the most vitaminaceous and hardy green—they are the hardest to soften up and make edible, too! On the other hand, try not to overcook it because that is a bad thing also. Got to catch that moment of perfection.

Chicory-endive—Chicory and endive are interchangeable in recipes. Chicory is "French endive" and endive is "Belgian endive" and then there's more than one kind of the chicory-French endive like witloof chicory which is the classic kind of Magdeburg chicory which is famous for the coffee making from the roots because it grows bigger roots. (For making coffee from chicory roots look in the Herbs and Flavorings chapter.) Chicory-endive can also be a hotweather substitute for head lettuce which gets buggy, rotten and stops growing when the real hot weather comes. You can eat chicory-endive raw in a salad or cook the tops like spinach. But one of its most famous uses is for winter salad that you get by digging the roots in the fall and setting them back in moist soil in warm cellar or in the southern United States they just bank the chicory row with soil for the winter right in the garden and harvest it right from there.

Chicory-endive will last easily in a root cellar for a couple of months if you take it up just before freezing with considerable soil still on the roots. Set the plants on the floor (a dirt floor of course) with the roots down and packed together as closely as possible. If your cellar is moderately moist the endive will do fine there. The leaves that grow in the cellar from these roots are your winter salad greens. Make sure if you're planning to do this that you don't start your chicory plants too early in the spring because if the plants have gone to seed before you move them to the cellar they can't be used for "forcing"— it doesn't work.

The way to keep chicory for winter right in the garden in a mild winter climate is when the first frost comes, first cut off the chicory tops without injuring the crowns. Now cover with dirt so that you end up scraping a ridge about 18 inches high. Leave it like that until around late December. Then take the dirt off one end of the row and cut off the white shoots. You cover the plants back up with dirt after this harvesting and mark with a stick to show how far down the row you harvested. You can keep coming back and working your way farther down the row. Be sure and harvest fairly often because if the chicory gets ahead of you and makes it through the ground it will get bitter. And be sure and cover it back up after your harvest because that way when you've come to the end of the row you can just go back and start harvesting at the first end again all winter long.

To braise chicory, remove any discolored outside leaves. Cover the remaining heads with boiling water and let stand for 5 minutes, then drain. Lay the head in a greased, shallow ovenproof dish. Sprinkle with salt and pepper and squeeze a little lemon juice in each one. Add ¾ cup stock and dot each head with butter. Cover and cook with moderate heat. The last 20 minutes remove the cover, turn the chicory over and let it brown.

For *endive salad* you can slice lengthwise or crosswise into a salad. Some people pick off the green outer leaves and use only the light-colored feathery leaves. I think they're all fine. Wash thoroughly and cut off discolored parts. Chill until crisp before making your salad. For a plain endive salad serve with a French dressing, garnish with paprika, parsley (and rings of green pepper if you have it).

Endive Potato Salad—Cut 2 cups boiled potatoes into slices and marinate 1 hour with salt and pepper, oil and vinegar (a vinegar and oil "dressing"). Get ready 4 hard-boiled eggs. Prepare the endive. Mix sliced marinated potatoes and endive. Arrange the boiled eggs in quarters over the top and pour French dressing over all.

To cook leave stalks whole unless very large, in which case split them. Place in a frying pan, add beef or chicken stock until ½ inch deep. Salt to taste, cover and cook gently until done. For variety you could serve butter or covered with white sauce.

Now here are some GREENS TO EAT COOKED.

Beet greens—I've found a green that I like tastewise even better than chard. I am putting about two-thirds chard and one-third beet greens into my freezer. I like the beety taste and the pretty red stems of the beet greens. So does Mike (whose idea this originally was). When harvested early and given plenty of water the beets recover and grow more tops or we can get greens from them when the big beets are harvested.

Turnip greens—In my garden anyway they are prickly, the bugs riddle the leaves, and the turnips can't recover if they lose their tops. I've seen baby turnips bundled and sold tops and all as "turnip greens." They'd be good that way, too.

Mustard greens are stronger in taste and tougher compared to spinach and chard. And they are worse than dill for turning into a weed. But I like the strong taste. They do grow rapidly and they make edible greens if you cut them before they get too big and tough. But they also rapidly go to seed, The seeds they shed take off immediately upon the next watering so I have had several generations of mustard greens growing by the end of the year.

Swiss chard doesn't "bolt." It grows and grows and grows if you let it into very large leaves with fleshy stalks. I like it stalk and all. When it is up 6 inches or more I go out with a bucket and knife and whack off everything about 1 inch above the root level. That's quick and easy and it doesn't harm the plant at all. (Spinach has to be cut one leaf at a time because the stalk is so tough.) The chard will grow again and depending on your soil and watering, in a few weeks or less you will have another crop, and another if you want after that, and so on. When I get all the chard I want in the freezer we till up the ground and plant in potatoes or some other late crop.

There are two distinct stages at which you could harvest your chard that gives you a different sort of green to cook. If you harvest while young and small, like 6 inches tall you get a tender, spinachy green with very little "rib." That's my favorite way to eat it. But if you keep watering and don't cut it will grow and grow into a tall, big leaf with a long, thick stem and that's the way some good friends of mine like to harvest it. If you harvest it like that you sort of get two vegetables for one. One is the spinach-type leaf and another dish can be made with the stem. Or you can use chard stems for a celery substitute. Chard is so much easier to grow than celery and the texture and crunchiness, when raw, are similar, although the chard stems are a bit milder in flavor. A reader, Celia Sorenson from Spokane, Washington, first gave me this idea and it works. You can chop them up in a lettuce salad or use in egg salad sandwiches, in cooking

too, especially soup. Anyplace it says "celery." But they cook more quickly than celery.

Spinach—I used to plant spinach, but I don't bother anymore. Spinach is a one-crop green. It is the earliest next to dandelion greens. I used to plant one row of spinach for our first spring garden greens, then Swiss chard for the major crop. Chard is preferable to spinach because it grows again after cutting. Spinach grows only once and you have to rush out there and harvest it before it starts to "bolt"—that means grow flower stalks.

Spinach gets bitter and tough when it bolts and stops making new leaves. All the plants' energy goes into stalk and flower. Spinach leaves never get near as big as chard leaves anyway. So the only good reason I can see for planting spinach is for an *early* greens crop because it does come on a couple of weeks before chard.

Spinach has its admirers though and Karin Webber wrote me from Reseda, California, to send this recipe for it.

Spinach Provençale—You'll need 2 pounds of fresh spinach, 1 large onion, 1 clove garlic, olive oil, butter, 2 beaten eggs, 1 cup freshly grated Parmesan cheese, salt and freshly ground black pepper. Wash the leaves carefully and the rest is easy as pie. Chop the onion and mince the garlic. Heat the olive oil in a very large kettle and sauté the onion and garlic in it for a few minutes. When the onion is transparent, add spinach and cover tightly. In about 3 minutes the spinach will be reduced to a fraction of its former bulk. Remove the lid and cook a few minutes longer. Remove from heat. Butter a medium-size baking dish. When spinach is somewhat cooled, stir in the 2 beaten eggs and ½ cup of the Parmesan cheese. Season with salt and pepper and pour mixture into the baking dish. Sprinkle the remaining Parmesan over the top and dot with butter. Bake the spinach in a 275° oven for about 10 to 15 minutes and serve steaming hot. It's delicious and it doubles easily.

To cook greens—For all these you wash your leaves before cooking. Boil with or without salt (I don't use it). To add flavor use water in which corned beef, salt pork or bacon has been cooked or use stock. Or serve buttered and peppered. Or with vinegar. Mustard, kale and turnip greens are specially good cooked in the water in which the meat has cooked and then serve with the meat.

SAVING YOUR OWN GREENS SEED—Spinach and lettuce are annuals. That means they make seed the first year they grow. In the case of spinach the plant stops putting energy into making leaves and instead puts up a long stalk. We say it is "bolting." It will flower on top of the stalk and where each flower was, seed will come. Maybe they call it "bolting" because with spinach and lettuce it seems to happen fast. It isn't any use trying to harvest greens if they have started to bolt. But when saving seed from spinach and lettuce plants, be choosy about which of the plants you save it from. You want one of the last to go to seed rather than one of the first, which is difficult to manage if you are basically raising it for a food crop rather than a seed crop. Spinach will not cross with New Zealand spinach but other spinach varieties will cross because spinach pollen is very fine and the wind carries it all over the place. Plant only one variety. Lettuce, on the other hand, has a self-fertilizing blossom, so even if you are growing several varieties in your own garden they generally don't cross-pollinate. You may need to stake the tall lettuce seed stalks so they don't fall over and let your seed get lost. When the seeds are fully developed cut the seed stalks and separate out the seeds from the stalk.

Lettuce is one of the seed makers that is triggered by the long daylight periods of early summer. That means if you live in a warm part of the country where they grow lettuce all winter and plant your seed in October you won't find your lettuce plant making seed until the following summer. On the other hand if you plant it in late spring in the North you'll find it soon making seed. For a longer harvest season and a delay of the seed making, therefore, plant as early in spring as you can, indoors or out.

On saving seeds in general remember no seed, wherever it's from, your garden or the professional seedsman, is going to germinate 100 percent. Fifty percent is more realistic so save more than just the bare minimum. Seeds are living things and can have all kinds of troubles of their own. Seeds get old and die and that affects germination rates too. All your greens seeds, however, have real good longevity. Lettuce, endive, kale, collard, Chinese cabbage seeds keep well for five years and chard and mustard green seeds keep well for four.

Collards, kale and Chinese cabbage are all of the cabbage family, biennial; and you follow the same procedure for saving seeds from them as for broccoli so look back there for your answers.

To freeze greens for winter, I bring them into the house by the 5-gallon bucket. Then wash in a sinkful of water. I then fish them out again leaf by leaf, having sloshed away the dirt. I pick out the weeds that accidentally came along and the bugs are generally left in the water. I have a large pan of water boiling on the stove. When the water boils up and the leaves wilt down they are ready to go into the baggies. I fish the greens out of the water using two potato mashers, the same way I do corn on the cob, one masher on each side. The experts say to blanch "2" minutes, cool immediately in ice water and drain as well as you can on towels. That's a waste of good dry towel and of ice. Greens keep better in the freezer than any other vegetable, whether they are cooled beforehand or not.

Here's a step-by-step version of how to freeze greens.

1. Wash off bugs and dust from leaves. Put a big pan of water on to boil.
2. Cut in 2½-inch lengths (about).
3. Drop a load of chard into the boiling water. Let boil 3 minutes.
4. Scoop it out into a colander to drain.
5. Hold under running cold water just long enough so you can handle it.

6. Pack in baggies, squeeze out most of the air and fasten the neck with one of those little wires or tie it in a knot. Pack enough chard in the baggie for one meal for your family.
7. Put immediately into the freezer.

To eat greens I just turn out the frozen lump into a little water. Thaw out and heat up. Then I either butter or serve with vinegar.

To dry greens—Freezing is the best way to keep them if you have a choice, I think, but more can be done with a dried green than you might think. Instead of trying to somehow make dried greens into wet ones again you're better off grinding your dried greens finely in a seed mill kind of thing, then add the powder to anything from soup to salad or use it mixed with other dried vegetable powders to make instant vegetable soup. You can use the powder like a seasoning powder too. To dry spinach, or beet tops, Swiss chard or any other greens, start by making sure they are well washed and the roots are cut away and discarded. You'll have better results with young leaves than with old ones. Slice both the leaf stalks and blades into sections about ¼ inch long, spread out on your drying screens or trays and dry.

To can greens, wash, sort out weeds and then wilt down in boiling water as described for freezing procedure. Then pack your hot wilted greens in your jar, cover with boiling water, leaving ½ inch head space. Add salt if you like. Put on your jar lids and process pints at 10 pounds pressure for 45 minutes, quarts for 70 minutes.

JERUSALEM ARTICHOKES are perennial tubers that grow wild in the eastern part of the United States and Canada or can be cultivated. The Indians used them for food. Being free from starch they can be eaten uncooked. Dig them anytime from after the first frost until spring, about October 1 to March 10, when the new growth starts. But don't dig up too many at one time because they don't keep well. The part you eat looks like small light brown little potatoes. You can substitute them for water chestnuts in any recipe.

Using a heavy mulch on them in the winter season will help prevent the ground freezing and make it easier for you when you want to dig some up. Freezing underground doesn't hurt the artichokes but it makes it kind of hard to dig them up. They are really prolific growers. Some people complain that they tend to take over in the garden like a weed. But you can make use of that abundance. Dig your extras and feed them to the chickens, or goats or pigs. They are so easy to grow that you might want to plant extras on purpose to serve as part of your animal feed. To store fresh artichokes wash but don't peel and keep in an airtight refrigerator-type container.

When spring comes your artichokes start multiplying. You either let them spread where they are or, if you like a neater garden, dig them and replant in rows. If you want to increase your artichoke crop fast you can cut them before planting like you do potatoes to increase your "seed" amount. Just lay them one by one on a cutting board and cut an X on each one which gives you four seeds. You can either plant them in rows in which case you plant one seed every foot with 2 or 3 feet between your rows or you can plant in "beds" like some flowers grow. Make your beds about 4 feet by 4 feet. Once the artichokes get going they'll pretty much choke out the weeds and you can just let them grow as much as they want to in there.

To bake before roasting, boil about 10 minutes, then peel and arrange around the meat the same as for potatoes, or put into a baking dish with dots of butter and salt and pepper.

To puree, cook until tender (in stock if you have it), peel and put through a sieve or mash with a little butter and seasoning.

To sauté, boil 15 minutes, cut into thick slices and fry in shallow oil until golden brown or slice thin as a penny and fry like potato chips in deep fat.

For **Artichoke Fritters** dip into a batter (egg, flour, milk, salt) and fry in deep fat until golden brown.

To peel or not to peel, that is the question— People can really get worked up over peelings. And so it is with Jerusalem artichokes, there are the pro-peelers and the anti-peelers. I don't think it makes a whole lot of difference since if you have 'em you have lots of 'em. But if you are an anti-peeler just scrub well and remove any dark blemish and slice off lumps.

Or, wash them thoroughly and peel thinly with a vegetable peeler. Have ready a bowl of cold water with some lemon juice or vinegar in it to drop them into if you're going to use them raw in salads. Otherwise they quickly turn black if exposed to the air. They can also be cooked in their skins and the skin removed after cooking. But if you boil them in the skins you should get those off while they are quite hot or you'll lose a lot of artichoke with them.

If you are going to boil them, cook them quickly since overcooking toughens them. Serve boiled artichokes with a white sauce or a butter-lemon juice-parsley sauce. Chives and parsley really get along with artichokes.

Raw Jerusalem artichokes are good grated or ground on a bed of lettuce with salad dressing and a bit of grated onion. Or served sliced and mixed in salads where they taste like water chestnuts. Use the leftover lemon juice that you marinated them in with your salad dressing.

KALE—Look under Greens, the part about "Greens That Grow in Winter."

KOHLRABI is the enlarged stem (with leaves growing out of it) of the kohlrabi plant. Don't use it larger than 2½ inches across or it will be woody textured and too strong in taste. If cooked when very young and tender, however, it is fine flavored and delicate.

Raw kohlrabi—You can wash, trim and eat like an apple. Or use like cabbage to make slaw salad.

Baked kohlrabi—Bake unpeeled kohlrabis until done. Peel. Slash in a few places and season with salt, paprika and butter.

Buttered and Sautéed Kohlrabi—Use only the bulb and remove the green skin. Slice or cut into fourths. Boil until tender. Then either serve with butter, salt and pepper to taste or brown the cooked kohlrabi in melted butter which has been seasoned with onion and curry powder.

Creamed Kohlrabi—Cut off the tops and roots of about 6 kohlrabis. Wash, peel and leave whole or dice. Cook in boiling water until tender. Make a white sauce of 2 tablespoons butter, 2 tablespoons flour, 2 cups milk, salt and paprika to taste and an egg yolk, and pour over the drained kohlrabi before serving. Kohlrabi can be served with a cheese or tomato sauce, too.

Bulb and Greens—Wash, peel and dice the bulb and cook in salted water until tender. Cook the greens in another pan of boiling water until tender. Drain the greens and chop fine. Make a paste of butter and flour, add soup stock to make a sauce and then the chopped greens, and finally the cooked kohlrabi. Another way to do it is to use the water in which the vegetable was cooked instead of stock and keep the chopped greens out of the sauce. In this case serve the kohlrabi with a border of the greens. Kohlrabi is good cooked with boiled beef.

To freeze, scald 1 minute, cool and package.

To can, cut off tops and roots. Wash, peel and leave whole or dice, as you prefer. Pack hot and cover with boiling water. Process pints 30 minutes and quarts 35 minutes at 10 pounds pressure.

To store in a root cellar, leave in the ground until late fall. The early frosts will do no harm and they keep better in the ground. At a time when the soil is relatively dry, dig your kohlrabis and cut off the tops about ½ inch above the crown. They keep best in layers between moist sand, peat or sphagnum moss. Keep as cool as possible, short of freezing. If they get too warm the roots will sprout new tops and become woody as all the strength goes into making leaves. If you don't bed them as described they will wither.

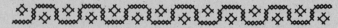

LEEKS are an onion variety. For me they take too long to grow and what they have to offer onionwise isn't worth the wait. I get our onions quicker and easier using multipliers and sets (see Onion). But here's the information, anyway, in case they do wonderfully well in your garden. The part used is the thick stem which corresponds to the familiar onion bulb. To prepare cut off the roots and remove the outer skin.

Boiled Leeks—Wash and trim, leaving about 1½ inches of the green top. You can use the green part that you trim off in your stock pot. Boil until tender. Drain. Serve with melted butter. Or cover the cooked stalks with salt, pepper and grated cheese and set under the broiler until the cheese is melted. Or serve on toast covered with a white sauce. Or drain, chill and serve as a salad covered with French dressing.

Baked Leeks—Parboil 5 minutes in boiling water. Drain. Cut into 2-inch pieces and put into an ovenproof dish with salt, pepper and enough meat stock or consommé to cover. Bake in a moderate oven, 325° for 30 minutes.

Leek Soup can be made in as many ways as onion soup. You can boil leeks with pork and potatoes or with beef and potatoes. You can also cut the white part of the leek into thin slices and precook by frying before adding to the soup or else make a cream soup and grate the leek before adding. Serve with crackers or croutons.

To store, you can leave the leeks in the ground and pull as needed if your climate is very mild. Otherwise store in your root cellar. But onions keep so well by comparison that I can't see bothering with leeks if your climate is such that you can't leave them in the garden.

LETTUCE—Look in this chapter under Greens, "The Five Lettuces."

LIMA BEANS—Look under "Beans" and inside there under L for Limas. I once saw directions in a book for how to freeze lima beans. It said they should be sorted for size and the large ones blanched for 4 minutes, the medium-sized ones 3, and the small ones 2 minutes. Those directions must have been written in a public library. Or else by a machine.

MUSHROOMS—Can be grown under your kitchen sink, or in a basement or cellar, in the dark, damp space between the floor of any building you have and the ground or in a building like a garage or barn. It's easier than most people think if you do the basics right. The easy-goingest mushroom grower I know is a remarkable Florida lady named Rachel Jackson. She lives on the Linger Longer Ranch at Barberville, Florida, and is always looking for sharecroppers who will come trailer and all and help garden her land in return for three-quarters of the produce. She throws old mushrooms on the compost pile and around the barn, often blending them first and sprinkling the water mixture to work like seed. One of the problems with that approach is you must be very careful what you plant and what you harvest. Edible mushrooms so much resemble deadly poisonous varieties and an unexpected variety could easily turn up in the middle of your outdoor crop. For example the jack-o'-lantern

mushroom much resembles the chanterelle, the only real difference being that the jack-o'-lantern has a near-golden-yellow flesh and is poisonous, and the chanterelle has almost whitish flesh and is good to eat. So one of the nice things about growing mushrooms under controlled conditions is that you know what you've got.

To plant, start out by buying spawn, which is the word for mushroom seed, from a seedsman like Gurney (Yankton, South Dakota) or Henry Field (Shenandoah, Iowa). If you really want to make it simple for yourself the next time around some seedsmen including Gurney sell preplanted mushroom kits. But all the kit really is, is your growing mixture already put together for you and sterilized. And if you are half the gardener I believe you are, you can do this for yourself. Once you have your own mushrooms growing you can even save your own spawn. Here's a step by step procedure to get your mushroom crop.

1. *Where and in what*—Decide where you're going to grow mushrooms—in cave, fallout shelter, under the kitchen sink or whatever. Your place will work best if it hovers around 45° to 60° but the mushrooms won't die unless they either freeze or get way too hot. You want a high humidity but you can create that artifically by regular watering, atomizer style, and using polyethylene or some such tents to cover the growing boxes if you don't have natural humidity. The growing boxes can be heavy, waxed cardboard but wooden boxes would hold up better in the long run. Make your boxes 5-11 inches deep at least. You can just spread them out or if short of space you can build a shelf arrangement for them. Remember this is the only crop in the Vegetables chapter that doesn't need light to grow. Mushrooms make food out of manure rather than from sunshine. But the humble origins don't matter much because mushrooms are a delicious and very nourishing food to say nothing of being an adventure to grow!

2. *The soil for them*—For sure you have to have manure, at least 20 percent. Horse manure is considered best. Horse manure with some chicken manure added is better yet. But you can make do with what you have as long as it is manure and as long as you have let the manure age enough so that it won't heat up to more than 85° or so which would harm your mushrooms. Now stretch your manure by

mixing it with composted (means old and partially rotted) hay or straw. Some old sawdust stirred in works fine too. Mix together the manure-hay-straw mixture and load the boxes 6 to 10 inches deep. Be a little choosy what you stir in—growing mushrooms pick up some flavors easily, like rancid olive oil flavor from olive oil accidentally in the soil.

3. *Baking the dirt*—This step is really important and please don't skip it. Mushrooms have quite a few natural enemies, bug things, worm things, mold things, and doing this step protects the mushrooms. This step also makes sure that you won't grow any kind of mushroom-toadstool-looking thing except exactly what you intend to. Box by box, bake box, dirt and all in your oven at 200° for at least 1 hour. Give it some time to get hot before you start timing the hour. Other ways to accomplish this are to compost the manure mixture beforehand and make sure it gets up to at least 170° or do like the professionals do and run hot steam through the mixture to pasteurize it.

4. *Planting the spawn*—After your soil has cooled down to normal make sure it is loose and not hard-packed. Now sprinkle spawn over the surface and either sprinkle more pasteurized manure-compost mixture over that thinly or else work the spawn flakes with your hands gently into the soil mixture no more than about 1 inch. Now sprinkle with lukewarm water and plan on keeping the mixture wet. It works best if you water with as fine a spray as you can manage and check often enough to make sure the mushroom bed doesn't dry out. If you let it dry clear out that could be the end of your hoped-for mushroom crop. It would help at first to put a damp cloth over the tray or rig up some constantly dripping water to keep humidity high in your mushroom-growing area. On the other hand you can drown out your mushrooms with too much water. If you can squeeze some of the growing mixture in your hand and no water comes out it's still on the OK side. The polyethylene tent over your growing boxes helps hold in humidity without having to keep the dirt itself oversoaked.

5. *Casing*—Three weeks after you planted your spawn in the boxes your mushroom crop is ready to flower. Believe it or not, the mushroom itself is a flower thing. The "casing" encourages it to do this. By now you've probably got the first sign of life from your mushrooms above ground (they do most of their early growing below ground where the food is). In fact, you shouldn't do this casing step until you see a sign of life above the ground. Now sprinkle on anywhere from ½ to 1 inch of compost or nice humusy soil (but *not* sand or clay soil). About a week or ten days after this casing you'll see mushrooms starting to form and ten days after that you'll be able to start picking. After finishing the harvest you can sprinkle on another inch of fresh growing mixture and start again with planting the spawn. This will work for a total of three crops or so before you have to start fresh with a whole new box of soil mixture for them. The old box of soil will be a good addition to your garden or to use for potted plants.

6. *To harvest*—Mushrooms don't all grow at the same speed and ones the same age aren't necessarily the same size. You may be harvesting as long as two to four months. Twist them out of the soil carefully and don't leave any little broken pieces behind if you can help it because those little pieces can rot and cause trouble for the rest of the crop. Pick them when closed and still white. Otherwise you have an overgrown mushroom. For fresh mushrooms don't wash and try not to bruise them and they'll keep fairly well about a week in an uncovered dish in the refrigerator.

7. *To raise your own spawn*—A box where mushrooms have been grown for several months has what is called "running spawn" all through at the level where you first planted spawn. You can use that dirt (unpasteurized, of course) to plant other boxes. If you dry that dirt in an airy, but shaded place, you can store it under dry, dark, cool but above freezing conditions for maybe up to ten years.

To cook, clean the mushrooms up. You'll find that homegrown mushrooms are better tasting and tenderer than store ones and can be eaten raw cut in slices and mixed in salads. To cook add only a little water, cook at a simmering temperature, and don't cook any longer than necessary or they will get tough. Add seasonings after cooking rather than before and that helps keep them tender. Ten or 15 minutes of cooking with a tight cover should do it. You can store cooked mushrooms in the refrigerator and use in other recipes for the next few days.

You can fry mushrooms in a little butter 3 to 8 minutes, add salt and pepper and then serve on toast or mix with other foods. Or you can broil them by brushing with melted butter, broiling, seasoning with salt, pepper and nutmeg and serving. If you add a cup of cooked mushrooms to any white sauce you can serve them that way alone as creamed mushrooms or as a sauce on cauliflower, or peas, or fish, ham, tongue or toast.

Homemade Mushroom Soup—Clean ½ pound of fresh mushrooms, and chop them up. Pour boiling water over them and then pour it off. Melt 4 tablespoons lard or drippings, add 4 tablespoons flour, mix together and brown the flour lightly. Add 1 minced clove garlic, 1 tablespoon chopped onion and 1 tablespoon chopped parsley and continue browning. Add mushrooms, cover and let simmer for 10 minutes. Add 2 medium-sized potatoes that have been cubed and cooked in 1½ quarts of water, a very small bay leaf, 1 tablespoon vinegar, dash of marjoram, salt and pepper to taste. Cook 10 minutes more. If you have sour cream around add a couple tablespoons of sour cream before serving to make it extra good. Or serve with Cheddar cheese grated on top. If all that sounds too complicated just chop up a cup of onion, a cup celery, 4 cups fresh mushrooms, sauté the mixture in butter, add 2 tablespoons flour, brown, add 7 cups milk, season with salt and pepper or whatever you like, simmer a half hour and serve.

Mushroom Burgers—Stir together in a bowl ¼ pound cleaned, finely chopped mushrooms, 1 large onion chopped fine, ¼ cup bread crumbs (the homemade kind), 2 beaten eggs, ¾ cups grated Cheddar cheese and salt, pepper, oregano as suits your taste. Form into hamburger-type patties and fry in a pan on very low heat. Tastes even better if you have some garlic slices floating around in the pan cooking with it. Done when crisp on the outside and moist inside.

To preserve—By the nature of them, unless you live in a drafty tent you have a chance of growing mushrooms fresh all year round. Nevertheless, they can be preserved by drying, freezing or canning.

To dry, clean the mushrooms, slice thin and dry until brittle. You can add dried mushrooms directly to soup or revive them by soaking in water.

To freeze, clean, cut into pieces no larger than an inch across. You can prevent darkening by soaking the mushrooms 5 minutes in a mixture of 1 pint of water with a teaspoon lemon juice (or ½ teaspoon citric acid powder). Drain. Steam or blanch 3 to 5 minutes. Dip in cold water. Drain, pack and freeze.

To can, clean mushrooms and pretreat by cooking 5 minutes in boiling water that contains 1 tablespoon of vinegar and 1 teaspoon salt per quart. Drain. Fill jars with mushrooms and cover with fresh boiling water. Add ½ tablespoon lemon juice (or citric acid) to preserve color. Process in pressure cooker 25 minutes at 10 pounds.

MUSTARD GREENS—Look under Greens in the "Greens to Eat Cooked" section.

OKRA—Okra is a famous Deep South vegetable. Outside the Gulf Coast area it really isn't much appreciated and the reason probably is because it grows best and easiest in the South and it is a vegetable that loses its best fast after being away from the garden, so store okra or preserved okra really doesn't taste too hot and doesn't let you know what you're missing. But you can grow it if you have a climate that can handle corn, tomatoes and squash and doesn't have cool, wet weather or unseasonable frosts. The other name for okra is "gumbo" and when you hear about a gumbo recipe that generally means a soup kind of thing with okra in it. It's a beautiful plant that's closely related to the beautiful hibiscus flower. Lots of okra growers plant it in their flower area rather than their vegetable areas because it grows up to 4 feet high, has leaves sometimes as much as a foot wide, and before making fruit bears lots of pretty yellow blossoms with red centers. After the flowers come the seed pods which are the part you eat.

To plant—As far as soil types, okra will grow in anything although it does better like most of the others if you've been composting or manuring or both faithfully. If you live in a hot summer, but short growing season area the answer would be to start it indoors and then transplant, but you have to start it in one of the kinds of pots where you put container and all out in the garden because otherwise it doesn't handle transplanting. In a northern garden plant it in as much wind shelter as you can. Set out or plant about the same time you would watermelon or squash, when you're sure the last frost has happened and the soil has warmed up. Plant an inch deep and about a foot apart if you are transplanting, closer if you aren't because the germination rate on okra seed is way

worse than the average. Rows should be about 3 feet apart, closer if you are planting a dwarf variety. "Dwarf" to okra means a plant that grows like 2 feet high instead of 3 or 4; the pods are basically the same size for your harvesting. Soaking seeds before planting helps some with that germination problem. Varieties differ but in general you'll have the start of your okra harvest 50 to 60 days after planting. While the plants are young keep the weeds out but don't till deep because you'll mess up their big root systems, and once they start to cover the ground no more cultivating.

To harvest—If your growing conditions are halfway right you'll be loaded with the stuff. Four or five plants can produce enough for a small family. Pick the long, green seed pods when they are 2 or 3 inches long. No more. That is the best-tasting stage. You should go through and collect pods at least every other day if possible. Not only to get pods at their prime but to keep the plants producing, because if you let pods mature on the plant it will stop producing new ones. Eat the okra as soon as possible after you pick it, because they get tough quickly once they are off the vine. If you keep on picking the okra will keep on making okras until killed by frost, but the best ones will be the first part of the crop.

Saving your own seed—Leave the okra pods on your chosen plant and let them become completely mature. That means they will be brittle, brown and up to a foot long. Then shell out the seeds like beans. (Before they get clear ripe these okra pod bean seeds make good eating.) Dry and store.

To cook—Inside the okra pod there is a kind of "slimy" stuff. If you're not familiar with it and realize this is the natural and proper way that okra is you can get turned off fast. If you like okra but not the "slimy" part cooking it with tomatoes or in soups cuts it. Trim off both ends of the pods before cooking. Then slice into ½-inch lengths, more or less. Very young and tender pods can be cooked whole. Okra is good in combination with peas, tomatoes, onions, peppers, corn, squash and eggplant all or any. If you do end up with some old woody okra it can still be added to your soup or stock pot to add flavor and then fished out later so you don't actually eat the woody part.

Boiled Okra—Cook the okra gently in salted boiling water until tender. Drain, add butter, seasoning, and simmer until the butter is absorbed. Some people like a dash of vinegar too.

Okra and Tomatoes—Cut the pods crosswise into slices. Cover with hot water and simmer 20 minutes or so. Then add peeled, cut-up garden tomatoes and cook about 10 minutes more. Season with butter, salt and pepper.

I've received several letters containing advice on cooking okra from readers. Geneva Travis wrote from Kell, Illinois, that when you boil okra it is less slimy if you "kinda steam it till barely fork tender—drain—set back on the turned-off burner" (she has a gas stove) "till ready to serve. This dries it out a little. When I cook okra and tomatoes, I put onion in it. To fry okra I let grow 5 or 6 inches long, wash, tip, slice, roll in salted cornmeal, brown in bacon fat or whatever.

"I fry okra kinda fast—no lid, stir often and watch carefully. Did you ever plant red okra! It's a beautiful red maroon color—bears sooner, tastes better and isn't near so slimy. I win a blue ribbon at the Fair every year I enter it." Geneva knows her okra way better than I do and I'm grateful she wrote.

Julia Reynolds wrote me from Galvin, Washington, that she likes okra cooked, sliced and fried with potatoes. Joyce Darling wrote me from Harrodsburg, Kentucky, that she likes to make fried okra by slicing it crossways, about ¼ inch thick or less, salting, and coating with cornmeal with a little flour in it. Then she dumps the bowl of coated slices into a little hot grease in a skillet and fries, turning as it browns. She adds a little shortening or lard to keep it from sticking.

Okra peas—The best okra is picked with the seeds no more than half grown. If the seed is still tender but fully grown you can shell it out separately and cook like peas.

Okra Gumbo—Here's one version of that famous southern dish made with okra. Wash, stem, about a pound of garden fresh okra and slice it into about ½-inch sections. In a big frying pan start the okra cooking in bacon drippings or cooking oil. Add a finely chopped green pepper, a chopped-up onion, a clove of crushed garlic, about 4 peeled and cut-up tomatoes, a can of tomato paste or equivalent or your homemade catsup, ½ cup water, ½ teaspoon cayenne pepper or crushed red pepper. Simmer about 20 minutes. Now add 1 pound shrimp and a cup of smoked ham or sausage (whichever, thinly sliced). Cook about 45 minutes. Good served poured over rice.

To preserve—Okra can be frozen, dried or canned, but whichever you choose be sure and do it quite soon after picking. Otherwise the pods turn woody the same way they do if left on the plant.

To freeze—You can freeze okra straight and it freezes very well by scalding 2 or 3 minutes, cooling and packaging. Just be sure and use young, tender pods. But it tastes even more like fresh okra if you do something a little different. You start out like you're cooking fried okra. Wash, tip, slice, season with salt and pepper and shake in a sack with cornmeal until all covered or else prepare whatever way you like best for frying. Then fry in deep oil or whatever you prefer only now you take it out when barely half-fried and let cool to room temperature. Then package and freeze. When you're ready to use this kind of frozen okra you can put it in the oven if you're cooking something in there or let it thaw out and finish browning in a skillet with little or no oil, as it seems to need.

To dry—The old timers dried a lot of okra and they did it by stringing small, tender pods on a thread and hanging them over the stove to dry, then giving one last good heating in the oven before putting into final storage. Larger pods they sliced and then strung up the same way, hanging the strings in an airy but shady place until dried. Or they sliced okra and spread it thinly out on some kind of drying surface on top of brown paper or white cloth in the sun (cover at night). You can oven-dry or dry in a dryer by cutting young, tender pods crosswise or lengthwise, spreading thinly on trays. Done when brittle.

To can, pack hot with hot liquid. Process at 10 pounds pressure, 40 minutes for pints, 50 minutes for quarts.

ONION—Everybody knows about onions . . . or do they? I suspect the onion is actually one of the least understood garden vegetables. First of all there are those people who think that the onion, in all its varieties, is a flavoring agent. I can get positively red-faced over that. The onion family is a big one and a various one which I'm going to spread out in this section as well as I can for you to understand. Some of them like garlic, shallots, chives are definitely flavoring agents and you'd scarcely encounter them as a main course. But the "green onion" and the big globe type onion to me are as respectable and important vegetables as okra or peas. This onion-as-vegetable is not merely important because it's food, but from my point of view it's even more important than that because it's one of the garden's easiest vegetables to grow and one of the easiest to preserve over winter if all you have is an attic and a sack. There's a very strong vein of tradition that believes eating onions helps keep you healthy and some growing scientific evidence to back that up too. Well, be it all as it may, to start with I am sure unless you're really an old hand with onions, that there are more kinds of them than you realized. This onion section is divided by how they reproduce—a really important angle if you're serious about being self-sufficient. So first come garlic and shallots because they reproduce by bulb division, and then come Egyptian or tree onions that I grew up calling multipliers that make sets or bulblets at the top of the stem. And then come the kinds of onions that make seed like chives and leeks and globe onions.

The bulb dividers—Shallots and garlic, in my opinion, truly do belong more in the Herbs and Flavorings chapter than here in the Vegetables chapter so that's where I've put the main discussion of them along with horseradish and chicory roots for coffee making and so on. But just to keep the perspective, shallots and garlic both are onion varieties that multiply underground, meaning that they divide and grow multiple sets underground instead of one big bulb like the winter onions you see in plastic net-type bags in the grocery store.

Bulblets that grow from the top of the green stem—That's a long title but it's hard to know just what to call these. Some people call it a "tree" onion though it little resembles a tree except to make sets at the top of each long hollow round green stem, instead of anywhere else. Some call them scallions but in common usage scallion generally just means green onion which is a stage of life every seed-making (next category) onion goes through and generally the "scallions" or "green onions" that you see in the store are just that, a seed-type onion picked early in its life cycle. Lots of people call them Egyptian onions but they are really a native of North America, the onion that was here when the white man arrived! I grew up calling them multiplier onions and still do and yet since I've got to the point of reading books about onions I'm discovering people talking about a multiplier onion that reproduces by bulb division like garlic or shallots

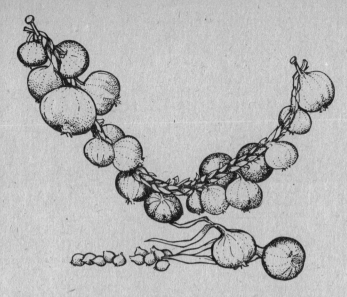

which is a variety I've never met in person. The plot gets even muddier because this variety of onion is just about nonexistent in seed catalogs—I would guess because once you buy some sets you'll never need more, in fact soon your whole neighborhood will be growing it from your generosity. Yet it is not commonly known or grown except in local areas here and there where some home gardeners are keeping it alive. Well, the Potlatch River valley is one of those areas and so, according to a letter I got from Violet Stewart, is Oklahoma. "I have multiplier onions. Everyone in Oklahoma does I think." Nichols Garden Nursery in Oregon lists them—I don't know if those are the same kind I mean or not. I've sold them off-and-onishly for years but mostly off because my garden simply can't keep up with the requests from people who've read this book and I hate to aggravate people by keeping them waiting for next year's crop.

They are a perennial onion—you plant a row and have it forevermore. They are the first edible thing in my spring garden. They'll take off way before the last frost—frosts don't bother them in the least. They are as persistent as chard. I go out and cut bunches of them for green onions and they immediately recommence growing. When you cut a multiplier onion you do not pull it up by the roots like you do a green onion raised from seed or a set of the commoner sort. You cut it off just above the ground leaving the root which promptly, as I said, grows you another green onion. And so on. They get bigger and bigger. Then their stalks become tough and inedible so farewell to green onions of the multiplier type, but then the root is growing big enough so you can pull the whole thing, cut off the top, peel, and use like any large onion. If you want well-developed bulbs you just keep whacking off the seed tips that try to grow and the strength will go into the bulb. When the summer heat comes on (if you don't keep them cut off) the multiplier onion flowers and then grows a cluster of sets on the tops of the long leaves, now easily 5 feet high if they've been generously watered. These are very like the regular sets of other types of onions except that they grow in thin air. If left alone the stalk will dry up, bend over, deposit the sets somewhere on the ground where you will have more multipliers next spring. But it's

best to pick them and plant in a row for more multipliers (plant in the fall for earliest growth next spring) or discard.

Multiplier onions don't make big onion bulbs for winter onions like the other types do. (But a person could go out and dig them up as needed through the winter since they are out there available all winter waiting for spring to take off again.)

Onions that grow from seed—Chives, leeks, globe onions and the seed onion kind of green onion all belong here. Leeks and globe onions are the two kinds of onions that you can take most seriously as a vegetable. Leeks are by far the harder to grow. Leeks don't make a bulb and aren't suitable for winter keeping by drying the same way as the big bulb onions. On the other hand they stand a fairly cold winter fairly well and you can leave them in the garden all winter, well mulched with straw or some such or transplant to a storage cold frame for winter eating. Leeks take about five months or more to reach maturity from planting the seed and that is one of their biggest drawbacks. Real hot weather or real cold weather either one hinders their growth. Unless you have a very long growing season you'll probably have to start them indoors 10 to 12 weeks before planting them outdoors. Plant any onion seed ¼ inch deep and ½ inch apart, but when setting leeks out in the garden set them 3 or 4 inches apart. And you don't have to wait until they are fully grown to use them. Leeks, like any onion, can be used onion-style at any stage.

But to have leeks, the real vegetable, they should be mature which means having a thick stem up to 2 inches wide and 4 to 6 inches long. You harvest by cutting off the roots at the base of the stem and can eat all the rest, including the leaves of young ones fresh from the garden. On not so young and not so fresh leeks you do avoid the leaves. Leeks can be used in cooking anyplace onions are but they are much milder than onions. They are very good sliced thin and cooked over low heat with thin sliced mushrooms. You can cook leeks by themselves as a vegetable and serve any way you would asparagus—good covered with any sort of sauce.

The globe-type onions—This is the commercial winter onion and there are all kinds of familiar ones here from the grocery store and lots more that gardeners raise.

Green onions—This is a young stage in the life of a globe-type onion or you can make multiplier onions do for it. When you read the seed catalogs you'll see them offering you seed, or sets or plants. Seed is by far the cheapest way to start, sets a little more expensive, and plants the most expensive but any of the three is cheaper than buying them at the store. Planting from seed you'll have green onions in 60-75 days, from sets sooner yet, and from plants in 25 or more days, quickest of all.

But my inclination is always to try to be as independent as possible so we plant onion seed to make green onions and sets and we plant sets to make onions and big onions—and don't buy plants at all. You can plant onion seed indoors as much as six weeks before the ground can be worked and transplant them out later but that's too much work for me. I just wait until the garden soil is more or less ready for some planting—as early as possible—and then plant them directly in the garden. You thin gradually as they grow by taking out the overcrowded ones and eating them. To plant sets just make a shallow trench, put the sets in there, neck up and cover to the neck with dirt. Sets should be planted 2 or 3 inches apart in the row. Either sets or seed enjoy the cool, wet spring weather to grow in. If your weather isn't wet at least keep the onions well watered. You'll get the best results if you keep the topsoil from drying clear out around them. When weeding be careful not to disturb the shallow onion roots because it may very much slow down their growth.

Onions really like wood ashes as well as the usual manure-compost stuff so you can in the off-season get rid of some of your ash-pan ashes where onions will grow. For green onions all summer long you can plant onion seed at intervals all spring, but they are much harder to get going once dry, hot weather sets in. Another way to get green onions is to plant sets in October and they will be giving you green onions about two weeks after they get going in the spring. What you're doing to get your green onions is harvesting globe-type onions before they get big enough to form the large bulbs. Onion varieties and individual onions have a lot of difference in their speed of growth or even if they'll grow at all—a certain part of the sets never do. You need to figure from two to four months from seed to good-sized green onions though you can be harvesting them younger. For store-type green onions the best seeds to plant are ones with "white" in the name like Evergreen Long White, White Spanish or Southport White Globe.

The big onions—They come in yellow, white, red, Bermuda and many other names. There are easily 50 different varieties of them. Ask the great gardeners in your neighborhood which ones they grow or just start experimenting. In the South the Yellow Bermuda, Granex and Grano-type onions do best. They are planted in the fall and harvested in the spring but they don't store well. In the middle between North and South, Sweet Spanish does well and it stores well. There are lots of hybrids developed for this climate zone but I'm not recommending them to you because I'm hoping you will be saving your own seed and not want them for that reason. In the Northeast and Midwest, Southport White Globe, Southport Yellow Globe, Ebenezer, Early Yellow Globe, Yellow Globe Danvers all do well and are very good long storing onions. In very northern regions Early Harvest does well but it's a hybrid. So you see the best winter storing onions are kinds that naturally grow best in places where you need them.

In order to develop big bulbs onions need long days. You can plant onions for bulbs either from seed or from sets. If planted from sets in the spring you can count on a good part of them making it to storing size by fall. My bulb onions never get as big as the store ones except for a few but that doesn't bother me a bit. Because they're practically free and I have as many as I want so there's just a little extra peeling. I've read

that to store onions for winter you should grow them from seed rather than from sets but that isn't so from my own experience and under the saving sets and seeds headings I'll tell you how to make it work. An easy way to raise winter onions is to plant seed the first summer to make sets, then save the sets and plant again the next spring to make bulbs. With the right climate and the right onion fall seeding makes it even easier. Walla Walla sweet onions are planted around August 25 to September 1. It's going through a cold winter that makes them sweet. Bermuda and Sweet Spanish onions are started in early September. Then the following spring they take off to make those big lovely onions. Remember they need long days to really put the growth on those bulbs. The Bermuda won't winter-keep as well as the Sweet Spanish. In general white varieties are milder and make more popular green onions and those are the kind you raise for the little "pickling onions." Red varieties are sweetest of all and winter keep the worst. Yellow varieties winter-keep the best.

Saving your own sets—With the seed-making onions you can save either seed or sets and in order of choice you get your first chance to save at the set stage which comes generally way before the seed stage. Figure you need a quart of sets to plant 100 feet of row and they'll shrink some over the winter and some won't grow. Plant your seed and let the onion plants grow until the root bulb is about marble-sized. Then they are cured by removing the tops and sun-drying the bottoms to be capable of wintering. Store cool and dry and well ventilated like in a pair of worn out panty hose. Plant next spring.

I got a letter from Mrs. Otto Kliewer of Frazer, Montana, who told me another way to make sets: "My mother-in-law tells me that if you have onions left over in the spring that you can cut them into sections and plant them and each section will produce an onion. I have done that and it works!"

To save your own seed—If you don't want your onions to make seed but to keep putting their energy into making bulb, when they start to make flowers just snap the flower stem off. Otherwise they are going to make seed and that's how they do it. They put up one slender stalk that flowers and then makes seed. Onion pollen is carried by insects and that means you can't have pure-bred seed unless you grow only one kind or have only one kind flowering at a time or keep your different kinds quite separate. On the other hand if they do cross the results will be edible and maybe have hybrid vigor! Onions are biennial if you're going from seed to set and then from set to bulb. You save good bulbs from the plants you choose to be parents and set them out the next spring. To keep from losing your onion seed by scattering before it is ripe on the plant, fasten a paper bag over the seed head with a rubber band. Then you can harvest, bag and all, when you're ready. But give the insects a chance to do their job completely first. Or you can gather your onion seed a little earlier and finish drying on a newspaper. Onion seeds will last for years if well dried and sealed in glass where humidity can't get at them, but they will die in just a few months if you have them in a warm, humid place. Getting them too dry by artificial heating will kill them too. They are one of the least long-lived seeds unless conditions are just right.

Weep no more—In an earlier edition of this book I mentioned crying over onions. Well, some thoughtful readers cured me of that. Frances Hanken wrote me from Lucerne Valley, California: "Please, Carla, weep no more—all you need do is keep a supply of them in the refrigerator first—then when you cut them up, you will find no tears at all. I've used onions in cooking for so many years and since I've 'cooled it' no tears for me!" Terry Bedard of Warner Robins, Georgia, wrote and told me her simple preventive: "Five to 10 minutes before using onions put them in the freezer. It has no effect on the onion's texture or flavor but it completely kills the strong fumes and just that easy, no more crying." Another reader told me: "I was told to hold a bread crust between my teeth. I figured out that meant to breathe through your mouth. It works!"

To cook, try peeling the paper skin off big ones, boiling until done and serving with a white sauce or cheesey sort of sauce poured over. Or bake big onions in their skins like potatoes, 30 to 40 minutes at 350°. Or slice a bunch of onions, sauté until golden in some cooking oil, add sliced apples, raisins, a dash of vinegar or lemon juice, cover and steam until the apples are softened. Salt and pepper to taste.

To preserve—I think there's no point in trying to can or freeze onions when they are the easiest thing in the whole garden to keep all year round in a virtually "fresh" state by drying whole. They get stronger dried whole (I don't mean sliced and dried . . . I mean just like the big onions you buy in the store) but you expect strongness in an onion anyway. Here's another argument against freezing onions. A lady wrote me from Springfield, New Jersey, "I have a small freezer chest and when onions were on sale I froze some chopped onions. I put them in freezer bags and then in aluminum foil wrapping, and still they filled my freezer with such an odor that I finally ended up throwing them all out. What did I do wrong? My little 'bargain' in onion didn't prove to be a bargain at all for me."

To dry in little pieces, you can slice onions up and down, same direction as from their stem to root ends about ¼ inch thick into fairly same-sized pieces and dry. Dry until light colored and brittle. For oven drying dry under 135° because they can't stand more heat.

To pickle, start out with bulbs that you have saved set-style from any sort of white rooted onion. Here's a recipe Fern Archibald sent me from Morgantown, Indiana. It's been in her family 200 years! "Select small white onions. Peel (if held under water will not affect eyes). After peeling, cover with a rather strong brine, keeping them under by laying a plate on top. Let stand for 2 days. Drain and place in a new brine for same length of time. Then boil in still another brine for 3-4 minutes. After boiling put them in clear cold water to fresh up, leaving them in cold water 4-5 hours. Drain, pack in jars. Scatter whole cloves, pepper and mace among them. Fill up the jars with scalding vinegar to each gallon of which has been added a cup of sugar. Seal while hot. Good in 4-5 weeks, but better in 3-4 months."

When the weather is hot enough to discourage growth or you are satisfied with the onion size or if they have started to dry up on top anyway walk along your row and twist the green tops over. Come back in a few days when you expect a spell of hot sunny weather and dig your onions. They are spread out on top of the ground. Ones that accidentally got cut with the spade go into the house to be used soon. Sets that for some reason didn't take off are cured and saved to try again next year. They often make it the second time they are planted.

I've read that you cannot save onions grown from sets for winter onions. Every summer we bring in onions from sets by the gunnysack full for our winter supply, so I think you really can. The trick is to cure especially well in the sun for three days or so before bringing in. Also rip off the "set" portion before drying if you can. The onion grown from a set has two parts. One is small and extends up into a stiff hollow stem. That is the part you should rip off.

After you bring your onions in from the field you should continue drying them. We have tried all sorts of systems for this. You can braid them by the dry stems and hang them up in bunches with wire or twine around the bunch. Or put them in an "onion"-type bag and hang them up or into old panty hose. My current and easiest yet system is to dump them into cardboard boxes and bring them into the kitchen. I check them occasionally by running my hands through the boxes and remove any that feel damp. Any onion that feels the least damp is on the verge of spoiling. When the rest are really bone, bone dry from the kitchen's heat (once that old wood cookstove starts going it really gives them the treatment) they can go under the bed or into the attic. Anywhere they won't freeze and will stay dry.

Slight freezing doesn't hurt them, provided you don't handle them while frozen. Good ventilation is very important to their storage place and that's why they should be in some sort of loosely woven bag or hanging basket or braided and hung up or some such. They do better dry and cool than they do stored hot and cool because with too much heat they have a tendency to sort of gradually dry away to layer upon layer of papery nothingness as your winter goes by.

When we are using our big winter onions we take the largest first, then gradually work our way down in size. That way if there are any left over, come spring they will be small ones suitable to use as sets in the spring planting.

OYSTER PLANT—See Salsify.

PARSNIPS are about the hardest to grow root vegetable but worth the trouble because of their winter-keeping ability. It's just a case of knowing what they need and giving it to them. They are a relative of the carrot and more than any other vegetable in the garden, even the carrot, can handle, and moreover, thrive on, being left in the garden all winter to be dug as needed. The problems come under soil, seed and season.

Soil—Parsnips need a deep and finely cultivated soil. If your soil is very sandy naturally that makes it easy. They'll love it. If it's not you have some work ahead of you. But the same manuring and composting treatment that benefits your other garden vegetables also helps parsnips. The parsnip place in your garden needs more though. It needs the soil worked thoroughly a foot or a foot and a half deep with stones and such gotten out that the roots would catch on and get deformed and discouraged. A heavy clay soil will be the hardest kind to get ready for parsnips. Working in extra cinders and compost will help make your soil loose and crumbly. You can do this working up of the soil without turning your good topsoil under and digging it to the bottom—it's good enough just to get the soil loose. Some people have grown parsnips 3 or 4 feet long for fun by digging the soil loose that deep and supplying plenty of manure-compost.

Planting seed—Parsnip seed doesn't keep well over a year so if it doesn't come up the problem may be old seed. But don't despair too soon because parsnip seed has the distinction of being slower to germinate even under the best conditions than any other kind of seed I know of. Figure 21 to 28 days from planting to seeing something green above the ground! It has to be planted very shallow and gently. It has trouble getting up if there is any sort of crust on your soil. Water well before you plant it, ideally plant ½ inch apart though you can't possibly do that in real life because the seed is so fine. Cover no more than ¼ inch deep, very lightly. If you feel like the seeds need extra protection like from birds or some such, protect with a ½-inch layer of peat moss or some such light mulch which you'll take off as soon as the parsnips are coming up. In a short summer climate the right time to plant is immediately after your last frost date since parsnips take 100 to 120 days to mature. In the South parsnips can't take the hot midsummer weather so you plant in the fall or early, early spring. The parsnip rows can be anywhere from 18 inches to 3 feet apart, if like 18 inches let's hope you got plenty of manure-compost into the soil.

Weeding and thinning—Because parsnips are so slow to come up you've got to do something extra to keep from losing them in weeds. So do like with carrots and mix radish seed with your parsnip seed. The radish seed comes up fast and shows you where the parsnip row will be and that makes it possible for you to cultivate and keep the weeds out without accidentally cultivating out your parsnips-to-be. After they get going you can thin to 3 to 6 inches apart depending on how much space you can spare and how rich your soil is. Or let them go as long as you can and figure on eating the thinnings. Keep weeding faithfully all summer long.

Freezing—If you've been reading this Vegetables chapter straight through remember how we rush sweet corn from its stalk to the cooking pot because it has lots of natural sugar in it that starts changing to starch the minute it leaves the stalk or is unhusked? Parsnips turn that exactly around. Parsnips have lots of starch in them which below freezing weather changes to sugar! That's why you're ahead tastewise to leave them outside in the ground until they have

been exposed to at least three weeks of frosty weather. You can leave them in the ground all winter. Freezing only improves them. The technical problem is that you can't dig anything out of frozen ground but must do your harvesting during thaws and if you want parsnips and no thaw comes, you're out of luck. That's the advantage of some alternative systems (see the Preserving section later on). Tastewise they are best if left in the ground until spring. But then you have to dig them out for sure or they will start to work on making seed and get completely woody and inedible.

To save your own seed—Same principle as other biennials (turn back to Carrot). The seed will be made the second summer of the parsnip's life. So leave in the ground the ones you want to make seed, collect the seed when it is mature and store for use. Collect generously on parsnips: because of its difficulties with staying alive and germinating, having lots of extra to plant is a sort of insurance. Parsnip seeds will only last halfway reliably one to two years.

To cook—You can catch parsnips generally speaking at any of three stages. In the first they are garden fresh and young, starchy rather than sweet, but tender all through without the woody center core that comes later. This is before they are full grown and have their frost treatment. The large, older parsnips may be better tasting but you've got a woody center core to get rid of as well as the peel. Old parsnips get too woody to eat—might as well let them go on and make seed.

Young parsnips—You can scrape rather than peel, wash, French fry or whatever. Some people like to eat parsnip tops . . . they taste a little bit like watercress and can be used in salads. Other people get a sort of allergic reaction from wet parsnip leaves that blisters tender skin like wrists. I don't know why.

Older parsnips—Boil unpeeled, washed parsnips until tender—takes about 10 minutes for a 1-inch-wide parsnip. Now peel by skinning like you would a potato or run a razor blade the parsnip's length just cutting the skin and roll out the parsnip. If the parsnip has a woody core now slit it lengthwise down to the core and get that out. Or if you are going to cut the parsnip into sections do that and then push the core out of each section. Boiled parsnips are good served cold with mayonnaise. Or creamed. Cut in slices and browned in butter. Or as part of any potato-turnip kind of stew or soup. Or mashed and served with salt, pepper and butter. Or mashed, seasoned, shaped into cakes, lightly floured, fried brown and served. Or glazed in a frying pan in a mixture of salt, pepper, butter, fruit juice and brown sugar or honey. Or instead of boiling them you can roast in the jacket with meat the same as potatoes.

To keep parsnips at their best in the garden, if you are in the northern United States, mulch lightly until outside temperatures are consistently low. Then remove the mulch until you figure the parsnips are thoroughly frozen. Then mulch deeply enough to keep them frozen. That keeps them but they aren't very diggable in frozen ground. They can be stored in a root pit: lay right on the ground, cover with soil then with straw or leaves and then a waterproof tarp or plastic. If you want to keep them in a root cellar pack in moist soil. They will soon start to develop again in the spring. Then the roots all become too woody to eat.

Or you can keep dug up parsnips between layers of damp sand in a tub affair in a cool outbuilding.

To freeze, cut into ½-inch cubes or lengthwise into slices about ¾ inch thick, scald 2 or 3 minutes. Cool, package, freeze.

To dry, avoid parsnips old enough to have a woody core. Slice, cut into chunks, or easiest of all—shred with a salad maker. Those shreds dry very quickly and evenly. Then you can reconstitute by overnight soaking, cook and eat, or add to soups, stews, casseroles or powder to be part of your instant vegetable soup.

PEAS are as easy as parsnips are hard, except for all that picking and shelling. But abundance isn't really a thing to complain about. Peas are a cheery thought to me all winter because they are the first thing I plant. I plant my peas about February 20. It doesn't matter if it's snowing or there is snow on the ground as long as the ground isn't frozen. That's long before my husband will even consider going into the garden. But not me. I'm just famished by then. I grab my jar of homegrown pea seed, and my pick, and head for the garden. I plant the peas near the edge of the garden and that way when Mike gets around to plowing he can just omit where I've already planted.

Peas don't mind cold. You could plant them in the late fall if you wanted to. They have some kind of wonderful instinct that tells them just when to wake up and start growing and they won't grow until then anyway. But the ones that I plant so early get off at the very first opportunity and so we have peas on our table two weeks before anybody else. There's another advantage to such early planting too. That is that early peas can be picked, shelled, put to sleep in the deepfreeze and the ground is available for the green beans which will be coming on a week later. It is just awful trying to put up both peas and beans at the same time.

So I go out in my winter coat while everybody in the house is either laughing or sighing in sorrow at my strangeness and I muck through the cold, muddy ground to the chosen spot. I eye it, calculate vaguely where my row will go, walk to one end and commence whacking with my pick. I used to spade the ground but that is a terrible struggle in this clay ground when it is wet. The peas don't care anyway. All they need is a head start and they'll beat the weeds anyway. So using the pick I manage to break open a row. (Last year I was seven months pregnant when I did it—in fact I've been pregnant come to think of it a lot of years when I planted peas. I have mostly spring babies—like the goats.) Then I walk back and commence planting pea seeds. I don't drop them in the least precisely, just sort of dribble them through my fingers. It doesn't hurt peas to be a little crowded. Then I walk back, kick clods back over them as best I can and go on to the next row. By three rows I'm either cold enough or tired enough to quit but from then on I get out to the garden every day if I can for at least a few minutes to sow a few more seeds.

It makes me happy to plant seeds. As long as I am putting seeds in the ground I know spring will come and by then I'm getting anxious for spring. So I plant peas until the peas are all planted (we need 12 rows or so) then put in some spinach—not that I'm crazy about spinach because I'm not but it's something else like peas that I can plant so very early. By the time I have those in it has warmed up enough for the onion sets and my husband has started taking walks to the garden on his own and the multipliers are up. When the multipliers come up spring has sprung.

The rows of peas that I planted with the pick always turn out to be crooked. Not merely curved but outright zigzag and too close together for the rototiller. My husband looks at them, sighs and gets on with the chard, carrots, beans and so on. Our garden is short on looks anyway. Nobody around here is decorator-minded. But it really does grow the food.

The kinds of peas—I always plant bush peas. But that isn't the only kind I could. There are pole peas just like there are pole beans, and sugar peas, and southern kinds of peas that some people swear are beans and some believe are peas. I think they are peas so I put them here instead of with the beans. Bush peas are the easiest to grow. Pole peas take longer to mature, you have to rig up something for them to climb on like brush stuck in the ground, or beanpole-type poles with chicken wire on them. The pole peas are supposed to bear more pods and longer once they get going than the bush peas but I really don't think it's enough to make up for the extra work they are and waiting for them since peas hate hot weather. Pole peas also take more space. Pole peas grow from 3 to 6 feet high. Bush peas will only get up between 1 and 2 feet high.

Then there are the edible pod or sugar or snow peas. It all means the same kind of pea. These are special in that you eat them pod and all as soon as you can see a slight swelling inside the pod. Sort of a special treat but not a kind you want to plant for a food staple for your family.

Regular green peas like cool nights and bright,

cool days and don't do well in the South (maybe one planting right in the earliest spring). The peas that do well in that climate are black-eyed peas, a hot-weather plant good for growing where green peas don't do well. Crowder peas like heat too. Black-eyed peas can be used green in the summer and dried for use like beans in the winter. (So can green peas.) Crowder peas can be used in the pod like snap beans or shelled. These southern peas need about four months of warm days and nights for a good crop. (Regular green peas make it in 60 to 70 days.)

On growing—Peas are easy to raise in cool weather and hard in hot weather. They hate dryness. Plant (more or less) an inch deep, and 2 to 3 inches apart. They are easy to space when planting so you don't need to thin later. They'll be ten days to two weeks coming up if they think the weather is warm enough to come up at all. If you want to rush them because you're trying to beat the heat or just want peas a week earlier soak them in a flat dish spread one pea deep with water halfway up the pea seed until little sprouts show and then plant right away before they rot. In the South they are sometimes planted in the fall. With luck, in a more northern climate you can plant in the later summer and get a fall crop. But my way of doing it is to plant a lot of them at the time when peas grow best and then freeze and dry enough for the rest of the year. Start harvesting as soon as the pods are decently filled out. If you pick too soon before the peas have gotten to their full size you'll be wasting your and the pea vine's effort. If you wait a few days too many the peas will be getting yellow and hard and losing their good taste although still fine to dry or make seed from. When picking pods treat the vines gently so you don't hurt them or pull out the roots and that way they'll go on producing for quite a while if you keep them picked (go through about every other day) and keep them well watered.

To save your own seed—Basically it's the same as saving bean seed so turn back to the Bean section for more detailed directions. I've heard that black-eyed peas will cross with green peas and if you plant to save your own seed they can't be grown together and be in bloom at the same time. In general you let peas for seed stay on the vine until the pods are well developed and later shell out of the pod. Black-eyed peas aren't done that way though. To save seed from black-eyed peas you should pick before the pods are well developed. That way they can be easily shelled before the pods begin to dry out. They are shelled out of the green pods and then dried.

Dried pea seed has a good livability. It should keep its germinating power three years easily and I have a friend who has homegrown and saved peas eight years old that will still sprout (and still make fine food too). You can figure a pint of seed will plant about 100 feet in your garden.

To cook—Peas are like corn in that on the vine they have lots of natural sugar which will start turning to starch after they are picked. Not as fast as with corn but fast enough that you'll find fresh garden peas the best you ever tasted if you've never tasted them before, and you'll want to get your peas from the plant to the pot or frozen or canned just as promptly as possible. They keep better in the shell than out of it (just like corn keeps better in the husk than out of it) so don't shell until just before cooking. Store in the refrigerator if you must keep them hanging around. Don't wash peas before cooking. Just shell them out of clean pods and that's good enough. I'm sure you already have lots of regular pea recipes. Maybe you could use some for those edible pod peas?

Plain Sugar Peas—To do this pick and wash but don't shell. Cook pods and all until tender. Drain and serve with Hollandaise or melted butter or chill and serve as a salad covered with French dressing.

Sugar Pea Soup—Cook a piece of ham in water or use meat stock instead. Add the sugar pods, and a small new onion and a batch of tiny new potatoes. Serve when pea pods and potatoes are tender.

Sweet and Sour Sugar Peas—Stir fry the peas in 2 or 3 tablespoons vegetable oil in a large pan with sliced onion and celery (1 or 2 cups each) for 5 to 15 minutes. Season with salt to taste and soy sauce. Can also be served with basic sweet and sour sauce (double recipe) over meatballs on a bed of brown rice.

To freeze—Most of the work is not in the freezing. For days on end we pick in the early morning or late evening to avoid sunstroke and shell the rest in our spare time. The emptied shells go to the pig. Peas are sorted as they are shelled. The ones that have already started to get too hard or dry are not shelled; they go into a special bucket for drying. (See Dried Peas and Beans.) It takes a lot of work and a lot of time to shell out a quart of peas. Everybody that comes along gets a batch of pea pods dumped in their lap and we all sit on the porch and work. Once a day's batch is shelled the water in a kettle is set to boiling. Then I lower a sieveful of peas into the boiling water. I leave it there until the water returns to a boil. A moment after that the peas have all changed color. I lift them out, cool under running water and pour into a bowl. I refill my sieve and put it in the boiling water. While that is in the process of coming to a boil again I am bagging up the first batch in baggies tied at the top with a twist of wire. Every five or so baggies are bagged again in a larger-sized baggie. That's because sometimes the baggies break and lose their peas. If you have them double bagged you can't lose any peas and the peas are easier to find in the freezer. It's usually about 11:00 at night when I get the last sieveful done. (But since I first published this, several people have written to me to say they blanch peas *in the pod*, then shell, then freeze, and that they shell easier that way.)

To can, pack hot with hot water, put lids on, process pints 35 minutes, quarts 40 minutes at 10 pounds pressure.

To dry—Basically it's the same as beans and you may get a lot of ideas from reading the section on how to dry beans. You can dry sugar peas pod and all by washing, cutting in 1/4-inch pieces and drying the same way you would string beans.

Dried peas—Soak these a whole 24 hours before cooking time.

Dried Pea Soup—Sauté 1 chopped onion in 2 tablespoons butter. Into a heavy pot put some bacon, ham or salt pork, the sautéed onion and a heaping cup of dried peas. Add water to cover and simmer 4 hours, stirring often, and adding more water about every hour, as much as needed. Salt, pepper and serve.

✿⊱⊰✿⊱⊰✿⊱⊰✿⊱⊰✿⊱⊰✿⊱⊰✿⊱⊰✿

PEPPERS—This is a big and various family with all sorts of shapes, colors and hotnesses. You have to be careful what kind you're buying. I have a neighbor who truck-gardens vegetables for sale. She bought 50 pepper plants at a nearby nursery only to discover come harvest time that she had a tremendous crop of cayenne peppers! Those are little hot red ones of which a tiny bit goes a long ways. Chili peppers and Tabasco peppers are some of the other famous hot kinds. Look in the Herbs and Flavorings chapter for more on them. What I'm going to talk about here are the table sorts of peppers that are generally eaten green, but ripen to yellow or red or dark purple or even white or brown in some unusual variations. They come in blocky shapes (the familiar store kind) or heart-shaped (the familiar pimento kind), tomato-shaped and long-shaped. I'd recommend blocky for a basic green pepper, the pimento pepper to grow for making home-canned pimentos, but that long kind called Sweet Banana or Sweet Hungarian is a heavier producer than the others. They are only 2 inches wide at the top, 6 to 8 inches long but set 30 or more fruits per plant. You can try out different varieties until you find what suits your climate and your cooking inclinations best. My favorite green pepper is the Yolo Wonder.

To grow—In most climates you'll have to start peppers from seed indoors. They would be killed by frost. Figure on planting them two weeks after your last frost date. Plant the seed indoors eight to ten weeks before that last frost date. Plant it ⅛ inch deep and 1 inch apart, more or less. When the peppers are about 2 inches tall transplant to flats 2 inches apart. When they are going to the garden they should be at least 5 or 6 inches tall and you set them out 1 to 2 feet apart in rows 2 or 3 feet apart. How many plants you grow depends on how many peppers you can use. You'll be able to pick the first peppers maybe ten weeks after transplanting to the garden. Each plant will ripen one fruit at a time as long as you keep picking them and frost doesn't kill it. You'll get a maximum of maybe eight or ten peppers per plant.

To get even that much production out of them the plants need ideal conditions which may not be easy for you to provide. They want a warm summer, plenty of watering, and a light rather than clay-type soil. (I have the heaviest clay imaginable. Our valley used to feature a brick factory using the native stuff and all the real old buildings on Main Street are made of Kendrick mud.) Be sure and harvest your green peppers, large or small, before they get touched by frost which will ruin them, same as it will tomatoes. If you can get them safely in the house they'll keep a while more in a cool place where the air is not too dry. To get them off the plants you just snap them off and carry into the house.

To save your own seed—Peppers are a fruited plant category. They should be as thoroughly ripe as possible before picking. That means red and rather soft in the case of pepper varieties that turn red when ripe. Gather just before frost and turn back to the Cucumber section for directions on handling a fruited plant.

To eat—Raw peppers are good chopped in a green salad. Whether you want them raw or cooked you always get rid of the seeds and white pulp inside. Just cut around the top stem with a sharp small knife as if you were going to make a lid for a jack-o'-lantern. Lift out the stem part, scoop out the seeds and pulp and you have whole peppers ready for stuffing. There isn't any practical reason for skinning a pepper except to can pimentos but it can be done by roasting the peppers in a hot oven until the skin blisters and blackens a little then while still hot put them in a pot with a tight lid and a little water to steam a few minutes. Then you can easily slip off the skins.

To freeze, cut up. Remove core and seeds. Cut any way you want them. You can freeze your nicest ones in halves for later stuffing and make the others into strips for winter salads and such. If you use green peppers in salads when only partly thawed they will still be crisp. You don't need to blanch. Just pack (double sacking is best) and freeze. Use in soups, casseroles, macaroni dishes, chicken dishes . . . To freeze red pimento peppers roast and skin as described under "To eat," then freeze as for green peppers.

To dry, cut in ½-inch strips or rings. Remove seeds. Spread on drying frames or thread on a string. Spread rings no more than two layers deep, strips no more than ½ inch deep. Dry until crisp and brittle.

To can green peppers, cut out stem ends and remove seeds and cores as above. You can leave them whole or cut into any number of shape of pieces you fancy. Preboil 5 minutes. Then pack hot with hot liquid. Put on jar lids and process 20 minutes for pints or 25 minutes for quarts under 10 pounds pressure. If you want to use a hot-water-bath canning method they only need 45 minutes.

To can pimentos, first roast in a 450° oven 5 minutes or until the skins blister. Then drop them into cold water. Then peel. Cut out stem ends, remove seeds and cores. Pack them flat in pint jars. Sprinkle in about ½ teaspoon salt. Put on your jar lid. Pimentos make their own liquid—don't add any. Process 20 minutes at 10 pounds or 40 minutes in a hot-water bath.

Canned Pickled Pimentos—Start out by seeding and slicing sweet red peppers until you have 2 quarts' worth. Cover them with boiling water for a minute. Drain and cover with ice water. Drain and pack into sterilized jars. Bring 1 cup vinegar to a boil and hold it for 2 minutes, add 1 cup olive oil and when it boils up again pour over the peppers and seal. If the vinegar-olive oil mixture wasn't enough to get your peppers covered make more.

Pimento Cheese—Judy Hohstadt wrote me from Cove, Oregon, with this recipe: "I've been trying to raise pimentos. They grow great except for turning red and that they will not do until after they're picked. By the time they are red there is not much meat left in them to can. We use them in this Pimento Cheese recipe. It's great in sandwiches or as a dip. Grate ¾ pound of medium sharp cheese. Add 1 can (used to be 21-cent size—boy that seems like a long time ago) or homemade equivalent of pimentos, juice too. Mash pimento and add to the cheese. Mix with mayonnaise—enough for a spreading consistency. Add 1 teaspoon onion juice and a little pepper. That's it."

Red and Green Pepper Relish—Start with a dozen each of sweet red peppers and sweet green peppers. Remove stem ends, get out the pulp and seeds. Peel 15 white onions and chop both onions and all the peppers fine. Cover with boiling water 5 minutes. Drain. Cover again with boiling water and let set 10 minutes. Combine 1½ cups sugar, 1 quart cider vinegar and ¼ cup salt and boil them 5 minutes. Add the vegetables, boil 15 minutes more, seal in sterilized jars.

POTATOES—A funny thing happened on the way from Peppers to Potatoes—I had a baby. Monday I wrote the seventh edition version of peppers, which is mostly like writing from scratch because I've been expanding it so much. Tuesday morning I woke up and my water broke (in exactly that sequence, I was still lying in bed). Well, my labor hadn't started but Mike took me to the hospital because I have a record for having babies on the fast side and he, even though he has pregnancy tested a cow, and has delivered umpteen farm babies, doesn't want to get stuck delivering one of mine. So I was taken to the labor room and lay there all day waiting to get on to Potatoes and feeling very bored and sort of guilty because Mike had work to do too and there we were and nothing happening. At 5:00 P.M. I had a contraction, at 5:15 another, one at 5:20 and one at 5:25. The nurse came in and I told her I thought maybe something was happening. She said I'd have to be more regular than that and went away. Then everything stopped for 30 minutes. Then it went another half hour, then stopped another half hour. From 7:00 to 8:00 it ambled along in a semiserious way. The nurse checked me and said I was 3 centimeters dilated. (I had been 2 when I checked in that morning.) I asked her to call the doctor who had repeatedly made me promise I'd let him know when "labor started" because he had a feeling I might go pretty fast once I got started. She thought it was early but did so for me. (This was my sixth child.)

At 8:30 Mike was seriously considering going for a walk. It's hard for him to sit anywhere very long but things started seeming more serious and he decided to stick around. At about 8:45 I asked him to please tell the nurse it was feeling more serious. She came in and checked me and said I was dilated 5 centimeters. That was at 8:48. As her shoulders were disappearing out the door I said, "Mike, you better tell her I feel like I'm getting ready to bear down." He dashed out into the hall after her. The two of them came back on the run with a cart to take me to the delivery room across the hall. They got me across before the next contraction hit me. As soon as I was on that table here it came and the contraction moved the baby out of the womb and well down the birth canal. The nurse was saying "Don't push! Don't push!" The next contraction the baby's head crowned and then was out almost to the shoulders. Enough so that Mike could see he was blue as blue ink. "Push! Push!" said the nurse. I tried and with the third contraction he came out all the way. The doctor had run in just as the baby crowned and moments later they could see the baby had a loop of cord around his neck and another around his chest. The doctor slipped his fingers under that loop of cord, gently loosened it and lifted it over the baby's head. The baby gasped, coughed and began to breathe and cry. I was sitting up trying to see every part of him at once, trying to really be able to believe that the baby I had carried unseen for so many months really was in every part and whole a fine healthy boy. And he was! The delivery time was 12 minutes after the moment the nurse had said I was 5 centimeters dilated. 9:00 P.M., February 15, 1977.

Today is Saturday, four days later. I got home from the hospital on Thursday.

Now I've just got to finish writing about potatoes and after that pumpkin, radish, rutabaga, salsify, squash, tomato, turnip and watercress. I've got orders waiting for this seventh edition to be finished and people are going to feel like I'm not very dependable if I take still longer. Besides there's a class of college students in Bellingham, Washington, that will be starting a course in two weeks called "The 5-Acre Farm" and want to use this book as a textbook and I want them to have it. Jacob Michael Emery is in his crib nearby and not at all sure he likes the sound of a typewriter. He weighs 7 pounds 8½ ounces, is 20 inches long and loves to sleep but never for too long at a time!

It isn't just because I live in Idaho, land of the famous baking spud, or because my husband spent many a childhood hour walking down the rows in southern Idaho, with a potato sack hooked from a belt around his waist and dragging between his legs, picking up potatoes. Nor is it just because I'm the daughter of a three-square-meals-a-day Pennsylvania Dutchman and all of those meals including potatoes. Nor is it just because I married another potato lover—potatoes are just naturally important. They are a starchy food. If you work hard that means they are a *food* food. You can grow them easily in large quantities in your own garden.

Potatoes are one of the native American food plants, like corn, tomatoes and pumpkins. Maybe you think they came from Ireland but they didn't. The Irish potato got to Ireland by way of first the Incas in South America, then to Spain around 1700, and gradually got up all through Europe (including Ireland), from which it came back to North America. Potatoes are important from the independence point of view because they are one of those wonderful root vegetables that winter so easily so simply. They are easy to save your own "seed" on because you plant potatoes to grow potatoes. They do better in the northern U.S. than in the South. Southerners love sweet potatoes

which are really no sort of potato at all except for having the name. Look under S for sweet potatoes in this chapter.

Soil—Like any root vegetable where the important action is underground potatoes do best in a sandy soil that spreads apart easily to let potatoes happen under there but will do fine in any soil that you've got loosened enough with compost-manure kinds of things to be a nice loam for them and that you've cultivated enough, deep enough so the growing little potatoes have stretching-out room. Potatoes are such a staple that you may want to really grow a bunch of them, maybe even a few in the garden for summer new potato eating fresh and then a really serious patch of them on one side of the garden or in a field elsewhere. Potatoes like wood ashes so the potato patch is another good place to spread your wood stove ashes. Rich ground helps them but go easy on the horse manure in your potato patch because that is one that can make a funny, "scabbed" skin on them, which is going to be a problem if your available gardening area is small.

Climate—Light frosts don't kill potatoes, so they can be planted very early in the spring. The problem for them in the South is that warm soil temperatures combined with a lot of moisture give potatoes a tendency to rot in the ground and they are much more subject to plant disorders and don't store as well. Potatoes do their best growing in weather that is fairly cool but with days that are long. In some mild climates, if you can solve the other problems, you can plant potatoes the year around. In cold weather climates you plant the first planting a month or two weeks before you've expected the last frost. If you do want to try potato growing in a hot climate look for the heat resistant varieties that have been developed. Chippewa is one, providing you keep it well watered.

Weeding and watering—Potatoes need a good soaking at least once a week, either by rainfall or your ingenuity and labor. As soon as your potatoes are up so you can see where the rows are, you can start fighting weeds. Keep that up all the while they are growing so they won't have competition for food and water.

What you use for seed—Potato plants will make seed but it doesn't breed true to variety. The plant sends up a stalk, flowers prettily above ground, but for our use the seed making job is finished underground where the plant finishes making potatoes with eyes. The next spring every eye has the capacity to sprout and grow a new potato plant. If you don't know what I mean by an eye get a potato and look at it. Each little round depression on the potato surface is an eye. The eyes are generally many on one end of the potato and scattered more thinly over the rest of it. Each potato piece that you plant must have at least one eye in it to grow a new plant and needs a sufficient-sized chunk of potato behind that eye to supply nourishment for the new plant to get up through the ground and reach the sunlight where it can make its own energy.

Where to get your seed—Regular store potatoes are cheaper than specially bagged-up "seed potatoes." Maybe you bought more potatoes than you can use before some start sprouting and then you can use the sprouted ones for some of your potato seed. The only problem there is you're not too clear what variety you have and maybe the store potatoes were treated with a chemical to inhibit their sprouting. If they don't grow for you that is probably what the trouble was. On the other hand the "sets" that you buy in seed catalogs are potatoes that have been cut into the smallest pieces they dare and have often been treated with chemicals too. You may be tempted to save the little bitty potatoes that are on your vines to be seed potatoes but don't do that because that means you are selecting plants with the worst hereditary characteristic available—failure to mature in time. I think the ideal start would be to buy seed potatoes of a known variety the first year or get them from a neighbor who knows what he has and then the years after save your own. To save seed potatoes you save them same as you would for eating like under dirt or in a root cellar over winter. Then each time you want to make a planting get the ones from storage that look most eager to sprout or that have sprouted and let them go ahead and make potato plants in your garden.

Potatoes are the poor man's friend and if need be you can make do with even less than that. As college researchers say that a large piece of potato with an eye grows better than a small piece, then a whole potato grows best of all. But many a desperate housewife has planted potato peelings that have eyes in them and gotten a fine crop of potatoes.

What kind of potato? There are basically two kinds—reds and whites. The whites winter-store best and bake best. The reds have the nicest taste when they are new potatoes and you eat them boiled. So I like to make early plantings of red potatoes for eating out of the garden and then plant white potatoes for winter storing. I think you're best off storing potatoes for either eating or planting on the dirt floor of your root cellar covered with dirt. Then come planting time plant most of the potatoes you have left. They won't look near as nice as they did when you put them there but they will grow new potatoes and that's the important thing. As you read seed catalogs you'll also discover there are early varieties and late varieties. If you plant an early variety early in the spring you'll have new potatoes mature and on your table sooner. Plant early potatoes as soon as you can get the ground worked, January in the extreme southern states, May in the cold states. "Late" potatoes don't work out in the South but do in the North because they are your best for storing—the later you harvest the less time you are asking your potato to keep. So you plant late potatoes in the North like in late May or all through June or even July depending on your kind of growing season. You can figure a peck of potatoes will plant 300 feet of row.

How to cut and cure for seed—Like I said before, you could plant 'em whole or you could plant peelings but the usual way to do it and the way we do it lies somewhere in between. We don't do the curing part here because our area has no trouble with potato diseases and our climate isn't generally very wet but in more southerly places, or soggy or sick, curing is a good idea. When you cut the potato make sure that each piece has at least one eye. Try not to cut through the middle of an eye because it may kill the sprout. You can get three, four or five squarish pieces out of an average potato. We like to have several good eyes on each chunk and that way you get less chunks out of each potato but hopefully more sprouts. To cure your seed let it just set around for 2 or 3 days until the fresh-cut surfaces have darkened and partially dried. That helps prevent it rotting in the ground. How much seed? Well, I think any family would want to plant at least 50 pounds.

To plant—There's more than one time-honored way besides just making a furrow and dropping your pieces into the bottom of it. That's the easiest way though to do a big field of potatoes. Make the rows 2½ feet apart or so. Put each potato piece down there 3 to 5 inches, on the shallow side if you have a clayey, heavy soil, on the deep side if you have a wonderfully sandy soil or are planting way before the last frost date. Then even if the ground freezes after you plant, as long as the freezing doesn't reach your seed potatoes they will be fine and will start growing as soon as the right time comes—which they can judge far better than you can. Space your seed from 6 to 18 inches apart, depending on how good your soil is and how cramped you are for space. I plant 'em 6 inches apart, I'm always trying to squeeze in just a few more plants. Plant with the eye pointing upward. In three or four weeks you'll be seeing the sprouts above ground.

If you want to hurry them up and your weather is warm, leaving the potatoes you'll use for seed lying out in the sun for a week or two before planting is supposed to help, but remember the green on potatoes is poisonous as are the sprouts. I've heard of a child dying from eating potatoes her dad had spread out in the yard to green up and sprout. The taste is so bad I don't see how anybody could be tempted but children will eat some strange-tasting things as every mother knows. So if you've got green or sprouting potatoes around be careful.

We plant the first crop of potatoes as early as we have the ground plowed and cultivated. Then we plant succession crops every few weeks until midsummer. By then every spare inch in the garden is in

potatoes including where we grew early crops like spinach, peas and greens. It is not a good idea to plant all your potatoes at once and early. Not if you want to store them through the winter. The late potatoes are easier to keep. So the first crops are for our household use through the summer. I leave them in the ground going out to dig every couple days or so.

I start my digging at one end of the first row and proceed systematically. That way I always have new potatoes which are the nicest and those left in the ground have the opportunity to keep on growing as long as they are willing and able.

Straw bed planting—This is an old time method that Mike likes because it simplifies the potato digging when harvest time comes. The potatoes grow fine in the straw and are easy to find and get out of it.

To plant the potatoes first dig a trench in your tilled ground with a spade. Make it around 8 inches deep. Great precision is not necessary, so dig it give or take some inches. Not too shallow though. Now in the bottom of the trench spread a layer of well-rotted manure unless you live in the South where this tends to cause potato scab. Next lay in your seed potatoes. Now cover with either dirt or straw. Or a little straw and then some dirt. If you don't have the manure they'll grow anyway. Manure is always good for the garden unless you get to unbelievable extremes so I put it on every excuse I get. Now give them a good soaking to get them started if you don't expect nature to do it for you.

Instant planting—This is one of Mike's methods too. (He likes finding easy ways to do things!) If your ground is sticky clay or needs manuring, the furrowing or straw bed methods will work better than this one. Go out into the garden with a box of seed potatoes, cut and ready to go, and a shovel. This is a good way to get in your very earliest potatoes. Force your garden spade straight down into the dirt, as far as you can get it if frost danger isn't past yet and you want them deep. Now lean forward on the spade handle until you've forced open a space in the dirt between the back of the spade blade and the dirt. Drop your seed potato in there, right into the open space you made. Pull the spade out, leaving the seed potato planted in the hole. Gently step on the ground with your foot to settle the dirt back again and walk to the next spot up your row where you're going to plant the next set.

To harvest—You can start getting potatoes before the plants are finished making them. You can dig up the whole plant and take everything it has or if you have nice loose or sandy soil or a straw bed you can just poke around until you find some potatoes near the surface. Gently get them out, firm up the soil around the plant again and the rest will keep growing. The main crop isn't ready until the leaves on the potato plants start to yellow or better yet the whole vine starts to wither. That will be about three full months from when you planted them. You could let them stay in the ground as long as a month but they should be dug before ground freezing time arrives. Be sure you make your potato digging a smooth well-planned operation that gets them from under the ground and into their dark storage place all in one day. Don't leave them lying out in the sunlight because remember that makes them taste awful and be poisonous in the peeling area and under it—everywhere they get that greenish tinge. Exposure to light, even if not direct sunlight, in storage will tend to have the same effect, though more gradually.

New potatoes—Fresh from the ground potatoes are a whole new eating experience if you haven't had them before. Delicious! Those tiny new potatoes are, I think, best and easiest served boiled in their jackets. Which can then easily be slipped off by the cook or you can eat them jackets and all. On young root vegetables in general a cloth, a scrub brush or especially one of those plastic orange Tuffy pads will do the job of getting off your garden dirt. Just scrub . . . a lot of the peel will come off with the dirt. It is exposure to the air that soon toughens the skin and makes it necessary to peel them off and makes them a hindrance to good taste. New potatoes will cook more quickly than ones that have been stored. You test for doneness with a fork, and if it penetrates to the center easily with a little pressure your potato is done. Boiled potatoes should be drained right away so they won't keep soaking up water and get mushy. Potato water is good for all kinds of things, gravy making, soup making, bread making and so you should save it.

Peelings—I've always got a slop bucket right under the sink and that's a good part of what the chickens and pigs live off of. If I didn't put something in it I'd have to feed them that much more store-bought food which would be more expensive. They get the peelings off of potatoes that have been stored long enough for them to toughen up and get that slightly bitter taste. There are people who think that's awful. They've heard that potatoes cooked with their skins are more nutritious than those cooked peeled. That may be true but if your family is growing a big garden you just aren't short of nutrition and personally I don't like the taste of potato peelings. I'm also always a little leery of getting one that may have accidentally had a chance to green up some and that's where the most greenness would be and that's going to taste even worse. But here's the voice of a reader who doesn't peel her potatoes to tell you how to do it that way. She's Celia Sorenson from Spokane, Washington:

"I've pretty much freed myself from potato peeling without making drastic changes in our own eating patterns. If you cook potatoes with fairly good skins whole, unskinned and unpricked in a small amount of water, the skin will split and loosen. Then you can remove it with your fingers and cut your potato to serve in chunks. As long as the skin can be scrubbed and pared clean you can make mashed potatoes without peeling too. Cook whole unskinned potatoes and press them through a ricer. Ricers cost about $2 these days. The skins are retained in the ricer's sievelike container, and the pulp comes out the holes. The riced potatoes are good as is or can be mashed with just a fork."

I've cooked more potatoes than any single other food item. I commonly fix them more different ways

too but my recipes are still all easy ones—bake, boil, mash, fry.

To bake potatoes you'll do better starting with a white potato. I hate to use foil at all but if you save it after each baking to be used again your conscience can feel better about it and it does make a nice potato. You get the potato real clean, rub it with butter, wrap it securely in the foil, bake at 350° until pokably tender. An underdone potato in Rocky Mountain talk is called "boney."

For *Mashed Potatoes* I cook the peeled potatoes until they are tender when pierced by a fork. Then drain off the potato water to use in making the gravy. Keep the potatoes on a very low heat for a moment if they are soggy. Add a lump of butter and a slosh of milk, less if they got soggy from overcooking. Mash thoroughly with a potato masher. Salt (and pepper if you want) to taste. Mound in a serving bowl, add a dash of paprika to the top for decoration and a dab of butter to melt in a hollow in the middle. Serve with gravy, available for the members of the family to combine as they please. When I make the supper spuds I usually try to have some left over for breakfast. For hash browns the next morning hold out some whole ones before you start mashing and leave them in the refrigerator overnight.

Hash Browns—Put just enough margarine or other grease in the frying pan and shine it. Grate the cold boiled mashed potatoes into the pan and press it down flat. Let fry until crisp on the bottom and then turn and let crisp on the other side or if the layer is very thin fold over like an omelet.

Julia Reynolds wrote me from Galvin, Washington, a hint on making hash browns. She says, "After you grate them, rinse in a colander under cold water, drain well, and you will have hash browns, after they are fried, just like what you get in a restaurant."

If your leftover potato is mashed rather than whole, you can fry it plain. Or you can make *Potato Cakes* for breakfast the next morning. Mix 2 cups cold mashed potato, 2 beaten eggs and some chopped onion, green or otherwise, and a little chopped green pepper if you have it. Mix well. Make into patties, and fry.

My family loves *Homemade French Fries*. I use a Dutch oven (any heavy kettle will do) half full of lard or heated oil. (You can save your kettle full of lard and use it over and over again for such things as onion rings, fried green pepper rings, fried green tomatoes or zucchini squash. In either case, dip in egg batter, then in flour and fry until the coating is golden.) If the grease gets strong, fry some potatoes in it to clear the taste and strain through a dishtowel. It helps if you are butchering your own pork because then lard is free.

Work quickly with your potatoes to prevent them turning pink. Pare, cut into strips (the smaller the strips the more we like them) and dry inside a towel. Drop the potatoes into the hot fat. You can test the fat temperature by dropping in one. If it sinks like a stone and stays there, the fat isn't hot enough. When the potatoes all float and look golden brown, dip them out and drain on a towel or absorbent paper or in a sieve. Salt if you want and serve immediately. We have homemade catsup on the table to go with them.

An Illinois reader wrote me that she likes potatoes cut same as for French fries, coated with cornmeal and fried.

Potato salad is a great hot summer dish when you're busy with the garden and food preserving and don't want to be cooking. It's a good way to use up leftover mashed potatoes and it's a good old standby dish to take to a potluck dinner or some such. Basically it's a cold boiled potatoes and hard-boiled eggs, onions and mayonnaise dish but you can vary with celery chopped, diced pickle or olives or pimento, season with celery seed, dill, garlic powder, paprika.

Here's a recipe for *Potluck Potato Salad.* Boil 10 pounds potatoes and a dozen eggs. Cool and peel eggs and potatoes. Dice up 4 large onions and eggs. Separately stir together 2 quarts of your homemade mayonnaise with 6 tablespoons sugar, 1½ cups vinegar, 1½ cups water and salt, pepper, etc. for seasonings to taste. Mix potatoes and eggs with the dressing. Give it a good chilling and time for the dressing to soak into the potatoes before serving. A wonderful lady named Mohrine Comstock wrote me from Westminster, Colorado, that the secret of her great potluck potato salad is to add a pinch or more of horseradish and mustard to the mayonnaise.

Potato Chips (called "Saratoga chips" in the old days) are made by paring the spuds, then slicing into thin shavings with a vegetable cutter: Let them soak in ice water for an hour, drain, and dry in a towel. Have ready your heated deep fat and fry until they curl and are delicately brown. Put them in a wire frying basket to immerse in the fat and shake them as free of fat as possible before lifting them from the kettle, then put to drain on absorbent paper. Dust with salt. Don't have the fat too hot or too cold. Let it reheat between batches. You can make up a big batch and they will last 20 days or so. Keep in a cool, dry place and reheat in the oven until crisp before serving.

Potato Pancakes—This is a famous dish with many different versions. Margaret Larsen sent me this one from Fields, Oregon. It was her mother's recipe. "She had chickens and grew plenty of potatoes. My mother considered this a one dish meal and we always put warm applesauce or sour cream on top of the pancakes. Grate 4 medium-sized peeled potatoes and 1 large onion on your smallest-sized grater. (Do not blend in blender.) Add the yolks of 4 eggs that you have gotten ready by separating and 1 table-spoon or less salt. Whip the whites of the eggs and add them. Fry brown on each side, turning only once. Fry in a skillet that has a lid."

Potato Whole Wheat Bread—Sometimes in my Newsletters I have an impossible-to-find recipes section. Somebody asked me to help them find a recipe for potato rolls. This is one of the recipes that came in answer to her request and I love it. It's from Mary Endrizzi of Denver, Colorado. You'll need 2 cups leftover mashed potatoes, ¼ cup brown sugar, 2 teaspoons salt, 1½ cups warm milk, ⅓ cup shortening, 7 cups whole wheat flour, 1 package or 1 tablespoon dry yeast, ½ cup lukewarm water and 1 beaten egg. Stir sugar, salt and shortening into warm milk until dissolved. Dissolve yeast in lukewarm water, add to milk mixture. Stir in half of whole wheat flour, beat until smooth. Add mashed potatoes. Gradually add remaining flour, mixing well to form soft ball. Knead on lightly floured board until smooth and satiny. Place ball of dough in greased bowl and brush top with additional melted shortening. Cover, let rise until double in warm place. Divide into loaves; place in greased bread pans. Let rise until double in bulk and bake in 375° oven about 1 hour.

Harvesting for storage—The potatoes that aren't for immediate kitchen use we leave in the ground until fall. Actually anytime after the vines have dropped and died the potatoes have stopped growing and are ready to dig but they keep better in that hot weather in the garden. When it's starting to stay cool we get out and dig potatoes. Mike spades and I feel around in the loosened dirt with my hands to find and bring up all the loosened potatoes. The children pop them into burlap bags. The very small ones and the ones that have been accidentally cut go into a special cardboard box to come directly into the kitchen.

The small ones should be used first like new potatoes. If the skin is allowed to harden on them they will scarcely be worth the peeling and can just move on to the pig trough. The potatoes for the next few months can go into the basement and the potatoes for the months after that should go into a root cellar or a pit in the garden. Potatoes must *not* be allowed to lie exposed to the sun. This causes a disagreeable greening under the skin. They will keep a couple months really no matter what you do as long as they are in a halfway dark dry place. After that check occasionally to see how they are doing. If they start to sprout (which warmth and light will promote but sooner or later they will try it anyway) snap the sprouts off if you are saving them for eating. Otherwise plant them sprout and all.

Even if it's potatoes you bought at the store you should store them in a cool dark place where there is ventilation like in cloth bags or bins where air can get to them. They'll spoil way faster in an air-stifled plastic sack than they will keep the better way. If you do end up digging more potatoes than what you need for your immediate use during the heated part of the summer, don't store them in a damp place. They'll keep best covered with straw in a cool, shady outbuilding and then when cold weather comes along you can move them to your root cellar or a pit in the ground. Potatoes keep best very cool, like between 36°

and 40° but they are one vegetable that *must not* be allowed to freeze. A good outdoor pit for potatoes is the same one described under Cabbage. The basics are to dig your hole to 2 feet below the frost line (that means the depth to which it freezes and you hope you figured it right). Put in the potatoes, cover with straw, pile dirt over that. Lay a piece of tin over that and it will help keep them dry. In your root cellar the potatoes can be stored in wooden boxes, basket, any bin kind of thing or right on the dirt floor so long as they are protected from light. (A good root cellar is lightproof except when you are actually in there getting stuff in or out.)

To freeze, you have to cook the potatoes first. You can freeze boiled or mashed or French fried potatoes. The freezer life of French fried potatoes isn't very long though.

To dry—I don't think drying potatoes is very practical when they store so well root-cellar style but if you want to you've got to cook them done first. (Peel first or after cooking.) Then put the cooked potatoes (they can be nearly done, just a trifle on the firm side is best) through a potato ricer or some such to get shreds or cut into thin slices, spread on trays and dry until brittle. If you leave out the peeling your dried potatoes will have a weird flavor.

To can potatoes is an entry I've never seen in any book of directions but my mother used to make a canned meat stew and had plenty of potatoes and carrots in it as well as meat, a real instant one-dish meal. All you did was warm it up and boil the recommended 15 minutes with the lid off. So if you may can potatoes in a stew, obviously you could can them separately. That might be useful to somebody. To can stew follow directions for canning meat. Since meat requires more canning time than anything else the rest would be safe too.

Since I wrote that paragraph Mrs. Durland wrote me from Plano, Illinois, to ask me what to do with goose feathers (I wasn't sure) and to send me her recipe for canning potatoes. "First you boil the potatoes in their skins about 10 minutes, peel, pack and cover with boiling water. Leave ½ inch head space. Add salt, 1 teaspoon per quart, ½ teaspoon per pint. Adjust lids. Process. In pressure cooked pints 35 minutes, quarts 40 minutes with 10 pounds pressure or in boiling-water bath 180 minutes."

PUMPKINS and the big winter squashes grow more pounds of flesh per plant than any other garden thing I can think of. You can easily grow endless pounds of pumpkins and they store relatively well, too. The problem for me has always been finding a way to use them up besides letting the children make six jack-o'-lanterns apiece. Jack-o'-lanterns are the first priority of the pumpkin crop in this family. When we harvest them the nicest ones are set aside to be jack-o'-lanterns. The ones that are so blemished they wouldn't store go to the pigs. After the jack-o'-lanterns have run their course they go to the pigs too.

But if you don't have more pumpkins than you can think of ways to use you can cook them and eat them after they are done being jack-o'-lanterns.

Pumpkins are really in the squash family and just about everything about growing, harvesting, curing and storing big winter squashes also applies to pumpkins. You plant them in early midsummer after the weather is for sure past the last frost and has warmed up comfortably. They are one of those hill, vine spreading-type crops that are wonderful if you have the room to put them. Plant pumpkin seeds an inch deep, about four seeds to a hill and make the hills about 3 feet apart each way. They'll be mature in 100 to 120 days. For more details look under Squash, winter.

To save your own seed—Pumpkins will cross with summer squashes very easily. They are insect-pollinated and if you have the two growing within ¼ mile of each other crosses are likely. If you have both in the same garden crosses are certain. I've grown squmpkins myself and they are edible, if peculiar. Depends how adventuresome you are in your eating. Pumpkins are very hardy so if you've got the acreage you could put them way off by themselves or as far as I'm concerned summer squashes are very unnecessary and you could just skip them. You get more for your effort in pounds of tasty and nourishing food and ease of winter capability from pumpkins than from summer squashes in my opinion. Pumpkins do not cross with winter squashes so you're safe growing the two of them together. One variety of pumpkin will cross with another kind so pick your favorite and stick with it. Then make sure your pumpkins for seed are completely ripe and remove the seeds from the hollow, wash them thoroughly, spread out to dry. Or proceed as under Cucumber if you want to do a really professional job. If you keep them from unnatural heat pumpkin seeds keep their power to grow very well, four years easily.

To harvest and store, leave the pumpkins out there under after the first frost or longer. Then go out and cut the stems about an inch from the pumpkin. Leave them where they are for a couple weeks more during which time they will be "curing." Now you can sort them and bring them in. They shouldn't suffer freezing in storage. If they do freeze, as soon as they start to thaw they will also start to spoil and your only alternative would be to cook them all on the spot, mash and freeze or can. Pumpkins are best off spread on a shelf or on a floor where they don't touch one another. They tend to go bad at the point where they touch one another. If your regular checks show that you have a pumpkin with a bad spot just cut it out and cook up the rest of it. Pumpkins in storage don't keep as well as squash or root vegetables. After a few months, especially if they are in a relatively warm place, they will be coarse and stringy and will get more so as time goes on. So although they are quite easy to keep free from rot that is an argument for freezing or canning them when you get a chance.

To cook—Here's where people generally run into problems. Pumpkins are generally found in supermarkets only around Halloween. Most gardening books don't tell how to grow them and most cookbooks don't tell how to cook them. That's a shame because they deserve better. There's a cookbook out called *The Pumpkin Eater Cook Book* by Phyllis E. Strohsahl, 64 pages long, sells for $1.95, that will give you many ideas. Write Cucamonga Enterprises, P.O. Box AL-Cucamonga, California 91730, for a copy. But basically you start any recipe by boiling, baking or pressure cooking. Then mash and you've got the equivalent of the canned pumpkin that is called for in most recipes. Just substitute from there.

To boil, halve the pumpkin and scoop out the seeds and stringy fibers that are mixed up with them. Peel and cut what's left into cookable-sized pieces. Boil until tender. Takes a half hour or so.

To bake arrange your peeled pieces cut side down in some sort of baking pan. Takes about an hour at 400°. Then you scoop out the part that stayed soft and mashable.

In the **pressure cooker** cook the peeled pieces 15 minutes at 15 pounds.

Or you can make instant mashed pumpkin to use in your cooking in a blender by blending 2 cups cut-up pumpkin with ½ cup water until smooth. If you aren't going to use your puree in a recipe where it will get cooked you can cook it plain in a pan but you'll have to stir constantly to keep it from burning.

Pumpkream Pie—It was a red-letter day for me when this one came in the mail! Esther Shuttleworth, the mother of that famous editor of the *Mother Earth News*, sent it to me. Here are her directions: Mix together 1 cup granulated sugar, 1 pinch salt, 1 teaspoon cinnamon, ¼ teaspoon cloves, ¼ teaspoon nutmeg. Beat in 2 eggs—then add 1 cup well-cooked-down (cooked-dry) pumpkin. Add 1 cup thick cream or whipping cream. Bake 20 minutes at 425°. Reduce that to 375°. Bake until it raises up, then makes small cracks around the edge. (Bake in an 8-inch pie pan which will be *full.*) Thank you, Esther, I really feel honored that you wrote me and shared that recipe. That reminds me of another red-letter day. I answered the telephone and a lady from California was there wanting to order a hardcover copy of the book for her grandchildren. The address she gave me was "Marian Anderson . . ." I said, "Marian Anderson, the great singer?" And she said "Yes!" She had a strong, lovely voice just talking over the telephone and was a thoroughly enjoyable lady to talk to.

Ivy's Pumpkin Pie from Scratch—Ivy Isaacson lives in Kendrick and has helped me a lot with the book mimeographing. I got a request in the mail for a pumpkin pie recipe from scratch and Ivy offered hers. Here it is for everybody: Cut pumpkin in pieces, peel and cook in small amount of water. Drain well, mash and put through strainer. Line a 9-inch pie pan with plain pastry. Set oven at 450°. Mix 1½ cups of your cooked and strained pumpkin, ⅓ cup brown sugar, ⅓ cup white sugar, 1 teaspoon cinnamon, ½ teaspoon ginger, ¼ teaspoon nutmeg, ½ teaspoon salt, 2 eggs slightly beaten, 1½ cups milk, ½ cup cream or evaporated milk. Pour into pie shell. Bake 10 minutes, then lower heat to 300° and bake until firm (about 45 minutes). For spicier filling add ¼ teaspoon cloves.

Cellar-type winter storage—Basically same as squash. Look under Squash, winter. Should be dry, above ground, frostproof, like in rows on shelves not touching one another. Be sure and cure them before putting into storage.

To freeze, wash, remove seeds (you can save them for seed or for snacks; see Seeds section), cut pumpkin into pieces and cook until soft in boiling water. Or steam in a pressure cooker. Or bake in the oven. Then remove the pulp from the rind and mash it. Package and freeze. There really isn't a good way to cool it but if you don't freeze too many pounds any one day the freezer can handle the cooling adequately. I really like this mashed pumpkin served as an occasional yellow vegetable. I merely thaw and serve with butter and seasoning. You could use it in pie or add to bread dough, too.

To can, cut into chunks and then peel the chunks. Cut the peeled chunks into smaller chunks and boil in the least water you can get away with. Then mash with a potato masher when tender or put through a rotary colander or mash through a sieve. If you don't have time to make pureed pumpkin you could just pour your hot cubed pumpkin into the jars and process it that way. Pack the pumpkin hot. Put on lids and process at 10 pounds pressure, 60 minutes for pints, 90 minutes for quarts.

To dry is not new under the sun—the pioneer Americans dried pumpkins a lot.

The pioneer method was generally to slice the pumpkin around in circles, scrape out the seeds and strings, peel it and let the circles hang in the air out of direct sunshine until they dried. Now the pumpkin is generally cut into smaller pieces like quartered, seeded, peeled, cut into 1-inch strips, and those cut ¼ inch thick. But that's a lot of slicing and you can dry bigger pieces like the pioneers did. Or you can shred the pumpkin and have smaller pieces easier. Dry until tough. Big hunks of dried pumpkin or small store well in a bag, take a long time to cook up (like several hours) but are fine eating.

RADISHES are the vegetable children love to grow because they're so easy. They're the one that spring-starved fanatics get out and plant because they're early and quick—you'll have the first ones to eat maybe as soon as three weeks after planting. They probably get more loving attention than they are worth foodwise. But they are useful to help mark your carrot rows. And you can plant them with parsnips to help those frail creatures break through the soil. They have to be pulled and used promptly when they reach their prime which is soon gone, leaving radishes too pithy and soft to be very good. You can preserve them by drying or canning or cellar style. There are many different colors and sizes but the usual sort is red and short rooted rather than long. You can plant them as soon as you can stir the soil. Poor soil or dryness slows up their growth and may get you tough roots that are too hot. There are winter varieties meant to be planted in the fall. Plant ½ inch deep, sort of an inch apart only they'll end up closer because the seed is so small and hard to control, and if you're cramped for space make your rows as close as a foot. Since they don't last long, if you want a steady supply of radishes you'll have to make successive plantings every two weeks or so, or else plant a combination of early maturing and late maturing varieties. You can find them with maturing dates anywhere from as little as 20 days up to as long as 50. Radishes like cool weather and will do best before the real heat is on. The white varieties tend to be milder and stay crisp longer if you can get used to the idea of a radish that isn't red and round. Winter radishes should be planted in midsummer. You can store them by leaving them in the ground, well mulched, or between layers of moist sand in a box or tub. Winter radishes are better cooked than the summer ones.

To save your own seed—Radishes are insect-pollinated and will cross between varieties so only have one kind in flower at once. Radishes that are left in the ground past their prime will soon send up a stalk, flower, then form seed pods. Let the seed pods develop, ripen and dry. If the stalk looks fragile you could stake it to keep from losing the seed if it fell over on the ground. Harvest the seed pods by breaking off the stalks. Don't open until you can rattle the seeds around in the pod. If they aren't dry enough to rattle continue drying the pods in a shady, airy place out of direct sunlight. Once they are dry enough to rattle you can open the seed pod, spread out the seeds from inside and continue drying them. When the seeds are completely dried you can store them in an envelope or whatever you want. Remember to mark the variety of radish, year you saved the seed, and store in a dry place. Radish seeds will live in storage five years or more.

Raw radishes to eat—My family enjoys occasional raw radishes, especially the first few batches. For the first exciting appearance of radishes at the table I go all out and make radish roses.

To make radish roses, choose round radishes without blemishes. Wash. Trim off the roots and part of the stalk—leave a few of the best-looking short leaves on. With a sharp knife, starting at the root end, peel the red skin down. Make about five of these "petals." Once you have the knack the petals will open right out as you peel—the trick is to get them the right thickness and width. Experiment!

Radishes are also good sliced thin in a tossed salad. Or grated.

You can add sliced raw radish to your cucumber or tomato sandwiches on homemade or dark store bread.

Cathy Tate is a super gardener from Keller, Washington, who knows how to get the most from her radish crops. Rosy Radish Relish and the next recipe, Braised Radishes, were both sent to me by her.

Rosy Radish Relish—Makes 2½ pints. Use 3 cups stemmed radishes, 2 large ribs celery, 1 large mild red onion, 2 teaspoons salt, 1 cup sugar, 1 tablespoon mustard seed, 2 tablespoons dill seed, ½ teaspoon celery salt and 1 cup cider vinegar. Put the radishes, celery and onion through the coarse blade of a grinder or chop them finely. Mix with the remaining ingredients and allow to stand for 3 hours. Bring to a boil in a large pan and cook 10 minutes. Pour into hot jars, leaving ½ inch head space. Seal and process in a boiling-water bath for 20 minutes.

Braised Radishes—Two tablespoons butter, 2 cups sliced radishes, 1 bouillon cube, ¼ cup hot water, ⅛ teaspoon ground marjoram, salt. Melt butter in saucepan, add radishes and cook 5 minutes. Stir frequently. Dissolve bouillon in hot water and add to radishes and simmer 3-4 minutes. Add marjoram and serve as a hot vegetable. (I use the same amount of beef broth.)

Creamed Radishes—If you're having trouble using up your radishes (I don't know of any families that could eat all the radishes they could grow) make Creamed Radishes. Wash, pare and slice the radishes to get about 1½ cups. You can do this also with your large strongly flavored radishes. Boil until tender. Make a white sauce from 2 tablespoons flour, 2 tablespoons fat, 1 cup milk, salt and pepper. Mix the sauce with the radishes and serve.

To can—Follow directions for turnips.

To dry, cut radishes thin, dry until brittle and store. Good broken up into small pieces and scattered over a salad. Or you can use them like "chips" for dipping.

RHUBARB is filed in the Sweets chapter. That may sound weird because rhubarb is some of the sourest stuff around but I figure the only way anybody eats it is with so much sweetening you might as well face it and call it a sweet.

RUTABAGA—I just love rutabagas! I love them best of all peeled and eaten straight like an apple. They taste good and are really good for you. If you don't know about rutabagas they are sort of a yellow turnip, milky flavored. They take about 90 days to mature. The earliest varieties of turnip take 35 days to mature, later ones take 60 so you see foot for foot in your garden you'll probably wait a month longer for rutabagas than if you had planted turnips there. Plant ½ inch deep and generally raised in the same way that you would a turnip. Except that rutabagas need more room to grow per plant than turnips and take longer to reach maturity. They don't like hot weather and are naturally a northern vegetable. You plant them in early spring and figure on your crop by fall and they'll probably do well for you unless you have a very hot summer. Like any root vegetable they like a well-worked-up, well-compost-manured soil. They are pretty tough about frost and so you should figure on leaving them grow until at least after your first frost unless you're hungry in which case you can go get them sooner. You save rutabaga seed same as for beets or turnips—they're a biennial too. Store them in an underground pit or root cellar same as turnips. Rutabagas have an odor in storage that celery will pick up so those two shouldn't be stored together for very long. Rutabagas store very well in any cool darkness, cellar, pit or a big box with sand or dirt in it. Cook and eat similar to turnips, only they take longer to cook. If, in the end, you have a crop and decide you don't like them, feed them to your cows, goats, etc. They will love them and the rutabagas can provide a substantial part of their winter nourishment.

To freeze, harvest rutabagas while very young, small and tender. Remove tops, wash, peel and cut into ½-inch cubes. Scald 2 minutes, cool and package. To cook just thaw and mash and serve with seasoning.

SALSIFY is also called oyster plant or vegetable oyster in old-time cookbooks. It is very like parsnips to grow and has all the same problems. The part you eat is the long tapering white root which when boiled, mashed and fried has an oyster flavor and that's where it gets its nickname. The roots at maturity are about 8 inches long and an inch thick. They don't have their best flavor until they've been through frost, though the youngness, freshness and tenderness of smaller ones right from the garden can make up for that. Salsify in southern gardens is planted in summer to get a winter crop. It takes 120 to 150 days of growing season. But if you plant before June or July in a warm climate you may get seed instead of root even though it is technically a biennial. In more northern gardens you can plant in the spring for it to grow all summer. Plant ½ inch deep, 2 inches apart, thin later to 6 inches apart. In a climate that salsify likes you may have a problem of overabundance if you let it get away from you and do some self-seeding—then it deserves the name of weed.

To cook—If the salsify is garden fresh just scrub the roots, scrape them and boil tender in a covered pan until they are fork tender (10 to 20 minutes). Old or store salsify can use a tablespoon of lemon juice in the boiling water to keep the roots from turning dark. You can cook the fresh slender leaves by any cooked greens recipe. After your salsify is boiled tender, drain, season with butter, salt and pepper and parsley if you have it. Or cover with a white sauce.

Quick Salsify Fritters—Mash cooked seasoned salsify and shape into cakes. Roll the cakes in flour and brown in butter.

Mock Fried Oysters—Wash, trim and cook a bunch of salsify in boiling salted water until tender. Drain and scrape off the skin. Mash. (If it is stringy you could put the mash through a colander.) For every 2 cups of mashed salsify add 1 teaspoon flour, 1 tablespoon butter, 1 beaten egg and salt and pepper. Take a spoonful and shape it into the size of an oyster. Dip the "oyster" in flour or cracker crumbs and brown on each side in the frying pan in butter.

Winter storage—You can store salsify the same as beets, carrots or parsnips but out of the ground it has a tendency to shrivel. The best way of all to store

salsify is right where it grew. It can last out the winter right out in the garden. But put a mulch over it like a bunch of straw. That's to keep the ground from freezing so hard you can't dig up your salsify. Or if you're leaving and want to take your salsify with you, dig up the roots, leave 1½ inches of stalk on them, store between layers of damp sand in a root cellar.

SPINACH—Look under Greens in this chapter.

SQUASH, SUMMER—First of all I've got to explain what's what among the many plants called squash. Summer squash and winter squash unfortunately share the name squash which results in a lot of confusion since they are generally listed together in gardening books as if they were varieties of the same thing. They are *not* and there are really radical differences in the way you grow, cook and preserve them. Because of the publicity the zucchini variety of squash has received, lots of people think that "zucchini" means summer squash and the summer squashes are all just varieties of zucchini. That's wrong, too. Zucchini is one of the many summer squash varieties. There is the dark green zucchini summer squash, and then there is white or yellow or the striped vegetable marrow and scalloped pattypan squash (or "white bush scallop" or "cymling"), cocozelle, yellow crookneck, yellow straightneck and so on.

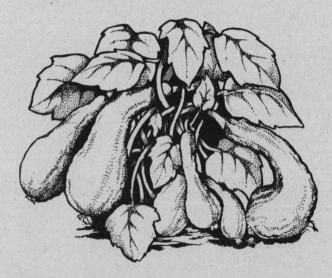

Summer squashes are prolific!—Especially zucchini! Even for small children it will grow and without fail it will bloom abundantly and produce abundantly. If you don't know about zucchini in particular and summer squash in general they can embarrass you with that abundance. Summer squash is a "low-calorie" vegetable and to me that means it's kind of an interesting extra to serve but not a staple that I could depend on to keep my family from starving. To me summer squash is not very exciting tastewise unless it's cooked with a bunch of other good things in which case you're tasting *them* and not the summer squash. Two plants would probably be enough for a small family, four plants provide some to give away to friends, eight plants give you a winter's supply.

If you plant a whole package of zucchini seed, alas! Prolific is hardly the word. Overwhelming seems more like it. It will grow and grow and grow. There will be no way to eat up or use up or give away all that summer squash. Desperate friends will be trying to give you some. We grow it for pig feed. But if you've never grown zucchini do so once at least for fun. It will be a new kind of trouble for you trying to figure out what to do with so much food. Pick your zucchini small. Then you'll be spared wondering how to use the extra 3 pounds that will grow if you leave it on the vine a few days longer. If you're desperate and your zucchini is still reproducing (which it will do as will all the summer squash as long as you keep picking and frost doesn't arrive) you could quit watering them or let them grow the last fruits for a seed crop or attack the plants with an ax screaming.

Climate and soil—I never heard of a place you couldn't grow summer squash. The longer the growing season, the longer they bear. In 40 to 55 days you have your first young summer squash ready to eat. There is no point in starting them indoors and transplanting because they can't take having the roots disturbed. Summer squashes want warm soil, well past frost, to be planted and warm weather to grow in. They like well-manured-composted soil and wood ashes. The weeds should be kept down.

To plant—There are so many different varieties, different in habits and requirements that this is one case you better just do whatever the package says, the first time anyway. But don't plant zucchini hillstyle. Plant in rows, 1 to 2 inches deep, and give your zucchini plants 4 feet between plants by thinning because they are going to get *big*.

To harvest—You'll have the tastiest, tenderest eating if you harvest them very young, not more than 4 to 6 inches in diameter for the kinds that grow wide, not more than 6 to 8 inches long for the kinds that grow long. The skin ought to be so tender that you can easily press your fingernail through it. As long as you keep picking your plants will keep producing. If you leave them on past the stage I described they get much bigger, the skin gets tougher and the seeds get big and tougher too. But they are still edible.

To save your own seed is practically impossible unless you live on a desert island. The problem is that pumpkins and squash are insect-pollinated and cross very easily. All pumpkins and squash and cushaws and gourds belong to one of the four species of the genus *Cucurbita*. Therefore to save seed you must plant only one variety from each of the following species:

Cucurbita pepo—All summer squash, crooknecks, cocozelles, zucchini, acorn, Delicata, Benning's, Green Tint, Vegetable Spaghetti, common orange Halloween pumpkins, ornamental gourds and two Japanese varieties, Hyuga Black and Kikuza White.

Cucurbita maxima—All Hubbards, giant types of pumpkins such as Hungarian Mammoths and Big Macs, Buttercup, Boston Marrow, Delicious, Turban and three Japanese varieties, Green Hokkaido, Orange Hokkaido and Red Kuri.

Butternut and the cushaws are in the other species. For this information I'm indebted to Kent Wheely, RFD 2, Princeton, Missouri 64673, who coordinates a wonderful organization of amateur seed savers called True Seed Exchange. New members welcome.

So when it comes to saving your own seed the odds are that somebody within ¼ mile (the approximate distance you need to safeguard your variety's seed purity) is probably raising pumpkins or another variety of squash. If you want to try anyway let the chosen fruits get thoroughly huge and ripe and then proceed by the directions under Cucumber. If you can get a good crop of pure seed, plant anything you want for the next five years. Your pure line seeds will keep the ability to grow that long or longer.

To cook summer squash that has been harvested young, frying, baking or steaming gives you better results than boiling because they are mostly water anyway. You don't have to peel 'em unless they're old and tough skinned. Try slicing the squash and cooking in a little butter for 10 minutes. Or boil in a little water until tender and then drain, season with butter and serve. Or mash, season and serve. Or slice, dip in egg batter, then flour and French fry. Or fry in butter in a pan with chopped onions. But if you want to get really serious about summer squash, especially zucchini, you'll need more recipes than that. There are two absolutely wonderful garden-to-table cookbooks in print, both of which have very good zucchini sections and recipes for every other vegetable too. One is *The Home Garden Cookbook, from Seed to Plate* by Ken and Pat Kraft, published by Wilshire Book Company, 12015 Sherman Road, North Hollywood, California 91605. The other is *The Kitchen Garden Book* by Stringfellow Barr and Stella Standard, published by Lancer Books, 1560 Broadway, New York, New York 10036. For an entire book of zucchini recipes try *The Zucchini Cookbook* by Paula Simmons, published by Pacific Search, 715 Harrison Street, Seattle, Washington 98109.

Mary Ann Shepherd wrote to me from Del Mar, California, about her zucchini: "Last year we really over-programmed on zucchini and one of our house guests reported that when you visit Shepherds you have zucchini for breakfast (bread), lunch (raw in salads and pickled), dinner (as a vegetable—grated and stir fried with mushrooms) and for dessert (chocolate cake) as well as for canapés (raw sticks marinated in salad dressing or raw sticks to dunk with) and she expected the furniture to be made from it this year!" Here are some things I do with it and some good recipes that have been sent to me.

To bake, slice summer squash into ½-inch slices put into a baking dish. Dot with butter, sprinkle with salt and finely chopped onion. Add just enough water to cover the bottom of the dish. Cover and bake until tender. Optionally you could add some cream at the last.

Cheese Summer Squash—Cut maybe 9 little squashes in half and steam in water 10 minutes. Then lay into a buttered ovenproof dish, sliced sides up. Sprinkle with salt and ½ teaspoon sage. Dot with butter. Sprinkle about ½ cup grated Cheddar cheese over the top and put in 325° oven until cheese is melted.

Sour Cream Summer Squash—Cut about 2 pounds of squash into 1-inch slices. Sprinkle them with ½ teaspoon salt. Let stand an hour and then drain. In a frying pan sauté squash in margarine or oil with ½ cup chopped onion. When squash is tender, add 1 cup sour cream mixed with 4 teaspoons flour. Bring to a boil. Sprinkle with paprika and serve.

Baked Squash Soufflé—This one was sent to me by Arlene Jackson of Santee, California, who is a famous cook in her town and justly so! Boil 3 or 4 zucchini squashes until tender. Mash. Brown 1 diced medium-sized onion in margarine. Add onion, grated cheese, 2 or 3 eggs, beaten, pinch of garlic, and salt and pepper to taste to mashed zucchini. Mix and pour into casserole. Dot with butter and, if desired, grated cheese. (Parmesan and cracker meal.) Bake about 1 hour at 350°. Slivered almonds browned in margarine can be added to topping.

When somebody tells you zucchini is Italian soul food, that's OK. But when they try to tell you the zucchini came over on the boat with Columbus they've got the direction just exactly backwards. Same story as with the Irish potato that actually started with the Incas in Peru. Both summer squash and winter squash are native Americans that migrated to Europe. But when you hear that fried squash blossoms are a traditional American Indian delicacy it's true! And the squash blossoms you should use are summer ones, not winter ones, because those are the ones you can best spare.

There are two kinds of blossoms on your zucchini plant in bloom. The bright yellow ones are girls and they have little squashes developing under the flower. The male blossoms are yellow, on long upright stems. Pick male flowers and you won't be depriving yourself of any squashes. This recipe is from Jan Franco of Hamden, Connecticut, who also wrote me these beautiful lines: "I used to work in a library and I love books and used to buy them when possible—being especially prone to succumb to anything with 'complete' in the title. Well, my husband says this is the first 'complete' book I have (*Old Fashioned Recipe Book*) because it's the only one that includes the most important topic: *the Lord*, in addition to all the self-sufficiency information, etc. After all, no matter how self-sufficient we may be, we're all dependent on Him.

"Squash Blossom Fritters—Pick a dozen or so male flowers. Pick at a time when the flowers are open to make sure there are no bees trapped inside. Make a batter from: 1 egg, ¾ cup whole wheat flour (or white), 1 teaspoon baking powder, a little milk. Coat the flowers with batter and fry in a little oil until lightly browned. Yum. Also can be frozen—warm in oven. We use zucchini or pattypan flowers. An Italian favorite!"

To cellar-store, let the squashes grow as big as they will, pick and store in a cool place. They'll keep a couple months or so.

To can, don't peel, just cut off the ends. Cut into ½-inch slices. Bring to a boil. Pack hot with hot water. Put on your lids. Process pints 30 minutes and quarts 40 minutes at 10 pounds pressure. I think you're

better off, though, just enjoying summer squash in season because it really isn't too good dried, frozen or canned.

It's easy *to freeze* summer squash. Just peel, let boil about 3 minutes, cool and package. Works fine with great huge summer squashes just as well as with little ones. I don't freeze more than a couple bucketfuls though because there just isn't that much desire for it in my family.

To dry, slice ⅛ inch thick and turn as necessary while drying so they won't mildew. These dried zucchini slices (or other summer squashes) are good used with dips instead of potato chips (and better for you!). Try them with a yogurt-based dip. Yellow straight-necked squash is another variety that makes good dipping material.

SQUASH, WINTER—You never use winter squash green and small, the way you do summer squash. You let winter squash thoroughly ripen on the vine. Winter squash tastes way different too. It's a very nourishing vegetable, different from summer squash that way too, and most resembles sweet potato in taste, texture and uses I think. Gardeners in other places seem to like to grow 5-pound Butternut or Buttercup squashes and think a 15-pound Hubbard a really big squash.

But 75- and 80-pound Marblehead squashes are commonplace up and down the Potlatch River valley. Several local farmers grow them commercially. I can't find Marblehead squash in any seed catalog. Maybe they figure you just don't want that much squash. But you can mail-order the seed from our local seedsman—Brocke and Sons, Kendrick, Idaho 83537. The Banana squashes get quite large too but not like that. Those big squashes are stored here in special barns where a fire is kept burning all the time in cold weather so they won't freeze until markets open up for them. Then they are cut into big chunks and trucked in a special insulated truck to market. The nearest other big-sized squash growers I know about are near Great Falls, Montana, where there are Amish farmers. It takes a specially large portion of faith and God's help to be a truck farmer!

The big winter squashes are useful as winter food for people and also for animals, especially goats. If you can't raise grain you can winter your goats on stock beets, carrots and squash, along with just a little purchased grain and hay. Cows will use winter squashes for winter feed, too, so they don't go to waste. Rotted ones or bad spots when you are cutting them can go to the pig. They have to be cut before you give them to the animals. That is really a job. The longer they are in storage the tougher the peel gets. Smaller varieties like acorn dry up quickest. That's why for winter keeping to grow bigger ones is better. You can open the tough squashes by literally hammering a butcher knife through the shells. Always cut lengthwise.

Among the small winter squashes I prefer the acorn and we grow a lot of them. It's the family's favorite eating squash. The trouble with acorn squashes, though, is that they commence in about two months of storage to get yellow and hard as rocks and rather dried up inside, though the flesh is still edible. For the next four months big squashes like Marblehead can be eaten fresh with the ones going bad being constantly supplied to the pig. After that frozen squash is the best thing. You can freeze squash in the late fall and all winter at your leisure.

On hill crops in general—Winter squash, some kinds of summer squash, and watermelons are your hill crops. They all love heat and can't be planted until the soil has really warmed up, around June 1 here. Hill crops are not very practical in a small garden because they are all space hogs, the small cucumber least so, the huge winter squashes that grow in rows 12 feet apart with 6 feet between hills the most so. Hilling is not so important in light soil but I'd do it anyway to help you see where you planted until the plants get going. Don't hill in extremely sandy soil because a hill of sand dries out too fast and your plants will probably die. In clay-type soil hilling really helps your plants grow. Here is how Mike makes a hill. He stands about where he wants the hill with a hoe and hoes the topsoil toward himself in a semicircle to make a "hill" about 6 inches high and about 1 to 1½ feet in diameter.

Nowadays you can find squashes in either "bush" or "vine" (running) varieties. The bush kinds have smaller fruits but don't spread out as far, which makes them better in a small garden. The vine varieties are best I think if you've got the room to grow them. Plant bush varieties in hills 4 feet apart and rows 4 feet apart. Plant runners in hills 6 to 8 feet apart and rows 6 to 8 feet apart. The old timers plant the seed upright, with the eye down, and cover 1 to 2 inches deep. The ideal is to grow about four plants to a hill. You can plant more and thin down to four once they get going. It will be a long time before they need all that space between the rows. You can make use of it by growing early beans or peas between the squash rows and then take out the plants after your harvest in June or July. Your winter squash won't be ready to harvest before 80 to 120 days after planting.

The hill crops are all vine-type plants that need to spread out over the ground. There's no use asking them to climb a pole unless you're going to sling nets to support each big fruit that will grow and that's unreal. So you give them plenty of ground to spread out on. They all need weeding which is easy at first when they are still confined to the hill. Then you can come breezing through with a rototiller. After the vines start to grow you've got to be careful not to hurt the vine and will have to come in with a hoe working around those vines to get out the bad guys. Winter squashes all need lots of water, especially once they start making their fruits.

To save your own seed—Winter squash are insect pollinated and cross very easily. See the entry on seed saving under Summer Squash for details. Save seed from fruits that are thoroughly ripe by the directions for cucumber. Your seed should hold its germinating power five years.

My family's winter squash favorite is **Acorn Squash Baked in the Shell**. I cut them in half and then remove the seeds. In the center of each half squash I sprinkle a little brown sugar and butter. Or

some cooked bacon bits and butter. Or I mix ½ cup orange juice concentrate, ½ cup honey, salt, 2 tablespoons butter, ⅛ teaspoon nutmeg and divide this among the squashes. Or combine prefried crumbled bacon (4 slices say), ½ small onion, cut up and fried, ½ cup brown sugar, a big pinch of ground cloves and 1½ cups peeled apple sections. In any case the bacon bits are sprinkled on top the last thing and the filled squashes are baked in a loaf pan at about 350° until fork tender. Then they are served. Since it is hard for any child or most adults to eat an entire half acorn squash we carve them up at the table and serve the pieces, trying hard not to lose much of the filling in the process. Then just spoon the squash off the rind into your mouth.

You can use mashed squash in any bread-type recipe (including cookies, cake and muffins).

Squash Stuffing—Mix together 2 cups mashed squash, 1 egg, 1 cup each finely chopped onion and celery, 1 tablespoon chopped parsley, 1 green pepper chopped up, 2 tablespoons melted butter, ½ teaspoon sage and a dash thyme.

To can, use the directions for pumpkin, either cubed or pureed.

To freeze, cut winter squash open and remove the seeds and stringy fibers. Then either bake it or boil it in as little water as possible. You can also bake whole Hubbard squash. Takes about 2 hours. Then you cut, remove seeds. Whether you bake or boil your squash when it is cooked scrape the squash off the rind and mash with a masher or rotary colander or by pushing through a sieve. (Mashing with the masher is by far the easiest way.) Then package and freeze. There's no good way to cool it so just don't put more in the freezer than it can handle a day.

I thaw a bag of frozen squash in a frying pan with a little water, butter and honey. Mix well—serve hot. Substitute for sweet potatoes on Thanksgiving or any other time. Squash is way cheaper and easier to grow than sweet potatoes around here.

To dry, follow directions for drying pumpkin.

Shelf storage for winter squash (and pumpkin)— Getting winter squashes to store as long as possible is a lot like handling pumpkins. Let them stay on the vine until frost time. Then cut from the vine *leaving some stem* on the squashes and let cure in the field another few days. Now bring them into the warmest room in your house for the next stage of curing. At temperatures of 80° to 85°, the rind will harden and the fruit will heal its own surface cuts. But handle gently because it is the bruised places that rot first and the fruit can't heal itself of a bruise. After they have spent about 10 days around my wood stove in the kitchen they go up into the attic where they are spread out on newspapers. Wooden shelves would work fine for them, too. They shouldn't be touching each other. Fortunately, I have a very large cool attic.

A university handout says that at over 60° they get too dry and at under 50° they get "chilling injury." Everybody around here simply does it the best they can to keep them from getting clear frozen. They absolutely can't stand freezing and you have to be sure and get them harvested out of the field before they freeze there. Everybody's system is different. You just have to think about all the nooks and crannies of your own set of buildings and don't put the squash in the root cellar (not onions, either, or pumpkins) because dampness is really harmful and will soon result in rot. With luck some of our Marblehead squash harvested in October will still be fine in late March.

SWEET POTATOES—What vegetable is one of the most nutritious in the garden, is planted something like a potato, has vines like a morning glory, is stored, cooked, and tastes quite like winter squash and is not a yam? It's a sweet potato! The sweet potato comes in moist varieties which do best in the South and in drier kinds which do better up North. The moist southerners are often called yams but true yams are a tropical plant that really isn't grown anywhere in the continental United States except Florida. Sweet potatoes hate cold and love hot weather, but by starting them indoors they can be grown as far north as southern New York, Michigan and the Midwest. The part you eat is the root and so they prefer a loose, even sandy soil, or if you don't have that, soil that you have already deeply and well cultivated to make it easy for those roots to get fat when the time comes. They appreciate some manure-compost but it needs to be well stirred in and not overdone or the growth will go to vine instead of root. The roots grow underground in the last few weeks of the sweet potatoes' productive life. What grows above ground is a long trailing morning-glory-type vine. If you're short of garden room you can run the vines up a garden fence or even grow sweet potatoes in a window box (at least a foot deep and well watered) and let the vines trail down.

To grow slips—The sweet potato, like the white potato, is not grown from seed but from growth off the last year's crop of sweet potatoes. You can also plant from cuttings. You need to be able to count on four or five warm months to have success with sweet potatoes. They won't make it on a cool summer either. Where you can expect a safely warm long growing season you can cut sweet potatoes into small pieces and plant them just like that. They will grow sprouts that become sweet potato plants. The plants should be about 14 inches apart in the row and the rows 2½ feet apart. They need good drainage and it may work best for you to plant them in a ridge of dirt about 4-8 inches or so high. Once the plants are up and making vines you can remove pieces of the vines and plant them in other rows, and if you are gentle and pick a rainy spell for making and planting the cuttings they will each one grow roots and give you that many more sweet potato plants.

Where your sweet potato growing season is shorter you can get extra time by starting your new plants in a hot bed. Or you can buy plants from a local nursery or one of the mail order seedsmen that carry them. If you aren't growing from homegrown sweet potatoes the first year it is possible you won't have much success trying to grow slips from store sweet potatoes because some of them are treated to discourage sprouting. When you have homegrown sweet potatoes you plant from the ones that were on the small side. Start them in the hot bed about five or six weeks before your expected planting date (safely past last frost). Set them close together in sand or a fine soil, covered about 2 inches and keep them warm, like at least 75° and moist. As you get nearer transplanting time start giving the plants more cool air to get them hardened off for going outdoors.

At transplanting time each root should have sent up a series of sprouts that have already started developing root structures of their own. You carefully pull off each sprout that has roots of its own like that and plant 14 inches apart in the raised row same as you would pieces. For each 25 plants you get growing with success you may be able to harvest about 30 pounds of sweet potatoes. Once the vines get going they'll be growing every which way and putting down new roots wherever they take a notion to do so you won't be able to cultivate in there. Don't tear the vines loose from the ground if you can help it because that hurts the plant and decreases your yield.

To harvest—In the North where you need every growing day you can get you will probably want to let them grow until the vines are actually nipped by frost. Then dig your sweet potatoes. In the South you can leave them in there until a handy day for harvest. In Florida or Texas you can, if you want to, leave them in the ground until you actually want to bring them in the kitchen and use them. Choose a sunny, dry day when the soil is not wet to dig them. Dig with a potato fork very carefully from the side, not from on top. You want to dig carefully because cut or bruised sweet potatoes are the ones that won't winter-keep and will rot first. The same goes for handling them after they are dug—*gently*, so as not to bruise. Gently separate each sweet potato from its root. Let them lie on the ground in the sunshine for two or three hours to dry thoroughly. Now pack them in cardboard boxes, no more than one or two layers deep if you can help it and continue the curing process in a warm, well-ventilated room for several days. Best is from 80° to 90° for this stage, like near your cookstove or furnace. Handle them as little as possible during the curing process and afterwards. A really good cure can take as long as two weeks. Then store them for the winter around 45° or 55°. I know you can't do that exactly but as long as they are in a dry place and don't freeze you've done your best. Set aside ones that were cut or bruised during harvesting to use up first and keep an eye on the rest because they don't keep nearly as dependably as white potatoes do.

To cook, keep in mind that the best eating is from sweet potatoes that have been through the whole curing process. Then they can be boiled, baked, broiled, glazed, served with cream or made into croquettes. You're better off boiling or baking them first and then skinning them because they are hard to peel before cooking, you lose some of the sweet potato and they want to turn black. To boil just scrub, cover with water and cook until just tender. Get the skins off and serve with melted butter. To bake, scrub them, bake until tender (about an hour). If you wrap them a few minutes in a towel after they come out of the oven the skin will get tender and easy to get off.

To can, cook in boiling water or steam for 20 to 30

minutes. Peel and cut into pieces. You can dry pack them by just filling your jar with the hot pieces of sweet potato and putting the lid on or wet pack by covering the potato pieces with boiling water. In either case process at 10 pounds pressure 65 minutes for quarts.

To freeze, wash, cook until nearly tender in water, steam or bake in the oven, then peel, cut in halves and package or slice, or mash and package. Then freeze.

To dry is very like working with pumpkin. You can just peel and slice and set out to dry. Or boil the sweet potatoes until tender. Then slip off the skins, slice and sun-dry. Dried sweet potato can be cooked up to tenderness and used in puddings, pies, breads and so on.

SWISS CHARD—Look under Greens in this chapter.

TOMATOES are wonderfully versatile things—half fruit, half vegetable. At some stage or another you can make practically anything out of them. Green, yellow and red are stages of ripeness. First they are green, then briefly yellowish, then red. At least that was the way they were in the old days. But tomatoes are big business for the seedsman, the most popular home garden vegetable there is (beans are next most popular). They easily develop new varieties and hybrids and as a result there are many, many kinds to choose from. One seed house was carrying 95 different tomato varieties last time I counted. You can have them in different colors when ripe—red, yellow, orange, pink, green, white; supersized 2-pound tomatoes, or small as a currant; sweet tasting or sour; in dwarf bushes a few inches high; "tree tomato" or in a vine-type climber that can make it up to a second-floor window; you can get varieties quick to mature, or slow or anything in between; any sort of shape that's a variation on times or procedures; and the usual choice of standards versus hybrids if you are considering saving your own seed. My choice is a standard, red, average-sized and -shaped high-acid type.

If you've never eaten anything but store tomatoes you truly don't know what you've missed. There is a world of difference in taste between a garden-raised,

vine-ripened tomato and the store tomato which is picked green so it won't bruise in shipping or spoil before it gets to the purchaser. Maybe that's why so many people grow their own. Or maybe it's because they are so easy to raise and produce so generously. I got a letter from a lady who lives in the city and in one year grew over 300 pounds of tomatoes (organically) in a 12 x 16-foot plot. You can grow tomatoes anywhere you have a warm summer with some 60° nights in August. Various varieties will give you fruit anywhere from 55 to 90 days from date of transplanting to the garden. The quickest-to-maturity varieties don't grow as big and don't get as tasty as the more leisurely ones. Tomatoes aren't very picky about their soil except they want it well cultivated and loose and with some nourishment in it but mainly they want all the sunshine they can get and plenty of water. Too much manure or any nitrogen-type fertilizer makes them run to leaves instead of fruit.

To plant—If you live in the southern part of Florida or Texas you can plant tomatoes right out in the place where they are to grow. Plant generously and then thin to the best ones for your crop. In somewhat more northerly but still mild wintered areas of the South you can start the plants outdoors in cold frames during cool weather and then transplant to your garden proper from there. In still colder climates than that, it will be necessary to start the plants indoors or in a hot frame and then transplant them to your garden when all danger of frost is over. It's easy to raise tomato plants from seed and they transplant without difficulty. The two pitfalls in tomato planting are getting too many and starting too early.

One ounce of tomato seed might produce 3,500 to 4,500 plants. I didn't count 'em. I read that in a book. But I do know that practically every spring tomato-from-seed growing friends of mine are hitting me up to please take a few dozen plants, or maybe a few hundred? Because they accidentally got way too many started and can't bear not to see them have a chance to come into production. Even 25 plants would give you a good crop of tomatoes with lots to put up for the winter and some for the neighbors too, if you have good soil, plenty of water and give them room. With 100 plants you can become a truck gardener and have a crop to sell. A half dozen plants gives you a good summer's eating.

Just exactly how many is right for you depends on how much room you have in your garden, how large your family is and how hard you're willing to work at putting them up for winter. You'll have to grow them a few summers to have those answers.

The other pitfall is to start tomatoes in the house too *early* in the spring. Planting seeds is such fun and tomatoes are so mouth-watering to think about . . . but if started too soon they will be tall and spindly plants that actually will be slower going into production out in the garden than if you have transplanted them at a younger stage in life. So don't start the seed until four weeks before you expect your last spring frost (or six to eight weeks before if you can't help yourself).

First get your dirt ready (one-third peat, one-third

sand, one-third garden dirt is a good combination—you can sterilize it in the oven at 180° for 45 minutes if you are worried about disease or bug problems in it). Put your seedbed dirt into shallow boxes with drainage holes on the bottom or into small growing pots or big tin cans with drainage holes (or small ones). Dirt should come up to about ¼ inch below the rim of the container. (Incidentally, these are good directions for most of the seeds you may want to start indoors.) About two hours before planting moisten your seedbed dirt well. Plant tomato seeds ¼ inch deep, 2 inches apart. Cover with newspaper, plastic or glass, leaving a small opening on a corner. Keep in a place at least 70° warm because that is the temperature that coaxes tomatoes, a tropical plant in origins, to come out. When the dirt feels dry to your touch water with a fine spray. When you can see seedlings, take off that cover and move the containers to a cooler room where they can have lots of light. Water regularly but try not to wet the leaves while you're doing it.

To transplant—When the seedlings have made it to 2 inches tall you transplant them to larger quarters like individual pots. Or you can transplant to a cold frame to grow until the weather is suitable for them to go into the garden. Or you could start them indoors on the six to eight weeks before last frost date, then when the plants are about two or three weeks old transplant them into the garden and put a Hotkap over each (a commercial product like a little private paper greenhouse).

Water your tomato plants before transplanting them. The dirt should be wet enough to cling to the roots. Dig the hole you're going to plant into before you take out the plant from its former home, and put plenty of water into the new hole. Set the plant in right up to its leaves. It will grow new roots along the part of the stem that ends up underground and that will help it grow and be healthy. Set the plants from 2 to 6 feet apart depending on the variety and how much garden room you have to spare. Rows should be 3 (or more) feet apart. Crowded tomato plants are no bargain—they tend to produce less fruit. Once the plants are in the holes, firm the dirt over them by gently stepping on it.

Of stakes and weeds and such—There are different varieties of tomatoes but the typical one can be let to run over the ground like any vine plant in which case it will take up a little more garden room or it can be staked up. I let mine run but lots of people stake. To stake them, plant a stake as high as the variety you choose is expected to grow. Using an old stocking or rag or some such tie a strip firmly to your stake, then make a loose loop with the cloth around the stem of the tomato plant. If you squeeze the stem you'll really hurt the plant. One way or another you've got to fight weeds. You can put down a good 2-inch mulch or come through regularly tilling the ground between plants until the vines cover the ground and prevent it.

If you grow tomatoes you may have to cope with tomato worms. I haven't ever had them but I've had neighbors all around who did. I credit my chickens with the help. Chickens also like tomatoes though, so I have a struggle either way. Shutting up the chickens from midsummer on works. A tomato worm is about 1½ inches long. A very fat, hairless green grub with one horn sticking out its tail. They can't sting with it though folklore says they do and they can't bite but they are revolting to pick up with your bare hands. You find them deep in the plant and have to pick them off by hand going out early each morning with gloves and a can. Personally I'd rather cope with the chickens. A reader in Berwyn, Illinois, wrote me that she was taught to take a stick that would bend but not break and use it to make a sort of pincher to pick the green tomato worms off with.

Cutworms are another problem. You set out your plants, come back the next day and all that is left is a little stem sticking out of the ground. Mae Wallace (the Berwyn reader) says she uses cornflake boxes or other similar boxes and cuts around them to make four or five narrow collars. She makes them about 3 inches tall and puts the dirt to within an inch of the top of the band. The cutworms don't crawl over and your plant is spared. That's a good idea. Cheaper than putting an aluminum foil collar around the stem (2 inches above the ground and 2 inches below) which was the way I knew to handle them.

To harvest—Your tomatoes will probably begin to ripen sometime in August and should be picked as fast as they get ready. Pick at the red moment of ripe taste perfection and then you can all make fools of yourselves eating them. Really—vine-ripened tomatoes are so good! Don't pick them off the vines early to let them ripen indoors. That's just robbing yourself of the best. That time comes all too soon. Your tomato vines will keep bearing until frost kills them and you keep picking to eat, can, freeze, sell, give away . . .

Then before you anticipate the first frost go out and pick all the big nice green ones as well as the ripe ones and bring them in the house for storage. If the frost doesn't happen that night wait until you fear again (either listen to the weather forecasts or become a weather predicter) and then go out again, and get all the good tomatoes that have grown since you last picked and so on. After the frost has finally come you can harvest every tomato left on the vines, good or bad. Tomatoes that got touched by frost will have translucent spots. But deep inside the vines, if it wasn't too heavy a frost, there will be lots of good ones. Now pick every last tomato, good or bad. The bad ones can go to the pigs or chickens.

To save your own seed—Many of those tomato varieties are hybrids—don't save their seed. Tomatoes are self-pollinated so the chances of crossing are slight even if you are saving seeds from several different varieties growing in your own small garden. Choose the fruits you want to save for seed, the best fruits from the best plants and let them stay on the plant until well past what you would consider overripe for table use. Follow the fermentation directions under Cucumber, Saving seed. Tomato seeds will live four years with care, or more.

Our summer tomatoes are usually eaten fresh, mouthful by mouthful of the whole tomato, or are served sliced at meals. I trim off the top and bottom ends for the animal bucket. The rest I serve in thick slices, skin and all. We like tomato sandwiches for lunch. Just homemade bread, sliced fresh tomatoes from the garden and mayonnaise. Sometimes garden cucumber slices on it too.

To peel, dip the tomato in boiling water for 1 minute, then into cold water and you can easily slip off the skin.

Tomato flowerets for salads are made by choosing small tomatoes of equal size. Cut across three or four times not quite to the base. The tomato should open up like a water lily. You can put a little blob of mayonnaise in the center with a pinch of chopped parsley on top and use to garnish a mixed green salad or serve individually on a lettuce bed.

I can tomato juice, catsup, taco sauce and stewed tomatoes while they are in season. Literally bushels of tomatoes go through my canner. Then we have the green tomatoes all fall. The recipes for catsup and taco sauce are in the Sours chapter. If some of the stored tomatoes ripen up but aren't nice enough for slicing I make them into stewed tomatoes, too.

Stewed Tomatoes #1—Slice and peel into a cooking pan. Cook for 5 minutes and season with salt and pepper. You can also serve on slices of homemade bread toasted and cut in cubes or plain.

Stewed Tomatoes #2—To make a fancier stewed tomato in quantity for canning, try this. My neighbor Laura Rishling invented the recipe. She can also grow peanuts in Idaho, probably cotton too if she cared to, so you see she is pretty talented. She and her husband, Don, sell hundreds of dollars worth of garden produce every summer besides keeping their own two deep freezers full of literally their backyard.

Prepare 2 cups chopped onion, 2 cups chopped green pepper, 2 cups chopped celery and combine with 1 whole chopped garlic. Peel about 12 quarts of tomatoes. Cold pack by layers in each quart jar—a layer of tomatoes, then a layer of the vegetables. Fill to within 1 inch of top. Add 1 teaspoon salt and ½ teaspoon oregano to each quart. Put lids on and process in a water bath 45 minutes.

Italian Gravy—This was a recipe sent to me and it goes with that delectable-sounding menu in the Eggplant section. Fry 1 medium onion, chopped, 1 clove garlic, chopped and 2 tablespoons chopped parsley in 4 tablespoons olive oil until light brown. Add ½ pound ground beef, 1½ teaspoons salt and a pinch of pepper and cook until the meat loses its redness. Blend in 1 can tomato paste and 1 small can of tomatoes or puree, simmer for 1 hour, stirring occasionally. If the gravy is cooked even longer than this it will taste even better, about 1½ hours is better. Chicken, sausage, meatballs, pork chops, steak or wieners may be added to the gravy while it is simmering to make an even better taste. You can use leftovers. The more types of meat put in the gravy the better it will taste. If you add ½ teaspoon sugar it will counteract acidity.

Raw Tomato Spaghetti Sauce—Make the sauce at least 1½ hours before you're going to be serving. After you have your sauce all made and it has rested the 1½ hours to get the flavors well merged add your cooked spaghetti (well drained) and mix it up with the sauce and serve right away. To make the sauce itself, combine ½ cup olive oil, about a dozen medium-sized fresh tomatoes, sliced very thin, 20 leaves fresh basil, torn across, 3 cloves mashed garlic, a teaspoon salt, a pinch or two of freshly ground pepper. Serve with freshly grated cheese.

GREEN TOMATOES—You're going to have them. You can either eat them green or try to get them to ripen. The green tomatoes will keep green best around 45°. They would ripen best at around 70°. Either way they should be where the light is dim.

To store green tomatoes spread them out somewhere where they won't freeze and won't be damp. You will have to check them every couple of days, especially at first. The reason you don't want to pile your green tomatoes in a box is that when they go bad they do so suddenly and make a repulsive slimy mess. A bad apple in a box just quietly shrivels and gets fuzzy. A bad tomato collapses all over its neighbors spreading the infection. So spread them out so they don't touch each other and that way you can quickly remove any bad ones and the rest will be unaffected.

If a tomato has a translucent spot on it—that is where it did get a touch of frost and it will rot first from the spot. If you catch it soon enough you can just trim out the spot and use the tomato in a green tomato dish. The tomatoes in storage will gradually ripen. They will taste like store tomatoes rather than vine ripened. But you'll have homegrown tomatoes for Thanksgiving dinner, fresh sliced on the table, and that's worth a lot too.

I like **Fried Green Tomatoes** and it's the easiest way to fix them. Slice your green tomatoes into about ½-inch slices. Combine flour, salt and pepper in a pie tin and then dip the tomato slices in it to get both sides well coated. Fry them in hot shortening on one side and then the other. Serve hot and right away. Or you can use an egg and flour coating. A little basil in the flour is also good.

Edna Andrews wrote me from Ravensdale, Washington, that she freezes sliced green tomatoes and that way has fried ones all winter. "I slice them thin and put in cartons, any kind to fit your family size and add nothing to them and freeze. Sometimes a few on top look dark when opened but they still taste good. They lose some of their hardness but when fried crisp they taste just like fresh ones."

Green Tomato Mincemeat—This is a true old time way of using green tomatoes. I like this recipe sent to me by Rebecca Coufal of Addy, Washington. "This is just like the meat mincemeat. Len doesn't like mincemeat so if I were to use meat to make it I would be shot but he doesn't care much what I do with all the green tomatoes we end up with. Scald 10 pounds green tomatoes, then grind and drain 3 times. Mix with 2 quarts chopped apples, 2 pounds raisins, 1 pound chopped suet, 4 pounds sugar (honey), 2 tablespoons salt, 2 tablespoons cinnamon, 1 tablespoon cloves, 1 tablespoon nutmeg. Boil slowly for 2 hours or simmer in oven until you get around to it. Add 1 orange ground whole (peel, too) and pack hot into 1-quart jars. I use quarts as that is just enough for 1 pie. It makes 7 quarts—about as many times as I'll have an excuse to make mincemeat pie in a year's time."

Baked Green Tomatoes—Cut your tomatoes in about ½-inch slices and arrange half of them in the bottom of a greased baking dish. Over that make a layer of small toasted bread cubes (homemade bread), salt, pepper and butter dots. Put a second layer of green tomatoes, then a second layer of everything else. Finally sprinkle grated Parmesan cheese on top. Bake at 350° until tender.

Green Tomato Pie is a classic green tomato dish. Cover with water 2 cups chopped green tomatoes and bring to a boil. Drain. Add ½ cup brown sugar, 2 tablespoons vinegar, ½ teaspoon cinnamon, ½ cup chopped raisins, 3 tablespoons melted butter, ½ teaspoon salt, 3 cloves and ¼ teaspoon mace. Use a pie plate lined with a bottom crust. Add your mock mince made with the green tomatoes. Put on a top crust and slash to let steam escape. Crimp crust edge. Bake at 375° about 40 minutes.

If you could use still more green tomato recipes get *The Green Tomato Cookbook* by Paula Simmons, $2.95, published by Pacific Search, 715 Harrison Street, Seattle, Washington 98109.

To can tomatoes used to be simple. You just peeled them and cooked them. Filled your jars, put lids on and processed 15 minutes in a plain old water bath canner. Progress has brought us the new low-acid varieties of tomato. The easiest thing is to make sure that's not what you're growing. And can your tomatoes at a peak of ripeness because that is when they are most acid. Before peak ripeness they are less acid and when they get overripe they become less acid again. If you're not sure what you have you could pressure can at 10 pounds pressure for 10 minutes and that's what you do if you are canning low-acid tomatoes. Don't use cracked or moldy tomatoes for canning. Even if you plan on cutting off the moldy places. Because mold spores are probably all through the tomato. Mold growing in an acid uses up the acid and then botulism spores could take off and grow.

To freeze stewed tomatoes, peel the tomatoes, then cut into quarters and boil the quarters 5 or 10 minutes. Cool, package and freeze. You can freeze in jars. I've done this and it works all right, but I like canned tomatoes better because you don't have to bother thawing and I think they taste better.

You can *freeze tomatoes raw* but then you must use them frozen or they will spoil. What you do is just drop the frozen chunk into the stew or whatever and that way it cooks up so quickly it can't spoil. I got a cute letter with a good recipe from Liz Zellhoefer of Albany, California. She's the lady who grew over 300 pounds of tomatoes in a 12 x 16-foot plot. Says she, "Well, I caught on real quick that if I canned all those tomatoes I might go bananas. So, I looked around for recipes and came up with the way to put up many pounds of tomatoes as easily as possible. In a huge kettle put 30-40 pounds of washed, cut in half tomatoes. Add 3 sticks of chopped celery, 3 carrots, 3 onions, a bunch of parsley and boil. Boil

hard until everything is mushy. Drain off 'water,' puree through a ricer. Bring to boil, cook until thick. Pour into containers and freeze. I had so many containers that for 1½ years I didn't have to buy any tomatoes or tomato sauce!"

Here's a recipe for *Tomato Paste* out of my mother's cookbook. I've never tried it. The cookbook is called *The American Woman's Cookbook.* I know the title by heart though the front pages are long gone. The recipe is on page 700. "Spread thick tomato puree on dry plates or flat granite pans that have been brushed with unsalted fat. As soon as a film forms over the top loosen the paste with a spatula and turn it on to a screen covered with cheesecloth. Dry it in the sun or a very slow oven. When it is so dry that it can be handled without sticking, roll it in paraffin paper, fold under the ends of the paper and store in a tin box or a glass jar." The paste may be used for soup, sauces, scalloped dishes and so on. "Paraffin paper" would be translated waxed paper I'd guess. One teaspoon of the paste makes 1 cup of soup. Though I haven't made this I've done a practically identical procedure with fruit purees so I think it would work.

Freezing tomatoes for salad—Another way to freeze tomatoes is to take firm tomatoes, dip in boiling water, slip skins and freeze whole. When wanting to use for salad take them out just before mealtime, cut in pieces and mix with your salad. They will be just right by the time you eat your salad.

Drying tomatoes is harder than with most other vegetables and you're best off doing it in a regular dehydrator. They must not be overripe or they tend to mold. Choose firm ones just at the peak of maturity. Slice from bottom to top ⅜ inch or less thick. Lay the sliced pieces directly on your drying tray with a little room between slices for air circulation, no more than one layer high. With care they can dry very nicely keeping their flavor and color.

Shed-stored tomatoes—Trudy Dorr wrote me from Lynden, Washington, a way of keeping tomatoes I'd never heard of. She says, "You can cover your tomatoes when you think a frost is coming and then when it does come pull the whole plant up, root and all, and hang in porch, shed etc., and the tomatoes will ripen. This way I have tomatoes until at least Thanksgiving and they taste the same as the ones from the plant all summer (vine ripened)."

TURNIPS—After two months of hard work I'm nearing the end of this Vegetables chapter rewrite. As of this moment I'm alternating typing with Jacob on my lap with not typing and holding him on my shoulder and patting him. He is just about the fussiest baby I've ever had. He has a bit of diarrhea which is getting better, a bit of a rash and sneezes several times a day. Enough to keep me a nervous wreck. He sure is husky though. The more they yell the quicker the lungs and limbs get strong. That's true, if limited comfort, when you're trying to make a squally baby happy.

Turnips are easy to grow and store well root cellar-style. They are a good vegetable for high altitudes and cold climates. In the South they make a good winter vegetable. You can eat the top for greens. This family really likes the taste of turnip, good raw or cooked. Turnips hate hot weather, especially hot nights so if you don't live like at 8,000 feet or in the chilly northland the answer is to plant either an early crop or a late one. If you try to grow turnips through a hot summer you'll be likely to get a stringy, strong-tasting root. The soil for them should be well and deeply cultivated like for any root vegetable, and well composted-manured. They like wood ashes too. They do best in a really loose sandy type soil but if you get enough compost-manure-type stuff they'll do fine in even a heavy clay. Turnips have maturing times anywhere from 35 to 70 days but most of the quicker maturing ones are recently developed hybrids.

To plant—Plant your seed ¼ inch deep, and an inch or so apart, expecting that you will thin later to about 6 inches apart. If you have really rich soil and are short of garden space you can put rows of turnips as close as a foot apart. If you want to plant an acre of them (they're good winter animal feed) you can sow broadcast and rake lightly to get the seed covered. If your weather is dry give the newly planted seeds a good wetting to help get them started. White varieties make a good spring-planted turnip. The yellow turnip is a good winter keeper and it's your turnips destined for root cellar storage that you want to plant late in July for a fall crop. The late turnips won't be bothered so much with wireworms either which are the one problem I know of that turnips can have. Maybe your soil doesn't have wireworms at all—better yet. Turnips can stand some frost and so they'll keep on growing if you have some decent weather after the first frost. If you live in a really mild-wintered area plant in late fall and then you'll have a winter crop.

Of harvesting, thinning and wireworms—When your turnips are 4 to 6 inches high or when they start to be crowding one another trying to grow, start thinning. You can eat the thinnings . . . or freeze or can them. Turnips are especially subject to a beastie called a wireworm. Wireworms are pure white, about ¼ inch long and not skinny. They have two little black eyes and get around very actively. They tunnel along the outside of the turnip and gradually get farther in, if they can. They are the larva of a fly. When we harvest turnips for freezing, wireworms are all over and it's part of the business. They do no harm to people, only to root vegetables. I once talked to a young woman who told me she had thrown out a whole big kettle of food waiting to be canned because she found a wireworm (long since deceased) floating on the top. That's just ridiculous. She should have fished out the wireworm and kept the vegetables. And if one accidentally got into a jar, that's OK too. Good for laughs and no harm at all.

To save your own seed—Turnips are insect pollinated which means different varieties cross easily if grown within ¼ mile of each other. Other than that they are biennials and you follow the same procedure as for beets. Turnip seed is very strong, should keep its germinating power five years or more with care.

Raw turnips are good sliced thin and dipped into a seasoned sour cream dressing (let each person do their own dipping) or served grated with such a dressing. If you serve carrot sticks and celery with the turnip slices it goes well because turnip is a sharp-tasting vegetable and combines with those blander ones very well. I also love turnip grated, added to a tossed green salad and served with a French dressing.

Turnip Slaw—Get ready 4 cups pared and shredded turnips, 2 cored and diced red apples. Mix with 2 tablespoons chopped parsley, 2 tablespoons minced onion. Stir together ½ cup sour cream, 1 tablespoon vinegar, 1 tablespoon honey, salt and pepper to taste and then combine dressing with vegetables.

Cooked turnips are easy and good pot-boiled with any sort of potato, cabbage or meat dish. Turnips can be eaten when only an inch or so in diameter if you want. Small ones can be cooked whole. Larger ones can be sliced about ½ inch thick. Cook until tender enough to pierce with a fork. Sliced cooked turnips and cream is good or a white sauce if you have more time. If you have extra stock or consommé, cook in just enough of that to cover the turnips and save your liquid when you take out the turnips to mash them. Then return them to the liquid along with some butter and simmer until it is all absorbed.

To bake, wash and wipe turnips, but don't peel. Bake until tender, peel and serve either mashed or with a white sauce.

Turnip greens—Look in the Greens section for recipe ideas.

To freeze—Because of my wireworm troubles, I harvest all my turnips early, peel, cut into chunks, blanch a few minutes, cool, bag and *freeze.* When I want them I just turn out of the bag into a little water, thaw and usually serve mashed with a little butter and seasoning.

To can, proceed as for beets.

To dry, use young, tender turnips. Peel, slice thin or shred and dry.

Ground, pit or cellar-type storage—I have neighbors who raise huge, lovely turnips and store them in a root cellar. To do this leave them in the ground until frost, then dig up and store in a vegetable pit or root cellar. You can leave turnips in the garden really late and they will still be all right. Turnips and rutabagas have an odor in storage which celery can be affected by. In very mild winter areas you can leave them in the ground and dig as needed until the weather gets warm enough that they start to grow again which ruins them for eating. Farther north, you can let them stay in the garden through the first light frosts, then dig, cut off the tops and store them in a place as cool, but not freezing, as you can manage. You can store them by any of the methods for potatoes. If your storage place is too warm they may start to grow and get pithy. (Turnips can stand top frosting but alternate freezing and thawing of the root will ruin them.)

WATERCRESS—And here I am at the end of Vegetables. Maybe I should have made it Artichoke to Zucchini but I got too enthused; I didn't wait and covered zucchini under S for Squash.

Watercress grows in cold deep springs. I only saw it anywhere but in a store once. On the road to Jackson Hole, Wyoming, coming in from the southwest. Near the side of the road there is a small cold spring and therein grows watercress. I was staying then with a cattle rancher down the road hefting hay bales for my keep and learning to make bread. His wife's name was Nita and I still have a cookbook she gave me. I've just picked it up to do a little sentimental reminiscing and notice that it is printed looseleaf and bound with rings just like my book. It's strange the paths our feet take. I wonder if Nita will ever know I remember her spring. Though it wasn't really hers. She took me there. But it really was anybody's. Just a spring alongside the highway. Free and giving to anyone who was looking for it. With all that wonderful watercress growing in it. We stopped and cut some and drove on home.

There was a Salt Lake City real estate developer lived on down the road used to hang around the ranch a lot. I wasn't a bit surprised at the end of that summer to hear that he had talked Lloyd into selling him the ranch. It sounded like a lot of money, but when a man is talked out of his land he is talked out of a good part of his soul. It depresses me to think about it. The developer broke it into small plots and sold it for recreation cabin sites to city folks.

There's $40,000 waiting for me in a trust account from the sale of my father's property which I may or may not live to see. It doesn't really matter. What matters was *his* farm then. And what matters now is *our* farm, such as it is, that we have managed to get started on by our own efforts. Daddy would respect that more, anyway.

I'm a Christian and I believe that God answers prayer. But He doesn't ordinarily just hand things out free. God gives us fruitful labors, and it is our job to do the laboring part. We show our faith in His will to bless us by working on, undismayed by the apparently uncrossable river or unclimbable mountain. If we work, really work—(you can pray and work at the same time and that's how I do a lot of mine)—and constantly search in your mind for God's will in your work, what you should work for and how you should work at it—then the Fruit is certain. Not just earthly fruits but even more important spiritual fruits of knowing how to love and experiencing love, both God's and man's, and the deep and lovely

satisfaction of seeing God make of your soul-self a beautiful and worthy one.

We get our water from a spring here. It has a peculiarity of moving around. About every three months there is no water, and Mike climbs down the canyon to find out where the spring went. He always finds it, digs it out enough to make the water flow easily, and resets the pipe that carries the spring water to the first tank, which is in the canyon, and from which it gets pumped up to the tank above our house, from which we have gravity flow down to the house. So it isn't really suitable for growing watercress. It also has a tendency to dry up to a trickle in hot weather just when we need the water most.

Last summer we had a terrible drought. The worst the old-timers had ever seen. We had to feed hay in August and most of my bees died before I realized they were starving to death in midsummer because no flowers were blooming. It finally rained in September and it was odd because then all the flowers started blooming that hadn't done so all summer. Since then we have been having the wettest fall on record.

In case I ever do have a good spring, I have a collection of watercress recipes and here they are for you.

Watercress Salad—Remove the roots. Pick over and wash the watercress thoroughly. Make sure there are no water bugs. Drain and chill. Arrange on chilled plates and serve with French dressing. Or add chilled cucumbers, cut in dice or in thin slices.

Watercress Nut Salad—Mix watercress, shredded lettuce and nut meats. Use lemon juice for a salad dressing.

Watercress Sandwiches—Strip watercress from the stems and sprinkle it with salt, paprika and lemon juice. Or mix seasoned cress with mayonnaise (about 1½ cups cress per ¼ cup mayonnaise). Good with whole wheat homemade bread.

Watercress is good, too, added to a tossed green salad and with sliced tomato.

Watercress Soup—Peel and slice a large onion or leek and about 1½ pounds potatoes and put them in a pan with 6 cups soup stock. Keep back about one-third of the leaves of a large bunch of watercress. Add the rest along with the stalks to the stock. Cook until the vegetables are soft and then sieve the whole thing. Add a little flour for thickening and when thickened add the chopped watercress leaves that you held back and simmer 5 minutes more before serving. Or make the soup with half milk and half water instead of the stock.

VEGETABLE JUICES

To get any vegetable juice except tomato or cucumber requires special equipment. (Rhubarb is really a vegetable but gets treated like a fruit.) The mail-order juicers are $60 to $150. The juicer has two products—juice and pulp. Carrot pulp is relished by rabbits. A blender liquefies the entire product by breaking down the tissue and suspending it in its own juice. You can get juices with a hand mill, too, but not very easily or efficiently—except cucumber juice. To make cucumber juice you just peel, grate and squeeze.

To prepare the vegetables for juice extraction, wash or scrub them clean. Then put them whole into the juicer.

To make juice from root vegetables it would be best for you to store the vegetable and make the juice as you need it. As a very general rule a pound of vegetable will yield about a cup of juice. Freshly made juices taste better. Don't store juices in a metal container.

Carrot is the only "sweet" vegetable juice. Incidentally don't drink more than one big glass of carrot juice per day or you may turn as yellow as the carrot! (Some friends of mine did!) Spinach, broccoli, cabbage, celery, green pepper, beet and watercress juices are most palatable in relatively small quantities combined with other juices—especially tomato and apple. The vegetable juice combinations you like are a very individual matter. You may not like these at all.

Cabbage Combination—Use ¾ cup cabbage juice and add ¼ cup celery juice or ¼ cup tomato juice or ¼ cup carrot juice.

Carrot, Beet, Lettuce—1½ cups carrot juice, half the remainder beet juice and half lettuce juice to make up to 2 cups.

Carrot, Celery, Apple—One-third part carrot juice, one-third part celery juice and one-third part apple juice.

Carrot, Celery, Spinach—Combine one-third part celery juice, one-third carrot juice and one-third spinach juice.

Carrot, Celery, Parsley—½ cup carrot juice, ½ cup celery juice and 1 tablespoon parsley juice.

Carrot Shake—½ cup carrot juice and ½ cup milk.

Celery (or Celeriac) Juice—Can be drunk alone, but don't use the leaves. They make it too bitter. Add a little lemon or grapefruit to hold color and improve the flavor.

Celery, Lettuce, Spinach—1 cup celery juice, ⅓ cup spinach juice, parsley juice for flavor (a tablespoon or 2 tablespoons).

Celery, Carrot—⅓ cup celery juice and ½ cup carrot juice.

Parsley Juice isn't drunk by itself. But you can combine it. Parsley juice is good especially with carrot, celery and lettuce juices.

Quick Beet Soup—Combine 2 cups milk, ½ cup beet juice and seasonings.

Quick Spinach Soup—Combine 2 cups milk, 1 cup spinach juice and your seasonings.

The Famous 8—If you have a juicer, you can experiment with blends of tomato, carrot, celery, beet, parsley, lettuce, watercress and spinach juice.

TOMATO JUICE

Once you make your tomato juice it can be used fresh, canned or frozen. Use vine-ripened tomatoes. The flavor is so much better. Cut away any large green portions. To get tomato juice from tomato pulp just put through a colander or some such to strain and break up the fibers.

To freeze—Low acid varieties and sound well-ripened tomatoes will freeze best. Quarter them. Place in a covered pan. Crush lightly to provide enough juice to cover the bottom of the pan. Heat rapidly to 185°-195° (below boiling). Then put them through a food press, a rotary colander or something to get the juice. If you want seeds in your juice, use something with large holes. Then cool the juice quickly by setting the pan in ice water. Add salt, 1 teaspoon per 1 quart juice. Pack in your containers and freeze immediately.

To can—Cut into parts and crush enough to get juice to cover the bottom of the pan. Simmer, stirring often. Then put through the strainer size of your preference. Season the juice to taste. (You could add 1 teaspoon salt per 1 quart of juice. Or you could have cooked an onion with about every 3 gallons of tomatoes and added 2 tablespoons honey per quart.) After the juice is seasoned, reheat to boiling, pour into hot jars and process in hot water at simmering (180°) for 10 minutes. Seal.

Tomato Juice Beverage—Plan on canning or freezing this recipe because it makes lots. Cook ½ bushel tomatoes, 10 large carrots, 4 green peppers, 4 large onions, ½ pound green beans, 3 kohlrabis, a bunch of celery and a bunch parsley until soft. Rub it all through a colander. Season with salt and pepper. To can, fill your jars, process 5 minutes and you're done. To freeze, cool as quickly as possible, package and freeze.

Quick Tomato #1—To 2½ cups tomato juice, add a trace of pepper, ¼ teaspoon salt, 1 tablespoon lemon juice, ½ teaspoon horseradish and ¼ teaspoon celery salt.

Quick Tomato #2—Combine equal amounts of tomato and celery juice. Add seasonings to taste.

Tomato-Grapefruit—Combine equal amounts of tomato and grapefruit juice. Add a squeeze of lemon juice and a dash of salt.

Tomato-Sauerkraut—Combine equal amounts of tomato and sauerkraut juice. Add a squeeze of lemon juice. Spice it up with Tabasco and Worcestershire if you have an iron stomach.

Vegetable juices in your breadstuffs—Viola Erickson wrote me from Newton, Illinois, to urge me to try using tomato juice for part of my liquid in bread making. She's right! Or tomato juice with carrot or celery juice or any sort of V-8ish vegetable juice mixture. It really gives a great flavor—all those good vitamins jumping out and hitting your taste buds. You can use vegetable juices in any sort of bread or rolls. Viola uses 1 cup tomato juice per 1 cup water. Along with eggs and the other stuff. She says it rises faster and comes out a lighter bread with a very fine texture.

SPROUTS

It's not really old fashioned, but I've tried to put into this book everything that people wanted, and I've had requests for how to make sprouts. Well, I'm not really a sprouter though I'm planning to catch up with the times. But a lady who has been helping me write this cookbook practically from the beginning, Pat Crim of Fort Collins, Colorado, wrote me this: "I sprout only alfalfa seeds and the advantage to me is that it gives my family a source of fresh greens all winter and they are amazingly cheap. I just use a widemouthed mason jar with several layers of nylon net over the mouth and a canning ring to hold them on. I put the seeds in the jar and leave them in a warm, dark closet, taking them out two or three times a day to rinse them, until they are sprouted. It takes less time than going to the store for a head of lettuce." When you sprout your seeds don't just leave them under water. It won't work, they'll spoil. Instead, do like Pat does. You can hurry bigger seeds by first soaking them in some warm water overnight. Some people lay them on several layers of wet paper towels. Give yourself about 5 days to get them sprouted. It may happen faster.

Then Ellen Hanshaw wrote me from Port Angeles, Washington, her way of sprouting: "I use an 8 x 8 x 2-inch glass baking dish lined with five layers of white terry cloth soaked with warm water. And 1½ teaspoons of alfalfa seeds sprinkled over. I lightly lay a plastic bag over the top, put the dish where it won't get direct sunlight and 4 days later have a full dish of sprouts, with no rinsing or watering in between time."

The juices left over from sprouting are nourishing and you can add them to gravy or stew or such. *Do not ever* eat potato or tomato sprouts. They are *poisonous.* Do not sprout seeds that are being sold for planting in the garden because they are often treated with poisonous fungicides. That's repeating myself but I'm worried maybe you didn't read it the first time. Don't put your sprouts in direct sunlight. Don't worry about little whiskers that grow on your sprouts. These are rootlets starting and are fine to eat. Beans, lentils, and so on have hulls that you can eat, or if you don't like them put the sprouts in a bowl of cold water, rub them gently and the hulls will come off and float and you can discard them. The general length your sprouts grow to really doesn't matter—it's just a matter of your personal preference.

You can sprout any beans, peas, lentils, sunflower seeds, and alfalfa seeds. You can also sprout soy, barley, buckwheat, fava, lima, pinto, garbanzos and actually just about anything. I've even heard of sprouting corn, dill, flax, fenugreek, pumpkin, beet and lettuce seeds. You can use the same general procedure for them all. The bigger seeds like bean, pea, and lentil are done when the sprout is more than an inch long. Smaller seeds make smaller sprouts, of course. Grown sprouts can be stored a week in the refrigerator, or a long time in the freezer.

Eating them—Don't cook the sprouts more than 5 or 6 minutes. Too much cooking takes away their prime. Except for soybean sprouts, which are tougher. You can mix them raw in salads. Rye and wheat sprouts can be eaten plain as a snack. You can add them to soups, casseroles, scrambled eggs, bread batters or stewed tomatoes, but remember to do it just at the end, 5 minutes before serving if it's a cooked dish. They make a good substitute in recipes calling for celery, which is something a lot of people (me included) can't grow. They have that nice crunchiness of celery. You can cook and serve plain as a "vegetable" dish. Just steam, fry quickly in a little oil, or bake.

Sprouted peas are good served with salt, pepper, and a pinch of basil leaves. Cook them a half hour or so to get them tender. Add butter and serve.

Wheat sprouts will help unleavened or leavened breads and taste good baked in. Ground wheat sprouts are good added to butter for a special spread.

Wheat grass—Start out by sprouting the regular way until the sprouts are as long as the seed. Then uncover, water once in a while. If you have them on something that will hold the dampness well like a sponge, the sprouts should keep growing until they look like grass. When they are between 1 and 2 inches long is the best time to eat them. You eat the entire seed and grass thing. Very full of vitamins!

For more information—The best book I know of on sprouting is called *Sprouting for All Seasons* by Bertha B. Larimore. It's a homely unknown put out by a small publisher written by a very plain speaking and honest lady—no colored pages, no cute illustrations, just very good and comprehensive directions for sprouting anything, any way and then a book full of good recipes to use the sprouts in. I recommend it. $3.50 from Horizon Publishers, P.O. Box 490, Bountiful, Utah 84010.

NUTS

If you live in California you can raise almonds and macadamia nuts. If you live in the Southwest you could grow pine nuts. California, Oregon and Washington grow fine English walnuts and filberts. Pecans, black walnuts, peanuts (not really a nut because they belong to the bean and pea family) and chestnuts are others that can be grown here in the United States.

Different trees have different climate needs, different fertilization needs. It is complex and I can't give you all the answers. But there are two organizations of amateur nut growers that do have answers and are glad to help you and I recommend you get in touch with them. They are Northern Nut Growers Association, 4518 Holston Hills Road, S.E., Knoxville, Tennessee 37914; and Illinois Nut Tree Association, 937 W. King Street, Decatur, Illinois 62522.

The good thing about having your own nut trees is that once started they go on quietly year after year producing very large nut crops with practically no care—as well as your bonus of beauty and shade. A paper-shell pecan tree can give you 100 pounds of pecans a year. An English walnut (the small kind) gives 4 or 5 bushels of nuts, as will a hickory. A mature black walnut tree can produce 30 to 40 bushels!

Store your nuts—They need protection both from air and from heat to prevent the oil in them from becoming rancid. Nuts keep best in the shell. If you have shelled nuts, they'll keep better whole than chopped. They'll keep better unroasted than roasted. Shelled nuts, if stored in a tightly closed container in the refrigerator, will keep for several months, which isn't bad if you can spare the refrigerator room. You can also freeze either shelled or unshelled nuts.

In cracking a bushel of nuts, the hard shells will be easier to crack and nut meats less fragile and liable to breakage if you first soak the nuts in warm water. After the soaked nuts are cracked, spread out the nut meats to dry for several hours before you put them away.

To roast nuts, heat your oven to 350°. Spread the nuts out on a cookie sheet or such and toast them for 6 to 12 minutes. Use your judgment—you want a light brown effect. Stir them at intervals to make sure they aren't burning and to get all the sides roasted. Another way is to roast nuts in heavy frying pans or Dutch ovens on top of your stove. It will take 10 to 15 minutes on a very moderate heat. Add 1 teaspoon salad oil per cup nut meats. Mix the oil in well before starting. It will help you get even browning. After the nuts are done, sprinkle salt over them if you want. If oiled, cool on absorbent paper.

Mixed Nut Butter—Prepare ¼ pound almonds, ½ pound pecans, ½ pound filberts or hazelnuts and ½ pound roasted peanuts. Put them all through a grinder and then mix well. Pack in a glass or some other straight-sided container and chill. When wanted for use, dip the container in hot water and the contents will spill out. Cut into slices. Good for vegetarians.

The little **ACORN** grows on the mighty oak (you knew that). White oak acorns are not as bitter as those on red oaks.

Here's how to make an *acorn flour.* Peel the acorns. Grind up. Soak the flour in warm water. The water will turn brown which is the tannin coming out. Throw away the water and repeat four times. Spread the paste on a tray in a slow oven until dry. Grind again.

ALMOND trees grow in California mostly. Sweet almonds that is. Almond extract is made from the bitter almond tree which grows in Europe and whose nuts contain enough prussic acid so you couldn't eat more than a few. I never had an almond tree. The Halls almond tree won't make nuts by itself. You have to plant a peach or nectarine near it for good pollination. The book *How to Grow Vegetables and Fruits by the Organic Method* edited by Rodale and Staff, has a good description of how to raise and harvest this and other nuts grown in the United States. On page 850 they say:

"The outer hulls of the nuts split open in fall when almonds are ripe. When most of the hulls in the center of the tree have split, nuts are shaken or knocked out of the branches and gathered from the ground. Heavy rubber mallets may be used for jarring the nuts loose without injury to the bark. After the harvest, almonds should be shelled and dried to prevent mildew. Kernels are spread for drying in a partially shaded place and are left until the meat is crisp. They are then stored in airtight containers in a cool place until used."

To blanch almonds (to "blanch" means get the papery outside skins off), pour boiling water over the nuts. Let them stand 5 minutes, or until the skins wrinkle. Drain away the water and slip off the skin.

To make slivered almonds, lay them, flat side down, on a cutting board and cut lengthwise with a sharp knife into slivers.

To toast them, put on a cookie sheet in a 350° oven until golden, about 15 minutes. Or mix in 1 tablespoon melted butter and 1 teaspoon salt per pound almonds and bake until lightly browned and crisp, stirring often. Or you can do it on top of the stove by first blanching, then heating butter in a small pan over low heat, adding nuts, and sautéing 5 minutes, or until lightly browned. Then drain on absorbent paper.

Almond Paste was a Victorian gourmet ingredient used to make macaroons, crescents and marzipan. (See Old Fashioned Candies for recipes.) To make it yourself pound in mortar, grind in a chopper or blend in blender shelled, skinned and dried almonds (not roasted). If need be run through the grinder several times until the nuts are really fine. For every 2 cups almonds, dissolve 1 cup sugar in ½ cup orange juice and then mix thoroughly with almonds. Another way to make almond paste is to mix 1 pound ground almonds with 1 pound sugar and 1 cup water, which has been cooked to the soft ball stage. Then add ½ cup orange juice. Almond paste improves with some storage. Wait a week at least before using. If you have lots of time and use white sugar, marzipan making is quite an art to take up.

BUTTERNUTS are the most northerly in range of the nut trees. They also are subject to a fungus problem. They have a relatively heavy shell. Are also known as "oilnuts" and "long walnuts." Butternut trees can be tapped in the spring just like maple trees and their sap boiled down to make a sweet syrup. Butternut roots give off a poison that kills evergreen trees so they can't be grown near together.

Butternuts are really hard to shell. You can wear a glove to protect your hand and stand the butternut on solid iron, like an anvil, then hit the pointed end with a hammer. In half an hour you might have a pint of nut meats. They are a little easier to shell if you first cover them with boiling water and let soak for 15 minutes.

These nuts grow on the tree in clusters inside a spongy, hairy husk. The husk is easy to get off. Inside the hard shell that you hammer off, the nut parts are almost, but not quite, separated by woody membranes like a walnut. You have to pick the nut meats out and they break in the process. Butternuts can be stored in a cool dry place for several months (longer if refrigerated). They are the fattiest of all nuts, good in cake or homemade bread. Just add to any recipe and cut back the shortening a trifle.

The **CHESTNUT** in America today is not the same one that old-timers meant except when they referred to the "chinquapin," which is our Southern native chestnut. All the American chestnuts have died of a blight. The ones growing now are imports from Europe (the Spanish chestnut) and the Orient (the Chinese chestnut). Chestnuts are an unusual nut because they are mostly starch with only a little fat so you can do vegetable kinds of things with them. Chestnuts imported from France are called "marrons" and are the biggest and best supposedly.

On the tree the chestnuts grow inside of "burrs," which split to spill out the nuts inside onto the ground in the fall. You must pick them up before they have a chance to get moldy or wormy. If you put them in water, bad ones will float. Store in airtight containers in a slightly damp atmosphere.

To shell chestnuts, rub with oil and bake in oven until shells crack. Then shell, soak in water until the skin loosens and peel. Or with a sharp knife cut a crisscross gash on the flat side of the shell of each chestnut. Cover with 1 inch of boiling water and let soak 10 minutes. Then you can lift the nuts out and peel off shell and inner skin both at once.

Chestnuts are perishable at room temperature even in the shell. Under refrigeration they'll keep several months. When you refrigerate chestnuts give

them air by packing them in loosely covered containers or in plastic bags that have holes in them. Shelled blanched chestnuts will keep even longer if frozen.

To freeze them, pack in containers that can be tightly closed and use in cooking without defrosting.

To make a **Chestnut Puree,** boil shelled chestnuts in lightly salted water until tender. Then mash and add a little butter, salt and pepper. To use the puree as a poultry stuffing base, just add bread crumbs, beaten eggs and a little of the juice in which the chestnuts were cooked.

Sliced chestnuts are good with Brussels sprouts. Chestnuts go well with chicken soup.

Chestnut Chicken Soup—Roast to remove shells and then cool. Cook 1 cup peeled chestnuts in 2 cups chicken soup until tender. Add about 6 cups more chicken soup. Season with salt and pepper and serve.

COCONUT—To make your own shredded coconut at home take the hull off the coconut, then shred it with a vegetable shredder. Put the shredded coconut in a flat pan and put the pan in the oven at about 300°. Stir occasionally until it is dried. You can also sun dry coconut. All you have to do is cut the meat in thin slices, spread it on your trays and put it in the sun until dry. Then store in airtight cans or jars. This can be added to pudding, eaten as a sweet or used in place of nuts.

FILBERTS—See Hazelnuts.

HAZELNUTS and filberts aren't the same thing but they belong to the same botanical family. Washington and Oregon grow filberts commercially. Pick up the nuts as soon as possible after they fall to the ground in the fall to prevent mold. Give them the water test—floaters are not good. Dry them by spreading out and stirring occasionally in a dry room. Then store in the shells where mice and rats won't be tempted.

For culinary purposes filberts may be toasted, ground and so forth. For baking purposes they are usually left unblanched for the pinkish skin adds much to the flavor and to their food value.

To remove the skins, spread the nuts on a cookie sheet or in a shallow baking pan. Bake at 300° for 15 minutes, stirring occasionally. After they have cooled enough to handle you can rub the skins off with your fingers. If you plan to chop filberts toast after chopping. Store toasted nuts in an airtight container.

HEARTNUTS—See Walnuts.

HICKORY nuts cross with pecans, pignuts and other hickory varieties. They grow wild in the eastern United States. It takes them as long as 5 years to start bearing nuts. The shells are very hard and the nut meats relatively small. They resemble pecans. They can be stored in the shell for months in a cool dry place. A hot-water bath beforehand helps make shelling easier.

MACADAMIA nuts (first grown in Australia, then Hawaii, now getting started in California) have a husk that ruptures itself when the nuts are ready and they fall to the ground. They should be thoroughly dried before storage. You need a special tool to crack the shells because they are so hard—like vise-grip pliers. Before you use the nutcracker, spread the nuts on a baking sheet and roast at 200° for 1 hour. Cool slightly and shell. Store shelled nuts in the refrigerator in a covered container.

PEANUTS are a southern plant that needs a long growing season. Varieties are differentiated by the shape when shelled. The Virginia peanut is long and slender, the Runner is small and stubby and the Spanish is round. You need four months of hot summer weather to have an easy time growing peanuts. That means that north of Arkansas you are starting to get out of their natural range and will have to try harder. It's worth the try though because they are such good food, good fun, and freshly dug and home roasted peanuts are delicious. Peanuts are an odd and interesting plant to watch growing. They have two sets of flowers, one showy yellow, then another set that forms the peanuts by bending over and growing into the ground. It is underground that the peanuts develop.

Virginia varieties of peanuts grow well in the warm climate gardens. Spanish peanut varieties are tougher for northern growing than the Virginia. The Tennessee Red variety offered by Parks Seed Company makes a good showing for itself in northern gardens too. If you're trying to grow peanuts in an area that really is too cold for them, it will probably be worth your while to prepare them a special planting area. You can make them long 4-foot wide beds each of which can hold 3 rows with the peanuts planted 1 foot apart and your rows 1 foot apart. Make sure your soil is very well nourished to encourage them to grow as fast as possible. If you don't have a loose textured soil add sand to help them. Sandy soil also helps lengthen their growing season because it warms up quickly. If their growing place is a sheltered site that slopes to the south you're better off yet.

To plant a peanut—Each healthy peanut plant with a chance to get its growing done will yield you about ½ cup of shelled nuts. You can plant your

peanuts either whole or shelled. Start with seed that you have bought from a seedsman rather than with store peanuts. Shelled peanuts grow quicker but you have to shell very carefully so that you don't break the papery inner skin. Don't plant until the ground is warm. Spanish peanuts grow a foot high but Tennessee Reds can grow 2 feet high. If you haven't prepared your peanuts a special richly-nourished and well-tilled seedbed plant them 18 inches apart with rows a couple feet apart.

To harvest, you must dig up the whole plant to get at the pods. Dig your peanuts before frost and then hang them on the vine to cure in an airy place like a shed, or a well-ventilated attic or on a piece of wire screening. They need to cure for about 2 months before you do anything more with them. You can save some of them for the next year's seed. The last time for digging is when the inside of the shell is showing color and veins. In more northerly areas you can leave the peanuts in the ground until mid-October because they need the time to finish developing. Shake the dirt off roots and peanut pods, and hang the plant up vine and all to begin curing in an airy place like a shed or well-ventilated attic. Let them cure like that two months. Or if you are short of time or space after two or three weeks of vine drying you can pull off the peanuts, pile them lightly into cardboard boxes or onto newspaper and let them dry like that another 2 or 3 weeks. Store them like that and roast only as needed since they taste best when freshly roasted.

To blanch peanuts, put them into boiling water and leave for 3 minutes. Pour off the water, skin and spread out the nuts to dry. But if you are planning to make peanut butter, *roasting* is preferable. In that case spread out the peanuts in a shallow pan or on a cookie sheet and roast at 350°. Stir frequently. To know when they are done the safest way is to remove and shell a nut at intervals. When the skin slips off easily and the nut itself is a light brown and tastes "roasted" they are done—probably 15 to 20 minutes. A properly roasted peanut ends up with a brittle shell and an inner skin that will come off easily.

Peanut flour is a commercial product made of the residue after the peanuts have been pressed for oil. I don't know any way to make it at home. It can be added in reasonable amounts to any cake or bread recipe.

Gorp—One part shelled, toasted peanuts ground (you can use an ordinary hand meat chopper with the small-hole plate) mixed with one part raisins. Put it all through the chopper about three times for the best flavor. Use more or less raisins to suit yourself. It's a sweet with no sugar. Works with walnuts, too, or almonds (put the almonds through the grater first). Add chocolate to make a concentrated trail food.

Peanut butter that you buy in the stores is protected against rancidity by the addition of an antioxidant so your homemade peanut butter wouldn't keep as well. You can solve that problem by either making it in small batches and keeping them in the refrigerator while they are being used up, or by canning your peanut butter. If the oil starts to separate and rise on your peanut butter, just turn the jar upside down. Peanut butter is simply ground, mashed or blended peanuts. Skin them first. You can use a grinder, a mortar and pestle or a blender.

Blender Peanut Butter—Put 1 cup peanuts in a blender. You can add a maximum of 1 cup more after it gets going. Add about 2 tablespoons vegetable oil per cup peanuts. Add salt, if you want (like ½ teaspoon salt per cup nuts).

Grinder or Mortar and Pestle Peanut Butter—Put the nuts in the same proportions as above through the grinder several times or mash them with the mortar and pestle until the consistency satisfies you. Mix in oil and salt in the later stages.

Crunchy peanut butter you can make yourself. If you are using a grinder, just put through a part of your peanuts on the coarse grind and then hold them out to add at the very end. Otherwise, cut up peanuts by hand or use a vegetable chopper and stir them in the last thing.

The ultimate peanut butter is supposed to be this blend. The Spanish peanuts contain a large amount of oil, which is offset by the texture of the Virginia peanuts. Use two parts of Virginia peanuts to one part Spanish peanuts, such as 1 cup Spanish peanuts and 2 cups Virginia peanuts. You can add salt, sugar or oil to any peanut butter recipe in the amounts that suit you. Tastes on salt really differ. In this recipe it shouldn't be necessary to add oil because the peanuts should have just the right amount themselves.

To can peanut butter, pack closely into clean jars, filling to within 1 inch of the top. Put your lid and screw band on and tighten. Process 1 hour at simmering (about 180°) in a water bath canner.

PECANS are a good nut, easy to grow all over the southern United States, and easy to shell. In the shell they will keep in a cool dry place for many months. Once shelled they keep best in the refrigerator. If you have trouble getting your nuts off the tree you can knock them from the branches with a pole.

PISTACHIOS grow in inland California. In the shell they will keep in a cool place for many months. Shelled they must be stored tightly covered, preferably in the refrigerator.

WALNUTS, Butternuts and Heartnuts are all related. If you are planting walnuts check on the sex life of your variety. Carpathian walnuts need two trees to make nuts. You can plant the Thomas black walnut tree by itself. It may matter because it's quite likely you don't have space for two of them! Black walnuts are comparatively difficult to crack and the nut meats are hard to get out whole from all the little chambers. But they sure do produce. Heartnuts are relatively easy to crack. Walnut trees grow to a great age (like 130 years!) and get very big. They are beautiful in your yard. When they do get old enough to die they are good for furniture making and smoking meats. Plant some for your grandchildren! We had a huge one in the front yard of our old home in Juliaetta (4 miles south down the road from Kendrick).

Walnuts fall off the tree when they get ready at summer's end and that's when your job begins. There is a thick yellowish-green husk covering them. Before they fall from the tree it's a grass green hull. There are recipes for a catsup made from those green walnuts in all the old-time recipe books. I never had the nerve to try one. I chomped into a green walnut once and was puckered up for the rest of the day. If they aren't poisonous I can't understand why not. Best way to get those hulls off is to gather up all the walnuts in their hulls and transport them to your driveway. Use gloves to make the change. The juice in the hulls that have been mashed by being walked on or some such will stain your fingers (it also makes a great home-grown furniture stain). So use gloves to handle them. Spread them out and let the cars run over them for a while. The tires will mash those husks away without harming the nuts. In about a week the job will be done. Get out your gloves again and move the walnuts indoors for stage two of their treatment. Don't leave them lie in the sun and wind. It will hurt the nutmeats inside. Don't dawdle around and delay harvesting them while the husks turn black and get maggots in them. That's bad for your walnuts too.

A cement floor of a sheltered building where you can spread them out and stir them around once in a while will be perfect. A cool, darkish, well-ventilated attic would work very well too. It's important to dry them not too quickly and not too dry.

To crack—The idea is to hit the walnut hard on that sharp point enough times that it will split from top to bottom into four neat sections. Practice helps. Once they have split that way use a wire cutter to make a longitudinal cut along the grain to open the shell and let you get out the nutmeat from that quarter.

To store—In the shell, properly cured, walnuts will store until next fall. You can bake the nutmeats right after cracking in a 215° oven for 15 minutes and they'll keep a good long while. Or you can freeze them, or merely keep them in the refrigerator.

SEEDS

Laura's Sunflower Seed Recipe—Leave the sunflower heads on the plant until after the first frost. Then pick the heads and spread out—seeds up—in the sunshine for a week. You could lay them on a wall or a roof or anything. Check occasionally to make sure they aren't molding. Then remove the seeds.

Put the seeds in the bottom of a 3-gallon crock or something comparable. Add enough water to fill the crock and half a box of salt (or use 2 gallons of water and a 1-pound 10-ounce box of salt). Stir, then leave to soak for 1 week.

Now spread the seeds on a tray and roast in your oven at 350°, stirring at least every 10 minutes to get the damp ones evenly distributed. It will take about an hour to dry them but test to make sure, observing and cracking samples. The development of a whitish color shows they are getting done and inside the shell they should be dry instead of still soggy.

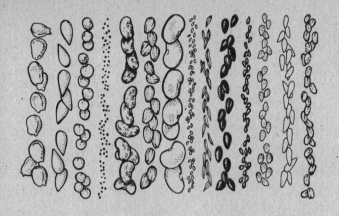

Watch carefully to prevent burning. After coming out of the oven the seeds are done and ready to eat. Store in a cool, dry place.

A while back a reader (now I forget who) asked me to help her find a recipe for a "sunflower loaf." I didn't know and asked Anna Baker, who must have one of the world's greatest collections of cookbooks, and who can cook too. She's helped me sleuth a good many difficult recipes in the past. Here are two recipes she sent me that she thought might be the ones the California reader was wanting:

Vegetable Seed Roast

4 medium-sized carrots—grated
6 medium-sized boiled potatoes—sliced
4 small onions—minced
1 tablespoon chopped parsley
½ cup chopped celery
½ cup chopped spinach or beet tops
1 cup chopped cabbage
1 cup chopped sunflower seeds (or leave whole)
1½ cups whole wheat bread crumbs
½ cup milk
4 eggs
1 minced clove garlic, or little garlic salt

Directions:

Mix all together well. Place in oiled pan. Dot top with butter or oil. Bake 2 hours, at 250°. This is the closest I've found to the California Casserole wanted.

Sunflower Loaf

2 cups cooked brown rice
1 cup chopped sunflower seeds
½ cup whole wheat bread crumbs (toasted)
Soy milk to moisten
2 tablespoons soy sauce
2 tablespoons chopped onion
2 tablespoons diced celery
Salt to taste

Directions:

Mix thoroughly. If too dry, add in more soy milk. Bake in 325° to 350° oven for 45 minutes.

Pumpkin Seeds—Open the pumpkin and remove the seeds. Let the seeds dry for 2 days. They can be spread on a tray or on newspaper. Just before roasting, rub the seeds between your fingers to remove that thin papery outer skin. Then roast under a low flame for about 15 minutes. When they start popping out of the tray, they're done. They're brown, too, when done. A moment before removing them from the oven, sprinkle soy sauce (the health food kind is much better tasting than the regular supermarket stuff) over them. Some people chew and eat the shells and all, but it's sort of a woody taste. Jeanie gave me this recipe. She used to live in the Bronx and now she lives down the road with her sister, mother, father, her husband and her sister's husband.

Plain Pumpkin Seeds—Prepare as above. Toast, then brush with melted butter and sprinkle with salt.

Banana Squash Seeds—These are very big seeds and fine roasted, too.

Salted Roasted Pumpkin or Squash Seeds—Wash seeds. Boil them in salted water (2-3 tablespoons salt per quart water) for about 15 minutes. Drain. Spread on a cookie sheet with a little oil or melted butter. Roast in a moderate oven (350°) until they are brown and crisp. Some people like them flavored with soy sauce.

Watermelon Seeds—One thing they haven't put on the market yet is watermelon seeds, but Alice Shattuck wrote me that when her grandmother (and she is a grandmother herself!) and her mother used to cook up a lot of watermelon for syrup, they would save all the seeds. They washed the seeds and then boiled them a little. After that, they dried them off and spread the watermelon seeds on wooden trays to dry in the sun.

Oil from Seeds—A number of people have asked me if there is any way to make the pressed oils at home. I don't know of a way. Cottonseeds are ground, then the oil pressed out and the residue used for fertilizer or as a food for cattle. Peanut oil is pressed from the nuts. Linseed (made from flaxseed) oil is gotten by first crushing the seeds and then pressing for the oil. Similar procedures apply for safflower and other oils. I've never been able to do more toward home extraction than just make a "butter" in the blender.

VEGETARIAN COOKING

There are whole shelves of wonderful recipe books available now that specialize in vegetarian recipes. When I first started writing this book I really didn't know anything about that way of eating having lived all my life on a farm and in a climate where meat and dairy products were a really important part of the diet. What I mean is as you go farther north or farther up in altitude you get into climates where fruits and vegetables are harder to grow but forage crops like brush and grass and hay do well and your diet tends to lean away from fruits and vegetables and to include more and more meat and dairy products. Melanie Kohler of Haleiwa, Hawaii, was my first

teacher on vegetarian eating and she has sent me so many wonderful recipes and knows so much more about the subject than I do that I've practically let her do this whole section for me.

One opinion I do hold about vegetarian eating is about that commercial meat substitute called TVP—textured vegetable protein. I'd avoid it. It's full of things like monosodium glutamate and chemicals I can't pronounce and I don't know what it is. It dehydrates well and when canned, keeps a very long time. That makes it a great product for somebody to sell and then comes the advertising to tell you it's a good thing. I think if you're going to be a vegetarian you'd do better to be like Melanie and make your stuff from scratch.

Now, here's Melanie.

"Dear Carla: Maybe you would like some background information before I start on the recipes. Both my husband and I were born and raised as Seventh-Day Adventists (my father-in-law is an SDA minister). Danny grew up in California, but I'm a native Hawaiian (although I don't have any Hawaiian blood—I'm Portuguese, Chinese, Spanish and Filipino). Danny's dad was transferred here to Hawaii to pastor our Church while we were both in high school, and we've been sweethearts since then. We're now 26 and 27 years old, have a 2½ year old miniature Danny, and live on 2⅓ acres of hilltop land about 40 miles from Honolulu.

"Now, not all Seventh-Day Adventists are vegetarians—I never have been one, but Danny was raised as one and got his eating habits changed while he was in the army. We are allowed to eat beef, lamb, chicken, turkey and fish, but not unclean food such as pork and shellfish. But, although we

aren't vegetarians, we do have vegetarian meals about two or three times a week—both because we feel that it is healthful and to keep the cost of our food down (since we don't raise any livestock). You really can't beat vegetarian dishes (if prepared the right way) for tasty and most of all economical food!

"The Cottage Cheese Patties recipe that I sent you earlier is one of our favorites. It's also my old standby to take to Church potlucks, and I never have to take home any leftovers!

"Cottage Cheese Patties—Combine 1 cup cottage cheese, 1 cup bread crumbs, 1 cup rolled oats, 1 onion, chopped fine, 2 tablespoons chopped parsley, 2 to 3 eggs, salt and sage to taste. Form into patties and fry. Place browned patties in baking dish, cover with tomato sauce. Bake at 350° for about 30 minutes, or until gravy bubbles. This recipe should serve about 4 to 5 people. I usually make several recipes of patties, cool them after frying, then place the patties in plastic bags and put in the freezer. Then, whenever we have unexpected guests, or get home late from work, or whatever, I can just take out however many patties I need, put them in a baking pan, pour tomato sauce over and bake until bubbly. You can also pour cream of mushroom soup over to make the gravy, or homemade brown gravy, or just eat the patties plain with a little catsup. The mixture can also be formed into balls, fried, added to spaghetti sauce and served over cooked spaghetti. Actually, you can fix up these patties just about any way you want—just use your imagination and whatever you have in your pantry!

"A couple of good recipes that I got while majoring in home economics at Walla Walla College in Washington state are for Walnut Cheese Patties and Imperial Roast.

"**Walnut Cheese Patties**—Mix together 6 hard-cooked eggs, chopped, 1 cup cottage cheese, 1 onion, ground, ¼ cup soft bread crumbs, 1 teaspoon salt, ½ cup ground nuts and 2 tablespoons chopped parsley. Shape into patties; dip into beaten eggs and dry bread crumbs to coat. Brown lightly in hot oil and place in baking dish. Pour desired gravy (tomato sauce or mushroom soup or brown gravy) over and bake at 350° for 1 hour.

"**Imperial Roast**—Mix together ¼ cup cooked brown rice (or white, if you don't have brown), 1 hard-cooked egg, chopped, 2 cups dry cubed bread, ½ cup chopped walnuts, 3 tablespoons evaporated milk, 1½ teaspoons salt and ½ teaspoon sage. Place in oiled pan to a depth of about 2 inches. Bake at 400° for about 1 hour. Serve with gravy.

"If you like **Eggplant** like I do, a very easy and tasty dish, that can be used either as an entrée or side vegetable can be made as follows: Slice eggplants (as many as needed to feed your family) into approximately ½-inch thick slices. Dip slices into beaten egg, then dredge in mixture of flour, salt and pepper. Fry slices in oil until golden brown and set aside. Chop 1 or 2 onions and fry in same pan until golden. Place a layer of eggplant slices in a greased baking dish, sprinkle with some of the sautéed onion and pour some tomato sauce over. Repeat layers until all of the onions and eggplant slices are used up; end with a layer of tomato sauce over all. Bake at 350° until bubbly (30-45 minutes).

"A meatlike substitute can be made from the gluten of hard-wheat flour.

"**Gluten**—Mix 8 cups gluten flour with 4 to 5 cups water (amount of water needed will vary according to flour—dough should be about the same consistency as drop biscuit dough). Knead mixture with hands for about 5 minutes, cover with water and let stand for a few hours or overnight. Wash dough carefully under running water (this washes out all of the starch and leaves behind the gluten, or protein part of the wheat). What you will have left is the raw gluten, which can now be formed into steaks or ground up to use in roasts, etc. What I usually do is form the raw gluten into a roll then slice off steaks from this roll. Boil these steaks in a broth that you make from onion, garlic, water, soy sauce, salt, brown sugar and some oil. Simmer for about 1 hour in the broth, then let cool and store (still in the broth) in your refrigerator until you're ready to use it. We like these steaks dipped in beaten egg, then in cornflake crumbs, fried until golden brown and served with catsup.

"After being cooked in the broth, the steaks may also be soaked in a teriyaki sauce made of *shoyu* (soy sauce), sugar, fresh garlic, ginger and water; and broiled right before serving. Or the teriyaki gluten steaks may be sliced, combined with your choice of fresh garden vegetables (onions, celery, green beans, broccoli, cauliflower, tomatoes, or whatever), and stir-fried over high heat until vegetables are just barely cooked and still crunchy. Serve immediately with hot steamed rice. A little bit of meat or gluten and whatever vegetables we happen to have on hand stir-fried together like that and served with rice

are an old faithful standby around our house. Of course, we eat rice with almost every meal instead of potatoes. There is a strong Oriental influence here in Hawaii along with the Western way of living that we have. The result is something uniquely Hawaiian, I think. I also have a large collection of Hawaiian and other local recipes, and would love to share them with you if you're ever interested.

"Now, back to vegetarian cookery. These next few recipes are some I've gotten at various times from different ladies in my Church.

"**Carrot and Nut Loaf**—2 cups ground raw carrots, 1½ cups dried breads crumbs, ⅓ cup milk (or more), 3 tablespoons oil, 1 onion, chopped, ½ cup chopped nuts and salt to taste. Mix all ingredients together, add 1 or 2 eggs, if needed to moisten. Put into a greased baking dish, cover and bake at 350° for 1 hour. Uncover for the last few minutes to brown top.

"**Princess Loaf**—Sauté ½ cup chopped onion and combine with ½ cup cooked brown rice, 2 beaten eggs, ½ cup evaporated milk, 1 cup bread crumbs, ½ cup sour cream, 2 tablespoons margarine, 1 cup chopped walnuts, ½ teaspoon sage and 1 teaspoon salt. Bake at 350° for about 45 minutes.

"**Pecan Loaf**—Mix together 4 eggs, 1 cup chopped pecans, ¼ cup chopped parsley, ¼ cup melted butter, ½ onion, chopped, 1 cup finely chopped celery, 2 cups oats, 3 cups milk and salt to taste. Bake at 350° for 45 to 60 minutes, or until loaf is set.

"As you know, soybeans are very good sources of protein, and they taste good, too. Here in Hawaii, we can get them either fresh or dried—I don't know how available they are on the Mainland. If fresh, I just boil them in some salted water (in the pods), then we just eat them as is, popping them from the pods into our mouths. The dried soybeans I soak and boil till tender just like any other dried bean, then use them in the following recipes:

"**Soybean Loaf**—Combine 2 cups soybeans (soaked, cooked and ground), 1 cup tomato sauce, 1 onion, ground, 1 cup cubed cheese, ½ cup cornmeal, ¼ cup chopped ripe olives, 3 eggs and salt and sage to taste. Bake at 350° for 1 to 1½ hours.

"**Baked Soybeans**—Mix together 6 cups cooked soybeans (2 cups dried), 3 tablespoons molasses, 1 can tomato soup, 1 cup liquid from beans, the juice of 1 lemon, 1 tablespoon oil and salt to taste. Place in bean pot or baking dish. Put a whole onion in the center of the beans and place several bay leaves on top. Bake at 325° for 1 hour or longer, adding more bean liquid or tomato juice as needed to keep moist.

"**Savory Soybean Patties**—Grind 6 cups cooked soybeans, add 1½ cups oats, ½ teaspoon garlic salt, 2 tablespoons soy sauce, ¼ teaspoon salt, 2 eggs and any other seasonings you may feel in the mood for. Allow mixture to stand for 10 minutes for the oats to absorb moisture. Drop by tablespoonfuls into oiled skillet and fry till brown. Serve with homemade tomato sauce.

"Another one of our old family favorites is **Egg Foo Young,** prepared very simply with whatever we happen to have in the refrigerator or in the garden. I don't have any particular quantities for anything in this recipe—just vary it according to whatever you have, and how many you plan to serve. I use home-sprouted mung bean sprouts, carrots (cut in slivers), green beans (sliced thin, diagonally), celery (cut same as beans), onions (sliced thinly), bell peppers (sliced thinly), etc. Canned bamboo shoots and water chestnuts may also be added for a more exotic touch, but they're really not necessary. Mix all ingredients (all vegetables are still raw) and add enough beaten eggs to hold together. Fry in large patties and serve hot with steamed rice and soy sauce. The vegetables should still be crunchy and the eggs a golden brown.

A sweet-sour sauce to serve with the patties may also be made from soy sauce, brown sugar, vinegar or lemon juice, a pinch of salt and cornstarch to thicken. This is a good dish to prepare ahead—have all of the vegetables sliced and mixed ahead of time, then add eggs right before dinner. Bring your electric skillet to the table and fry the egg patties right there at the dining table so your family can have them piping hot as they are ready for them.

"Well, Carla, I've been typing this straight through, and I'm pooped! After doing these few pages, it's even more of an amazement to me how you managed to ever do all of those 600-plus pages! And especially with five little children around the place—I know what kind of trouble my little one can get into the minute that I turn my back, and to multiply that by five just boggles my imagination!

"Love and aloha!"

Top, left:
Here is Art Johns and his tall, tall corn.
Art and his wife, Ruth, have a beautiful farm just
midway between Kendrick and Juliaetta. From their
house you can look out the windows on one side and
see Kendrick and out the windows on the other side
and see Juliaetta (about four miles between the
two towns). Ethel and Carroll Groseclose live right
across the canyon and they are good friends.

Top, right:
Carroll Groseclose is our next-door neighbor.
His house is only a half mile or so from ours
if you take the path straight up through
the woods. Danny likes to walk up there and
listen to Carroll's fishing stories or watch
him make trout flies out of colored bird feathers
and nylon thread. The girls often stop by too
because it seems like there's always something
yummy happening in the kitchen that his wife
Ethel is sure to invite them to sample.

Bottom, left:
Here are Ethel's hands showing you how
the "sets" grow at the end of a multiplier
onion stem. Can you distinguish the single big
stem that grew the bulblets from the smaller
stems going every which way where the bulblets
are trying to become onion plants themselves,
without any ground to live in yet?

Imogene is one of the best gardeners in the valley—and that's saying a lot because the valley has many good ones. Here she is by her Oregon Giant pole beans. She has spring water brought down the hill in a pipe and then she gets it around the garden by running it down little ditches she makes along the plant rows. She doesn't own a freezer. Cans enough vegetables to see her family of three through the winter. Imogene goes to the store less than anybody I know.

Imogene makes carrot juice regularly in the winter time for her family, using this old juicer and the carrots she has stored in the root cellar. Here she is making carrot juice in her kitchen. In the background you can see her wood cook stove. It's called a "Home Comfort."

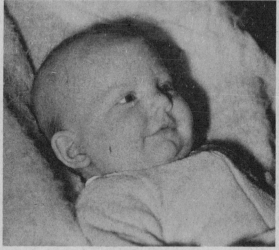

Jacob Michael Emery.

Here is Mike driving his rototiller down the onion and lettuce row, digging out the weeds. A rototiller has a small gasoline engine and the tines turn around kind of lawn mower-style and dig up the ground. It's a favorite tool of home gardeners who don't have enough land to warrant a tractor but still appreciate mechanical help.

SWEETS

INTRODUCTION

Maybe seeing a grumpy, tired, teething baby close its eyes in sleep is the sweetest thing in the world. Maybe it's hearing the man you've been married to for so many years say "I Love You" and mean it. Maybe it's finding out something you've been worried sick about is all right after all. I'm sure it isn't anything in the recipes in this chapter. Most true sweets have their bitter side. The sweet is so sweet because it's such a relief after what comes before. For culinary bittersweets you'd have to look in the Sours chapter under Spiced Fruit—that's a bittersweet where you get vinegar and sugar at once. Sugar is a sweet where the bitter comes afterward—when you get a big pain in the hole in your tooth about the third bite into the once easy goody. When I think of food sweets my favorite thing to think of is fruits and berries. Those are the best tasting of all to me, never caused a cavity that I know of, and don't need a thing extra in season to make them a joy to eat.

TREE FRUITS

So if you don't have one, plant a big, diversified orchard. That way every year, although frost will probably catch some of your trees in bloom, lots of others will still make it through. The different kinds of fruit and different varieties of the same fruit have different blossoming dates—earlier and later. If it happens to freeze while the flowers are blooming there will be no crop of fruit. You'd probably be surprised at the amount of fruit your family could use if they had all they wanted. I canned 100 quarts of cherries last summer and here it is February 1st and I only have one quart left. But I still have apricots, plums, grape and tomato juice, apple plum butter and a lone jar of applesauce, too, so we aren't clear to the end. The cherries are my family's favorite fruit and I haven't been too strict on the rationing. As the year wears on and the favorite fruits like cherries, peaches and pears are eaten up, the others start looking better and tasting better to them.

WHAT FRUITS TO GROW depends mainly on your climate. The farther north you live, the higher in altitude you are, the shorter your frost-free season. In colder areas you may be limited to apples and cherries, colder than that to crabapples, and colder than that you will really have to go into berries for your fruit crop. The farther south you live, the more fruits you can add to the list. But cold-climate fruits won't do as well where the bananas grow. Deciduous trees need a cold winter for their normal annual cycle. I don't know much about real warm climate growing, but if you live in a place like Florida, here's a letter that's bound to set you dreaming! "Dear Carla, We decided that it was just as easy to raise vegetables as flowers and grass, and fruit trees instead of shade trees. We took out all our areca palms and planted about 10 varieties of bananas. Also, put in orange, grapefruit, tangerine, avocado, mango, Key lime, lemon, calamondin and carambola trees. After three years of gardening, we know what vegetables we can produce with greatest success. Our tomatoes have been most successful and I've canned them in every form. Rabbits are our source of fertilizer besides a source of meat." That's from Ella Hupman who lives in Fort Lauderdale, Florida. You see she didn't plant any apple, cherry, apricot, plum, peach, nectarine or pear trees! That's what I can grow. So you can be blessed with fruit wherever you live though not necessarily the same fruit. Other kinds of tree fruits are figs, mulberries and quince.

HOW FRUIT TREES GET BORN—Orchard keeping is more complex than vegetable gardening. So first off, abandon the notion that it is all going to be simple, unless you can just buy somebody else's established orchard and learn enough to keep it going. The trees will probably outlive you. But you can start trees from fruit seeds you save if you are careful to take seeds from the fruit when it is ripe rather than letting them stand in fermenting fruit juice or some such an overly long time which kills the embryo. Dry the seeds and store until late autumn. Plant 3 inches deep. The winter chill and freezing will break the seed's dormancy and next spring it will grow.

Still, you won't have much luck trying to start an orchard from seed. You have to buy young trees from a nursery. It makes me sad to say it because it seems unnatural and wrong, but if you plant a pit from your prized cherry or apple tree the chances are greatest that the offspring will have little in common with the tree you know and love, and the offspring fruit, if any, may be very small and sour. Apples, cherries and plums will start from seed though and there are lots of wild volunteers of those three around here, even an occasional wild pear and some apricots gone wild from long abandoned orchards. The reason they don't grow true is because they are the hybrids of hybrids. The top of the tree is grafted onto a hardier rootstock, but one whose seed doesn't have the fruiting capacity of your present treetop.

Grafting and budding are arts that you should really learn in person, or at the very least, get a whole book on the subject and study it. You can order rootstocks from Grootendorst Nurseries, Lakeside, Michigan 49116, minimum order $10 for 10. They sell rootstocks for apples, pears, plums, peaches and cherry. They sell an "amateur grafting kit" for $17.50 that includes a budding and grafting knife, 8 ounces of grafting wax, 60 yards of ¼-inch grafting tape, 250-300 rubber budding strips in four sizes and "full instructions." That gives you a notion what you would be getting into. Not that I'm trying to discourage you! Grafting is a regrettably rare skill and I'd like to see many more people master it. Grootendorst Nurseries is associated with Southmeadow Fruit Gardens, 2363 Tilbury Place, Birmingham, Michigan 48009, which has the distinction of being the only place I know of in this country where you can mail-order bayberry plants. That's the natural wax bearing plant that is the only homestead (nonindustrial) vegetarian way of making candles. (See the Candles section of Home Industries.)

You also need expert advice about what combinations to buy. Some fruit trees can't make fruit by themselves (are not self-fruitful) and need another tree to be a pollinizer for them. For example, the Delicious apple and its red relatives are not self-fruitful and a pollinizer is required. Jonathan, Golden Delicious, Winter Banana, Yellow Transparent and Lodi would all do the job. Mutzu wouldn't. Nectarines don't need a pollinizer. Some apricots do and some don't. Hale, Candoka, and Earlihale peaches do and Early Elberta is the best. Bartlett and Anjou pears can usually make it without a pollinizer but they will do better with one present. Cherries need one except for the sour cherry Montmorency and so on it goes. So trees have sex. If your peach tree has small hard fruits that never seem to ripen, that's probably because it is a boy. The pollen carriers are insects. Without that, you would have no fruit.

You'll also have to choose between dwarf, semidwarf and standard-sized trees. Thirty years ago dwarf trees were more expensive. That was when they were becoming popular and demand was greater than supply. Now at the nursery I go to, dwarf, semidwarf and standards are exactly the same price. The only difference in the trees' constitution is the rootstock. When you get ready to do your own grafting, you will be offered a choice of dwarf, semidwarf or standard rootstocks, and as the rootstock is chosen so the tree will grow. There is a lot more difference than merely the name. Recently I got a question in the mail—"What trees produce the fastest and largest quantities?" The answer is not the same ones. That's the whole thing in dwarf versus standard. Dwarf trees bear fruit sooner. A standard apple tree may not produce fruit for 6 to 8 years. A dwarf may in 2 to 4 years. (Apple takes the most time.) Dwarfs are easier to get to so you can spray or prune or pick fruit easier. The fruit is the same size on either tree. The other side of it is that standards produce the largest quantities of fruit per year per tree once they get going and they live longer than dwarf varieties. A dwarf tree will live for maybe 25 years, a standard tree for maybe 40. Semidwarfs are a compromise in between the two extremes. So you really have to make your own personal decision based on your goals for your family and your orchard and then get the appropriate kind of tree.

We get half standards and half semidwarfs. But we already have a good-sized orchard with just about every kind of fruit in it so waiting doesn't matter. And we have lots of room to expand the orchard. There's a factor I didn't mention. That dwarfs don't need near as much room as standards. If you have a small yard in a city, the obvious choice would be to divide the area between different kinds of dwarf fruit trees for as much variety as you could get for the given area. Dwarf apple trees can be spaced as close as 8 feet by 10 feet apart. A standard-sized apple needs more like a spacing of 40 feet by 40 feet. Standard apples take more room than any of the other standard fruit trees. Check the alphabetical section below for details on each one.

If you planted half standards and half dwarfs you could be enjoying the fruit of your dwarfs while waiting for your standards to mature. I like the idea of planting for your grandchildren. Plan on planting some fruit and nut trees every spring and more every fall as long as you can find the room even if you already have an orchard. It takes a long time for a tree to grow and some of them may not make it. Sooner or later some of the grown trees will die of old age. It's a wonderful thing to plant a tree. Each tree is a living thing that will share the rest of your life. It will grow and give you shade and elegant beauty and food to eat, a place for the birds to nest and the children to climb and for you to hang your hammock. In summer when the fruit starts the children and I quit cooking breakfasts. We just get up in the morning and head for the orchard. Who needs any other start to the day when there are trees loaded with heavenly ripe cherries waiting to be eaten! It's fun to gather round the tree, big ones handing down fruit to the smaller ones, mother pulling down low hanging branches for smaller children to hang onto and strip. That's the easy part. Then we've got to put up the winter supply.

Avoid buying fruit trees mail-order. The catalog salesmanship is great but in the long run I think you'll be happier with what you buy in person from a local nursery. The mail-order trees are cheaper. They are also smaller and in worse condition and get off to a much poorer start. Your local plant nursery knows expertly what trees are most suitable for your area. Their trees are already acclimated, and if your tree should die they will quite likely replace it for you at no charge if you ask (and save your receipt!). Buy the biggest (oldest) trees you can afford. It takes them long enough to grow anyway. If you want to mail-order I recommend Van Well Nursery, P.O. Box 1339, Wenatchee, Washington 98801. They have a free catalog and prices so low you will gasp. Good especially to check into if you are planting a whole orchard—their specialty is volume business. They have berries, too. Minimum order, $8.

You can plant either in the early spring or in the late fall. Plant where they will have enough room—more for standards than dwarfs, not under telephone lines, and where they'll have sunshine and shelter from wind if they aren't hardy. Dig your hole. Cut off the metal pot with tin snips or tear if off if it's made of paper to avoid disturbing the roots. Set the tree in the hole and replace the dirt around it. Stomp dirt all around it to be firm and create a depression into which water can settle. But don't ever cover the root-stock scar. You can see where the top part of your tree was grafted onto the root part. If that scar gets covered, it will sprout a tree of its own and eventually would take over from the top that you want to grow. Remove any grass around for 3 or 4 feet in diameter. Keep the grass and other weeds rooted out from around your little tree from then on. Water at least twice a week.

Don't prune any the first year. After that, you can prune once in the spring and again in the fall. Prune when the leaves are off the tree. If some kinds of trees are cut during their growing season (walnut, American elm), they may bleed to death. To prune a young tree means to cut off 2 or 3 inches from the end of each branch. Don't remove the lower branches of dwarf trees. There won't be any higher ones. Dwarf trees eventually develop a whole bunch of shoots that reach for the sky like an African bush haircut. Keep cutting those top ones off to get more like a crew cut on top. Prune with hand shears, "lopping shears" or a pruning saw.

Older trees are pruned to remove dead or diseased wood, to make harvesting more convenient, to let light in where branches are overcrowded, and to control vertical top growth that is impossible to harvest anyway. If the branch taken off an older tree is ½ inch or less in diameter, you don't need to paint the wound. Painting protects against disease until the cambium bark can seal it up. Summer rainfalls make problems more likely. You can buy special paint with an asphalt base and spread it on with a putty knife. Or use ordinary paint. Or roofing cement.

Pruning is a complex subject. It's not the same for every tree. A good guide on the subject that takes it separately for each variety of trees is *How to Prune Fruit Trees*, available for $2.50 from the author R. Sanford Martin, 10535 Las Lunitas Ave., Tujunga, California 91042. I've had the pleasure of meeting Mr. Martin and this fruit section is indebted to his patient answers to my many questions.

TO SPRAY OR NOT TO SPRAY—I don't spray my trees at all. That isn't to say there is no disease in my orchard because there is. I don't know what it is but the leaves curl up and the whole tree will look pretty sick. But they generally don't die and they get over it and seem to become immune for at least several years afterwards. I have a big enough orchard that the temporary outing of some trees is no problem to total supply. I'm probably lucky. I've heard from people who were suffering with things like peach tree borers. (There's more on peach tree borers under "peaches.") When you don't spray, and if you're lucky enough not to get a major disease problem or insect problem in your orchard about the worst you have to put up with is scars on the sides of the fruit sometimes or an occasional worm. I don't mind. I take my biggest losses to birds. They love cherries. Some years they are hungrier than others. I've never quite figured it out.

TREE FRUITS— APPLE TO POMEGRANATE

APPLES are a real staple for me. They grow easily, store well and have so many uses. Standard apples are 6 to 8 years to first fruiting and need to be spaced 40 feet by 40 feet. Dwarf apples fruit in 2 to 4 years and are spaced 8 feet by 10 feet. You can choose apple varieties to ripen early, middle or late. There is lots more about apples scattered here and there in this book. For the best storing, pick them before they're dead ripe. Don't pick right after rain. They should be dry. Cool storage is vital. It just amazes me how fast they start to shrivel, lose that crisp nice texture and flavor, and plain old rot when we bring in a box from the storage shed to the kitchen—literally within a couple of days. The secret is keeping them cold but not frozen. In warmish weather they tend to rot first at the bottom of the box. Adjacent apples won't catch the rot very fast but over longish periods of time they'll soak up a noxious rotten flavor so pick-

ing over the apples—but carefully not to bruise them—is a good idea once in a while. Apples on top that have been touched by frost will be brown and then bad in the frosted place.

The keeping qualities of raw apples vary. In our orchard we have early apples that come on same time as the apricots and of course you don't worry about storing them. What we don't eat we can as applesauce or apple butter. They are better applesauce apples than storing apples anyway. Ditto for the next crop of apples. The last crop consists of apples that don't turn red until fall is really on and they aren't picked until after frost. It is October as I write this and I have only just begun to harvest these red apples. These are the ones we store for winter. Obviously the later you put them into storage, the later you have them. They keep better on the tree than in the basement. Only when they really show a determination to fall from the tree do I pick in earnest.

We also have a big green late apple. It gets very large, never does turn red, and is very good. These apples are so good we always just eat them up. I wish I could tell you what kind they all are but I don't know. Your local nursery can tell you what varieties do best in your area and when they ripen. Although I don't know what kind of trees I personally have I can quote you some names from my reading. The best apples for storing are said to be Yellow Newtown, Winesap, Arkansas and York Imperial.

A way to help keep your apples cold is to give the cellar access to frosty night air and then shut it up tight during the daytime. With the best of luck they will even keep till spring. But the apples shouldn't freeze. You could insulate your boxes under straw in the barn, or underground under straw and dirt inside barrels. Another way to keep apples stored is to line a big box with crumpled newspapers. Put your box of apples inside that. Cover all with more newspaper and then a heavy quilt or some such. My apples are stored in cardboard boxes in the bunkhouse under an old mattress. The children enjoy fresh raw fruit so much when the rest is out of season. I bring apples into the house as needed. We generally eat them peeled—with breakfast or between meals. Or baked served with thick cream.

I sort the apples while picking, taking out bruised, very ripe and soft ones, and ones with wormholes to make into applesauce or for the animals. When storing green apples, put the very greenest and soundest ones into storage. Don't throw them around. If an apple falls off the tree instead of being picked, put it into the box for quick use since even if it doesn't show, it has been bruised and will spoil quicker. If your wasps are active, pick late in the day to avoid grabbing a wasp along with the apple.

I make lots of **applesauce.** It's a good way to preserve apples that wouldn't keep otherwise. Applesauce is hard to keep from spoiling in the jar. Even in a sealed jar, because it is so dense and a dense mass is difficult to heat to boiling throughout. Unsweetened applesauce doesn't have such a severe tendency this way, and it's very easy to stir in sweetening after you open the jar when you need it. So to make applesauce peel and core your apples, boil and mash until you have a sauce.

You can also **freeze apples** to use in making pies and so on. Just wash, peel, core, slice, scald, drain, chill, cover with a thin syrup and freeze. Or you can do without the syrup. Just peel and slice into salted water, then pack into baggies and freeze. The slices break apart quite easily while still frozen for making apple pie or crisp or you can add a small amount of water and make applesauce.

Apples are one fruit that you will have raw for a very considerable time out of season. That gives you so many great possibilities for ways to use them. I like apples in salads, apples in puddings, apples in any dessert, fried apples and baked apples.

To bake apples peel and core the apples (or don't peel if they're on the small side). Place in a shallow pan with a piece of butter and a dab of honey in the center of each apple. Sprinkle generously with cinnamon. Put 3 cups water in the pan and cook until the apples are nearly done, basting often. Then put in the oven and bake. The apples will be nearly transparent when done. Serve with whipped cream. For a really special dish stuff the apple center with 2 tablespoons pitted, mashed or blended dates. Or raisins. Or nuts. Bake, covered, at 375° until tender and juicy.

Boiled Apples—Don't peel the apples for this. Flavor and pectin come from the peelings. Put cored apples (especially good with fair skinned kinds) in a saucepan with about half an inch of water. Pour ½ cup sugar or equivalent sweetening over and boil until the apples are quite tender. While the apples are cooking turn them several times and keep boiling until the liquid turns thick like a jelly. Now serve. You'll love them.

APRICOTS, either standard or dwarf, take three years to first fruiting. Space standards 20 feet by 20 feet, dwarfs 12 feet by 12 feet. Apricots shouldn't be picked green because they won't ripen off the tree. Instead they would just shrivel and get bitter. Pears, on the other hand, should be picked before quite ripe and allowed to finish in the box. If left on the tree until dead ripe more likely than not they will be rotten by the core. I canned about 60 quarts of apricots last year, maybe more. The ones I had pitted were really popular. The ones I got in a hurry and didn't pit for some reason don't have a clear syrup and aren't nearly as popular with the children so I've been putting them in the bread. Next year I'll take the time to pit all the apricots I can.

To can apricots just wash, cut them in half and take the pit out. Put into jars, add hot syrup and process in a hot water bath 25 minutes for pints, 30 minutes for quarts.

To freeze apricots just wash, cut in half, take out the pit, cover with syrup and freeze.

Apricots are subject to a fungus disease that we call "scab." That's what it looks like and all unsprayed ones have more or less of it, domestics often more than wild trees, for some strange reason. You can cut off the scab if you want or go ahead and can the fruit up scab and all. Given a good cooking it does no harm, softens up and is hardly noticeable for family use.

CHERRIES—Standards take 6 to 7 years to first fruit, need 25 feet by 25 feet. Dwarfs take 4 to 5 years, need 12 feet by 12 feet. That's sweet cherries. Sour cherries fruit a couple of years sooner and require less room.

Cherries can be **canned** with or without pits. But I think it's insane to go to all the work to take out the pits when the kids can spit them out so easily and the flavor is fine. I read somewhere you should prick each cherry with a sterilized needle. That's insane, too. Just fill your jars (remove stems and leaves), pour over hot syrup and process in hot water bath for 15 minutes. Cherries can easier and nicer than any other fruit except maybe peaches. I give canned cherries as gifts sometimes to visitors—I'm that pleased with the product. That's sweet cherries. Now there's a little sour kind of cherry called a pie cherry that isn't so hot canned unless you do something extra with it like stick it into a pie.

To freeze cherries wash them. Pit cherries you'll want for salads or cooking. Leave some unpitted for eating. Best frozen covered with apple or pineapple juice. Or any sweet syrup. You can freeze plain—makes good snacking.

Maraschino Cherries—I've never made these but it's a recipe so hard to come by that I'm including it more for curiosity's sake. Wash 2 pounds good ripe, but not overripe, Royal Ann cherries. Next you need limewater and you can get the basics for that at your drugstore. Combine 1 cup limewater with 4 cups cold water, pour over the cherries and let soak 6 hours. Now drain cherries, rinse well and pit them. Combine 3 cups sugar, 1½ cups hot water and 2 tablespoons red food coloring. Heat to boiling and add the pitted cherries. Let it cook on low heat for about 10 minutes. Cool and let rest in the refrigerator until the next day. Now reheat to boiling and stir in 1 tablespoon almond extract. Then hot pack the cherries together with enough syrup to cover into hot sterilized jars and seal. Can in small jars because you won't want to use too many at a time. (The FDA has recently found that some red food coloring is cancer-causing. So leave it out and don't worry about color.)

FIGS don't grow in Idaho but they do in Southern California. Those fortunate people! To *freeze* figs just put fully ripe, large ones in plastic bags and freeze. You can pick figs all summer long. They don't blossom. The fruit just appears along the branches.

To bake fresh figs, wash them and cut off both ends. For about two dozen large figs set them in a glass baking pan and pour a nice fruit juice over—apple is best. While they are baking (moderate oven) stir in the juice every once in a while to get them moistened and roll them over. Give them at least 40 minutes. Good with whipped cream.

Special Figs—Put in the oven (350°) as for baked figs with the contents of a 16-ounce can apple juice concentrate. After the first 40 minutes turn heat down to 150° and dry 30 minutes more. They come out "candied."

LOQUATS can grow in California or the Gulf states. They are the earliest fruiting fruit I know of. The variety called "Early Red" is ready to eat in January. "Advance" ripens March to May. "Champagne" has a big fruit with the best flavor. Loquats grow tall where it's warm and wet, shorter under less favorable conditions. Have top flavor when fully ripe but make better jelly and preserves when the fruit is somewhat on the green side. Loquat is an evergreen of the rose family! Sort of like eating super-sized rose hips.

PEACHES and **NECTARINES** are my favorite fruits in the world to eat out of hand. I have a nectarine tree growing in the orchard. Last year a neighbor ran over it with his pickup and practically broke my heart but one branch survived and I've hopes for it yet.

Peach tree borers are a bad problem in places like Pennsylvania. They not only attack peach trees but also wild and cultivated cherry trees, plum, prune, nectarine and apricot. You've got them if you find masses of tree gum that contain red-brown larval droppings and sawdust on the tree trunks near the ground. The borers destroy the inner tree bark from below the soil surface to 10 inches above it. The trees first do poorly and the leaves get off-color. Then they die. The borers themselves are about an inch long. They look like worms that have brown heads and cream-colored bodies. The best cure is prevention. Paint your newly planted trees with exterior white latex and add a sticking agent for longer lasting protection. Keep the tree growing at the proper rate with plenty of water and fertilizer. Any tree weakened by injury, drought, hunger or sunburn will be more subject to attack by borers. If your tree does get infected you can worm by hand by digging out the dirt down 6 inches. Find the wormholes by making cuts around the damaged areas. Use a flexible wire in the burrows to skewer the worms. Do it again in two weeks. Fill up the holes and replace the dirt. Put mothballs or lots of ashes on the ground around the tree trunk to try to discourage a return visit.

To can peaches you wash them, dip them in boiling water, then quickly into cold water. That loosens the skins so you can slip them off. Now cut the peaches in halves and take out the pits. If you're slow you can drop the fruit into water containing 2 tablespoons *each* salt and vinegar per gallon water to prevent darkening. I don't do that. I just work fast. I pack the raw fruit into jars getting as much in as I can, cover with hot syrup, put on lids and process in hot water bath 30 minutes. You can **freeze** peaches by going through the same preparation only you put them in the freezer with cold syrup instead of processing. Or you can freeze whole peaches and save on sugar. Use *ripe* unpeeled peaches. Freeze first and then pack in plastic bags for long-term storage. To serve these frozen whole peaches hold under running water till the skins will slide off. Slice. You still won't need sugar. They'll keep their natural sweetness. Or you can freeze peeled, sliced peaches in pineapple or apple juice with a little ascorbic acid or lemon juice added.

PEARS are picked green and stored to ripen. If you left them on the tree to ripen they would have a tendency to go bad at the center or to fall off and rot on the ground. Pick the pears when they are fully grown but still hard and green, when they change from deep green to pale green. Bartlett pears ripen the quickest—in a couple of weeks. Keiffer pears are fast, too. When the pears get ripe you need to go ahead and can or otherwise preserve them. Store them where it is cool. Don't put any bad ones in the storage box. (Keep below 75°.) I haven't personally been lucky with pears. One year it was blight, one drought, once an early freeze.

PERSIMMONS are another Southern fruit. They grow both wild and tame. Green ones are awful. Make sure you don't have any, or they'll sour your whole batch. Native persimmons are small and orange, Japanese persimmons are big and red. You can freeze the Japanese ones whole. Freeze unpeeled, separately. Store in plastic bags after they are frozen. To serve, peel (the skin will slip if you hold the fruit under running water). Dice and serve with cream. The cream freezes as the fruit thaws. The pulp can be made into leather (sieve out seeds). To can pulp pack in small jars, process in hot water bath for 30 minutes. You can also freeze the pulp.

PLUMS come in so many different colors and sizes— purple, red, green—smaller than an apricot to almost as big as a peach. Take your choice. They are easy to grow. My family though will ask for cherries, peaches, nectarines, pears, apricots or berries before they will plums. Sad but true. You dry a certain kind of plum and you have a prune. You dry any other kind of plum and you have a dried plum. Pit them before you dry them—don't try to make them look like the store-bought prunes. You can freeze plums whole. Just wash, bag up and freeze. To serve the frozen plums just rinse off, slice into dishes and let defrost enough so you can get your teeth into them. Can hot packs. Process in hot water bath 20 minutes for pints, 25 for quarts.

POMEGRANATES start from a bush rather than a seed. They are hardy in the Las Vegas area and have no insect problems. Beautiful flowers for a good two months that are brilliant coral and trumpet shaped. The pomegranate is ripe for sure when it starts to split. (You can't tell by the outside color.) Will *really* stain your kids' clothes.

BERRIES AND GRAPES

It's a good idea to have a variety of berries as well as a good orchard. Your first strawberries will bear in June. Raspberries mature in July. Blackberries and wild berries are on in August and September. That will give you berries all summer long. When you pick berries that have thorns, wear long stockings with the feet whacked off—not nylons—or some similar heavy protection on your arms so you won't get too badly scratched. A leather belt around your waist with a half-gallon can hanging on it is handy and then you can empty the berries into a big bucket when the little one is full. Don't worry about leaves and such when you're picking. You can put the berries in water when you get home and leaves and such will float to the top and you can just scoop them away.

Strawberries and raspberries and many other berries reproduce by "runners." Strawberry runners travel on top of the ground, then stop about a foot away from the parent plant, put down roots and become a new and independent strawberry plant. You just whack the connection, dig up the independent plant and reset it in your ground where you want it. Other berry runners travel under the ground like the nuisance lilac "suckers" and then pop up anywhere to reach for the precious light. In the spring you just dig up these sticklike shoots, replant where you want them and they'll go ahead and grow. These new runners bear no fruit the first year, they will bear fruit the second year.

So when you want some berry or grape plants or more berry or grape plants you don't plant a seed— you plant a "cutting" of some sort. A "cutting" is a piece of a parent plant that when planted on its own can develop into an independent plant. You can plant a cutting taken from the branches (a "stem cutting") or a piece of root ("root cutting") or in some cases you can even use a single leaf ("leaf cutting"). You can take a cutting from a dormant plant or from one that is actively growing in the spring and early summer. Later than that you are past the time for planting cuttings. Your planted cuttings need halfway agreeable weather, protection from getting dried out—keep them well watered until they take—and protection from curious children who would pull them up to see if they've got roots yet!

When gardening neighbors are cleaning out unwanted berry runners in the spring and cutting back

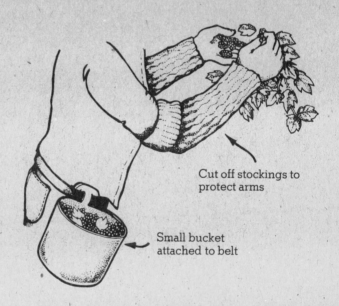

Cut off stockings to protect arms

Small bucket attached to belt

perennials they can give you all the good starts you'll need if you just give them advance notice that you would like to have them. They have to dig them out anyway from between their rows and if they didn't give them to you then they would throw the starts away. If you can't get berry and grape starts from neighbors, buy from your local nurseryman rather than by mail-order. If you live someplace where there are no plant nurseries and mail-order is the only answer, you won't have any trouble finding a choice. Almost all the big catalog seed houses carry a wide selection of berry cuttings, too. There is at least one that specializes in berries. You can write for *Brittingham's Berry Book* to Brittingham Plant Farms, Ocean City Road, Salisbury, Maryland 21801. It's a free catalog. It makes educational reading for anyone who is interested in berries.

The Complete Guide to Growing Berries and Grapes pulls together most of the basic details about these small fruits. It's written by Louise Riotte and published by Garden Way, Charlotte, Vermont 05445.

Recipes—If you have some unusual kind of berries or small fruit for which you can't find specific recipes (there are umpteen different kinds of berries), just substitute in recipes that call for a similar fruit because they are very similar except for the sweetness/tartness which you can taste test and add more or less sweetening as needed.

To can berries process them as soon as possible after picking. Get them ready by hulling or stemming. Put in a sieve and wash by swishing them through a pan of cold water several times. Strawberries tend to lose their color and aren't as nice canned as frozen but it can be done. The trouble with freezing everything is that you then have everything in one big vulnerable basket. Blackberries, blueberries, gooseberries and huckleberries can nicely. If you freeze huckleberries make sure your jars are sealed and you wash the outsides because they tend to give off an odor that other foods pick up. My friend Imogene open kettle cans all her berries. More conservatively, I'd recommend you fill your jars, then add boiling water, sweetened or otherwise as you please, to within a half inch of the top. And then process in a hot water bath for 10 minutes.

Omelets with Berries—Beat up 2 or 3 eggs until just blended but not frothy. Melt 1 tablespoon butter in a clean frying pan. Pour half the egg mixture into skillet for your first omelet. Stir around once and then stir by shaking the pan. When the omelet is done put it on a serving dish. Pour ½ cup fresh berries onto it. Fold over. Top with whipped cream and a few more berries and do your other omelet with another ½ cup berries and whipped cream.

Basic Berry Syrup—In a nonaluminum pan mix together 2 cups berry juice and 3 cups sugar. Cook over low heat until all the sugar is in solution. In a separate small saucepan combine ½ cup water with ½ bottle liquid pectin or ½ box pectin. Boil 3 to 5 minutes, stirring constantly. Stir pectin mixture into the juice mixture and refrigerate until ready to use. Your result will be a basic pancake-type syrup.

Basic Berry Jam—Weigh hulled and washed berries. Weigh out an equal amount of sugar. Mash berries and set to cook over low heat—not in an aluminum pan. Bring to boil slowly with frequent stirring. Add sugar. Simmer until thick, stirring often enough so jam doesn't start to stick and burn on the bottom. Seal in hot clean jars.

THROUGH THE BERRY AND GRAPE ALPHABET

BLACKBERRIES—They grow wild and they grow tame. They are called "blackberries" and they are called umpteen other names like "dewberry" and "thimbleberry," "black raspberry," "flymboy," "wineberry," "nagoonberry," "cloudberry," "wild raspberry," "salmonberry," "blackcap," "bake-apple." The line of distinction between blackberries and raspberries in the wild isn't very clear, and there are so many different varieties with so many different sizes and colors that suffice it they are all good to eat. If you live where they grow abundantly you have a wonderful ready-made free source of small fruit. Blackberries make good out-of-hand eating and good jam and jelly. You can make a hedge of blackberries. If you pick them prematurely they won't be as sweet as later on. Let them stay on the bush until they are really, really ripe and then they will be sweet and not sour tasting. The "dewberry" variety of blackberry has huge beautiful berries but it isn't as winter hardy as some others. You can propagate blackberries by the volunteer suckers that grow or by root cuttings. Vine-type blackberries like youngberries, boysenberries, dewberries and loganberries seldom sucker but can be propagated by leaf bud cuttings, except for some fancy thornless varieties. What would happen if you took a root cutting of an improved thornless variety is the new plant would revert to the old thorny kind. A 2-inch segment is enough for a root cutting to plant.

BLUEBERRIES need an acid soil. If they have that you have a wonderful berry that may bear fruit the first year and for the next 50, but if they don't have an acid soil they will die and that's that.

CHOKECHERRIES grew wild where I lived as a little girl. People who haven't grown up with chokecherries generally don't appreciate them much at first. They grow on a bushy sort of tree in places cold enough that you really appreciate *any* kind of fruit. They come on in the fall after the frosts and for weeks on end on the way to and from school, walking or riding my pony (it was always one or the other for the two-mile stretch) a pause to refresh at the chokecherry grove made the trip easier. The pit is very large in relation to the tiny cherry-like flesh around it. You spit out the pits. The leaves of the tree are quite poisonous so don't try to make tea out of them like you can from raspberry leaves. The flavor is so sour ("choke") that it will pucker you up, but once you've learned to love chokecherries you eat them anyway, pucker up, spit out the seed and reach for another handful! They make a wonderful unusual tasting pancake and waffle syrup which was one of my mother's specialties. Nothing special to it—just sweeten with sugar and cook down until thick enough. You can buy started chokecherry trees from some mail-order nurseries and hometown nurseries.

CURRANTS went through a time of trouble in the 1920's when bushes were uprooted and became very rare as a result. Certain varieties of currants and gooseberries were supposed to carry white-pine blister rust, a disease that destroyed white pine trees. Many states passed laws banning currants and gooseberries and seed catalogs stopped carrying them. Now currants are making a comeback. Legal restrictions on them are being lifted and increasing numbers of seedsmen and nurseries are carrying them again. That's good because currants and gooseberries are among the hardiest of the berries and important to folks who have to live on mountainsides. Currants are a firm berry as compared to the blackberry. They are easy to propagate by stem cut-

tings, and I know people who have raised them from seed. Take cuttings about 8 inches long anytime during the fall, winter or very early spring. They won't do quite as well if you start them after growth has got going in the spring. They do good in a clay soil. It's still a good idea not to plant currants if there are white pines (pines with needles growing in clusters of five) within 300 yards. And check your local laws to make sure you aren't in an area where it's still illegal to plant them.

ELDERBERRIES resemble chokecherries in being a tree fruit. Only they are very small, smaller even than a chokecherry. Under natural conditions elderberries grow at lower elevations, chokecherries at higher ones, but they both like mountains and canyonsides. Elderberries are on the sour side. They have a lot of seed which you sort of collect in your mouth until there is enough to bother spitting it out. Or go ahead and swallow them. Elderberry blossoms are listed in the Herbs chapter for tea making. Here is what Criss Wilhite wrote me from Fresno, California, about elderberries: "Another thing we dry is elderberries. We go to the mountains in August and cut bushels of elderberries and elderblow. We dry the elderblow for tea. We dry the berries on their stems. It takes only a few days. Then we remove the woody stems and forget about the smaller ones. The berries this way are great in homegrown and -ground cornmeal mush or muffins or any baked goods. Elderberry juice is great to mix with apple juice or sauce. It tastes like cranapple. We also make elderberry-gooseberry juice. The tart elderberries compensate for the too-sweet gooseberries."

GOOSEBERRIES went through the same thing as currants and became very uncommon. Berry gooseberries grow on a low berry-type bush. Chinese gooseberries are something else entirely. They started out in China, then got to New Zealand and finally to California. Chinese gooseberries grow on a grape-type vine, are large as a lemon and have no connection with the regular gooseberry. The first importers of the fruit renamed them "kiwi fruit" and that's what they are called in California supermarkets. So far California is the only place in the United States where Chinese gooseberries are being grown. Regular gooseberries are another tiny berry type fruit. In my experience they either have to be picked before the berries get too ripe or you have to cope with worms in them. It's the same deal as peas. The insects "sting" them—make black spots on the outside which if left long enough hatch into worms. If you have a sturdy stomach you can use the wormy gooseberries. I set them on to cook in plenty of water. As the berries heat, the worms rise to the top and can be skimmed off.

To make Gooseberry Jam cook 4½ cups gooseberries in 2 tablespoons water over medium low heat until yellow. Add 2 cups sugar. Bring to a boil again and boil 5 minutes. Pour in jars and seal. You get 2 pints of jam.

When gooseberries are green they are still underripe. They turn kind of purple red at the moment of ripeness. There is a wide variety of sizes from tiny on up.

Gooseberry Pie—Cook 3 cups fresh gooseberries just long enough so they pop. Add 1½ cups sugar, ½ teaspoon ground nutmeg and 4 tablespoons flour. Pour into a prepared unbaked piecrust. Put second crust on and seal well to keep from boiling over. Put slits in top. Brush top with cream and sprinkle sugar on it. Bake about 45 minutes at 425°, or until it looks cooked. Good with plain cream.

GRAPES—Quite likely you can get started with grapes with cuttings from a neighbor who has them. You cut in the early spring before the sap has started to run when it looks all dead. Don't prune grapes after the sap is running because they'll bleed like crazy. Cut off a length of stem with at least five bud spots on it. This is where the leaves will develop later. Stick it in your chosen place with two or three spots underground and the other three above. Roots will grow from those underground and leaves from those above. Keep the ground soaked around them all that first summer. You may have grapes from them even the first year. If you're planting in a row, set cuttings about 2 feet apart. They can be by the side of a building if you want. Pick a sunny side. Supply a pole for climbing. When choosing grape starts be careful to take slips off a good productive plant rather than just anything.

Grapes, like pears, are a late summer crop—at least around here. If you pick only good ones and keep them in a cold, moderately moist place they will keep a month or two. Catawba keep the best. Ours are some little green kind with seeds. You can get a lot of useful information on grapes out of the Henry Field Seed Company catalog. Don't get in a hurry for production. Generally you'll have no grapes the first year you plant, very few the second, a little the third and then in the fourth year you'll start to get into real production—depending on how you prune. That's true of cold weather type grapes. You see there are two basic kinds of grapes. One is your *vinifera* or California wine type. They are most common in warm climates. Thompson's Seedless, also this type, is a good table grape. With these warm climate grapes you can have grapes growing by the second year after planting. Your *labrusca* varieties have slip-skins and are your cold weather kinds of grapes. Concord is one. The Concord grape is a *good* producer. These do better in cold climates where they will give you a heavier production than your warm weather types will. Cold weather types will do fine in New York. But they take at least three years to bear fruit. They bear fruit from the third, fourth and fifth buds from the base of the vine. When you are pruning you have to be careful you don't cut away that fruiting wood.

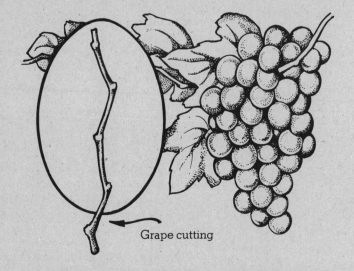

Grape cutting

Green grapes make nice table grapes, but purple salad grapes are better for preserves and juice. The green grapes can be made into homemade fruit cocktail. Just cut your fruits small—whatever you have like strawberries, peaches and so on. Combine with a honey syrup and can or freeze. Although you never see grapes listed in regular canning lists they can be canned.

To can them just remove the stems, pack in your jars, pour over hot syrup or even plain water. Process in a hot water bath 15 minutes.

I generally juice mine. That means I heat them just enough to get the juice ready (see juicing), mash out the juice and can it. When serving the juice I dilute half and half with water. Early in the season the children don't care much for grape juice but by about February when the apples are gone they start to really relish it and I do too.

HUCKLEBERRIES are cousins of the blueberry with a small firm berry.

Basic Huckleberry Sauce—1 cup huckleberries, ¼ cup sugar, 1 tablespoon water, 2 tablespoons light corn syrup, 2 tablespoons berry juice, 1 tablespoon cornstarch and 2 teaspoons lemon juice. Place berries in a pan. Add sugar, water and corn syrup. Bring to a boil. Blend berry juice and cornstarch and stir into berries, stirring constantly. Cook until thickened. Stir in lemon juice and remove from heat. Chill. Good for jelly roll, open face pie, cooked pie shell or sauce, or topping for ice cream.

Huckleberry Pie—Get ready dough for a two-crust pie. Boil, drain and rinse 2 cups huckleberries, then cook again with a very little water until tender. Add sweetening to taste and 2 tablespoons flour. Bake in a 425° oven.

You can get two whole pages of huckleberry recipes by writing "Dorothy Dean's Homemakers Service" at the *Spokesman-Review*, Spokane, Washington 99210, and asking for "Huckleberry Hits."

Huckleberry Cake—Barbara Stone wrote me from Stites, Idaho, with this one. "I don't care for huckleberries raw but in a cake is something else. Separate 3 eggs. Beat the whites until stiff and set aside. Beat the egg yolks and blend with ¼ cup milk. Blend in 1 cup sugar and ½ cup butter or other shortening. Sift 1½ cups flour with 1 teaspoon baking powder, ¼ teaspoon nutmeg, ½ teaspoon cinnamon and add to egg yolk mixture. The batter will be unusually stiff. Put berries into flat dish and roll in flour. Up to this point an electric beater can be used, but now the berries are folded into the batter with a spoon. Then fold in the beaten egg whites. Bake in a greased and floured 8 x 8-inch pan. A loaf pan is better so the batter doesn't spread too thin. Sprinkle the entire top of the cake with a thin coating of sugar. This will form a glaze. No frosting is necessary. Bake in a moderate oven (350°) until done. Depending on the oven it usually takes 50-60 minutes."

RASPBERRIES, like blackberries, are a very soft berry. The soft berries do better frozen than canned because they cook up so easily. They make good jam, jelly, sauce and juice, too, but are nicest of all fresh. Raspberry plants don't last forever. A started raspberry row will last maybe 7 to 10 years. So after the fifth year start a new row so it will be growing berries when the old one starts slowing up. Raspberries come in both black and red. Most varieties will only bear once on a cane so you prune by cutting out old canes after they have fruited. But there is one kind of raspberry now that will bear fruit two years in a row before stopping on any particular cane.

STRAWBERRY plants want lots of moisture and a sort of shady location like on the shady side of your house or under an orchard. To can strawberries just let them boil up once, then pour into jars and seal. That's Imogene's way and she cans umpteen quarts every summer. Imogene is a favorite neighbor of mine. She is about 60 years old. She has one arm sort of paralyzed from a childhood case of polio and she sees only well enough to read newspaper headlines. She lives on about three acres with her husband, who has been a total invalid for several years now with a bad heart condition, and with her widowed mother, who doesn't get around too actively due to arthritis. She was not blessed with children. Imogene milks goats and has a big garden. Her family lives more nearly totally off their own produce than any other I know.

But the important thing about Imogene is that she is the most cheerful, friendly, giving person I know—I'd even risk it to say in the whole wide world. She's always got a big smile and a hello. She loves company any day but her precious Sabbath, which she truly regards for rest and prayer as she feels God wants her to. And seems like she's always calling me up wanting to give me something. The country people trade as much for the love of giving as for getting something accomplished. And sure enough I'll end up with a big sack of carrots and another of spuds or some such. I'd rather eat Imogene's vegetables than my own. Hers are raised with such love there just have to be more vitamins in them! I don't believe she owns a cookbook. She cooks on a wood stove and does all her canning water bath the old-time way. There are some recipes of hers in the Sauerkraut section.

If you want to can strawberries the university way pack them hot, cover with hot juice and process 15 minutes. I freeze them. Imogene doesn't have a freezer so that's why she cans everything—even things they say you can't. Personally though I like my fruits canned and my berries frozen from the point of view of taste and texture. I just pick, bag and freeze—no syrup or liquid at all. Same for any berry, not just strawberries. It saves work and mess, too.

GARDEN FRUITS

CANTALOUPES are raised truck garden scale all up and down the bottom of our valley along the railroad tracks. The bottom, of course, is the warmest place of all. And the railroad company doesn't seem to mind if people farm the ground practically up to the tracks. Somebody from New York saw that and was surprised and said that in New York the railroad company wouldn't let them do that. One more good point for this country over New York, I guess.

If you live in a middling sort of climate plant your cantaloupe and watermelon seeds as early as you dare. If the seeds rot, plant again and if those seeds rot, plant again. The longer season you can manage for your plants the better off you'll be. Give them plenty of room between plants. Keep the weeds out and give them plenty of water and they'll set fine crops for you. When wasps are eating on your melons here's a solution. You know the way the wasps do it—they will nibble at the shell until they get a hole and then eat out a chamber inside the hole causing the melon to rot inside. Just wrap each melon, still on the vine, in net (Heloise's famous nylon net) and that will protect them and you can use it over and over again every year. Or keep an eye on them and harvest any that are under attack. They are ready to pick when the skin starts to get yellowish and they soften up a little. American melons also usually crack away from the stem a little when they are ripe and ready. Nichols Garden Nursery carries a lot of interesting foreign varieties (1190 North Pacific Highway, Albany, Oregon 97321). They can be frozen and there are directions in Food Preservation.

For a really exotic dessert in season serve *Cantaloupe Delmonico.* Pick cantaloupes of middling size. Cut in half and scoop out the seeds and pulp. Put red raspberries into the cavity. If you have them, mix red raspberries with red currants or other fruit like blackberries. Chill and serve with whipped cream.

RHUBARB leaves are poisonous. Don't confuse them with the variety of Swiss chard called "rhubarb chard" because the stalks look red like rhubarb. It's supposed to be a good kind of chard. The rhubarb leaves on the other hand, aren't. Rhubarb will grow almost anywhere. You can revive an old plant in the early spring by dividing and transplanting part of it. That's because rhubarb plants get kind of root bound. Till around the old plant to loosen the soil. If you have set out a young plant that you bought from your plant nursery, don't cut the first year and only a little the second year. By the third you can take the outside two-thirds of the stalks. Leave the center ones. If you keep your rhubarb plant's roots wet it will keep producing for you all summer and you can keep harvesting. Since rhubarb is mostly water, anyway, it doesn't need much water for cooking, just enough to cover the bottom of the pan. Early rhubarb can be washed and cut into pieces, then covered and cooked until tender. Peeling isn't necessary—it just removes the color. The problem with cooking rhubarb is it's so sour that you have to add great amounts of sweetening to make it edible. If you make rhubarb leather though, you avoid that problem. You can make a good sauce by cooking rhubarb in a little orange juice and adding nutmeg and grated orange peel and honey.

To freeze rhubarb, wash, trim and cut into pieces. Pack tightly into frozen food containers. Cover, label, if you want, and put in the freezer. It's like berries, you don't have to blanch. (I don't label unless I can't see and don't expect to remember what is in the package.) Mike would happily label for me but there's no telling what he'd put on them. He finished packaging a batch of chickens for me one afternoon when between us we did up about 24 chickens from hen house to freezer. I go to the freezer now and if

Mike labeled there's no telling what the message is going to be. I've even had to thaw out things called "Surprise."

To can rhubarb pack hot, cover with hot juice and process 10 minutes in a hot water bath. Good seasoned with cinnamon and lemon juice.

Orange and rhubarb are good flavors together anytime.

Make a **Rhubarb Pie** by putting about 1 pint of 1-inch rhubarb sections into an unbaked pie shell. Scatter ½ orange, peeled and cut into little pieces, over the top. Now sprinkle 1 cup of sweetening over that—like a cup of brown sugar. And scatter a little tapioca around, too. It will take up the juice and add a niceness of its own. Now put the top crust on and bake in a moderate oven.

Rhubarb Bread Pudding—Combine 2 cups bread cubes, 2 cups cubed rhubarb, 2 egg yolks, ½ cup sugar and 2 cups milk. Sprinkle nutmeg and sugar over the mixture and bake. From Mrs. Goodspeed of Kent, Washington.

Rhubarb Cake—From Gaylee Pysitt of Hemmingford, Nevada: "2 cups flour, ½ cup shortening, 1½ cups sugar, 1 cup sour milk, 1 egg, 1 teaspoon soda, a pinch of salt, 1 teaspoon vanilla and 2 cups rhubarb. I throw all this together and then sprinkle on the topping after I put it in a 9 x 13-inch pan. Topping is ½ cup sugar and 1 teaspoon cinnamon, mixed together and sprinkled on top of the cake. Bake at 350° to 375° for 30 to 40 minutes."

WATERMELON—Seems like some people can grow them and some can't. I have neighbors who grow fields of watermelon to sell on a truck garden basis. One of them never waters his melons. He claims it spoils the natural sweetness to water them artificially. And his melons are just heavenly. I can't seem to grow a good big watermelon. I've just about decided to quit wasting my time and stick to cantaloupes which are much easier for me to grow. If you can grow melons, include the Crenshaw on your list. That is colloquially called the "winter melon" because you can store it until late fall. There are so many different good melon varieties it will really pay you to get to know them—the sort of cantaloupe-watermelon crosses. We never run short of melons because I have so many gardening friends that grow more than they know what to do with. I have the word from these friends that you can freeze watermelon, too, and how to is in Food Preservation. The best way to eat a watermelon is to cut it in pieces and start eating and continue until you're full. The hard part is figuring when it's ripe. The thump test is to rap it with your knuckles and if it sounds hollow it is ready. The plug test is surer. With a pocketknife you cut a round cork-shaped plug out of the side of the watermelon, pull it out, and actually have a look at what's inside. If it's white you've been way over-eager, if it's pink it's coming but not clear ready, if it's bright pink you can eat the plug. Otherwise slip the plug back in the melon and go away for a while yet. Another way is to look and see if the place where it is lying on the ground has turned kind of white—then it's ripe.

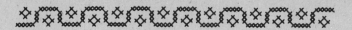

FRUIT JUICES

Fruit juices can be made without special equipment. But cider, grape juice and other juices in quantity are most happily gotten with the aid of a fruit press. Or with a Mehu-Maija, which is a brand name of a very fine Finnish juice extractor. You can buy "juicers" at health food type stores, but they are on the expensive side. A juicer or fruit press makes juice without cooking the fruit. The Mehu-Maija is a steaming method of juice extraction.

The old fashioned way to get fruit juice is to cook the fruit (or some berries can simply be mashed) and put it through anything from a colander (such as for tomato juice with some seeds) to a cloth. (For directions on making a jelly bag, see Definitions.) Prop the sieve up in a pan and go do something else while it drops, or use a rotary colander and rub the pulp around with your wooden pestle. If you are using a cloth, make it a sturdy one. You can "wring" the juice out, or pin the cloth to the sides of the colander with clothespins and let it drop. A first treatment often yields a juice with floating pulp in it. If you want a clear juice for jelly making or your beverage, give the juice a second straining through a clean cloth, or let it set overnight and pour off the top. You can often get extra juice from berries by taking the pulp of your first squeezing and putting it back on the stove with some water. Boil 5 minutes and then squeeze again.

When directions call for crushing the fruit, a wire potato masher, pastry fork or slotted spoon can be used for soft fruits. Firm fruits can be crushed with a food chopper. A colander, food press or strainer will give you a puree. Don't use galvanized ware in direct contact with fruit or fruit juices because the acid in fruit forms poisonous salts with the zinc. Metallic off-flavors may result from the use of iron utensils, chipped enamelware or tinware that is not well tinned.

Your juices, once extracted, can be easily canned (water bath time is 5 or 10 minutes), frozen, drunk on the spot or made into syrup or frozen concentrate to be diluted when wanted. Freezing liquids isn't hard. Put a plastic baggie into a pint jar, quart jar or tin can you've saved. Pour in the fluid and fold the baggie over the top of the fluid. The airspace at the bottom of the baggie protects jars from breaking. If it is a widemouthed jar or if you don't fill near the neck, you can freeze liquids in glass without a baggie. When the juice is thawed out again it will probably be more diluted near the top and oversweet near the bottom. Just stir it up.

Homegrown fruits vary widely in sweetness and flavor. Fully ripe fruits are best for making fruit juices (except for jelly making). Use your own judgment as to the thinning and sweetening desirable for your own juice. Berries, sweet cherries, apples, melons, pineapples, peaches and apricots have a relatively sweet juice. Cranberries, plums, currants, rhubarb, sour cherries and tart grapes have a tart juice. The tart juices can be drunk sweetened and make fine additions to other juices or to mix with ginger ale. The amount to dilute sour cherry, plum, grape and berry juices is generally one-third to one-half. You can use water or a bland juice or ginger ale to dilute. The "citrus" juices are orange, lemon, lime and grapefruit. These are generally thinned with water, sweetened, and often combined with other juices.

Juices like apricot, berry, melon, peach, pear, and plum are categorized as the ones that make "nectars." They are best thinned with water or added to other juices.

CANNING—Heat high acid fruit juices—from apricots, berries, red cherries, red grapes, peaches, plums and rhubarb—to 190° to inactivate enzymes and deepen color. If you do it in the top of a double boiler, you'll get a fresher fruit flavor. Don't let the temperature reach the boiling point. Once it has reached 190°, cool it quickly to keep your fresh flavor. If you have a choice, don't heat apple, light colored cherry, light grape and citrus juices. Store in freshly sterilized bottles. (They should be sterilized by boiling, covered with water, for 20 minutes.) Cap with corklined metal caps and turn upside down for 5 minutes. Leave bottles in a dark place. If you haven't one, put the jars in paper bags or cardboard cartons. To hold flavor, color and vitamins, have a storage place that doesn't get above 70°.

MORE ABOUT FREEZING—Although you can freeze juice in almost anything, you'll have a better tasting long-term product if you manage to make it something you can seal. Leave plenty of head space—

Widemouthed pint jar	½ inch head space
Narrow-mouthed pint jar	¾ inch head space
Widemouthed quart jar	1 inch head space
Narrow-mouthed quart jar	1½ inches head space

HOMEMADE FROZEN JUICE CONCENTRATE—To make a homemade frozen juice concentrate just like the store one (and you can!), you only need a large, narrow-necked container, like a gallon jug, and a freezer. Pour your juice into the container. Plastic works good. If you aren't using plastic be sure and fill no more than three-fourths full so you won't risk breaking the jug when the liquid expands in freezing. Cap and freeze. After it is all frozen remove the cap and turn the jug upside down. Suspend it by the "shoulders" over a lower container, such as a widemouthed gallon jar, so the drips won't make a mess and because the drips are the good part. Don't try to rush the draining process with heat. You'll mess up the process if you do because then the ice would melt and run down and dilute your juice concentrate. The principle involved is that for some reason the juicier bits melt before the plain water crystals. When the drips running off are no longer sweet and colored take away the jug. Finish melting the ice in it and throw the ice water out. Now repeat your freezing and dripping procedure two more times for a total of three altogether. You now have a fine concentrate. Go ahead and store it in the freezer. Since so many recipes are written assuming you have frozen concentrates and there are so many fun things you can do with them, anyway, and since they are really so easy to make—try it!

APPLE JUICE—If you want to make large amounts of cider, a press is helpful. Companies that carry supplies for home winemaking carry them. The press can also be used for crushing large amounts of other heavy fruits to make juices from grapes, peaches and pears. If you want to just make an occasional 2- or 3-gallon batch a press isn't essential. You'll need about a bushel of apples to make each 2 to 2½ gallons of cider. Any kind of apples can be used, but if you have more than one kind you can try different blends for the sweetness-tartness qualities you prefer. In general good eating apples are also the best cider apples. Don't use sprayed, partly rotten apples, or apples that have been lying on the ground very long.

One type of cider press is a tub with a metal cylinder in the middle. You wash your apples and cut out the wormholes. Usually it's handiest to cut all the apples in two as you go in order to get at the wormholes. Cut out whatever is not good apple— rotten spots, or scarred places where it rubbed against the tree. But it isn't necessary to take out the seeds. The apples should be chopped to a real fine pulp or mashed before squeezing. The ground apple is called "pomace." You can use a hand food chopper or a meat grinder. The press I have will not extract juice from apples very well if they are whole or even in chunks. You put the mashed fruit in a cloth bag and then put the bag into the press. I think Jonathans make the best apple cider. Mellow apples like Golden Delicious make the worst. For serious cider making you can get into more expense. Morgan Brothers has a small wooden and metal cider press for about $25.60. That's the kind I have. For $140 they have an electric grinder for making large quantities of apple pomace which I haven't. You can do the same thing with a meat grinder. If you do use an electric grinder reduce the speed to put apples through. They have

maybe you won't want to bother with this step at all. But here's an interesting oddment for your thoughts. Pesticides tend to concentrate in the pomace. So if you have a batch of apples you're concerned have been sprayed or sprayed too much, cider is the thing to make out of them. To have your cider really pomace free, pour the juice through a cheesecloth or diaper or some such into a settling container. This should be a pan or bowl made of crockery, stainless steel, glass or unchipped enamel because the juice is acid. Keep the juice below 40° for 12 to 36 hours—long enough to get the cider clear enough to suit you. It won't ferment at that temperature.

OK you have cider. You can drink it fresh. If you keep it refrigerated, below 36°, it will stay fresh as long as two weeks but sooner or later if you don't use it up you will have first fizzy cider and then apple wine. Or you can freeze it.

To freeze cider you don't need any heat treatment. Just pack in containers and put in your freezer. Figure that it will expand about 10 percent when frozen so you don't break your container. Plastic containers or glass jars with plenty of head space are all right. You can line tin cans by putting a plastic baggie inside them and twist and tie the baggie over the top of the juice and freeze it that way too. It will keep frozen as long as a year.

To can cider is more complicated. First you want to pasteurize it. Use your dairy thermometer to get your temperature right. You can order a metal stemmed thermometer that isn't so breakable for $1.95 from Fleischmann's Yeast, Box 82, Arden, North Carolina 28764. Heat it to 170° and keep it there for 10 minutes. If a scum rises, skim it off. You don't want to get it hotter or keep it hot longer because you'll get a cooked flavor and it won't be cider to be excited about. Have ready your canning jars or jugs and caps. Pour the hot cider immediately from your pan into the preheated jar or jug and lid or cap at once with scalded lids or caps. Now lay the jar or jug on its side for 10 minutes to make sure the cap gets hot enough. The experts now move the jugs to a tub or sink containing lukewarm water for a few minutes then let them finish cooling in the air. The reason for such gradual heating and cooling is so your containers won't break. The best caps for your jugs are screw caps fitted with rubber gaskets rather than cardboard linings. The rubber gaskets give you a much better seal. If you want to home can cider in tin cans, you have to use a special kind of metal, not your regular cans.

Cider Tea—Half cider and half tea, flavored with lemon juice and sweetened to taste. Or combine 4 cups cider, 2 cups tea and juice of 2 oranges and 1 lemon. Sweeten to taste.

Half and Half—Cider blends well half and half with plum, pear, cherry or raspberry juice. Combine before freezing if possible.

Cider Nog—Separate 4 eggs. Beat the yolks creamy and the whites stiff. Mix 4 cups cider and the yolks and sweeten to taste. Stir in half the whites and season lightly with nutmeg. Chill. To serve spoon the rest of the meringue on top.

wooden pestles for sale to use for followers on the grinder contents rather than risking your fingers. The top A-1 maker of cider making equipment though is MacKay's Wood Products, P.O. Box 1023, Bellingham, Washington 93225. I've met Mr. MacKay and I've seen his cider presses and if you write him he'll send you literature on different models. Write him whether you need a press for family use or want to make cider on a commercial scale. He has all sizes. His $43 size is called a "fruit press" and is *not* for apples. Apples would break it *unless* you pregrind them (which is what a lot of people do). The fruit press is good for juicing berries, cherries, soft fruit or precrushed fruit. This is the model you usually see sold as a "cider press" by retailers. His proper cider press is $220 and has an electric motor. It can make 30 gallons of cider an hour. A grinder is part of the machine. A manually operated cider press with grinding attachment (also manual) is $152. The apples go through MacKay's cider presses whole, leaves, worms and all, and do no awful harm, "Gives you more protein," says the gentleman himself.

Put the cleaned and cut apples into the metal cylinder and press. There is a crank device to put the pressure on. Have a nonmetal container ready to catch the juice. You could use it then strained or unstrained. If you don't strain it the bottom couple inches will have visible pulp collect in them. If you want to strain just pour the juice through a couple thicknesses of cheesecloth. Rinse your cloth whenever the holes clog.

Even if you don't have a cider press you can make cider. Clean and cut your apples. Put them through a grinder or chopper saving all the juice and then squeeze your grindings through a strong cloth bag. Cider isn't intended to be sweetened. Before canning or freezing cider let the freshly pressed juice stand until the pulp settles. Now people are learning to drink apple juice with some sediment in it so

Cider Ale—Combine 1 cup orange juice, ¼ cup lemon juice, 2 cups cider and 2 cups ginger ale. Sweetens to taste.

Cider Punch—Combine 8 cups cider, 2 cups cranberry juice, the juice of ½ lemon and 4 cups ginger ale. Sweeten to taste.

APRICOT JUICE—Pit and quarter the apricots. Bring to the boiling point in just enough water to prevent scorching. When tender mash with a potato masher and then press through a sieve or colander. This is a "puree." (Optional, 1 tablespoon lemon juice per 3 cups puree.) For a juice strain again through something finer. Sweeten, if desired. Incidentally 1 pound apricots is approximately 10 whole ones or 2 cups chopped or crushed apricots. To can the apricot nectar process 20 minutes in a simmering water bath (180°)—apricot juice dilutes to taste very successfully, same as grape.

Apricot Nectar from Canned Apricots—Blend or puree 1 quart canned apricots. Add water to thin, if needed. Serve right away.

Apricot-Citrus Juice—Combine half apricot puree and half orange or grapefruit juice.

Apricot Punch—Combine one-third apricot juice or puree and two-thirds any other juice.

BARBERRY JUICE—Use cranberry recipe.

BERRY JUICE—The general rule—except for strawberries (which aren't heated)—is to wash, crush, heat to 175° and extract the juice.

Busy Woman's Berry Juice—(Blackberry, raspberry, gooseberry and the like.) This stretches the berries as far as possible. Put your berries in a kettle. Cover with water and boil 5 minutes. Drain off the juice and save it. Cover the berries again with water, boil 5 minutes. Drain off the juice and save it. Cover the berries again with water, boil 5 minutes more, drain again and save the juice. Squeeze the seeds and stuff left if you want. Boil again if you think it would help. You can use your busy woman's berry juice as a base for jelly or for juice. Each successive boiling will make a lighter colored juice. Sweeten to taste.

Wonderful Berry Drink—Boil 2 quarts water with 1½ cups sugar or ¾ cup honey for 3 minutes. Then crush 2 quarts raspberries, blackberries or strawberries and pour the hot syrup over the fruit. Cool. Strain. Add 1 cup lemon juice, ice cubes and serve.

CHERRY JUICE—Stem, sort and wash. Drain and pit. If your cherries are red, crush them, heat to 165° (don't boil) and strain the juice through a jelly bag. If they are a white variety, grind and press for juice without heating. Cool, let stand overnight and pour off the clear juice to be your cherry juice or else strain through a bag. Sweeten if you think it needs it. Sweet cherry juice doesn't have the flavor and tartness of sour cherry juice. Adding some sour cherry juice will improve your product if you are working with sweet cherries.

Quick Cherry Drink—Mash through a colander 1 quart very ripe pitted cherries. Add 1 quart water and the juice of 1 lemon. Sweeten to taste. Strain and chill. Serve with ice.

Cherry Punch—Combine 9 cups water and 9 mint leaves. Simmer 5 minutes and strain. Add sweetening and cook 5 minutes. Cool. Combine the mint tea, 2 cups orange juice, 2 cups lemon juice, 2 cups cherry juice, 2 cups pineapple juice and 4 cups regular tea. Mix and let rest an hour. Serve chilled. It makes a lot.

CITRUS JUICE (Orange, grapefruit, lemon, lime)— Tree-ripened fruit, if you can get it, makes the best juice. Don't heat citrus juice and don't strain it. Just halve your fruit and extract the juice on a lemon drill (see Definitions) or what-have-you. Don't press the oil from the rind and do remove the seeds. Don't sweeten the juice unless it is for lemonade and limeade. I've heard that navel oranges don't make good juice for canning or bottling but I don't know why. Cut away the navel ends before you juice them. If you want to strain the juice use something with big holes. To get the maximum juice from the fruit, quickly heat it in hot water for several minutes before squeezing or roll to soften.

When juicing oranges you can figure that a dozen large ones will give you 7 or 8 (8-ounce) glasses of juice. A dozen medium-sized ones would give you 6 or more glasses and a dozen small ones would give you 4½ to 5 glasses. It's a good idea to work as rapidly as possible to preserve nutritive values.

You can mail-order unparaffined oranges, grapefruit and lemons from Ehrlich Date Garden, 868 Avenue B, Yuma, Arizona 85364. Those and tangerines, too, from Valley Cove Ranch, P.O. Box 603, Springville, California 93265. Nightingale Organic Grower and Nursery, Route 1, Box 847, Punta Gorda, Florida 33950, ships unparaffined oranges and grapefruit. Ira D. Ebersole, 25295 S.W. 194th Avenue, Route 2, Homestead, Florida 33030, ships limes (and mangoes and papayas).

Limes are more acid than lemons. They can be substituted in almost any recipe calling for lemon, using two-thirds as much lime juice as lemon juice.

Citrus Combination—Two-thirds grapefruit or orange juice combined with one-third other juice: it can be apricot, peach, nectarine juice or purees, or any other juice you want to experiment with.

Grapefruit-Grape—Half grapefruit juice and half grape juice. Serve over ice cubes.

Orangeade—Combine sweetening, 1 cup water and the grated rind of 1 orange in a saucepan. Boil 5 minutes. Cool. Add 2 cups orange juice and 2 cups cold water. Serve chilled over ice.

Lemonade—For each serving mix 4 tablespoons lemon juice, 2 tablespoons sugar or other sweetener and 1 glass ice water. For a batch, juice 5 lemons. Add 5 cups water and sweeten to taste. Serve with a slice of lemon in each glass.

Pink Lemonade—Add to a pint of lemonade prepared in the usual way a cup or less of strawberry, red raspberry, currant or cranberry juice. (A little cranberry juice goes a long way.)

Limeade—For each glass use 3 tablespoons lime juice, fill up with water and sweeten to taste. Serve a slice of the lime in each glass.

Rinds—If your rinds are unparaffined save a reasonable amount, grate and store tightly covered in the refrigerator for appropriate dishes.

CRANBERRY JUICE—Cook 1 pound of cranberries in 1 quart water until soft. Crush and drain through cheesecloth for a nice clear juice.

Cranberry Cocktail from Scratch—Grind 4 cups cranberries in your food chopper. Add 1 cup sugar to 6 cups water. Add the ground cranberries and their juice and boil all for 5 minutes. Cool and strain. Add 1 cup orange juice and the juice of 1 lemon. Chill.

CURRANT JUICE—Choose fully ripe bright red currants. Wash in cold water and remove stems. Crush the currants and warm to 165° to start the flow of juice. Don't boil. Press the hot fruit in a jelly bag to extract juice. Sweeten to taste.

Black Currant Punch—To each cup of currant juice add 2 cups weak green tea. Sweeten to taste. Serve in glasses half filled with chopped ice and garnish with a sprig of mint.

GRAPE JUICE—(For good readable advice on grapes see *Organic Gardening*, February 1972, p. 72.) The Concord and Catawba varieties are especially fine for juice but you can make it from the others, too. The key to enjoying homemade grape juice is knowing that you want to dilute your juice with water to taste when you serve it. The floating crystals are tartrate (cream of tartar). In grape juice you have a natural concentrate. If the grapes are ripe and sweet you don't need to add sugar. If you add more sugar to your grape juice you get the equivalent of a syrup.

Use only sound, ripe grapes. Let them ripen on the vine and after you pick them keep them out of the sun until you have a chance to pick off the stems and wash them. Mash the grapes with a potato masher or in a press. Cover the red grapes and Concord grapes with water and heat to 145°. Don't heat white grapes. Put the pan contents in a cloth or fruit press. Work the sack gently so that you extract all the juice or just let it hang all night. If you want clearer juice let the extracted juice stand overnight in a cool place. Then pour off the top. The pulp will have settled to the bottom.

To can the juice, process at 190° for 20 minutes. Or boil 5 minutes and then process 5 minutes, but this method affects the taste some. If you have white grapes be careful not to crush the seeds.

Simple Canned Grape Juice—Into a clean sterile quart jar put 1 cup any kind of grapes. Add 1 cup sugar or ½ cup hot honey. Fill the jar on up with boiling hot water and seal it! Takes about a month to be ready. Tastes good.

Grape Punch—Combine juice of 2 lemons and 1 orange, 2 cups grape juice and 2 cups water. Sweeten to taste.

LOGANBERRY JUICE

Loganberry Ale—Combine 1 cup loganberry juice, juice and grated rind of 4 lemons, 1 cup sugar, 2 cups ginger ale and 3 cups water. Let stand a couple hours to mellow. Garnish each glass with a mint sprig and lemon slice.

Loganberry Special—Combine 2 cups loganberry juice, 1 cup raspberry juice, 1 cup lemon juice and 3 crushed mint leaves. Mix and serve over crushed ice.

Also see BERRY JUICE.

PEACH JUICE—Heat before extracting juice. (But my preference is to can rather than juice peaches because they are the perfect canning fruit.)

Peach Special—Combine half peach juice and half orange or grapefruit juice.

PEAR JUICE—Follow directions for apple juice.

PLUM JUICE—Tree-ripened plums of deep color are best. Wash, mash and simmer until soft in enough water to barely cover. Press and strain. Sweeten if the fruit was tart enough to need it.

RASPBERRY JUICE—Use fully ripe, juicy berries. Wash in cold water and drain. Crush and heat the berries slightly to start the flow of juice. Strain in a jelly bag to get the juice.

Raspberry-Apple Juice—Combine half raspberry juice and half apple juice.

Delicious Raspberry-Mint Drink—Combine 1 cup sugar or ½ cup honey, 1 cup water and the grated rind of 2 lemons. Cook, stirring, over low heat until your sweetening is dissolved. Boil 5 minutes more. Cool. Add 2 cups crushed raspberries, 1 cup lemon juice and 4 more cups water. Serve with some mint leaves in the bottom of the glass (and in the pitcher) and one on top.

RHUBARB JUICE—To each 5 pounds of red rhubarb, cut in small pieces, add 1 quart water. Cook until the fruit is soft and then squeeze through a cloth.

Rhubarb Ale—Combine 6 cups rhubarb juice and ½ cup sugar. Heat until the sugar is dissolved. Cool. Add ⅓ cup orange juice, 4 tablespoons lemon juice and 4 cups ginger ale. Serve with ice.

Rhubarb Punch #1—Boil 1 cup sugar and ½ cup water for 3 minutes. Cool. To the syrup add 3 cups rhubarb juice, 1 cup pineapple juice, the juice of 2 lemons and 1 cup crushed strawberries. Mix. Serve with crushed ice and mint leaves.

Rhubarb Punch #2—Combine ½ cup grape juice, ½ cup sugar, 1 cup orange juice, 1 cup rhubarb juice and 2 cups water.

STRAWBERRY JUICE—Use fully ripe berries. Wash in cold water. Drain. Remove anything green. Crush and strain the juice through a jelly bag.

Strawberry Punch from Scratch—Mash 1 quart strawberries. Add the juice of 1 lemon, 2 tablespoon orange juice, 6 cups of water and let the mixture stand 3 hours. Strain. Sweeten to taste. Serve with ice.

Strawberry-Pineapple Juice—Combine 2 cups strawberry juice, 1 cup pineapple juice, 4 cups water, ½ cup lemon juice and ⅓ cup honey. Mix well and serve with ice.

BEVERAGE-BASE SYRUPS

Homemade syrups are handy to make drinks on camping trips and at picnics. They keep well in the refrigerator and a little syrup poured into a glass three-quarters full of cold water (or to taste) makes an easy, quick drink that the children can fix for themselves. Just about any fruit juice can be made into a syrup in a similar manner—cherry, raspberry and the like. Add ice, if possible, when serving. Dilute with ginger ale for variety. You can store unsealed syrup in bottles or a covered fruit jar. Children can handle the bottles better than the jars. I would think you could make these with honey too, instead of sugar. My recipe testing hasn't caught up here. I'll test these out this summer using honey.

Plain Sugar Syrup (Simple Syrup)—Boil 2 cups sugar with 2 cups water for 5 minutes. Chill and store in a covered jar. This was popular with Great-grandmother for flavoring summer drinks because the sugar was already in solution and she didn't have trouble with sugar settling in the bottom of the glass.

Standard Recipe Meant to Be Sealed—Wash currants, black or red raspberries, blueberries, grapes, elderberries and so forth. Simmer in water to cover until soft. Drain juice and strain it. For every 2 cups juice, add 1¾ cups sugar. Boil 15 minutes. Skim and pour into sterilized bottles. Bottle hot and seal. Or cork.

Orange Syrup—Strain the juice of 24 oranges and 6 lemons. For each pint of juice add 1¾ cups sugar. Boil the juice-sugar mixture, skim, strain and chill.

Strawberry Syrup—Take ripe strawberries, crush in a cloth and press out the juice. For each 2 cups of strawberry juice add 2 cups of the Plain Sugar Syrup. Boil gently for 15 minutes. Bottle.

Currant Syrup—Boil 3 cups sugar with 4 cups water until the sugar is dissolved, then add 4 cups cooked, strained currant juice and the juice of 6 lemons. Cool and bottle. This is nice to add color to other drinks.

Irene's Lemonade Syrup—Combine 2 cups sugar, 1 cup water and 2 lemon peels, cut in small pieces. Boil 5 minutes. Add the juice of 6 lemons. You can

either strain the syrup or just leave the cooked peel in it. Keep it refrigerated.

SHRUB (A VINEGAR BEVERAGE)

The base for shrub is a vinegar-fruit mix. To serve it is diluted to taste with water or ginger ale. Great-grandmother liked it served hot for coughs and colds in winter and as a chilled beverage in summer. When bottled it will keep for years.

Blackcurrant, Raspberry or Blackberry Shrub—Wash 2 pounds of berries. Remove stalks and stems. Put into a crockery bowl and crush very thoroughly with a potato masher or pestle. Pour over the fruit mush 2 cups of white vinegar and let stand for 5 days, stirring every day. Strain through a cloth. Measure the resulting juice and for every 2 cups add 1 pound of sugar. Boil very gently for 10 minutes, removing any scum. Strain again. Pour into bottles, cork and seal with paraffin. (Stores that handle beverage-making supplies carry corks. The grocery store has paraffin.)

Raspberry or Strawberry Shrub—Add enough vinegar to cover 1 gallon red raspberries or strawberries. Let them stand 24 hours, scald and then strain. Measure the juice. Add 1 pound of sugar per 2 cups juice. Boil 20 minutes and bottle.

Spiced Raspberry Shrub—Put your raspberries in a crock or jar. Cover with cider vinegar. Mash. Let stand overnight. Strain. For every 2 cups juice, add 2 cups sugar, 1 cinnamon stick and 6 whole cloves. Boil 10 minutes. Bottle and seal while hot.

SUMMER ICES

I think of an "ice" as sort of a frozen beverage. A "frappé" is one that is expected to be frozen only to a coarse mushy stage. Sherbets made with milk or cream are under Ice Cream (Dairy). Here "sherbet" is a water ice to which can be added a small quantity of dissolved gelatin or beaten egg whites. These recipes are a good way to satisfy your hot weather ice eaters with something homemade.

Homemade popsicles are cheap, easy and even more fun for the children than going to the store. You can use wooden sticks for handles and sturdy small bowls or cans for containers—work up a collection. Or buy popsicle molds—Tupperware carries them and so

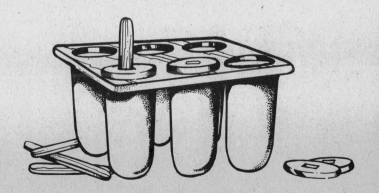

does Maid of Scandinavia. The latter has an 8-unit mold with plastic holders for $1.10 (3245 Raleigh Ave., Minneapolis, Minnesota 55416). The holders get lost and fall apart to boot but you can substitute sticks after they disintegrate. If you have a big family or lots of small friends I recommend getting at least two molds so you can have one freezing while they are consuming the other. Or cut one in half.

Fill the molds not quite full, insert your holder and freeze. Don't let the gremlins pull the holders until you're sure the center of the popsicle is solidly frozen and you have loosened the sides by running hot water over the back of the mold. Otherwise they might pull out the holder prematurely leaving a hole that it won't freeze back into.

You don't have to unmold all the popsicles at once. Just loosen as many as you need. Refill the emptied units and return to the freezer. Children like strong, sweet juice like grape and cranberry for popsicles—but when they're hot anything will do. The regular here is goat's milk popsicles. Popsicle making is a nice way to use leftover juices from canned fruit, too, and you can even make them of plain old water or herb tea. You can make parfait popsicles by freezing a layer of one color, then a layer of another color.

Basic Fruit Popsicles—Puree 1 cup any kind of fruit or a mixture of fruits and mix with 1 cup water. Pour into your ice cube tray. When they are starting to freeze add a wooden stick or toothpick to each section.

Banana Popsicles—Mrs. Linda Crabtree of Kettering, Ohio, sent me this recipe on February 11, 1974. I finally am adding it to this book May 17, 1976. You'll need firm but ripe bananas and popsicle sticks or popsicle-type sticks, some chilled strained honey and chopped salted peanuts. Cut the bananas in half crosswise so you now have two bananas for each one you had before. Stick the popsicle stick into one end of the banana to be a handle. Coat each banana half with honey and then roll it in the nuts. Freeze unwrapped until solid.

Pudding Popsicles—Susan Staley was in Germany when she sent me this recipe. She said, "If your children love the fudgesicle-type popsicle you can easily make them. Just make up a batch of pudding and freeze it in your popsicle molds. They're delicious and you can make different kinds besides chocolate. Butterscotch is very good. In fact any flavor of pudding your children love hot they're bound to like cold in hot summer weather."

The following recipes are good for popsicles or "frappés" (that's a dessert ice). To have a frappé, just eat it before it is frozen clear solid. (If you get a dessert ice frozen too hard to serve, just let it thaw again until it has the consistency of thick mush and *then* serve.) Feel free to change the sweetening type and amount to suit your preference.

Strawberry or Raspberry Ice—Remove the green stem end from the fruit, enough to make 3 or 4 cups. Pour ½ cup honey over the fruit. Mash the mixture with a potato masher until you have it pulped as finely and mixed as well as you can. (Optional, strain the seeds out.) Add 1 cup water and the juice of 1 lemon. Freeze, stirring occasionally. This is a delicious summer dessert and my favorite ice to make. I serve before it's frozen clear solid.

Cherry Ice—Stone 1½ quarts cherries. Mash them with a potato masher until you have them mushed as well as you can. Add ¼ cup honey and the juice of 1 lemon. Mix well. Freeze, stirring occasionally since it freezes first on the sides of the bowl and you'll want to pull that to the center. Serve with homemade whipped cream, slightly sweetened.

Grape Ice—Pulp 3 pounds of grapes. I like the little green seedless ones. Then you can keep the pulps and skins in the syrup. If you are using seeded grapes you'll have to pick the seeds out and put the grapes through a sieve in which case you'll lose a lot of good stuff. Add ¼ cup honey and mash well. Freeze, stirring occasionally. This recipe takes considerably longer to freeze than the two above. This is nice with a whipped cream topping or plain. Serve when it is barely beyond the "slush" stage.

Any Fruit Ice—You could juice pomegranates or barberries or red currants or cook and strain quinces, or grate pineapple, or boil and pulp apples or rhubarb—whatever you have. Sweeten to taste, add lemon juice, if the flavor needs it, and freeze it.

Cider Ice—Dissolve 1½ cups sugar in 4 cups cider. Add 1 cup orange juice and ¼ cup lemon juice. Mix and freeze.

Ginger Ale Ice—Combine ¾ cup sugar and 2 cups water. Heat and boil 5 minutes. Cool. Add 1 cup orange juice, ½ cup lemon juice and 2 bottles ginger ale. Freeze.

Root Beer Ice—Combine 1 bottle root beer, 1 tablespoon lemon juice, 1 tablespoon brown sugar and a few grains salt. Freeze.

You don't have to have a crank freezer for any of these although if you do, then by all means use it.

Cranberry Ice—Heat 1 quart cranberries and 2 cups water together, boiling until the cranberries are soft. Run through a sieve. Add 2 cups brown sugar to puree. Heat again stirring until the sugar is dissolved. Add juice of 1 orange. Remove from heat. Cool. Pour into tray and freeze firm. Remove to chilled bowl and beat until light. Return to tray and finish freezing without stirring.

Frozen Fruits—Strawberries, raspberries, fresh peaches or crushed pineapple (as well as canned fruits, especially pears and peaches in syrup) can be frozen. Mash the fruit, add sweetening to taste and let stand until a syrup is formed. Then use your crank freezer or freeze in trays, stirring occasionally. It can be served in slices or dished up casually. Good with whipped cream on top.

Lemon Ice—Cook ¾ cup sugar and 2 cups water slowly for 10 minutes. Cool. Add to ½ cup strained lemon juice. Add trace (1/16 teaspoon) salt. Pour into tray and freeze firm. Remove to chilled bowl and beat until very light. Fold in 2 stiffly beaten egg whites to which a trace of salt has been added. Quickly return to finish freezing without further stirring.

Lime Ice—Cook ⅔ cup sugar and 2 cups water slowly for 10 minutes. Add to ½ cup strained lime juice. Cool. Pour into freezing tray and freeze firm. Remove to chilled bowl and beat until very light. Fold in 2 stiffly beaten egg whites to which a trace of salt has been added. Finish freezing.

Strawberry Sherbet—Soften 1 envelope unflavored gelatin in 1 cup orange juice in a small pan. Combine 1 quart washed, hulled, crushed strawberries with ½ cup sugar and then stir in gelatin-orange juice mixture. Pour into your freezer tray. Freeze, stirring once or twice, until almost firm. Remove to chilled bowl, break up with a fork and then beat until smooth but not melted. Fold in 2 stiffly beaten egg whites, blend and return to refrigerator. Freeze, stirring once in a while with a fork, until firm.

Orange Sherbet—Combine 1½ cups water (use milk if you want a richer sherbet) with ¾ cup sugar, ¼ cup light corn syrup and a pinch of salt in a pan and cook, stirring constantly, over low heat until the sugar is dissolved. Cool. Add 1 cup orange juice and ¼ cup lemon juice. Pour into your refrigerator tray and freeze, stirring once in a great while, until almost firm. Then remove to a chilled bowl, break up with a fork, beat until smooth but not melted. Fold in 2 stiffly beaten egg whites and return to the refrigerator tray. Freeze until firm.

DRIED FRUIT

Dried fruit is really an important subject. It is easy to make if you have the fruit to start with. It requires nothing but the fruit and sunshine. It keeps well and is a delicious food with a "candy-like treat" quality. When a recipe calls for the classic "raisins" or "currants" you can substitute any sort of home-dried fruit chopped up a little. It will probably turn out to be tastier and more digestible than if you used the raisins. In my experience there is something in regular store raisins that is quite irritating to the digestive tract. Home-dried fruits are much more digestible. You can also use your home-dried fruit whenever you need "prunes," "dried figs," "dried apricots" or any other dried or concentrated fruit in a recipe. You need it to make fruitcake or mincemeat, and you'll enjoy using it in any bread, pancake or cookie, to make winter breakfast cereals more interesting, in poultry stuffings or in salads (like grated carrot, chopped dried fruit and dressing—a midwinter regular of mine). You can dry any fruit except berries. They turn out too tough, dry, and full of seeds. Better to freeze or can berries.

Basically you can choose one of three ways to dry your fruit. You can:

1. Dry it whole or in halves as appropriate.
2. Pulp it and dry in sheets—that's called "fruit leather."
3. Juice it, dry the pulp in sheets to make fruit leather and can the juice.

DRYING WHOLE FRUIT

Just be sure and take the pit out whether it be a cherry or a peach so it isn't really "whole." You'll have trouble getting them dry all the way if you don't.

You have the choice of drying in the sun or in the oven, or drying with or without a sulfur dioxide processing and with or without sugar. Personally, I dry mine in the sun without a sulfur treatment and without sugar. It comes out plenty sweet for my taste. I live in a region where when fruit is in season the days are very dry and very hot so conditions are just right for sun drying.

The drying process removes the water and stops the chemical change of "ripening" that eventually results in "rotten." Your fruit is suspended in its moment of glory for you to enjoy all winter long. You can soak and then cook your home-dried fruit just like the store fruit whenever you want to use it or gnaw on it for a healthy sweet treat. Some fruits dry better than others—the easiest to dry are apples, apricots, cherries, coconut, dates, figs, guava, nectarines, peaches, pears, plums and prunes. Avocado, bananas, and berries don't dry well. For best results don't over-

whelm the system—it has its limits. Keep dust and dirt eliminated as much as possible by washing the fruit before drying it and protecting the trays of fruit from bugs.

Not all climates are suitable for sun drying. If you have high humidity and it rains every day it will be hard to sun dry food. Hot days when the sun is shining brightly all day long are the best for sun drying—quick drying is best for the food. Have good air circulation around the food. Lay it on a screen that is held off the ground and set each fruit separately with airspace between it and the next one. Turn the fruit often enough to keep it from sticking. I usually don't take the fruit in at night because we have virtually no dew and rain is woefully unlikely in August.

Fruit should be just perfectly ripe to be dried. Don't dry green fruit. Don't dry fruit with rotten spots, cut them out and dry the rest of the fruit. I sort when canning—nicest ones for sun drying—rest into the jars.

If the fruit is very big you may want to slice into thin pieces. The thick pieces dry very slowly. The fruit is dried when you can squeeze a handful and have no moisture left on your hand and the fruit springs apart when you open your hand. The fruit should be pliable and leathery—not crisp.

An extra insurance after sun drying is to put the fruit into a wide container for about a week. Stir 2 or 3 times a day and keep covered with a wire screen or cloth fastened around the rim with a rubber band or string to keep out bugs. Then you can put the dried fruit in containers which should be moisture proof, bug proof and dust proof. On the other hand the reality is that you can use almost anything for a while— even a dry gourd, a paper bag, a glass jar, a tin box with a tight-fitting lid. Store in a dry, dark cool place for maximum keeping. I prefer storing in glass jars with the lids on tight so I can keep an eye on what's going on in there.

For absolute security, store it in the freezer. Or put your dried fruit in clean glass fruit jars. Put these (unlidded) into the oven and heat 20 minutes at 150°. Remove, screw your sealing lids on tight and put away. Once you have opened one of them you can keep it in the refrigerator for extra security though I haven't had any trouble. The main thing is to get it good and dry to start with. Otherwise you risk mold.

Prepare your fruit early in the morning of a day that promises to be hot and sunny. This is in order to get in a full day of sun drying before night falls. You can get the prepared fruit out on a cookie sheet, a cardboard sheet covered with aluminum foil or a cheesecloth. My preference is a screen made like a window screen with a wooden frame, if the wasps aren't around yet. These screens are then best set up on posts or some such outside so that air circulates through the mesh and all around your fruit. Very thick and moist fruits, such as peach halves, need to be turned occasionally—enough so they don't stick to the screen since they are very hard to get separated from the screen if they dry entirely in one position. Apple slices can be strung on thread and dried in your kitchen or attic. Cherry halves, on the other hand, should be placed sticky side up and don't need to be turned. They come out sort of like raisins incidentally. Small thin fruits, like cherry halves, don't need as long as fat fleshy ones like peach halves. Three days is a good general average.

Once August arrives, we are afflicted by wasps with some child or other getting stung almost every day. I intensely dislike the things as does everyone else. They eat meat and fruit especially and so fruit set out to dry not only attracts hordes of them, which is dangerous for the children, but they actually will eat it up themselves so it requires different planning.

Cherries and apricots usually come before the wasps (that's tick season which has problems of another sort) so I can just lay them out plain with at most a dish towel over the top—they'll go ahead and dry underneath it.

If you are worried about the possibilities of insect infestation all you have to do is put the dried fruit in the oven, get it up to a temperature of at least 150° and keep it there 10 minutes. Then pack in containers that don't allow air circulation or insect passage. It should be all right. Check it once in a while anyway throughout the winter, and if it shows signs of bugs just give it another heat treatment.

The quicker you can get your fruits dried the better off they are. When you spread them out set them separately so they don't touch each other. Turn the larger fruits daily, large fruits such as apples, pears and peaches should be pared, divided and the seeds or stones removed. One method is to "scald" very juicy fruits first in a hot oven. This forms a film over the cut surfaces. I've also heard it recommended that fruit be precooked but I don't do that either. If the rains come while you are in the middle of your drying you can finish off in the oven: 110°-150° is OK and oven drying is generally quicker than sun drying— about one day from morning to night or less would do it even starting from scratch. Sun drying takes longer than oven drying because it happens at lower temperature. Sun drying tastes better. With oven drying you must be very careful not to scorch the fruit.

Commercially dried fruit usually says on the label "sulfur dioxide," which means that the fruit has been exposed to sulfur dioxide fumes. The purpose is to prevent darkening of light-colored fruits. Sulfur dioxide is said to be harmless and to disappear in the steam when the fruit is cooked, but we eat the better part of our dried fruit raw as chewy snacks, so color is the least of my worries foodwise, and I avoid nonfoods whenever possible as a matter of principle. I'm convinced I can taste the sulfur dioxide in dried fruit processed with it. For more on all this, see the Food Drying section in the Food Preservation chapter.

APPLES aren't dried whole. Use fully ripe sweet apples (like Gravensteins). Usually they are peeled and cored and what's left is made into doughnut-type rings about ⅛ inch thick. Let the slices fall into cold water while you are working to prevent "rusting." Adding ¼ cup lemon juice or 1 teaspoon ascorbic acid per 2 cups cold water will help. The slices then can be strung on a thread or even basted to a large piece of cheesecloth. If your apples are small, wormy or too mealy to make doughnut rings from, cut into slices of whatever shape you can. String the apple sections on a long thread and then hang up or lay out to dry in the hot sun. It's much harder to dry fruit in the southern parts of the United States. There is more trouble there with humidity, insects and mold. If you are finding it too hard to dry fruit outdoors there is always the oven. A USDA pamphlet AWI-59, available for free from your county extension agent, covers the subject of oven drying very thoroughly on both fruits and vegetables. It suggests dipping fruit into a brine (5 tablespoons salt per 5 gallons water) before drying. To oven dry you can use thicker slices—up to

¼ inch. Drain thoroughly. Dry at 140° on a cookie sheet. Turn once in a while. The dried apples will be light colored and soft. You can dry apple shreds same as banana shreds.

BANANA shreds can be dried. Peel your bananas. Using a coarse shredder shred right into your oven frying pan. Cook 1 minute under the broiler, if you have one. Then dry at 140° for 6 to 8 hours, stirring once in a while so they don't stick. Or slice peeled bananas ¼ inch thick onto a drying tray and dry until crisp. Or cut in half crosswise, quarter each half and dry.

CURRANTS—Put your currants into a large bowl and add some flour (about ½ cup per pound of currants). Mix the flour with the currants and then rub the currants between your hands to get the stems off. After the stems are off, put the currants in a colander and let water stream through them until you have nothing left but currants. Then scald them a half minute, chill by drenching again with cold water. Drain. Spread on pie dishes, trays and so on, and put out in the sun or on your screen or into the oven to dry. They are like little raisins when done.

FIGS—Pick several days before they fully ripen. Wear gloves because the juice is irritating. Cut off stem and blossom ends. Steam for 20 minutes. Dry. To store dried figs brush outside lightly with honey. Pack in plastic and keep in refrigerator or freeze.

GRAPES—When grapes dry you have raisins. I used to think that raisins were some kind of fruit that grew in California. It was a real surprise to me to learn that raisins are dried grapes and prunes were dried plums!

Grapes are one of the harder fruits to dry—harder than any of the large pitted sorts which are the easiest. Any sweet grape can be dried. Seedless varieties are best. Good raisin varieties are the Thompson Seedless, Black Malaga, Black Thompson Seedless and Muscat. Let your grapes ripen on the vines until they are as sweet as you'd expect them to be before they start going bad. Then pick the branches, cluster by cluster. Spread them out in the sun to dry and turn them over occasionally. It may take a couple of weeks or so. Once the raisins are dried you can remove them from the stems for storage or store them on the stems as you prefer. Or you can dry seedless green grapes at 170° for at least 24 hours in an oven.

Well, I used to think that drying grapes to make raisins was hard. Then I got this letter from Criss Wilhite, from Fresno, California, the "raisin capital of the world." Says Criss, "We cut the grapes, lay them on newspaper next to the vines. Ten days later, we turn them over. Ten days after that, we roll them up in the newspaper. Since there is no dew here in summer, we don't have to cover them up. The *hard* part is stemming them! Last summer, we dried so many grapes that we ended up with 100 pounds of raisins. I put the raisins in baskets and sorted them out from the big stems and stuff. Then I bagged them in 2-pound bags and stuck them in the freezer. (Since this is the agribusiness and grape center of the country, every grape-loving, pesticide-resistant bug imaginable winters over in raisins. Freezing is easier

than oven-heating.) Whenever we need raisins I spill a bag out and empty it into a colander. I sort of knead the raisins around in it and the stems rub off and fall out. I do this until about 70 percent are stemmed. Then, I put them in a damp terry cloth towel, roll them up and rub them around a bit. I do that twice. It gets a few more stems out, washes and moistens the fruit. It all takes 20 minutes maximum. We eat three or four pounds a week! A hundred pounds a year isn't enough for us."

PEACHES—To dry peaches, peel, halve and pit. Cut each half into fourths and dry, turning occasionally.

PEARS—Use sweet ones. Boil until skins will slip. Cool. Remove skins. Cut in halves. Scoop out core (use a teaspoon). Lay out pear halves on trays or cookie sheets for oven drying. Dry at 140° with oven door propped ½ inch open. Turn once in a while. Store these dried pears in refrigerator or freezer.

PLUMS—A prune is a kind of plum, the freestone. It is blue black and oval with firm flesh. Most commercial prunes are "nectarized." That means they are cooked under pressure in their own juice before drying. If you want to imitate that you could soak in hot water 20 minutes before drying. But that isn't necessary. If you can get the pit out easily take it out and dry your prune halves the regular way. The half prunes won't look like store prunes exactly but you'll find them a lot easier to get dry. If not, pick the prunes when they are ripe and then let them dry whole. They must be kept very dry. To oven dry prunes start at 250° for 15 minutes, finish at 140°, turning occasionally. It takes about 2 days. Plums dried without pits are good for pies.

SUGAR-DRIED FRUITS—Sugar acts in a preserving way and this combines methods. To make a half-dried crock preserve, pit, peel and cut up peaches or apples. Then dry partly and pack in a crock with sugar spread thickly between each layer. It takes about 80 percent sugar to have an absolutely sure preserving effect. Another way to do it is to halve peaches, remove the pits, sprinkle the cavities with granulated sugar and dry in an oven. Currants and cherries can be boiled with ½ pound sugar per pound fruit for 15 minutes, then spread out to dry. But to me the whole point of drying is to get that delicious healthy sugar-free sweet so I don't use this method.

COOKING DRIED FRUIT—Less sugar is needed for dried than fresh fruit, probably none. That's because the drying process changes the starch in the fruit to sugar. The dryness and the sugar content were the forces combined to preserve it. A little lemon juice though usually improves the flavor. Soak before cooking—6 hours or more.

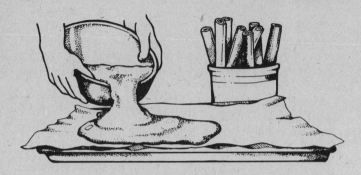

FRUIT LEATHER

Another way to dry fruit, or squash, sweet potato or pumpkin, is to leather it. If you do the vegetables this way you have to precook them and then sweeten and spice to taste. For the fruit basically you just rinse it off, then grind or force through a sieve or mash with a potato masher. You get out pits and seeds at whatever stage is appropriate. Then you make a thin layer of your pulp on a tray or in a wide, flat pan, or what-have-you and let it dry. The thinner your layer is the quicker and easier it will dry. I recommend ⅛ inch. Get it too thick and you'll have trouble with it spoiling or you'll just plain get tired of having it around before it finally dries. You can sun dry or oven dry. Sun drying tastes better and lasts longer. Oven drying runs the risk of scorching. It takes longer to oven dry fruit leather than plain fruit. When your fruit leather is dry cut in strips about 1¼ by 2 inches or into squares. If you made strips roll each one up tightly into a ball and then store in a tightly-covered tin box or some similar moisture and bug proof container. Or you can just bag them up and store in the deep freezer.

When oven drying try not to get the heat above 120° and figure on 15 to 20 hours to do the job. You can cook it up like dried fruit if you like but the children enjoy snacking on it so much that is generally the way mine goes. You can make a kind of candy by sprinkling a breadboard with powdered sugar and working leather strips on it patting and rolling until about ⅛ inch thick. You can mash your fruit and store it in the freezer until you can get around to making leather of it and it will be all right. You can also use overripe fruit for leather. Apricots and peaches make the nicest leathers but you can make good ones out of pears, plums, rhubarb or even berries.

APRICOT LEATHER—Wash and pit the fruit. Puree your apricot halves however you're going to do it (leave the skins on). To each cup of mashed apricot, add 1 tablespoon honey and ¼ teaspoon cinnamon (or any other sweetening or spice that suits you, like a dash of nutmeg or nothing at all). Spread your drying tray or whatever it is with plastic or oil it. If you use plastic make sure some hangs out at the edges. Spread your fruit paste on the surface and set it out to dry. When it's done you can just peel the plastic backing away.

APPLE LEATHER—Early summer apples work better than the crisp hard late apples. If they need sweetening add it. Cinnamon or coconut are good mixed in: ¼ teaspoon cinnamon or ½ cup coconut per 2 cups puree.

To make leather out of the crisp, hard apples you peel, core, section and grind in your grinder. Be sure and catch the juice that runs out. Add 2½ cups cider per gallon ground apple and then cook the whole mixture over low heat. When it is boiling and has cleared some, sweeten it if needed and then spread on your sheets to dry.

BERRY LEATHER—Puree your berries some way or another. Putting them in a blender works. Add 1 tablespoon honey per 1½ cups of berry puree and proceed with your drying.

PEACH LEATHER—Get the fuzz off either by washing or peeling. Cinnamon and nutmeg go well with it. Peaches are so sweet you certainly don't need to add any sugar.

PEAR LEATHER—Peel them and core them. Don't sweeten.

RHUBARB LEATHER—In general rhubarb is more of a trial than a blessing to me because it seems to require so much sweetening to make it edible. But you can make rhubarb leather by washing and cutting up your rhubarb pulp. Rhubarb and raspberries go very well together to make a mixed fruit leather. Rhubarb is so acid that you can't dry it straight on any metal surface like a cookie sheet. You'll have to use plastic underneath and be careful not to let the pulp get under the plastic.

LEATHER-JUICE COMBINATION

The essence of this method is that you steam or precook your pitted fruit. Then put the whole works into a sieve. What stays in the sieve gets made into fruit leather by the above recipes. What runs through without a struggle gets made into juice. This is really a great way to make your fruit juice without struggle and without waste.

APRICOT LEATHER AND JUICE—Steam or cook slightly 1 gallon of pitted apricots. Add 1½ cups pineapple juice. Drain off the juice. You know the more juice you get off, the quicker what's left will dry. Sweeten the pulp that's left if you want. Almond extract is a good flavoring—3 teaspoons. Can the leftover juice. Spread out your pulp to dry.

PRUNE LEATHER AND JUICE—Steam or cook a gallon of prunes with a couple cups of water. Then drain to get your juice off and can the juice. It will be a pretty concentrated juice and should be diluted for serving. Pulp your pulp. You can add almond extract and honey for a good taste and then dry.

FRUIT PASTE CANDY—Another use for your fruit pulp. The pulp of two or more kinds of fruit can be combined, too, or you could start from scratch with fresh or canned fruit. Just put the pulp through a fine strainer. Then measure it. For each pint pulp add 1⅓ cups sugar. Cook, stirring constantly, until thick and clear. Then turn out on an oiled platter. Let dry until a good tough film is formed on the top. Then turn it out onto a wire screen to finish drying—until it loses its stickiness. The sooner you can get it dried the better. I recommend the open air and sunshine for the job.

FRUIT SAUCES

If you have a batch of fruit that is going bad, and you want to get it put up the quickest, easiest, cheapest way possible—make a sauce of it!

Applesauce isn't the only member of this family. You can make something similar from cherries, peaches, rhubarb or the famous cranberry. Berries make fine special sauces to go on desserts. Apricots, and even prunes, can be made into a sauce. The sauces aren't meant to be supersweet and can be sweetened with brown sugar or honey if you like, to suit your own taste. Just the right amount depends a lot on you and on the fruit—cherries come sweet and sour and so do apples. The basic sauce recipe is to prepare your fruit (peel, core, or whatever is appropriate), add to boiling water (a third part or less of your fruit amount), cover and simmer gently until tender. Remove from heat. If needed put the fruit through a strainer to make a smooth sauce. Add sweetening and mix well. Always use a wooden spoon to stir and a really heavy pan to cook it in.

To can it return to the heat and boil again. Have ready jars. Boil some lids in a pan of water. Using a widemouthed funnel quickly pour the very hot sauce into the jar. Then put on the first lid and then the screw one on. Now give it 15 minutes of hard boiling in a water bath. Lift out, tighten and set aside to cool.

To freeze, cool your sauce as rapidly as possible. Put into your container and chill.

Applesauce—For 2 pounds apples use about ⅓ cup water and even less of sugar.

Pink Applesauce—Use red apples and leave the skins on while cooking. Proceed as above. Strain.

Dried Apricot Sauce—Chop up 1 cup of your dried apricots. Cook them with about 2 cups water until tender. Then add 1 teaspoon lemon juice and sweeten to taste. Add a little more water if it turned out too thick or cook some more if too thin. Or use any other dried fruit.

Blueberry Sauce—Start with 1 cup blueberries. Put half the blueberries and ½ cup water into a pan. Simmer 3 minutes. Add 1 teaspoon cornstarch and stir thoroughly. Continue cooking, stirring constantly, until thick. Then add the other half of the berries and cook 3 minutes more. Add 2 tablespoons lemon juice.

Cherry Sauce—Use about ⅔ cup water per original 1 pound cherries. You'll only need to cook them about 5 minutes.

Gooseberry Sauce—Stew ½ pound gooseberries in ½ cup water until soft. Rub through a sieve. Return to pan. Add sweetening to taste and 1 tablespoon butter if you are planning to serve it as a relish with roast goose, duck or mutton.

Gooseberry Fool—Simmer green gooseberries, starting with cold water, until tender, adding a little salt (optional) to preserve the color. Strain and puree. Put the puree on the heat with sugar to taste and cook until sugar is dissolved. To serve mix with cream.

Peach Sauce—Use about ⅔ cup water per original 1 pound peaches. They need cook only 5 minutes or so. Optional, add cinnamon and nutmeg.

Plum Sauce—Cook plums in about ½ cup water per original 1 pound plums. They'll need 7 to 10 minutes. Put through strainer. Sweeten to taste. Add 1 tablespoon lemon juice.

Rhubarb Sauce—Cut trimmed stalks into about 1½-inch sections. Most rhubarb, if put on over very gentle heat, will make its own juice and needs no added water at all. Simmer until you have a nice looking sauce. Sweeten to taste. Rhubarb needs quite a bit of sweetening.

Basic Raw Fruit Sauce—Crush your fruits such as peaches, raspberries or strawberries. Sweeten it to taste and serve over your ice cream, pudding or cake.

FRUIT BUTTERS

It is February 1, 1974, and I have to write up this Butters section, the Honey section, the Introduction and Fruits—Apple to Pomegranate—and the middle of the Dairy chapter and I'm done with this first draft of the book. All five children are at home as they have been since mid-December when Dolly first got sick. They still haven't decided what's wrong with her. First they thought it was rheumatic fever. Now they say maybe rheumatoid arthritis but they're not sure. If you think that because I've written a book and I'm a Christian and I don't use white sugar (not to imply equality among the various named) I never had my troubles let me tell you different. You don't know half of it. But I've had my miracles, too. And that's the important thing. And just making it—just having gotten one foot in front of the other and kept moving all day long no matter how heavy the foot and the heart felt—can be miracle enough in some situations. . . .

Really being this near to finishing the first draft of the book is a miracle. A year and a half ago I had made up my mind not to take it up again. My husband's preferred choice with regard to the book from the very start had been that I would refund the money on all those early orders I took. And I would have, only I never had the money again or the time, especially the money. Then we came to one of those great marital shakeups that have to happen once every five years or so I guess, and I got thoroughly shook up and swore off everything except what could make me a better housekeeper and wife and mother. Not a bad decision. I really did need strengthening in that direction. And so I swore off the book and regarded it as a selfish desire and any further involvement with it on my part on the order of being tempted into sin. And for one full year I never touched the manuscript. And for most of that year I really didn't think about it much because I was really busy just trying to get the housekeeping in my head done and become somebody that God and I could be satisfied with.

But about last August thoughts of the book started coming to me again. First in terms of responsibility to the people whose money I had taken and spent, to whom I had promised so much by sending them first of all that ambitious table of contents to which they were now holding me, and to whom I had sent parts of the book in three separate mailings and then left them hanging without a refund or further word. I've always been an almost painfully responsible person and although I've had my fantasies of disappearing in the Underground or becoming a waitress in Tahiti I don't expect it will ever happen. So I started to try to plan how to refund the money and get a letter out to everybody explaining why I had given up. But I just couldn't seem to get it done, even though that meant typing only one stencil and mimeographing it and mailing it out. I did decide that since I had kept no records of who paid me that I'd write everybody and ask them to bill me for what they figured I owed them and that would give me time to gradually get them all paid off. But again I couldn't seem to even get that done.

And the notion of finishing the book kept cropping up in my head oftener and oftener no matter how hard I tried to put it down. I regarded that oft-upcropping thought with almost tearful frustration—we had less money than ever, Mike had been laid off from his part-time job. I had less time than ever. (When I started the book, I had two children and now I had five.) How could I buy all the rest of the paper, buy the postage, get the mimeographing done since I no longer had access to the machine I had been borrowing. It broke down. But the urge to write again just got worse and worse even though it seemed like all I could do to get through the chores I had. I'm not a lazy or puny person. I had my fifth baby on a Thursday morning, left the hospital Friday evening, went home and commenced to catch up on the dishes and wash. But it *seemed* like I was at my limit and being nagged by the urge to write seemed to make me even tireder. (And that's one of those curious things because once I

actually started writing that sensation of weariness gradually left.) Anyway—

When you become a Christian one of the first things you learn to look for is God's will in your life. God promised in the Bible that all things work to the good of them that love the Lord. He has a wonderful and beautiful life plan waiting for everyone who will belong to Him and let Him help them. From the time I first discovered God I have been, maybe exceptionally, dependent upon His prompting. By that I mean the clues He gave me in my mind to what He wanted me to do. I was feeling so totally lost and overwhelmed by my difficulties I clung to God with the fierceness of desperation. He was my only hope in difficulties that I'm not going to detail here. I had no idea how to save myself from my problems. God took me in hand then and literally led me minute by minute from task to task. When I woke up in the morning the first thing I said was, "Good morning, God." His comfort and advice in my mind was almost a constant experience in those dark days and sometimes I think it would be worth all the other agonies to have Him so close again. Because like a parent letting a growing child go I have not been led so tightly by Him since I gained strength of my own.

God's will? You might ask. That's a hard idea if maybe you don't even believe in God. But the faith thing is at the middle of it all. If you make even a feeble effort, the classical mustard seed, toward God, you'll experience God reaching out to meet your effort at faith. And the more you trust in Him the mightier He rewards your trust. So I wanted God to lead me and I laid myself in His hands and He came through. Ever since the day I first gave Him my life, and frankly, at the time I didn't realize I was giving Him my life—I was just reaching out to Him in great trouble because I had exhausted everything human, by looking back now over the span of time I can see the steady climb upward toward goals I could scarcely have visualized at that time. The fulfilling of God's beautiful plan for my life. And His promise that all things work to the good of them that love the Lord. I've stood on that promise through some dark, dark hours. And it has always turned out to be true. That's the faith thing again. When you stand on one of God's promises out of the Bible, stubbornly, like the Gospel song "I would not be denied." Then in the end God fulfills it. So when you try to know God's will, and if you feel anything that *might* be His will give it a chance on the important possibility that maybe it *is* His will that you've asked for, then you're learning to be prompted by God.

I was about halfway into the book when I had this tremendous personal finding of God. It was part of the big shakeup I told you about. At that time the book work had kind of petered out too. I worked but I wasn't getting anywhere. Which isn't surprising because I never finished anything of significance in my life before. Not finishing things was a dominant feature of my character it seemed. Anytime something got rough or was around too long I gave up and looked for something else. Now here I am about to have my 8th wedding anniversary, and about to finish this book and that's what *God* accomplished.

But for a year I hadn't touched the book. Instead I sorted out my values and learned that the most important thing for me was serving the ones I loved, my husband and my children. That I should always put their needs ahead of my own, willingly. I was learning the basic Jesus principle of Give and it shall be Given unto you. I was learning love your enemy and that's a rough one. I was learning give, give, give and love, love, love, which is the upside down and opposite from the way I had been living before. And in return I was joyful in the blessings that I discovered following these laws of God brought me. Because so fast not only God was loving me but so many other people too that it was a springtime and a renaissance and a dawning in my soul as the new self, the reborn self discovered itself and was discovered by new sisters and brothers in Christ, finding myself part of a family with God the Father at the head, part of a brethren whose fellowship would do for one another whatever needed, found myself with new weapons against new enemies, weapons of prayer and song, and love, and Bible reading against the whole gamut of miseries. And they worked! I saw new enemies because I know now the old enemy was myself and getting that one taken care of I was really freed to take the battle where it could matter.

So I hadn't even desired to finish the book for a whole year. And anyway it was glaringly obvious to me that I could not finish the book from the money point of view, this trying to print it myself which I was committed to, and because the limits of my own time and strength, and because of the stress on my marriage which taking it up again seemed bound to cause. To desire to finish the book seemed very much like desiring financial, physical and emotional suicide for those reasons. But was the desire all mine? Because for a year I hadn't desired it. And it was more like me to give up when it got rough than to struggle on. And in my experience with God's way of leading me the thought that comes and nags me, patiently, relentlessly, the "do this, do this, do this," is one way God has of showing me His will. And that's the way the thought of finishing the book came to me, more and more.

So one day I almost literally broke down. I remember kneeling on my living room floor, crying, with lifted hands, and saying to God—"OK, Lord, this seems to be Your will. God, I can't see the way through, but if it's Your will I know You have a way through for me and I've just got to go ahead and trust You." So I did. I secretly went back to work on the book. I sought for God's leading with regard to the project constantly and followed it explicitly. I had no hope outside of His Power to do miracles. I worked on the book during daytime hours while my husband was at work and did the displaced housework in the evenings, scrubbing floors and ironing shirts usually until 11:00 at night. God gave me the strength and that was His first miracle for me. I was able to do twice as much work as I had been able to do before.

When weeks later I finally felt it was time to tell Mike, he was really good about it and that was a second miracle because for the years past he had grown to hate everything relating to the book and my

work on it with almost a passion. But ever since then he's been very patient and he didn't ask me where I was going to find enough money, or how much that we needed to pay bills I was instead using for the book. When it finally did reach the point where I needed outside help I found it from people who were willing to wait to be paid until after the book was done and printed and sold. When it came time to buy paper and a mimeograph machine, stencils, ink, and typewriters I went down to Lewiston with the pickup and just started charging where I could, buying and signing checks when I had to. I knew I didn't have a cent in the bank. But I also knew that I was supposed to finish the book and that I had to have these materials to do so. So I kept writing checks until my checkbook read minus $550 and then I went home with my pickup load. I didn't tell Mike. I went to bed that night and believe it or not I slept.

The next day was Tuesday. That's prayer meeting day for me. Usually it's at my house but that day it was at my friend Pat's—a very gentle and beautiful soul, once widowed, and the mother of 8 children. I was scared to death what I had done and went to that prayer meeting in a spirit of desperation. I called a friend from Pat's house who was supposed to be rich and tried to borrow money. He told me that his finances were at an all-time low and the best he could do for me was $100, which I must repay in two months. That completed my list of people I thought I had a chance of borrowing from. Everybody else I knew was as tight for money as we were.

I was almost scared to pray. But finally I managed. I wish I could recreate for you here that time of prayer because it was a precious experience, but I can't. Suffice it that I prayed, very hard, very sincerely, and my Christian Sisters saw my agony of spirit and prayed with me. And then came that moment that we call "getting through" when you know with a mysterious kind of spiritual discernment that God has heard. There comes a beautiful peace and calm. "It's done," said Pat. "Yes, I know," I nodded. "You're going to get all you asked for and more," she said.

Well, I went home and made plans for the next day. Opal would come and babysit for me while I went out to get the money. I slept again. Next day Opal came and I got dressed up in my one and only good outfit. The one I bought on charge account at our local two-room department store. I fixed my hair, put on some makeup and got ready to drive off trying to look as if needing money were the last thing on my mind. Opal regarded me a little anxiously. She knew what was up. "Opal," I said, "I know God's got that money out there waiting for me. It's just a problem of finding out where."

I went to my bank. Not with much expectations but I thought I'd try. I remembered trying to get a loan from another bank when we bought this farm. We never yet have managed to borrow money from a bank. At that time it didn't look too bad though until I mentioned to the man that I was writing a book and immediately that was a mistake. He stopped writing, pushed the paper away from him, and I knew the interview was over. To him anyone admitting to writing a book couldn't possibly be a good risk. Well, this time the bank interview didn't close quite so disastrously. The bank man couldn't loan any money on anything so nebulous as an unfinished book. "What if you should die?" But he suggested that maybe I could get it from a private party.

I'd heard that there were some elderly brothers who sometimes loaned money for interest living down the road. I headed first to their house. Found it after some inquiry. They weren't at home. I went to another party. He wouldn't loan me so much as a dollar.

I heard that the brothers were in Kendrick. So I drove there and parked my car by the grocery store where I usually do. Instead of going around the corner to Main Street I opened the back door of the grocery store which lets you in the meat department. I was going to shortcut through the store. The grocer was standing there so I said, "I'm looking for the brothers. Do you have any idea where I could find them?" He answered, "Yes, I just saw them. But what do you want them for?" And within fifteen minutes more I had deposited a loan from the *grocer* at the bank and indeed the total amount with the $100 I had borrowed Tuesday on the phone, did add up to $60 more than what I actually had to have, as Pat had predicted.

I had money in the bank to cover those checks. The very next place I went was back to Pat's. I knocked on the door. "I got the money," I said to her, "and like you said. I've come to say thanks." She understood and we went into the kitchen and prayed and I thanked God for what He had done for me. I wanted to be like the leper that remembered to go back and thank Christ for His healing.

Dolly is much, much better now than she was in the middle of January when there were days when she could not use her hands even to turn the pages of a book or feed herself. In fact she seems very nearly well again. The doctors predict she is almost certain to suffer another and worse attack within a relatively short time. But that's doctor thinking for you. As far as I'm concerned with it's over and done. Dolly is well now and she's going to stay well. I'm going to take such good care of her that the old bug, whatever it is, doesn't have a chance. And this isn't the first time my opinion parted company with the doctor's and I won. There's too much at stake here for me to agree with something like that. God will guide my hand in nursing her and He's the greatest Physician of them all.

Well, sooner or later I've got to say something about fruit butters.

FRUIT BUTTERS—Technically a butter is a thick smooth sauce, made by straining fruit or vegetables. I think jams and jellies are too sweet. Sauces and butters I like. And you can use a butter just like a jam to spread on pancakes or bread but it doesn't have nearly as much sweetness. Just cook up the food with enough sweetening to suit you, and other seasoning if you want and can and you're done. Personally I think the tarter fruits make better butters. Peach or sweet cherry butter is too sweet. But apple and apple cider

butter made with a tart variety of apple is good and apple-plum butter is our all-time family favorite.

We first started out making apple-plum butter at our first home in Juliaetta four miles down the road from here. The nearest thing that place had to an orchard was the big walnut tree in the front yard. So when fruit season came I scavenged up and down the highways and byways. This region is unusual in that everywhere pioneers and people all down the years stopped to lunch or picnic and left apple cores and plum pits. The volunteer apple and plum trees generally have a smaller fruit but they are loaded almost every year and free for the picking. So the children and I would drive down the road with a backseat full of cardboard boxes and then go home and make apple-plum butter, one-third plum to two-thirds apple.

A butter is basically made by long cooking over very mild heat. On top of the stove you have to keep a close eye on it, stirring very frequently. For fruits use an enamel or stainless-steel pan and use a wooden spoon to stir. Cook on low heat slowly for a long time. If you are very busy, cook it instead in the oven in a covered kettle at a temperature of 300°-350°. Then you don't have to stir it and it doesn't burn on the bottom. If your sauce doesn't get smooth enough to suit you can put it through a rotary colander after the cooking. A "rotary colander" is a cone-shaped colander with a wooden mallet to help work the stuff through. You fill it with goop and then turn the wooden mallet, rolling it around the sides of the colander. Don't just stomp with the mallet—gets you nowhere. Season your finished butter with cinnamon, cloves, nutmeg, allspice or what you like.

To can a butter you can do open kettle canning. Have the butter boiling on the stove and proceed by my directions in the section on Canning in the Food Preservation chapter. But for extra safety I recommend that you process it in a hot water bath for 10 minutes at least. You don't want all your hard work to be in vain because the stuff molded. The reason you have to be so careful is because the thick sauce is *hard* to heat clear through.

To freeze just pour into a container, cool and put in the freezer. Can or freeze butters in half pints or pints because a butter that isn't heavily sweetened will mold in a couple weeks, even if refrigerated, unless you can depend on your family to eat it up faster than that.

Old Fashioned Apple and Apple Cider Butter— This is the traditional apple butter made of pared apples boiled down with cider. Boil 6 cups of apple cider in an enamel or stainless-steel pan. (Optional, for extra redness start with 12 cups cider and boil it down to 6 cups.) While the cider is boiling down, core and quarter about 10 pounds of apples. Add apples when the cider is ready and continue cooking slowly until tender. Put it through your colander. Put your butter back into the pan and add 1½ cups brown sugar (or more to taste—it depends some on the sweetness of your apple variety). Optional, add ½ teaspoon ground cinnamon, ¼ teaspoon allspice, ¼ teaspoon cloves and a pinch of salt. Continue cooking over very low heat, stirring a lot, until the cider and sauce do not separate when a spoonful is placed on a plate. Then pour into containers for canning or freezing.

Apple-Plum Butter—Use from twice to three times as many apples as plums. Cut up the fruit and cook in a little water until tender. Then put through the colander. Add sweetening. Continue cooking until the butter is thick enough to deserve the name. This is Mike's favorite kind. He likes it on waffles or pancakes or toast and so do I and the children.

Peach Butter—Scald, peel, stone and slice 7 pounds of whole peaches. Cook in ½ cup water very slowly until soft—about 3 hours. Then sieve. Add 1½ cups brown sugar.

JAMS AND JELLIES

Jam is fruit boiled thick with sugar. It's just too sweet for me. Most jam recipes call for a two to one ratio sugar to fruit by weight or volume. Some jam recipes that are really trying to hold down the sugar content call for a one to one ratio. Jelly generally has a one to one ratio, 1 cup juice to 1 cup sugar. Jams and jellies preserve easily because the sugar itself acts as a preservative. Old-timers would turn narrow necked wine type bottles into jam holders by tying strings soaked in kerosene around the shoulders. Then they set the strings on fire. That cracked the necks so they could be knocked off and the edges filed smooth. The bottles were washed, sterilized, the hot jam poured in and sealed with two or three thicknesses of that good old-time brown paper, well pasted together, and tied strongly with string. The new-time way to seal them is with paraffin. But in the case of paraffin you have to let your jelly set up (jell) and cool clear down first before you add the paraffin.

The key to jelly is pectin. It's a natural substance in some fruits, especially underripe ones, that when heated and combined with *acid* from the fruit and *sugar* "jells." Apples usually are rich in pectin. Natural ripening causes the pectin to break down. So if your fruit is overripe, your jelly will never get firm no matter how long you boil it. Peaches, strawberries and cherries don't have much pectin. You can combine pectin-rich fruits with pectin-poor fruits, or use commercially prepared pectin or make your own.

There's an old-time test you can use to tell whether or not you have enough pectin present for good jellying. Into a glass container put 1 tablespoon of juice and with this mix 1 tablespoon of alcohol. If you have enough pectin there, the fruit juice will turn into a jelly-like mass that you can gather up with a spoon. If not enough pectin is present, it won't jell when you add the alcohol and that tells you to add some more pectin. If you are short of pectin, adding sour apples, crab apples, currants, lemons, cranberries, sour plums, loganberries or green gooseberries will be sure to provide it. Ripe apples, blackberries, oranges, grapefruit, sour cherries and grapes have a sort of average pectin content. Fruits that don't jell well on their own because of low pectin content are apricots, peaches, pears, strawberries and raspberries. You must also have a big enough acid content for jellying. Taste the juice for tartness. If it isn't very tart add lemon juice for extra acid. Jelly making depends on having proper amounts of fruits, pectin, acid and sugar. It's a chemical change.

Altitude also affects your jelly making. Martha Mohan, who lives over 6,000 feet up near Hotchkiss, Colorado, wrote me, "To make jelly from wild berries at altitudes over 6,000 feet, I have found that the wild berries should be boiled at least three times and preferably four times as long. At 6,500 feet I cook all jellies three times as long as cooking charts show, until it sheets off the spoon. An old-timer, a lady we know,

who lives at 8,300 feet elevation told me this and it works for me. These jellies are really worth the extra effort and are really great with any wild meat."

JELLY TEST—To see if the jelly is ready for canning, take a little up in a spoon and then let it drop from the side of the spoon. When the drops flow together and sheet from the spoon your jelly is done.

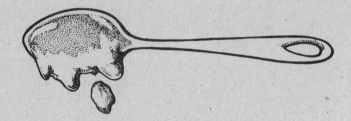

There is a lot more than this to jelly making and I recommend that you send for one of the canning books mentioned in the Food Preservation section or get the USDA Home and Garden Bulletin No. 56, *How to Make Jellies, Jams, and Preserves at Home,* which you can probably obtain free from your county extension agent.

Jelly is generally canned. You can use baby food jars with their own lids if it is the kind with a tight seal that will preserve it OK and is of a handy size.

HOMEMADE PECTIN from apples. You can use skins and cores of cut up apples to make this or whole apples or apple pulp. Boil 2 pounds of your apples with 4 cups water for about 45 minutes. Get the juice first through a cloth with pressure, then strain that juice again through another cloth or jelly bag without pressure. Boil the resulting juice 15 minutes and can it if you won't be using it right away. Add 1 cup of this apple pectin per cup of pectin-weak fruit juice. When making jellies using this apple pectin juice— other fruit juice combination, ¾ cup sugar per cup liquid is usually correct.

If you use the commercially prepared pectin you have the option of freezing your jams and jellies. Cottage cheese containers are handy for this purpose. With each package of Sure-Jell or Jam and Jelly Pectin, or whatever the product is called in your parts, come good general instructions for both canned and frozen jams and jellies. The frozen ones are nice in that they are uncooked and preserve that fresh fruit flavor. To make jelly the fruit has to be cooked— cooking brings out the pectin in the right form for jelly making. Only with commercial pectin can you jelly uncooked fruit. To jell with natural pectin the fruit is generally cleaned, cooked, mashed and put through a jelly bag or two to get the juice that is the jelly base. If you squeeze the bag you will get pulp too which is OK unless you want a clear jelly—in that case don't squeeze the bag.

Loquat Jelly—Remove blossom and cut fruit in half. Add water to cover. Simmer until tender. Strain and measure juice. Boil juice 5 minutes, then add ¾ cup sugar per cup juice. Cook until jelly test works, then pour into jars and seal.

Quince Jelly—Make it using 2 parts apple juice to 1 part quince; or 1 part cranberry juice, 1 part quince and 1 part apple juice. Use two-thirds as much sugar as juice. Save the pulp for a butter.

Chokecherry Jelly—To 3 cups chokecherry juice add the juice of 2 lemons and 3 cups sugar. Boil at least 25 minutes, or until a drop of juice on a saucer will jell. Pour into jars and seal. Half crab apple, half chokecherry also works nicely. And those are two fruits that go together, those and gooseberries will grow in the high mountain country where fruit is hard to come by.

Corncob Jelly—Break 12 corncobs into small pieces. Boil in 3 pints water for 30 minutes. Then strain. To 3 cups corn juice, add the juice of 1 lemon and a box of commercial pectin. Bring to a boil. Add 3 cups sugar and boil 3 minutes longer. Pour into jars and seal.

Lemon-Honey Jelly—This is a favorite recipe from Nanci Falley of Lockhart, Texas. Combine ¾ cup lemon juice and 2½ cups honey. Bring to a full rolling boil. Add ½ cup liquid fruit pectin, stir vigorously and boil about 2 minutes. Pour into hot sterilized jars. Cover with paraffin to seal.

No-Sugar Jelly—To 1 cup fruit juice, take 1 to 2 tablespoons unflavored gelatin which has been dissolved in 1 to 2 tablespoons cold water. (Stir the gelatin into the cold water until well dissolved. Let stand a few minutes.) Now add hot juice steadily and stir well. Set aside to cool in your refrigerator. Because there is no extra sugar in this kind of jelly it won't keep without refrigeration and you must use it up within two weeks.

Honey-Fruit Jelly—Combine 2 cups high or medium pectin fruit juice, ½ cup mild-flavored honey and 2 teaspoons lemon juice. Bring to a boil and stir in all at once 2 tablespoons powdered pectin. Let boil 10 minutes and pour into your jelly glasses. For low pectin fruit juices use 4 teaspoons lemon juice and 3 tablespoons powdered pectin. If you want to use homemade pectin, substitute 2 cups homemade pectin for both the lemon juice and powdered pectin.

SEALING JELLY WITH PARAFFIN—If you do this it makes it possible to use odds and ends of jars other than regular canning jars and stretches your jar supply. You simply pour a ¼- to ½-inch layer of melted paraffin onto the top of the jelly after the jelly has cooled enough to set up. And you can wash these little disks of paraffin as you use the jelly, toss them in a box and melt them down again the next year for reuse.

Simple Orange Marmalade—Cut 6 oranges into quarters and then cut each quarter into thin slices. Discard the seeds. Measure your resulting fruit and then add 3 cups water per cup fruit and let soak overnight. The next day simmer until the rind is tender. Then add 1 cup sugar for each cup of fruit. Cook until fruit is clear and the syrup sheets from a spoon (222°). Pour into glasses and seal.

Dried Fruit Jam—This is great because it's a jam that doesn't even need honey for an extra sweetener. Use dried fruit in any combination that suits your tastes—½ cup dried apricots with ¼ cup dates is good. Make it in a blender and moisten with a fruit juice to spreadability. One cup pineapple juice does it in the apricot-date recipe. It helps to soak the dried fruit overnight in the juice before blending. You can use this dried fruit jam like a syrup on pancakes and waffles, too.

Sunshine Preserves—You can make this out of apricot halves, nectarine or peach slices, or whole berries. The fruits keep their shape and color well. Use 3 cups sugar and 2 tablespoons lemon juice to 4 cups fruit. Combine fruit, lemon juice and sugar in a saucepan. Stir gently to blend the ingredients. Now cover and let set at room temperature 1 hour. This is to get some juice out to cook it in. Now put it on the heat. Stir until it boils. Then let it boil hard 4 minutes without stirring. Now cool, uncovered. Pour your preserves out into glass or plastic pans or trays so that it is between ⅓ and ¾ inch deep. Set in direct sunlight. If bugs or dust will be a problem, cover with a pane of glass or clear plastic, leaving a 1-inch opening along the side. Once every hour stir the preserves a little bit. It is done when the fruit is plump (turn them over as needed) and the juice is about as thick as corn syrup. It will get thicker when cold. It takes longer to do this in a humid climate like on the coast where it rains a lot than in a desert climate where evaporation is really fast.

Overnight Strawberry Preserves—Mrs. Ora J. Rees donated this recipe to her Grange cookbook and I found it there. Wash and hull firm choice berries. Combine 2 cups sugar with 1 cup water and boil until it will spin a thread when you hold a spoon up that has been dipped into the liquid. Now gently add 4 cups strawberries, ¼ cup lemon juice and 2 cups more sugar and boil 12 minutes without stirring.

If you get a scum skim it off. Pour the mixture out into a shallow pan and let set 24 hours. Put into jars cold and seal with paraffin. The berries keep their shape and color.

Crab Apple Preserves—Core the crab apples with a sharp small knife through the blossom-end leaving the stems on. Take 1 pound granulated sugar and 1 cup water for each pound of prepared fruit. Put sugar and water over the heat, and boil to dissolve sugar. Skim and then drop the apples in. Let them boil gently until clear and the skins begin to break. Take the apples out with a perforated skimmer and pack them in jars. Pour the syrup over and seal. Optional, slices of lemon boiled with the fruit, 1 lemon per 3 pounds of fruit. You might as well seal, it's safer that way.

Citron Preserves #1—Get rid of the peel and seeds. Make pieces about 3 inches long. Soak in water until tender enough to pierce with a straw. Remove the citron with a perforated skimmer to a plate. Add sugar to the juice—2½ cups per 2 cups juice. Cook until scum quits rising. Return citron again and boil juice until citron is clear. (It takes about an hour.) Remove citron again and boil juice 15 minutes more. Add 3 sliced lemons (without seeds, of course) per gallon juice during this last boiling. Put citron into jars. Pour juice in over to near top and seal.

Citron Preserves #2—You'll need 2 oranges, pulp and chopped peel, 2 lemons, pulp and chopped peel, 10 cups seeded citron and sugar. Peel the oranges and lemons and cut the pulp fine. Run the peelings through your grinder and cover with boiling water. Let stand until cold. Put all the ingredients in together and measure. Add an equal amount of sugar. Let stand overnight. In the morning cook until thick, stirring often.

SYRUPS

If you are avoiding sugar, white or brown, get two small syrup pitchers. Fill one with honey and one with molasses. If you have it, or can afford it, you could keep a third with real maple syrup in it. You could substitute sorghum for the molasses, but molasses is better tasting as a table syrup by far. The only thing I really prefer sorghum for is rubbing the top and sides of a ham before I bake it. Or a plain pork roast. That's all I do and it comes out just delicious. Keep the pitcher filled with honey in a warm spot in your kitchen—over the pilot light or on the warming shelf of your wood stove and serve both pitchers whenever they are appropriate. If you want to serve brown sugar in a bowl you can, but you'd better wrap it back up when the meal is over so it doesn't dry in rock type lumps. If it does get hard you can pound it fine again with a hammer.

Homemade syrup was one of the delights of my childhood. Usually it was chokecherry syrup poured over pancakes. Sometimes it was honey syrup. We had bees on the place and more honey than we knew what to do with. The first money I ever made was peddling buckets of chokecherries in our local metropolis—Livingston, Montana. I took my pony, Shorty Bill, laden with buckets a couple of miles on up the mountain from our home to a little canyon where the chokecherry bushes were thick. I worked hard all day picking into those metal buckets. Rode home, tired but satisfied, with the fruit of my labors. The next day was Mama's day to drive the 30 miles into town to do a few weeks' shopping. She took me and my buckets of chokecherries. I went from door to door, knocking on doors, offering my chokecherries for sale.

I think I charged about a dollar a bucket. My last customer gave me a beautiful bouquet of flowers from her garden as well as the money for chokecherries. I took the flowers to the hospital and told them to give them to a sick person. The receptionist was very nice about it. I wonder if she really did. Then Mama came back from her shopping and found me sitting on the hospital steps. She took me to the bank and I opened a savings account with my five dollars earned from selling chokecherries. Now I guess door-to-door selling is illegal everywhere—"the Green River ordinance." But as I remember those housewives were really pleased to see buckets of chokecherries like the ones they had picked when *they* were little. Something that wasn't sold in stores.

I'd like to sound virtuously thrifty at this point but it wouldn't be true. That savings account, like all the ones that followed it, soon showed the minimum balance. By now I've quit bothering trying to keep one. I'm not even sure if saving money is a virtue. I've been more inclined to store what extra dollars there were in things like a home and now a farm and that's probably technically a better place to put them anyway.

One lesson that I did learn well in those days and from that pony though was *trust*. There's more on Shorty Bill somewhere in this book—maybe Sours? Anyway, I rode him every day to a country school two miles down the road. One late fall day I took a notion to ride home from school directly over the mountain instead of going by the road. I let myself through the gate across from the little schoolhouse and Shorty and I didn't have another fence from there to home. We were on what you might call open range. We slowly rode up out of the Bracket Creek Canyon where the school was into the treeless exposed top of the mountain that lay between the school and my home. As I rode dusk fell early and without warning out of the gray sky came a true blizzard. The snow began to fall thicker and thicker. Big white flakes and with them utter black darkness. The wind howled pushing against my pony's body and mine and whined in my ears. I couldn't even see my pony's ears ahead of me. Though I was, as always, warmly dressed I started to feel a real chill on my face.

There was no light, no road, no fence to follow. No sound but the wind. I was a little girl about eight with no hope in the world but my pony. I knew those blizzards. It might snow for days and nights and when it stopped there could be easily four feet of snow on the ground. I had gone with my father when a band of sheep got caught in a blizzard and had watched as he sought for rounded mounds in the surface of the snow and then dug down to find the all too often dead sheep and lambs underneath. For a moment I was very frightened. Then I seemed to remember my daddy once saying to me that if I ever got lost with Shorty Bill, I was to let the horse have his head, that he had senses which I did not and could not understand, and that he would take me home. So I let him have his head. That means I simply let the reins hang slack instead of putting any pressure on him to tell him what way he should go. And I concentrated all my own efforts on keeping warm. And hanging on. I

made myself as small as I could, hunching over his back with my head low and snuggled as deep into my own wraps as I could get, trying to shelter my face from the wind. It seemed that we went on a very long time like that. Shorty wasn't one to hurry if he wasn't being urged. He moved along steadily though and I felt soothed by his steady rocking motion, almost sleepy, except I had to hang on tight. Suddenly he stopped. That did scare me. I peered up and out and then I could just barely see the shine of a light outside the barn. My daddy was there. He must have been waiting for us. He lifted me off the horse and hugged me. Whenever I think of that I think that going home to Heaven must be like that. You trust because there is nothing else to do anyway. And your trust brings you safely home. I've felt like I was in darkness many times since that ride. But there's a hand that holds mine and an invisible light that goes before me. Guiding, guarding all the way. Though it be even the valley of the shadow of death.

Well, back to syrup. The old-time syrups were not only used on hot breads like biscuits and pancakes and on ice cream but also on puddings and pound cakes, as flavorings in sauces and sherbets and as beverage bases. One or two spoonfuls of a fruit syrup in a glass of cold water with shaved ice makes a nice summer beverage. Most of these recipes name white sugar but you can substitute honey. The trouble with honey in this case is that it has such a distinctive flavor of its own, and if you use it in everything you get tired of honey flavor pretty soon.

General fruit syrup recipe—Fruits vary in natural sweetness or tartness, chokecherries probably being at one extreme and dark sweet cherries probably the other. So the amount of sugar to add involves your judgment. But in general get the juice from the strawberries, raspberries, currants, grapes, or what you want as directed for fruit juices. After the juice is brought to a boil add sweetening and boil down to the density you want. Then can.

Whole Fruit Syrup—Wash, core, pit the fruit and peel if you think the peels wouldn't make it through the blender or wire mesh strainer or wouldn't be nice. Now blend or force through a wire strainer. For every 1 cup mashed fruit add ¼ cup water, 2 teaspoons lemon juice and ½ cup honey. Boil together 5 minutes, stirring constantly. Now take your syrup off the stove. Skim off the foam. Pour into hot jars and seal or cool for serving.

Quick Berry Syrup—If you haven't time for all the boiling down do this. For each 4 cups berry juice stir in 2 cups sugar and 2 cups light corn syrup. If it is strawberry or raspberry juice, add 2 tablespoons lemon juice (the others don't need it). Boil. Skim if needed. To can it, process 10 minutes for pints or quarts.

Resourceful Woman's Syrup—Take any leftover fruit syrup or juice. Sweeten as needed and boil down until it is syrup-like.

Virginia's Chokecherry Syrup—Combine equal parts of berries and boiling water. Mash berries thoroughly with wooden mallet or spoon. Squeeze pulp through a cloth supported by a colander. Combine equal parts juice and sugar. Bring to a boil. If you like it thicker boil it down to the density you want. Another way is to combine water and berries and cook a few minutes, then mash with a mallet and proceed as above. Some cooks add pectin to the pulp—½ box to 6 cups juice, boil and then add sugar. It hastens the process. Get it thick enough and you'll have jelly.

Egg Butter—Beat 3 eggs well. Add 2 cups molasses and boil until thickened.

Maple-Honey Syrup—Combine ½ cup maple syrup, 1 cup honey and ¼ cup butter.

Blueberry Syrup—Combine 1 cup fresh (or frozen or canned) blueberries, ½ cup water and ¼ cup sugar and bring to a boil. Crush berries. Simmer 2 or 3 minutes more. Serve this syrup hot.

Blackberry Syrup—Crush well-ripened blackberries and add one-fourth as much boiling water as you have berries. Let stand 24 hours, stirring frequently. Strain. Add 1 cup sugar for each quart of juice and boil slowly for 15 minutes, or until you have the density you want and then can it.

Phony Maple Syrup—Boil for 5 minutes 1 cup dark brown sugar with ½ cup water. Add ¼ teaspoon maple flavoring and 2 tablespoons butter. Serve *warm*.

Honey Syrup—To use straight honey for syrup, warm in a pan of hot water before serving so it will pour easily or else mix with about one-fifth water. A honey-butter syrup for immediate use can be made by melting about 3 tablespoons butter per ½ cup honey. Serve while hot and stir when necessary to redistribute butter which will tend to float. Or swirl before each pouring to mix. You can stretch your honey by mixing 1 cup honey with ½ cup sugar and ¼ cup water. Heat and mix together. Serve warm. Stretch it even further, if need be, by combining ½ cup water and 1 cup brown sugar per cup of honey.

Cream and Sugar Syrup—Mix in a pan ½ cup cream, 1 cup brown sugar and ½ cup dark corn syrup. Bring to a boil and serve warm.

Corn Syrup—12 cobs eating corn (a little old for eating like corn on cob). Take knife and run down cob every so often around cob then place in kettle with 1 gallon water. Boil for about 1 hour until water is milky. Strain and add enough water to make 1 gallon if needs be. Then add 8 pounds brown sugar and 1 whole lemon. Boil until desired consistency and add 1 teaspoon or so of maple flavoring. This was sent in by Shirley Empey from Mesa, Washington.

Uncooked Chokecherry Syrup—Mrs. Nielson of Walla Walla, Washington sent me this one. She said, "Here is a syrup recipe I've used for many years and it keeps in old syrup bottles and is very good. Grind in food grinder 12 pounds chokecherries, pits and all. Add 3 ounces tartaric acid and 2 quarts cold water and stir well. Let stand 48 hours. Strain through a clean cloth and keep only the juice. Add 1½ cups sugar for each cup of juice. Stir until it's clear and all sugar is dissolved. Need not reheat. Put into jars or bottles and seal." (You get the tartaric acid at the drugstore.)

AND SAUCES

Great-grandmother was strong on sauces. She made her own and lots of different kinds. The "pudding" (really a steamed bread) was always served with a sauce. The calf's-foot jelly also usually had a sauce. I like coffee jelly with a simple brown-sugar-dissolved-in-rich-cream sauce. (These jelly recipes are in the Meat chapter under Gelatin.) Sauces generally run in three types—what you put on meat, what you put on pudding and what you put on fruit. To go with meat at table it's usually a homemade fruit catsup for me (Sours chapter). My sauces for fruit generally are based on whipped cream. The other kind I make a lot is a barbecue sauce which to me means some form of tomatoes, plus molasses, plus a dash of vinegar and some chopped onion, which I mix together and pour over the meat when it's about one-third to half done. (Use a Dutch oven.) Barbecued meat is a favorite with the children. Alas, anything sweet is a favorite with the children.

Honey-Cream Sauce—Whip ½ cup cream, then beat in ½ cup honey and 1 teaspoon lemon juice.

Shortcake Sauce—Whip 1 cup cream. Add 2 egg yolks, one at a time, and beat more. Add 3 tablespoons honey and 2 tablespoons lemon juice.

Fruit and Cream Sauce—Whip 1 cup cream and sweeten with about ¼ cup honey. Put the whipped cream on your pudding or whatnot and then pour a spoonful of fruit on top.

Orange Sauce—Combine ½ cup butter, ⅔ cup honey, 1 tablespoon orange juice and 1 teaspoon grated orange rind.

Quick Molasses Sauce—Boil 1 cup molasses with 2 tablespoons butter for 5 minutes. Cool. Add 2 tablespoons lemon juice.

Mostly Molasses Sauce—Boil together for 15 or 20 minutes 1 cup molasses, ½ cup water, 1 tablespoon butter, a pinch each of salt and cinnamon and 1 tablespoon vinegar.

Raisin Sauce—Cook ½ cup raisins in a little over ¼ cup water. When the raisins are soft, strain and reserve ¼ cup water drained from them. Combine ¾ cup brown sugar and the raisin water and cook together 5 minutes. Then add 2 teaspoons butter and ½ teaspoon vanilla. Mix, add raisins or not as you prefer, and serve warm.

Maple Cream Sauce—Combine 1 cup maple syrup and ½ cup cream. Boil to soft ball. Beat 1 minute. Add 1 teaspoon vanilla.

Or use a Fruit Sauce on your pudding.

HOMEGROWN SUGARS

In Colonial America dried pumpkin, maple sugar and honey were used for sweetening agents. My mother bought plain old white sugar in 25- or 50-pound bags and then transferred it to a bin in the kitchen. There was a bin for flour, too. They didn't go to town too often from the ranch. It was a long day's proposition so when they did the car really came home loaded. The sugar lasted for a long time. Mama wasn't much of a sweets maker. Fudge and Divinity at Christmas time was her candy repertoire. Oatmeal cookies for everyday. I've got a real sweet tooth and I practically ruined my teeth and health with candy bars and pop once I got away from Mama. Now I'm a mother too and fighting the same battle. I prefer using honey though and I can make a 5-gallon can last all winter. There are four kinds of sugar. Fructose is found in fruits and honey. Glucose is also found in fruits and in the blood. It's the sugar they give in hospitals. Lactose is a kind of sugar found in milk. Your whey from cheese making is rich in it and will sweeten your bread. If you boil down the whey you get a more concentrated lactose syrup. Sucrose comes from sugarcane and sugar beets.

SUGAR BEETS

Commercial white sugar comes mainly from sugarcane and some from sugar beets. Beet sugar production is just about impossible as a home industry. There are a lot of sugar beets grown around Colorado. I remember the smell of those processing plants. Really rank. At the factory the top and small part of the neck of the beet are cut off, the beet washed, cut into very thin slices and exposed to running water which dissolves the sugar. The beet juice containing it is black. Lime is added to precipitate unwanted stuff. The remaining clear juice is then centrifuged to get molasses and raw beet sugar. And then put through several more procedures to get the sugar white.

If you wanted to try **GROWING YOUR OWN SUGAR BEETS** you'd have to contact a commercial seedsman and I don't know one personally that carries them. We don't grow them around here. They aren't in the garden seed catalogs. The sugar beet is a remarkable plant. Its taproot can be as much as 6 to 7 feet deep and smaller roots reach out in all directions. When you pull it out to harvest, the lower part of the taproot and the tiny rootlets remain. So they aerate the soil and draw food from lower levels than your usual crop. They are said to grow in any climate in the United States. They like sunshine. You should seed in rows 18 inches apart and thin the seedlings to stand 9 inches apart in the row. Keep out the weeds. You can plant when frost danger is past and harvest around October first. But beets can't compete with cane in terms of yield, and you can't make beet sugar without

a factory. Raw beets don't even have a sweet taste. Factory beet sugar is made by grinding, crushing, heat, pressure and chemicals. And the beets aren't good people food. Fine animal feed though, but don't feed the animals spoiled beets—it would make them sick.

TO MAKE A BEET SYRUP—Scrub the beets well. Slice like cucumbers. Cover with boiling water and bring to a boil. Drain. Now you have thin raw beet syrup. Evaporate the water to thicken it using low heat. You can use the green leaves that you cut off for animal food or compost them.

Sugar from beets is too hard. Maybe you could raise cane. *Countryside Magazine*, issue of February-March, had a couple letters about sorghum which might be helpful to you. If you aren't familiar with it, *Countryside* is a kind of clean-cut little homesteaders' magazine. Last I heard you could subscribe for $9 a year by writing Jerome D. Belanger, Route 1, Box 239, Waterloo, Wisconsin 53594. Better known as "Jerry," he prints a lot of the letters he gets in the magazine. People write in questions and other people reading it write in answers. They have some articles, too, and Jerry is the ever-eloquent hero of it all. It's his own thing and like me he can say just what he thinks. That's worth a lot in your reading material.

SORGHUM CANE AND SUGARCANE

Sorghum cane and sugarcane are relatives with all the varieties of silage cane and are all similar in growth and nature. Cane is grown commercially in Hawaii, Louisiana and Florida. Canes are all to some extent warm climate plants, but they can grow farther north than many people think. A few years ago a lady right in our valley planted a nice stand of sorghum cane and made herself some syrup. Cane is a thirsty plant and you've got to give it *lots* of water. In the old days in places where lots of sorghum grew it was cut and hauled to a special syrup mill. There a mule pulled the press to get the juice out. He walked round and round and when he got tired they would feed him tidbits of the cane and lead him around his circle some more. Then the juice was cooked down until it was the proper consistency. Then stored in buckets with tight lids.

Some of your sugarcane is sure to be gnawed on plain by the children. They cut off a stick a foot or so long. Then peel off enough peeling so they can get their teeth into the softer inside. Take a bite, chew and suck until all the sweetness is out. Then spit out the tough fibers that would noways chew up and get another bite. At its best cane is a giant grass that can grow as high as 18 feet. It likes lots of sun and water—you can irrigate. You can make your own sugar from cane. You press the juice out, collect it, boil and stir it and eventually solid pieces of sugar will form. They won't be "granulated" like your store sugar. The lumps will be like small stones or gravel. If you ground your lumps very fine you'd have confectioners' sugar.

You can't get sorghum syrup from sugarcane or vice versa. (Hazel is my expert on sorghum and I'm quoting freely.) You get a thin but very tasty table syrup from sugarcane. Sorghum is processed both for table use and for animals. It is used in horse feed and for dairy cows and usually mixed in small amounts of one or two tons since it will dry out in the summer. Hazel says they get two tons mixed at a time for their one milk cow and five goats. The formula for their feed mix is as follows: 3 sacks (100 pounds each) cottonseed hulls; 2 sacks (100 pounds each) cottonseed meal; salt; calcium; 100 pounds of sorghum syrup; the rest of the weight of dry corn (shuck, cob and all).

The distinction between sorghum and molasses is that the molasses is the strong part that is scraped from the bottom of the barrels when cane syrup is made. The dregs and leavings you might say. So to make homemade sorghum syrup first you have to plant your sorghum cane. You can mail-order it from H. G. Hastings Co., Box 4088, Atlanta, Georgia 30302. See if your local seedsman knows a nearer, cheaper source. Then you raise it, cut it, and you are up to the pressing problem. Some other folks use "sorghum" to mean homemade molasses.

Without a real sorghum press you'll have to improvise something. You could grind and then squeeze for juice cider style. Then boil down your juice until it seems thick enough to be called a syrup. The sorghum making process is the same as to make maple syrup. The cane that has been pressed dry of juice is good winter feed for cattle. So are the skimmings from your boiling off. You boil down the syrup in a big evaporator tray over a fire. Keep an eye on the evaporating, skim off the surface foam. Figure about 3 hours to boil it down. It's "sorghum" whenever you decide you're done. The color will brown.

7th Edition, June 18, 1976. I've discovered that there is one of those wonderful old-time USDA Farmers' Bulletins (No. 135) on the subject of "Sorghum Sirup Manufacture" (1901). You get a copy by writing Homestead General Store, Box 1112, Woodstock, Georgia 30188. (Have to buy it—not free.) And Raymond Weaver, a professional sorghum maker from Sale Creek, Tennessee, wrote to explain all about sorghum making. I bet maybe you could order some of that fine honey or sorghum from Raymond!

"Dear Carla: I specialize in honey and sorghum and my wife is a fantastic baker. Quite naturally I checked out your article on sorghum and seems like you could use some meat to go on those bones. Maybe the most helpful thing I can do is to give the task some perspective by giving you some yardsticks to go by.

"A person might start by writing to: U.S. Sugar Crops Field Station, Route 10, Box 152, Meridian, Mississippi 39301. Tell them your situation and ask about recommended varieties. You might ask for Agriculture Handbook 441 which is the main publication on sorghum—also the bulletin on whichever varieties they recommend. We planted Dale, theirs and Honey Drip—Dale being far superior to the other two. Sorghum does not come up good in cold ground. I recommend planting two weeks after the last frost. You need *four full frost-free months* after you plant it.

"How much to plant? The standard is 100 gallons per acre. Yields of over 400 gallons have been recorded though. If you can estimate the bushels of corn a piece of ground will produce, a good rule of thumb is 2 gallons of syrup for each bushel of corn. Another rule of thumb is 1 gallon for each 100 feet of row (approximately 13,020 feet per acre or 130 gallons). For the beginner, I recommend a plot 50 x 50 feet. This will give you enough to cut your teeth on, and you'll be glad you didn't get in any deeper (750 feet of row or 7½ gallons). Shake the seed in a row letting it dribble out the side of your hand between thumb and index finger. You want a seed about every 2 inches. This will give you a good sure stand. When 1 inch high thin to 6 to 8 inches apart and weed. It's really important not to have it too thick. A good big stalk will produce as much syrup as 15 little thin whips with only a small fraction of the work. I intend to remove my suckers (tillers) when cane is 24 inches high.

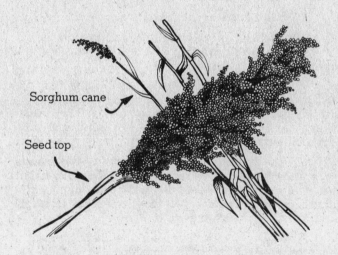

Sorghum cane

Seed top

"Cane is ripe when the seed is in hard dough (hard to cut with the thumbnail). We make strippers out of old saws by removing the handle and putting our own homemade one on. It should be light but strong and shaped like a hoe handle. The toothed edge is good to knock off the leaves. The first 6 inches of the back edge can be sharpened like a sickle blade to cut off stalks and head. Start stripping as soon as the cane reaches hard dough. One hour per 100 feet of row is a good rule of thumb. It is better to get it a little early than a little late. If you wait longer the syrup will get darker and stronger. Haul to the mill and protect from rain, cattle and frost.

"If you have more than a few feet of row you better have a sorghum mill. The cider press is going to get old pretty fast. Your 50 x 50-foot patch is likely to produce 60 to 80 gallons of juice. That will be a very good day's work with a cider press—maybe more. If you have a three-roller horse-drawn mill you should get about 15 gallons an hour (green juice). It takes one man sticking cane and one man carrying cane in, removing pomace (crushed stalk) and staying after the horse. Juice should not be ground more than 24 hours in advance. In my case we start grinding Saturday morning and grind all day, counting late starts, breakdowns, tired horses and low yield we usually end up with about 80 gallons. They finish grinding about noon Sunday just as we are pulling off the first molasses. That way we know just how much juice we are going to have and most important we are not likely to run out of juice.

"Cooking syrup is the most challenging thing I have ever done in my life. I recommend that the beginner start out with five people on the pan: the syrup maker, two skimmers, a backup syrup maker and a relief skimmer. When you're learning it's better to have too much help and cut down than to have too little and be run ragged. The syrup maker has a tremendous amount of responsibility. He must see that:

"1. Plenty of juice is on hand so that he doesn't have to shut down unexpectedly and wait for juice. This is when the syrup is most likely to scorch.

"2. The proper amount of juice is in the pan. Too much can cause it to boil over and make it finish slowly. Too little will make it scorch.

"3. The skimmers are doing a good job.

"4. The proper amount of fire is under the pan. Too much fire will make it boil over. With not enough it takes forever to finish.

"5. The syrup doesn't cook back. That is, the syrup in each successive section must be a little thicker than that in the preceding section. If one section gets ahead of the section in front of it, it will scorch before it gets to the spout.

"6. The syrup tends to chalk near the end. This is a white coating of starch which looks like white paint. As it builds up the bottom side will brown then char. Later, pieces of this charred chalk will break loose giving the syrup a scorched taste.

"The syrup maker must keep the chalk scraped off the bottom of the pan with something like a spatula or cut off the syrup flow, empty the last few sections and scrub them out good before continuing. This past year I had a scorch so I cut off the syrup flow with a rag and we scrubbed the last four sections good. They were badly chalked. Even though the chalk was not charred we noticed a definite improvement in the quality of the syrup when we resumed.

"7. The most important job of all for the syrup maker is judging when to pull the syrup. One old saying is that it's ready when the bubbles get as big as a bull's eye. A better way is to pull it when it begins to thread. Dip your pusher into the finishing syrup and hold it up in the air letting the syrup drip back into the pan. If it immediately breaks into a stream of little drops then it needs to cook a little more. If it falls about 6 inches in a smooth stream then breaks into little drops you have a light syrup (226°) just right for pancakes. City folks tend to prefer a thin mild syrup like this which is easy to pour.

"If the stream falls about a foot before it breaks into drops it's getting pretty thick. This is the way old-timer country people usually like it. The thicker it gets the richer (stronger) the flavor. The best way of all to know when to pull your syrup is to use a candy thermometer. I prefer the kind in a glass tube with the pencil clip on it. This can give the beginner a

big edge on the experienced syrup maker. You want 226°-230° depending on how thick and strong flavored you want it.

"Don't take your thermometer out of hot syrup and wash it off. It will crack. Let it cool a minute first. Don't let it get water inside the tube. It will fog up so bad you can't read it. Don't pull your syrup too fast. If you do you'll leave a bare spot behind your pusher which will scorch before the syrup can run in and cover it. Be sure and strain your syrup through cheesecloth. It will have a few yellow jackets and honeybees in it. You don't want to bottle that. I use aluminum screen under the cheesecloth for support.

"Avoid the galvanized pans with soldered seams. This puts hot syrup in direct contact with zinc and lead. The galvanize eventually wears off and you know where it goes! I use black iron with beaded seams. It would be better with welded seams. I'm not that skilled a welder, though. Stainless and copper are too expensive. You should get 1 gallon of syrup for each 10 gallons of juice you put in the pan. We got 35 gallons of syrup from 275 gallons of juice or about 7.5 to 1. This was from heavily green manured land.

"Watch your hot syrup. It will cook you to the bone. *Never! never! never!* pick up a pan full of hot syrup. One slip could be fatal. I wish I could tell you that sorghum is a breeze but it's not. It's a lot of hard work and long hours especially until you find out what you're doing. Estimates of stripping time and pan crew should improve with experience. By the way the beginner should make about 2 gallons of syrup an hour and I guess every syrup maker has had some scorches.

"I'm not sure feed molasses is sorghum. Sorghum is not a true molasses. It is a syrup. A true molasses is a syrup from which at least some of the sugar has been removed.

"Five varieties of seed can be had from: Foundation Seed Stocks, University of Mississippi, P.O.B. 5267, Mississippi State, Mississippi 39762.

"By the way, orange is not a recommended variety. The recommended rate is usually about 3 pounds per acre. At this rate a few ounces would plant your 50 x 50-foot plot. If you need translations or clarifications or anything else just say the word. You're doing a fantastic job, Carla. On behalf of all homesteaders thanks!!

"P.S. You'll need about 100 gallons of water. We carried ours until we got the shed built over the pan. Now we just set two drums under the low end a month or so before we make. 'Stripping time' is both cutting and stripping and topping."

SUGAR MAPLE

Sugar beets and sorghum cane having been discussed, that leaves maple trees and bees if you want to be sweetly self-sufficient. If you live in a state bordering any one of the Great Lakes or in the Northeast, you should be able to grow sugar maples. You can grow them other places, too. Your altitude is an important factor. Between 600 feet and 2,500 feet is best

for the trees. I have a neighbor that grew a beautiful big sugar maple from a sapling in her front yard. I hope within a year or so when I can afford it to put in a fair-sized grove of them on our place. But it's not the kind of crop that you can cash in on very fast. I'll be planting them more for my children than for me because they take a long time to grow. In general, figure that a tree is mature enough for tapping when it is at least 40 years old, a foot in diameter, and 60 feet high. Sometimes they grow faster though.

If you are so lucky as to have inherited mature sugar maple trees on your land or have access to them, Agriculture Handbook No. 134, "Maple Syrup Producers Manual," put out by the U.S. Department of Agriculture and available from the Superintendent of Documents, Washington, D.C., tells in complete detail everything you could want to know about producing maple syrup. *Organic Gardening*, January 1972, page 67, has an article on it. And from Schocken Books, Inc., 200 Madison Avenue, New York, New York 10016, for $2.75 you can order *The Maple Sugar Book* by Helen and Scott Nearing.

You tap your maple trees around the first March thaw. The right weather is warm days and freezing nights. Then the sap rises in the trees. The trunks are tapped as soon as the sap begins to run and shows in the end of the twigs, usually in late winter if the winter was mild or in the earliest spring. The hole in the tree is bored with an auger. New tapholes are drilled every year and into each hole you insert a hollow metal spout and from that you hang a bucket. A really big old tree can have as many as four buckets on it. A modern method is to use plastic tubing that stretches from tree to tree and carries the sap all the way to the sugarhouse, but varmints have a tendency to chew holes in it. So the sap goes up the tree trunk and out the spout and down into your old-time bucket and then every day you should collect the drippings from each tree and take them to the sugarhouse for boiling down. If you've only got one tree go ahead and tap it. Boil the sap down on your kitchen stove and you'll have about a pint of maple syrup. It takes a *lot* of sap to make syrup.

The sap you've collected looks and tastes like sugared water. In fact you can drink it straight, or use it to sweeten other drinks or in cooking. Boiling it down is a long process. You can test your boiling sap for density by the regular sugaring tests (see Measures near the back of this book). After your syrup is dense enough to suit you pour into any sterilized container that you can get a real tight lid on. Use a paraffin dip for extra safety.

7th Edition. Jean Nance wrote me from Neoga, Illinois, about syrup making. "We make maple syrup in small batches, from 10 maple trees. You say that the sap must be watched all the time, which would discourage many people. Of course, if you have a fancy evaporator, you do have to watch it all the time. However, on the kitchen stove, you just put as many quarts of sap as you have in your largest kettle. If you have 8 quarts, you are going to get about 8 *ounces* of syrup. Until the volume is down to perhaps 16 ounces, you are essentially boiling water, and don't have to watch it at all. The last bit of boiling down does have to be watched carefully. The main problem is steaming up the house—everything drips!"

And Marlissa Carrion wrote me from New York about her childhood in Ohio. "We used to run out in the yard in the winter with a big roaster pan, scoop up fresh-fallen snow, and Mom and my aunt would be heating maple syrup. Then we'd trail ribbons of maple syrup in the cold snow and it would harden to a kind of candy."

HONEY

Shakespeare said, "Where the bee sucks there suck I" or something like it and to me that means honeysuckle. That's a wild vine with pretty trumpet-shaped orange flowers that grows up the trunks of trees and flowers among their branches. The children love honeysuckle time. To get the nectar you pick some of the pretty, long orange flowers when they are fully developed. Pick them with the tiny green bulb on their base intact. Then nip off that green bulb with your fingernail. Put your mouth to the opening you made at the base of the flower and suck. You will get a tiny taste of honey. Some flowers will have more of it and some less.

To buy honey from stores is getting more and more expensive. It's been bad for bees in our part of the country two summers in a row. If you buy your honey try to get it wholesale direct from the bee man. Buy by the 5-gallon can. You'll save money and that can should be a whole year's supply for you. Even if you do set out to raise bees they won't be able to spare you a significant amount of honey probably until the third year allowing one year for them to get going, and one year for you to make mistakes.

LEARNING TO BEEKEEP—Of all the subjects in this book, beekeeping is the one I feel worst about teaching in a book. You really need to learn it in person. So try real hard to find a local beekeeper who will let you visit him and take you through a hive and show you his workshop where he makes hives and how he extracts. Helpful texts for new beekeepers are *The Art and Adventure of Beekeeping* by Ormond and Harry Aebi, 1975, available for $4.95 from Unity Press, Box 1037, Santa Cruz, California 95061. Also, *The Hive and the Honey Bee*, edited by Roy A. Grout, published by Dadant & Sons, Inc., Hamilton, Illinois 62341. This is often used as a college entomology and apiculture (beekeeping) text and is *good*. The grand-daddy of them all is the *ABC and XYZ of Bee Culture* by A. I. Root. It is encyclopedic and very complete. There's so much information in there I'm afraid you'd just feel lost. I'd also recommend *Beekeeping for Beginners* by G. H. Cale Jr., published in 1964 by the Journal Printing Company, Carthage, Illinois 62321, and I can't remember who I bought it from. Maybe Garden Way. *Honey for Health* is a kind of fun paperback available at health food stores.

Bee supply catalogs are fun and will help you find what you need. The largest is Dadant & Sons, Inc., Hamilton, Illinois 62341. But check out the competition too—like Strauser Bee Supply, Box 991, Walla Walla, Washington 99362, and Forbes and Johnston, P.O. Box 212, Homerville, Georgia 31634. The Bee Supplies catalog put out by the A. I. Root Co., 623 West Liberty Street, Medina, Ohio 44256 is free and contains everything the Root Company thinks they might be able to sell you relative to bees, which is very educational of itself.

If you order mail-order bees like from Montgomery Ward you'll get a really useful pamphlet called "How to Handle Your Package Bee Colony." And you'll probably want to subscribe to the *American Bee Journal* which you can get for $4 a year from Vern E. Sisson, *American Bee Journal*, Hamilton, Illinois 62341. But better than anything you can read would be the opportunity to look into a beehive with an experienced bee man. You can watch his technique and he will show you the different kinds of cells and bees. And you'll catch his calm. If he gets stung he takes a half minute out to cuss and then proceeds with the job.

STINGS—The notion that you can work with bees and never get stung is a kind of romantic fiction, perpetrated by bee people for fun. Two bee men in the presence of an innocent have a traditional conversation that goes like this: First bee man—"Have you ever got stung?" Second bee man—"No, never. Have you?" First bee man—"Never." The fact is even with the best preparation you're almost certain to get stung about once for every trip to the beehives you make and much more if you don't have the right kind of bee costume on. It's really important to have a good bee costume worked up so you don't have to be nervous. That way you can just go in there and do what you have to do. The worst things that can happen when working with bees are panic or an itchy nose.

Some people if they get stung too many times get allergic to bee stings and that can be dangerous. This can happen to you if you don't wear your protective clothing at all times. So don't get any more stings than you can help. I have a friend who worked once with such a bee man. A bee got into his helmet and stung him. He turned deathly pale and immediately had to go and lie down for about half an hour on the grass near the hives. Such people if they get stung once too often it will kill them. There is a pill you can take to counteract and they carry these pills with them all the time. It's Benadryl—a doctor's prescription drug for bee stings.

There are other people who get almost immune to the stings and it doesn't bother them much more than a mosquito bite. Bee venom is the same kind of stuff as rattlesnake venom. Bees can only sting once. They leave their stinger in you and die. A wasp can sting again and again. So bees are really good guys to me. They don't usually sting unless you are actually opening up the hive, moving around the frames and robbing honey. That gets them upset enough to lay down their lives. If you are merely peacefully watching bees come and go in their doorway there's very little chance of being stung. A bee sting itches like crazy because of the stinger in it.

BEE COSTUME—A really safe one is *hot* inside. You take your choice. White seems to repel bees so the more white you wear the better. Your *hands and arms* should be protected by very heavy work gloves or bee-proof gloves that you order from Ward's or a bee supplier. And a homemade gauntlet (an artificial sleeve). They don't sell gauntlets. Make the gauntlet puffy and sew it on at the top of the work gloves. Make it long enough to reach high above your elbow with elastic at the top to hold it firmly on. Or buy store bee gloves which are one piece long gloves with elastic at the top. A favorite spot the bees sting is right at the top of your gauntlet or long gloves where the elastic presses them close to your arm. And they'll really try to sting your hands. Getting gloves even of the toughest leather isn't absolute protection. Sometimes they can sting through leather, too. The bees will crawl around on you and keep poking their stinger down trying to hit pay dirt. If you make a gauntlet use canvas which is stiff and bags out good and is thick. The bagging out is your best protection.

Your *feet and ankles* should be protected by wearing work boots (or cowboy boots). Both are absolutely bee proof but work boots are better. Tie your pants tight to them with a strip of inner-tube rubber or elastic so the bees can't crawl up your legs. Or use the top cut away from an old army combat boot—the canvas wrap around that straps tight to hold your pant leg close against your boot. Bees crawl up. They won't just sting you on your ankles if they get in. They'll go way up so fast it'll amaze you. That's the voice of experience. Don't assume they can't find the gap. That's really underestimating bees. And bees just naturally crawl up. Early in my beekeeping I went out to the hives with my pants tied down but I was wearing a winter coat rather than coveralls. I figured that would be good enough. Suddenly they found a way up under that coat clear up under my shirt and I ran all the way back to the house slapping

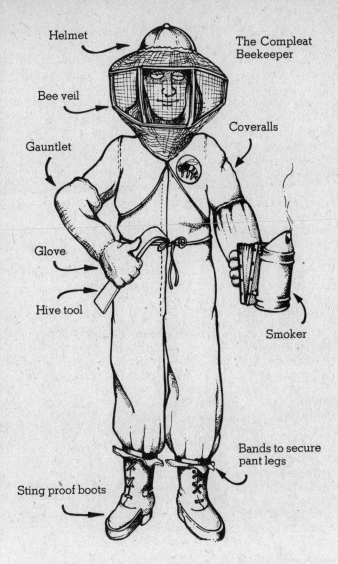

The Compleat
Beekeeper

Helmet

Bee veil

Gauntlet

Glove

Hive tool

Sting proof boots

Coveralls

Smoker

Bands to secure
pant legs

bees all the way and I had about 12 mean stings around my waist and above on my back and front.

White one piece coveralls, complete with long sleeves and on the baggy side fastened firmly around the outside of your high footwear protect your legs and middle. Now your costume needs a *helmet and veil* to be complete. I kid you not—it takes as long to get ready to go to the bees as it does to work them. And it's miserably hot inside all this stuff but that beats getting stung. You put it all on in this order: 1. Coverall. 2. Boots. 3. Rubbers or leggings. 4. Bee helmet and veil. 5. Gloves and gauntlets.

To protect your head you start with a tropical type helmet (construction hard hat) or a straw hat or felt or some such that has a *firm* brim. Now you need a bee veil which you can mail-order. The bee veil top fits around the inner brim of your hat. It covers over the outer brim. The crown of the helmet fits up through the top hole of the bee veil. You tie it firmly around the crown by a drawstring. So turn up your collar. Tuck your hair inside. Draw the bottom drawstrings tight around the base of the collar. Have it so there isn't even a small hole. Then bring the strings down, cross them over, draw them around to your back, cross them there and bring on around to your front again where you tie them firmly. Why? So that when

you lean over your bee helmet doesn't flop off taking veil and all with it.

SMOKERS AND BEE GO are two methods for trying to make the bees go away. To make your smoker work you put some dry grass or a piece of rag in there or some such that will smoke rather than burn well. You set it on fire just before you're ready to go out to the hives (after your bee costume is on), screw the top on and go. After you get the hive lid off blow lots of smoke at the bees. My personal impression though is that the things don't work worth a hoot, and I usually don't even bother with them. Bee Go is used by professional beekeepers when they get ready to take the supers for extracting the honey. It is sprinkled on the very top of the hive. It repels the bees and they move down about one super. Then the bee man takes off that top super, replaces the hive lid and sprinkles it on again and waits again for the bees to go and so on until they have all the supers they want. That's because you don't want a bunch of bees going along with you to wherever you're going to extract. A few bees will hang around anyway, though, especially drones. It's important not to get any of the stuff on the honey.

You can make a homemade Bee Go out of carbolic acid. Make a solution of the acid. Put it in a bottle that has a shaker top like for clothes sprinkling. Cut a cloth to be just the size to fit right over a super. Shake some acid solution on your cloth. Pry the lid off the super. Lay the cloth over the hive. Wait a few minutes. The fumes will drive the bees down. Then take the super. Don't use too much. It would ruin the honey or wax if it got in it.

GETTING STARTED IN BEES can be done in any of three ways. You can buy mail-order type bees. Or you can buy hives from an established beehive keeper in your area. The professional bee men have a workshop and make their own hives as they need them. But you'll have to stick with the one you start with because components from one source generally won't fit with those from another. Bee men make their own frames too but they usually buy their comb foundation. Montgomery Ward has it and the bee journals advertise it, too. Or you can beg, buy or borrow a couple frames with a queen cell, some workers and a little honey in them from a neighborly beekeeper and start a hive with them. I would recommend that you start by buying hives from an established beekeeper. Early spring is the time to do it. They will cost you anywhere from $25 to $50. You will have an already established hive in which everything is going right, one that has lots of workers ready to go and a fine producing queen. You'll probably get the bottom two boxes—your brood chambers—and would have to pay extra, around $5 each, for supers.

A hive is like this: The bees live in the bottom box which is usually called a "brood chamber." There the queen stays and lays eggs and most of the cells in there have baby bees in them rather than honey. The next layer up usually ends up being mostly brood cells, too, with maybe some honey around the sides and top. A layer is called a "super." Those two bottom boxes are what you get when you buy bees from a bee man and you never want to break up that comb to try to get any honey. Just leave it alone. The supers are mostly shallower boxes that you lay on top of these bottom two brood chambers. They are the ones that the bees store extra honey in. The bees work from the bottom up and that's why you need more supers in a good honey year and less in a bad one. The bee men make their own supers and if you start out buying hives from a bee man you're well advised to either buy supers from him or make your own because the supers *must* be the same size as the bottom boxes, and I've never met any two men yet that used the same size boxes.

Supers that you buy come in 8-inch or 10-inch heights. The deeper ones aren't really desirable because if they do get full of honey they are almost too heavy to carry.

Each super or brood chamber holds six parallel *frames,* hung vertically so that they don't touch the bottom or sides of the box. It is the frame on which the bees make beeswax cells to contain brood or honey or pollen (bee bread).

You can get a good hive going the mail-order way, too. I've done it. Montgomery Ward's catalog carries bees and Sears might too. Costs about $50 or more to get the basics. It comes disassembled and you put it together yourself. Nothing to that. You don't get near as many bees to start with and you don't have any finished comb to start with buying mail-order and those are the drawbacks. But given enough time, good conditions and good care, mail-order bees will establish themselves and do fine. You can't get a hive going just by putting out a hive and hoping. I've tried that too. And if you're a beginner catching a swarm is asking a lot of yourself awful fast. Not that it's hard. But when you see a swarm of bees and everybody around in a panic over them and

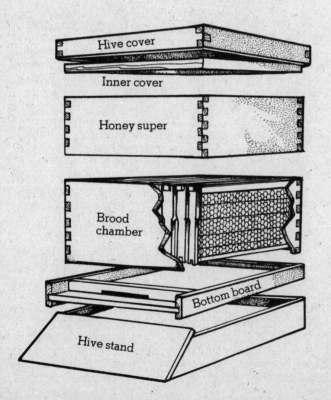

Hive cover

Inner cover

Honey super

Brood chamber

Bottom board

Hive stand

you've never handled bees before, you'd find it hard to believe me.

A brood chamber to start with before the bees arrive consists of a.) the floor of the hive, b.) the sides of the first box which are fastened together at the corners somehow and c.) the top. Those pieces are the basics of the hive and a, b and c are detachable from each other just by lifting them apart. Inside are the "frames." Most beehives are made to take six frames. There are grooves on the inside of the walls to slide the wooden sides of the frames in and out. They are equidistant apart all across the inside of the box. The middle of the frame is made, if you're just starting, of *"comb foundation."* This you have to buy to start with. Foundation is a thin sheet of beeswax. When you put the foundation into the frames you need to use either wires or string to hold it up. Wires are best. Professional bee men have a special machine for sinking the wires into the foundation. It sends a jolt of electricity through the wire that heats it and causes it to sink into the wax.

You can make do with strings though, putting them through the hole and drawing them tight. If you don't use wire or string the foundation will wilt in the summer heat and get out of place. The result will be you can't raise frames efficiently to look for queen or queen cells because the frames will get stuck together by the bees. If you put the foundation in right the bees will build a neat sheet of cells along the side of the foundation and leave themselves an open air walkway between the sheets that helps you too when you want to go into your hives to look for the queen or queen cells. At the end of summer hopefully the frame has been built into comb by the bees and is dripping with honey. Then you pull those frames out again to uncap the honey cells. Don't destroy the comb. It is precious to you and the bees to maximize your honey crop next year. Just carefully take off the tips of the honey chambers—the "caps"—with a hot knife. And try to keep the rest of the frame as undamaged as possible. When the honey is out you will replace the empty frames (which are now what we called drawn comb) in the super and give it back to the bees to be refilled. You can mail-order an electric knife that is perfect for that uncapping.

STARTING ADDITIONAL HIVES—Once you have a start of bees you can get all the other hives you want off your own bees and I think you'd be foolish to buy more when you could start your own. This is a little-known piece of information and I consider it the jewel of my whole bee section. Get ready a brood chamber about May 1. You can make your own out of an apple box or saw one out and nail it together. Now go into your best established hive: that's the one with the most bees, because it will be on the verge of swarming anyway. If you're able to, find the queen in the hive (and to do this you pull out frames and look them over carefully one by one until you locate the queen bee). You want to be sure *not* to move her.

The queen bee doesn't look like any other bee at all. She's about an inch long and tapers clear from her front to her tail. The other bees will be kind of spread out away from her. They don't crowd her round. If you aren't wanting to start new hives, pinch out all those big queen cells to prevent swarming. The more workers populate your hive the more honey they will bring home. The queen cells are the biggest. The next biggest ones are drone cells. The smallest are the worker cells. Anyway, to start a new hive take four frames out of one of your best established hives. Choose frames that have brood cells, some honey and some bee bread (pollen), which means cells filled with a sort of yellowish grainy stuff. And dump lots of worker bees in there. You can scrape them off other frames. Put the lid on and stuff up the entrance loosely with grass to give them a chance to feel at home. The worker bees will make a queen out of one of the brood cells if you didn't give them a queen cell. They'll make a queen by feeding a special food.

If you go into a hive and find queen cells but no queen that probably means the old queen swarmed. When the first queen hatches out she'll go around and sting the others to death right in their cells. There can be only one queen in a hive. A queen bee won't sting you. The only stinging she would do during her life is other queen bees. The drones haven't even got a stinger. Only the workers sting you. The drones are big fat bees. There are two popular kinds of queens. The black ones are called "Black Italian" and the light ones are called "Caucasian."

When you look at a frame the cells that are capped dark brown are brood cells. Those are the ones the bees hatch out of. The ones that are capped light colored contain honey. They'll be in sections of either one or the other. Queen cells are very easy to find, about an inch long, kind of hanging away from the rest of the comb. Drone cells stick out but not near like that. Drone cells stick out like little lumps. The worker cells are just right level with the rest of the comb.

You can make a hive with every queen cell. There is usually more than one queen cell per frame if they're making them at all. You can cut them out from the frame if need be and stick each one into a new frame. Add a frame with some honey cells in it and some brood cells that worker bees will hatch out of. The frames will almost certainly have some workers crawling around on them when you install them in the new hive. Put the lid on and go away and leave them alone. The workers will do the rest. That's another way to make a new hive. Or you can mail-order a package of bees and a queen. Just make sure you have them by May 1 so they'll be ready when the flowers are on. Bees can only make honey when flowers are in season. The rest of the year they have to eat their stored honey to keep alive.

The queen bee is a marvelous creature. A queen can live for seven or eight years which is a long time for a bug. They are really good though for only about three and that's why they talk about "replacing" the queen. Your honey crop depends in part on the vigor of your queen. The more eggs she lays, the more workers there are to make honey. It also depends on the weather. During a coldish spring she may not lay much of a brood. Then with luck you can harvest a honey crop in August. You'll get a gallon or maybe two gallons or maybe more of honey per hive per summer. As long as there are blossoms the bees will

make honey. Around here they are done with most of their honey making by the end of August when everything dries up and that's the time to go get the honey. We use two brood chambers and two supers. Take one super for us and leave the bottom honey super for the bees to winter on. You'll have to decide how much honey they need to winter on and just take what's over that. Different parts of the country have a longer or shorter cold season. If the bees don't have enough of a winter supply of honey they will die of starvation and you'll go out in the spring to look at them and just find a bunch of dried up little bodies. Check them in cold weather, too. You won't even need a bee suit. They'll be huddled in the brood chamber trying to keep alive by buzzing to make warmth. If they seem short of food dump a bunch of brown sugar right in there by them. They'll survive on it.

My general impression is that people are usually expecting more honey than they actually get. Maybe in the south it's better but in these more northern climates it takes a couple years to get built up to where your bees will be keeping you in honey—at least. And it takes at least six hives. I'd say work up to a dozen if you can. And visit your bees at least every three weeks to check for signs of trouble.

Queen excluders are generally made to sound like a necessity but they really aren't. If your hive is overcrowded and you have a bunch of queen cells in the bottom about to hatch out you could put the queen into the second story and the queen excluder between so they won't fight. It takes 21 days for workers to hatch, 16 days for a queen to hatch, 24 days for a drone to hatch. The queen excluder is a metal sheet with holes punched in it just the size workers can go through but a queen can't. Then you can put the extra queens with more workers into another hive and have new hives and then you don't need the queen excluder any more. I'd say don't use one. Edwin P. Arthur wrote me from Fullerton, California, that he finds a woven wire excluder located above the brood chamber helpful during heavy honey flow but doesn't have luck with excluders with punched holes—metal or plastic.

A PLATFORM is needed under your beehives if tall grass is interfering with their flight patterns. Also to level them and keep out ants. If you can help it don't put hives in the same pasture with horses or cows because sooner or later one of the big animals will get rambunctious and knock over a hive. If this happens in cold weather and you don't notice right away you'll have a hive of dead bees. They need the shelter their hive's enclosure provides. Skunks will take bees. They get outside a hive and thump a foot. As the bees come out they eat them.

To move a hive of bees plug up the door with cloth or grass. Grass is better because if you plug it airtight you'll smother bees. It depends on how far you move them. If you move them at night when they're all inside you can even leave the door open. To move them in the daytime, plug it up because they'll start flying as soon as you stop. For a long trip a piece of wire screen is great to plug it up. As long as you're moving they'll stay in the hive. But if you stop and then start moving and it is unplugged you leave a lot of bees behind.

FOUL BROOD is a bee disease. It is present when the larvae rot in their cells. If you were to stick a straw in and draw it out you'd just have a white stringy substance. If the state bee inspector finds foul brood in any hive of a commercial operator he condemns his entire stock. The preventative of it is a medicine the bees eat. It is a Terramycin stuff that you sprinkle on pepper style and about as thickly on top of the brood chamber. In the fall after you take the honey out you sprinkle 2 tablespoons of the stuff on each brood chamber and then do it again in spring. Foul brood can be contracted by your bees if there is a herd of wild bees nearby in some old building or tree that are suffering from it. If your bees get it the only remedy is to give them extra frequent treatments of the medicine until they straighten out.

TO MAKE COMB HONEY you put little square boxes into the hive instead of regular frames. The boxes for comb honey are made out of cottonwood because it has no resin in it. It grows wild around here. With no resin it can't taint the honey. If you want to make them yourself you would have to dry the wood clear out before working with it.

Plastic comb—A new development on the bee scene, which may be a great help, is a one piece frame-foundation-half drawed honeycomb made of plastic. You can put these in and out just like the regular frame and foundation and use them in an extractor. For free brochures you can write Croan Engineering Company, 5582 McFadden Avenue, Huntington Beach, California 92649. Mrs. Croan's daughter Suzanne is married to Jerry Zaslaw, who is Mike's boss at the North Idaho Children's home in Lewiston where he makes the cash crop and that's how I came by the information. Minimum order is a carton of 20 combs at $1.50 each and 2 pairs of spacers at $1 a pair. They fit a standard 16¼ x 20 x 6⅝-inch super.

HONEY FLAVORS—Bees gather what they find. They can only work when flowers are in bloom. So they have more chance to gather honey in climates where flowers blossom more months. Their honey is invariably flavored to reflect where the honey came from. In southern California where bee pasture is available nearly year-round it's not unusual to take as much as 40 pounds of honey from one 10-inch super twice a year. Bees can make honey from flowers on the eucalyptus trees or from citrus and others, which are in flower in winter, like the lemon. But if the bees get their honey from wild flowers, carob trees and oxalis it may be rich dark honey that the USDA would grade Number Four—meaning not fit for human use. Commercial standards prefer the sort of honey you get from a big sweet clover or alfalfa field, which is pale.

GOING INTO THE HIVES means to open up the hive and carefully remove and look over every single frame to find the queen, look for queen cells, and generally assess how many bees there are, how many and what type of brood cells, how much honey is coming in, and whether the bee colony needs more supers or not. You want to give them plenty of supers

if they need them because overcrowding stimulates swarming. (Sometimes they swarm anyway.) If you're very lucky you may need five or six supers by summer's end. More likely less. It will depend on the hive. Each hive has its own history each summer and there's seldom any two just alike.

Get into your bee costume, get your smoker going, take either a hive tool or a screwdriver with you to the hives. Use it to pry apart the lid from hive and supers from brood chamber. The nearer you get to the bottom the harder it will be to get things apart as the comb gets bigger and firmer. You can set the supers on the grass while you are working in the brood chamber. To put a super back on the brood chamber do it so as to kill no more bees than necessary. Start it at one end and slide the super slowly into the brood chamber so that you slowly shove the bees that are on top over the sides. They'll find their way around to the door again. This is one business where there's really no substitute for going to the hives with an experienced bee man no matter how well written or illustrated your manual.

SWARMING is common in the first half of June. There can be only one queen in the hive. If extras hatch out there go so many of your bees flying off with the young queens to make a home and a new hive wherever they can that what's left won't give you much of a honey crop. And you'll hear from the neighbors. Bees like to move into house walls. They can get between the outside walls or between upper and lower floors. About the only way to get them out if they do that, short of tearing the house down, is to poison them. You can get stuff in a spray can in a hardware store. Black Flag I think. It's a general insect killer. There's really no way to know whose bees are whose once they've left the hive, but once you get a reputation as a beekeeper about swarming time the phone is sure to ring with a sort of hysterical voice on the other end—something like, "Your bees have swarmed to a bush in my yard and nobody dares leave the house." You can try telling her that swarming bees don't sting. It's true. When they take the photos of somebody with his face covered with bees that's the kind they are using.

Well, if they swarm onto a branch they are easy to get, all clustered up like that. You can even do it without your protective gloves on. Just cut off the branch with the bees on it. Hold it over a brood chamber and shake or lightly brush the bees off the branch into the brood chamber. You can do it with a brush or a leafy limb. Bee professionals carry around an extra brood chamber in the pickup just in case they see a swarm they can catch. When swarming bees cluster they all just hang there— solid bees, a little over a foot long with lots of extras flying around outside.

The thing to remember is they're all ladies and whatever they've made up their mind to do they're going to do. I know a case where they clustered on a branch only a few feet off the ground. The beekeeper set a hive that was left open on top right underneath the swarm and even put some honey in it. Then he gently brushed the swarm with a limb into the hive which is just the way you're supposed to do it. (You can set the hive on a stepladder if it's a higher branch.) Then he went away for the night and the next morning all the bees had taken off for who knows where. If they had been in the hive he would have put the lid on, blocked the entrance and taken them home. On the other hand I know a case where the cluster was on a limb 40 feet high. The property owner was pretty insistent about getting rid of them though so the bee man, mostly to oblige her, left a hive sitting underneath the limb and by throwing a rope with a weight on the end over the branch managed to shake a few off and get them scattered on the ground below. Lo and behold the bees moved into his hive.

EXTRACTING HONEY—Wait until the major nectar flow is over. That's when the flowers are mostly gone, about August. Then get your supers. If you've already made the acquaintance of a commercial operator he may quite likely be willing to extract your honey for you for a reasonable fee. His equipment probably consists of an electric knife to uncap the frames or else a hollow knife with steam run through it so the knife is hot. It slices the caps off the honey cells real easy. Keep the honey in a warm room before extracting so it will come out easier. He has a special vat for the slicings to fall into. By means of heated coils it separates wax from the honey sticking to it. A little stream of melted wax comes out one side and the honey comes out the other. That is the only wax the beekeeper harvests—from the caps. Because he keeps the rest to use again. Why, when the price of wax is so high? Because a frame made with plain foundation will yield say 30 pounds of honey. But a frame on which bees in a former summer have "drawed" or "pulled" out those long wax honey chambers will produce 90 pounds of honey, three times as much! This is because the bees don't have to spend time and energy building comb and can go right to work gathering honey and filling the comb. All they have to do is cap it. That means put a lid back on the wax tube.

Then the bee man puts the whole uncapped frame in his extractor. The commercial extractor is a big round drum that will hold 50 frames at once. The uncapped frames are pinched into wire grippers in there and then the machine commences to whirl them

around very fast. The honey flows out by centrifugal force. The force flings it against the wall of the drum. It flows down the wall and is collected at the bottom, being piped directly to a big holding tank. Smaller versions of an extractor can be bought out of the Root Catalog but you don't have to have one.

To get honey without an extractor cut off the tops of the honey cells, hang the frames up over a heat source like a wood stove. The honey will melt and drip down. Have something there to catch it, of course. You have to do one side and then the other. If the honey looks messy you can heat and strain it before using it in cooking. Then pour it into jars and seal. Don't heat that honey in an iron kettle. It will cause it to darken. If you have wax mixed in with your honey melt it in a double boiler with gentle heat and take off the scum with a skimmer as it appears. If you have leftover wax you can put it beside the hive and the bees will eventually reuse it if it is left there long enough. I have heard of squeezing honey out from the wax by hand but it seems to me that would be an awful waste of drawed comb. Or make a Rube Goldberg contraption with an electric drill top and a "barrel" bottom that will grip and spin your uncapped frame.

On the other hand, if you need the wax for candlemaking anyway the easiest way of all to get honey without an extractor is to melt the whole thing down together. Just make sure you use frames that are clean and don't have baby bees in them—they'll mess up the taste of the honey. You need frames that are solid honey. You can put the rest back to feed the bees in winter.

Day before yesterday I went out to the hives and got two nice full frames because I was out of honey. I like that better than having one big honey making session in August like the professionals do. Two frames make a good gallon of honey. (There are six frames to a super or a brood chamber. We use about 10 gallons of honey a year so you can see with three or four hives a family need only take one super a year for their needs.) I cut the honey, comb and all, into a great big frying pan. Melted it. Skimmed the whitish wax off the top and strained it into a separate frying pan. I strained the rest of the honey through a cloth set over a deep pan and then poured the strained honey into quart jars. The honey with all the wax in it I let cool. The wax rose to the top and I could easily take it off. The rest of the honey there I reheated and poured into another jar. It was all that simple. Of course, it wrecked the drawed comb but my bees have been established long enough and there are enough hives so that isn't any big problem. I even have a hive living two feet away from the back door in the old refrigerator that used to be a smoker. It's a beehive now since they moved in. But I kind of enjoy them.

RECYCLING THE FRAMES—You put comb foundation against the frame wires and put the frames back into the hive. Somebody discovered way back when that if the bees were given frames with foundation made of beeswax just exactly that distance apart they would make a comb on each side of the frame built on the base of the foundation and then leave them-

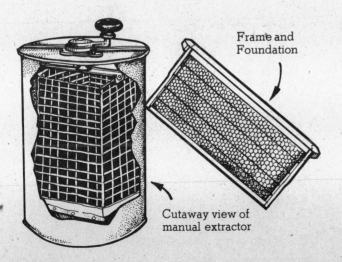

Frame and Foundation

Cutaway view of manual extractor

selves a walkway between each frame. Which is perfect too for beekeepers because to get the honey out all we need to do is pop out a frame and there you are. You can buy foundation from all the bee suppliers like the A. I. Root Company. The old-timers used to make their own. In those days the Root Company made rollers for rolling the wax into foundation. Now you can't buy rollers anywhere that I know of unless you can find one as an antique. You can only buy the foundation from the Root Company. Progress I guess. The old-time rollers were made of hardwood maple and carved by hand. The foundation has to be rolled to have a certain type of impressions in it otherwise the bees won't build it into honey anyway. The way the old-timers made the sheets of wax for rolling was they took an 8- or 10-inch board and dipped it into hot beeswax once or twice, then let it cool. When the wax was firm they slit it on the side and peeled it off.

WAX CANDLES—As recently as when I last went over the Candles section in this book I still believed that you can't make candles from beeswax unless you work with it in a solid state by pinching and pressing. Now I know different. Here's how to make lovely pure beeswax candles. First, you want to clean your wax if it is dirty looking. Wax melts at 130°. Add a little cider vinegar to the wax and some water and hold it at 135°-140° for two or three days, if possible. The dirt settles to the bottom, the honey collects in a layer just below the wax, which floats on top. In factories they force it through canvas under great pressure, but this works fine if not better. When your wax is clean you are ready to make dipped candles or mold candles, whatever you like. To make mold candles just proceed the regular way. Have a mold with a wick in it. Melt the wax and pour it in around the wick. Pour your wax into the molds at from 190° to 200°. That gives a nice sheen on the outside and you're less likely to get bubbles. *But don't get burnt.* To make dipped candles, which are more economical of the beeswax, you have ready two containers. One has your melted wax in it. The other contains ice water. You can dip six or eight at a time if you have a holder that will suspend that many wicks at once. You dip in the wax and then dip in the ice water. Then dip in the wax again, then in the ice water again and so on until you have your candle where you want it.

STORING HONEY—Honey keeps easier, better than just about anything. If it gets sugary on top all you have to do is put the can on the back of the stove or on very low heat and the sugar will go back into solution as it warms. You can store honey in a deep freeze but I don't see any point in it since it does keep fine outside. The typical storage container, a 5-gallon can with a 2-inch opening, is impractical though because if it sugars you have to melt the whole supply every time you need a quart and it is so heavy to handle. Better to pack your honey in the first place in 1-gallon jars and keep a 1-quart container in your kitchen for current use. Store your honey where it won't get over 75° since above that temperature it will lose flavor and color—the higher above the faster the change. But keep your kitchen container in a warm place or the honey won't mix with other ingredients very easily.

If you want to preserve some of your honey in the comb save your nicest combs and stand them edgewise in a crock or metal can and cover with extracted honey.

COOKING WITH HONEY—Once you get the swing of it it's really fun using honey, molasses, sorghum and maple syrup instead of white sugar. Tastier too. You can substitute sweeteners freely. The only difference is that you have to stir honey for a while to get it to dissolve. And you use half as much honey as the amount of sugar the recipe calls for and reduce the amount of liquid slightly. You won't get an equivalent amount of *real* sweetness because honey *tastes* sweeter than the same amount of sugar. Maple sugar, brown sugar, molasses and corn syrup are all less sweet than white sugar figured on a pound for pound comparison—meaning they have fewer calories per pound.

Marilyn Gordon and her husband raise and sell honey at Boone, Colorado. She really knows what she's talking about and here's her advice: "To substitute honey for sugar in a baking recipe use ¾ cup honey for 1 cup sugar and reduce liquid in the recipe by ¼ cup—like in cakes. If liquid isn't called for in your recipe, add 4 tablespoons additional flour for each ¾ cup honey used in cookies. Bake at a temperature 25° lower than called for, as baked goods with honey will brown faster. Cakes, cookies and breads will be moist and stay fresh longer."

Freezing fruit with honey—Don't make a heavy syrup. One cup honey to 2 cups water is as much honey as you'd want to use. That will give you what the recipes call a "medium" syrup. For a "thin" or "light" syrup use 1 cup honey with 3 cups water. Then allow ¾ to 1 cup syrup per quart freezer container. Measure your syrup into the container. Slice fruit directly into it and freeze. You won't need any ascorbic acid when you freeze fruit in honey syrup. The syrup itself will prevent the fruit from changing color. Add a crumpled piece of freezer paper to keep the fruit forced down under the syrup. Peaches and strawberries are especially good this way.

Honey Fruit Jam—To make Doris's gooseberry jam combine 3 cups green gooseberries and 2 cups clover honey. Cook slowly until mixture jellies on a cold dish. Put in jars and seal with paraffin. Simple and very good and you can apply the same principle to other fruits.

Honey Fruit Jelly—Measure 1 cup prepared fruit juice into a pan. Add 3 cups honey, mixing well. Bring to a boil, stirring constantly. At once stir in ½ bottle liquid pectin. Boil hard 1 minute more. Remove from heat. Skim off foam with a metal spoon. Pour quickly into sterilized jars and seal at once. You'll need about 5 glasses. Good made with orange juice.

Honey Tea—A bee man taught me this one. Put water on to boil. When it's boiling add 3 teaspoons honey per 4 cups water and boil a few minutes more until thoroughly in solution. Add tea leaves to make tea. Steep, strain and serve. For iced honey tea, make as above then chill.

Uncooked Berry-Honey Jam—Mash fresh berries

(raspberries or strawberries very good in this). Put the mashed berries in a blender with a package of pectin and blend. Taste. Now add as much honey as you think it needs to be sweet enough and blend again. You can only make a little bit of this at a time because blenders don't hold much. Store it in the refrigerator.

Honey Dressing for Fruit Salad—Combine half honey and half lemon juice. Store, covered, in the refrigerator.

Alaska Honey—Larry Malcolm wrote me from Eagle River, Alaska, to supply this recipe "for people who for reasons cannot have bees but still want to make honey! Boil together 10 cups sugar and 2 cups water for 10 minutes. Remove from heat and add 1 teaspoon alum and 25 fireweed flowers, 45 pink clover flowers, 45 white clover flowers (or 90 clover of any color). Let stand 5 minutes. Strain and pour into jars. Simple, isn't it? And it comes out nice and thick and wonderfully *good!* We're having a taffy pull this weekend. Hooray! Went dog-sledding yesterday for the first time. Beats sno-machines hands-down! So *quiet*, with a full moon!"

Cracker Jacks Made with Honey—From Marilyn: "Blend ½ cup melted butter with ½ cup honey. Heat until well blended. Pour over a mixture of 3 quarts popped corn and 1 cup chopped nuts. Mix well. Spread over cookie sheet in thin layer. Bake in preheated 350° oven for 10 to 15 minutes until crisp. Be careful, mixture is very hot."

Broiled Honey Topping—More from Marilyn: "Mix ¼ cup soft margarine or butter with ½ cup honey, ½ cup shredded coconut and ½ cup chopped walnuts. Spread over top of hot 9-inch square cake. Broil until topping is bubbly. Tastes best served warm. Or heat ingredients in saucepan, thin with several spoons of milk, serve over ice cream or pudding."

CANDIES

We have candy on Halloween, Thanksgiving, Christmas, Easter and birthdays. After supper and homemade, if possible. I'm not thrifty, either, when it comes to all that store-type candy that comes home with the children on Halloween and Christmas. The next day what's left over gets either given away, thrown away or put away for the next special occasion if it's something that will keep.

What's basic to making candy is to know *the candy stages:*

Soft Ball—234°-240°. A few drops in a cup of cold water are firm enough to hold together so you can pick it up.

Hard Ball—250°-266°. When a few drops in a cup of cold water form a firm ball.

Soft Crack—270°-290°. When a few drops in the bottom of a cup of cold water are a little too hard to form into a ball.

Hard Crack (or brittle)—300°-310°. When a few drops in a cup of cold water form immediately into crisp, firm drops in the bottom of the cup.

Caramel Stage—310°-338°. This can be told by the color—the boiling mass begins to turn a little yellow.

On all the candy stages except caramel you drop a few drops of your candy mixture off the end of a spoon into a cup of cold water. Then stick your fingers in there and feel what happened to the drops—soft, hard, and so on.

TAFFY

In the in-many-ways-wonderful Old Days entertainment consisted of getting together and making something—a barn, a quilt, and for the little ones, taffy! As candies go, I like taffy. You won't eat as much of this as you will fudge and such stuff because it's sticky. You put it in your mouth and roll it around and around and it gradually dissolves. I don't eat much candy now because it gets in my cavities and reminds me dramatically that sweets dissolve teeth but lest the art be lost forever here's how to make it.

TO MAKE TAFFY mix your ingredients and then cook, stirring frequently, to the hard ball stage. That means every once in a while hold up your spoon and watch how the syrup drips from it. At first it just drops off like any liquid. Then it drops more slowly. Next thing there is a little thread between the drops. This is called the "thread" stage and now you test for the hard ball condition.

Into some cold water in a cup drop about ¼ teaspoon of the syrup. Work it with your fingers into a ball. If the ball is soft the taffy isn't ready yet—although by the time you are done with your first testing, try testing again because by *now* it may be! When the taffy can be pushed together into a hard ball (it clicks when you take it out and rap it against the edge of the cup), it is ready to be poured out into a very generously buttered pan or platter.

DON'T COOL YOUR TAFFY TOO FAST by putting it out in the cold or into the refrigerator. The outside edges would set up into the hard ball stage while the inside would still be too hot to work (and once it's hard ball you can't do anything with it). Stir occasionally as the taffy cools in order to get the outside edge to the center and to keep the cooling throughout the mass as uniform as possible. But don't stir any more than necessary to do that, or it will "sugar"—get sugar granules. Merely lift the outside edges and bring them to the center.

WHEN SHOULD YOU START PULLING? As soon as the taffy is cool enough that it won't burn your hands. It has to be done quickly. Once the taffy sets it is hard to do much with. If some gets hard in the pan before anyone has a change to start pulling it the case is hopeless. Get ready by washing hands and then butter your hands. (Some people prefer to dip their hands in cornstarch—you don't have such a buttery final product.) Take the taffy from the outside of the

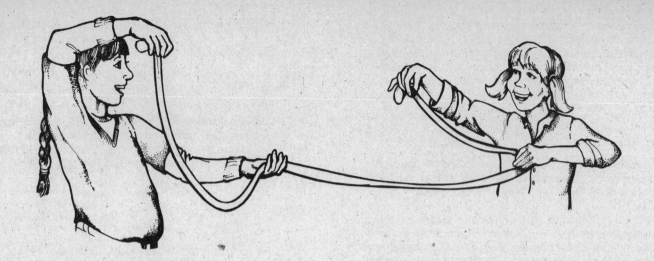

pan first since there it is the coolest. If you are having a jolly old fashioned taffy pull for family and friends and kids, divide the taffy up into several gobs. Pull the gob out into a long strand and then fold it back into a single gob again. Pull out and fold back over and over again. As you pull the taffy gets lighter in color because more air is getting included in it.

WHEN SHOULD YOU STOP PULLING? When it is hard to make the taffy stick back together again after pulling it, or when it is cracking as you start to pull it out, or when it is just too hard to pull. (*Note:* In very hot summer weather when the temperature is 100° or above your taffy may *never* get brittle.)

WHAT MAKES TAFFY PULLING A PARTY? See who can pull it the longest. Make different kinds of ropes or designs with it—funny little animals, or spell your name with it. And eat some. Divide the taffy into several sections and color them differently. Braid different colors together. Or make a basket by winding strands around the bottom or outside of a cup or bowl. Butter the cup or bowl on the outside before you start. Put a handle on your basket and set it to cool. When it is cool you can easily remove it from the mold.

WHAT DO YOU DO WHEN YOU'RE DONE PULLING? Have ready a tabletop sprinkled with powdered sugar. Lay the taffy down and arrange it in the final shape you desire, such as a twisted rope, figure eights and so on. You make long pieces into ropes and twists. If you want to make letters, numbers and so forth, you have to use short pieces, of course. Let the long pieces rest until they are hard and crisp. Then you can crack them by hand into shorter sections or cut with a knife.

THE OLD FASHIONED TAFFY "HOOK" was an aid to a one-person taffy making operation. It was a large iron hook screwed into the wall. At taffy time it was buttered. The candy was pulled by hand just enough to fit over the hook with ends left to be grasped in each hand and pulled. Then the ends of the taffy were slapped together. The "old" middle was removed from the hook and the "new" middle put on it and it was pulled again. And again and again until the candy was done.

If you want to **VARY THE FLAVORING OR COLOR** remember to add it while the candy is still in the pot.

For peppermint or striped candy divide the candy before pulling and color to suit: one portion red, one portion green and the remainder white is a good combination. Pull each color separately. Then make each color into long strands. Put together the strands of various colors as you desire until your stick is as thick as you want it lightly rolling the new "rope" on a firm surface to make it adhere well. Then cut lengths with scissors or knife.

If you want, you can shape your short lengths into something special like a candy cane or figure eight. You can flavor taffy for candy canes with peppermint extract available in some grocery stores—or from your peppermint patch. Delicate flavorings such as peppermint or lemon juice should be added at the very end just as the taffy is taken from the stove. Individual wax paper wrappings work fine if you want to keep the pulled taffy awhile.

Chopped nuts can be added to the taffy by putting them in the bottom of the buttered pan, then pour the taffy over them, cool and pull as usual.

Pure Honey Taffy—Heat 2 cups honey to boiling. Add a pinch of baking soda, 1 tablespoon butter, 1 tablespoon lemon juice and a few grains salt. Boil to hard ball stage. Pour into buttered pan. Cool. Pull.

Salt-Water Taffy—Mix 1 cup sugar, 3 tablespoons cornstarch and a few grains salt. Add ½ cup water and ⅔ cup honey. Cook to the hard ball stage. Pour into buttered pan. Cool. Pull.

Vinegar Taffy—Combine 1 cup sugar, ⅛ teaspoon cream of tartar, 2 tablespoons butter, ½ cup vinegar and a few grains salt. Boil to hard ball stage. Cool. Pull.

Molasses Taffy—Combine 1 cup white sugar, 1 cup brown sugar, 2 cups light molasses and ¾ cup water in a pan. Cook to hard ball stage. Pour into buttered pan. Cool. Pull.

Taffy with Cream—Combine 1 cup sugar, ½ cup light brown sugar, 1 cup molasses, ¾ cup corn syrup, ½ cup cream and ½ cup water. Boil to the hard ball stage. Remove from heat. Add a pinch each of salt and soda, ¼ cup butter and ½ teaspoon vanilla. Beat this all up well and then pour into buttered pan. Cool. Pull.

MARSHMALLOWS

Marshmallows and marshmallow cream of a sort can be made at home. Before the time of store gelatin, marshmallows were a confectioners' specialty made with gum acacia (also known as gum arabic). Gum acacia is available through drugstores at about $2.25 a pound. It makes passable marshmallow cream but it has a tendency to separate. Modern marshmallow recipes use gelatin or Jell-o for their results. A hint is to avoid making them on rainy, damp days. They can be dusted with cornstarch or powdered sugar when cut. Your results won't be just like the store ones. I don't think they're worth the trouble. Too sweet and too much cooking. But I once got interested in the subject and researched it and here's what I found out. Also homemade marshmallows don't keep well. Dry out too fast. Unless you wrap and freeze them. The aplets and cotlets are very good though and a famous fruit country candy.

Plain Marshmallows—Dissolve 1 tablespoon gelatin in ¼ cup cold water and set aside. Combine 1 cup sugar and ½ cup hot water and boil to the soft ball stage. Add the softened gelatin, a dash of salt and 1 teaspoon vanilla to the syrup. Beat until stiff (takes about 10 minutes). This is an instance where an electric mixer is a must. Pour into buttered pan. Refrigerate overnight before cutting up. When cold cut into squares and roll in a mixture of powdered sugar and cornstarch, if you want to hold down the sweetness of powdered sugar alone. These will dry hard by the next day if you don't wrap in plastic or paper.

Pastel Marshmallows—Combine 1 (3-ounce) package of Jell-o, any flavor, 1 cup sugar and ⅔ cup boiling water. Put it on the stove and simmer, stirring, until it's clear and thoroughly dissolved. Then add 3 tablespoons light corn syrup. Refrigerate 30 minutes. Beat until it's thick and stiff. Takes about 7 minutes with an electric beater. Put into buttered pan or drop by spoonfuls on waxed paper. Refrigerate overnight before cutting up.

Aplets Candy—You'll need 2⅓ cups cold homemade applesauce, 4 cups sugar, 4 envelopes unflavored gelatin, and the juice and grated rind of 1 orange and 1 lemon. Combine the applesauce and sugar in a saucepan and bring to a boil. Add dissolved gelatin and cook 15 minutes, stirring constantly. Add the orange and lemon juice and rind. Pour into a flat pan. Let stand overnight but do not refrigerate. Next day cut into squares and dust with powdered sugar. This keeps well and can be made a week or two ahead of the holidays.

Cotlets Candy—Use the aplets recipe substituting the same quantity cooked and sieved dried apricots for the applesauce.

Marshmallow Powder—It certainly isn't do-it-yourselfing, but probably your marshmallows will turn out more like the store-bought ones if you use the "Marshmallow Powder" that you can mail-order from Maid of Scandinavia, 1 pound for $1.80 (see Herbs introduction for address).

CANDIES THAT DON'T USE WHITE SUGAR

Virginia's Quick Good Honey Bars—Grind raisins until you have a cupful. You can finish the grinding with a piece of bread (½ slice). It gets the last of the raisins out of the grinder and doesn't hurt the candy a bit. Combine with ½ cup peanut butter, ½ cup powdered milk, ½ teaspoon flavoring (coconut, vanilla, etc. as you wish) and 2 tablespoons honey. Mix. Then knead with your hands. Make into a log shape. Chill and then slice. Chilling makes it slice better. If you want it sweeter, work in some powdered sugar. Nuts, coconut and the like can be added. Kids can make it and the ingredients are very flexible. Try substituting some of your other home-dried fruits for the raisins.

Raisin-Nut Bars—Grind together 2 cups raisins and 1 cup nuts (whatever kind you like). Mix the raisins-nuts with ¼ cup honey and press into a ½-inch sheet. Cover and put a weight on top for a day and a night. Then cut the candy into bars and roll each bar in coconut shreds.

Judith's Good Quick Honey Bars—I got this recipe as part of a beautiful letter. Mix 2 cups powdered milk, 1 cup peanut butter and 1 cup honey (or molasses). Roll in nuts. Roll into balls and chill. Good with some corn syrup or cocoa mixed in, too.

FAMOUS OLD FASHIONED CANDIES

For horehound candy recipes see the Herbs chapter under "horehound."

Caramel—The old-timers used homemade caramel for coloring and flavoring. It keeps indefinitely. To make it just put sugar in a pan and melt it slowly. Then cook until the color is dark brown. But don't scorch! In this recipe you are starting out with white sugar. Now add as much boiling water as the amount of sugar and slowly continue cooking until you have a thick syrup. Pour into a jar and put a lid on it.

Cream Caramels—You'll need 4 cups white sugar, 4 cups of quite thick cream, 1 cup light corn syrup, a pinch of salt and 1 cup chopped walnuts. Remember to stir all the time you boil. Put the sugar, 1 cup of the cream, the corn syrup, and salt into a pan and bring to a good boil. Add another cup of cream and bring to a good boil again—and do this twice more until all the cream is used. Then boil to the soft ball stage (234°-240°). It will be quite thick. Add the chopped walnuts. Beat at once until thick and pour into buttered platters. It will make two platters.

Pralines—Combine 1⅞ cups powdered sugar, 1 cup maple syrup and ½ cup cream. Boil to the soft ball stage (234°-240°). Remove from heat. Beat until creamy. Add 2 cups chopped nuts (pecans are good). Pour into a buttered pan and cut into squares.

Lemon Drops—Pour just enough lemon juice to dissolve the sugar over 2 cups powdered sugar. Then boil to a thick syrup. Drop on plates and put away to harden.

Cracker Jacks—Combine 2 cups sugar, 1 cup molasses and 2 tablespoons vinegar. Boil to the crack stage. Remove from heat. Add ½ teaspoon soda. Beat well and pour over popcorn and chopped peanuts.

Kisses—Beat 2 egg whites stiff. Add a pinch of salt, ½ cup powdered sugar and ½ teaspoon vanilla. Drop from a teaspoon onto a lightly oiled cookie sheet. Bake in a 300° oven about 30 minutes until firm and dry. Optional, ¼ cup coconut or 1 square chocolate, melted and combined.

Pecan Macaroons—(Almond ones are actually the more traditional.) Beat 1 egg white stiff. Then gradually beat in ⅓ cup pecan nut meats (chopped fine). Drop mixture by teaspoonfuls on a baking sheet covered with buttered paper. Make smooth rounds of your drops. Sift powdered sugar over the top. Bake at about 350°.

True Macaroons from Scratch—Blanch ½ pound almonds and pound them to a paste in a mortar, or put through a grinder, set on fine, several times, or blend. Add ½ pound powdered sugar and 2 stiffly beaten egg whites. Work it all together, then form balls about the size of a whole nutmeg. Bake at 250° until light brown.

Macaroons with Almond Paste—To make almond paste see Nuts. Add gradually to ½ pound of almond paste, ¾ cup sugar and 3 beaten egg whites. Mix well and add ¼ cup powdered sugar and 2 tablespoons flour. Put teaspoonfuls on a paper on your cookie sheet. Flatten the shapes a little. Bake at 250°-300° for about 30 minutes.

MOLDED CANDIES

Marzipan (also known in the old days as "toy candy")—Mix 1 cup almond paste, 1 cup powdered sugar and ½ teaspoon orange extract or vanilla, for flavoring (rose water is the traditional one if you can get it or make it). Knead it a long time—20 minutes maybe and then set on a rack to dry. Marzipan was a traditional special holiday candy. It was shaped into tiny replicas of fruits or whatever took the maker's fancy.

Sometimes the replicas were painted with food coloring or dipped into it Easter-egg style. Don't paint until the marzipan figures have dried overnight. You can paint with food colors using a small paintbrush.

Then give it time to dry. Sometimes they were given accessories such as cloves for stems and leaves made of bits of angelica.

The figures could be glazed by leaving covered with syrup 8 hours, then draining and letting dry again. The syrup is made by cooking 5 pounds sugar and 2½ cups water to the soft ball stage (234°-240°). Remove syrup from heat and let it get cold. Add marzipan in a single layer. It is important throughout to avoid disturbing the syrup as much as possible.

Phony Marzipan—If you make a dough with ½ cup butter, ¼ cup sugar, 1 teaspoon vanilla and 1¼ cups flour, divide it into parts, and color each part with food coloring—Well, then you can shape dough pieces into fruit shapes or what you like. And roll them in colored sugar. And bake at 350°.

You can buy special marzipan molds for making fruit shapes from Maid of Scandinavia if you don't want to mold your own. They have food colors, too.

Homemade colored sugars for ornamenting—You start out with white sugar. Just take a little of the fresh juice of cranberries, red raspberries, currants, black raspberries, grapes or juice of any other colored fruits. Thicken the juice stiff with the sugar. Then spread the sugar out on a plate to dry, or use at once. It may be colored yellow with orange peel strained through a cloth or green with the juice of spinach.

The whole candy thing belongs more to arts and crafts than truly to cooking. I can't really reconcile myself to the notion of spending all that time and labor to make something so beautiful and then open my mouth and wipe it out. Same for cake decorating. I enjoy the fancy decorated cookies grandmas around here make for Christmas. But when people have the creative urge you just have to get out of their way and let them go. I used to write poetry and maybe that's just as useless a product as a cookie or cake decoration and maybe more so because it isn't even edible. I tried to offer my poems mail-order once and out of a mailing of several hundred two dear people responded—more to keep my morale up, I think, than for the sake of the poems.

When Mike was a student in the big city I used to take my poems down to a street corner in Greenwich Village (along with a baby or two), put on a great big sandwich board that said "Poems for Sale" on each side and sell copies for 25 to 50 cents apiece. (Mike priced them for me.) I barely made enough to pay my bus fare and buy lunch but it was really beautiful just standing there sharing my work all day with people who came to read my notebooks and pick out one or two that really were going to go home and live with them and be a part of their lives. That was the only thing I've ever missed about New York—selling poems. I never was one to write in an Ivory Tower. I needed people to be reacting to what I was doing. Providing kind of a sonar for me as I swam through the literary waters to guide me to a better and better result. Better because it meant more to them. And though I've always written something or other it means the most when there is a real human being on the receiving end that can laugh, and care, and learn something they really want to know.

Me and the bees.

A bee in Art's marigold.

Here is Art Johns in his watermelon patch.

This is Imogene's beautiful hand showing
you some grapes she has raised.

Here are Ivy (left) and Shirley (right) making sauerkraut for you to see, along with some others that you can't see in this picture. They're a little camera embarrassed. You move the cabbage head back and forth across a kraut cutter board with a blade set in it so that the cabbage is sliced just the right thickness. Then the shredded cabbage is put into the crock and salted layer by layer.

That's Lillian Peavey on the left. She's a World War II bride from France. Ivy Isaacson is on the right. They've been pounding the kraut to get some juice out.

Now Darlene and Lillian are holding the finished canned kraut. Darlene looked at this picture with me and said, "Boy, they're sure going to think we're all well fed around here!"

SOURS

INTRODUCTION

There's a sort of philosophical question here. All the "sour" foods that I'm talking about in this chapter do not occur that way in nature. You make them sour by adding salt or by adding vinegar or both. Or by getting plenty of acid in there, which is what makes vinegar vinegar rather than apple juice. Or you can use lye which is a base instead of an acid and that's how you make olives (and pretzels and bagels and soap). Then there's a tendency for strong seasonings like mustard seed and cinnamon to get added in. And a further tendency to pour in enough sugar to cover up all the salt and vinegar and insist to the taste buds that the stuff really is food. The salt and vinegar (or alcohol) are in there because little living microbe beasties can't stand to be in the same place after it gets so strong. It's a good preservation thing. (Except there's that one kind of self-fermenting, no-salt sauerkraut, that is an exception to all this.)

What I'm trying to say is I can really see a reason for vinegar and salt in sauerkraut and pickles, even if the stronger combinations are somewhat on the indigestible side, but I really start to feel uncomfortable with the recipes that throw in lots of sugar too. Sugar is a "poison" and therefore a food preserver as well, but for the health of your family I think you'd probably be better off to go easy on that kind of combination sweet-sour food. What you would be eating is a sugar-vinegar-salt syrup seasoned and served soaked up in what was originally a cucumber or some such and now is not much more than a container for the syrup.

Dear, well-meaning people have sent me their favorite recipes and I've reprinted them here. Use your own judgment as you pick and choose. And have fun!

CROCK PICKLES

Since I first published this book I've received three letters from people who tried the crock pickles. One fellow was ecstatic. He had them a little beyond the half-cured stage and declared they were the best pickles he had ever tasted. But one lady told me they were way too salty—and another fellow wrote me a desperate SOS that he had a terrible scum and the cukes were going soft which means they rotted and should be thrown out. So please read all this advice before you try a crock pickle recipe to avoid the pitfalls.

Not very many people make crock pickles nowadays. Not because it's hard to do. Mainly because we've been overconditioned against our fellow creatures—the microorganisms—and crock pickles are characterized by yukky-looking stuff on top that will hereafter be referred to as the "scum." There are other problems too.

Old fashioned crock pickles are cured by fermenting. That's why they have a scum. Don't worry when they get a powerful odor. They're supposed to. They have to be in the crock at least three weeks to complete the process of fermentation. During that time they will change in color from bright green to an olive or yellow green and the white inside will become translucent. Before that they are "half-cured" pickles—my favorite stage. When the pickles get to your preferred stage of curing, you can take them out and can them. Or you may keep them in the crock all winter which is what Great-grandmother did and also the way they were stored down at the general store in the pickle barrel. Pickle barrel pickles are very salty and spicy. They have to be so as not to spoil. Half-cured pickles are mild.

Don't overwhelm the capacity of the salt and vinegar to control the microorganisms by letting dirt get in the pickle barrel. The pickle brine doesn't act by killing the way canning does. Instead its effect is to drive the organisms into a nonreproductive state—spores. The more beasties there are in the food at the moment you put it into the pickling solution, the greater your risk.

If you make your pickles according to all this advice then be brave when you see the scum arrive on them. Organisms called "false yeasts" grow on top of pickle brine. They are eating the organic acid formed during the initial fermentation. Even mold doesn't hurt *unless it touches the pickle* so just don't let the fluid get too low. Your pickled food must *always* be kept completely covered by the protective brine, preferably by a safety margin of *at least 2 inches*. The water will be slowly evaporating as the winter passes so you *must* add more at intervals.

I put up 15 gallons of crock pickles a year for this family and don't have any left over come spring. As the year wears on they aren't as tasty as canned pickles but it might be worth it to you in the jars saved and the time saved during the frantic harvest season when you don't know whether to snap, pop, can or cuss. And then maybe you'll just eat all your crock pickles up at the half-cured stage and can pickles for use later in the year.

You can't make crock pickles from waxed store cucumbers. The brine cannot penetrate the wax. So you'll be using cucumbers from your own or a friend's garden. "Midgets" are those up to 3 inches. They go into your midget crock—a glass gallon jar will do. "Dills" are those 3 to 6 inches long. Cucumbers over 6 inches long are "slicers" to be used in your kitchen to make cucumber sandwiches (slice peeled cucumbers and mayonnaise on homemade bread) or instant pickles (thinly sliced peeled cucumbers in a salt, vinegar, water brine) or however you like fresh cucumbers. The real big ones won't make good pickles anyway because they get too hollow in the middle.

In former editions of this book I said not to use cucumbers that have turned yellow. If all you've ever seen is store cucumbers you may not know about yellow ones, but the life cycle of a cucumber is first a blossom, then a tiny green cucumber, then a big green one, then a real big green one, and then a yellow one. I used to think the yellow ones were "over-ripe" and recommended that they be fed to cows or pigs or chickens. But a couple of readers wrote and set me straight. They said you could make good canned pickles out of the yellow ones and sent me recipes. So look in the next section of canned pickle recipes for what to do with the yellow ones.

Bitter cucumbers come from not watering your cucumber vines regularly while they are producing. A severe shortage of water will cause bitter tasting cucumbers. Even if you recommence watering, every cucumber that started to grow during the drought will have that bitter taste. So if you're going on a trip make arrangements with someone to keep the cucumbers watered!

If you're planning to make both canned pickles and crock pickles make the canned pickles first, then your crock pickles. That way you make your crock pickles about September, adding more cucumbers as they become ready in the garden. This is because *it helps if they don't ferment at warm temperatures.* It's a good general rule anyway to keep all your pickles on dark cool shelves or in the coolest spot in the house. If possible get the cucumbers into the brine quite soon after picking in the garden. If you have to hold them any time, refrigerate or at least keep them in the shade with a wet cloth over them. Cucumbers deteriorate rapidly, especially at warm temperatures. Wash them well to make sure you aren't including any more of those small creatures than you can help but handle gently to avoid bruising since bruised places decay easier. Remove any *blossoms* because they are a source of enzymes that cause unwanted softening during fermentation. *Don't soak cucumbers in water* before pickling. They would fill with water and couldn't soak up the brine.

Use pure granulated salt ("pickling salt"), not iodized table salt. For the best flavor use fresh spices. Grind your own when possible and you can raise your own dill. By the time your cucumbers are ready for pickling the dill should have matured its seed heads and be ready for cutting. You use stems, heads, seeds and all, either fresh from the garden or dried. Don't make the pickles using heavily chlorinated water. For the container a "crock" is traditional but glass jars, gallon or larger, unchipped enamel, plastic or wood containers work fine. You'll also need a lid such as a plate which can fit snugly inside the container to cover the pickles and hold them under the brine. Use a weight on the cover like a glass jar filled with water to overcome their urge to float up. The jar is easier to manage than the traditional stone which should be sterilized before being put on the brine and is mighty unhandy to cook. (The real, real modern way is to weight down the plate with a plastic bag filled with water and tied shut.) Over the top of it all you'll need a cloth to keep dust out and prevent flies and such from expiring in the juice. The plate

should be well below the top of the fluid so that your pickles are under 2 inches of brine.

If you really feel the scum on your fermenting crock passes the limits of housewifely tolerance here are some tricks. Take the cloth off once a week to wash it and let it rest in the brine the last day before you wash it. Some of the scum will travel to the top of the cloth and can be transported away. Or you can skim the brine once a week. If you think your crock is *sick,* carefully pour off all the brine and bring it to a boil, then pour hot back onto the pickles. *Remove any pickles with soft spots.* Do this every day for three days. If you can't win that way, beef up the brine with *more salt and vinegar.* That will hold down on the scum but will also result in real strong pickles.

Actually I don't think you'll need to resort to such drastic measures because the scum is on the *top* and your pickles are fine 2 inches underneath—honest they are! Take one out, rinse it off and offer it to your husband. He'll offer to go pick more cucumbers for you immediately to make another crock of such fine pickles!

As the year wears on your crock pickles get stronger in vinegar and salt and the taste of the lactic acid bacteria that cured them. Then it won't do to just rinse them off. Soak the pickles 24 hours in clean water, changing it several times, until their taste is acceptably freshened. Then make a fresh brine to keep them in the refrigerator. I keep a gallon jar in the refrigerator all winter long with these freshened pickles, rescued from the big crock, ready for snacking, to pack lunches and for table use. But I don't freshen pickles from the pure vinegar crocks. They don't turn out well. It's better to just slice those thin and serve like a relish. They are *hot* and a few slices is plenty.

Crock Dill Pickles—This recipe makes fine tasting crock pickles somewhat like kosher dills. If you want to make fermented pickles and can them I recommend the mild version of this recipe. But the relatively weaker brine will give more trouble if you try to store pickles in it all winter. Don't try this recipe until you've read all the introductory stuff on crock pickles please because I want you to be successful.

Start with a 5-gallon crock and 20 pounds (about a half bushel) of dill cucumbers. Get ready ¾ cup whole mixed pickling spice, which you can buy at any grocery store, and a few bunches of dill. Put half the spices and a layer of dill on the bottom of your crock. Add cucumbers to within about 5 inches of the top. Put the rest of the dill and spices on top of the cucumbers. Now decide if this crock is to be all eaten up or canned within six weeks or if you're making a long-term crock. In the former case make a brine of 2½ cups vinegar, 1¾ cups salt and 2½ gallons water. In the latter case double the salt and vinegar. Be sure the cucumbers are covered by at least 2 inches of brine. If need be you can make more brine or take out some cucumbers. Don't jam them down, since it bruises them. Now cover, weight, and put your cloth over the top. Scum will begin forming in a few days.

To can these pickles just pack in the canning jars when they are done fermenting. Add some new dill to each jar. Cover with boiling brine, the old or newly made as you prefer. Adjust jar lid. Place jar in boiling water and keep there 15 minutes. Remove, tighten lid and you're done.

No-Scum Crock Dill Pickles—My wonderful friend Gertrude Johnson, from Lamont, Washington (population 91—her husband is the mayor!), guarantees this recipe. Start with 1 peck 4- to 6-inch cucumbers. Wash and place in 4-gallon crock with grape (or horseradish) leaves and dill weed. Boil together 6 quarts water, 1½ pints vinegar, 1½ cups canning salt and 2 tablespoons alum (from the grocery or drugstore) for at least 5 minutes. Cool and pour over the cucumbers. Weight with plate to keep cucumbers covered with brining solution and cure for 10 days. You may add garlic after the eighth day. "This does not scum over the top as the usual crock dills are apt to do. Let cure in a cool place."

The Anything Dill Crock—Using the same principle as with cucumbers you can pickle other vegetables, such as purple cabbage, nasturtium buds, beans, baby onions, cauliflower flowerets and green tomatoes. They all go in raw except beans which

are boiled 2 minutes first. Mix in lots of dill. Beans are my favorite.

Firewater Dills—Ulcer gulch. Same as any crock dill only add red peppers.

Pickles Fermented in Quart Jars—Brine: 8 cups cold water, ¾ cup pickling salt (scant) and 2 cups 4% to 6% cider vinegar. To each quart add fresh dill (4 large sprays), ¼ teaspoon powdered alum or 2 lumps solid alum and ¼ teaspoon cream of tartar. Rinse pickles off; put 2 dill sprays in a clean jar, add pickles, alum, cream of tartar and 2 dill sprays on top. Now add the brine to cover. Put lid on tight and keep at room temperature for 6 days. Pickles must work in the jars, they won't spoil. Store in cool dark place. Ready to use in 8 weeks.

PURE VINEGAR CROCKS

Strong, Spicy Crock Dills—This uses pure wine vinegar. Brine about a gallon of medium-sized cucumbers overnight. Dry them off. Get ready peppercorns, chopped fresh tarragon (or dried if you must), dill and cloves. Place a layer of cucumbers in your crock, then sprinkle it with a few peppercorns, a bit of tarragon, a few cloves and lay on a spray of dill. Continue in layers like that to near the top. Cover the whole works with boiling wine vinegar (2 inches to spare of course). Cover with a plate, weight it and cover with a cloth.

Strong, Sweet Midget Pickles—You'll never get a scum on these crock pickles because the liquid is pure vinegar. Brine about a gallon of midget cucumbers overnight. Combine 4 quarts cider vinegar, 2 onions, peeled and sliced, 3½ tablespoons dry mustard, 4 tablespoons salt, 4 tablespoons whole cloves, 3 sticks cinnamon, broken up, 2 tablespoons peppercorns, 2 tablespoons ground cloves, 1 pound raw sugar and 2 tablespoons molasses. Add midget cucumbers until you only have 2 inches to the top of the brine. Cover, weight and throw over the cloth.

CANNED AND SEALED CUCUMBER PICKLES

Crock pickles in brine are best at their prime—when they're freshly made. But as pickles go they are the worst as the year wears on. They are very little work at first compared to canned pickles but more later on as you keep checking the crock, and when you go through all that freshening and rebrining to serve. So maybe that's why all the country cooks I know quit keeping crock pickles when canning jars and lids became available and started making canned and sealed pickles. You don't have the trouble I mentioned with the pure vinegar crocks but those pickles are *strong*. Canned pickles don't have to be strong at all—you can even make them with no vinegar at all if you process in boiling water long enough to make sure the beasties are all dead.

The same general rules as for crock pickles work here too. Don't use store cucumbers. Don't use iodized salt. Don't use that flavorless white kind of vinegar. "Pickling spice" is a ready-mix you can buy at spice departments of grocery stores. Use fresh firm cucumbers and remove blossom ends. Cucumbers to make canned pickles should be about 3 to 5 inches long. Don't presoak them. Make sure the ends are rubbed smooth and the whole cuke is clean. If you use garden dill, or grape leaves or such as that—rinse them off good before you start. You may can your cucumbers whole or slice them into fourths, or sixths (or eighths—depending on how big the cucumber is). Dill

pickles are sliced lengthwise. It's your bread-and-butter pickles (later on in this chapter) that are often sliced crosswise. "Canned" doesn't necessarily mean "cooked" in this section—depends on the recipe. When canning, make sure your vegetables are all *under* the liquid. Choose the recipe that matches best with what you think you want to make and what ingredients you have. I recommend them all!

Store your canned dill pickles in a *cool* place. They are ready to eat when they've turned sort of transparent. Give your jars a boiling before you fill them.

Canned Dill Pickles Made Without Vinegar—
Have ready 2 gallons of cucumbers and a batch of
canning jars (like maybe 8). Put a grape leaf and a
stalk of dill or ½ teaspoon of dill seed in the bottom of
the jar. Now pack in cucumbers to fill it up. Put more
dill weed or another ½ teaspoon of seed on top.
When your jars are all packed make a brine by combining 8 cups water (if you can afford it, the pickles
will taste even better if you use 6 cups water and 2
cups lemon juice here) and ⅓ cup salt and get it up to
boiling. Have your water bath canner ready to go.
Pour the hot salty water over the pickles up to the
neck of the jar. Put another grape leaf on top. Then
your lids and boil in the canner at least 10 minutes.

Garlic Dills—These are another kind of canned
dill pickle with a long tradition behind them. You
pack your cucumbers in the jar with dill and garlic—
use plenty for really flavorful pickles. Make a brine by
combining 3 quarts water, 1 quart vinegar (at least 5%
acid), 1 cup canning salt and ½ teaspoon powdered
alum. You can double or triple that brine as
needed. Pour the boiling brine over the cucumbers
in the jars and seal.

Cold Packed Vinegary-Spicy Canned Dills—
Make a brine by combining 2 quarts water, 1 quart
vinegar, about 3/5 (not quite ⅔ cup) uniodized salt
and a pinch of alum powder. Boil it for 5 minutes.
Cool. Have ready jars that have already been boiled
and cooled. In each quart jar pack 6 slices of peeled
white onion (use more or less of any of these seasonings if you prefer), 4 or 5 2-inch stems of dill (leaves,
seeds and all), 1 dried chili pod, 1 clove garlic and
your cucumbers. Now pour the brine over. Heat your
jar lids and then put them on tightly to seal the jars.

The great thing about using white onion, dill, chili
and garlic cloves for pickle seasonings (any pickle you
want) besides the good flavor is that all four can easily be raised right in your own garden.

BREAD-AND-BUTTER PICKLES
AND MUSTARD PICKLES

At first I didn't have a section in this book on
bread-and-butter pickles and mustard pickles. I
thought everybody already had good pickle recipes,
and I wasn't going to load your bookshelves with
more of the same old stuff. But people wrote me and

asked for them—I guess they aren't as common as I
thought—so here goes. "Bread-and-butter" pickles
mean generally sweet pickles—I mean really sweet if
you measure by the amount of sugar used, though
you don't realize it so much because the sourness of
the vinegar and spices covers it up some. They are
generally made by slicing your cukes thinly across
(*not* lengthwise) so you get little circles. If you are
using extra large cucumbers and the skins are rough,
peel them first. But you can make them using real
small whole cucumbers (a pure vinegar sweet crock
pickle for example). Mustard pickles are another
distinct variety of pickle that uses a combination of
vegetables and a very significant amount of mustard
in the recipe.

Sugar Free Bread-and-Butter Pickles—In almost
any recipe you can substitute frozen apple concentrate for the sugar called for—cup for cup—and get a
passable result. That's what this recipe does. Slice
and combine 1 gallon cucumbers, 8 white onions, 2
green peppers and 2 red peppers. Lightly toss with ¼
cup uniodized salt and let rest with the salt on them
for 3 hours in a cool place (like inside your refrigerator). Now dissolve 2 cups apple juice concentrate in 2 cups water (or you can use 2 cups brown
sugar). Add 2 cups lemon juice and 2 tablespoons
celery seed. Boil 2 minutes (or so). Now pour in your
sliced, salted vegetables and bring just to the boiling
point, but get it off the heat before it really does boil.
Pour into jars that you've got hot and ready, put your
hot lids on and seal.

Fermented Sweet Pickles—This recipe is a lot of
work, but it's an interesting combination of a fermented dill-type pickle and the flavor of a spiced
sweet pickle. Start out with freshly picked 4- or 5-inch
cucumbers. Wash, dry and lay them in a crock or a
big glass jar or a big deep earthenware bowl. Make
enough brine to cover them with 2 inches over (1½
cups uniodized salt per 1 gallon water). Cover with
cloth, plate and weight. Let work 2 weeks. Remove
the scum and wash the cloth every day.

By the end of your 2 weeks the cucumbers should
be sort of clear and dark green. Take them out of the
crock, rinse well in cold water and cut into 1-inch
chunks. Now cover the chunks with a new solution of
1 tablespoon powdered alum per each quart of water.
They stay in the alum solution for 12 to 18 hours.

Then take them out, drain, rinse, drain again, put back in the crock and cover them with a real hot syrup (2 cups sugar to each cup vinegar). Put in there too 1 teaspoon of whole cloves and 2 teaspoons of stick cinnamon for each quart of cucumbers—all tied up in a hankie so you can get rid of it when the pickles are spicy enough. Twenty-four hours later pour the syrup off your pickles into the pot. Boil it. Pour back over pickles. Do this for two more days. Now drain the syrup back into your pot. Pack the pickles into sterilized jars. Boil the syrup. Get rid of the spices in the hankie. Pour boiling syrup to cover the pickles and seal up right away.

Honey and Curry Bread-and-Butter Pickles—Slice about 30 small cucumbers. Soak 4 to 8 hours in a brine (½ cup uniodized salt and water to cover). Make a syrup of 1 cup honey, 4 cups sugar, 1 tablespoon curry powder, ¼ cup mustard seed, 1 quart vinegar and bring to a boil. Drain the brine off your cucumber slices and dump them into the boiling syrup. Boil 5 minutes, then pour into your jars and seal.

Quick Bread-and-Butter Pickles—Make ready a syrup of 3½ cups sugar, 1½ teaspoons turmeric, 3 cups vinegar and 2 cups water. Tie up 2 tablespoons mustard seed in a thin hankie and drop it in there. Now slice up 1 gallon cucumbers, 8 onions and 2 sweet red peppers (may substitute green). Toss lightly with ½ cup uniodized salt and some ice cubes, if you have them, and chill for 3 hours. Now put your syrup on to boil. Drain the vegetables real good in a strainer or colander and dump into the syrup. Get it all up to a boil again. Pour into clean jars and seal. (Not with the hankie with the mustard seeds in it though.)

You can use sliced small white (pickling) onions in this recipe just as good as big ones. Half green and half red peppers is good, too. For a spicier, stronger syrup combine 5 cups sugar, 2 tablespoons mustard seed (not in a hankie), 2 teaspoons celery seed, ½ teaspoon ground cloves, 1¼ teaspoons turmeric and 5 cups cider vinegar. Proceed as directed above.

If you can't find turmeric, substitute 1 teaspoon dill for 1 teaspoon turmeric.

✿✿✿✿✿✿✿✿✿✿✿✿✿✿✿

LAZY HOUSEWIFE PICKLES

The first five years I was working on this book I took a very disapproving attitude toward quicky recipes. I was a full-time housewife (and mother and homesteader and book writer) and had more time than money, and doing it the long way was good for economy generally and for quality, too. Now I'm back adding some material for the 7th edition, and I can really understand how a woman can be grateful for a shorter version of any recipe.

So many people have asked if my life has changed because I wrote this book. Yes, it really has. I don't have a milk cow anymore. Nelly is over at the School of Country Living for the students to practice milking on. Mike tries every year for a garden, but it's really more of a token thing. My deep-freeze is empty. My cellar shelves are empty. I seldom cook at all. We eat at the School at lot. That's where the garden is now and the homemade butter and food preserving. I'm generally on the telephone or worrying over the checking accounts or trying to solve a problem or trying to get another inch of progress for the School. I've put so much time and love and money and effort into that School. I won't venture to decide whether I should have or not. I've done what I had such a deep urging to do. I'm still doing it. As of this writing there are no answers. Is the School going to be good enough? Will students come? Can it support itself? We're getting ready for the second opening, just 10 days away. Somebody made a mistake in the checking account, and I've written about $2,500 more in checks on the school account than I have money. Honest I didn't realize it was that bad. Well, you see not that much has changed really. It has and yet it hasn't. The atmosphere of crisis, the struggle, the hand-to-mouth existence, the questing after a dream and battling with windmills . . . it's still me.

Except, for better or for worse, a whole bunch more people have gotten married into my struggles, which is beautiful except sometimes it feels so heavy having so many people who trust me to be responsible for them. I'm not that positive I'm right about most things. I have a wonderful husband and we love each other. Five children. And Darlene who types and Diann who mimeographs. But also so many others. Maybe as many as 30 or 40 when things get really busy. When I started writing this book I was desperately lonely. I think I was trying to find some way to reach out and touch some other human beings. I wanted to give something of myself that might be barter for a friendship and it worked because there resulted the letters that meant so much to me through those years of writing. Well, I sure am blessed with people now. I wish I had the time to really introduce you to each one of them.

Back to pickles. This is a recipe that a lady wrote and asked me for. I didn't know it but published her request in our *Newsletter* that goes out twice a year to people who have mail-ordered the book from us. Ben Bischoff who lives in Blackfoot, Idaho (that's quite near where Mike grew up and went to high school at Arco), had the recipe. He sent one copy to the lady who had originally requested it and one to me so I could share it with you: Start out with 4 quarts small cucumbers. Wash and examine the cucumbers, then pack in glass jars. Mix 1 cup mustard, 1 cup sugar and 1 cup salt together. Add 1 gallon vinegar slowly, stirring well. Pour the mustard-sugar-salt-vinegar brine over the pickles in the jars and seal. You don't even have to heat the brine. Let your lazy housewife pickles stand for at least a week and then you can start eating them.

No Cook–No Vinegar Canned Dill Pickle Recipe—This recipe was sent to me as part of a beautiful letter from a wonderful person. Darlene Thompson is her name and she signed her letter to me "Yours in Christ." That makes her doubly a sister to me—once for the brotherhood of man and again in the body of Christ. These are her own words:

"My grandmother's family was one of the first two to settle the North Dakota territory. . . . Here is a prized old pickle recipe. Am not a pickle lover—but could eat a whole jar of these. This recipe is one brought from Germany to the Russian Ukraine area where our family was one of many German farming families that turned the steppes into a rich productive area. When they sought refuge in the country of America, the same recipe was used on the German farms in the Dakotas. Hope you'll try at least a few quarts of these:

"Wash cucumbers. Place washed fresh dill on the bottom of jar with: 1 teaspoon pickling spice, 1 tablespoon salt, 2 cloves garlic, dash alum (1 or 2 hot peppers may be added too). Fill jar with cucumbers and add more dill to top. Fill with cold water to within ¼ inch of top. Seal tightly and shake to dissolve salt. This is a no-cook pickle."

YELLOW CUCUMBER PICKLES

There are some people out there in pickle-lover land who believe that yellow cucumbers make the very best pickles of all. They wrote to tell me so! Pat Finley of Harrisburg, Oregon, told me this recipe of hers is "sweet and real crunchy and delicious."

First day—Use 9 pounds (about 12 large ones) ripe yellow cucumbers, the more meat inside the better. Peel cukes and scrape the seeds out, then slice lengthwise and put in a stone jar. Now mix 2 gallons cold water with 3 cups hydrated lime in a separate container. Finally, pour the lime water over your cucumbers and let set 24 hours.

Second day—Drain and wash *thoroughly*. Soak in clear water 4 hours or overnight. (I recommend overnight so you'll have more time for the next steps.)

Third day (or 4 hours later)—First drain and rinse, and put back into crock. Now make a syrup in a large container by combining 5 pounds sugar, 3 pints vinegar, 2 tablespoons salt and 1 teaspoon *each* of the following spices all tied up in a cloth bag—cloves, cinnamon, ginger, mace and celery seed. When your syrup comes to a boil you go ahead and pour it over the cucumbers while still hot. *Let set 4 hours.* Now heat the syrup and cucumber mixture in a large covered container. Remember it should be enameled or stainless steel—not aluminum. Cook slowly 1½ to 2 hours with frequent, gentle stirring. Cook until the cucumbers are very clear. You can add green food coloring while cooking if you're concerned about the color. Seal while hot. Store on a coolish shelf for a week and then they are ready to start eating!

OTHER PICKLES

Actually you could pickle just about anything. Cured meat like ham and bacon and corned beef is just another salt and sugar recipe except for having saltpeter added (makes it red). Dill-type pickles use salt and vinegar, leave the sweetness out. Spiced fruits leave the salt out, have sugar, vinegar and spices in. Krauts and salted down vegetables are just vegetables and salt. Mustard pickles depend on a hefty addition of mustard. These ingredients aren't there just for flavoring. They are the original chemical preservatives. So there are just about infinite different ways to pickle infinite different foods depending on your choice of picklers, how strong they are, which vegetables you use and just how you go about it. There are some great big books just on some aspect or other of the pickling subject. *Note:* I tried to keep the various pickled such and suches in alphabetical order to help you find what you want. But first comes miscellaneous.

Slightly Pickled Vegetables—Kathy Ellington of Danville, California, wrote me that she often uses this recipe and enjoys it. She says the only drawback is that the mixture must be refrigerated. Combine and boil 5 tablespoons salt, 10 cups water, 3⅓ cups cider vinegar and 1 clove garlic or 1 fresh chili pepper. After you have it boiling, remove from the heat, add 1 teaspoon pickling spice and set aside to cool and get its flavor. Now in large glass jars layer and tightly pack vegetables of your choice. Cauliflower would be good, and/or celery, rutabaga, beans, mushrooms, cabbage, carrots, broccoli, asparagus—just do your own thing with it. Now pour the pickling juice over the vegetables. Close the jars with lids and refrigerate overnight. It sounds wonderful.

This pickle section owes a lot to the great pickle makers of western Washington's Palouse Prairie, which fortunately is right next to Idaho's panhandle where I live. It seems like nobody can ever find Kendrick when they look on a map. It's about 27 miles north of Lewiston, which is the largest city in northern

Idaho. And it's about 28 miles east of Moscow and that's where the University of Idaho is and I'm sure it's on your map. The "panhandle" is what we call that narrow northern neck of Idaho squeezed in between Washington and Montana. My special favorite Palouse lady is Gertrude Johnson. Once I SOSed her for a "true old-time mustard pickle recipe" and that's how I first heard about

Eloise Pott's Mixed Mustard Pickle—Use 2 quarts very green and solid tomatoes, 6 green peppers, 1 quart pickling onions (if you don't have them use 6 onions sliced), 24 small cucumbers (use more if they're tiny ones), 1 head cauliflower, 3½ quarts vinegar, 1 cup sugar, 5½ teaspoons turmeric, 1 cup dry mustard and ¾ cup flour. Break cauliflower into small pieces. Cut tomatoes in small wedges. Slice green peppers. Add cucumbers (leave the tiny ones whole). Put it all in a crock and cover with brine made in proportion of 1 cup salt to 1 quart water. Let set overnight. The next morning drain and scald. Make sauce by combining vinegar, sugar, turmeric and mustard. Make a paste of the flour and a little vinegar, add to your sauce and cook about 20 minutes. You'll have to stir diligently to keep it from scorching. Add your vegetables now, heat to the boiling point and hold there at a simmer 5 minutes. Now you can pour the mustard pickles into hot sterilized jars and seal them.

Pickled Beets—Cook small beets until tender. Then cover them with cold water and you can slip the skins right off. Mix 2 cups vinegar, 2 cups brown sugar, ½ teaspoon salt, ½ teaspoon whole cloves, ½ tablespoon broken-up whole cinnamon and ½ teaspoon whole allspice. Cover the beets with the vinegar mixture and simmer 15 minutes. Then dip out the beets. Pack in clean, hot jars. Cover with the hot spiced vinegar and seal.

Paprika Beets—Same as above only replace cinnamon and allspice with a pinch each of pepper and paprika and add 1 chopped green pepper.

Cabbage Mustard Pickles—Mustard pickles are really an interesting mixture and another way to make use of green tomatoes. Here's one that uses a head of cabbage instead of one of cauliflower. Stir 1 cup uniodized salt into 1 gallon water in a crock or glass. Cut up pretty fine 1 quart of cucumbers, 1 quart of green tomatoes, 1 head of cabbage and 4 sweet peppers and put them in the brine for 24 hours. Drain thoroughly. Combine vegetables with 2 quarts vinegar, 1 cup flour, 1 tablespoon turmeric and ½ cup mustard. Boil 3 minutes, pour into jars and seal.

Pickled Red Cabbage—Choose 1 hard red cabbage. Trim off the coarse outside leaves. Cut it in quarters, core and remove the thickest stalks. Then shred the cabbage finely. Put the shreds in layers on a dish, sprinkling each layer with salt, and leave until the following day. Boil 1 tablespoon mixed pickling spice in 1 quart vinegar for 5 minutes. Then leave until cold. Drain off all moisture from the cabbage and put into jars. Pour the cold spiced vinegar over the cabbage. It should come to at least 1 inch above the cabbage. Weight the cabbage and cover the whole. It will be ready to use after 2 weeks. It won't keep well over 2 months since it tends to soften.

Carrot and Pepper and Cucumber Pickles—Make 2-inch long chunks of about 10 medium-sized cucumbers. Soak them in a brine overnight (½ cup uniodized salt per 1 quart water). Pare 6 large carrots, cut into 2-inch strips and cook 5 minutes in salted water. Get the seeds out of 6 red peppers and 6 green peppers and cut them into strips. Drain the cucumbers and carrots well. In a pan combine 6 cups sugar, 3 tablespoons celery seed, 3 tablespoons mustard seeds, 2 teaspoons turmeric, 1 tablespoon salt and 4 cups cider vinegar. Dump in your drained vegetables. When boiling, pour into jars and seal.

Pickled Okra—Okra is a southern plant and pickling is a real southern art, maybe because it once played such a serious food preservation role there. My mother was from Alabama. She traveled to Montana to be a country schoolteacher when fresh out of the University of Alabama. She graduated in English. Her real name was Irma Ferne and her maiden name was Thrasher, descended from one of four English brothers who got off the boat at Colonial Virginia, so I'm told. Most people called her Ferne and a few old friends teased her with "Alabam." I learned about okra from her and developed a taste for it. Delphia Myrl Stubbs from Kansas City, Kansas, sent me this recipe on a "here's what's cookin'" card: Combine 1 quart white vinegar, 1 cup water, ½ cup salt and bring them to a boil. Put 1 clove garlic, 1 hot pepper and 1 teaspoon of dill seed in the bottom of each glass jar and then fill it with okra. Pour your hot brine over that and seal while hot. Let rest 3 weeks and chill before serving.

Mustard Pickled Eggs—Boil the eggs, cool and remove shells. Boil 1 quart vinegar, 1 teaspoon dry mustard, 1 teaspoon salt and 1 teaspoon pepper together. Pour the cooled brine into your pickling jar and add the eggs. Cover and let cure at least 10 days before they're ready.

Spiced Pickled Eggs—Hard boil the eggs, cool and remove shells. Make a brine of ½ cup salt to 2 cups water. Soak the eggs in the brine 2 days. Then pour off the brine and make a new brine by heating 1 quart vinegar, ¼ cup pickling spices, 2 cloves garlic and 1 tablespoon sugar to boiling. Pour it over the eggs.

Clove Pickled Eggs—Stick a few cloves in each egg in either recipe above.

Pickled Onions—Small button onions are best. Get them as near the same size as possible and not too big. Peel until the white is reached. When peeled, put them into a strong brine of salt and water for 24 hours, then boil. Strain out and dry the onions. Put them into jars or bottles and cover with boiled and cooled vinegar. Flavor with peppercorns, white

mustard, sliced horseradish, a little mace—any or all. And cover.

Green Tomato Pickle—This is very good with cheese sandwiches. Take 8 pounds of green tomatoes, chopped fine or ground, and add 4 pounds of brown sugar. Boil down for 3 hours. Add 1 quart vinegar, 1 teaspoon *each* mace, cinnamon and cloves and boil for 15 minutes. Let cool and pack into jars.

Sliced Tomato Pickle—This recipe came from Mrs. Goodspeed of Kent, Washington: 1 peck green tomatoes, 12 onions and 6 green peppers. Slice fine, sprinkle with salt, and let stand overnight. Drain very dry. Take half water and half vinegar—enough to cover the pickles and scald, then drain again.

Boil 6 pints good vinegar, 1½ pounds brown sugar and ½ cup mixed pickle spice, pour over the pickles and seal while very hot.

Zucchini is really in style. I received quite a number of letters this last year sending me either zucchini pickle-relish recipes or zucchini bread recipes, both heavy in sugar. Zucchini is not a real high nourishment vegetable. It's one that grows profusely with practically no effort on the grower's part. Then you can work real hard to try to find uses for it. Some buttered boiled zucchini is good food and I like it, but it really worries me that people in the name of "economizing" and "living out of the garden" would manage to get a bunch of zucchini eaten by mixing it with sugar. You could pulp grass and mix it with sugar—or liver or earthworms—and somebody would eat it. But I'd rather see you put in that effort earlier in the season buying seed and toiling in your garden to grow some other vegetables that require more effort but put more nourishment on your table in the long run and don't require a bunch of sugar to make them palatable.

SAUERKRAUT

To make real homestead kraut, first you grow your cabbage. There's lots more on that in the Vegetables chapter. But "kraut" is a process, not just a one-vegetable thing. It's shredding and salting and letting go through a natural process of fermentation. So you could put down green beans with your cabbage kraut, or sliced apples, green tomatoes or cucumbers. Or you can make kraut out of shredded turnips with no cabbage in there at all. Or out of green beans alone. But most often sauerkraut means cabbage and salt. You can add extra flavor with a few grains of coriander or juniper berries, but I don't do any of these extras because we like our kraut plain. There are so many other things to do that time of year, it's good to be able to *not* do something.

Salted Kraut—If you have a cold place like a dugout cellar to keep your kraut in, and if you make it in the fall after the worst heat is over, you can keep it all winter. But don't wait too long to make it because your cabbage will dry out some and the juice will be hard to get. If you are making sauerkraut in hot weather you may want to can the sauerkraut after it has finished fermenting.

Sauerkraut is a self-fermented, cured product like crock pickles. You'll need the same kind of container as for crock pickles, one big enough to hold at least 5 gallons and sturdy enough to stand a hearty pounding—crock, glass, plastic or wood. About 7 heads of cabbage will make you 3 gallons of sauerkraut. Technically you'll need 3 tablespoons pickling salt (not iodized salt) for every 5 pounds of shredded cabbage. The old-timers salted to taste, I mean *really* stopped and tasted it, and you can learn to do that after you get used to knowing what taste to look for.

Hack away the buggy leaves from your cabbage until you get down to the nice solid center. (Incidentally, scattering dill seeds over the young cabbage head practically eliminates insect damage for me—they just don't like a house with dill in it. Or plant thyme alongside it in a row about 6 inches away. Bugs hate thyme.) Then cut the cabbage into quarters and discard the hard core. If you used the core it would make your kraut very bitter. Shred the cabbage finely. I shred it using a butcher knife on a wooden cutting board but someday I'm going to splurge on an old-time slaw cutter (about $4.10 from Maid of Scandinavia or Morgan Brothers, Inc.). The cabbage shreds should be about the thickness of a dime, long and thin.

If you aren't brave enough to guess at the amounts like Great-grandmother always did, weigh 5 pounds of the shredded cabbage on a food scale, measure 3 tablespoons salt and sprinkle over the cabbage. Mix with your hands a bit and then tamp. If you are brave enough, put cabbage into your 5-gallon crock to make about a 2-inch layer in the bottom. Tamp it down. Add 1 or 2 tablespoons of salt to taste, and tamp down again. To "tamp" means to stomp the heck out of it with a heavy blunt object.

Wood seems to work the best. I use a whittled down cedar fence post. You are done tamping when you've stomped so much the juice has come out of the cabbage and just covers it. Pack each layer in, salt, and then tamp until the juice is out enough to cover the shredded cabbage.

You need to get fairly near the right amount of salt and get it well mixed in. Too little or uneven distribution of the salt can result in a soft kraut. Too much salt or uneven distribution of it can cause a pink-colored kraut caused by the growth of certain types of yeast.

When you've shredded, salted and tamped your way through all your heads of cabbage or to the top of your crock, cover the cabbage. Everybody has their own system. Mine is to use a cloth over the sauerkraut, then a plate just a little smaller than the diameter of the container and a jar filled with water (with a lid on) on top of that. Hopefully the end result is that the brine comes to just the cover but not over it. The cabbage, same as with crock pickles, needs to be thoroughly under the juice. And it needs to be covered sufficiently to shut out air from the surface. Even so your top layer may turn brown, in which case just throw away the off-color part when you get ready to use the crock. (Animals can eat it.) The rest of the kraut will be fine.

Now leave your kraut to ferment. It will start making gas bubbles and that tells you it's fermenting. Fermenting takes from 2 to 6 weeks, depending on how warm your weather is. You know when the kraut is ready by taking a taste of it. Some people just leave it all alone during this time. Others wash the cloth, the sides of the crock and the lid every week. Home-fermented cabbage is fairly strong stuff. But I like it strong.

Salt-Free Kraut—I've had a request for a salt-free kraut recipe. Here it is. For each head of cabbage use ½ teaspoon dill seed, ½ teaspoon caraway seed, ½ teaspoon celery seed and 1 teaspoon ground sea kelp. Pulverize the seeds and kelp with a mortar and pestle and then just scatter them over the top after you have shredded your cabbage. Add water enough to cover. Put a plate on top with a weight on it. Scrape off the scum as it ferments. It takes 7 to 10 days in a warmish room. It's ready when it tastes ready. Now drain off the liquid. You may can this kraut by processing 20 minutes in quart jars.

Quick Kraut in Jars—A friend of mine packs, pounds and salts her shredded cabbage right in the jars. She lets it rest 3 days and then seals without heating. She declares that way makes fine sauerkraut.

Turnip Kraut—Grate, salt and tamp the turnips. Pack in quart jars. Pour boiling water over and seal.

Green Bean Kraut—Don't try this with yellow beans. They're too soft. (I don't care much for yellow beans, anyway. They don't taste as nourishing to me.) Slice your beans lengthwise two or three times. Layer them in a crock with salt, about a 2-inch layer of sliced beans and then a small handful of salt. As many layers as you want to go but don't tamp them down like you do for sauerkraut. Then lay on a clean cloth like a piece of sheet. Then a plate, then a jar of water for weight. If within 24 hours the beans don't make enough juice to cover themselves you'll have to make one for them. Make a brine strong enough to float an egg and pour enough of it into the beans to get them covered. You can add beans to your crock as they come on in the garden until it is full. Clean them off once a week same as you would for kraut. Give them a month to six weeks to get done fermenting. To cook them first rinse off in cold water. Cover with more water and boil 30 minutes to get the salt out. Change the water again and finish cooking. Good with meat. Wm. J. Zeit taught me how to make these.

Salted Down Green Beans—Get the beans ready just as if for your table—bud off the two tips and snap into about 1-inch lengths. Rinse and then cook in water until table ready. Now pour off the hot water. Cool them off with a sloshing of cold water. Now layer them with salt in a *real* clean crock. (Don't stomp or you'd have soup.) Use plenty of salt (uniodized). Add enough water to get the beans covered with liquid. Finish with plate and weight.

Salted Down Corn—Boil sweet corn on the cob. Cut off the cob just as you would to make frozen or canned corn. Layer into a clean crock with sprinkled salt layers. Add liquid as needed. Cover with plate and weight. When you're ready, eat it straight or fry it in bacon grease or serve hot and buttered. You could leave it on the cob but you sure would be wasting precious crock space.

RECIPES USING SAUERKRAUT

Sauerkraut Casserole. Sauerkraut makes for quick and easy one-dish type meals. This recipe came from Kay Arnold who lives in Colorado and writes a recipe column for some area newspapers called "The Hangin' Skillet." When a group of tourists from Holland came through her town she interviewed the group leader and got this recipe: Rinse a quart of sauerkraut once or twice and place in a greased casserole. Cover with a layer of sautéed, crumbled bacon or cooked sausage "pennies." Then make fluffy mashed potatoes and season with salt, pepper and *nutmeg*. Sprinkle bread crumbs over. Now dot with butter. Bake in a 350° oven until it has a brown crust. Good with a salad.

Grandpa Smith's Mess—It's a complete meal-in-one sent to me by Eleanor Seberger of Cozad, Nevada. She says to boil potatoes with the skins on. Then make enough sausage cakes—with a few extras—as your family would need. Fry a batch of onions, chopped fine. Take up the sausage and heat your sauerkraut in the sausage skillet. Let each person take a serving of each ingredient—sausage cakes, potatoes, onions and sauerkraut. Cut with a knife, mix and down with hot garlic bread or toast.

Sauerkraut doesn't have to mean sausage though. Here's a vegetarian sauerkraut recipe.

Sauerkraut Onion Biscuits—Everybody in my family loves these! When you bake bread, while you are letting your dough have its first rising, drain the juice off a pint of sauerkraut and then fry the sauerkraut and an equal (or smaller) amount of onion in a greased pan. When the dough has risen, roll it out with a rolling pin to less than ½ inch—as thin as you can get it. Cut the dough into squares 6 to 8 inches on a side. Put a nice big heaping spoonful of the cooked mix in the middle of each one. Pinch together, let rise and bake. If they come out just in time for supper—perfect! Imogene taught me how to make these. She and her family are vegetarians, but that doesn't mean they don't eat hearty meals!

Imogene's one of my favorite people. She's a lady who doesn't go to town very often. She's never used a recipe book. She hasn't bought any detergents for at least 50 years because she makes all her own soap. I took her with me once to a cafeteria. She had a glass of ice water and asked what the ashtray was for. She's my ideal. I wish I didn't know what they were for. Not that I smoke, because I don't. But just to be that truly innocent of worldliness! Imogene and her family are Seventh-Day Adventists. They believe in staying away from the "world" and worldliness as much as possible. I'm in real sympathy with that point of view. An old English poet said "The world is too much with us. Late and soon, getting and spending we lay waste our powers." (Or something like that—I'm quoting from memory.)

Imogene's Sauerkraut Dumplings—Put water on in a kettle. Let it boil up. Get out a quart of sauerkraut, drain the juice off and fry it in a little oil. Make a dough of flour, water, and salt to the consistency of bread dough. With a sharp knife cut off pieces 1 inch long and about ⅓ inch thick. Put into the boiling water and let boil. When the dumplings are boiled down to where there isn't any water left or very little left add the kraut. Mix and serve.

Cold Kraut Salad—Just mix some chopped green pepper and as much onion as you want with the kraut. Add a dash of salad oil (optional).

Fancy Kraut Salad—Stir in grated apple, a dribble of honey, salt and pepper to the above.

Baked Sauerkraut, Onion, Apple—Combine sauerkraut, cored apple slices, and sautéed onion in a greased ovenproof dish. Dribble a tablespoon of molasses over the top and scatter a fat pinch of dry mustard over. Bake at 350° for 30 minutes.

Pork Bones and Kraut—Kraut goes well with any pork. It's a good way to use your pork bones if you don't want to bother with gelatin making. Boil the pork bones (such as the backbone or ribs) until done. Cool enough to separate the meat from the bones and discard them. Add kraut and cook until done.

Steak Stuffed with Kraut—Salt and pepper a big round steak, add a layer of bacon. Then lots of kraut. Roll it up and tie it with a string. Bake in your roaster in a moderate oven for an hour.

Fancy Ribs and Kraut—Brown your ribs. Cook them until about half done in your Dutch oven. Add a quart of kraut and potatoes, then water to cover. Add drop dumplings. Cook until potatoes and dumplings are done.

OLIVES

Lots of people in California really want to know how to cure their own olives. As an Idahoan, I am not of much help. Maybe somebody or bodies who have tried it will send me their experience to share in this section. I sure would appreciate it. You know—this book is sort of an encyclopedia. No one person has or can experience everything in an encyclopedia. But on the other hand, there isn't a person alive who doesn't know at least one useful and important thing that I don't. If you'd all share that one or more things with me to put in this book— What a great book it will be!

That's about what I had for "olives" through the 6th edition. Now for the 7th I can share with you some *real* answers because so many people that had experience curing olives *did* write to tell us.

Olive trees will grow in at least some parts of California, Florida, Arizona, New Mexico and Texas. The tree doesn't mind some drought and can handle temperatures as low as 15° briefly. For good production though, you need to be able to get a reasonable amount of water by rain or irrigation. It needs good drainage and fertile soil. The tree takes four years to begin to bear. It's an evergreen with pretty silvery leaves. These are the kinds in order of size of fruit: Sevillano, Manzanillo and Mission. Mission are the biggest.

You can use the olive fruit to make cured olives, green or black, or to press for oil. You can't eat them raw. They are so high in acid, trying to eat one raw would really shake up your mouth. That's why they are treated with lye which neutralizes the acid as part of their curing process. But lye is even more of a risk to you than uncured olives so be very careful when using it. Read the caution on the label. If you splash some lye water on your skin, washing it with water and vinegar or any acid fruit will help. If you get it in your eye, you're going to be blind and if your kid swallows it he won't have an esophagus or stomach anymore whether you call the doctor immediately or not so be *careful*.

The middle of October is when your olive crop will generally be ready. Pick them while still firm. For most recipes pick while still green, don't wait and let the olives get black on the tree. You should start the cure within a few days after the olives come off the tree because sitting around doesn't improve them. For more extensive information write the University of California Agricultural Extension Service or Mary E. Hall, Extension Nutrition Specialist, Morgan Hall, University of California, Berkeley, California 94720, for a booklet called "Home Pickling of Olives," HXT-29, 1966.

HOME-CURED GREEN OLIVES

Here is a letter I received. It isn't signed but it sounds like the writer really has lots of experience with olives. "Home-cured olives are such a treat. They are easily done, but you have to follow instructions closely or you will fail. First have everything you're going to use ready and clean. The olives should be freshly picked and I always make the green ones. I worked in an olive curing plant and the black ones are more difficult to get just right. The olives should be graded so all are the same size so as to cure at the same rate. Throw away all bruised or cut ones. This recipe is to cure 40 or 50 pounds of olives. A wooden keg is best but you can use a crock jar. Only you need a drain hole at the bottom and you do not naturally have that in a crock. I used to use an old wooden washing machine. Dissolve 1 can of lye in 5 gallons cold water. (Soft water works better. Do not use fluoridated water.) Stir with a long wooden stick so the lye fumes don't burn your hands. Now gently pour olives into lye solution. Water will cover olives. Stir gently every few hours to get them all well soaked

in the solution. Keep them in there until the lye almost reaches the pit. The water turns lighter. You can cut one in half and see if it is still bitter. You can taste it but do not let it stay in your mouth. Spit it out and rinse your mouth. When the lye has almost reached the pit, drain and cover with fresh water. Change the water every 12 hours for 2 days and be careful not to bruise any of the olives. If you see slick or cut ones take them out.

"Now place your olives in a second lye solution using 1 pound of lye to 6 gallons of water. Always use cold water. Allow olives to remain in this solution for 4 to 5 hours, or until the lye reaches the pit. You will know when you cut them open. Drain off the lye and cover with cold water. Change water every 12 hours for a week. Then cover with brine. To make the first brine, use 2 tablespoons salt per 1 gallon water and let stand 1 day. For a second brine, use 2 tablespoons salt to 4 gallons cold water. Allow to stand 1 day. For your third brine, use 2 tablespoons salt to 6 gallons of water and allow to stand 2 days. For your fourth brine, use 2 tablespoons salt to 8 gallons of water and allow to stand 3 days. Now make a final brine using 10 tablespoons salt to 10 gallons of water. Bring this to a rolling boil. Skim scum, let cool and cover the olives. Have the last brine ready to go over the olives right after you drain them of the next to last brine. If you are going to keep them for several weeks they should be pressure cooked or you can get poisoned. Fill jars with olives and add brine to cover. Seal and pressure. Keep under 240° for 60 minutes. I know this sounds like a lot of work but it is worth it if you like olives and have them."

I'm going to supply you with still more olive curing recipes because I think by comparing different people's methods you're going to understand what it's all about a whole lot better.

Green Olives—Warren E. Brown of Lafayette, California, sent me this recipe for green olives that his father had used years ago. "He used to make the olives in sausage barrels, which gave them an unusual flavor. 1.) Dissolve 1 can of any kind of lye and 1 pound of salt in 6 gallons of water. 2.) Add 6 gallons of half-ripe olives. 3.) Stir frequently for 2½ days, or until the lye penetrates nearly to the pit. Test by cutting to seed. If lye has penetrated almost to seed, pour off solution and replace with clear water. 4.) Change water twice daily, or oftener, until lye taste is entirely gone. 5.) Cover with weak brine (1 pound salt to 6 gallons water) for 2 or 3 days then replace with a strong brine solution (3 pounds salt to 6 gallons water) until olives taste right. *Note:* Some olives fail to take the lye. These may be removed by covering with clear water. The ones that float are to be skimmed off. *Important:* Brine that is too strong will cause olives to wrinkle and become tough. In rare cases the lye does not penetrate the olives in 3 days. In such an event the old solution may be removed and a new solution added."

Never-a-Miss Green Olives—Mrs. Alyne Carnes of Cottonwood, California, writes: "We don't have any olive trees on our place, but our grandson lives at Rancho Cordova near Sacramento and we found plenty down there. They canned around 75 quarts. I put up 57 quarts this year. Delicious. I use this recipe for curing green olives. I have never cured the ripe ones. I have used this recipe for years with good results, never a miss, and am glad to pass it on.

"I always put mine in either glass or plastic jars, this last year we bought plastic 5-gallon buckets. Make a solution of 1 gallon of water and 4 tablespoons of lye. Cover the olives and let stand 24 hours. Drain. Cover again with a solution of 1 gallon water and 2 tablespoons lye. Let stand 48 hours. Be sure that olives are covered with the water. I put a large plate or plastic lid to cover them. Drain and start with salt solution. The first 24 hours cover with 1 gallon water and 2 tablespoons salt. Drain. Next day cover with 1 gallon water and 3 tablespoons salt and let stand 24 hours. Drain. Next 4 tablespoons to 1 gallon of water. Drain. Next 5 tablespoons salt per gallon water. Now they should be ready to eat. If you taste any lye, keep in same solution until satisfied. Can be canned in same solution. Bring to a boil and boil for 5 minutes. Fill sterilized jars and seal."

Not everybody agrees on the canning directions. The first recipe said to pressure cook them an hour. I have a letter from Lucile Gray, Extension Home Economist at the University of Idaho in which she says, "A pressure canner is required. Therefore hot water bath canning of olives would *not* be safe." On most of these back to the land subjects I can trust my own judgment, but on olives I don't know a thing so am faithfully presenting you with the best sources I've been able to find.

You may be wondering why I skim over easy-to-find recipes (one lady wrote and complained because I didn't have a recipe for spaghetti sauce, so I'm adding one to this edition), and then go on at such length about how to cure olives. But there's a method to my madness. I don't want this to be just another cookbook on your shelf with the same old set of recipes. It wouldn't be a good enough excuse to make a tree into paper if I did that. This book assumes you've already got a good spaghetti sauce recipe—it's trying to supply the ones I think you may *not* have in your other cookbooks.

Here are some other green olive making hints I've been able to turn up. When treating your olives with the lye solution, it's the same rules as making soap. Place the olives in a stone crock or glass jar or wooden barrel but never, never in anything metal. Stir with a wooden spoon. When testing for how far the lye has soaked in, the olive's inside will be a yellowish-green color where the lye has penetrated but it's hard to see the line of separation between penetrated and not penetrated. If you keep an uncured olive handy to compare colors it will help you. How long it takes the lye to reach the pit depends in part on the weather and temperature. It can be from 8 to 48 hours. Some people strongly recommend that you don't let olives sit in lye solution overnight. If they aren't ready by the time you are sleepy and want to go to bed, pour off the lye and replace it with fresh water, then start again the next day. The reason for such caution is that if the lye gets into the olive pits, it's next to impossible to get it out again. After the lye

stage you have that long rinsing stage. Then comes the brining period in general. And then you eat or can them. The reason pressure canning is recommended is because all that lye makes the olives very low in acid and that means there are potential botulism problems just like with canned beets and corn. Fill jars with olives, hot water and maybe just a little vinegar and process 60 minutes at 10 pounds pressure. Don't start counting them until you have the pressure up to 10 pounds.

BLACK OLIVES

Here's an explanation of curing black olives. Nobody has recommended you try it, but then again olive trees bear heavily and have very long lives, so you will have lots of opportunities to practice if you have any at all. The black olive procedure takes longer. The big difference is that the olives have to be exposed to the air as part of the process.

1. Mix 3 level tablespoons lye per gallon of water and soak your olives in it until it merely penetrates the skins. As little as 3 hours may do it. Check often so you don't have an overdose.
2. When the lye has just penetrated the skin and not the flesh, pour off the lye solution and let the olives lay out in the air for a day. Stir them every few hours.
3. Now give your olives another lye bath until the lye has soaked in another 1/36th-1/16th inch. Then pour off the lye water and let the olives lay in the air again, stirring every few hours.
4. Again lye bathe them until the lye has gone in 1/8-3/16 inch. (No wonder everybody thinks this procedure is too hard!)
5. Now give them a new solution of 4 level tablespoons lye per gallon water. Leave them in there until it soaks to the pits. Pour off solution and give the olives another day of fresh air.
6. Now cover with fresh water, changing every few hours all day long until the lye taste is gone. Freshening will take about a week.
7. Now give them the brining treatment and can them like green olives.

Greek Olives—This kind of olive isn't familiar to most Americans who have always had olives out of cans from the supermarket. It's a European style and the usefulness of it here is that it's a way of curing ripe olives that doesn't require lye and can be done by the amateur successfully. Greek olives are "stronger" tasting than the ones we're used to, but they are edible and can be really good in a mixture like tamale pie or spaghetti. Once you acquire the taste you may find yourself eating them straight. You start by picking black olives from the tree instead of the green ones you picked before. Use a crock or watertight wooden box or widemouthed glass jar. Stir together 2 pounds of olives to be cured with ½ pound of salt and then pour another ¼ pound of salt (more or less doesn't matter much) over the top. Every 3 days or so, pour the olive-salt mixture out of its first container into another one and then back again to stir things up as gently as possibly. Remove any olives that have gotten soft or broken. It will take about a month to six weeks to get the job done. Then you can sift out or brush off the salt. Dip into olive oil and store in the refrigerator. If you are living without a refrigerator and need another storage method, shake off the excess salt, dip olives in a colander into boiling water for a few seconds, drain and let dry overnight. Now mix 1 pound salt per 10 pounds olives and keep in a cool place. But without refrigeration even this method may not hold them for more than a month. Don't worry because they look all shriveled up and wrinkled. That's how Greek olives always look!

HOMEMADE OLIVE OIL

This really doesn't fit under "sours" but I don't know where else it fits either and at least it's here with olives. Many people have asked me how they can make their own cooking oils. This is the only one I've ever been able to find that seems halfway possible for someone to do on their own. The recipe was written by the late W. V. Cruess, who was Professor of Food Technology at the College of Agriculture, Berkeley, California.

There is no thoroughly satisfactory way of making olive oil upon a very small scale without expensive machinery. The necessary utensils to follow this recipe can be found on any farm.

EXTRACTION OF OIL WITHOUT PRESSURE—A pound or two or ordinary lye, such as Rax, Babbit's Red Seal or Greenbank's, will be needed. Make up a solution of ½ pound of the lye per 1 gallon of water, using an agateware or iron pot. Do not use your aluminum ware; it will dissolve in the lye. A small basket of wire screen such as is used for making French-fried potatoes, will be needed or a piece of cheesecloth can be used. Heat the lye solution to boiling and while it is boiling, dip the olives in it for about 20 seconds. The time will vary with the toughness of the skins. Leave the olives in the lye until the skins are softened; that is, practically dissolved. Then plunge them into cold water for a few seconds to check the action of the lye. Place the lye-treated olives on a piece of fly screen tacked to a frame over a large dishpan. Rub them on the screen until the flesh has separated from the pits and dropped through the screen into the pan. A heavy pair of rubber gloves is useful in this process to prevent the hands becoming badly stained and roughened by the lye and olive juice.

Place the pulp, which should now be of a pasty or mushy consistency, in a pot with about two or three times its own volume of water. Heat while stirring to the simmering point for about ½ hour. Set aside for several days to permit the oil to rise to the surface. Usually a fair yield of oil can be obtained by skimming it with more water and allowing it to stand again. The process should be repeated several times. By this process, we have obtained about two-thirds the yield of oil that can be obtained by the use of a commercial press. The secret of success lies in rubbing the olive flesh to a fine-grained pulp on a screen.

The oil obtained by this process must be washed and should be filtered as described later. It has been found that the yield of oil is sometimes increased by adding about ¼ pound of salt per gallon of water used with the pulp. Always use a large excess of water with the pulp, as this facilitates separation of the oil.

HOMEMADE OLIVE PRESS—Materials needed: a heavy auto jack, 2 lengths of steel cable or chain or heavy rope, 1 shallow wooden watertight tray, 1 piece heavy burlap material to hold the crushed fruit, two 2" x 10" x 16" boards for the bottom, two 2" x 4" x 20" for braces, 4 threaded eyebolts with nuts. Start by nailing the bottom together and put the two 2" x 10" x 16" side by side and nail them onto the edge of the 2"

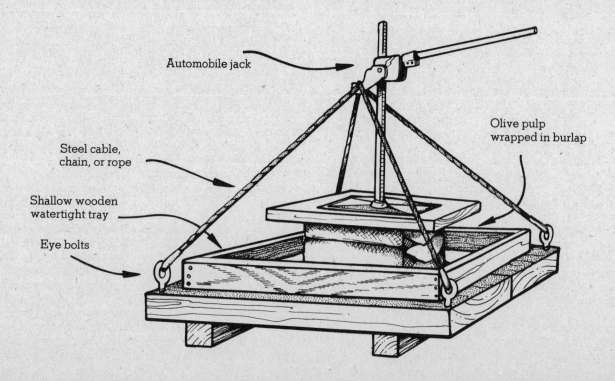

Automobile jack

Olive pulp
wrapped in burlap

Steel cable,
chain, or rope

Shallow wooden
watertight tray

Eye bolts

x 4" x 20" as shown. Next build a tray or simple box and caulk all joints to insure watertightness. And set this on the bottom. Then drill holes for eyebolts in the four corners at the bottom as shown, and insert eyebolts. All that is left is to set the jack up and measure and attach the cable.

One of the greatest difficulties will be the crushing of the fruit. This may be done as described above. If that method is used, return pits to the olives before pressing. The olives may also be crushed by placing them in a strong sack and hammering the sack with the broad side of an ax or with a heavy board in the same way that ice is crushed in a sack. The fruit must be thoroughly broken up. It will crush better if it is boiled for a short time to soften it. Place the crushed fruit and pits in a piece of heavy burlap and fold the edge of the burlap in to give a press cake about 10 x 10 inches and about 4 inches thick. Make two of these and place them in the press. Press slowly until no more juice can be obtained. Save all juice and oil pressed from the fruit. The pressed pulp should now be boiled with an equal volume of water and pressed a second time. Repeat boiling and pressing again. Usually a fourth heating and pressing will pay. Combine all of this pressed liquid and allow it to stand in a tub or barrel overnight. The oil can then be skimmed off.

WASHING THE OIL—Oil obtained by either of the above methods will be bitter and not clear. It must be washed with water to remove the bitterness and rough flavor. To do this, first prepare a bucket or 5-gallon can with a hole and faucet or cork near the bottom. Place the oil in this container and add an equal quantity, or more, of warm water. Mix oil and water by stirring for several minutes. Allow water to settle for several hours. Draw off the water and replace it with fresh warm water. Stir, settle and draw off after several hours. Repeat until the oil no longer has a bitter taste. Usually two days' washing will be sufficient.

FILTERING THE OIL—The oil will be cloudy and mixed with a little water. It can be made clear by filtration. A tin funnel can always be bought from the hardware store. One about 7 inches in diameter is a convenient size. Filter paper can be bought from the drugstore. Ask the druggist to fold the paper for you and tell you how to place it in the funnel.

Place the funnel in a widemouthed bottle, or place a 1 x 3-inch piece of wood over a bucket and bore a large hole in the wood to take the stem of the funnel easily. Pour the oil into the filter paper in the funnel and allow to filter. Oil filters slowly. Do not become discouraged if it requires several days for it to run through the filter.

Olive oil is not of very good flavor right after it is made. It should be kept for several months before it can be expected to have the proper flavor. Keep it in well cleaned bottles away from bright light. Too much light will cause it to lose color and flavor. A warm room will cause it to age more rapidly. The oil will also age more rapidly if the bottles are only three-fourths full and if a small piece of cotton is used to close the bottle.

CATSUPS

A catsup is something pulped and preserved with some combination of salt, vinegar, spices and sugar. Just which of those and how many can vary a lot. It can be made out of tomatoes, grapes, cucumbers, peaches—lots of things. The consistency is the key. It's a cooked, strained fruit or vegetable that is highly spiced to make a smooth, thick sauce. Don't worry about the color of your homemade catsups. They won't turn out like the commercial preparations, but color isn't everything. The spices can be varied to taste—add or subtract as you please. I'm in the process of trying to convert all my recipes to honey or molasses sweetening, but I haven't gotten to these yet.

Peach Catsup—My husband's favorite. He likes it with game or ham, as a dipping sauce or in the gravy. Combine 1 quart stoned, sectioned peaches, 1 chopped onion, 1 cup sugar, ½ cup vinegar, ¼ teaspoon salt, ¼ teaspoon allspice, ½ teaspoon cloves and ½ teaspoon cinnamon. Boil 1 hour. Fill jars and seal.

Instant Catsup—Put 3 teaspoons cornstarch in pan over medium heat and make a paste by gradually adding 2 cups tomato juice. Flavor with ½ teaspoon salt, 1 teaspoon honey, a little onion and garlic salt and a pinch of red pepper (optional).

Uncooked Tomato Sauce—We use this for a taco sauce. It keeps at least a year without sealing. It doesn't have to be refrigerated either. You mix without any cooking and keep it in a jar or small crock in a cool dry place—in other words, it's a crock tomato sauce without even any fermentation it's so strong. Combine 2 quarts peeled, chopped or ground tomatoes (ripe), 4 tablespoons chopped or ground onion, 1¾ cups celery, cut in small pieces, 1 tablespoon cayenne pepper, ½ teaspoon ground cloves, ½ teaspoon ground cinnamon, 1 teaspoon grated or ground nutmeg, 6 tablespoons sugar, 4 tablespoons salt, 6 tablespoons mustard seed and 1¾ cups vinegar.

Old Fashioned Canned Tomato Catsup—Make this when you have lots of time. You boil and boil and boil—maybe 4, 5, or 6 hours. And you have to keep it stirred. Wash and slice a peck (about 12½ pounds) of ripe red tomatoes (the redder the better to have a catsup with good color). Immerse the tomatoes in boiling water a few at a time for about a minute—or until the skin is ready to come off. You can tell by gouging up a little corner of skin with your fingernail and pulling on it. Then take off the skin and stem ends and section the tomatoes. Boil all the tomatoes about 15 minutes (until soft). Slice 2 medium-sized onions and fry them until soft in another pan. Put the cooked onion and tomato through a sieve to pulp them. Combine onion and tomato pulp. Add ¼ teaspoon cayenne pepper and boil until the mixture is reduced to one-half its original volume. (This is the point at which you boil and boil and boil.) While the tomato-onion pulp is boiling, spice your vinegar. Pour 2 cups cider vinegar into an enamel pan. Make a spice bag out of a handkerchief or cheesecloth and put in 1½ tablespoons broken-up stick cinnamon, 1 tablespoon whole cloves and 3 finely chopped cloves garlic. Immerse the spice bag in the vinegar and cook it slowly for ½ hour, then cover and set aside with the spice bag still in it until needed.

When the tomato pulp is reduced by half, remove the spice bag and measure the vinegar. You want 1¼ cups of it. Add more, if needed, then combine vinegar with pulp. Add 1 cup sugar (white, raw or brown), 2½ teaspoons salt and 1 tablespoon paprika. If it is still too thin to suit you, boil and boil again until the consistency satisfies you. Otherwise just boil 10 minutes more and pour while boiling hot into presterilized canning jars and seal.

Marie's Blender Catsup—In the earlier editions of this book the only catsup recipe was Old Fashioned Canned Tomato Catsup. Eleanor Seberger, who writes a number of cooking columns for various Midwestern newspapers and did a beautiful review of this book, wrote to Darlene while I was off on a book-selling trip. "I'm enclosing a catsup recipe I want Carla to try. I felt sorry for her in the catsup making pages, for this is so easy and quick . . . and my family *loves* it. Boys won't eat the boughten stuff if this is on the table. Note that the blender even uses unpeeled tomatoes. Don't try to double the recipe though for most roasters will not hold the larger amount. This cooks down easily in 3 to 4 hours, and I always end up with the 5 pints it promises." My children *love* homemade catsup too, Eleanor. To make Marie's Blender Catsup you wash and quarter 8 pounds ripe tomatoes, add 2 red peppers, seeded, 2 green peppers, seeded, and 4 medium-sized onions. Whirl in blender, using 3 cups white vinegar as needed for liquid (draining it partially off and reusing). Put all into a shallow roaster, adding 3 cups sugar, 3 tablespoons salt, 1½ teaspoons allspice, 3 teaspoons dry mustard, ¼ teaspoon cloves, 1½ teaspoons cinnamon and ½ teaspoon hot red pepper. Bake, uncovered, at 325° until volume is reduced by half, stirring occasionally. It will take about 4 hours. Seal while hot. Makes 5 pints.

Chili Sauce—Peel and cut up 4 quarts ripe tomatoes. Finely grind white onions until you have 3 cups. Remove the seeds from 1 green pepper and 1 red pepper. Grind separately until you have 1 cup of each. Put vegetables in a heavy pot and add 2 cups sugar, 2 tablespoons salt and ¼ teaspoon cayenne pepper. Put on low heat and cook, stirring, until the sugar is dissolved. Then cook slowly, stirring occasionally, about 2 hours, or until the mixture thickens. Now add (tied in a hankie) 1 tablespoon whole cloves, 3 sticks whole cinnamon and 1 tablespoon mustard seed. Also 3 cups vinegar. Cook until very thick. Remove bag of spices and pour immediately into hot sterilized jars. Seal.

Cranberry Catsup—Wash and pick over 2½ pounds cranberries. Cover with vinegar and cook until they burst. Force through a sieve. Add 2⅔ cups sugar, 1 tablespoon cinnamon and 1 teaspoon ground cloves. Return to heat and simmer until thick. Pour into hot sterilized jars and seal.

Currant Catsup—4 pounds ripe currants, 2 cups vinegar, 1 tablespoon cinnamon, 1 teaspoon salt, 3½ cups sugar, 1 tablespoon cloves and 1 teaspoon pepper. Mix, boil down to a thick sauce and bottle.

Apple, Plum or Grape Catsup—Start with 1 quart applesauce. Or for grape sauce cook grapes in an enamel kettle slowly until soft (about 25 minutes). Then put through colander to get the grape puree. Cook plums and colander them for plum sauce. Combine 1 quart any sauce with 1 teaspoon ginger, 1 teaspoon cinnamon, 1 teaspoon cloves, 2 cups vinegar, 1 teaspoon pepper, 1 teaspoon mustard, 1 teaspoon onion juice and 2 teaspoons salt. Simmer slowly until thick. Bottle and seal. If you like sweet sauce, add brown sugar or molasses to taste.

Apple Catsup—Peel and quarter a dozen round, tart apples. Stew until soft in as little water as possible. Sieve them. For every quart of sieved apple, add ½ cup sugar, 1 teaspoon pepper, 1 teaspoon cloves, 1 teaspoon mustard, 2 teaspoons cinnamon, 2 medium-sized onions, chopped very fine, 1 tablespoon salt and 2 cups vinegar.

VINEGAR

Vinegar is something I never have managed to do. And not for the lack of trying. And not because it can't be done. A dear old lady in Juliaetta named Mrs. Eggers took my recipe and made wonderful vinegar out of it. The absolute best wine-type vinegar I ever tasted. And she ended up with a "mother" just like you're supposed to that was like a colored firm but clear gelatin. She even gave me the mother after she got done making vinegar and I brought it home and tried to make vinegar out of it and still no luck. So I'm going to tell you how Mrs. Eggers makes vinegar instead of how I do it. All kinds of things happened while I was trying to make vinegar and for the time being I've given up.

My last attempted batches were in the living room. One was a jar of mixed grape and peach wine. One a big crock of malt stuff hopefully becoming malt vinegar. And, oh yes, there was also a yet larger crock of rotting apple peels and cores on the way to becoming cider vinegar. But it all smelled so bad that it got to be a social problem. Like Dolly's music teacher got a funny look on his face and gave a very short lesson (the piano was in the same room and I never told him about the crocks). Then one fine day soon afterward Dolly was sitting on top of the stove playing and she fell off splat right into the biggest crock of all. She gave out with an anguished cry— half embarrassment and half pain. By the time we got her fished out all the containers were either spilled or contaminated so I called it quits for the time being.

But I can give you all the theory about how you can make vinegar. It's a two-step fermentation. First, one kind of organism turns the sugar into alcohol. Then another takes over and turns the alcohol into acetic acid. Acetic acid is the textbook name for vinegar, only what we put on the Swiss chard at dinnertime isn't near as strong as what they use in the laboratory. Adding yeast makes the alcohol stage get going faster. Adding the mother helps the acid formation from the alcohol because that adds the right kind of organism for *that* change. If you don't use either yeast or acid eventually the right kind of critters will just fall in from the air and I know that's true because Mrs. Eggers did it that way.

A lady who read what I had written before this wrote: "When I was a child some 50 years ago, the apples were ground in an old outside cider mill, then the juice was pressed out with a wooden press, yielding 50-gallon barrels. They were wooden barrels with wooden lids. A large cloth was tied over the top of the barrel and the lid propped open to let in air. The barrels were stored in the smokehouse to ferment all summer. The smokehouse was made of hewn oak logs, with a solid door and one cat hole large enough for the family cat to enter to catch all the mice that might enter. It had no windows and a dirt floor. It was always cool and damp even on the hottest day. An old iron pot was in the middle of the building where a fire was built to cure the ham and sausage in winter. The fire was always smothered to a smoke and Daddy watched it very closely. Before cold weather the vinegar was stored in big barrels that lay on their side with a large stopper in a hole in the top side. We sold gallons of vinegar to everyone in the community all year round. The barrels were never used for anything but vinegar and were washed with fresh well water each year, removing the mother, and refilled with fresh apple cider. All the kraut and salt pickles were made in the same building. There was an attic above the smokehouse with a ladder to climb. We stored apples and Keiffer pears and jars of canned fruit and vegetables in the attic. Daddy always bought a small barrel of salt fish for the smokehouse every winter, and we had a leg of dried beef."

You want to know how they make "cider vinegar" nowadays? Commercial cider vinegar starts with apple wastes, peels and cores, which is really not all

bad. You can do the same thing. The cider company presses the apple wastes to get the juice out. It adds water and sugar, heats it to cause fermentation and then it is rapidly oxidized to produce the acetic acid content. The vinegar is diluted and labeled and it was less than 48 hours from apple core to finished product.

Here's how you can make vinegar like Mrs. Eggers:

WHAT YOU START WITH—Vinegar flavors and acidities vary according to the kind of juice you start with. Cider vinegar means you started with apple juice (cider) or some apple product like peelings and corings. White vinegar starts out from grain. Malt vinegar is made from barley, but for you it would be easier to buy a can of malt extract to start it. (Make sure you don't buy the kind of canned malt extract that's meant for beermaking. That has hops in it and you would have bitter hop-flavored vinegar. The vinegarmaking kind of malt is much rarer than the hop-flavored kind. Morgan Brothers in Lewiston has it though.) You can make vinegar from any homemade wine but not from most store bought wines because those contain preservatives that would prevent the second step fermentation you need. Some imported wines can be used because they don't have preservatives in them, but it's almost impossible to judge from the container whether it's got preservatives in it or not. You can make vinegar from fruit juices like pear, grape, cherry, or even the leftovers from your fruit canning—the peelings and corings of peaches, pears, apples, grape hulls and whole cherries. Mrs. Eggers made hers from apple peels and cores. You can't use store vinegar to hurry your vinegar makers on their way because if you add vinegar in the first step while you are making wine the vinegar will tend to mess up or stop that reaction, and adding it when you want the wine to turn to acetic acid will do you no good because the store vinegar is all pasteurized and the needed beasties in it are dead. So find something sweet to start the fermentation. You can add sugar or molasses to beef it up. Anything sweet—leftover sweetened tea, leftover canned fruit juices, jellies, sugarbowl rinsings. You can add such makings every day for a while, adding a little more water each time. If it seems to stop working before the vinegar comes, try adding more of whatever sweetener you're using. If it won't bubble for you, or if you want to hurry it up, add 1 tablespoon of yeast to get it working.

THE WORKING PERIOD—Put your starters in a crock, wooden container or widemouthed glass jar. Never ferment in metal or chipped enamel. Leave from a half to a fourth of your crock space empty for later additions, should you so decide, and general bubbling up. Cover with a clean cloth and tie that good around the neck of your container with a string to keep bugs from falling in and dying. That crock is going to be sitting there a long time, and if you aren't careful the contents will get dirty. Wash and replace the cloth once a week. Set the crock in a warm place—80° is a good temperature. It will work at a cooler temperature—but the cooler the temperature the longer you have to wait for it to get done. During the first fermentation stage it bubbles. As long as that is going on, bubbles will be coming up and you can hold a match over the surface and see them coming up. When it gets done bubbling it's ready for the second stage.

How long stage two will take really depends on if you've got some "mother." Mother is a thick, clear, jelly-like sort of amber substance made by the kind of beasties that make vinegar and they live in it. If you've got some to add to your crock when you're ready to get stage two going, you'll have the nicest vinegar you ever tasted in four to six weeks. But if you don't have any mother to add, it will take as long as six months to have your first batch of vinegar. You must wait for the right kind of beastie to float by in the air, drop into your crock and decide this is a good place to bring up a family! When that does happen the crock surface will gradually start to show a thin grayish film. This is your mother getting started. *Don't disturb it.* It's important that the mother stay on top until its work is done. It will settle to the bottom of your crock, heavy and thick, later on. Taste occasionally to see how sour your vinegar-to-be is becoming.

FINISHING UP YOUR VINEGAR—Commercial vinegars have a standardized acid content. (They are diluted to be just so and then pasteurized and bottled.) Homemade ones don't unless you are a chemist. They generally end up being stronger than commercial ones. That's why some old-time recipes that were meant for homemade vinegar don't work very well with the modern kind and vice versa. I mean store vinegar doesn't have the pure food preserving zap that homemade does. So that has to be taken into consideration when you are cooking or pickling with your homemade vinegar. And don't lose your mother now you've got her! I don't know anywhere you can buy or get a start of mother unless you have a vinegarmaking neighbor like Mrs. Eggers down the road. Store some mother in glass jars so that next apple cider making season you'll be ready or keep a batch going continually. To store just put the mother in a jar, cover with vinegar and cap the bottle.

The vinegar out of your crock should be strained until it's "clean" enough to suit you. Pack the vinegar in a stone crock or glass jar and seal it tightly. Or bottle and cork or cap. From the time of sealing the vinegar will gradually become more mellow and of a distinctive flavor although you could use it immediately if you want. This homemade vinegar can be used as a "starter" for your next batch. But it will keep best if you pasteurize it.

TO PASTEURIZE VINEGAR—Put the bottles or jugs of vinegar into a pan filled with cold water. Heat the water gradually until the vinegar is about 145°. Hold the vinegar at that temperature about a half an hour. Cool it. Be sure the bottles are loosely corked or unsealed while pasteurizing. The pasteurization will keep your vinegar from clouding through formation of mother. (If you pasteurize your vinegar it can't be used as a starter.) If you don't want to pasteurize the vinegar strain it through a wet doubled cheesecloth before bottling and then store in a cool dry place.

TO STRENGTHEN VINEGAR—Let it freeze on top. Then take the ice off the top since only the water portion freezes.

Pure Cider Vinegar—Let homemade cider stand exposed to the air in a warm room for a month or two and it will turn to vinegar. Tart apples make the best vinegar.

Cider Vinegar—Put 1 gallon of good sweet natural cider and 1 quart of molasses into a crockery or glass container. Cover the top with cloth and set it in the sun. Cover it when it rains. When it stops bubbling, add some mother if you can and in a month or so it should be good strong vinegar. You can dilute it if it is stronger than you wanted.

Homely Vinegar—When you are processing a bunch of apples, peaches, pears, grapes or cherries, wash them thoroughly before preparing for use and save the peelings, hulls, cores or seeds as appropriate. Place these in a crock. Sweeten well. Add enough water to cover them. You can sweeten with honey, molasses or sugar. Let stand several days keeping the top covered with a cloth. You can add fresh peelings, now and then. The scum (mother) on top will gradually thicken. When the vinegar tastes right, strain and bottle. Another way to do is to let your peelings, water and sweetening stand several days, then strain and let the juice resulting stand until you have table vinegar.

Wine Vinegar—You can make your own wine vinegar by taking homemade grape or dark berry juice. Dilute, sweeten and mix, if desired, with a lighter juice such as peach. Keep in a warm place, covered. First it will ferment. You'll see the bubbles of carbon dioxide rising poetically as it works. Then it will go flat and your vinegar making begins, which takes much longer and is less dramatic. You don't have to have mother to start. It speeds things but unless you live in the frozen north mother is all around us. In the south you may end up with father, aunt and uncle, too.

Apple Combo Vinegar—Combine a fruit juice with a tart apple juice. Pear is good. If you don't have a juicer, it will be easiest for you to just wash and mash the fruit by stomping with your kraut stomper. Then let it work until you like the vinegar flavor. Strain and store in glass in a cool dark place.

HERB FLAVORED VINEGARS

Vinegars can be flavored with leaf herbs, with seeds, or combinations thereof. In general figure 3 tablespoons seeds per quart vinegar or 2 handfuls leaves. Gather your leaves fresh, if possible—the flavor will be more pungent. If you must use dried leaves moisten them with a little hot water in a bowl before proceeding. In the case of leaves, combine them with the vinegar by boiling gently 5 minutes in an enamel kettle. Then let the mixture stand 2 or 3 weeks in a warm place such as your kitchen. Or in a sunny window. Shake the bottle twice a day. If you are using seeds, crush them with a mortar and pestle (or if you don't have that, crush them in a wide-mouthed jar with a wooden spoon). Then add them to the vinegar, boil and proceed as above. At the end or before the recommended period taste the vinegar. If it doesn't seem flavorful enough strain and start over

with more seeds or leaves. When straining first use a sieve, then a cloth. When the vinegar suits you, bottle it. You can start with storebought cider or wine vinegar or with your homemade.

Caraway, Mustard, Celery or Cardamom Seed Vinegar—Combine 3 tablespoons seeds and 1 quart white wine vinegar.

Tarragon Vinegar—Combine 4 cups tarragon leaves and smaller stalks, 1 quart wine vinegar, 3 cloves and 1 small clove garlic (remove garlic after 24 hours). Gather the tarragon just before it blossoms. Discard the larger stalks. Mash the leaves some. Takes 2 months to really get good.

Mint Vinegar—Combine 2 cups mint leaves, 1 cup sugar and 1 quart cider vinegar. Another way to do it is to pack the leaves into a pint jar and fill the jar with wine vinegar. Let stand 2 weeks or more, then strain. Bottle.

Basil Vinegar—Combine ¾ cup leaves and 1 quart wine vinegar.

Garlic Vinegar—Combine 4 cloves garlic, peeled and chopped, ½ teaspoon salt, 2 teaspoons ground cloves, 1 teaspoon freshly ground peppercorns, 1 teaspoon caraway seeds and 1 quart wine vinegar. Give it 2 or 3 weeks before you strain and use.

Burnet (leaves or seeds)—Marjoram, dill, lemon balm, chives are other possibilities. Mix and match to suit yourself.

Chervil Vinegar (good in salad dressings)—Half fill a bottle with fresh or dry leaves. Fill the bottle with good vinegar and heat it gently by placing in warm water. Bring water to boiling point. Take off heat. When cool cap. Let steep 2 weeks. Then it's ready.

Celery Vinegar—Combine ¼ pound celery seed or 1 quart fresh celery, chopped fine, 1 quart vinegar, 1 tablespoon salt and 1 tablespoon sugar. Put celery in a jar, heat the vinegar, sugar and salt, pour in boiling hot over celery. Let cool, cover tightly and set away. In 2 weeks strain and bottle.

Spiced Vinegar—Combine 1 quart cider vinegar, ½ ounce celery seed, ⅓ ounce dried parsley, 1 clove garlic, 3 small onions, grated, 2 whole cloves, 1 teaspoon peppercorns, 1 teaspoon nutmeg, salt to taste, 1 tablespoon sugar and 1 tablespoon good brandy. Cover in jar. Let stand 3 weeks, strain and bottle.

Plain Onion or Garlic or Celery Leaf Vinegar—24 green onions (shallots are best if you have them) or 4 cloves garlic or 2 cups celery leaves, peeled and chopped. Two or 3 weeks in 1 quart vinegar. Strain and use.

Hot, Hot Vinegar—Add horseradish, onion, paprika, pepper, chili peppers, cayenne pepper, curry powder—any or all as suits you. Strain and bottle when you like the taste. These aren't for me but some people love anything that will scald their gullet.

SPICED FRUIT

For some reason I'm having a hard time concentrating this morning. Dolly is playing the piano. She had a sleighing accident day before yesterday and still isn't able to walk. We tried to get her to the doctor yesterday, but it is the first week in January with unusually heavy snows. After struggling about an hour we gave up and decided to wait until today. I'll try again this afternoon. The pickup is all chained up (no heater in the beast) and then Dolly and I will try to get to Troy and our wonderful Dr. Drury. Maybe by then the sun will have melted some of the snow and black ice off the highway. Looking out my living room window right now I see the highway where it runs along the other side of the canyon and it is still snow covered. I'll have chains on this time though and that ought to help a lot.

The worst is getting off our personal mountainside and down to the highway. Worse still is trying to get home again up our mountainside. About a week ago Mike and I were driving in and we literally started to slide off the cliffside. It's a good 200 feet to the bottom. I chickened out first. Opened the car door and said, "Mike, I'm leaving." He lasted about ten seconds more and then left too. The car hung there until the next day. He got the crawler tractor (a cat type with tracks instead of wheels) going and I had to sit in that car and steer while he pushed me back onto the road.

In a way I enjoy the snow. It reminds me of winters when I was a little girl. On the sheep ranch in Montana we were really on top of the world. The lowest point on the ranch was 6,000 feet. The buildings were located at that point. If I rode my horse on up to a high point I could easily see 75 miles on a clear day and days were mostly clear in summer. ("Oh, give me a home where the buffalo roam, and the deer and the antelope play. Where seldom is heard a discouraging word and the skies are not cloudy all day.")

So today I have all five of them home instead of the usual four. I'm trying to keep them usefully occupied. Danny and Dolly are working in arithmetic workbooks. Becca is working in a preprimary reading workbook. Luke is in the basement playing with the pumpkins and Sara is discovering she can crawl under chairs. When I was a little girl I spent a lot of time studying at home with my parents—usually Jan-

uary and February. When I did go to school from that mountain ranch I rode horseback for two miles each way.

It wasn't really a "one room" school. We had a cloakroom in front and a teacherage in the back so the teacher could live there when the snow got too deep for her to easily drive back and forth from the ranch where she lived with her husband in the Shields River Valley below between Clyde Park and Wilsall. Our creek, our school and our community were all called Bracket Creek and that is home in my heart though long gone in the world of reality. On cold days like today Mrs. Carroll would fix us some hot canned soup on the potbellied wood stove in the classroom to complement the basket lunches we carried. We had hearty appetites. Everybody rode horseback to school. Some rode five miles each way. You can make fast time on a good horse and when you're used to it.

There was a little barn behind the schoolhouse where the animals waited patiently for school to be out and then the merry race to the crossroads began. I always lost. I rode a not so young half Shetland gelding called "Shorty Bill" who was probably my childhood's closest friend. I would go out to the field to get that horse after breakfast—a little kid running with bridle in hand. He would run across the field to meet me.

We'd go down to the big red barn with its vast mow full of hay and its underparts full of a complicated wonderland of stalls, pens, grain and harness rooms, where Shorty would have his breakfast of rolled oats, and I'd saddle him up.

On summer days when the business at hand wasn't serious I would often ride him with no saddle or bridle. I could pull myself up by a handful of his mane. (It got sparser and sparser at the point where I grabbed.) I'd push on his neck to show him the direc-

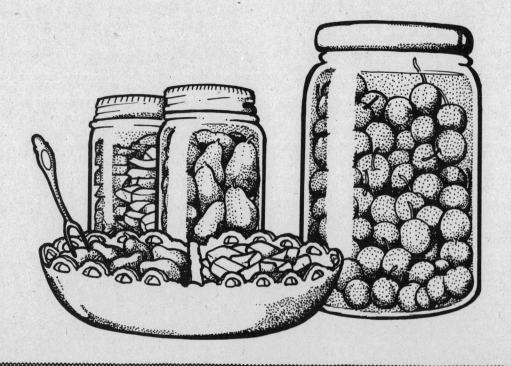

tion I wanted him to go, kick him to make him go and slide to the side to tell him I wanted to stop. In summer there was hard work to do on horseback though and Shorty had no part of that. That was for the five big horses we had, the largest being a great big pink-eyed Appaloosa that could pick his way down a cliffside with 200 pounds of pack rattling on his back like there was nothing to it.

Once every week we had to take the Appaloosa and the others, loaded with food and general supplies, up to the sheep camp to help move the sheepherder's camp. We'd take down his tent and sack up his pots and pans and sleeping bag and gun and then the horses would carry it all to the new spot. It was most generally miserable. Horseflies were all over and drove everybody crazy, man and beast. They are the biggest meanest fly in the world I think and they bite so hard they leave a bloody mark where they've been. If they happen to bite your horse in a tender place you've suddenly got a very insecure seat atop there.

Well, that ought to be enough digression to get my head organized. Digressions are easier and more fun to write than the rest of it. Spiced fruit.

Spiced fruit is something you can make like crock pickles—without canning or sealing and the real old-time recipes don't spoil—they just get spicier and spicier. I can't eat much of it because all that spice is too much for my digestive tract, but I can promise you that in small amounts they are very tasty—like spiced crab apples that you can get in the store only much more so. Not the kind of thing that you would eat in large quantities though so you shouldn't look upon this method of preserving to result in a staple type food. Just a holiday goody.

If your fruit does show signs of fermentation pour off the liquid, boil it awhile and then pour back over the fruit. Brandied fruit has an alcohol content but spiced fruit doesn't. For a milder version you can cut back on sugar, vinegar and spices and then can the results. The real thing can be left in a bowl with a plate on top all winter. I've done it. Whenever you want some just fork it out. Don't be bothered by floating mold and scum. Your fruit is below the level of the fluid's surface. Rinse the fruit before serving in case any top glop came along as you fished it out.

In general, use 7 pounds of fruit, 4 pounds of sugar, 2 to 4 cups of vinegar, 1 tablespoon each of cinnamon, cloves and allspice. Pare peaches and pears. Prick plums and tomatoes with a needle in several places to help the preservatives get inside. Boil the fruit in the syrup 5 minutes. Remove the fruit and boil the syrup until it has thickened some. Put the fruit in jars and pour the boiling syrup over it. You can spice blackberries, currants, gooseberries, peaches, pears, plums, tomatoes, cherries, crab apples, watermelon rind, pieces of almost green cantaloupe, apricots, nectarines, prunes, quinces, citron and so on. Let your spiced fruit stand at least several weeks before using it.

These recipes all use sugar. I went through my spiced fruit phase before I was a beekeeper. In the Middle East fruit is preserved in a syrup made of honey and vinegar and I'm sure you could do the same thing with these recipes.

Spiced Plums—Decide how many plums you want to spice and weigh them. For every pound of plums use 1 pound of sugar (1¾ cups). For every pound of sugar, use ⅔ cup vinegar. For every gallon of plums use ½ ounce each of ground cinnamon, cloves, mace and allspice. Prick each plum in several places with a big needle. Add the spices to the syrup and boil it. Pour the boiling mixture over the plums. Let them rest three days; then pour off the syrup and reboil it. Boil it down until thick but still enough to cover your plums. Pour hot over the plums in the jar in which they are to be kept. Cover the jar well to keep out the dust and insects. Makes plums very special.

Spiced Watermelon Rind—This recipe is canned. Use a watermelon with a good thick rind. Pare off the hard green surface as well as the pink inner pulp. Great-grandmother's watermelon had a much thicker rind than ours. That's because the people who have been doing the watermelon seed selection have been selecting for more pink inside and less rind with no thought to us spiced watermelon rind makers. So you now have to use more watermelons for an equivalent amount of pickle. Those old-time seeds aren't clear extinct because I know one watermelon pickle lover down the road who has cherished her seed supply for many years now and can still grow a thick rinded watermelon. That's good because I hate to see anything become extinct. Except I wish wasps, ticks, horseflies and mosquitoes would. I can't imagine what *they* are good for.

Cube 3 pounds of the white portion of the rind. Soak overnight in a brine made of 2 tablespoons salt to 4 cups water. Drain. Cover with fresh water and cook until tender. Drain. Combine 5 cups sugar, 2 cups cider vinegar and 1 tablespoon whole cloves. In a bag tie up 1 tablespoon whole allspice, 1 tablespoon broken-up cinnamon stick and 1 lemon, sliced, and add to syrup. Boil 5 minutes. Add watermelon and cook until transparent (45 minutes maybe). Pack in sterilized hot jars and seal (open kettle type canning).

Sweet Pickled Crab Apples—Wash the crab apples and remove blossom ends. You'll need a peck (about 2 gallons) of them. Make a syrup of 1 quart vinegar, 3 pounds brown sugar, 1 teaspoon whole cloves and 1 stick cinnamon. Boil. Add apples and cook in this syrup 10 minutes. Put into jars. Boil down the syrup and pour over the fruit. Seal. Additional good tasting things to add to your syrup are cider, allspice, ginger, nutmeg and lemon juice.

Pickled Citron—Pare the citrons and cut in medium thin slices. Use about 2 pounds of citron for this recipe. Soak overnight in brine (the same as for watermelon rind). Drain. Cook in clear water until tender. Add citron to a hot mixture of 2 cups vinegar, 2 cups water, 1 lemon, sliced, 1 tablespoon cinnamon, 1 teaspoon cloves and 1 teaspoon allspice. Boil rapidly until citron becomes clear. It really does turn sort of transparent. Then seal in hot jars open kettle canning style.

Cantaloupe Sweet Pickles—Cut 12 unripe melons into quarters. Peel tough outer rind and the mushy, stringy inner surface. Place them in a jar in vinegar to cover and leave overnight. In the morning to each pint of vinegar add ¾ pound sugar, 1 tablespoon cloves, ½ tablespoon mace and 4 large sticks of cinnamon, broken into small pieces. Boil the vinegar and spices, remove the melons to jars. Boil the syrup 30 minutes longer. Pour it hot over the fruit in jars and seal.

Pickled Peaches or Pears—You can easily skin peaches by dipping quickly into hot water and then sliding the skins off. Pears have to be peeled. For about a gallon of peaches or pears boil 3½ cups sugar with 2 cups vinegar and ½ ounce stick cinnamon. Put a few peaches or pears at a time into the syrup and cook until tender. Then pack the fruit into jars, putting a few cloves into each jar. Pour the hot syrup over them and seal.

Ginger Pears—Peel and quarter 2 pounds hard late pears, removing cores. They shouldn't be too ripe for best results. Slice thin. Squeeze 1 lemon to get its juice. Grate the rind. Combine lemon juice, lemon rind, ½ cup water and 2 pounds sugar in a kettle. Add 2 ounces ginger root or crystallized ginger and simmer about 45 minutes by which time the fruit should be transparent. When the syrup is thick pour into jars.

❖❖❖❖❖❖❖❖❖❖❖❖❖❖❖❖

BRANDIED FRUIT

Becca (short for Rebecca) just crawled down from my lap to go hold a bunny. Santa brought her two little half pounders for Christmas. They make great pets. Are fearless now and hop all over the place. Makes January a little livelier for the household set. Luke, his silver pistol and his little toy crawler tractor are all in my lap (replacing Rebecca who was there before she got interested in the rabbits) and on we go to brandied fruit.

This is really a hard subject and I've put it off to the last minute. Not that it is hard to write up. But many people hold very strong opinions for or against the use of alcohol including in my own community. The Church I go to has a very firm anti-alcohol stance and most of my best friends wouldn't let the stuff in their homes in tutti-frutti or any other form. I've great sympathy with that point of view. I don't see any excuse for debauching because it is invariably damaging to something somebody should care about.

The use of alcohol I think is also an impediment to our ability to perceive the prompting of the Holy Spirit. Our minds are made like delicate instruments. You can think of it on the same principle as a radio receiver picking up a signal through the air. So we are able to receive the Spirit and to be shown His will for us and knowing that is the best thing that can happen to you because He wants to and can help with all your problems. So His prompting is an important thing to be able to receive because it's the best advice you'll ever get and from someone who knows exactly what the problems are all about better than any human friend you've got. Alcohol or any other drug messes up the reception.

But I'll part with my denomination to consider that it is possible there may be a time in your life for alcohol. That would be if there is a reason and if the reason is that God said you should have it, how much, and when. There is no doubt in my mind that many of the people I've met who love Jesus and who are in denominations where the use of alcoholic beverages is permitted—like Catholics—do indeed know the same Jesus I do and the same Holy Spirit. I have a specially warm place in my heart for those Catholic sisters because I've been very close to some through trying times and I know what tough Christian stuff they can be made of. And they also know what it is to be having a large family in times when some people think that's a criminal act and many more disapprove either vaguely or specifically.

So the most significant thing about brandied fruit for better or for worse is that it has an alcohol content. It makes a heady dessert and not one that children can have very much of so you don't need much for a winter's supply. Tutti-frutti is the most common and versatile sort because you can eat it straight or use it for an ice cream or general dessert topping or make a sort of fruit cake out of it (actually better than eating it straight).

Earlen's Tutti-Frutti—You can start out with 1½ cups fruit and 1½ cups sugar. For your first mixture half-drained crushed pineapple and half-drained chopped canned peaches are good along with 6 chopped maraschino cherries. A package of dry yeast stirred in helps to get the fermentation off to a quick start. Stir it several times the first day. At least every two weeks after that add 1 more cup of sugar and 1 more cup of fruit. Alternate your fruit so you don't end up with all the same thing. Don't put it in the refrigerator, but don't have it too near the heat either.

Once you get it going you can give a cup of "starter" to friends who can soon work up their own supply of tutti-frutti from it. The mixture is at its best after four weeks have passed. You can take out fruit to use as needed, but try not to let what's left get below 1 cup. To have more of it just add more fruit and sugar ahead of schedule. You can use fresh, canned or frozen fruits such as Bing cherries, raspberries, blueberries, apples, pears, or fruit cocktail as well as the first ones I mentioned. But if pears and fruit cocktail are used, treat them gently so they don't become too mushy. Don't use bananas.

Be sure and keep the fruit under the liquid. You can use a weighted saucer to hold it down. Fruit exposed to air will darken in color and taste *too* fermented.

Old-Time Tutti-Frutti—The recipe I first gave you is quite common around the country now and implies some city-type living with the maraschino cherries and pineapple. Here's a way to make tutti-frutti off your own garden and orchard, a sack of sugar and a cup of brandy. Start this at the beginning of the fruit season. Strawberries are probably the first you have

Tutti-frutti

and are great for the purpose. You can start in a jar and transfer to a crock as your supply grows. For this recipe I'd suggest keeping it in as cool a place as you can find during the summer. As the season goes on add cherries, apricots, plums, nectarines and peaches. Avoid apples, pears, melons and blackberries.

Into the jar put 1 cup of very good brandy, rum or cognac, 1 cup of sugar and 1 cup of the fruit. Stir and let rest. Don't refrigerate. Cover to keep the dust out but don't seal. As each new fruit comes along add it and more sugar, at the rate of 1 cup sugar per 1 cup fruit. You don't need more brandy. Cut large fruit into small pieces and stir well at each addition. Take out pits and seeds where appropriate.

If you figure three months for it to mature, it will be about ready for Christmas time. Serve over plain pudding, or cake or ice cream. Or make a fruitcake with it, or a holiday fruit bread. The baking action will evaporate all the alcohol.

Almost Instant Brandied Fruit—Use canned fruit. Apricots, peaches, pears and so on are all right. Save the juice off the fruit and boil it down to half the original amount. Add one-third part brandy to two-thirds part your boiled down syrup and pour that over the fruit. Let it rest at least 24 hours before serving to let the fruit absorb the flavor.

You can also make brandied fruit using rum. Mix 2 cups well-drained fruit with 2 cups sugar. Cover well with rum. It takes about 1½ cups. Then just as in the other recipes you can add more fruit and sugar every week or two to keep it going.

Tutti-Frutti Ice Cream—Soften store-bought vanilla ice cream or make your own. At the very end add tutti-frutti and refreeze or freeze.

Tutti-Frutti Fruitcake—Mash ½ cup butter together with 1 cup sugar until well mixed. Add 4 eggs, 3 cups flour, 2 teaspoons soda, 1 teaspoon cloves, 1 teaspoon allspice, 2 cups of your brandied fruit of any sort, 1½ cups applesauce, 1 cup raisins and 1 cup nuts. This bakes best in an angel-food type pan because it is very moist—a buttered 9-inch tube pan

would be right. It takes a long time to bake—70 or 80 minutes or more in a moderate oven (350°).

I saw this version of fruitcake in a little magazine called *Mail Box News*. It's put out by Maid of Scandinavia Company, comes every month and a subscription doesn't cost very much. It's quite small and mostly deals with cake decorating, but every so often they come up with something very good of another sort. I would guess the tutti-frutti recipe also was first printed by them although I was first given a copy by a Sister Rebekah at a Lodge meeting in Juliaetta. Later I was reading a back issue of *Mail Box News* and saw the same recipe in there. Something good gets around the country fast. The better mousetrap theory really works.

Combination Spicing and Brandying—Peel about 4 pounds of peaches. Dissolve 4 pounds of sugar in 3 cups of water. To spice with cloves alone insert 2 whole cloves in each peach. To spice with cinnamon and cloves put 1 tablespoon of stick cinnamon and 1 tablespoon of whole cloves into a spice bag and boil with the syrup. Put in the fruit a little at a time and boil each 5 minutes. When done, remove the fruit to jars and boil the syrup about 10 minutes, or until thick. Pour syrup over the fruit to fill the jar two-thirds full and then finish filling with brandy. Remove the spice bag when the syrup suits your taste test for spiciness.

Rummed Blackberry Juice—Steam 4½ quarts blackberries until the juice starts to flow. Strain in a cheesecloth bag until you get all the juice you can. Add the juice of 3 lemons and 4 oranges to the blackberry juice. Bring to a boil what you have left of the blackberries with 6 cups water, strain again and add that to your juice. Add 2 cups sugar. Now bring juice just to a boil and add 2 cups rum. Can or bottle it. (You could substitute brandy.)

Brandied Cherries—Boil 5 cups sugar with 2 cups water for 12 minutes, or until you have a clear syrup. Pour that syrup over 5 pounds of cherries (the small sour kind) and let stand overnight. Drain the syrup off and boil it again. Add cherries and boil about 5 minutes more. Take out cherries with a skimmer (the kind with holes in it to let the juice drain away) and put the cherries into canning jars. Boil the syrup down 15 minutes more. It should be getting pretty thick. Add 2 cups brandy. Remove from heat. Pour over cherries and seal.

Buried Brandied Peaches—I think the very best brandied fruit of all is made by this recipe. I found it in an antique book and Mike and I tried it out of curiosity. I imagine it would work with any fruit though we used peaches. Peaches brandy best, and after them cherries. This recipe needs *no* brandy. Only fruit and sugar. Choose fine, ripe, very sweet peaches. They must not have bad spots. Peel them. Cover the bottom of something you can bury with whole peaches. Pour in enough sugar to cover them. Add more peaches and then more sugar in the same manner until you are out of peaches or room in your container. Cover very tightly, but not absolutely airtight and bury in the ground for 4 months or more. We put ours about 3 feet down which made the top of it about 2 feet down. Mark the spot so you'll know where to dig it up.

I was really afraid dirt would get into it but not one speck did. We put it down in peach season just outside the backdoor and dug it up for Thanksgiving. Which isn't a full 4 months. The floating top layer, the part that was out of the liquid was spoiled. We threw it away. What was left was a sort of brandied peaches of quality the likes of which I'd never seen before, with the peaches perfectly preserved in color like the day we put them in there.

But it darkened very fast when exposed to air—within 24 hours we could see and taste the difference as it commenced to deteriorate. Apparently the exposure to air was causing the trouble. If I had it to do over I'd reseal it in smaller jars as soon as we dug it up and just open them up as needed, so there would be as little exposure to air before serving as possible. You absolutely must keep any brandied (or spiced) fruit below the liquid and out of the air but this stuff was even affected by the exposure of the liquid to the air.

I think the temperature control also helped make it good. I imagine if you sealed a crock of tutti-frutti and buried it the same way for 3 months it would do as well because the temperature underground is evenly cool but not too cold. Especially early in the season when above ground is hot. Brandied fruit made from scratch needs a cool temperature since you don't have the help of preservatives in store-bought foods.

I managed to get to the doctor and back with Dolly. She has crutches to walk with now and she thinks it's great fun. Can't wait to go to school and show them off. Dolly is my eldest, nine years old. She can change a baby, cook a meal, iron a dress, and coax a two-year-old out of the grumps. A real mother's right hand and a willing worker to do it too. But Mother's right hand is one legged now. Or three with the crutches. . . .

(February 1975—I wrote the above paragraph not knowing the next morning Dolly would be unable to walk on the remaining good leg. Subsequently both arms went bad, then neck and back. It all turned out happily in the end but the end was much longer to be waited for than I had expected.)

DAIRY

GETTING STARTED

(Dedicated to the Discriminating Woman Who Would Rather Own a Cow—Or Goat!)

Marietta, the Shorthorn cow, got mastitis on Christmas Eve. So from then till now (April 4) there was no milking cow. We finally squeezed out enough money and bought a Jersey carrying her third calf, due to calve in August, for $350 from a nearby dairy. She was number 108. I had a notion I'd go out and milk her for the first time and use it for the first paragraph of this chapter. I figured it would really be rapturous and poetical.

Well, it happened that morning I couldn't get out the door without an entourage of Becca, 4, Luke, 2, and Baby Sara, 11 months. And for some reason they were all three in a bad mood and Sara was crying more on than off. We appeared at the barn accompanied by Thor—who not only chases chickens but also thinks he has a mission to impress milk cows with his importance—and by a cast of about 30 chickens (they're not nearly as dumb as people think), who had it all figured in their heads how they were going to share the milk cow's grain. Number 108 apparently had never been in the presence of whining, crying children, or a barking dog, or cackling, crowing, thieving chickens before. She wouldn't go when I tried to chase her and turned out to have a solid distaste for stanchions. Fifteen minutes later I was squatting in the middle of the barn holding crying Sara with one arm, trying to milk with the other, and admonishing the children and the dog by turns to be quiet. The chickens were occupied in the manger eating the cow's grain. At that moment Dolly yelled from the house that I was wanted on the telephone and I thanked God for mercifully giving me a release from my suffering.

When I went back out after the phone call, I had the baby asleep in her crib and the other children happily occupied elsewhere. The chickens had their tummies already full so they went off to look for something more exciting than grain—like a fat bug—and I locked the dog in the house. By the time the milking was over, number 108 had such a feeling for me that she followed me back to the house and walked around it for the next two hours mooing mournfully. The homesteading literature is somewhat slanted toward goats. Goats are small, and they are playful, mischievous and fun. But I've had experience with both cows and goats and let me tell you cows don't jump around but still water runs deep and they sure enough have an emotional life. This morning I was back out milking number 108, now renamed Nelly. I've submitted to her disinclination for stanchions and discovered it a blessing. I finally realized that I couldn't drive her anyplace because her notion is to follow me, and if I get behind her she's just going to stand there. There's always a period of adjustment when a new animal joins your family. A cow has a different mentality from a goat. They're a very, very steady kind of animal. Once the cow gets a notion of how things are supposed to be that's the way she's going to continue and it's unreal for any mere human beings to think they're going to have her doing it a different way. But if you learn to give a little, a cow that cares is really loving and giving in her own way.

So now I gather up the milk bucket. I use a plastic bucket because it's so much quieter—doesn't rattle and ping and startle the animals or me out of our reveries. And I fill a jar or pitcher part way with warm water and put a rag in it and go directly from the house through the gate into the field. Nelly sees me and comes right away. It's not good for milk cows to run. My father drilled that into me—never, never run a milk cow. Nelly used to run when she saw me, but that was when she was new and so nervous. Run to me I mean. And when a 700-pound cow runs to you that's too much love—you'd really rather she'd walk up. So now as soon as she sees me she starts coming, following up to wherever I decide to stop, which will be a flat spot inside the barn or in the field depending on the weather. If I bring grain and the chickens follow, Nelly starts eating the grain along with the chickens. She's used to them now. She has a way bigger mouth than they do so they don't really get away with that much. I take my bucket and go to the rear and start milking.

It's so nice out there in the sunshine. The children are there and the dog is there but Nelly is used to them now. Nelly, being a Jersey, isn't so high off the ground, and I can even sit on the ground to milk. She's very careful not to move around while I'm milking. Instinct tells her she must be still and her whole psychology is such a beautiful mixture of inborn wiseness about how she will take care of me (or a calf) and I will take care of her that it's virtually a spiritual experience being near her. And there she is with her belly hanging low because she's full of calf again. I think any animal that goes through being pregnant, bearing young and then uses her own body to make food, enough food for her baby and mine too, deserves a lot of respect and affection whether it be goat, cow, reindeer or yak. When I started writing this book I had goats. Now I have cows. They're both wonderful.

COWS VERSUS GOATS

A dairy animal is absolutely efficient. Grass, vegetables, grain, water and salt go in at one end. Milk, baby animals (meat) and manure to build up your garden soil come out at various other locations. There is no waste. She can be purchased reasonably, easily moved from location to location, and will love you. Any cow eats much more than a goat and requires hay in quantity in winter, whereas goats can get along on less hay and quite a bit of vegetable food and brush. Cows give more milk per animal by far and their cream can be more easily separated to be made into butter and whipping cream. And plain cream. A milk cow can be bred annually to a beef-type bull in order to have a beefy calf for eventual slaughter. (Incidentally, you can milk sheep, too. They can produce 1½ to 2½ quarts of milk a day, often have inconveniently short tits, and younger ones hate to stand still. But the milk is good tasting and it *can* be done.)

EXPENSES—You can keep about five goats to one milk cow as far as the expense of feeding goes. You won't have near the struggle to keep the cow out of the garden you would with the goat. On the other hand, with goats if one dies you haven't lost every-thing. Around here a super cow could sell for $400. Lesser cows would cost less, but inflation is driving animal prices steadily upwards. A super cow would be one that isn't too old and gives 6 gallons a day. An average cow is $350. That would be one bred and in at least her second lactation. Incidentally, by the time you get a cow or goat home, through the period of adjustment and allow for exaggerations on the part of the man who sold her to you, she'll probably turn out to be giving a little more than half of what he prom-ised. Which is still a lot of milk.

The price of cows through the years has climbed slowly compared to the price of goats. Three years ago around here milking nannies changed hands for $5 a head, when you could get somebody to take one. Kids were generally given away. Then goats became fashionable and within a year and a half a milking nanny of good quality (not pedigreed but well-mannered and giving plenty of milk, I mean) sold for as high as $50. I don't know what they'd sell for today because they aren't changing hands at all. Anybody that has a goat is hanging on for dear life. There is such a demand from people trying to get started in them that there aren't enough goats to go around.

A correspondent from Minnesota who raises regis-tered goats wrote me a couple of years ago that half purebred doe kids sold for $15 and registered kids for $60. She wrote me a month ago that now one-month-old doe kids, registerable, were selling for $150. That's very good for people who are selling goats. But I bought a registered Shorthorn cow, bred, and on her second calf, which is just prime, last fall for less than $400. Actually the cash didn't change hands. We traded hay for her. So I think the relative price of goats is not going to hold up this high when the demand finally catches up with the supply. Since cows generally have one baby at a time but goats have often multiples like two, three or four, it won't be too long until it does catch up. A nearby dairy owner sells newborn dairy-type bull calves for $50, half beef-type bull calves for $90, half beef-type heifer calves for $100, and an all dairy-type heifer calf for $125. A cow grows up to weigh between 700 and 1,500 pounds depending on the breed. A bull can weigh around 3,000 pounds. That's a lot of meat compared to a goat.

One and three titted goats or a two or three titted cow are bargains. A one titted goat is one whose one side never developed normally or that was injured on one side. A good one can give almost as much milk as the regular kind. Same for the cows.

February 1, 1974. Since the bottom dropped out of the beef market in early 1974, calves as well as cows are selling for much lower than I've quoted them. Beef-type bull calves have been selling for under $10, others up to $35. A real good time to invest in some for yourself.

June 21, 1976. Update on prices. Milk cow prices have held fairly steady through the years if the cows were in good health and sold privately. When sold through the livestock auction ring they are affected by the great fluctuations in beef cow prices, sell for per-pound prices, and it can be low. Beef prices are slowly recovering but calf prices are still $20-$25 for a dairy-type calf, way below the $95-$100 you could get before the market peaked and broke.

There is a lot more to all these topics than this and maybe some of the things I say here would be argued with by other people. Whether you have a cow or a milk goat (or goats) is a very individual mat-ter and depends a lot on what kind of land you have, as well as what you have in the way of money to get started, and your personal preferences. Some people get really hot arguing one against the other. I started out with goats because I started out poverty-stricken on 3 acres and had a chance to get the goats at $5 a head. I've had as many as 20 at one time.

If you have a brushy cliff back of your house and just enough flat land for a vegetable garden, I'd say get a goat—it will thrive. If you are planning to home-stead in dense timber where there is no natural open grassy meadow, don't buy a cow. You'd have to buy hay year-round for her because there's not enough grass. Get goats. Their instinctive feeding habits are like deer. They eat twigs by preference rather than grass, anyway, and they'll be delighted with the forest as well as help make a clearing for you. If you have a nice alfalfa pasture and plenty of capital and you'd like to raise baby calves and pigs and lots of chickens, a cow would be very sensible. If you get goats you will end up eating goat meat. If you get a cow you will be raising calves to be beefsteak.

GOAT'S MILK VERSUS COW'S MILK—Like I said I think any animal that shares the fruit of its body with us, be it milk or meat, is wonderful. I think it's disre-spectful to cows to get too prejudiced toward goats. And by the time you're done reading this dairy section you'll see that I love goats, too, just as much as any other confirmed goat lover. Now for the facts. Milk is milk and it's food and that's the important thing.

A poor goat in her first lactation may give only a couple cups a day. A prime milk goat may give as much as 5 quarts a day. A small Jersey cow will give 2 to 4 gallons a day. A big cow will give 4 to 7 gallons a day.

Goat's milk is prehomogenized like the store milk although given enough time some cream will finally rise to the top and you can skim it off with a dipper and have it on something for a real treat. Cow's milk is fun because the cream rises fast and clearly to the top so you just skim it off and there's your whipping cream and cream for butter making and cream to go in a pitcher on the table to use over the strawberries. Some people struggle to make butter from goat's milk. I did, too, and made it. But I think the most sensible thing, if you're going to use goat's milk, is to just plan the menu around whole milk the same way you would if you were living on reconstituted powdered milk and you couldn't afford to buy cream or butter. Only it's so much better because the cream and butter is there—you're eating it—only it's just not separated out so you can see it.

On the farm either goat's milk or cow's milk should be drunk fresh. When you've got it coming every 12 hours there's no reason to use milk over 24 hours old for plain table milk. You can use older milk for baking. Real fresh goat's milk tastes very like cow's milk. It does have the characteristic of developing a strong taste more rapidly after that, but there's no need to drink old goat's milk unless you're trying to get cream to rise to the top of it. In that case you need to let it rest a few days. Don't judge goat's milk from that canned goat's milk. It's pretty awful stuff.

GOATS

I've just read a book that said goats could starve on grass. It's not that simple. Goats need some brush in their diet but they can get along on brush and grass just fine. Vegetables can take the place of brush. But grain can't. They don't do well just on grain and grass.

Goats can eat grain, stock beets, corn fodder, carrot tops, lettuce, nice second cutting alfalfa (they don't care for the coarse stuff), melon rinds—anything from the garden. They like brush, rose bushes and

apple branches, so if you have fruit trees, roses and berry bushes, you'll have to protect them.

Chicken layers' mash will kill goats. It's loaded with methedrine—the same stuff as in "speed" dope. Grain or alfalfa will founder them (or a cow or a horse) if they aren't used to it. In fact, any major sudden change of diet can be rough on your goats. To "founder" means they will get full of gas and die. It's also called "the bloat." So if you are living near somebody's alfalfa field you'll have to have especially good fencing. (See the Animal Doctoring section for more details on this.)

Goats don't need fancy quarters. Just a good dry place to get in out of the rain or snow and they've plenty of sense to know when to go in it—goats or a milk cow, either one. An indoor home with an open door to pasture is perfect and they can choose for themselves where they want to be when. A quick and easy shelter from rain and sun can be made by putting four posts in the ground and roofing them with a sheet of tin and wrapping some around three sides. As for keeping a billy goat in a special little house— some folks do, but I always let mine run with the herd. That way I don't have to worry about trying to tell when the nannies are ready for him.

Words I've heard you shouldn't use are "billy" and "nanny"—you should use "buck" and "doe" instead. Well either is all right with me. I hate to hear a nonpedigreed goat called a "scrub," though, because I think it really puts her down unnecessarily. The country people around here call them billies and nannies and that's good earth talk to me. The word "chevon" means goat intended for meat. A "wether" is a castrated boy goat.

You know the trouble with most of the books I read on how to do things like take care of animals and garden is they make it so hard when it's really not, and they tell you to do all kinds of things you don't need to do and buy all kinds of things you don't need to buy. Like dehorning. I always just let my goats that were going to grow horns go ahead and grow them. Horns don't bother me a bit. Neither do testicles on a boy goat so we don't have to castrate. It's bad enough having to butcher them without going through all that other stuff too.

HOW MANY GOATS?—Let me deal in conservative figures in case your goats turn out to be average or worse. Such a goat gives about 3 quarts a day. You'll need a quart a day to feed her kid, more later, leaving only 1½ quarts or so for your family. Yearlings won't give even that much. You can tell yearlings because they aren't as large as full-grown goats, and their teats and bags are smaller. At one time I milked two mature nans and two yearlings. I got about 1½ gallons a day and that barely supplied the two nan kids that I was feeding plus our four children, me and Pa. Now I'm milking seven goats and that includes some really good ones. I get about 6 gallons a day. With this supply I always have plenty for the family, make butter and cheese, and am raising two pigs. You really can't have too many nan goats. You can get them to adopt a calf or a bum lamb or let them raise their own kids for meat or market crop, if you don't want to bother milking them. If you feed a milk goat really well, including vegetables and grain, she'll give more milk and can be milked for as long as two years on one freshening.

BREEDS—Among the goat breeds that I've had experience with Toggenburgs far and away impressed me the most. Mine were persnickety aristocrats. It was an old Toggenburg that usually bossed the herd. Toggenburgs had very definite notions as to how I ought to handle them and were more independent than the rest but, wow, did they ever give the milk. They were also in the front line when it came to fighting coyotes. The Toggenburgs always got the most blood on their horns. French Alpines were also very good milk producers for me. Saanens I found stood out for their dispositions. They are the people-lovingest goats, for somebody who needs their goat to really love them as well as give milk, Saanen would be the thing. I've seen enough of Nubians and La Manchas to love and respect them, too. Nubians are African bred and withstand heat well.

I don't think there are significant differences in the milk composition itself. Experts go on a lot about percentage differences in butterfat between various varieties of goat, but it really isn't a perceptible difference to you who are milking and cooking with the milk.

Still, you're going to want to know what kind of goat you've got. Here's a process of elimination. A goat with very long whitish hair that sheds in the spring is an Angora. Not one of the recognized dairy goat breeds, but they've been milked. On the wild side but they've been tamed. The hair is called mohair and spins, dyes and weaves very well. An adult goat that never gets more than 20 inches high is a Pygmy. They can be milked, are uncommon, and the best source of further information about them is to write the National Pygmy Goat Association, Route 2, Box 62, Monmouth, Oregon 97361. If it's not Angora or Pygmy check the ears. Long and drooping ears mean a Nubian. No ears means a La Mancha. Erect ears mean it's either a Toggenburg, Saanen or French Alpine. Saanens are always pure white. Toggenburgs are always some shade of brown with white markings on the face and rump. Alpines come in a variety of colors and patterns. Or you could have a cross between any two or more of the above breeds.

SOME QUESTIONS TO ASK BEFORE YOU BUY A GOAT—How old is she? Is she bred? To what kind of goat? When will she freshen? How many times has she kidded before? How many kids? (They can have anywhere from one to four. I have a goat who has three every time.) Or how long has she been milking? What is it like to milk her? (Try it yourself, if possible.) How much milk does she give? How many teats does she have? Does she jump fences? Is she hard to catch? Does she bite or butt other goats? Will she lead? Has she had a distemper shot? What breed or combination is she? Are there tumors or abscesses in her udder? (If there are you can feel them as large, very hard areas.) Goats frequently have benign tumors that don't seem to do any harm. However, an abscess is a red tender swelling of the entire side. You can't milk that. You'll have to dry her up and

she'll have a tendency to abscess again next time around. That's called "mastitis." (More on it in the Animal Doctoring section.)

When you buy a goat find out how they get it places. Do they lead her with a rope or shake a can of grain in front of her nose? This information immediately becomes very important. It's nicest if they are broken to lead. All my new or naughty goats wear collars with a short rope attached. It makes it easier to grab them and get them started leading. I don't like the grain-can bit because with a big herd and some calves and horses in there too, I'm liable to get trampled. But for just a few goats it's a good technique to train them to follow as you walk along holding the can and occasionally shaking it so they can hear the scrumptious noise. Stop and give them just a bite before they start or whenever they look like they're losing faith in you and the can. Or you can grab the horns and just drag them along with somebody behind to push. A place where horns are useful but a desperation measure. Or you can carry them—another desperation measure.

GETTING HER BRED—Do you want to get a billy of your own? If you don't have your own you can probably take your nan to someone who does when she needs him. However, if you don't have access to a billy you'll have to get your own. They are unpopular inside city limits and in crowded neighborhoods because a mature billy goat has a tremendously strong odor. Every time you handle him you'll walk away with a tremendously strong odor too. If they aren't always handled carefully and gently, they will develop some very bad butting habits. If horned, they can be quite dangerous to small children, since a point of one of those horns could come up and get an eye. I've rescued my two-year-old from being butted against the chicken house wall after a friend played at "wrestling" with our billy and awakened his butting instinct. I had to get rid of the billy. Unfortunately, no matter how careful you are sooner or later billies will get that instinct awakened.

Don't count on artificial insemination. It is more a cattle procedure than a goat one. If you can correctly tell when your doe is wanting the buck you can take her and bring her back the same day and the thing will be accomplished. Some goat owners with registered herds charge a lot of money for their buck's service. A friendly neighbor may let you use his buck for a few dollars. If the price is too high, then that's a good reason to keep your own buck. Buy a young one cheap in the spring. He'll be able to do the job by fall breeding time.

GOAT FACTS OF LIFE—Goats are in their prime generally from 3 to 6 years of age. It is best to breed young does from 15 to 18 months old, or *at least* 10 months old. Too early breeding will stunt growth and cause dead babies and poor milk production. They come into heat from September to January for 1 to 2 days and the period in between heats is 17 to 21 days. They make their condition known by uneasiness and constant wagging of the tail. Gestation period ranges from 146 to 152 days (about 5 months). The usual number of kids for a mature doe is two—or one—or even three or four. Keep records on your does. They will tend to repeat themselves.

RUNAWAY GOATS—The biggest problem with any goats, billies or nans, is controlling them. They can jump over, crawl through, or squeeze between—and they can do terrible damage terribly fast if they get where they don't belong. Goats need companionship to be happy. But it doesn't have to be another goat. A sheep, a cow, or your children can serve the purpose. Poultry can't, though. A chicken just does not have *it* except to another bird. But companionship alone won't keep goats where they belong.

JUMPING GOATS—If a goat knows it can and wants to, it can jump over a 5-foot, or even a 6-foot, fence. If I get a goat that has a bad jumping habit I sell it on to somebody who has the kind of situation where they have to picket a goat anyway. To picket the goat put on a collar or halter and attach a light link chain. The chain is attached to a metal stake that you can drive into the ground with a mallet where you want her to browse. Or use a "stay." That's an old tire or a heavy piece of iron instead of a stake. You can move the stay occasionally without the trouble of pounding in the stake. None of my goats have

to be picketed because we have plenty of room here. I do sometimes use a yoke though. If a young goat starts going through or over fences Mike finds a forked tree branch shaped like a "Y." The goat's neck goes into the "V" and the ends of the stick are tied above its neck with leather or something. It can't squeeze through fence holes anymore and jumping isn't convenient either. If a goat grows up thinking it can't do those things it will give up trying. After six weeks you can take off the yoke and it won't be a problem again. If it should happen again just put the yoke on as a reminder. That's how you raise goats that don't test your fences.

Wrap the trunks of fruit trees with chicken wire 6 feet high. That keeps them from eating the bark. If the goats are sticking their heads through and getting stuff they shouldn't, fence with chicken wire. Keep them well fed so the garden won't look so tempting.

How do you deal with a goat that jumped the fence and is happily eating your neighbor's roses and doesn't want to be caught?

1. Try the grain-shaken-in-a-can bit. Turn the grain so he can see it.
2. If he's leery, walk past him with the grain completely ignoring him. Go pick up some curious object beyond him and examine it. Then put down the object and walk back past the goat carefully ignoring it. Whistle if you can. The goat will be overcome with curiosity and follow you. Slow down. At a point of closest intersection dive for legs or horns, whichever you think you can have a better chance with. I love horned goats because in desperation I can usually catch them there. Then yell for help.
3. If that doesn't work, rope him and put him up for sale.
4. If you can't rope him, shoot him and make goat sausage.

THE BUTTING ORDER—Goats are rough on each other. They occasionally even bite each other. A big goat with big horns will bully a new goat, especially a small one, and keep it away from the food. If you're planning to have just two goats and have small quarters for them to live and eat in, it would make sense to get two goats that are dehorned or naturally hornless. And make that either two yearlings or two adults while you're at it. There are exceptions, though. I had a yearling once that was so mean to the big goats I had to sell her. But generally once a herd gets established and used to each other they live together fairly peaceably. I mean by that any combination of goats given time will become pals. A boss goat always emerges, too, usually a big, older nanny. She will lead the herd out to feed in the morning and back home at night. But they aren't necessarily charitable to the weak so if a goat seems hurt or sick put it in a pen by itself with water, straw or hay bedding and good food. The other goats probably wouldn't let the sick one get its share of food and might persecute it to boot.

FOR MORE INFORMATION ON GOATS—Subscribe to the *Dairy Goat Journal*, P.O. Box 1908, Scottsdale, Arizona 85252 ($7 a year). Buy a copy of *Raising Milk*

Goats the Modern Way by Jerry Belanger, published by Garden Way Publishing Co., Charlotte, Vermont. Another *very fine* source is *The Best of Capri*, selections from newsletters of the Illinois Dairy Goat Association, edited by Jerry Belanger, Judith Kapture and Elsie Evelsizer and published by *Countryside* magazine, Waterloo, Wisconsin 53594.

COWS

BREEDS—A Holstein cow is a big, lean black-and-white animal that gives up to 6 gallons a day of low cream-content milk. A Guernsey is yellow and white and a Brown Swiss is tan colored. A Jersey is an animal that gives about 3 or 4 gallons a day of comparatively high-cream content milk. The Jersey costs less to keep because it is smaller and eats less, but it gives less milk. Jerseys and Shorthorns have the reputation of easiest calving. Jerseys and Guernseys, Brown Swiss and Holsteins are the gentlest and friendliest breeds I've known. Not all beef breed cows are to be milked by ordinary mortals. Angus, for example, are very excitable animals. You'd never be able to catch one to milk her. And yet somebody somewhere has made a milk cow at some time out of every beef breed there is.

Shorthorns are volume milk producers, but in my experience have more disease problems, especially pinkeye, than the average. Pure white Shorthorn heifers sometimes have an inherited defect that prevents them from conceiving. Irish Dexters are the smallest dairy breed—both in size and numbers—in the U.S. Like the Shorthorn white heifers, they too may carry a defective gene. In the case of Irish Dexters it means a stillborn "bulldog" calf for their fourth or fifth calf. Ayrshire is another fine basic dairy breed. There are literally several hundred cow breeds worldwide and at least 35 *common* ones—including both dairy and beef—in the United States.

In choosing a family milk cow, it's the total volume of milk and cream together you'll get and the amount you'll have to feed the cow—hence the upkeep cost—that really matters. Jerseys are half the size of Devons and so they eat half as much. A Jersey in her prime will give 4 gallons a day, and there aren't many families that that isn't enough for. Guernsey is the next biggest breed after Jersey. They have a reputation of being very docile and manageable but so are Jerseys. Milking Shorthorns, Brown Swiss and Holsteins are next up in size. Milking Shorthorns and Brown Swiss are two of the dual-purpose breeds, stocky builds for meaty calves, but easy calving and good milk production which are dairy characteristics. Holsteins are big, bony, and pure dairy types. All the big cows give lots of milk, up to 6 gallons per day and sometimes more on champion ones. Red Poll and Devon cows are also dual-purpose breeds. They are exotics and the biggest I'm going to mention. To a certain extent your cow will be priced by the pound and that makes the larger breeds more expensive. Rare breeds are highest priced of all.

TO GET A COW you could watch the ads or advertise for a "family milk cow." Don't buy a milk cow at a livestock auction if you can help it. If you have a chance to ask questions here are some things you want to find out: What breed is she? How old is she? How many seasons has she been milked? How many calves did she have—twins? Any delivery complications? Is she milking now? How long has she been milking? Or when will she come fresh (give birth)? How much money do you want for her? How much milk does she give? (Or did she give last year?) Any health problems with her? Or behavior problems? Is she breechy? (That means does she go through fences?)

A cow can be milked until she is 10 to 12 years old. After that age you may find it impossible to get her bred again. So a 4-year-old cow is a fine buy. A "heifer" means a cow that hasn't yet had a second calf. They sell cheaper but they are unaccustomed to the calving and milking routine—which may be a problem if you are too. They may have trouble calving their first calves and cows, like goats, only give half as much milk the first year they are fresh as they will later on. If a cow is going to have trouble calving it will be her first one she'll have trouble with. Charolais cows tend to have trouble with their first calves because their calves are so big. Brown Swiss do too. A farmer nearby who raises them loses about one in five calves born to his Charolais heifers. (A way to avoid this calving difficulty is to breed to a bull of a *small dairy* breed like Jersey or to a bull of a *small beef* breed like Black Angus which was deliberately selected for small calves—hence easy calvings.)

If you are just shopping for a calf to raise for meat, a male calf of a dairy breed is your best buy. Jersey bull calves are especially cheap because Jersey fat is yellow. On the market this is confused with old bull fat so feeders won't touch them. But for homestead use they make fine meat. When you buy a dairy-type animal you're buying a greater percentage of bone but the lower price will compensate for it.

COW BODIES AND COW PSYCHOLOGY—A cow has 360-degree panoramic vision. That means she can put her hind foot into the bucket or kick it over on you and it's *not* a lucky accident for her. Cows can't see color. Everything is black and white to them, so it doesn't matter what you wear. They *are* very sensitive to stark black-white contrasts and have poor depth perception. White lines painted across a road can look like a cattle guard to them. It's hard for a cow to tell the difference between a shadow and a hole in the ground. She doesn't like glaring light bulbs very much. A cow's best sense is her smelling. She can smell her calf 3 or 4 miles away. She has good hearing, too. Hold down on the yelling. She was designed to eat with her head down. If your feed trough isn't low enough, her saliva won't run good. Cattle herds will form smaller subherds with an order of dominance in each group. So there will be a boss cow same as your boss goat. Unlike goats cows have long tails with hair on the end of them.

COW FACTS OF LIFE—Don't let a heifer get bred as soon as she is capable of it or you will have a cow stunted for life, always a poor milk producer. They can conceive as young as 3 months. Don't let them conceive until at least 13 months old.

COW FEED—Mainly grass or hay. Any kind of grain is a good protein supplement. A cow needs two kinds of food in her diet to be healthy: roughage, which can be supplied by any kinds of grass, even straw, and protein. Alfalfa hay has both. Straw is high roughage, low protein. You would have to supplement straw with grain or good alfalfa hay which is a high protein hay. Straight grain isn't a good feed because there's not enough roughage. Cows can use silage, cabbage, turnips, beet pulp, squash, pumpkins and so on as part of their feed, too. If you can supply your cow good green leafy alfalfa hay almost any mixture of homegrown grains will be a fine protein supplement. There are people who will tell you you must feed a commercial dairy ration. It's true it may contain items that boost production a little. But not enough to justify your loss of the knowledge and capacity for independence in my opinion. Heifers on their first calf need extra grain because they are still growing. You can also feed cows grasses, pasture legumes, corn, sorghum, milo, kafir, soybeans, peas, oats, barley, and other greens, grains and suchlike.

THE REALITIES
(For the Very Uninitiated)

You can't just buy an animal, walk out to the field and milk it. Milk comes from female animals (mammals) that have recently given birth and have either been previously milked cr been nursed by their young or the young of some other species. (You can put bum lambs or a calf on a goat.) So to have a milking cow there has to have been a bull in her life about 285 days ago and likewise with a goat (5 months ago). Even if you buy an animal that is already "fresh" (milking), time is going to run out on you. You can't just keep milking her forever. She will gradually dry up. You have to again give the cow access to the bull or the artificial inseminator at a time when she is receptive (in heat).

Then she has a gestation (pregnancy) of 9 months, calves, and comes fresh (gives milk). Your cow is milking again but you also have a hungry calf. A cow usually has plenty of milk for everybody, though if it's her first calf she won't be giving as much as she will after subsequent calvings. You can separate the calf from the cow, do all the milking yourself and feed the calf its share out of a pan, then turn the cow in with the calf until your family runs out of milk again. Or you can keep the calf shut away from the cow all night, milk in the morning and then let them run together the rest of the day—meaning there will be no evening milking for you.

A milk cow can very neatly be put on an annual schedule. Gestation is 285 days. Dry her up 6 weeks before she is due to calve. That way you are only milkless 6 weeks of the year. The second time she comes into season after calving put her with the bull. It probably won't take. Put her with the bull again the next month and that probably will settle her or better yet just let her and the bull run together that month. That way she will be due to calve again at the same time next year and you can get one calf a year from her plus all that milk.

If you don't dry up your cow that last 6 weeks it's rather hard on her and the milk may get "strong" tasting. The rest of the time you'll have more milk than at first you know what to do with. You can use the extra milk in new recipes and I've collected all I could here.

Or use it to raise the calf and young pigs for your meat supply and to feed the hens. You can make cheese and feed the pigs and chickens the whey that is left from cheesemaking.

If you are milking goats and have yearlings, or a poor milker, or they all have triplets you don't have much choice—you're going to have to kill some kids to insure your family milk supply or else find homes for them elsewhere. You can't afford to buy milk for them. They are only worth a few dollars, if you can find somebody to take them. They aren't as important as having milk for your own children. If you try to raise them on that cheap milk substitute they'll be scouring and sick most of the time and you'll spend whatever you saved on kaopectate and antibiotics trying to help them hang on. Goat babies don't do well on anything but goat's milk.

I try never to kill a nan kid because it is a waste, but when I have more billy kids than I have extra milk for, and nobody wants them, I kill them. This is hard to talk about and hard to do, but I'm going to tell you how because I'm writing this book for real people trying to do real things in real difficult situations and sometime you may need to know this. If I'm going to maybe kill the kid I get there as soon after birth as possible. I check for sex. Then I take the little billy out of earshot of the mother and get a hammer. I hit it as hard as I can on the head with a hammer. That blow probably suffices. The newborns don't have much stamina, but I hit it a couple more times to make sure. Better have it quick, certain, and complete if it has to be done.

If you do have extra milk, then by all means raise your extra billy goats for meat. If you don't have a market for them—and the market can stand only so many billy goats unless you're selling them at $5 a head for meat (which has been done around here) you might as well eat them yourself. Since goats typically have two or three or even four kids at a time, and they can even kid twice a year, you have extras pretty fast once you get started. Male kids and bull calves are supposed to be castrated to make for better meat and gentler handling. This is done by cutting off the testicles with a knife or putting a tight rubber band around the place where the testicles connect to the body. But we really don't believe that it improves the meat any and on young animals, well brought up, I don't think it makes much difference to their handling so we don't castrate.

The animals can be butchered when big enough to suit you. Even a kid 6 weeks old will add 15 pounds of meat to your supply. But the longer you wait the more meat you'll get—up to a point. Calves keep growing until they are about 2 years old and the same with goats. Cull nans are also used for meat. Those are nans that can't be bred, or don't give enough milk to bother, or can't be milked or can't be controlled. Calves are never killed like kids. Even a newborn calf is worth at least $75.

SOME DEFINITIONS

freshen—to give birth to a kid or calf and have her milk come in

spring—the lips of the vulva swell, a sure sign that the birthing is coming

to kid—to give birth, of a goat

to calve—to give birth to a calf, of a cow

heifer—a female cow before her second calving

bull—a mature uncastrated male cow

steer—castrated male cow, raised for beef or draft service

calf—any cow, sometimes used until they are nearly 1½ years old

in season—when the female is ovulating and will stand still to receive the male and get bred

in heat—same as "in season"

gestation—pregnancy

service—breeding, "to service" an animal means to breed her, get her pregnant

artificial insemination—when a cow is bred with a metal tube inserted while she's in a chute and given bull semen when you can't manage or don't want to provide a bull

sire—a bull

dam—a mother cow

udder—her "breast" milk bag

BODY TEMPERATURE—The normal average temperature of a goat is 103.8°, but it can range from 101.7° to 105.3° without meaning that anything is wrong. This is rectal temperature. The normal average rectal temperature of a dairy cow is 101.5°, but it can range from 100.4° to 102.8° normally. Incidentally, the normal body temperature of a chicken in the day-

time is 107°. You must buy a special veterinary thermometer to take these.

HEAT PERIODS—A cow comes into heat from 8 to 30 hours, on the average about 16 hours. Usually her heat period is every 21 days, but individual animals can have a cycle as short as 18 days or as long as 24. Her first heat period after giving birth will be in 30 to 60 days. You can tell she's in heat by her restlessness and she'll be doing a lot of bawling. If you have other cows (even females), they'll be riding her in the manner of a bull. If she lays down any time in the latter part of her heat period she'll go out of heat. If a normally peaceable heifer goes through your fence it probably also means she's in heat. If the neighbor's bull comes through your fence and breeds her that's an absolute proof.

I've read in the authorities where a goat is supposed to be in season 2 to 3 days but mine only stay in for a day. They come in about every 21 days, too. You can tell when a nanny is in heat because she bleats all day long, runs up and down the fence looking longingly out and wiggles her tail provocatively. She is spotting blood if you look closely, and the labia of the vagina are swelled up and red looking. Because goats and cows are only in for a day you have to notice them fast and get them bred fast. A bull or billy goat is always ready. All you have to do is put them together and he does the rest. A half hour should do it.

Young goats may vary about when they come into heat the first time, but older ones that have birthed in the spring won't come into season again until fall. In that case, the first chill frosts of September will bring it on. Don't bother looking for heat signs in summer unless the goat went through the fall and winter without a chance to conceive. I've known goats that were running with the billy to conceive in midsummer. Goats naturally get bred between September and November but there are exceptions. I had a goat that didn't conceive then and by the following summer still hadn't kidded. I was just about to consign her to the meat supply when she began to make bag and bulge as if pregnant and in August she kidded.

A female goat has her first heat at about 6 months and can get bred then if you have her running with a billy. If you let her get bred then rather than when she is 11 months old you'll have an emaciated little goat half the size of a full-grown goat, whose single kid may or may not live and who will lovingly give you her all of about a quart of milk a day (a full-grown milker gives around 3 or 4) as she gets more and more rundown looking. So try to let her get bigger before she gets bred. If you do find yourself with a child bride give her extra good care, lots of grain and Tender Loving Care. Milk her long enough to teach her the routine and develop her teats and bag some. Then let her run with her kids or dry her up.

Some other animals: a mare (female horse) stays in heat for 2 to 11 days, usually around 6, and comes in about every 22 days. She will be in heat again in from 3 to 15 days after giving birth to a colt. A sow comes in heat again in from 1 to 8 weeks after pigging (which means to have a litter of babies). A ewe (female sheep) comes in heat for about 35 hours every 16 days. A lady dog will stay in heat for 9 days, more or less, and a cat can stay in even longer. After a large animal is bred and out of heat she is said to be "settled." She won't feel that good again for a long time.

PERIODS OF PREGNANCY (GESTATION PERIODS)— These vary somewhat but in general a cow will calve 285 days from her date of service, a goat will kid 151 days after, a mare will foal 336 to 340 days after, a sow will pig 112 to 113 days after, a ewe will lamb 150 to 152 days after breeding, a dog has her litter in 60 days and a cat in 64. In other words a mare bred on September 4 would be due to foal on August 7 the next year. A sow bred on September 4 would be due to pig on the 25th of December. All those days confuse me so I just figure that a cow takes 9 months and a goat takes 5 months and then watch for them to spring.

KIDDING—When the lips of the vulva swell up and the opening becomes longer and larger the nanny is springing and delivery is nearing but not imminent. When hollows appear under the tail above and to the left and right of her vagina, delivery will take place within two hours. The kid will come out first. She almost certainly won't need any help from you. The afterbirth follows. It may take a long time to finish coming out. Leave it alone. I know how miserable it is when the doctor gets in a rush about afterbirth. It will come out in time. Or pull just a little if you must, but if it makes her bleed quit for sure. When she gets done she may or may not eat it. If she does it's recycling. If she doesn't—well, after all she's not a meat eater by nature.

A drink of warm water with some blackstrap molasses in it is a help to a goat that is kidding. She may drink as much as a gallon. If she seems chilled and seems to be having difficulty expelling the afterbirth the drink of warm water also helps. When you know a goat is near kidding check on her every morning. If she doesn't show up, go find her.

There is no reason for you to think you have got to get there and tie the cord. My advice would be in fact don't. Leave that part of it up to nature. You

probably won't find the babies until after nature has taken care of that part, anyway.

Your important role with goats that are running free in the open, and this is important, is to discover the mother with her kids as soon after kidding as possible. Kids are usually born in the early morning hours. Goats in my experience aren't super picky about where they have their kids. If she kidded in cold weather out in the open, the kids will die if you don't help them. Just pick up those little babies in your arms, if you find them chilled and weak or prostrate-looking, and carry them into the house. Keep them wrapped in warm covers and near a source of heat.

Now go back out and move the mother goat into a good sheltered place like inside a shed or barn. If your facilities are very limited you can even provide a large-sized doghouse and it will work. Have a dry cover on the floor, such as straw, hay or sawdust. Give her some grain and milk her. If you haven't milked her or handled her much before, you'll find birthing has made her completely gentle and she'll cooperate fine with you.

Take the milk to the house, put some into a small pop bottle, using a lamb nipple on the end of it, and feed it to the baby. Just get the nipple in its mouth and it'll get the idea. Never feed cold milk. After a few feedings and a real good warming that baby goat will be fine and can go back out to the barn to live. Or if it still seems to be doing poorly, you could keep it in the house until you feel sure it's strong. If the kid is too weak even to nurse the long, soft lamb nipple, you can feed it with an infant syringe, available at drugstores (the rubber bulb you use to clean newborn baby's snotty nose) or a spoon.

Baby lambs are treated exactly the same way. Don't use a baby bottle with them. It's the wrong style nipple. You should have your calf nipple on hand well before the birthing because it's terribly important to get that first good nourishment into a chilled newborn animal. You'll be amazed at the change that takes place. I've found kid goats that looked almost dead but after they were warmed up and had a meal in their tummy, they stood up, bleated, wagged their tail and within two hours and another meal they were

just fine. Same thing with lambs. A good way to avoid this problem is to confine the mother in a good birthing place when you see she's that close, but you don't always know for sure.

If you don't know a place in your vicinity to buy a lamb nipple (or calf bottle or calf feeder) you can mail-order from United Pharmacal Company, 306 Cherokee Street, St. Joseph, Missouri 64504. Lamb nipples (that also work for baby goats and pigs) are 20 cents each—a dozen for $2 last I heard. A plastic calf bottle with nipple and rack is $3.50. They also carry animal antibiotics, grooming equipment and so on. A catalog is available on request.

CALVING—The same principles apply. Prevention is the best cure. A heifer that hasn't had a calf before, or for safety's sake, that hasn't had *two*, shouldn't be bred to a bull of a larger breed than her own. Goat breeds are generally the same size and though I've seen declarations to the contrary the fact is that you can breed a goat of any one breed to a goat of any other breed and the results will be goat and will be fine. But cow breeds vary so much in size. An unbred Jersey cow might weigh 600 pounds or even less before her first calving. On the other hand a Devon cow could weigh 1,600 pounds. So you see you wouldn't want to breed your Jersey heifer to a Devon bull because the resulting calf would probably be so big she couldn't bear it naturally. Breed her to a Jersey bull the first couple of times. Then you could try something bigger. Shorthorn is fine for a middle course because although the Shorthorn cow weighs about 1,200 pounds or even 1,500 on some of the Australian Illawarrs exotics, the calf is not large. The dairy breeds of cows all calve easily anyway, as they are selected for that. It's some of the smallest and largest beef breeds that have the reputation of calving difficulty.

Ordinarily your cow will calve and be standing there nuzzling her baby and you won't have to do a thing except provide the usual necessities of food, water and shelter. She may very likely calve in the open. That isn't near the problem it can be with goats and sheep because calves generally are hardier at birth. If your cow is obviously in trouble the first thing I'd do is ask an experienced neighbor for advice if you live in the country. Most experienced farmers can help you judge what is happening very competently. If need be you'll load her up in your truck and take her to the vet. A cow is worth a lot of money and well worth what you'd pay the vet to get her fixed up. And then you have the value of the calf, too.

WEANING CALVES—You can take a calf from the mother anytime from birth on. If you take the calf away immediately, you get it without prejudices about how it should eat and without too much energy to fight your ministrations. If you wait 2 or 3 days, however, it has been well started by the mother although the mother's milk production in the long run may benefit more if you take the calf off her immediately and milk her out twice a day.

You feed the calf the first milk you get from the mother, but do not use it yourself since it is at first brownish and later yellowish colostrum milk. Some people say wait 10 days but I usually start sooner when the colostrum taste is completely out because it seems like I always need the milk. The colostrum milk is *fine* for pigs and chickens as well as the calf so you don't need to throw any away.

How much milk should a calf have? A quart or so to start with, then work up to 2 quarts a day at 2 weeks, then 3 quarts a day at 3 weeks. Depends also on what it will take. You can give more of the cow's milk than of fake milk or goat's milk. Calves of different breeds, hence different weights, will take relatively more or less. The older the calf, the more it will take. Too much causes scours. A big calf would happily drink much more milk than is ordinarily given it. We force the calf to share his milk with us because we need it too.

When calves are raised to set records for weight gain and final size—registered championship-type animals—they are usually left on the mother because the plain fact is that given all the milk they desire on a demand schedule, as they are with the mother, they gain faster and end up being bigger and better looking than they do on the bucket. But they get along with the bucket and our children have milk, too, and within a few months they will be eating grass or hay or grain. You can kind of watch to see when they start taking other kinds of feed. You can wean a calf from milk completely at a surprisingly young age and it will survive but it will be stunted.

DEHORNING—I don't dehorn goats. I think a fine set of horns is a glorious sight and furthermore in our situation the goats need their horns for self-defense. With horns, goats have more capacity to protect themselves from predators on our property. We've had the goats come home with blood on their horns and spots of blood on their heads but no goats missing. That's absolute proof that the predators got the worst of it! Mike says when goats are attacked by coyotes they get in a circle with the kids in the middle and their horns facing outside.

However, we have lost newborn kids to predators. So I would advise that if you're near the woods, keep a goat about to kid near the buildings until she has kidded and her kids are able to run as fast as the rest of the herd—they'll develop jumping and running abilities very fast. Predators seldom come in where the man smell is heavy.

But if you are wanting "show" goats that can win county fair prizes they must be dehorned. Or if your goats will be playing with small children, especially in the case of a billy that you intend to keep on into adulthood you might want to do it. My children never have been hurt by a goat but I've been lucky. An easy alternative to dehorning in this case might be to buy "muley" goats that are naturally hornless. (Naturally hornless cows are called "polled" and a lot of the breeds have polled strains.)

If you're going to dehorn it's much, much better to do the job on the kid when it's 3 days old than later on when the horns are big. On a baby goat you can dehorn using a caustic paste or by a burning treatment. Goats with horns that have already started to grow out are dehorned by nipping. A baby muley goat has straight hair around its horn buttons. Don't do anything. A baby that is going to grow horns will have curly hair there.

The burning way—You can buy a special tool for this or use any make-do iron rod as long as the base is about the size of a nickel. You heat the make-do rod in a fire, branding-iron style, until it is *really* hot. Then press the hot end to the horn button. You have to have a tremendous solid hold on the kid so it can't wiggle. It only takes about 15 seconds.

Caustic comes in sticks or as a paste. The sticks are easier to use. Caustic is a problem either way because it eats indiscriminately wherever it lands. A kid goat with caustic on can't be out in the rain because if the caustic runs into its eyes it could go blind. If you're going to use caustic you also have to start on a very young goat, like 3 days old, before the horn has started to grow out. And you've got to do it *right* or what you end up with is ugly deformed horns, but horns anyway. Do this:

1. Trim hair off from around horn buttons.
2. Put vaseline around the area of the horn button. (If you stick adhesive on the button itself it won't get vaseline on it while you're doing this.)
3. Put the caustic on the button. Don't get it on your skin either. It really eats.
4. You're going to have to figure out something for the next little while so the goat doesn't spread that stuff around. You could have somebody sit and hold it for a half hour or put it in a very confining cage.
5. You've got to go through this every day until you're sure you've won. If the horns get ahead of the paste, forget it. It's no use. Go on to the next method.

Nipping—You can get dehorning nippers that cost between $3 and $5. Get some "Blood Stop" from the vet, too. It's a purple powder. You shake the powder on the horn right where you have cut and it will seal it in a hurry. (Incidentally, regular pruning nippers won't work.)

Young horns can be gotten with nippers. Make sure the edge of the nippers is almost even with the skull. The animal will struggle, screaming, and will bleed. Have help to sit on it while you're nipping. Put the nippers carefully where you want them and then do it quickly and firmly. Then shake the powder on. The hole in the horn goes right down to the nostrils. You can look down there and see them breathe. But the Blood Stop seals it up in a hurry.

Big, old horns have to be taken off by sawing with a meat saw. It's a hard job. You need at least three men. Two sitting on the goat and one sawing. They bleed like the dickens but the Blood Stop will help. If you have a goat who is making himself dangerous with his horns this treatment will gentle him down.

CASTRATING is something we don't do with sheep or pigs or goats. There truly is no need to do it because the males are butchered before they get big enough to be a problem. But with calves there are two real arguments in favor of it. One is that a bull calf is ready to breed well before he is ready to

butcher. Cows are very strong and can go through fences if they want to bad enough. If you have a Jersey bull calf and your neighbor has registered Herefords and your bull calf goes through the fence and breeds some of his cows he is going to be just furious.

The other problem is that bull calves grow sufficiently big that they can become dangerous before the age of butchering. Nature meant the bull to protect the herd from predators and it has very reckless, aggressive instincts. It's supposed to be willing to risk itself on the slightest provocation. But that can really backfire in a homestead situation. I got a letter only a couple of weeks ago from a friend homesteading in Mexico whose eight-year-old boy was run down by a Charolais bull that escaped from his pen. The boy's leg was broken and they are lucky nothing worse happened.

Bulls with horns are even more dangerous. It's no joke when your bull calves are in the alfalfa and you are trying to chase them out before they bloat themselves to death. The next thing you know they are taking the whole thing wrong and have decided to charge you—which they can do even though you've bottle or bucket fed them from a day old up.

This is laying out for you the grim reality so you won't be too horrified by what follows. Don't think that because milk cows are so gentle, milk-breed bulls will also be gentle. In fact it is just the opposite. For some reason the worst bulls of all for disposition are those of the dairy breeds.

There are several different ways to castrate. For the first time it would be a good idea to have somebody who has done it before help you, but if there isn't anybody like that I'll give you the best directions I can. The traditional way but also the most traumatic is with the knife. On big ranches the calves get cut, branded, and have their shots all at once when they are moved. The February calves go to spring pasture in April (more or less depending on where you live) and that's when they are handled. The fall calves are done when the animals are brought back to their winter feeding place. So the typical age is 6 to 8 weeks on a calf.

It is important to do the castrating after the animal is well-established but before it is too old. Don't castrate too late. I've heard of people who had five or six big yearling calves bleed to death because they were too old when it was done. A year is way too old.

Castrating with a knife—You have to throw the animal, of course, and tie its legs and have plenty of help with sitting on it to hold it still. Slit the scrotum right down the middle belly line. There are about three layers of tissue, one of which is pretty hard to get through. Have your knife razor sharp. Put your hand now around the outside of the scrotum so you squeeze the testicles clear out. There's a cord attached to each one. You cut that away and it's done. Have the gear ready to give a shot of Combiotic or some other animal antibiotic. Some Blood Stop helps, too.

Now if you think that's awful let me tell you something absolutely true. The old-time Rocky Mountain sheepherders used to cut the string by biting it with their teeth. They'd spit the round balls out into a bucket and have them next morning for breakfast with eggs. In country talk they are called Rocky Mountain oysters. To cook them you just bread and fry like oysters. Store in the deep freeze like any other meat while you're working up your nerve.

Using an emasculator—This is one you buy from a veterinary or vet supply house. It's probably a better method for a beginner. Maybe better all around. In this case, it's an instrument that puts a tough rubber band around the base of the scrotum where it joins the abdomen. Eventually it drops off for lack of blood. Use this on a bull calf when it's about 1 week old. *Don't wait.* I recommend you buy one from a vet and ask his advice on using it. Watch for infection.

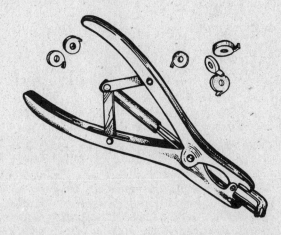

Docking tool—This is sold by Sears, Montgomery Ward, Ranchrite and so on. It's a combination dehorning and castrating tool. It's the quickest way to do it there is but they bleed the worst and that's my objection to it. You wouldn't want to use it on a very big calf—one over 250 pounds—or he'll bleed to death. The docking tool is a round circle with sharp blades around the inside. You put it up over the scrotum and squeeze. The blades close in a pincer-like action and take the whole thing right off.

TOENAILS—Some goats never seem to have toenail problems. Others have toenails that grow and

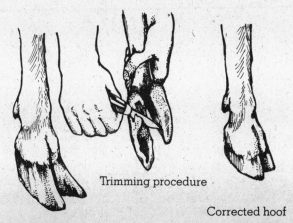

Trimming procedure

Corrected hoof

Badly overgrown hoof

grow and you have to cut them off to keep these goats from becoming virtual cripples trying to get around with all that nail on each hoof.

A young goat has fairly soft hooves and you can trim them with a knife. Just don't go far enough back to get into the quick and though it may make them nervous it doesn't hurt. On an old goat the hooves are very hard and you'll need a meat saw or regular hoof nippers to do the job. I bought an old doe once who had 5 inches of toenail that had to be sawed off from the front of each hoof.

BLEATING—Some goats are very noisy. If you have no choice but to have a silent goat or no goat at all, get a goat and if the bleating becomes a problem you can have it debleated at the vet's. Keeping the kids and mama out of sight of one another and separating them before they have a chance to get really attached helps. A nan in season will be noisy and actually that's a convenience because it lets you know when she is ready to be with the billy. To me debleating is a last resort but I know some of you have special problems with having to live with lots of neighbors and critical municipal authorities.

TATTOOING—Registered cows or goats have to have their ears tattooed. You buy a tattoo set or borrow one. "Place the figures or letters which you wish to use to identify the animal into the slotted jaw of the marker, close the lock, and before punching the ear, try the marker on a piece of cardboard so as to assure yourself that the figures or letters are in the order desired." Clean inside the ear with a cloth dampened with alcohol or kerosene. Tattoo in the ear away from hair, dark skin, and the ear cords or ribs. Be sure you get the tattoo pins forced deep into the ear surface. Now get a glob of ink on your fingers and rub it well into all the holes you punched. A disagreeable job.

BARNKEEPING—Milking stimulates contractions of other parts. Just be prepared when your cow spreads her legs and starts to squat and get yourself and the milk bucket clear away fast because it tends to splash all over. Goats are so much nicer that way. At regular intervals, like every few days, shovel the scrapings out of the barn into a pile where it can age and get ripe and ready for the garden. It makes the barn nice to scatter straw on the barn floor after you have it shoveled out.

MAIL-ORDER SUPPLIES—Whether you have a goat or cow, I'm sure you'd be really interested to browse through the catalog of American Supply House, P.O. Box 1114, Columbia, Missouri 65201. They specialize in supplies for the goat owner and dairyman, and they carry a number of hard-to-find items like dehorning paste and an iron for burning the baby horns away. And they carry things you wouldn't expect to find in a dairy supply catalog like electric drills and grinders, but they're trying to make a living, too. And things that you would hope to find there and do like old-time square butter molds made of maple and old-time butter paddles, which aren't really necessary for butter-making but aren't so expensive that you couldn't buy one sometime for fun—$1.50. Course then you know you've got to buy the small aluminum seamless milk strainer to use them in for $7.95.

MILKING

When you milk an animal you're getting into her emotional life. You can't help it, so adjust gracefully. If she's upset about anything, if something scared her, if she doesn't know you or doesn't like you she won't have the bag contraction that lets the milk down. If in the midst of milking something scares her, or if she has a sore teat and hurts, the milk may momentarily stop coming down. Once she has decided to adopt you she'll baa and run to you when you call her. You're her baby and she's going to sustain you. Have a can of grain handy. She'll follow you to the barn. Scatter some grain in the stanchion feeder. She'll stick her head in there and eat. Close the stanchion and milk her. When you're done open the stanchion. Pat her and say a kind word like, "Thanks, old bag," and then chase her out of the barn. She'll be feeling a lot more comfortable with the tension off her bag since you emptied it. If you ever nursed a baby you understand how she felt. A full mammary gland (breast on you, udder on her) is misery, and an over-full one is hell. She was desperate to be milked to relieve the discomfort.

That's why, if you're going to milk an animal, you're going to have to be completely reliable. As reliable as a baby that has no other source of food. You also have to be reliable because an animal's ability to give milk is a long-term investment, and if you skip a milking the animal starts to dry up to say nothing of her suffering and pain. If you don't milk her regularly, or if you don't milk her completely dry, you trigger another natural reaction called "drying up." Nature makes automatic adjustments for the baby's demands. If you milk her completely dry regularly (twice a day), nature says to that udder that the baby is big and hungry—he's eating all you have and wants more so keep making that much and more if you can. So she produces as much milk as she possibly can. On the other hand, if milk is left in the udder nature says to her the baby is eating other food and isn't so hungry now, conserve your strength and make less milk. So the next day she produces less milk.

What happens when you milk? Your stimulation of the teat (pronounced "tit") causes a contraction reaction to occur in the milk storing area of her bag. That's why when you first handle the teats of a nervous goat nothing happens. Each teat is like a syringe bulb and the bulbs are empty when the milk is held up high, so no matter how you squeeze none will come out. If the animal is happy and relaxed, if she expected to give her milk to you anyway, as soon as you handle her teats the upper part of the bag forces milk down. Now when you squeeze the teat something comes out.

Now you've got to milk for all you're worth. The contraction reflexes in the bag won't go on forever. You've got to get the milk out while it is on. You empty the filled cavity of the teat by squeezing the milk in there out the hole in the end. Then open your hand long enough to let it fill up again from the pressure above and squeeze it out again. On one of my goats it takes about 167 squeezes on each side plus stripping to get all the milk out. In effect you block off

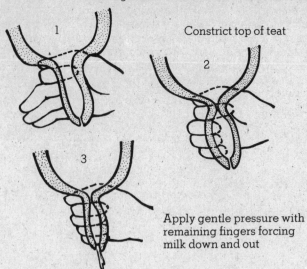

Grab high on teat near udder

Constrict top of teat

Apply gentle pressure with remaining fingers forcing milk down and out

the space above the teat with your fingers so it doesn't go back up and then squeeze on the rest of it to empty it out the hole. Then open up at the top again to let more milk down. Once you get going you can really move the milk out if her hole is big enough.

The reactions on each side are separate. After you've milked one teat you might still have to work a little to get the next one going. Just how you squeeze the milk out of the nipple depends on the shape of the teat that she has. A yearling goat with very small short teats is hard to milk and it takes a long time even though she doesn't give much. You milk those short teats by blocking off with your thumb and index finger and then adding your next two fingers (one at a time) to force the milk on out. Or you can "strip" by starting at the top of the nipple and pulling your hand down to force it between your thumb and forefinger. This will also help to enlarge a small nipple.

You have to keep your hand above or away from the nipple hole or the milk will go everywhere but the bucket. On a good-sized teat you can use your whole hand then it's easy. Just block with your thumb and index finger as high on the nipple as you can get and then add your other fingers one at a time to gradually force the milk out. Within a few days you can be pretty fast and comfortable with it though at first your wrists will get tired.

Danny could milk a goat when he was four. He fired both barrels at once. Then sat and waited for them to refill. But the usual way is to alternate hands, squeezing with one while the other is filling with new milk. So while your left hand is blocking off at the top and then squeezing your right hand is relaxing. Then your left hand is relaxing while your right hand is blocking off at the top and then squeezing.

When the flow of milk slows very perceptibly and the sinus takes longer and longer to fill it is time to switch to the stripping motion. Use your thumb and index finger and pull them down over the teat so the teat is pulled through your fingers from top to bottom and you have the last drop. You may strip each teat about five times.

How do you turn on a goat that doesn't want to be milked? You seduce her. Take a pot of warm water and a fuzzy rag to the barn with you when you go out to milk. It's a good idea to always do that anyway. Not only may you get more milk if you wash the udder and teats but also if she's been lying in the mud it keeps it out of the milk. Dirt in the milk means a high bacteria count—which means it sours quicker. The combination of warmth, wetness and manipulation (like the baby that butts her udder) will go a long way toward overcoming her hostility and nervousness. An udder that hasn't been washed isn't as easy to grip as a damp one either. And mud that got into the milk, dust actually, will go right through your straining cloth. You'll discover it as a sort of dark sediment at the bottom of your milk jar after it has set 12 hours or more.

If that didn't work and you're still squeezing and nothing is coming out and you're afraid she's going to dry up on you I know an absolutely surefire way to get her to relax and let that milk down. Maybe she's upset because she's new in your family or has just been separated from an old buddy or because you just knocked her kids in the head and she heard them cry out. Just take the teat in your own mouth and suck a little. She can't resist that—it's too real. Nature will get her and the milk will come. Once the bag contraction is started you'll have no need to resort to that again. If you'd rather find some more artificial technique use a syringe from a snakebite kit and it will have somewhat the same effect. So as soon as you taste the milk coming or can tell it's started just go ahead and finish the regular way.

PROBLEMS—A three titted goat, that is a goat with one normal side and the other with two nipples instead of one isn't uncommon. Nor is a four titter with two nipples on each side. You can use them just for brood goats—that means you let them rear kids and don't try to milk them. Or you can try to make them into a family milk goat anyway. The third nipple may or may not release milk. If it does you may have to develop a special way of milking that double tit to compensate for the problem of two nozzles. I had one that I milked from behind between her legs because somehow when I grabbed her from that angle I had more luck getting both squirts in the bucket. I wouldn't use the son of such a goat for a breeding billy for fear the trait could be passed on through him.

If your cow or goat puts her manury foot right in the middle of your milk bucket just as you are finishing milking her, don't kill her. You aren't the first one it ever happened to. Some of them really make a habit of it. In that case you'll have to develop a defense. An animal that does that or kicks the bucket or dances around can be hobbled. Or in the case of a goat you can hold one foot while you're milking with the other hand. A big, tall flat-bottom bucket is more stable and it's harder for them to get a foot into it. If she does succeed just consign that portion of the milk to the animals and try again.

Some goats kneel on their front feet when you try to milk them. Some have the habit of trying to lie down completely. In the former case you can learn to

milk her on her knees. In the latter you can either rig up a body sling or make hamburger out of her. In the case of any bad habit part of breaking her of it is to refuse to stop milking—even if you have to milk on the ground. Then she may give it up as ineffectual.

One thing that a cow can do to you that a goat can't is switch you right in the eye with a manury old tail. If she's got that habit just include her tail in the hobble or get it under your arm and keep it there for the duration. In October you can trim it as short as possible for the winter but let it grow out again by summer to help against the flies.

Nerves can really affect the amount of milk she gives you. You may get some, but not as much as you'd expect, and when you feel the bag you can tell that it's still round and not slack as it should be when emptied. Try milking into something plastic because it is less noisy. Keep everything routine and keep children and strangers away from her, especially at milking time. If other goats are harassing her, isolate her. Speak softly to her, if at all, and be patient. (Animals are milked on the right. That means on the animal's right. You mount a horse on its left.)

Other facts could be affecting her milk production though. If she is standing out in a cold rain with no shelter not only might she get pneumonia but her milk production will go down. Goats must have shelter available. If she isn't getting a variety of good food—ample brushy range and a little grain supplement in summer; hay, grain and vegetables in winter—her milk production will go down. She's a wonderful conversion machine. Grass goes in one end and meat, milk and garden manure come out at various other points, but if you don't supply her with adequate raw materials she can't do her thing with them.

Milking is done every 12 hours to get the most out with the least effort on your part. Milk early before the animals scatter to feed. Milk early in the evening and that way in winter you'll still have some daylight to do it. Milking is usually done all by hand but some people raising a calf leave calf and cow together all night. Then separate them in the morning and milk for the household supply in the evening.

If somebody sells you a doe with a kid 6 weeks old and keeps the kid you are going to have a very hard time switching her over to hand milking. It's much better to plan ahead and do it all one way or the other. The speed with which you can milk a goat is, other factors being equal (her state of mind and the quantity of milk in there), probably directly proportionate to the size, both length and width, of her teat. It takes a long time to milk a yearling or a goat that hasn't been hand milked before because her teats aren't enlarged.

A good family milker isn't a natural thing. Her udder is abnormally large to cope with saving all that milk for 12 hours when nature meant her to feed her calf or kid much more frequently. Her teats are long and large from hours of being pulled on during hand milking. When you see a goat with a big udder and big long teats she'll probably be a good family milk goat. One reason she's so expensive is because she didn't get like that overnight.

The doe with kid at side probably gets milked out a minimum of eight times a day. By the time the kid is 6 weeks old she is producing a lot of milk but she never has very much in her udder at any one time. Her teats are short and small because that works fine for the kid. He sucks it out instead of manipulating it out the way we have to. If you try to suddenly put her on an every 12 hours milking basis she's almost certain to abscess on you or at least be terribly sore and miserable. Her udder isn't used to holding all that milk that long. By the time you're ready to milk she'll be so tight and sore her teats will be hard as rock and she'll jump and tremble every time you touch her. By the time you've tried to milk out a half gallon, 10 ccs. at a time, she'll be both bruised and have a very bad attitude. If it has to be done phase her over gradually by milking rather frequently at first and then making it less and less often all the time. It's a good idea to plan on milking one or two new nans every year along with the rest of your herd. It takes about 6 months to get them broken in good. Then let them conceive and kid again and you'll have a real good milk goat.

A cow has four teats whereas a goat has two. When one teat seems to be empty move on with that hand to another. Then go back a couple of times before you finish for the stripping to get what's left. It should take you about 10 minutes to milk her. A good milk cow is a gentle creature. After a while she'll come when she sees you or knows that you want her. You can tie her up to milk her (have a halter on her). Eventually you could probably walk up to her in the field and milk her as she stands. Before milking her bag and teats will be full looking and round. As you milk the teats get a wrinkled shriveled appearance and the udder develops two big folds on the backside. A sturdy stool about a foot high will suit you and you can milk into a bucket—one with a bail (handle) for easy carrying. If she kicks or is otherwise hard to control you'll have to milk in a stanchion for sure. And use hobbles on her hind legs. You might think the front end is so far away it couldn't know what the hind end is doing but a mad cow can kick with hind foot forward, to the side or back and she can put that foot right where she aims it and it can really hurt. So use hobbles while you're making friends.

TO CHANGE MILKING SCHEDULES—If you bought a cow that is used to being milked at 6:00 A.M. and you sleep till 9:00 A.M. that's OK. Milk her 15 minutes to a half hour later each morning and evening until you get her on the schedule you want to keep. That way you minimize the drying-up tendency. And give her lots of grain in the meantime to help keep up the milk production. If you bought a cow and she is being separated from her calf for the first time, keep a good eye on her for the first 12 hours because she is going to be very emotionally upset—enough so to go wandering all over the country mooing if you leave a gate open. Cows are very home oriented, but she doesn't know yet that your place is home now.

A "STANCHION" is a frame to hold a goat or cow by its neck while it's being milked. You can make a goat stanchion out of a cow one just by nailing a board on it to narrow its grip. There is a manger where the animal's head will be in which grain or hay is placed. The animal sticks its head in to feed in the manger. Then the movable slat is moved over at its neck and fastened so she cannot pull her big head back through until allowed to. Some animals just hate stanchions and will let down their milk better if you milk them in the open. But if you're milking a big herd or have some horny animals it really helps. A stool for you to sit on while milking is needed to milk a big cow. But goats and Jersey cows are built nearer the ground. Some people have little goat stanchions built on a raised platform or milk them on the porch. I just sit on the barn floor anyway to milk. I usually have a child or two sitting on my legs while I'm milking. Or you could squat to milk the goat.

BOTTLE AND BUCKET BABIES

THE MIRACLE—Our white Saanen buck goat is named Miracle. His mother's name was Mary. He was the first goat born on our farm. He was Mary's first baby and neither she nor I had gotten into the farm kidding routine yet. She gave birth to him on a miserable rainy day in late February on the manure pile. Mike and I had been through that rather recently ourselves when he was with me in the delivery room and I cried with the wonder of it when he and I found them and that's why I named the kid "Miracle." There isn't that much difference in the basics. The miracle of life is the same whether it begins among sterile sheets and bad-tempered nurses or in the rain on a manure pile. And I always cry with joy when it's over whether it's goat, cow, or me.

When a goat kids in the cold weather and the kid seems to be inactive it is probably chilled. Take the kid into the house. Wrap it in a cloth and put it in a cardboard box near the heat source until it dries off and gets warm. (Getting born is a wet business.) When the kid climbs out of your box and wobbles all over the house nuzzling at everybody optimistically it is doing fine for a six-hour-old baby. Its little tail will wag and its disposition already demonstrates the incurable curiosity of goat or antelope.

One school of thought advocates taking the kid away from the mother immediately so she won't get

attached to it and be harder to milk later. Another is to leave the kid with the mother for three days and then separate them. I like to separate them right away because I think it's easier to get the kid drinking from a rubber nipple if it hasn't had a chance to nurse the mother. You can't change your mind in the middle because if the kid is taken away from her for 6 hours she may well butt it viciously and refuse to mother it.

SEXING KIDS—What you plan for the kid may depend on its sex. Boy kid goats have small feelable hanging testicles on their tummy, just to the front of their hind legs. They pee from the middle of the tummy so it runs straight down as they stand. Girl goats don't have those testicles and they pee from the rear, squatting backwards as they do so. (I'm writing this for beginners—we all have a first time to learn those things maybe when you're 3 and maybe when you're 33.)

COLOSTRUM MILK—It's very important to get the mother's first milk into the kid or calf. It has a special name—the colostrum milk—and it looks special. It is thick and darker in color than regular milk. This milk contains precious immunizations the mother is passing on to her kid and the kid may be sickly without it. *Don't* heat the colostrum milk more than barely lukewarm because it will turn hard as cheese and be useless.

This means you have to go out within a couple hours after the goat has kidded, take the kid and put it in a warm dry place and milk the nanny mother for her colostrum and then get her comfortably settled if you are planning to separate them. You can freeze extra colostrum milk (it's best frozen in a sterilized glass container). Then you can thaw and warm it to feed multiple births or an orphan that may happen later.

FEEDING—Feed the kid every 2 hours the first day, then at about 4-hour intervals, then 8-hour intervals, and then morning and evening. Two hours the first day, 4 hours the second day, 8 hours the third day, then morning, noon and night for about 10 days, and from then on morning and night after you milk. Notice how much they are able to take at a feeding. At first they take only an ounce or two. By the end they'll empty a big pop bottle.

Lamb nipples don't have an internal air supply

like baby bottles that feed air in through the rim. The kid has to learn to let go of the nipple every so often so air can rush in and equalize the pressure otherwise the milk will stop coming.

Here's how you give a bottle to a resistant kid or calf or one who doesn't know what he's supposed to do. Force his mouth open. Put the nipple in. Be holding his body to prevent him backing away from you. Once the nipple is in hold your hand around the sides and bottom of his mouth to prevent him from spitting it out. Once he gets some swallows of good milk down he'll get the idea. Kid goats are easier to bottle break than calves.

NEWBORN CALVES—In the case of a newborn calf take out a big towel or blanket to dry off the calf with a good rubbing. Check to make sure it's in a relatively nice place. Calves are tougher than kids. If you want the pair moved just pick up the calf and carry it in your arms. The cow will follow. She'll try to hide it as soon as she can though. That's called "brushing up" and it's an instinct cows have. She'll go to the hiding place several times a day to feed and check on it. Goats on the other hand will stay right by their babies.

We usually give the newborn calf its Bose vaccine and maybe some A and D and Combiotic and hang around until it stands and finds its first meal. Even if you leave the calf with the cow you've still got to milk her out yourself at least once a day. That's because any milk cow in her second (or more) lactation gives much more milk than a newborn calf can use and she will be miserable and risking mastitis if you don't take the extra milk.

AUCTION CALVES—To start a calf the rule of colostrum also applies. If you buy a baby calf at a livestock auction you have special problems. The calf probably either has never eaten or else it has been nursing the cow and is not pan broken. In the former case ranchers often take the calf to the sale ring while it is still practically wet if the sale day happens to fall that soon after it is born. Or the brood cow might have died in calving and he doesn't want to bother with an orphan. By the time you get such a calf home it will seem weak and listless.

If you plan to buy a baby calf at auction do these things. Take a blanket to the sales yard if the weather is cold. A long chilly ride home in the back of a pickup is going to weaken your calf even more. When you get it home give it a place indoors—in the barn with lots of hay or straw bedding and a blanket over it if it is shivering or wet or weak. Then give it a "calf starter" pill. This contains an antibiotic—Terramycin—and will help the calf fight germs until it can get stronger since it can't have mother's colostrum. You can get the pills from a vet or veterinary supplier. (See the instructions on how to give a pill in the Animal Doctoring section.)

His first meal is warm milk with egg yolk beaten into it. Cold milk can kill a calf. The egg yolk makes the first meal a little richer and thicker—kind of like the colostrum. I don't know why it's done, but it's the custom here and usually there is a very good reason for anything that is the custom. You can continue to give him the milk and egg yolk mixture for several meals and revert to it if he does poorly.

Calves are not necessarily bottle babies. You feed them either out of a pan or from a calf bottle or calf feeder. A calf feeder is a bucket with a nipple attached to the bottom. If you're going to use the calf feeder you've got to start with it—the very first time you try to feed the calf. He'll get a fix on whatever he is sucking when he gets his first good swig of milk and will be hard to change over. You coax the nipple into his mouth the first time. Same with a calf bottle, which is a big plastic bottle with the right-sized nipple. Try to stay with small calves drinking out of a calf bottle. Otherwise they may yank the nipple off, end up inhaling their dinner, and get clinical pneumonia. Or use a stainless-steel pan (but any kind will do) about 6 inches deep and about 1 foot across. I warm my milk and egg mix right in the pan. Make it a little extra warm to compensate for chilling on the trip to the barn. The calf has two strong natural instincts that you have to consider when you're breaking him to a pan feed. One is to reach up to feed and the other is to suck on a nipple type object. So do this:

Cup your left hand slightly. Dip your hand in the warm milk. Slip your middle fingers into his mouth. With your other hand scoop up milk and pour it into your feeding hand. Some of it will run down the grooves between your fingers and get into his mouth. You need somebody to hold the pan while you are doing this. And the calf needs to be lying down to make it easier for you. You may have to spend a long time just doing this. Now try to gradually lower your hand into the milk. He'll suck up the milk and it will go into his mouth. Wiggle your fingers in his mouth a little if he seems to be losing interest. It takes a little effort to get him pan broken, but once he is, all you have to do is take his pan and set it down and get out of the way. That's helpful when he gets to 200 pounds. *Note:* It's actually healthier for a calf to nurse with his head up than down because that's the way he's designed so there's another advantage to the bottle method.

Feed the calf every few hours until you're sure you are getting food down him. Then feed him morning, noon and night for a few days, then twice a day. He will be a ravenous glutton but don't give him all he can drink as it will make him sick. Incidentally big goats that are still nursing tug so hard they are liable to pull the rubber nipple off. You'll have to hold it on the bottle as they suck. A calf can be weaned partially when he is eating other foods and completely when he is able to sustain himself on other foods—about 4 months. A goat can be tapered off when he is eating other feeds and weaned completely at 4 months, too.

SCOURS—The turds of the goats should be round and firm, miniatures of mama's. When goat kids or calves get a loose diarrhea it's called "scours." Sometimes they scour their way and finally get over it, but sometimes it can kill them. Chilling and overfeeding are the two greatest dangers. When we have a baby calf with scours we put him in the warmest, dryest place possible, give an extra calf starter pill if it is

very bad and give him half a 12-ounce bottle of Kaopectate. Kaopectate is a mixture of real fruit pectin and kaolin—a natural clay. It really helps. Then I give less milk and sometimes make it less strong by watering it. You just have to experiment around trying to figure out what the individual animal needs in this individual case. If a goat kid on anything but goat's milk is scouring, a bottle or even a half a bottle of goat's milk or, if need be, goat's milk for several feedings will usually clear it up. Goat kids have a hard time on any milk but their natural milk.

That powdered fake stuff is the worst I know, powdered milk is next worst, cow's milk is best for them. I am always very reluctant to sell unweaned kids to people who don't have goat's milk to give them because I know they'll have a hard time keeping the kids healthy. Bigger kids can handle cow's milk better than little ones.

It isn't the same with calves, though. If they scour on a diet of goat's milk you can't change to cow's milk—the change in formula will make them even sicker. Just give kaopectate and give them *less* of what you're giving them. Some baby cereal or scorched flour with the kaopectate may also help. And so will shots of vitamins and antibiotics.

THE LAST RESORT—If you find a calf prostrate, shivering, with tongue slightly protruding and eyes sunk in—one that cannot get up or eat due to the chill on an unseasonably cold night—carry it into the house. Lay a towel in the bathtub. Lay the calf on the towel and a blanket on top and draw in enough hot water to stop the shivering. In the meantime get a hot place ready for it after it comes out of the tub so it doesn't get chilled again. Keep it warm even when it seems to be pulling out of it. A chill may give it a fatal setback.

MUSICAL MOTHERS—It takes about two good goats to support one calf. Get your goats milking good first and then you can acquire the calf. One really good goat can support a calf if she can be persuaded to adopt it and let it nurse her. To put a calf on a cow that's not its natural mother put vinegar on the calf and on the cow—on their noses and other places. Then they think they belong together.

BRINGING THEM UP RIGHT—The best animals are the ones you raise yourself because they know what to expect, are fond of you, and vice versa. Their lifetime habits are laid down early. A hand-fed kid or calf remains your baby all its life even if it grows up to be a big stinking billy goat gruff with a foot-long beard or a cow. The animals learn to come when you call because you first called them to eat.

You also want to break an animal to lead while it is a baby, small enough to manage. You can't break an 800-pound bull to do anything. So put a collar on it. Let the children tie something to the collar and lead it around and around and around until it gets the idea. Keep this up regularly and when it's big you will still be able to put the rope through the halter ring, give it a little tug, and your 800-pound beast will follow docilely.

I suppose this is self-evident, but maybe it isn't:

Always be gentle and kind to your animals and be patient. Don't force a bottle into the mouth if you can help it. Don't drag or carry the animals if you can help it. Take the time to coax and teach good habits. Don't make the animals afraid of you. A goat or cow with good manners, friendly feelings toward human beings, and well trained in what is expected is worth the top price. An angry (mean) animal that won't cooperate is a cull and worth the bottom price only. To say nothing of all the grief it's going to cause you. Whatever you do to that frail little animal, if it's wrong, you're going to pay for tenfold when it grows up. That's the same as raising children.

ANIMAL DOCTORING

Here are some common troubles I know from personal experience.

HARDWARE SICKNESS—(That's what the old-timers call it.) Our vet tells me that he gets around 200 cows a year with this. It means that your cow has eaten a piece of metal. Cows, unlike goats, aren't picky about what they eat. They munch mechanically along, and if there is a nail in the food, or susceptibly close, it goes down too. I had a neighbor whose cow ate baling wire. That's a bad one, and she eventually had to be operated on by the vet. But nails, bolts, even hinges, can be survived if you know how. The old-timers came up with the remedy and it's still used for hardware sickness. Of course prevention is the best remedy of all so check your feeding places and keep your eyes open when you're walking around in your pasture to pick up any small loose metal pieces you see. Once in a great while a goat gets hardware sickness, too.

Symptoms—The animal stops eating. It gets a miserable look in its eyes and will stop going out to browse with the herd. It just lies around by the barn being reluctant but not impossible to get up. There is no fever.

Treatment—The old-timers went to town, bought a magnet and forced the animal to swallow it. If the metal has not progressed beyond the big stomach region this will save your cow. The magnet grabs the

metal and pulls it to the bottom of the cow's stomach. It doesn't ever pass out. She has magnet and metal for the rest of her life. But the important thing is she doesn't die. When she starts eating again, you can relax and feel safe. There are now small, very heavy, smooth oval-shaped magnets sold for this very purpose through veterinary suppliers.

If you can get to a vet it will make it easier. In the first place he can make a surer diagnosis than you. Both you and he can take the cow's temperature by putting the animal thermometer up her behind just like you do a baby. (The above symptoms with no fever lead you to suspect hardware sickness.) But he also has a metal detector. He puts the earphones on and runs the rod around under her belly. If it screeches in his ears he knows she does for sure have hardware sickness and he knows where in her the metal is. If it goes on too far it may be tearing up her insides. He will probably give her a dose of medicine to stimulate her bowels since the hardware sickness makes them stop moving. It will make her have diarrhea for a couple days but in this sickness that's a good thing. Then he will make her swallow the magnet. And he may give her a shot of antibiotic and send some home with you to give to her two more consecutive days.

The vet tells me that they only have to operate on about two of those 200 cows a year with hardware sickness. If the cow doesn't recommence eating and doesn't seem perfectly all right by 5 days after the onset, take her for surgery, which is expensive but not as expensive as a $400 or $500 cow.

GIVING SHOTS—Practically everybody that's any part a farmer gives their own shots. It is cheaper and more convenient. You can buy in bulk from vet suppliers that specialize in mail-order business to farmers. But it's better yet to buy from your own vet or vet supply center because of all the free advice you can get with your purchase and the promptness with which you can get it home. There's no way to know in advance for sure who is going to be sick with what. You can get needles, antibiotic and immunizer. We give all our calves immunity shots.

I had a beautiful registered Shorthorn bull calf die of white muscle disease. Much as I hate to stick a needle in anything (I really have to pray hard to get the courage) it's better than seeing them sick. I used to think this business of shots all the time was just a scheme to make doctors money. I still think they give too many shots. But after almost losing a child to whooping cough, I've learned that lesson very well and my babies get shots against diphtheria, tetanus, whooping cough (the famous DPTs), the oral medicine against polio and the three-in-one against hard measles, German measles and mumps.

Newborn calves get 2 ccs. of vitamin A and D solution and 2 ccs. of Bose (which is the immunizer against white muscle disease) as soon as possible after they are born. At three months they each get 5 ccs. of black leg vaccine. The vaccines keep a long time so you can buy and store a supply. Combiotic is a veterinary antibiotic that will store in your refrigerator and is a good thing to have on hand. It keeps a couple years anyway. Some people give their cows 4 ccs. of A and D solution in the fall plus 2 ccs. of Lepto in a muscle and 4 ounces of a flea powder shaken on each cow's back for routine upkeep.

So sick animals that need an antibiotic can get shots. Usually one a day for 3 days, or more if necessary—2½ to 3 ccs. for a baby calf. Penicillin and its descendants are very precious stuff for man, beast or even insect. (The bees can get a variety of Terramycin in an edible powder.) Cows don't like shots any more than you and they have a lot more fight. Lock her head in a stanchion with the lure of some grain. Hobble or tie at least one hind foot very securely.

With goats you can have someone sitting on the head and someone on the behind. Same for a calf. If your cow isn't gentle and won't come into a stanchion, you need the kind of squeeze chute used for loading cows (a tight corridor that can be locked off in front and behind the animal so it can't go anywhere). Or you will have to rope and tie it unless you're so expert you can give a shot practically on the run. (The needle is liable to bend or break out.)

Find a bulge of pure muscle in the front shoulder or rear thigh. Don't stick into a bone. Aim that needle right in the middle of the muscle. You won't have to jab as hard as you think—the needles are really sharp. The hard thing is to get the plunger pushed carefully all the way down and the needle removed while the animal is carrying on like crazy. Those plastic disposable needles have a tendency to break off at the neck. Then you've got to go back and get the needle out of the cow or she will bleed through the hole in the needle. Practice helps. But I still prefer the plastic needles. You can reuse them several times.

Boil your needles between uses. The plastic needles can be boiled, too. To fill a needle peel off the little foil cover in the middle of the metal cap on the medicine bottle. That exposes a rubber area. Just force the needle point right through the middle of the rubber into the bottle. (Turn the bottle upside down.) Force the air out of your needle before you put it in the bottle by pushing the plunger clear down. Fill your needle with as much as you need measuring by the calibrations on the body of the needle as you pull back on the plunger. (If you accidentally pull it all the way out you have to start over.) Pull it back out of the bottle. Have a look at it to make sure that you don't have air in it. Squeeze a drop out the end to make sure. Air inside a cow is unhealthy.

Fill your needles on the site. Don't let children carry them with bare tips. I've had the experience of falling with a needle in my coat pocket. It rammed right into my innards. I'm lucky it wasn't an eye. So get your animal ready *first*. Then get the needle.

Here's a letter I got from Bobbi McCollum, Pietown, New Mexico. She's given many more shots than I have and has some advice for us: "On giving shots (I'm a nurse and this is from experience), when you pull medicine out of the bottle do this first—draw plunger back to where you want to fill and inject an equal quantity of air into the bottle as medicine you're removing. If you don't you create a vacuum in the bottle. I assisted in a surgery on glass removal from a nurse who had a bottle shatter in her face for just this reason."

TO FEED A PILL—Cow pills seem huge. Here are the basics for giving pills to calf, cow, goat or horse. For a calf have somebody to help you hold it. For a cow or goat put it in the stanchion. A good horse should just stand there and accept anything, but you may need someone in front but not in back. Push your fingers into the mouth up at the corner where there are no teeth and the animal will open up the teeth part. (You open a horse's mouth to put the bit in the same way if he won't just do it for you.)

Get one arm firmly around the neck and with the hand you've got in its mouth just push that big bolus pill right down the animal's throat hole as fast as you can. Don't worry about choking it. You won't. Don't worry about making it uncomfortable. If the animal is sick enough to need the pill at all a moment's discomfort is unimportant. When you think the pill is shoved down far enough pull your hand out and with both hands try to hold the animal's mouth shut.

What the animal will now try to do is get the pill up and spit it out. One of three things will happen. It will either swallow the pill on down. Or it will urp it up, chew a moment, and swallow half of it back down (that's why you're holding the mouth shut) and spit out the other half when you finally let the mouth open. Or it will spit the whole thing out. If it spits out half or all you simply have to start again and try to poke it down farther this time, over and over until you finally get that pill down your animal. The usual beginner's problem is not poking it far enough down.

FOUNDERING—This and hardware sickness are the two most common animal ailments I've observed. And they are both due to human carelessness rather than to germs. That is something to contemplate. Foundering is indigestion quite often unto death.

For example, we had a nice 5-month-old billy kid. Company came to visit the farm. The children thought it would be nice to give grain to the little goat and unbeknownst to me gave it a terrible quantity. The goat was not accustomed to grain in its diet at all. That evening it could not stand up. The following morning it was dead. You will almost always be certain of this diagnosis because you'll know when your animal was under conditions to be foundered. They can founder from two things—grain or green alfalfa in the field (or other rich green food, if the animal is used to hay). Foundering kills any size. It can take a 3,000-pound bull just as easily as it did my billy kid. It kills quickly. You have to find and treat it fast.

These animals have no natural judgment about what to eat, how much, and when. In other words, they will eat as much of the richest feed as they can find as fast as they can. Not too long ago I accidentally left both the door to the grain room in the barn and the people door of the barn open. My beloved and enterprising milk cow, named Buttercup, climbed up and went in that people door, walked down the corridor into the grain room and there nearly polished off a 50-pound bag of chopped barley. Needless to say she promptly foundered.

She was a big cow and used to grain in lesser quantities, which is what saved her life. But when I found her she was suffering terrible diarrhea and looking very, very sick. Foundering can hit in one of two ways—either by diarrhea or by bloat. Diarrhea is much the preferable. We got her to the vet right away and he dosed her and sent her home with follow-up pills for us to give her. She took the pill nicely for two days. The third day she was feeling better than we realized and when my husband tried to give her the pill she simply turned her head suddenly, and firmly pressing him between her head and the stanchion broke three ribs on him. We pronounced her well enough and she never did get that last pill.

Buttercup got so dehydrated from her diarrhea that she dried up and I had to abruptly wean her little calf. After she got over it, her milk came back a little but it was still way down from where it had been. I sold her and used the money to buy a fresh cow.

Foundering is caused by a relatively great change in diet. In other words, if I started Buttercup out on a cup of grain a day and gradually worked her up, she could digest big quantities without harmful effect (although I doubt 50 pounds a meal). When we had an alfalfa field and kept the cows pastured in it from very earliest spring on they got fat on alfalfa and thrived. This is because when the first little starts of alfalfa came on slowly with the spring they ate them. As more alfalfa plants grew the cows got accustomed to the richness of the feed until when the alfalfa was waist high and chock with food value the cows could eat a bellyful of it as often as they wanted and they thrived.

But if those same cows had been pastured in the field next to the alfalfa, on plain old grass or on dry baled hay and a child came to tell me they were through the fence into the hay (the green alfalfa), I would run knowing time was precious and hoping they hadn't already been in there long enough to eat themselves to death.

The worst foundering is a bloat. The animal's sides swell up and up. At first it passes quantities of gas. When it stops passing gas the disease is turning fatal. It cannot rise. It will soon die. It's green alfalfa that's so dangerous. When the alfalfa is cut and dried in the sun it becomes hay and won't have the same effect on animals.

So the lesson in all this is watch your animal's diet. If you buy an animal ask how much grain and what green feed it has been on. Drill it into your children that animals may slurp up grain like crazy, but it can kill in the amounts that the animal isn't used to. Prevention is by far the best cure.

If you do get a case call your vet. There are two tried and tested home remedies for foundering. One treatment is to push a garden hose down the animal's throat morning and evening for three or four days. Take the hardware off the hose and thread it into the cow gently. It may help, too, to run a bunch of water into the cow's stomach through that hose. Another treatment is to get the animal's upper body higher than their lower end like by having it lay in a ditch.

As a very last resort you can stick a knife in the guts to try and let some gas out. The vet does use this treatment, but if you can't get your animal to the vet or not in time it's a last resort that sometimes does work. To save the cow's life you've got to let some of that gas out. Stick the knife in right behind the rib cage, below the spine, in that swayback spot where it sort of caves in naturally. Have the knife point pointing forward toward the head of the animal and toward the middle of its insides. You know what really happens in a grain bloat? All that mash is fermenting inside of it.

7th edition, June 21, 1976. Bloat is so common that lots of people have experience with it to add to mine. Some very good advice, too—read on! From Bob Runk of Simi Valley, California: "I noticed when you spoke of bloat you mentioned that one might relieve the pressure by puncturing the rumen with a knife. If I may, I have a helpful suggestion. It's imperative that this is *only* done on the left side. Danger of puncturing vital organs exists if a knife is pressed into the right side." The Bantam copy editor had a reaction to the subject of sticking to let out gas. She thought I ought to say that you should only do it if you had somebody experienced there by you. I've never tried it. But I watched a favorite goat of mine die of bloat years ago when I had much less experience and much less nerve. If I ever had an animal that sick with bloat again—obviously near death—I'd try *something,* and if that didn't work I'd try something else!

The garden hose method has as many advocates as the knife method. Barbara Stone wrote me this from Stites, Idaho: "I do not know if this method will work for sheep or goats as we don't have any goats. You mentioned that you should stick them, but that is the last resort if nothing else helps. Here is the method to use in 'letting a cow down,' letting the gas out of their stomach without sticking.

"First, get a piece of garden hose approximately 4-5 feet long. Next get a piece of 1½-2-inch black plastic pipe, the kind used for irrigation. Make sure both pieces are thoroughly cleaned. If the hose is the hard plastic kind take a bucket of boiling hot water to the area where you are working. Take the garden hose

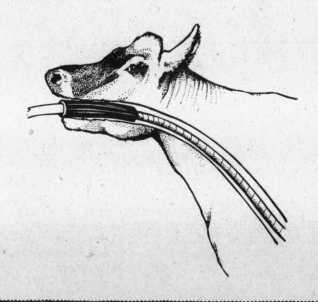

and put it in the pail of water, let it set for a few minutes, then drain completely. If possible, use ¾-inch rubber hose rather than plastic hose. Take the end of the hose and carefully cut all the rough edges off. It may hurt them if left sharp. Place the black pipe in the mouth and carefully put the garden hose through it down the throat. Depending on the size of the animal, on a cow you may have to go 3-4 feet before hitting the air pocket. When you hit it, they will immediately start burping or belching but keep this out of line of your face, as it will just about knock you off your feet. Keep this hose in the stomach until all the gas is out. By putting the hose to your ear, you can hear if there is any more left. Take the hose out and they should be on their feet in just a few minutes. If not work with the animal until you can get it up. If the cow has her head laying flat on the ground try to get her on her knees otherwise it doesn't go in the right places. Our big Holstein cow went clear down during the night over the holidays and she was down for almost 3 days, but she had somehow hurt herself and couldn't get up. We had to have the vet come down and he had no idea what she had done, but it is important if you have a cow down to prevent her from getting pneumonia. As cold as it was at that time and we couldn't get her in the barn, we just had to keep old blankets and straw around her for the time she was down. We put feed and water in front of her and she ate and drank, and she finally did get up to everyone's joy.

"I forgot to mention that you use the black pipe in the cow's mouth to prevent the animal from chewing on the hose, so you can get it down. Sometimes an animal becomes plugged and cannot have a bowel movement, then mineral oil should be given to the animal. Contact your vet as to how much for the individual cow. Ours didn't have to have any so I don't know the amount to use. After the animal is up make sure it stays up. Sometimes if the animal is in the barn or is up on its feet you can use the same method, but hold the head back slightly so the hose will slip down easily. This works on calves as well as cows.

"If you don't have a hose handy a person can use a regular rope. Stanchion the animal and take the rope in both hands placing it sideways in the mouth over the teeth. Put this as far back in the mouth as possible, this makes the animal chew and gag, and start belching. Continue this until the gas is out. But as in the other method stay out of the line of fire. Don't put the rope down the throat. As you said in the book find out what made the animal bloat. With the cow we think she just didn't feel well and laid down and couldn't get back up.

"We also had a cow that had just calved, but she had laid in such a position that she couldn't get up. She was in the middle of the field, but she found a place where she had her head downhill and her back area uphill. This had never happened to us before, so we didn't know exactly what to do, but we knew she couldn't stay there too long. With the help of a neighbor we got her feet dragged around with both areas on the same level. Put her on her knees and held her so she'd stay there. Within just a few hours she was

up as if nothing happened. If this happens again, and it probably will sometime, we'll know what to do. If no one is around to help, use the tractor or the pickup, tie a rope around the front legs and carefully roll them around until they are straight. Watch the neck that it doesn't get hurt. All of these things a person has to learn sometimes the hard way."

CUTS most often seem to come on the teats. Clean the cut. Don't break your milking schedule even if it takes a long time to milk that cut teat and the cow suffers and you agonize in sympathy. She'd suffer more if the milk built up, swelling in that teat under the cut and abscessing above it. You may have to hobble her to keep her from kicking if it hurts. Then treat the cut with a product called Bag Balm, which is available from veterinary outlets. Bag Balm is also good for humans, and other cuts on your animals can be cleaned and treated with it. But use separate cans of Bag Balm for man and beast. For badly infected wounds give Combiotic.

MASTITIS is an infection in the udder and unfortunately common in both goats and cows. Best prevention is regular milking. An overfull udder can bruise itself and bring on trouble. A part of the udder that has had mastitis before will be especially susceptible to it again.

Prevention is the best cure for mastitis. It is *very hard* to cure even using antibiotics, which are about the only hope you have. If you use antibiotics you won't be able to use the milk. So as you milk, morning and night, be aware of the possibility and check for symptoms. If you can't prevent it you can at least catch it early. Mastitis can also happen in dry cows that are not being milked so if you have a sick cow check to see what you can squeeze out of each teat even if you expect her to be plumb dry.

Mastitis will only happen one quarter at a time (a cow's udder has four separate quarters, each with its own faucet-teat). If you can catch it while it is confined to one quarter you can prevent it spreading to the others. That quarter (or half on a goat) will be feeling warmer than usual from the fever in it and be harder than usual. It will seem hard to milk out and you won't get as much milk as usual. As the mastitis

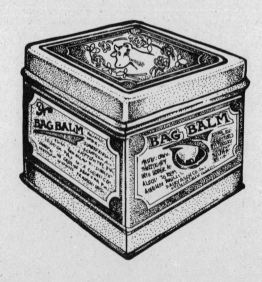

worsens the milk will become thicker and thicker until it is a struggle to squeeze it out and it comes out like toothpaste out of a tube. It will turn from pure white to a yellowish, which is pus in it, or brownish or pinkish color, which is blood in it. Obviously your family stops drinking the milk until you get it straightened out. Just throw it away. But be careful where you throw it because it is full of infection. And *please* remember to wash your hands very thoroughly after you milk a mastitis animal and before you milk another animal or you can spread the mastitis germs to every animal in your herd. Mastitis is not just a threat to the animal's milk producing capacity (any milking animal can get it), which is threat enough. I've seen cows near death when it sets into a general systemic blood poisoning.

Mastitis is not due to any one particular bug. It is an infection of the tender udder tissue that has entered through the cow's teat hole. There are at least 20 different organisms that can cause it. Under normal conditions the cow has enough resistance to these bugs that are all around her always not to get an infection. An injury to the udder or the kind of internal bruising caused by her not getting milked out when she needs to be makes her more susceptible.

For a suspected case the vet can test a milk sample. Your dairy can also test for bacteria count. For a sure case you can buy a mastitis powder that comes in a little tube like a needleless shot giver. You gently put the open end of the tube into the hole where the milk comes out and push the plunger to force up as much of the medicine as the directions say. Do this after you have milked the cow out. Do it again after each milking until she is well. (Don't use the milk. If you even suspect mastitis, of course, you won't use the milk.) The tube contains an antibiotic. It is lethal to a fetus within 3 months of term so you can't use it on a cow that is due to deliver within 3 or 4 months.

Now from my personal experience I don't think it works very well. Daily shots of Combiotic instead give me the best results. Check with your vet by telephone for the amount in cc.s. Combiotic ends up being a cheaper treatment since the teat tubes are $1.50 each and you need one per teat per milking. It is vital with mastitis to get it knocked out as fast as possible before the animal's current and future milk production is jeopardized. So get on it the day you detect or suspect mastitis and stay on it until it's gone. Your animal will more than likely have dried herself up a lot before it's over though. A good dollop of *real* rich feed may help bring her back but probably not much.

MAGGOTS are caused by flies that lay their eggs in a wound. When the eggs hatch the little worms live in the animal's living flesh. It is a terrible sight. When I was little we had a lot of trouble with bears getting into the sheep. Often the bears only succeeded in getting part of a sheep. I remember vividly helping my daddy. He would hold the wounded sheep down while I poured the oil all over where the worms were writhing in its exposed flesh. So be forewarned. If your animal has an open wound in the fly season you must keep a salve on it or else pour an antimaggot solution on there.

CANCER—If it is where you can see it there is a hard protruding lump that just grows and grows while the rest of the animal does poorly. Make sure you have a cancer lump and not merely an infection. You do this by jabbing it with a knife. An infection runs pus. A cancer is hard clear through. If it is a cancer take the animal away, shoot, and dispose of the body. An animal that does very poorly and you don't know why, is not meat you want to eat.

TUBERCULOSIS—Nowadays it isn't very common because of the long vigilance practiced by dairymen. It's smart to have your dairy goats and dairy cows checked for TB by a vet. You take them to him and he gives the skin test. You take them back three days later and he reads it for the results. It's worth the money to be sure the milk is safe.

BANGS—Cows that carry it don't show it. But their babies are born dead, and you and your children can catch a human form of Bangs called undulant fever which is a very grim disease. A friend of mine in the dairy business nursed one of her daughters through it. To prevent Bangs give your heifers shots at six months to vaccinate them. If you buy a new cow give her a Bangs shot. If she has it the shot will kill her.

INFECTIONS—Lance the wound by cutting it to let it drain. Put a healing salve on it, like Bag Balm. If that isn't good enough use antibiotic shots.

RINGWORM—Ringworm is a fungus. They claim the animal kind can't spread to humans. But first I got a spot on my arm. It kept breaking out again on my arm. We couldn't figure out where it was coming from. Then we discovered patches on Marietta. That was the milk cow at the time and I'm the only one in the family that milks usually. Mike runs them in at night and feeds them and I come along with the bucket and do my thing. So I think it has to be more than coincidence that Marietta and I had ringworm at the same time. The doctors have a new treatment now for people ringworm which is a one-shot painting that wipes it out. On me it took my skin right off. The ringworm—not the treatment. The ringworm eventually spread to all the cows. It took the hair off in roundish—but not necessarily so—areas leaving a kind of whitish scaly surface. A good medicine for it is iodine dissolved in glycerin that you should be able to purchase from your vet. You paint it on once and that's fine until you find the next spot. In the old days they just left it alone and it seemed to be a winter affliction that the cows sloughed off in their spring molt. The old-time remedy is to get an old rag and tie it on a stick. Dip the rag into a can of used motor oil and run it over the ringworm areas (not near eyes).

WHITE MUSCLE DISEASE—We had a calf die of this. It was very stiff in the joints, moved little, slowly, and with obvious difficulty, and was in poor health generally. It couldn't follow its mother and so didn't get enough to eat. There is a lot of white muscle disease in our area and it's important that we get a calf immunized against it as soon after birth as possible because it's just about impossible to cure once it sets in. We figure on giving it the immunization shot the same day it's born. You can mail-order these and other serums or buy from your vet or vet supply source.

PNEUMONIA—Calves and goats get this. It is similar to what you'd expect in humans. They have a very snotty nose. Maybe runny eyes. Are running a fever, and are weak and obviously very sick. The breathing is unnatural. Keep the animal in as warm and dry a place as you can. Give daily Combiotic shots and try to get some good warm food into it. It should be better within a few days. Don't get too brave. Coddle it a while more because they can relapse.

FOOT ROT—Barbara Stone from Stites, Idaho, has a wonderful "Glenn's grandpa" who has been around cows all his life and passed on this remedy through her. "Foot rot can happen to just about any animal with hooves. This is quite painful to the animal. The symptoms are limping and sometimes holding the foot up off the ground. Either rope or stanchion the animal before beginning the treatment. Using a stick or a horse-hoof pick, clean all the manure, rocks and whatever else is in the area between the toes. Pick up the foot and just stick it in a pail of used motor oil. Leave it in there for a few minutes or as long as the animal will allow you to have it there. Sometimes it is not too easy. This treatment should be done once a day for as long as needed. Usually it won't take more than two or three times. Try to keep the animal in a floored place that is not too wet or full of manure so that hoof can dry off. If nothing else lock it in the barn."

PINKEYE—People pinkeye, kitten pinkeye, rabbit pinkeye are all disagreeable. We take the kids to the doctor for a prescription or get some Murine eyedrops and it works for kittens and baby rabbits. Bovine pinkeye is in a class by itself. We have a lot of it in this part of the country. It starts right after the face flies do. That's in late June or so when it dries off and starts to turn hot and the face flies turn up to hang around a cow's eyes and drive her crazy. We try to help by soaking rags in a face-fly discourager and hanging them up on a rope so the cows can scratch themselves on it. But your best preventive to pinkeye is your breed of cow. Breeders have paid a lot of attention to resistance to this disease. Black Angus cows can list among their fine selling points that they are pinkeye resistant. Shorthorns are not—from personal experience. Charolais are supposed to be resistant, but it's not 100 percent. Herefords are more susceptible than Black Angus.

Pinkeye comes on very fast. It generally happens on only one side at a time. The eye turns white all over and looks ulcerated and *awful.* You'll know the instant you see the cow that something is terribly wrong. If you don't have pinkeye treating experience, or even if you do, the best thing to do is load the sick animal up and get her to the vet *immediately* because every hour really matters with this rapidly progressive disease. If you're in doubt phone him up first to discuss if it is what you think it is. It's a good idea to check all your cows' eyes morning and night in face-fly season as a matter of routine to catch any pinkeye getting started. In some cases, with quick action the vet may be able to save the eye. Or you may lose the sight in that eye but prevent it from spreading to the other eye. Then you've got a one-eyed cow but otherwise she will be functional. If you lose both eyes

to pinkeye you'll have to sell her for hamburger or eat her yourself because she'll starve anyway. Our vet's treatment is a shot in the affected eye and then he sews the eye shut. I know an old-timer who says the way to treat it is get a handful of salt and rub the affected eye with all your might.

LICE can turn up on practically anything, man or beast. And don't let anybody kid you and tell you that animal lice leave human beings alone. I know several people who have gotten horrible cases of lice, them and their whole households, off animals, in one case a neighbor's milk cow. Animal lice don't make the jump to people generally unless you do get really intimate—like leaning your head against the cow. But once you've got 'em you have a fight on your hands. If you can help it don't go home. Get a hot shower. Wash your hair with a strong soap. Wash all the clothes you were wearing in detergent and hot water. If still in doubt buy a can of garden spray that's good for flying bugs (terrible strong stuff I know but nothing lesser that I know is *really* effective) and spray your car out. Take off your shoes and spray them. If the infestation of lice is in your whole family and/or your house you're going to have to go through this battle again and again. It won't be easy but in the end you'll win. I've been through it. Wash all the clothes, bedding. Shampoo and bathe the children. Fumigate the house thoroughly. If it didn't work do it again. And you have my sincerest sympathy. That's one of the most miserable afflictions I can think of. The same for the cow or chickens or other critters that have 'em. Malathion is an effective spray but it's terrible inorganic stuff. A new treatment of whitewash in your animal shelter and crankcase oil on the roosts, in the case of chickens, has been known to work. Makes me itch and scratch just to write about it.

MAIL-ORDER MEDICINES AND SUPPLIES—United Pharmacal Company, 306 Cherokee Street, St. Joseph, Missouri 64504, specializes in mail-order veterinary supplies. They have a free catalog you can ask for.

LOCAL KNOWLEDGE—Ask neighbors or your vet what diseases are prevalent in your area so you can take preventive measures or be on the lookout for them. I just discovered a new one here. It's a fly called the heel fly that lays eggs one summer under the heel of a cow. The eggs hatch and the larvae crawl clear up the leg of the cow to live on her back. The next summer they bore an opening and change into flies again and leave the cow to find another host. I've got one cow that has this (she had it when I bought her) and the vet tells me at this stage there is nothing to be done. The preventive has to be given in the fall of the year. It's an internal medicine. He says anything strong enough to kill them at this stage would kill her too. Oh, yuk!

TRAVELING WITH ANIMALS

You need to be prepared to travel with your animals. Even if the man you buy it from agrees to deliver the animal two days later you may need to take it to the vet or be mad enough at it to want to take it back to the previous owner. A half-ton pickup can hold any smaller animal and a small-type cow like a Jersey. It

can hold a bigger cow, but it's a real struggle. You'd have to bend a big Shorthorn cow pretty near to an S-shape to get her in. A three-quarter-ton pickup bed will hold any big cow or bull easily. You'll need stock racks, of course, to haul cows. You can make your own. A one-ton truck can transport three big cows plus one or more calves tucked in around the sides.

You can transport a goat in the back of a pickup most comfortably by tying a rope to each side of its collar and fastening the ends to each side of the pickup. That holds it in the pickup without danger of it jumping over the side. Or you can tie it to the middle right behind the cab on a very short lead. You can tie the legs of a calf or goat and put it in a car trunk with the door a little open, but I don't care for the method much. If you can spread out a big sheet of plastic so your upholstery is perfectly protected you can move one or more goats or small pigs or sheep in the back of a car. Just don't try to eat anything in the front seat during your trip or you'll have goats in your lap.

I once traveled sixty miles in a small car with five goats, three young children, and myself very largely expectant. The humans and goats were fine but it took the car a while to recover. You can bring a newborn calf or smallish pig home in a gunnysack tied around its body leaving the head out.

WINTERING

WINTERING GOATS is not the same as wintering cows, but in a pinch you can winter goats purely on hay because I've done it. But to keep milk production up and to keep them happiest they need some vegetables, a grain ration and access to brush. Goats are related to deer and they are naturally twig eaters. They like to eat the young tips, just the way you'd prune a tree, only they don't know when enough is enough and can kill a tree. That's fine if you're afflicted with lots of dense brush. They'll keep it back.

Just what quantity it takes to winter goats depends on the quality of your feed and the method you use to feed. Feeding in a manger does go farther than throwing feed on the ground. And have your hay stored so they can't get in and walk around on top of it because they've no judgment and will get it in such

a foul condition that then they don't want to eat it. A good winter ration in an average winter around here—which is no real rough winter—is 6 to 9 bales of real good hay, that's second cutting alfalfa, for the whole winter—you just ration it out to them—plus a handful of chopped grain apiece per day. They like squash and mangel beets and carrots. That's a good liberal diet for a milking nanny. Some people feed them skimpier.

I read in a very popular recent book that goats are "wasteful" eaters. The same book directed you to give them what seemed to me an amazing quantity of grain per day. Well, if you gave any goat that much grain, of course it would "waste it" because they can't eat that much. It also described goats as "finicky" eaters. They can be. Goats are a lot like cats and dogs. Everyone has heard of an Aunt Minnie's tiger tomcat that won't touch anything but chopped liver and she has to buy it fresh every day for him. You can do that to a goat if you work at it. Goats that aren't being milked don't need any grain at all.

WINTERING COWS takes a lot of hay. You don't need to give anything else but water and a salt block to nonmilking cows, but cows that are milking and getting ready to come fresh should be getting some grain every day. Cows have the kind of digestive tract that needs a lot of roughage but also some protein. Alfalfa hay is ideal for them because it has both. But if you haven't got and can't afford alfalfa hay you could use a poorer hay with a grain supplement to supply protein. If you use a straw, like barley straw or oat straw which are real cheap because they are just the stalks left after the combine has taken the grain heads, you should also give them some higher quality hay. The straw is roughage but there isn't enough food value in it to keep them in good shape. Grains differ in food value. Barley is richer than oats, but it's also more expensive than oats.

A good feed for the milk cow is a mixture of half chopped oats and half chopped barley. That's what we use. For winter hay we use part alfalfa and part oat and pea hay. We plant a mixture of oat and pea seed and then cut it for hay when it's grown up. It's very nourishing for the animals and I like it because it has grain right in there for the cows and chickens. That way I don't have to buy winter grain, which is almost prohibitively expensive, for them. The chickens get in there and scratch around all winter long for their own grain and do fine. Must be. I didn't feed my chickens all winter long and they're giving me 15 eggs a day now, plus the ones being set on.

Any grain that you buy for your animals you should ask to have chopped. They can digest it better that way and they'll get much more food value for your dollar. If you raise your own grain rigging up your own chopper is almost a must. Or you can use the real coarse grind on your home flour grinder. The whole grain is cheaper so you can save yourself money by doing your own grinding. If you raise your own grain and so have it cheaply available, you can start feeding chopped grain to calves as soon as they will take it. This makes them grow a little faster than they would otherwise. We don't grain the calves, but I give the milk cows about a half gallon grain morning and night. That's really more than necessary. I give the rest some grain once in a while for love and to keep them gentle.

To winter a cow you figure two tons of hay per cow per average winter. It isn't certain. "Winter" means how many days the ground is covered with snow or for some other reason there is no grass. Summer drought may dry up all the grass and have you feeding hay long before the snow comes. Or your pasture may be too small to supply grass for the number of animals you have and then you'll have to supplement even in summer. Hay prices here were around $80 a ton last fall.

HAY MAKING—There isn't anything complicated to it. Hay is just dried grass or other green leafy stuff that is food for animals. But it's really vital to have it because with hay you can keep your cows, goats, sheep, rabbits, horses—and chickens, too, if there's some grain heads in it—alive through the winter. And they'll be making milk, meat and eggs for you in the time when vegetables and fruit don't grow. You can cut any grass for hay and in time of terrible drought I've seen farmers get out and mow every open field an owner would give them permission to, trying to get something together to keep the animals alive through the winter.

The important thing with hay making is not to let it get rained on. You cut the grass when it is tall, rich looking and green. You let it lay in the sun for a few days until it has dried out (doesn't have to be all bone dry). Then gather it up and get it under cover. And you pray from the time you cut it until the time you can get it under cover that it won't rain. Because if it does get wet, a significant amount of food value will be lost from it. You'll have to wait again for it to dry out and it'll take longer this time with it laying in a mass on the ground.

So if it rains all the time you can't harvest hay. The reason I'm moved to remark this is because this summer it has rained practically three weeks in a row here where we normally have hot, dry summers and our first hay cutting is ruined. If hay is cut and then lays on the ground in the rain (and you can't finish harvesting if it is wet) the rain washes out the nutrients and the color. Instead of being nice and green it is yellow like straw. Hay like that is called "bleached" and it's no good. Even so you've got to get it up off the field so the grass can grow back again. If you left it laying there it would act like a mulch and stifle the plants underneath. So now we've got that bleached hay to get rid of—whenever it dries out enough to get into the field and work. Rain is always a threat to hay making. You want rain when the stuff is growing. But then when you are ready to harvest—and you want to get it harvested when it is good and tall but the stalks have not turned real tough—you want sunshine. If you have good hot sunshine you should be able to get your hay cut and out of the field in four days. Then it can rain again and you'll be glad because that gets your next crop started growing. If you're rich and can afford a swather you can harvest that hay even quicker. You could swath on a Monday and if it's hot, you could bale on Wednesday.

Nowadays haying is very mechanized. Before balers they mowed the hay, like with a horse-drawn mower. And then used a horse-drawn dump rake or forked it up into piles or rows by hand to dry. And then pitched those piles into a wagon. And then pitched the hay from the wagon into a big net that hung from a rope on the end of a derrick. And then turned the derrick around and pitched it from the net into the haymow. Before that they used a scythe, with a special kind of cradle that put the hay in a windrow (which is a long pile of hay) and did the whole thing by hand. Here at Kendrick, Idaho, on unirrigated land two hay crops is a good year. On irrigated land here in the river valley with plenty of good hot sunshine I've seen an enterprising farmer down the Potlatch River harvest as many as five cuttings of hay off a single field. In irrigated country in California, where they grow hay all year round, they could get ten crops. It takes both moisture and heat to make hay.

"Hay" means a harvest of grasses or legumes—like alfalfa or clover or peas. The best hay for horses is what's left over after you've fed the other animals like cows and goats and rabbits. Because horses can get by with anything. And the others can't. Milk cows won't hold up so well on grass hay, and goats and rabbits need good green alfalfa. Foodwise hay has two parts for cows. Protein feeds them and there's lots of protein in alfalfa and pea hays and not so much in clover hay. And then the roughage part that they need to make their systems work right. Roughage is the grasses or stalks. Alfalfa hay is a good hay because it has both. Grain supplies protein if you're feeding a hay like clover, or a grass that is short in it. In the spring the grass grows again and the hay feeding season is over, and then the cows can go out on that good green stuff and get fat. Alfalfa is even better pasture for cows than grass if you can spare it for them. But don't start animals on alfalfa that aren't used to it or they'll bloat. Especially on wet alfalfa—that's the most dangerous of all!

We've got that situation now. A whole field of wet, soaking wet for three weeks, alfalfa with a layer of bleached hay on top of it. Mike says we'll just give up and turn the animals in there. But they aren't used to alfalfa to say nothing of wet alfalfa. So first we must wait until it dries off. And then we'll let them in there for an hour. And a couple hours the next day, and so on until they get used to it. And we'll buy hay from somebody who had better luck for this winter's feed. If very many people had the kind of weather we did in haying time you can expect the price of hay will be up this fall!

Hay has a little trick of setting itself (and your barn) on fire by spontaneous combustion. It has this tendency if it is piled up in storage incompletely cured. That means too wet. Now I know it doesn't make any sense that damp hay is more likely to catch on fire than dry hay but it's true—heavy, leafy legume hays are more likely to do that to you than grass hay. If you twist a wisp of hay and it feels tough, if you break a stem and it feels tough, if you break a stem and there is evidence of moisture, if you can scrape the epidermis off a stem with your fingernail—that probably means you haven't got it safely dry yet.

When the hay is acting sort of brittle, and there's no wetness when you twist a stem, and the epidermis doesn't peel off the stem when you scrape it with your fingernail, then it's probably cured enough. For the very best hay—the kind you can feed your cows and need no grain supplement at all—cut legumes when they are beginning to blossom. Grow your hay on a well-manured field and cure it as fast as possible. The best hay is green in color and will have *leaves* on the stems. This green, leafy hay is great feed for goats and rabbits too. But you can even cut the straw stubble (or pasture it) that is left after grain crops are harvested and they can be *part* of your winter feed for big animals. The straw provides roughage which they need but doesn't have protein which they also need.

A mower blade is the most efficient way to gather hay up and store it, but I've helped my daddy stack hay loose in haystacks. People with balers that use wire to tie bales are really lucky because we have the kind of baler that ties with twine. Mike and a neighbor make hay all summer. Mike has a baler and Doug has a mower. They get our hay and Doug's, and then put up hay all up and down the valley for people who don't, or can't, do it for themselves on shares. Then comes second cutting when the hay has grown high enough again and they go through all the fields making hay again.

We've usually had plenty of hay for ourselves, some to sell and some to trade. With the cost of machinery and everything else nowadays you just can't afford to own everything yourself for one farm. So neighbors here trade machinery and they trade labor, too. And they don't make a big deal out of what they're going to get out of it. It's more like a giving contest: "I can do more for you than you can do for me." It's a good game that works to the benefit of everybody, but it really baffles some people. They have notions of capital and labor and how they're supposed to be at each other's throats. I've seen people come out here and be given a job more out of charity than because they were needed and then turn around and act vicious because they thought they got paid two dollars less than they should have been. Then they wonder why they couldn't find another job. That's a terrible breach of country etiquette and the bush telegraph is almost as inexorable as the credit companies' files for carrying ratings on people's character. City people are used to anonymity. That doesn't exist in the country. You are what you are and everybody knows what you are for better or for worse.

7th edition, June 21, 1976. Lynn Wehn of Bemidji, Minnesota, wrote about the oat and pea hay I mentioned Mike made. She wanted to know at what point we harvest it and how. You harvest the planting of mixed oat and pea seed just as the oats start to turn. If you wait longer the oats will be too ripe and won't make good hay. Peas-oats are good protein and the pea vines and oat straw are good roughage.

MILK

The best way to keep milk utensils sweet smelling and clean is to wash them with lukewarm water in which you have dissolved 1 teaspoon of washing soda per quart of water. Then rinse and scald with very hot water. Strain your milk through four thicknesses of dish towel put over a large wire strainer. This won't catch soluble impurities. They settle as a kind of "dust" in the bottom of your jar and do no harm I know of. Or you can buy a specially designed milk strainer and throwaway strainer pads.

You'll have less to strain out if the udder is washed before milking—or at least wiped off to get rid of dried mud and manure that might fall into the milk. Washing with warm water also helps a nervous cow to let her milk down. Straining helps to get rid of hair, dirt and so on which cause off-flavors and a high bacteria count. (Milk with a high bacteria count will sour fast.) It helps avoid "strong" tasting goat's milk if you strain and refrigerate right after milking. A regular commercial milk strainer is like a large metal bowl with holes in the bottom. A ring fits in the bottom to hold down a paper filter disk. The gunk is trapped on the disk, which is thrown away after the straining. Quick cooling and clean utensils make a big difference in the flavor of your milk.

"Whole milk" is milk in which the normal amount of cream is mixed throughout the milk by shaking it up. This is always a temporary situation with home milk as you can't duplicate the dairy homogenization that shakes it up never to return. If all the cream has been skimmed or separated out of the milk it is called "skimmed milk." Skimmed milk is fine food for chickens, pigs and the like. Sour milk can be achieved naturally by waiting or hurriedly by adding 1 tablespoon lemon juice or vinegar per cup of milk.

Raw milk does not taste like pasteurized milk from the dairy and goat's milk does not taste like either, and the more it ages the more pronounced the difference becomes. You may have trouble changing your family over from any one to any other of those. I can remember as a child how awful the store milk tasted to me when we sold our last cow and then how awful

the raw milk seemed to taste for a while when several years later we again had a milk cow.

So to get your family on a new type of milk, serve it in eggnogs, Postum (⅓ milk) and such like at first. Once they get used to the idea of drinking it, drinking it straight will soon follow. Give babies a gradual transition, starting out with one-fifth of the new type and working up gradually. There may be a period of either constipation or looseness until they make the adjustment. If you try to switch a baby over without this gradual introduction you can end up in terrible trouble. I kid you not. Cow's milk is very constipating for babies that have been on those canned formulas. If you tried to make an immediate changeover that baby might not be able to have one single bowel movement again, and you might end up with something drastic like surgery on it as the cow's milk builds up inside. So if you set out to change a baby's milk type—even what you think is a "big" baby—watch the subsequent bowel movements carefully. Give that one-fifth part of the new milk. And wait to see if the baby's next few bowel movements come as you would normally expect. If they don't—don't give any more of the new milk until you get baby straightened out again and then try less.

SEPARATORS—Some people like them. Mostly they're the people who milk a lot of cows, sell their milk and cream, have an electric one and are used to it. Or else it's people who have a number of goats because their separator makes it possible for them to enjoy goat cream and butter. For years it was impossible to find a hand-cranked cream separator except at an auction. Now you can order a plain hand-cranked model ($120.50) or a combination hand-crank and electric model ($149.50) from Bruce Weaver, Box 917, McCook, Nebraska 69001. I bought one of his and it has given me good service. You have to take them apart, wash all the parts and dry them after each use. That is a lot of work. There are 18 disks, 17 other parts, the wrench, plus jars and milk pails to wash morning and night. You can get cow's cream so much easier by just letting your milk set in a gallon jar for 24 hours and then skimming it off with a dipper. I used to separate but I don't bother now.

A table-type separator has to be bolted to a very sturdy tabletop. The hand-cranked ones won't separate properly unless you have the crank moving at the proper speed. It is supposed to click. You keep going faster until it just quits clicking and stays at that speed. If you go too fast you're going to throw away a rather high percentage of your cream. Don't go by the clicks of somebody else's separator unless it is the same model and the same make. Different ones require different speeds.

Goat's milk is hard to separate even with a cream separator. Make sure you have a model that can be set specially for goat's milk. Otherwise it won't work. You can save your milk for several milkings and then separate it all at once. It even works with cold milk if you have the right setting on the cream percentage. The special thing about goat's milk is that the fat globules are so much smaller.

TO CAN MILK strain your fresh milk and cool it.

Then pour into clean jars to within ½ inch of the jar top. Put on your lids firmly. Process in a pressure cooker for 10 minutes at 10 pounds pressure or 60 minutes in a water bath canner.

MILK AND CHICKENS—The old-timers didn't feed their chickens grain. Maybe with the price of grain up that's something to reconsider. They fed them clabbered milk. That means milk soured until the curds and whey have separated. Chickens do very well on a steady diet of this sour milk. But *don't* give them fresh milk—it can cause diarrhea and throw off your egg production. And *do* make sure that they have plain water in addition to the clabbered milk.

MILK SOUPS

Cream soups are so easy and good. We just finished a lunch of tomato soup. I made it by thickening some of my V-7 juice with flour. Then I added salt, a little pour of molasses, and gradually stirred in milk. I was going to add some soda but couldn't find any. It came out good, anyway.

My mother believed that milk or cream soups should never be boiled. She said it ruined the flavor and made a mean scum to clean out of the kettle. She always added the hot milk to the other ingredients at the last minute. You can make a milk soup really out of any vegetable following the same general formula as in the following recipes. But here's a little competition to "ummmmmm good."

Cream of Fresh Mushroom Soup—The old-timers around here go out in the spring and come back with pans of mushrooms. Some of the ones they find are really good. They sauté them in butter, can them, or make soup. Wash a half pound of fresh mushrooms, bruising them lightly if necessary, but do not peel. Chop rather fine. Brown them slightly in 6 tablespoons butter. Then blend in 4 tablespoons flour and gradually stir in 6 cups milk. Cook in the top of a double boiler for 20 minutes, stirring frequently. Season with salt and pepper. Serve with crackers.

Onion Soup—Chop about a pound of onions. I do more crying over onions than anything else. The best answer I know is to get away from the onions, give my nose a good blowing, wipe my eyes, wash my hands, and go back when I've sufficiently recovered to finish the job. I can chop onions with my eyes closed but it gets up my nose. Then cook the onions with a couple of tablespoons butter over a gentle heat for a few minutes without browning. Add 4 cups chicken stock, salt and pepper to taste, and cook 30 minutes more. Add a little flour and milk paste for thickening and 2 cups milk. Cook, stirring, until thickened. Good with bread and cheese.

Cream of Onion and Potato Soup—Boil about 4 cubed potatoes and 4 sliced onions together in water until tender. Drain, saving the water. Rub the vegetables through a coarse strainer or blend them into a puree. Melt 2 tablespoons butter and then mix into it 2 tablespoons flour, ½ teaspoon salt and a pinch of pepper. Add 3 cups scalded milk and the potato water gradually. Stir constantly as you add the liquids. Add the potatoes and onion puree, stir, cook 3 minutes and serve.

Cream of Corn Soup—This was an old pioneer standby. Combine 2½ cups of corn cut from the cob (you can use frozen or canned), a slice of onion and 2 cups milk in the top of a double boiler and heat to scalding. Melt 3 tablespoons butter and mash in 3 tablespoons flour, ½ teaspoon salt and a pinch of pepper. Gradually add 3 more cups of milk, stirring constantly. Heat to boiling and cook for 3 minutes. Force the corn-milk mix you first made through a sieve and/or puree in a blender, if you want it really creamy.

Cream of Pea Soup—Cook 2 cups peas (fresh, canned or frozen) with 1½ cups water, ½ teaspoon salt and 1 slice onion for 15 minutes. Press through a sieve or blend and add to a thin white sauce made by melting 2 tablespoons butter and blending in 2 tablespoons flour, a pinch of pepper and 2 cups milk. You can make this really elegant by serving it garnished with a few whole peas, some minced chervil, chives, or parsley and passing around croutons fried in butter. It also improves it to use meat stock instead of water.

Cream of Spinach Soup—Puree ¾ cup cooked greens in a blender or chop fine or rub through a sieve. Combine 2 cups milk, 1 bay leaf, 2 sprigs parsley and 1 teaspoon minced onion and heat to boiling. Melt 3 tablespoons butter, blend in 3 tablespoons flour, a pinch of paprika, 1 teaspoon salt and the milk mixture. Simmer 5 minutes, stirring constantly. Add the spinach to the mixture and ¼ cup cream. Reheat and serve.

Cream of Tomato Soup—Peel about 6 tomatoes and cook, or use about 2 cups canned tomatoes. Simmer for 15 minutes after you have mashed them to break up large pieces. Now cool and then puree in a blender or just finish mashing. Add ½ teaspoon soda, 1 tablespoon honey and 1 teaspoon salt. In a separate pan melt 2 tablespoons butter. Mash in 2 tablespoons flour. Then gradually stir in 2 cups milk, stirring constantly until it thickens. Now stir in your tomato mixture, 2 cups more of milk and 1 tablespoon of finely chopped parsley, if you have it. Heat and serve.

Thickened Milk—Mrs. Lillie R. Balph wrote me from Beaver Falls, Pennsylvania, and she isn't the only one I've heard from about this though my mother never made it. "My mother served this to us as a breakfast cereal. It isn't a soup. She used flour to thicken the milk to a pudding consistency. She put butter and salt in it and heated it until it was very smooth and creamy. She served it in cereal dishes. She ate it with sugar and more butter but Father and us children used cream and sugar. My aunt made hers lumpy as did other women in the community. Sometimes I make it for myself."

MILK BEVERAGES

Almost Instant Breakfast—Combine 2 eggs, 1 cup or more milk and a pour of molasses (or some instant cocoa, or a little honey and vanilla). Beat it up with the eggbeater or put into the blender. Pour into a glass and serve. You can sprinkle nutmeg on top, if you want. Serve with toasted homemade bread. If you beat the yolks and whites separately and then fold the whites in last, you'll have a fluffy eggnog. If you use scalding milk, you'll have a nice hot one (now add the nutmeg for sure).

Banana Milk Shake—Slice 2 bananas and beat until creamy, or put through a coarse sieve, or blend. Add 2 cups cold milk, mix thoroughly and serve at once.

Banana-Pineapple Eggnog—Add 1 beaten egg and 2 tablespoons pineapple juice to the above recipe.

Eggnog for a Group—Beat 3 egg whites, then 3 egg yolks, then beat in 3 cups rich milk (some cream in it), 2 tablespoons brown sugar and 2 tablespoons vanilla. Sprinkle nutmeg on the top of each serving.

A Real Strawberry Milk Shake—Crush about 1 quart strawberries and press through a coarse sieve in order to get at least 1⅔ cups puree. Or blend. Combine the strawberry puree with 5 cups milk and ½ cup cream. Add ½ cup honey, ½ teaspoon salt and 2½ teaspoons lemon juice. Mix well and chill. Top each glass with a spoonful of whipped cream.

Banana-Strawberry Shake—Mash 2 medium-ripe bananas and combine with 1 cup slightly sweetened, crushed strawberries. Mix in 1 tablespoon lemon juice, 1 quart milk and 1 quart slightly softened vanilla ice cream with a whisk. You could garnish each serving with a fresh strawberry.

Lemon Shake—Combine 2 beaten eggs, ½ cup ice water, ⅓ cup lemon juice and sweetening. Mix it thoroughly. Then beat slowly into 3 cups milk.

Apricot Milk—Put 1 cup cooked apricots and their juice through a sieve, or blend. Mix the pulp with 3 cups milk. Put ½ pint vanilla ice cream in a pitcher and pour the milk mixture over it. Stir slightly.

Prune Milk—Pit and mash the prunes until you have 1 cup pulp. Add that to 3 cups chilled milk and beat them together or shake in a jar. Pour into glasses and top with whipped cream.

Orange Juice and Milk—Combine 2 cups milk, 1 cup orange juice and 1 tablespoon honey in a jar. Tighten the lid and shake vigorously, or blend. If you can shake it with ice it will be even nicer. You may want more sweetening.

Pear and Ginger Ale Milk—Press 1 cup cooked or canned pears (not the juice) through a sieve, or blend. Mix with 1 quart milk. Pour into glasses and to each glass add a dollop of fizzy ginger ale.

Maple and Ginger Ale Milk—Add ½ cup maple syrup to 1 quart milk and mix well. Pour the milk into tall glasses and add a dollop of ginger ale (recipe in Herbs) to taste.

Milk Lassie—Stir 1 tablespoon molasses into a cup of milk, hot or cold. Easy and nice.

Banana Lassie—Mash 1 ripe banana until smooth. Stir in 1 tablespoon molasses and a pinch of salt. Add ¾ cup milk and mix well.

Koumiss—A popular old-time fermented milk beverage, this was originally of mare's milk. It is easy to make. Put milk fresh from the cow into a scalded pop bottle. Fill it almost up to the top and cork it tightly. Shake it up thoroughly every day for 10 days. At the end of that time it is koumiss and ready to drink.

Shaker Syllabub—The Shakers heavily sweetened a gallon of warmed apple cider with maple sugar or syrup and grated a nutmeg on top. Then milked the cow right into the mixture and served it at the table while still hot and foamy. Some winter I'm going to try that just for adventure!

CUSTARD

Custard can be made by baking or boiling, or can be thickened with rennet which causes a yogurt-like result. Custards have to be cooked at a low temperature and not too long or they will curdle. But frankly I'm always in such a muddle my custards "curdle" more often than not, and they are still delicious. All "curdle" means is that some water separates out. I just pour it off and serve what's left. The best way to regulate the cooking temperature of baked custards is to surround with water. Set the individual custard dishes in a pan of hot water. Make all boiled custards in the top of a double boiler. Milk that is a little sour can also cause curdling.

The authorities say if the custard does start to separate remove it immediately from the heat, set the custard pan in a pan of cold water and beat to redistribute the particles. Any acid such as lemon juice would reinforce the tendency to curdle. Baked custards come out firmer than boiled custards. You know it is done when the blade of a knife run into the center of the custard comes out clean. The firmness of the custard is also a result of the amount of egg in it. The more egg in your custard, the firmer it will be. Two eggs per cup of liquid is a good general guide. One egg per cup of liquid makes a soft custard all right for baking in small cups.

Baked Custard—Combine 3 lightly beaten eggs, ¼ teaspoon salt and ⅓ cup sugar. Add 3 cups scalded milk slowly, stirring constantly. Add ½ teaspoon vanilla. Pour into custard cups. Sprinkle with nutmeg. Place the filled custard cups in a pan of hot water and bake in a moderate oven (325°) for 45 minutes, or until a knife inserted in the center of the custard comes out clean.

For *chocolate custard:* Add 1½ ounces (squares) of chocolate to the milk and heat until melted. You can't use that instant chocolate stuff.

For *coconut custard:* Add ½ cup shredded coconut to the mixture.

For *coffee custard:* Scald 2 tablespoons ground coffee with the milk, strain, and proceed as for the baked custard.

For *date custard:* Add ½ cup chopped dates to the custard before baking.

For *honey custard:* Use ½ cup honey instead of sugar.

For *rum custard:* Leave out the vanilla and add 2 tablespoons rum.

Boiled Custard—Combine 2 lightly beaten eggs, ⅛ teaspoon salt and ¼ cup sugar. Add slowly 2 cups scalded milk and cook in the top of a double boiler until the mixture coats a spoon. Add ½ teaspoon vanilla and chill.

For *almond custard:* Use almond extract instead of the vanilla and top with shaved toasted almonds when ready to serve.

For *caramel custard:* Use brown sugar instead of white.

For *chocolate custard:* Melt 1 ounce (square) chocolate in the milk.

Vanilla Rennet Custard—Combine 2 cups milk, 2 tablespoons sugar and dash of salt in small pan. Cook, stirring constantly, over low heat, until lukewarm. Remove from heat and add 1 teaspoon vanilla. Crush 1 rennet tablet in cold water in a cup, stirring until dissolved. Add it quickly to the milk mixture, stirring only once or twice. Pour immediately into a quart dish or into individual dishes. Let stand at room temperature until the mixture is set (do not move) then chill. The custard will set in 10 to 30 minutes, depending on the temperature of the room. The higher the room temperature the longer the time is needed. Sprinkle top of custard lightly with nutmeg or cinnamon just before serving. Rennet is sometimes available at grocery stores.

Custard making is so simple and yet such an art. My mother's custards were carefully made in little individual dishes. They always came out just perfect and were such a gift of love it makes me both hungry and homesick just to remember them. Here's a letter from two more ladies who really take custard seriously. Mrs. Edgar R. Bilbert wrote me from Kennewick, Washington: "I am writing this to tell you of a recipe my neighbor, Mrs. Farrell Clontz, gave me. She gave me permission to give it to you. Maybe it isn't a recipe. She adds 2 white crackers, broken up, to each 5-inch-across-the-top custard dish. This takes up the water that often forms in the custard. I think it even makes a nice topping. Mrs. Clontz also adds white crackers to her scrambled eggs when she adds milk."

QUICK MILK CULTURES

Store buttermilk, kefir and yogurt are the three common cultures in use but they are not the only ones. The mention of store buttermilk may confuse you. Farm buttermilk is the liquid left over after you've churned butter. It is delicious and good to use in cooking or to drink straight. Commercial dairy buttermilk never was near a butter churn. It is made by adding a culture to milk to thicken it. Then dots of butter are sprayed into the cultured milk and the buttermilk is ready for sale. Kefir is milk cultured by a combination of lactic bacteria (yogurt culture) plus yeast cells which produce alcohol and carbon dioxide. That means the kefir culture will have everything yogurt does plus an alcohol content ranging from 1 to 4 percent. Procedure for kefir is basically the same as for buttermilk or yogurt cultures except that incubation temperature can be lower. (Be sure not to put the milk in a sealed container to ferment or you may have an explosion because of the gas being produced.) There are two really good books on the whole general subject of these quick milk cultures. One is *Making Your Own Cheese and Yogurt* by Max Alth, published by Funk and Wagnalls, New York, 1973 (also good on cheese making). The other is *Yogurt, Kefir, and Other Milk Cultures* by Beatrice Trum Hunter that can be ordered from Keats Publishing Company, 212 Elm St., New Canaan, Connecticut 06840.

BUTTERMILK CULTURED MILK—Mix 2 cups raw milk or homegrown milk with ¼ cup store buttermilk. Cover and set in a warmish place for 24 hours. You can use ¼ cup of your resulting thick milk to start a new batch and so on. You can make cottage cheese out of the results. Both curd and whey are good and nourishing to eat if you want. Any little mold that forms on top can simply be scraped off and given to the animals. Buttermilk culture is the least sour tasting of the three. Sourness also depends on how soon you eat it. The sooner you eat any of these three the less sour they will be. The longer you wait to eat your cultured milk the more sour it will be—up to a certain maximum point.

KEFIR—If you can buy store cultured kefir, start by combining 2 cups raw or homegrown milk with ¼ cup unflavored kefir. Cover and let rest for 48 hours. Good to drink mixed with fruit juice, fresh fruit or frozen fruit, or sweetened with honey or sorghum cane syrup or molasses. Or you can buy kefir starter in "grains." Here's a letter from Mrs. George O. Nordmann of Topton, North Carolina, about how she makes kefir. "First, obtain some kefir grains. These are available from R.A.J. Biological Laboratory, 35 Park Avenue, Blue Point, New York 11715. One half unit will culture 1 cup of milk, one full unit will culture 1 pint of milk. No need to order any but the half unit as kefir grains multiply quite rapidly. (The surplus may be dried, frozen or held over for a short period in the refrigerator.)

The grains may be used with any good quality milk: powdered, skim, goat's, cow's or soya milk. When using powdered milk, avoid chlorinated and/or fluoridated water.

"Place the grains (after rinsing in cold water) in the amount of whatever kind of milk you use in a quart jar and leave set at room temperature overnight. Next day, strain out grains, rinse them and place in more milk in another container. The milk from which the grains were removed is now ready to drink. The sourness depends on the length of time the grains were allowed to stand in the milk. Always rinse the grains in cold water before reusing. The proportion of grains to milk should be about 1 cup of grains to 1 quart of milk. They multiply fastest in skim or low-fat milk at about 68°-70°. Freeze-dried grains may be ordered from Continental Culture Specialists, 1354 E. Colorado St., Glendale, California 91025. Those from R.A.J. are active."

Here's a letter from Alan Clute of Sunnyvale, California, who got some kefir culture from a friend: "Ours is a gelatinous blob, about ½ inch across, which we recently got from a friend. You just plunk it into some barely warm milk and let it sit, covered and wrapped, at a warm room temperature—no need for special heat as with yogurt. Next day you fish it out and repeat, sort of like milking a cow. When the blob grows big enough it can be divided and shared. Our friend said the culture needs to be used every couple of days or so which means that, as with a cow, somebody else has to care for it while you're away." But, Alan, you can't put a cow in the freezer to wait out your trip—and you can your blob!

YOGURT is milk soured by a selected variety of bacteria. The best way to get started with the right kind is to buy a pint in the dairy case and add 3 tablespoons of that to a quart of your own milk. You can use cow, goat, soybean milk, or even powdered skim milk. Or you could use a commercial yogurt culture for a starter—check at your health food store. Yogurt is thickened because the bacteria consumes the milk sugar and changes some of it to lactic acid. Once you have made a yogurt culture at home you can keep making more by using a little of your last culture to make each new batch, but eventually the mixture gets invaded by an off-breed of bacteria. In that case you could start over with some dairy yogurt. This happens about once a month. You can't make your own culture (starter) unless you're a bacteriologist because that involves isolating a batch of one kind of invisible bacteria from all the others and growing it.

You can make rennet puddings from scratch, though, and they are similar to yogurt. When Little Miss Muffet ate "curds and whey" I figure she was either eating homemade cottage cheese or else a junket pudding. They used "essence of pepsin" or "liquid rennet" or a "junket tablet" to make them and that's the same rennet that is now used in cheesemaking. (See Cheese section for how to make rennet.) To make rennet pudding just stir in the acid, let the milk stand at room temperature for about 20 minutes and then refrigerate. Serve with cream and sweetening or fruit. It's very bland. You can buy rennet tablets or junket tablets (same thing) in a grocery store.

Basic Yogurt—I think the type of milk used has a lot to do with yogurt being too runny and not setting up, and I have to use noninstant nonfat dry milk. You could try it using skim milk; a friend did and said it was perfect. This yogurt recipe was sent to me by Connie Hughes.

Use 1½ cups canned milk, 2⅔ cups skim milk and 1 teaspoon unflavored gelatin. Put the milk in a 2-quart pan and sprinkle on gelatin. Let soak 5 minutes or so then stir with a wire whisk while heating to almost boiling (to pasteurize). Cool to warm (I set the pan in a dishpan with cold water and watch it till it's just warm). Add ¼ cup commercial yogurt (unflavored) and whisk in well. Rinse out small jars with hot water and fill with warm yogurt mixture. Set in a warm place overnight till set. Taste it to see if it's ready or not. Then refrigerate.

Heat milk to 150° to pasteurize, cool to 110°

Add milk powder if desired for extra thickness and nutrition

Stir in starter and maintain at 110° until thickened. Disturb as little as possible

Thick Yogurt—To thicken the above recipe add anywhere from 2 tablespoons to 1 cup powdered milk. From scratch with powdered milk use 2½ cups dry milk powder with 3¾ cups water.

Christine's Yogurt—From Christine Roelke of Manchester, Pennsylvania. "I have a yogurt maker/warming tray. Use 1 quart whole or skim milk and add ⅓ or ½ cup powdered milk (optional for a firmer or pudding-like consistency). Scald, then let cool until it feels lukewarm to the touch. Add vanilla (1 teaspoon) and honey (less than ¼ teaspoon). Mix in 2 to 3 tablespoons plain yogurt. Let sit on warm surface for 2 to 4 hours. Cover the containers with a cookie sheet to keep the warmth down where the yogurt is. Note: I found out honey can be added before the milk has turned to yogurt. I just discovered this and am so thrilled with it."

Yogurt for a Big Family—Heat 1 gallon milk to 110°. Add 1 cup yogurt. Let set until it is cultured. Chill and eat.

Flavored Yogurt—Blend in with the finished yogurt, berries that have been put through a sieve or blended, or any fruit juice. Use about ¼ to ¾ cup flavoring per 2 cups yogurt. Sweeten with honey or sharpen the flavor with lemon juice as you prefer. Rhubarb sauce and yogurt go well together. Or serve it with any whole fruit. Use it for a vegetable salad dressing combined with seasonings like parsley, horseradish, tomato juice, onion or Roquefort cheese.

The American Taste—so called. Mix ½ teaspoon vanilla flavoring into your quart of milk that's going to be yogurt.

Yogurt and Cucumbers—Peel 3 large cucumbers and slice into ⅛-inch thick pieces. Combine 4 cups yogurt, 1 clove garlic, ground or finely chopped, and 1 teaspoon salt. Pour over the cucumbers and serve cold.

Yogurt-Fruit Drink—In a blender combine 1 cup fruit juice, 1 cup yogurt, a little honey, if you need more sweetening, and ½ cup ice, if you want it *really* cold.

Banana-Yogurt Drink—1 cup yogurt, ½ cup milk, 1 banana, honey to taste and ice, if wanted. Combine in a blender.

Yogurt Salad Dressing—Combine 4 cloves minced garlic (*really fine*), 4 tablespoons lemon juice, ¼ cup cooking oil and 4 tablespoons grated onion with 2½ cups yogurt, 2 teaspoons salt, ¼ cup chopped parsley and a pinch of red paprika. Serve chilled.

Frozen Yogurt—Soft frozen yogurt is good topped with nuts, honey, or granola, fruit, fruit juice or any other fruit or sweetening thing. Mix yogurt with fruit (1 cup yogurt to 1 cup fruit). Use fresh fruit cut fine. Procedure is to first freeze yogurt to a soft mush, then beat it up with fruit, freeze again and serve.

Cardamom Fruit Yogurt—3 cups yogurt mixed with 1 cup fruit and 1¼ teaspoon ground cardomom.

For your next batch—Just save about ¼ cup of your first batch. Keep it in the refrigerator or in a covered container. Use it within 5 days to start another batch of yogurt. And so on until your yogurt gets that off-taste that shows you that some sort of bacteria has moved in on the original variety. That's when you have to get some of the store kind again. You could also buy yogurt culture direct from a dairy supplier if you had any use for so much at once.

Yogurt makers—Those $12 items sold in the health food stores are nice but not necessary.

CREAM CHEESE

Cream cheese and yogurt are actually very similar. Yogurt is skim milk cultured the way the dairies make it. Cream cheese can be made from more or less rich cream which gives you, in turn, a higher or lower calorie cream cheese. It will soon spoil, unlike your hard cheeses, and so it has to be kept protected from air after it's made, refrigerated, and eaten relatively soon.

You can substitute your homemade cream cheese

in all those good recipes. A 3-ounce package means 6 tablespoons of your own. The 8-ounce package means 1 cup of your own cream cheese. Don't store cream cheese in your freezer. You'll cause weeping and destroy the texture because when the ice crystals form they break up the fine consistency. This cream cheese takes 15 to 18 hours to set up right. You can use yogurt culture or a regular cheese culture or a cultured buttermilk culture.

You can make it from regular cream which contains 24-35 percent fat, but it really improves it to add skim milk powder to increase the milk solids and reduce the fat. Pure cream cheese is very buttery. Store cream cheese isn't very much cream in fact. Although it isn't necessary, dairies add a gelatin "stabilizer."

Here are some of the old fashioned ways to make something like cream cheese without using gelatin or powdered milk.

Yogurt Cream Cheese—Pour yogurt into a cloth, gather the corners and sides in your hands and tie firmly. Hang this on a clothesline in a cool airy place to drip for a day or two. Then scrape what you have left from the cloth and place it in a jar.

Sour Cream Cheese #1—Salt to taste sour cream and stir well. Pour into a cloth which has been wrung out in cold water and proceed as above. This has a really sour taste.

Sour Cream Cheese #2—Take 1 quart of cream (the lighter the better to avoid the buttery taste). Set the dish in a pan of hot water and warm almost to the boiling point. Remove and cool to lukewarm. Add rennet. Let stand until thick. Break the curds slightly with a spoon and then tie up in a cloth. Press the cloth lightly with a weight for a half day so the pressed-out whey will drain away. Then retie in a clean cloth, rub salt over the outside and let hang to drip for a day or so more.

Devonshire Cream or "Clotted Cream"—This is just delicious and I really recommend your trying it if you have lots of milk and cream to play with. Combine 2 quarts milk and 1 quart heavy cream and refrigerate overnight. The next day heat to a temperature of about 90° and hold there for about 3 to 5 hours, or until a wrinkled, leathery look appears on the surface, this containing little pockets filled with a liquid resembling melted butter. Don't stir or shake the contents. Don't let it get too hot. When it is very wrinkled and drawn-looking, cool and again refrigerate overnight.

The next day skim off the thick top cream. That is your Devonshire cream. It is good with canned fruit or fresh strawberries. You'll get about 1 pint of Devonshire cream.

COTTAGE CHEESE AND FARMER CHEESE

These can be made of skim milk, buttermilk, whole milk or goat's milk, but not very well of pasteurized milk because the natural souring process is one key to good cottage cheese. If you must use pasteurized (store) milk warm the milk to about 75° and then add 1 cup cultured buttermilk from the store.

It will help also to use rennet (½ tablet to 1 gallon of milk), or preferably a junket tablet which has a milder action than rennet. Goat's milk does not thicken as easily and has a softer curd than cow's milk so to make cottage cheese with it, it helps to mix in one-half or one-third cow's milk. Otherwise it takes about 5 days to get goat milk sour enough for cottage cheese.

One quart of milk will make about 1 cup of cottage cheese. You can work with any convenient amount since there are no other ingredients except salt "to taste" in the final stage. The best container in which to "set" the milk is a wide, coverable one. Sour the milk in the same container in which you will make the cottage cheese. A covered enamel roaster, or canning kettle or a heavy crockery or stainless steel bowl would all be fine. Do not use aluminum.

The more milk you work with the easier it will be to control the temperature—75° to 85° is the temperature to strive for through the clabbering process. Leave the milk on the warming shelf of your wood stove or some other warm but not hot place, similar to one you would use to raise yeast bread. (If you are using milk that is already sour you would skip this step, of course.) Temperatures that are too low allow the proliferation of less desirable bacteria. Temperatures that are too high will kill your bacteria and stop their creation of the lactic acid that you need to clabber the milk. They will also toughen the curd.

The clabbering may take a few hours or a few days depending on temperature and bacteria count. When the milk is "set" it will have a consistency something like jelly. The solids will have formed one large curd which floats on whey in the bottom. When the milk is sour and clabbered you are ready to cut the curd.

Cut the curd using a clean butcher knife with a blade long enough to reach from the surface of the curd to the bottom of the pan. Make parallel cuts across the curd one way and then perpendicular parallel cuts across the other way to create squares between ½ inch and 1 inch on the side. If you are using a deep pan, rig up a galvanized wire to cut the curd horizontally at intervals between the top and the bottom of the pan. Now stir the curd very slowly and gently, endeavoring not to break up the curd but to keep it from clumping. The clumping tendency will be most pronounced at first and less so as the curd gets firmer with your final heating.

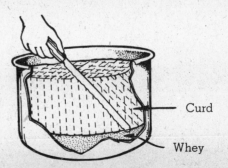

Cut clabbered curd into ½ inch to 1 inch square chunks

Now the curd is heated a little more to get it to just the right firmness. This is more art than science and depends on how you like your cottage cheese. The lower the temperature at which you stop, the softer curded will be your cheese, the higher the temperature the firmer your curd will be. Don't let the milk heat over 110° for traditional soft-curd cheese. Up to 120° gives you the tougher curded "farmer" style cheese. One system is to take a half hour heating at the rate of about 2° every 5 minutes to a final temperature of 100° or so, and then hold it at that temperature until it has developed the desired firmness. That's the laboratory ideal and really can't be duplicated in the kitchen but have courage—many a fine bowl of cottage cheese has been made under less than perfect conditions!

Heat very slowly to desired temperature, stirring gently

To test the curd pinch a little between thumb and finger. If a tiny bit remains on the ball of your thumb it is about ready. When you are satisfied that all the curd would pass the pinch test you are ready to drain the whey. Dump the curd and whey into a cheesecloth-covered colander or a colander having very coarse holes and substantial interstices to hold back the curd as the whey drains away (save the whey for your animals). You can make something suitable by punching holes in a metal pan or can from the inside out.

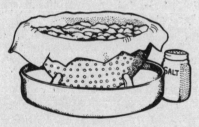

Drain whey from curd; salt to taste

If the milk was very sour you could rinse the curd with cold water and drain again. At this point you may want to break up the curd with cold water and drain again. Sprinkle salt over the curd, work it in thoroughly and let the cottage cheese continue to drain for at least an hour. You could tie the end of the cloth together and hang it from a nail until all the whey has drained off.

You now have dry cottage cheese. It will keep about a week or 10 days in the refrigerator (covered). The usual commercial product is "creamed." You can add cream to yours at this time or before serving, but it makes more sense to do so shortly before serving because creamed cottage cheese does not keep nearly as well as the dry.

If you blend some "dry" cottage cheese with water and add tomato sauce and seasonings you can make a salad dressing. With blue cheese in it, it's blue cheese dressing, with vanilla and sweetening added, it's a low-calorie imitation whipped cream.

Other ways to serve the cottage cheese are to press it into a dish and then cut off slices or roll it into balls. You could add ½ teaspoon each grated onion, minced green onion tops or minced chives per cup of cottage cheese. Or you could mix in ¼ cup chopped stuffed olives and 2 tablespoons mayonnaise per cup. We like it with cream and honey on the top, but I've seen the horrified faces of enough cottage cheese-with-salt-and-pepper eaters to know it's all a matter of preference. You can also serve it mixed with celery seed or caraway seeds. Health food people would like their cottage cheese mixed with sea salt, garlic and chives.

Easy Curds and Cream (one of infinite varieties)—Set your milk in a bowl until it becomes clabbered. Pour the clabbered milk slowly into a curd press (see Hard Cheese). Let the press drain overnight. Turn the curds out into a flat dish. Grate nutmeg freely over the top and serve with heavy sweet cream, more grated nutmeg and sweetening.

Doris Gronewold's Goat Milk Cottage Cheese—1 gallon freshly drawn goat's milk—should be at 100°. Dissolve ⅛ of a Hansen's cheese rennet tablet in 2 tablespoons warm water. Stir in the milk. This will set in ½ hour. Stir the mixture to break the whey from the curds. Squeeze. Salt, chill and serve. I sometimes add chives to mine.

Cottage Cheese Blintzes—Blintzes are a Jewish pancake dessert. I traded a copy of the Recipe Book for this recipe.

Beat 1 egg with a rotary beater until white and yolk are blended. Sift together 1 cup sifted all-purpose flour and ½ teaspoon salt. Alternately add flour and 1 cup water, a little at a time, to the egg. Beat until smooth and free from lumps. Break the surface air bubbles with a fork. Heat a 6-inch skillet over medium heat. Grease lightly. Using a ¼-cup measure, pour 3 tablespoons of the batter into the pan all at once. Tilt the pan quickly so that the entire bottom is covered with a thin layer of the batter. Cook until the pancake is firm, but not browned. Cook on one side only. Invert on a clean tea towel. The pancake will slip out easily when it is done. Place a heaping tablespoon of the filling on the pancake. Fold the four sides over the center and invert on the cloth. Continue with the remaining batter and filling and grease the pan from time to time as needed. This much preparation may be done in advance, and the blintzes wrapped in a tea towel and stored in the refrigerator; or they may be wrapped in foil and frozen.

At serving time, heat 4 tablespoons oil in a large skillet or shallow baking pan. Place the blintzes in the pan, side by side without crowding. Brown over medium heat or bake at 350° for 30 minutes (allow slightly longer if the blintzes were still frozen when placed in the pan). Turn over once during cooking, to brown both sides. This makes 11.

Filling—Mix 1 pound dry cottage cheese, 1 slightly beaten egg, 1 tablespoon sugar, ½ tablespoon ground cinnamon and ¼ tablespoon salt until blended. This makes 2 cups, enough for the above recipe. If served as a dessert, ½ teaspoon vanilla extract and ½ cup seedless raisins may be added (optional). Serve with sour cream, or both sour cream and jam.

Cottage Cheese Sandwich Spreads—Mix cottage cheese with finely chopped beet pickles, or nuts and cherries, or chopped green beans and green peppers, or finely cut nuts and pimento bits, or cucumber and celery bits, onion and paprika, or finely chopped Swiss chard and onion and pickle, or tomato chunks and chopped olives or lemon juice and lettuce or cucumber slices and tomato slices!

Cottage Cheese Pancakes—Sent by Bobbi McCollum from Canyon Country, California. Combine 4 beaten eggs, 1 cup sour cream or yogurt, 1 cup cottage cheese, 1 cup flour, a dash of salt and 1 tablespoon sugar or honey. Fry on medium hot griddle same as any pancake. You can thin it down and add fruit, or add vanilla to make it cakier tasting.

HOMEMADE CHEESE SPREADS

American cheese, the familiar processed cheese from the store, is a blend of fresh and aged cheeses that have been melted, pasteurized and mixed with an emulsifier. This makes the texture uniform and soft and also destroys some of the flavor. The pasteurization discourages further ripening. Commercial cheese spreads also usually have extra moisture and a "stabilizer" added.

From Homemade Cheese—Grate 1 pound of basic cheese, like Cheddar. Combine with ½ cup butter, 4 tablespoons dry mustard and ¼ cup milk. Cut up some pimentos to mix in or stir in caraway seeds or shake in garlic salt or onion salt for your flavoring.

Delicious Cheese—Ina Fidler, who is a true country gentlewoman, as well as mistress of all the true country culinary arts, gave me this recipe. She is a grandmother and lives up the road from me in a big white house just where a sign by the road says "Two Miles to Troy." Ina told me that the person who gave her the recipe said you can make it in a big supply, paraffin it, and it will keep a long time, but she couldn't vouch for that part of it because it had never lasted long enough around her home to test its keeping qualities.

Scald 2 gallons of sour (clabbered) milk. That means milk that has gotten sort of firm. Strain off the whey. Be sure and get as much of the whey out of the curds as you can or else the cheese will come out soupy or too soft. If you aren't familiar with these processes use the detailed directions for cottage cheese making. It's the same up to the point of straining off the whey. Now add ½ teaspoon soda and ½ cup butter to the curd. That's what you have left after you pour off the whey. Stir up and let stand for 2 hours. Now put it in a double boiler and add 1 teaspoon butter coloring and 2 teaspoons salt. A big, wide double boiler will do the job quicker and easier than a small

one because you have the cheese more evenly spread out over the hot bottom. Stir and add 1 cup of very sour cream. The sourer the cream you add the more your results will taste like an aged cheese. Best of all use homemade butter and home soured cream. You can skip the butter coloring, if you want. Now cook in the double boiler until the curds melt together, stirring some. It's about the consistency of melted store cheese when you get done. Now rub the bottom and sides of a mold with butter. Your mold can be any old bowl, either square or round in shape. Now pour your cheese right into the mold and let it cool and set up.

Cup Cheese—Start with about 4 quarts of thick sour milk. Cut the milk through several times with a long sharp knife, then heat slowly to 90°, or scald until the curd is very dry. Remove from the heat and place in a wet cheesecloth bag. Press under a heavy weight for 12 to 24 hours, or until the cheese is dry. Force through a cheese sieve or grate fine. Place in a wooden bowl, cover with a heavy cloth and keep in a warm place for 3 to 7 days, or until soft and ripe, stirring occasionally. Then place in a frying pan and cook, stirring constantly until all the lumps are dissolved. Add 1 teaspoon salt and 3 tablespoons butter, mix well, and pour into cups or bowls. It will make about 3 cups of cheese.

Dutch Cheese Spread—Pour 1 quart of milk into a crockery bowl and let stand in a warm place to thicken. When the milk is quite thick, pour boiling water over it, place in a cheesecloth bag and let drain for 12 hours. Rub the cheese through a fine sieve. Work in 2 tablespoons milk and 2 tablespoons cream with a spoon until it is all the consistency of apple butter. Season with ½ teaspoon salt and a very little pepper, if desired. Serve on buttered bread with apple butter.

Potted Cheese—This is an old recipe that a friend sent me. I haven't tried it but it sounds good. Cheese that has gone dry or begun to mold can be turned into a very delicious compound by the following process:

Remove all the moldy portions. If dry, grate it. If not, pound smooth. Add a wineglass of sherry and 1 teaspoon of white sugar for each pound. When the whole is a smooth paste, press down tight in small pots or jars and lay a paper dipped in brandy on the top or turn hot melted suet over it until the surface is completely covered. One tablespoonful of butter added to each pound of cheese, while rubbing smooth, will make the compound rich. It will keep several years. This cheese is better when a year old than when freshly made. Keep in a cool dry place.

HARD CHEESES

The two parts of this book about which I have the biggest sense of accomplishment are the descriptions of home butchering and this cheese section of the Dairy chapter. The home butchering is described as a homesteader would do it, using simple language and is something I simply wrote down as we did it. I did my best because I don't believe similar information is available anywhere else and now it is here.

The cheesemaking was a different sort of hunt. Professionals wouldn't tell me. They said things like you couldn't make cheese without a big factory and lots of expensive equipment and very controlled conditions. Of course, I had that famous cheese recipe that comes with the rennet tablets and has been reworded and reprinted all too many times. I ordered a government book called *Cheese Varieties* that is full of what appear to be cheese recipes. Every time I and friends tried them—and in total that was a lot of times and a lot of different recipes in the book—it turned out to be a moldy disaster. A regular publisher has reprinted this book word for word, calling it *Cheeses of the World* and it is still just as useless from the cooking point of view.

Finally I got a recipe from Mary Simeone, who at the time was 9-months pregnant, living in a tent two-thirds up the side of an Idaho mountain, while her husband built a log cabin. She was milking two goats and her finished cheese tasted very like the good strong Greek and Italian cheeses that usually you can only find in city gourmet shops. Hers is the recipe I called "Basic Cheese" and I like it because it spares you all the useless detail of the rennet company recipe. She aged her cheese by hanging it on the end of a string under the biggest bull pine she could find and that's to encourage any of you who think you can't make cheese without a factory. The fact is factories were very recent arrivals on the cheese scene. Mary and her husband are from some Italian part of New York City and they are making it fine now in Elk River, Idaho, which is really out of the way, even for Idaho.

My big breakthrough was meeting John E. Montoure, Associate Professor of Bacteriology-Biochemistry at the University of Idaho, at a meeting of the Idaho Purebred Dairy Cattle Association where my husband and I sort of stuck out like sore teats. A speaker got up and told us how we should be counting our blessings because we belonged to the upper classes and were in the lap of luxury. He must have meant all those guys with 150 head of milking Holsteins home in the dairy barn, but I thought of our three head of registered Shorthorns that we traded hay for to a desperate man and practically got hysterical and fell out of my chair.

Anyway, there I met John Montoure, who was head of probably the biggest and best university-type cheesemaking laboratory at the University of Idaho before somebody in Boise decided that grammar and such like were more important than the science of making a cheese and wiped out his funding 100 percent. That's really a sad thing. Because here is somebody who knows as much and maybe more about making cheese as anybody in the United States and he can't make cheese anymore. Well, he's gone back to teaching biochemistry and he's hoping someday maybe he'll get his funding back.

When I talked to him and asked *him* about making cheese homestead style he didn't say, "Oh no, you have to have a factory." That man just sat down and started working. He knew every recipe I asked for by heart. I spent two long afternoons with him writing as fast as I could and when I get a chance I'm going back for more because what he knows is too good to be just kept in one man's head. And he hadn't the slightest hesitation about sharing his information with me though I told him what it was for and he wasn't getting anything for it.

On each recipe he'd have to start out figuring from 1,000 pounds of milk because that was what he was used to working with. Then he'd convert every ingredient down to household quantity for me in proportion.

GALLONS AND POUNDS—Dairy operations measure milk by the pound rather than the gallon. Five gallons of milk equals 42 pounds and that amount of milk should yield you 4 to 4½ pounds of finished cheese. That's 10 pounds of cheese per 100 pounds of milk, or approximately 1 pound cheese per 10 pounds of milk.

CHEESE COLORING—They used to make it from coal tars and then discovered it was a carcinogenic substance. The cheese coloring that is now sold is OK. To buy cheese coloring (or rennet, or starter for cultured buttermilk), you can mail-order from Dairy Laboratories, 2300 Locust Street, Philadelphia, Pennsylvania 19103; Chr. Hansen's Laboratory, 9015 West Maple Street, Milwaukee, Wisconsin 53214; Klenzade Products, Beloit, Wisconsin 53511; Marschall Dairy Laboratory, 14 Proudfit Street, Madison, Wisconsin 53703; or New Jersey Dairy Laboratories, P.O. Box 748, New Brunswick, New Jersey 08903.

RENNET is used to make these cheeses rather than the natural souring that you use for cottage cheese because the use of rennet allows you to get out more water and that gives you a different kind and a nicer cheese. Even 3 percent less water makes a big difference in the final product. You can order rennet from the addresses I gave above.

If you cared to, or had to, you could make your

own rennet since it is the salt extract of a suckling calf (that means one that has eaten no grass or solid food). You just take the stomach of a suckling calf (a *suckling* calf has only one stomach compared to the four of an adult). Add salt to it and dry it in strips as if you were making jerky. To make cheese with it, cut off a 1-inch square and add it to milk. That would be the equivalent of 2 drops of liquid rennet. If you have trouble clabbering your milk use more liquid rennet. Better too much than too little. Your basic store rennet rule is to dissolve ¼ rennet tablet for each 2 gallons milk in ½ cup cool water. Add with the milk at 86°-90°. Stir well. Cover and let rest an hour, or until curd is well formed.

CULTURE you're familiar with from yogurt, cultured buttermilk and cultured cream cheese. Culture is a bacterial organism that you can order in a dried form from the same addresses. Before 1940 they thought you couldn't make cheese with pasteurized milk. They soured milk the natural way you do for cottage cheese and some cheesemakers made good cheese and some didn't, just as a matter of luck depending on what kind of bacteria were plentiful in their cheesery. Some organisms will make a bitter cheese. Bad ones break down protein. Good ones make an acid and the enzymes will break down some protein, but in a desired way so you get the flavor you want. Since 1940 cheesemakers have learned to pasteurize the milk to destroy the bad bacteria and then add back the good bacteria in their "culture." When you use culture you actually have a choice to add or not add rennet because given time the good organisms will clabber the milk anyway.

Factory cheese operations order frozen cultures which are shipped by express in an ice chest with dry ice around them. You can also order freeze-dried cultures and that's the kind you would prefer.

The Hansen cultures 40 and 41 are basic for making any cheese except Swiss cheese which uses a different one. Swiss cheese is one kind that you can't make at home anyway. The 40 and 41 cultures come in a small vial and run around $3. Ask for "Cheddar cheese culture."

To get the most from your dry cheese culture you can keep it going same as you would yogurt. In fact make yogurt with it and then you have both. Add some to a quart of milk. Let set at 70°. Every two or three days take out 1 teaspoon and add it to another quart of milk to keep it going. Use a clean container and boiled milk. Or pasteurized—that's milk held at 145° for 30 minutes. Or scalded to save time. That's holding it at 161° for 1 minute.

But most homesteaders avoid all this struggle and use cultured buttermilk from the store dairy case to get their starter. They add ¼ cup buttermilk starter to 1 quart milk. Let work 24 hours at room temperature. Add your quart of home cultured buttermilk to 3 to 5 gallons milk, warmed to 86°-90° and let ripen 1 or 2 hours. Now you're ready to add rennet. If you skip this step your cheese may swell and not ripen properly. These are the "good" microorganisms that you want to ripen your cheese. If you don't fill your milk with them you will have less desirable ones.

MOISTURE CONTENT—Most cheeses are made of the same thing—milk, usually skim milk. The different results are achieved by slight differences in either dryness, acid content or temperature. At home you can control the amount of moisture in the final product. The temperature at which you cook it and the length of time you cook it controls the moisture content. More moisture gives you a softer body and a sharper taste. There is a tendency to develop off-flavors faster but also it cures faster. The use of rennet rather than natural souring enables you to get out more of the water.

TEMPERATURE is really important! If you can't control the cooking temperature you're going to end up with a different cheese each time. That doesn't mean it has to be a bad cheese though. In making these hard cheeses if you go much above 100° or 102°, you will kill off the good organisms, which you don't want to do ever. This is where hard cheese is different from cottage cheese. Hard cheese is made as much by the curing process as by what you do at the beginning and it's the organisms that give you the cure working gradually in there.

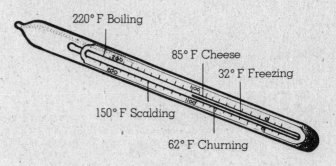

Curing temperature is the second one that matters in hard cheese making—45° is best. Then the cure happens slowly and you take a chance on the quality of the cheese—things might happen in there that you'd rather not from off-breeds of bacteria. At lower temperatures it just means a longer curing time and you'll get tired of waiting. If you cure at 45° a Cheddar cheese will have the right kind of flavor in 6 to 9 months. Curing at 48°-52° can give you an entirely different cheese. This is the place where making cheese at home is rough compared to having the "factory conditions" which means having controlled temperatures and humidity. Turn your cheese over every day or so for the first month. Grease the bandage and rub it at that time, too.

To get around this problem: First, don't worry about getting your cheese precisely like the store version. It will still be good food and good cheese. Second, do your major cheesemaking in the fall after the worst of the heat is over. Third, figure out the coolest place you have—the most nearly suitable. (Same problem as with storing apples.) For good quality cheese 60° is too high. Your root cellar might be a good place although you risk the cheese picking up an off-flavor from the vegetables there. You know the vital thing with root cellars is that they have no windows and that prevents entrance of *light* and you keep that door *closed* except when you must pass through and that as seldom as possible. This keeps the temperature and humidity right so your carrots and potatoes don't wither. So if you wait until late enough in the summer so your root cellar won't be above 60° you could use it. Before then you could use your refrigerator. You must be *very* careful to keep all flies out of your curing place or you may get maggots in the cheese.

The size of your cheese also matters. Smaller cheeses have a greater tendency to dry out. Starting with at least 5 gallons of milk will help you here. But the milk shouldn't be more than two days old if you can help it. It's OK to skim it.

PRESSING—The traditional press for homemade cheese is a coffee can with nail holes punched through the bottom and sides. Be sure and punch from the inside out. That's harder to do but if you punch from the outside in you'll have sharp edges inside that will tear your cheesecloth, make it hard to get the cheese back out, and leave pockmarks on the surface of the cheese. It's important to get the curds into the press (wrapped in a cloth) while they are hot. Then you put your round wooden follower on top and weights on that. The combination of heat and pressure drives off the whey and causes the curds to change from individual pieces to a solid mass that won't spoil inside.

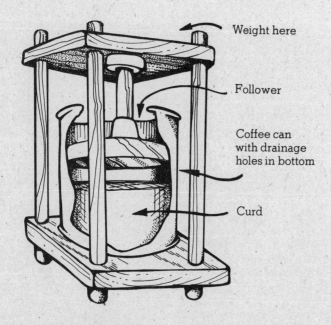

Weight here

Follower

Coffee can with drainage holes in bottom

Curd

SALTING THE CURD—It's a good idea to add the salt in three portions. Add the first third, stir, then add the second, stir again, and so on.

WRAPPING THE CHEESE—Professionals use a foil coated with wax into which the cheese ball is really sealed. You could use foil inside of butcher paper. Vinegar cloth is easiest though. You have to freshen the vinegar at intervals. Paraffin dip is a good mold preventer. Just melt your paraffin, dip the cheese all around into it and cool. You may also can cheese, if you have a way of creating a vacuum, because mold can't grow without air and it's mold that we're trying to prevent at this stage. You can't can and create a vacuum though because you're not a factory so paraffin or use the vinegar cloth or foil.

REFERENCES—When I first tried to write about cheese you couldn't find recipes anywhere. Now there is a little book called *Cheese Making* by Charles J. Hunt sold by Country Things, 42985 Texas Ave., Palm Desert, California 92260, which is really quite good and fills a much needed place. Also *Cheese Making at Home* by Don Radke (Doubleday, 1974). Then there is a four-volume series of totally professional cheesemaking books called the "Pfizer Cheese Monographs" by Norman F. Olson, Ph.D., recently published by Chas. Pfizer and Co., New York, New York. I wouldn't bother ordering them unless you are really planning to go into cheesemaking business practically at factory level because that's what they are written for.

Swiss Cheese is a very delicate cheese for which everything has to be just right and it is the only one that it would be useless to even attempt at home. The normal procedure is to start out with 3,000 pounds of milk. You just can't make it in small quantities because to get the good eye formation (that's the holes in it) you need a *very* large cheese. They cut it up in little pieces to sell it but when it's made if you get a ball of less than 40 pounds (60 gallons of milk that would require) the eyes wouldn't form right. You also have to have very little temperature change and that's the other thing that is next to impossible to manage at home. The genuine outer rind is really tough on a Swiss cheese in the making. Take any book that claims to tell you how to make Swiss cheese at home with a few dozen grains of salt.

Sometimes even in the factory Swiss cheese goes a little wrong and the gas inside explodes and cheese goes all over the room. Other times it makes no eye at all and that's the troubles they have even under controlled conditions. Swiss cheese also uses a special culture, not the general Cheddar culture but a half and half mixture of *Streptococcus thermophilis* and *Lactobacillus bulgaricus*. You can also add another kind of bacteria called an "eye former" (this is *Propiono bacterium shermanii*) during the cooking operation. If you insist on trying you can order it all from Hansen. The "eye former" has to be kept refrigerated.

Basic Farm Cheese (Works Fine with Goat's Milk)

1. Fill a 9-quart enamel bucket (looks like a chamber pot) or stainless steel but never aluminum to within about an inch of the top with whole milk.

2. Warm it to 86°. Use a dairy thermometer to tell.

3. Add ¼ rennet tablet (or a whole junket tablet) crushed with 1 teaspoon of water. Stir it in. (Your drugstore can order rennet for you.)

4. Let set very quietly until it curds, about 20 minutes maybe.

5. Cut into approximately ½-inch squares by cutting one way and then cutting the other (to make a pattern of squares on the top) and then by reaching in to cut across from top to bottom of the bucket.

6. "Bathe" the curds for 2 minutes with your hands. That means to gently and slowly move the curds around in the whey. (Even more so than "swish.")

7. Set your enamel bucket in a dishpan of water back on the stove. Keep it covered with a cloth so specks and flies won't fall in or crawl in.

8. Slowly warm to 102° (use a dairy thermometer again), stirring occasionally to keep contents at an even temperature. It will tend to get hotter at the bottom of the pan.

9. Take it off the stove and let it set an hour, stirring occasionally very gently.

10. Put cheesecloth over a colander. (Your department store may have to order cheesecloth specially for you.) Fasten the edges with clothespins. Pour the cheese in there. Save the whey. You can feed it to the animals or make bread with it. All the vitamins are in the whey now.

11. Add 1 tablespoon salt and mix with hands. Add 1 tablespoon salt and mix again (total of 2).

12. Tie ends of cheesecloth together to make a bag. Hang it up where you can let it drip for the rest of the day.

13. Put a holding band around the edge of the cheese bag made of cheesecloth like a headband or belt. Put a paper plate with the fluted edge trimmed off over the cheese and one under it and a heavy weight over it and a hard flat smooth thing underneath and let it press like that all night. Something flat

and iron is good to press it or a piece of wood with bricks on top.

14. After it has been pressed all night, let it dry in an airy, cool place, turning it every few days until it forms a hard rind. If it molds cut the mold away.

15. Paraffin it. To do that you heat a block of store paraffin in a pan to almost boiling (210°), then brush the hot wax over your cheese or dip parts of the cheese in until you have it all covered. Attach a string in there and you can hang it up in a cool place to age. At first your cheese will be tasteless and have the consistency of a rubber eraser. The flavor comes with aging. Give it two months at least. Be careful you have it thoroughly paraffined or it may get wormy.

Colby Cheese—Pasteurize 12 gallons of milk. Cool to 88° to 90°. Add 2 cups of your culture (I told you how to make this under the heading of Culture). Let it set for 30 minutes. Now add 2 drops of liquid rennet which has been diluted in 1 cup of water. If you use tablets follow the manufacturer's directions. They'll say how much for 12 gallons. Mix the rennet into the milk thoroughly for 3 minutes and then stop. It will take about 30 minutes to set up.

Put your finger into the milk at a 45-degree angle. If the curd will break real clean on a nice straight line it is ready. Your finger won't have goop on it and the curd can be picked straight up. Now cut the curd. The more uniform the pieces you cut it into the better because small ones will cook too fast and big ones will be undercooked, meaning they will still be fragile and will shatter. Cut as for cottage cheese.

Let it rest 15 minutes. This is to "heal" the curd so it doesn't break up when you start to stir it. Now heat it very slowly. The professionals go up 1° the first 5 minutes, 2° with the second 5 minutes and so on (100° to 102° is the very highest you should go). If you go higher your organisms will start to die and the cheese won't develop as you want. Use a cheese thermometer (same as a dairy thermometer). It will take about half an hour to get the temperature up if you are doing it just right. Set up some kind of a double boiler—like a 5-gallon pail in a canning kettle with water that comes half way up the side. That will keep the temperature right.

After you have gotten the temperature up to 100° in this gradual way, drain off the whey and stir the curd so it doesn't form a single mass. Add salt to taste—maybe 3 to 4 tablespoons for 10 pounds of curd. If you are on a low-salt diet you can substitute a potassium salt. If you didn't salt at all you would get a bland type cheese and a different type of fermentation because the salt holds back some organisms. Thoroughly mix. Put it in a sterilized cheesecloth and press. Start with 5 pounds of pressure for the first half hour to give it a chance to knit together. Gradually increase the pressure to 20 to 25 pounds. It will be of a spongy texture now, not solid like a Cheddar. The cheesecloth closes up the surface of the cheese and gives you a nice product. (Resist the temptation to nibble.) The cloth also acts as a wick and draws moisture out of the inside giving it a path to travel out of the press. So use a cloth whatever else your pressing arrangements. Press overnight—12 to 16 hours. Wrap the cheese in the way I told you.

Now cure the Colby below 45°. Curing above that temperature speeds up the process but you risk a poor taste. If you cured it in your refrigerator it would take 9 to 12 months assuming the temperature in there is 38°-42°. For the first month it would taste like "green curd." At about 3 months you start to pick up a reasonable amount of Colby taste.

Monterey Cheese—Same as Colby, only you "cook" at 100° for 1 hour and 45 minutes before proceeding.

Cheddar Cheese—To make Cheddar cheese proceed as directed for the Colby-type cheese until the end of the curd heating process. The curd should be contracted to about one-half the starting size, firm, and without a tendency to stick when pressed together. Use an ordinary flatiron or a piece of heavy iron bar to make a hot iron test. The curds when rubbed on the clean hot iron and then drawn away should show fine threads about ⅛ inch long. When the curd passes this test dip or pour off the whey, keeping the curd stirred with your hands as you do so.

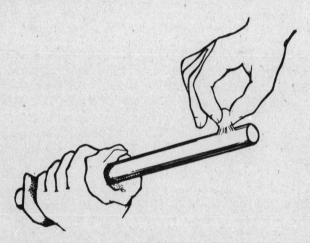

When the whey is off put the curd in a deep, more-or-less-rectangular pan that has a hole punched in the bottom to let whey escape. The top or bottom of an old fashioned roasting pan will work fine for a moderate amount of curd. Don't let the curd cool off while you are draining and transferring it. Pile it evenly in the roasting pan and cut a channel through the cheese to help the whey drain toward the hole in the bottom of the pan. It is handy to have the hole at one end of the pan and then you could keep the pan slightly tilted. Put the pan in your oven. You'll want just enough heat in the oven to keep the cheese at a temperature of 98° to 100°. Put a pan underneath to catch the whey. This is the Cheddaring process and will probably require some experimentation for you. Avoid too much heat.

After about 20 minutes the curd would be firmly matted. Then cut the curd into blocks 6 inches long and turn them over so that what was the top of the curd is now underneath and next to the bottom of the pan. Continue the heating—throughout try not to let the temperature of the curd get below 90°. You'll need

a thermometer inserted in the curd to keep you informed. Turn the curd pieces about every 15 minutes. At the end of the third turning pile the curd blocks two deep. In 15 minutes more repile them three deep if they seem dry enough. The Cheddaring process is done when the hot iron test shows you strings from ½ to 1½ inches long. There is an easier acidity test but you would have to use special equipment.

Next cut the curd with a butcher knife into small pieces about ½ inch wide and 1½ inches long. Then stir thoroughly for about 15 minutes before salting. Add 2 to 3 ounces of salt for every 5 gallons of milk that you started with. The best salt is cheese salt obtainable from a dairy supply or maybe from your drugstore. Its coarse flaky consistency makes it more readily absorbed by the cheese. Spread out the curd, sprinkle the salt on, let cool to 86° to 90°, sprinkle on another bit of salt, stir thoroughly and wait for the salt to dissolve. The curd isn't ready for the press until it is dissolved. Maintain your temperature throughout and when you're ready to press, put the curd in the press at a temperature of about 85°. Now turn back to the directions for Colby cheese and press and finish the cheese according to that. This Cheddaring process will take about 2½ hours in all. When you're done the curd is all in little strings that look almost like a cooked chicken breast.

Grating Cheese—This is a firmer cheese that you grate and use the way you do Parmesan. Make it from skim milk. Clabber, cut and cook in the whey same as Colby. Only don't cook a half hour. Cook for 2 or 3 hours. After it is nicely cured go ahead and grate it. You can add additional seasoning to suit yourself.

Professor Montoure's Deep Fat Fried Cheese—Fry chunks of pressed curd. The pieces are cut ½ inch to 1 inch long similar to French fries. They keep their shape and have a nice flavor. Do this with "green curd" meaning freshly made cheese. You can't do it with aged cheese.

Mrs. Carl Sandburg's and Doris Gronewold's Neufchâtel Cheese—1 gallon freshly-drawn goat's milk, ½ junket or rennet tablet thoroughly dissolved in ¼ cup cold water, ⅓ cup smoothly coagulated sour milk (you can use sour cream or kefir or yogurt starters). Nuts, olives, onions, chives, etc. Cool milk to 75°. Add ⅓ cup sour milk. Stir for 1 minute. Add rennet tablet and stir again for 1 minute. Do not disturb again and keep in a warm room for 18 hours. Dip the curd into cheesecloth and hang to drip. Drain but not until the curd looks dry, as the mixture doesn't seem to stick together when pressed. Put curd in bowl, salt to taste, add nuts or whatever you like (Doris loves it with olives and nuts). For pressing use a coffee can (1-pound size). Have bottom and sides perforated with nail holes. Be sure rough edges of the holes are to the outside. Line with cheesecloth and ladle in cheese. Draw cheesecloth over top. Place a wooden follower on cheese and apply a 50-pound weight. Length of time required to press cheese depends on temperature and weight (around 2-3 days for the cheese).

Roquefort Cheese—You can't make Roquefort really unless you've got sheep's milk. If you did have sheep's milk you could blend sheep's and cow's milk to stretch it and you'd still get the right flavor. Even one part sheep's milk to nine parts cow's is OK. "Roquefort" is sort of a trademark. Blue cheese is very similar except you can use cow's or goat's milk to make it.

Blue (or Bleu) Cheese—Blue mold is the most common one. You may have some around the house right now. It's a penicillin-type mold. It is also used to develop Tilsit, Roquefort and Gorgonzola cheeses. This is another case of not being afraid of mold. Unless it's unbelievably foul you don't discourage the mold in this case. One problem with making this, though, is the mold tends to spread and you may find it on other things besides your blue cheese, especially if you have a humid environment. A cloth soaked in vinegar discourages it. Use a fairly heavy cloth, like good cotton flannel. This is to protect your other cheeses. But the vinegar will evaporate so you must keep it freshened. Paraffin would protect them completely and mold *must* have air to grow. If another kind of cheese does get moldy, scrub the mold off with vinegar. Wait until it dries. Then dip into paraffin and it should keep. Some mold on the outside doesn't hurt the inside a bit. Even if it is in a thick layer out there.

Start to make your blue cheese with 5 gallons of milk. That will give you 3½ to 4 pounds of cheese. Use raw milk—don't pasteurize it. Shake part of the milk to get air bubbles in it. You can put a quart in a blender for 5 minutes and then add it to the other milk. Or shake some in a half-gallon fruit jar or use an electric mixer. Just a portion of it thus shook will do. Now add your culture. The same as with Colby. Use 1 cup of culture. Now have your milk lukewarm and add rennet, 1 drop of the liquid or an appropriate amount of the tablet kind, or a half-square inch of the calf's stomach. When it has set up, cut the curd. Mix well but don't agitate more than 3 minutes. Cut 1-inch square chunks. These are larger than for Colby. You want a softer curd in this case. Let set 15 minutes. Now turn the curd slowly. You don't want to break up the curds. You don't want dry blue cheese.

Now bring the temperature up gradually and cook for 2 hours at 100° in your double boiler. Drain. Add your blue mold. You could buy a pound of the freeze-dried mold from a dairy supplier. That costs $18 to $20 and they don't sell it in lesser amounts though you could ask and maybe they would for you. It will keep practically forever. And all you need to make your batch of blue cheese is just a pinch stirred in.

Or you could grow your own by getting some blue cheese or Roquefort from the grocery store. Then you set some of the cheese on a damp slice of bread. Any kind of bread will do. And put it in a jar with holes punched in the top lid or with a cloth over the top. In one or two days, or maybe even as much as a week, your bread with the cheese on top will also be good and moldy. Then you remove one-fourth of your slice of bread, dry it, crumble it, and you have enough blue cheese mold to make one batch of this cheese. Save the other three-quarters and each one of them could make a batch, too. Remember when you dry the bread don't do it in an oven. Just leave it out at room temperature because you don't want the mold

spores to die. You can keep your culture going by taking one-quarter of the molded bread and putting it on a fresh damp slice of bread again. In the good old days even your commercial dairies used this method for growing mold spores.

Now mix in ½ teaspoon salt and get ready to drain the cheese. In this case you don't wrap in cloth. And you don't put pressure. Make a cheese hoop by taking a straight-sided can that is about 6 inches in diameter and 6 inches or so deep, like a 6-inch stovepipe, and poke nail holes in the sides from the inside out so you won't have rough edges inside. Make the holes about every 1 or 2 inches on the sides. Make a follower for each end. Any piece of board that was the right size and shape to barely fit into the can or pipe would be fine. Now put the first follower on the table. The pipe on top of that. The cheese into the pipe. And the last follower on top of the cheese and turn upside down. Keep doing this every half hour for 2 hours. The cheese will be cooling off. Water will be running out. The central mass will be holding its shape well enough.

Now take the cheese off the follower and set it instead on heavy burlap, a towel, or three or four thicknesses of sheeting. But not on paper—that would cause the cheese to get soggy on the bottom. And let it set like that for 12 to 16 hours. Now rub 1½ tablespoons salt on the surface (iodized table salt is fine). It won't all go on at first. Do it once a day for 5 to 7 days. You're salting the curd from the outside. The moisture will come out, grab the salt and go back in. After the week of salting comes the poking.

Take a ⅛-inch knitting needle and poke holes in the side of the cheese, 1 inch apart all over the surface and deep enough so you come clear out the other side. Then tip over the cheese and do the same from the other side. This is to allow air inside so mold can grow inside because mold must have air. Then let the cheese set at 45° in a humid place. You don't wrap it, of course. If you set it in the refrigerator you'd probably make everything else mold. Incidentally, this blue mold won't make you healthy eating it—it's different from the one the doctor prescribes. It takes 4 to 6 weeks to get right. You want mold on the surface as well as in the center. The mold colors will vary from blue to gray. If you get black, wash that off with vinegar and then let it go again. Or use a mild salt solution and a soft brush. At a higher temperature it would be ready even sooner. After it has arrived at the flavor and ripeness you like you can wax it or put it in a cold place to store. But if you freeze it, it will turn crumbly.

Italian Cheese (a cheese made especially for grating)—Heat 10 quarts fresh milk to 85°. Add ½ rennet tablet dissolved in cold water. Wait 40 minutes to let the curd get firm. Then break up the curd with your hands and heat it in the whey until it is as hot as your hand can stand. Gather the curd with your hands and mat it together until it is firm. Remove the curd from the whey and put it in the cheese press. Press one side, then reverse it in the press and squeeze some more. Put the curd in its sack back into the whey and heat to below boiling (don't let it boil). Remove from the heat and let the cheese stay in the whey until all is cold. Remove and let drain for 24 hours. You could now eat the cheese but for the proper grating cheese rub it with salt and let dry in your curing room for 3 days or so. When it is dry put it in a jar of salt brine for another 3 days. Make the brine so strong that there is salt undissolved in the bottom. Then put the cheese in your curing room to dry again for 3 days and rub the cheese lightly with salt every other day until dry. Put the cheese in a crock. Cover the crock with a cloth. Rub it lightly with salt once a week for a month. Then just leave it in the crock for 3 to 6 months. Now your cheese is completely cured and ready for grating.

The next two recipes (Twenty-Minute Cheese and Cheese à L'Obispo) are taken from a pamphlet called "Home Cheesemaking with Goat Milk," which is put out by Dairy Goat Journal, Box 836, Columbia, Missouri 65201. Doris Gronewold recommended the recipes to me from her own experience and Kent Leach, editor of the *Dairy Goat Journal*, gave me permission to quote anything I wanted as long as I gave credit which is herewith given. And incidentally that *Dairy Goat Journal* is a little magazine that you would really enjoy subscribing to if you are a goat owner—$3 a year.

Twenty-Minute Cheese—To 3 quarts fresh goat's milk at blood heat add ½ teaspoon liquid rennet. Stir gently. As it thickens, which is almost immediately, add 1 quart boiling water and continue to stir gently, separating the curd from the whey and firming the curd so it can be handled at once.

Place a reed cheese basket in a colander and dip the curd into it, pressing down. When all the curd is in the basket turn the basket over, slip the curd out and replace it with the bottom side up. Thus the reeds will mark the cheese on all sides.

If an unsalted, uncured cheese is liked it may be eaten now.

To cure the cheese leave it in the basket for 36 hours, or until firm enough to keep its shape. During this time keep it in the kitchen or other warm, dry place and slip it out of the basket twice a day and turn it over. When firm enough, remove from the basket and keep on a plate in the kitchen or pantry. Sprinkle dry salt on the side that is up. Continue to turn as before, each time salting the upper surface and the rim and using a dry plate. When no more moisture sweats out it can be placed in a stone crock in the cellar or springhouse. If it molds wipe with a cloth dampened with salty water.

While the cheese may now be eaten or kept for a year, it is perhaps at its best when about 6 months old.

The color is white, but a yellow cheese may be made by adding a few drops of cheese coloring when the rennet is added to the milk.

Cheese à L'Obispo—Get a bottle of rennet tablets for cheese (not junket). Use about 8 pounds milk; put in rather more rennet than suggested in the instructions that come with the rennet. Let it set an hour. Cut curd and heat to 98°, no higher. Stir gently every few minutes. Cover and set away for an hour longer. Drain on sieve lined with muslin and pack into a mold, salting away for 24 hours.

For a mold you could use a 1-pound coffee can. Cut out the bottom, punch holes in the lid and use it as a bottom. A circular piece of stout tin should fit inside the can for a follower. For weight use a quart jar filled with sand. Line the mold with thin muslin.

Take out of the mold and set on a screen tray in an airy place, with a soft folded cloth under the cheese, and a bit of muslin over it to keep off the dust. Turn daily for 10 or 12 days, changing the cloth underneath each time.

It is now sufficiently cured to eat. Melt paraffin in a tin lid and turn the cheese carefully in it until it is well coated.

Cheese can be eaten now, or cured for as much as 6 months. In damp weather the cheese will mold on the outside before cured enough. If it molds, clean off with a cloth dampened in vinegar, and wipe dry.

CREAM

This is where goat's milk and cow's milk are so different, and I prefer cow's milk because I enjoy homemade butter and whipped cream. I like having a little pitcher of cream to pour over the strawberries, or a big one of cream to make ice cream. Goat's milk doesn't come in very large quantities, anyway. You can get some cream if you separate mechanically, but it isn't worth all that disk washing. You can get some cream if you let it set long enough but by then it's almost sour. Goat's butter is white rather than yellow and has a different taste than cow's butter—doesn't taste as buttery to me. There's a difference in cow's milk, too, but not nearly so much as between cow's and goat's.

Of cows, the Jersey gives the most cream in its milk, the Guernsey next, and the Holstein least (but Holsteins give a high total milk quantity). Shorthorns have plenty of cream but it isn't as yellow. Cream technically is globules of fat which have been held in suspension throughout the liquid. In cow's milk they soon rise to the top due to their comparative lightness. (Oil floats on water.) The longer the milk sets quietly the more cream there will be technically for the first 36 hours, but you can get lots after 12 hours and most after 24. The heaviest cream, which is called "whip-" ping" or "spoon" cream, is nearest the top in a thick layer. You find goat's cream on the top in the same way only it takes longer to rise and there is never as much.

I keep my milk in gallon jars or 5-gallon buckets (when I have that much) in the refrigerator. I skim the cream off at the end of the 24 hours unless I need it sooner. The best thing is a regular skimmer. Mine are antiques. I don't know if you can still buy them or not. A skimmer is a long-handled utensil with a cup fastened on the end. You set the cup into the cream so that the rim is just barely below the liquid's surface. That way the part of the liquid that slips over into the cup of the skimmer is the top cream and not the milk underneath.

When you get used to it you can really do a very precise job of separating the cream from the milk and getting the cream out. Your jar, of course, has to have a wide enough mouth so the skimmer can easily get in and out. Old fashioned recipe books often say to let the cream rise in a shallow, wide container. I can't understand why. I find the cream much easier to skim off from a tall, deep container.

Cream separators work on a centrifugal principle. The milk is supposed to be put through while still warm, at least 90°. For separating in winter, you could flush some warm water through the separator first. But I know people who put it through cold and it seems to work all right. It separates cow's milk very thoroughly. The separator is set to deliver cream at a certain percent butterfat, for example 30 percent butterfat.

It is possible to freeze cream. Forty percent butterfat or higher, pasteurized, freezes best and will whip up after freezing. To pasteurize cream, milk, or a combination thereof, you can either put the cream

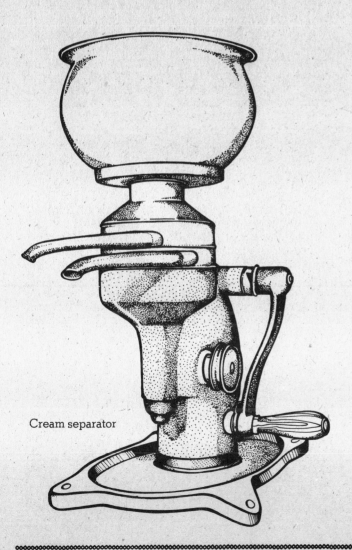

Cream separator

into a double boiler, covered, and heat to 160°-165°, hold for 1 minute, then cool. Or heat to 140°-150° and hold for 30 minutes. But frankly I've never had any reason to pasteurize milk or to freeze cream. I like raw milk. The cream does have a tendency to get ahead of me when the milk is really in season—in spring after the babies come. But I prefer to make butter and freeze the *butter* in that situation.

SOUR CREAM—Home-soured cream is different from dairy soured cream the same way home-soured milk or buttermilk is different from dairy yogurt or cultured buttermilk. Home-soured cream has more of a tendency to separate into curds and whey. Just pour off the whey or stir it up and proceed with your recipe. If you have a culture on hand for your yogurt you can use it to make cultured sour cream, too.

If you are baking and the recipe calls for sour cream and you don't have any, you can make do by adding 1 tablespoon lemon juice or vinegar per cup cream and mixing well. Most recipe books today mean dairy sour cream when they call for sour cream in recipes, and you can't always substitute home-soured cream with success unless you have a very smooth, mild-flavored one.

Sour Cream Gravy—Use this as a basic "stroganoff" sauce with "chicken paprika" Hungarian style. It is also good with chicken, veal cutlets, liver, kidney, tripe, rabbit or any game. Cook a chopped onion or more in butter or in the grease left from cooking in your pan. Blend in flour enough to take up the grease. Season with salt, paprika. Add mushrooms, if you have them, and their juice, if canned. When the base is ready add sour cream gradually, stirring constantly. Heat just to boiling. Don't overcook! Stir while you are heating and as it is thickening. Then remove, pour over the meat and serve immediately.

WHIPPING CREAM—There's lots of lore on the subject. Some say it depends on your cow. Some say that your top cream will be too thick to whip and you should add some milk before whipping. Some say fresh cream doesn't whip well. Cool the cream because warmth thins it and age from 12 to 24 hours before whipping and you should be fine. Don't add your sweetening if it is a liquid, like honey or molasses, until you have your cream whipped. One half cup whipping cream gives you about one cup whipped cream but you need a big deep bowl to whip in to keep it from splashing all over. If your cream really doesn't want to whip, add the white of an egg to it. Chill, and then it will whip. For a very sweet dessert you can use unsweetened whipped cream and it will taste fine. A couple drops of vanilla improves whipped cream.

BUTTER

Butter making is affected by your cream's whipping ability. You may find that your particular cow's cream is harder than the average to make butter from. Sometimes the farther a cow gets into her time of milking, the harder it is to get the butter. The cream may churn easier if you wait until it is not too sweet. The taste of your butter is affected also by how sour the cream is that you use. I prefer butter made from sour cream, but not so sour that it has three colors of mold on it. I've heard that the feed your cow has been on can also affect the churning, that cottonseed meal and timothy hay for some reason give trouble. Sweet cream also takes longer to churn and doesn't give as much butter proportionately.

If you don't have a butter churn the simplest way is probably to put your cream in a quart or half-gallon jar and give it to the children to roll back and forth across the floor. It takes about 15 to 30 minutes for the butter to churn. Don't ever fill up a container in which you want to churn, because as it whips it doubles in bulk and will slop out the top. Leave it at least half empty. It churns easiest when the container is only one-third full.

A large homemade churn could be made from a barrel with a rod put through about three-fourths of the way across the diameter. Hang the barrel on the rod and work out a system to rotate it. If your container is sealed you might want to stop two or three times and let the gas out.

There is an electric drill attachment for stirring paint that could be adapted to churn butter. You could also churn by simply putting an electric drill through a hole in the metal top of a widemouthed gallon (or larger) jar and rigging up paddles to fit and fasten on the drill.

Butter can be churned using an electric mixer but you have to watch carefully and remove the mixer just before the butter starts to come. Finish by beating it with a spoon or churning it in a jar as first mentioned. Otherwise the mixer would shred the butter and it would be very hard to gather together again.

Sears and Roebuck's Farm Catalog here carries two electric churns. The smaller comes with a one-gallon jar (it will churn three quarts) for $24.50. The larger is a motor and dasher which could be fitted onto a two-, three- or five-gallon jar or used on a crock for $26.95. Sears sells a three-gallon jar for $6.19. Nonelectric churns appear to be practically

extinct except in antique stores—which is a shame. A familiar sight in the antique stores is the tall, upright crock churn with a lid through which is run a wooden dasher. You stand or sit by the churn and work the dasher up and down until the butter comes.

Morgan Brothers in Lewiston, Idaho, has some manual churns for sale. These are big crock-type ones with a lid and wooden dasher that you work up and down by hand. I still don't know where you can buy a gear-driven manual churn. A four-gallon crock churn is $13.23 plus shipping charges. A three-gallon one is $10.79, a two-gallon one is $9.25. You can buy a very small electric churn there for $29.75.

Anything from whole milk to "spoon cream" (so thick it won't pour), either sweet or sour, can be churned for butter. However, churning whole milk is hardly worth your while since a quart of milk only makes about a teaspoon of butter. For the average paddle churn of three-gallon size use about one gallon of cream at about 60°. If the cream is too warm, the butter is long in coming and is too soft to handle. If it is too cold, it also takes too long to come and only part of the butterfat separates from the cream, leaving a very thick buttermilk. Shake, beat or agitate the cream until the butterfat has separated out and formed a big glob.

The churning should be done at a set rate and not too fast. It takes about 20 minutes of steady churning until you first hear the splash of butter and feel the stiffness in churning. It is well to churn past the first coming of butter to be sure you get all the butterfat from the cream. If you are using a big barrel churn with a bunghole to let out the buttermilk, stop turning when the granules are the size of wheat grains. You can tell with experience because the sound of the cream in the churn changes. Let the buttermilk out through the hole and run it through a strainer to catch any particles of butter.

The next project is to wash and gather the butter. Some wash first and gather after. Some do both at once. If you are working with a large churn that has a bunghole you could add pure clean water, twice as much as the buttermilk you drew off, after replacing the cork, and rotate the churn about four times. Then drain that wash water and repeat with clean water. Then commence to work the butter. There is an old-time machine called a "worker" that was rinsed with hot water and then with cold and used to press the butter into a thin layer, then fold it into a pile and press again. It was great for large quantities of butter and for mixing the salt into the butter. About ¾ ounce of salt is added per pound of butter, or according to your taste.

To work the butter by hand pull the bung on a paddle churn and drain off the buttermilk. With a spoon remove the butter to a bowl, and scrape the butter from the paddle. Remove pieces of butter in the buttermilk. You will get 2½ to 3 quarts buttermilk and about 1 pound of butter from 1 gallon of cream. If the temperature is 80° or so, you can't work butter until you've chilled it. Pour cold water on it to chill it. Now gather it into a ball, press it into a thin layer and then gather into a ball again, ad infinitum until all the salt is well worked in and the buttermilk is worked out.

To wash and work the butter at the same time put the butter from the buttermilk into a large bowl of ice water and squeeze it gently between your fingers until it feels smooth and waxy. It should go through several bowls of cool water. When the water stays clear, repeat one more time. Then shape into a cake and pat to remove the extra water. Next salt to taste and work the salt in well. The habit of salting butter originated from the preserving power of salt. Unsalted butter does not keep as well. In some countries like Australia all butter is unsalted. Butter can absorb odors if it isn't kept covered. But ours usually doesn't last that long.

The color of cow's butter may vary. There is a coloring product on the market for butter and cheese. It isn't the kind that was dangerous to health. But color never did matter that much to me.

STORING BUTTER—Make sure all the buttermilk is out. You can brine it by making butter balls the size of a baseball. Cover them with brine strong enough to float an egg. Cover and store in a cool place. This is good for months or even longer. If you have the salt you can cover them with layers of pure salt.

GOAT'S BUTTER—It's not impossible. I used to make it and found it not as hard as some say. Goat's butter is very soft at room temperature, has a slightly goaty taste, is white and won't give vegetables and corn bread the butter flavor you're accustomed to. I substituted meat drippings on vegetables when I was using goat butter. My way of making it was to beat with a hand beater for a minute, pour into a jar one-half or less full, shake the jar to the tune of "Yankee Doodle" and in about 7 minutes once I had butter. The butter was in soft, little slippery curds sticking up like icebergs from the buttermilk.

BUTTER MOLDS—Before using a butter mold scald it, then soak in cold water for an hour. Pack it solidly with butter and level off the top surface. When the butter is molded it can be pressed out.

BUTTER BALLS—Scald a pair of wooden butter paddles, then soak them in cold water for about an hour. Measure the butter by teaspoonfuls to have the balls about the same size. Have the butter firm but not hard and roll each spoonful lightly between the paddles to form the balls. Drop onto a chilled plate, cracked ice, or into ice water. Or press each ball slightly to make it round on the side and flat on the top and bottom.

BUTTER PATS—Shape your butter into a rectangle the shape of the commercial quarter pound. Let it cool to firm. Cut neat squares off the end to be your pats. To decorate you could dip a fork in hot water and draw on them or put a little sprig of parsley on each one.

BUTTER CURLS were traditionally made with a "butter curler." It was dipped into hot water and then drawn lightly and quickly toward you across the butter. This made a thin shaving of butter which curled up. The butter curler was dipped into hot water between each curl.

Lemon Butter—Cream butter until fluffy and add a few drops lemon juice. Use for sandwiches, canapés and fish.

Herbed Butter—For each half a cup butter add about 1 teaspoon of your choice of dried herbs (basil, thyme, marjoram, dill are fine) or chopped fresh herbs. A dash of garlic salt is good, too.

Whipped Butter—The wife of a professional dairyman gave me this recipe at that Idaho Purebred meeting. She says it makes a soft, fluffy spread. Bring ¼ pound butter and ¼ pound water to room temperature. (The pounds aren't weird to dairy types—they're all the time weighing milk anyway.) Whip it together with the mixer. You might need more water. That's all there is to it.

BUTTERMILK

CHURNED BUTTERMILK is just the milk substance left after you have churned your butter. It may have an acid flavor and it may not. It depends on how sour the cream was when you churned. Sour cream makes a sour flavored buttermilk. If you want nice buttermilk don't let your cream get too rank before you churn.

CULTURED BUTTERMILK is skim milk that has been cultured with a variety of bacteria in the same way you make yogurt. It is let set for 12 to 14 hours after the culture is introduced. Then it is stirred to break up the mass and that's why it doesn't have a yogurt-like consistency. Then to make it look like churned buttermilk they take melted butterfat and spray it into the buttermilk. That makes the little butter specks in it that make you a believer. They add 1 or 2 percent butter that way—whatever they think the customers want. So you can substitute your homemade yogurt plus a dab of butter in any recipe where it calls for cultured buttermilk.

DRIED BUTTERMILK, on the other hand, that you can buy in the grocery store is the real thing.

HOMEMADE CULTURED BUTTERMILK—Mix 1 quart of skim milk with ½ cup or so of commercial buttermilk in a glass container, such as a jar or bottle. Check the yogurt section because it's the same procedure. You can keep the culture going until it gets contaminated in the same way yogurt does.

BUTTERMILK RECIPES—There are so many great things you can do with buttermilk. In any of the following recipes you can use store buttermilk or the yogurt-butter mix I mentioned, or your homemade buttermilk left over from churning if you have a nice-tasting one. In baking you can use even a pretty strong tasting buttermilk and it will still turn out deliciously. It makes a fine gravy.

Buttermilk Cheese—Go through the usual steps. It will make the best cottage cheese or hard cheese of all!

Strawberry-Banana Buttermilk—Mash and beat together 1 or 2 cups strawberries, 1 banana and 2 cups buttermilk. A very special beverage.

Orange-Honey Buttermilk—Combine 4 cups buttermilk, juice of 2 oranges and 2 tablespoons honey.

Buttermilk Coleslaw Dressing—Combine 1½ tablespoons sugar, 1 cup cold buttermilk, ½ teaspoon mustard, 1½ tablespoons lemon juice or vinegar and ¼ teaspoon salt.

Buttermilk Vegetable Soup—Slice 2 medium-sized cooked potatoes. Chop 3 green onions (the white part very fine, the green part not so). Mix with 1 quart of churned buttermilk. Add salt and pepper to taste. Heat to serving temperature and serve (don't boil it). You can use big onions instead of the green ones by chopping and prefrying them. Bacon bits are good, too.

Buttermilk Raisin Soup—Moisten 1 tablespoon flour with 1 tablespoon buttermilk and heat 1 quart buttermilk to scalding temperature. Add the flour and beat with your eggbeater until it is well distributed. Add ½ cup seedless raisins, 1 piece stick cinnamon and a pinch of salt. Cook until the raisins are puffed. When ready to serve, add sweetening and ¼ cup heavy cream, whipped.

Buttermilk Porridge—Boil ½ cup barley slowly in 3 cups water for about 2 hours. Add 1½ quarts buttermilk, stirring until it boils, cook a few minutes, then add ½ teaspoon salt. Serve with syrup or other sweetening.

Buttermilk Biscuits—Sift 2 cups flour, 2¼ teaspoons baking powder, 1 teaspoon salt and ¼ teaspoon baking soda together. Cut 6 tablespoons butter with two knives into the dry ingredients. Add ¾ cup buttermilk and mix quickly but thoroughly. Turn onto floured board, knead lightly for a few seconds. Roll out to about a ½-inch thickness and cut with your biscuit cutter. Place the biscuits on a buttered baking sheet and brush with milk. Bake at about 450° for 12 to 15 minutes, or until brown.

Buttermilk Waffles—Sift 2 cups flour, 2 teaspoons baking powder, ½ teaspoon salt, ½ teaspoon baking soda and 3 tablespoons sugar together. Combine 2 beaten egg yolks, 2 cups buttermilk and ¼ cup melted butter. Add liquid to dry ingredients and beat well. Fold in the 2 stiffly beaten egg whites and bake on your waffle iron.

ICE CREAM

The old-time name for ice cream was "cream." Old recipes usually contained lots of cream and eggs. It was considered a confection and manufactured by the same people who made bonbons. It can be made in your refrigerator's freezing compartment or in a crank freezer. The stirring is to break up ice crystals and improve the texture. "Refrigerator" ice cream contains so much cream, eggs and/or gelatin that ice crystals and texture aren't a problem. But even if the dessert is to be frozen in the refrigerator or freezer, it helps to remove it when it is at the mushy stage, put it in a chilled bowl and beat vigorously. A second beating later on would improve it even more.

The freezing time in the refrigerator freezing compartment depends on the mixture, its depth, and the refrigerator. It averages around 2 hours. The temperature should be under 20°. It helps to use cold ingredients and to chill the mixture well before putting it in the freezer. Don't try to make ice cubes at the same time. The sweeter the mixture the more difficult it will be to freeze. It's best to freeze at the coldest setting you have—the quicker the desserts freeze the better they hold their lightness. But after freezing is accomplished they are improved by resting to mellow for a couple of hours. It helps the flavor and the texture.

If you are getting a buttery taste it may be either that the cream was overwhipped or that it is too rich in butterfat. You can fix that simply by using a more thorough skimming so the cream won't be quite so rich. It is better not to use absolutely fresh cream. Good cream will double in bulk while freezing.

Fresh fruit for frozen desserts should be very ripe. If it doesn't seem ripe enough, cook it with a little water. A fruit puree can be cooked fruit put through a sieve or raw fruit grated or pulped, as in the case of ripe fleshy fruits like apricots and strawberries.

Refrigerator ice creams usually contain whipped cream and/or beaten egg white to give them their lightness. Crank freezer ice creams can get it from the cranking process. If you buy a crank freezer, directions will come with it. The crank freezer will consist of a bucket of wood or metal that holds the ice and salt freezing mixture and a nonrusting metal can with a tight-fitting lid for holding the cream to be frozen. The ice cream is stirred by a paddle inside the can which is turned by a crank outside—or in some cases by an electric motor.

You usually need about 12 pounds of ice for a batch. You could freeze milk cartons full of water in your freezer and then dump out the ice into a bag and pound it to chips with a wooden mallet. You need rock salt, too, for the freezer. The recommended proportions vary. Usually you can use just one part rock salt to eight parts crushed ice during the freezing process. Alternate layers of ice and salt to a point higher than your ice cream will be in the can. After freezing the ice cream you can repack it for mellowing—use four parts ice to one part rock salt. Then cover the freezer with newspapers or a piece of rug. In winter you could use snow instead of ice. If the salt doesn't act rapidly enough on it add a cup of cold water.

But I never bother mellowing our homemade ice cream. The children are so anxious and it tastes fine enough to me when it's first done. I don't worry about measuring proportions of salt and ice either. I just pour in ice and then pour on salt. The can shouldn't be more than two-thirds full. Turn the crank slowly at first until the ice cream is mush, then more rapidly until it is too stiff to turn. You might want to take off the lid occasionally to scrape the harder ice cream off the sides of the can and back into the middle. Be careful to wipe off the top of the freezer can each time you open it since even a little of the rock salt brine getting in could spoil your batch. If your recipe contains nuts or fruit, it will work better if you don't add them until the mixture is mush.

For storing ice cream 0° is a good temperature. Use it within two weeks. Don't let it thaw and then try to refreeze because it will get hard and not be nearly as nice. To keep your ice cream, repack it in nonmetal containers as it deteriorates very rapidly in metallic ones.

Carla's Basic Ice Cream Recipe—This we make in the ice cream freezer, though before we had an ice cream freezer we just froze it in bowls in the freezer compartment. (We stirred it occasionally while it was freezing.) It came out harder that way but I served it before it got totally hard and in hot summer weather it was still a big hit. I start out with 6 eggs beaten as light as I can manage. Now add ¼ teaspoon vanilla extract and 1½ to 2 cups fruit. My favorite for big occasions is a mixture of 1 mashed ripe banana, 1 cup crushed pineapple and 1 orange with the peel and the seeds discarded. More fruit makes it better. At the last I fold in 1 cup of cream that has been whipped. More of that doesn't hurt either. This really doesn't make very much ice cream. I usually double this recipe. They'll love every minute of it. I forgot the honey. Maybe ¼ cup of that, if your fruit needs it. For peach, apricot or quince ice cream use some almond extract rather than vanilla. To stretch your ice cream add some milk.

The fact is when you're using an ice cream freezer you can freeze almost any mixture and as long as the results are cold your children will be happy.

Apricot Mousse—Mix about 2¼ cups of pulped cooked apricots with ¼ cup honey. Chill in a freezing tray for a half hour or so. Then remove from the tray and combine in a bowl with 2 egg whites, beating until light and fluffy. Then whip 1½ cups cream. When the cream is ready, fold it into the beaten apricots and egg whites. Return to the tray and freeze without stirring.

Fruit Mousse—Whip 2 cups heavy cream. Combine with 1 cup of any pulped fruit. Add a trace of vanilla, sweeten if needed, and freeze.

Ice Cream Sandwiches—Between thin slices of devil's food cake (or whatever you like) place a serving of vanilla ice cream (or whatever you like). You can make your own paper cases and store them in the freezer.

Neapolitan Ice Cream—Pack a mold in salt and ice or have ready a mold to go in your freezer. Spread the first variety of ice cream smoothly over the bottom. (You'll need to have ready your three preferred varieties—strawberry, vanilla and chocolate are traditional but you can vary that.) If it is not very firm, cover and let it freeze a few minutes. Then spread a good layer of the next variety upon it, and as soon as this hardens, spread over the last kind. Cover and freeze. (Spumoni is made with lemon ice or French vanilla ice cream, bisque ice cream and chocolate mousse.)

Applesauce Ice Cream—Combine 1 cup applesauce, a pinch of cinnamon, a pinch of nutmeg, 1 teaspoon melted butter and 2 teaspoons lemon juice. Chill. Fold in 1 cup whipped cream and toasted flaked coconut or chopped nuts, if you want it extra rich, and freeze until firm.

Milk Shake—Mash fruit, fresh or frozen, such as strawberries. Add ice cream and some milk and continue mashing. Add more milk and mix gradually until your milk shake is thinned as much as you like it.

Maple Parfait—Pour 1 cup hot maple syrup slowly over 4 slightly beaten egg yolks. Add a pinch of salt, cook until thickened and chill. Whip 2 cups heavy cream to the soft peak stage and then fold into the chilled syrup mixture. Fold in 4 stiffly beaten egg whites and freeze until firm. For "maple nut" fold in ½ cup chopped walnuts or pecans before the egg whites are added.

SNOW ICE CREAM—To make snow ice cream the children must go out with a bowl and find some clean snow. Mine are usually out gathering snow when the first flakes fall and I have to dump the first batches trying to explain to the tearful little ones that, yes, I really will make snow ice cream for them just as soon as I get some clean snow. When I get clean snow, the dryer the better, I put a glob of snow in the blender along with a couple eggs, a tablespoon or two of honey, maybe a fourth teaspoon of vanilla extract, and some milk (maybe a cup), blend it together and what they really have then is snow milk shake. You can add any kind of fruit, too. Or cocoa. Or molasses. If you use canned milk it has a richer taste and it's thicker. The important thing is it has *their* snow in it and that makes this recipe a winner every time. You don't have to use a blender. You can just stir it together. Snow ice cream doesn't refreeze well at all. It turns to ice. So don't make more than what will be eaten right away.

Nancy's Snow Ice Cream—"I was glad to see the recipes for Snow Ice Cream. That is one of my most cherished girlhood memories and our children love making it too. I doubt if my mother ever used a 'recipe' for it, but the one I always use is similar to one of yours. We beat up the basic recipe (usually doubled) and chill it; then the kids bring in a huge 6-quart pan full of the lovely dry, white, fluffy snow and we make it.

"Basic recipe: Mix together in large bowl 1 egg, ½ cup granulated sugar, ½ cup milk or cream or evaporated milk (I like to use a little cream if I have it because we always drink 1% milk) and 1 teaspoon vanilla. We always just stir in the snow with a spoon until the right consistency. The kids like it just as well plain, but our variations are (added to the basic recipe before the snow): about ½ to 1 cup of crushed pineapple, or a spoonful or two of chocolate syrup, or a big slurp of maple syrup. My mother used to use maple syrup a lot to flavor ice cream made by any method. (She was raised on a farm in Ohio where they had some sugar maple trees.) In regular ice cream recipes they substituted maple syrup for the sugar (½ cup of maple syrup for 1 cup sugar)."

Homemade Snow Cones—My neighbor Kay Morey, a very dear friend who has dug me out of many a hole, gathers clean snow and packs it into cups. She pours fruit juice or syrup over and the children love it.

THE ICE HARVEST AND VANILLA ICE CREAM—I received this letter from Margaret Kerrick of West Roxbury, Massachusetts.

"I grew up on a farm in Pennsylvania and lived through most of the stuff you have in your book. The only thing I find missing is the ice harvest. There was no refrigeration when I was a child, and so when the ponds froze over, all the men in the community would gather with their teams and sleighs and saws, and cut ice from the ponds. They would haul out huge cakes of ice after sawing it; they must have measured

two-feet square or more, and anywhere from nine inches to a foot thick. Everyone had an icehouse where the ice was stored, between layers of sawdust. It was pulled up a long chute, by means of ice tongs and a rope, from the sleigh to the icehouse, and there it kept perfectly all winter.

I wrote and asked Margaret to tell me more—

"Our men in Spring Hill, Pennsylvania, where I grew up, didn't have any power saws, so they chopped a hole in the ice and then got the crosscut saw in and sawed the cakes out. Then they fitted an ice tongs onto the free cake, tied a rope to it, and it was then hauled out of the water by a team of horses, and pulled up into a sleigh. When the sleigh was loaded it was drawn by horses to the icehouse of the particular farm which was being served that day. On arrival at the icehouse, the tongs were attached to each cake of ice in turn, and this ice was pulled up into the icehouse and covered with sawdust, brought in usually from a local sawmill. It was hard cold work, and the men came in for dinner with huge appetites. My mother cooked gargantuan meals, and delicious ones too, huge slabs of salt ham, mashed potatoes, squash, pickles, jelly, bread and apple pie. Those men would consume about three loaves of bread at a meal. I can remember one very taciturn man who never said anything except 'more bread.' He didn't say that when he could spear a slice with his fork. The ice lasted very well until the next year's harvest. We used one cake every day to put in the milk vat to cool the milk, and on Sunday, my father would get out an extra cake to make ice cream with. Also we used half a cake at a time in our old wooden house refrigerator. The ice cake was placed in the top compartment which was lined with tin or zinc. As it melted a small pipe carried the water to a container in the cellar. This kept the food cool, but nothing like today's refrigerators.

"While I'm writing I might as well include our family recipe for vanilla ice cream, which we made in the hand crank freezer. I have one of those freezers and I use it quite often.

Vanilla Ice Cream—Mix 1 quart light cream, 1½ tablespoons vanilla, ¾ cup sugar. To freeze in a hand crank freezer, you have to smash the ice first, or buy crushed ice. Use three parts of ice to one of rock salt. First put the cream mixture into the freezer can, set the can in the freezer, adjust the top, and fill in around the can with ice and rock salt in layers. Then turn the handle of the crank, slowly at first, then faster as it begins to freeze. This makes for a smoother ice cream. When you feel that it is becoming harder to turn, you can open it up and see if it is done. Then you can lick the paddle. Pull it out and gather around with spoons and dig in. If there isn't enough for everyone to have a taste from the paddle, let them eat from the freezer. We always made the ice cream before we went to church. After we had our licks, my father packed it, poured off the water from the melting ice, added fresh ice and salt and covered the freezer with a burlap bag with the remains of the ice in it. Then after we came home from church and had our dinner, we unpacked the freezer and ate huge dishes of ice cream."

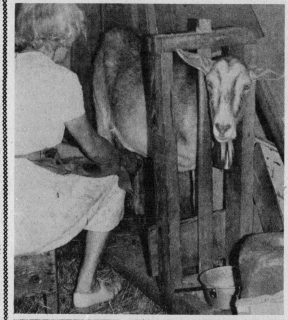

Imogene has a nice little stanchion to milk
her goats in. She puts some grain or other goodies
in the pan and then shuts the movable slat to
hold the goat's head in there so it can't leave
if it gets done eating before she gets done
milking. Cow stanchions work on the same
principle, only are bigger for a bigger animal.

These two goats are Imogene's.
She can keep a goat milking fine for
two years. She takes such good care of them.
The directions for feeding a goat in winter
in this book are from her and Mrs. Harless.

Whenever you go to visit Imogene and her husband, Ralph, and mother, Mrs. McLain,
you get a real country welcome. Here they are coming to the door to meet us.

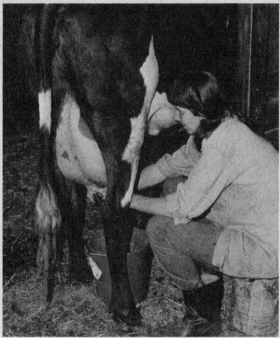

One way to raise a calf is using this big plastic bottle with a nipple on the end called a calf bottle. You pour the milk in, put the nipple on, and hang it up somewhere by its wire holder. In this picture Mike has just put the calf bottle up on the fence.

Here I am milking our big shorthorn cow, Marietta. Her head is in a stanchion and she is eating something good. I'm sitting on a bucket instead of the ground. Marietta's bag is higher off the ground than Nelly's. Marietta is a barn cow. She'd never believe I was serious about it if I tried to milk her out in the pasture.

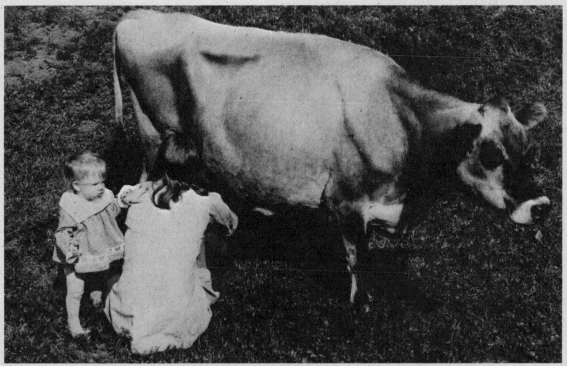

This is Carla with baby Sara out milking Nelly right on the green grass (into a bucket) where Nelly and I decided would be a good place to be.

POULTRY

Although my mother could turn out good food on the old wood cook stove and wasn't discouraged by all sorts of country problems, no part of the barnyard was ever really her thing except the chicken house. She loved her chickens and they seemed to love her. I really love all the animals, including the big ones, but Mother was terrified of them. I remember one time Daddy had to be away overnight. Mother assured him that just for once she could manage to milk the cow. Well, I awoke the next morning to hear her hollering desperately outside the window. I ran to look and there she was perched on the very top of the fence post, balancing up there in some mysterious way while our gentle milk cow stood patiently at the bottom of the post waiting to be taken on into the barn. Mother was positive she was under attack. I'll never forget that scene because although I'm lean like the Harshbarger side of the family (my father's—my complete maiden name was Carlotta Louise Harshbarger, "Carla" is a nickname) Mother always packed quite a bit of weight and her on top of that fence post was an achievement. If you don't believe me just go out and try to stand on top of a wooden fence post—no matter how much you weigh.

Anyway, the chickens loved my mother. They got all her kitchen scraps and Daddy could feed the pigs on whatever else there was—the chickens had first rights. And all this seemed to be appreciated by them. They laid eggs aplenty for us. And I'll never forget the taste of Mother's fried chicken. She'd have me go out and catch and kill a couple birds (she never could bring herself to come out of the house until that was all over with). Then she'd appear with a big bucket of scalding water and we'd pick and clean and cut up the birds together. That very night for supper we'd eat them. Mother turned up her nose at chicken that was over 12 hours from the hoof to the pan. She didn't have a deep freeze. She canned lots of venison but her chicken was always fresh. That was one of the wonderful things about chicken.

If Mother went to town shopping and stayed too long, the chickens would get restless and manage somehow to get the front door open. Then Mother would come home, walk in and find chickens roosting all over—on the kitchen stove, the table, the cupboards. When we walked in they would all fly up and squawk at once and feathers and droppings would go every which way. Every spring she had baby chickens living in a cardboard box back of the wood stove, and after Daddy built a bathroom with a tub in it onto the house, Mother would keep the baby chicks in the bathtub after they outgrew the cardboard box until it was warm enough for them to be outside—and you took your spring baths out of a tin tub just like before we had the plumbing. Mother had a wonderful healing touch with sick animals. I've seen her revive an almost-dead baby chick that had suffered some crisis of illness or injury. She would work the stiff little legs and wings up and down until circulation was restored. Then wrap the chick in a soft white dish towel (white from being boiled in lye water on top of the stove), and put it in a little box or pan wherever in the stove's vicinity a wave of her experienced arm told her the brooding temperature was just right.

My mother was wonderful. She had a master's degree in English from the University of Alabama and it never got in her way in the least. Right after that she left Alabama where her growing up as a drunkard's daughter had left her mostly bad memories and took a job teaching school in a tiny western town. Years later she met my father at a country dance. They had a short courtship and married. Mother was in her late 30's then. She had been widowed as the result of a tragic car wreck seven years earlier and had a little boy, my brother Dick, who was mostly raised by his grandmother as a result of Mother being widowed shortly after he was born and him being the only grandchild on that side.

When I grew up and left home and went to college I was by historical record part of the first generation on my father's side to go to college. Some of my cousins did too. In fact a lot of them. They became mostly missionaries or ministers or the wives thereof. When I was living in Chicago going to school at the Chicago Division of the University of Illinois it just used to infuriate me to hear fellow classmates use the tired phrase "a dumb farmer." My father is a farmer and he's not a bit dumb I'd answer, and it didn't seem to help a bit. Then I'd try to explain how my father could wire a house, or plumb it, how he could break a horse, or weld a broken plow, or fix an engine, or a sick cow. That he could run a farm which is just like running a business only you have to be able to predict weather, too, and are always looking for people to help you only they usually turn out to be from the city and they don't do anything but break the machinery and make mistakes in general. I tried to say that Daddy could rope a calf, hunt, and kill and butcher all the meat his family needed if there were nothing else to eat, that he was willing to get up at 5 in the morning, and work like a dog till past dark to make an honest and independent living, that he could read and write, too, and he just wasn't dumb. Daddy had a series of heart attacks in his 40's and the doctor said he was overworked and that he'd kill himself if he tried to continue farming. Daddy loafed around for a few years and Mama went back to teaching. Then Daddy decided to go to college. It was as simple as that. He enrolled at Montana State College and in three years he had a B.A. degree in English. Then he went on to the University of Washington and got an M.A. He was teaching school when he finally died twenty years later. So maybe then those people would believe he wasn't dumb. You know IQ is mostly a measure of vocabulary and the Rocky Mountain people don't do a whole lot of trade in big words. So maybe they come out looking not so good on the IQ tests. But if it was a test of grim survival I'd rather be lost in the mountains or anyplace else with one of our Idaho or Montana loggers or cowboys than I would with a city man with an IQ of 200, or whatever you want to quote.

And that's the kind of thing this book is about. Not trying to shove a lot of big words at you, but trying to help you know all the real things about making it that the country people know. It's been frustrating for me all my life because I'm typical rural Rocky Mountain style and nobody could ever believe I had a brain in my head to look at me or listen. I talked to a lady the other day, and she said she would be willing to help me with this book, to edit it, and show me my run on sentences and how I could fix them. I told her sure fine but somebody else got to her before I did, bless her heart. They told her that I was talking Rocky Mountain because we all preferred that to English and it did the job better.

Now we've got the problem which should come first, the chicken or the egg! I'm going to start with the egg.

OF EGGS

Your homegrown eggs may vary considerably in size and color and freshness. The first "pullet eggs" that a young hen lays are smaller. Small breeds such as Banty lay small eggs. Leghorns lay white eggs. Rhode Island Reds lay brown eggs. If you have a small flock you'll learn to recognize each hen's egg—they are each a unique combination of size, shape and color—you'll know who's laying and who isn't.

You may get an egg with two yolks. You may get an egg covered with chicken poop—just wash it off. Your egg yolk may seem darker in color and have a stronger taste and the egg white be thicker and firmer and the whole egg hold together more firmly than what you're used to. That's because your chickens have had access to a richer, more natural diet than commercial laying chickens do and the egg shows it. Your egg may have a dark spot in it with even a speck of blood. If it's not too far gone it's edible—that just shows that it was a fertile egg and given the right conditions would have become a chick. Your egg may have a half developed chick in it or may be full of a rotten yellow yuk. With experience you'll learn to tell that kind beforehand. You're bound to get surprised once in a while, though—an egg that looks dirty and old will turn out to be just fine— or vice versa.

It's best to gather the eggs every day and store them in a cool place like the refrigerator or cellar. But if your chickens are running loose, and especially if you have Bantys, you're certain sooner or later to discover a nest that some old hen hid and laid 25 eggs

in, and then the problem is to figure out if they are fresh enough to use or not. The easiest way of all is to keep those eggs in a special pan and put scrambled eggs on the menu for next morning. Into a small dish break the first egg. Usually a bad egg you can tell without even breaking it clear open. It's hard to crack because the membrane inside the shell has become tough. That's if a chick has been developing inside. If you start to crack the shell and yellow yuk starts to ooze out it's rotten. But then you have to deal with the marginal cases. Depends on how egg hungry you are and how finicky you are. If the egg doesn't have a funny smell and looks all right I'd say go ahead and use it. Pour it out of the small bowl into your mixing bowl and go on to the next. Incidentially, if the last one was rotten, be sure and rinse the small bowl well before you pour another egg into it.

If you want to know about the egg without opening it here's another way. Again, if your egg was laid within the last few days and you know it because you emptied the nest day before yesterday, you don't have to bother with this. Put the eggs in a pan of water. If fresh each egg will lie on its side on the bottom

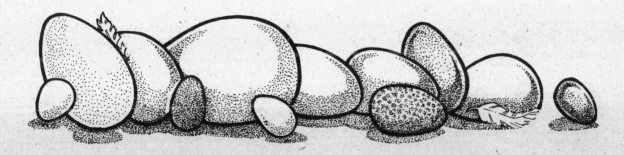

of the pan. If a few days old, one end will tip upwards. If stale an egg will stand on end. If plumb rotten it will float. This is because an egg contains an air cell. The air cell is at the large end of the egg. Eggshells are perforated right through by minute holes needed by the chick for breathing. Thus with time a part of the liquid content of the egg will evaporate. The white and yolk shrink and the resulting space is filled by an enlarged air space. But let me warn you—this float test is not completely dependable.

CANDLING—Or you could "candle" the eggs. But you can't candle dark-shelled eggs—only white ones. Take a candle, or an electric light, or lamp into an otherwise dark room. Make a candling chimney from two pieces of cardboard. The first is a cylinder large enough to surround the candle or light and the other is a tube inserted through a hole at right angles and somewhat smaller in diameter than an ordinary egg. It should be inserted at about the level of the light. Through this the egg can be observed against the light.

To test eggs hold each one up against the opening, broad end upward, and look through it at the light. If the contents do not fill the shell, the egg is not perfectly fresh. The larger the airspace the older the egg. The yolk should be perfectly clear and round in outline. If, beside the air space, there is a dark haze or cloud in the egg it has spoiled. If the cloud contains a black spot give it to the kids to take somewhere far away and throw. An egg that has been stored awhile will show some shrinkage however.

Another candling sign is yolk movement. In an older egg the yolk moves about more freely.

HATCHING—Chicken eggs, all breeds, take 21 days to hatch. That's exactly three weeks. The proper brooding temperature is 99¾°, which is just what it's like under a mama hen. Turn the eggs from 90 to 180 degrees (that's a fourth to halfway) two or three times a day. The way to tell where you're at is to mark an X on the egg and turn the X up one time and down the

next. Don't turn the eggs after the 19th day. Incubator hatching is at best a very risky proposition. You're bound to have eggs that don't hatch. If you didn't have a rooster with your chickens none of them will. You need that daddy chicken for fertile eggs. (This is elementary birds and bees but I've met city folks who've never stopped to consider these things.) The best incubator is a mother hen, especially a Banty. This is the most famous breed of chicken for mothering. But all your store baby chicks come from mechanical incubators and there are a number of homestead-style incubators available, some better than others. The most primitive is a bucket with eggs in it wrapped in a cloth and a light bulb suspended over. It's the least likely to work and yet I know people who have hatched chicks with exactly that arrangement. Humidity helps your eggs to hatch, too. Pans of water evaporating in the bottom of your incubator can supply that. You need some ventilation because the developing baby chicks are breathing out carbon dioxide and taking in oxygen. It goes right through the shell through tiny holes. Don't let your incubator sit in the sunshine or in a draft because either one might be more than the heat control system could handle. If it gets turned off for a while don't panic. The mother hen leaves the eggs once a day to get herself some food and water. Quite likely the eggs will be all right, maybe a day later in hatching. If you're really serious about using your own incubator I recommend a paperback book called *A Guide to Better Hatching* by Janet Stromberg. For a copy write Strombergs, Box 717, Fort Dodge, Iowa 50501. While you're writing ask for their "Chicks and Pets Unlimited Catalog." It's 48 pages of fascinating reading. You can buy anything from a $750 buffalo or a $3,950 zebra to your choice of almost 60 different varieties of pigeons at about $10 a pair and up.

MAIL-ORDER CHICKS—You can buy all pullets which will grow up to be hens, or all cockerels which will become fryers, or "straight run" and then you've got to figure out for yourself which is which when they get big enough and treat them accordingly. If you get little chicks in April they will start laying in October or November—providing they are hen chickens and not cockerels that merely learn to crow and chase hens. But if you get them that early you need a really warm place to keep them. The ideal time for chick survival is July 15. Then you can probably raise 100 chicks without even a heat lamp if your nights are warm. Don't put more than 25 together under heat lamp conditions or they'll huddle up to try to get warm and some will suffocate.

CHICK CARE—When mail-order chicks arrive, give food and water immediately in a container with edges not over 1 inch high. Commercial chick starter is good. Cornmeal alone will give them diarrhea. Cooked egg, bread crumbs and cooked oatmeal are good homegrown foods. Keep them warm back of the stove or buy a heat lamp for them. To make a chick waterer fill a quart jar with water. Put a shallow bowl upside down on it like a lid. Turn the whole thing upside down outside the chick pen. (The jar will slop for a moment.) Slip a match or toothpick under one edge of the jar to keep the water flowing as the chicks need it and set it down in there. Newly hatched chicks

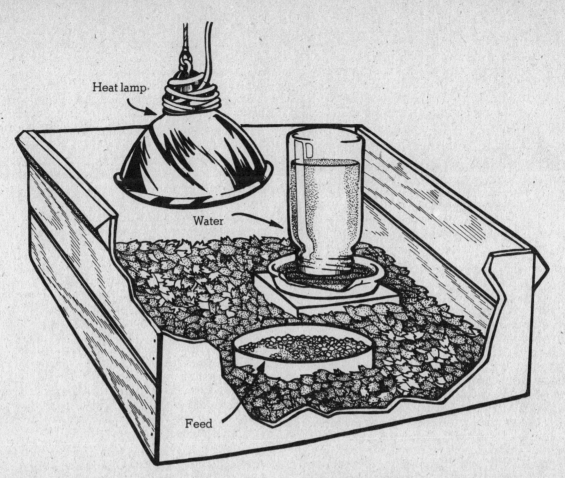

Heat lamp

Water

Feed

can't be put behind chicken wire. They're so little they'll walk right through it. A box with high sides is a fine start.

It takes at least 3 months for them to get to edible size. To a certain extent the more you feed them the faster they will be ready for the frying pan.

The young hens that have not yet begun to lay eggs or are just starting are called "pullets." You can tell when a pullet starts to lay eggs because she gets broad across the behind (same thing happened to me having babies).

Whenever possible I let my hens set and raise their own families. You can start out with just two Bantys, male and female, and they'll do the rest. If you have layers, too, you can put their eggs under the Bantys and get a bonus. Hens like to lay where there are eggs already. Mark with a crayon the ones she's setting on (like with a big X) and then you can gather new ones. The survival instinct of chickens will cause them to try to hide their nest if you keep emptying it completely of eggs. If you leave one egg in each time it helps some. That's the biggest trouble with letting them run loose. Then sometimes you can't find the eggs.

The best way to keep chickens laying in the hen house, besides shutting them up completely, is to feed them in the chicken house last thing in the afternoon when it is about their bedtime (well before true dark) and then shut them up for the night. They will lay their eggs first thing in the morning and then you can open the doors and let them go on their foraging way.

It helps if you have a roomy, nice chicken house with lots of nesting boxes made the way hens like them (read on) and lots of nice clean straw bedding in those nesting boxes. Incidentally have you ever seen a chicken lay an egg? It is by nature rather a private act. When I was a little girl about 6 or so, I got a terrible desire to see the egg come out. I patiently waited days behind a little red hen who laid her eggs in a rather exposed nest and finally one day it happened —I saw the egg come out! Not as dramatic as watching kittens or puppies or baby goats and so on come out but a wonderful moment nonetheless. I was really impressed with the serious effort it required from the hen and her immense relief when the act was all over. When you stop to think about it you know that has to be something of an accomplishment. And then she jumped up from the nest and walked in a happy and excited way all about cackling her head off over the accomplishment of it all! So if you want to meditate on where eggs come from that's where and you can be rightfully grateful to the hen because she worked at it.

SETTING means when a chicken stops just laying her eggs and walking away and instead stays to sit on them, keep them warm, turn them over twice a day and so incubate out a family. It's desirable or undesirable, depending on whether you want chicks or eggs more. To discourage a setting hen just keep taking her eggs away.

When a hen is setting she is *supposed* to hatch in 21 days. Mine always seem to take much longer, like 28 days or more. If she continued laying a few days after she started setting, chicken babies will appear for several days. Don't try to rush them. Let the chick come out of the egg at its own pace. If you peel the shell off for it thinking to help, the chick is certain to die. It has an umbilical cord attached to the shell inside that has to dry up naturally. If possible leave Banty chicks with the mother and let her roam. She will do a good job.

MOLT—Hens can be thrown into a "molt" the latter part of July or the first of August. They lose some feathers and quit laying. Young hens started as chicks before April or May go into a molt in early winter. If you're lucky the ones that went into the late summer molt will snap out of it in October or November and lay through the winter. Winter is a big problem anyway, eggwise.

In my own experience chickens that roam at least some of the time are by far the happiest chickens and the best-looking ones in the summertime. When I plant the beans and corn (and then have to shut up the chickens for a while) at first it's pleasant not having to hunt all over creation for eggs. I usually buy a couple bags of laying mash for the duration to try to keep the egg production up and give the hen house an extra good going over with lots of fresh straw in the nesting boxes. But even so within a couple weeks egg production starts to decline some, the hens start to look ratty, like they're going into a molt, and then worst of all some of them will start to eat eggs. Chickens running around where they aren't overcrowded don't eat eggs usually, but locked up in a chicken house they sure learn it fast. All I know to do in that case is start gathering eggs four times a day. Take them out even from under hens that are in the process of laying another one. When I catch an egg eater in the act or else can identify one by the yolk on her beak I evict her from the hen house and eat her.

It's a great relief to be able to let them all out again—for the chickens and for me. But in winter if you let your chickens out where they will get their feet cold and wet it's the end of your egg production. They have a built-in system to measure hours of daylight and temperature, and lay best when days are long. Big egg producers keep them shut in and keep lights on. It works, too, and if you didn't manage to get enough eggs put away in the spring you'd better try to keep them laying as long as you can.

Everybody has a different formula for making hens lay in winter. Great-grandmother says that she fed them a teaspoon of cayenne pepper every other day. The University gives them hormones and then they not only lay all winter but they lay two eggs a day! They like a heat lamp, and light until 10 or 11 at night helps (you could leave it on all night if turning it off is a nuisance to you). And you can feed aplenty of rich feed like grain, and laying mash and table scraps and give them plenty of water. There's a gal in Alaska who hangs a kerosene lantern in her hen house just about dusk during the winter. She allows only enough oil in the base to burn 3 to 4 hours to supply a total 14 hours of daylight. That's the magic number for egg laying.

But if you don't have the money or electricity to do it that way don't worry. My chickens don't lay worth a darn during the winter months. I comfort myself that God didn't design them to. That's where knowing how to preserve eggs comes in. Those University birds lose their feathers, look wretched and die young. My hens go on laying to ages that amaze people. I'd rather let them have the winter rest and then they lay twice as good when spring comes again and there's no real loss.

HOUSING YOUR CHICKENS—Art Boe is an ex-Alaska fisherman, off and on building contractor, ex-high school science teacher, South Dakota farm boy, cow milker and dear friend. His wife is the second grade teacher and has an Emery in her class about every other year. Here is Art's recipe for the ideal chicken house.

First level your ground. Allow 5 to 7 square feet per chicken. A simple pole building, shed type, is adequate. You'll need windows on the south side in northern climates, with enough roof overhang to keep *out* the summer sun and let *in* the winter sun. Have a third to a quarter of the south side in windows, made so that you can remove the glass in summer for ventilation. (Have chicken wire on the inside to hold in the chickens when you take the windows out.) Slope the roof, say from 7 feet in front to 6 feet in the back. The rule of thumb is 1 foot of drop for each 8 feet of roof—more if you live in snow country, where piled up snow could collapse your roof.

You'll need electricity in there for a light bulb if you live where winter nights are long and you want to push your chickens to maximum year-round production. You won't need heat in winter if you insulate your chicken house and it is small enough with a low enough roof to keep the warm air near the chickens, who make quite a bit of heat themselves. But you will need some ventilation even in winter, at least some cracks. The ammonia builds up awfully strong from their manure.

You can get along with a dirt floor, but you're better off with a wooden floor built up off the ground. It is warmer and will dry from underneath. Chickens make *a lot* of moisture. Add a foot of sawdust or shavings. Stir together the sawdust or shavings and manure once in a while. Shovel the whole sawdust-manure mixture out and start fresh as needed. If you have a generous sawdust layer to begin with, you'll maybe need to do this only twice a year. Wood shavings or sawdust are especially good because the turpentine in them repels lice. Lice *love* straw.

If you're not going to let your chickens forage, they'll need a fenced chicken yard to scratch around in and get some air. Fence it 6 feet high. You may have to clip their wings on one side too if they are determined to fly over. Have plenty of 1/32-inch (more or less) small gravel in there for their gizzards so they can grind up their food.

Besides feeders and waterers in your hen house, you'll need roosts and nesting boxes. A roost is a long pole set about 4 or 5 feet off the chicken house floor. The chickens will fly up there to sleep. You can't put roosts right on top of each other. Chickens, like any other creatures, don't like to be pooped upon. If they don't have a chicken house they will fly up in trees or onto rafters as soon as they get big enough to fly that high. Since they sleep unbelievably soundly they have an instinct to pick a very protected place to park in.

A *nesting box* is something (anything) like a wooden box, open at the side, with hay or straw inside for the hen to use to make her nest. Nail it up, 3 feet high or so, on your chicken house wall. A whole row of them will keep your layers happy. They like dark, comfy, private places to do their thing in.

FEEDING THEM—Banty chickens are smaller than the regular laying and fried-chicken type breeds, but they make up for that in self-sufficiency. Mine don't need any feed except in the dead of winter. In the summer they range all over the farm with their families picking up bugs. The people up the road will be telling me about the grasshopper situation—that the hoppers are stripping the fruit trees and berry bushes and I'll honestly say I haven't seen a hopper all summer. That's because of all my chickens ranging around. They take a toll by pecking tomatoes and strawberries and I have to confine them after planting corn, beans, peas and beets until the young plants are well started to keep them from scratching up and eating the seed, but otherwise they get the run of the place. I plant plenty of lettuce so I have enough for the chickens and us, too. If the chickens don't have enough room to run in they'll kill all the green stuff in sight by eating it to the ground. They need green stuff.

I simply couldn't afford to keep this many chickens if I had to keep them confined all the time, to say nothing of the trouble it would be hauling food and water. The average number here is about 50 layers. That isn't just Bantys, includes my heavy meat breeds. I buy cockerels at the $12 per hundred special rate and raise them for fryers, so they don't stay around more than about three months. I have Leghorns and Rhode Island Reds and all kinds of strange combina-

tions. It would be nice to have big chickens with the resourcefulness of Bantys.

Don't leave them completely on their own though, not your Bantys or any other chickens. Give them some table scraps in the chicken house to remind them where they are supposed to lay their eggs. Give them some cracked grain for love and encouragement, egg laying and growth. In winter when snow is on the ground, you'll have to feed them a complete diet. You can't get something for nothing. Encourage them to forage all you can but don't turn them into wild things.

If you are raising chickens in town compromise by just letting them out the last few hours before sundown. That way they get a chance to pick up a little natural food and don't range too far from home.

It's no problem at all to keep big chickens on homegrown food. They'll eat anything except white sugar. They spend a lot of time in the barn in winter. Chickens will eat good alfalfa hay and get all the grass and weed seeds mixed in there. They'll eat all your kitchen scraps, peelings, leftovers, sour or sweet milk, pickles, meat scraps and rancid lard. Little chickens need lots of good food and clean water. They can be fed the same scrambled eggs and bread diet as under Goose. But the truth is chicks will do best on commercial chick starter or being mothered by a hen. There's really no in-between.

Now as far as raising foods specially to feed chickens goes, I've fed mine sunflower seeds and corn and dried peas and beans. If you have it, grain is handiest and a good rich feed that they do well on, but you can't just confine chickens and feed them grain. They've got to have a chance to pick up pebbles for their gizzard. A chicken has no teeth. He swallows down into the first stomach in his neck called his crop. Then as he needs it he swallows on down from there into his chewing stomach—the gizzard. In that tough old gizzard the grain is pushed around amongst those pebbles until it is literally smashed. But there is a certain attrition by pooping of the pebble supply. Scattering fine gravel in the hen house will do it. It helps confined hens too if you save the eggshells, crush them with a rolling pin, and return them for recycling. Hens can and happily will eat whole eggshells but the problem with that is they may develop into egg eaters.

ROOSTERS—You should change roosters at least every two years or you run a risk of some birth defects in your chickens from inbreeding. So consign homegrown roosters to the pot or sell or exchange them for roosters from some other person's chicken flock. Chickens are the only animals I've seen really come to harm from inbreeding. Doesn't matter whether you have Banty chickens or some other breed. Roosters can be castrated. It's called caponizing them. But it's hardly worth the trouble.

Roosters are aggressive, as are all males, and may chase and peck small children. They won't bother a child big enough not to care. It's your toddlers and two-year-olds they go for. The best thing to do with a rooster that has attacked your child is to take it to the chopping block. You almost certainly

have more. Many a time I've run out of the house because I heard a child screaming in the yard and there was a rooster flying up and pecking at the child's face. I wondered if somehow it was my private nightmare until I received the following letter from another mother, Becky Jacobson of Felton, Delaware: "Dear Carla, You said that roosters were aggressive and may chase and peck small children, but you never heard of one doing real damage. Let me share my sad experience with an aggressive rooster and I hope it will save some other family much grief. We had a small rooster who would fly at people once in a while but we never thought much about it. Our few chickens are usually kept penned up in the chicken yard.

"One afternoon they were out and my 20-month-old daughter was playing and following her father around. She walked past the rooster and must have stopped in front of him. Before we knew what happened he flew up and spurred her in the eye. She is now blind in her left eye and the eyeball is disfigured. When she is four or five, if her eye doesn't have to be taken out, she'll be fitted with a lens that will make her eyes look the same. It's cost us thousands of dollars and much heartache to learn this lesson. If anyone has a rooster that flies at anyone, have him for dinner, and any rooster that has spurs, if you have young children, cut them off."

CHICKEN BREEDS—Every different size and coloring of chicken, or bird for that matter, that can be passed down consistently can be considered a "breed." There are so many you can get very confused. You don't need "fancy" breeds. They are for people who want what nobody else has and can pay a high price for the privilege. Here are some general categories to guide you. White chickens generally lay white eggs. Dark-feathered breeds generally lay brown eggs. There is a pure black breed that lays pure white eggs. The well-known Araucanas lay greenish or pinkish or bluish eggs. An individual Araucana hen won't change colors. Whatever color she lays, that's what you get. White-feathered birds are easier to prepare for the table because if you've missed a few feathers at picking time the family will probably eat them and never know the difference. No such luck with dark-feathered breeds. And then chickens come in heavy, light and bantam weight. That makes a difference at fryer time. Heavy chickens are the best fryers and roasters. They eat more and lay slightly bigger eggs. Rhode Island Reds and White Rocks are brown and white egg layers respectively of the heavy breeds. Leghorns are light. Their roosters make passable fryers, though smaller than Reds or Rocks. They eat less and lay a white, smaller egg, but still marketably large.

A Banty is a real small bird, smaller even than a Leghorn. But their great advantage is they are so healthy, they can make it through almost anything. They are cute with lots of personality, are great foragers, are good incubating machines for yours or anybody else's fertile eggs and good mothers, too, even if you put the ugly duckling himself under her. Their disadvantage is that the Banty roosters are so wonderful doing their thing that soon you'd have all half Bantys which is not good from the meat point of view. For this reason I butcher most of the Banty roosters so the others have a chance to do something too. Bantys are too small to be proper fryers. They stew OK, lay eggs almost too small to make presentable single egg servings but scramble fine.

The Leghorn is the accepted favorite for commercial laying operations. There is virtually no competition. The white eggs sell better and color better at Easter. The smaller size means the chicken eats less for the per egg production (though the eggs are slightly smaller). They are kept in huge chicken houses, debeaked (the ends of their beaks cut off to make them blunt instead of pointed) so they won't peck at each other's mites, and fed food chemically designed to encourage egg production. When they get three years old they are sold for 25 cents or so each to become chicken soup or some such. In my experience Leghorns haven't wintered as well as Rhode Island Reds or even White Rocks and they don't seem to have quite the ability to forage of some other breeds. But that's my opinion and there are homesteading folks out there who have had nothing but good experiences with their Leghorns so please don't let what I've said prejudice you out of giving them an equal chance among the breeds you may be looking into.

USING EGGS WHEN YOU HAVE LOTS

When spring comes and you are gathering eggs by the kettleful don't forget to preserve some of them. But you can still enjoy your bounty. You can have scrambled eggs for lunch as well as breakfast, make deviled eggs, French toast, crepes suzettes, eggnogs, ice cream and keep a bowl of plain old hard-boiled eggs on hand for snacking, packed lunches and potato salad. Homegrown eggs make better home-made mayonnaise than store eggs. They make good leavened-with-egg batters.

Instant Breakfast—This is my standby for sleep-in mornings. Two eggs (or 3—or 1, if I'm short), 1 cup cold milk in summer (hot milk in winter served in a warm mug with nutmeg sprinkled on top and hot homemade bread buttered and shoved under the broiler a moment to melt it) and enough honey or molasses or sorghum or brown sugar to sweeten it to taste for the one I'm making it for. Beat it up with the eggbeater and serve. Sometimes I make it with some chocolate or vanilla malt (Carnation), or fruit syrup or some fresh berries or fruit beat up in it too (in which case I adjust the sweetening). We make these as part of any easy lunch or for between-meal snacks, too.

Crepes—A French sounding name for a tender pancake, but I actually got into this type of recipe from a very antique and common cookbook. Combine 6 eggs, 1½ cups unbleached flour (or whole wheat), ¼ cup loosely packed brown sugar or a couple tablespoons honey, and 1 cup milk. Drop by tablespoonfuls onto a greased frying pan or griddle over medium low heat, turning when one side is done. Serve with honey, homemade butter and fruit sauce or syrup. Roll up and eat. Some people like to fill them up with Devonshire cream (a kind of cream cheese—recipe in Dairy).

Shirred Eggs—Melt 4 tablespoons butter and distribute among 6 small custard dishes or muffin containers. (There used to be a regular product for this called an "egg shirrer.") Dust the buttered bottoms with dry bread crumbs. Break 2 eggs into each one. Don't stir. Sprinkle with salt and pepper and set them into a moderate oven until thoroughly set.

Ice Cream—This homemade ice cream tends to be either a little too soft or a little too hard, but it's quick and easy to make and so nourishing. In spring when cows and chickens are at top production we make lots of it. You will need 1 cup whipping cream, 6 eggs, 1 cup crushed pineapple, 1 mashed banana and the diced sections of 1 orange. Whip the cream and eggs separately. Add ¼ teaspoon vanilla extract. Then gently fold together and fold in the fruit. Freeze in your refrigerator freezer compartment with occasional stirring to get the fruit off the bottom as it thickens. To vary the recipe, use 1½ to 2 cups of any fruit, adding honey as needed for sweetening.

How to boil eggs—In pioneer days the women used to sprinkle a little salt in with the boiling eggs to keep them from cracking and to help them peel easier. A method highly recommended nowadays is to put the eggs into cold water, bring to a boil, cover tightly and let set off the stove for 25 minutes. Put them into very cold water when done and let set for 5 minutes and then peel.

Deviled Eggs—Cut hard-boiled eggs neatly into halves. Remove and mash the yolks and season them with salt, pepper, mustard, grated onion or what you prefer. Then roll the mashed, seasoned yolk into balls of the appropriate size and put one ball into each half white. Serve on a platter.

Flower Eggs—To really dress up a potato salad or macaroni salad. Use a nicely peeled boiled egg. Holding the larger end of the egg downwards in your left hand, and using a sharp knife, peel down from the smaller end in petal-like shapes just to the hard-boiled yolk, stopping where the egg starts to flatten at the larger end. Open the egg and press the petal shapes out flat and sprinkle with paprika.

PRESERVING EGGS

Under natural conditions more hens' eggs are laid during the months of March, April, May and June than during the other eight months combined. The commercial method of preserving eggs is by cold storage at around 40°. Eggs preserved by any method aren't as nice as fresh ones, but they're better than eating somebody else's eggs.

Rotate your egg supply to use the oldest or most doubtful first. The eggs you preserve should be the ones that you are sure are fresh. Gather every day to make sure they are. Leave one egg in the nest but change that one regularly so you don't end up wasting an egg.

FROZEN EGGS—First decide how you need your eggs—whole, as for scrambling, yolks separate, or whites separate. I never make any meringues and fancy stuff so all my eggs go in whole. The freezer life of an egg is 8 months. Use clean eggs. Wash them if need be so you can be sure no dirt particles get in. Now decide how many you need in a package. You have to use these up within 12 hours of thawing so you don't want more than one day's worth in a package or it will be wasted. That's six eggs for me. To freeze whole eggs take them out of the shell and put into your freezer containers. Baby food jars work best. Freeze egg whites in your recipe amount. Don't include even a speck of yolk. Don't add anything. Freeze egg yolks with either salt or honey: 1 teaspoon honey or ¼ teaspoon salt per ½ cup yolks. You'll want to have these labeled as to whether they are whole or yolks and are salty or sweet.

1½ tablespoons thawed yolk equals one fresh egg yolk

2 tablespoons thawed egg white equals one fresh egg white

3 tablespoons thawed whole egg equals one fresh egg (sort of—because homegrown eggs aren't all that standardized anyway)

The other egg preserving methods are in the shell. For these methods don't wash the egg. If an egg is dirty just put into the daily supply to be used up soon. An eggshell is naturally covered by a gelatinous film which washing removes. That film helps seal the shell pores. Without it the egg is more susceptible to bacteria and evaporation. Don't use cracked eggs either. For some reason eggs laid during March, April and May seem to keep better than later eggs. Maybe because it takes time for water glass to seal the pores and if they are at a low temperature while it's working, it helps.

WATER-GLASS METHOD (This is what I use mostly)—Pack them when they are between 24 hours and 4 days old. Older eggs won't keep so well. Eggs from hens that have no roosters running with them will keep longer than fertile eggs. But mine are fertile. You can get the water glass (sodium silicate) at your drugstore or the druggist can help you locate it. It's getting more expensive all the time. It's about $1.05 a pint now. Use 1 pint of water glass to 9 or 10 pints of water. For larger or smaller quantities use the same proportion—any one part water glass to nine parts water.

Have your crock scalded clean to start with (I use deep plastic cans). Boil the water and let it cool before you add the water glass. Pour the solution into the crock. Add the eggs. Make sure there is an extra 2 inches of solution covering them and to allow for evaporation. Store in a cool place like your cellar. Add more boiled and cooled water as the solution evaporates to maintain your 2 inches of fluid above the eggs. It evaporates pretty fast in hot weather. Earthenware, enamel, glass or plastic containers all will work. Cover the container as tightly as you can. Flies just love to drown in there. Don't let it freeze. When you first make up the water glass it is a clear liquid. It gradually turns into a milk-colored sort of jelly. Incidentally, when you put in your water-glass solution don't fill the crock over half full because when you put in the eggs it will rise. Water glass isn't poisonous and it won't hurt you if it gets on your hands or clothes. It just seals the eggshell. One gallon of water glass will make enough solution to preserve from 75 to 100 dozen eggs. The most practical approach is just make more solution as you have more eggs to add. Add them about every 3 days along with enough solution to cover them. If you're lucky they will keep as long as a year. If you boil these eggs, prick the small end with a pin first or they will pop open. You'll have to rub or wash the water glass off before you crack the eggs. Otherwise it will fall off into the omelet.

MINERAL OIL—If you can't get water glass anything to prevent the evaporation of the egg's contents will help preserve them. Eggs have on occasion been packed in lard, or painted with a gum arabic solution, or greased with lard or butter and then packed in sawdust or oatmeal. To coat them with mineral oil wash the shells. Then apply the oil by dipping the eggs. Warm the oil a little to thin it but have it no hotter than your hand can stand. Try to oil the eggs within 24 hours after they were laid. Let the excess oil drain off. Pack the oiled eggs in clean boxes and store them in the coolest place you have. Mineral-oiled eggs get thick whites. They are slippery to peel when hard boiled.

THE BARREL METHOD—During cold weather you can pack eggs in a barrel or crock or plastic can in sawdust or oatmeal, small end down.

PRESERVING BY BOILING—This is a new one to me but Barbara Rogers wrote me from Carlsbad, California, that you can preserve eggs by submerging them (in the shell) in boiling water for *exactly* 5 seconds and then pull them out. They'll keep at room temperature for 6 months or refrigerated for up to a year.

BRINED EGGS—Put clean eggs in a crockery, wood or plastic container. Cover with a mixture of 3 gallons water, 1 pint quicklime (from lumberyards or drugstores) and 1 cup salt. Weight enough to hold eggs under the solution. You can add more eggs later but be careful that they don't crack going in. Store in a cool place.

HOMEMADE EASTER EGGS

Once I advertised in my Newsletter for advice on how to color Easter eggs a homemade way. Here are some of the wonderful answers that arrived:

ONION SKINS AND FOOD COLORING AND VINEGAR—Wrap the eggs in onion skins, then a cloth and tie with string. Onion skins are a natural dye and the string presses it against the egg making patterns also. Boil these eggs (they can start out uncooked) and then unwrap for lovely surprises. Also can be dyed again with food coloring for further beauty. To dye with food coloring submerge a cooked egg in a cup of water that has a little vinegar in it. Vinegar sets the color. Using a dropper, drop the food color onto the egg. It spreads and makes amazing patterns. Rinse the eggs afterwards to remove excess color. From Carol Kahn of Vernonia, Oregon.

COLORS AND DYESTUFFS—Dyeing is dyeing whether it's eggs or wool. The stem, leaves and flowers of goldenrod, pear leaves, tanglewood stems, apple bark, hickory bark, all make a yellow color. Sassafras roots make pink. Red onion skins, bloodroot, fresh beet juice, madder root, and logwood make red. Birch leaves, Spanish onion skins—outer leaves only, elderberry leaves and rhubarb leaves make green. Walnut hulls make brown. Catherine Lancaster wrote me from Hico, West Virginia, to tell me that.

PRECOOKED DYES—"I don't know how you celebrate Easter, but we always color eggs. And what better way than with natural dyes. The colors turn out much softer looking than commercial egg dyes and often give a spotty or speckled finish. Dyes should be cooled before using, preferably overnight. You should add just a little vinegar to the dye to fix the color. (Don't boil vinegar in aluminum.) Examples: 5 red cabbage leaves plus 4 cups water equals aqua color and an egg pattern like tie-dye material. Or boil the outer dry skins of 2 medium onions for an orange dye. Orange peel gives you a light yellow dye. Yellow Delicious apple peelings make lavender with soft rust flakes. Thyme boiled makes a pale graying yellow-orange dye. The possibilities are only limited by your imagination and willingness to give it some effort." From Mrs. Linda Crabtree, Kettering, Ohio.

DANDELION AND PINE NEEDLE EGGS—"We dye Easter eggs this way: First send the children out to gather lots of large leaves, daffodils and dandelions and other leaves or needles from fir or pine trees. Then take your eggs and wrap them with the leaves putting the flowers and pine needles under the big leaves. Cover the whole egg by wrapping the leaves around the whole thing. Then we tie string around the leaves to hold them on. Boil until eggs are hard cooked. Remove from water and take off the string and unwrap the leaves. You will have a beautiful design. The pine or fir needles will produce a design on the egg. The green leaves produce yellow. Daffodils and dandelions produce deeper orangish yellow coloring. Also for deep dark blues and purples, squash canned blackberries or blueberries on the egg and then cover with leaves or onion skin. Leaves can be used again and again. Boiling longer produces richer, darker shades. The eggs are beautiful and each egg is different. Also we like to dye the big goose eggs. They lay about Easter time and it's fun to have the big eggs. They are delicious too." Nancy Dyer of Corbett, Oregon, sent me that one. Makes me want Easter to hurry round again so I can try it all!

FLOWER PATTERNED EGGS—"Here's a good way to color Easter eggs. My great-grandmother taught my mother this. You need brown onion skins, small spring flowers like buttercups, grass flowers, raw white eggs, small squares of soft cloth and string. Lay flowers next to eggs, petals spread out. Next position onion skins on top of flowers. Wrap gently in soft cloth and tie with string. Cook in gently simmering water about 25 minutes. Unwrap cloth, peel off onion skin and flowers and they are truly beautiful." From Mrs. Karen Hayes, St. John, Washington.

CHICKEN FOR MEAT

SIZES—A 1½-pound chicken is big enough to cook as a *broiler*. From about 2 pounds on up it could be cooked as a *fryer*. A *stewing* chicken is not necessarily a heavy one—it means a chicken no longer tender—a year or more old. A healthy chicken has bright eyes and a red comb. A fryer has soft cartilage at the end of the breastbone and pinfeathers. An older stewing type has a rigid breastbone and long hairs on its skin.

TO CATCH a chicken enter the chickens' sleeping quarters well after dark equipped with twine or a burlap bag. Carry a flashlight. Quietly grasp the one you want by its skinny legs and tie twine around them. Or put it in the bag and tie the mouth of that or put it in a rabbit hutch. It will be ready when you want it in the morning for killing. To catch a chicken in the daytime that can't be walked up to (when you feed them) or cornered in the chicken house, make a chicken hook out of a length of wire (clothes hanger) with a miniature shepherd's crook at the end. Holding the other end of the wire suddenly stretch out the wire and hook the chicken's leg in the crook. It is easier to catch the chicken while it's sleeping and that way you won't have to contend with a full crop (the first and highest up "stomach") when cleaning it.

TO KILL the chicken grasp it firmly by the ankles and both wing tips with the left hand and place its body on the chopping block so that the neck is stretched out across the block. This may require a bit of maneuvering. The chicken may retract its head just when you're all set. Have the chopping block well away from the house because the chicken's body will flop around and scatter blood. (A chopping block is a large flat-topped and flat-bottomed piece of tree, with the grain running perpendicular to the ground.) Have a sharpened ax or hatchet ready in your right hand and with one hard blow sever head from neck. Cut it as near the head and far from the body as you can in order to save the neck for cooking and to avoid cutting the crop located at the base of its neck.

Some people prefer to wring the chicken's neck. This may be done by grasping the chicken firmly by the upper part of the neck or head. Then get the body swinging rapidly as you would twirl a heavy object on the end of a string until the body separates from the portion you are holding. And it *will*. A more professional method is to pierce the brain with a knife run through the roof of the mouth or to stun the bird by a blow on the head. Then the blood vessels in the neck can be cut by severing the artery which is reached in the neck back of the earlobe. Another way to cut that artery is by running the knife through the mouth into the back part of the throat. But I've never known anybody who used this method—only read about it. That always gets up my suspicion a little. Be sure to let your bird bleed thoroughly since this will improve its eating and keeping qualities. Besides no way can you accomplish anything with it until it's done its flapping around.

Since I first wrote this section I've gotten some interesting advice from readers. Especially on making that chicken hold still while you're trying to chop its head off. One writer told me that she "hypnotizes" the chicken by putting the chicken's head under its wing, then swings it around, then chops the head off. Betty Lawrence from White Swan, Washington, wrote me that she hammers two nails about one inch apart on the surface of her chopping block. She leaves part of the nails sticking up and then when she's ready to chop the head off she lays that chicken's neck between the nails and pulls back gently until the head is next to the nails. This is all so they don't move their head and necks out of place just as you're aimed and ready to bring down the blade. Of course, if you use this system you've got to be careful *not* to hit those two nails as well as *not* to hit the crop and *to* hit the chicken's neck clear across. Because hitting nails is very bad for ax blades.

When I was a little girl chopping for my mama I used to say a prayer for the chicken before I raised my ax that if God had a place in heaven for the souls of chickens He should please take this one. In the animal graveyard at the side of the garden where beloved departed cats and dogs and field mice lay, brother Dick and I also buried not a few chicken heads with full honors as best we could manage. And, oh, Mother's fresh fried chicken! With mashed potatoes and lots of gravy made with milk! Dick and I would eat and eat. The wishbones were saved and dried near the stove for a day or two. Then we each took hold of a side and got our wish in mind (you couldn't say out loud what it was) and pulled. The one who ended up with the longest piece of bone would get his wish—or so we claimed.

TO PICK the bird first determine if you want to "dry pick" or "scald." Some people claim that a dry picked bird tastes better and is in better shape for selling. I doubt this unless the scalded bird has been overscalded. However, if you want to save the feathers for stuffing you may want to dry pick. Dry picking is more difficult than scalding because the feathers are harder to pull out.

Dry picking should be begun immediately after killing (even before the bird stops bleeding) before the flesh has a chance to become cold which would set the feathers in tightly. Be careful not to tear the skin.

Pick up the breast and up the side. Then do the wings, back, and finally the pinfeathers which can be removed with a tweezers or with a knife blade (you catch the pinfeather between the blade and your thumb and pull).

To scald—Have a bucket or big pan of water on to boil before you kill the bird. A canner is good. While the chicken is flopping and bleeding bring your water outside to your work area. Spread out newspapers to do the picking on. You can roll them up afterwards with the feathers inside to keep them from flying all over your yard. If you are using a flattish pan you can dip the breast and then the back into the water, holding the bird by the ankles. Make sure the wing and tail feathers get a good scalding because they are the toughest to pull out. If you are using a bucket be sure you get the bird in far enough to scald the feathered portion of the "knees." But don't overscald since this will cause the outer surface of the skin to rub off. Less than 30 seconds should do it. You can scald several birds in the same water as long as it doesn't cool below about 120°. Commence picking immediately after pulling the bird out of the water, starting with the wing and tail feathers, then leg feathers, then body feathers, and finally pinfeathers. Rebecca Coufel and her husband do 70 or 80 chickens at a time. They wet them with a hose or bucket of cold water before scalding—claim the hot water gets under their feathers better for the prewetting.

Singeing—After the pinfeathers have been removed you will still have down and very fine long hairs, especially on an older bird. These are burned off by singeing. Do it in the yard where you won't set anything else on fire. The bird is held by the ankles over a flame (from natural gas or burning paper) and its position constantly changed until all parts having these hairs have been exposed enough to singe them away. The most convenient flame is probably made by rolling newspaper or brown paper into a cone shape, tight at one end (to be the handle) and wide enough at the other to flame readily. A burning paper bag won't blacken the bird as much as newspaper. Don't touch the paper to the bird since that would dirty it with ashes. Hold the chicken up by the ankles with your left hand and hold the ignited newspaper with your right (if you're right-handed). It won't take long to singe all the chicken. With practice you can do several chickens with one "cone."

Or you can use a wood grain alcohol—preferably not rubbing alcohol as the flame doesn't last as long. You can use extracts as a last resort but there isn't as much flame and it is more expensive. The advantage of using wood alcohol is it does a thorough job and doesn't leave black on the bird like burning paper does. Just pour alcohol in a small amount (⅛ cup) into a shallow saucer and light. And then turn your chicken around over the fire until all the hairs are singed off.

Now the chicken is ready to clean.

TO CLEAN or "draw" the chicken means remove innards, head and feet. Put it into very cold water in order to cool the entire body. This "plumps" it. You will also need a bowl of clean cold water to rinse the pieces in, a very sharp knife and an empty bowl to hold the finished chicken pieces. Have a thick layer of newspaper spread out to clean the chicken on. You can remove grubby layers as you need to and wrap innards up in them to dispose of by burying in the garden or a trip to the garbage dump.

If the head is still attached, cut it off. With your fingers carefully feel for the knee joint. Bend the knee and cut across the joint until the feet are off. (Incidentally, you can stew the chicken feet to make stock. Scald with boiling water and the skin and claw cases will peel off. To cook place in cold salted water and cook slowly.) Then cut off the oil bag at the end of the back on the "pope's nose," or "the north end going south," which the chicken used to preen its feathers.

Now cut carefully across the abdomen from thigh to thigh making sure you do not cut any of the intestines in the cavity. (Some people make the incision from below the breastbone to the tail—it doesn't matter.) Reach carefully under the breastbone into the body until the heart is reached. Loosen the membranes between the innards and the body wall and remove the entrails. The gizzard, heart and liver will be embedded in the mass. Be especially careful of the gallbladder, a greenish sac embedded in the undersurface of the right lobe of the liver. If it should break, the bile which it contains would make bitter and undesirable any part of the chicken that it touched.

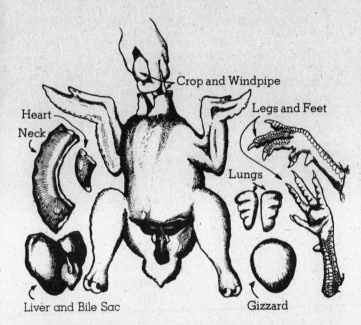

Save the giblets—heart, liver and gizzard. Cut off the part of the liver containing the gallbladder and discard it. Cut the gizzard open like a pocketbook three-quarters of the way around. Inside will be food and grit the chicken swallowed to be its grinding mechanism. Empty that out. Carefully peel off and discard the yellowish inner lining of the gizzard. Cut away the heart from its attached arteries and rinse heart, gizzard, and liver—the giblets are ready.

Finish separating the innards by cutting *around* the excretory vent so that it is discarded with the intestines. The kidneys in the back cavity and the lungs in the chest cavity adhere closely to the body wall and

should now be removed. It is impossible to get all the kidney out. Don't worry about it. Now get back to the chicken's front end. Cut the skin on the under part of the throat and remove windpipe, esophagus and crop by grasping one part and pulling the rest through. The crop tears very easily. You must gently separate it from the skin next to it before pulling. Finally, wash the drawn bird by allowing cold water to run through it or by immersing in water a bit. Don't soak.

TO PREPARE A BROILER split the bird into two halves down one side of the backbone and along the breastbone. (Optional, cut along the other side of the backbone and remove it.) To freeze the broiler, place two pieces of freezer paper between the halves to make it easy to separate them, then wrap well in a plastic bag or freezer paper. Label with date of freezing, and "broiler."

TO PREPARE A ROASTER for freezing wrap the giblets in freezer paper. Put the bird and giblets in a plastic bag and lower the bag into a pan of lukewarm water being careful not to let any water get inside the bag. The water will press the plastic against the bird and expel all air. Twist the part of the bag remaining out of the water tight. Then loop it double and fasten with a strong rubber band or wire.

A roasting bird may be frozen with the stuffing in it for up to two months but be sure the stuffing is thoroughly chilled before stuffing and freezing the bird. The bird may be stuffed both through the opening you made to remove the crop and in the abdominal cavity. Stuff sufficiently to fill the skin. When the body is full sew up the skin or close with a combination of skewers and thread. If the sides are very slack skewers alone could do the job.

A roasting bird is "trussed" by drawing the thighs and wings close against the body and fastening securely with skewers or tying with string. Keeps those appendages from drying up while the thicker parts of the bird are baking. If the neck has been removed, the skin of the neck is drawn over the cavity to the back and fastened with a skewer. (Wooden skewers are nicer than metal ones if you can get them.)

TO PREPARE A FRYER, it is easiest to cut off both legs and wings before opening the abdomen to remove the entrails. Separate each drumstick from the thigh by carefully feeling out the joint and then cutting the tendons at that point with a sharp knife. You take the drumstick off before taking the thigh off for better leverage. Cut the skin between the thigh and abdomen. Bend the thigh sharply away from the body cavity and cut it away along the line where it joins the abdomen and through the joint.

Pull one wing upward to expose the joint connecting it to the body and cut through the joint. Do the other wing.

Separate the breast from the back by cutting clear down both sides of the bird. Cut back and breast into two pieces each, cutting crosswise. The wishbone may be separated by inserting a knife under the tip and cutting downward, the knife following the bone. For a very big bird you may wish to further divide the back and breast.

Chicken Liver Pâté—The livers of about 5 or 6 average-sized chickens will give you ½ pound of chicken liver. If you just do in a couple every Saturday for Sunday dinner, you could add the fresh ones to your supply in the freezer until you have enough. Then cook the livers slowly in 2 tablespoons butter with 2 chopped onions until the onion is soft and the pink in the liver has disappeared. Remove the liver and mash with a fork or masher or pestle and force through a sieve after chopping. Then add ¼ cup sour cream, salt and pepper. You can store the pâté in a very small crock or bowl.

GOOD RECIPES FOR OLD HENS!

Chicken and Dressing—Cook the chicken and the giblets until you can easily separate the meat from the bones. That will require at least several hours or more, depending on how tough your old bird is. Let cool. Remove bones and cartilage. Grind the chicken skin and giblets. The chicken meat is nicest diced. Make a bread dressing base by gathering up your stock of bread crumbs or crumbling about a half loaf of homemade whole wheat bread (I don't like store bread for dressing—it's too salty). Add a dash of sage, 4 beaten eggs, and enough of the broth you cooked the chicken in and some milk, too, to moisten the dressing appropriately. Optional are chopped onion and celery and other seasonings. In an oven pan put a layer of dressing, then a layer of chicken, a layer of dressing again and so on. Bake, covered for 40 minutes at 350°.

Chicken and Noodles—This recipe warms up well so if you're expecting a bad day make it the day before. Put your stewing hen in a deep pan. Cover with water and add ½ teaspoon salt for each pound of chicken. Add 1 carrot, 1 small onion, 2 pieces of celery, 1 clove and 3 peppercorns. Bring to a boil, reduce heat and simmer until the meat will easily come off the bones and is very tender—2½ to 4 hours. Cool

enough to work with. Take the chicken off the bones and discard the bones. Return the meat to the broth. I always serve this with homemade egg noodles.

Chicken Stew—Prepare the chicken as for Chicken and Noodles, but instead of adding noodles add potatoes, carrots and onions and cook until tender.

Chicken Potpie—Make either Chicken Stew or Chicken and Noodles without the noodles. Then brown 4 tablespoons flour in a frying pan with 4 tablespoons butter. Gradually add enough broth to make a good gravy (about 2½ cups). Butter a baking dish. Mince the giblets. Put your meat in the dish. Pour the gravy over it.

Make dumpling dough by sifting together 2 cups whole wheat flour, a pinch of salt, 3 tablespoons baking powder, then adding ½ cup milk and 2 beaten eggs. Drop the dumpling dough by teaspoonfuls on top of the meat and gravy. Bake at 450° until the dumplings are done. (Save the leftover chicken stock for future use.)

Chicken Lunchmeat—Paula West wrote me another good way to use old stringy chickens is to make them into lunchmeat. "Grind them up with a pound of ground pork and some ground ham (I grind the last leavings of everything and put it in the freezer), add a little garlic and salt and thyme and bake in loaf pans until the thermometer says 180°. I slice and freeze in usable-size packages."

Chicken Loaf—Ivy Isaacson is a beautiful person, a real old-timer. Her husband Dick is the only person I know who has experience driving oxen and knows how to make an ox yoke starting with the right size tree. This is Ivy's recipe.

First of all boil your old hen until it is so tender you can pick out the bones and discard them. Keep the chicken broth. Mix 1 small loaf bread torn into pieces with 4 cups corn bread and add enough of the chicken broth to moisten the breads thoroughly. Now add ½ to 1 cup chopped celery, ½ to 1 cup chopped onion, salt, pepper and sage to taste. Place mixture in a buttered 12 x 15-inch pan. Cover with the chicken meat. Mix ¼ cup melted butter with ¾ cup flour. Add 2 cups milk. Cook same as any white sauce until thickened. Cool. Add 6 eggs, beaten. Pour over chicken. Sprinkle with buttered bread crumbs. Bake at 350° for 1 hour. Ivy recommends that when first cooking the chicken you add a carrot, celery stalk and a slice of onion. Then grate the cooked carrot and leave it in the broth to be mixed with the breads. This will give you 15 to 20 servings. Good to take to a potluck!

Unborn eggs—When you are butchering old hens you are going to encounter clusters of eggs of all sizes from almost regular egg size down to soybean size and smaller. Save those. They are good food. You can cook them in the chicken broth for soup. Scramble them with regular eggs. Or stir into any rice-vegetable type mixture that you could make into a fried rice kind of thing.

GOOSE

Geese and ducks are the water loving poultry. In general geese are big and ducks are smaller. The best source I know for detailed information about them is *Successful Duck and Goose Raising* by Darrel Sheraw and Loyl Stromberg, published by that same Stromberg Publishing Company that is so active all over the poultry field. I really recommend this book to give you a quality and detail of information that I can't here.

You've probably seen the advertisements of geese as great "weeders." That needs to be clarified. You can put geese into a cornfield after the corn is grown up tall and the ears are almost ready to pick for corn on the cob. They will get the weeds and leave the corn. But if you put them in there with young corn plants the geese would wipe them out. They are the same in a field of sunflowers. They like to eat thistles and burr weeds. Large-scale goose raising is said to be profitable—that means by the ten thousand. Market profit can be around $1.50 per bird. The riskiest area is with the young geese, which are very tender and must almost literally be babysat the first six weeks. If you have your goose mothers doing their own hatching same as chickens they will take good care of the children too, but incubator babies are a whole different thing. Newly-hatched goslings need to be kept at 90° for the first week and then you can gradually work it down to a normal temperature. The first six weeks until they are feathered out good is the critical period. This may surprise you but the baby geese can't stand getting wet until they are feathered out. So if you have them out eating grass which is a good thing to do and it looks like rain you have to bring them in. Geese herd pretty good and you can make one of your children into a little goose girl to take care of them. Start on a small scale and then if they work out for you and you want to you can get into bigger numbers.

Goose families are a pleasure to behold. They mate two by two and they mate for life. In spring after the babies are hatched you see them proudly walking about looking for good green things to eat—mama, daddy, and children.

People argue about getting the feathers off geese and ducks while they are still alive. The nicest feathers for pillow and mattress making are the ones from live birds there's no doubt. And there can be some method to the madness because you see in the spring the birds grow lots of lovely little feathers and then pull them out themselves and use them to create their wonderful downy nests. So what human beings are trying to do is share in the feather crop that's going to come off anyway. The point isn't to pull big feathers off, only the "down." It does cause momentary discomfort to the bird, but then you get into the whole question of trade-offs. In geese you don't have extra males to eat like you do with chickens—it takes two to bring up a family. But geese are much longer lived than chickens, too. So it's a whole different life cycle kind of thing. What I'm trying to say is humans and their domestic animals have real interdependencies, and if he or she could talk I'm sure your goose would much prefer to have some feathers pulled a couple times a year and the rest of the time have a soft life and a good winter grain ration than have people feel they've got a moral obligation to kill him before they get some feathers! If you pluck the down and short body feathers at the time they would normally be shedding them the feathers will release a little easier than at other times. Plucking is an art, too. You must pull the feathers the "wrong way—against the grain." You must be firm and quick. Get it over with and treat them good the rest of the time. They'll stay friends with you and kind of get used to it.

Another problem people have with geese is trying to decide which are boys and which are girls. Some breeds you can tell by appearance but most you have to do a rabbit-style close anatomical observation. Get somebody to help you. Pick one up, turn it upside down and start hunting around. There isn't much to see but with practice you can learn the difference. The female has a little round hole and the male has a round hole with a nubbin sticking out. If you can get a friend who has done it before to help you the first time it's a help. The easiest way of all though is to wait until spring. You may not know but the geese sure do. Off they will go two by two and the one who ends up laying eggs and sitting on the nest is the female.

DIFFERENT KINDS OF GEESE—The White Chinese is my favorite breed of goose. It's only about half the size of the other common breeds—Embden or Toulouse or African—but still plenty big for a Thanksgiving or Christmas dinner. We like them better than turkey. These geese will eat greens as long as they are available and thrive on alfalfa, needing only a chopped grain supplement in winter. They go for some weeds, too—dandelions, morning glory and pigweed—but their favorites are lettuce, chard, young peas, beans and corn. They'll even eat onions. If they get into the garden very often they can wipe you out, so you'll have to put up chicken wire to keep free-running goslings and geese outside. Geese are quite vulnerable to predators. My last summer's batch went down to the crick and something got every one of them.

All the geese are grass eaters. Toulouse is the best goose for reproducing itself. Goose eggs don't hatch as well if the geese are crossbred. In many kinds of animals you get a hardier, better animal by crossbreeding, but that's not true of geese. The White Chinese and Embden geese also go broody very well. The Embden is your big meat bird. Vendors will give you $7.50 on the hoof for them. They'll weigh 20 to 24 pounds by Thanksgiving. But don't let your geese go broody in January because none of their eggs will hatch. Our spring-hatched geese are ready by Thanksgiving when the bulk of them go into the freezer. Geese can live to a great age, but I wouldn't eat one over 3 years old—they get tough as shoe leather. It's easier to tell a young goose from an old one than to tell a hen from a gander. A young goose has down on its legs, which are soft and yellow.

The White Chinese not only do all their own foraging, but also reproduce like rabbits. A pair will produce about 20 goslings per spring, and your breeders may live as long as 15 years. A hogwire fence will hold adults, though a henless gander may occasionally fly over and need to be caught. A lonely gander has a rotten personality and will bite small children or you—when your back is turned. A whole flock can turn mean if abused, so be careful.

Goslings are hard to get started, so don't have them delivered until you have really warm weather, at least June or even later. Order from the supplier nearest you and pick them up personally if you can. Otherwise have them sent air express even though it's expensive. Goslings are not cheap. From my mail-order supply source, the White Chinese are about $1.75 each, and they are the least expensive variety. Freight is charged on top of that. My local hatchery charges $2.50 each. It isn't practical to buy eggs from mail-order sources and try to hatch them yourself. You're likely to have bad luck. You can get goslings or breeding pairs by mail-order from Northwest Farms, Inc., Box 3003, Portland, Oregon 97208 (they also have young ostriches for $550 and a very interesting catalog), and from the Heart of Missouri Poultry Farm, P.O. Box 954, Columbia, Missouri 39429. Goslings are much frailer than baby chicks, and are especially susceptible to chilling—they soak themselves every time they eat. I keep mine in a little room off the kitchen. There they don't need a heat lamp; but if kept in a chillier place, I'd supply a heat lamp for them to huddle under when they feel cold. For large numbers of goslings provide more than one lamp so they won't smother each other trying to reach the warmth.

You cannot feed goslings or ducklings regular chick starter because they can't handle the medication in there. So I worked up a system for starting them on homegrown food, which they like. Feed them three times a day at first—all they will eat. (They are water-type creatures and need a very wet diet.)

Morning—Cooked oatmeal covered with a little water.
Lunch—Scrambled eggs covered with a little water.
Supper—Homemade whole wheat bread covered with a little water.

Supply greens at all three meals, not grass or tough stems at first, because all that goslings can manage at this stage are very tender green leaves. Cut the greens up with a knife or scissors. After the first week, reduce their grain-egg supplement to two meals a day and offer more and more greens. Their bills will be stronger and they can manage weeds better. By the time they are down to one grain meal a day, they are ready to try life outside in the wonderful green world. I let them have a few hours of total freedom with my daughter (the goose girl) to follow along until they are returned to the cage for bed. When they are 6 weeks old, they can sleep outside, too, unless there is a long spell of chilling rain. By 8 weeks old they can pretty well take care of themselves. But geese that wander down a creek into the woods will most likely be gone by the next day—skunks, coons or weasels will do the job.

TO CLIP GOOSE WINGS—If they fly take off the wing 5 inches from the tip on one side. Just cut with scissors. It unbalances them. If you were to cut off both sides, they still could fly as they would be balanced.

TO CATCH A GOOSE at slaughter-time, especially an aggressive gander, remember that he may have lots of fight but his coordination is lousy. When he comes hissing at you, bend over toward him, reach out and grab his neck. Keeping one hand behind his head, hang on so that he can't bite and with the other arm, just scoop up his body, pinning the wings by tucking him under your arm and pressing him to your side. Holding his neck in one hand and his body under your other arm, you can carry him safely. Some friends have been continuing my education about geese. They say they shoot a goose in the head with a .22, then skin it out rather than pick it. Well, meat's meat.

Dry picking the goose makes the best feathers for stuffing pillows and quilts. If you plan to use the feathers, have cheesecloth bags and string ready before you start. Carefully pick while still warm. Be sure to free the feathers of any skin that may adhere to them so they won't be tainted. Separate the ones over 2 inches long, especially the large wing and tail feathers. These should be cut with a scissors or stripped off the quill which is discarded. The cheesecloth bags full of feathers can be closed at the top with a string. Later when you have time, clean and dry the feathers. See how in the Home Industries chapter.

After the feathers are taken off, the down is removed by brushing the body with your hand moistened in water. It's difficult to dry pick in cold weather, however, when the feathers are harder to pull and the flesh is likely to tear. Scald the geese in boiling water and the picking will be easier. Clean the same as for chicken.

Incidentally, goose eggs are fine eating. Use them the same way you would a chicken egg. They taste just the same to me, but are much bigger. One goose egg will make an omelet; fry one and it fills the pan.

Here are some of my favorite goose recipes:

Braised Gosling—Use a roaster with a rack in the bottom of it. Put chunks of a carrot, an onion, a turnip, a pared apple and a stalk of celery on the grating. Lay the birds on that. Rub salt, pepper and a little sage on them. Pour some boiling water in the side. Cover and roast at 350°—15 minutes to the pound. Baste with butter. To make the gravy remove the goslings, mashing the vegetables by pouring them and the cooking liquid through a sieve into a bowl. Skim as much of the grease as possible after it has set a moment. Add the cooked giblets. Put about 3 tablespoons of the goose grease in a frying pan. Thicken with flour, add the broth gradually, stirring the lumps out before adding more liquid until it has all been added. Applesauce and green peas or lima beans are good with the goslings.

Goose Giblet Gravy—I use the neck, gizzard and heart. (The famous pâté de foie gras is made of goose liver.) Precook the giblets by boiling them until the gizzard is fork tender. Put the giblets on at the same time you put the roast in, because it often takes a long time to get that gizzard tender! If you want to use the giblets in the stuffing instead of the gravy, you'll have to start them the night before. Check about every hour and add more water as needed. Season the cooking water with 1 teaspoon salt, 2 peppercorns, 1 clove, a bit of bay leaf, a sectioned carrot, a sectioned celery stalk and an onion. After the giblets are cooked, cool

and then mince. Make a gravy of goose grease from your goose roast, flour, and the broth the giblets were cooked in. Add the minced meat. Make lots of gravy and refrigerate what's left over. Reheat the leftover gravy. Add sufficient water to get the right consistency. It thickens while stored. Add sliced leftover goose meat. It's a tasty, easy way to have goose.

Goose Stuffed with Sauerkraut—This is my Thanksgiving favorite, especially timely because the geese and the sauerkraut are both at their prime. Fill the goose with homemade sauerkraut. Sew up, tie into shape and place in a large kettle. Cover with about 2 quarts more sauerkraut and add boiling water. Simmer gently for 3 hours. At the end of this time, take out the goose and put it in your roaster. Rub the skin with butter. Bake in a 400° oven about 1 hour, or until nicely browned. Serve on a bed of the boiled sauerkraut. Salt and season with pepper, or butter the boiled sauerkraut since the boiling weakens the flavor.

DUCK

For best eating ducks should be not more than one year old. I'm talking about domestic ducks. We don't eat game birds. I don't want any mercury in the diet if I can help it. A ten-week-old duck that weighs about 5 or 6 pounds is ready for frying or roasting and is technically called "duckling." Domestic duck is quite fatty. A good reason for eating duckling rather than duck is that the pinfeathers of a duckling are just starting to grow.

For people who have a small farm and want eggs, ducks are also a good thing. The Khaki Campbell variety is raved about by everybody I know who has them. They are said to be healthy, cold weather hardy and will continue laying in cold weather. Like the Sex-link chickens, which are real steady layers, the Khaki Campbells don't go broody easy. To "go broody" means to set on a nest of eggs in which case, of course, they lay a nestful and then stop laying for a couple months which is bad for your egg production. When birds have no mother instinct to go broody they can just go on laying eggs practically forever and these ducks will do that. They've been recorded to lay nearly 365 eggs per year and that's better than any chicken on record. The Khaki Campbell bird weighs about 4 pounds and looks like a wild mallard. If you buy young ones (or any other kind of baby duck for that matter) don't feed them straight chick starter. They would get deformed wings or worse because it's just not a natural feed for them. Feed them the diet given under "goose." If you are trying to raise your own ducks from eggs, your duck parents need to be at least one and preferably nearer two years of age for it to work. Before then their eggs don't have good hatchability. That means that the eggs are fertile but the babies inside aren't hardy enough to make it. Which sounds strange to me but somebody who ought to know told me so and it's for sure I don't know different. The same thing is supposed to be true of goose eggs, that they don't have good hatchability until the parents are 2½ years old. If you have trouble eating duck eggs because of the unfamiliar "strongness" make bread and custards out of them.

If you want to raise ducks for meat the Khaki Campbell is not quite so good because it is a small bird. The best meat varieties of duck are the White Pekin, Aylesbury and Muscovy. The Muscovy is best for reproducing itself. The big ones are fat. An adult can weigh 16 pounds. But the right butcher size is about 8 pounds. The Muscovy will lay about 100 eggs a year, which is still not too bad.

If you want to keep a nonbroody bird like the Khaki Campbell duck or Sex-link chicken you can use your Banty chickens to set on their eggs and mother the chicks and still reproduce them fine. If baby ducks are being raised by their mothers near any body of water that is halfway natural you'll take some hard losses. Bullfrogs and other such things like baby ducks to eat. You'll do better bringing them into the house to raise.

TO KILL a duck chop off its head. Or stun it with a sharp blow on the head and then stick through the throat or just back of the eye with a narrow-bladed knife.

TO PICK a duck soak it in cold water until thoroughly wet. Remove from the water and roll in a towel. Then pour boiling water over the duck, let stand a few minutes and the feathers can be easily and quickly removed. If you are doing commercial numbers of birds, dry pick the tail and wing and steam the ducks 1½ to 2 minutes. You can hang 6 or 8 ducks at a time on hooks in the barrel, running a hook in the mouth and out the nostril. Then pluck.

If you aren't using the feathers for pillows you can put hot paraffin on top of your scalding water to make the removal of the down very simple. Or if you object to paraffin (I do) you can singe the down off and then wash the duck.

Remove the oil sac on the tip of the "north end going south." For fried duckling peel off the skin and fat from the body and legs (the wings will be hard to do). Clean the same as chicken. If the duck is to be cut, it is conventional also to split the bird down the back and remove the backbone.

Roast Duck with Orange Juice—Rub the duck inside and out with salt and pepper. Put a whole onion and some chopped celery inside the duck or stuff it with a bread stuffing. Rub the outside of the duck with oil. A duckling can be roasted at 500° for 15 minutes, then at 350° until done (about 20 minutes more). A

full-grown duck should be roasted at 350° for about 25 minutes per pound, uncovered, and basted once in a while with the pan drippings or with orange juice. When the duck is done make a sauce by adding 2 tablespoons flour to the drippings in the pan (or if you burnt the bottom pour the drippings into a frying pan), blending, adding a cup each of water and orange juice. Don't boil. Pour over duck and garnish with orange sections.

Fried Duck—Cook the gizzard, heart, neck and rib bones the same as to make goose giblet gravy. Or fry the first three alone with the other pieces. If you saved the skin and fat from the body and legs when you were cleaning the bird, cut it into small pieces and render out the duck grease. Remove the crack-

lings. Beat 1 egg with a fork and add 3 tablespoons milk, salt and pepper. (You may find you need still more dipping batter than this.) Dip each piece of duck into the batter, then roll in fine dry bread crumbs. Brown the duck pieces in the rendered duck fat. When browned pour off most of the fat, add 2 tablespoons water, cover and bake at 350° for 45 minutes. Remove cover during the last 10 minutes. A Dutch oven works very nicely with this recipe.

Doris's Duck Tip—When you have duck with a fishy or wild flavor, put the whole duck in salt water and add onions. Bring just to boil and drain off. Then prepare the duck as usual. Another lady said her system was to stuff the duck with an apple and onion, each chopped, and seasonings.

TURKEY

My mother used to raise turkeys and they chased me. They come in different kinds and sizes. The Nicholas Mammoth white turkeys have toms that weigh 50 to 60 pounds at maturity. At five months they weigh 20 to 25 pounds. The hens weigh 15 to 18 pounds. All that is a lot of bird. One place you can buy turkey poults—that's just-hatched turkeys—is Montana Hatcheries, Inc., 400 South 4th Street, Great Falls, Montana 54905. Another is Phinney Hatcheries, Walla Walla, Washington 99362. The latter is my favorite place to buy chicks. But when buying turkey poults you need to get your order in early, like midwinter. And check on delivery schedules because they are only hatched during a couple months of the year. One year I was going to have some and couldn't because I got my order in too late.

Turkey toms (that's the male) are big and they are aggressive. That can be a problem if you have small children. I've known a band of gobblers to sneak up and attack my husband Mike when they were free ranging. They didn't remain free ranging.

Unlike most other kinds of poultry there are as far as I know only a few kinds of turkeys. The most common are the white and the two brown kinds called "bronze breasted." One of the bronze breasted is a new strain that is resistant to a common turkey disease and the other is the older one. I'd advise you to buy bronze. In my own experience white turkeys don't winter as well as bronze. My white turkeys had trouble with toes freezing off. They were more subject to sickness in general. For in-depth information on turkey raising there is a book called *Starting Right with Turkeys*, written by G. T. Klein, published by the Garden Way Publishing Co., Charlotte, Vermont 05445. It's a paperback, price around $3.50.

Turkey hens are good mothers. Give them a turkey-sized A-frame in their pen, one for each hen and an extra or so with straw inside to help make a nest. She'll lay eggs in there and set and raise a fine family. You can feed turkeys chicken-type rations with plenty of water. When you decide to start with turkeys don't get just one. Turkeys don't like being alone and a single one may refuse to eat and die of starvation. Turkeys are supposed to be subject to disease from mingling with chickens but apparently it doesn't always happen because I don't know any turkey-chicken owners who keep their turkeys in above ground type cages and completely isolated from the chickens and none of them have had a disease problem. My turkeys are caged in a big long run with posts set into the corners and high wire sides. To start mail-order baby turkeys on homegrown food use the same rations as for goslings, only leave out the water

poured over the food. Give them water to drink separately. Add a combination of cracked corn, wheat, oats and greens gradually. You can buy a commercial turkey starter mash but most feed stores don't carry it and chick starter will work if you supplement with scrambled eggs or bugs. I know people who believe that for the first three days anyway the home-grown ration does even better. Turkeys have a little trouble figuring out what is food when they don't have a mother to show them. Old-timers put some bright colored marbles in with their food to attract them, or laid it out on a clean sheet of newspaper. Later you can use a regular metal feeder. They'll be very hard

on your garden if they get in there, same as geese. It's not worth it. Turkeys have strange personalities. A full-grown gobbler is an amazingly ugly creature. They will follow you around if they are loose making a racket and you may think you're being persecuted and then one day you realize that they like you and are hanging around in friendship and hoping for a handout.

TO KILL a turkey first catch the bird and tie its legs. The turkey may then be beheaded with an ax (a two-man job, one to hold the turkey and one to chop). Another method is to suspend a cord or wire from a beam or some object above the head so that the lower end comes even to about your shoulder. Hang the bird from this by its legs—head downward. Give it a sharp blow on the back of its head to stun it, then reach a sharp knife through its mouth and out crosswise to sever the arteries in the throat. Allow the bird to bleed. The feathers can then be removed.

If the bird is to be dry picked begin immediately. Be careful not to tear the flesh. Pull the wing feathers and the main tail feathers by yanking them straight out. Remove the breast feathers next because the skin of the breast is tender and likely to tear if cold. Jerk them straight outward from the bird as it hangs, a few at a time. After plucking the breast move up over the body and then to the back. Finish on the neck. If you prefer to scald proceed as for a chicken. To clean proceed as for chicken.

TO EAT a turkey can be a real challenge for a small family. This is not a one-time happening so you might well do some advance planning. Figure on roast turkey for its first appearance on the table. Serve with baked or mashed potatoes, stuffing, green vegetable, hot giblet gravy, homemade bread and dessert. A real feast. Now it's not so simple. For the second appearance you could have turkey à la king with white sauce that substitutes chicken broth for the milk. Add pieces of turkey, pimento and peas and serve over toast. Next day have turkey sandwiches with mayonnaise, salt, pepper, lettuce or whatever. Next day serve turkey bone soup.

TO ROAST a turkey figure out how you're going to get it into the oven. And hopefully you've got a young enough bird so it won't be tough. It probably won't fit in your roaster. You can wrap the whole thing in aluminum foil and set it on anything that will fit in the oven and won't burn—like a cookie sheet. For dressing, giblet gravy and seasoning proceed as for chicken except everything is on a larger scale. The problem with turkey is keeping it from drying out. So you want a nice moist dressing, and gravy to pour over and a way to try to keep from losing moisture while it's baking like the foil around it—or a paper bag. Basting with fat and juices is another way to try to keep it moist but it doesn't work quite as well as the covering.

Turkey Bone Soup—Break up your leftover cooked turkey when it is getting pretty near the end. Put bones, meat, and your leftover stuffing, carrot chunks and some onion and maybe celery into a kettle with plenty of water. Add a few peppercorns, salt and a bay leaf. Cook an hour or until you can get the remaining meat off the bones. Discard the bones. Now add rice or barley and cook on low heat until the grain is ready.

PIGEON

Pigeons bought to be pets or food animals will go wild at the slightest opportunity. If a pair get out of your cage you'll have pigeons in your chicken house, pigeons in your garage, pigeons in your machine shed. This can be a mixed blessing. You can always invite your friends in for a shotgun hunt if you live isolated in the country. You can pat yourself on the back because the pigeons are foraging and making it quite well on food they steal from your other animals and find on their own. But they will turn every building they sleep and nest in into a chicken house full of smelly droppings. If they are roosting over your car you will have a fresh set of droppings on the hood every morning. They reproduce really effectively and in a few years your place may have more pigeons than are welcome. Moral of the story is to keep them in their cages. Cities are famous for their downtown pigeons which is exactly the same situation. Remember though that they are edible and can be caught with effort in traps. You can make pigeon potpie, or pigeon boiled with celery and onions, or pigeon baked in barbecue sauce. If you're interested in having pigeons there's a good little booklet called *Pigeons for Pleasure and Profit: A Complete Guide to Pigeon Raising* by Charles Foy. You can order from Northwest Farms, Inc., P.O. Box 3003, Portland, Oregon 97208. If you want to *really* go into it, send $6 for *Making Pigeons Pay* by Wendell Lewis (owner of Palmetto Squab Ranch) to the Levi Publishing Co., P.O. Drawer 730-A, Sumter, South Carolina 29150.

Northwest Farms and Strombergs Pets Unlimited (Box 717, Fort Dodge, Iowa 50501) have the two widest selections of poultry for sale that I know. Northwest Farms also has a very interesting catalog you can write for.

In general you build a nice roomy cage for pigeons, on legs so it is above the ground. The bottom and back side should be wood. The rest can be wire in spring, summer and fall. If your winters are cold, put up some plywood to shelter them more. On the wooden back side put sheltered chicken-style, but pigeon-sized, nesting boxes. You can get a start for $10 a pair, more or less. Allow two nesting boxes for each pair of pigeons you have in the cage. Feed cracked grain and seed mixture with some pea and bean kinds of things in there. Crushed oyster shells or eggshells and clean water and a little salt should also be available.

Catch the pigeons in their nests or on their roosts at night. Confine them overnight. Chop off the heads on a meat board. Some people skin them rather than pick them. Some people say only the breast is worth the trouble but I use the whole bird. If they are shot with a shotgun and full of pellets some meat gets ruined.

Young pigeons have tender, pink legs and light red flesh on the breast. In old ones it is very dark.

Squabs are the young tame pigeons. They are as large as old birds but are soft and plump and covered with pinfeathers. (An older pigeon, like any other old bird, needs long, slow cooking to make it tender.) Squabs, being tender, are usually broiled. Prepare the same as chicken.

Broiled Squab—Split the birds down the back and flatten the breast. Sprinkle with salt and pepper and broil until browned, basting with butter. Serve on toast.

Pigeon Stew—Cut up the pigeons and sauté them in a bit of grease in a heavy pan. Then add 2 cups stock or leftover gravy, ½ cup chopped mushrooms, salt and pepper and sage. Cook until tender.

Boiled Stuffed Pigeon—Use about 6 pigeons, stuff them with a bread, celery and sage stuffing, sew up, and put them in the pot. Add 3 slices bacon, a cut up carrot and a cut up onion. Cover with hot water or stock and cook 2 or 3 hours until tender. Thicken the remaining liquid in the pan for a gravy and serve with toast, mashed potatoes or rice.

Pigeon Potpie—Boil until tender. Pick out bones. Make a gravy and add a pie crust.

ZOO BIRDS

COTURNIX QUAIL have received a lot of publicity. I wonder if they are really that much better than other birds. I've had them and never done as well as the glowing published reports. I have friends who have had them. They found them rather sensitive to handle. A person with a real soul kinship to poultry could do well with them, but other people have a hard time getting very many eggs. They are a very small bird with a very small egg.

PHEASANTS AND OTHER GAME BIRDS—These are sometimes strikingly beautiful birds but I don't recommend them for food production. They are the most timid "domesticated" bird there is. They will absolutely suffer in crowded quarters with lots of commotion around. They need to be in a big pen where they can get away from you. It has to have a roofed top to prevent them flying away. If they get out after belonging to you awhile they may hang around, roosting on a board fence or some such until hunting season. Then they will disappear. They can generally take care of themselves in the wilds OK but to harvest them you may need luck and a .22. Raising game-type pheasants is under the control of your state game commission. It is true in the states I know of now that you must have a permit to raise them in captivity. In Idaho there are unannounced visits by an inspector making sure that certain requirements with regard to their housing and so on are enforced. This isn't true of the "show" pheasants—the goldens and silvers. For more information on pheasants you can order *Raising a Brood of Pheasants*, Oregon State Game Commission Wildlife Bulletin No. 6 from Northwest Farms, Inc., P.O. Box 3003, Portland, Oregon 97208.

GUINEA HENS come in two colors, white and silver. They are famous for the racket they make when strangers come. I like the silver ones best because white animals, other than Arctic foxes, remind me of laboratories and humans tampering with nature. The pearl gray guineas are pretty in a homely sort of way. They are a little bigger than a chicken and have similar habits. They are much harder to catch than a chicken though. Interesting to have around. They are very good to eat but must be under a year old or they will be tough. They lay lots of eggs which are also fine to eat.

PEACOCKS are not strictly the zoo bird you may think. Lots of homesteaders keep them and are really enthusiastic about their advantages. Besides those lovely feathers on the male they are excellent to eat. The meat is fine-grained and tenderest when they are about 6 to 8 months old. They are as fine watchdogs as the guinea hens as well as beautiful. They are like a pheasant and can thrive in the woods, like a turkey in the diseases they are subject to. They are cheap to feed because of their foraging ability if you have them running loose. In summer they don't need any food. In winter 25 pounds of corn will keep a pair right through. There are drawbacks, too. They don't become able to reproduce until 2 years old. The male doesn't finish developing his beautiful plumage until 4 or even 5 years old. If you need to keep them caged they require a big run because they are big birds. It has to have a wire top because they are strong flyers and love to roost on places like the barn roof. The run must also be very tight to the ground or they will squeeze under even at the cost of injuring themselves. That period of adjustment before they decide to belong to you and your place can be risky. If they escape from you they will be almost impossible to catch again. They only lay once a year and not very many eggs. They will brood their own eggs given the chance.

There just aren't any quick and easy answers to all the big questions of life. There is no way to seal yourself off from trouble, pain, difficulty. No philosophy of life is really going to work for you that doesn't accept those things and find a productive use for them. Yes, I mean it—really, find a way to turn trouble and suffering into something worthwhile. And you can by directing yourself with all your heart to struggle for really worthwhile goals. Then naturally the troubles you have are for something good and you're going to win in the end. But when you win you can't just sit there and live on past glory. Look around and find something new and even bigger and better to be having troubles for.

Life is a river. When it is lived right it's a quick clear river rushing over and around the rocks in its path down to the sea of eternity. I see so many people though letting their beautiful river turn into a sluggish muddy swamp with a whole bunch of mosquitoes growing on the top. Reality is harsh. Like I said it's full of pain that you can't escape. But it's also marvelous. Frightening and wonderful as being in love. It's hard to be in love. But if you always ran away from being in love and never loved what would you have? Life is so often like being in love with somebody who doesn't love you back and yet you have to keep loving and loving anyway and in the end you are loved back and it's all worthwhile. The biggest pitfall—the place where the wonderful life rivers most often get dammed up is in illusion. That and trying to avoid pain. The use of alcohol, drugs, and a whole lot of modern times in general—the perpetually blaring radio or TV, the world of the media—creates illusion and dams up rivers.

It's terribly important to be able to hear yourself think. You can't do that if you're listening to something else. Yet you can't do any really important thinking, just staring at your big toes. The river by nature flows. You can turn it into a rotten swamp but you can't stop it flowing. You can't get any very worthwhile meditations off in a swamp though. It's some more of those strange paradoxes but the really great breakthrough kind of understandings come in those lulls between the battle scenes. They are born of action. You can't go off and contemplate dandelions and have anything important happen in your head unless you are first bone tired from doing something you think is really important. But on the other hand, you can't get along on pure action either. There's got to be some time with the dandelions. Or in the garden. Or with the milk cow. Beautiful quiet times when your head has a chance to tell you a few things you were needing to be told. Your very own head is your best friend if you'll only give it a chance to work.

Here is my mother holding me when I was little. It looks in the picture like we love each other and that was always so.

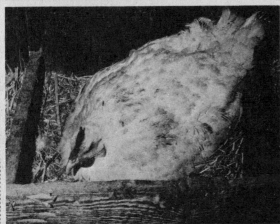

Here is a hen setting on her eggs. She intends to raise a family. She'll sit there day after day only leaving a few minutes each day or run and get a drink of water and grab a bite of food if any is handy, then back to her precious eggs. But beware! A setting hen is a "broody" hen and that means a moody hen. If you reach close as if to steal an egg you're going to get pecked.

These eggs are being preserved in waterglass.

Here is a family of baby chicks. Only I'm the mama. They came mail order from the incubator at a hatchery. You can see the infrared heat lamp that keeps them warm at night and the plastic gallon jug turned upside-down waterer. That way they can't get in it and drown or get a chill.

Here are chickens doing what comes natural, scratching around in the barnyard looking for bugs to eat.

Meet our old white turkey gobbler! The end of his nose decoration froze off last winter but he's still a proud bird and a grand sight as he puffs out his feathers and struts that handsomeness for whoever will see.

I love geese and ducks more than any other poultry. Most of them pair off in their own breed, mated for life. They are very undemanding, generally peaceable, and a lovely sight if you've a pond or river for them to swim around on.

MEAT

INTRODUCTION

OF KILLING—God made the tiger to eat nothing but meat, and man to have a diet of part meat which, like the tiger, we have to kill to get. I don't think much of people who say they like to eat meat, but they want somebody else to do the killing of the animal and go "ick" at the sight of its bleeding body. That is simple irreverence and wanting something for nothing. If I were trying to devise a way of life that would keep men as close to their Creator as possible, I would stipulate that each family would only eat meat they had killed themselves. Doing our own killing keeps us close to God's reality. I mean the *real* world He made for us to live in, not our illusions about it. It teaches us humility and reminds us of our interdependence with other species. My husband says, too, that there would be fewer wars if people were doing their own killing and knew what it was to have to cause death to a living creature. I'm sad, humble and grateful for each animal that perishes for the sake of nourishing my family. If the good Lord has a place in His heaven for the souls of chickens, cows and pigs, I hope He has taken and will take every one of them.

Killing that is acceptable to nature provides for the ample continuation of the species. In other words, we may eat the extra males, the females that are past reproductive age or even younger females, if the herd has grown to a size where its natural environment couldn't support it anyway. Killing for the sake of sport is unnatural. Don't kill in a species that doesn't have extras.

OF BUTCHERING—This chapter is not fancy butchering. But the essential is to get your meat from animal to pan *yourself*, and I hope it will accomplish that. There are cuts here that you don't see in the store, but they have lots of expensive power-cutting equipment that you don't want or need to buy. In most families the men butcher and cut up and the women wrap, but I know some country women who take great pride in cutting up the meat themselves. Some people send their cows to a custom cutting house where they are butchered, cut, wrapped and quick frozen for a fee per pound. Some people do their own hog butchering but send out the hams and bacons to the custom cutting house to be cured for them. You have to decide what's the best way for your own family to do it. Around here the best months for butchering are late October, early November and late February. The "best" means the weather's cold enough so the meat will keep but not so cold that everything keeps freezing on you.

This chapter is just like any textbook—you'll understand it a lot better after you try it a few times. The school that really teaches you something is the one where you *do* it. And you've got to do it a few times to get comfortable with it. The biggest hurdle is getting started, getting the notion that you can butcher. You can read this chapter from beginning to end 15 times and still the only way you'll get proficient with these procedures is by doing it a few times. And even better than reading this chapter would be if you can get a chance to do it with somebody who knows what he's doing.

CUTTING IT UP—Once you get started the rest follows easier. And it's OK if you don't get it just right the first time. You're going to eat the meat yourself, so if your steaks are triangular it will just give you a good laugh every time you eat steaks this winter. If you are careful with your basic preparation—don't shoot the animal if it's in a fever (excited), get it bled out right, get it cool, keep it clean and don't let the meat spoil—you really can't go too far wrong in the cutting up. It will all end up getting eaten.

COOKING AND EATING IT—When you have a whole big animal to eat it may be quite an adjustment. Maybe in the past you've learned to cook hamburger 365 ways. Now you have every different cut of the animal to contend with. Don't be worried. Big hunks are roasts. Little tiny hunks are stewing meat. Medium-sized flat pieces of meat are steaks. Very thick pieces of meat are also roasts. Bones with a very little meat on them are soup bones and the ribs are "spareribs" for baking with a barbecue sauce on them. With a Dutch oven and a frying pan you'll have no trouble consuming an entire cow given a freezer or locker (which is a big public freezer that you can rent space in) to store it in while you're gradually eating it up. Cook the roasts and ribs in the Dutch oven with the lid on, the soups and stews in it with the lid off. Cook the flat meat in your frying pan. If you don't have a freezer or access to a locker you'll have to bone out and can all your meat.

Try not to eat steaks every day the first three weeks—you'll end up eating hamburger every day the last three! Rotate. Have steak one day, then hamburger, a roast the next, then a stew, soup or ribs, then back to steak. That system comes out about even. You can be using the leftover supper meat for cold cuts and hash and ground meat sandwiches at lunchtime. If you have a pig in your freezer, too, so much the better. Most of the pig makes good breakfast meat. Rotate sausage, ham, bacon and pork chops for breakfast. Add a couple of nights of pork roast, ribs or chops to your evening meal rotation. You can eat about four pigs while you are eating up one cow using this system.

If they ever drop the bomb don't eat any internal organs or bone marrow or animal skin. The muscle meat would be all right if you keep it dirt free. I don't eat nonmuscle organ meats much, anyway. If there are any poisons in the animal's system that's where they end up getting concentrated—in the brain, liver and kidneys. It's true what people say about liver being great food but that was in the good old days before the earth, air and water were filled with poison. Better if you can raise it yourself, though.

TENDERNESS—A homemade meat tenderizer is a mixture of vinegar and lemon juice. Or you can marinate tough cuts in grated onions and oil. But my favorite tenderizer is the Dutch oven with the lid on—cook in a 300° oven for as long as it takes, with plenty of moisture. And better yet butcher your animal at the proper age to be tender or else make hamburger or sausage out of the whole thing.

Frank Womack Jr. wrote me from Pomeroy, Washington, about another meat tenderizer—coffee! He says: "It is a means of tenderizing about the toughest meat you can get—buffalo or especially chuck roasts. You do not need a knife to cut roast cooked in this way. It falls apart simply using a fork. I use it making stews, also. Simply substitute leftover (or fresh) coffee for an equal amount of whatever fluid you use cooking the roast. There is no taste of coffee in the meat and the remaining fluid after cooking makes excellent gravies."

ON PEDIGREED ANIMALS

If you can only afford to buy a small piece of land that won't run enough animals to support your family, and yet you wish you could be full-time, you'd have to raise your profit margin per animal. There are two ways I know to do that. One is the organic meat market where you get paid much more for your carcasses than you would otherwise, so you could make it with fewer animals. The other is the registered animal market. Both of these are somewhat risky and both depend a lot on your ability to sell yourself and your animals and also on getting in with the groups that promote these products.

A registered animal is an animal with known characteristics. It is recorded who his parents were, and grandparents and so on. When he is bred to another animal with known characteristics you know what sort of offspring you are going to get. What do I mean by "characteristics"? Well, take cows. The Hereford is a small cow with a terrific foraging ability. (The famous red-and-white ones.) The small-boned structure is relatively more efficient at food conversion. A Shorthorn would starve to death on the deserts of south Idaho and Wyoming where Herefords can wander and grow fat. "Polled" animals are cow and

goat breeds that have been developed to be naturally hornless. Now if you're worried about pinkeye you can get Black Angus instead. They are small, good foragers and very disease resistant. The trouble with both Herefords and Angus is their small build causes calving problems and you'll have to get good at recognizing and helping with calving problems. And, of course, they're not so big. And the Angus are as wild as the proverbial March Hare. So they don't make good family milk cows. Charolais, Limousine, Simmental and a whole list of new breeds called the "exotics" are simply huge beef animals. The Shorthorn and the Brown Swiss are a beef-dairy combination. Holsteins are the dairy breed that gives lots of milk with not such a high butterfat percentage. Holsteins are very big and there is actually a whole *lot* of beef on a Holstein bull which shows you some of the unrealities of trying to divide up the characteristics so finely. Jerseys are small dairy-type cows that give lots of milk with a high butterfat content, and so on it goes.

If you decide to raise registered cows you can pay a sizable price for your start. That would be as many cows as you can afford and a bull. Or else you'll plan to artificially inseminate (A-I) and buy frozen semen from the champion bulls of your breed. Then you build up your herd. You aren't going to eat *any* of the offspring. That's a point for you to bear in mind. The registered stock is much too valuable financially to be wasted on your dinner table. You'll have to raise some cheaper animals to be your family's food. And you can't sell your product through the regular outlet—like a stockyard on regular sale days. You'll have to wait for a special sale of registered Herefords and you might have to truck your animals quite a ways to do it. Each animal must be carefully and well halter broke, in tip-top condition and it's almost a must that you take your best ones around to all the stock shows you've got the time and money to go to because the more ribbons they win the higher prices you can charge for them. You'll also join your state and national associations for your particular breed of registered animal. You'll get a monthly publication and your dues will partly go to the advertising which keeps up the national image of your breed.

If you happen into a breed with troubles in its organization, one that isn't really meeting the competition advertising-wise in the national market, you'll have trouble getting the top price for your animals. For example, the Shorthorn is one of the oldest registered cow breeds. It combines the characteristics of a beef animal and a dairy animal. Duke Darius, one of the national champions, is now about four years old and weighs nearly a ton and a half. That's as big as the exotic breeds. The cows calve easily, are good mothers and produce enough milk to be good dairy animals. The second highest milk-producing herd per cow in Idaho is a herd of Milking Shorthorns. (The best is a Holstein herd.) Yet fifty years ago the national association had a big internal fight between the owners and, as a result, divided into the Beef Shorthorn Association and the Dairy Shorthorn Association. So it has been ever since, and that's one good reason you've probably heard of Hereford and Angus, and probably not of Shorthorn. The Idaho Shorthorn

Association is not active, has no state advertising program, and as a result the saleability of Shorthorns in Idaho is not near what it could be.

Who will you sell to? To people who think that a registered animal is that much better an animal and who want to pay the higher price for it. And to people like yourself who hope to make money off selling registered animals and are trying to get their own start. And to parents of 4-H'ers and FFA boys who want an animal that can win a prize for them at the county fair. They'll favor certain breeds, though. Right now they are going for the real big cows like Charolais, Limousine and Simmental or crosses with them. You'll sell to people who have the money and like the notion of owning a registered animal as being somehow an upper-class kind of thing. And to big dairies and stock raisers who want a bull with particular kinds of characteristics. For example, dairy owners generally breed their cows to big meat-type bulls so that the bull calves can be sold at the higher prices that beef characteristics would bring. They mostly A-I them now, though, so you'll have to try to get into the semen market.

If you, yourself, set out to buy a registered animal, remember that you're being exposed to an expert at person-to-person salesmanship. And there have been cases where people misrepresented their animals. Claimed them to be bred when they weren't. Or said they gave more milk than they really did. At such a high price it will pay you to be very, very careful. Remember also he is selling his own culls. An owner of registered animals is trying all the time to improve the characteristics of his herd, how much milk the animal gives if it's a dairy herd, how fast the calf gains weight if it's a beef herd. The ones he sells are the ones that don't meet his standards. They are not his best ones, unless you're prepared to pay fantastic prices.

So it's interesting and potentially useful to have a notion of the purebred lines, but unless you actually are going to try to make money from raising purebred stock I'd say the wisest way to spend your dollar is on the regular kind. The purebred associations spend a lot of money for advertising in all your stock magazines, and the purebred owners are good subscribers so the stock magazines print articles on purebred animals a lot. But out in the real country world it's not typical for somebody to own a registered cow and virtually unheard of to own other kinds of registered animals. And that doesn't mean the farmers don't have good animals. You can buy animals in the newspaper classified or from neighbors or, if need be, at the livestock auction—you can't do such careful buying at an auction, though you may get a bargain. (The purebred owners advertise in the animal magazines.) They'll be described as a some-kind-or-other but they won't be registered unless the ad specifically states so. And they'll possibly be very fine and adequate animals that give milk and make meat as good as any registered one you can afford to buy.

I've had goats, as many as 20 at a time, roaming around this farm and none of them were ever registered. Yet some of them gave milk as good as registered ones I've been told about. My personal experience with goats is that the best milkers in my herd were always Toggenburg-looking animals. Yet I read a goat book the other day in which Toggenburgs weren't even considered worthy of rating. I found French Alpines to come in second and Saanens about third on my milk scale and again that's just opposite of the national standards. But the local strains of goats may have their own distinct comparative levels.

So think twice before you drive 150 miles to buy a registered animal. It might grow up to be a real bummer. And there might be a perfectly adequate one up the road at half the price only it isn't registered.

RABBIT

Rabbits need but one mature male to keep the supply going. If you have more, you can eat the others. Or you can keep two—just in case. If you are buying rabbits to get started a buck (male) and two does (female) will do fine. When the does aren't bred they can room together. To breed her just put the doe with the buck. Don't put the buck in with the doe. It's a fast way to lose a good buck, since the doe will fiercely fight him. (This because the doe has a motherly instinct to be protective of her hutch, so much so that even if it is another doe put in there after she has lived there awhile, she may attack the new doe.) It only takes about one minute. You can watch to be certain, but I'm sure you may now consider your doe a mother-to-be. Write down the date for future reference. In 30 to 31 days, she'll be a mother. As such she needs separate quarters in a pen with a nesting box and plenty of room for the growing litter she will have. The nesting box should be like a separate little room. You can set a wooden box inside the hutch for that. It should be at least 1½ feet long and 1 foot wide with top, bottom and sides and a doorway for her to go in and out. Ordinary rabbit hutches have a wire bottom so the droppings can just fall through. (Galvanized wire with 1 x ½-inch spaces is best for smaller breeds such as New Zealands or smaller. The best to use for big breeds is 1 x 1-inch wire, 14-gauge.) If you don't provide her with a nesting box the babies will just fall through the wire, too, and she'll be so nervous and upset at being out in the open with them she is liable to eat some of them.

So fix her up with the box and supply straw, hay and calm. She'll make just a dandy little nest in there using the fur off her own body to line it. Get her moved in well before the delivery date. With a good box into which you have put hay and maybe some cotton rags she can have young that will survive even in the coldest weather. The entrance to the box should be raised a couple inches off the box floor so that the blind, helpless young don't accidentally roll out the doorway. When they are big enough to hop over on their own they'll be all right out there anyway. The rabbit is a mammal and feeds the babies milk from her own body until they are large enough to come out and share her feed. Once I had a mother rabbit jump out of her hutch and get killed by a dog when her litter was very young. I saved them by feeding them regularly with milk in an eyedropper until they were big enough to lap milk out of a saucer like a kitten. Another way to handle orphans is to put them in with another litter of about the same size. The foster mother will generally adopt them. Bigger young rabbits and their parents like to eat very green, leafy hay as well as grain. To buy that kind ask for "second cutting alfalfa." Chopped grain is better than whole grain. In the winter, it's handy to have stock beets and cabbage, too. In summer they like anything green that isn't poisonous. I plant extra rows of lettuce for them. And when I weed in summer I take along a bucket to put the pulled weeds in for the rabbits. Feeding this way you never have to buy a rabbit pellet and they do fine.

First-time rabbit mamas sometimes don't catch on in time. They don't make a nest or don't have their babies in it (and then the babies die of exposure or fall through the wire). Or if very emotionally upset (which happens easily to rabbits—a dog that scares the kids at kindling time, change in feed, water shortage) they may even eat the babies. Give her two more chances to raise a family. If she still doesn't, eat her and replace her.

My rabbits have always been wonderfully healthy even though I've had up to 30 at a time. The only sickness I ever had out there is infected eyes, which the babies tend to get. Same problem the neighborhood cats have. I treat it by putting drops of Murine that I buy at the drugstore in their eyes two or three times a day until they get over it. Same treatment for kittens and children with eye problems.

An important thing to know about rabbits is that they are an animal that can't stand heat. Too much will kill them. So the best hutch is a large airy one set up on legs or posts for air to circulate under and around with chicken wire sides and bottom except to the nesting box area. The top should be made of wood with an overhanging eave to help shelter from the sun. If, in addition, you can set the whole arrangement under a big tree or where a large building will shelter it from afternoon sunlight, this will also help. If you get into real terrible hot "dog days" in August, take your hose and soak the roof of the rabbit hutch a couple of times an afternoon. If you aren't aware of these precautions, you can lose a batch of

very nice rabbits real fast. When they die of heat they look fine in the morning and in the evening when you look again they are dead. I've had it happen to me. On any hot day cut down on feed and feed at night.

There's more than one exclusive way to raise rabbits. I got a letter from a lady who has about 80 rabbits living in her garage. The garage has a dirt floor. She said most of her does run loose on the floor and each time they kindle they have a burrow ready. Trouble is, I wonder how she catches them.

They must be kept supplied with clean water. If you use the bottom half of a coffee can, or some such, you can punch holes through the side and wire it to the side of the hutch so it can't be tipped over. You can set their food in free or use a bowl. In the winter, when their water freezes, go out once a day with warm water to give them a chance for a drink. In summer clean out the hutch occasionally when it gets too manured up. All animal manure needs to be left piled someplace for at least six months. When it is fresh it is "hot" and would kill plants. After it has aged—a whole year is best—then it is just wonderful for the garden.

The young rabbits can be weaned at 6 to 8 weeks or left in with the mother, if you want. The best kinds for meat are any of the Giant varieties, like Checkered Giant, Flemish Giant or the Californian. They are kind of big when they're born and grow up real fast. They will gain faster on a diet of rabbit pellets and hay than on the diet I outlined. Your big breeds are selected for fast growth that is expected to be fostered by a high-nourishment food like the pellets. With luck a breed like Flemish Giants might butcher out a 3-pound carcass at 10 weeks—shortly later a 5-pound carcass. You'll be able to kill average-sized rabbits at 2 months and each one would dress out to 2 pounds, but you still don't come out moneywise because the price of the pellets is so high. Here it's $6.30 for an 80-pound bag and rabbit meat sells for 80 cents a pound, which works out to $1.60 per rabbit dressed out—you only about break even. So I like to feed homegrown stuff and let them grow a little slower.

Then there are rabbit breeds noted for fur production, and the ones called "show" breeds, which are kind of pets, and the Angora rabbits which must be plucked. There are something like 50 recognized rabbit breeds. The best listing of rabbit breeds I know is the *Official Guide Book of the American Rabbit Breeders Association*. It's free if you join the American Rabbit Breeders Association ($7 a year), 2401B East Oakland Ave., Bloomington, Illinois 61701. You don't have to have rabbits to join. Other good general sources of rabbit information are *Raising Rabbits the Modern Way* by Robert Bennett, $3.95 from Garden Way Publishing, Charlotte, Vermont 05445, and *Domestic Rabbit Production*, a scholarly work by George B. Templeton, Director, U.S. Rabbit Experimental Station, published by the Interstate Printers and Publishers Inc., Danville, Illinois 61832. *Countryside* magazine carries a directory of rabbit breeders, which will be useful to you if you need someone to sell your rabbits. You can get an interesting rabbitry supply catalog for 50 cents from Morgan Enterprises, Rt. 2, Box 200, Liberal, Kansas 67901, or a free catalog from Bass Rabbitry and Small Stock Equipment, R.F.D. #1, Monett, Missouri 65708. Another free catalog on rabbits, bees and worms can be gotten from Ludo, 850 Evans Road, Milpitas, California 95035.

Any rabbit you don't want to keep for breeding should be butchered when it tips the scale at 2 pounds, to be a potential fryer unless it is a big breed. An old rabbit can be stewed like an old chicken. Young rabbits are distinguished by their soft ears and paws—stiffness is a sign of age.

TO CATCH the rabbit, grab it by the scruff of the neck with your right hand and by the legs with your left. Hold the feet firmly in your left hand so it won't struggle. Sex the rabbit because it's your extra males you especially want to eat. Hold the rabbit upside down and pull back the skin between its legs. The boy rabbit has a blunt nubbin in there and the girl rabbit has a slit.

TO KILL the rabbit first stun it with a hard blow on the head, right back of its ears. Or you can snap the neck by stretching it with your hands. The head is then chopped off on your chopping block as close to the head as possible.

TO SKIN the rabbit (same for a squirrel) first slit the skin between the legs with a very sharp small knife. Start with the hock joint on the inside of one hind leg, cut up to the pelvic median point of the rab-

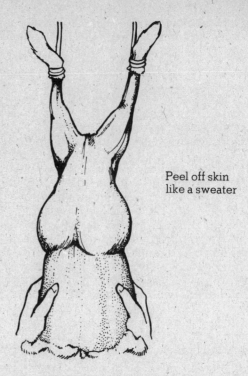

Peel off skin like a sweater

Slit the skin between the legs from hock joints to root of tail (dotted line)

bit and then back down the inside of the other hind leg to the hock joint. Cut the skin off at the hock joint of each hind leg and peel it back enough to expose the two Achilles tendons. It will be handy if you have ready a gambrel, suspended about chest high. You can make one out of a piece of stiff wire about 1 foot long. Make a hook at each end to hook the exposed Achilles tendons of the rabbit and suspend from a tree branch or some such. Or a rope thrown over a tree branch with a hook on each end will work. After the

rabbit is suspended, cut the front feet off at the hock joint. Now cut the tail off. You can give that to the children to enjoy. Then peel the skin down off the body to the front feet. When the skin has peeled down enough to expose the joint next to the front foot, cut the foot off at that joint and the skin will be free.

TO CLEAN (DRESS) a rabbit cut around the anal vent and down the abdomen being very careful not to sever the intestines. You might keep your finger inside as you are cutting down so the knife will come to your finger rather than a gut. Cut right through the breastbone or "brisket" to the neck. Help the innards fall free from the connective tissue into a pan or newspaper which you have ready. You may save the

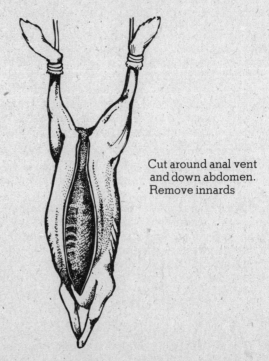

Cut around anal vent and down abdomen. Remove innards

heart and liver (separate it from the gallbladder). You will have to help the lungs out, as they stick in the cavity. Take down the rabbit from the gambrel and rinse off the blood and dirt if any.

If the liver has many white-filled spots on it you have coccidiosis disease on your farm. Chickens get it too, as well as other kinds of poultry and sheep. You may not know it is present until you butcher and see the liver spots. Birds roosting above your rabbit pens can leave droppings in the rabbits' water and make them sick so don't let the birds do that. The best treatment for rabbit coccidiosis is prevention. You can give them a medicine like Sulmet in their water, ½ cupful to about 1 quart water for 14 days, but be sure and discontinue for 14 days before butchering. Coccidiosis symptoms in your rabbits would be sleepiness or lack of energy. Kill and burn infected rabbits. Do not eat the meat. And remember the livers need not be fully spotted. Any slight discoloration is a sign of infection.

CUT UP similarly to a chicken that is to be fried except that the back, being so long, is divided into an extra piece and the breast and upper chest, having already been severed on the breastbone, are divided completely by cutting along the backbone making two pieces.

Buttermilk Rabbit—Place your rabbit in a casserole dish. Pour 2 tablespoons melted butter over 2 cups bread crumbs and spread the buttered crumbs over the rabbit in the casserole dish. Add salt, pepper and paprika, if you like it. Cover rabbit and crumbs with 2 cups buttermilk. Top with 3 bacon strips. Bake at 350° for 1½ hours.

Sour Cream Rabbit—Cut rabbit as for frying. Brown in butter. Add 2 cups sour cream and simmer until tender. You can season with salt, pepper, minced onion and parsley that has been cooked in butter 2 minutes before being added. Add a little cayenne, if you like things hot.

Doris's Rabbit Stew—Cut rabbit up. Dredge in flour. Brown all sides. Fry until tender. Cool. Remove bones and chunk meat. Dice white potatoes and cook with thinly sliced carrots. Season. When partially done, add peas, parsley and sliced onions. Cook very slowly for 2 hours. Now take your skillet with the rabbit drippings (where you previously fried the rabbit) and make a light gravy. Pour this over your done, but not too juicy, stew. Add 2 tablespoons butter and finish seasoning, if needed. This eliminates all wild taste in rabbit.

Fried Rabbit—If the rabbit is very big boil 10 minutes, drain and then proceed when cool enough to handle. Dip in egg, then in crumbs and sprinkle with salt (or into salted flour) and place in hot frying pan which contains plenty of fat. Cover and get the rabbit well done on the first side before you turn to brown it on the other side. If you want to make gravy 1 cup of milk or cream will go well in it.

Rabbit and Biscuits—Cut up the rabbit, cover with cold water and put on to boil. Add 1 teaspoon salt and cook until tender. Have biscuits ready (buttermilk biscuits are wonderful!). Break open a biscuit on each plate. Put a piece of rabbit on the biscuit. Thicken a reasonable amount of the broth with flour, add 1 cup of milk or cream, stirring, and pour some over each piece of rabbit and biscuit. Serve at once!

Roast Rabbit—Stuff the rabbit with a regular stuffing or line with sausage. Sew up and truss the shoulders and legs closely to the body or they'll cook to a crisp. Rub the skin with butter, add a little water to the pan, and baste often with butter unless you can use a Dutch oven with a tight-fitting lid. Make a gravy of the drippings with a little currant or wild plum jelly added and serve with mashed potatoes.

Barbecue Sauce Rabbit—Brown your cut up rabbit in a heavy frying pan that has a lid. Make a barbecue sauce of 1 teaspoon salt, pepper to taste, ½ cup water, 1 small onion, chopped, a shake of garlic powder, ¾ cup tomato paste, ½ cup catsup, ¾ cup brown sugar, ½ cup vinegar and 2 tablespoons prepared mustard. Pour the barbecue sauce over the browned rabbit, put the lid on the pan and bake in a 350° oven until done (an hour or so).

Chicken or Rabbit in Pot—Brown meat in small amount of oil in skillet or Dutch oven. Add onions, tomatoes (stewed or fresh), wine, mushrooms (if on hand), carrots or other vegetables as desired. Cook until tender and sauce is thick.

These recipes are from Nancy Cramer, Kent, Washington:

Basic Sweet and Sour Sauce—Dissolve 1 bouillon cube in 1 cup boiling water. Add 2 tablespoons vinegar and 1 tablespoon brown sugar. Heat. Thicken with a flour and water paste (thin) or whatever to desired thickness. Can be used with baked chicken or rabbit.

Rabbit and Dumplings are even better than chicken and dumplings. Cook rabbit pieces in water (to almost cover) with salt and a bay leaf until tender. Remove bay leaf. Forty-five minutes before serving add 2 large onions and 4 or 5 (however many you need for your size family) carrots in thick slices (½ inch or more). Also a couple of pinches of sweet basil and parsley. When done, drop dumplings (any good recipe) on top and cook following directions until done. (I cook dumplings 5 minutes more than directions to be sure and avoid gumminess.) Just discovered recently that dumplings must always rest on meat and vegetables above water and not in water to be good. When done fish out dumplings—carrot and onion mixture (serve this separately as vegetables) with slotted spoon and rabbit. Thicken gravy with flour and water and serve over dumplings. Makes a nice one-dish meal.

Bunny Sausage—6 pounds uncooked rabbit meat, ground, 2 small onions, minced, 2 level tablespoons salt, 2 level teaspoons pepper, ½ cup ground cracker or bread crumbs, ¾ cup sweet milk, ¼ teaspoon paprika, 1 bay leaf, ½ teaspoon ground sage and 1 or 2 eggs, well beaten.

Mix the ingredients well together. Mold into small cakes and fry until nicely browned. Pack into clean canning jars to within 1 inch of top of jar and add 3 or 4 tablespoons of the grease in which the cakes were fried. Put on cap, screwing the band tight. Process according to regular directions for meat. Or you could freeze it.

EARTHWORMS really do go with rabbits. The ideal worm farm is a box under the wire bottom of your hutch. But worms also like paper, garbage, and to have the soil turned over once in a while. If they're under rabbit cages you don't have to feed your worms anything else. You can use plywood for the worm box sides. You don't need a floor. The best worm book I know is *Earthworms for Ecology and Profit* by Ronald E. Gaddie Sr. and Donald E. Douglas, published by Bookworm Publishing, 1207 South Palmetto, Ontario, California 91761. Earthworms are good to fish with, good for your birds and good in your garden.

GENERAL ADVICE ON CUTTING UP LARGE ANIMALS

Technically "butchering" is when you kill, skin, gut and quarter the animal. Then you hang the quarters up to age, in the case of most animals, or merely to cool overnight in the case of pig. Then, "cutting up" is when you take the quarters into the house to the table and cut them up the rest of the way into cooking-type pieces. The same principles apply as with butchering. First of all, relax, you're going to eat it yourself so it doesn't have to be beautifully done. It doesn't even have to be correct. In fact, as hard as I tried to write you down a good set of directions for cutting up pig, beef, deer and so on, I still don't know if you can *actually* figure out what I'm trying to tell you. Unless you've had a college course in comparative anatomy or dissected a cat or two in a zoology course you may not be able to distinguish one muscle bundle from another. But I tried to write it on the assumption that you can tell bone from meat from fat and not necessarily any more.

It was really kind of interesting for me to get it all down. When I was a little girl my mother believed that every situation could be made to have educational value so whenever she cleaned a chicken she would call me over and have me identify all the various abdominal components. I really did end up being kind of fascinated with it and tried very hard to become a doctor. I struggled through three years of premed at the University of Illinois, Chicago Division. Through comparative anatomy, zoology, embryology, and through all that chemistry up through organic. My grades were mostly good but chemistry was my downfall. That and trigonometry and physics. I really wasn't educationally prepared well enough for those subjects and I had a fatal lack of enthusiasm for them—hard as I tried to discipline myself. The final semester my counselor advised me that the combination of my feminine gender, poverty and chemical mediocrity meant I had about a zero chance of getting accepted into a medical school. So that ended that since I didn't know any better at the time than to take his word for it, but I'll have you know I got straight A's in all the anatomy and dissecting type subjects and, like the teachers of subjects like "Hellenistic Marketing" and "Music of Ancient China" are always saying, it's bound to be useful sooner or later—you might be surprised just when. So it was with me and I have just listed for you my credentials for writing about meat cutting, above and beyond having done it, and I hope you're satisfied.

If you do need more help, try *Butchering, Processing and Preservation of Meat* by Frank G. Ashbrook, Van Nostrand Reinhold Co., 450 West 33d Street, New York, New York 10001—about $4.95. There's a good government booklet on slaughtering beef, No. 2209, but last I heard it was out of print. *Meat on the Farm: Butchering, Curing and Keeping* is a 1903 government bulletin available from Homestead General Store, Box 1112, Woodstock, Georgia 30188.

WHAT'S DEAD AND FIT TO EAT—If you know an animal has just died and you know why, here is your rule. Don't eat an animal that died of disease, except a nonmicrobial type disease like foundering. Do eat an animal that died of an injury like getting hit by a car. It would be a shame to waste the meat. If you don't know why the animal died or it has been dead a while *do not* eat it. Animals are never killed by strangling. As soon as possible as much of the blood as possible is drained out onto the ground. The only exception to this that I know is blood sausage (recipe later on) which some Christians strongly object to on scriptural grounds.

SUPPLIES—Before you start to cut up a large animal have handy a few very sharp knives, a meat saw and a regular wood-cutting saw for cutting the animal in halves. The meat saw blade is too thin for that job. It helps to have a knife sharpener or whetstone handy to keep your knives sharp. Razor sharp knives minimize waste by enabling you to trim closely and precisely. If you're planning to freeze the meat, you'll need freezer paper and freezer tape, which you can get at a grocery store or from a local butcher. Have handy, too, a crayon or marker to label your packages.

Have three containers ready, such as cardboard boxes or dishpans, and a fourth if you plan to set aside some of the meat for jerky. One is for the unusable trimmings that you will give your cat, dog,

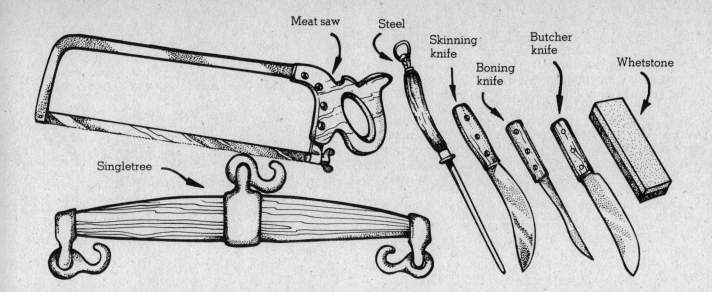

Meat saw

Steel

Skinning knife

Boning knife

Butcher knife

Whetstone

Singletree

chickens or pigs to eat. The second is for pieces of meat that you intend to grind up for hamburger. The third holds long lean strips (at least 3 inches long) without too much gristle and with every bit of the fat cut away that make the best jerky. You can sort these out from among the general hamburger pile. The fourth box is handy for the bones and ribs, which are bulky and would crowd your tabletop until you have a chance to wrap them and put them away in the freezer.

A big sturdy table is a good place to do the work. Everybody I know uses the kitchen table. We have a piece of plywood cut to fit the top of it for cutting up times. You could cover your table with butcher paper before starting.

TRIMMING—When cutting up game you have to contend with the shot area unless you're lucky and the hunter got the animal in the head. Wherever the bullet passed through, the meat will be messed up, torn and bloodshot. The meat containing hard black bits is what we mean by "bloodshot." You'll just have to salvage what you can, the bloodshot meat must be all trimmed off or else throw away the whole piece. It doesn't look good or taste good, and it spoils very easily. Get rid of all the black bits, too. A well-bled animal shouldn't have too much of that.

It helps to have one person trim the cuts as another carves them off. "Trimming" means to cut off unwanted fat. (On wild meat that's as much of it as possible. This is because the wild taste is concentrated in the fat.) And also cut off unwanted bone, moldy, bloodshot or dried-up areas. You can save the fat for candle or soap making.

Mold can get a hold, usually along the bone, when an animal was killed so far back that it took like a week in warm weather to get it out of the woods. Halving and quartering the animal right after it is killed and cleaned helps in such situations. Also keep the meat cool. The mold doesn't ruin the rest of the meat. If some of the meat has started to spoil, just trim off the moldy areas or the parts that don't smell good and then go ahead and wrap and freeze the rest.

Such meat, however, must be cooked very promptly and thoroughly upon thawing.

If hair on the meat is a problem, try wiping the meat with a damp cloth. If that doesn't get it all don't waste good meat trying to get rid of all of it now. Go ahead and wrap the meat, hair and all, but wash it in water with a little vinegar just before cooking to take the hair off. (The meat should not be washed before freezing.)

On wild meat trim away the tough paperlike outer skin from your steaks. You can cut it at each end and just rip it off across the middle.

CUTTING—Always try to cut either outside the muscle bundle or across the grain (across the muscle fibers). A commercial butcher works with frozen meat and power saws. He can saw out all his cuts. It's best for you to first cut with the knife through the meat part, then saw with the meat saw across the remaining bone if you want to include the bone. You may prefer though to just bone out all the meat. Meat is almost impossible to saw because it's wobbly and won't hold still. If you freeze it before butchering that problem is eliminated but then it's a lot harder to find your way around in the carcass and harder to cut it.

Before you start cutting ask the cook about her preference. Your animal is going to become spareribs, hamburger, stew meat, steaks, roasts and soup bones. But spareribs can be cut into smaller chunks to be stewing meat. Stewing meat and even steaks and roasts can be hamburger, if you want to grind them up. Roasts can be made into steaks, if you just cut them into slices. The usual rule is to make the more tender cuts into steaks. You can learn to tell the difference—steaks are a lighter color. And ask the cook how thick she wants her steaks and chops—½ inch, or more, or less? Wild meat is usually cut about half the thickness of beef.

It is sad, but true, that most work comes from the least desirable cuts.

WRAPPING—Get ready a pile of "sheets" of your freezer paper. To cut across the big roll of butcher paper, take a couple good snips with your scissors, then, holding the paper firmly, just push the scissors on across and it will cut like a razor. An even faster way is to measure out the length of paper needed, place the rolled paper on the edge of the kitchen counter or table and pull it across the edge. It will tear straight across. Check with the cook about how many steaks or chops the family needs per meal and wrap just that number in each package. Remember, venison chops are usually cut thinner than beef and so you need more of them per person. Ask her, too, how many pounds of hamburger she wants per package? Or sausage? And how much stew meat per package?

Freezer paper is shiny on one side, plain on the other. Put the meat on the shiny side—that's to keep it from sticking and from soaking the paper. Put the meat into the center of the sheet a little nearer one corner. Fold that corner over the meat, fold in both sides and roll the meat over and over until the paper is used up. Fasten the loose end with a strip of freezer tape. (Freezer tape is needed because regular tape doesn't hold well under freezing temperatures.) Write on the package the kind of animal (elk, beef or whatever) and the kind of cut (steak, stew and the like).

❧❧❧❧❧❧❧❧❧❧❧❧❧❧❧

HAMBURGER AND SAUSAGE—To make hamburger from your scraps, simply put them through your meat grinder along with the amount of fat you prefer. (I don't add any fat to venison.) If fat is added use pork or beef fat, not wild fat. Make sure the fat and meat are well mixed before you package the sausage or hamburger. You can knead the mixture with your hands until you have it distributed evenly. To make sausage as distinguished from hamburger, start out with your beef, goat, venison, etc. scraps, grind them as if to make burger, and simply add one-third pork fat and seasonings or add one-third pre-seasoned pork sausage.

DIVIDING THE MEAT—Hunter's etiquette is that the meat is divided equally among all male members of the hunting party, no matter who actually killed the animal. If two, each gets half. If more, it is divided up equally. There is a sound reason for this. In hunting every member of the party works to maintain camp, flush the game and drive it into the rifleman's sights. If you think somebody is worthless, don't take him along.

THE WAY I USE WORDS

"*Chop*" is veal and pork terminology, used generally for deer, too—equivalent to "steak" on a beef or elk.

"*Inside*" means inside the chest and abdominal cavity.

"*Outside*" means on the side where the skin was attached.

"*Front*" means toward the head end of the animal.

"*Back*" or "*rear*" means toward the tail end of the animal.

"*Butchering*" is technically when you kill, skin, gut and quarter the animal.

"*Cutting up*" is cutting the animal into cooking-type pieces.

"*Boning out*" is removing the muscle bundles from the bone to cut up.

"*Tips*" are ministeaks.

MAKING HALVES—You have already skinned the animal and gutted it. (Full instructions on this under each animal below.) A big carcass should be hung 5 to 6 days in a cool place before cutting up. The meat flavor is improved by this aging (except pork). The meat is cut into halves before hanging. Big animals like beef or elk are quartered before hanging. To make the halves, saw with your wood-type saw from one end to the other right down the middle of the backbone. Start with the highest point and saw downward as it is hanging. This is the hardest work you'll have in the whole job. It takes time and it helps if a couple men can take turns sawing. As you approach the middle of the animal get helpers to pull the sides of the carcass apart so that they don't press on the sides of the saw and bind it.

MAKING QUARTERS—Now you want to divide each half to make your quarters. Starting from the rear end of the half, find where the ribs start by feeling for them. Count each rib until you get to three. Cut between the third and fourth ribs to make your quarters. You'll need your meat or wood saw to finish the cut. Even on a big beef this system should give quarters within a pound or two of the same weight. This really helps if you are packing meat out of the woods since it gives each packer an equal weight to carry.

You now have two front quarters and two hindquarters. Later I'll describe how to cut up the hindquarter and then the front quarter and you can read through it twice, once for each half of your animal.

PIG

For the second time this week my two-year-old, Lukie, has mysteriously eliminated a page of this book. I just finished trying to remember and rewrite what was on the Peanut Butter and Pecan page in the Vegetables chapter only to immediately discover that this page of Pig was also missing. Hence the leanness of what will follow because I threw away all my notes on the subject after I typed the first draft.

Pigs are important because they eat garbage. We keep a slop bucket in the kitchen for the pigs. Into the slop bucket go peelings, leftovers, extra milk, spoiled foods from the root cellar, jars of canned fruit that got moldy, bread crusts—if I burned the bottom of the loaf

or if I accidentally baked it 2 hours instead of 40 minutes—and so on. People have asked me if you can feed chickens scraps of chicken meat or pigs scraps of pig meat. Yes, you can. They don't mind a bit. They both eat meat leftovers although our cat and

dog get first pick of the meat scraps. They will eat leftover grease, too. I don't give them bones. The chickens can pick on them though. I do give seeds to the pigs when I am working on fruit in the summer. Pigs are tremendously efficient food converters into meat and lard. They gain weight very fast. If you get a little pig in the spring, 6 months later it will weigh 200 pounds, which is the butchering size. If you feed a good grain mixture they grow to 200 pounds in as little as 4 months. Corn is the richest food for them. But use the cheapest possible pig feed for your area. Here that means oats, which aren't really as rich as corn, and pea "screenings," the weed seed the harvester separates out from the peas. If you keep food in front of them constantly, that's when you get your fastest gain. They would go on up to 400 pounds, if you let them, but after 200 the bacon just keeps getting fatter, and there is proportionately more lard and less meat, which is not what most people need.

Mike told me that in the big cities there is a law that garbage can't be fed to pigs. That just boggles my mind. It is so inefficient. Just where there are hungry people who would be so glad for cheap pork chops. It seems to me that it should be just the opposite. Most of our people live in cities. There they are, so many people, eating so much food and having so many potato peelings and leftovers. When this garbage food is poured down a sewer it simply multiplies the general sewage problem. And when it is taken out to a dump with metals and papers and buried or burned that is a total disgraceful waste of a valuable recyclable material—food. It should be just the opposite. All those people should be saving their recyclable food just like the country people do. They could keep a whole army of pigs and chickens growing!

The notion that "garbage" of itself is unclean is nonsense. We feed our pigs and chickens the leftovers from our homegrown fruits and vegetables. That means our pork, eggs and chicken have the same high standard of composition as the other food this family eats—"organic," if you want to use the term. Garbage only looks unpalatable because the peelings and the leftovers, gravy and grease are all poured together.

Pigs are the most civilized barnyard animal there is and probably the ugliest. If you get orphaned pig-

gies you can raise them in the house. Spread some straw in your basement and provide some dirt in a box the same way you would for a kitty. A pig will use his litter box just the way he's supposed to. You can start out feeding him with teaspoons of milk thickened with a little farina and with a little light corn syrup to sweeten it. Soon he can move on to cream of wheat and oatmeal. If your little pig isn't doing well on this diet, or if you have a sick one, the best special diet of all for little pigs is eggs—just plain shelled eggs in a bowl. Anywhere from 2 eggs on up to 7 eggs or so. Offer them 3 times a day. If you want to bottle feed a pig, use any quart bottle with a lamb nipple, less for a smaller pig. But cow's milk can give them diarrhea.

You don't want to keep pigs in the house too long, though. Not at all if when you get them they are not sick and weaner sized. "Weaner" size means big enough to leave their mother. Weaner pigs are now selling for $35 a head here. A couple years ago it was $15 each. Pig prices, like cow prices, fluctuate over the years with supply and demand. The lady who used to own this house told me how once she had an orphaned litter of six pigs living in the basement. One day a salesman came to call upstairs at the front door. She rushed up the stairs to let him in and forgot to shut the basement door behind her. The six now-not-so-little pigs charged up the stairs behind her. When the door opened and the salesman saw her and then the six pigs came charging up behind her, he looked really worried and said, "Oh, I must have the wrong house," and ran away. You've got to be made of tough stuff to work door-to-door in the country!

Margie Stroupe from Weingarten, Missouri, wrote me her pig raising story. She says: "I'll take a baby pig and let it have room #7 for its home. Had to when our mother sow had 15, came down with milk fever and almost died. She squashed nine because she couldn't handle herself and before I got nerve enough to get in with her and take the six living ones. Andy was down on his back and all he could do was storm because he was afraid she'd 'get' me. But she couldn't even get to her feet. We called the vet and spent $15 for the sow's shot and the vet said if she wasn't better by morning to knock her in the head and put her on a brush pile. Well, his medicine did her no good and we wound up giving her 7 ccs. Combiotic night and morning for 4 days. She got well, we fed her out and on May 11, 1974, she butchered out 306 pounds, without head, feet, skin and the like. So though we hated to do without a brood sow, she wound up feeding us almost a year. The baby pigs, well, that's another story. The milk I fed them wasn't the right formula and I lost 4 with scours and getting them too hot."

Ruth Proctor wrote me from New Plymouth, Idaho, with her pig story. "I can identify with you as I, too, take on seemingly insurmountable tasks—the only difference being that I have (as yet) not written a book. But once I got the bright idea of asking a potato processing plant for their trimmings and peelings to feed to our 50 hogs and ended up getting 2 tons every day. The only catch being that we had to furnish the truck and keep them hauled off. Now, as we found out, there is no way 50 hogs can consume 2 tons of spuds every day, but it made wonderful fertilizer for our fields—though somewhat stinky."

Barb Ingram from Santa, Idaho, sent me her advice on pig raising: "On bringing your pig home, worm it. Then feed it all the slag coal it wants and there is never any need to worm again. Never feed a pig large quantities of milk without grain mixed in. They may bloat and die. Never hose a pig with cold water when it is hot. It will put them into shock and they will die. Corn feeding makes for lots of fat. Peas, barley, oats all make for a leaner meat. But be sure and soak all grains that have a husk, such as whole oats, for at least 2 days."

My husband Mike is a firm believer in having pigs weed the garden. We suffer from morning glory and after the stuff has irrevocably taken over one area he fences it off for the pigs to pasture in. You know you can pasture pigs rather than feed them grains if you have enough land. If they are in a small area like your garden they will plow and fertilize it as well as pasture it for you!

Anyway, pigs, like goats, need a shelter such as a little house with a wooden floor so that they can get up out of their mud. Especially in the winter. You can either keep them confined in this indoor quarters all the time, which could be one end of a shed or a section of your barn, or you can connect the indoor quarters zoo-style with a fenced outdoor run. You have to fence any area for a pig very carefully. Pigs are rooters. That snout is pure bone and cartilage. Wherever they have ground they'll keep it thoroughly churned up, muddy and manury. It makes no sense to give a pig a small grassy pasture. They'd ruin it for other grass eaters by rooting up and killing all the grass. (If you can pasture your pigs on at least 1 acre per pig—depending on the lushness of the ground cover, the more weeds the better—they'll graze on grass and get fat and have enough room so they won't ruin the pasture. But keep giving garbage, too. It helps.) If you have an area of rocky ground it would be a good place to put a small outdoor pig run since you can't use it for much else and they can't tear it up. Or another answer to this problem is to put a ring in the pig's nose. If you give them an outdoor run, a space 20 feet on the side is fine for one pig. You could give more for more pigs.

Fence with hog wire if you're going to use wire. This is a woven wire. Pigs don't need as high a fence as cows. But it must be strong. And it must be protected along the ground. You can either dig a trench and set your fence in concrete, or bury the bottom part of your wire at least 6 inches underground. Or you can stretch barbed wire along the bottom of your posts.

But I'll tell you from experience that even hog wire is liable not to work. The pigs will go through that wire more and more as they get bigger. They'll break holes even in the hog wire and you'll have to go out with pliers to try to twist the broken ends back together.

The problem with using wire can be solved by putting a 2 x 10-inch board between the posts real tight right along the bottom. If you've got soft dirt they can dig under it. Choose rocky or hard ground. Nail up a board also between the posts along the top of the fence and that way they can't pull the fence wire down by climbing onto it. An entire fence made of wood panels works better than wire but it's more expensive. Steel panel fencing is the best of all, but that's even more expensive.

CATCHING A PIG—There's an old saying—"As independent as a hog on ice." If your pigs are broke to the slop bucket—that means if they know you and look forward to your visits with buckets of that good garbage—all you have to do if they do get out is run get the bucket and they'll follow you anywhere, even right back into the pen. On catching a pig that isn't slop bucket broke, well, they're "as independent as a hog on ice" and as hard to get ahold of as the one in a "catch the greased pig" contest. You just find yourself a few neighborly football players and try to tackle the pig. Then you carry it or drag it back by the heels or whatever your imagination suggests. But it's still best to have good fences because if pigs have a few hours in the garden while you're not home they'll wipe out your root vegetables.

NAMES—A "gilt" is a female that hasn't had babies. After that she is called a "sow." An "old gilt" is a female that got to be 1 or 2 years old and never bred. A "barrow" is a castrated boy pig. A "boar" is a male for breeding, one that has been allowed to grow up and isn't castrated. Some farmers cut off the tails of their pigs and castrate the males. We don't. Mike says he doesn't know a good reason for doing either one of them if you're just going to have a few pigs and you're going to have them controlled. It really isn't necessary when you're going to butcher at 200 pounds. There are different kinds of pigs but they're all pig. There isn't any point in going to extra trouble or expense to buy pedigreed animals.

WORMING—Whether your pigs have ever had worms or not, it's best to give worming medicine immediately upon bringing new pigs of any age to your property and every six weeks thereafter. Because pigs are so prone to worm problems. Get a bottle of liquid worm medicine from your veterinary supplier. The exact instructions are on the bottle. You withhold food and water for 24 hours, then mix the appropriate amount of medicine with water and serve in their food through the next day. They drink it down willingly.

BEDDING—If you're going to keep them in a small enclosed pen you need to provide bedding. Straw or sawdust is best. Every time it gets yukky enough—change it. (Save it for the garden!) Sunshine is important, too, in season.

BUTCHERING THE PIG

You'll need more than one worker. Unless you're going to skin it out—in which case one person can handle the job, not happily but adequately. But if you skin the pig your bacon won't have a rind, your hams won't have a skin. Even worse you're likely to lose a significant amount of lard and bacon because the bacon is right under the skin which does not strip away cleanly as other animals. Pigskin, unlike the skin of other animals, is edible. You can add some pigskin to boiled potatoes or milk gravy, or to baked beans, or make cracklings and lard and cook with the cracklings. And to skin a pig is a miserable job, especially around the head.

You can use everything but the squeal of the pig is the old saying. If you scrape rather than skin. But to get the skin scraped rather than skinned you need to make arrangements to scald it. That also isn't instant or easy. Maybe you can find out about a neighbor who has such a setup and can get permission to butcher your pig at his house. Or maybe you can bring over your pig when he is doing his (most everybody butchers in the late fall), and he'll help you in return for your helping him. Or maybe you'll hear of a hog butchering bee in your area. Otherwise you'll have to find a friend, follow these directions and do the best you can—which will still be all right. You'll end up with your meat and that's the important thing. It will take about 1½ hours to kill, scrape and gut the pig. (About 4 hours to cut it up.)

Up at a ranch on a nearby "ridge," which means on the land up out of our canyon (where there is gently rolling ground called "ridges"), there is a big hog butchering bee held each fall. Last year when we went there were 19 hogs butchered in one day by 10 men. The women brought food for lunch, potluck style, and in the toolshed where we lunched there was coffee and a fire going all day for hand and food warming. The men who scalded and scraped and sprayed the pigs (they had a hose attachment) wore rubber raincoats, rubber waders and woolen hats, since they couldn't help but get wet in those freezing temperatures. (Hog butchering bees are usually held between December 9 and February 12.)

So first you must decide if you are going to skin or scald your pig. In either case don't feed or water it for 24 hours beforehand to have the innards as light as possible and to save yourself feed. To skin, all you have to do is kill it and commence skinning. Try not to lose the fat on the belly because that's your bacon. Practice helps.

TO KILL A HOG—Make a mental X from its left ear to right eye and from right ear to left eye and where it crosses shoot. Shoot straight in because the brain is small. A pistol is by far the best for this job, which is one good reason why country people don't want their pistols taken away. Get the right angle so you'll do the job the first time because it's much harder to get it right if the pig is wounded and jumping around. A .22-caliber is the most economic on meat because it doesn't destroy much and is still big enough to do the job.

Now immediately, using a long narrow-bladed sharp knife (at least 7 inches long) cut open the hog's throat until you get the jugular vein or the aorta. You'll know because then the blood will pour out. If you haven't got it just right, keep cutting until you do find it. Killing them is no fun, anyway. Do it right. The animal has to be well bled and the sooner it dies after you first shoot it the better for you both. For a knife you can use a large hunting knife or a good stiff

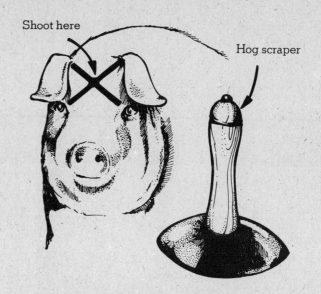

Shoot here

Hog scraper

butcher knife. The best place to cut is right back of the jaws in the center of the throat. Cut toward the pig's left side to get the aorta. Now wait and let it bleed. Adjust the head so the opening is downhill from the body and so the jugular opening is not covered.

GETTING READY TO SCALD—If, after you kill it, you let it lay too long in the cold air before getting it into the vat, the body heat starts out of it and that will make it harder when you scald. If the pigs of more than one owner are being butchered together, you cut an ear of the dead pig to distinguish your own. One notch for his and two for yours, for example.

To scald it you must have yourself all set up beforehand. Start early in the morning to prepare your water. You can use snow. It's nice and clean to butcher on the snow, anyway. Have a good-sized scalding vat. You can use a 50-gallon steel barrel, if it's clean inside (sometimes they have held insecticides—you need to know the history of the barrel), that is set up so you can heat the water in it with a fire under it or around it. You have to get the pig in, then pull it out, turn it around, and get the other end in to scald it. That's almost impossible for one person to do alone and not easy for two. A big hog won't fit in the barrel. About 240 pounds is tops.

The best thing is to make a permanent vat. The nicest ones are made out of sheet metal. This is set up with plenty of space underneath to build a fire and with a platform on each side, made of something like old bridge timbers, that won't catch on fire easily. The platform is for the men to stand on while they are rolling the pig in the water. An old steam-engine boiler also makes a good vat. Ours is made from half of an old steel hot water tank. To make a really nifty vat, you can pick up some used firebrick (or even find some for free for hauling them away), dig a pit, line with the brick and place your vat over the top. Be sure to leave enough room at both ends to be able to start your fire and to add more wood to keep the water hot.

Make a hole in the lower end of your scalding vat that you can plug with a whittled cork or some such. It helps mightily if the vat is located where you can get at it with a hose line from the house or some other water outlet. Rinse water through the cavity to clean it out a little. Then put water in it. You want to have a big enough vat and enough water in it so the pig is almost covered with water. Allow for losing some water by sloshing out at the side if you are doing more than one pig. You can't add more water because then it will be too cool for the next pig—unless you're willing to wait while it heats up again.

It's handy to have a dairy thermometer to get the water's temperature. Between 150° and 165° is right. But from 140° to 180° works. Supposedly if you dip your hand through the water three times and the third pass it's so hot you can hardly stand it—it should be just right. (If your hands are cold to start with.) If you get the water too hot you'll cook the hog and, worse yet, the hair will set and be very hard to get out.

Put in about ½ can lye to 200 gallons water. Makes it clean up easier. The old-timers used a couple shovelfuls of wood ashes for their lye solution. (Stir well.) When your water is the right temperature, kill the pig.

GETTING THE PIG TO THE HOT WATER—At the big butchering bee they have two tractors with forklifts ("farmhand," "frontend lift," "buckrake") working to move the carcasses around. If you don't have a forklift I hope you can find an old-time hay hook to help move it. Put the hook point in through the open mouth, then out through the jaw so that it comes right out of the skin. Drag the animal over to your scalding vat. (Hay hooks are invaluable also at haying time. They are just right for moving bales of hay and I've used them on untold hundreds, ever since I was a little girl. There's a knack to it that you soon get so that you can slip that hook into the bale and lift the bale wherever you want it, bracing the other end of the bale against your body.)

If you have to use a barrel vat and have a forklift, you can hook the pig's head end up with the hay hook that way to scald its rear end. You'll want to have it on a gambrel anyway to gut it. A singletree or gambrel stick can be any straight stick with metal rings at the end and a chain in the middle to hang it by. (A singletree is actually a piece of old-time horse harness that people found out made a great gambrel. Nobody around here knows what the word gambrel means. They all use a singletree and call it a single-tree.) We've used a neck yoke, too, and wired the legs onto it. An excellent investment if you are going to do home butchering of anything larger than a chicken or rabbit. The gambrel has to be long enough to spread the hind legs real tight. For the average hog, that's about 30 inches. Use a wire or rope or chain around the center to hang it to your forklift, or to a tree limb, or a tripod, or a rafter beam when time comes to gut the animal after scalding.

SCALDING IN A VAT—Lay pig on platform by scalding vat. You now need two 30-foot ropes (more or less). Half-inch rope is fine. You can make do with one but two are much better. Smaller rope is harder to get hold of and to work with.

Using one rope—Rope the pig up before you put it into the vat. Double the rear legs. Throw one free end across the vat and have somebody over there to hold it. Put the pig into the vat slowly so as not to splash. With one rope this can be a two man job. With two ropes you can use four people to roll the pig. Roll the pig gently back and forth. Now turn it over. Continue the rolling in the water. Keep the rope just snug enough to see if its hair is "slipping" yet. If you can pull it out that's what "slipping" means. Now hand over both rope ends to one side and both guys get over on that side to haul the pig out.

Using two ropes

1. Make each rope have a U shape.
2. Lay the pig on ropes across the U shape.
3. Bring the two free ends of the U over the pig and through the inside of the U.
4. Now take those free U ends back to where they were.

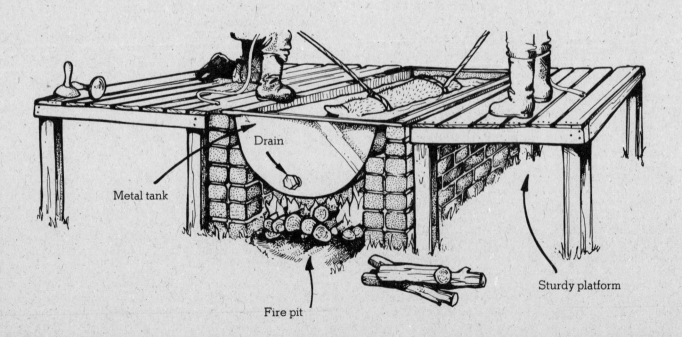

Metal tank

Drain

Fire pit

Sturdy platform

It would be a double half hitch if you pulled it tight. Have two people take hold of the bottom of the U's. And two other people take the loose ends. You now have four people, each with a grip on the ropes which cross the pig behind its front legs and in front of its hind legs. Two are on the platform on one side of the vat and two are on the platform on the other side. With the pig inside the rope. This way you can let it into the vat, roll it around in there. Turn it over and get it out again when both sides are scalded and the hair is slipping.

Then it's ready to scrape. If the hair is worn off where the ropes are around the pig it's getting pretty close to ready. If you can grab a handful of hair and the scarfskin comes off with it then it's ready. Or better yet, take a hog scraper or a knife and just scrape on part of it while it's still in the vat. If it scrapes good, it's ready.

If you leave the pig in the vat too long at too high a temperature the hair will set which makes for quite a problem. The answer once the mischief is done is to scrape as hard as you can and mutter a lot.

PIG'S FEET—If you are planning to save the pig's feet for pickling or some such, if the dew claws will snap off they are scalded enough. You use a hay hook or a knife to chop off the hooves. The feet are hardest to scrape. Do them first while hot. If you start to scrape and find out you actually didn't scald the pig long enough you can put it back in.

SCRAPING—You'll need a hog scraper or several knives. If you have the sharpest scraping knife, you'll be the fastest scraper, but you'll also make the most cuts. It doesn't take long for a knife to get dull scraping on that hair though. You can mail-order a hog scraper for $4.27 (last I heard) from Morgan Brothers in Lewiston, Idaho. If you have hot water to spare, it helps when scraping older hogs (which get really tough to scrape, especially red-haired ones) to pour more hot water over them out of a bucket, then take your fingers and pull hair out as if you were pulling chicken feathers. Then do the head around the eyes, nose and jaw. As you scrape you get not only hair but also dirt and the scarfskin. Try not to cut through the hide. Work over the whole body this way. On an old hog there will be bristles on the snout (whiskers). You can shave them off with a sharp knife barber-style or singe off as you would a chicken.

The best scraping motion with a knife is to hold the knife on both ends. Don't pull the way you would slice, that cuts the skins. Pull across (sideways). When you get one side of the pig done roll him over. Scoop more water up in your bucket and pour over to keep the pores hot and soft so the hair will keep coming loose. About one-fourth to one-third of your scraping time will be spent around the head because it's hard to get around the parts of it. Save the ears. They are good to flavor a mess of beans or with kraut. There is a couple of pounds of meat in the jowl (cheeks) that will make good scrapple, headcheese, salt pork or side meat.

You scraped your pig right by the barrel or the vat so that you could get hot water for pouring over it. Now it's time to hang it up in order to gut it.

GETTING THE HAMSTRINGS—They are located in the back of the hind legs, the Achilles tendons. Make an up and down slit. Don't cut crosswise there. There are actually two cords there. Get *both* of them, especially on a heavy hog. You use a singletree (or gambrel) to hang the pig by the hamstrings. Put one hook from each end of the gambrel under each hamstring. If you are using just a stick, put each end through one hamstring. At the butchering bee the hogs are put on a singletree hung from a forklift after the scraping is finished and so moved to the gutting area which is the back of a pickup truck. They are suspended over the truck bed while being gutted. Then they are moved on to the hanging area where a loop of chain is hung around the rafter beam and the singletree then shifted from the forklift and fastened to that chain.

The gambrel, if you are making your own out of wood, needs a V-shaped notch on the topside near each end so the hamstrings won't slip off the end to the middle.

GUTTING THE PIG—When you butcher a pig you discard about 20 percent of its weight. This is the stage at which most of that goes.

After the pig is hung, now is your chance to put the final touches on your scraping job. Scrape up. Pour the water over where it is needed. It makes a difference whether you are butchering a male pig or a female. Have some twine ready or heavy string.

A male—Cut around the penis which is in the middle of the pig's belly and slip on up to around the rectum. Notice a cord running from the penis right under the skin up (all directions assume that the pig is hanging from its hind feet and that you are standing facing the belly side of it) to the rectum. That cord runs right into the gut. Pick up the penis area and tie off the cord which connects to it with your twine. Cut the cord on out. Cut all around the anus to free the end of the gut and tie that. That's to prevent what's inside that part of the gut, which is not nice, from coming out on your meat at any stage of your work. When you cut around it keep your knife sloping toward the meat and away from the anus so you don't cut the gut.

A female—Start by cutting around the anus so you can get hold of the end of the gut and tie that off with twine the same as for a male.

NEXT ON MALE OR FEMALE

1. Cut down the belly midline until you have the skin parted from up at the top to the jaw at the bottom. Be careful not to cut into an intestine.

2. Split the brisket or breastbone. Hammer on your knife to drive it through. The brisket is right in the center between the shoulders where the ribs join together in front of the heart, lungs and liver. You're aiming to cut that pig into two separate and distinct halves and the brisket is the hard part in the front to get through to accomplish that.

3. Cut between the hind legs starting on the midline.

4. Finish cutting on the belly by putting your

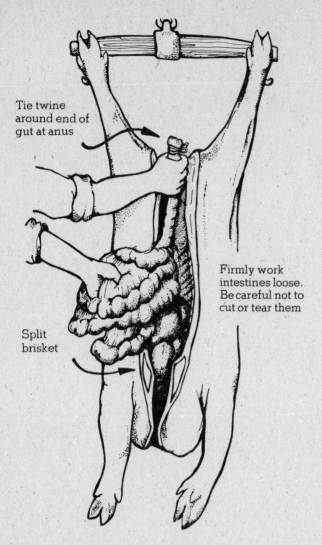

Tie twine around end of gut at anus

Split brisket

Firmly work intestines loose. Be careful not to cut or tear them

bring out the windpipe and esophagus. Get the tongue out whether you plan to eat it or not because if you don't, blood will collect there.

7. You have to cut the head off before you can make halves. Cut the head off about an inch behind the ears. Once you have the meat cut all the way around, twist the head around and around until it just snaps off.

8. Make halves by sawing with a meat saw right down through the middle of the backbone from top to bottom.

9. Now let the meat hang to cool. Don't cut it up while it is warm. Pork, unlike beef or goat, is not aged so by the next day you could proceed to cut it up. It is not harmed though by a reasonable wait—even as long as one week if you have *really* cold weather. It doesn't keep as well as beef.

For a much more professional description of everything relevant to pig processing order "Slaughtering, Cutting, and Processing Pork on the Farm," Farmers' Bulletin No. 2138, U.S. Department of Agriculture from your county extension agent or from the Superintendent of Documents, U.S. Government Printing Office, Washington, D.C. 20025 (20 cents). There are similar pamphlets available on butchering cow, beef, game and sheep. The descriptions are detailed professionally, and there are lots of illustrations.

SUCKLING PIG was a gourmet dish in the old days. Nobody eats it now because it makes no sense to eat a little pig when you could have all the meat of a big pig by waiting 5 months. But in case you got mad at your piggies here is the recipe. They are killed, scalded, scraped and gutted on the same basic principles. After cleaning out the innards, rinse the pig in warm soda water. Leave on the head but clean the passages of the head and throat with a wooden skewer wrapped in a small piece of soft cloth.

To cook a suckling pig fill with a stuffing. Sew and truss. Bend the forefeet backward from the knee and the hind legs forward. Make deep cuts in the skin in three places. Put a potato or apple in the mouth to hold it open. Roast at 350° until the meat thermometer reaches 185° (3 to 4 hours). To stuff a 12-pound suckling you might use 3 cups diced celery, 2 cups chopped onion, ½ cup minced parsley all sautéed in plenty of butter and then combined with about 7 cups dry bread crumbs.

Before freezers the pig's fat was rendered into lard, taking care not to overbrown the cracklings so they could be a people snack or animal feed. The hams, shoulders and bacon were cured and smoked so they would not spoil and the lean meat was cut and ground for sausage. The choice parts were eaten fresh. That general plan is still followed though it doesn't have to be. You could actually cure any part of the pig or make sausage of all of it. Or use it uncured as roasts, chops and side meat (uncured bacon). On an old sow you generally save the ham, bacon and tenderloin and make all the rest into sausage including the whole front shoulder.

hand inside, being careful that your hand is between the knife and the intestines. Believe it or not, it would be better to cut yourself than the intestines but you won't. Now start to bring the innards out of the hog starting from the top. Have a big washbasin ready for the organs that you want to save, heart and liver.

5. Cut the diaphragm to bring out the rest of the organs. The diaphragm is a muscle layer separating the intestines area from the heart-lungs area.

6. Organ meats—Trim off the top of the heart. Heart, trimmed, goes into dishpan. Get off gallbladder from liver. If you are going to cut, then cut through the liver. If you accidentally cut into the gallbladder, the bile escaping will ruin your meat. Old-timers just peel it out and they follow the duct up a ways and peel that out, too. The sweetbread looks like brains. It is attached between the stomach and liver. Leave the kidneys in until you cut up the meat. The long narrow liver-looking thing is the spleen and isn't used.

On a large, old well-fattened hog the entrails will carry several pounds of fat which you can save for lard. Young hogs don't have enough to fool with. The "leaf lard" is inside the body cavity from midline to rear on each side. Peel it out. Don't leave it on the bacon because it's just pure lard.

The last to come out will be the tongue as you

CUTTING UP THE PIG

TRIM off the dirty and bloodshot spots—everything that doesn't look like what you would want to eat.

HAVE READY CONTAINERS. I use 4- and 5-gallon plastic buckets bought from Perma-Pak. One holds meat to be cured. One holds pieces that are to be ground for sausage. One holds bones for gelatin making or to cook up with sauerkraut or beans. One holds fat that will be rendered into lard. I also have ready meat-type wrapping paper and freezer tape with which to wrap the roasts, chops and ribs that go directly into the freezer.

THE HEAD is already cut off if you've been following my directions. Prepare it according to the directions for headcheese and scrapple.

Or cut off the jowl, which is the chin area, and make it into bacon (your curing bucket) with the trimmings (you want your bacon slab fairly neat looking) going into the sausage can. Save the ears, too, to flavor a mess of beans and you can discard the rest.

Or cut off all the meat you can get at and put it into your sausage can and discard the rest.

Or clean out the ears, nose and mouth passages real well with a cloth on a stick or just a cloth on your finger and by rinsing well with water. Then in a big kettle (I use my canner) cook the whole head for hours and hours and hours until the meat falls off the bones. Then remove the bones and the more strange looking stuff like eyes and the lining of the mouth. Skim off every bit of the grease you can get to go with your lard renderings. Divide and package in jars and freeze what's left to go with kraut or beans. That is my favorite way of preparing the head.

For supper tonight we had kidney beans (the recipe under kidney beans in the Vegetables chapter) helped along with some head meat fished out of the kettle where I'm cooking up some from a pig we butchered last weekend. That and milk and a dessert made of whipped cream, crumbled heels of homemade bread loaves and some home-canned cherries and apricots. It put me to thinking. Certainly wasn't a gourmet dinner. People have sometimes eaten at our home and really gone away raving when they happened onto us when we were having homemade ice cream made the old-fashioned way (mostly whipping cream and fruit), or homemade bread with so much applesauce in it that it was about half cake only no sugar, or sirloin steaks.

But at that meal of kidney beans, head meat and dessert I imagine most folks would turn up their noses. Yet it was really special to me because all the ingredients came off our farm. I read in the woman's section of our area newspaper (*The Lewiston Tribune*) just this afternoon an article about a lady who grew much of her own food. Read and approved. But then it went on to give her recipes and only one ingredient per recipe could possibly have been homegrown. The recipes called for things like margarine, brown sugar, vanilla, baking powder, nutmeg, exotic nuts, raisins, cake mix, confectioners' sugar, lemon rind, miniature marshmallows, cocoa and so on.

I'm afraid she and many other good people are getting off on a really wrong track. They get a big garden, a cow for milk, and do some butchering, and that's all great. But they don't change their cooking or eating style. They still make cakes that call for exotic nuts, raisins, baking powder and sugar—none of which they can grow. If one of the ingredients is homegrown that's a great start, but it's a long ways from winning the game.

This noon for lunch we had a soup made of carrots, potatoes, onions and milk, along with hamburgers (homemade bread and cut up onion in them). Breakfast was homemade bread and butter and an eggnog flavored with store-bought molasses. My grocery bill the last few months has been averaging around $20 a month and that's not bad for a family of seven. If we could grow light bulbs and spray starch we'd have it made, but I haven't given up electricity or ironed shirts and dresses yet. It's that cheap when everything on the farm is producing just perfect—corn, chickens, garden, orchard. Any slip sends the bill soaring up. Like if the cow dries up I'm shorted on dairy products. None of us can stand reconstituted powdered milk. So suddenly I'm spending $50 a month additional on dairy products. My favorite month foodwise is June. New potatoes and peas and turnips and lettuce, fresh strawberries, raspberries, and cherries, lots of milk and eggs. The winter food bill depends precisely on how much food is in the deep freeze and in storage otherwise. And remember there's a lot of expenses to producing the food that people who live strictly out of the grocery store don't have. Well, that's a digression but you probably enjoyed reading about something besides meat for a moment.

THE BODY—Directions (front, back, and so on) are generally as if the animal were standing up. Some people start cutting it up while it is still hanging but we bring the carcass in, one half at a time, and lay it on our big plywood cutting board which is scrubbed in the tub with a scrub brush and then laid across the kitchen table. A pig is actually easy to cut up. I'll theoretically divide it into thirds. The front third is figured as if the head were still on.

The hind third—Meaning the hind leg.

1. Saw off the hind foot through the ankle (hock) about a foot up from the hoof. The foot you can either set aside to make pickled pigs' feet or trim off the meat for sausage and put the rest into the gelatin bucket. If you don't want to make gelatin or pickled pigs' feet give the feet to the hog.

2. Now cut the hind leg (ham) away from the body. You'll have the tail end of the backbone included in your piece which you can trim out later to make your ham look nice. You're cutting in front of the pig's hip bone and getting off all the hind leg with this cut. Cut the meaty areas with a knife. Finish going through the bone with a meat saw. On a sow you'll have two tits included plus about two inches. In person talk we'd call it the pig's thigh. On a young pig it will weigh about 20 pounds. On an old sow it will weigh about 30 pounds.

3. Trim it around the top to make it look neat.

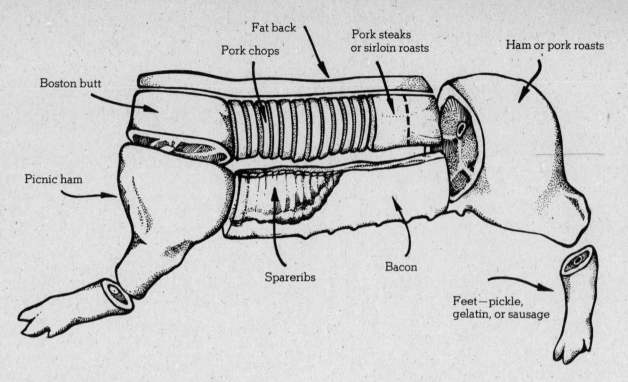

Fat back

Pork chops

Pork steaks
or sirloin roasts

Ham or pork roasts

Boston butt

Picnic ham

Spareribs

Bacon

Feet—pickle,
gelatin, or sausage

Make sausage or lard of the trimmings (depending on whether they are meat and fat, or mostly fat). Sausage trimmings are generally cut into approximately 1-inch strips to go through the grinder better. If you are planning to cure the ham, the skin is generally left on. Put the ham into your curing bucket. If you don't want to cure it then it will become pork roasts. In that case trim the skin off and put it into your sausage bucket. Cut the ham into roast-sized pieces. Check with your cook about how large she likes her roasts. The only rigid rule is that a roast has to be small enough to fit into the pan with the lid on. Other than that a chunk of meat is a chunk of meat no matter what the experts say. Incidentally, if you plan to cure your hams and bacons with the skin on and you have a propane torch you can use it to burn any remaining hairs off them.

The front third

1. Cut off the foot at the ankle—about 8 inches above the hoof. Put it in the same place you did the hind foot.

2. Now cut the leg plus the front shoulder off. You'll find the right spot by cutting behind the third rib. You'll need your meat saw. You're cutting it off just back of the shoulder blade straight up and down the body. If you are making hams to be cured take the big piece that you cut off (minus the foot that you cut off) and divide it in half horizontally to the ground just below the lower edge of the shoulder blade. The resulting half that has backbone in it is called the Boston butt ham or shoulder roast and the lower half is called the picnic ham. If you would rather make roasts than hams out of your Boston butt and picnic hams, again cut them on down into roaster-sized pieces.

3. Now trim out the backbone. Trim off the meat left around the backbone for sausage and put the backbone itself into your gelatin pile or bones pile.

4. The three front ribs that get included in the cut can be packaged for short ribs. Saw them away from the rest.

5. That flapping flap of meat attached to the lower half of the front leg is bacon (or sausage or side meat if you'd rather). For bacon cut away and make the edges nice. For sausage cut into strips. For side meat leave plain and don't cure.

Here is a way of double wrapping meat that some people use. We don't because we're frugal of paper and use up the meat relatively soon, but for a really sure long-term way of wrapping that pushes the air out and protects your meat from freezer burn do this:

a. Put in center of paper a pile of meat the size for one meal.

b. Wipe hands on apron, or pants, or whatever.

c. Bring paper tops together and fold over. Tuck under ends as for Christmas package.

d. Get second sheet of paper. Double wrap, tape and write on it what is inside.

The above directions on front third are designed for a young pig, the 200-pound kind. On an old hog you take that whole front third and cut up most of the meat to go through your grinder for sausage.

The middle third—That's what's left. Separate the ribs from the bacon. You can see where the ribs are. The bacon is the boneless flap of "skin" behind the ribs. *Stay out of the thick, meaty pork chop area* along the backbone. You can peel the meat off the outside of the ribs, too, and make bacon out of it. Or leave it on for very meaty spareribs. That's what I like to do.

THE BACON—You can take the skin off the bacon or not. If you plan to cut the skin off, whacking the whole bacon section on the table as hard as you can, skin side down, several times before you start makes it a little easier. I like the bacon cut into squarish sections about 6 inches on the side. You can make them bigger—it doesn't matter. Put the trimmings into the sausage pile. I've made triangular bacon but it slices up nicer if it is square. Personally I like the skin off. If you don't cure this meat for bacon then it is called "pork side meat" and you can slice and fry it just the same for breakfast only it won't have the cured taste. Slice like bacon only thicker, season and fry. Don't flour. Cook through.

THE FATBACK is the fat on the back of the pig which you trim off with the skin for your lard pail, leaving only just the amount you like on your pork chops—¼ to ½ inch is plenty.

CHOPS—What's left looks like backbone. It includes the muscles that run right alongside of it. You can either bone the chops out or saw them out. I don't like bones out of chops though that is easier to do. Boned-out chops don't look like chops anymore and though you only lose a little meat in the boning out process, on a chop that's a noticeable loss.

To bone them out, cut the muscle away from the bone. Slice across the grain and package for the freezer in meal-sized numbers—about five for us. The little muscle on the other side of the bone can be pulled out and cut across the grain into "tips," which means a minichop. The vertebrae can go into your bones department—the best thing I know for making gelatin.

To saw them out—The butcher does it with a power saw, which makes it easier for him, but you can do it by cutting the meat part with a knife and then finishing with a meat saw. Cut across the grain of the tenderloin the same way you would for boned-out chops.

The rear third of the "backbone" can be sawed into pork steaks (cut across the grain) or cut into a couple sirloin roasts.

HEADCHEESE AND SCRAPPLE

There are four good ways to use the meat of the pig's head. They all require similar preparatory steps. You can make 1) pork mincemeat, 2) sausage, 3) headcheese or 4) scrapple (or you can just fry the sliced scraps like side meat).

First you can decide if you want to make the headcheese or the scrapple. In case you've never eaten either I'll tell you what they're like. Headcheese is a homemade luncheon meat. It's quick and easy compared to scrapple. It's an all-meat product. You can add in the pig's tongue, skin, heart and other scraps while you're making the headcheese, if you want to. Headcheese makes a fine cold snack when cut in slices and served with hot mustard or horseradish. Or it can be dipped in egg and crumbs and fried like scrapple for your meat dish. Or you can make a kind of sausage out of it if you know where to get casings (or how). Like all pork products it's on the bland side so either while cooking or when serving you'll want to spice it up some.

Jowl

Scrapple, on the other hand, is a meat and meat soup mixture made firm by thickening with a cereal and spiced to taste. Almost everybody likes headcheese. Some people like scrapple and some don't. Scrapple makes a good quick breakfast or lunch. You can cut it into sections sized appropriately for one meal for your family, package it in a baggie and freeze. To serve the scrapple, thaw, if frozen. Cut into ½-inch slices. Some people like it dipped in egg or in egg and crumbs before frying. Fry it like cornmeal mush in a lightly buttered pan, about 10 minutes per side, over medium to low heat until browned on each side and crisp. Serve with maple syrup.

Still another way to use the pig's head is a combination of headcheese and *panhas*. You go ahead and make your headcheese. After making headcheese you have a soup broth left over anyway to use as you please or throw out. Add cornmeal and seasonings to that meat broth just as for scrapple and you get the meatless scrapple called *panhas*.

If you'd like to make a trial run of something like scrapple, to see if you're going to like it, use some leftover ham to make it. Prepare 1½ cups ground cooked ham. Then mix together 1 cup cornmeal, ½ teaspoon salt, pepper to taste and 1 cup cold water. Boil 1¾ cups water and then slowly add the cold cornmeal mixture. Cook on low heat until the scrapple has thickened and is boiling, stirring all the time. Add the ground ham, mix it up good, and pour out into pans to set up. That takes at least several hours in a chilly place. Then you can turn it out of the pan, slice off some and fry as described earlier.

Now that you've decided whether you're going to make headcheese, or scrapple or headcheese and *panhas*, there's the problem of what you're going to make it out of. If you have or are going to have a hog's head, that's fine. If you don't, you can actually make these out of any pork sausage type scraps. If you don't have your own pig, some farmers don't want to bother with their hogs' heads and will sell them to you. Heads vary considerably in size depending on how old the animal is. An old brood sow can have a head almost twice as big as that of a pig of the usual butchering age. A reasonable price for a hog's head is $3.50.

If you are starting with just a head, I hope for your sake that when the pig was butchered they scalded it and scraped off all the hair with knives or hog scrapers. That way you can use the skin, too, and don't have to bother with skinning. There's nothing worse to skin than a pig. If the head is a hairy one, you'll have to skin it which is an awful, tedious, frustrating job and you have my sympathy.

If you are doing your own butchering and are thus starting with the whole pig, here's the order of the doing.

1. Shoot, scald, scrape off the hair, and then gut the pig. When you're going to use the head it's nicest if when the pig is gutted the cut is made clear down to the jaw. Then when the innards fall out you can pull out the whole mess from the neck, including trachea, esophagus, jugular, and ending up with the tongue (save that). After the animal has been gutted and has hung long enough to be completely cooled, cut off the head right behind the ears. Use the biggest, sharpest knife you have. Cut all around the neck until you have exposed the bone. Then grab the head and twist it firmly around and around until the bones snap apart and the head separates from the body.

2. Take the head out to your chopping block and split it in half with the ax. If it looks like mincemeat before you finally manage to get the halves separated don't despair—that won't hurt the final product any. Just collect the pieces off the chopping block and carry them back to the kitchen.

3. Remove and discard the eyes, nasal passages and eardrums. You can use the ears, lips and snout if they are well cleaned. Scrape the ears to get them clean. Usually the jowl isn't used because it's so fatty. The "jowl" is the neck-cheek area. Remove all the fat you can and save it to render for cooking lard or soap. Make deep cuts in the thick meat pieces.

4. Put the meat in your kettle. A cast-iron kettle is best because it heats most evenly (so is an old fashioned wood or coal burning range for the same reason). For one hog's head you'll need the equivalent of a canner or big 8-quart pressure cooker to make this recipe. Cover the meat with water and simmer until it is ready to fall off the bones.

5. Remove the meat from the broth. Pick it over and separate the meat from most of the fat, all of the bones, and from the broth. Grind the meat.

Up to this point the recipe is the same whether you are making headcheese or scrapple. Now it separates.

Headcheese—Mix the ground meat mass with seasonings to taste: salt, pepper, red pepper, ground cloves, coriander and sweet marjoram are all possibilities. Take a little sample, spice it, and then taste to see if you like your combination. Keep testing until you get it right and then spice the whole mass accordingly. Red pepper is good in it if you have a cast-iron stomach. I grind my own but be sure you get it fine because if somebody bites into a speck-sized bit of it it'll take the top of his head off.

Pack the seasoned headcheese tightly in a bowl or loaf pan and press into as compact a mass as you

can in the bottom of the bowl. For extra firmness, cover it with a weighted plate. Refrigerate. When it is very firm it is ready to slice and eat. The textbooks say wait two days but I've used it as soon as a few hours.

Headcheese Sausage—This is a variation you can try sometime. After the headcheese is seasoned to taste, stuff it into casings instead of pressing it into a bowl. Then recook the sausages in the pork soup until they float, 10 to 30 minutes. After they float chill them in cold water. Store in a cool place. You can add a smoke flavor by giving them 4 hours in the smokehouse.

Scrapple—Skim every bit of fat from the broth. Add to the broth 1 (2-pound 10-ounce) box of old fashioned oatmeal. Don't use the instant kind since it won't make good scrapple for some reason. Or add enough cornmeal to make a soft mush. Or add half cornmeal and half buckwheat flour. Or seven parts cornmeal and three parts buckwheat flour to make a soft mush. I prefer the oatmeal but you can vary the specific grain combination to suit yourself. If you are working with a large quantity of meat, rather than just one head, figure one part dry cereal and three parts soup to seven parts ground cooked meat. If you use cornmeal, cool some of the broth and moisten the cornmeal with it before adding to prevent lumps.

Now season the scrapple. For the basic one pig's head and one box oatmeal recipe, add ½ tablespoon ground pepper and 2 tablespoons salt or vary the seasonings to suit yourself the same as with headcheese. Marjoram, sage, nutmeg, mace and onions are all good in it. If you use onions, grind them first and add at the beginning of the time the cereal will cook.

After your scrapple is thickened and seasoned it has to be cooked about half an hour very slowly. Don't let it burn on the bottom. When it is done pour into chilled, wet loaf-type (or other shallow) pans.

That's all there is to it.

Hazel in Georgia wrote me how her mother made a pressed meat out of a head meat, liver and cornmeal. It turns out like liver luncheon meat but has a special flavor you can only get homemade. She freezes the pressed meat in squares, ready to thaw, and eats as is or heats in hot grease. I wrote her for the recipe because it sounded really good but she didn't get around to it. I'm not really griping. Hazel's done a lot more for me already than I'll ever be able to do for her and she's a great lady.

From Ellen Currans of Douglas, Oregon, comes a recipe for scrapple without a pig's head. "One pound pork sausage, browned in a skillet with 1 large onion, chopped. Add 3 cups boiling water and 3 cups oatmeal. Salt and pepper to taste. Cook, stirring, until oatmeal has absorbed the water and tastes cooked. Our family eats as is, or it can be packed in a loaf pan, refrigerated and then sliced and fried in butter for breakfast. Makes a great first breakfast to take on camping trips."

The Johnsons of Wheaton, Illinois, sent me their Sylta Headcheese recipe which is as follows:

"Sylta Headcheese—(serves 20 to 25 when served with other meats). A hog's head is used to prepare this meat loaf. Today, it is nearly impossible to get a head; so the following meat adjustment has been made:

    4 to 5 pounds pork shoulder, with some fat and
        bone (pork butt may be used)
    2 to 3 pounds veal shoulder, with bone
    4 large pork hocks

"To Make a Hog's Head—Use ½ hog's head (5 pounds), 2 pounds lean pork and 2½ pounds veal shoulder. Clean and singe off hair and bristles. Clean teeth with a stiff brush and cut off ears. Soak in cold water for 6 to 12 hours, changing water. Place meat and hocks in boiling water to which has been added 4 teaspoons salt, 30 peppercorns and 20 whole allspice. Simmer 2 to 3 hours, or until tender. Remove meat from broth, save broth and cut meat in slices. Spread cloth or towel, wrung out in hot water, in a deep bowl. Line with cooked rind from pork hocks, right side down. To sliced meat, add 3 to 4 tablespoons crushed whole allspice (measure after crushing with rolling pin). Add 3 to 4 tablespoons salt. Arrange in cloth. Cover with rind if any is available. Pull cloth together tightly and tie with string. Put back in broth. Cook slowly 5 to 10 minutes. Lift out so it doesn't stick to the bottom. Remove to a platter, cover with a board and put weight on for 24 hours. Set in a cool place. Remove cloth after that time and wrap in a fresh cloth that has been soaked in salted water. Put in a plastic bag and refrigerate. Serve sliced thin with pickled beets."

Old-Time Barbecued Pig with the Head On—If you have occasion to cook for a huge family reunion or some such you could roast a smallish pig whole. You give it a real good scraping, clean it and scrape inside and out under running water an extra time. Now if you want to, you can make a dressing to stuff the pig. Takes maybe 2 gallons. There's a gentleman over in the nearby town of Genesee who is famous for his barbecued pig on a spit. The feet and ears are foil wrapped to keep them from burning. The whole roasting takes 5 hours for a real smallish pig (like 40 pounds) and more for a bigger one. Use a meat thermometer to find out what's happening way inside. Remember you've got to keep turning it on the spit. (A motorized spit is the ideal. That's what they have at Genesee.)

MAKING LARD

The first step in making lard is to feed the pig. Then comes the question of how fat you want your pig to be. If you pen an animal up and keep rich food like grain in front of it constantly (that's the commercially ideal way to raise them) you're going to have more fat and softer meat than if you let it rustle by letting it "graze" in a weedy field. Also older pigs have relatively more fat on them. That's the reason for the 200-pound rule. When you butcher at not more than 200 pounds you get more meat proportionately as well as more tender. Pig breeds have been deliberately pushed in the direction of an animal that will be fatter and fatter. Mike really disagrees with that. Your old-time wild pigs, which new breeds are supposed to be such an improvement on, were as lean as any other wild animal. We have a friend who hunted and killed one of their descendants that roam in a herd in California and he says that was by far the best pork he had ever tasted. It makes you want to ask when progress is maybe not really progress. Where can you buy now a breed of pig that will make lean meat if you don't happen to care for lard?

A certain amount of lard is really very handy. You almost have to have lard to make piecrusts and good soap. You can use it to replace vegetable oil in a whole lot of other places. I like vegetable oil better, as do most people probably, but I also like the idea of something virtually free—which is lard from pigs raised on garbage and something that I don't have to be dependent on the store for. You can use lard almost anyplace you would use oil once you get used to it. It makes a fine frying grease. You can use lard to substitute for oil in any recipe to be baked. The only problem area for substituting it I can think of is salad dressings. My mother's regular salad dressing was wilted lettuce dressing. That's because she had lard but not oil and that's one kind of salad dressing that uses lard. It's a delicious salad dressing and one that you can vary in many ways. You can fry bacon to get your lard and then crumble the bacon bits into the salad. That's the best tasting. But you can start out with straight lard, too. I usually thicken my wilted lettuce dressing with egg yolks. If you make a small amount of dressing it doesn't actually wilt the lettuce. Just dresses it. If you make a lot and pour it over hot it does wilt the lettuce but it tastes good that way, too.

I personally render lard in a big pan in the oven, takes me over 24 hours of slow heat. Then I dip the melted lard off the top into bowls with my cream dipper and put it into the refrigerator to chill. Then I cut the hardened lard into sections and put each one into a plastic baggie and into the freezer. Or else if I have enough coffee cans, I chill it in coffee cans. Then I put a baggie over the top of them for a lid and put can and all in the freezer. It would probably keep OK outside the freezer but I'm a shade surer that way. If you aren't going to freeze your lard, the basic rule is to chill it quickly (to get a fine-grained lard) and store immediately in the coolest place you have. Seal tightly and keep in the dark. Air and light cause rancid lard. Rancid lard tastes bad and isn't good for you. Rancid lard does make fine soap.

I take out one can at a time and it lives on a shelf beside the kitchen stove until I've emptied it and am ready for another one. Incidentally, when I'm getting ready to render lard, I cut the fat and skin into strips—any sort of shape but I try to get them not more than ½ inch wide. I bag up the cracklings and save them, too. Now for the details.

White creamy lard comes from high-quality lard stock that was trimmed and rendered pretty soon after the butchering. The fats that you got from around the internal organs of the pig are called the "caul" and "ruffle" fats. If they were washed promptly, and if none of the contents of the innards were spilled on them, they can also be made into lard, except their lard is a darker color. Besides your own butchering you could probably get fat from a butcher shop for a cheap price, if you wanted it. Just leave word that you are interested in buying. They'll probably give it to you. It's best, as with all butchering-type things, to do this during cool weather. Work with about 15 pounds or so at a time.

The grease will separate more easily from the tissue fibers if you cut the fat into pieces before putting it in your kettle. Some people even grind it through a meat chopper using a two- or three-blade knife and plate with a hole ¾ inch or larger. But that ruins your chance for cracklings. Cracklings are the little pieces of meat tissue that are left after you melt out the lard, like frying bacon. Some people like cracklings and some don't. They are packaged commercially and sold as a snack called "pork rinds." I remember vividly as a little girl my father's hog butchering and lard rendering and how good those fresh cracklings tasted. But now that I'm older I don't care for them—too greasy no matter how hard I try and what's left beyond the grease is sort of crusty and indigestible in my opinion. Strong systems really love them though—like my husband's.

So if you want proper cracklings, cut your lard into strips. You can put pure fat in the kettle or else start out with a little water in the bottom. An iron kettle is fine. Burning is a problem. It's safest to render in the oven. Or on the back of a wood cook stove because they have such a gentle even heat. If you don't get done one day you can just let it set and go on the next day when you get the stove going again. In any case use moderate heat. And don't stick your face in the kettle for a close examination. There is an occasional "pop" as some moisture in the fat turns to steam and you might get a grease burn in the eye. Remember the stuff is hot grease so make sure the pan is at the back of the stove and the children stay away.

Do not fill the kettle to the top so that there won't be any danger of it boiling over. Add ½ teaspoon baking soda to the fat when rendering is begun, which will darken the cracklings but whiten the lard. Be careful not to scorch. It happens so easily. The fat should be stirred frequently and cooking should be very slow until the fat begins to melt and the mass can be stirred easily in the kettle. If you have a dairy thermometer you can watch the temperature.

At the beginning of the process of rendering the temperature will be 212°. As the water contained in the fat tissue evaporates, the temperature will rise slowly until it reaches 245° to 255° and that is the highest it should go. As rendering proceeds the cracklings will first float and then gradually sink to the bottom and this is where trouble can really begin because they go down there and scorch. So if you stop the rendering while the cracklings are still floating you are safer. And if you are saving the cracklings scoop them out before they sink.

The more water left in your lard the less well it will keep. That doesn't matter though if you're going to freeze or can your lard. I freeze it. If you want really waterfree lard without struggling on to the bitter and potentially scorchy end, skim your lard off.

the top with a dairy skimmer since the water will all be on the bottom. By "dairy skimmer" I mean a plain old soup ladle which is what I skim the cream off my milk with.

CRACKLINGS—As the lard renders out into a clear liquid in your pan the cracklings turn brown, shrivel and float to the top. Don't stir excessively if you want them for snacking or they'll break up. Be sure they're done—that all the grease is rendered out. When they get visible bubbles in them they're about done. Then scoop them out and finish them off separately. You can put them to drain in a hot place or in your oven in a colander set in a pan and they'll drip awhile more. I freeze them loose in baggies, about half a cup in each. They can be added to corn bread for an old-time dish "crackling corn bread." Use any good recipe for corn bread. Only leave out any shortening in the recipe because the cracklings contribute enough grease of their own. Make sure that cracklings are broken into small pieces.

Here's a letter from Donna Joehn of Blaine, Washington. "Cracklings are my very favorite breakfast accompaniment with eggs. Cracklings are not the skin or rind. They are what is left after rendering out ground-up lard (or hog fat). They are crumbly looking things—like coarse graham cracker crumbs. To eat, you reheat till bubbly and crisp, then press dry of fat in a potato ricer or with a spoon in a strainer. Salt and pepper and enjoy in place of bacon. We can even buy them in grocery stores in British Columbia (we live near the border) where there is a large Mennonite settlement and people speak 'low German' on the streets. Of the skins my folks made 'rulchis' (little rolls). They cut the skins in strips (all fat removed) approximately 2 x 6 inches, rolled them up tightly, tied with string, then cooked and pickled them with the pigs' feet. These were later enjoyed especially by us kids. If you wanted the crisp fried rinds you'd have to strip off all fat before frying them and cut in narrow strips. I do this with bacon rinds."

If you want your lard to keep just as it is, without canning or freezing it, then continue rendering, stirring occasionally to make sure no sediment is scorching on the kettle bottom. In this case it is important that all the water be evaporated unless you skim your lard off which is a disagreeable job. When the cracklings are a deep golden brown the lard should be done. You can test for moisture by placing a lid on the kettle to see if moisture will accumulate on it. Remove from heat and let the sediment get quiet.

Get ready your containers in which to pour the rendered lard. Clean gallon tin cans are good, even if you don't have lids, or widemouthed jars, especially half gallons and gallons. Or the tall juice-type cans. You can freeze lard wrapped just in freezer paper if you can get it solid enough to wrap first. Cool it, for example, in a big metal bucket. Then cut and repackage in double layers of freezer paper or white butcher paper and freeze until wanted. It takes a lot of containers to store the lard from even one pig so be prepared.

When your lard liquid is cooled down to only warm it is ready to be put through a lard press, if you have one. They were common among the old-timers. I don't have one and don't know where you or I could find one except maybe as an expensive antique. I spread cloth in a wire sieve and strain through that into a bucket and from the bucket I pour into containers. When you get near the bottom of your rendering pan the sediment gets thicker. You should stop and switch cloths, this time adding a couple extra layers. Then you can pour it all out and squeeze heartily to get every last drop.

For the whitest homemade lard you can possibly make, add a raw potato in the bucket and stir it for a while. Then remove the potato. When your lard is ready to store get it cooled down as soon as you can. It should be protected from light, air and moisture. So if you are storing plain, put your lids on as tightly as if you were sealing them. Store on shelves in a dark cellar or inside brown paper bags if your containers are glass.

USING LARD—If you're using it for a cooking oil, it's handy to keep most of it in the freezer, one large container in the refrigerator and a small one by the stove, which you can refill from the one in the refrigerator as needed. When substituting pure lard for "shortening" in baking add an extra ¼ cup flour for every ½ cup lard used because lard is "shorter" and needs more flour to take it up.

Cheap homemade lard makes deep fat frying a reasonable way to prepare some foods. Deep fat fried foods are a favorite item with my family. My standard recipe is to thoroughly batter whatever I deep fry with beaten egg and flour and then fry it in grease hot enough to smoke. If the grease is hot enough before you start frying the batter casing will immediately seal up and the food won't absorb excessive grease. It's frying at too low a temperature that results in greasy foods.

That lard for deep fat frying can be used and re-used. I sometimes just leave it in the kettle between

uses. Or I strain it through a cloth or fine sieve to remove food particles and then store it in the refrigerator. After frying strongly flavored food, like fish or onions, a few slices of potatoes put in the cold lard and then heated until well browned will absorb the flavor. Then strain the hot lard.

I make no cakes or pastries and use cooking oil to make bread so deep fat frying and pan frying are the ways my lard gets used up (and soap making). Some people don't like the saturated fats. But I'm not afraid of them. I would be if I sat at my table all day but in truth I almost literally run from morning to night. It all gets burned up. I read a very expert report by a group of physicians researching heart disease. They discovered that the diet of their subjects in Ireland was much higher in saturated fats than the diet of their subjects in the United States, yet the rate of heart disease was much, much higher in the States, including arteries clogged by fat. They concluded that the Irish were staying healthy no matter what they ate because they lived a life that involved so much hard physical labor, whereas their American counterparts (Irish descendants in Boston were used in the study) did scarcely any. So eat what you want if you have a genuine hunger for it and are going to get up from the table and work it off before it has a chance to settle on you.

Each time I have a new baby my eldest daughter invariably looks through the literature and brings me a page of those "exercises" supposed to give you your shape back. At which point I get hysterical and rave about how picking up the floor and hanging up the laundry for umpteen children is sure to take care of my slack muscles. It's really true. I recommend having babies to keep you young and healthy. But that's another book.

FRITTERS

Fritters are a food dipped in batter and then fried in generous fat. You can make fritters out of just about anything—chicken, oysters, vegetables (of any kind), or fruits such as bananas, pineapples and apples. They were very popular around the turn of the century. If you've got lots of lard, these are fun to experiment with.

Fritter Batter—Combine 1 cup flour, ¼ teaspoon salt, slowly add ½ cup milk, then 1 tablespoon cooking oil, and finally 2 well-beaten eggs.

Baking Powder Fritter Batter—Combine 1 cup flour, ¼ teaspoon salt and 1½ teaspoons baking powder. Slowly add ½ cup milk, then 1 tablespoon cooking oil, and finally 2 well-beaten eggs. This gets puffier, but I like the plain batter best for taste.

To cook fritters use clear oil or lard for frying, about 3 inches deep. Heat the fat hot enough that a bit of batter dropped in will immediately rise to the surface and begin to brown. Don't put in too many fritters at once. Brown first one side and then turn and do the other. Drain well and serve quickly.

Vegetable Fritters—Cook, drain and cut into convenient-sized pieces before coating with the batter.

Apple Fritters—Peel, core tart apples and cut in round, thin slices. Marinate briefly in mixture of brandy, lemon juice and sugar, if you want to give it the gourmet treatment. Drain and dust with flour. Fry on both sides in butter, drain and sprinkle with powdered sugar and cinnamon. Serve hot.

Banana Fritters—Peel, cut in halves and split each piece lengthwise. Sprinkle with lemon juice before coating.

Meat Fritters—Use cooked, cold meats. Parboil oysters and other shellfish.

Corn Fritters—Combine leftover corn (1 cup more or less), 3 beaten eggs, 3 tablespoons flour, seasoning and 1 teaspoon baking powder. Skip the above batter. You made your own. Drop by spoonfuls into the hot fat. You can substitute other leftover vegetables in this.

HOME MEAT CURING

The ultimate to home meat curing, if you are going to use the commercial products put out by the Morton Salt Company, is their little book called *A Complete Guide to Home Meat Curing*. They also describe how to butcher and cut up not only pig, but also beef, veal and lamb. Also lard rendering, sausage making, jerky and so on—but always with an eye to moving the company's product. To order one of these send $1.25 along with the name of the book to Morton Salt Company, 110 North Wacker Drive, Chicago, Illinois 60606. You can order Tenderquick, Sugar Cure, with and without smoke flavor, sausage seasoning, a meat pump and needle from the same address. The meat pump is $4. The Tenderquick is $2.15 for 2 pounds. Sugar Cure with smoke flavor is $3.05 for 7½ pounds. Morgan Brothers in Lewiston also carries meat pumps and Sugar Cure as well as a selection of really good butcher knives (the kind you can shave with).

Here are some basics to the subject of cured meats. One is that you don't have to do your own curing even if you do your own butchering and cutting up. You can take just the hams and bacons to be cured at any professional cutting house where they will do a beautiful job. Their hams and bacons are meant to be stored frozen though rather than buried in the barn under the hay like grandpa did his. If you want hams that you can just hang on your porch or leave under the hay you've got to do your own cure and give it the strongest one you can. You'll get hams that germs can't live in. The trouble with these old-time cured hams (and that's what you make by the real old-time recipes) is that the only way they are edible is when you cut off a piece to flavor something like a pot of beans and let it boil hours (don't salt the beans) until enough of that curing solution works back out. There's no way to just slice some off and fry it for breakfast the way you can with modern hams. If you simmer 12 hours in a Dutch oven with about an inch of water in the bottom of the pan it will draw the salt out. That's the way you cook that famous $5-a-pound Smithfield or Virginia-style ham. It takes two months to cure them and it's quite a process but more than that nobody will tell me.

So whereas once the cure was functional as a way to keep meat—and not just pork—from spoiling, now the freezer does the job easier and we don't have to fight the salt inside. The cured hams and bacons that we eat now are a tasty reminder of those old-time hams. Not the real thing but much better eating. They should more properly be called half-cured. They are cured enough to have that special flavor but not enough to be stored anywhere but in the freezer. Trying to make home-cured hams that have just the right flavor and not too much of a cure is very difficult. I speak from experience. Mine have never yet turned out to suit me and I've tried everything. The thing that works best for me is either taking them to the custom cutter or just making pork roasts out of them and forgetting about curing. That only applies to the hams though—I can make home-cured bacon. Maybe with some more practice I could make good hams, too, but I hate to practice much on something as valuable as meat. I can make the old-time full-cured hams, but I don't have that much use for them in my modern style of cooking. The ironic thing is that the half-cured hams and bacons actually don't keep as well in the freezer as the plain uncured pork. Usually though, a pig is small enough that you eat it up before that's a problem.

If you take hams and bacons to a professional you can mark them with your initials by carving the letters using two lines as if you were going to shade the area between them and then pull out the strips to make the mark. It's getting harder and harder to find small meat cutting houses since the Meat Inspection Act (MIA) was passed. Whether or not it was a conspiracy by the big meat packing houses it resulted in the closing up of many of the small custom cutting houses and sausage makers in this part of the country (and elsewhere, too, I would guess) because it required arrangements of a complexity and resultant expensiveness that were just too much for small operations. As a result farmers around here have had trouble finding a place to butcher their chickens and cows when they didn't want to do it themselves and there has been a lot of bad feeling against the law. It has also created a bootleg sausage business.

The problems created by the Meat Inspection Act are also passed on to us as consumers because when we go to a custom cutting house that has managed to stay open we find that prices now are what we'd call outrageous because of all the stuff they had to buy under the Act. There's no doubt in my mind that the biggest single threat to individual freedom in this country comes from the Health, Education, and Welfare people. We took two young bulls to be butchered at summer's end and it cost us 65 pounds of hamburger, plus the hide, organ meats and $16. That was just when beef was short and so high priced. It's a great argument for doing it yourself. I've got a pig hanging out in the toolshed that I've got to either take someplace or cut up myself tomorrow. My husband is on a business trip and he said if the weather was too warm I'd have to go ahead and cut it up. Well, it's too warm.

My other problem with home-cured meats is that I have a longtime tendency toward tummy trouble. This is one thing that encouraged me to try raising all our food in the first place because almost all store foods have enough preservatives in them to give me trouble whereas I could eat and digest very peacefully any equivalent in homegrown and prepared food. The Tenderquick curing mix put out by Morton Salt contains not only salt, brown sugar and saltpeter, as do all curing mixtures, but also spices which make it appealing to most palates but make it indigestible for me. So unless I'm curing the meat for the other members of my family exclusively I make my own curing mixture. But though that gives me less trouble it is *still* rough on the system because of the saltpeter.

Recently I was looking over a 1917 "Farmers' Bulletin 913, USDA—Killing Hogs and Curing Pork," which has been reprinted and is sold by Homestead General Store, Box 1112, Woodstock, Georgia 30188. The most fascinating thing about that booklet is its numerous sausage recipes that do not contain *any* saltpeter, depending merely on salt and spices. It also contains the first recipe for making Smithfield ham I've ever seen and the only directions for making an icehouse I've ever seen.

Not just hams and bacon but also corned beef and jerky and usually any "smoked" meats are meats that have been through this curing process with the three—salt, brown sugar and saltpeter. "Smoked" meats are all actually cured first and smoked afterwards. Pickled pigs' feet may or may not be cured first. In the old days they did cure first but it's easier not to so people don't nowadays. The basic curing pickle for them all is similar but since the handling for each one is a little different I am doing them separately. You can actually "cure" meat with salt alone but it comes out hard as a rock and about as tasty. The brown sugar, saltpeter and spices thus help quality and taste—and repel flies.

A "sugar cure" means a curing mixture with a relatively high proportion of sugar. A "dry" cure means that the curing mixture is rubbed on the meat and then it is left in a container. At intervals the liquid that the curing mixture draws out of the meat is drained and more curing mixture is added. The more juice that comes out of your hams and bacon in a dry cure the saltier and more "cured" they are getting. The "brine" cure means that you dissolve the curing mixture in water and soak your hams or bacons (or beef to make corned beef or whatever) in there until they are cured enough to suit you. Brining is very temperamental but dry cure is worse. Dry cure will almost invariably make hams too salty. Dry cure is OK for bacon.

The curing process is a race against the bacteria. So it's best to start as soon as possible after butchering while the bacteria count in the meat is as low as it can be—even while the meat is still warm. Then keep it cool while curing. Temperatures around 36°-40° are recommended. I use a cool place. It's about impossible to control the temperature so exactly unless you cure in the refrigerator—which you can do and some people do so. Or have a walk-in cooler. But if you waited until cold weather to butcher, your outside temperature ought to make it near enough that cool. At temperatures below 36° the curing process actually

slows up because the salt doesn't go into the meat as well. Too warm a temperature encourages bacteria. You can tell if your meat has failed and the meat is spoiling instead because it smells and looks spoiled. At worst hams turn green along the bone. Such meat should be thrown out. I've never personally had such bad luck though. The nearest I've come to spoiled meat was when I got my cure so strong I couldn't stand it and tried to soak the cure back out by leaving the meat in water in the bathtub for two days. Well, what happened was the cure came soaking out of the outside edge of the meat fairly promptly and then that part began to spoil while the middle still was too salty. So I ended up trimming off the outside edges and doing the best I could to use up the middle, salt and all.

When cured pork, jerky and the like are smoked after curing, that is to give it the smoked flavor and drive out excess moisture. Corned beef isn't smoked. I never had smoked our home-cured pork either. On the hams I'm always in trouble before I ever get to that stage with having them too strong and on the bacons I like them just fine without. Smoking has a drying effect and kills any bacteria on the outside of the meat I am told. Smoke is no substitute for curing—just an added flavoring. The USDA is considering a ruling that a "country ham" be dried out and salty to a specific degree—dried out to 18% below the weight of raw meat with a salt content of at least 4%. Honey, other sweeteners and spices are optional. That gives you a good perspective on where you're trying to get.

So first you decide if you want to cure anything at home or if you want to take it to a custom cutter for curing. (Look under "Meats" in your Yellow Pages.) Any place that slaughters probably also cures. If you decide to try your own curing decide how much you want to cure. It might be more discreet to just try curing one of the hams and a couple slabs of the bacon first time around to see how it goes for you. If it works out fine you can do all your meat that way next time. If not you haven't lost so much. Now decide if you want to make your own curing mixture or if you want to use the store one. The store kind is available at most grocery stores and big discount-type stores around here as well as by mail-order. If you decide to make your own here's a basic recipe for a **Curing Mixture or Brine.**

7 pounds of salt—*not iodized*
3 pounds brown sugar
4 tablespoons (level) saltpeter (buy at drugstore)
7 gallons water

For a dry cure mix the dry ingredients together and take a flour sifter and sift the mixture three times together to blend them evenly.

"Saltpeter" means a mixture of $NaNO_3$ (sodium nitrate) and $NaNO_2$ (sodium nitrite). Read on your bottle and if the concentration is more than 6.25% reduce the amount you use accordingly. This is one of those "preservatives" and if you use too much the results will taste like soap and furthermore will poison you. This is the stuff that makes the ham pink. You could have all the salt and sugar in the world and it wouldn't give you a pink ham.

CURING HAMS—First you pump up your ham with brine using a meat pump. The meat pump needle has holes all along its length for saturation. Load your meat pump with the brine recipe I gave you and inject. Get in around the bone from the cut ends and through the muscle to the bone in the middle. Inject from both ends about one shot per square inch. It's a very messy job, leaks all over, so do it someplace that's not too bad to clean up. After using the meat pump be sure to wash and dry it thoroughly before putting it away. Pump brine in until it really swells up.

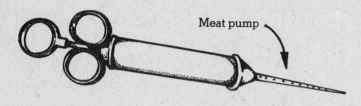

Meat pump

Meat workers call this injecting with the meat pump "stitching" it. You'll get best results by injecting according to the weight of your ham. When you butcher a pig you usually get about 60 pounds worth of curing meat, but weigh to make sure. Inject hams with brine in amount equivalent to 10 percent of weight, bacon equivalent to 6 percent of weight. Inject about once every square inch like I said and especially around the bone from both ends. After injecting rub some dry mix of the cure recipe I gave you on the outside of your hams and pack in a barrel, crock or plastic can for a week. Then wash the salt, etc., off and soak in fresh water for at least 2 hours. Some people soak 8 to 12 hours, starting with warm water. You don't have to change the water. Now smoke the ham. Smoke at 100°-140° for 24 hours.

Here is a recipe for a longer cure.

1. Pump up.
2. Pat on dry cure.
3. Let rest three days.
4. Pour off liquid and discard.
5. Pat on more cure and pack.
6. Rest seven days more.
7. Repeat #4 and #5.
8. Go till done (25 days plus how many days it was below freezing).

Here's a recipe that was sent me.

"Sugar Cure for Ham

2 cups coarse salt
1 cup brown sugar
2 tablespoons black pepper
1 tablespoon red pepper (I use 1 teaspoon)
1 tablespoon saltpeter
1 teaspoon ground cloves

"Use freshly butchered pork, not thoroughly cooled. Meat should feel warm. Mix all ingredients together well. Lay ham on piece of brown wrapping paper large enough to wrap it. Rub ham with small amounts of mixture until mixture begins to melt. Lift ham.

Cover paper under ham with thin coat of mixture. Lay it, skin side down, on paper. Pack remaining mixture on cut side, and as much as possible under skin and around knee joint. Draw paper tightly around meat, without disturbing mixture. Hold some of mixture directly on the joint while drawing over paper with other hand. Tie tightly. Sew muslin tightly around meat. Lay, skin side down, 24 hours. Drop ham in cloth bag and hang with knee down in a dark, well-ventilated, tightly screened room. Hang approximately 6 months (I hung mine until it completely stopped dripping. It shrinks about one-fourth).

"P.S. I forgot. Mine quit dripping at about three months."

That recipe is a dry cure and sounds like some of the old-time ones. In the old days after the ham was done it was wrapped in clean flour sacks, then in several layers of newspaper, and buried in wheat bins where it would keep for a year or more. Or wrapped well in cheesecloth and hung in the root cellar. That person's recipe doesn't use a meat pump. I've always used one in curing ham.

You know all these hams need to be cooked before eating because unlike the ones the cutting house makes they are not "precooked." You can give the outside a good scrubbing with a stiff brush and soak the whole thing in water overnight before cooking to lessen the saltiness.

If you want a precooked ham like they have in the stores poke a meat thermometer into the middle of it and bring up to a center temperature of 160° gradually.

BACON is a happier subject for me than hams. The sides and belly are the parts made into bacon. Using the homemade curing mixture you can rub the curing mixture on all surfaces of the meat putting more on heavier cuts. Then leave them set in a plastic can or crock. That's dry cure. If you dissolve curing mixture in water as for the meat pump you have a brine cure. Just set your bacon slabs in it. I cut my bacon into sections about 6 inches on the side. That makes about two breakfasts for us. The bacon is done

to suit me after only about 2 or 3 days of either curing method. Then I bag it up in individual plastic baggies, tie with wire and put in the freezer.

This doesn't have a heavy enough cure to keep outside the freezer. I take the skin off before curing and that helps give a faster cure, too. The skin can be used to flavor a mess of beans. If you cure with the skin on you'll then have to either cut with the rind on, which is hard, or take it off afterwards. On some of them if you get it started you can grab the rind with a pliers and peel it on off—on others you have to cut it all the way off. If you cook that rind in the oven to get all the grease out you can eat what's left for a snack. I cut homemade bacon on a wooden board with a long sharp knife, fry it in a little lard.

SALT PORK is made from the lower half of the sides when they aren't wanted for bacon. They don't make the best bacon, anyway. The meat for salt pork is cut into sections and each piece rubbed with salt. Then pack it in a crock and let stand overnight. In the morning pour the brine over the meat and put a weighted cover on the meat to keep it down in the brine. Use a plate with a big glass jar filled with water and a lid on it to hold down the plate. The pork can be kept in the brine until wanted.

Salt pork can be used to flavor other dishes or served alone like in this *Salt Pork and Milk Gravy:* About 30 minutes before serving cut ¾ pound salt pork into ⅛-inch slices. Soak them in hot water for 10 minutes then drain well. Flour the salt pork slices.

Now fry in some bacon drippings until brown and crisp. Remove meat from frying pan. Pour off all but enough grease to make your gravy. Add flour and blend until smooth. Now add milk until your gravy is made. Pour over meat and serve.

PIGS' FEET—Clean the feet, make sure the toes and dew claws are removed and also the glandular tissue between the toes, the hair and any dirt.

Pickled Pigs' Feet—Cover with boiling water and simmer until tender, 2½ to 3 hours. In a large enamel pan combine 1 quart vinegar, 6 whole cloves, 2 bay leaves, 1 stick cinnamon, 2 tablespoons salt, ¼ teaspoon pepper, ¼ cup brown sugar and 1 onion, sliced. Simmer 1 hour. Strain liquid to remove spices. Add 2 to 4 cups liquid in which pigs' feet have been cooked. Pour over feet and chill 2 days, if possible. This is right for 8 pigs' feet.

Cured Pickled Pigs' Feet—A fine brine to cure them is made by dissolving 1 pound uniodized salt, ¼ pound sugar and ¼ ounce saltpeter in 9 cups of water. Keep them in the brine at least 15 days. Put a weighted plate over them to make sure that the meat is under the brine as long as 3 weeks. When you want them for pickling remove and cook slowly until tender. Then chill and put in a jar with moderately strong vinegar. You can spice the vinegar to taste—bay leaves or allspice are fine, or spice as above. They will keep in the vinegar at least 3 weeks more and I'm sure you'll have them eaten by then.

BEEF

Most of the information about cows is in the Dairy chapter. Cows, at their best, are really two or more purpose animals—milk and manure as well as meat. Yogurt and all the milk by-products, like cheese and butter are an extra added bonus. And then you use the extra milk to raise more meat and eggs by feeding it to the pigs, baby calves and chickens. I think the most efficient way to get your beef is to have a milk cow and use the extra milk to raise a couple calves a year bought day-old which is cheapest.

It used to be that most farmers had a few calves and finished them on their own grass and grain for market. Now the beef industry has become really industrialized and has divided into brood cow-calf operations and feeder operations. The brood cows calve every year and the farmer sells the calves when they are between 400 and 800 pounds. They are sold at so many cents per pound through the auction ring. They may either be bought by a middleman, who puts them on his grass and puts some more weight on them before returning them to the auction ring, or they may go directly to the feedlot operator. He feeds them to an acceptable grade of beef and profitable size and takes them back to the auction ring where this time they are sold to the meat packer. The Lewiston auction ring handles hundreds of animals every time it is in session. It's a sight to see. I was there once when they brought a Charolais bull through. Charolais is one of the new beef breeds. They are an off-white and very big—a bull can be over 3,000 pounds. This was a big bull and he had horns and he was in a horrible mood. It really had us nervous for a while because he was charging everybody in sight and they couldn't even get into the ring to open the gate to let him out. Finally a brave man dodged out one side of the ring and let the bull charge him while another one just managed to get the gate open somewhat before the bull saw him and charged him too.

The commercial standard for beef is that it should be fat. The fatter an animal is the higher its meat will grade by the USDA inspector. So feedlots pour the grain into them to make fat, which most people will cut away from their meat and not eat—but which makes the meat more expensive and has the animals standing around in feedlots creating pollution problems instead of out on the range eating grass. Our cows for eating are grass-fed bulls. They've never tasted grain. They've never been castrated. According to University type lore the meat of bulls is supposed to be "strong." That's simply not true. According to the standards of the U.S. Government the fatter the meat is the better it is supposed to be. Yet like I said maybe Jack Sprat's wife would eat the fat, but nobody else I know of does.

You can take some beef tallow on the end of a fork and use it to grease a pancake griddle. You could make soap with it. You can grind a little bit in with your beef hamburger (although I prefer not to) but in general it is one animal product that there isn't that much use for. You'd be better off having something else done with that grain. Now that the nation is experiencing shortages this is another place that we could really be using our resources more wisely. The high price of grain is bound to really change the feedlots' business.

OF BEEF AND MARBLING
AND THE WORD "CHOICE"

I can appreciate the argument that cereal grains can produce more protein in bread than as food for animals which become meat. But not all the land can raise cereal grains. And there are ways to raise meat animals that give you edible proteins off of land you can't do anything else with—hillsides, woods, real dry places, real short growing season places. I call those natural forage areas. So it would be equally wasteful if there were no cows or goats to graze natural forage areas that grow enough cheap grass or some such to fatten a cow in spring or brush to maintain goats and couldn't raise vegetables or grains, anyway. Natural forage areas are the right kind of land for cow-calf farms. So having cows and feeding them grass is no problem.

That brings us to the marbling question. Historically there was a time of grain surplus. In the 1950's there was so much more grain being harvested than there was a market for that they even talked about throwing grain in the ocean to get rid of it. Cowmen bought that cheap grain. They raised their cows cheaper and faster on it than they could have otherwise and they liked having a grading system that appreciated the grain feed since they were getting it cheap. And the grain farmer really backed the grading system that legislated a couple of hundred extra pounds of grain into every cow that was destined for the supermarket because he so badly wanted to sell all the grain he was able to produce. It got written into the law of the land. Marbled beef.

What "marbled" beef means is what the law and the supermarkets call "choice beef" and remember "choice" is just a label and doesn't necessarily mean

what it sounds like. A normal beef animal has red meat with no fat on it. Its body carefully separates fat from meat. That is a very good thing for human beings because beef fat is high in cholesterol, higher than any other meat, and we don't want to eat that fat. "Graining" the animal means making it stand around where it doesn't get any exercise and pouring the calories into it in the form of grain or in other rich feed, like corn and molasses. Soon the capacity of that cow's body to separate fat from meat, as it normally would, is overcome. The red meat starts to have fat scattered throughout it, more and more. This kind of meat is called "marbled." Marbled is the same as "choice." To me the right word for that animal would be "obese." And to me "obese" is the same as "unhealthy." But an advertising system developed out of the grading system. Through advertising "choice" beef became accepted as the best beef, and more than one generation of people who must eat out of supermarkets have never seen anything else.

Now feed grains have become scarce and expensive. If cattlemen must continue to raise cattle as they did they may well go broke. And the price of beef is going to rise and rise. So now there is pressure from the cattlemen to drop the present grading system and accept grass-fed beef in the supermarket because it can be produced cheaper. And feedlot interests, whose occupation is marbling the grass-fed beef, are fighting them because that would eliminate their profitable position as one of the middlemen between the beef grower and the consumer. Unfortunately, change in the meat grading system is also being fought by consumer groups who have been so indoctrinated by the previous advertising campaigns into believing that choice beef is actually better stuff that they are opposing "lowering" standards.

What is grass-fed beef? It is a normal animal that hasn't crowned his preslaughter experience by standing in a feedlot being inactive and getting obese. He is an animal that represents a better utilization of all our resources taken as a whole because in him we have used the grassland for cows and the farmland to raise bread. And you get more protein per acre that way. What happens now when a grass-fed cow goes to market? He is the same age as the corresponding "finished" or grain-fed cow—18 to 20 months, up to 24 months. And no 18-to-20-month old cow is going to be tough. Grass-fed meat is what the country people have always eaten and still eat. I'll tell you from years of personal experience—grass-fed beef is tender and delicious. But what happens when that fine, completely healthy, young grass-fed animal goes to market?

Well, I'll tell you. The inspector, following the legal grading system inspects the carcass. "Fine carcass," he says. "Perfectly healthy." And he inspects the liver. "Fine liver," he says. "Perfectly healthy." And then he grades the grass-fed animal high, fair or low "good" instead of "choice" or anything near it because that's the highest he can grade a grass-fed animal, no matter how healthy. And what happens to beef that is graded "high" or "low good" instead of "choice"? It will be used for dog food, or maybe jerky or sausage.

I think it would be a very good thing if the USDA changed its grading system.

OF BULLS, STEERING AND MEAT

Is bull meat bad to eat? The reason "steer"—which means a castrated bull—has become practically synonymous with "beef" is because extra bulls are hard to keep. With a lot of young bulls around (and they mature fast sexually) you are liable to have five-month-old heifers bred. If a heifer (a young female cow) gets bred too young not only is she bound to have trouble in calving, possibly meaning a choice between her life and that of the calf, or she'll just plain have a dead calf. She may not be able to make much milk and her full growth may be stunted by the premature calving.

Bulls also tear down fences. A bull is a big husky animal, even a very young one. And whether they're ever near a cow before doesn't matter the first time they smell a cow in heat. The fact that there is a fence between them is no more important to the bull than if it was two stakes with a string between that you used to mark out a garden row. He will be inclined to just walk through, over or under the fence scarcely showing bewilderment at why that thing happens to be there just then. Bulls, with horns or without, can be dangerous. They are more aggressive than cows, more likely to attack if they think they are provoked. I have a friend whose seven-year-old boy was attacked by a Charolais bull and got his leg broke. Some bulls are gentle and friendly, regular family pets. But if you are raising fifty of them you are going to have all kinds.

I'm not trying to either defend steering or argue against it. I'm just trying to explain the little-known facts that surround the issue. The steer is a product of technology, but it's a technology that has been around a few thousand years. The facts I've stated are why cattle ranchers, as a matter of routine, have made steers out of all their bull calves except that certain few they mean to raise and keep or sell especially for breeding sires. Genetically speaking you have a lot more control over what's happening in your herd if you are only breeding from known sires at known times. And if you have bull calves of one breed on your place and your neighbor across the fence has let's say registered cows of another breed he is going to be worse than furious if some of your bulls go through the fence and breed his cows, which they are bound to do if you are keeping them anywhere but locked up in your barn or at a real tough corral. He would owe you the same consideration if your situation were reversed.

So steers aren't made because steer meat is better. That's a myth. For a long time the thought was perpetrated that steers grow faster and their meat is better. Both ideas are wrong. In fact steers don't grow as fast as bulls and the meat probably isn't as good.

Castrating used to have to be done with the knife. It was a bloody and disgusting business. Cowmen did it at branding time. They branded, gave shots, steered and so got all that stuff over with at one time.

Now there's a tool out called a docking tool and that is, if anything, an even bloodier business but very fast and efficient to work with. You have to use it on a young calf because an older one will bleed too much. Elastrators have simplified this matter of to steer or not because using them there is not a drop of blood and the animals don't seem to suffer excessively. The elastrator is a special tool that holds open a tough rubber band. You pull the testicles through the band. Then you release the band and it stifles the blood supply to the testicles. Most folks now agree that if it has to be done to any farm animal (or a sheep's tail) the elastrator is the most acceptable method. Yet this last year both we and a neighbor had bad calf trouble using the elastrator. I don't know if they tried to make the band out of some new stuff that wasn't as good or what.

If bull calves would only mature in size before they matured in sexual capability and aggressive instincts there wouldn't be this problem. But unfortunately it just isn't so; when they are less than half grown they think and act like any full-grown bull.

SELECTING YOUR COW BREED—If you really want to get involved, these are factors to judge your cow breed on: Foraging ability; longevity; disease resistance; food conversion; polled (naturally hornless) or horned; calving ease; gentleness; northern-southern adaptation; milk volume; size of animal; length of lactation period; amount of beef ("beef characteristic"); draft usefulness; availability (is there a breed association?); cream content; price; tendency to genetic defects. This list can be applied to either a dairy, beef or dual-purpose breed.

The main difference between beef and dairy breeds is milk production. A good beef cow has enough milk to raise one healthy calf without a grain supplement. A dairy cow can easily raise two or three fine calves (which you can generally persuade her to adopt by shutting them up in the barn together for a while) with a grain supplement. There is also a difference in build—"conformation." The dairy cow is lean, bony, has less muscle in places that would make high priced steaks and roasts. A "dual-purpose" breed has a beef conformation with a dairy-type ability to produce milk.

Worldwide there are literally hundreds of beef and dairy or dual-purpose breeds. In addition, there are many variations of the related water-buffalo-type animal most common in Asia. In the most heavily populated parts of the world cattle are the main source of power that pulls the plow and furnishes power for cereal production to keep people there alive. Milk production is incidental and the meat often not used at all. In the Western world, cattle are used for milk and meat, rarely now for draft animals. If you are interested in cattle (I am!) you'd be fascinated to read the two-volume research work called *World Cattle* by John E. Rouse, University of Oklahoma Press, Norman, Oklahoma, $25. The author is really firmly convinced that we must stop the practice of feeding grain to cattle for the production of fat beef.

Like I said, all the beef my family eats is from grass-fed bulls, and everyone who has eaten that meat says it is just simply *delicious*. All the females, of course, are saved to be milk cows unless they are not up to par in some way, such as having a birth defect. We have a heifer (young female) out here now that was born without a tail and missing the last couple of humps of her backbone. Otherwise she's fine but we won't use her for a brood cow since the trait might pass on. I had a four-titted nanny goat once (they should have two—cows have four) who had four-titted nanny kids. I wouldn't keep her billies for breeding either since they might carry it, too.

If you artifically inseminate you can have a calf that's half anything. The people who artificially inseminate are certified by the state. I guess they have to take a course. Around here it costs from $5 to $15 to get the inseminator to come. In their kit they carry all kinds of frozen semen for you to choose from. Very fancy stuff—it can be from champion bulls of any breed you choose. The semen will cost you anywhere from $2.50 to $20 per ampule, and the cow has to be in heat for it to work—that's the hard part—getting the right time.

FEEDING YOUR COW—The animal needs grass or hay, water and salt. (If you have a milk cow feed some grain or other *rich* feed, too.) That's all and don't let anybody tell you different. You can get various kinds of salt blocks. Some of them have minerals added. There is even a kind that contains a medicine to help them fight the burrowing flies that make worms in their backs. (Can't give that one to milk cows.) Cows need lots of clean water. If you have trouble with it freezing in winter you can buy an electric deal that plugs in and keeps the tank warm enough so the water doesn't freeze. Mike just goes out every day and chops a hole with the ax so they can drink and hopes for warm weather and a thaw. You don't need to give beef animals any grain. Some kinds of hay have more food value for them than others. Timothy hay is good for horses but not for cows.

"VEAL"—Well, "veal" means young beef and in Victorian days when they really went in for a big variety of exotic meats for the tables of the rich, blackbirds in a pie and all the gamut to haunch of venison, veal was a delicate and delicious regular. But from the point of view of somebody raising their own, veal meat is an uneconomical meat because that last eight months your calf will put on so much weight that to butcher him before is to be woefully inefficient. However, if you've got a reason like you sold the farm you *can* butcher a calf any time from the day he's born and meat's meat.

But I would recommend butchering no earlier than 15 months for that efficiency I was talking about. You get a spring calf the first summer. You give him milk and he's costing you milk and trouble. Throughout the winter you have to feed him hay and that's money and trouble again. If you butcher him the next spring, well OK—but wait. If you let him go he'll feed on all that good free summer grass all the second summer of his life and on through the fall up to the time you have to start feeding hay again when the ground gets covered with snow. (And that's the natural time to butcher him.) He'll put on weight at an amazing rate now that his basic frame is built and cheap and easy to you. If you let him go even to 24 months old, he will continue growing all that time. A cow does not become actually full grown until then, although like most other animals they are sexually mature at half that.

BUTCHERING THE COW

It takes about 3 hours for us to butcher a cow and 2½ hours longer to cut up each quarter. If we took it to a custom butcher he would charge about $45 or more to do a cow and keep the hide and organ meats. (A pig is $25 or so, and prices are going up fast!) It goes faster if you have a way to get the animal up off the ground. It helps, too, if you've had experience skinning and gutting some smaller animals like goat or deer. I'd hate to see somebody start on an 800-pound calf for their first experience. Butchering a cow is very hard work. The more experienced help you can call in the better. Their hide is *tough*—it is leather in the making. They are big and hard to shift around. Even the innards are heavy, and there is such a weight of them it presents quite a challenge.

So *before you start* have a few friends on hand. Have ready too, a gun to shoot the animal, a bucket or pan to hold the heart and liver, sharp hunting knives or skinning knives or butcher knives—plenty of them plus a stone you rub the blade edge across to sharpen it because you'll have to keep stopping and sharpening your knife. (You probably knew that but I'm trying to assume nothing. I've had people ask me if they should pasteurize the eggs, or why their chickens wouldn't sleep in the nests but kept climbing up to the hen house rafters or if a heifer and a Hereford were the same thing.) Getting a cow skinned is the hardest single butchering job I can think of. Just plain hard work and a long time of it. That's why you butcher a cow first and skin afterwards. If you skinned first those innards might wait in there too long for the meat's good.

You also need a big washtub for the guts. Even so they will have a tendency to overflow it. And have a plan for what you're going to do with all those innards—bury them in the garden or give them to the chickens or push them over a cliff or feed them to the pigs. All possibilities. It takes chickens a long time to get them eaten up. In warmish weather the innards get stinky pretty fast. You need about a 4-gallon bucket to hold the heart, liver and tongue. And it is nice to have a bucket full of warm water with a heavy dash of vinegar in it in which to wash your hands when they get sticky and especially after you've been handling the innards before you go back to work on the meat.

If you're planning on driving somewhere else with the butchered quarters, like in the back of your pickup, you'll want some clean old sheets to wrap the meat in so it doesn't get dirty. You also need a meat saw for making the halves and quarters. You could use a chain saw for the job, but it is far from necessary, maybe not even preferable. The saw you use is a regular crosscut or carpenter's-type saw.

OLD FASHIONED RECIPE BOOK

As I said, it will help a lot if you have an arrangement for hanging the animal up while skinning and gutting it. It's hard to do it with the animal lying on the ground, though not impossible and we've done it that way. It's the same thing you do when you've killed an elk in the woods. The elk is a game animal that is comparable in size to a cow. A deer is about a quarter the size of an elk and more like cutting up a goat or sheep. A tractor with a forklift (hoist) is the handiest thing for moving and raising your carcass.

TO KILL THE COW—Don't kill the animal when it is excited or has been running. If you've just had a big struggle getting it moved to where you want to kill it, go away for a few hours and let it calm down before shooting. That will help the final quality of your meat. You could use a .22, but a 3030 or bigger is surer. Try very hard to get it right with the first shot. If you miss with the first shot the animal may either go on a rampage and hurt somebody (come right through the side of your corral) or it may just run around and make it even harder to get another shot into it right. We had a really wild Angus heifer that it took Mike three shots to get down. She turned just at the last and wrong moment on the first shot so you see it can happen to anybody, no matter how you try because Mike is a great shot.

He says I'm the best shot on the place, which is very generous of him since the only shooting I do nowadays is when the dog makes me just furious chasing my chickens. . . . I was raised with guns and this summer, I just can't help telling you, when Grandpa Emery was here visiting he and Mike were out target practicing, and sighting in the big game rifle and a pistol. Mike invited me to come out and try my luck. I don't get away from the babies much so it was fun for me to shoot and I had good luck—got a good group on the rifle and the nearest dead center and did well with the .22 and pistol, too. My father usually had about three guns behind the kitchen door and more elsewhere. Guns and meat are synonymous among the Rocky Mountain country people.

My best talent is for shooting things I can't even see. I went charging out the front door to go boom off the porch (all Thor, the dog, has to do is hear the boom and he runs into the house and crawls under the bed). I pointed the gun at the tops of a big batch of timber where I figured the bullet wouldn't go anywhere to accomplish any real harm. Boom, I shot, and Lo, a bird fell out of a tree, shot through the head! A few weeks earlier I ran out and shot the gun to try to scare away a bunch of robins who were eating cherries. I thought I was shooting to miss them all. Boom and one fell with a broken neck. That sort of disturbed me because I really love robins and wouldn't ever kill one on purpose. Well, maybe that's the reason Thor gets under the bed so fast when he even sees me pick up the gun! I've given up going Boom for the sake of either Thor or the robins though. They're both incurable.

Anyway, shoot your cow by mentally making an X with the top points on each ear and the bottom points on each eye. Shoot where the lines cross. Tie the cow up if you can and one shot will be enough. Shoot straight in. You'll have to move around to do it

or wait until the cow turns to face you. Take your time and do it right. If you get it right the cow will drop to the ground instantly, exactly where it was standing when you shot it. As soon as the cow drops, you should start running toward it with your best knife to cut the throat. You want to get that opened up while the heart is still beating so it will pump the blood out well.

So shoot the cow in the forehead and then as soon as possible cut its throat. Cut under the ears or an inch or so back. Cut really deep and wide so the head is about half cut off. Start cutting from the chin side and cut up to both sides. Work the front leg back and forth for a while as if the animal were walking to help expel the blood.

Shoot here

IF YOU HAVE TO MOVE THE COW NOW—If the cow didn't drop where it was handiest for you and you have a tractor or other strong vehicle, you can drag it where you want it. Use a towing-type chain. Fasten the chain to the cow through the cut neck and around its neck. Fasten the chain's other end to a tractor or some such vehicle and drag the cow to the place you want to skin and gut it—where you have a way to hoist it preferably.

TO HOIST THE COW—Wait until it gets completely quiet. Last kicking reflexes will go on for a while and could hurt somebody. Keep the head downhill and the flow of blood unobstructed while you're waiting. Now cut a place to hook the singletree ends under the tendons of the rear legs. Cut on each hind leg just inside the back of the "knee." Do it just above the joint. You will be over two feet up from the hoof. Don't cut the tendon. Hook up the singletree with the tendons. If you have a tractor with a forklift you can now drive the forklift over the singletree. Fasten the singletree chain to the forklift and raise the animal. If you are working with a pulley or a "come-along," which is a one-man pulley, hook that up to your singletree and haul away to get that animal raised off the ground.

CUTTING THE HEAD OFF—Usually a cow is gutted before being fully skinned whereas sheep, rabbits or goats are skinned first. Finish cutting around the neck. Turn the head with a hard twist around and around until you feel the neck break. Then cut it all off. You'll have to finish with the saw. Some people use beef head meat to make sausage. Most people discard it except for the tongue. Cut out the tongue and put it in your organs bucket.

Now here I am saying, "Hello" as I retype some stencils for the fourth edition, having already sold 1,500 of these books, and I just discovered that I forgot to tell how to get the innards of the cow out in all those books. I can forgive myself printing pages upside down but this is awful! All those people depending on me and I've told them to get the animal raised up off the ground and then commence sawing off steak. In the first and second issues they could have turned to the pig section for help since it is very similar (and you can do that now, too) but in the third issue we forgot to print a page of the pig butchering, too, so it said at the bottom of one page to hang up the pig on the gambrel stick and then at the top of next page it commenced that you should take out the leaf lard and the tongue and you're now done. Oh, dear.

OK, so here we are ready to gut the cow and according to my previous directions you have her all hung up. But what if you're in really primitive circumstances and there was no way to get that cow up? You can still butcher. Mike and I did our first cow that way. If the cow is lying on the ground you go ahead and cut the head off. When you have the skin and meat all cut through give the neck a hard twist around and around until you feel it break. Then finish. Now you maneuver the animal onto its back exposing the full extent of belly topside. Just doing that with a big cow is quite an undertaking. Propping up one side with a stick for a brace may help. Then you can proceed by the directions given below except with the cow on the ground the innards will not fall out by themselves—you'll have to help them out.

GUTTING THE COW—If you have a male you start by cutting around the male genitalia, including a patch of skin around it. Then you slit up the midline (I'm assuming the animal is hanging by its heels so "up" means toward the anus), cutting the hide first and then around the anus so that you free the gut for tying off with a twine so nothing in there will come out. You lift free the genitalia along with the cord and then proceed to open the hide on down the belly line. The animal isn't skinned. You'll skin it after you gut it. Most folks run their hand inside the skin as they are cutting down from the outside to push back the intestines and prevent the knife accidentally cutting them open since they are right underneath. If you hear a hiss you did it. But don't despair. That happens a lot to amateurs. It's happened to us and it needn't harm the meat. Just struggle on. Saw through the H-shaped bone which is called the "aitch" bone. It's between the hind legs in front of the rectum. Cut all the way down the front before starting to pull the innards out. Have your washtub ready, they are big and heavy. After they are halfway out and the part that's out is in your washtub, you can take time out to find the liver and heart.

Beef heart is really good food. But to find it you'll have to look hard. It's encased in tissue and fat and

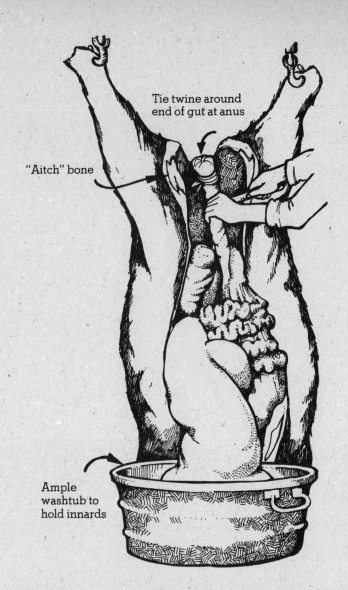

Tie twine around end of gut at anus

"Aitch" bone

Ample washtub to hold innards

you'll have to cut it free and then put it in your organ pail. (Later back at the house I give it a good rinsing under cold water, slice and bag up for freezing.)

The *liver* is big and easy to see. Like I always say, remember to get the gall sac off the liver. You have to cut through the liver to do it safely but there will be plenty of liver left. Back at the house you give the liver a good rinsing under cold water and then slice it real thin and freeze in meal-size baggies. Remember to eat up the heart and liver fairly quickly because they don't keep as well as the rest of the meat. If you don't have refrigeration you'll have to have the liver for dinner that night because it doesn't cure or can well.

Back to the cow. You'll have to cut through the breastbone now on down to the throat to finish opening up the belly side of the animal from tail to throat. That will make it easy for you to finish taking out all the innards and the tongue which is very good to eat and also will go into your organs bucket. After you have the innards all out, stop and give your hands a good washing in the bucket with vinegar water. Sharpen your knives, if they need it, and then go back to work on skinning the animal. That is a long, hard job. The hardest skinning job I can think of but stick with it because the cooler the animal gets as the body heat leaves it the harder the skinning gets. If you cut off the tail and skin the top part of it, what's left inside is the makings for oxtail soup! In the tanning section are good directions for handling your hide. When you have the cow all skinned, you are ready to halve and quarter it and age it. Pork is usually hung in halves and best just overnight because aging doesn't improve it, but beef is so big you need smaller sections just to be able to carry it around and to help it cool quicker and aging does improve it very much.

If you do this right each quarter will turn out to be from 90 to 140 pounds, depending on the age of finishing and all four pieces will be nearly of the same weight. Saw down the middle of the backbone to divide the animal into two equal halves. Use a wood saw or a chain saw or whatever you can lay hands on. It's a mean job and it helps if there is more than one person so you can take turns with one resting while the other is working. Now standing on the "belly" side and starting with the rear end of the cow, look inside the chest cavity to see where the ribs begin and count them. Between the third and fourth rib from the rear cut. When you get them cut partway apart, make a slit between the fourth and fifth ribs and tie a rope through there. That's getting ready so the front quarters can be hung by that rope in whatever place you have ready for hanging the quarters. Which should be someplace catproof, dogproof and flyproof, if possible (you can use meat bags—even make your own out of old sheets or some such—to help with the fly problem or else preferably you are butchering out of fly season). You need a cool place, too, and if you haven't butchered in cool weather you'll want to put the animal in a neighbor's or butcher's walk-in cooler. But a lot of butchers won't let

you use their walk-in cooler now because the Federal laws have made it illegal to have uninspected homestead-type meat in there with the high-class corporation-type meat.

Anyway you are still cutting one front quarter away from the hindquarter. Have one person hold the front quarter off the ground while you finish separating it and then carry it to the hanging place and hang there by your rope from a rafter or whatever. Now get the other front quarter the same way. Now let the hoist down enough so you can untie the two hindquarters and then move them to your hanging place.

AGING THE BEEF—Tenderizing it improves the taste. How I don't know, but it really does. Age it at least a few days and preferably a week or even a little more. Aging just means letting it wait before you go ahead and cut it up, wrap, and freeze or can. The meat doesn't rot right away because there aren't any microbe seeds in there. It was just alive. When it does start to go bad, it'll start from the outside and work in so you have plenty of warning and can trim off any bad parts. But handle the tallow (fat that you want to make special use of like for soap) and hide promptly because once they start going it's impossible to get the bad odor out. When the time does come for cutting up the quarters, it's a good idea to do it no faster than a quarter at a time. I mean a quarter per day. Another day of aging will improve the remaining beef. But a day of defrosting won't help the vegetables in your freezer at all and that's what will happen if you suddenly put a whole beef in there. In my own experience it takes very near 24 hours to get one beef quarter all frozen. Then you can go on to the next.

CUTTING UP THE HINDQUARTERS OF YOUR BEEF—Forschner knives are German products that are very

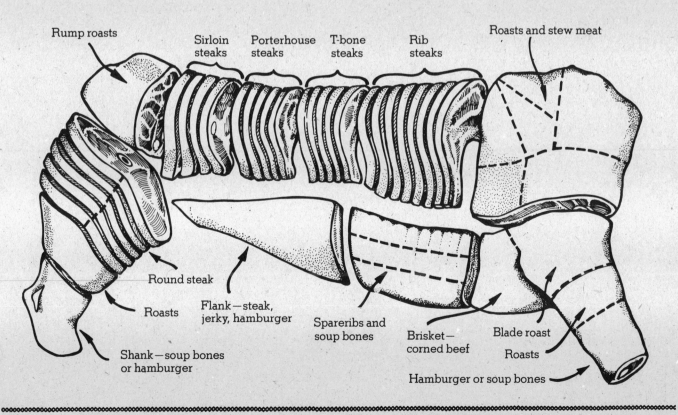

Rump roasts — Sirloin steaks — Porterhouse steaks — T-bone steaks — Rib steaks — Roasts and stew meat — Round steak — Roasts — Flank—steak, jerky, hamburger — Spareribs and soup bones — Brisket—corned beef — Blade roast — Roasts — Shank—soup bones or hamburger — Hamburger or soup bones

good. They are available only from butcher supply houses. To cut up something like a beef it really helps if you have a band saw. But they are very expensive. We don't have one. Sometimes you could find a small one secondhand for $500 or so. Maybe even for $250. Some people make their own. In general on cutting up I'd say make steak of the wide ends, roasts out of the narrow ones and hamburger out of the mistakes. Here is an attempt at more precise directions.

1. Cut the leg from the body.

2. Starting from the top of the leg, you can slice off the round steaks clear down to the "knee" joint. To package you can cut the round steak in half. If you do they will be easier to thaw.

3. The next portion of the leg working down will become roasts. If you make them about 2 inches thick or more it's fine. You are slicing it off the same as a steak only much thicker and that makes it a roast. If you trim out the bone that can be a soup bone for you.

4. When you get down to where there isn't so much meat, cut the rest of the lower leg into chunks for soup bones that are called "shank boil." Or you can trim off the meat and put it in your hamburger pile, if you want.

5. Cut the belly abdominal muscle flap away from the rest. That goes into the hamburger pile.

6. On the piece that's left you can start from the "front" end taking off rib steaks. There will be 11 to 14 inches of rib steak on a big beef, 6 or 7 on a smaller one. The big hind end of the loin is the rump roasts. Saw it off. It will be sort of triangle shaped.

7. Now start taking off sirloin steaks. The porterhouse is in the middle. The T-bones are clear to the front. Three-quarters of an inch is a nice thickness for steaks. One-half inch is really too thin for any steak except maybe round. Any steak with a bone in it should be at least three-quarters of an inch thick. Some people cut them an inch or even an inch and a quarter, but that's too thick.

CUTTING UP THE FRONT QUARTERS OF YOUR BEEF—To saw out steak, cut with your knife all around the backbone, then saw through the bone. The tenderloin is the tenderest steak. The round is the toughest. The muscles the cow uses the most (round—hind leg) are the toughest. Don't trim off *all* the fat—you want some around the edges of your steaks for flavor.

1. Remove the "arm" at the joint. Have one person cut from underneath as the other pulls the arm upwards. You've got to force it on up and out under and around that shoulder blade. You now have an arm and the rest. Cut off the top one-third of the arm for a "blade roast" and trim off some of the fat. Don't trim the roast completely clean either. Some fat around it helps the taste when it's cooking.

The next 6 inches can be a roast. And so can the next. Make it into what you like. It could be a big roast or one small one plus some stew meat. You can make the rest of the leg into stew bones or trim the meat away from the bone for hamburger.

2. With the meat saw separate the ribs from the backbone and its accompanying muscle bundles—the tenderloin and backstrap. Saw about 8 inches from where the ribs connect with the backbone. You can see what your steaks are going to look like now. Cut off the steaks. You waste less if you saw each one out but that requires tremendous time and effort. If you're not up to that you can bone out the two muscle bundles and make rib eyes of the larger muscle and tips of the smaller backstrap.

The neck end, which you can identify because it curves a little upwards, can be made into roasts and stew meat. The remaining rib area is one vast ordeal of spareribs and soup bones. You have the most work for the least desirable cuts. Starting from the rear, cut between one rib and the next all the way until they are completely separated. Then between the next and the next all the way and so on. Then saw across the individual ribs at 6-inch intervals or as your cook likes them. You'll end up probably sawing each rib thus into thirds.

CORNED BEEF—Use the recipes and procedures under Hams and Bacons.

DRIED BEEF—Do it according to the jerky recipes.

SHEEP AND GOAT

At one time my father was in the sheep business and had around a thousand head of them. You'd think therefore that I would know something about sheep but I don't. My first business venture, if you can call it that, had to do with sheep. In the spring every few days we would hear the bleating baas of bands of sheep going by our home near Clyde Park, Montana. The sheepherders were driving them off the valley bottom where the sheep were wintered up into the mountains where the snow was melting and the grass coming on green and beautiful. When we heard that sound Mother would give me a bag of cookies and a thermos of something good and warm to drink (it was spring but by no means warm in Montana) and I would run down our long lane to find the sheepherder who drove the flock.

Sheepherders are a very special sort of people. There are lots of jokes about them, but my childhood was peopled with them since we generally had one or more working for us. I'm about half sheepherder myself because I was raised an only child on a big ranch way up in the mountains with mostly nobody to talk to but my horse and God in the sky. The herders always were happy to stop and never failed to share with me the cookies and cocoa that I had brought them. We'd sit in the warm sheepwagon, which was the vehicle that they lived in, or on the back steps of that little rolling home, and I'd slowly get around to asking if there were any bums.

A bum lamb means a baby sheep that is orphaned and needs to be fed with a bottle or that is sick or injured and can't travel like it needs to for the long drive. Often enough I came home with one or more bums so that by spring's end I had a flock of about seven lambs that I fed cow's milk in a pop bottle with a rubber nipple. They all thrived. I had blind ones and lame ones, but they all knew who I was and I sure wasn't lonesome that summer. We were milking about five cows and there was plenty of milk for them. I was about seven years old.

So I have a lot of lovely but somewhat vague memories of days back on the sheep ranch like when the Mormon shearers came up to shear in our sheep sheds. How they wrestled with them to give them that barber job, sweating in their trousers and long underwear tops. How the wool was packed into long (like 15 feet) blue cloth bags hung from a special tripod and one man worked in the bag stomping the wool down until he could walk on top. A very ticky job. And how every evening Daddy would take off his long underwear, very privately in the bedroom with Mama, and she would pull the day's accumulation of ticks off of him. Ticks really thrive on sheep in the mountains in the spring.

But some of my sheep memories are sad ones, like how a hired man carelessly rubbed out his cigarette on the side of a tractor he had just filled at the gas pumps and it caused a fire that burned not only the tractor but also took the work shed adjacent to it wherein were those seven bum lambs and my precious little goat—my first goat, which I had gotten on Christmas morning. (I heard a funny sound in the living room. I jumped out of bed and ran in there and there was a little goat tied to the Christmas tree and it was trying to eat the tinsel.) I couldn't believe they were dead for a long time. I climbed up the big butte back of the house and called them evening after evening hoping the fire had merely frightened them off. Finally Daddy showed me bones that he had found in the debris.

You can use sheep for milk, but they are wild and don't give as much as a goat. They need to be sheared fall and spring. If you don't shear them and the weather gets hot they may get worms or be sick. To shear a sheep is not a job for an amateur. If you cut the wool in the middle you ruin the fleece for spinning and if you cut too close you have a bleeding sheep. Ask around for a professional sheepshearer. He will spread a tarp on the ground to keep the fleece clean. Get the sheep on it and sort of twirl the sheep and shear it at the same time. He must be very well coordinated and know sheep anatomy blindfolded. He will inevitably make a few nicks no matter how careful he is which he will treat with a disinfectant before he leaves.

There are various breeds of sheep. Black sheep wool brings the highest price now—$2.50 to $5 a pound—because it is rare and preferred by home spinners. White sheep wool sells for about 30¢ a pound. Black sheep wool can't be dyed. White and silver (from an old black sheep) can. Karakul and Corriedale sheep are white sheep with a higher quality wool for hand spinning that you can get a premium price for. Finn sheep have three to six babies at a time. Be careful you don't let a Finn ewe get bred by a ram of a larger breed. It could result in dead babies or a dead mama. Suffolk and Columbia are common meat-type breeds.

Mike thinks mutton is inedible. He and some friends stole a sheep when they were kids, butchered it, and tried to cook and eat it. Made them all deathly ill and he hasn't been able to eat sheep meat since! You could use the butchering directions for venison (in the Wild Meat section below) and get by. Just remember to skin the hide off before you gut it and don't let the wool touch the meat if you can help it. These butchering directions are sort of repetitive anyway because the basics are the same.

Something most city folks don't know about sheep is that their tails are generally cut off when they are young. By the knife or better by putting rubber bands around them. If you don't, they store fat in the tail and it gets pretty big. I've seen sheep with their tails though. I don't know if I'd do it now or not. I hate to mutilate an animal unnecessarily.

You can order an adequate looking booklet, "Slaughtering, Cutting, and Processing Lamb and Mutton on the Farm," Farmers' Bulletin No. 2152, U.S. Department of Agriculture, from the Superintendent of Documents, Washington, D.C. 20402, for 10 cents. Morton's *A Complete Guide to Home Meat Curing* (see "Home Meat Curing" under Pig) also has a guide to cutting up a sheep.

Sheep is "lamb" until it's about 8 months old. Then it becomes "mutton." If you are a candle maker save your mutton fat since it has the highest melting point of all the fats. Mutton is often a strong meat. If you're not used to it, use wild-type recipes. Don't eat it rare. Causes awful indigestion and I don't know why.

The meat of either sheep or goat is cut up pretty much like rabbit. Peel the shoulders right off the body. Cut through the thigh joint to separate the hind legs from the body. If you are careful you can get some steak off the back from the strip along the backbone, from the hams (the hind "thigh") and the shoulders. You can grind odds and ends for sausage, make big chunks into roasts. You can corn the meat by substituting in any corned beef recipe. You can make the sausage plain, but if one-third pork is added it will bind the meat together while cooking and improve its flavor.

GOAT IN PARTICULAR—We've eaten a lot of goats. Since we decided that the billies were more nuisance than value, we just eat up all the males in the fall. In the spring there is a new crop of kids and by fall the first male born will be able to breed all the nannies again. A goat is pregnant for 5 months. A billy can do the job at the age of 6 months. That's how it works. Lots more about goats in the Dairy chapter.

Goat meat is "wild" flavored. I've made goat stew, goat steaks and fried my goatburger pretty much on the same basic plan I do other meats. We never have cut roasts off our goats. I'd rather serve and eat the meat fried, or in burger, or sausage so everything is either sliced or ground. *Dairy Goat*

Journal, Columbia, Missouri 65201, has made up a little booklet about how to butcher a goat called "Butchering, Chevon, and Goat Hides." They also have one called "Goat Products Cook Book." I've forgotten how much they cost. Not too much. Like maybe 35 cents each. Goats are easy to butcher and cut up. Read some of the detailed butchering sections, especially deer.

KIDS (goat)—You butcher a kid goat the same way you do an adult basically. Only the whole thing is quicker because there is less of everything. After the kid is skinned and gutted you can roast it whole as in a barbecue on a spit like for the 4th of July when you have lots of guests . . . or quarter it for barbecuing or roasting for less people . . . or bone out the whole thing for sausage. A lot depends on the size of your kid. You wouldn't want to butcher before 12 weeks of age because you wouldn't get enough meat to make it worthwhile. A "kid" that is 6 to 9 months old is the age at which we usually butcher and then you have an animal big enough to make small steaks and roasts. So you have to use a lot of judgment and cut your meat according to the size of the animal and the use you need of it. It also depends on whether you have power meat-cutting equipment available. If you have a band saw, cutting meat is so easy that ministeaks are fine. But if you had to saw out every one the hard way there would be hardly enough meat on it to make it worth the trouble.

Kid is also on the "wild" side tastewise to those who aren't used to it and I refer you to my Wild Meat section where there are lots of good recipes for all the different cuts.

⊰⊱⊰⊱⊰⊱⊰⊱⊰⊱⊰⊱⊰⊱⊰⊱⊰⊱⊰⊱⊰⊱⊰⊱⊰⊱⊰⊱⊰⊱

WILD MEAT

Wild meat has generally more lean than fat, bear in the prehibernation season being the big exception. And the lean of such animals as deer, elk, antelope, moose, caribou, reindeer or small game is of greater density than the flesh of domesticated animals. Maybe because they get more exercise. The age range is greater, too, since domestic animals are almost always butchered in their young prime—except for hamburger-type cows or sausage pigs in which case it is ground up and you don't know.

So wild meat may be on the tough side. Also more care is potentially taken of domestic meat when butchering than of wild meat. What I mean is, if an animal has been running for two hours during a peak hunting day as it encounters hunter after hunter, and then it is cut down with a whole batch of bullets that hit in meaty prime places like the front shoulder or hind hip. Then if the animal is let lay a couple of hours before being gutted and the testicles are forgotten to be removed. Then if it has to wait another 5 days or so in warmish weather before being cut up and getting to the freezer while the rest of the hunting party has a chance to get "theirs," I wouldn't be surprised if the meat didn't compare very favorably to beefsteak.

You don't use wild fat except in the case of bear, if you have a choice, because the wild taste is concentrated there. When you want to roast a heavy chunk of meat you can lard it with salt pork to keep it

from becoming dry and tough. But a Dutch oven is even better insurance. A couple tablespoons of a tart jelly—like currant, barberry, wild plum—in the gravy or on the plate help any wild meat. Bland vegetables go well with wild meat—like cabbage, cauliflower, asparagus and breaded tomatoes. You can prepare a young or grain-fed game animal (other than bear or rabbit) rare. Grain-fed deer are ones that have been feeding in farmers' fields. Any meat is easier to cut when it is cold because cold fat is firmer. Cutting wild meat is especially hard because it has so little fat that it is wobbly. So chill as much as you can before cutting up.

TO FREEZE wild meat, first remove all visible fat except with bear. Boning helps, too. Make sure there are no hairs on the meat. The hair carries an off taste. If you need to clean the meat do so with a cloth dipped in vinegar. Vinegar helps dissolve clotted blood and pick up stray hairs.

MARINADES—Some people really believe in marinating their wild meat. They soak the meat for an hour or longer in water to which 1 tablespoon vinegar and 1 tablespoon salt have been added. Or soak it overnight in strong coffee.

QUANTITY OF MEAT—A big buck deer will dress out to about 200 or 225 pounds, an elk to 800 pounds.

FIELD CARE OF LARGE GAME

These directions are most suitable for deer and the other deerlike game animals—elk, antelope and moose. No matter where you shot, cut its throat. Then put the animal with its head downhill. Make sure it is thoroughly bled out. If it is male remove the genital organs and a large patch of hide from around them. Clean off your knife before proceeding. Then carefully cut around the anal vent and up to the neck, cutting through the rib cage. Be careful not to cut the intestines. Roll the innards out and separate from the body. You will have to cut the muscular diaphragm in order to get the lungs and heart. Carefully cut through the pelvic bone to get the rear gut and anus and the genitals of a female animal. Open the neck and take out the windpipe. If you want to wipe the body use cloths, not water. You can save the heart, liver, kidney, tongue and brain of the animal.

To get the hide off, cut around each of the four knee joints. Then slit along the inside of the leg clear up to the center cut. Using a sharp knife when necessary, work the skin back from the slits being careful that the hair doesn't touch the meat because it will give it an undesirable flavor. You can take the head off and discard it. If you want the antlers for a trophy, you could cut them off together with enough of the skull to hold them properly. However, if you're planning to use the services of a taxidermist he could probably do a better job than you and you'd best take him the whole head.

Split the body completely, working quickly to help cool it and avoid any spoiling. Any animal can be handled more conveniently if quartered. Quarter by cutting between the second and third rib from the rear and the vertebrae. Split down the backbone to make halfs of the halfs. To do this quartering you need a meat saw or sharp ax. Some sporting goods stores sell a light portable meat saw for this purpose. And hopefully you brought along some cheesecloth sacks to put the quarters in. You can buy them at sporting goods stores or make them. Salt, too. Not iodized salt—pickling salt. Because even if you don't want the hide you can give it to someone who can use it or sell it to a buyer. If it will be more than a day or two before reaching your home again salt the hide. Rub the salt all over, more on thicker places, and get into all the corners. Roll the hide and get it to the person who will tan it as soon as possible.

Until you can get the meat home keep it as cool as possible. Quartering and hanging with air circulating around it will help. On the way home your animal is better off on the trunk than the hood of the car. The engine heat promotes spoilage. Before you cut the animal into ribs and steaks, let it hang about ten

days at 35°-40°, if you have room or can get the facilities. Some butchers will let you use their cooling room for a fee. A few people have their own walk-in coolers. If the weather is cool enough let it hang in one of your own outbuildings with the door shut so wandering canines won't help themselves. The aging tenderizes the meat by allowing enzymes to work on the muscle a little. But if you don't have facilities to hang it that long, or if it's getting hot, by all means go ahead and cut it up. It won't be tender but it will at least be edible.

Because a deer is a relatively small game animal, boning out has been popularized for it. Very complete details, including lots of photographs, are available in a pamphlet sold by Oregon State University at Corvallis, Oregon 97331 ("Boning Out Your Deer"), Extension Bulletin 819. Personally I think this method like most "methods" is rather extreme. We bone out a few appropriate cuts and don't the rest.

TO HOLD DOWN ON THE "WILD" FLAVOR—The musk glands of deer are between the hocks and hoofs. Try to avoid handling them. Try to avoid killing the animal when feverish, that is when it has been running and is very upset. Such meat will be "bloodshot" and have an off taste. Be sure and cut it completely and as soon as possible and don't forget to remove the testicles of a male. Then halve and quarter and hang up to cool if you aren't going anywhere for a while. Use the organs for camp meat since they won't keep as well as the muscle meat.

CUTTING UP THE HINDQUARTERS

HAUNCH—This is the quarter containing the Achilles tendon by which you were hanging the animal and the big rear "haunch." "Haunch" means the whole hind leg of the animal. Cut off the haunch at the hip joint. It begins just below where the ribs end and you'll have to guess at just the right spot. You'll need your meat saw to get through the bone. Now cut across the haunch in two places to make thirds from top to bottom.

The top (widest) third is your round steak. To make big round steaks cut right across the grain of the entire haunch, sawing across the bone for each steak. An easier way that avoids having to saw across that bone for every steak is to separate the muscle bundles. The largest bundles are the "top round" and "bottom round" cuts. You can separate these two bundles, if you want, and cut across into steaks or leave them attached together and cut into steaks (depending on the size of your animal and your preference). The other muscle bundle is the sirloin. Cut across the grain for your sirloin steaks.

The middle third of the haunch is generally made into a roast. Some people, however, strip it off the bone and make hamburger or jerky out of it. The long, nice strips are good for jerky. The bottom third is generally stripped of meat and the meat put into the hamburger or jerky pile. The bone can be a soup bone.

RIBS AND BACKSTRAP—What you have left of the hindquarter is the ribs and backstrap. There are two strips of muscle along the backbone. The strip along the outside is the backstrap (tenderloin) and is the choicest, tenderest meat in the animal. You can either "bone out" these two muscles by cutting them away from the backbone and slice them into steaks or you can cut across the backbone for each steak and have both muscles represented in each steak.

If you sawed each one out you would have (using beef terminology), starting from the front end of the animal, club steaks, then T-bone steaks and finally sirloin steaks. You can see the "T"-shaped bone in the T-bone steaks. As a general guide the first third of the backstrap will be club steaks, the middle third T-bone and the last third sirloin. Some people make a roast of the last third instead of cutting it up for steaks. To make a roast just leave it in one piece.

On a small animal such as a deer (a deer is about one-fourth the meat of an elk or cow) all that sawing is a nuisance for the amount of meat you get out of it and the two long muscles are generally boned out. The small inside strip is the one that would be the small piece of meat on the inside of your T-bone steak. If you bone it out you can slice and make "tips" of it, which are fine floured and fried. You lose a little on your chop size from the boning out process but not too much. Cut as close to the ribs and backbone as you can to minimize loss. If you decide to bone out the tenderloin then just cut across it to make the steaks. On a small deer, they're very small, but good. Allow 2 or 3 for each person per meal. Some people make a roast of the sirloin instead of steaks. If you want *two* roasts, just cut it across the middle.

You can saw across the ribs and backbone to suit yourself for soup bones, spareribs and dog food. A small deer doesn't make very good spareribs— there is so very little meat on the ribs—but you could try if you want.

CUTTING UP THE FRONT QUARTERS

ARM—Cut the front leg from the ribs as you would a chicken thigh, pulling the bone away from the body in the joint as you cut until it is severed across the line where it joins the chest. It should pop right out of the joint. In butchering terminology the front leg is called the "arm."

Saw the arm into thirds from top to bottom with your meat saw. The top third is called a "blade roast." Some people make it into hamburger because it's a hard roast to serve and eat, especially if the animal is small. The middle third is made into an "arm roast." Trim what meat you can from the bottom third of the leg and put it into the pile for hamburger or jerky. Put the bone of that bottom third into your bone box.

REMAINDER OF FRONT QUARTERS—The meat along the outside of the backbone is the extension of the tenderloin muscle. Slice steak or tips out of it just like you did on the hindquarters. The rest is pretty much bone. Saw off the backbone and make soup bones or what you want of it. Section up the ribs for spareribs or stew meat using the meat saw where needed.

WILD STEAK

My husband likes our wild steak salted, floured and fried. I make my gravy plain or with a tablespoon of tart jelly, like currant or wild plum. Or I serve the meat plain with a spicy fruit catsup—like peach. But for something fancy or for people who aren't used to the wild taste and want a recipe that disguises it— here are some other ideas. Try these recipes, too, for any other meat whose taste you are having trouble with—rabbit, goat, old milk cow, hedgehog, or what have you. Any recipe that involves a barbecue sauce will also camouflage an unpleasant or unfamiliar meat.

Actually this extra effort is for the most discriminating taste. I was raised a large part on wild meat and our deerburger was all deer. There are better ways to fix it though and canned deer stew was a childhood favorite of mine. My father was hurt one fall in a logging accident in Oregon and had to be laid off for the rest of the winter. The little cash the folks had went for baby milk and the rest of the diet was venison. We never knocked venison.

Another possible problem with wild meat is it varies a lot in tenderness. Tame meat is usually butchered relatively young. But wild meat might be any age—and correspondingly tough or tender. You'll soon know the kind you have and can make cooking adaptations accordingly.

FOR TENDER ONES

Fried Wild Meat—Sprinkle the meat with salt and pepper and dip it into flour before frying. Fry quickly in butter or oil to preserve its moisture. Remove the meat from the pan. Thicken the pan drippings with 1 tablespoon (or so) flour, add water until it is of a suitable gravy consistency and 2 tablespoons currant (or other tart) jelly. Season the gravy if your taste buds say it is needed.

Wild Steak, Oriental—Mix together ½ cup cooking oil, 2 cloves garlic, chopped and 2 tablespoons soy sauce. Cut about a pound of wild steak into cubes or strips. Let first mixture rest about an hour to get well flavored. Cut up a green pepper into strips, removing and discarding seeds. Chop an onion, add a cup of chopped celery, if you have it, and get ready a couple fresh tomatoes by slicing into chunks. This is a good one to make near the end of the garden season when you have this stuff. Now brown the steak bits in your oil mixture, then add green pepper, onion and celery and cook about 7 minutes more. Dissolve 1 teaspoon cornstarch in a little water and stir it into the mixture. Salt and pepper to taste. Add a little homemade catsup or tomato sauce, if you have it, your fresh tomatoes and a little more water, if you need it to make the mixture of a manageable consistency. Serve with cooked rice.

Wild Meat, Hawaiian—Cube about 1 pound of wild steak or cut into strips. Shake the meat in a paper bag with some flour until the pieces are all coated. Brown them in enough butter to do the job. Then add ½ cup boiling water, salt to taste and simmer until tender. Hollow out and slice 2 green peppers. (Optional, ½ cup pineapple chunks.) In a separate pan make a sauce of 2 tablespoons cornstarch, ¼ cup vinegar, 2 tablespoons soy sauce, 2 tablespoons brown sugar and ½ cup pineapple juice if you are using pineapple or water if you aren't.) When the sauce is thick pour it over the meat. Cook the entire mixture about 3 more minutes and then serve with rice.

FOR TOUGH ONES

Mustard Steaks—Brush both sides of 4 good-sized wild steaks with mustard. Use about 2 tablespoons mustard for this. Sprinkle both sides of the meat with salt and pepper, then dip both sides in flour. Brown in melted butter in your Dutch oven. Set aside. In a saucepan combine 2 tablespoons brown sugar, 1 teaspoon salt, 2 tablespoons mustard, a dash each chili powder and cayenne, if you have a strong digestive tract, 2 tablespoons Worcestershire sauce, ¼ cup vinegar, ½ cup water and 1 cup of your homemade tomato juice or ½ cup homemade catsup and ½ cup water. When the sauce seems well mixed pour it over your meat. Put the lid on the Dutch oven and bake at 350° until done.

Wild Steak, Hungarian—Start out with enough steak for 6 people. Dip it lightly in flour, then shake off the excess. Brown in a little fat. Put into your Dutch oven. Brown several large onions, sliced, in some oil. When they're cooked to transparency pour over the meat. Add 1 teaspoon salt, ½ teaspoon paprika, ½ cup sour cream, ¾ cup water and 1 bay leaf. Bake at 325° about 2 hours.

Steak and Water—Brown steaks in 2 tablespoons shortening. Remove meat from pan. Make a gravy by adding 2 tablespoons flour, salt and pepper to taste and 2 cups water, after your flour has absorbed all the drippings and browned. Return steaks to pan in gravy. Cook, covered, in the oven at 300° until tender (about 45 minutes).

WILD ROASTS

I cook in a Dutch oven, usually with the lid on, usually at about 350°, but sometimes less, and usually brown the meat before commencing roasting. You can substitute your favorite roasting pan for my "Dutch oven." Trim all the fat away from your wild roast before commencing.

Wild Roast with Dressing—Brown your roast in a little bacon grease or other fat. Sprinkle it with salt and pepper to suit yourself. Bake in a Dutch oven, covered for 2 hours at 300° (assuming about a 2½-pound roast). Make about 1 pound of bread crumbs. Combine them in a bowl with 1½ teaspoons sage, 2 eggs, ¾ cup chopped onion and 1 bay leaf. Add enough milk to moisten the mixture and mix it well. Get your roast out of the oven. There will be juice in the bottom of the pan. Skim off any grease floating on top of it as best you can. Then spoon your dressing right down into the meat juice all around the roast. Cover and continue baking at 350° for 1 hour more. To serve, remove the roast and carve it. Serve the dressing in a separate bowl. This is a favorite of mine.

Coffee Wild Roast—In a wild roast make slits big enough to put sliced onions in. Slice 2 onions and fit them into the roast. Make a marinade of ⅓ cup vinegar and ⅔ cup water and pour that over the roast. Marinate overnight in the refrigerator or other cool place. When ready to cook drain off the marinade, brown in bacon fat or other oil, lay a few bacon strips across the top of the roast, sprinkle salt and pepper over it and set it in your Dutch oven or roaster. Add a mixture of half coffee and half water (about 2 cups of each); keep the lid on your roaster, and cook at 350° until done.

Green Pepper Wild Roast—I like this one a lot, too. Put your wild roast, a sprinkle of salt and pepper, and 4 cloves garlic, chopped (or less if you aren't a garlic lover), into your Dutch oven. Pour in 1 cup water, cover, and cook until done. Remove the seeds from 3 green peppers, cut them into slices and sauté in a little cooking oil, about 10 minutes. Add some of your homemade tomato catsup or canned tomatoes, or tomato juice if you like the flavor. Pour the green pepper sauce over the meat, carve and serve.

Herbed Wild Roast—Combine ½ cup flour, 2 teaspoons marjoram, 1 teaspoon thyme, 2 teaspoons rosemary, and 1 clove garlic, cut up. Rub your wild roast with a little cooking oil. Sprinkle salt and pepper on it, then apply your herb mixture onto it. Put the roast into your Dutch oven, add 1 cup water and 1 cup apple juice. Bake, basting occasionally, until done.

OTHER WILD CUTS

Wild stew isn't that different from any other stew. The first recipe is "regular." The next is more flavorful. To can stew first cook the meat. Add vegetables and seasonings. Fill jars, put lids on, and can as described below. Or you could make mincemeat out of it. For other wild burger ideas see the Sausage section below. There are 365 ways to fix hamburger, as a familiar cookbook avers, but fortunately when you raise or hunt your animals and do your own butchering I don't think you'll ever need that many.

If you want to eat kidney, wash well, slice and fry as with liver and heart. Personally, I don't care for it. Our family doesn't eat any nonmuscle organ meats but I can tell you how. The reason is because pollution in the animal's body is most likely to show up in those places. Even when we're raising our own and hunting our own in this polluted world we live in I figure you can't be too careful and muscle meat *is* the safest.

STEWING MEAT

Regular Stew—Cut your wild meat into 1-inch cubes, trimming away all fat. Use about 1½ pounds of meat. Sprinkle with salt and pepper, dredge in flour, brown in some shortening along with a chopped large onion. Add water enough to cover and cook until nearly tender. Then add 6 carrots, in chunks, and several potatoes, cut in sections. Add a couple cups of your fresh or home-canned tomatoes and peas, if you have them. Serve when the vegetables are tender but not overcooked.

Old-Time Wild Meat Stew—Brown chunks of meat (cut into 1½-inch cubes and with all fat trimmed away) in a little fat such as bacon grease, lard or oil. Use about 1½ pounds of meat (or less). After it is browned put in about 4 cups water. Add 1 teaspoon Worcestershire sauce, 1 clove garlic, minced, 1 medium slice onion, 2 bay leaves, 1 teaspoon salt, ½ teaspoon pepper and a dash of ground cloves. (Optional, ½ teaspoon paprika.) Simmer this mixture for 2 hours. Then add about 8 carrots, 1 small head cabbage, cut into sections (you could substitute 6 potatoes for the cabbage or use 3 potatoes *with* the cabbage), and about ½ pound onions, whatever size you have. If you like a juicy stew add a little more water. Cook until the vegetables are just done enough.

TO CAN wild meat, use clean, fresh, well-bled meat if possible. Chill as soon as possible after the kill. But do not freeze it if you are going to can. Don't wash the meat. Wipe it off with a damp cloth if it needs it. Cut into pieces that will fit easily into the jars. Bone it all, of course. You don't need fat either. Save those bones to make broth.

Put ½ teaspoon salt into each clean quart jar for seasoning. Put the meat in a large shallow pan with a little water to keep it from sticking. Cover and heat until the pink color is about gone from the center of the meat, stirring occasionally so that the meat will heat evenly throughout the pan.

Then pack your hot meat in the jars and cover with the hot broth that you cooked it in, adding water if necessary. Leave 1 inch head space over meat and broth. Adjust the lids and process at once in a pressure canner at 10 pounds pressure (240°) pints 75 minutes, quarts 90 minutes.

WILD BURGER

Wild Chili—This is good and you can easily make it as mild or strong as your family likes. Brown 1 pound ground wild meat with salt and pepper to taste

and ½ onion, cut up. Then add 1½ cups of your tomato juice and a couple cups of cooked kidney beans. Mix in chili powder to taste. Simmer 20 minutes and serve.

Wild Tacos—Brown your ground wild meat with salt and pepper to taste. Fry and fold in half the taco shells. Put a couple spoonfuls of the meat inside each shell. Have available shredded lettuce, tomato chunks and grated cheese. The spicy tomato sauce in the Sours chapter makes a good taco sauce. Let the members of your family finish filling the taco shells to suit themselves. Mothers in Mexico actually feed their children better than vendors of so-called "Mexican food" would have us think. They stuff tacos with a mixture of cooked and minced potatoes and meat as well as adding shredded lettuce and cheese on top. The meat and potatoes are boiled.

ORGANS

Liver or Heart—Cut into ½-inch slices, dip in flour and fry in bacon grease. Or boil and serve with a breadcrumb dressing.

Tongue—Scrape and boil thoroughly in salted water. Then peel off the outer skin and serve. Or salt for a day, boil and peel as above, then smoke another day (or 2 nights) and serve cold, sliced. The tongue of a very young wild animal is so tender it will cook up to a mush if you're not careful.

Brain—Salt the fresh brain lightly, keep overnight and the next day dip into hot water. The outer membrane will peel off easily then. Dip the brains in beaten egg and then in crumbs and fry in bacon drippings. Season to taste. Or mince them, add chopped green onion tops, beaten eggs and scramble the whole works.

WILD LEFTOVERS

Use wild leftovers the same as beef. Slice your leftover roast for sandwiches (mustard is good on them). Cold cuts are good warmed with leftover gravy. Or grind for luncheon meat or hash.

BEAR

The old-timers cleaned a bear by sticking one hand in his mouth, grabbing his tail with the other and turning him inside out. Nowadays we lesser mortals have to go the regular way by slitting and skin-

ning of the hide. Unless you find one without his skin. I did once. I was walking down a little canyon near my home as a little girl and came upon a large bear lying on the ground. I could see no wound. He appeared to be asleep. Strangest thing though was he was minus his hide. I touched one leg tentatively and uncertainly and he kicked me. Well I took off yelling for the house. My daddy was there sharpening his knife blade. I said, "Daddy, Daddy, there's a bear alive in the canyon and he hasn't got his skin on." My daddy just laughed. You know there are reflexes in animals' limbs for a little while even after they are dead.

You treat bear like you do pork. You can't make jerky out of bear meat because it can carry trichinosis just like pig and must always be well cooked before eating. A female bear is called a "sow." A young bear is a "shoat." The important thing about female bears and young bears though is not their name but their disposition. The only animal that I would tell you outright is aggressive and dangerous is a female bear with cubs. When I was a little girl we had a man walking around town on one leg and he was lucky to be walking at all. He made it up a tree with that one leg. Bears have the capacity to keep coming even with a bullet in the brain. You don't want to shoot one unless you're sure it can't get to you before it drops. Don't ever be one of those foolish Yellowstone Park tourist types that tries to get close and photograph that kind of bear.

If you do kill a bear you can gut and quarter it and then take the meat to a custom cutter to be cleaned and cured. Or you can do it yourself following my directions for pig. The hams and front shoulder are the parts that can be cured nicest. You could make bacon of the side meat. "Bear grease" means bear lard and some people declare it's better grease than any other you'll find. You render it out the same as for pork lard. There are only four or five states in the Union now where you can kill a bear (or an elk) anymore.

Colonial Mince Pie—If you want to thoroughly recreate an early Colonial Thanksgiving dessert make a mince pie with filling of bear's meat and dried pumpkin. Sweeten it with maple sugar and have a cornmeal crust.

Roasted Bear Meat #1—Rub a roast on the top and sides with sorghum and roast in a Dutch oven with about ½ inch water. This is my favorite way of making plain old pork roast, too.

Roasted Bear Meat #2—Rub a bear roast with vinegar and then dry with a cloth. Rub with a mixture of bacon grease, ½ teaspoon poultry seasoning, ½ teaspoon savory salt, ½ teaspoon garlic powder and ¼ teaspoon salt. Put the meat in your Dutch oven or roaster with a little water. Cover tightly and bake at medium heat until tender. That's if you want to be able to taste everything but the bear.

SMALL GAME

SQUIRREL, POSSUM AND COON have "kernels." They are situated around the neck and under the forelegs. You want to gut the animal *immediately*, remove the hide and those kernels. Then cool as soon as you can. You can cool somewhat by carrying by hand, uncovered or hanging. Otherwise, squirrel is cleaned similar to rabbit and can be cooked similarly, too. We ate them one poverty stricken year in North Carolina.

Real Brunswick Stew starts out with 2 cleaned squirrels. Cut them in pieces. Add 1 tablespoon salt to a gallon of water and set it to boil. Then add 1 chopped onion, 1 pint lima beans, 6 ears of corn, ½ pound salt pork, peeled potatoes, 1 teaspoon pepper and the squirrel pieces. Cover and simmer 2 hours. Then add 2 teaspoons sugar and 1 quart of sliced tomatoes. Simmer 1 hour longer.

Doris's Coon—Clean and skin. Remove kernels behind legs. Soak in salted water quite a few hours or overnight. Coon is good barbecued, but it can also be browned off after being cut up and then baked. Just be sure and use a younger coon. Use a basic barbecue sauce as for pork ribs. Baste your meat every hour. Do this until the meat is tender—4 to 6 hours.

PORCUPINE is one kind of animal that my daddy would never hunt. He said that was the only kind of meat a man lost in the forest without a gun had a chance of catching because they are so slow moving though prickly. He wanted them saved to be plentiful for such a desperate man.

Now it seems like nothing is plentiful but coyotes. I've lost a lot of my taste for wild meat since I started writing this book four years ago. There are too many hunters—too many of them from out of state coming in just for the sport. And too many people getting more than the limit. Mike and I didn't get any wild meat this last year. We were going to keep the deer on our place kind of for pets. We got a rude awakening there. Somebody came on our place and shot them. The same guy got the buck, the doe and the fawn. We know because he bragged about it to a friend of ours. Kind of makes you feel like posting your property isn't such a wicked and unsociable thing to do after all!

TROUT

Keep the trout out of the water and away from the bank long enough to make sure it is dead. There are various ways to clean it. Start from the two fins behind the anal vent. Cut them off around the vent and cut forward to the neck. Then pull out and discard the internal organs and scrape out the bloody membrane tissue along the backbone with your fingernail. That tissue is the fish's kidney. Rinse in water.

The head is handy if you want to carry the fish with you on a forked stick with one branch through gill flap and out the mouth or if you have an almost-too-small-to-be-legal fish. If you want to take the head off, cut it right back of the gill flaps. I don't think there is any need to scale trout. Put them on ice, if possible, while you're waiting to either cook or freeze them.

TO FREEZE—Put them in a milk carton or similar container full of water and freeze it all together. The water keeps them from drying out.

TO EAT—Peel the skin off the top side (it's tasty, too!). Very carefully, and in the best light you have, separate meat from bones—each person for himself. But do it for the smaller children and don't give any trout to toddlers lest you goof and get a tiny bone in it on which they might choke. Peel the meat slowly and carefully from the side using your fingers for best results or a fork if you're squeamish. Peel from the head toward the tail and from above the backbone moving down and cut along the ribs in order to avoid dislodging the fine rib bones from their connection with the backbone. If they do get loose with the meat it's a real nuisance trying to pick them out one by one and very easy to miss one. With practice you can lift the whole side of flesh up off the little rib bones. Do the same to the other side of the fish and you have your good eating ready.

Wilderness trout—I once fried 3 small trout on a flat rock heated in my campfire. I had no salt, pepper, flour or anything else to add but I remember those trout from an isolated mountain lake as one of the best meals of my life. I was sixteen years old. I had ridden fifteen miles before that meal and had fifteen miles yet to go.

Quick Trout—Season inside and out with salt and pepper. Roll in flour or cornmeal until coated inside and out or dip in beaten egg and crumbs. Fry in oil or lard. It will cook very quickly. Turn once. Watch to prevent burning.

Dutch Oven Trout—Partly precook 5 slices of bacon in a frying pan. Preheat your Dutch oven and pour the bacon grease into the bottom of it. Put the trout in a layer to cover the bottom (about 4 medium-sized ones). Sprinkle with salt and pepper to taste. Lay the bacon over the trout. Put the lid on and cook in the oven at medium heat about 15 minutes. Serve with lemon wedges, if you can get them.

Planking Large Trout—Place fish whole on hot greased plank (hickory, oak, or ash—1½ inches thick). Sprinkle with salt, pepper and melted butter. Bake at 400° an average of 15 minutes per pound for whole fish. When almost done, arrange a border of hot mashed potatoes around it. Brown under broiler. Surround with hot vegetables. Garnish. Serve on plank at the table.

SOME OTHERS

BULLFROGS, LEOPARD FROGS AND GREEN MARSH FROGS are all edible, that is, the front and hind legs. In Oregon the bullfrog is classified as a game fish and the bag limit is 12 per day. The hind legs are preferred and the frogs are generally considered at their best from June to October or later.

To prepare frog's legs, cut off the legs, loosen the outer skin, and then cut off the skin and toes. Wash the legs in lightly salted water (1 teaspoon to 1 quart water).

Fried Frog's Legs—Season the legs with salt, pepper and lemon juice. They are nicest if you then dip the legs into beaten eggs and into crumbs or flour before frying. They will fry very quickly—about 3 minutes in deep fat if you have it (a wire frying basket preserves their crust). If you are pan frying them turn the heat low and cook 5 to 10 minutes until the meat separates easily from the bones, turning as needed. You can make a gravy from the pan grease by adding flour and water.

HAZEL'S RATTLER RECIPE—The diamondback rattler is the best kind for eating. It should be killed by cutting off the head. Be careful not to touch the fangs as the poison is in them and can enter the bloodstream through a cut or scratch in the skin. There is no poison in the meat, which is very white and tender. To skin the snake nail it down or have someone hold it by the head end with a pair of pliers. Peel the skin off like you would peel a banana. Take it from 3 or 4 inches behind the head to within 3 or 4 inches of the rear elimination vent (on the underside about 6 or 7 inches from the rattler). Gut the snake. Cut the middle section that you skinned into 4- or 5-inch portions. *Batter* as for chicken and fry—either pan fry or deep fry. Or bake (wrapped to keep it from drying out). It should be split down the backbone to make it lie flat.

DORIS'S TURTLE—Kill and let hang with head off (downward) to bleed. Use a small hatchet to cleave away the shell. Then cut up as you would chicken. Soak 8 hours in cold salt water. *(Important.)* Now flour in unbleached white flour, salt, and pepper, and brown off. Bake 4 hours in a slow oven.

For soup do the same as above, then cool meat and remove bones. Chunk the meat and cook with small whole new potatoes, corn, peas, carrots, celery, bay leaves, curry, lima beans and fresh snap beans until done. Season. (Optional, tomatoes.)

CRAWDAD—I'll bet this is the only cookbook on your shelf that tells you what to do with crawdad. Little creeks around here have them. Now to catch them

you grab the crawdad in the middle with two fingers. Press the front pinchers together and drop it into a bag. For plain crawdad just boil them 10 minutes in salted water. Then serve. You pick off the shell and pick out the meat using toothpicks. You can also fry in deep fat. Or boil them and peel off the shell before serving. Serve with biscuits. They taste like lobster.

You think eating crawdad is bad? I once tried serving a batch of French fried grasshoppers. Nobody would eat them.

CARP—Clean it and cut into pieces. Sprinkle the pieces with lemon juice. Broil, turning once, for 25 minutes. Sprinkle salt on it and serve.

SAUSAGE

Sausage is a basic food. It is to pork what hamburger is to beef—a way to use all the scraps. On wild meat and small animals like goat you get so many odds and ends of meat pieces, especially if you are boning the meat out, that sausage is really a tasty way to fix them. "Sausage" can mean ground pork, or a mixture of one-third ground pork and two-thirds any other kind of meat.

You can make sausage by using the butcher's help with the grinding and no other equipment. Or you can invest in a sausage grinder and stuffer. Sausage, seasoned and frozen in breakfast-sized packages that you just thaw and make up into patties and fry, or sausage fried and then canned, is just as much sausage when it comes to using up those meat scraps and enjoying eating them, as sausage stuffed into casings and smoked.

Classic "sausage" is made of pork trimmings, one-third fat to two-thirds lean. Or of ground beef and pork mixed which is "bologna," or of lamb, mutton, or goat bound with one-third pork to help hold it together and improve flavor. (Though we just grind our goat meat plain and treat it like hamburger.) Or it can be made of part liver which gives you liver sausage. In very old recipes sausage was made from cured meat and highly seasoned to aid in its preservation. Now since everybody makes sausage for the freezer (or to can) you can season as lightly or as heavily as it suits you. Sausage can be smoked if you like the smoked flavor. Smoking is not necessary to sausage making. We don't smoke ours. If you want to smoke your sausage see the Smoking section for details.

Sausage making is really an important country art in this part of Idaho. Maybe everywhere in the country. The arrival of late fall and butchering time on the farm means sausage time. Often it is made twice a year. In late fall and again in early spring when some more butchering is done. In most of the small towns around here it is not only a private operation but also a public one. The communities have an annual sausage making bee and then a big sausage feed afterwards.

The hog butchering bee that I was telling you about is also a sausage making bee. The small intestines are cleaned by the women while the men are butchering. Those become the sausage casings. When they cut up the pigs they make sausage and stuff the casings and then smoke them in a little smokehouse right there.

GRINDING—The thing you must have or have access to to make sausage is a meat grinder. The best

grinder for sausage is one with a coarse (½-inch holes) and a fine (⅛-inch holes) choice of plates. Don't plan on using one of those small home-style meat grinders to make your sausage. I made that mistake. They just can't handle the job. Even if you keep the screw as tight as it will go, which helps, you end up getting some steel flavor in your meat. You have to keep tightening the screw because it keeps slipping. And sooner or later the grinder starts getting stringy ligaments wound around the outlet and finally gums up completely and is immobilized. It helps some to trim out as much of the ligaments as possible but there's no way to get them all.

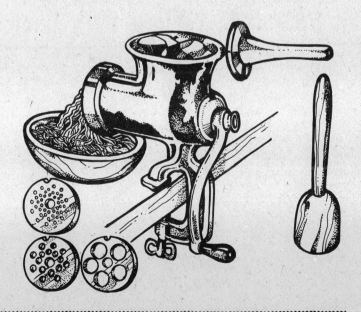

Better than to try to grind sausage in a little home grinder is to take a dishpan or two of it to your local butcher. But check with him first to see if he feels able to do it for you. There are so many new laws now that discriminate against home butchered meats that he may feel he can't take the chance.

You can mail-order yourself a sausage grinder and stuffer from Maid of Scandinavia for $20.45. It has the two disks for fine or coarse grinding and a ⅞-inch stuffer attachment. It's crank operated. The nicest of all are power grinders if you have the kind of handyman who can hook up a washing machine motor to anything. Maid of Scandinavia Company is at 3245 Raleigh Avenue, Minneapolis, Minnesota 55416. Add $1.10 for handling.

Before you grind the meat trim it all from the bones and cut away all gristle and blood clots. Cut the meat into strips, whether it is fat or lean. Put your fat in one pile and your lean in another to help you have a notion of proportions. You're supposed to use one-third fat and two-thirds lean and you can kind of judge that with your eye but I don't see much use in the fat part so I generally just use whatever fat comes along of its own accord and the fat that I can cut clean out easily goes into the rendering pail.

SEASONING—Some people grind their meat coarse, then add the seasoning and grind again. But it's too much struggle to grind more than once and easier to mix the seasoning with the meat before grinding than after. So do it like this. Cut the meat in strips. Lay it out on a mixing surface like a sheet of freezer paper with the wax side up. Sprinkle the seasoning over and mix with your hands. Sprinkle again and mix again until you have it well mixed. You can season about 20 pounds at a time this way. Much easier than working with it ground.

Now grind. If you have a real good grinder you could form your ground sausage into fist-sized balls and put them through the grinder again. It really helps to have a wooden follower to hold the sausage in the grinder. I don't know where you could buy one unless maybe from Morgan Brothers.

If you aren't sure of your seasoning amounts make a little sausage cake up on the spot, fry it and eat it. Then you can adjust the seasoning of the rest accordingly. You don't taste raw pork because it's been known to carry trichinosis, which is a disagreeable disease. There was a girl in college who ate several hot dogs in Chicago and got it. She got really sick and had to quit school. I can't imagine our homegrown pork having any such thing because pigs get it from eating infected meat and I know where everything that our pigs eat comes from. Nevertheless it's a good habit not to taste raw pork.

If you decide to add more seasoning to your already ground meat mix it in a big kettle. Get ready by washing both hands clear up to your elbows and then plunge in. Knead as for bread dough, picking up from the bottom, pulling up over the side to the top and punching into the center. In a moment give the kettle a quarter turn and continue. Some people grind the meat coarse, add the seasoning then grind it fine. That's OK if you have a good power grinder.

The seasoning can be as simple as salt and pepper. Or a very, very complex mixture. Morton Bros. (the salt people) carries a sausage seasoning. You can buy packages of it in our local grocery stores. Some people use a little Tenderquick in with their seasonings. Some make it all from scratch. The commercial seasonings contain a lot of spices blended with salt and also monosodium glutamate and preservatives. Use 8 ounces per 24 pounds meat for strongly seasoned sausage. Eight ounces for 35 pounds of meat gives you a milder sausage. I've tried just grinding and freezing the sausage plain and then seasoning it right before I cook it. It doesn't have the best flavor that way. The seasoning needs a chance to work in.

PACKAGING AND CASINGS—It is extra work and expense or time (if you clean your own) to stuff casings. At home I usually just wrap my sausage in freezer paper, enough per package for a meal, and that's it. But at the big hog butchering and sausage making bees I've enjoyed doing the real thing and maybe in years to come when I'm not so busy with the little children I'll do the real thing at home, too.

You can use plastic, muslin or gut casings. Plastic casings used to be readily available but are hard to get now. They were sold in 1-inch, 2-inch and 4-inch sizes. Two-inch was generally the most satisfactory. You don't eat the plastic casings, of course. Or the muslin ones. To shop for casings ask the custom butcher in your area. In larger cities there are sometimes stores that specialize in sausage. Or your local market might order them from his wholesaler. If that doesn't work check the Yellow Pages under "Meats, Custom Cutting" and "Meats, Wholesale." Casings are sold by the "hank" which is a 1½-pound package that is supposed to stuff about 100 pounds of sausage. When you buy sausage made of the natural gut you eat the casing, too. The last I heard these natural casings were about $7.50 a hank.

There are three kinds of natural casings. And a really good sausage stuffer has three nozzle sizes. Little pig size (what they call link sausage) is about 2 inches long and ½ inch wide and is a sheep casing. Beef casings are used to hold salami-type sausages. Pork casings make traditional "sausage" sausages. A hank of pork casings is supposed to stuff 100 pounds of pig—about 85 actually. Sheep casing will take 50 pounds. Beef casing will take a lot. You can buy natural casings in quantity and keep them in your freezer. I have a friend who kept hers there for 3 years before they were all used up and kept fine. Soak them in warm water before stuffing.

Muslin sausage casings you can make yourself. Don't dry sausage in them. You have to strip the muslin off first. Sew strips of muslin 8 inches wide by 18 inches long. This allows for a ½-inch seam. Fold and sew up one end and turn inside out. Firmly pack the sausage in there. Be sure there are no air pockets because air pockets would cause potential mold on the inside of the casings. Tie the top with a heavy cord and give it a loop to hang up the sausage. Be sure and dip your muslin casings in water and wring them out before starting to stuff them. If you don't have a sausage stuffer you can spoon sausage into big casings like these.

Making your own natural casings is cold, tedious, *hard* work and not for the squeamish. You need a fairly low faucet or hose that runs water on the ground, a knife to cut the gut when it shows a hole or tears, and a set of knitting needles. If you are going to clean casings it's doubly important that the animal not be fed for 24 hours before butchering. The casing is made from the animal's (sheep, cow or pig) small intestine. If there is food in there it makes a lot of unnecessary work getting it out.

If you are planning to save casings it is a good idea to keep your pigs especially well wormed. (The worm medicine is a liquid that you mix with a gallon of water and they drink it.) Not only is it disagreeable being in the same vicinity as a bunch of 6-inch long and husky writhing white worms, but also they make holes in the intestine and a really infested pig will have a gut like a sieve.

Here's what you do:

1. Cut the small intestine off where it starts below the stomach and cut it on the other end where it is about to connect up with the large intestine. You'll have to rescue it from the general pile of innards. Put it in a big dishpan.

2. Carry it over to where your faucet or hose is. Strip it between your fingers to remove as much of the contents as possible—food, worms or whatever—just let it spill out on the ground. This is where the agony starts because sausage and butchering weather is cold weather. But you have to do all this work with your bare hands because the gut is delicate and the job is delicate. Cold, wet hands will be in a state of near paralysis after the first 10 minutes. Not so bad if you're just doing one gut. If you're doing more than one you can take turns under the running water and standing thawing out your hands at the nearest fire.

3. Now you're going to turn the entire gut inside out. You have got the contents stripped out as best you can and the outside rinsed off under your faucet. There's a neat trick to this. Practice beforehand in the house where your hands are warm and dry with something like a sock till you feel you can do it even with your hands wet and frozen and with a slippery gut.

a. Get your sock.

b. Hold it upside down.

c. Start turning it inside out.

d. When it's a gut rather than a sock it's about 25 feet long and slippery. The way to get it turned inside out is by water pressure. The hard part is getting it started. Returning to the sock, if you turn socks inside out like I do you have your thumbs in a sort of pocket you've made all the way around. Now you're going to run your water into that pocket. Since the gut is waterproof the water pressure going into the pocket will push on it and draw more and more of the gut inside out until you're clear to the end. If you run into a wormhole or the gut starts to tear you lose your water pressure as the water starts to leak out the hole. In

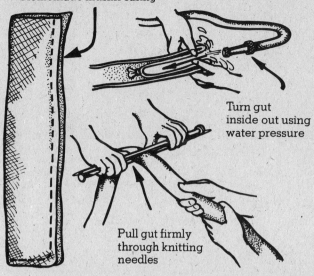

Homemade muslin casing

Turn gut inside out using water pressure

Pull gut firmly through knitting needles

that case cut the gut at the point of the leakage and start over again with the part that hasn't been turned yet.

e. You can do this indoors or out.

Put your turned cleaned casings in a pan. Now get two knitting needles. Put one end of the cleaned gut between the knitting needles. Have somebody hold the needles tightly together while another pulls the casing through between them. Rinse them some more. Now store in cold water if you're going to use them in a reasonable time. Otherwise freeze them. Soak in warm water before using.

Chitterlings is a Southern name for the casings used as a meat dish. Having gotten them this far you soak them in vinegar to remove the smell and then cook.

Stuffing the casings—The stuffer basically is a nozzle with a container on top fixed so you can put pressure on the contents. The pressure forces the sausage out through the nozzle and into the casing. The simplest sort is just a funnel. You hold the casing under the funnel and push it through with your hand. For the exorbitant price of $6.25 plus $1.10 handling you can buy a metal nozzle plus wooden follower mail-order from Maid of Scandinavia. The sausage grinder that they sell that I mentioned before has a stuffer attachment. In this case you turn the crank to force the sausage out of the nozzle into the casing until it is full. Pack the casing as tightly as possible. At the sausage making bees they have a special big crank operated sausage stuffer, but that's not likely for just a private person.

If you're only going to have one stuffer size it's better to have it too small than too large. Really nice stuffers have three nozzles for the three basic casing sizes but ordinary ones are ⅞ inch in diameter. It has to be small enough for the smallest casing to slip over the end of the nozzle easily.

Here's how to do it.

1. Separate out a length of casing.

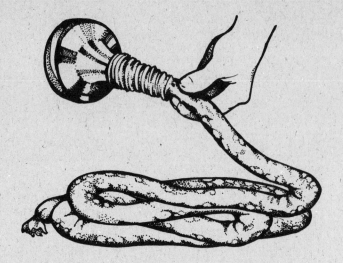

2. Put the entire casing over the nozzle of the stuffer.

3. Pinch the free end shut with your left hand.

4. Have a helper run the stuffer. The casing will unfold itself as the sausage is forced into it. To make a round sausage let about an 18-inch to 2-foot length fill. To stop the stuffer crank it quickly backward a half turn of the crank.

5. Pull off a little empty length of casing. Cut the casing.

6. Put the two loose ends of the sausage casing together forming a ring. Tie the ends together with twine or a stout soft white string. If you plan to hang the sausage to smoke it, tie another knot between the two free ends of your twine so you have a little string ring to hang it up by. Your sausage should be long enough to make a comfortable circle and touch end to end. Round sausages smoke best because they can't stick together, twist or flip.

If a casing breaks with the sausage in it set aside for the time being and you can restuff it later.

To make short links rather than rings start as before. Let fill about 5 inches, or as long as you prefer. Stop filling. Twist casing several times around to make a thorough obstruction. Commence filling again and so on. Cut off when you have enough to tie in a circle. (Takes about three.) Tie as before. If you don't tie them in a circle you'll have to tie between each link. Three inches long is nicest but you have to be pretty good at it to make them. A butcher doesn't even need to stop his machine. He can just keep the links flowing across the table.

Another way to do it is to make very long links and freeze them. Then you can just break off what you need.

To stuff using a plain old funnel—Use a funnel with a ¾-inch opening. Put the wet casing over the funnel end. Push meat down the funnel into the casing regulating the thickness as it goes in. Make 5 inches long. Twist funnel around to form link. Continue pushing meat in until used up. Puncture with a skewer to let air out.

Carla's Sausage—I'm always in a rush so we just grind the sausage, season it, bag up in the usual meal-sized lot and put it in the freezer. Since the hot spices give me indigestion, yet I'm a great lover of sausage, I created a recipe that tastes like fine sausage but won't give anybody indigestion. I recommend it to you all. I add hefty amounts of salt, garlic salt, dried parsley, sage and thyme. Onion salt, too, if I have it. It's the pepper, red pepper, cinnamon and so on in recipes that makes typical sausage indigestible. You stick to the "herb"-type seasonings and your sausage will taste absolutely sausagey and won't give the tenderest system bad after effects. All our sausage eaters like it, too. I never seem to be able to keep sausage on hand. It gets used up faster than any other part of the pig.

Plain Plain—Just grind up your pork trimmings. About one-fourth fat is my personal preference over the classical one-third. Season with salt, pepper, sage, and (optional) red pepper.

Seasoned Plain—For each 8 pounds of pork add 10 teaspoons salt, 8 teaspoons sage, 4 teaspoons ground pepper, 1 teaspoon ground cloves or whatever variation on that that you prefer like thyme or allspice or nutmeg. This is hot.

Another Seasoned Uncured Recipe—First mix your seasonings and then mix seasonings into meat. For each 2½ pounds of ground meat combine 2½ teaspoons sage, ¼ teaspoon thyme, ½ teaspoon cayenne, ¾ teaspoon pepper, ¼ teaspoon garlic powder, ¼ bay leaf, crushed, and a dash of celery seed.

Cured Pork Sausage—Before you grind the meat put your pork scraps into a brine using 2 pounds homemade cure per gallon water. Leave it in there 3 days. Then grind and stuff. Season some more if you think it needs it. Too strong for me.

Pizza Sausage—10 pounds pork, almost all lean if you can manage it, ¼ cup salt, 1 teaspoon pepper, 1 teaspoon crushed chili pepper and 3 teaspoons fennel seeds. Mix in seasonings. Grind, it will keep in refrigerator about 2 weeks. To cook, cut into patties and fry slowly or bake in 350° oven for 45 minutes. Good with tomato sauce and spaghetti. Crumble as it fries to put on pizza.

Bologna Sausage is made of a mixture of ground beef and ground pork. You could make this if you were butchering both a beef and a pig. That's a pretty natural thing to do come weather cold enough for slaughtering. By then we're low on all kinds of meat. You can substitute mutton or lamb for beef in this type of recipe. The proportion of pork lean and fat to beef can vary according to taste and convenience from as little as 5 pounds of pork to 20 pounds of beef to as much as 15 pounds of pork to 20 pounds of beef. So to a certain extent it can just be a matter of how many pounds of beef and pork scraps you have. You might want to save out a lot of your beef hamburger though to be plain old hamburger and the same of pork. The nicest mixture is probably 2 pounds of lean beef to 2 pounds of lean pork and some fat pork thrown in, not more than 1 pound. Season with sausage seasonings and grind. One teaspoon seasoning per pound meat. If you want to put together your own seasoning try salt, pepper, garlic, onion, coriander and mace. Water is added in the proportion of 3 or 4 pints per 25 pounds meat. Bologna is traditionally stuffed into beef casings, smoked and then cooked. Remember to soak the casings before stuffing them. Smoke the bologna from 2 to 3 hours. (See Smoking section p. 410.) Then simmer below the boiling point until it floats—15 to 30 minutes. Chill in cold water and hang to drip in a cool place. Then you can freeze it.

Liver Sausage—Along with seasoned pork sausage and blood sausage, this is one of the most popular country sausage recipes around here. To make liver sausage boil 5 pounds pork liver for 1 hour. Strain and discard broth. Cover 5 pounds lean pork and 5 pounds pork skin with water. Add 3 bay leaves, 6 whole cloves and 1 onion. Boil for 2 hours. Skim the fat from the broth. Remove the meat and cool the broth. Grind the liver and the meat. Add salt, pepper and garlic salt to taste. Add enough of the broth to moisten the mixture well. Stuff into casings and boil 1 hour. Then keep in refrigerator or freezer. This recipe only makes enough to stuff about 6 casings. Don't smoke liver sausage.

The above recipe is pretty heavy on the liver side. Most liver sausage contains only 10 to 20 percent liver. You can add your pork head, tongue, and the like to it. In that case you go ahead and cook all the meat except the liver just the way you would for scrapple—until it can be easily separated from the bones. Then cut the livers deeply with a knife and add them for the last 10 minutes. Don't overcook the variety meats. It all gets cooked again in the casings anyway. For 100 pounds of meat use 2 pounds salt, 2 ounces pepper, 1 ounce sage, ½ ounce red pepper and 1 ounce allspice. Mix the seasonings in and grind the meat until it's ready for stuffing into the soaked casings. Stuff, tie and simmer in water until it floats (10 to 30 minutes). Cool, chill and hang up to drain. Freeze.

Salami is made from meat like wild meats or goat that might be tough and needs grinding or tastes like a wild meat you aren't used to. The spiciness covers the taste. Don't use any fat from wild meat, except bear, since the others have the wild flavor concentrated in the fat. Wild sausage that's part pork or pork sausage makes a fine breakfast sausage. Wild meat is generally extremely lean. So you can combine it with really fatty pieces of pork and it will benefit. You can use one-fourth to one-third pork. Season and grind up. Then I just bag it up in baggies, tie with the wires and freeze. Each bag holds enough for a breakfast. When we have plenty of wild meat and pork I make it by the kettleful. Season with the commercial seasoning, 1 teaspoonful per pound or use your own formula. You can add black whole peppers after your grinding to make it authentic. Sage, allspice, garlic, ground cardamom seed and onion salt are all good in it. After the meat is seasoned, if you want, you can stuff it into casings. Smoke about 48 hours. Smoking is no substitute for cooking. Freeze it and cook it when you are ready for a sausage meal.

Potato Sausage—This recipe was sent to me by the Johnsons of Wheaton, Illinois. Use 4 pounds

ground beef and 2 pounds ground pork. Peel and grate potatoes until you get about a quart of grated potato. Use some of the liquid that drains off the grated potatoes so that the mixture is like a soft meatloaf. Grind 3 large onions and add. Add salt, pepper and ground allspice to taste—½ to 1 teaspoon—the flavor should be subtle. Put this mixture in sausage casings. Don't pack too tightly. Tie the ends. Simmer in salted boiling water for ½ to 1 hour. Freeze. To cook put in a shallow pan in the oven and brown at 375° for about 10 minutes.

Blood Sausage—This recipe will make about 30 pounds. It is probably better to use beef blood and beef or lamb casings. The meat used should be mostly pork, and a little beef can be added. Fresh pork hocks, shanks, shoulder or meat from hog's head works great. Fat must be left with it as it is needed. All ingredients should be ready ahead of time. Blood should be caught in a manner to keep it clean and a little salt added to keep it from setting or you can stir it.

The best way to get a pig's blood is to shoot it, then quickly hoist pig. Cut the jugular vein in the neck—or if you're a real expert you'll go straight to the aorta coming out of the heart. Press the neck of a jar to the pig's neck to catch blood as it pours out. To get blood from an unhoisted beef or pig just hold the pan so as to catch blood after cutting open. One hog will give about 1½ to 2 gallons of blood. Don't get blood from nose or mouth.

Keep pan under pig, keep stirring for at least 5 minutes; otherwise the blood will congeal into a lump and you want to keep it liquid. If you have snow pack the jar with snow to cool it.

Seven pounds fresh pork (cook the day before and save broth), 1 bundle casings (well washed and soaked in water), 3 pounds of rice (cooked almost done), 2 pounds barley (also precooked the day of use), ¼ cup cinnamon, 1 teaspoon cloves, 1½ teaspoons allspice, ¼ cup marjoram, 3 tablespoons pepper, ½ cup salt and 2 quarts fresh beef or pork blood. (Better tasting sausage if you can get beef. Same principles apply to getting beef blood as to pork.) Grind meat and fat. Warm broth. Mix meat, broth, warm rice, barley and blood. If blood has set, grind it and then mix in. Add spices. Mix thoroughly. Mixture must be quite warm to put in casings. Don't pack casings too full. Have a kettle of water boiling. Tie casings, leaving room for expansion. Drop a few at a time into the water. Cook about 10 minutes. Test by pricking it with a needle. If juice is clear take out and cool. Wrap for freezer.

My family enjoys it fried crisp or put on cookie sheet or shallow pan in hot oven until crisp. We use it for either breakfast or dinner. It is very expensive to buy and what we have bought never seems very good.

Pepperoni—4 pounds pork (but coarsely ground), 1 pound salt pork, 3 pounds beef, 2 tablespoons crushed chili pepper, 1 tablespoon pepper, 3 cloves (crushed), garlic or garlic salt, 1 teaspoon saltpeter, ½ pound small pork casings. Grind meat and salt pork, mix all ingredients in an enamel pan, stuff into small casings and tie off every 8 inches. Prick well with fork. Hang and dry three weeks in cool, airy room. Arrange them so none touch in drying.

German Franks—5 pounds veal, without bones, 5 pounds pork, no fat, 8 pounds lard, 13 grams salt per pound meat used; 3 grams pepper per pound meat used and ½ nutmeg or mace per pound meat used. All meat is ground very fine together with ice and salt and pepper and seasoning. Mix well after the grinding. Put into clean intestines and make 6-inch pieces. Prick with fork and will keep awhile in refrigerator or hang to dry.

Kielbasa (Polish Sausage)—1½ pounds pork loin or Boston butt, ½ pound veal, salt and pepper, 1 clove garlic (crushed), 1 teaspoon crushed marjoram, if wanted. Run meat through coarse grinder. Add 3 or 4 tablespoons water, garlic, salt and pepper to taste and marjoram. Mix thoroughly and stuff casing. It is now ready to smoke. If you do not have facilities to smoke, place in baking dish and cover with water. Bake at 325° to 350° until water is absorbed.

Brakkory—3 pounds pork butt, 3 pounds beef, 1½ pounds salt pork, 5 pounds potatoes (boiled), 1 quart milk, 3 tablespoons sugar, 3 tablespoons black pepper, 4 teaspoons cayenne pepper, 4 teaspoons saltpeter. Grind boiled potatoes and salt pork through 3/16-inch plate. Grind potatoes, salt pork, beef and pork butt 2 or 3 times. Add seasonings and saltpeter. Mix well. Boil milk. When cool, add to meat-potato mix and blend well. Stuff casings and twist into links. Smoke 3 or 4 hours at 100° to 110°. Take out, let cool and dry and refrigerate.

Dry Italian Sausage—5 pounds freshly butchered ground pork butt, 2 teaspoons black pepper, 1 clove garlic (chopped), 1 wineglass red table wine, 1 tablespoon salt, 1 tablespoon fennel seed, 1 teaspoon ground hot pepper. Blend well and store in refrigerator overnight. Next day stuff in casings. Can be frozen or hung to dry in cool ventilated room for 1 week, then frozen. Some add ground onions to sausage.

Rosemary Sausage—1 pound pork, 1 pound beef, 1 pound veal, 1 pound suet, 1 tablespoon salt, 1 teaspoon black pepper, 2 teaspoons rosemary (ground or chopped), ½ teaspoon thyme, ½ teaspoon marjoram, ½ teaspoon freshly grated nutmeg, and casings.

Finely grind first four ingredients. Add remaining ingredients and mix well. Put into casing and tie every 4 inches or form into patties and refrigerate.

Dutch "Poutden"—Use a Dutch oven or a large pan with a cover. Cut or chop up the following ingredients working from the bottom of the pan up. On the bottom make a layer of potatoes, then carrots, then onions, then apples, then cabbage, cut in chunks, then mettwurst or any good smoked sausage, cut in small pieces. Boil with 1 to 2 cups water added and salt and pepper. Boil until mushy. Can be served as it comes or it is good mashed together.

JERKY

"Jerky" basically means strips of raw meat seasoned in salt and pepper brine and dried. It's a homemade snack that anyone can enjoy. It's tasty and nourishing. I send Grandpa Emery a big jar of it with a red ribbon around the neck at Christmas because he really likes that kind of thing. It's good for company. But like many other old fashioned arts you have to make it a couple of times to get comfortable with the procedures and to find out just how dry and how spicy your particular family likes its jerky. Modern commercial jerky is so heavily treated with seasonings and preservatives that trying to eat it as a basic food would make you sick. Meat jerked to use as a basic food should be in thin strips, ¼ inch thick, prepared without any salt or spices, and dried in the sun a couple days. To eat use in stews and soups.

CUTTING—Use lean, red meat. The flesh of any large wild animal such as deer, elk or moose is fine. Beef, goat and mutton can also be jerked, but don't jerk pork or bear because these two may carry trichinosis. Veteran meat jerkers use the poorest meat for salami and better cuts such as the loin and round steak for jerking. Frozen meat can be thawed and jerked at any time in its locker life, if you get it into the locker fairly promptly in the first place. About 5 pounds of raw meat will yield 1 pound of jerky.

To prepare the meat for jerking first remove all fat, bone and visible connective tissue. Cut the remainder into strips about 5 inches long, 1 inch wide and ½ inch or less thick. Cut lengthwise along the muscle, not against the grain, to make the long strips. (Or 6 inches long and ¾ inch across or 9 inches long or what you like—but remember that any piece over ½ inch thick will be hard to get dry.)

SEASONING—After the strips are cut, and before they are dried, you season them. There are as many possible ways to do this as there are recipes for jerky and really they all work OK. You'll probably experiment. Mike and I never have agreed about it. The simplest method of "seasoning" is to dip the meat into salted water, but people usually want a stronger flavor. You can soak the meat in a seasoned brine for 24 hours. Rinse briefly, and then hang up to dry. Or else rub or pound the seasoning in by hand, let the seasoned meat rest a few hours, then rinse it off under the faucet. Jerked meat will usually take more seasoning than you might think because the heat of the drying process weakens the spices.

But just how much you want is very much a matter of taste and you'll have to make jerky a few times to find out what your particular family's tastes are (they probably won't all agree). If possible don't use iodized salt to make your brine—some people told me it gave their jerky an off flavor. Morton's Sugar Cure is a prepared mix for this purpose that you can buy and use. But I don't like some of their ingredients. You can mix your own seasonings. Salt, pepper, brown sugar, allspice, oregano, marjoram, basil, thyme, garlic powder and Tabasco are all possibilities. Some people, when making oven-dried jerky rather than smoked jerky, fake with that store stuff called liquid smoke.

Pure Salt Brine—Make a brine of ½ to 1½ pounds pickling salt in 1 gallon water. Proceed as below.

A Seasoned Brine—Dissolve 1 pound pickling salt, 1 pound brown sugar, 1 teaspoon ground allspice and 2 tablespoons black pepper in 1 gallon water. Use a granite canner, crock or plastic bucket. Soak the jerky strips in the brine for 12 hours. Weight the meat with a plate and a quart jar of water on top of the plate so that the liquid stays over it. Then rinse off in clear water. My husband prefers this recipe but I think it is *very* strong. To weaken it leave the meat in the seasoned brine a shorter time.

An Easy Dry Method—Have ready a suitable-sized granite canner, crock or plastic bucket. Sprinkle the bottom with salt, pepper, garlic powder and brown sugar. Put in a layer of meat and sprinkle again. Put in another layer and so on until you are done. Place the container in the refrigerator or some cool place and let rest 18 hours. Then remove, drain the meat thoroughly of the extracted juice and proceed to dry it. For a mild jerky, rinse the meat before drying it. This is my favorite recipe. It makes a comparatively sweet jerky.

Another Dry Method—Lay the meat strips on a towel, mix thoroughly ⅓ cup brown (or white) sugar, ¾ cup salt and 1 teaspoon crushed black pepper (or use Morton's Sugar Cure). Or use ½ cup salt and ⅔ cup brown sugar. Rub the seasoning in. Juice will be coming out. Turn the strips over and repeat on the other side. Some people do this on a wooden board and pound it in. Then roll the strips in a damp (wet and then wring out) towel and leave them in the refrigerator for 8 hours. Take them out of the towel. Rinse each piece thoroughly under running water. Lay on a dry towel for 2 or 3 hours.

DRYING—After the strips of meat are seasoned they are ready to dry. This can be done "in the field" by the heat of the sun during the day and the smoke of your campfire by night or in your smokehouse or in your oven depending on your preference and your facilities. Just exactly how dry you want it is also a matter of preference. For simple food preservation the dryer the better. You can stew the jerky to eat it, but people usually make it for smoking and plan to use it up soon and don't dry it clear out. As a snack it's nicer with some moisture left in. If some moisture is left you'll have to keep it stored in the refrigerator. If you get your jerky too dry to suit you, you can wrap it in a damp towel and keep it in a tightly lidded gallon jar in the refrigerator to recover a little moisture.

Completely dry jerky for long-term storage can be stored in an airtight container and will keep very well. I use quart jars. Just screw the lid on tight. The dryer the jerky and the more heavily seasoned, the more keeping power it has. The salt and sugar here have the same preservative effect as when making old fashioned home cured hams and bacon.

In the field—The meat strips can be spread on rocks or bushes on a hot day. If insects are a problem they can be covered with a muslin or build a smudge fire or you could stand there waving your arms all day and pray for a wind. If the weather changes to rain before you're done you'll have to take your meat indoors and wait to finish when the sun shines again. It will take about 3 days to do it this way, more or less, depending on your weather (the dryness and hotness).

Over a wood stove is a fine method for wintertime when you are using the stove a lot. Just run wires like a clothesline so that the meat can be suspended in the hot air around and above the stove. The little metal fasteners sold for hanging Christmas tree balls work fine for fastening a strip of jerky to a clothes hanger or wire.

Smoking and drying at the same time—Whether or not you smoke jerky is a matter of taste and convenience. If you want to stop smoking and the meat is still not dry, you can finish it in the oven. The thicker the pieces of jerky the longer it will take. It may get a crust on the outside and fail to dry in the middle if it's too thick or if you are smoking at too high a temperature. The meat should be drained and dried thoroughly before being placed in the smoker. The smoker temperature should be 90° to 120°. Smoking doesn't have to go on day and night but it should be completed as rapidly as possible. As to how long to smoke—I have heard of estimates anywhere from a few hours to several days. It mostly depends on how you like it and on your smoker. There's more on smoking meats in the special section with that name. We don't smoke our jerky. Just make and eat it out, seasoned and dried in the oven.

Oven-Dried Jerky—Set the oven temperature at about 120°. Remove your oven racks and lay the seasoned jerky strips across them. Leave a little room for the heat to circulate. You can put lots of jerky in the oven but don't have it any closer to the top or bottom of the oven than 4 inches. You can leave the jerky in as is the whole time or you can visit in the middle and turn the meat over. Make a small batch the first time and keep an eye on it till you become acquainted with your oven's peculiarities. It takes about 11 hours in my oven. A layer of aluminum foil on the bottom of the oven will catch the fat drips. If the oven door is left open a crack it lets the moisture out better. If you like your jerky moister than the dark brittle absolutely dry final stage, then stop at whatever stage you like. For muddy tasting fish like Kokanee salmon (a landlocked salmon) soak in salt water overnight before jerking.

PEMMICAN

Real old-time pemmican was made by the pioneers from lean portions of venison, buffalo and so on. Remove the fat from the lean. Sun dry the lean meat in thin jerky-like strips. Put the lean pieces

loosely in a jar. Render fat into tallow and pour it in hot over the lean dried meat until the spaces are filled. When you need it cook like sausage or else eat as dried beef.

Pemmican also was a pioneer trail food. It was light to carry and self-preserving because of the lard. This kind was made from jerky, dried berries (raisins can be substituted), suet and a little optional sweetening. For every pound of jerky use 2 tablespoons of sweetening, 2 ounces of dried berries or raisins and 1 pound of suet. Grind up the jerky (traditionally it was pounded into a powder). Mix the sweetening and dried berries in with the jerky. Melt the suet and when melted mix it thoroughly with the meat mix. Allow the pemmican to cool enough for the fat to be firm again and then pack as you like. Plastic bags work all right.

SMOKING MEAT AND FISH

I'm really not very expert on this subject. But I have some neighbors that have made smoking a highly developed part of their way of eating and they answered my questions for about two hours one evening. We have a smoker which we use occasionally. So between my own limited experience and what I've gleaned from other people's here goes.

Before meat is smoked it is cured the same as you do for jerky, bacon or hams. So you might look at those sections which I wrote up in considerable detail and have done a lot of. But you can actually smoke any meat. Poultry, fish, Cornish game hens, anything. You can buy meat at the store and take it home and smoke it. You can smoke cuts of meat like pork chops, if you really like the taste and enjoy doing it. To cure the meat the basics are the same as for jerky—a dry cure or a brine cure. If you want extra smoke flavor you can rub on that product called "liquid smoke" just before drying for the final stage.

SEASONING—Before the meat is smoked it is brined and seasoned similarly to the preparations for making jerky. A pamphlet offered free by Luhr Jensen and Sons, Hood River, Oregon 97031, contains detailed recipes for every variety of animal, fish and bird. (They sell smokers.) However, the seasoning and smoking are a matter of taste and the amounts and length of time given in that pamphlet for smoking tend to be more of a maximum than an average. Brining is the fastest way to prepare foods for smoking and curing and is the method used commercially. Morton's Sugar Cure is a commercial mix for the brining. You can make your own of half sugar (use white or brown) and half salt. Pepper and other spices are optional. Let it soak in the brine 7 or 8 hours, don't use an aluminum container or chipped enamels for brining. (Stainless steel is bright and shiny—aluminum is dull.) Be sure and rinse after brining.

BIRDS are hung with the cavity opening down and fastened to the top of the meat rack. They should be smoked about 2 hours to the pound. They can be

kept up to 2 weeks in the refrigerator after being smoked. They should be cooked before being eaten in a 250° oven, 15 minutes to the pound, or barbecued. Poultry is quite dark colored when it has been smoked. If desired, rub lightly with a garlic clove before smoking.

Fish—split down the back leaving belly skin intact. Spread out flat

Sausage—hang by string loop

Poultry—hang with body cavity down

FISH should be well cleaned and rinsed. You can leave the head on but you must remove the gills. If the fish is very large you had better fillet it or chunk it. Or at least split it down the back so it can be laid out flat. If the head is left on it's handy because you can hang the fish up by the head. To chunk a big fish like a salmon, cut lengthwise along the backbone, leaving two fillets. Then make sections out of them that are about 5 inches square.

A do-it-yourself method of seasoning that is good with salmon especially is to sprinkle the filleted pieces with smoke salt and then let them rest overnight, one on top of the other, with a plate on top to weight them. Keep in a cool place—not over 50°. Make sure you get the seasoning both inside and outside the fish. In the morning rinse them and pat dry with toweling or a cloth. Now sprinkle with lemon pepper, garlic salt, dill, cayenne, chili powder and paprika. That ought to make it hot enough. And then smoke for about 4½ to 5 hours, or until it feels firm. Trout should come out a golden brown.

You can prepare fish in a *plain brine* instead of all that hot stuff by just leaving them in a solution made of 1½ cups salt per gallon water. Soak 12 to 18 hours for small fish; as long as 36 hours for large ones or large pieces. Move the fish around in the solution occasionally. Then just take them out of the brine and let them dry and commence smoking. Turn every hour unless they are hanging. Smoke about 3 hours at 130° for very small fish like trout—up to 10 hours at 150° for large fish. The ideal is a moist and slightly oily effect when you're done.

Smoked fish can be used flaked or in fish stews, mixed in a salad with hard-boiled eggs, onion and so on, or combined with scrambled eggs.

RED MEAT—You can use the recipes given under jerky to cure red meat. Or you can use the straight brine cure given just above for fish. The meat has to be cut into jerky-type strips. In fact, smoked red meat is just another way of saying jerky. Smoke at 140°. You want to get the full flavor through but not burn it. Keep tasting until it suits you.

SAUSAGE is smoked about 4 hours. (Some people prefer as much as 8 hours.) You can tell by the color how it's coming. Some people don't like too much of a smoky flavor. You can taste test to see if it's where you want. Just fry up a sample, taste test, and then decide whether to take the rest out or leave them to continue smoking. To hang them in a smokehouse make crossbar sticks nearly the width of your smokehouse. Hang the sausages on them by the loop you made in the string. Don't crowd them. Leave a little space between so the smoke can get at them evenly. Let them hang at least a day after the smoking to give the smoke a chance to soak in. If you have really cool weather it would be good to let them hang there for as long as a week. Then put the sausages in the freezer.

HAM AND BACON—See "Dry Curing Hams and Bacon," in the Pig section.

A SMOKEHOUSE OR VERSION THEREOF—I've heard tell of all kinds of contraptions to do the job like a box rigged up that connects with a stovepipe and a completely homemade cabinet-sized plywood one. The latter is described in the Oregon State University (Corvallis, Oregon 97331) Extension Bulletin No. 788 titled "A Smokehouse for the Sportsman and Hobbyist." The University of Idaho (Moscow, Idaho 83843—about 27 miles from here) has more ideas in its Bulletin No. 373 of the College of Agriculture, Extension Service, titled "Game Cookery Guide." You can write and order either of those pamphlets.

There is a ready-made smoker on the market available mail-order from Luhr Jensen and Sons, Hood River, Oregon 97031. Last I knew it was $30. Probably more now. You can write them and get literature on it.

The smokehouse at the Jack Lohman ranch where I went to the butchering bee was about 4 feet by 8 feet with a door on one side. It had plywood sides and roof with a layer of tin over that. Inside there was a 2-foot-high section of metal barrel sitting on the ground with a tin sheet covering that loosely. The fire was inside the barrel. If you have access to an old outdoor privy that hasn't been used for at least 20 years you could make a smokehouse of this type out of it.

A number of neighbors of ours have smokers made out of old refrigerators and that's the kind we have, too. You sit a hot plate in the bottom with an extension cord running out the back door. That works fine when you burn sawdust or chips. The sawdust or chips should be in a drying pan or other container placed on the hot plate. Don't put them right on the element because that will shorten its life. The sawdust and chips can be bought commercially. Hickory Flavor is the product's name.

A refrigerator is handy because it has ready-made racks. The first rack should be 10 inches off the smoker floor. Then they need to be at least 10 inches

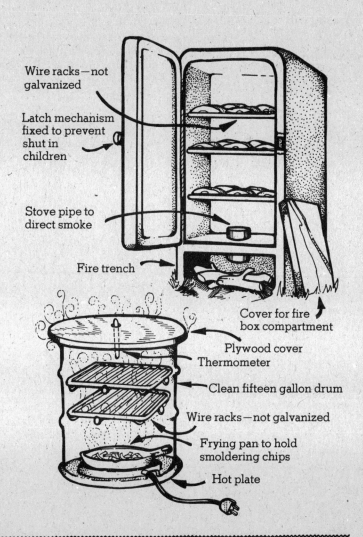

Wire racks—not galvanized

Latch mechanism fixed to prevent shut in children

Stove pipe to direct smoke

Fire trench

Cover for fire box compartment

Plywood cover
Thermometer

Clean fifteen gallon drum

Wire racks—not galvanized

Frying pan to hold smoldering chips

Hot plate

apart with plenty of room for the smoke to circulate between and around the meat. But like anything jerry-rigged, you'll have trouble with a refrigerator smoker. It's hard to keep it cool enough and it is important to do your smoking at fairly near the recommended temperature. You can try disconnecting all but one ring of your hot plate. Our other big problem is with gremlins pulling the plug.

If you are going to make a smokehouse out of an abandoned refrigerator (or freezer) be sure and fix the door so the children can't shut themselves in there and suffocate—yours or anybody's. Or you can punch vents in the tops. You can make a better smoker than the one I described above by removing the compressor and works, then cutting a hole in the bottom and putting a stovepipe between the refrigerator compartment and the underneath part where you can dig a fire trench. Tin cans can be used for stovepipe. Don't lay meat on galvanized racks. Use stainless steel or hooks. These old refrigerators nowadays are much easier to come by than barrels which is one way the old-timers used to do it.

Details for a frame smokehouse and for a cement-block one for old-time hams and bacons are in the government booklet on pig butchering mentioned under Pig. The way the store-type hams and the ones from custom cutters are smoked though is in a big fancy machine made of metal—a big box with a smoke maker underneath that gives that absolutely precise control of their temperature and amount of smoke. I know without asking that real people can't afford it. I've seen two and they seemed identical. About 5 x 5 feet large. Set up indoors.

One of the nearest living relatives I have on my mother's side is a red-haired (so am I) cousin named Liz, who is just about my age and she lives in Seattle with her family. Her husband can really smoke meat right and here's how he describes his method. He uses a 15-gallon drum with a plywood board over the top for a lid after he has cut the top out. He drills a small hole in the center of the plywood and that's to

hang a meat thermometer down in there. He puts a hot plate on the bottom of the drum with a frying pan on top of that. A couple handfuls of chips in the frying pan (that's the commercial smoke chips)—enough to cover the bottom. He adds more later as he needs to. He has wire racks above. The kind with legs on them that you use to cool cakes. He uses three altogether, one on top of the other and the meat is on the racks. The hot plate is adjusted for the meat thermometer to show a temperature of 135° or 140°. Have it warmed up good before you put the meat in there. He smokes salmon for 6 to 8 hours. To get his salmon ready for smoking, he soaks it overnight in a brine made by mixing half salt and half brown sugar until it is syrupy (in water, of course). For salmon you can take the bone out but leave the skin on and then smoke it, skin side down, and don't turn it over at all. Don't worry about it and keep pulling the lid off to see how it's doing. The only thing you need to worry about is the chips disappearing.

Smoking is done for the flavor. It really doesn't enhance the meat's keeping power much except as it dries it.

The wood you burn to make your smoke can't be just any. Fruit wood is best—apple, pear or cherry. Use a green wood, one that is freshly cut down and not yet dry. That way it will smolder rather than burn. You don't want it to really burn. Just smoke. Wild maple is good but take the bark off before you use it. How much wood you'll need depends on how fresh (green) it is, on the size of your smokehouse building and how long you're going to smoke. Around here apple wood for smokers is usually advertised in the classified section of the newspaper.

If you want to use your own wood, oak, apple, hickory, willow, cottonwood, birch, ash, maple or any other fruit and knot woods are all right. Don't use the resinous (evergreen) woods. Pine gives the meat a turpentine flavor. Cedar, fir and spruce make it taste medicated. Keep the smoke coming but it needn't be dense.

HOMEMADE GELATIN

I make homemade gelatin as often as I can get the makings. We butcher here at home fairly often and friends that butcher often let me have the feet. I can't buy feet to make jelly. Our local custom butcher is compelled by law, in the name of our health, to put all cow's feet from the knee down into a barrel and pour creosote over them, so he can't sell them to me to make gelatin or even give the bones to a neighbor lady's dog for gnawing. I think that law is the same everywhere now. But it's stupid and wasteful because by the time you've boiled the feet 4 to 7 hours to make gelatin, I'm sure no germs can survive.

After trying homemade gelatin I really could notice the acid bite and heavy sweetness of the presweetened, preflavored commercial gelatin powder. Homemade gelatin hasn't been bleached or preserved or excessively sugared so I'm sure it's better for me and I prefer the *taste*, too. Homemade gelatin is very mild with a bit of the taste of the animal. Personally I prefer beef and pork jelly. I think chicken jelly is a bit too chickeny but I make it, too, and add extra flavoring to disguise the chicken. It was a real research job for me learning how to do it. I started out with recipes such as the following and had to experiment for a long time to figure out what it was all about. But

here, for you, is everything I've learned about making homemade gelatin.

By "jelly" the old-time recipe writers meant gelatin. Now, we call pectin jellied preserves "jelly" and animal jellies "gelatin." To Great-grandmother they were both "jelly." "Stock" means the soup broth. Homemade gelatin is strained, clarified meat stock flavored any way you like. It sets up (jells) when it is chilled. It melts when it gets warm. To firm it just chill again and it will set up again. Gelatin seems to come out of the bones and ligaments. Feet are the boniest, ligamentiest part of all the animal and not good for anything else in the kitchen. If you don't have "4 calf's feet" (which is a sensible number if you just butchered a calf) substitute 2 or more pounds of soup bones. "Calf's-foot jelly" is famous but you can actually make homemade gelatin from cow's heels, too, which is in the same family only a little more grown up, beef soup bones, sheep or goat legs, pig's feet or backbone, chicken necks, heads, backs, feet, or any other bony pieces you can get hold of.

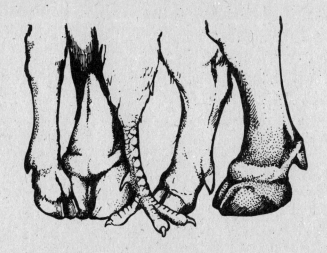

The stiffness of your jelly depends on what part of the animal you make it from, how long you boiled to concentrate it, and how much liquid you added while preparing it for table consumption. The stiffer you make it to start with, the more possibilities you have for adding flavoring later. Once you have your jelly you can divide it, using one part in one recipe and one part in another. If you're tasting as you go, be reassured, it tastes more like a proper gelatin after it has set up. Start your jelly at least the day before you plan to use it. The natural time is when convenient after butchering. You can keep the feet, skin and all, and other bones for jelly making in big paper bags in your freezer until you have time to work with them. I'll forewarn you—you don't get an awful lot for your work. This is a rare and precious delicacy.

Here's an outline of how to proceed:

1. Prepare bones. (If you're the independent type that means butcher.)

2. Cover them with water and simmer until reduced by at least one-half (4 hours or more) to get your concentrated stock. (For specific directions for each kind of animal see the following section.)

3. Chill enough to set up firmly. Remove fat from top and sediment from bottom of gelatin.

4. Clarify. (Complete directions given later.)

5. Flavor to suit yourself. (Recipes later.)

6. Reset, serve, and enjoy!

CALF'S-FOOT JELLY (OR COW HEEL)—Start with 4 calf or cow legs (or 3 or 5, if your cow is odd that way). Cut the foot off of each one at the first joint above the hoof. Use a sharp knife and a lot of elbow grease (depends on how good you are at finding joints). If you cook the leg bones, too, you'll have even

more gelatin but you'd need a *big* kettle or to saw them in chunks with a meat saw. Put the feet in a pan of hot water and boil 15 minutes. Remove. Slit the skin with a sharp knife and peel it off. You can cut the skin away from the hoof through the top portion of the hoof which you'll discover is soft. Cut in two between the "toes" and right on up through so that each foot is now in two pieces. Remove as much of the fat from between the toes as is practicable. Rinse them. Put into a big pan with a gallon of cold water. Bring it gradually to a boil. Boil uncovered, gently 6 or 7 hours. Skim off the scum that rises to the top several times as they are cooking. When the water is down to about 1 quart take the feet out of the pan.

Strain the liquid through a cloth or fine sieve. Measure it. Put it in the refrigerator or in a cool place and let it set up. In the morning take off the fat that has accumulated on the top and quickly rinse the outside of the pan in a little hot water for a moment to loosen the jelly. Then turn it over and the jelly will slip out. Trim off the sediment from the bottom. Clarify.

PIG JELLY—For some reason you get more gelatin from pig bones than from any other animal. Use the whole foot from the knee joint down. The backbone is very good for jelly making, too. Leave the skin on if the hair has been scraped off. Otherwise, skin the feet. No need to cut or trim. Cover with water and boil gently 4 to 7 hours; skin, toes and all. Skim off scum and fat several times while it cooks. Strain through a sieve to get out the bones and meat (save *that* for other dishes). Chill overnight. If your broth doesn't jelly firm enough to suit you boil it down some more.

MUTTON OR GOAT JELLY—Boil leg (shank) bones of sheep or goat for 6 or 7 hours.

CHICKEN "FOOT" JELLY—Use the head, feet, necks and backs, if you don't need them for something else. Or if you're a purist use just the smooth legs of birds less than a year old. With luck about three pair of feet will make a pint of jelly. Scald with boiling water and cook slowly a long time.

CLARIFYING THE JELLY—The clearer you can get your jelly the more attractive the final result will be and the better it will combine with other foods in recipes. Clarifying also reduces the animal flavor. But homemade gelatin, even when well clarified, is still a little on the milky order and not crystal clear like store gelatin. For every quart of gelatin in your pan add ½ cup sugar, white or brown, or honey, and the shells and slightly beaten whites of 5 eggs (less if you're short, but it won't turn out quite as clear). Stir in the sweetening, shells and egg whites as soon as the jelly is melted. You can leave out the sweetening if you want; it will still clarify. The following recipes are based on sweetened gelatin. Don't stir the jelly after it begins to get really warm. Let it boil 10 minutes, add ½ cup cold water and let boil 5 minutes longer. Take the pan off the fire, cover tightly, and let stand for a half hour in a warm place. Strain through several thicknesses of cloth. If you dip the cloth in hot water and wring it out it will help prevent the jelly from setting in the cloth during the straining process. Strain while hot—otherwise it will jell in the bag. You'll probably have to apply some pressure. Wring the loose ends of the bag to force the broth through. If it isn't clear enough the first time you can put it through the cloths again.

In the following jelly recipes set the homemade jelly in your *final* serving molds, preferably individual ones like custard dishes. This is because it doesn't transfer well once set—tends to lose shape and shine. Use *cold* sauces only. It melts easily. Serve *chilled*. It melts at room temperature. If it should start to melt on you or get broken up, just finish melting, return to refrigerator, and it will set up very nicely for you.

My Favorite Gelatin—Let jelly melt over low heat in pan. Add grape or orange juice frozen concentrate (I can make my own frozen concentrates) and lemon juice to taste. Cool the jelly. Add chopped, peeled apple and let set up again.

Coffee Jelly—Melt 1 cup jelly. Combine 2 teaspoons instant coffee with 2 tablespoons water. Add to jelly. Pour into mold and let chill to set. To make this with regular coffee, combine a *very firm* jelly with enough *strong* coffee to flavor. Add extra sweetening, if desired.

Lemon Jelly—Combine 1 cup jelly and the juice of 1½ lemons. Strain the lemon juice through a cloth before adding it to keep the gelatin as clear as possible. Chill.

Old Fashioned Wine Jellies—Start with a very stiff jelly. Add lemon juice and either red or white wine to taste (I prefer red). To a white wine jelly you could add some orange juice and grated (unparaffined) orange and lemon peel. To red wine jelly you could add red berries, such as raspberries, strawberries and currants.

Fruit Jelly—A thick gelatin can take the fruit directly and it will remain in suspension. Let it partly set up, then add the fruit. In a diluted gelatin the fruit sinks to the bottom. In the latter case chill a bottom layer until firm, then add a layer of fruit, then more melted gelatin. Chill until firm again, add another fruit layer and so on. Fresh peaches, apricots, plums and apples are good if cooked in a little sweetened water before going into the jelly. (Drain thoroughly before adding.) Strawberries, raspberries, grapes, cherries, chopped peeled apples and currants can go in raw. Your own sun- or oven-dried fruits and brandied cherries are fine, too, if you divide the larger pieces before adding to the jelly.

Sauce for Jelly—Great-grandmother served animal jellies with a sauce when she was able (just as she did the bread varieties she called "pudding"). The easiest is whipped cream. For salad-type jellies (make with raw vegetables, home sun-dried fruit and fruit juices) serve homemade mayonnaise, sour cream or yogurt dressing. The following vanilla sauce is nice on a dessert jelly and will use up some of those egg yolks left over from the clarifying process: Scald 1 cup milk. Add a little sweetening, 2 or more egg yolks and ½ teaspoon cornstarch. Cook, stirring constantly, in your double boiler until it thickens. Add a bit of real vanilla flavoring and stir until cool.

To substitute your gelatin in modern recipes use 2 cups of homemade gelatin for "one envelope" commercial gelatin and cut back on the fluid.

OTHER GELATIN PRODUCTS

HOMEMADE MEAT GLAZE is handy for adding color and flavor to soups, sauces and gravies. To put on meat, melt the glaze over hot water and apply with a pastry brush. To make it, start out with your bone stock as for homemade gelatin and boil until greatly reduced, keeping it well skimmed. Do not clarify. Figure on boiling 1 quart of bone stock down to a cup or less, transferring it to a smaller pan as it reduces. To get a darker color simmer the concentrated stock with caramelized sugar until it becomes like a syrup.

HOMEMADE BOUILLON "CUBES"—Make your stock and concentrate but do not clarify. Whatever type meat you used will be the flavor cube you get. Remove fat but not sediment. When you have a well-jellied stock you're ready for bouillon cube making.

1. Melt the jelly.

2. Season it *strong* with your favorite soup seasonings.

3. Pour the seasoned jelly 1 inch deep into some containers you can get along without, like cans, the smaller the better.

4. Set the cans in a water bath that reaches about one-third up the side of the can. Cook on low heat at least 8 hours more, refilling the water bath as needed.

5. Chill.

6. Separate concentrate from container.

7. Wrap in paper squares cut from grocery bags, or in foil.

8. Pack in jars with tight-fitting lids. Keep out of damp.

CROCK MINCEMEAT

Mincemeat belongs to the same family as fruitcakes and plum pudding—a little goes a long way. If you are making old fashioned crock mincemeat make it in late November, or whenever your weather turns cold and will stay that way a few months, and it should keep fine through the winter on your porch or anywhere outside. Mike and I kept a crock of it on a wide windowsill of our 7th-floor married-student housing in Manhattan during one frustrated urban winter and it was somehow a spiritual comfort.

Homemade mincemeat doesn't taste like store mincemeat at first. But the more it ages, the more it does. You can use any leftover liquid or fruit juice (such as the juice left after you've opened canned fruit) or even bits of leftover cooked meat by adding them to your mincemeat crock and stirring in once you've got it going. And it's a good idea to add a little more liquor or juice such as grape or orange just before baking a mincemeat pie. Each time you take out some to make pies, cookies and so forth, stir the whole crockful up thoroughly. A mincemeat pie is always made with two crusts. Bake 10 minutes at about 450°, then 30 minutes longer at a slightly lower temperature.

"True" mincemeat is probably the variety containing beef and suet, specifically that made from beef neck, but it can also be made from pork and wild meat. Of course, there are the mock varieties made from green tomatoes and raisins, and rhubarb and raisins. The latter two require special recipes.

Any mincemeat recipe can be stretched at the moment you want to bake with it by adding chopped apple. The apple is best if it is a tart one such as Winesap, Transparent or Jonathan. Crock mincemeats are very concentrated for the sake of easy preservation. A cup or more chopped apples to a pint of mincemeat really improves the mixture when you go to bake with it.

Old-time crock mincemeat contains sugar, spices, vinegar, molasses and alcohol, alone or in such combinations as to make it self-preserving. More modern recipes aren't as strong and must be canned or frozen for long-term storage. If you are going to can your mincemeat you might want to leave out the spices and add them just before using it since spices darken the mincemeat. To can mincemeat process 30 minutes in a hot water bath or 10 minutes at 10 pounds in a pressure cooker. To freeze just put in cartons and place in the freezer. If you have leftover crock mincemeat and spring is coming just package it up and freeze.

In any mincemeat recipe I'd recommend using homemade candied fruits, and home-dried raisins, if you can. Homemade citron is so much nicer than the store kind which is loaded with preservatives. You'll taste the difference!

Easy Crock Mincemeat—Mix 2 cups chopped or ground cooked beef, 4 cups sugar, 1 whole nutmeg, 2 cups cider (boiled down from 4 cups), juice of 2 lemons (and grated rinds if unparaffined), 4 teaspoons salt, 4 teaspoons cinnamon, 4 cups fruit (your preferred mixture of raisins, candied citron, currants), 1 teaspoon cloves and 1 cup suet (beef fat), finely chopped. Bring it all to boiling. Boil 10 minutes, then pack in a small crock and pour a little brandy on top. When you want to use, add more chopped apple and some raisins.

Crock Mincemeat with Brandy—Boil 4 pounds lean beef until quite tender, cool and chop or grind fine. Peel, core, and chop fine 1 peck (11 pounds) apples. Mix beef and apples, then add 2 pounds seeded raisins, 2 pounds currants, ½ pound candied citron, chopped, 1½ pounds beef suet, chopped or ground while cold, 6 cups sweet apple cider, 1 cup dark molasses, 1 teaspoon cinnamon, 1 teaspoon ground cloves, 1 tablespoon salt and 5 pounds sugar. (Increase the spices if you like it spicier.) Mix in a kettle, cook slowly for 5 hours and cool. Add 1 cup good brandy. Pack in your crock, cover and set in a cool place. To use in baking, add 1 cup chopped apple per cup mincemeat.

Teetotalers Crock Mincemeat—Stew 2 pounds lean beef until tender, cool and chop or grind fine. Add 1 pound chopped beef suet. Pare, core and chop 4 pounds tart apples and add. Then add 3 pounds sugar, 2 pounds currants, 2 pounds seeded raisins, 1 whole nutmeg, ½ teaspoon ground mace, juice of 2 oranges and of 2 lemons (and the grated peels, if unparaffined), ½ pound candied citron and 1 tablespoon salt. Cook an hour and pack into a stone crock of appropriate size. Cover with a plate and set in a cold place.

Pork Mincemeat—If you are doing your own butchering this is one good way to use the hog's head (another is headcheese) and backbone. Boil until tender. Then skin the head, bone out the meat and grind it up. Don't use all the fat. For each 8 pounds of pork add 2½ pounds dried apples, ground and then cooked, and 3 pounds of green apples, if you can get them (or 3 pounds of fresh *tart* apples). Put 4 whole lemons and 4 peeled oranges through the grinder. Combine ground fruit, pork, 3 pounds of raisins, 1 quart vinegar, 2¾ pounds sugar, 1 tablespoon allspice and 1 tablespoon cinnamon. Cook for 1 hour.

Wild Mincemeat—If you want to make mincemeat out of venison bones and scraps, trim away as much fat as possible and simmer the remainder until tender. Then refrigerate in the cooking liquid overnight (or until you can remove any remaining fat from the top of the liquid). Bone the meat and coarsely grind it. For 2 quarts venison (or 4 pounds) combine 3 pounds peeled, cored, ground apples, and ½ pound ground beef suet. Then add 2 pounds seedless raisins, 1 pound seeded raisins, ½ pound currants, 1 tablespoon salt, 1 tablespoon cinnamon, 1 tablespoon ground ginger, 1 tablespoon ground cloves, 1 tablespoon ground nutmeg, 1 teaspoon allspice, 2 quarts fruit juice (such as cider or grape) and 1 pound brown sugar. Simmer 2 hours being careful not to let it stick. Can or freeze.

Deer or Elk Mincemeat—Combine 8 pounds cooked deer or elk meat (ground—trim away all fat first), 4 pounds raisins, 2 pounds currants, 8 quarts chopped apples, 1 pound ground beef suet, 1 cup molasses, 2 cups vinegar, juice of 1 lemon and 1 orange and ground rinds, 2 cups citron, 5 pounds sugar, 3 tablespoons cinnamon, 2 tablespoons allspice, 1 tablespoon cloves, 1 teaspoon nutmeg and salt to taste. Cook the ingredients until well blended and of the right consistency. Can (makes about 8 quarts) or freeze.

RECIPES USING HOMEMADE MINCEMEAT

Thanksgiving Pie—Mix 1 pint mincemeat with 2 cups peeled, cored, chopped tart apples. Fill an unbaked pastry shell. Top with pastry. Bake 10 minutes at about 450°, then 30 minutes at a lower temperature.

Filled Mincemeat Cookies—Blend ½ cup soft shortening, 1 cup sugar and 2 eggs. Stir in 2 tablespoons thick cream and 1 teaspoon vanilla. Sift together 2½ cups flour, ¼ teaspoon soda and ½ teaspoon salt. Add to shortening mixture. Gather dough into a round ball and chill for 1 hour. Then roll out to about 1/16 inch thick. Cut 3-inch rounds or squares. Put a rounded teaspoonful of mincemeat on each dough round. Fold the dough over pressing edges together with the floured tines of a fork or with fingertip (a square would thus become a triangle). Put the filled cookies on a greased cookie sheet. Bake at 400° 8 to 10 minutes.

Mincemeat Cookies—Cream 1 cup shortening. Add ½ cup brown sugar and blend well. Add 2 eggs and beat thoroughly. Mix ½ teaspoon salt and 1 teaspoon soda with 3¼ cups flour. Alternately add 1½ cups mincemeat and the flour mixture to the liquid mixture. The liquid amount depends how liquid your mincemeat is. You might want to add a little more or less flour to get the right cookie consistency. Finally, add ½ cup chopped nuts (more or less depending on if you have them). Mix. Drop with a spoon onto your greased cookie sheet. Bake 10 minutes in a 375° oven.

Mincemeat Jelly Roll—Combine 2 cups sifted flour, ¼ cup sugar, 1 teaspoon salt and ¼ cup milk. Add 1 tablespoon dry yeast dissolved in ⅓ cup lukewarm water and a beaten egg. Let rise. Punch down. Let rise again.

Divide dough in half. Roll out each half to a ½-inch thickness. Spread a layer of your mincemeat over each half. Roll it up jelly-roll style. Pinch edges to seal. Let rise once more. Bake at 350° about 30 minutes, or until nicely browned and crusty on outside.

Mincemeat Muffins—Beat 1 egg with 1¾ cups milk. Add 2 teaspoons melted butter. Combine 3 cups whole wheat flour, 3 teaspoons baking powder, 1 teaspoon soda, 1 tablespoon sugar, and 1 teaspoon salt and then add to liquid. Add 1 cup mincemeat and 2 teaspoons fruit juice or water. Mix it all together well. Grease your muffin tin and fill the cavities two-thirds full. Bake at 375° for 25 minutes.

Cranberry Mincemeat Pie—Combine 1½ cups mincemeat-chopped apple combination, 1½ cups cranberry sauce (preferably homemade and not too sweet), ¼ cup orange juice and 3 tablespoons flour. Mix and pour into an unbaked shell. Cover with a top crust. Pinch sides and brush the top with milk. Bake at 400° 50 minutes.

Mincemeat-Oatmeal Cookies—Sift together 1½ cups plus 2 tablespoons flour, ¾ teaspoon soda and ½ teaspoon salt. Cream ½ cup lard and then gradually add 1 cup brown sugar. Add 1 well-beaten egg and 1⅓ cups mincemeat. Add flour mixture gradually and then 1½ cups rolled oats. Drop by spoonfuls onto greased cookie sheet. Bake at 350° about 15 minutes.

Mincemeat Apples—Try baking apples with the cores out and the cavity stuffed with mincemeat.

Mincemeat Brown Betty—Make 2 cups bread crumbs, preferably of homemade whole wheat bread. Butter a bread pan. Put one-third of the crumbs in it. Add a layer of 2 peeled, sliced apples, then a layer of ½ cup mincemeat. Sprinkle over a pinch of cinnamon. Add another layer of crumbs, 2 more sliced apples, another ½ cup mincemeat, another sprinkle of cinnamon, and the remaining crumbs. Pour ¼ cup orange juice over all. Dot with butter. Bake at 350° for 30 minutes. Good with cream.

GRAVY

Good gravy to go on the potatoes can be made anytime you fry or roast meat. When your meat is done remove it from the pan. Estimate how much gravy your family can use. If you want 1 cup, pour off the grease until you have about 2 tablespoons left, 4 for 2 cups, and so on. If you don't have that much add a little melted butter, bacon drippings or lard. Loosen all the good brown bits in the bottom of your pan (assuming you don't have a burnt mess in which case salvage some grease by pouring off the top and start over in another pan) and add 2 tablespoons whole wheat or unbleached flour per 2 tablespoons grease.

For heaven's sake don't stop to actually "measure" the hot grease and flour. You can learn to estimate close enough by looking at it and really it doesn't make that much difference if you use a little more or less of either. Just don't have a whole lot of extra grease because it will float on top of your gravy and look and taste yuk!

Over medium heat make a paste of the brown bits, grease and flour with your fork and let it cook a couple minutes, stirring constantly. This accomplishes the browning and cooking of your flour and gives you almost an "instant" gravy. Your mashing action with the fork will break up potential lumps. Now add a little pour of liquid. Stir it in until the lumps are gone, then add more and stir again until the lumps are out and again until your liquid is all added. You can add more liquid each time but start with a very little. Stop adding liquid when your gravy is thinned to where you want it.

For liquid use your potato water or water off another cooked vegetable or milk. I drain the vegetable waters into the gravy (or else add them to the animal pail) then cook that down to the wanted density. Pork chop gravy is good with half milk and half water or all milk. Chicken gravy is good with half or all milk. Beef gravy is good made with part milk or just your vegetable water. Deer, elk, and other game gravies don't get along good with milk. Game gravies are much improved by adding a couple tablespoons of currant, wild plum or some other tart jelly. For roast turkey, duck or goose, use no milk, but add the chopped cooked giblets and the giblet broth for a delicious gravy.

If you get the gravy too thin and watery, you can boil it until it thickens again enough to suit you. Finally salt and pepper to taste. Really taste it until it seems right, but don't burn your tongue! Then serve to go on your meat and mashed potatoes, or rice, or thick slices of bread in a sturdy bowl with a good dipper. And put the pan to soak in the sink so it won't be a chore to wash.

If you want to thicken a broth as from a stew or to make gravy when a lot of good meat juices are in the pan one way is to skim most of the excess grease, get out your eggbeater, sprinkle some flour on the top, and then quickly grab the beater and beat as hard as you can until the lumps are sort of out. Keep adding more flour in this way until you get your gravy the consistency you want. If you scattered the flour too thickly or lost the race to get it beaten in before the lumps got set you can still strain the gravy through a sieve and strain out or mash out the lumps.

Gravy Trick—Put flour in a jar that has a tight-fitting lid. Add cold water, about 1½ times by volume. Shake by hand. Never fill jar over three-fourths full. Add to the gravy or stew slowly, stirring the whole time. Howard Perkins (Pennsauken, New Jersey) told me this one.

Roux—But here's a better way to thicken the stew. It was sent to me by Virginia Boegli, the high school friend who drew some of the illustrations for the early editions of this book. Virginia and I went to high school together one year in Bozeman, Montana. She made good gravy and good bread, too.

"I've discovered a great little French technique that really simplifies gravy. It's called roux. A roux is a paste of about equal parts fat and flour. The fat may be drippings or butter or so forth. A roux can be blended into hot liquid without all that lumpiness. When my roasting pan has a hard brown coating after roasting meat I like to put water in it and simmer to get all that goody. Then stir in a roux and seasoning—Voilà, it's gravy. If you want you can make a jar of roux and keep it in the refrigerator. A glob the size of a walnut thickens about a quart of gravy or a large pot of stew. If in doubt, it's easy to add a little at a time."

White Sauce is a meatless white gravy. It's good poured over bland vegetables such as boiled onions, cauliflower or asparagus. I use it mixed with diced leftover ham (omit the salt for home-cured ham) to get an extra meal out of the ham. To make white sauce, melt some butter in your frying pan. Soak it up with an equal measure of flour and brown a couple minutes, stirring constantly. Now gradually dilute with *milk*, stirring constantly. Season and it's ready to be poured over your vegetables.

MAKING LEFTOVER MEAT INTO SANDWICH FILLINGS

These sandwich fillings are meant to be spread on homemade bread. Store bread is too salty and generally "strong" tasting for them. Any leftover meat can be made into a fine sandwich filling. Just do this—

1. Remove bone and fat (except for old-time potted ham).

2. Slice or grind the meat.

3. Moisten it with a salad dressing, such as mayonnaise or tartar sauce.

You can make plain meat fillings this way or with the variations below. Croquettes are another good way to use meat leftovers. So is sliced meat warmed up in leftover gravy and served with rice or sliced boiled spuds sautéed in a little butter with some chopped fresh green onion.

Ham and Egg—Grind the ham with chopped hard-cooked egg. Moisten with mayonnaise or cream dressing. Add finely chopped red or green pepper and mustard.

Ham and Pickle—Grind 2 cups ham. Mix smooth with 1 small ground pickle, 2 teaspoons prepared mustard, 2 tablespoons butter and ½ teaspoon pepper.

Ham and Everything—Mix together 1 cup chopped ham, 1 chopped hard-cooked egg, 2 tablespoons chopped green pepper, 2 tablespoons chopped sour pickle and a pinch of pepper. Moisten with mayonnaise. Add thin pickle slices and strips of green pepper, if desired.

Old-Time Potted Ham—Grind one-third fat and two-thirds lean to a smooth paste. Add salt and cayenne pepper to taste. Heat and pack in small pots.

Ham and Chicken—Grind 1 cup cooked chicken meat, white or dark, and ¼ cup cooked ham. Mince ½ cup celery, 1 tablespoon green pepper and mix with meat. Moisten with about ¼ cup mayonnaise.

Chicken Salad Sandwich Filling—Grind cooked chicken and moisten with mayonnaise. Add crumbled crisp bacon or chopped celery.

Chopped Veal—Grind about 1¼ cups veal and season with 1 teaspoon salt, 1 tablespoon lemon juice and a little pepper and mustard, if desired.

Chopped Mutton—Grind cold mutton or lamb, about 1¼ cups of it, until fine. Season with 1 teaspoon salt, 1 tablespoon pickled nasturtium seeds, if you have them, 1 teaspoon chopped fresh mint, if you have it, a pinch of pepper and 1 tablespoon lemon juice. This is good on whole wheat bread with lettuce.

Beef Sandwich Spread—Grind the meat, add mayonnaise to moisten, salt and pepper to taste, and stir in some chopped green onion or green pepper or pickle. Doesn't keep well, so eat it all up.

HASH

The basic hash recipe is to cut up cooked meat (mutton, beef, corned beef, or what-have-you) into small pieces (or grind it) and add diced cold boiled spuds. The usual proportion is half meat and half potato. Some people stretch it with more potato. You could add chopped onion, too. Moisten with leftover gravy, soup stock, egg, or even milk or water. Season with salt and pepper. I usually make it with leftover gravy.

When wanted to eat turn into an oiled frying pan, and bake in a hot oven until brown, or fry on the top of the stove, turning once. Slightly beaten eggs mixed with the hash will make it stick together better if you don't use gravy. If you cook an especially moist hash slowly in a covered pan for about half an hour, until there is a rich crust on the bottom, you can fold it like an omelet and serve that way. Hash is a good breakfast (or lunch) dish with eggs on the side and good for using up leftovers.

German Hash—Mix 1 cup chopped cooked beef, 1 cup chopped tart apples, 1 cup chopped boiled potatoes, 1 teaspoon salt and a pinch of paprika. Sauté 1 small onion, chopped fine, in 3 tablespoons butter until transparent. Add the other ingredients to the onion and butter and heat until very hot, stirring often.

A Corned Beef Hash from Scratch—Simmer 4 pounds corned beef until tender. Keep meat covered with water throughout. Remove meat (save water) and chop fine. Cook a quartered cabbage, 3 potatoes and 2 onions in the beef water. Cool and chop vegetables and combine with beef. Add pepper and salt to taste. Let the hash blend at least 12 hours before cooking. Bake in the oven (about 400°) in a well-buttered shallow pan until brown.

MEAT SOUP

Consommé—Get ready a 4-pound or so chicken for the pot. Saw some beef bones into pieces—about 2 pounds worth. Cut up 2 pounds of beef. Put them all in a covered kettle and add water to cover. Let it all soak an hour and then put over the fire and bring quickly to the boiling point. Reduce heat at once to simmering and cook 6 or 7 hours. In the last hour of cooking add 1 tablespoon salt, ½ cup carrots, ½ cup onion, ½ cup celery, 1 teaspoon peppercorns, 2 whole cloves, 1 allspice berry, 1 small bay leaf, 2 sprigs parsley, 1 sprig thyme, 1 sprig savory and 1 sprig marjoram. Cut the vegetables into reasonable-sized pieces. At the end of the last hour of cooking, strain the soup. Then chill it and when cold remove any fat that has solidified on the surface. Clarify by reheating with 2 slightly beaten egg whites, stirring constantly until it boils. Boil 5 minutes. Then let stand until it settles. Strain through two thicknesses of cheesecloth.

Bouillon—Use 3½ pounds beef. Put in a pan with water and let stand an hour. Then put over heat in covered pot and bring to boiling point. Skim off scum. Reduce heat and simmer 3 hours. Chop 1 onion, 1 carrot, 1 sprig parsley, and 2 stalks celery and add to soup with ½ bay leaf, 2 cloves, 6 peppercorns and 1 teaspoon salt. Let simmer an hour more. Strain into a bowl and chill. Remove fat when it is firm and clarify as for consommé.

Scotch Broth (a mutton soup)—Trim all the fat from about a 1½-pound neck of mutton or some other piece. Put it in your pan, cover with water and bring slowly to a boil. Skim off the scum and then add salt and pepper and about 2 ounces of pearl barley. Simmer 1 hour. Add 1 onion, diced, 2 leeks, if you have them, some chopped parsley, 1 large carrot, 1 small turnip and a few sticks of celery. Continue cooking another hour. Now cool enough to work with. Take out the meat, remove the bone, cut up the meat and return it to the broth. Reheat, add a little chopped parsley and you have your soup.

Mock Turtle Soup (Calf's Head Soup)—Boil a beef or veal head (and feet, if you want) until the meat separates from the bones. Remove bones. Cut meat into 1-inch pieces. Boil an hour more (until tender) with an onion and bay leaf. Add 8 sliced small onions, 1 tablespoon parsley, and season to taste with mace, cloves and salt. (Great-grandmother added the chopped brains and soup balls made of butter and cracker crumbs mixed, and veal forcemeat balls near the end.)

To can soup stock make it fairly concentrated. Cook your bones, chicken, etc., until tender in lightly salted water. Then chill. Remove fat and bones. Keep the meat and sediment. Reheat and pour your boiling soup into jars, leaving 1 inch head space. Put on lids and process in a pressure canner at 10 pounds pressure (240°) 20 minutes for pint jars, 25 minutes for quart jars. This is a good way to settle your soup stock supply problem and to get the most of the bones when butchering has happened and you have a lot of them. Don't use bones from pork, burned pieces, smoked or corned meats, or fatty lamb to make stock. If you don't like canning you could freeze your stock.

Dolly and the rabbit love each other. Farm children learn to love the animals, and yet to let them go when it becomes necessary. But this rabbit will be a mama many times and doesn't have to be butchered.

Pierre Champeaux is teaching the rabbit-butchering class at the School of Country Living, and the students have mixed reactions to what's happening!

This calf is only about 20 minutes old and is getting his shots. Mike has the needle, Carla is sympathizing, and Danny is learning.

In this picture you see a 2,000-pound bull-to-be trying to find his very first drink of milk. He hasn't quite made the connection yet. Both he and his mother are still kind of wet. An older calf is looking curiously through the fence at them.

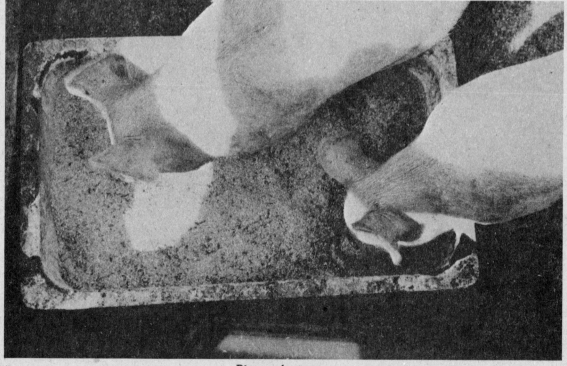

Pigs prefer to eat.

HERBS, SPICES, FORMULAS AND REMEDIES

"HERBS" AND "SPICES"

"Herbs" technically mean the leaves or other parts of aromatic plants grown in the temperate zone whereas "spices" are the stems, leaves, roots, seeds, flowers, buds or bark of aromatic plants grown in the tropics. Because we can grow them ourselves, the herbs, as contrasted with the spices, can be used fresh from the garden.

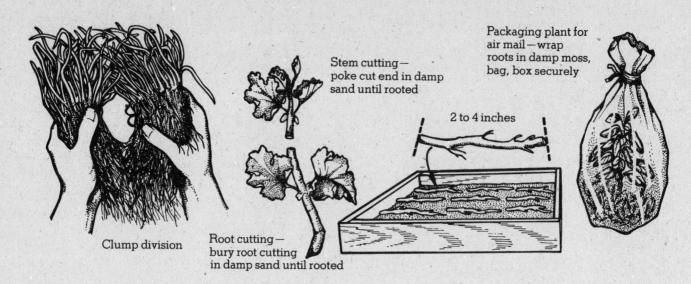

Stem cutting—
poke cut end in damp
sand until rooted

Packaging plant for
air mail—wrap
roots in damp moss,
bag, box securely

2 to 4 inches

Clump division

Root cutting—
bury root cutting
in damp sand until rooted

Herbs are or aren't a necessity of life depending on your convictions, but for sure they're a pleasant luxury and comfort that comes so naturally to country living that I'm including them in this book. We use three herb teas mainly. That's camomile that we gather growing in open places all over the farm, wild mint that grows down along Brady Gulch Creek that runs along the bottom of our canyon, and wild strawberry leaves that we gather from the tender little plants that grow in the timbered places. Honey complements the taste of any herb-type tea just perfectly, really helps bring out the flavor. I'll have lots of honey this summer. I even have a batch of bees living two feet away from the back door in the old refrigerator that used to be a smoker. It's a beehive now since they moved in. But I kind of enjoy their neighborly buzzing. Anyway, herbs and honey go together.

Some people doctor with herbs a lot. I know comfrey is indeed a comforting drink no matter what ails you. Healthwise though I recommend a Seventh-Day Adventist doctor as providing the best of both worlds. Once when I went to my Adventist doctor full of mysterious problems he first gave me a couple prescriptions, then some marital advice and then he prayed for me. Now that's doctoring! And that was before I became a Christian even. The gist of his advice was I should quit trying to write this book. He continued to offer it at every visit and as you see I didn't obey so any health problems I end up with are no fault of his! Fact is, though, I feel great.

PROPAGATION—A lot of the herbs are perennials and you can get yourself more of the same kind of plant ("propagation") by digging up a plant that is at least two years old and dividing the root clumps (costmary, for example). Be gentle and let the plant find its own natural separations. Try not to tear the roots as you pull them apart. *Don't* use a knife. If you're having a real hard time leave the roots in a bucket of water overnight. That will help relax them and make it easier for you.

Lemon balm, comfrey, mint and horseradish are some of the herbs you can propagate by root cuttings. For a root cutting you literally cut off a piece of root from an established plant (at least two years old) and then plant it in a new place to make a new plant. The piece of root you cut off for replanting should be at least 2 inches long. If the root is small, thin and just not husky-looking take more than 2 inches—like 4 inches.

BUYING—An interesting catalog for you to get is *The Herb and Rare Seed Catalog* put out by Nichols Garden Nursery, 1190 North Pacific Highway, Albany, Oregon 97321. This is a homemade-looking black and white catalog. Nichols carries things like black sweet corn that the Aztecs were growing when Cortez came along; red beans from Guatemala with a 3,000-year history and Santa Maria ninquito beans from Portugal that are tiny and pink. French varieties of carrots. Italian onions. Melons from Persia and France (the Charantais is a good one but you have to pick it at just the moment of ripeness—you can tell when it's ripe by the smell) and many, many herb varieties.

Seeds from herbs grown in places other than your hometown often fail. The safest seeds for you are those grown in your own or neighbors' gardens since these are acclimated. You'll have better success with outside seeds if you "stratify" them before planting. In fact some seeds will not grow at all without this treatment. That means freezing and thawing them. Put them in your freezer in a paper or plastic package and leave them there at least overnight. Now take them out and let them thaw completely. Do this at least three times with the package.

A lot of the herbs you can't start from seed and a lot of them are still rare enough that local nurseries don't carry them. More common ones are listed in the major seed catalogs as seeds. Burpee has anise, basil, borage, caraway, catnip, chicory, dill, flax, horehound, horseradish, lavender, marjoram, nasturtium, parsley, rosemary, sage, savory and thyme. Gurney carries many of these as well as chokecherry and mint. Many herbs do fine even in a window box or potted through the wintertime—parsley, chives, mint, rosemary, tarragon, oregano, sage, sweet marjoram and savory are all in this class. For extensive information about herb gardening and descriptions of many kinds that this chapter omits as well as further hints on how to preserve and use them I refer you to Sections 34 and 35 of Rodale and Staff's *How to Grow Vegetables and Fruits by the Organic Method.* You can mail-order it from Rodale Press, Emmaus, Pennsylvania 18049 or from me here in Kendrick, Idaho, for $12.50 plus postage.

You can also mail-order herb seeds, plants, flower oils, herb books, kits, rose jars, rose beads and so on from Shuttle Hill Herb Shop, 256B Delaware Avenue, Delmar, New York 12054. And they have a fine herb catalog. Kiehl Pharmacy, Inc., 109 Third Avenue, New York, New York 10003 has books, herbs, gums, oils and so on. They sell only one-pound amounts and want no orders less than $20. Indiana Botanic Gardens, 626 Seventeenth Street, Hammond, Indiana 46325, is also a good source for herbs and oils.

And then there's Borchelt Herb Gardens, 474 Carriage Shop Road, East Falmouth, Massachusetts 02536. They have things like flaxseed, lavender flowers and orrisroot powder, but they don't ship live plants. Medicine Wheel Family, P.O. Box 1121, Idyllwild, California 92349, wholesales bulk herbs and has an interesting list you can write for. Spend $1.25 on *The Herb Buyer's Guide* (write Pyramid Publications, Inc., 919 Third Avenue, New York, New York 10022) and you get 27 pages of addresses for mail-order herbs plus other herb information.

GRINDING—Equip yourself with an old fashioned mortar and pestle and spice mill. With those you can mash seeds, crush dried herbs, peppercorns and so forth, and add them fresh when wanted. The old-time implements for grinding spice were called "spice mortars" and "spice mills" or they used a mortar and pestle. The spices are ground in a mortar by crushing with the pestle—just pure elbow grease.

You can mail-order a mortar and pestle set from Maid of Scandinavia, 3245 Raleigh Avenue, Minneapolis, Minnesota 55416. They also have a supply of hard-to-find whole and ground spices and extracts that includes whole Jamaica ginger, cardamom seeds, juniper berries, saffron, white peppercorns, vanilla beans, ground fennel seeds, fenugreek, gumbo filé (sassafras leaves), arrowroot, chicory, oil of wintergreen and oil of spearmint. You can grind herbs in your blender or juicer too, but I prefer them the old fashioned ways. Ginger root was once invariably sold intact and people grated their own. They also crushed their cinnamon bark and ground the cloves. Now you can take your choice, but the rule is the more freshly

ground the better tasting so when buying, figure the wholer the better and take it home and grind it yourself. If you don't believe me I suggest the sniff test! Grind some whole allspice or peppercorns. Sniff. Then sniff your kitchen container of preground spice.

STORING—To store herbs I use baby food jars, cleaned, dried, filled and with lid on tightly. Keeping them in airtight containers helps prevent flavor deterioration. And try to keep them in a dark, dry place away from heat—not on a shelf right over your stove. The cool storage is to inhibit evaporation of the flavoring oil in the herb and the dark is to protect the color which fades when exposed to light.

HARVESTING

Gather herbs on a dry day, early in the morning but after the dew is off. The season to harvest varies with the species. Parsley and chervil are dried in May, June and July. Burnet and tarragon are gathered in June, July and August; marjoram and mint in July; summer savory and lemon thyme at the end of July and August. The tender young leaves that appear before the flowering are usually best. Get them before they are showing signs of going to seed. That happens after they blossom. The blossoms turn into seed clusters. Then their energy goes into making seed and the plant gets bitter or at best not at its prime. If you are gathering wild herbs remember that roadsides and some fields and meadows get heavy doses of insecticide. Harvest somewhere else. Cut the herbs with scissors and put them into clean pillowcases or flour sacks or some such. Then take them home and carefully pick over. If dust is a problem rinse in cool water, shake and drain.

You can either dry or freeze your leafy herbs for winter use. **TO DRY,** you can spread individual leaves on sheets of paper or screens to dry in the shade in an attic, or in the slow oven if you prefer. Direct hot sunlight would ruin them by burning or browning. A little sun early or late in the day is OK. Don't let them get rained or dewed on. Or you can cut off the top 6

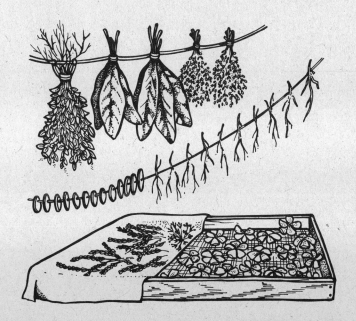

inches of the plant, or even use whole plants, bunch them and hang up the root end upward in a shady airy place. Tie them in bundles with a string and allow at least two weeks for drying. Hanging works well with anise, basil, marigold, marjoram, mint, oregano, parsley, rosemary, sage, savory, tarragon and thyme.

Some herbs are huge (like 6-foot-high) plants with real big leaves. With comfrey, borage and costmary you can tear the midrib away from the rest of the leaf and then tear the rest of the leaf into smaller pieces. That helps the leaves dry better and prevents mold. Or hang these big leaves individually to dry. Mint, lemon balm and most other small-leaved kitchen herbs will easily dry in the shade within three days, but if you tear the small leaves away from the plant stem and discard it that will speed it up. The problem with tearing the leaves is they don't hold their flavor as well. Drying the big moist-leaved plants is harder. Turn all drying leaves once or twice a day. Keep good air circulation. The aromatic herbs shouldn't be exposed to too much heat. If you want to oven dry, spread in shallow pans in a 140° oven with the door ajar for 1 or 2 hours. After drying you can store the leaves in a glass jar with a tight lid.

TO FREEZE dip in and out of boiling water, dry, pack in small amounts in a plastic bag and freeze. The cheaper "baggies" work fine. Herbs that freeze well are anise, basil, chives, coriander, marigold, mint, oregano, rosemary, sage, savory, tarragon and thyme. Take out of the freezer only the amount you intend to use. Whether freezing or drying label all containers. Frozen and dried the herbs tend to look alike and you may not be able to smell the difference.

ROOTS—Herb roots are generally preferable in the fresh rather than the dry state. Dig in the fall after the roots and leaves are dead or mature or dig before they start growing in the spring. Wash in cool water quickly. You can then string them up in a place where they will be warm enough to dry soon but not exposed to the sun, such as in an attic, or expose them to sun, or to an oven's heat if you aren't confident that you can dry them completely otherwise. Or you can slice and dry in the shade where air circulation is good. Store when thoroughly dry and brittle. If protected from extremes of heat and cold the roots will keep fine for years. Store so as to protect from the air as much as possible.

SEEDS—To save herb seeds pick the entire stalk when the seedpods are fully formed but not yet burst. Spread the pods on a cloth in the sun to dry. If it takes more than one day bring them in at night and stir occasionally while they are outside. When dry, shell and store your seeds in a tightly covered container in a cool, dry place.

FLOWERS—Don't bruise or overheat. Collect just after they have bloomed. Don't pile them up. Dry on a screen if possible. Harvest orange flowers and elderberry flowers in May, June and July.

My head just does not want to work this morning. I have so many things to do and my brains are moving like molasses in January. Mike said an angry word as he went out the door to work and I'm not going to be right all day. Dear God, make that be a lesson to me to really watch my tongue and speak only kind and loving things. God, if I deserved it make me better. Guide me, Lord. Sometimes things get so confusing. Sometimes I'm not sure what it is You really do want me to do. Help me to get everything done this morning that I've got to do. Thank You, God. Thank You for the joy to come.

You know there's always pain and trouble in life. In fact the harder people try to run away from it the worse they're going to end up with it. The best thing to do is figure out what it's good for. God promised that when you let Him take care of you all things work to your good.

That's a promise I really depend on. I know no matter how bad things look, He's going to make it turn into such a blessing for me that I'll be glad it all happened. God doesn't send His people into battle to get wounded. When God sends you into a struggle it's because there's a victory He wants you to win and if you just hang in there and keep trusting Him and struggling on and don't let yourself start thinking that even God couldn't turn this one into a victory it will all come out so *happily*.

HERB RECIPES AND PRODUCTS

TO USE YOUR DRIED HERBS—If you dried your herbs whole, when you want to use them crumble or rub through a sieve to remove the stems and midribs. (They hold the flavor better when not powdered.) If you soak them in lemon juice or wine before adding to a dish the flavor will come out better. The dried leaves by quantity are at least three times as strong as the fresh. Figure ½ teaspoon dried (¼ teaspoon powdered) herb is equivalent to a 1 heaping tablespoon of chopped fresh herbs. Another way to figure it is about ¼ teaspoon dried herb in a dish for four.

HERB BUTTER—To make herb butters soften the butter and cream into it finely chopped herbs to your taste. Chives or watercress are fine. You may want to add a little lemon juice. Use 1 tablespoon (well packed) of fresh herbs or ½ teaspoon dried ones per ¼ cup butter. Use the herb butter on bread, on hot meats, or with eggs.

HERB VINEGAR—Recipes are in the Sours chapter.

TO MAKE AN EXTRACT—Gather fresh herbs and pound to a pulp with a mortar and pestle. Let the plant parts concerned stand in pure distilled vinegar or corn, sunflower or olive oil or alcohol. (Getting 180-proof edible alcohol to make an alcohol-based extract is not so simple for us as it was for Great-grandmother. But you can substitute vodka. It's half water and half alcohol, equal volumes in 100 proof.) Use 2 tablespoons pounded herb to ¾ cup liquid. The liquid then absorbs the soluble parts of the plant. Shake daily for 3 weeks. Keep at a warmish temperature, like in the sun.

Herbal extracts and oils are used to make scented

candles, soaps, cosmetics like peppermint-flavored toothpaste, and for flavoring candies and baked goods. Certain ones are also used in mixture to repel insects from people and plants. Look toward the end of this chapter for recipes for homemade cosmetics, insect repellents and home remedies.

TO MAKE AN HERBAL "OIL" OR "ESSENCE" throw flowers, leaves or bark into a kettle and simmer in water about 24 hours over a slow fire. Then slowly cool and skim the oil that rises to the top of the water. If you're using this method put your materials into a bag to cook them because they almost invariably float and it's easier to get the oil separated that way. You squeeze the bag to help get the oil out. You can even put it through a clothes wringer or use a cider press. For pine oil use pieces of wood cut fine. For birch use the inner part of the tree, for cedar use the tips of the branches. To make a sunflower seed oil throw seeds in whole but premashed to help the oil come out. Rose, lavender, violet and lemon balm make good oils. If you did it right the oil should have a strong scent of the plant and you can use it like perfume.

Some herbal oils are "distilled." Boil your materials in a teakettle. Fit a tube, preferably copper, over the spout and run it through a pan of cold water. The steam, condensed, will be your oil. The principle is that you are separating out substances that vaporize at a lower temperature than water and when they reach the cold copper coil they condense.

SPIRIT—A solution made with brandy is called an herb spirit. The basic recipe for herb spirit is to use fresh herbs, picking just before flowering or when otherwise appropriate. Strip the leaves from the stems and pack lightly in a jar. Fill the jar with brandy and cover tightly. Let rest for a month. Strain and bottle.

A useful herb spirit for seasoning soups is equal parts of sweet marjoram, basil, thyme, savory and parsley. Measure and mix before filling the jar.

POWDER—An herb powder is simply bark or dried herbs pulverized to a powder in your mortar.

SYRUP—An herbal syrup used as a beverage or medicine base is made by adding simple syrup (sugar and water) to the herbal infusion when hot and somewhat evaporated. Bottle and seal when hot.

SACHETS AND HERB PILLOWS—These are cloth "pillows" made to hold dried and crushed herbs and flowers. Sachets can be put with wearing apparel, household linen or stationery to scent it. Herb pillows were traditionally used to overcome a sickroom smell and soothe nerves. You can experiment to get your favorite scent. Lavender is traditional, but don't be afraid to try other mixtures. Lilac, rose petals, sweet peas, mint, rosemary and thyme are all suitable. Or use lavender, sage, peppermint and lemon balm in some combination, or sage, peppermint and lemon balm without lavender. (For more ideas, see Potpourris under Rose in Herbs and Flavorings list below.)

Choose a dry morning to collect the herbs and flowers—after the dew has dried. Collect about four times as much as you expect to need because they will shrink in drying. Use the petals of flowers only. Dry them away from light, spread out shallow on

clean paper or cloth. Stir a couple of times a day. When dry, strip herb leaves from stems and ribs. Mix all ingredients and grind to a powder in your spice mill or with your mortar. Add a fixative like orrisroot. If you are making a quantity of powder at once—more than you need to fill your sachets or pillows—store in a small tightly-lidded bottle in a cool place and protect from light.

Now pack the powder into "pillowcases" of cotton, and then sew up the open side. (Make a large herb pillow by sewing together two men's handkerchiefs.) You can cover the inner pillow with velvet, gingham, percale, or ribbon-trimmed lace—or any scrap material you have. To hang or pin in place, sew a loop of ribbon or bias tape into one corner as the fourth side is sewn.

Here's a Midwestern pioneer recipe for a *Headache Pillow:* Mix together 2 ounces *each* lavender, marjoram, rose petals, betony rose leaf and ½ ounce cloves. You're supposed to sniff it to cure your headache.

To Ease Melancholy and Put You to Sleep Pillow—Mix 2 ounces rose petals, 1 ounce mint and ¼ ounce crushed clove.

PASTILLES—Also called scent balls. Same as the stuff to go in a sachet or herb pillow or potpourri only it's melted together with a gum resin that will make it all go together and be hard. Any size from like a tiny bead up. Can be polished on a lathe. To make beads pierce with a needle while still soft. Can be sculpted into jewelry and so on. Pound your ingredients in a smooth-sided mortar together with ribbon variety gum tragacanth and moisten with a little rose-water until you have a mixture that is like a dough. Shape and dry.

SEASONING MIXTURES

Lamb Seasoning—In a bowl combine ¼ cup dried onion flakes and 1 tablespoon *each* ground cumin seed, garlic powder, pepper and basil. Store in an airtight container and use it to season lamb.

Herbed Salt—In a bowl combine 1 cup salt and 1 teaspoon *each* dried parsley, chives, onion flakes and summer savory. Store in an airtight container and use it for roll or bread dough and to season salads.

Sesame Salt—Put into a frying pan and heat gently until the seeds begin to brown (do not overheat): 8 parts raw sesame seeds and 1 part sea salt (available at health food stores). Remove and allow to cool. Mix well and grind. Sprinkle this on foods at the table—soups, salads, entrées, but when you do, don't use too much salt in the cooking.

Herb Bags—In each of several 4-inch squares of cheesecloth combine ½ teaspoon thyme, ¼ teaspoon *each* basil and marjoram, 1 bay leaf, crumbled, and 5 peppercorns. Tie the squares into bags with string. Store in an airtight container and use to season soups and stews.

Simple Kitchen Pepper—Keep a shaker of mixed salt and pepper near the stove if you want to use salt and pepper in practically everything like some folks do. Three parts salt to one part of pepper.

Spiced Pepper—In a bowl combine ¼ cup coarsely ground black pepper, 2 tablespoons thyme, 1 tablespoon *each* ground caraway seed and sweet Hungarian paprika, and 1 teaspoon garlic powder. Store the pepper in an airtight container and use it to season roasts and steaks.

Cinnamon Sugar—Combine ¼ cup sugar with ½ teaspoon cinnamon. Mix well and store in a covered jar.

Dessert Spice Blend—This blend is nicely balanced in flavor and good for spice cakes, cookies and pies. Combine 2 teaspoons powdered cinnamon, 2 teaspoons ground nutmeg, 1 teaspoon powdered ginger, ½ teaspoon powdered allspice and ½ teaspoon powdered cloves. Optional are ½ teaspoon mace, ½ teaspoon ground coriander and ½ teaspoon ground cardamom.

Homemade Pumpkin Pie Spice—In a bowl combine 1 tablespoon *each* cinnamon and ground ginger, 1½ teaspoons *each* ground allspice and nutmeg and 1 teaspoon ground cloves. Store in an airtight container and use to flavor gingerbread, pies and other desserts.

Pickling Spice #1—In a bowl combine 2 tablespoons *each* whole allspice and whole coriander, 1 tablespoon mustard seed, 2 bay leaves, crumbled, and a 1-inch piece of dried ginger root, peeled and chopped. Store the spice in an airtight container and use it for pickling fruits and vegetables, making preserves and braising meat.

Pickling Spice #2—Combine whole cassia buds, white peppercorns, black peppercorns, allspice, bay leaves, mustard seeds, dried sliced ginger and chili pods.

Curry Powder—Curry powder is a mixture of spices. You can make your own. Have the ingredients well powdered using a mortar and pestle to grind. Sift together and keep in a tightly corked bottle.

Curry powders may be a combination of just a few spices or as many as fifty. The curry powders sold in grocery stores are usually a combination of fifteen or twenty herbs, seeds and spices, but people who really know about curry have special combinations of spices to go with various dishes, some of which need mild subtle seasonings and others hotter ones. The strength of a curry depends on how much chili is used. Here are the principal possibilities of curry powder: allspice, anise, bay leaves, cayenne pepper, cinnamon, caraway, celery seeds, cloves, coriander, cumin seeds, curry leaves, dill, fennel, fenugreek (seeds and leaves), garlic, ginger, mace, mustard, nutmeg, oregano, pepper (white and black), paprika, poppy seeds, saffron, turmeric, mint, cubeb berries, juniper berries and salt. One mixture could be: 3 ounces turmeric, 4 ounces coriander seed, 2 ounces black pepper, 1 ounce fenugreek, 1 ounce ginger and ¼ ounce cayenne pepper.

My Favorite Curry Mixture—This recipe is from Zubaidah Ismail, Penang, Malaysia. Combine 1 teaspoon ground turmeric, 1 teaspoon chili powder, 1 teaspoon ground ginger, 1 teaspoon coriander seeds and 2 teaspoons powdered cinnamon. Mix all together and there's your curry powder.

From-scratch Curry Powder—Grind with mortar and pestle until a fine powder 6 tablespoons coriander seed, ⅛ teaspoon cayenne pepper, 1½ tablespoons turmeric, ½ tablespoon whole cloves, 1½ tablespoons fenugreek seeds, ½ tablespoon cardamom seed and 1½ tablespoons cumin seeds.

Spice bag—When a recipe calls for a spice bag put the whole spices listed in the recipe into a handkerchief-sized piece of cheesecloth or some such, tie firmly and cook right with the dish to be flavored. Remove the bag before serving. It prevents your friend with the ulcer from accidentally biting down on a peppercorn.

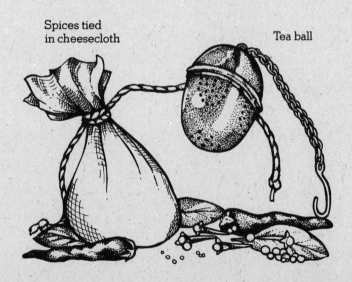

Spices tied in cheesecloth

Tea ball

HERBS AND FLAVORINGS
Alfalfa to Wintergreen—
Garden to Table

ALFALFA—A prime grass used for making hay. A tea is made from the leaves and one also from the seeds. Sometimes it is combined with peppermint. Harvest your leaves when the plant is in early bloom. Separate out the stems and discard. Cure in the shade. Pour boiling water over the dried alfalfa to make the tea. You can also eat the young tips for greens. A super tea mix is 40% alfalfa, 40% comfrey and 20% mint.

Violet Stewart writes: "I go out in a field of fresh alfalfa where there is new growth. Cut an arm load and bring home. Put into a tub and wash thoroughly. Shake water out and lay on trays to sun dry. When dampness is gone I strip tender leaves off and lay the leaves on trays and dry in 200° oven to kill any bug eggs left and when thoroughly dry put into a tight can. There is my alfalfa leaves for tea. I think it keeps arthritis in check. I drink it every day instead of coffee or tea."

ALLSPICE—"Berries" means the whole allspice. It can be ground in a mortar with a pestle. It is not grown in the United States.

ANGELICA—A biennial, very like celery in its growing requirements. Does best in soil kept constantly moist with partial shade. Leaves and stems are used in the kitchen.

ANISE—Seeds must be planted as soon as ripe or they lose their power to germinate. Or propagate by dividing older roots and planting them in fall or early spring. Space plants 18 inches apart. Anise grows to 6 feet tall. Plant indoors in the fall in very moist soil or start in a greenhouse and then transplant outdoors in spring unless you have the 120-day season. The whole root can be chewed on. Or candied. Dry, loosen seeds and separate from chaff. Cut when the anise seeds are dark gray. The stalk and leaves, if you get them while still young and tender, can be chopped and added to a salad. Oil of anise is used nowadays in some commercial cough medicines.

BASIL (Sweet)—A basic seasoning herb. You can also make a medicinal-type tea from it and flavor vinegar. Set out greenhouse plants after frost danger is over. Bush basil is hardier than sweet basil. Annual. Space 15 inches. Pinch off tops so plants will bush. Harvest when buds appear—both leaves and buds. It will grow a second crop if you don't cut all the way to the ground. Tie in bunches to dry.

BORAGE—An annual herb with cucumber-flavored leaves. Mince the fuzzy little leaves fine and add to an early spring salad. Plant seed in spring or early summer. Self-sowing after first year. Harvest when young leaves develop.

BURNET (Salad Burnet)—Cucumber flavor when you use leaves in salads or to flavor vinegar. Use leaves only. A very hardy plant. Propagate by root division in early spring. Once started you'll have it for years.

CACTUS—Marion Stick is a lady of Indian descent who lives in Phoenix, Arizona. The Indians make use of many desert plants. They pick the fruit from cactus and make jelly and candy. Here's how Marion says to do it:

Cactus Candy—Make it from the small barrel cactus. Take off spines and outer skin. Cut pulp across in 1-inch slices. Soak overnight in cold water. In the morning cut into 1-inch pieces and boil until tender. Drain and cook slowly in a syrup until syrup is almost gone. Watch so the pieces do not scorch. To make syrup for about 2 quarts of cactus pieces, combine 3 cups sugar, 1 cup water, 2 tablespoons orange juice and 1 tablespoon lemon juice. Bring to a boil and add cactus. When syrup is almost gone, remove cactus pieces. You may cover with powdered or granulated sugar.

Cactus Prickly Pear Jelly—Pick prickly pears with leather gloves. Take off spines. Rinse the fruit and place in kettle, adding enough water to cover. Boil until quite tender, squeeze through jelly bag or jelly press. To every 2½ cups of juice add 1 (1¾-ounce) package powdered pectin and boil for a couple minutes. Then add 3 tablespoons lemon juice and 3½ cups sugar. Stir often and boil hard for 5 minutes. Pour in jelly glasses and seal with paraffin.

Camomile

CAMOMILE TEA—Gather the yellow flower heads, tender branches and stems when in full bloom and dry. Pour boiling water over them and steep to make tea. Peter Rabbit had some. It's supposed to be good for indigestion, chills and nervousness, and he had all three. I love it for everyday now that I've gotten used to it. We gather wild camomile but you can grow your own. It's an annual. You plant the seed in fall or early spring.

CARAWAY—A biennial. You plant it one year; it makes seed the second. Plant 8 inches apart in the spring. When seed clusters ripen the second year, cut plants off 1 foot above ground. Dry laying flat on paper or cloth. Then thresh off seeds by hitting with a stick. Blow off chaff and store seeds for planting or eating.

CATNIP—A perennial. Cut the tops when the plant is in full blossom. When they have been dried you can make a tea for colds or stuff a toy for somebody's cat. Discard the stems. You can make a tea from the leaves (fresh or dried) that is soothing—good at bedtime. Easy to propagate by dividing clumps of older plants and replanting. A catnip plant has to be at least two years old to interest your cat. When drying catnip keep it high above the ground or you'll have every cat in the neighborhood come to call! They don't seem to smell it if it's high off the floor. Then you can sew little gingham or felt mice come winter, stuff them with catnip and give for Christmas presents to all your friends who have cats!

CELERY—The leaves are for winter use the same as described for parsley and can be dried.

Celery Salt—Combine ¾ cup salt and ¼ cup celery seed, both toasted lightly in a dry skillet. Pulverize the mixture and sieve it into a small bowl. Store in airtight container and use to season soups, chowders and salads.

CHERVIL can be used fresh, frozen or dried. It's a hardy plant. Use the tender young leaves cut from 2-month-old seedlings to freeze. You can use older leaves to dry. Dry as for herb flowers. It's an annual similar to dill—it volunteers. Or you can harvest the ripe seed and replant in spring. The roots are edible. But must cook a *long* time—boil, cool, boil again, now serve.

Herb Soup, seasoned with chervil, can be varied indefinitely as to the green vegetables. But for a start take sorrel, spinach and lettuce, fresh from your garden, and get rid of any tough midribs. Wash and shred. Use 1 cup finely shredded spinach, ½ cup shredded sorrel and ½ cup of the white heart leaves of head lettuce. Use about ¼ cup butter and sauté (don't brown). Add 4 peeled potatoes, 1 tablespoon salt and 2 quarts boiling water. Let the soup then simmer gently for 1 hour. Crush the potatoes, add 1 tablespoon chervil and simmer 5 minutes more. Add a cup of croutons before serving.

CHICORY—Root is dried, ground and mixed with coffee to stretch it or added to oven-browned barley for a coffee substitute. The green leaves can be used like spinach but boil in two waters to get rid of the bitter taste. The roots, if planted in a cellar or outside under a cover to exclude light, will produce blanched leaves which you can eat raw as a salad or boil to use as greens in the wintertime.

CHIVE—A hardy perennial of the onion family. Cut off the plant top when leaves develop and add to salads or soups. Good with Jerusalem artichokes. Chives don't dry well but you can freeze them in little individual packages. Or they will grow indoors potted for you in the wintertime. Plant seed or bulbs in the early spring. Divide at least every three years.

CHOKECHERRY is not the "wild cherry" referred to in old cookbooks. The bark of true wild cherry trees can be used in homemade root beer. When broken into bits, boiled, strained and sweetened with honey, it makes an old-time cough remedy. Chokecherry berries make wonderful pancake syrup and jelly. The leaves contain a deadly poison.

CITRON looks like a small, round watermelon. Inside the flesh is uniformly green with green seeds. There is no hollow cavity as with cantaloupe or pumpkin. It's solid clean through. Citron is only eaten pickled or preserved in sugar syrup or candied. You can substitute citron melon preserves for store-bought citron in fruit cakes, plum puddings and mincemeat. Remove the strips of citron from the syrup, cut them into smaller pieces, and toss the pieces with flour until they are no longer sticky. See Sweets for preserving and candying citron.

CLOVE TEA—Follow recipe for tea but add 3 whole cloves for each person to be served.

CLOVER BLOOM VINEGAR—Combine 6 pounds brown sugar, ½ bushel clover bloom, 4 quarts molasses and 9 gallons boiling water. Let cool. Add 3 tablespoons dry yeast dissolved in ¼ cup water. Let stand 14 days, strain and store until it tastes like vinegar.

COLORING FOOD—Caramel provides a brown color. Green can be made from spinach, red from red beets. To get spinach green wash some spinach, boil it until tender and pour off the juice for your coloring extract. Or for a stronger green let the spinach cool, squeeze dry, mash by pounding and then put through sieve. Green peas give a lighter shade of green. The coral of a lobster pounded and put through a sieve will give red as will vinegar or water that has stood on sliced boiled beets.

COMFREY cannot be raised from seed. It has to be propagated by root cuttings. Plant a 2-inch root cutting 4 inches deep any time of the year. Fast growing. Some people roll the leaves and tape them on as a poultice for sores. Others grind it. It is also good to eat in salads when young and when a little larger, eat like spinach. Dry the leaves for winter use. I'm told that a dose of comfrey tea will cure scours in baby goats. Good for people too. It's also recommended as a hair rinse. For 4 cups of tea use ¼ cup dried comfrey leaves. To dry them just gather, wash and dry in oven or other warm place. Crumble and store. Comfrey-peppermint is a good tea combination. Comfrey is said to be good for itchy places, too. Just rub fresh leaves over the afflicted area. The medicinal plant of all medicinal plants. Highly respectable medical researchers have agreed that it does have a heal-

ing effect. A good livestock feed, too, because it's high in protein (like alfalfa).

CORIANDER—An annual that you should plant in late spring. It should be planted ½ inch deep. Harvest when seed tops ripen and proceed same as for caraway. Mash seeds with a rolling pin. Put in apple pie and apple butter.

COSTMARY—A perennial. Use the young tender leaves, gathered in very early spring (they are bitter if you wait too long), fresh or dried, to flavor fish, lamb or poultry. A little dried costmary goes a long way. Needs partial shade and mulching to keep ground moist.

DANDELION—Mildred Beitzel of Palouse, Washington, gave me these recipes and more. A great lady and a dandy-lion expert! I love those shining little flower suns too.

Dandelion Blossom Fritters #1—¼ cup milk, ½ cup flour, 1 egg, beaten, 2 tablespoons powdered milk, 1 teaspoon baking powder, a pinch of salt and 16 large fresh dandelion blossoms (no stems). Mix all ingredients except blossoms. Wash the blossoms lightly, drain and dip immediately into batter. Fry until golden brown. Yield: 4 servings.

Dandelion Blossom Fritters #2—1½ cups whole wheat flour, 2 teaspoons baking powder, 1 tablespoon sugar, 1 teaspoon salt, ½ cup milk, 1 egg, beaten, 1 tablespoon melted butter or oil and 2 cups dandelion blossoms. Mix dry ingredients; add milk, egg and butter. Mix well, add blossoms which have been rinsed under cold water. Drop by spoonfuls onto greased griddle and fry until golden brown. Yield: 3-4 servings.

These are tasty and delicious, although it may sound strange to someone who thinks of dandelions only as a bad weed to be pulled up and thrown away.

Tasty Dandelion Blossoms—Gather blossoms in early morning and rinse in cold water. Soak 2 hours in salted water. Roll in egg batter, then flour and fry until golden brown. (We omitted the 2-hour soaking

and they tasted fine prepared this much simpler method.) Some people gather only the buds instead of the flowers and boil them a few minutes to remove some of the bitterness. Mix with egg and fry in patties. The Japanese often cooked dandelion flowers during the food shortage of World War II.

Dandelion Jelly—Pick 1 quart of blossoms in the morning. Hold each flower by its calyx (the green base) and snip off the golden blossoms with scissors into your saucepan. Discard calyx. Boil blossoms in 1 quart water for 3 minutes. Drain off 3 cups liquid. Add 1 (1¾-ounce) package powdered pectin to the liquid and 2 tablespoons lemon juice. When it comes to a rolling boil, add 4½ cups sugar and a few drops of yellow food coloring. Boil about 3 minutes, or to the jelly stage.

Dandelion Root Vegetable—Use like parsnips or salsify. Peel, slice and simmer with a pinch of soda until almost fork tender. Drain, then simmer until completely tender. Drain again. Season with salt, pepper and butter.

Dandelion Greens—Use young, tender leaves. Wash. Add salad dressing. Good done wilted-lettuce style with a hard-boiled egg. Or steam and season with salt, pepper and butter.

Dandelion Root Coffee—Dandelion coffee makes a surprisingly good substitute. Gather roots in the fall (October) when they have stored up their food reserve of inulin (not insulin), or in the early spring before blooming. Scrub unpeeled roots with a stiff brush. Dry them in the oven (150°) until they are brittle and snap easily. Then roast them at about 375° for 15 to 20 minutes, or until they are dark brown inside. Grind in the blender until they look like coffee, or use a rolling pin to grind to a coarse powder. Store in glass jars and use just as you would coffee. We boil about 1 teaspoon for each cup and stir it into the cup. Your brew will have a flavor all its own, vaguely chocolaty and pleasing. You'll like it better every time the price of coffee goes up.

DILL—Heads, seeds and stems, are used to make dill pickles. You use them fresh or dried. To dry for winter use, cut the plants, after the seed heads have formed, on a dry summer day. Tie in bunches and hang in an airy but shady place. Frames covered with cheesecloth or netting are fine for large quantities. Or just lay them on newspaper like I do. When the heads are dry you can shell off the seeds and store in covered glass jars. Or fold up stalks and all in your newspaper and they will keep fine. You could also freeze dill or grow it in a kitchen pot through the winter. Dill is amazing stuff. A friend of mine poured the brine from a jar of dill pickles on the ground by her garbage cans and "Lo!"—a crop of dill grew.

This recipe was sent to me by Ellie Allers of Eureka, Montana. "It is my grandmother's wash day standby. I have eight grandchildren myself so it's no recent one. Those were days when meat wasn't an everyday commodity.

"Dill Soup—This consisted of every vegetable available. Tomato sauce or catsup, a handful of rice or whatever, 2 or 3 sprigs of dill, salt, pepper, 2 or 3

hefty tablespoons bacon fat carefully saved from day to day and, if you had it, a bit of chopped bacon. It simmered on the stove all morning. It sounds horrible, tastes marvelous. My husband loves it, and I have canned it for future emergency needs. Best served with hefty chunks of homemade bread and butter."

DITTANY—A perennial. It will make a brilliant flash of light if you hold a match under its flower cluster on a quiet summer evening. The dried leaves make a good tea. Hard to grow. Start with two-year-old plants.

ELDERBERRY—There are lots of elderberry trees around here. The berries are tiny and kind of bitter. For tea, use 4 cups fresh ripe berries and 2 cups water. Stir, mash well and strain, squeezing to get all the juice you can. Freeze or can. When wanted, let simmer a bit. Sweeten with honey. Dilute to taste.

Elderberry Flower Tea—Pick blossoms in full bloom. Dry in the sun. When completely dry, put in a jar. At cold or flu time, put 1 or 2 teaspoons in a cup. Pour boiling water over as for regular tea. Strain. Add honey to sweeten. Optional, a shot of whiskey in it! After drinking the tea, go to bed. Stay covered and sweat the cold out. You make this using fresh flowers, too.

Elderberry Blossom Fritters—Start with 10 elderberry blossoms with stems. Dip the blossoms in clean water for a few minutes. Shake off the water. Mix ¾ cup flour, ¼ teaspoon salt, 3 beaten egg yolks and ½ cup milk. A tablespoon rum or brandy adds flavor. Beat until smooth. Fold in slightly beaten whites of the 3 eggs. Heat frying pan with 1 inch oil. Dip each blossom into flour and egg mixture, fry and serve. Good with a green salad.

FENNEL—An annual that grows like a weed and has a small white daisy-like bloom. Gather the plant when the blossoms are just starting to open. Use like camomile for tea. It's a close relative. Combine with sage for a sore throat. Stalks can also be eaten.

FLAXSEED—The seed of the common flax plant, now sold as a flower, but once common because household linen was made from its fibers. When using the seeds be careful not to crush them as internal oil will make the whole decoction nauseating.

Flaxseed Lemonade—Pour 1 quart of boiling water over 4 tablespoons flaxseed and let it steep 3 hours. Strain, sweeten to taste and add the juice of 2 lemons. If too thick, add more water. Soothing for colds. Another way to make it is to boil 3 tablespoons of the seed in 6 cups water until it reduces to about 3 cups of water. Then add lemon and sugar and strain before serving. You can keep a coffeepot of it on the back of the stove and drink as often as you like.

GARLIC looks like a grass from the top, but if you try to pull some up you can smell the garlic. The bulbs grow underground and are made up of a cluster of smaller ones, each called a "clove." To use the garlic clove, peel papery outer layer, and then use whole, chopped or crushed in a garlic press. Garlic is hardy and can be left in the garden over the winter or dug up and stored like onions. Plant garlic bulbs in Octo-

ber and leave until August. After digging let them dry in the shade or in the sun if below 100°. A hotter sun will burn them. When dry, dust off and store.

Garlic powder is made by drying and then grinding the cloves.

Garlic salt is a mixture of table salt and garlic powder. To make it, split a clove of garlic and crush it with 1 teaspoon salt in a small mortar or on a board with the tip of a knife.

GERANIUM (scented)—Use in sachets and for flavoring.

GINGER ROOT—If you can get fresh ginger root, wash, dry, bag and store in your freezer. You can just grate the frozen root when needed. Or use fresh root and grate, slice, mince or press in a garlic press. An old-time horse trading trick was to poke some ginger up the tail end of a tired old horse right before sale time and it would really act young!

Ginger Sugar—Into a bowl sift together 2 cups sugar and ¼ cup ground ginger and combine the mixture well. Transfer the mixture to an airtight container and let stand for at least 3 days. Use the sugar to flavor cakes, puddings, squash and applesauce and for glazing hams.

GINSENG—The roots are dug in mid-October of the sixth or seventh year after planting. Dig the roots with their forks intact. Don't scrape or scrub. To cure dry between 60° and 80° for three days then at 90°. Have them spread thinly and well ventilated. Turn frequently. Roots over 2 inches in diameter will need 6 weeks at 90° to cure, smaller ones less time.

GOLDENROD tea is a new one to me but Elsie Christiansen of Idleyld Park, Oregon, wrote me special to tell me it's good not only for drinking but as an antiseptic for burns, bee stings and mosquito bites. But she didn't say how she harvests it.

HELIOTROPE—A perennial. Propagate by cuttings taken in early spring and set in clean sand. Tricky to raise. Very fragrant and blooms all winter if brought indoors. Needs humidity when potted, to be watered daily and a temperature around 50°. Likes to be in a hanging basket.

HOPS—A perennial. For tea, I use 1 teaspoon hops per 2 cups water. Steep until red. Strain. Sweeten to taste. Horribly bitter so maybe it's medicinal. You need to plant male and female hops (they won't thrive without marriage).

HOREHOUND—The leaves are used for flavoring beer, cough drops, honey and for making tea. They are best gathered just before flowers open and can be dried, preferably in a warm, shaded, airy place. Pick the smaller stems near the ground, the tops of the larger ones. Propagate by clump divisions.

Horehound Candy—Steep 2 heaping teaspoons dried horehound in 1 cup water for half an hour. Strain. Put the leaves in a cloth and press or twist to get every last drop. Add 3½ pounds brown sugar. Boil to the ball stage. Pour out into flat, well-greased pans and mark with a knife into sticks or small squares as soon as candy is cool enough to retain its shape. The amount of herb can be varied to taste. If you are uncertain, make the rest of the batch first, then add the tea gradually until you have the desired flavor. Or add tea to 2 cups brown sugar, ½ cup Karo Syrup and 1 teaspoon butter. Or boil down and add as flavoring to any mild taffy recipe.

HORSERADISH when homegrown will be more crooked than the commercial variety which is uprooted, trimmed and then replanted. You can dig from September until the ground freezes. But keep in mind it makes its greatest growth in late summer and early fall. Three or four days before harvesting, remove tops as near to the ground as possible. Store like any other root.

Horseradish is strong stuff and a comparatively few hills of it will suffice for your family use. It is perennial. You can also dig the roots in the early spring before the leaves start. Tender, young, early spring horseradish leaves will add a mustard-like taste to a ham or cheese sandwich.

To prepare the horseradish scrub the roots clean. Then peel off the brown outer skin (you can use a vegetable peeler). If you drop it into cold water right after peeling you can prevent discoloration. Put it in the blender, through the food grinder or grate. (Makes you cry.) Put the ground horseradish in a half pint or pint jar. Baby food jars work great! Add vinegar to moisten. The best is white wine vinegar or distilled vinegar of a 4½- to 5-percent strength. Cider vinegar causes the grated horseradish to turn dark within a comparatively short time. Bottle and tightly cap the horseradish as soon as possible after grating. Over long usage the vinegar will gradually evaporate so replace as needed. The vinegar keeps your grated horseradish from turning color. Some people add a bit of sugar. Some add salt. Some grind in a little beet to make it red. This is generally served with hot roast beef, or cold meats, or even just homemade dark buttered bread. Refrigerate the prepared horseradish to keep it "hot." Horseradish may also be dried, ground to a powder and put up in bottles in dry form. Prepared this way it will keep much longer, but it does not make as good a relish as when grated fresh.

Here are precise amounts for people who prefer them: 1 cup grated horseradish, ½ cup white vinegar, and ¼ teaspoon salt. Mix and pack in jars.

Sour Cream Horseradish—Take 2 tablespoons of your prepared horseradish. Chill ½ cup sour cream thoroughly and then whip it until stiff. Add ½ teaspoon sugar and whip some more. Fold in the horseradish and serve with meat loaf or ham. You can use a pinch of salt in place of the sugar. Optional, 1 tablespoon chopped chives or parsley, 1 tablespoon vinegar, or a little cayenne pepper, or ½ teaspoon prepared mustard, or a dash of Tabasco, or ¼ teaspoon pepper, or combinations thereof.

Horseradish Sandwich Filling—Mix equal quantities of finely grated horseradish and mayonnaise. The horseradish can be topped with thinly sliced tomato, cucumber, radish or chopped watercress. Spread between thin slices of buttered brown bread.

Horseradish Sauce—Melt 1 tablespoon butter and blend in 1 tablespoon flour. Add 1 cup soup stock or water. Cover and heat to boiling. Stir in ½ cup freshly grated horseradish, 1 tablespoon lemon juice, salt and pepper to taste. Simmer 2 minutes and serve. This is especially good with tongue.

Horseradish Milk Sauce—You can make a cooked sauce with milk in the top of your double boiler. Mix 3 tablespoons cracker crumbs, ⅓ cup grated horseradish and 1½ cups milk. Cook over simmering water 20 minutes. Add 3 tablespoons butter, ½ teaspoon salt and ⅛ teaspoon pepper and you have your sauce.

HYSSOP (Anise Hyssop) makes a medicinal tea. Great for bees since it blooms all summer until frost. Birds like the seeds.

LAVENDER—Honeybees love lavender. It is used as a tea herb, to make fragrances, in jellies, wine vinegars, to scent soap and to keep moths out of the cupboard. You can distill a good and useful lavender oil that improves with age. Flowers that are cut off when first opened and dried are for sachets. The dried flowers are light blue and have a lovely fragrance. The lavender flowers can be combined with dried orrisroot to improve their lasting power, or with

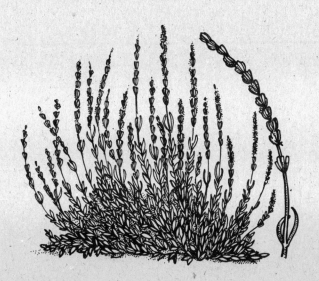

rose petals, orange peel, rose geranium leaves or spices for various scents. A lavender hedge blooms from June to August and really gives your gardens fragrance. There are many different varieties of lavender. *Lavandula vera* and *Lavandula officinalis* have the strongest scents (the deeper the calyx color the stronger the scent you'll get).

I've met a lady who wants to be called Catherine Shirley who knows an amazing amount about lavender. I asked her to write it down to share with all of us and here is what she said:

"First I want to tell you about lavender. The Latin name for it is *Lavandula*. The true lavender is a small shrubby plant native to southern Europe. It is widely cultivated for its fragrant flowerets and for the oil distilled from the fresh flowering tops. The plant thrives best in light and rather dry soils well supplied with lime. Mine is well fertilized and I add crushed egg shells to the soil. On low and wet land it is certain to winterkill. It also should be loosely covered to prevent the snow from getting inside the branches which freezes and thus winterkills.

"The plant can be started from seed but it grows very slowly. It is more readily propagated from cuttings or by division especially if first treated with hormone for rooting. The hormone develops roots faster and they are stronger. Cuttings should be set in well-prepared soil in early spring, 12 to 15 inches apart in rows spaced to suit the cultivation intended. Lavender can be grown as a hedge to give plenty of flowers for harvesting. Frequent and thorough cultivation is desirable. Growth is slow and plants do not produce any considerable quantity of flowers for several years, but full crops may be expected for some time thereafter if the plants are given proper care. The plants should not be watered very much. Lavender when grown in poor soil that is limy and gravelly produces stronger scented flowers. The flowering tops, soon as in full bloom, are harvested. If used for production of oil they are distilled at once without drying. If dry flowers are wanted for sachets, the tops are carefully dried in the shade and flowers later stripped from the stems by hand.

"Soon as spikes of lavender are in bloom they should be cut. Otherwise a lot of fragrance can be lost if left standing too long, especially if rain falls on them. If the plant got wet already, then they can be cut without waiting for all buds to bloom. The spikes can be partly bloomed. Shake the spikes over spread out paper as some buds will fall off. Dropped flowers and buds can be picked up after they have dried and put in a glass jar with a lid on. These can be used to make balls, sachets or added to potpourris.

"*Book marks*—Real short lavender spikes with flower and buds can be artistically arranged between two small squares of nylon tulle, nylon organdy or any stiff transparent material in a sandwich-like fashion. Secure the spikes with glue that dries clear or a few small staples so the spikes do not move around. Then sew patches of pretty braid or tapes around the edge on all sides to suit your fancy. Makes a good gift for people who like to read a lot."

Lavender Sachet Powder—Mix ½ ounce dried powdered lavender flowers with ½ teaspoon powdered cloves. Sew it up tightly in a little cloth pillow and leave that pillow in a bureau drawer to perfume the clothes. That's an old-time elegance.

Lavender Water—Dissolve 3 drops oil of lavender in 2 cups distilled water. Age at least a week. Better with a lump of sugar in it but then it has a tendency to ferment and go bad. A perfume.

Lavender Potpourris—Turn to the Rose entry of this herbal dictionary.

LEMON BALM—A hardy perennial with a lemony mint fragrance. Use fresh leaves in salads. Leaves are used commercially in perfumes, toilet waters and to flavor Benedictine. Makes a great herb tea. You can serve as a plain iced tea in summer and a hot tea in winter. Also good to scent your soap. Harvest just before the buds flower. The lemon flavor is really very strong and clear. Good for homesteaders who can't get lemons. You really can substitute the dried lemons of the lemon balm for fresh lemons. To get more, divide mature plants and replant in moist soil.

Lemon Balmade—Combine ½ cup lemon balm that has been cut fine, ½ cup mint, also cut fine, ½ cup sugar, ¼ cup honey diluted with ¼ cup water, ½ cup lemon juice and ¼ cup orange juice. Let stand an hour. Now add 4 quarts ginger ale—homemade or store-bought. This is a fine drink for guests. Will serve about 16.

LEMON VERBENA is not hardy! Plant after last frost. Repot and bring indoors before last warm summer evenings are over. The lemon verbena leaves are at their best during early apple harvest season. You can dry leaves for winter use or use fresh to make tea. Makes a soothing tea, good at bedtime. For lemon flavoring, add fresh lemon verbena leaves to drinks or fruit desserts.

LOVAGE—Leaves and stalks are used like celery. Use dried leaves in soups, meats and salads for a celery taste.

MARJORAM—If you live in warmer climates this plant grows as a perennial. Cut fresh leaves anytime after the plant is up 5 inches, but it's best to take the top 4 inches when the plant begins to bloom. In colder climates it is unable to withstand frost and snow and must be grown as an annual. Cut off the whole plant in the fall, dry and then strip leaves from stems. To propagate, use division or let parent plants self-sow. Marjoram plants prefer partial shade. This is a basic herb in Italian cooking and in sausages.

MESQUITE BEAN—Soak the seeds in water for several hours to get a sweet lemon-flavored drink. Or grind the seeds and mix that powder with water to get your beverage.

MINT—A very hardy perennial you can propagate by digging up and replanting runners, plantlets or root divisions. The little plantlets grow just below the dirt surface. Be careful to cut between rather than through any baby or adult plant. Easy to get started with, and the most all-around useful herb I can think of. To use fresh, cut off plant tips, wash, dry and cut off the leaves with your scissors. For winter use you can freeze or dry the mint. Frozen mint will keep its strength better. To freeze just wash, dry and wrap a few tips at a time in freezer paper or a baggie. Keep dried mint leaves out of the light. When you are ready to use the dried leaves pour boiling water over them. In general, 2 tablespoons of fresh chopped mint would be equivalent to 1½ teaspoons dry mint or 1 teaspoon mint extract. The mint taste goes especially well with lamb or mutton. There are many mint flavors. Spearmint is most common. Orange and apple mint exist, even pineapple flavored mint! Mint does well in sand. Needs to be divided regularly. Thin by using.

Basic Mint Tea—Steep 4 tablespoons of fresh mint leaves for 5 minutes (less if desired). Serve with honey and affection.

Mint Jelly—1 cup fresh mint leaves, ¼ cup boiling water, 2¾ cups sugar and 1 quart apple juice. Wash mint leaves, snip from stems, then add boiling water and 2½ cups sugar. Let stand a few hours. Bring to boiling point and strain through several layers of cheesecloth. Add the remaining ¼ cup sugar to apple juice and stir until it reacts to jelly test (see Jelly in Sweets chapter). Skim and pour into hot sterilized jelly glasses. Seal with paraffin. If the color is too pale, add a little green food coloring.

Mint Cup—Put several mint leaves into a tall glass; fill full of shaved ice; add the juice of 1 lemon and 2 slices of orange; sweeten to taste; fill the glass with water.

Minted Green Peas or New Potatoes—Add some sprigs of mint while boiling. Figure about 6 leaves per 4 cups vegetables plus 1 tablespoon of butter.

Pineapple-Mint Drink—In a blender combine 1 cup mint leaves with 1 cup pineapple juice. Add more pineapple juice to dilute to taste (like 3 cups more). Serve over ice cubes.

Mint Vinegar Sauce—For roast lamb or chops. Wash and then chop very fine 1 cup mint leaves. Dissolve 1 tablespoon sugar in 1 cup vinegar. Add the mint and let stand in the liquid 1 hour. Optional, 1 tablespoon lemon juice and a dash each of salt and pepper.

Mint Jelly Sauce—Combine 1 tablespoon chopped mint with 1 cup currant jelly in a saucepan over low heat. Serve hot with lamb or mutton.

Baked Pears with Mint—Place 3 large, thinly sliced pears in rows in a greased baking dish. Sprinkle with ¼ teaspoon salt and 2 tablespoons sugar. Dot with butter. Cover and bake at 300° for 30 minutes, or until tender. Garnish with mint sprigs and serve hot.

Mintade—Boil ½ cup water and ½ cup sugar for 5 minutes. Add 6 tablespoons chopped mint leaves and ⅔ cup lemon juice. Let stand overnight. Strain. Color green with food coloring, if you want. Put into jar and store in refrigerator. Add to iced tea, lemonade, punch and the like for mint flavor. Garnish with a fresh sprig.

Mint Shake—Combine 1 well beaten egg, ½ cup cold water and the juice of ½ lemon. Add mintade and sweetening to taste.

Fruit Salad Dressing—Combine 2 tablespoons mint vinegar (Sours chapter), 2 tablespoons cream and 1 cup mayonnaise.

MUGWORT—Also called *Lactiflora*. When dried makes a good homemade moth repellent in cedar chest and closet.

MUSTARD—There's more than one kind. White mustard has reddish yellow seeds. Black mustard has smaller blackish red seeds. Wild mustard has oil seeds that in the old days were sometimes used to stretch the first two named kinds. The store-bought mustard is made from white mustard plant. White mustard isn't the wild mustard we know but a more tropical plant. To make white mustard seeds into dry mustard you grind them in a mortar. Sift and discard the papery hulls. Wet mustard is dry mustard moistened with vinegar or water. You can gather unopened wild mustard buds in the early spring and serve them like broccoli with a cheese sauce. Lots of wild mustard in Oregon and Idaho valleys.

Hot Mustard—Combine 3 tablespoons dry mustard, 4 tablespoons white flour, 1 tablespoon sugar, 2 teaspoons salt and ¼ teaspoon pepper with enough vinegar to make a soft paste. Beat by hand or with an electric mixer on low speed until smooth and creamy. Keep in a covered container.

Spiced Mustard is made by first spicing the vinegar and then adding other ingredients. Put 2 tablespoons finely chopped onion, 3 bay leaves and 1 clove chopped garlic into 1½ cups vinegar. Cover an heat in a moderate oven (325°) for about 20 minutes. Strain out the solids. In another container mix the amount of dry mustard you want to make up with a pinch each powdered cinnamon and cloves and a bit of sugar. Gradually stir in hot vinegar until it is the consistency you want. Save the rest of the spiced vinegar for making salad dressing or more spiced mustard when you want it. Pack the mustard mix into small jars and cover when cooled.

Mustard Plaster—A favorite home remedy for chest colds. Mix one part mustard with eight or ten parts flour. Add lukewarm water until you have a smooth paste, then spread between two pieces of cloth such as muslin, old sheet scraps or flannel. Rub the chest well with vaseline before applying to prevent blistering and don't leave it on after the skin is well reddened. Keep away from mouth and eyes. See Home Remedies near the end of this chapter for more mustard plaster information.

NASTURTIUM—An annual with pretty flowers. The leaves have a peppery taste and are good in sandwiches and salads. Seeds are picked green and pickled to be a substitute for capers. Pick after the flower has dried off.

Nasturtium Blossom Sandwiches—Wash and dry the blossoms. Lay on buttered white or brown bread. Cut in fancy shapes and add a blossom to the top of each sandwich.

Pickled Capers—Brine seeds in salt water for 2 days, then in cold water for 1 day, drain and pack with a hot vinegar solution. Or dry them in a warm oven, and then pour over the vinegar solution. You can make fine spiced vinegar to preserve them in by putting 1 cup white vinegar in a pan, adding ½ teaspoon salt, 1 bay leaf and a few peppercorns. Let it boil. Remove from heat and let stand 2 hours. Strain. Another way is combine ½ cup cider vinegar and ½ cup sugar. If your nasturtium seeds are appearing over an inconvenient period of time, pick them as they are ready and keep in a brine of ½ cup salt to 4 cups water. Change it every 3 days. When you have all the seeds you are going to get or that you want you can go ahead and pickle them.

NETTLE—A common weed used to make an herb tea. Use the young first leaves. Boil them. Use gloves to pick them!

ONION—Onions should be left in the ground until they are so mature that the tops dry up. Pull out of the ground and let them sun cure for 3 days. Store in a warm dry place such as an upstairs floor or on a netting. You can dry onions grown from sets if you rip off the old "set" and then cure thoroughly. Lots more on onions in the Vegetables chapter.

Onion juice—Cut a slice from the root end of the onion and scrape out the juice with the edge of a teaspoon, or squeeze on a lemon squeezer that you keep especially for this purpose.

Onion powder—Grind finely dried onion chips.

Onion salt—Mix table salt and onion powder.

ORANGE FLOWER WATER—Combine 1 pound orange flowers, 1 ounce grated orange peel (not any white pulp) with 4 cups water. Let soak 24 hours. Distill 2 cups. Or dissolve 1 ounce orange essence from an herbal supplier in 1 gallon distilled water.

OREGANO—A perennial if your winters aren't too severe. (Winter it in the house in a pot if they are.) Propagate from cuttings or root divisions. Set plants out after frost danger. Flavor of leaves grown outside is much better than that of leaves grown inside. It thrives potted but you can keep it cut back by adding to any Italian dish.

ORRIS is made from the root of the blue flag (iris)

plant. It is a substance to hold the perfume of fragrant plants. Dig up the roots of as many iris plants as you think you'll need. Remember these roots and the orris you'll make from them are *not* to be eaten. *Poisonous!* Wash the dirt off the roots with running water and dry them off. Dry like other roots. When absolutely dry and brittle cut the roots into very fine chips and dry those chips about 3 more days. Store in a paper bag in a dark, dry place and it will keep fine for years. Better label "Poisonous." The orris chips (or you can powder it with a mortar and pestle) will help keep potpourris and sachets fragrant for years because it is a fragrance preservative. Use ¼ cup chipped or powdered orris to 4 cups of fragrant materials (like lavender, rose petals, mint).

PAPRIKA—Dry and grind the outer shell of the sweet red pepper.

PARSLEY—This is a biennial that can be planted from seed in early spring. Harvest all you want the first year but the second let it make seed. Cuttings from a plant going to seed would be bitter and worthless for cooking anyway. For you apartment dwellers parsley works well as a potted plant. But keep it in a glazed pot to help keep it moist all the time.

To chop fresh parsley pinch the tufts of parsley tightly between the thumb and forefinger of the left hand, then cut finely with your kitchen scissors. Try parsley added to fresh corn in place of salt.

To dry, harvest in dry weather, spread thinly on a plate and then bake in a 350° oven with the door open until the dampness is out. Then close the oven door and bake at 400° for 5 minutes more. Don't let it get brown. Turn the heat off and let the parsley remain until completely dry. The parsley leaves can either be stripped from the stem before drying or rubbed through a coarse sieve afterwards to remove the stalks. Put the dried leaves or powder in a glass jar with a tight lid and keep in a dry place. Celery leaves can also be done this way.

But the easiest way of all to preserve parsley is to shove a bunch into a quart jar, put a lid on and freeze. Remove as needed.

Parsley Butter is made by adding the juice of 2 lemons, drop by drop, to 1 cup softened butter. Keep stirring as you add it—it takes quite a while. Then add 2 tablespoons crumbled dried parsley. A clam dip.

Parsley-Dill Potato Salad—Peel and cook 5 pounds potatoes in boiling water with 1 teaspoon salt until tender. Drain and cool. Dice or slice. Add 3 apples, chopped, and 2 celery stalks, chopped, if you have them. Combine 1 cup sour cream with ¾ cup mayonnaise. Add 2 tablespoons dill seed, 2 tablespoons minced parsley and 2 tablespoons vinegar. Combine potatoes and mayonnaise mixture. Chill. Optional, 6 chopped hard-boiled eggs.

Quick Parsley Flavor—When you have lots of extra parsley, grind it and make ice cubes out of the juice. Wrap each cube separately in foil or in a baggie and store in freezer for flavoring soup, sauces and gravies.

PENNYROYAL—Makes a good fly repellent when planted around doors and windows.

PEPPER—

Black pepper is ground peppercorns. You can't grow your own but you can grind your own in a mortar or spice mill or in a tabletop-type pepper grinder. White pepper is made from the pepper berry by removing the outer husk before grinding. If you cut a peppercorn in half you'll see the black husk and the white center—grind your own and get both at once.

Cayenne pepper (red)—The Burpee catalog has tabasco and cayenne peppers. There are very distinct varieties of peppers so don't get them confused. They vary tremendously in hotness. Tabasco is the hottest. The famous tabasco sauce is a very old-time recipe that is aged naturally for 3 years before bottling. When you grind any hot pepper in a mortar be sure you get it crushed really fine. Otherwise somebody may take a bite of your food and it'll take the top of his head off if he gets an oversized bit of that stuff.

Pull up the whole plant before frost time. Hang upside down in an airy place to dry. Peppers are easiest to store after they are dry. Or just the pods can be harvested and strung on strings to dry. These peppers when dried are dark to light red, have yellow seeds, and the pods are from 1 to 2½ inches long.

If you are freezing food mixtures that contain chili peppers, remove the chili before freezing or the stuff will get hotter and *hotter!*

Cayenne is made by removing the seeds and grinding the dried shell.

Tabasco pepper—Dry the small fruits when they are pale yellow turning orange-scarlet and grind for tabasco sauce.

Chili Powder—To make it from scratch mix ground cayenne peppers, cumin seed and oregano. Experiment with small quantities to get the proportions you prefer. Or use this Portland, Oregon, lady's wonderful recipe: Combine 3 dried ancho chilies and 3 or 4 dried pequin chilies, all with stems removed, seeded, and crumbled, 1½ teaspoons cumin seed, 1 teaspoon oregano and ½ teaspoon garlic powder. Pulverize the mixture. Store the powder in airtight container and use it to season chili sauces.

PEPPERMINT—A variety of mint. Half peppermint and half rose hips is a good tea mix.

POKE SALET—My friend Hazel, in Georgia, wrote me: "Poke salet is a wild plant with large dark red berries which some say are poison. Gather in early spring around wet swampy places. Use the first tender green leaves. It's the first thing 'fresh' we can get around here so when we see it in the early part of the year we know spring has arrived. The stems are good fried like okra."

I've got another friend who loves poke salet greens. She's Violet Stewart, a lady of Indian descent from Okay, Oklahoma. She writes me long newsy letters and she's been teaching me a *lot*. It's wonderful givers like her and Col. Bill Rogers in Wyoming and Hazel and so many, many others that have made this book as special as it is. Violet makes crocheted pillows for sale. And she likes poke salet which she spells "polk salid." Violet told me that the ripe poke salet berries make a deep red dye. They are ripe in the fall. And the Indians in Oklahoma still use them to dye clay, wood, cloth, wool and feathers. She sent me a batch to try for myself. I appreciate that!

Poke Salet Dumplings are made with cornmeal. "Shape into balls and drop into the pot of boiling poke salet. Be sure to use hot water for the dumplings." I've heard another way to fix the poke salet greens is to mix them with mustard leaves, cress or whatever other greens you have. Add a dash salt and some ham or bacon. Keep covered while cooking. *Gardening in the South* has a section on it. But *Gardening in the South* is out of print now which is a shame because it was a great book.

POPPY was raised a lot in the old days for the tiny seeds. Good for flavoring cakes and rolls. Or for birdseed.

ROSE—You can do more with roses than you ever guessed!

Rose Brandy—You can order starts of the old fashioned very fragrant roses for potpourris, rose jars, beads and eating from Tillotson's Roses, Brown's Valley Road, Watsonville, California 95076. To flavor sauces for cakes and puddings—gather rose leaves while the dew is on them. Fill a bottle with them. Then pour into the bottle a good brandy. Steep 3 to 4 weeks. Strain. Rebottle.

Potpourris—That word is pronounced "popurrees" the way I understand it. It's French. The reason I've got potpourris filed here under roses is because although they may contain many different ingredients rose petals are always the main ingredient. The purpose is fragrance. The container should be china or pottery and have a lid you can close tightly. You keep that lid on tight after the potpourri is made except when you want to scent a room and then uncorking for half an hour should do it. The reason you don't want to use a glass container is because light deteriorates your potpourri.

The potpourri mixture to go into the jar should be at least four-fifths rose petals. You can make the other one-fifth any kind of sweet smelling flower or skip it if you want and use straight rose petals. Lavender, hyacinth, lemon verbena, heliotrope, lilac, calendula, pinks or any other one or combination of ones you want to try. A tablespoon or two of fragrant herbs would add to your potpourri's interest but be cautious of using more because it may get overwhelming. Rosemary, bay leaf, marjoram, cedar or balsam needles, basil, mint, sage and thyme are all good herb possibilities. Two or 3 teaspoons of crushed spices would add fragrance too, but again heed the caution not to make it more. Good spices to use are cloves, cinnamon, nutmeg, mace or allspice. Or you could put in a slice of lemon or orange peel stuck full of cloves. You could also add a few drops (add 1 drop at a time, stir with a wooden spoon) of a fragrant oil like eucalyptus oil, or lemon verbena, peppermint, rose geranium or rosemary oils—or a few drops of another strong scent like brandy or attar of roses. Now you want to add a fixative which can be orrisroot that you can grow and process yourself or 1 tablespoon each of gum benzoin and gum storax for each 5 cups of potpourri. You can order gum benzoin and gum storax from your drugstore and orrisroot in a powdered form for as little as $1 from Indiana Botanic Gardens, Inc., 626 Seventeenth Street, Hammond, Indiana 46325. After your ingredients are mixed, packed into jars and corked tightly, let them rest 2 or 3 weeks before you consider it finished.

All Rose Jar—This potpourri has a prettier color but it doesn't stay near as fragrant as long as the moist one. Gather your fragrant roses in the early morning just after the dew is off. Use roses between three-quarters and full bloom. Snip off the green calyx (that is the base of the petals) with a scissors holding the rose so you don't lose petals. Dry your petals on a screen or cloth out of direct sunlight. When dry combine with powdered orrisroot and set out in an open-topped jar. Or use in a sachet.

A Damp Potpourri—Dry the rose petals just until they feel leathery—8 hours or overnight. Use ice cream-type salt that is coarse and not iodized. Put the salt and the petals down in layers in the bottom of a glass jar—¼ cup salt to 2 cups petals. Add some orrisroot, too. Keep a lid on the jar and open only when you want to let some fragrance out.

Attar of Roses—Fill a large glass jar with rose petals, carefully separated from the rest of the plant. Add just enough water to cover them and let the jar set in the sun 2 or 3 days, bringing it indoors overnight. At the end of the third or fourth day small particles of yellow oil will be seen floating on the surface of the water. In the course of a week it will have increased to a thin scum. The scum is attar of roses. Take it up with a little cotton tied to the end of a stick and squeeze it into a small container.

To make *Rosewater* put petals into a wide-mouthed bottle and pour some pure alcohol over. Let stand until ready for use. Or combine some attar of roses with 1 part alcohol and 10 parts distilled water. You have to shake a long time, slowly at first, to get a solution. Or combine 1 ounce essence of roses that

you can buy from herbal suppliers with 1 gallon distilled water and age 2 weeks.

Rose Petal Honey was a favorite of Martha Washington's. Bring 2 pints of honey to a boil. Add 1 pint rose petals. Let stand 4 hours. Heat again. Strain into jars.

Rose Petal Jam—Gently rinse the petals and remove the white petal ends. Pack your petals firmly into a measuring cup. You'll need 2 cups for this recipe. Cover the 2 cups of petals with 2 cups boiling water in a pan and simmer 10 minutes. Strain the liquid and reserve the petals. Add 2¾ cups sugar and 3 tablespoons honey to the water in which the petals were cooked and simmer, uncovered, 30 minutes. Add 1 teaspoon lemon juice and the reserved petals and simmer 30 minutes more. The rose petals will have dissolved. Have ready your jelly jars. Bottle and seal.

Rose Petal Jelly—Things have got to where I can't answer a lot of mail personally or properly since the first six editions of this book have come out but I can still enjoy reading it:

"Dear Carla: The recipe book I bought has been given to a friend—who lives on top of Green Peter Mountain, and who shot a bear (a real, live bear) that was getting honey from the hives. Not only did she shoot it, she skinned it and put both hide and meat into the deep freeze. Perhaps you would like to have this:

"*Sara's Rose Petal Jelly:* 2 quarts pink rose petals, 3 cups boiling water, 3 cups sugar, ¼ cup lemon juice and 1 package M.C.P. pectin. Gather rose petals in early morning just after the dew has left. Yellow petals may be added if you are short of your quarts. Red rose petals may also be used but be careful since they have a much stronger flavor. Pour the boiling water over the petals and steep until all color is absorbed. Measure sugar into a dish to add later. Measure rosewater and lemon juice into a 6- or 8-quart kettle. Add pectin and stir well. Place on hottest fire and bring to a boil. Add measured sugar and mix well. Continue stirring and bring to a full rolling boil. Boil exactly 2 minutes. Skim and pour into prepared glasses and seal.

"And Sara's the one who shot the bear!"

I got that letter from Corean Morgan of Sweet Home, Oregon.

Rosebud Ice Cubes—Freeze a tiny rosebud in each cube to float in special summer drinks.

Rose Petal Bread—Add 1 cup lightly packed rose petals, 1 teaspoon rose extract (Maid of Scandinavia has it), 3 teaspoons lemon extract and extra sweetening to a regular 2-loaf white bread recipe.

Catherine Shirley really knows her roses as well as her lavender. Here are some rose recipes she sent me.

"Crystallized Rose Petals—I pick a few first roses. They are dark pink fragrant ones of the old fashioned kind. They have thorns, this project is rather tedious and time consuming, but makes nice gifts when put in nice containers at Christmas time. They are also pleasant to eat. I picked a few roses with short stems. This makes the roots get stronger. I cut off the white part which is the base of the rose, because it is bitter. I take the petals apart and wash each carefully under running water, or if water is not plentiful I swish each petal in a pan of water and change the water quite often. Put on paper towel to dry. Then take an egg white, add a little cold water and beat slightly. I dip each petal in the egg white and lift it out with a fork and lay on granulated sugar, press gently and carefully turn it over and treat same way and lift and lay on piece of waxed paper. Let dry thoroughly, turn over, let other side dry thoroughly. Then pack in a dark jar so they will keep their color. Damask or cabbage roses are especially good for confection."

Rose Beads—This is Catherine Shirley's recipe that Darlene tried. Darlene's lovely eldest daughter won Junior Miss this year at Kendrick and got 5 dozen roses. "I pick enough roses to make a heaping full cast-iron skillet after bases are cut off. A rusty skillet makes beads velvety black. As a rule black beads are preferred. I pour in enough rainwater to reach almost to the top. Then bring it up with low heat to a simmer or preferably just under simmering stage, and keep it thus for 1 hour. Then take it off until the next day. Next day stir up the petals and simmer for 1 hour. Then take it off until the next day. Next day again stir up the petals and simmer same way for 1 hour. Third day stir up the petals again and simmer same way again. By this time it should be like a stiff dough that is all black. If a little too dry add a little more rainwater which is nature's distilled water. If a little too moist, then simmer a little longer. I should say under simmer.

"In order to get the beads practically one size I take a piece of an old hose, press the bead dough into it so it is full and take a piece of dowel just round enough to get in the piece of hose and push the dough out of the other end on a marked surface in order to get them the same lengths. Cut with a knife, even lengths as marked. Then take each cut piece and roll in the palm of the hands until nice and round.

"The hose size would make them about three times as large as the size they should be because they shrink a lot. After the bead is rolled, then stick a rustproof straight pin in and let dry. Before they get too dry pins should be turned so the dough does not stick on the pins and so they can be removed easily. After the pins are removed the beads should be left to dry the pin holes more thoroughly. If they are preferred to be velvety black they do not need any more treatments. Otherwise the palms can be oiled with sweet oil and rub the beads between the oiled palms to make the beads shiny. Then they are ready to string with gold or crystal beads or both."

"The best roses are still the old fashioned kind such as cabbage, Chrysler Imperial, moss roses, dog rose which the more the petals dry the more intense the fragrance, and their fragrance lasts more permanently. Hybrid roses are fragrant while growing but lose their fragrance after being simmered. You can pick leaves for fresh or dried anytime after the plant is mature. Use in sachets or to flavor jelly, cake, etc.

"P.S. I make crystallized pinks or carnations called 'pinks' and they taste nice like clove-flavored candy."

ROSE GERANIUM isn't hardy. Don't plant outside until sunny early summer days. Repot and bring indoors before frost. To propagate make root cuttings.

Rose Geranium Jelly is made by flavoring apple jelly. Wash the apples but do not peel or core. Quarter the apples and barely cover with water. Simmer until tender. Get the juice and put it through a jelly bag, measure apple juice and return it to the stove. When it is boiling add ¾ cup sugar per cup juice. Boil on to jelly stage. When almost done put a few rose geranium leaves into the boiling jelly. They quickly give off their flavor. Dip them up and down until you have the desired taste and fragrant smell. Use 2 or 3 leaves for each pint. Tint a rose color with food coloring. Remove the leaves. Pour the jelly into your jars and seal.

Rose Geranium Leaf Cake Flavoring—Put a leaf in the bottom of a cake pan and pour the cake batter over it.

Rose Geranium Cake—Sift together 2 cups flour, ½ teaspoon salt and 1 teaspoon baking powder. Cream ½ cup butter and 1 cup sugar. Add alternately the flour and ⅔ cup water. Last add the unbeaten whites of 4 eggs. Whip hard for 5 minutes. Line a loaf pan with buttered paper and rose geranium leaves. Pour in batter. Bake in a 350° oven for 30 to 45 minutes. Pull the leaves off with the paper when the cake is done.

ROSE HIP is the round reddish "fruit" (also called "haw") formed after the flowers of the wild rose have bloomed. The hip is the seedpod of the plant. Tea can be brewed from the rose hips. They can be dried for winter use. When picking rose hips be sure they have not been sprayed. Those growing along railroad tracks and major highways probably have been sprayed and should be avoided. Gather them in the late fall or all winter long when they are bright red after the first frost. Keep cool until you can prepare them or dry and store. Wash and cut both ends of hips with scissors. Cover if you cook them. Use wooden spoons and earthenware or china bowls. Cook in glass or enamel pans or stainless steel.

Three of them have more vitamin C than the average orange! A single cup of pared rose hips may contain as much vitamin C as 10 to 12 dozen oranges. The *Rosa rugosa* species is best because its hips are about 1 inch across—much easier to work with. But you can use any hips that grow handy.

Dried Rose Hips—Dry in a slow oven (150°) until they are hard and brittle. Then store when thoroughly dry in airtight jars. If not real dry, they will mold. When ready to use cover with water and simmer until soft. Use the pulp to make jam or jelly. It mixes good with other fruits like apple or cranberry.

Rose Hip Tea—Boil dried coarse ground rose hips with water, about 1 tablespoonful for each cup of tea. The longer you boil the stronger your tea. Strain. Sweeten with brown sugar or honey.

Doris's Rose Hip Tea—Stem the hips. Dry them. Grind. Mix dried ground hips with mint and well-dried strawberry leaves. Use ¼ rose hips, ¼ mint and the rest wild strawberry leaves. Or leave out the mint.

Rose Hip Syrup—Wash fresh hips and remove stems. Put 2 pounds through food chopper using medium blade. Cover with 6 cups boiling water and boil 2 minutes. Strain through sieve and put remainder in a jelly bag to drain. There should be 1½ pints of liquid. If more, boil down. Add ¾ cup sugar and boil 5 minutes. Bottle.

Rose Hip Jam—Try to preserve the hips the same day you pick them. Boil 4 cups berries with 2½ cups water until berries are tender. Put through sieve to remove seeds. Add 1 cup sugar for every 2 cups pulp. Add 1 teaspoon lemon juice. Mix thoroughly and bring slowly to a simmer. Cook about 20 minutes. Seal.

Rose Hip Extract—Lila Morris of Beavercreek, Oregon, sent me this one. She says to add it to breakfast juice, gelatin, desserts, meat sauces, soups or

sherbet for lots of vitamin C. Gather rose hips, chill and remove blossom ends, stems and leaves. Rinse off. For each cup of hips bring to a rolling boil 1½ cups water. Add the cup of rose hips. Cover and simmer 15 minutes. Mash with fork or potato masher and let set 24 hours. Strain off liquid part. That's your extract. Bring extract to a good boil. Add 2 tablespoons vinegar or lemon juice for each pint. Pour hot into jars and seal.

Rose Hip Jelly—Wash, stem and chop your hips. For every 4 cups of hips boil 2 cups water 5 minutes and then let hang overnight in a jelly bag to get the juice. For every 1 cup of rose hip juice add 3 cups of apple juice. Boil 10 minutes. Gradually add 1 cup sugar for every cup of juice you are working with and boil until it jells.

ROSELLE JELLY—Cover the roselles with water and cook until tender. Strain through a jelly bag. Measure the juice. Boil it 5 minutes. Add 1½ cups sugar and 2 teaspoons lemon juice per 2 cups roselle juice. Cook until it sheets from the spoon. Skim. Pour into your jelly jars and seal.

ROSEMARY—A tender perennial whose leaves are somewhat like evergreen needles. It looks like a tiny pine tree. Harvest when in full bloom. It can be used fresh or dried for seasoning. Grows fine in a pot. Pluck some needles to add to boiling potatoes or broiled lamb chops. Add some to spaghetti sauce.

Herbal Hamburger—Melt 1 tablespoon butter with ½ teaspoon dried rosemary in frying pan. Stir a bit to let rosemary flavor butter. (Don't brown butter.) Add about 1 pound of hamburger shaped into patties and cook. Remove hamburgers when done. Add another tablespoon butter to pan drippings together with ½ teaspoon dry mustard and a dash of Worcestershire sauce. Stir a minute. Pour over hamburgers.

Rosemary Tea—Pour boiling water over the needles and steep until strong enough.

RUE—Harvest in the early summer. The leaves can be steeped for a tea. The flavor is bitter as the name implies.

SAGE—A perennial that you can order from the larger seed catalogs. It is fine seasoning for sausage and poultry stuffings. Cut the stems just before flowering or when the crop is matured as you prefer.
Tie in bunches and hang up to dry. It grows fine in a pot. You propagate by stem cuttings and root division in early spring.

If you want just a few leaves go out and pick them anytime but be kind to your new plants until they are pretty well started. The best leaves are from the tips of the branches. Cull the old woody plants.

Stuffing—If you are using fresh sage for flavoring stuffing, soak it for 5 minutes in boiling water, then dry carefully before chopping.

Sage Bread—This is a good sandwich bread. If your milk is raw scald it first. Use 2 cups milk, ¼ cup sugar, 2 teaspoons salt, 2 teaspoons celery seed and 1 teaspoon ground sage. Add ¼ cup cooking oil, 2 eggs and 2 tablespoons yeast. Mix it all well. Add enough flour to make a kneadable dough. Knead, let rise, punch down and divide into two loaves. Put loaves into greased bread pans, let rise again until doubled in bulk. Bake at 400° until loaf sounds hollow when rapped. (Some people let this bread have an extra rising and punching down before making into loaves.)

Sage Tea—Steep sage leaves in boiling water as you would for store-bought tea. Strain. Sweeten with honey. For a medicinal gargle brew until dark green in color.

Clary sage is a fragrance fixative same as orris-root. Good with rose petals, lavenders and mints in potpourri—which you *smell*, don't eat!

SASSAFRAS—A tree that can be grown in mild climates like Texas and Arkansas. The leaves are made into filé. The wood, root and bark can all be used for teamaking. The FDA took it off the market. I know there is something in it very strong because it always gave me indigestion. Maybe the problem is they use the wrong part of it. Mrs. Marv Renwald, Lake Village, Indiana, wrote me: "My grandpa told me to use only the bark and to gather it when the leaves are as big as a thumb joint in the spring."

Filé is a traditional gumbo ingredient. To make it dry young sassafras leaves in the shade and pulverize them with a few leaves of the sweet bay. When added to soup (gumbo) they add a distinctive flavoring and thickening effect. If you don't have sassafras you can substitute young okra pods for the filé.

Sassafras Gumbo #1—Sassafras leaves, dried and powdered—1 large spoonful to a pot of beef soup. Put in a few minutes before taking from fire.

Sassafras Gumbo #2—6 squirrels or 2 chickens, cut up small and cooked until flesh falls from bones. Put in a handful of sassafras buds per gallon (either green or dried in a bag). One quart okra, 2 onions, cut fine, 6 white potatoes, diced, grated carrot, a little cabbage, pepper and salt. Remove sassafras bag before serving. Add pod of red pepper. Thicken with browned flour.

Sassafras Tea Wood—Really stretches—you can brew and brew and brew with it. Chop roots into bits for your tea wood and boil. (Don't let an aluminum pan stand with sassafras tea in it—it coats and won't

come off.) It's also good iced, sweetened with brown sugar. You can reuse the sassafras roots several times although the first brew has the finest flavor. In general use 1 ounce of sassafras to 2 cups of water for a strong tea.

SAVORY—An annual planted from seed in the early spring. Harvest when tips begin to bloom. Dried leaves good in poultry stuffing, with meats and green beans. Grows fine in a pot.

SLIPPERY ELM—The inner bark was once broken into bits to make the famous tea. They poured 1 cup of boiling water over 1 teaspoonful of slippery elm bark and let it steep until cold. When cold, it was strained, lemon juice added and sweetened to taste. But since the elms are having such a hard time anyway, I'd leave them alone and try something else.

SORREL—French sorrel and miniature sorrel are two different sorrels, yet very similar in many ways. The French sorrel will grow ten times larger than the little sorrel. However, children especially love the tangy, fresh miniature sorrel greens. This miniature sorrel can be served year-round as a salad green. Eat raw or cooked. Use young leaves in soups and green salads. Mince and use with or without chives or young onions in cottage cheese. Grows from a bulb which you can transplant to your own garden if you find it growing wild. Or it will self-sow once you have a plant for two years.

TARRAGON—Grows fine in a pot. The fresh leaves are good with beets. Sauté them in butter or oil and baste the chicken with it. Tarragon is a perennial propagated by stem cuttings or root division in the early spring. Harvest when tips begin to bloom. A mixture of finely chopped tarragon, onion and parsley is good in an omelet or scrambled eggs.

THYME—A perennial. "Common thyme," the variety you want for eating, is easily grown. Propagate by root cluster division starting the second year. The dried leaves are a seasoning ingredient for many soups and sauces. To use, cut the tender new leaves and flowering tips. To keep, dry and store in *glass* jars with tight lids. You can make tea from the dried leaves or flavor meats, soups, poultry and gravies. Use fresh leaves in salads. Thyme grows well in a pot, too. Plant it in a hanging basket and keep it moist.

VANILLA—The whole bean from which the genuine extract is made can be ordered from Lekvar-by-the-Barrel, 1577 First Avenue, New York, New York 10028.

Vanilla Extract—Use 4 ounces vanilla beans, 16 ounces edible alcohol and 16 ounces water. Slice the beans and cut into fine pieces with a sharp knife. Thoroughly powder them in a mortar with 1 or 2 ounces granulated sugar. Put the powder into the alcohol and water mixture. If you don't have pure alcohol and are substituting a strong whisky blend or brandy use correspondingly less water. Let the vanilla soak in the liquid for 4 weeks. Strain. The liquid is your extract. You can add the old dregs to a new batch for extra economy. Old-time imitation vanilla extract was sometimes made using half or all tonka beans in place of vanilla beans to make it cheaper.

Easy Vanilla Extract—Violet Stewart of Okay, Oklahoma, wrote me that she simply takes 1 quart of any good 80-proof brandy, splits 2 vanilla beans and drops them in. Cork and let sit for 2 months before using.

WINTERGREEN—A little evergreen plant with small white flowers. It grows wild in Minnesota, Wisconsin, New York and Connecticut. It will grow between 1,000 and 3,000 feet but 2,000 is ideal for it. To get some in your garden you have to do it by root division in the fall before frost or spring. Harvest in early September or October. A lathe shelter to grow it in is a good idea since it must have partial shade to grow well. Wintergreen or some wintergreen extract is a must in homemade root beer. Wintergreen leaves are nice to chew on fresh. Dried or fresh they make a fragrant tea. Use a cupful of the fresh leaves per quart of water.

TEAS AND COFFEES

In colonial America when tea drinking became unpatriotic during the Revolutionary War (remember the Boston Tea Party!) the conventional China tea leaves were replaced by raspberry leaves, loosestrife, hardtack, goldenrod, dittany, blackberry leaves, sage and many others. Some other homemade drinks enjoyed on the frontier were teas made from wild rose hips, mint, oat straw, sarsaparilla and the marrow from beef bones. Rye and chestnuts, ground and roasted, or roasted crushed barley alone, were made into "coffees." Look under the "Herbs and Flavorings" list for more information about all the different kinds of plants you can make a tea out of. Regular China tea and South American coffee contain caffeine and really aren't good for you. These alternative teas and coffees do no harm. So you can drink teas and coffees made from the dried leaves and stems of many plants, from barks and nuts, and grains too.

"Infusions" and "decoctions" aren't the same thing. A decoction is made by boiling the herb in water (an average of 10 minutes) and straining while hot. Coffee is a familiar decoction. An infusion is made by pouring hot water over the herb and then letting it steep. Tea is an infusion.

Leaf teas are easy to make. Boil water. Pour in leaves, take off the stove and let set for a while. (Don't boil herbs.) Use from 1 teaspoon to ¼ cup herbs per quart water or thereabouts. You really must experiment to get it just right. Every herb is a little different and so are tastes. Get to know your teas and you'll be able to judge by the color when you have the desired strength. Sweeten with brown sugar or honey to really complement the taste of herb tea. In general leaves and flowers are steeped; roots and seeds are boiled. You can freeze your leftover tea to use for quick servings but strain out the herbs first or it will get stronger and stronger and stronger! To serve put a little strainer over your cup and pour through that.

East Indian Tea—Make black tea, add milk and honey and keep heating. Add ginger, cinnamon and ground cardamom to taste.

Health Tea—One pound fresh (or 2 ounces dried) Russian comfrey, 1 bunch lemon balm (or ½ to 1 ounce dried) or ½ cup lemon juice and 1 bunch spearmint (or small amount dried). Put 5 quarts hard boiling water in a 16-quart enamel kettle with cover. Add comfrey, lemon balm and spearmint to the boiling water. Cover and steep 20 minutes. Add honey to taste—we prefer clover honey. If lemon juice is used instead of lemon balm, add it before honey. Stir well. Put in jugs in the refrigerator and drink as wanted, like lemonade.

Herbed Lemonade—Add any concentrated herb tea to lemonade and chill for a nice different drink.

Sun Tea—Fill a gallon jar with water. Add your herbs. Screw on a lid tightly. Shake a moment. Let set in the hot sun for 4 or 5 hours. Or more. Like a day. Or two. Or three. Shake again occasionally. Now strain out the herbs. Add honey—or lemon juice. Teas made this way are less bitter. Tannin out of store-bought tea (Far East kind) won't go into solution as much when treated this way. This is a good way to fix dried fruit, too—like prunes, plums or apples. Just combine fruit, water, sweetening, cinnamon and let it set in the sun all afternoon. I got these recipes at a phone-in radio program in Wichita, Kansas, January 1975.

Folks there in Wichita also recommended mint leaves in lemonade, raspberry leaves for when you're in labor and sarsaparilla for any fellow who needs more manhood!

COFFEES THAT AREN'T COFFEE

You can buy one at the store called Postum. Mike and I have drunk it for years and enjoy it. Postum is made from ground roasted grain. Mike drinks a teaspoon of Postum in a cup of hot water. That's too strong for me. I like it with honey and milk, about one-third or one-fourth milk. I often make a whole coffeepot of it that way and share it with the children for breakfast. Unlike real coffee, I can share coffees that aren't coffee all I want to. It's more comfortable than saying to a child "that's not good for you; you can't have any" and they are standing there watching me drink it. The wise psychologists say our children imitate what we do and not what we say. In their innocent devotion they are trying to follow the true form of our behavior. You can drink Postum in all milk or in milk with a dash of cocoa or made into an eggnog with milk or with milk flavored with molasses. Another store noncoffee is called Yannoh. It is made from barley, wheat, soya, chickpeas, rice, dandelion and burdock roots. You perk it just like coffee. If the grocer doesn't have it you can ask him to order it for you. Yannoh can be bought at health food stores.

Homemade Roasted Grain Coffee—Combine 8 cups wheat bran, 3 beaten eggs, 2 cups cornmeal and 1 cup molasses or sorghum. Spread the mixture on a cookie sheet and bake slowly at about 200°, stirring often. Boil with water to serve.

Acorn Coffee—Select plump, round, sweet acorns. Shell and brown in oven. Grind in a coffee mill and use as ordinary coffee. Or do this: Hull out ½ cup of small acorns. Add ½ cup cracked wheat. Mix. Roast in your oven. Pound in a mortar. Boil with water to get your coffee. Add honey, molasses or brown sugar to sweeten.

Dandelion Root Coffee is another common substitute. Look in the preceding herb list under "D" for dandelion for your recipe.

Chicory is a real multiple use plant. Use young, tender leaves for salads or boil as greens. Dry the roots, grind and use as a substitute for coffee. First grow your chicory (no raw manure—it encourages crooked roots). Cut off the green tops (make salad). Scrub or scrape the roots, slice them and string on a thread your little circles or strips of chicory. Hang up to dry. When completely dry, spread on cookie sheet and roast at a low temperature until a very dark brown—they start to smell like a chocolate cake. Taste to sample for the moment of roasted perfection. Now cool the chicory. Grind it with mortar and pestle. Serve it by first boiling a pot of water, then drop in a spoonful of chicory, stir, let steep a few minutes and there you are. Chicory is stronger than coffee so use less. Serve plain or with honey and cream. You can make more chicory coffee out of the same grounds.

Cocoa that isn't cocoa—If you live in the right place you could grow a carob tree. The carob "fruit" when ground is amazingly similar to cocoa and universally agreed to be better for you. You can buy a commercial preparation of it called Cara-coa at health food stores.

WILD FOOD FORAGING

May 25, 1976. Last summer a forest ranger near here sat down to eat his packed lunch out in the woodsy open. He spotted an interesting looking plant nearby, broke off a leaf and added it to the inside of his sandwich experimentally and ate his lunch. He was dead within two hours. A little boy 25 miles down the road from us at Lapwai, Idaho, spotted a big reedy plant that looked just right for whistle making. He carved himself a very fine whistle out of it, blew on it to see if it worked . . . and died. Those are true stories. They both happened in the summer of 1975 and in both cases hemlock was involved. Hemlock is one of the most poisonous plants in the world. It's the same plant family that they fed to Socrates in a cup and he drank it and died. They gave him water hemlock which is native to Greece and causes death within five minutes. Hemlock has migrated from Europe to the United States and is spreading all over North America. It likes to grow in shady places and spreads along river and creek banks. The North American kind takes from a half hour to two hours to kill you.

Wild hemlock

Hemlock is a member of the carrot family. It is a biennial. The first year it grows low and has a very carroty looking top. It is making a sturdy root which is the most poisonous part of it. The next year energy from that big root pours up into building a sturdy tall stalk, five or six feet high, perfect looking whistle material. Then it flowers and makes seed at the top of the stalk. Flowers and seeds are poisonous, too. Some neighbors down the road with a lot of the stuff chopped it all down, gathered it into a pile and set fire to it. The smoke made their whole family sick. The county weed control agent told them that fumes from burning hemlock were also poisonous. His name is Homer Fudder and he has a personal campaign to try to stop the hemlock and to stop people from dying of it. He told me you can even die if you try to pull out the plant and have a cut on your hand and get hemlock juice into it.

But you say you've got a book that tells you which wild foods are edible and which aren't. Well, right in front of me I have an article called "Principal Food Plants of the United States" published in an utterly respectable wilderness and country living magazine. It says "HEMLOCK—(all year) young tips used for tea and formerly in root beer; inner bark used for breadstuff; sap, potable." It doesn't distinguish between the nonpoisoning hemlock *tree* and the poisonous hemlock *plant*. If that one entry in a list of a couple hundred "food plants" is *that* potentially misleading, how much can the others be trusted?

And then again could a person make a mistake in their plant identification? Could someone who had lived in the country all his life make a mistake between hemlock and Indian celery? They are actually very similar and that exact mistake did apparently happen here just a month ago. The people who ate hemlock thinking it was something else didn't die. They took ipecac which is a medicine to make you throw up. Then they were rushed to the hospital, had their stomachs pumped and were then given a medicine to clean them out from the other end. Maybe it really wasn't hemlock in the first place. But the plant expert at the University of Idaho that they took a sample to said it was.

What about the books that discuss plants that have "medicinal uses"? I found hemlock in one of those. It said it was good to strengthen male potency. You just can't believe everything you read and I've written enough pages of this book myself to understand how often authors end up simply collecting information already in print with the danger ever present of passing on somebody else's error. That isn't terribly criminal when the intentions are good—except maybe when the results could be fatal. That's why this book doesn't have a real wild foods section. You'll find wild foods mentioned here and there in it, nettle tea, poke salet from the South, dandelion root and greens, elderberries and chokecherries, but only when I know from personal experience or from common experience of friends and neighbors that it really is edible. Please don't get mad at me. I don't mean to put down the bulk of the wonderful research that has been done on wild foods and I'm sure it's true that

dandelions, for example, have more vitamins and minerals in them than any garden plant. But just be cautious what you make a sandwich of.

While we're talking about poisonous plants here are some more to look out for. Hyacinth, daffodil and narcissus all have bulbs. If you eat the bulb it will cause nausea, vomiting, diarrhea and may be fatal. Oleander leaves and branches are extremely poisonous. They affect the heart, produce severe digestive upset and have been known to cause death. Poinsettia is so poisonous that even one leaf can kill a child. All parts of dieffenbachia cause intense burning and irritation of the mouth and tongue. Death can occur if the tongue swells enough to close the throat so air cannot get through. Rosary pea and castor bean seeds are fatal. A single rosary pea seed has caused death. One or two castor bean seeds are a near fatal dose to an adult let alone a child. Mistletoe berries are fatal to both children and adults. Larksonia seeds can be fatal. The fleshy roots of monkshood are poisonous.

And that's not all. Autumn crocus bulbs cause trouble. Lily of the valley leaves and flowers affect the heartbeat, stomach and mind badly. Foxglove leaves are one of the sources of the drug digitalis used to stimulate the heart. In large amounts it can be fatal. Bleeding heart leaves and roots may be poisonous in large amounts. Rhubarb leaves eaten in large amounts, even when cooked, can cause convulsions and coma rapidly followed by death. A few daphne berries can kill a child. All parts of laurels, azaleas and rhododendron are fatal, producing nausea and vomiting, depression, difficulty in breathing, prostration and coma. Jessamine berries are fatal. Yew berries and leaves are fatal with the leaves being more so than the berries. Death is sudden with no warning symptoms. This list was sent to me by my dear friend Violet Stewart who has taught me as much about wild food foraging as anyone. Violet said to me, "I hope you can find a space for this in your book sometime. I'll feel I may have had a part in saving one life."

HOME-BOTTLED BEVERAGES

If you've been reading this book just to see what strange and irrelevant thing I'm going to say next, this chapter once wasn't such good pickings for you. It is one of the oldest chapters of my book—written before my readers finally got the message through to me that I was supposed to sound like myself instead of like a book. The way that happened was with the first two issues of the book that I mailed out to the "subscribers" I also sent cover letters to explain a few things I thought needed explaining. Enough people wrote me back to say that my book would do but they really enjoyed the cover letters. That got me to thinking and I ended up doing all my writing the same way as those cover letters. I've been leafing through those old letters. Here's a copy of one I wrote in February 1971.

"Thank you very much for your check and order for the *Old Fashioned Recipe Book!* I will send it as soon as possible, but I must beg your patience because that may be as long as a month yet." No kidding, I said that. On January 18, 1972 (my 33rd birthday), I was in the process of mailing out the first issue (chapters Definitions and Measures, Home Industries except Candles, and Herbs and Flavorings) and this is an excerpt from that cover letter.

"Then I was informed by a friend that I may be breaking the law by advertising and selling a book of which I have not got all. I started having melancholy fantasies of myself pining away in jail and the children crying for their mother and every time somebody drove up to the house I worried that it might be the sheriff coming to get me. I suggested to Mike that we just send everybody's money back. He said that after all he had gone through with me on this book if I quit now he'd disapprove so much that it wouldn't be worth it to me. He added that the book was ruining our life together and what I had better do was just finish it."

The next issue of the book was maybe half of Meats and the Beverage chapter. The cover letter is dated May 31, 1972, which is probably within a month or so. It says things like this: "On a recent infrequent trip to our local metropolis of Lewiston (24 miles, 30,000 people metropolitan area) to take a sick baby to the doctor I got stopped by a State Patrolman. Turned out I was missing one license plate, didn't have my driver's license or registration for the car, didn't know my social security number or the car's make or year. That's what country living and having babies and trying to write a book can do to you!

"If your second issue of the book smells funny it's because the chapters were stored in a chick house. That smell is your certification of homestead genuineness. Quite a few of the envelopes got chicken droppings on them because one batch of chicks learned to fly higher than I expected and took to roosting on a box of envelopes. If your envelope has the stamp on upside down, is somewhat illegible, or otherwise strange it's probably because my children are big wheels in the mail department."

OF BEVERAGES—The quickest and easiest way I know to keep working men and women happy in hot weather is to keep gallon jars of cool liquid in the refrigerator and a plastic gallon jar of ice cubes in the freezer compartment. I make lots of tea (wild strawberry leaf is Mike's favorite and camomile is mine . . . we use a lot of wild mint too). I sweeten the tea with honey, chill it and serve plain or with ice cubes for a special treat. I also keep our plain old spring water chilled in the refrigerator in summer for drinks, too. And the children enjoy the juices canned up from the previous summer's fruit crop, thinned with cold water.

Way back in the times I was just writing about, when the book was first getting made, I had hopes of finding a girl to come and work with me. I only got two inquiries that summer. The first was somebody's sister whose sister I think was more enthused than she was. She called me up long distance from Michigan and when I told her we worked about a 12-hour day in the summer she decided she wasn't interested. Then an Oregon girl got interested and drove all the way over here. She stayed an hour declared our place was "'just like my mother-in-law's" and left. By the next summer I was getting some real solid inquiries but by then Mike and I had decided to not try to take on any extras. But it's really not so bad around here in the summer—12-hour days and all—and part of what makes it tolerable is having good things to drink.

HOW TO BOTTLE BEVERAGES THAT ARE INTENDED TO FERMENT IN THE BOTTLE

This includes ginger ale, root beer and whatever else you want to try.

First start collecting bottles. Up to 25 quart bottles or up to 75 small bottles is a good supply. The best are returnable soft drink bottles. Beer bottles can't stand nearly as much pressure and are dangerous and unreliable—one could blow up in your face. It is almost impossible to get the pressure equal in all bottles. It always seems that more yeast and/or sugar end up in some bottles than in others resulting in varying pressures. I've used nonreturnable bottles but have had some scary incidents with them so there's fair warning. Don't save screw top bottles because they can't be capped.

Clean your bottles—the bathtub is a good place. A bottle brush is handy. Put water in the tub, fill each bottle with water, shake and empty. Repeat a couple of times. Then hold it up to the light to make sure that somebody didn't use it for an ashtray—cigarette butts and ashes stick to the bottom and resist soaking— might as well discard it. It is easiest of all if you cleaned the bottles right after they were used. Box up the clean bottles and carry them out to your working area. For beer, pour the required amount of sugar into each bottle before you begin bottling.

You need a siphon. That is essentially a rubber tube about four feet in length. You may have to buy a shower attachment at the drugstore and rob it of its tube. (It has a spray nozzle on one end, tube, and mouth to fit on the faucet at the other end. Remove nozzle and mouth if you can. But a narrower tube would give you more efficiency.) To use the siphon put one end of it in the beverage container. The beverage has to be sitting higher than the area where you will be filling bottles at the other end of the siphon. Station somebody at the beverage container to make sure the opening of the siphon tube stays under the fluid but above the sediment. I usually put the crock on my kitchen counter and sit in a chair beside it with the free end of the siphon in my lap. I hold a big bowl between my knees to catch the inevitable stray squirts between bottles and have the empty bottles in a box on the floor within easy reach. With my little daughter holding the top end of the siphon under the liquid and my little son handing me bottles together we can do a whole bottling job. If you can't find a siphon at all, use a dipper and funnel and fill each bottle that way.

Suck on the tube from the low end as you would through a straw but hard until the fluid starts running. It won't stop then until the crock is empty unless the upper end comes out of the fluid. (If it does you'll have to suck to get it flowing again.) Put your thumb over the opening in the hose to hold back the fluid until you have a bottle in place (or bend the hose) and get a bottle with your other hand. Hold the bottle in the bowl in your lap, get the siphon into the neck of the bottle and let it fill, then plug the nozzle with your thumb again, set the full bottle on the floor, reach for another empty—on and on until you've used up your beverage. If the fluid won't come check your tube carefully for a crack or hole. If you find one it may work to cover it tighly by wrapping adhesive around the tube (make sure it's dry when you do it). Now put the full bottles on the table. Adjust the fluid level so that it is within a half inch of the top. Have ready your bottle capper and box of caps. The bottle capper and bottles you can use over and over. The caps you have to buy fresh every time. The capper should cost around $8. You can buy one from Sears, Roebuck, Montgomery Ward, some local hardware stores, and also by mail order from Herter's (Waseca, Minnesota 56093) and Maid of Scandinavia. The caps are available at many grocery stores in boxes of 144 for about 50¢ or by mail-order from the above companies (for more). If you are trying to cap shorter beer bottles you'll have to put a block of wood under the bottle because the capper won't screw down that far. To cap press the lid on very firmly. Look at it to make sure you got it on right. The sides should be folded down with a slight pressure indentation in the center of the cap.

Rinse the bottles to clean off spilled beverage. Put them away. Devise a method of distinguishing your batches in storage. You could alternate by storing one batch on its sides and the next batch perpendicularly. If you stack horizontally you can make very efficient use of a limited storage space. Don't try to make home-bottled beverages more than ten days ahead because a hot spell may have you scurrying to put the whole batch in the refrigerator lest the pressure get too high and your refrigerator can only hold so many bottles. But hot spells also increase consumption. It's a good idea to boil the water before making any of the home-bottled beverages in order to discourage the wild yeast that can cause excessive fermentation and bottle pressure. Set your pan in a sink full of cold water for quick cooling of the water to lukewarm.

Fermentation rate is related to heat. In winter your crock or bottle may ferment all day and stop at night. In summer with hot days and hot nights it will race along and you may find yourself with bottles blowing up. A cold spell can put the yeast into a sort of hibernation from which it awakens when the weather gets warm again. The yeast will ferment as long as it has sugar to feed on. If it does not run out of sugar and stop growing it will continue until it produces enough alcohol to kill it. A little fermentation gives you a fizzy fun beverage that everyone will enjoy. A lot gives a strong tasting alcoholic beverage.

Store the bottles in a quiet place. If a bottle blows up it probably means you used too fragile a bottle or let it work too long considering the temperature. If you are afraid the pressures are getting too high in your bottles, immediately put them in the refrigerator and fermentation will slow down a lot, pressure will reduce somewhat with chilling, and all will be well for a while more. When you open a bottle and half the contents come foaming out—that means the pressure is dangerously high. If you follow recipes closely as to the amount of yeast and sugar, stir your ingredients well, don't bottle the sediment, use returnable soft drink bottles and *boil* the beverage before cooling and adding yeast—hot weather spells should be your only problem. When the temperature stays up day and night over 70° I would consider reducing the yeast and keep a close watch on the pressure developing. Plan on regular checking of sample bottles to keep you informed.

BOTTLING FOR CHILDREN—For small children's beverages I think half the fun for them is helping with the bottling and the other half is drinking it out of the bottle. Take any punch recipe or juice. Dilute it to save yourself money. Out of the bottle it will taste good anyway and then you can let them drink all they want in hot weather. If you are planning to add a little fizz by letting some yeast work briefly, be sure and dilute the juice because otherwise it will taste too strong. (Yeast always exaggerates flavor besides adding a very definite taste of its own.) To make completely unfizzed drinks and thus avoid the yeast taste, have instant servability, and time before pressure and fermentation become problems—boil your beverage, bottle as hot as you can stand it, add no yeast, keep refrigerated and if you have children I guarantee you won't have any left around to get too cold. If you use a trace of yeast and then refrigerate after about 18 hours, you'll have plenty of fizz and a trace of alcohol content. A two-gallon batch makes around 21 bottles varying some according to just what size bottles you have.

BOTTLING WITH A CORK—This is all right for fruit syrups, vinegars and alcoholic beverages. Pare the cork to fit. Ram it in and tip into melted paraffin the whole head and neck of the bottle if you want an additional seal. If you are having trouble with getting corks in, try twisting the cork to get it in further or driving it in with a mallet. Fill the bottles to within an inch of where you figure the cork will touch. If you are trying to keep a sterile solution sterilize your bottles. Boil your solution 5 to 15 minutes. Steam the cork to sterilize it and work with it all hot. When it has cooled, go ahead and dip in paraffin.

CORKERS—Or you can buy a corker. Lewiston's Morgan Brothers carries two kinds of them. One is a wooden corker, imported from Germany for $3.80. You have to use your own hammer or wooden mallet (he has those, too) to help ram the cork through. The other is a $7.95 all metal corker. It's somewhat similar to a bottle capper and you don't need to hammer to make it work. To use either of these:

1. Soak the cork overnight in water.

2. Put the cork in the corker and fit the corker over the bottle.

3. Force the cork into the bottle mouth. (The corker squeezes the cork to narrow it temporarily and provides a follower so you can ram the cork in without fracturing the bottle. The wet cork slips in easily and then expands to stay firmly in place.)

Capper

Corker

SERVING—When you are ready to serve a beverage fermented with yeast let it stand quietly upright in the refrigerator for at least several hours and preferably longer. Then decant carefully into some other container to avoid the yeast sediment in the bottom half inch or so. This will help the taste. But none of these beverages will give you the "lift" of commercial cola drinks. The commercial drinks contain caffeine and/or theobromine, which are stimulants. The former is found naturally in coffee and tea, the latter in cocoa.

CHARGED WATER—Certain mineral springs contain considerable quantities of carbon dioxide in solution. Such springs at Vichy, France, and Seltzer, Germany, were the origin of the antique terms

"Vichy" water and "Seltzer" water. Similar springs at Saratoga Springs, New York, and Manitou Springs, Colorado, were also famous. "Soft drinks" are charged by forcing carbon dioxide into the beverages under increased pressure. When the bottles are opened and the excess pressure is released, bubbles of carbon dioxide rapidly escape from the liquid. Soda water in fountains is charged with carbon dioxide. The gas is forced into solution under a pressure of several atmospheres. When the beverage was first manufactured, soda (sodium carbonate) was used with an acid to produce the carbon dioxide. That's how it became known as "soda water."

If you decide it isn't worth the struggle to make drinks with yeast I'll tell you that you can buy containers of charged water ($3 for 20) and a charger to use them in ($20) from Maid of Scandinavia Company, 3245 Raleigh Avenue, Minneapolis, Minnesota 55416. With a charger you could make your own soda waters and sodas on the spot. (I don't though.)

SUPPLIES. You can mail-order a number of beverage making supplies from Nichols Garden Nursery, 1190 North Pacific Highway, Albany, Oregon 97321, such as corks, plastic screw-on caps so you can reuse screw type bottles, and ready-made jelly bags (ask for a "nylon straining bag"). Morgan Brothers, 1305 Main, Lewiston, Idaho 83501, has all kinds of beverage making supplies as well as other things. It's a fascinating store. There are all sorts of crocks, barrels, cast-iron kettles and other wonderful stuff. You can buy three sizes of old-fashioned potato ricers, old-time tin washbasins for 35¢ each, tin water dippers for 39¢ each and tin cups, two for 25¢. They carry plain malt syrup for $1.17 for a three-pound can and I don't know of anyplace else where you can find it. That's the kind you use for cooking and vinegar making. Most places that have malt syrup carry the hop flavored kind for beer making and that makes vinegar bitter. Morgan Brothers also has hog scrapers, sausage making equipment of all sorts and *real* butcher knives (the kind you can shave with). And the elderly Mr. Morgan himself is an experience you're not likely to forget. He is a walking storehouse of all sorts of do-it-yourselfing lore and he loves to discuss it with people and to show them around the store. If you are looking for some peculiar old-time implement I'll bet Mr. Morgan can help you find it if you write him. And if you ever happen to drive through Lewiston, stop and tour the store yourself. It's on the highway and it doesn't look like much from the outside, just got a few crocks in a show window.

GINGER ALE

Ginger ale is a good base for a lot of other drinks when mixed with various fruit juices. If you like it stronger, just add more ginger or vice versa. If your weather is cold, add more yeast. If hot be prepared to refrigerate all your bottles as soon as you have the desired amount of fizz. It only takes a couple of days for it to work enough to be a real "pop" beverage.

Dissolve 2½ to 3 cups honey or 5¼ cups sugar in 2 gallons of water. Add the beaten whites of 3 eggs and 1 tablespoon ginger moistened with water. Put into a large pan and bring to the boiling point. Skim and set aside to cool. (You'll feel like you're losing all the ginger, but don't worry, even though a lot of it gets caught in this skimming, the flavor is there.) When lukewarm, add the juice of 4 lemons and ¼ teaspoon dry yeast. Stir well. Let stand a few moments, strain through a cloth and bottle. In 48 hours it will be ready to drink. If the pressure in your bottles builds up too much, refrigerate to stop fermentation. You will need about 22 bottles for this recipe.

Another Ginger Ale Recipe—Pound 3 tablespoons ginger root. Pour 4 quarts *boiling* water over it. Add the juice of 1 lime, 3 cups sugar or the equivalent in another sweetening and 3 tablespoons cream of tartar. Cover with a cloth so flies don't drop in. Cool to lukewarm. Add 1 tablespoon yeast. Let rest 6 hours and then chill and serve or bottle.

Unfermented Ginger Ale—Cut 4 ounces ginger root into small pieces and mix with 4 lemons, cut into strips as thin as you can manage. Pour 2 quarts boiling water over the mixture and let set 5 minutes. Strain out the solids and chill your liquid. Add 2 cups lemon juice and sweeten to taste. Dilute with cold water if it tastes strong or if intended for small children. Serve with ice and mint leaves in the glass for a hot weather special.

Mint Gingerade—Pour 2 cups sweetened boiling water (with a dash of salt in it, helps draw out the mint flavor) over 2 cups finely chopped mint leaves. Let stand until cool. Strain out the leaves. Add 2 quarts ginger ale or gingerade and serve very cold garnished with a pretty mint sprig.

Now here are some recipes for nice beverages you can make once your ginger ale is done.

Ginger Spiced Apple—Combine 1 quart apple juice, 6 cinnamon sticks, 16 whole cloves, ¼ teaspoon nutmeg and bring to a slow boil for 10 minutes. Strain. Chill. Add 1 quart chilled ginger ale.

Ginger Grape—4 cups ginger ale, 2 cups grape juice (or grapefruit juice, or orange juice) and 3 tablespoons lemon juice. Optional, sprig of mint. Add the ginger ale just before serving over ice.

Ginger, Grape, Grapefruit—Combine 3 cups ginger ale, 2 cups grapefruit juice and 2 cups grape juice.

Ginger Mint Lemon—Gather a bunch of mint, discarding the stems. Bruise the leaves and cover with ½ cup water and 1 cup lemon juice. Let soak an hour. Add 6 cups ginger ale, sweeten to taste and serve over ice.

Ginger Punch—Cook ¾ cup sugar (or ½ cup honey) in 4 cups water for 3 minutes. Add ½ cup lemon juice, 1 cup orange juice, grated rind of ½ orange and 1 tablespoon grated lemon rind. Cool. Add 1 quart ginger ale (or 1 quart tea).

ROOT BEER

You can either make your own root beer from scratch or make it using a commercial extract. It's harder to make now than it was though because the FDA has taken sassafras off the market. The most common store extract around here and the one with which I have experience is Hires. Our store charges 29¢ for a 3-ounce bottle. You can mail-order the extract from the Hires Company, 2201 Main Street, Evanston, Illinois 60202. Each bottle of extract will make up into 5 gallons of root beer. There are recipes and instructions with each bottle. The Herter's catalog (Herter's Inc., Waseca, Minnesota 56093) also carries a line of root beer extract ($1.39 for a 12-ounce bottle). So does Maid of Scandinavia. Some California markets carry a "McCormick Root Beer Concentrate."

You will also need a collection of returnable soft drink bottles, a bottle capper and a supply of bottle caps, as well as your extract, sweetening and yeast. You can serve the root beer "instant" without bottling but the best flavor will only come after the yeast works. For some reason you don't need to worry as much about bottles blowing up with the commercial extract. I've never known one to get up a real serious head of steam (though yours might be different). It somehow combines agreeably with the yeast flavor. You can also use your root beer extract, commercial or homemade, to flavor homemade popsicles, ice cream milk shakes, candy or lemonade.

Postscript on root beer—The commercial extract gets up a big fizz and tastes like a dark beer given time enough. I've really gone into a lot of detail about bottling. Mike and the children think it's so much fun to bottle and to drink out of the bottles, but as the years have gone by I've been doing less and less of that. Now I generally make my root beer from the commercial extract in a 5-gallon can in the hottest summer weather. Then anybody can dip it out to drink as they want and I serve it by the pitcherful for meals and between-meal refreshments. It doesn't have any fizz but I also don't have to buy bottle caps and bother with bottling and unbottling.

Jo Gunnerson, a minister's wife and a lovely lady, sent me these two quick root beer recipes:

Root Beer for the Family (1 gallon)—Combine 2 tablespoons root beer extract, 2½ cups sugar, 1 teaspoon yeast and 1 gallon warm water. Let stand at room temperature for 12 to 15 hours. Chill. Better the second day. Even better the third if it lasts that long.

Sunday School Picnic Root Beer—Combine in a large container (bucket or tub) 7½ cups sugar, 4 gallons plus 3 cups water, 5/6 bottle of extract (I used the whole thing!) and 5 pounds *dry ice*. Mix 30 to 45 minutes before serving. Stir occasionally to carbonate. The kids love to watch this—the dry ice smokes and looks spooky! (But make sure none of the ice gets into their hands or into servings of root beer. It *burns*.)

HOMEMADE EXTRACTS—Here are some root beer recipes from scratch but frankly the commercial extracts are cheaper, milder on the stomach and better tasting than any of my formulas. So I'll offer my recipes only for folks who insist on doing it *all* themselves!

Formula Root Beer—Make your tea of roots, leaves or what you like. Dilute to taste leaving it a little on the weak side. Add 1¾ cups sugar per gallon liquid (or 1 cup honey) and a pinch of dry yeast for 2 gallons of liquid or ¼ teaspoon for 5 gallons (more in cold weather). Boil the liquid and cool before adding the yeast and bottling. This will work as long as your original tea has no sweetenings such as fruit juice, molasses or brown sugar. If it does have sweetenings reduce sugar proportionately.

Easy Root Beer—Combine 3 tablespoons sarsaparilla, 1 tablespoon sassafras, 1 heaping teaspoon hops and ¼ teaspoon coriander, ground with a rolling pin. Add 2 cups water. Bring to a boil in an enameled pan and simmer, covered, 12 hours or more. Strain out the solids. To the tea add 2 gallons boiled water, 3 cups sugar (or 1½ cups honey) and ¼ teaspoon wintergreen extract. Cool. Add ¼ teaspoon yeast. Stir into the solution. Bottle.

Root Beer from Scratch—If you can't get fresh wintergreen (it's almost impossible unless you live where it grows wild), substitute ¼ teaspoon wintergreen extract from grocery stores or mail-order sources at the time you add the sugar.

1 ounce sassafras (see Herbs chapter on gathering it)
1 ounce yellow-dock (the root, if you can find the plant and dig it, or buy at health food store)
1 ounce whole allspice (grocery store)
½ ounce wild cherry bark (don't girdle on the tree or it will die—or buy at health food store)
1 ounce fresh wintergreen (green leaves of the plant)
¼ ounce dried hops (health food store or home-grown)

Add ample water to cover in an enameled pan. Boil at least 12 hours. Strain out solids. What you have left is your extract.

Boil 2 gallons water. Cool to lukewarm. Add 3 cups sugar (or 1½ cups honey), ¼ teaspoon yeast and enough of your extract to give you the strength of flavor you want. Bottle.

Another from Scratch Root Beer Recipe—This was sent to me by a reader. I haven't tried it. I don't know where you'd find oil of spruce or sassafras now.

For each gallon water to be used, take ½ ounce each hops, burdock, yellow-dock, sarsaparilla, dandelion and spikenard roots, bruised. Boil about 30 minutes. Strain while hot. Add 8 or 10 drops of oil of spruce and sassafras mixed in equal proportions. When cool enough not to scald your hand put in 2 tablespoons dry yeast and ⅔ pint molasses (or white sugar equaling 1 pound—that gives it about the right sweetness). Keep these proportions for as many gallons as you wish to make. You can adjust to use more or less roots to suit your taste after trying it. It is best to get the dry roots or dig them and let them dry. Of course, you can add any other desired root known to possess medicinal properties to the beer. After all is mixed let it stand in a jar with a cloth thrown over it to work about 2 hours, then bottle and set in a cool place.

Birch beer—In some places you can buy a "Baker's Birch Beer Extract" which people tell me makes the best tasting drink of all!

MULLED BEVERAGES

You can mull any juice by adding sugar and spices and heating to a boil. Then simmer 10 minutes, strain and serve hot. Grape juice, orange juice, cider and red wines mull especially well. Spices invariably include cloves and cinnamon sticks. Whole allspice, nutmeg and ginger are other possibilities. Lemon juice and lemon slices are good in the drink. Sweeten with your favorite sweetener. Be sure to strain unless all will be consumed immediately. The drink gets stronger the longer the whole spices are in it and will soon become distasteful.

Spiced Lemonade—Put 2 quarts water, 4 tablespoons sugar, 3 cloves and about 2 inches of stick cinnamon into a pan. Bring slowly to a boil, strain, add the juice of 4 lemons and reboil. Serve with a slice of lemon in each glass.

Mulled Red Wine—Use the cheapest red wine you can find (it will still be good). Heat 1 quart wine and add 1 piece stick cinnamon, juice of 1 lemon, ½ cup sugar, 8 cloves and ½ lemon sliced into sections. Strain. Serve with a slice of the lemon in each cup. Good for the old, cold, weary and disheartened—a medicinal substance. Mull port or sweet wines without adding sugar.

Mulled Cranberry Cider—Mix 4 cups cider (or grape juice), 4 cups cranberry juice, 6 cloves, 1 stick of cinnamon, 4 whole allspice and ½ cup brown sugar. Heat until the sugar dissolves and serve hot.

Spiced Cider—Mix 4 cups cider, 2 whole allspice, 2 whole cloves, about 3 inches of stick cinnamon and

boil 5 minutes. Add ½ cup brown sugar, boil 5 minutes more and serve hot.

Cider Punch for a Crowd—Squeeze 1 orange and 1 lemon. Combine the chopped peels, ½ cup sugar, 1 stick of cinnamon, ½ teaspoon whole allspice and 4 cups water. Boil gently 30 minutes. Strain, add the orange and lemon juice and 2 quarts cider. Reheat and serve.

Mulled Grape Juice—Combine 4 cups grape juice (dilute if it is very strong), 4 sticks of cinnamon, dash each nutmeg, cloves, ginger and powdered cinnamon and about ¼ cup sugar. Bring to a boil and serve hot.

Hot Spiced Tea for a Crowd—Combine 3 quarts boiling water, 3 tablespoons tea leaves, 2 sticks of cinnamon and 1 teaspoon whole cloves. When your tea is strong enough, strain, and add ¾ cup sugar, ⅓ cup lemon juice and 1 cup orange juice. Reheat. The "tea" leaves can be whatever kind you prefer— raspberry, strawberry, rose hip and so forth.

HOUSEHOLD FORMULAS

Window Washing Solution—½ cup ammonia, ⅛ cup vinegar, 1 quart warm water. (Also good on mirrors.)

Painted Wall, Woodwork, Venetian Blind Washing Solution—½ cup ammonia, ½ cup vinegar, ¼ cup baking soda, 1 gallon warm water.

Strong Cleaner and Wax Stripper—1 gallon hot water, 1 cup sudsy ammonia, ½ cup vinegar, ¼ cup baking soda. Use gloves and do not mix with any household cleaners, especially chlorine ones, because you'll have poisonous fumes. To use on painted surfaces, test a small patch first to make sure it's not too strong. (Donna Park wrote me this hint.)

Mild Cleaner for Waxed Surfaces—1 gallon hot water, ¼ cup sudsy ammonia, ¼ cup vinegar, 1 tablespoon baking soda. (From Lin Shoemaker and Mabel Cox.)

To remove paint from furniture—Dissolve ½ pound laundry starch in a little water. Dissolve 4 tablespoons lye in 6 cups of water. Combine. Put on with an old brush. Leave on 5 to 10 minutes. Scrape and wipe off. Rinse with watered down vinegar.

To remove paint stains from glass—Wipe with hot vinegar.

To clean tarnished jewelry—Soak for a few minutes in lemon juice concentrate. All the tarnish will wipe off. (Mrs. Arlene Jackson of Santee, California, sent me this one.)

To polish silver—Martha Mohan of Hotchkiss, Colorado, wrote me too. She said, "Someone told me that cigarette ashes would polish silver. I tried making a paste of water and wood ashes from my cook stove and it really polishes silver and also copper." That water and ash combination could work for some other hard cleaning jobs too, because water plus any ashes makes lye!

Furniture Polish—Make and bottle for future use. Three tablespoons linseed oil, 1 tablespoon turpentine, 1 quart hot water. Apply to furniture. Dry at once with a soft cloth. Rub to a polish. Or equal parts cooking oil and vinegar boiled 10 minutes. Rub in until well polished.

To clean paneling—Combine 4 tablespoons vinegar, 2 tablespoons olive oil and 1 pint warm water. After cleaning a small area, you rub it dry with clean soft cloth. If especially dirty use triple 0 steel wool inside a wet cloth and rub paneling with grain of wood so as not to scratch finish. "Our house was rented for five years and we thought the paneling was ruined. A friend gave me this recipe and told me to try it. We had to use the steel wool and mix up several fresh jars of it as the water got so dirty but the paneling is now nice and clean." (Mrs. Charles N. Abee of Antioch, Tennessee, sent me this recipe.)

Refrigerator Cleaning Solution—Weak solution of baking soda.

To deodorize jars and bottles—Pour a solution of water and dry mustard into them, then let stand for several hours.

Boot Grease—Cook bear grease and pitch in a pot, stirring good all the time. Take off fire to cool, stirring all the time. Then heat up shoes by fire and put on lots of grease to keep out water. Another way to waterproof shoes is to warm beeswax and sheep fat until the mixture is melted and then rub it on the bottoms and tops, especially everywhere it is sewed together to close all those little holes.

Another Window Cleaning Solution—Combine 1 cup rubbing alcohol, 1 cup cold water, 1 tablespoon white vinegar. Use in a spray-type bottle.

Old-Time Sealing Wax—1 pound resin, 2 ounces beeswax, 1½ ounces tallow. To cover corks use a brush to cover and as they cool, dip the corked mouth into the melted wax.

To make old-time quill pens—The second, third and fourth quills of the wing are the best. If you want them to be clear, put the feather into boiling alum water for 5 to 10 minutes, then scrape the outer skin off. After this dry them in hot sand, in a stove or before the fire.

A Homemade Green Ink—Half fill a glass with wine vinegar. Heat it in a double boiler. Add verdigris until no more dissolves. That's the green "rust" old copper gets. (Poisonous.) In order to keep the verdigris from crystallizing, add 6 to 8 parts gum arabic for each part of verdigris that you use. Heat again. Do not heat on direct fire or the green color is lost. Cool before using.

Wallpaper Cleaner Dough—Mix 4 tablespoons baking soda and 2 cups flour. Mix 2½ tablespoons ammonia and 1¼ cups water. Then combine these two mixtures and beat until smooth. Put in top of double boiler, cover and set over bottom part filled partially with boiling water and let steam over *very low* heat for 1½ hours. Lift cover and remove from off steam and let cool till room temperature. Spoon or take out and knead until soft dough. Start at top of

wall with small portion kneaded and roll down to absorb and remove soil. Knead dirty part inside to make clean dough outside and use like this until whole dough is soiled. For larger expanses of wall more dough can be made.

To remove labels from glass jars and plastics use warm salad oil.

ESPECIALLY FOR PARENTS OF CHILDREN AND DOGS

If you have to look at the back of a kid's throat for some reason (usually to see if tonsils are inflamed) it is a good idea to use a lollipop as it overcomes the child's fear of that woodenish taste and gives them a reward after the ordeal. Catherine Liott wrote me from New Zealand with that one!

To get rid of skunk smell a good soaking in vinegar followed by a good soapy scrubbing does it for clothes. Or wash several times in vinegar. To get the smell off a dog bathe him in tomato juice. By the time you've got all the tomato juice off him again you'll have the skunk odor off too.

What to do if your dog gets ahold of poison—Mix equal parts of kerosene and milk, about a tablespoon of each, shake well and pour down the dog's throat. It really works, even when the dog has had the first fit. And it is much less severe than some other home methods. Naturally if you live near a vet . . .

Should your puppy have an accident on your new living room rug, cover soiled area (liquid that is) with wheat germ and allow to dry—no stain and no smell.

To get fresh paint off children rub with cooking oil. The kids painted a birdhouse and I thought I'd never have them anything but blue again until Becca discovered that cooking oil dissolves the paint easily.

DO-IT-YOURSELF COSMETICS

I didn't used to have a section like this in the book. I was raised to believe that beauty was on the inside. That it consisted of glowing health and a fine character. I was brought up that makeup and paying a lot of attention to fixing yourself up, like curlers and such, was wrong and same for fussing over clothes beyond what was practical. I've never changed very much from that. I don't use any makeup at all and I don't curl my hair. At home I wear what's comfortable and doesn't show the dirt. Church once, and now for better or for worse, Church and TV shows are the times when I dress up. Generally a long dress. I just love velvet. And there's one style especially I love, a jumper sort of thing and I wear it with a sweater or blouse. I've got four of them made in that same identical favorite style of mine in different colors and that's what I always wear. I'm not much at getting together accessories. The shoes have a tendency to be tennis

shoes in summer . . . or sandals . . . and snow boots in winter. I'm hatless, gloveless, and have a hard time keeping track of a purse so often I tuck my money into my bra and go like that. Yes. I still do wear one of those. Could never get used to flopping around and I'm at that stage in life where I would flop in a major way. Can't bear new ones though. Too uncomfortable. So I wear my oldies that have been through the wash so much the elastic is practically dead in them and that suits me just fine. In practical terms it means though that I sort of sag and my sticking out doesn't happen quite up in the place where the dress designers expect it to, and it really frustrates the dress lady in our little department store here at Kendrick on those rare occasions when I do try to shop for something to wear. She really wants me to look nice. Well, I'm just telling you how I am. And I do love long velvet dresses and pretty ruffly negligees so you see I'm human too. But somebody else had to tell me to put some cosmetics in the book. I'm glad they did and here are some formulas I've found.

Steaming is a good treatment for skin problems or a general need for a pick-me-up. I've enjoyed it many times. It deep cleans your facial pores. But don't do it if you have broken veins on your face or break out very easily. To experts steaming means having your face in a hot towel tent. To me it means spending 5 or 10 minutes with a few hot washrags on your face. You can pour an herb tea over the washrags and then you have an herbal facial—like camomile, or nettle, or rosemary, or peppermint or comfrey. Then when you're done wash out any dirt that's left and close the pores with cold washrags or an astringent.

Instant Skin Cleanser—Get a lather up with mild soap. Sprinkle some kitchen-type cornmeal in the lather and rub and scrub your face with the mixture.

Yogurt Cleanser—Yogurt with a tiny dash of salt. Not for dry skin.

Natural Astringents—Peeled cucumbers, or lemon juice and water or rose water.

For Oily Skin—Cold parsley tea dabbed on several times a day.

Skin Freshener—A strong mint tea facial.

Treatment for Large Pores—Put 4 tablespoons bran mixed with the chopped skins of 2 lemons into a jelly bag. Dip into boiling water, apply to face with enough pressure on bag contents to squeeze out a little of the lemon quality. Repeat for a while. Don't use any heat treatment on a face that has broken veins since it can make them worse.

Facial Mask #1—Mix 2 tablespoons slightly warmed honey with 1 teaspoon lemon juice. Put on your face and leave for about a half hour.

Facial Mask #2—This is to help drag blackheads and whiteheads out of your pores. Slightly beat an egg white and then spread it fairly thick over your face. Let it dry. Do the same thing with another egg white right on top of the first. Let it stay there a half day. This is a good time to take a nap. Rinse off the egg white.

Makeup—A drop of food coloring mixed with a fingerful of petroleum jelly for some homemade lip gloss, rouge or eye shadow. Kids have fun with it and it won't hurt your skin.

Bathing in Vinegar—Now I like Dial soap and so does Mike, unless it's homemade soap which we like better because it's homemade, but a lady wrote me and said she agreed with my dad that a nightly bath was bad for your skin and knew a 70-year-old woman "with skin like a 16 year old. Her secret is 1 cup apple cider vinegar in about 6 to 8 inches warm water. Scrub with a rough cloth or body brush. Don't use anything else and in about a month you can see the difference and feel it also."

Bath Salts—Epsom salts with a few drops of your favorite fragrance mixed in and bottled special.

Herb Bath Salts—In with Epsom salts mix sage, thyme and pennyroyal. Or lavender, rosemary and pennyroyal. Or lemon balm and peppermint. Or whatever combination pleases you.

Camomile Shampoo—Barb Ingram, who is part Blackfoot Indian and lives at Santa, Idaho, a little ways north of me sent me some really good recipes. She says she uses this recipe and it works beautifully. Put 1 tablespoon soap flakes, 1 teaspoon borax and 1 ounce camomile flowers (powdered) into basin. Add ½ pint hot water and heat until thick lather is formed. Wet hair with warm water, massage, rinse and wash again.

Hair Rinse—3 tablespoons vinegar per half gallon water.

Herbal Hair Rinse—Rinse your hair in herb tea. Camomile is supposed to be best for blondes. Rosemary for brunettes! Or pound a quart of balsam fir needles with a hammer to release the oils. Soak in cold water overnight. Then rub in 2 tablespoons balsam rinse after shampooing and rinsing. Rinse well again.

Squeeze-Style Toothpaste—Combine ¼ teaspoon mineral oil, 2 teaspoons distilled water, 2 teaspoons glycerin, 1 tablet crushed saccharin, ¼ teaspoon gum tragacanth, ¼ teaspoon white powder soap, 1 tablespoon plus ¼ teaspoon precipitated chalk and 5 teaspoons milk of magnesia. Add flavoring oil to taste.

Toothpaste—You can use common table salt for a toothpaste. It's rougher on your teeth and doesn't taste as good but it's cheaper and more available. Takes care of bad breath, too. Or use plain baking soda. Or baking soda with a drop of oil of spearmint, peppermint, cinnamon or cloves in it. Or a mixture of three parts baking soda and one part salt.

Cucumber Cold Cream—Barb sent me this one, too. Shred ½ ounce of white wax into a jar and add 2 ounces almond oil. Stand jar in a saucepan of boiling water and stir occasionally until wax is dissolved. Peel a ripe cucumber and chop very finely. Add just enough to jar to be covered by the wax. Cover and leave in pan of water. Simmer slowly for at least an hour. Remove from heat, stir thoroughly and allow to get cold. For everyday use.

Cleansing Cream—In a double boiler melt and mix into ½ cup safflower oil (or avocado or sweet almond), 1 tablespoon cocoa butter and 1 tablespoon of anhydrous lanolin. Take off the heat, beat until partly cooled and store in a jar. Shake before using.

Elderberry Cleansing Cream—We have lots of elderberry trees around here. They grow on steep canyon sides. The pretty blossoms are a pleasure in the spring and the small tart berries are on in the fall. The flowers have an ancient fame for being good for the skin. You can dry them to have year-round. Drop a few in your bathwater and make this special cleansing cream: In a double boiler heat 1 cup homemade buttermilk and ¼ cup elderberry flowers for half an hour. Then take it off the heat and let rest for a few hours. Heat again. Strain out the flowers. Add 2 tablespoons honey. Store in a really cool place.

Homemade Sun Lotion—For *before*—olive oil with a little vinegar in it. Rub it on where the sun will be hitting you. A wide-brimmed hat and long sleeves work even better.

Homemade Lanolin—Boil a batch of sheep wool and drain the oil. The lanolin is the oil. If you handle newly sheared wool you get your hands loaded with lanolin. It's very soothing and healing to the skin.

Hand Lotion—This formula was sent to me by a lady in Turkey. She got it from her mother-in-law who she says has the softest, whitest hands of any 70 year old she has ever seen. Combine ½ kilo rubbing alcohol (17.6 ounces), 250 grams hydrogen peroxide (8.8 ounces), ½ kilo rosewater (17.6 ounces), 50 grams glycerin (1.8 ounces) and 10 grams benzoin (0.4 ounce).

Who Has a Quince Seed Hand Lotion Recipe?
Mrs. Marion Walkling, Centralia, Washington, wrote me this letter: "When I was a girl in the 1930's we had a friend whose family had a tougher time than ours even, surviving the depression. She had a quince tree, and my grandparents gave us cull oranges from the packinghouse. My mom made the most delicious quince and orange marmalade. Our friend made a real good gooey soothing hand lotion from the quince seed. I flew home this month and saw her but she is very feeble and cannot recall the recipe. Have you ever come across a recipe for hand lotion from quince seeds?" If you have write me so I can put it in the next edition of this book!

ART AND FUN FORMULAS

Library Paste—This is from the *Women's Circle Cook Book*. Mix together in a pan and cook over a low flame, stirring constantly, until thick: ½ cup sugar and ½ cup flour, 2 cups water, ½ teaspoon powdered alum. Remove from heat and add 15 drops oil of cloves to prevent spoilage and give paste a nice odor. Pour into jars. Makes 1 pint. Will keep several months.

Quick Paste—White flour and water worked to a pasty consistency.

For Blowing Bubbles—Mix 1 quart water, 12 teaspoons glycerin, 8 teaspoons tincture of green soap (can use castile soap ground and measured the same). Mix it well and then add 1 drop of ammonia.

Homemade Modeling Clay for Children—1 cup flour, 1 cup salt, 1 tablespoon powdered alum, 1 cup water. Combine flour, salt and alum in a large mixing bowl. Add most of the water and mix well. If the dough is too stiff to work easily with your hands add a little more water. If desired mix in a preferred shade of food coloring. When you are not using the dough keep it in a jar with a tight lid so it won't dry out.

A Clay to Make Jewelry and Toys—In the top of a double boiler thoroughly mix 1 cup cornstarch with 1 pound bicarbonate of soda. Mix in 1¼ cups cold water and stir constantly over medium heat for about 4 minutes. When it is like mashed potatoes turn out onto a plate and let cool covered with a damp cloth. After cooling knead it like dough. But don't knead it all at once. Put the unused portion in a plastic baggie type thing so it won't dry out. Just knead the part you are going to use. If you knead in a few drops of white glue (like Elmer's) it will give it extra strength. Mold your shapes by hand or cut with a cookie cutter. When you have the shape you want dry the piece for about 36 hours (or until really hard). You can paint with tempera, and after that is dry, coat with shellac for shine and protection.

Imitation Marble—Mix 5 pounds Portland cement, 2 pounds plaster of paris, 5 pounds very fine sawdust and 1 pound powdered alum with water until it is thoroughly mixed and of a creamy consistency. Color by adding umber or ocher or what you prefer. Use this to make decorative items or toys by pouring into well oiled molds and spreading with a trowel. It ends up very hard and easy to polish.

To-Keep-Young-Children-Occupied-on-a-Rainy-Day—Sprinkle powdered Bon Ami in a fruit jar lid (that's what comes on mayonnaise). Mix enough water in to make it very like thick cream. Add food coloring. Make one of each color. Spread newspapers on the floor in front of your largest window and let the children finger paint on the glass. When they are through it's a simple matter to wipe off and Presto— you have a clean window! Grace Brown of Rainier, Washington, sent me that one. She raised 9 children and has 33 grandchildren so she knows a lot of child pleasers like this one.

CHRISTMAS ON THE HOMESTEAD!

My Daddy, Mama and I always went out by foot or pickup to pick out and cut down a Christmas tree. We had a farm all the years I can remember, so trespassing was no problem. The world would be white and still and very cold, the snow up to seven feet high in drifts—which on days I wasn't helping find the Christmas tree, I walked safely over on thick snow crusts or burrowed into through long, dazzling, warm tunnels. Daddy always picked a perfect tree, just the right height to stand in a calf bucket, wired to the sides, and still leave the silver Christmas star honorably marking the peak of the tree, yet not scraping the ceiling. The whole family worked together to decorate the tree with hundreds of tinsel "icicles" which had to be gently and carefully separated from their brethren and draped in even distribution all over the tree. Fragile, shiny-colored globes went on the ends of branches, colored, fuzzy tinsel garlands went round and round and then the wonderful colored lights. Underneath the tree were layers of white tissue paper on which holiday wrapped presents accumulated daily until Christmas.

That was the joy of the Christmas tree. The sorrow was that there were so few of us to share it. My mother's mother had only one child—Irma Ferne Thresher—who became first Mrs. Charlie Hoff, mother of a son Dick, then a widow, then Mrs. Carl Harshbarger, then my mother. Brother Dick was eight years older than me and mostly seemed to live with his relatives. He had two aunts, childless throughout their lifetimes, and his widowed grandmother clung to him all the more earnestly having lost her husband and her only son. Instead of more children after me there was a heartbreaking miscarriage of a fine five-month fetus. Daddy was deeply hurt. He had dreamed of a large family like his own and those of all his brothers and sisters. There was never another living baby. They never understood why not. I longed for a sister to play with.

Now like playing detective, I can perhaps explain their problem. I'm Rh-negative. It is only thanks to modern science—a substance called Rhogam—that I am able to have child after child. The Rh-negative factor in blood was not discovered until World War II. That's after my parents gave up. I would guess my mother and her mother both had that problem. My first child is Rh-negative, too—a daughter, which means she will also have this problem. The rest are all positive, which means that without Rhogam I would probably have aborted all but the first and possibly even him.

To me now, as from early childhood, the conception and birth of a well child is a precious miracle. And that of course is also what Christmas is all about, the often unacknowledged reason behind the presents and feasting and gaiety, the birth of that very special Child.

Salt Dough for Christmas Tree Ornaments—We are ardent Christmas do-it-ourselfers. It means more that way. Mike and the children find, chop down and bring home the Christmas tree. We decorate it over the following two weeks with paper chains, garlands of popped popcorn and cranberries, and with ornaments made of salt dough or cookies. When it comes time to take the tree down we save the prettiest salt dough ornaments for the next year. The salt dough is an inedible cookie dough. You mix it, roll it out, cut into the shapes you want and bake. When the ornaments have cooled you get out the plain old watercolor paints (or more professional ones) and decorate them to suit yourselves. They aren't very fragile. Just remember to make a hole for the ribbon or string before you bake it. They are very hard and bitter when finished so your Christmas tree decorations won't suffer loss by nibbling. That's their big advantage over regular cookie ornaments.

To make the salt dough just mix together 1 cup salt, 4 cups flour and 1½ cups water. This is a very stiff dough. Knead until smooth. Then roll to a one-fourth inch thickness and cut with cookie cutters or imagination. (Or you can mold little figures.) If you poke with a nail before you bake, you'll get about the right size hole to hang it in the tree. Don't make them too big and heavy or they'll weigh down your branches. Bake at 225° for 30 minutes—keep checking them so that they don't scorch. Another way to do it is to color the dough with food coloring. Another formula is 4 cups salt, 2 cups cornstarch and 2 cups water. This one gets baked at 200°, or if you have the time you can just leave them set out to dry. With either recipe, setting out to dry takes about 48 hours to dry completely through.

Making Your Own Christmas Wrapping Paper—"Cook up a thick batch of clothes starch. Cool until you can put your hands into it. Separate into pans to add color (dividing for as many colors as you want to make). Add poster paints (tempera) and mix well. Take a roll of shelf or butcher paper and cut into desired lengths. Spread out on a picnic or long table for long pieces. Pour color on and work with hands like finger paints. To make designs, raid your kitchen drawers and cupboards for any item of plastic or metal that will leave its unique design, i.e., fork tines, cookie cutters, bottles with molded designs, pastry blenders, apple corers, butter cutters, bottles and so

forth. Don't forget finger designs. Gold spray paint can be added for interest—also glitter, beads, stones and initials, or names to personalize your paper. Spread out on the floor to dry. The year we made our own wrap, it drew more oohs and ahs than any other for appearance and originality. We also use old Christmas cards (cut up into small sizes) for tags. This we do, always, since then. These wrappings are sturdy, not see-through too." This recipe was sent to me and the recipe got separated from the name so I can't give credit.

BUG AND WORM FORMULAS

So many people have asked me please did I know a way to worm animals organically. And I didn't used to have an answer for them. But about a year ago I met Pete Jacobs who lives up on the ridge above Kendrick. He was raised in Louisiana, farmed there with mules. Now he raises green beans and is an electrician on the side. He's really exciting to talk to. He knows a lot and he remembers a lot and he tells it well. He's the only person I know could get anybody excited about the life cycle of the string bean.

For worming animals—Pete says in the old days they wormed dogs with a copper penny. Nowadays pennies aren't made of copper anymore and if you have a real copper penny chances are you wouldn't want to use it this way anyhow. But this is what the old-timers did. For a small dog they cut the copper penny in half because a whole penny would have made him sick and they just wanted to do in the worms not the dog. They wadded that half copper penny up with bread and fed it to the little dog. And that's all there was to it. He was wormed. For an average-sized dog they used the whole copper penny wadded up with bread and fed it to him.

Violet Stewart says a small amount of garlic in your dog's food will keep him wormed. To worm children, the old-timers gave a mixture of sulfur and molasses.

Tobacco was a great old-time wormer Pete told me. You can put it in horse feed and they'll eat it right down and it will worm them. Good for worming hogs, too. Buy a can of Prince Albert or some such brand at the grocery store and feed one can to a couple of hogs.

Coal is another natural wormer. Pigs just love coal. Pete said he used to take a bucket of coal and dump it over the fence right into the hog pen—the very same kind of coal you'd use in your wood cook stove to hold the fire after you got it going good with wood. The pigs would run up and eat those chunks of coal. Just chomp them up as if they were food and swallow it right down as if they knew it was something good for them. And eating the coal would worm them.

Tobacco drives off insects, too. If you live someplace where you can get cheap tobacco dust sweepings they really have a use. Put them in a duster and dust your animals that are bothered with bugs. There are so many mean insects that go after the cows especially. And if your dog is threatened by fleas the tobacco dust will take care of them. If you can't find tobacco dust and talcum powder is handier you can soak a dog's fur with talcum powder and that will take care of the fleas.

Salve to keep off red bugs and mosquitoes— Hazel lives in Georgia. I treasure her because she knows more about eating from scratch than any other one human being I know. She knows how to catch, kill, skin, clean, cook and eat a rattlesnake and how to make blackbird pie fit for a king. I haven't tried any of those myself but I respect the proposition that Hazel knows how. Hazel also knows what to do for yourself about bugs. She goes fishing and berry gathering a lot. And then she rubs on her ankles and exposed skin with a salve she makes herself to keep off "red bugs" and mosquitoes. To make it she buys flowers of sulfur at the drugstore. If they don't have them in stock they can order them for you. Now you need clean lard, plain old lard. Mix the flowers of sulfur with the lard until the mixture is a good deep yellow. That's all there is to it. Store your salve in small jars with tight lids. This is also good for old or stubborn sores on either man or beast. But be sure you mark and keep separate jars that are for man as opposed to beast use!

Bug in your ear?—If a bug flies in somebody's ear don't try to dig it out because you might end up really hurting them. Hold a flashlight or lightbulb on an extension cord near the ear and the bug should come out to the light the same way they revolve around light bulbs on your porch at night. Oh, forgot to mention better have the patient in an otherwise dark place, like the backyard at night.

Mosquito bites, bee and hornet stings—Mrs. Sylvia Allen of Kent, Washington, wrote me this: "An excellent remedy for bee stings is unseasoned meat tenderizer. I use the Adolph's unseasoned—put small amount in a spoon, add enough water to make a paste and apply to the bee or wasp sting area. I have never failed to have this work for me; and my daughter and I are extremely allergic to stings. We carry a bottle everywhere we go. I have heard it is the papaya enzyme in the tenderizer that neutralizes the bee's poison."

Mrs. J. L. Martin of Covina, California, wrote to tell me she once put cotton saturated with witch hazel on a bee sting and had instant relief and no swelling. Trudy Rohler of Kettering, Ohio, wrote me: "For the sting of a bee, wasp or other stinging insect remove stinger if any and go to the garden and grab a tomato leaf and rub it on the stung area until the leaf is a pulpy mess that you can't hold onto. It will relieve the pain or itching and take the swelling down or prevent swelling."

Virginia Nelson from Naples, Idaho, told me she dissolves two aspirin tablets in ¼ cup rubbing alcohol. Keeps it in a bottle and dabs the solution on bites with cotton or fingers. Somebody else I know cuts a slice of "hot" onion and lays that on the sting. Doctor Spock says to apply a paste of baking soda and water. Some other people say vinegar for a hornet sting. Vitamin types say vitamin E helps.

I've seen prayer cause the red flush from an acute reaction to a wasp sting to disappear completely. Maybe it's all a matter of what you put your faith in.

Repelling bugs from houses—Bugs are supposed to not like certain plants like pennyroyal and garlic. That's the premise that many organic bug sprays are made on. (More on that in the Vegetables chapter.) So planting pennyroyal and garlic around doors and windows may help. They don't like dill either. Tropical bugs must be tougher though. Peace Sullivan, a freelance journalist living with her UPI correspondent husband just outside Rio de Janeiro, Brazil, wrote me this: "We live in a tiny house on a hill overlooking the ocean. It's beautiful. We're in the middle of the jungle, with a huge avocado tree that is dripping with fruit outside our door. We also have bananas and papayas. The jungle is full of beautiful plants and birds who sing to us. We have a tiny vegetable garden, but have had very little luck with it. The worst problem is the bugs, and a potent spray of garlic, onion and very hot pepper seems to have no effect on them. We do, however, grow a lot of basil, including two window boxes full. We read it helped keep flies away, thus the window boxes, and sure enough, no flies in the house."

Wasps from a picnic—Mrs. Harvey Thompson of Yelm, Washington, tells me she uses a dish one-third full of plain old cider vinegar to drive off yellow jackets.

Flies from goats—Terry Bedard of Warner Robbins, Georgia, wrote me: "Here's something you might like to try. Add apple cider vinegar when you feed your goats (approximately ¼ cup per goat). They love the taste and it will cut down tremendously on the flies they attract not only to their body but also to their manure."

Attracting bugs—You can lead some bugs to their doom with things they *do* like—molasses for example. Make a homemade flypaper by mixing pine tar and molasses. Spread the mixture on something light and hangable like paper, cloth or a piece of screen. Hang it up where your flies are the worst.

A flea destroyer—Mary Alice Ames from Anacortes, Washington, wrote me: "Here's a little something for you. I love animals and have as many of them as possible, but in the spring, summer and fall there is always a flea problem. If you don't want your children to be exposed to the discomforts of flea bites, and if you don't like 'chemicals' try talcum powder. Saturate the animals' fur with the powder. This doesn't get rid of every last one always but it helps. When you have so much talcum powder in the fur that when you pat him a cloud of talc comes up that's good. The talc clogs the flea's breathing tubes. It makes people sneeze too so do it outside and then let the animal run. Also, bay leaves under the mattress pad on the children's bed repel fleas. Cedar boughs put between the box spring and mattress repel fleas, too."

Pinworm remedy—Violet Stewart from Oklahoma has written me a lot of answers from her rich experience in life. Here's Violet Stewart's advice on pinworms: "Unless you are familiar with the symptoms you might not know what was wrong. Children scratch their backside continually. It is a great source of annoyance and more dangerous than one can imagine. The worms are so small they cannot be seen and they multiply fast in the soft tissues. Especially with little girls they can become a very bad thing as they will enter in the vagina and cause trouble. Scratching can break the skin and complicate things with an infection. A good way to stop them is to scald a couple cloves of garlic, or the equivalent powder after crushing, with hot water. Let cool and strain. Have patient lay on left side with knees drawn to chest. Give an enema with the garlic solution. Do not try to give all at once. Be patient. Get a cup or so into the child and let them hold it a few moments. Then potty. Repeat until you have used all your garlic water. Then wash all areas with soap and water.

"All clothing should be clean. Even beds have to be washed well and the child taught to wash hands after each trip to the bathroom because the adult worms can come on outside and get on hands and fingers if the child scratches where they are. Give the garlic enema again the next day and then every three days for at least nine more days. Keep changing and washing the child's linens and clothes. Don't quit even if the itching subsides because the larva will be hatching out and they become adults in 24 hours ready to reproduce. You can also give the child garlic to eat or garlic pills from the drugstore if she can stand them."

HOME REMEDIES

Please don't think that I'm proposing this list as a substitute for a good doctor, penicillin or needed medical treatment. It's an interesting collection and sometime it might come in useful to you but that's all it is. The old-timers in the good old days had a lot of babies and a lot of them didn't live to grow up. They didn't have shots to prevent measles (both kinds), and mumps, and whooping cough, and tetanus, and polio, and diphtheria like all the children routinely have now. "Strep throat" was a dread disease then often leading into rheumatic fever or scarlet fever that now we can get under practically instant control with antibiotics. Great-grandmother practiced a lot more preventive medicine than we do now. I worry that if there ever was a crisis that made impossible the practice of the type of modern medicine we are used to, young mothers would lose many more of their children than Great-grandmother did because of the things we have forgotten or ceased to practice. For one, quarantine. Before there were shots to immunize there was quarantine. Now shots haven't "wiped out" these dread diseases in the sense of making them extinct. They all make their rounds among the children every winter just like they used to. Only the children get them in such a mild form that they are scarcely noticeable. That means that as soon as we stopped immunizing all those diseases would be just as much a threat to the unprotected children as they ever were.

The first line of defense for an unimmunized child was not to get exposed. Diseases in which you break out are actively infectious during the period in which the victim is broken out even though they are starting to feel better. Our public school system is based on a system which has very high development of immunization and medical care. You'd never dare throw together every child from the surrounding countryside every day under any other circumstances. The second line of defense was to have the child constantly in as good health as possible. Great-grandmother worried continually over things like mittens and rubbers and neck scarves and not going out too soon into the cold after you were sick and not getting too tired or getting caught in the rain because she wanted to keep up her child's natural resistance to disease.

If that didn't work and the child did get sick, Great-grandmother was a master nurse and she took no chances with her patient. The patient stayed quiet and indoors and warm and ate well and slept well— as well as Great-grandmother could manage. All this with the idea of helping the little natural body soldiers have all the energy possible to fight the enemy since she had no better medicine than the capacity for resistance in her child's own body. Great-grandmother knew her childhood diseases about as well as if she'd been to nursing school. She knew the symptoms and she knew how to nurse them. And she nursed with the loving, infinite faith and patience that only a mother has.

Burns—This is the most important advice you'll read in this whole section. Burns are inevitable. Hot grease and hot honey give the worst kitchen-type burns. The hotter the stuff is when it hits the skin, the worse the burn. So keep boiling liquids on the back of the stove with handles turned inwards. Don't leave little children alone in a kitchen with something boiling if you can help it. When the child does overturn a pot of something hot like fudge or soup or whatever, as he will sooner or later no matter how careful you are, just leap over there, grab him or her up in your arms and plop her or him into the sink. Start running cold water in as great a quantity as you can get it over all the affected places. If you get there quick enough with enough cold water you may escape with no bad burns at all.

Sunburn—Once the book here simply answered "Vaseline" but then at a friend's home I got introduced to *Aloe vera*, the "burn plant" (sometimes called the "Texas Healer"). You can buy one from a florist they told me or get a start from a neighbor. To use snap off the tip of one of its fat, cactus-type leaves (but it is completely smooth and has no prickles at all). Squeeze out the natural salve from inside the leaf right onto your burn. It's also good for heat burns. The plant will heal its broken off tip and be ready for the next time you need it.

High fever (When you can't reach a doctor)—Aspirin and a wet rubdown (water, not alcohol).

Constipation—Enema with ½ teaspoon salt and 1 teaspoon baking soda for each cup water. You can get the gear at the drugstore.

Itching hives—Hot bath with baking soda. Use 1 cup soda in a small tub, 2 cups for a large tub.

Bleaching and germicidal agent—Here's one I'm positive about. Sunshine!

Earache (When you can't reach a doctor)—Aspirin and warmth on the ear. Any hot compress, or a warm pancake rolled and pressed against the ear, or a few drops of warmed olive oil dropped in the ear, or a hot water bottle.

"Never-fail" nose cork pat. 1893

Nosebleed—It used to say in this Recipe Book "Don't blow or squeeze nose. Apply cold (such as a cold compress with ice or ice water) to back of neck, forehead and upper lip." Then I got a letter from "JW" at Loring AFB, Maine. (There is really a lot of reader interest in this home remedies section!) And JW disagreed. JW said: "Having had a high surface vein in my nose (till I had it cauterized) I have bled quarts! It took an internist to tell me how to stop it. And this is the *only* thing that works for a real gusher. The ice or pad under the lip—none of that works if it's an active nosebleed (odds are the minor ones stopped because the person sat still)." And JW said to do this. "1.) Blow the nose gently to remove excess blood . . . a large amount of blood will take longer to clot, plus the clot will break off later and it will bleed again. 2.) Hold your nose for 7 or 8 minutes. Time it. Sit while you do this. (Don't lie down. The blood will merely continue down the throat.) Get occupied—TV or something, and don't peek every 2 seconds—it releases the pressure. Pressure should be *gentle* but *firm*."

Small cuts and scratches—Wash with soap and water, rinse with hydrogen peroxide, if needed.

Dressing for Skin Infection—One teaspoon Epsom salts or salt in 1 cup boiled water. Use a thick bandage and keep it moist with solution. Or many people really recommend keeping the sore wrapped with clean cloth that has been soaked in turpentine. Or mixed Epsom salts and glycerin. For more good poultice and salve recipes see the special section on them just a bit farther on.

For anything—A cup of comfrey tea, hot, with each meal—three times a day.

For cracks under toes—Take some white wool yarn or just a washed strip of wool from the sheep (best because of the lanolin present), put a tiny bit of Vaseline on it and tie around toe—not tight. It will almost heal overnight.

Canker sores—Gregory A. Oberg, a doctor of chiropractic in Richland, Washington, sent me his grandfather's remedy for canker sores. He says first of all check your diet to make sure it is balanced and then get some copper sulfate (blue vitriol) at your drugstore. "It comes in many forms, powder, crystal, etc., and any form is all right. You won't need much, only a few grams will do. Take a small bottle (an old pill bottle will do) and fill it about three-fourths full of water. Dissolve enough copper sulfate in the water so that there is still some left undissolved in the bottom of the jar. Use a Q-tip and take some of this saturated solution and rub it on the canker sore. Spit out any left in your mouth and you can rinse out your mouth if you want to be extra sure. Swallowing the copper sulfate won't hurt. Use only once a day and for not more than two days. That treatment is also good for cauterizing other cuts and bites in the mouth. This treatment will burn like crazy but works better and faster than anything I've come across."

A gargle—Pinch of salt in ¼ cup warm water.

For smallpox sores—This is a genuine old-time pharmacy formula that a lady in Wichita, Kansas, went to a lot of trouble to get me. Mix 1 ounce oil of eucalyptus, 7 ounces olive oil, 8 ounces lime water and apply well to affected places.

Asafetida—Southern drugstores may still carry it. As a waxy substance it was sewed into a cloth bag which children wore around their necks in winter to keep them healthy. Or you can buy it in a liquid form and add 1 or 2 drops in the baby's milk bottle. That's all I know about it except I sure have met a lot of believers!

Slivers—This recipe was sent to me too but I've mislaid the name of who sent it. Anyway "Use a bottle of household turpentine. Dab the sliver a couple times. It sorta makes the skin transparent so you can see it. Then clamp down firmly with a tweezer or a knife blade and hold firmly with finger as close to skin as can be done. Pull firmly, slowly, and do not jerk on the end you can get hold of. Put your finger on the turpentine bottle and dab over the spot again. If you have not gotten it all you may have to use a sterilized needle to dig it out. But the turpentine will help it come clean most of the time. By applying the turpentine first it will cause the sliver to come out whole most of the time." I really appreciate your sending me that recipe.

FOR COLITIS AND OTHER DIGESTIVE PROBLEMS

1. Don't wear clothes that are tight fitting around the waist and abdomen. (They also cause hemorrhoids.)

2. Don't eat any seasonings except salt, onion and garlic. Don't drink tea, coffee, sodas (pop) or any herbal teas except wild strawberry, comfrey, camomile and rose hip. Especially not sassafras.

3. Get a homestead and grow your own vegetables, meat, fruit, eggs, milk. The chemicals in store food are almost certainly aggravating your problem. When you get it do eat plenty of that good homegrown food.

4. You've got to have some bran in your food every single day. Use whole wheat flour instead of white. Avoid white sugar. Use granola or wheat germ. Turnips and cabbage are great for you, too.

5. Don't take medicine, drugs or laxatives if you can help it.

6. Be happy. Even if that requires some drastic rearranging of your life-style. You'll pay more attention to taking care of yourself when you are peaceful. Stress goes to the digestive system and to the heart.

7. If you are dieting you can't go entirely without food. The plain digestive juices would damage your innards' delicate lining without some food in there.

8. Avoid an overdose of things like tiny nuts and seeds, seedy fruits like blackberries and fruit peels like apple. And here are some helpful recipes.

The Gentlest Beverage—Hot water, honey and lemon juice. Juice of ¼ lemon (strained), 1½ cups hot water and honey to taste. If you're trying to break the coffee habit try drinking two-thirds boiled water combined with one-third (or more) milk. Stir in molasses to taste. Comfrey or camomile tea sweetened with honey is also good. In summer try ice water with a dash of lemon juice. It's refreshing!

Custard—2 cups milk and 2 eggs beaten together. Preheat oven to 350°. Put a loaf pan half full of water into the oven. Pour your custard into ovenproof custard dishes and carefully set them in the water. Bake until a knife inserted can be pulled out with the blade free of adhering globs of custard. Serve with a bit of molasses or warmed honey.

Flannel Cakes—Combine 5 eggs, 1 cup whole wheat flour and 1½ cups milk. This is a very fluid batter. Heat a cast-iron frying pan and add just enough oil to shine it. Warm it to medium. Add about ¼ cup batter. Turn pan if necessary to let batter cover bottom. Let it cook slowly as you would a fried egg. Turn it pancake style when the bottom is cooked and let the top cook. You can eat these with real butter and honey.

If you live on the above recipes for a day or two and follow the general good advice above you will be on the way I hope to feeling good again. And get plenty of sleep and take a nap every day after lunch.

POULTICES AND SALVES

This is old fashioned medicine. I've been very choosy about what recipes I've included here so I'm sure you won't come to any harm trying these and they may help. These are all recipes that people known to me, often many of them, have been using for years and really have confidence in. Using poultices and making salves is a little more complex than some of the other mixtures we've been talking about so I'm going into more detail here about just how you do it. When preparing any herb product use glass, Pyrex, Corning ware or stainless steel because contact with metals may harm your product.

Poultices—Plantain or comfrey leaves—either one—are said to make a really healing poultice. So is a bowl of hops mixed with a cup of hot vinegar. A poultice of boiled mullein leaves is good for cuts on animals. In any herb poultice use four times as much if your leaves are green and fresh than if they are dried. Chop green leaves finely, soak them a bit in almost boiling water and then put them on the hurt place. Let them cool before you put them up so they don't burn the patient and don't leave a cold poultice on. Don't reuse the herbs, if possible. Have a fresh poultice ready to go on when you take the cooling one off. They may sound spendthrift of herbs but comfrey which is the number one healing herb grows huge and hardy so you'll have all to work with you want once it gets a good start in your garden. You can make the poultice stay on and do its job by putting a cloth over it or wrapping the whole thing in a clean cloth to apply.

Mustard Plaster—The mustard can be mixed with boiling water, vinegar, the white of an egg, flour or cornmeal. The white of an egg is best because it doesn't blister. Otherwise I'd use flour or cornmeal. Mix to a consistency the same as for the table. That would take about one part dry mustard to four parts flour. The strongest application is to spread the mixture evenly and thinly on a thin muslin cloth (or gauze or a threadbare diaper), cover that with another cloth of the same type and size and then apply the plaster to the chest. After about 10 minutes the skin will be

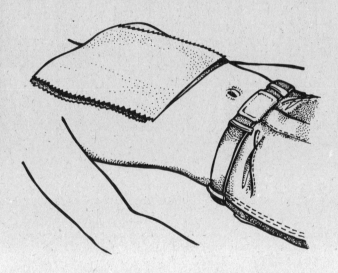

turning pink. Don't let it stay on long enough to make a blister. Take it off. Wash the chest skin gently and apply a little sweet cream or oil. And cover the chest again and keep it so. This is for a chest cold. Emma Jones, Eltopia, Washington, wrote to tell me that if you add 1 teaspoon baking powder in with the flour and mustard you will not blister anybody. Even though it can become a little red on the chest it will not burn and this way you can leave the mustard plaster on as long as you want.

"Drawing Salve"—Hal Berger, who lives with his wife, children, and goats on a 400-acre farm outside Leavenworth, Washington, sent me his grandma's recipe to heal cuts and draw out splinters, dirt, poisons and so on. You'll need ½ cup sweet oil, ½ cup white or yellow beeswax, ½ cup sheep fat and ½ cup pork leaf lard. Heat each of these ingredients separately, then combine and boil together for 10 minutes. Now add 1 tablespoon turpentine (unheated) and 3 drops carbolic acid which won't be easy for you to find nowadays.

Balm of Gilead Salve—For cuts, scrapes, chapped hands. The main ingredient is the sticky, brownish buds of the cottonwood tree (Northern Black Cottonwood—*Populus trichocarpa*—common name "Balm of Gilead") found in the western United States and Canada. Pick the buds in spring before the green leaves form. Make sure you get the buds at the sticky stage. Cook this in a big tin can because it's almost impossible to clean out and it will be easier if you can just throw out the container. Add enough lard to cover the buds when it has melted. If you use any cooking oil instead you get liquid salve instead of a solid one. Simmer on low heat 2 or 3 hours. Strain into sterilized jars or cans. You'll end up throwing out the straining cloth so make it something you can do without.

TRADITIONAL BEVERAGES FOR INVALIDS

For the herb teas such as flaxseed, slippery elm, camomile, etc., look under Herbs. For more milk beverages see the Dairy chapter, otherwise, when colds, flu, and general miseries strike in your family that the doctor can't do anything about anyway, try these.

Hot Toddy—One cup hot water. Whiskey to flavor. Teaspoon brown sugar.

Barley Water #1—Wash a cup of barley. Soak it for 30 minutes. Put it on to boil with 6 cups of water and let the whole boil down to about 3 cups. Add salt and a pat of butter and strain through a sieve. Or you can flavor with any tart fruit syrup, juice or jelly.

Barley Water #2—This one is more diluted. Soak 3 tablespoons barley overnight in 4 cups cold water. Strain and serve with salt, lemon juice or sugar. Serve hot or cold.

"Tea" for Children—In ½ cup of boiling water dissolve some hard candy or a teaspoon of sugar, honey or molasses. In another pan heat a mixture of milk and cream—a half cup. You can serve the hot milk in a pitcher and let the child pour it into the "tea."

Black Currant (or what have you)—Put a heaping tablespoon of black currant jam or whatever berry jam you prefer into a pan with 1 cup water. Simmer 5 minutes and then strain. Add a little lemon juice and honey, if the drink needs more sweetening. Strain and serve hot.

Eggnog—Beat the yolk of 1 egg, add 1 tablespoon sugar and beat until light. Add ½ cup milk. Beat the white of the egg well and fold it in lightly.

Milk Punch—Separate an egg. Beat the yolk until very light with 1 teaspoon sugar. Add white, beaten stiff, and 1 teaspoon brandy. Fill up the glass with hot milk. Sprinkle a little nutmeg on top. Serve hot for colds.

Egg Lemonade—Beat 1 egg with 1 tablespoon sugar until light. Add 3 tablespoons cold water and the juice of a small lemon. Serve with ice and straw.

Albumen Milk—Put into a quart bottle 2 cups milk, the whites of 2 eggs and a pinch of salt. Cover and shake for 5 minutes.

Albumen Water—Add the white of an egg to a cup of water. Stir slowly for 5 minutes. Strain through cheesecloth. Sweeten and flavor to suit the child. A teaspoon of brandy may be added. Can be given by bottle. Traditional for an upset stomach.

White Wine Soup—Boil 2 cups white wine and pour very gradually over 2 egg yolks, beaten very light. Add croutons and serve at once. The boiling eliminates the alcohol from these soups.

Red Wine Soup—Boil 1 cup red wine, ½ cup water, 3 whole cloves and 3 small sticks of cinnamon for 10 minutes. Gradually pour boiling hot over the well beaten yolk of 1 egg. Serve hot or cold. Not good for a digestive complaint because of the spices.

Spoon Syrup—Chop 1 unparaffined lemon and add to 1 cup honey. Heat and stir. Administer as often as the invalid likes. Traditional cough remedy.

Hot Lemonade—Juice of half a lemon and a thin slice of it if unparaffined. Add 1½ cups boiling water and honey to taste. My favorite winter bedtime drink. Quick, easy, and nice.

Beef Tea—Grind 1 pound of lean beef (like round steak or neck bone meat) and put in a quart jar with 1 cup cold water and ½ teaspoon salt. Cover the jar and put it on a cloth in a pan of cold water. Bring the water to a gentle boil and continue for about 1 hour. Cool the jar on a rack and strain the juice. Serve hot. A liquid food for the seriously ill.

Mrs. McLain, Imogene's mother, is well into her 80s. She sits at her old sewing machine and makes quilts out of cut-up, donated old clothes. She gives the quilts to her church to send on to disaster victims around the world.

Imogene believes in comfrey's healing power. She has a tall patch growing back of her house where she comes out and harvests whenever it's wanted.

Becca, Dolly, and Danny (left to right) on our hillside are picking camomile to dry for the winter's tea-making.

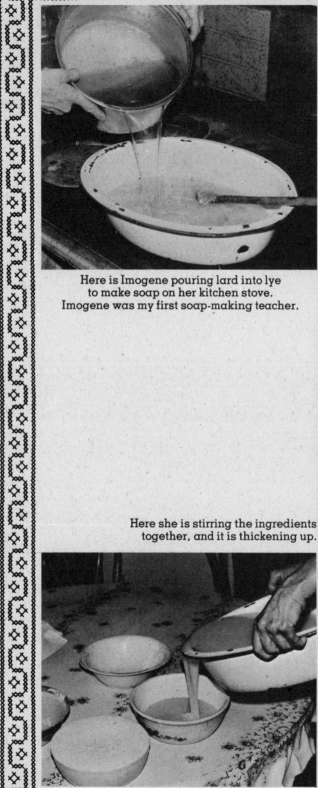

Here is Imogene pouring lard into lye
to make soap on her kitchen stove.
Imogene was my first soap-making teacher.

Here she is stirring the ingredients
together, and it is thickening up.

Now the soap is ready to harden
and she pours it into bowls.

Imogene's finished soap-aged, grated into chips,
and ready for the washing machine. She doesn't
use any soap that hasn't aged at least five years.

DEFINITIONS AND MEASURES

INTRODUCTION

Many friends have written to ask me to expand this chapter. They want detailed directions for spinning and weaving, knitting, rag rug making, basket making, flax culture, chemical tanning, blacksmithing, building plans for farm outbuildings, pottery and brick making. I just don't know all that. This chapter isn't very big, but it really represents the limits of my knowledge. Nobody knows everything and neither do I. The whole question of home industries is so broad. It can mean things you can do at home to make a living. But to me this chapter is a loose end from the others—because your extra lard makes fine soap and your wild animal and goat fat, which isn't pleasantly edible, makes excellent candles, especially with some beeswax mixed in. Feathers from your poultry can become ticks and pillows and quilts. Skins from the animals you have butchered shouldn't be wasted. They can become moccasins and rugs, shirts, trousers and blankets—if you know how. I'm not much of a tanner myself, but I sure respect people who are. So I've told you what I do know and hope it helps at least some.

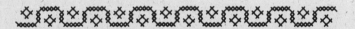

STUFFING WITH CORNHUSKS, HAIR, WOOL, FEATHERS AND COTTON

CORNHUSKS—To make the very best possible husk beds, save the husks from the green corn as it is used daily (corn on the cob). The husks are coarse and should be slit. Drive a few large nails through a board, file them sharp and draw the husks across these to slit them into shreds an inch or less wide. Or use an old carving fork. Then put them out to dry in an attic or the loft of an outbuilding. If the corn is not green, reject the weatherworn outer husks taking only the thin papery ones. When a sufficient amount has been prepared buy your ticking. That should be a heavy, very tough twill ticking weave made especially for making pillows and mattresses. Fill the tick as desired. The fuller it is the stiffer it will be. The husk mattress is not washable but the tick could be taken off and washed, the husks sunned, and then put back in the tick.

CATTAIL FIBERS—The fibers of cattail down (from the seed head) make excellent cushion stuffing. Start with a sackful and make your pillows same as with any other stuffing.

ANGORA FUR comes from Angora rabbits. You pull it off them same as they pull it off themselves to make wonderful nests to have babies in. It's fine for spinning or stuffing, but it takes a lot of rabbits. They are cute, cuddly things.

Angora wool comes from the Angora goat, which looks quite a bit like a dairy goat but isn't just the same. Angora goats are not very common except in Texas where there is a small Angora wool industry. The Angora hair is long, long goat hair that they grow in the fall to cope with cold winter weather. In the spring you have to cut or pull it off and save for spinning or stuffing. If you don't get it by late spring they will shed it all off onto the ground and fences and suchlike and you'll lose the whole crop. They look short-haired and regular all through the early summer until their hair gets started growing again. We have a mamma, daddy and baby. They are much more timid than our other goats.

Mohair is the proper name for the Angora goat hair. For real production you shear your Angora goats like sheep twice a year, in spring and fall. Then you give the hair a good washing in soap and water which takes out the dirt and lanolin. Squeeze it and dry it. You can skim and save the lanolin for soaps and lotions. You can dye the mohair as the next step after washing, or after carding and spinning, or after your cloth is made—it doesn't matter which. It takes a color very nicely. Once your mohair cloth is made you have a fire resistant cloth that won't flame, is warm, tough, shrugs off dirt and looks nice. Angora goats originated in the Himalayas and they look kind of exotic with big horns. I really like them.

HAIR from hides is removed by the liming process described under tanning. If wanted for upholstering, wash the hair through several waters until clean and dry in a warm place. It may then be stuffed as desired.

FEATHERS—Goose feathers were obtained in Colonial days three or four times a year by stripping them from the live birds—except for the quills which were used for pens and never pulled but once from a goose. Some people only picked them in springtime and harvest time. A stocking was pulled over the bird's head to keep it from biting or else the head was thrust down a long, narrow necked "goose basket." The pickers have to wear old clothes and tie covers over their hair because the down flies everywhere. Goose feathers make fine feather beds and pillows, very soft and warm.

Duck feathers have the problem of an odor which is difficult to remove completely. Duck and goose feathers are softer, fluffier and more moisture proof (don't absorb sweat) than chicken feathers. But you can make do with chicken feathers.

Before killing the birds have ready paper bags or cheesecloth bags. Carefully pick the bird as soon as it is killed, while still warm. Be careful to free the feathers of any skin or flesh that may adhere to them while being picked or they will be tainted. Separate the feathers over two inches long, especially the large wing and tail feathers. They should be cut with a scissors or stripped off the quill and the quill discarded. The paper bags full of feathers can be closed at the top with string, staples or folded tightly. They are put into a slow oven for about half an hour, then removed then put back in the oven two or three times. The oven must not be too hot. Some people say before putting the feathers in the oven they should be put loosely into a dry tub or basket and shaken up daily so that all may in turn be exposed to the air. Others recommend, as an easier plan, merely suspending the bag from the ceiling of a warm kitchen, or on the wall behind a fireplace, wherever it is most practical. In this case the feathers will take longer to dry. Perhaps the nicest way of all is to put them into cheesecloth bags. The feathers inside the cheesecloth bag can then be washed in soap and water and hung out between the lines. But dry them in the shade because the sun will bake the life out of them.

To make a feather quilt lay the feathers, still in their cheesecloth bags, upon the bottom layer of the quilt as it is stretched out on the quilting frame. Then put your quilt cover on, tack it down and sew or tie. Or the feathers could be placed directly between layers of cheesecloth and then the quilt made over that. If this method is to be used sew over the entire cheesecloth and feather layer (and quilt, too, if you wish) to create an effect of "diamonds" or "squares." This will keep the feathers from shifting out of place and bunching. Such a quilt can be washed very occasionally if care is used, but it is preferable to have a removable cover to protect the feathers as much as possible. To make pillows and ticks use commercial ticking and fill them as slack or full as you like, but the first time make them fuller than you think you want because they will gradually pack.

You won't get good results from what's called "dead" feathers. That means the ones that the chickens lose in their regular molting process and your children find in the yard or on the chicken house floor. They will be full of straw or even pebbles and chicken droppings and will be real hard to clean. They are not as lively and nice as freshly plucked ones. If somebody gives you a mess of feathers that are not in good shape (and that's the way you'll usually get them)—I mean containing lice and other creepy-crawlers along with dirt, droppings, and so on—here is what you do. By hand you'll have to pick out rocks, straw, sticks and major globs of glop. Now if there are no bugs go ahead and strip the wing and other large feathers to get those big quills out of the way. It takes a *long* time to strip feathers. And cut off the sharp tips on the shorter feathers. If there are bugs you might want to give it all a somewhat antiseptic laundering. The way you do that is sew or tie the feathers into a bag. If you've got something like old scrim curtains, the kind you can look through, that's perfect because it lets the dirt out. But any loosely woven cloth material will do. Then you put the whole thing in the washing machine and keep putting it through until you're satisfied. Or wash in the bag by hand squeezing and letting fill again and again. You can use a soap suitable for wool, even some bleach if you want, and water warm but not boiling hot unless the bug problem is bad. In that case a dose of boiling water in a pan on the stove may be the only answer for your "presoak" cycle. Personally I wouldn't bring home a batch of feathers that had critters because next thing you'll have them all over your own farm. Just tell them to keep their feathers. But anyway Pat Woods from Sedro Woolley, Washington, wrote me that a neighboring chicken farmer just presented her with six great big sacks of feathers in this condition and what should she do so I'm writing her and writing it up for the book at the same time. (I'm always

glad to get questions from people because it tells me what people are needing to know and helps me make this book a more useful one for its readers. So if you've got questions too, do write me—don't feel embarrassed about it.) If you have a dryer put your sack of feathers inside a pillowcase for extra coverage and then just go ahead and dry them. If not hang the feathers inside the lighter bag in the shade on your line.

To make a feather bed use regular twill ticking. Sew double seams so you won't have feathers creeping out. Leave one end open. Pour in 10 to 20 pounds of dry clean feathers and sew it up. You can make feather quilts to go on top of your bed. The feather "bed" is the layer that is meant to go underneath you. With feathers above and below in that manner you can sleep warm even in 50° below temperatures and I kid you not. That's what the pioneers who had no heat in their homes at night in places like Vermont used for bedding.

When making chicken feather quilts you also must make sure you have the feathers in a special inside layer because you don't want to have to pull a needle through the feather section as you quilt the top. It will pull feathers out with it every time.

WOOL—In the spring when the warmer weather has come to stay, take the wool from the sheep by shearing. Sheep are delicate and unless you have shelter for them and have them in it, one night out immediately after shearing in an unseasonal storm can take an awful toll. (That's speaking from experience.) But do shear even if you must sell the wool rather than use it yourself. If you don't shear they shed some of it anyway and are miserably hot wearing the rest.

The sheep's wool, if you work right, will come off all in one piece and that's the fleece. Get the sheep firmly between your knees with his head pointing toward your behind and on its side or back. Start clipping, have your shears really sharp. You can use garden-type shears. Clip away, turning the sheep's body as needed. Clip as near the body as you can. Have ready a bag such as a gunnysack. Gather up the fleece and put it into the bag. Turn that sheep out and grab the next. Do your shearing in a small pen so that if your animal does get away from you, you don't have to chase it all over creation to finish.

When you're done have your wife check you all over for ticks. The best way to kill a tick, I think, is to drop him into the flame of your wood stove or put him on an electric burner or a gas flame until you're sure he's dead. They don't crush easily. Or else pull the head part away from the body part or tear open the body part. To remove a tick that isn't just walking around (one that is feeding) use a tweezers or your fingers, and get a firm hold on the head part. Otherwise you may just pull him apart. Don't assume that just because you've got his head in the tweezers he's dead—he isn't. If you think this is brutal to my fellow critters you've never worn a tick. Tick season is May. We have to check dogs and kids every day and have gotten as many as 20 off a dog. They only eat twice in their lives, but when they feed they feast—on your blood. They always go to the head end though, so that helps in finding them.

Now for the fleece. It is probably dirty and has seeds and the like in it. Put it in a tub with lukewarm water and a very mild detergent and wash, pulling it apart with your hands. If the water is too hot the wool will shrink and wad up into little knots and you can't even card it. And make sure you don't use too much soap. Wool isn't that different fresh from the sheep or in the sweater. And remember you've got 100 percent wool! Dry the wool in the shade not in the sun. Don't let the wind blow it away.

In the past it was possible to send the wool away to have it cleaned and carded by Utah Woolen Mills. They've quit advertising in the *Idaho Farmer* and I don't know if they still have that service. In St. Peter, Minnesota, there is a working woolen mill. Most people in the old days carded their own. Wool cards are rectangular pieces of thin board with a simple handle on the back or at the side. To this board is fastened a smaller rectangle of strong leather, set thick with slightly bent wire teeth, like a coarse brush or currycomb. The carder takes one card with her left hand, and resting it on her knees draws a tuft of wool across it several times until a sufficient quantity of fiber has been caught upon the wire teeth. She then draws the second wool card across the first several times until the fibers are brushed parallel. Then by a motion the wool is rolled or "carded" into small fleecy rolls which are ready for spinning or to fill quilts. (In early days the leather back of the wool card was pierced with an awl by hand, the wire teeth cut off from a length of wire, slightly bent, and set one by one.)

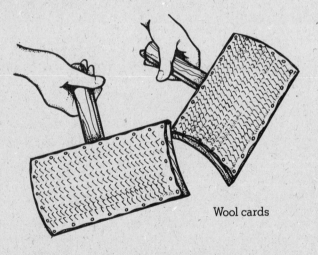

Wool cards

You can buy a catalog for $4 plus postage from the Whole Earth Truck Store, 558 Santa Cruz, Menlo Park, California 94025, that tells where you can order wool, looms, spinning wheels and all kinds of do-it-yourselfing stuff. It's called *Whole Earth Epilog*.

To make the wool into a warm quilt start with a layer of cheesecloth. Put the wool on the cheesecloth. It should be ½ inch thick for a regular quilt, but for a thick comforter the wool layer can be 1, 2 or even 3 inches, or as thick as you wish. Put a layer of cheesecloth on top and coarsely stitch it into place with a pattern of diamonds or squares. This prevents

the wool from shifting to one corner. The prepared layer can then be covered with cotton, sateen, outing flannel, satin, or whatever is desired. It can be tied with yarn or baby ribbon or coarsely stitched—however, the cover should be removable as you do not want to wash the wool much. I guarantee, if you keep the cover clean, the wool inside the cheesecloth won't get dirty in 25 years. Wool makes a fluffy, light and warm quilt.

PLANTS TO GROW FOR SPINNING—Flax is the classic one. Nettles make a fine, white, linen-type fiber nearly as strong as flax. Nettles were commonly used to make a linen in Europe years ago all the way back to the caveman days. Flax used to be a very common crop right here in Idaho. Now most of the world's supply is grown in Russia. Flax is coming back a little. It's also good for making linseed oil from the seeds. To make linen out of flax you must "ret" it by soaking in water to rot the pith and "bark." How long it takes to ret depends on your climate. In a warm climate and warm weather 3 weeks can be enough. In a cooler area it may take 1½ months or longer. The flax-soaking vat should be of wood or clay construction. Metal drums color the fiber—which doesn't matter if it is to be used for rough sacking material or to spin into rope but does matter if you want to make something nice out of it.

To preserve the total length of the fiber and to prevent discolored ends, pull your flax roots and all. Then pull or shell the seeds off the stems. You treat flax different from wheat. Don't beat the seeds off. After retting is done you break the rotted pith out of the stem and knock loose the "bark" with a wooden mallet or stone, or a stick across the edge of a wooden bench. Starting at one end of a handful or bundle you beat and turn the bundle, working toward the middle, then change ends and finish the bundle, working from ends to the middle again. The fibers are then combed and spun. You can comb it with regular wool-carding combs or hair-type combs. You'll end up with short fibers called "tow" and long fibers called "streak." Spin and weave it, make rope and sacks and tablecloths.

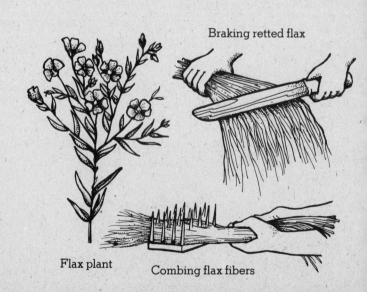

Braking retted flax

Flax plant   Combing flax fibers

And then, of course, there's king cotton! You need a warmish climate like Alabama or California. Grow it until the "bolls" break open and you can see the beautiful cotton in there. Card it with wood cards and go ahead and stuff with it.

OF QUILTING

The classic quilt style and the only one I care about, being of a practical mind, is the "crazy" quilt. This means the quilt cover is made by fitting and sewing together pieces of every size, shape and kind of material. The results are usually very interesting! The total should be blanket-sized to fit the bed you have in mind. A quilt is a total of three ingredients. The stuff in the middle is wool, feathers, commercial bat, or old blankets. The easiest is the latter. When I have old blankets with holes or that have shrunk out of shape I make a quilt of them. The crazy top covers whatever is providing the real warmth and a bottom layer is made of any material you prefer. I like flannel because it's cozy in bed. (I'm an advocate of sheet blankets which are practically extinct except for Montgomery Ward's—they are so warm and nice if you're in a house that doesn't have any heat at night.) Some people use cotton, sometimes plain, sometimes a pretty print. I strongly advise against the commercial bat, which is the "in" thing to use these days. It's not awfully warm and after about three washings it starts to wad up and fall apart. The three layers of the traditional quilt are put together on a quilt frame to be tied. The frame stretches the quilt and gets it off the floor.

HOW TO MAKE A QUILTING FRAME—You need four boards to make a rectangular shape somewhat bigger than you want your quilt to be. You fasten them together at the four corners with "C" clamps that you can buy at a hardware store. Or nail them or tie

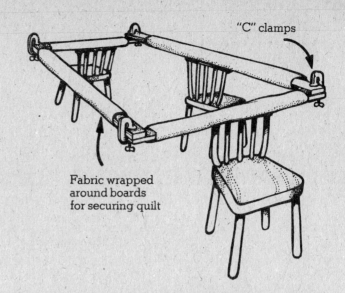

"C" clamps

Fabric wrapped around boards for securing quilt

them. You double over a long strip of cloth, like one torn from an old sheet and staple it the whole length of each board so you have something to pin your quilt top to. Now you want to get the quilting frame up off the ground so you set it on chair tops or on boxes or whatever else seems handy.

TYING means when the layers are fastened together with wool yarn sewn through at intervals back and forth across the quilt and tied above each stitch with the little ends left dangling on the top side for appearance's sake. About eight people can tie a quilt in an hour to an hour and a half. If your quilt is the sort that you can't readily wash the center layer (wool or feathers) don't tie—instead make a fitted "bag" to be a cover with just big loose stitches on one side so you can get it off when you need to wash the cover and stitch it up again afterwards with the unwashable filling in its own cover inside the bag.

SOAP MAKING

First, let me disillusion you. In my experience homemade soap doesn't work very well to wash dishes or clothes in *cold* water because it doesn't dissolve easily, even if you make it into soap flakes. If you use it to wash dishes in hard water, it *will* leave a ring around the sink. It is good for washing clothes if you are able to wash them in hot water. Make sure the soap is dissolved before you add clothes or dishes. Use water as hot as your hands can stand—or hotter. Great-grandmother boiled her clothes in a big iron pot with the homemade soap over a fire in the backyard on washday. If you want to use homemade soap and your hot water is limited, dissolve your soap first in a pan on the stove and then add it to your washing water. Stir or beat the water if necessary to finish the dissolving. Be sure the soap is all dissolved before you add the clothes. Otherwise you risk having little particles of undissolved soap left among your clothes. A really good hand rinse will easily get rid of those particles but automatic washers aren't built to handle the problem. Homemade soap is fine for human bodies if it is properly aged. We wash our faces and take baths with it.

Homemade soap doesn't contain the bleach that is present in so many detergents now so your clothes won't look "white" unless you add a bleaching agent separately to the water. Or you can make it with bleach in it. Homemade soap won't work well in a very hard water unless you use some borax to hold down the "curding." I put borax in when I make the soap. Using Purex (liquid bleach) will also help hold down the curds. If you can get it into solution 3 cups to a washing machine full of water will do a good job, and you can put up to 12 batches of clothes through that same water. Of course, you start with the white, then do the colored loads, finally the overalls. You put them through two rinses in the same order and that way you get the most mileage out of the soap, water and the fuel you heat it with, if you have an old-style washing machine rather than an "automatic."

OF LYE

READ THIS: Lye is caustic soda. It *burns*. Keep children and animals away from it. Don't put it in aluminum containers because it will react with the aluminum. Don't put it in iron or stainless steel. Utensils exposed to lye should be enamel, crockery, glass or wood. Rinse utensils after they have been in a lye solution. Never use anything but a *wooden spoon*—a slotted one is good for stirring. Never add hot or even warm water to the canned store lye crystals. They heat up anyway when combined with water and the hot water will cause spattering. Lye in the eyes, on skin, or clothing can cause severe burns. Obviously you don't swallow it.

FIRST AID FOR LYE BURNS—Learn these now. If you ever need to use the information you won't have time to look it up. Act *immediately*.

Lye on your skin—Flood with water for 15 minutes, then wash with vinegar or lemon juice. (For protection when making soap, keep a bowl of vinegar near, so if you spatter lye on your hands you can dip them immediately into the vinegar to neutralize it.)

Lye that is swallowed—Get the person to drink vinegar or lemon, orange, rhubarb or grapefruit juice, as much as the victim will take. Then follow with olive oil, butter or cooking oil. Then call the doctor.

Lye in the eyes—Flood with water for at least 15 minutes. One way is to have the victim lie down and you pour water over the eye, cup after cup, holding the eye open to make sure the water is rinsing it. Then rinse the eye with a 5 percent boric acid solution. Then call the doctor.

MAKING LYE—Use hardwood ashes, if possible, such as oak, walnut, or fruit wood, since they make a stronger lye. Pine, fir, and other evergreens are soft woods.

To make lye put the wood ashes in a barrel with a small opening near the base to let the water "leach" through. If your wooden tub or barrel doesn't have a hole, bore one with a drill on the side near the bottom of the barrel. Before putting your ashes in put several clean rocks or bricks inside the container by the hole, then a generous layer of straw if you have it (or hay or grass if you don't). Then you can add your ashes. You can just let them accumulate until you want lye or until your container is full. The most efficient way of proceeding is then to add water to your barrel until water begins to run from the tap, then plug the tap hole with a cork plug (home brewer's supply houses carry them) or something and let it soak a few days. If you have extra ashes you can add more ashes and water as the first layer settles in the barrel from the wetting. In three days open the plug and have a wooden tub, crock or glass container ready to catch the trickle of lye water emerging from the opening.

Wooden barrels—But you say wooden tubs and barrels are extinct! Yes, they're hard to come by although you can buy oak barrels from Herter's, Inc., Waseca, Minnesota 56093. Use a peach basket to hold the ashes if you have a container large enough to sit underneath and catch the lye or make out of wood a V-shaped hopper to keep your ashes in until wanted with a hole in the bottom to get your lye water when you want it. Here's where you can buy new wooden barrels if you're interested: Inland Cooperage Company, 1005 South Cedar, Spokane, Washington 99204. Prices used to be 5-gallon barrel $6.50, 10-gallon $8.50, 15-gallon $9.70, 30-gallon $13.50, and 50-gallon $19. The barrel business is run by a man named Conrad Schneider. He is an elderly German gentleman. Barrels are useful for all kinds of things when you get into the old-time arts. Most people think of wood barrels as made of oak. Maybe they used to be. But these are made of fir. They are paraffin lined inside.

Test the concentration of your lye by putting in an egg or potato. If it floats enough that a piece about the size of a quarter is exposed on the surface, the lye is about right for soap making. If it sinks, the lye water needs to be leached another time through fresh ashes or else boiled down until the concentration is strong enough. If your lye isn't strong enough, you'll make soft soap like the pioneers used.

You can use lye as a cleaning fluid for washing garbage cans, hog, dairy, poultry quarters and such like problem areas. Use about 2½ cups liquid lye or 1 can commercial crystals per 10 gallons warm water, or as you like it.

Using homemade lye to make soap would require experience to know how much to use. Store lye is sold in cans, usually containing about 13 ounces, under several different brand names. Note the sodium hydroxide content. It should be 94%-98%. There is usually a soap recipe on the lye can. Most lye companies will send further information on soap making upon request.

Excess lye makes a coarse, flinty soap that will crumble when shaved. Soap should have a smooth, velvety texture that curls when shaved. If any free lye is present, the soap "bites" when touched with the tongue.

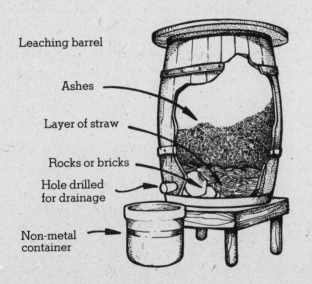

Leaching barrel

Ashes

Layer of straw

Rocks or bricks

Hole drilled for drainage

Non-metal container

FATS FOR SOAP

The grease must be pure and clean to obtain soap with a clean wholesome odor. Six pounds of fat and 1 can of lye can be made into 9 pounds of soap.

Mutton (sheep) or goat tallow (fat) is the hardest of all animal fats, having the highest melting point. Used alone it makes a hard, dry soap unless additional water is added or unless it is mixed with softer fats such as lard, goose grease or chicken fat.

Beef tallow is next in hardness and also should be mixed with softer fat or have additional water added.

Lard (pig fat) makes fine soap.

Poultry fat is too soft when used alone so should be mixed with harder fats.

Meat fryings, cracklings, meat trimmings and other refuse fat must be clarified and desalted.

You can use any animal or vegetable fat but not mineral oil. The soap made from vegetable oils or soft fats requires less water and needs to dry longer than soap made from tallow. Cottonseed oil is difficult to saponify and results in a rather soft soap. Store your fat in a cool dry place while accumulating enough for soap making. When you do have enough make it into soap promptly because fat will become rancid over time and rancid fat has to be re-treated before it can be used. Soap improves with age; fat does not. Olive oil is better than other vegetable oils for soap making. The vegetable oils are the least desirable fats to use.

TO PREPARE (RENDER) FAT FROM BUTCHERING AND MEAT TRIMMINGS—Instead of storing rinds and meat scraps, render and store extracted fat in tightly-covered containers in a cool, dry place. Grind the fat or cut it into pieces. Put the fat into a large kettle on top of the stove or in a large pan in the oven. Add about 1 quart of water for each 10 pounds of fat. Use a moderate temperature and stir occasionally. When the fat is liquefied and the solids (cracklings) are brown and settling, carefully strain the fat. You may want to do this more than once. Your soap will be as white as your fat is. If you do not want to strain the fat, scrape the sediment off its bottom, pour off the liquid and repeat as necessary. Old-timers, years ago, had a "fat press" that was an iron kettle about 1½ feet in diameter with a sieve in the bottom and a big dasher that fit over it and could be screwed down tight to put pressure on the cracklings. This was for pressing out lard or tallow.

To clarify drippings and remove salt put the left-over cooking grease into a kettle with an equal amount of water. Bring to a boil, stir, and add 1 quart of cold water for each gallon of the drippings. Again stir. Then cool and skim fat from surface with skimmer or refrigerate and clean the cake of fat as described above or strain. Repeat these procedures until you are satisfied with the condition of your grease. (Soft fats that won't get firm even when refrigerated have to be skimmed, of course.)

To remove rancidity boil the sour or rancid fat in a mixture of five parts of water to one part of vinegar.

Cool and skim fat or refrigerate and remove fat cake. Remelt the fat and for each gallon of fat add 1 quart cold water. Stir slightly. Cool and skim fat or remove fat cake. Repeat as necessary. Fat that is rancid is fine for soap making but not for eating ever again.

PERFUME

Oil of sassafras, oil of lavender or oil of lemon may be added to soap. They used to be cheap but are now expensive. Oil of citronella is sometimes suggested but I wouldn't use it. It's an excellent insect repellent, however. Never use perfumes containing alcohol—they will not last and may cause separation. Experiment to learn just how strong you want your smell. For a start you might use per 15 pounds of tallow, 4 teaspoons oil of sassafras, 2 teaspoons oil of lavender, 1 teaspoon oil of lemon, 1 teaspoon oil of cloves, 1 teaspoon oil of almond, 2 teaspoons oil of pine or ½ teaspoon rose geranium oil. You can make your own rose geranium perfume by making a tea of the rose geranium leaves and adding it to the soap. All soap readily absorbs odors, desirable or undesirable. It can be perfumed simply by placing with it the petals of a favorite flower or a perfume if it has not been added previously.

COLORING

Uncolored soap is fine. A light yellow or marbled effect can be made with liquid butter coloring. You can make your own pink coloring by adding an extract of the blossoms of pink roses or tulips. A green color can be had by pounding the tops of beets to extract a few drops of the juice and adding it to the water (also from spinach, parsley, and the like—see Food Coloring section). Your druggist might be able to suggest other coloring materials.

OTHER OPTIONAL INGREDIENTS AND SPECIAL SOAPS

Borax will quicken the sudsing action of soap. Two tablespoons dissolved in the lye solution (can of lye) will be sufficient.

Floating soap is made by folding air into any soap when it begins to have a creamy consistency. Test for floating by dropping a few drops on cold water. The air is folded in as egg white would be folded into a cake mixture.

Abrasive Soap—Pumice stone, emery dust, or Tripoli powder is added to make a regular mechanics soap. Castor oil or some other light mineral oil is needed to prevent the abrasive from settling.

Method: Dissolve 3 pounds homemade soap in 6 cups of water (more if the soap is very dry). Add 1 tablespoon borax and 3 ounces castor oil or other light mineral oil. When cooled to a creamy consistency work in 5 pounds of pumice stone powder. Pour into widemouthed jars or cans, cover tightly and use as a paste. Or pour into a mold and when hard cut into cakes. You can also add 5 to 6 pounds of the abrasive

Making soap is a chemical process. When lye and fat are brought together under the right conditions, they react to make soap and glycerin. The process is called "saponification." It may take several weeks for complete saponification to take place. This is one reason aging is so important in soap making. Soon after it is made soap actually contains some free lye but the longer it ages the less chance there is of free lye being present. Soap made from lard or soap that has been boiled requires longer aging before it becomes hard and ready for use. Once it is saponified the soap will never separate into fat and lye again. In homemade soap the glycerin is left in. Commercially it is separated and sold as glycerin. Perfume, coloring, abrasives or ingredients that influence the sudsing action could be added as you prefer.

To make the very best soap (mine is not), use exact weights, measures and temperatures. A dairy (floating) thermometer and household scales are useful. Dairy thermometers are almost essential in home cheese making, too. (You can buy one mail-order for $2.50 from American Supply House, P.O. Box 1114, Columbia, Missouri 65201.) Add the lye slowly to your water when making a solution from the store-bought crystals, and then add the lye solution *slowly* to the melted fat. Stir evenly, preferably only in one direction. Rapid addition of the lye to your fat or of the fat to the lye can cause separation. So can jerky, uneven stirring. Boiled soap is probably superior to the kind I describe here, but it's a lot trickier to make. Use an iron or enameled kettle.

You're confused already? Then get this in mind before you go farther. To make soap you—

1. Slowly add 1 can lye to 5 cups cold water in an earthenware, ovenproof glass (Pyrex) or unchipped enameled container. Do it outdoors or open the windows. Mixing lye and water produces *heat*. The solution will reach almost 200°. There will be strong fumes. You can see them. Try not to breathe them. They'll make you cough. Don't use anything but a wooden spoon to stir. Be careful not to splash it on your skin. Stir constantly until the lye crystals are all dissolved. Now let it cool. Cool the lye solution to 70°-75° if your fat is lard (pig fat), 90°-95° for an all tallow soap. You can throw the empty lye can into your wood burner.

2. Heat 10 cups melted fat to 80° or 85° for soft fat such as lard, 100°-110° for half lard and half tallow or 120°-130° for an all tallow soap. A relatively large proportion of fat gives you a milder soap.

3. Pour the fat slowly into the lye water when you have each at the right temperature.

4. Add 3 cups borax or any other extras you want. (You can get borax at the grocery store.) Yes, I do mean 3 cups of borax. That's what I put in but actually the amount of borax can be completely flexible. It depends on how hard your water is. You could make a batch this way and see how it washes, then either add or subtract borax next time accordingly. Or you could leave out the borax and add it at the time

to the regular soap mixture when it thickens and stir until thoroughly blended.

Coconut oil produces a fine sudsing soap similar to a "shaving" soap. Add 6 ounces coconut oil per can lye (per 6 pounds fat). A similar effect is achieved by using all lard for the fat. A pure coconut oil soap gives a very profuse but thin lather. For a thicker lather use part tallow. Pure coconut oil soap is made by using 1 can lye, 4½ pounds coconut oil and 2½ pints water. Have lye solution at 70°, oil at 130°.

Tar soap is frequently used as a shampoo. As any plain lard or tallow soap becomes creamy, add 8 ounces oil of tar and work in well by stirring to prevent small lumps from forming.

"Toilet" soap simply means that the fat used was from butchering rather than drippings, giving whiter, better quality soap.

Ammonia, kerosene, carbolic acid, motor oil are not desirable additives. Either the lye neutralizes them or they make soap harsh on skin and increase cost.

"Saddle" soap means an all mutton or beef tallow soap. Such a soap is valuable as a cleaner and preserver of leather.

"Castile" soap is a very high-grade soap: 24 ounces olive oil, 38 ounces good grade tallow and 24 ounces coconut oil. Have fats at 90°. Use 1 can lye and 2 pints water cooled to 90°.

Old fashioned soap jelly is used in washing machines and for washing dishes because it melts in hot water and makes thick suds. Cut 1 pound hard soap into fine shavings and add 1 gallon water. Boil about 10 minutes, then cool. Keep covered to prevent drying out.

Rosin added to soap increases its lathering ability but makes the soap darker and softer. OK for a laundry soap. Add 8 ounces crushed rosin to 5½ pounds fat and heat until the rosin melts or is dissolved in the fat. Cool fat to 100° and add 90° lye solution made of 1 can lye dissolved in 2½ pints water.

you wash clothes. That will give you a good notion just how much borax to include in your soap recipe. The borax helps to hold down the tendency of homemade soap to curd in hard water. Since chemically it doesn't play any role in the soap recipe—it's just a physical additive—using more or less doesn't affect the quality of your soap a bit. Hard water means water with minerals dissolved in it. Rainwater isn't hard but almost all water from springs, wells or rivers is in varying degrees. Detergents already contain additives to hold down the curding. The curding is caused by solids that precipitate out of your water in combination with the soap.

5. Stir in one direction for 15 minutes. Soap starts out dark colored and as you stir gets some lighter in color. It is ready to pour when it is like thick pea soup and drops trailed from the spoon will stand momentarily on the surface.

6. Pour into molds (see below).

There are infinite variations on this recipe, but it's the one I know best and a relatively simple one. Makes a good basic soap for soap flakes to wash dishes and clothes. This is a "raw" soap as opposed to recipes for "cooked" soaps.

FOR SOAP TO BE MADE INTO FLAKES you can use anything except metal surfaces for a mold—serving bowls, enamel pans, cottage cheese cartons (handy because you can cut them off when you're done). Have your molds ready before you start. Pour the soap carefully into the mold. It takes several days for the soap to harden enough to be removed. To get it out of the mold slip a paring knife around the edge and pry some. The longer it sets the easier it is to get out.

Let your soap age as long as possible before making flakes. Age your soap in open air in an open box 8 or 10 months or a year if you can. Don't allow the soap to freeze for at least the first two weeks. The best curing is at room temperature. The soap, if you're desperate, could be used at the end of the month. Your attic is a fine place for storage. The longer the soap has aged the better it will crumble.

Five-year-old soap makes something very like de-

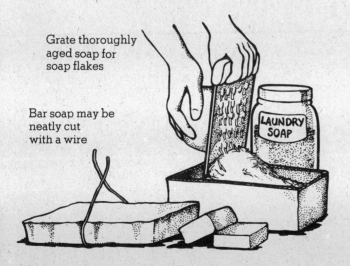

Grate thoroughly aged soap for soap flakes

Bar soap may be neatly cut with a wire

tergent in consistency. If you grate it prematurely it has enough moisture in it that it might be lumpy. A way to rush the soap, however, is to first flake it and then dry it in a 150° oven. When thoroughly dry, pulverize it. To make flakes use a grater, or put the soap through a food chopper, or shave with a knife. You can store your soap flakes in a cardboard box, paper box or what-have-you.

FOR BAR SOAP you could pour the soap that is ready to mold into a soaked wooden box lined with a cotton cloth wetted and then wrung as dry as possible. When well set remove the soap and cut into convenient-sized cakes. Pile so air circulates around each cake. If you have molds the size of soap bars it would be convenient. Or you could use glass pans lined with wax paper. Milk cartons will also work. Cover with cardboard, then with a rug or blanket to retain the heat while it is texturing out. Leave it undisturbed at least 24 hours before cutting and piling. To remove the soap from a mold made of a damp box lined with cotton just lift it by the ends of the overhanging lining. The soap can be neatly cut by wrapping it once with a fine wire or string, crossing ends and pulling.

Homemade soap leaves clothes with a lovely clean smell. Use about 1½ cups per load or 3 cups if you're planning on putting a lot of clothes through the same water.

I like homemade soap for dishwashing—here's my testimonial—My glasses have been shinier and my silverware has been sparkling since I started washing dishes with homemade soap . . . I can also see the soap in the rinse water for the dishes which turns gray very quickly. An advantage over detergents which you think you have got rid of and end up eating! Homemade soap works OK in lukewarm water if you can give a halfway ample hot rinse.

If you wonder what using homemade soap flakes would be like just buy some White King. As far as I can tell it's the identical same stuff. Homemade soap flakes work best in hot water. You'll have to agitate the water to get the flakes into solution and have suds.

SOAP WITH BLEACH—Gertrude Johnson of Lamont, Washington, wrote me:

"I've made soap for years but mine never turned out to my satisfaction until I ran across this recipe. Start with 10 cups melted fat (lard and suet is a good combination) and stir into this 1 cup liquid bleach (Clorox, Purex, etc.). Dissolve 1 can lye in 6 quarts water and dump in the fat and bleach mixture. Stir thoroughly. Set 4 to 5 days, stirring frequently. It will start out thin and watery but by the fourth or fifth day will be solid to the bottom of your old canner (my soap kettle). Then put on the stove and melt, pour into mold and cut when cool. It should dry for several months to cure. I just melt this to use in my automatic washer and my clothes are clean smelling and white. Besides, the suds don't ruin the soil and water as detergents do."

Since I first published Gertrude's recipe lots of people have written to tell me what good soap it made for them.

VIOLET'S SOAP MAKING TECHNIQUE—Violet

Stewart is a wonderful pioneer lady from Okay, Oklahoma, who has helped me a lot with the writing of this book. Here's what she says about her soap making: "This is the method I used to make my homemade soap. It is a carryover from my mother, who is now gone. Each day I save my fats of all kinds. If I boil meat I cool the pot of liquid and remove the fat. Then I put it on and melt it and cook it long enough to get all water out. If you do not get all the water out it will mold or spoil. Then I fold several thicknesses of cheesecloth, or any loose weave cotton and strain the melted fat. Always be sure you are careful when handling hot fat since it can burn you. I keep all fat in a tightly lidded pail until I am ready to make soap. The day before soap making I usually do this step. I use a large pot so it will not be apt to boil over. So do not fill it too full of water. Now put the fat in and let it melt. Stir once in a while to break up any lumps. When the water boils let it set and settle. This process is to remove any salt in the fat and a settling will be in the bottom of the pot and the congealed fat will come on top.

"Lift off fat and weigh. I make only small batches at a time since it is easier to handle. Granite pots are best to use. Do not use glass or aluminum. Aluminum will turn soap dark—besides it ruins the aluminum. Lye eats it. Melt the fat and do not let it get hot, just melted. Set aside and measure out 2½ pints cold water for 6 pounds melted fat. Measure water into granite pot large enough to hold the amount. Add 1 can of commercial lye slowly and stir with a wooden stick long enough to not spatter on your hand. Stir gently until lye dissolves. Pour in your 6 pounds of melted fat, stirring gently while pouring in the fat. Fat must never be hot or it can explode when added to lye. Keep moving gently for about 20 minutes and it will get about like honey. The fat should be so it feels warm to the hand. Have granite pans or light wooden boxes ready. If pans are used, wet with cold water. Pour soap in pans and put where draft will not hit it. Cover up with blanket and in a couple hours go back. Then you can take a knife and cut it into bars. Let it set overnight and by then you can turn it out on a board and finish breaking the cuts so it will separate nicely. I let it cure for another week or so by piling the bars up on one another so the air can circulate around them. In six weeks it will be completely cured. Then it is ready for use.

"I put bars into a few gallon glass jars, and pour hot water over. Every day or so I drain off the liquid into a plastic pail. When I get ready to wash I fill machine with hot water and add soap liquid and start machine. When it suds real good I know I have it right. Then I add the clothes. This lye soap will not hurt your hands. I once had detergent poisoning in my hand and it cost me. I use homemade soap all the time now. But remember you always have to add hot water to it, before cooling it down to hand temperature. You can use the leftover water to irrigate garden or flowers. Works like fertilizer. If you have hard water to use add a cup full of borax to soap while stirring. You can use any kind of fat. The more tallow (beef fat) you use the harder the soap. Soap will be a little dark when first made but will turn white in a week. This sounds like a lot of work but it isn't after you make a couple batches. All these little things will soon come naturally. Each batch makes 9 pounds of finished soap. I make it every time I get 6 pounds of clean fat."

TANNING

Tanning is a long hard process. Sometimes you may be more successful than others. Some techniques may suit you better than others. There are a lot of different ways to do it, and as varying end products.

TANNING SUPPLIES may be unavailable in your local stores. You can order by mail almost anything you may encounter relating to the field of tanning and taxidermy from Van Dyke's, Woonsocket, South Dakota 57385. Order Catalog 17-T if you want to see what they have available. Van Dyke's carries glycerin, lactic acid, neat's-foot oil, salinometers, sack salt and beeswax. Herter's, Inc., Waseca, Minnesota 56093, also has tanning supplies although not as wide a selection. But they carry some items that you can't get from Van Dyke's. They have a catalog which includes their entire line as well as taxidermy supplies, for $1. Herter's carries nylon thread in three sizes, which is good for sewing up skins since cotton has a tendency to rot, and taxidermists' needles that have a triangular point for easier penetration (curved or straight as you prefer), skinning and fleshing knives, and premixed tanning compounds. Another good source is the J. W. Elwood Supply Co. at 1202 Harney St., Omaha, Nebraska 68103. They are associated with the Northwest School of Taxidermy (same address) which has a good correspondence course in tanning. If you make rawhide like the pioneers did or buckskin like the Indians did you don't have to go to anybody for supplies.

DEFINITIONS

BATING SOLUTION—A solution to neutralize the hide after dehairing in limewater.

BUCKSKIN—A dehaired leather tanned by Indian methods.

DEHAIRING—The process by which you remove hair from the hide. You have a choice of several.

FLESHING—Scraping off every bit of meat and "flesh" from the hide.

GREEN HIDE—An untanned one.

HIDE—The skin of a large, adult animal.

HIDE RELAXING COMPOUND—A do-it-yourself formula is to wash and soak hide in hot borax solution until you can feel that it is not so stiff.

NEAT'S-FOOT OIL—Oil skimmed off after hoofs and hide trimmings have been boiled down in water for so many hours that it will set solid as a "gelatin."

PELT—A sheepskin.

PRIME—Of skins that you want to keep the hair on, killed during the cold months.

RAWHIDE—A leather produced without chemicals. Not truly tanned because it is never very pliable except when wet.

SALINOMETER—An instrument that can measure the salt concentration in your solution.

SCALPS—Skins.

SCARF SKINS (striffin)—The outer layer of the skin. It cannot be tanned.

SCORES—Cuts.

SKIN—The skin of a smaller animal (as contrasted with hide).

SLEEKER—An instrument for smoothing the hide.

UNPRIME—Of skins that you want to keep the hair on, killed during the warm season.

SKINNING—Getting homemade leather or fur starts with skinning your animal right. If you want to do hair-on tanning be careful not to get blood on the fur. If you are skinning in the woods in winter you can wipe bloody places on the fur with snow to get them clean. If you can get the animal hung up it makes it easier to skin it. A "skinning knife" has a curved blade. You can make do with any sharp hunting or butcher knife. Have some flour or cornmeal handy so that if by accident you cut into the flesh and blood starts to get on the fur, you can apply it to the fresh cut areas to stanch it. If you plan to make a rug, the traditional way is to cut the animal's skin first down the center of the belly from the throat below the mouth to the base of the tail. Then cut along the inside of each leg from the foot straight up to your belly cut and remove the skin in one piece.

When you are doing your own skinning remember to do it right away before the skin is set on firmly. The skin on a cold animal must be cut away and that really increases the risk of your accidentally getting holes in the hide, whereas on a warm, freshly killed carcass the skin can almost be pulled away and it takes just a few minutes with practically no knife needed.

FLESHING AND SALTING—Once the animal is skinned you must scrape all pieces of flesh and fat from the skin. If they are left on the salt won't penetrate and the hair will slip while in the later curing process. That's a first aid kind of operation as distinguished from the real serious scraping that comes later. To cure the skin you rub salt liberally into the flesh side of the skin and fold the skin flesh side to flesh side. Then you can roll up tight and store the skin in a cool, dry place. Or if you have a deep freeze you can just pop it in there until you're ready to commence with it. But I've known these plain old salted down skins to keep just like that a surprisingly long time. The thing is if it spoils you've lost your skin because it's just about impossible to get the bad smell out again. The salted skin will keep better if it is dried completely in the sun but if you do that you must resoak it from one to six hours in water and then give it a good scraping on the flesh side to remove the glaze that otherwise would prevent your tanning solution from soaking into the hide. The salting actually set up the skin so that you can get right down to the hair roots when you flesh. However, if you are planning to make home-cured rawhide or buckskin as described below, do not salt the skin.

WHAT IT'S ALL ABOUT—You're converting an easily decomposed substance, skin, to one that resists putrefaction—leather. Animal skin when fresh and unworked consists of three layers—the outer skin called by tanners the "scarf skin" which comes off with the hair, the middle skin called "grain," and the underskin which is called the "flesh." The scarf skin cannot be tanned. The grain is what combines with tannin or other substances to produce leather. It is made up of interlaced bundles of gelatinous fibers more or less filled with fluid matter. In the tanning process the fluid is eliminated leaving only the fibrous portion that can be affected by the tanning materials. The loss of this fluid is what reduces the weight of the skin.

SKIN WEIGHTS—The kind of leather that you can make depends on the size and weight of the skin you start with. Commercial tanneries have equipment that can split a heavy hide into layers of lighter leather but you can't do that without a special shaving tool available from tanning suppliers. So if you want light leather for gloves, bags or garments you have to start with the skin of a small animal such as sheep, calf, goat or deer. The thickness of the finished leather is generally just a bit more than that of an untanned hide. The hide of a full-grown steer or cow will start out weighing 60 pounds or more, which is a word to the wise about just what sort of a job it is hefting one of those around to tan it. To make heavy belting, shoe sole or harness leather you must start out with a hide weighing over 50 pounds. Lace leather, small belting and straps are made from a hide of 20 to 40 pounds, which would be the skin from a light- to medium-sized cow. Calf skins, which average around 7 or 8 pounds in weight, are used for boot and shoe uppers and heavy gloves.

SPECIES AND SEASON—The species of animal affects the ultimate use of the skin, too. A fine furbearing skin would be tanned to take advantage of the fur. The best leather comes from animals taken in the summer and fall. Winter hides are less firm, are weakened by having grown all that hair, and all that hair is just an extra chore if you don't want it. On the other hand, the best hair-on skins are those taken during the winter when the animal has its heavier winter coat of fur. I don't recommend deer for hair-on tanning because the hair becomes brittle and it sheds.

Angora goatskins are often tanned with the fleece on for rugs. With the hair and scarf skin off they make a fine light leather. Use regular tanning directions.

Cowhides—Rather than struggle with such a heavy hide all in one piece, big cowhides are traditionally made into four separate strips for tanning. The hide is cut down the back to make two halves. Then each half is cut again in the nose-to-tail fashion. The back strips are heavier leather when finished than the belly strips. The splitting of the back strip from the belly strip is generally done at the break of the flank which makes the back strip about twice as wide as the belly one.

SEWING LEATHER THINGS—You need a special sewing machine with real heavy-duty capacity. There are places you can take leather things to have the

sewing done for you. Check around with the shoe repair shops and the taxidermists. If somebody in town
works with leather and makes things like saddles that
is the best of all for you.

The next two sections are on making rawhide and
buckskin, the two processes that are most appropriate
in a really primitive situation. The biggest drawback
of rawhide is that after you're all done if it happens to
get soaked again it can lose its shape. The biggest
problem with the buckskin (home-tanned leather) is
that it smells bad.

RAWHIDE

Properly speaking, rawhide isn't "leather" but it is
a potentially very useful material. You can't use a skin
that has been salted to make rawhide. You can make
rawhide entirely of easily available natural materials.
Rawhide is shaped when wet and then dried. Once it
dries it holds the shape and will be tight and hard. If
something made of wood cracks or if you want to fasten wood pieces together with a nonmetal material,
bind them with damp rawhide and then let it dry out.
Rawhide can be made into a rope by cutting in strips
and plaiting. Soak the strips until soft. Keep them
damp while you're plaiting, and grease the rope after
you're done to keep it from getting too stiff. To make
containers of rawhide, such as buckets and baskets,
cut the rawhide to the shape you need. Then soak
until soft, sew up, using thin strips of rawhide for
thread. Fill with dry sand and let dry or put over
a wooden form that is the shape you want it to
be and let dry. When dry your rawhide container
will be really sturdy!

Now that you know what rawhide is good for you
might want to make some.

1. Get your hide. It's most convenient to work
with that of a small animal such as a calf. You can't
use a hide that has been salted. If your skin has already been dried you'll have to soak and scrape it
until soft before proceeding.

2. Trim off unwanted flesh and fat with a sharp
knife (don't cut the skin!). Then lay the skin, hair side
up, on a clean surface and sprinkle about an inch of
dry wood ashes over every part of it. Work the ashes
well into the hair and then wet by sprinkling with the
softest water you can get hold of—rainwater, if possible. Fold the hide, paste and all, hair side in, into a
tight bundle. Tie the bundle with a rope and wrap
with wet burlap that you can keep wet or bury your
hide bundle in moist earth. It will take about three
days for the hair to get loose enough for the next step.

If you have a wooden or crockery container big
enough for the job you could soak the hide instead of
making paste as in the above method. Soak in caustic
lime or a weak lye made by mixing wood ashes and
water and leave it there until the hair is slipping.

3. Rinse the hide thoroughly. Proceed to unhair
and flesh it. You need a surface to put the hide on
and a scraper. You could buy a fleshing tool or make
one. A table knife blade is the right kind of blade.
(You don't want too sharp a knife for fear you'll cut

your hide.) If you can remove the knife from its handle
and set it into a piece of wood so you can have a
handle on each side of the blade, you have a perfect
fleshing tool. Lacking that even a rib bone will work
as a scraper. But if you're going to get serious about
tanning, a good farrier's tool for fleshing is worth having. Fix yourself a beam to work the hide on. A log or
half log (the round edges are the really important
part) or even a 2 x 8-inch plank rounded off will do.
Set the beam on legs at a 45° angle, bracing it well.
One end can rest on the ground. Equip yourself with
a bucket of water for rinsing. Throw the hide over the
beam with the end falling off the tip so you can press
your body against it and hold it on the beam while
your hands are occupied with the fleshing tool. Have
the *tail end* of the skin toward you as you scrape to
avoid catching your fleshing tool on the hair roots and
cutting into the skin. Wear a waterproof apron and
scrape downwards. Scrape the flesh side with your
scraper, moving the hide around as necessary to
flesh it all. Then turn it over to the hair side (with the
neck end toward you) and scrape off the hair and
scarf skin at the same time.

4. Wash the dehaired hide thoroughly, stretch to
its full extent and fasten for drying. You can nail it to
the side of a building, but get it high enough that
animals can't get at it. Or if you're planning to make
a lot of rawhide or buckskin rig yourself up a frame to
lace it on. Make the frame out of wood strong enough
to hold up against a good bit of pull, and big enough
to go around the outside of your stretched out hide
with room to spare. Then thread a ¼-inch rope or
what-have-you through the edge of the hide, then
around the outside of the frame, back in and through
the hide, around the frame again, and so on until
you have the whole skin stretched. Put your frame
where animals can't get at it. If you find the hide
stretching, keep taking up the slack until it is tight
as a drum. Don't dry your rawhide in direct sunlight. Find a shady spot where air can circulate
around it for best results.

5. When the skin is bone dry you have *rawhide*.
For an optional extra finishing touch you could go

over both sides of the skin with sandpaper, pumice or sandstone to smooth down rough spots and give it an even texture. When you want to use some, just cut off what you want, soak 10 to 12 hours until workable, and shape as already described. Another way is to soften rawhide by making a mixture of neat's-foot oil and tallow, half and half, or use any animal grease and work it into the rawhide as you work it on your beam.

BUCKSKIN

Buckskin, like rawhide, is not properly speaking either "tanned" or a "leather." It's useless for harness and binding because it stretches so badly if wetted. It tends to have an odor. On the other hand, it can be made relatively quickly without any store stuff. It's soft as chamois but stronger, warmer than cloth, and protects your skin as well as denim against briars. You can wash it like cloth, squeezing the soapy water right through. Indians, hunters and pioneers wore buckskin moccasins and clothes the year-around, but it was considered low-class stuff.

You could make buckskin from deer, calf, sheep or goat, but sheep isn't too desirable because it doesn't wear as well as the others. Deer and elk are the easiest to handle. Technically "buckskin" means the grain fibers have been separated and softened by continuous pulling and stretching while drying, rather than by chemical action, and that they are preserved in that separated and softened condition by grease and having been smoked. If buckskin gets wet it stiffens up again, but it can be re-softened by working with the hands.

TO MAKE BUCKSKIN

1. Don't salt skins to be made into buckskin. Soak the skin in plain water until the hair will come off. Keep the water in a warm place, if possible, and keep an eye on the skins so you'll know when they're ready. Stir at least once a day. If your hair won't slip, add wood ashes to make a weak lye solution. In this case remember to rinse *well* before proceeding. Don't try to take the hair off until it comes out easily. (You won't rot your skin by soaking it a little longer.) The hair ought to just rub off with your hand when it's ready.

2. When the hair is slipping throw your skin over the beam that was described under Rawhide and commence working with your fleshing tool. Have the hide neck up toward you and work the flesher down the beam away from you.

3. Make a paste with warm water and the skull contents (the brain) of the animal. You can add any animal grease if you're afraid you won't have enough for the job, but generally each animal has enough brain to treat its size of hide. The brain paste is applied warm to the hide, to both sides. If you are worried that the brains won't keep while the hide is soaking mix them with moss, make into patty shapes and dry out by sun, fire or oven. To get the paste on both sides you'll need to lace your skin in a frame the same way you do for rawhide. Apply paste. Remove

from frame, roll flesh side in, and store in a cool place for 2 days. Rinse well and wring as dry as possible.

Or instead of the brain use soft soap for this stage. Soft soap is soap made with a weak lye solution. If you aren't a soap maker shave up a bar of yellow laundry soap and dissolve it in water. For 2 cups of soft soap or 1 bar of laundry soap use about 2½ to 3 gallons of hot water. Soak the skin in it 4 or 5 days.

4. The hide must now be continuously worked while it is drying. If you let the hide get dry in the middle of the job it will get stiff and you'll have to dampen it again. Try not to get it too wet or you'll have to wait for the extra water to dry out. It can be pulled over the end of your beam or a stump and scraped with sharp stones or shells if you don't have metal tools. Or pull back and forth over a fence post with a wedge-shaped top. A small hide could be worked entirely by hand. A large one just about requires some system such as two people pulling it back and forth over a beam. The important thing is somehow to pull, twist and stretch that hide in every possible direction to loosen the fibers of the grain. It is *this* procedure that makes buckskin buckskin. You're done when the buckskin is almost as flexible as cloth.

If you are using the soft soap procedure for number three rather than the traditional brain one, do as follows: a) Rinse well. b) Work your hide as it dries. c) Grease it with an animal fat. d) Put skin into warm soft soap solution. e) Remove skin and rinse again. f) Work while drying again. By now it should be possible to squeeze water easily right through the skin. If it isn't soft or if you have hard spots moisten and work while drying again until you are satisfied. Optional, before smoking go over the flesh side with sandpaper to get any roughness.

5. The final step is to smoke the buckskin. This improves both its durability and appearance. There isn't any one absolutely fixed and necessary way to do this. If you have a regular smokehouse, spread your skin out in that by stretching it horizontally. You can smoke several skins at once by arranging them in layers. Or you can fasten large hides together in a

Arrange poles in tipi shape, drape skins over. Smoke gently with little heat

tent shape and build a small fire right under them. Burn green hardwood if you can get it. Don't use soft woods (pitchy ones). Willow, birch or alder are OK. The Indians used green willow, which makes the buckskin yellow. You can figure the smoking process will take 1 or 2 days. For the "tent," make a cone of small poles tied around the neck at the top tipi style. Then arrange your hides over that. Don't scorch the skin. You'll have to turn them over and smoke the other side when the inside is done. The buckskin is finished when it is colored a deep yellow or light brown.

A MORE SOPHISTICATED
DO-IT-YOURSELF TAN

(Uses Unslaked Lime and Sulfuric Acid)

After a preliminary fleshing to remove large hunks of flesh and fat, the skin should be rolled up in salt (see Skinning section) for 2 weeks in warm weather, 3 in winter. Then flesh it right down to the root hairs to remove all the tissue-paper-like membrane. If you want your hide tanned without the hair, the next step is to remove the hair or fur. Otherwise this step can be skipped. Hair is removed by soaking the pelt in a milk of lime solution. Take 6 to 8 pounds of unslaked (caustic) lime and put it in a wooden barrel or plastic garbage can. Do not use air lime. Add 1 quart of water slowly and stir. Do not add so much water at one time as to stop the slaking action, and don't let the solution splash on your skin or eyes. (This will cause a burn.) And if working in plastic don't let the heat build up enough to melt the container. After slaking is complete, add 2 gallons clear cold water, mix thoroughly, submerge hide and cover container. Stir 3 or 4 times daily and test hair each day. When the hair can be rubbed off, not pulled off, the process is complete. About 3 days is required for a deerskin. Remove the skin from the solution and scrape in the direction of the hair with a square-edged tool, such as the back of a knife. Scrape the hide uniformly and wash all lime out with fresh water. You cannot overwash it at this point. If you don't get the lime solution out it will continue to eat up your hide. If you live along a crick the ideal way to get rid of the lime is to hang the hide out in the riffle for 3-4 days. You can further neutralize it by soaking in a solution of ½ gallon vinegar to 20 gallons of water.

The pickling solution is prepared by first filling a plastic container with as much water as necessary to cover the hide without crowding it. Next add slowly, while stirring, 1½ liquid ounces of commercial sulfuric acid (65% to 70%) for each gallon of water in the container. (The Indians used urine as a pickling acid.) Do not pour water into the acid, which causes a violent reaction. (If any of the acid splashes on you, wash it off *immediately*.) Now stir in all the rock salt the solution will dissolve. Place the hide in the solution and move it around so that the solution reaches every part of it. Let it soak, stirring it daily for 4 or 5 days, or for as long as necessary to bleach the skin white. Test by cutting off a small strip of the hide along one edge to see if it is white clear through. Then wash it thoroughly and press it dry. (You can squeegee it out on your fleshing beam.)

Now take the amount of water that will completely cover the hide and mix in as much baking or washing soda as the water will hold in solution. Soak the hide in this for an hour to completely neutralize the acid. When this is done, rinse out the soda solution thoroughly, wring the hide out as much as possible by hand.

Thoroughly rub the flesh side of the hide with a mixture of neat's-foot oil (from a shoe store) and beef tallow. Then wash the skin with cold water and detergent, and hang to dry again.

When it is almost dry and still somewhat flexible work the skin back and forth over the edge of a board or square iron bar, flesh side down, to soften it. Pull and stretch the leather in every direction until it is white, dry and pliable. If the skin feels too oily, fine hardwood sawdust can be worked into it and then brushed off.

Charlie Wilkes of Hillside, New Jersey, sent me that recipe.

ALUM METHOD—I recommend using this method of tanning for smaller skins, especially if you want the hair left on. Proceed with the tanning steps above, leaving out the dehairing process and substituting the following solution for the sulfuric acid pickling solution:

Use a total of 10 gallons of water. Dissolve two pounds of alum (available from the drugstore) in a small amount of boiling water. Let this stand while you dissolve 5 pounds of rock salt in the rest of the water. Then add the alum solution to the salt bath and stir the whole thing until the salt and alum have been thoroughly mixed and dissolved. If you need more solution for a large skin, increase the amounts of alum and salt proportionally.

Soak, rinse and work as above. You may not need to oil very small skins that contain a good deal of natural oil. If they are too oily, you can rinse in gasoline to dissolve the oil.

BARK TANNED LEATHER—Old fashioned bark tanned sole and harness leather is the finest leather known but requires 120 pounds of finely ground oak or hemlock bark for each cowhide treated. If you have access to such a quantity of bark see Farmers Bulletin #1334, USDA, for detailed directions.

TANNING KITS—If you want to try one of the more sophisticated chemical tans probably the best way to start is either with one of Herter's premixed pickling mixtures or else one of Van Dyke's tanning kits. PLEASE NOTE: Many of the tanning chemicals are very dangerous. Don't breath the dust, keep them off your skin and out of your mouth. Some have very pretty colors—*don't let your children get hold of them!*

TO HAVE YOUR SKIN
COMMERCIALLY TANNED

If you plan to have the actual tanning done elsewhere, the hide should first be fleshed, salted, dried, marked and bagged for mailing to the tannery.

The finished hide is returned to you for final working up into your rug, vest or whatever. A lot of the commercial taxidermists use these tanneries rather than doing their own tanning. Some of the tanneries will do only hair-on tanning. Some are also willing to make "buckskin" which in this case means hairless leather suitable for making gloves and the like.

Fleshing—This means scraping all the fat and meat off. There are special tools advertised in tanning supply catalogs such as Herter's and Van Dyke's, but you can use a knife. (Be careful not to make holes in your hide.)

Salting—It's good to have a half-inch layer of salt all over the hide. Be sure and get salt into all the crannies and especially in places where the hide is thick. If you have several hides you can salt them in layers. That is, you could spread out a hide, salt it, then put another on top, salt it, and so on. Then roll them all up together. The best salt is hay salt or "mill run salt." It is sold in 50-pound bags by suppliers here. It's a rock salt. For hair-on tanning the mill run salt is especially to be preferred. When salting the general rule is that you can't use too much salt. Leave the salt on at least 4 days, 7 is better and even longer won't hurt—such as 2 weeks. When you are done salting give the hide a good shake.

Drying—For hair-on tanning don't let the sun ever get on your hide. Hang the hide to dry somewhere under cover. You can make a hole in your hide and put a rope through it to hang it or just hang it over a fence post if you are making buckskin for leather garments. After it has hung to dry a while it turns white and gets progressively harder. You have to roll it to send to a tannery before it gets too hard to roll.

Shipping—Mark in a way that you can recognize to make sure you get your hide back. If you punch the hide do so after it has dried so it will leave a distinctive mark. Punching a soft hide leaves a shapeless hole. A three cornered screw driver with the tip off, for example, would make a distinctive mark. Roll with the hair side in.

Put the hide in a burlap bag or what you prefer, and send by motor freight to the tannery of your choice.

Tannery—An untanned hide is called a "green" hide. The tannery price depends on the size and type of hide. For example a bear cub hide would be tanned cheaper than a big bear hide. Wholesale price is generally a third less than retail. Some tanneries that I know about are:

Colorado Tanning
1787-93 S. Broadway
Denver, Colorado 80210

Custom Tanning
1170 Martin Avenue
Santa Clara, California 95050

American Fur Dressing Company
P.O. Box 7719
10816 Newport Highway
Spokane, Washington 99208

Clearfield Taxidermy
Dept. AT-1
608-605 Hannah Street
Clearfield, Pennsylvania 16830

Colorado Tanning is the only one I know will do hair-off tanning for buckskin. They'll also do snakeskins, etc.

BLANKETS, RUGS AND CLOTHES FROM SKINS

Cutting skins—If the hair is on, always cut from the hairless side and let the knife ride through the hair so you don't shorten it. Use a sharp knife or scalpel depending on how heavy your hide is.

Sewing skins—You can sew together several small skins to make a robe, a parka, cap or whatever you want. You could sew fur to the back of woolen mittens for extra warmth, make a cap or vest. If you have a bullet hole cut away enough skin to change the shape of the hole from round to diamond. It will sew up better looking that way. Check your skin for cuts and mend them. Use nylon thread or dental floss. Where it will show use the clear nylon that is like a fishing leader. If you have a bad spot in your fur you can patch it using a baseball stitch over the top and back through again. However, when sewing a skin onto a backing of felt use a heavy colored thread to match the felt color. Special taxidermist's needles help. It's hard on a regular sewing machine to stitch heavy leathers. You can get heavy-duty leather sewing machines such as the shoe repair people use.

Rugs and robes are probably the easiest things you can make. Cut the skin to your preferred shape and trim off the ragged edges. Draw around the skin to get your pattern and then cut a piece of felt about 1½ inches larger than the skin all around. The edges of the felt are generally cut in a zigzag with a pinking shears for attractiveness. For extra warmth you can put in a layer of quilting bat between the skin and the felt. Attach the felt to the skin by catch-stitching along the edges. Sew from the back. If you can, try to keep your stitches from going clear through the hide. If your rug has a tail with it, that is usually not bordered unless it is a short one, like that of a mountain lion. For really sophisticated rug-making directions get the booklet on "Rug Making" from Van Dyke's.

A robe is usually around 60 by 70 inches. One horsehide, one cowhide, two or three yearling cowhides, eight calf hides, or six to ten sheepskins or goatskins will give you a robe. You can use either sheared or unsheared sheepskins. You'll want to make sure that the fur or wool is clean and that tangles and burrs are brushed out. A robe can be unlined, but it is nicer with a flannel or felt lining sewed on the same as you would for a rug.

Woven blanket—You can make a blanket from many small skins such as rabbit skin by tanning them and cutting into strips about 2 inches wide. Sew together end to end until you have strips long enough to form the warp and woof of a basket-style woven blanket. Join the ends with the overhand baseball stitch and make sure that the fur is running the same way along each strip. The more strips you have the bigger your blanket can be. When you have enough fasten into place on a frame the strips that will form the warp. Interweave the woof, not too tight. Put a piece of outing flannel on the back and stitch together as if you were making a quilt.

BROOMCORN

I didn't used to know anything about this until some Midwestern friends taught me. Illinois is the place where most of the broomcorn grows but that doesn't mean you couldn't grow it elsewhere. Brooms are made in Arcola, Illinois, by the Libman and Warren Broom companies. And at Mattoon, Illinois, by the Century Broom Company and three others. Broom making used to be a much bigger industry there than it is now but enough broomcorn is still grown there to keep about a dozen broom companies going. You can buy the seed from some seed companies like Henry Field Seed and Nursery Co., Shenandoah, Iowa 51602, and from Gurney Seed, Yankton, South Dakota 57078, and Grace's Gardens, Autumn Lane, Hacketts-town, New Jersey 07840. Plant your seed in rows 30 to 40 inches apart, 1½ inches deep and 3 inches apart in the row. Sounds like any other corn, huh! Care as for sweet corn, weeding and such. Grows 6 to 7 feet tall. But no ears! When plants are in the late bloom stage,

the top brush should be cut leaving 6 inches of stalk below the brush. Dry brush for 3 weeks. If you don't harvest your broom corn for broommaking, the plant will finish maturing, the brush will turn yellow and the seed forms. Seeds are excellent for birdfeed. Broomcorn first came to the United States when Ben Franklin went traveling and saw it in Hungary, or so the tale is told. He brought back seeds and began a new-style broom. It's actually derived from a variety of sorghum. Like I said above, the part you are growing it for is that stiff-branched, elongated top and that is what is used to make brooms and brushes. There are different varieties of broomcorn with different heights. Some grow 10 to 15 feet high and make carpet brooms. Some only get 2 to 6 feet high and resemble corn. The seed clusters grow at the tip of the stem re-

sembling corn tassels. You should dry the strawlike branches for several weeks at least before you try to make a broom. You can copy the store model of broom you like best to make your broom and save some of the seed for your next year's crop. It really isn't awfully hard.

GOURDS

Gourd shells can be put to practical use in the kitchen, but they soon wear out. They can be made into bowls, skimmers, dippers, bottles, seed holders and birdhouses. In a pinch you could use big ones to store grain and seeds in. They make fine children's toys, little dishes and doll bathtubs. More along the ornamental line they can be flower vases and cen-terpieces. The gourds come in an amazing array of sizes and styles. In desperation you could use them for dishes but you can't put them on a fire. You can drop heated stones in them though to make a sort of cooking vessel.

Gourds are the fruit of rapid-growing vines that will climb trellises and fences or spread over the ground. They are annuals and must be planted in the spring although they can be started indoors and transplanted to your garden if you have a short grow-ing season. A variety of seeds are generally listed in garden catalogs, including both the small and large varieties. To start with you could plant one of the "mixed" packets and then the next season choose the particular varieties you preferred to plant again. People who live in the Southwest have the easiest time with gourds because they both grow and dry so well in that climate, but you can enjoy gourds any-where if you know how.

Leave your gourds on the vine until near frost time. When you cut them off leave a few inches of stem attached. Always remove your gourds from the vine with a sharp knife. Any attempt to wrench and twist them off invariably results in damage, and the keeping quality may be severely impaired. Don't leave them on the ground or they'll rot. Now put the gourds in a dry place like on a high shelf in your kitchen or a room with a heat source in it so that humidity is as low as possible. Keep them there 3 weeks. Now wash the skins with a solution of nonbleaching disinfectant, using a fine but strong brush to remove all dust and grease, giving particular attention to this with the warted varieties. After a thorough wiping set the gourds to dry for a few hours.

To ensure that they will keep well and still retain their natural shine you use a wax polish. A good wax car polish looks fine or they may be varnished or sprayed with a clear cellulose lacquer. How long will decorative gourds keep? Temperature and humidity play an important part, but several years at least, though during this period they will lose some of their natural color.

For craft purposes, they should be fully ripened but not waxed, varnished or painted, as the skin and the interior of the fruit must be removed. When each gourd is ripe and hard a small hole can be made to get out seeds and flesh. The hole should be located at

the top or bottom ends. After boring the hole set the gourds in a warm place for another few days before removing the seeds, and don't scrape the inside of the gourd too hard at any particular point, otherwise the shell will become thin and may shrivel. After taking out the seeds wash the inside of the gourds and stand them in a fairly warm place for a few days. Then take the outer papery skins off by giving them a quick scalding in boiling water. A light scraping will finish getting it all off.

CUTTING GOURDS—Gourds are hard to cut. Brace the gourd and hammer the knife through or chop with a hatchet. Or for more precision use a drill, saber saw or keyhole saw. Make your first cut where you want it because it's very difficult to trim. Some gourd varieties are harder than others. Choose your gourd for the end result you want.

WHOLE GOURDS—In the Southwest a whole gourd will dry in about a month. You can tell because it gets light and the seeds rattle and the skin is leathery. You can hang them to display by punching a hole in the top and running string or leather through. They are also decorative displayed in bowls on tables. And a big burlap bag full of them makes marvelous winter entertainment for the children.

Rattle—Just let the gourd dry without cutting it open. Hang it so it doesn't touch other gourds. As it dries the seeds will get loose. A rattle makes a fine toy or child's musical instrument.

Bowl—For a bowl choose a round gourd and cut off one end or across the middle—depending on if you want a wide mouth or tapered shape. To make yourself a "set," choose matching gourds.

Dipper—For a dipper choose a gourd with a long, nicely shaped neck. The neck will be your handle. Lay the gourd on its side. Cut off the top half from the base of the neck to the other end of the gourd. If one side is flatter than the other let that be the bottom of your dipper.

Skimmer—Proceed as for dipper. Then perforate the bottom and sides of the dipper with a nail in many, many places. Finish drying. Then you can dip up scum from your stewpot with it and the juice will flow back into the kettle through the holes. Or you can scoop vegetables out of a soup or use the gourd for a sieve.

Bottle or vase—Choose a gourd with the appropriate shape. Test it to see if it can stand up on its bottom. Cut off the neck to make the shape you desire. You'll have to remove seeds, pulp and fibers through the neck hole as it softens up. Another style vase is made by cutting in half lengthwise, hollowing out, and using like a centerpiece with flowers in it.

Bird feeder—Let the gourd dry first or cut the hole and then let it dry. Make your entrance for the birds and hollow it out. Then put some birdseed in it, hang it up and they'll climb in and eat if it's fixed fairly securely.

Birdhouses—The big round pumpkin-sized gourds are good for this. Cut a big enough hole so you can hollow out the gourd. Hang it in a tree by punching a hole and putting leather through. For a lot more detail and the exact size entrances should be to attract different types of birds look up "Gourds Make Attractive Birdhouses," p. 54 in the August 1971 issue of *Organic Gardening*.

Toys—Bathtubs for dolls, cups for dolls to drink out of. Gourds come in all shapes and sizes so your imagination is your only real limit.

Lantern—Use a really big gourd. Cut out one whole side leaving neck intact and base intact so it will stand up. Hollow out. You can put the candle inside it. If you choose a gourd too small the sides will scorch and get kind of stinky. Or put flowers in for a table decoration.

CANDLES

When I was a little girl we used a kerosene lamp for light. Later we got electricity into the buildings. Light bulbs really give a better light. More of it with no odor and no lamps to fill or wicks to turn up or lamp glasses to break. Coleman lanterns were good to take to the barn and I remember my daddy and the sheepherder making the rounds at night with a Coleman lantern and a big quart jar of iodine to dab on the babies' cord ends. When sheep have babies they have them all at once. A flock of a thousand will all lamb out within 3 days or so, and it really keeps the shepherd busy giving help where it's needed. Like to help baby lambs when the mother doesn't want to let them nurse. I remember Daddy stationing me with a big stick by a penned up mother and baby with instructions to hit that old ewe as hard as I could with my stick every time she refused to let that baby suck. I wasn't big enough to hit awfully hard.

Coleman lanterns are still the best thing I know of for outdoor light and if you're farming or camping or hunting I wouldn't be without them. They throw out a lot of light and they are very portable in the lighted state. Any hardware store carries them. You have to buy a special fuel to go with them but a little of it goes a long way. You also have to buy a "mantle" which has the function of wick and lasts pretty good unless a little or curious finger pokes at it in which case it shatters into ashes. Don't throw away your instruction booklet because they are complicated to get started with. Or find a friend who knows.

I notice that kerosene lamps are back in the hardware stores now, too. At least at my local store. You can make an instant candle out of a string on some cooking oil in a dish. You get more light if you use seven or eight strings. Mike and I were in New York during the famous blackout when Manhattan was dark for twelve hours or so. I simply went to sleep early. Mike went to a classmate's house with a band of fellows and there were strings in cooking oil. (Let the string hang over the edge of the dish.) That was before we met. This Montana farmer's daughter met her Idaho cowboy on Amsterdam Avenue in Manhattan, New York City. He started taking me around just to prove to his friends there was somebody else like him. He was wearing his cowboy boots when I first laid eyes on him and by the next morning I knew I was in love. I was 27 years old. We've been married nine years now and have five children. It was the real thing.

There are all kinds of ways to make light and from this book's point of view those blocks of paraffin you buy at the hobby shops are the least interesting. Paraffin is a waxy fraction of petroleum and not the kind of thing you can do yourself unless you have a few oil wells and a refinery. You can make candles out of beeswax though, if you have enough beehives and they are doing well enough so that you have extra wax. Or you can use tallow like the old-timers did. Or you can use bayberries if you live where they grow. Once you have a formula for your "wax" you need wicks that you can make out of string and then you can either dip or melt your wax and cool it in molds for the final results. Candles are easy to make and lots of people are doing it for fun nowadays.

The different kinds of "waxes" will have different melting points and that is important to your candle. A melting point of 125° to 165° is supposed to be best. If you're hard up for light anything will do, even bacon grease with a string in it. Bacon grease smokes, as does oil, but you wouldn't use that anyway unless you needed it, in which case smoke would be secondary. Tallow candles tend to lose their shape in hot weather. Your big problem is to get the hardest wax you can with the materials you have to work with. Bacon grease is harder than cooking oil. Cow fat is harder yet. So make candles out of the latter if you have the choice. The deer and elk fats that shouldn't be used for making soap (they are too hard and cause curds) are great for candle making. The reason one kind of fat is harder than another is because it has more stearic acid in it naturally.

So if you have no choice but animal fat use your

hardest one. If you also have beeswax you can add it in any proportion. Like half melted, strained sheep fat mixed with half melted, strained beeswax. Beeswax improves the animal fat but is much harder to come by. Alum and saltpeter and stearic acid are said to make fat harder. You can buy stearic acid from candle material suppliers. Alum and saltpeter you get at most drugstores. If the druggist doesn't have it, he can order it for you. The old-timers in wagon-train days could get alum but not stearic acid. They made candles, for example, by dissolving 5 pounds alum in 10 gallons of water and boiling it until dissolved. Then they added 20 pounds of tallow and boiled an hour more. Then they stirred well and skimmed to take the wax off the top. When cool it was strained through thick muslin into molds, or candles were made by the dipping method.

You can make a wick out of string or cloth strings. A wick too narrow for the diameter of your candle will not be strong enough and will let the flame get drowned in the melting wax. A wick that is too thick will smoke. You can buy wicking or make your own. It helps to braid it. A wire center makes it burn brighter. Cotton cloth should have a good boiling before being made into wicks to get out the dyes and various additives.

For people who live where the mullein leaf grows you can make a primitive candle using the mullein leaf for wicking. Put mud in the bottom of a small flat can. Roll a dry mullein leaf and bury partially in the center of the mud. Let the mud dry completely. Pour hot bacon grease or some other tallow around the mullein leaf and let harden. When needed simply light the mullein leaf and it will burn. The mullein leaf will also burn by simply being placed in a dish or shell of bacon grease. Roll the leaf tightly and proceed the same as above.

If you buy store candle stuff you'll generally save money by buying directly from one of the big wholesalers like Pourette Mfg. Co., 6818 Roosevelt Way N.E., Seattle, Washington 98115. They used to sell candle wax 11-pound slabs for $2.25, 55-pound slabs for $11.25, and 110 pounds or more for approximately 17¢ per pound. It's probably more now being a petroleum product. They carry everything you can think of relating to candle making including stearic acid, sheets of beeswax, and citronella for making insect repellent candles. They also have candlewicking. In other parts of the country candle making supplies are handled by Hazel Pearson Handicrafts, 4128 Temple City Blvd., Rosemead, California 91770, Mangelsen's Distributors, 8718 L. St., Omaha, Nebraska 68127 and Utah Craft and Novelty Co., 3220 So. State, Salt Lake City, Utah 84115.

To make tallow candles save your firm, clean hunks of fat from butchering—from the high melting point animals if you can, like deer, elk, sheep and goat. Cow next down the list. Figure about 2 pounds of tallow per dozen candles. Render out the tallow similar to lard making by heating to melt it. After melting strain it through a cloth. Then skim your good tallow off the top. It helps to go through the whole procedure again with your skimmed tallow—melt, strain and skim for your final tallow. You can color your candles and scent them the same way as for soap, but with even more freedom since you aren't going to use the results on your skin. Alum or stearic acid or beeswax melted in with your tallow will raise its melting point and generally improve it.

A candle wax for vegetarians can be made from the waxy berries of the *bayberry* bush (as well as from beeswax) which grows in the wet soil near the sea on the East Coast. Gather when ripe late in the autumn. Throw into a copper kettle full of boiling water. When the fat melts out of them and floats at the top of the water skim it off into another container. Remelt that fat and strain in order to achieve wax of a fine transparent green color. (You won't get the lovely green color unless you use a copper kettle.)

Primitive wicks can be made by tearing cotton rags to get long cotton wicks. Or you could loosely spin hemp, tow, cotton or milkweed "silk" if you are a spinner. Or just twist it together tightly as best you can. The cotton is improved by being boiled beforehand to get the commercial dyes and chemicals out. Then for either the cotton or the hemp, tow, or milkweed silk, soak in limewater and saltpeter. Or limewater alone. Or vinegar. Or saltpeter alone. And then dry and it will improve the final action. You can also make wicks out of common rushes by stripping part of the outer bark from them leaving the pith bare.

Beeswax candles are the absolute best and really the easiest to make for pure do-it-yourselfing. But getting the beeswax isn't that easy. Big honey producers nowadays feed their bees thousands of pounds of sugar every year to carry them through the winter and dry seasons and to help with the honey crop. If you aren't feeding your bees sugar it takes them a lot longer to accomplish anything. That's assuming that you have good enough years with mild winters and no drought so that they don't all die on you. Raising bees is a lot trickier than the manuals make it out to be and I speak from sad experience.

Furthermore, your wax is valuable first of all as a basis for honey production. Beginning beekeepers don't realize that they can't have honey until they have honeycomb. Every day the bees spend making the honeycomb they can't be gathering and making honey. That is why honey production is so low the first few years you have bees, until they have a chance to build lots of honeycomb. Then they can use the same honeycomb year after year to store honey in.

The experienced honey producer doesn't take the honeycomb from the bees. He just slices the end off the chambers and makes the honey pour out of the inside by centrifugal force in an extractor. Then he gives the comb back to the bees. Because if you are raising bees for either the food or sale value of the honey—that ready-made comb is your honey crop. It spells the difference between a surplus of honey, where you can take the top couple frames for your own use, and such a poor honey crop that your bees will barely have enough to keep themselves alive through a mild winter because they've been busy building comb. Southern bee growers have a longer flower season and so a better chance for extra hon-

eycomb. For lots more explanation on this subject see the Honey section in the Sweets chapter.

If you do have beeswax for candles that has come fresh from the hives it will have a lot of honey and stuff in it. The best way to do the initial cleaning is to lay it on the ground by your beehives. The bees will very promptly come and within a day they'll have every last speck of honey cleaned off it. If you don't come and take it away again they'll carry off all the wax back into the hive for reuse, too.

You can cut beeswax with a knife if you slightly warm the knife beforehand. You can press the beeswax around the wick in the shape you prefer. Warmed slightly beeswax is very pliable. You can buy thin flat sheets of beeswax from regular candle suppliers. You make candles out of the sheets by rolling the sheet up around the wick. Beeswax candles are better in hot weather than the tallow ones. They don't drip or smell and they take a long time to burn. There is a lot more about cleaning beeswax and making dipped candles from it in the Honey section.

Commercial wax candles—Parawax was the cheapest the last time I looked. You can save all your old candle ends and remelt for the new ones. Heat this paraffin wax over *low* heat. Wax is volatile and explodes easily when overheated. Use a coffee can or big vegetable can or a very heavy old-time pitcher. A pot with handle and spout to pour out of is the nicest of all. Put the wax in the can and put the can into a bucket of water to create a double boiler effect. *Never* put wax directly on a heating element or it will blow sky-high. For wicking you can use pipe cleaners, old wicks from used candles, string or commercial wicking from the candle suppliers. For coloring you can use crayons. You can't use food coloring because it is water based and won't combine with the wax. Special candle wax colorings, scentings and all kinds of arty possibilities can be bought from said suppliers if you want to make your candles very, very nice to sell or give away.

The parawax is usually fixed in a *mold*. You can buy all kinds and shapes of molds, metal or plastic, from the suppliers. The large molded candles are their own base and last longer. Tapered candles re-

quire a candleholder to burn as do dipped candles. If you are working with homemade candle wax (tallow) you can test it for the melting point with a dairy or candy thermometer and it will give you a notion how your candles will hold up through the warm weather. You can make homemade molds out of yogurt or cottage-cheese containers. They can then be peeled off when you're done. Milk cartons will work, too. If you use tin-can molds you have to jam the candle on through after it has set up hard.

Traditional candle molds were made of metal. They were molds but they made candles that were long and narrow like dipped ones. To get the wick into place in a molded candle you attach it to a wire or nail across the open top of the mold to hang down the center. Then the melted tallow is poured in carefully around the wick. You can put more than one wick into a big candle if you want to—like three. After the tallow is poured into the mold let it stay overnight to cool, then warm a little to loosen. Slip the candle out and store in a dry, cool, dark place.

If you are working with *commercial wax* you can pour wax first and then put the wick in. If you are using string, first dip it in wax and then pull out long and straight. To add a wick to a candle in a mold let the wax set a few minutes, then stick the wick down in because the wax is still liquid in the middle. Don't cool candles in the refrigerator or freezer. They crack and become brittle. Leave at room temperature well before you plan to burn them—they will burn slower and won't drip. Don't store tapered candles upright because they may bend. Store them on their sides.

Dipping candles is very time consuming and it tends to make a mess. Lay sheets of paper under the candle rods and all over where you expect to be working to protect the floors. To work with a small amount of tallow or wax you need a tall container since you can't make an 8-inch candle from a 6-inch container. A 2-inch diameter would be sufficient for a start. Metal if possible. If you were a Colonial housewife making a whole winter's supply of dipped candles, you would use a large kettle, preferably one about 2 feet across containing half hot water and half rendered tallow. If you had them you would add beeswax and powdered alum to make the candles harden better. You would keep the tallow hot in your kettle and add more tallow and water as fast as the other was used up. To phase out you would just keep adding more hot water as the tallow got used up.

But to make *dipped candles with the commercial paraffin wax* you have to have a double boiler type arrangement with your tube that holds the wax being in a pan of water. This should also be tall, if possible.

If you are working with commercial wax you can also use a cooling tube of lukewarm water. This is to dip your candle in after it comes out of the hot wax. Stroke, blow, or pat the water with a cloth if it clings to the wax after in the cooling tube. For really good and more detailed directions on making dipped candles from commercial waxes you can order a booklet called "Secrets of Candle Dipping" from the Village Candle Store, Box 486, Marshfield, Wisconsin 54449.

To make *dipped tallow candles* you tie a wick to a stick and dip into melted tallow. Let harden, then dip again. Continue in this way until your candle is big enough to suit you. You can make more than one candle at a time by tying several wicks to a stick and dipping them all at once. In Colonial days two long poles were laid between two chairs. Across these poles at regular intervals were laid smaller sticks 15 to 18 inches long called candle rods. To each candle rod were attached six to eight carefully straightened candlewicks. The wicking was twisted strongly one way, then doubled, the loop was then slipped over the candle rod and the two ends twisted the other way around each other to make a really firm wick.

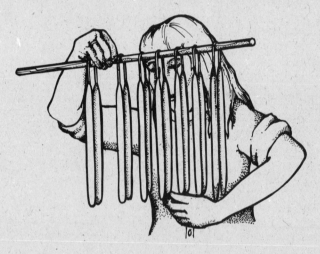

A rod with its row of wicks was dipped into the melted tallow in the pot, then returned to its place across the poles. Each candle rod was dipped in regular turn thus having time to cool and harden between dips. For the first dip wet your wicks in the tallow. They will probably want to float and you'll have to help them into it. When cool, straighten and smooth them. Then dip again. It is better if they go in obliquely rather than perpendicularly. If the bottoms get too large, hold them in the hot grease until a part melts off. After they have hung all night to cool you can cut off the bottom and trim around the base to get a nice bottom that will fit into your candleholder.

DEFINITIONS AND MEASURES

ON USING VERY OLD RECIPES

This isn't the only recipe book that believes you get your eggs and meat from your own barnyard and your fruit and vegetables from your very own garden. Great-grandmother had the same problems you do. (You know I didn't really know any great-grandmother of mine—I wish I could have. The "Great-grandmother" in this book is a pleasant figment of my imagination.) She needed cookbooks that told how to preserve homegrown produce, that listed from-scratch ingredients rather than processed, premixed ones, and that didn't assume she lived near all the specialty shops in New York City. And her cookbooks will work for *you*—if you know how to use them! This section is designed to help you make your own antique recipe books a useful part of the kitchen library, not just sentimental curiosities on the shelf.

LEAVENING is invariably a problem in old-time recipes. What's "old"? Well, 1900 is, 1870 more so. If baking powder is mentioned you may want to reduce the amount by one-half or one-third because modern baking powder is "double-acting" and raises two or three times as much as the first versions (depending on which brand you use). If soda is in the recipe it's quite likely the proportions aren't correct. For every cup of molasses, sour milk or buttermilk, or for every tablespoon of vinegar or lemon juice, ½ teaspoon of soda is appropriate. More soda won't react completely with the acid in the batter and you run the risk of a soda taste. There may even be soda included in the recipe without any acid. Someone thought soda was somehow a good thing and should be included. If you find soda listed without a corresponding acid (cream of tartar is an acid and sourdough starters and liquid yeasts all contain acid), omit the soda unless it's tomato soup! Soda and cream of tartar combined in a recipe are a form of "baking powder." They react together and release bubbles of carbon dioxide gas which leaven the mixture. The soda should be exactly half the amount of cream of tartar unless there is another acid present. "Saleratus" meant an old-time coarse-grained baking soda.

IF THE RECIPE CALLS FOR YEAST BY THE "TEACUP" or some such strong amount, liquid yeast is meant. Use any sourdough starter or homemade yeast recipe or substitute dry yeast. How much? For less than 6 cups of flour use 1 tablespoon dry yeast, from 6 to 11 cups of flour use 2 tablespoons and from 11 cups to 26 cups use 3 tablespoons. Then fill the "teacup" with water to keep your liquid quantity right. If the recipe calls for a yeast "cake," that means compressed yeast. Those pressed cakes of moist yeast and filler material are now rapidly disappearing from the marketplace since the introduction of dry yeast. For each cake of yeast substitute 1 tablespoon dry yeast.

"TEASPOON" AND "CUP" may not be what you think. "Teaspoon" has changed from the old-time ratio of four per tablespoon to our present three per tablespoon. Worse yet, in some old books "teaspoon" and "tablespoon," when applied to dry materials, were understood to be a "rounded" quantity, meaning as much heaped above the rim of the spoon as below. "Heaping" meant as much of a dry ingredient as could be piled on the spoon without falling off. A "dessertspoon" was half a tablespoon. That means it was the equivalent of two teaspoons when four teaspoons equalled one tablespoon. A "saltspoon" contained an eighth of a teaspoon.

"CUP" in old recipe books means about one-fifth less than our present 8-ounce cup. "Teacup" means what we would call a half-cup and "wineglass" is the equivalent of our one-fourth cup. When a recipe calls for "bowls," as some old mincemeat recipes do, use the same bowl consistently and guess from the quantity of ingredients how large a bowl is needed. (Three-cup capacity is a good average guess.) Ounces were figured 12 fluid and 16 dry per pound. Thus, a "pound" of molasses is 12 fluid ounces, about 1½ cups. Recipe amounts were often given by weight rather than volume. You can buy an adequate kitchen scale in most hardware stores. A "hen's egg of butter" is 3 to 4 tablespoons. A "walnut-sized lump of butter" is 2 tablespoons. For "tumbler," "large coffee cup" and "glassful" you can substitute 1 cup. "Dash" means one shake of the shaker. "Pinch" is as much as can be taken between the tip of your finger and thumb. Substitute a dash or a pinch for any "⅛ teaspoon."

FLOUR CONSISTENCIES have varied over the years and with the brand, but it is always safe to add flour on the assumption that a crepe suzette batter should be watery, a pancake batter thin, a waffle batter thin enough to pour and thick enough to clump voluntarily on the waffle iron and not run over. Quick bread batters should be thick with just enough thinness to pour into the pan and kneaded bread doughs should be thick and dry enough to handle without stickiness. If you need something more definite than that when it says "flour" and doesn't say how much, try using 1 measure liquid to 1 measure flour for pour batters, 1 measure liquid to about 2 measures flour for drop batters and 1 measure liquid to about 3 measures flour for dough. One-fourth teaspoon salt per 2 cups flour is fairly safe if you're not comfortable with "to taste."

WHOLE WHEAT FLOUR was formerly sold in two grades. "Graham" flour was the heavier, containing more bran and coarse particles and was considered the lowest class of brown flour. "Entire wheat flour" was the other grade. The entire wheat flour was usually intended when whole wheat flour was mentioned in a recipe unless graham flour was specifically named. In old recipe books "1 cup flour" means unsifted unless it says to sift it. You can substitute one kind of wheat flour freely for any other. It changes the color and the taste a little and that's all.

"LOAF SUGAR" was sugar purchased in hard loaves or cones that averaged about nine to ten pounds apiece in weight. That's way back when. One cone would last thrifty people a year. The sugar cone was cut into lumps of equal size and regular shape with special "sugar shears." For "1 lump loaf sugar" substitute a modern sugar cube. For loaf sugar "crushed" substitute granulated sugar. Loaf sugar "ground in a mortar" meant loaf sugar crushed only to a particle size similar to that of sand or fine gravel.

WHEN YOU SEE "SYRUP 32 DEG." or some such number, it refers to a saccharometer reading. Saccharometers measure sweetness and were commonly used in candymaking as well as home brewing. You can still buy a saccharometer from some big mail-order suppliers. "Powdered sugar" in the old recipe books meant a grade of fineness between granulated and confectioners' sugar. Granulated sugar had a weight of 2 cups per pound, powdered sugar a weight of 2⅔ cups per pound.

FRUITS AND VEGETABLES—Our great-grandmothers used a larger variety of wild and homegrown fruits, berries, nuts and herbs than we do—and used some vegetables that are not now usually sold in grocery stores. You can look for the names in your garden seed catalog and plant your own salsify, sorrel, leeks and the like. In some cases the plant is the same but over the years the name has changed. "Pieplant" means rhubarb, "vegetable marrow" means summer squash and "oyster plant" is salsify. "Filé" means sassafras leaves dried, powdered and used as a seasoning and for their thickening ability in soups. "Marron" means chestnut.

Here are some other terms that may have puzzled you. "Brine that will bear an egg" means with enough salt in it that an egg will float when placed into it. "Boiled until it will spin" means syrup boiled to the thread stage when you hold up your spoon and one drop is attached to the next by a thread. "Gem irons" were iron muffin pans. An "ice cave" was a special pan used to make ice cream and other frozen desserts. It was usually of copper or tin, either round or square, from one to two feet in diameter and about as deep, and with a tight-fitting lid, flanged, so that ice could be put on the top. It was buried in a tub filled with pounded ice and salt. "Lemon drill" means an old-time glass lemon and orange squeezer. Press half a lemon or orange down over the "hill" and twist to get your juice.

FLAVORING—You are safest if you learn to use judgment in flavoring. Lemons and eggs are not always of the same size anyway nor fruits of the same degree of sweetness or acidity. When your old-time cookbook was written adulteration of flavoring ingredients was common. You may need to reduce the quantity of spices given. If the recipe calls for ginger and the amount seems large, they meant the ginger root which was purchased whole and ground at home as needed. Home ground ginger is not as strong as the powdered commercial product. To substitute store ground ginger for ground root, reduce the amount to one-fourth of the quantity given. For "1 grated nutmeg" substitute 2¾ tablespoons store ground. They ground their own nutmeg then, too.

Get in the habit of tasting a pinch of mixture now and then and you'll learn what to expect and be forewarned when all is not well. Be prepared to try an old recipe several times before getting all the kinks out of it. If the recipe is for a large amount scale it down until your experimenting is done. After each trial think about where the measures may have been off and write down your guesses of what they should be. To be a *real* old-time cook get to know what a teaspoon and tablespoon of a dry ingredient look like in the palm of your hand. Know how stiff or runny and how sweet, sour, or spicy you want your dish to be and then *trust* your taste buds!

DICTIONARY OF ANTIQUE COOKBOOK WORDS

This dictionary attempts to cover the most puzzling cookbook vocabulary from Colonial times on. That covers a range from the spartan dishes of pioneer America through the extravagant all-in-French menus of the Victorian era (when "dyspepsia" was the national ailment), on into the early decades of this century. Listings are made by the first word of a natural combination no matter what part of speech it is. Appropriate recipes are included occasionally.

A

À L', À LA, AU, AUX—Food served in a certain style.

À LA CRÉOLE—With tomatoes.

À LA JARDINIÈRE—A dish garnished with vegetables, diced or in natural small pieces—such as peas and tiny sprigs of cauliflower.

À LA JULIENNE—Garnished with cooked carrot, turnip, onion, celery and the like, cut into matchlike strips.

À LA KING—Prepared in a rich cream sauce.

À LA MODE—"in the fashion." Beef à la mode is beef larded and braised. Pie à la mode is pie served with ice cream.

À L'ITALIENNE—Garnished with cooked macaroni, cut into rings (or vermicelli, spaghetti, etc.).

ABSINTHE—A green liqueur containing oils of wormwood and anise and other aromatics.

ACIDULATED WATER—Water to which vinegar or lemon juice is added: 1 tablespoon acid per 1 quart water.

AGATE KETTLE—An enameled iron or steel cooking utensil mottled and veined to resemble agate.

ALLIGATOR PEAR—Avocado.

ALUM—Used to keep pickles crisp. An astringent obtainable from the alum root, a North American herb, or from your grocery store.

AMANDINE—With almonds.

AMERICAN ICE CREAM—Combination of custard and cream, sometimes also flour or cornstarch. Meant to be stirred while freezing.

ANDIRONS—Iron fireplace furnishings used to help hold the logs and cooking utensils.

ANGELICA—A biennial herb that you can grow if you have a moist soil and cool climate. The top few inches of each young stem were formerly candied as a confection. Also at one time the name of a sweet California wine.

ANTIPASTO—Assortment of Italian appetizers such as sardines, anchovies, olives and the like.

APOLLINARIS—Brand name of a soda water, now off the market.

APOTHECARY—Old term for druggist.

ARROWROOT—A starch obtained by drying and powdering the root stocks of a plant that thrives on tidal flats, used for food, as a thickening agent and once widely used in baby formulas. Available at health food stores.

ASPIC—Clear unsweetened gelatin molded to garnish cold dishes.

ATTAR—Also called "otto." The fragrant essential oil extracted from rose petals. (Recipe in Herbs chapter.)

AU BEURRE—Cooked in or with butter.

AU GRATIN—Any dish covered with a sauce and topped with bread crumbs of cheese and afterwards browned under the grill or in the upper part of the oven. A shallow dish is usually used and the food served in the dish in which it is cooked.

AUBERGINE—Eggplant.

AVENA—Rolled oats.

B

BAIL—The handle of a pail or pot made of a wire looped over at either end around the vessel's "ears."

BAKE KETTLE—Dutch oven.

BAKERS' YEAST—Yeast used for making bread.

BALSAM OF PERU—An aromatic, oily preparation from a tropical American tree formerly used in perfume and medicine.

BALSAM OF TOLU—A Tennessee plant product, formerly used for making chewing gum, now off the market.

BARBECUE—To roast an animal slowly on a gridiron, spit, or over coals in a specially prepared trench. The animal, either whole or cut in pieces, is basted during cooking with a highly seasoned sauce. Now, a meal cooked in the open or on a spit.

BARBERRY—A shrub native to Europe and naturalized in the eastern U.S. Its oblong red berries are made into a preserve. The bark makes a fine yellow dye.

BARCELONA NUTS—A variety of filberts, kiln dried for better keeping.

BASTE—To moisten meat or other food while cooking to add flavor and to prevent drying of the surface. The liquid is usually melted fat, meat drippings, water or a sauce.

BATTER CAKES—Pancakes.

BATTER PUDDING—Custard, originally boiled in a bag.

BAVARIAN CREAM—A pudding made of flavored liquid, fruit pulp, gelatin, plus whipped cream.

BEATING—Food is beaten when the motion in mixing brings the contents at the bottom of the bowl to the top and there is a continual turning over and over of a considerable part of the contents of the bowl. Purpose is to enclose a large amount of air.

BELL PEPPERS—The large hollow green or red peppers.

BENNE—Wild sesame seed.

BERGAMOT—A variety of pear. Also, a pear-shaped orange that furnishes an oil formerly used in perfumery.

BEURRE NOIR—"Black butter." Use the fat remaining in the pan after frying meat and add enough melted butter to measure ⅓ cup. Add 1 teaspoon lemon juice or vinegar, salt and pepper to taste.

BILL-OF-FARE—Menu.

BISCUIT—Combination of whipped cream, sugar, flavoring and, often, macaroon or other crumbs. Frozen in individual forms, unstirred. Also, a quick-type bread.

BISQUE—A type of soup thickened by the addition of minced meat and crumbs. It often refers to a cream soup made from fish with the fish diced or mashed through a strainer.

BLACK TEA—Made from tea leaves withered, sweated, fermented, rolled and then fired.

BLADE OF MACE—The unground inner envelope of nutmegs.

BLANCH—To dip in boiling water, drain and rinse in cold water. Or to boil for a brief period only. Used to remove skins from nuts and fruits and to prepare vegetables for freezing.

BLANCHING BASKET—A long-handled colander for immersing in hot water and then lifting out to quickly drain and cool the contents.

BLANQUETTE—White meat in cream sauce that has been thickened with eggs.

BLOW—"Boil sugar to the blow" means to 240°, on a candy thermometer.

BOHEA TEA—A black tea, once applied to the choicest, then to the medium, finally to the poorest grade.

BOILER—A large, metal, oval container used for washing clothes, canning, making cheese and so forth.

BOMBE—Combination of two or more mixtures frozen in a melon-shaped or other fancy mold. The bombe is then hardened in a freezer. (Recipe in Dairy chapter.)

BONBON—A candy with a center of nut, fruit or rolled fondant which is then dipped into melted fondant and cooled to harden.

BONING—Removing bones from meat or fish, leaving the flesh nearly in its original shape.

BONING KNIFE—A narrow-bladed knife, the narrower the better.

BOUCHÉES—Small pastry shells or cases filled with creamed meat or fish.

BOUILLON—A hot beef stock made from lean beef, which is then clarified and seasoned. (Recipe in Meat chapter.)

BOUQUET GARNI—3 sprigs parsley, 1 small stalk celery, 1 leek, ½ bay leaf, 1 sprig dry thyme, all tied together or tied in a cheesecloth bag and added to stews and sauces. Or some variation thereof.

BRAISE (Braize)—To brown meat in a small amount of fat, then cook slowly in a covered utensil in a small amount of liquid.

BRAMBLE—Blackberry.

BRAN—The outer covering of the grain, rich in minerals, protein and vitamin B. Substitute wheat germ.

BRAZIER—An open pan for holding live coals.

BREAD—To roll cutlets, croquettes or other foods in crumbs. Or the familiar loaf.

BRINE—A strong salt and water solution.

BRINE THAT WILL BEAR AN EGG—Water containing enough salt so that an egg will float when placed in it.

BRIOCHE—A roll made of a sweet yeast dough.

BRISKET—Breastbone or breastbone area—in butchering.

BROCHETTE—A skewer. The skewer method of cooking.

BROIL—To cook by subjecting food to the direct heat of a fire of live coals (not smoky) or of a gas or electric burner or other direct heat.

BROILER—A 1½- to 2-pound chicken.

BROTH—A soup of meat, vegetables, and perhaps cereal but without other thickening.

BROWN SAUCE—A gravy made of milk, water or brown stock thickened with browned or plain flour. Usually contains meat drippings.

BROWN SOUP STOCK—Soup stock made from beef and highly seasoned with vegetables, spices and herbs.

BROWNED FLOUR—Made by lightly browning wheat flour in oven or on top of stove in a dry pan. This browned flour was preferred by old-time cooks for gravy making.

BRUISE—To pound small or crush such as in a mortar.

BRUNSWICK STEW—Originally squirrel, corn and lima beans.

BULGUR WHEAT—Precooked and dried wheat. It cooks more rapidly than whole or cracked wheat.

BUNG—A stopper for the large hole through which a cask is filled or the name of the hole itself.

BURGOO—A thick vegetable soup made with beef and chicken which is cooked a long time.

BUTTER BEANS—The yellow kind of string beans.

BUTTER FRUIT (to)—The whole fruit is cooked until tender and then rubbed through a sieve. Sugar and spices are added and then all cooked together until smooth and thick.

BUTTERINE—Artificial butter, oleomargarine.

BUTTERMILK—Liquid remaining after the butter has come and been removed.

BUTTERSCOTCH—Flavored with brown sugar.

C

CAFÉ AU LAIT—Made by pouring equal amounts of hot milk and hot coffee (double strength) together in a cup.

CAFÉ NOIR—Strong black coffee served in a demitasse in the living room after dinner. Made by using twice the quantity of coffee or half the amount of water.

CAMOMILE TEA—Tea brewed from the yellow flowers of the bitter herb of the aster family.

CAMPHENE—A form of camphor.

CANAPÉ—Tiny pieces of toast on which little savories were served. Made by cutting slices of bread into squares, diamonds or circles. These pieces were then covered lightly with butter and browned in the oven or fried in deep fat until golden brown. Then they were covered with seasoned mixtures and served hot or cold. In modern usage, a small open-faced sandwich.

CASTOR SUGAR—I didn't know what this was until I got a letter from Margaret C. Bergstrom, Bellingham, Washington: "My grandmother (and I am 57) always referred to granulated sugar as 'castor sugar,' and I presume that this was because when she was a young woman sugar was still sold in a loaf. The fine granulated was somewhat of a luxury and used for serving in the 'sugar shaker' or from the 'castor.' A lot of old cookbooks instruct you to break off so much loaf sugar and then beat the daylights out of it until it is workable as required for baking purposes." So there's the answer to *that* mystery.

"Castor" is the old-time word for a sort of sugar shaker and if you look on page 447 of the 1897 Sears catalog which has been reprinted and is such a wonderful adventure to read through there it is . . . "Special Drive in Quadruple Silver Plated Castors . . . the best selling pieces in hollow silverware."

And so I thought I had it all understood about castor sugar until I got another letter from David Streeter of Pomona, California, who told me that it was an English term that meant *superfine* granulated sugar. And then Hedy Herrick of Pullman, Washington wrote me that "castor" means a container for powders (Webster's dictionary no less she quoted as the source) and "hence, castor means powdered sugar."

CHAUD-FROID—Literally "hot-cold." A jellied sauce.

CHILI PEPPERS—Tiny red peppers with a very hot pungent flavor.

CHINE—Part of the pig corresponding to the loin in lamb and veal.

CHINESE CANE—Sorghum plant.

CHINQUAPIN—A dwarf species of chestnut, native to the southern U.S.

CHOUX PASTE—Basic dough for cream puffs, éclairs and the like, made of flour, butter, eggs, water, salt and vanilla.

CHOWCHOW—A mixture, especially a pickle made of mixed vegetables and mustard.

CHOWDER—Pieces of different vegetables or of fish and potatoes and various seasonings cooked in milk. A New England fish stew.

CHURN—To make butter by agitating to separate the oily globules and gather them. A container for doing this.

CHUTNEY—A spicy condiment or acid sauce made from apples, raisins, tomatoes, red pepper, ginger, garlic, lemons, vinegar, salt and sugar.

CITRIC ACID—One-half ounce is equivalent to the juice of 4 lemons usually.

CITRON—A variety of melon which is pickled and candied for use in fruitcakes.

CLABBERED—Separated into curds and whey.

Castor sugar

CLARIFY—To remove impurities from fat or liquid. To render fat. To clarify butter means to melt and strain or skim it. To clarify soup or gelatin add egg white which, after cooking, solidifies and collects foreign matter which may then be strained out.

CLEAVER—A butcher's chopper.

CLOCK-JACK—A device run by clockwork which turned the roast on its spit with regularity as it cooked over an open fire.

CLOTTED CREAM—Devonshire cream. See Cream Cheeses in Dairy chapter.

COAT—To dip in flour, crumbs and the like before frying.

COB IRONS—Andirons that supported the spit, sometimes having hooks to hold a dripping pan.

COCHINEAL—A small red Mediterranean insect. In the olden days it was crushed with a rolling pin to make a red food coloring.

COCOA BUTTER—The fat obtained from pressure on the cocoa bean.

COCOA NIBS—Broken beans of cocoa, after roasting. They were prepared by boiling in water for 2 hours, then strained.

COCOA SHELLS—The outer covering of the cocoa beans, removed after roasting. Sometimes used to make a beverage by boiling 3 hours, straining, and sweetening.

CODDLED EGG—1.) Scrambled in the top of a double boiler. 2.) A fresh egg in the shell is placed in boiling water which is then immediately removed from the heat. The egg will cook slowly in the water for 7 to 8 minutes when the white should be about the consistency of jelly.

COFFEE MILL—Hand mill for grinding coffee at home as needed.

COFFEE SUGAR—A partially refined light brown sugar, coarse grained and moist.

COLANDER—A pan with holes in it for straining liquids or draining solids.

COMFIT—A dry sweetmeat. Any kind of fruit, root or seed preserved with sugar and dried.

COMPOTE—Fresh fruit cooked in syrup, or a combination of two or more fresh or cooked fruits. The fruit is whole or in large pieces.

COMPOTIER—A dish for serving compotes.

CONDENSED MILK—Canned milk from which more than half the water has been removed. It is heavily sweetened with sugar.

CONDIMENTS—Salt, spices and various items used to flavor food.

CONFECTIONER—One who made or sold candy, sweetmeats and formerly also ice creams, sherbets, nuts, pickles and gelatin dishes.

CONFECTIONERS' SUGAR—A grade of sugar finer than powdered. There are 3½ cups confectioners' sugar per pound versus 2⅔ cups powdered sugar or 2 cups granulated sugar.

CONFITURES—Preserves.

CONSERVE—Jam made from a mixture of fruits, usually including citrus fruit, often with raisins and nuts added.

CONSOMMÉ—Clarified beef stock. Or a clarified soup made from two or three kinds of meat and highly seasoned with vegetables, spices and herbs. (Recipe under Meat Soups in Meat chapter.)

COOPER—One who made barrels, tubs and casks.

CORDIAL—A sweet and aromatic alcoholic beverage in the liqueur class.

CORN (to)—To salt beef in brine and saltpeter. Same identical process as for making hams and bacons only you're using beef instead of pork. The saltpeter gives it the red color (same as hams).

CORN FLOUR—Finely ground corn. Available at health food stores if you can't make your own. A finer grind than regular cornmeal.

CORN SALAD—A plant used in salad or cooked for greens. Listed in some seed catalogs.

COURT BOUILLON—Simmered stock of white wine, water, herbs, fish bones or vegetables. Victorians used it in poaching fish and making fish sauces.

CRACKED COCOA—See Cocoa Nibs.

CRACKLINGS—The parts left that get brown and float (are French fried) when lard is rendered. Be careful not to burn them. They are edible and make a nice snack, especially the ones made from strips of pig skin.

CREAM—Old-time name for ice cream.

CREAM (to)—Of fat and sugar. Put warm but not melted fat into a mixing bowl (lard usually or butter). Add sugar and work with hands or spoon until soft and completely incorporated.

CREAM A DISH (to)—Means to mix it with white sauce. To each cup of medium-to-thick white sauce add 1 to 1½ cups vegetables, meat, fish or hard-cooked eggs, cut in pieces.

CREAM CANDIES—Simple fondant with nuts, fruits and so on.

CREAM ICE—A frozen custard or frozen pudding.

CRÊPES—Very thin pancakes that have lots of eggs in them.

CRESS—Upland cress or peppergrass. Not the same as watercress. Found in some seed catalogs. Ready in ten days for use in green salads.

CRESS-SEED—Mustard seed.

CROISSANT—A rich, flaky, crescent-shaped roll.

CROQUETTES—Grind or separate into shreds cooked meat, fish, hard-cooked egg or vegetables. Make a thick white sauce. Add 1 cup sauce to each 1 or 2 cups ground food. Mix. Chill. Allow 1 or 2 tablespoons of that mixture for each croquette. Form into cylinders, cones and the like. Dip into slightly beaten egg diluted with 1 tablespoon water. Then dip into crumbs, then again into the egg. Fry in deep, hot fat until brown. Drain on absorbent material. Or anything dipped in beaten egg, rolled in crumbs and fried in hot fat until well browned.

CROUSTADES—Cut slices of bread 3 inches thick. Remove crusts. Cut slices into squares or rounds. Remove the inside portion leaving the sides and bottom ¼ inch thick. Brush inside and outside with melted butter. Brown in hot oven. Use as cases for serving creamed vegetables, fish, poultry or meats.

CROUTONS—Cut bread in slices ⅓ inch thick. Remove crusts. Spread both sides lightly with butter. Cut slices in ⅓-inch strips. Cut again to make ⅓-inch cubes. Toast until lightly browned. Used as a garnish for soups or salads.

CRULLER—An elongated doughnut.

CRUMPET—A raised muffin baked on a griddle.

CURE—To preserve meat by salting, corning and so on.

CURRIED—Seasoned with curry powder. (Recipe for curry powder in Herbs chapter.)

CUSTARD—A mixture containing raw eggs. When it is heated the egg particles become solidified and the mixture is thickened. (See Dairy chapter.)

CUTTING IN—A process used to blend fat with flour. It consists of cutting the fat into the flour with a knife or two knives or forks until it is distributed in as small particles as desired.

CYMLING—A summer squash variety.

D

DAMSON—A kind of plum.

DANZIG—A liqueur.

DARK RAISINS—Anything but the golden kind.

DASH—One-eighth of a teaspoon approximately. One shake of the container.

DAUB (to)—To force large lardoons through meat from surface to surface.

DECOCTION—A liquid preparation made by boiling a substance. (Coffee is one.)

DELMONICO STEAK—The rib eye.

DEMERARA SUGAR—Coarse, raw, kind of a tan color.

DEMIJOHN—A juglike glass vessel enclosed in wickerwork, and holding from 1 to 10 gallons.

DEMITASSE—Literally half a cup. Used to mean a small cup of black coffee generally served at the end of a luncheon or dinner.

DESSERTSPOON—Two teaspoons or half a tablespoon in the days when four teaspoons equaled one tablespoon.

DEVIL—Use spicy seasoning or sauce to flavor.

DEVONSHIRE CREAM—See Dairy chapter under Cream Cheese.

DEWBERRY—A blackberry-like fruit of trailing and climbing habit. About ten days ahead of any blackberry and twice as large. Also called the "low blackberry."

DICE—To cut into cubes about ¼ inch on a side.

DIJON MUSTARD—This used to be a word I didn't have a definition for and said so in this chapter. Then a reader sent me this answer: "Loosely, any of the descendants, direct or otherwise, of the famous compound of mustard perfected and preserved in the Dijon area of France. Alexandre Dumas's *Grand Dictionnaire* gives the Dijonnais credit for giving us their version of Palladius's 4th-century recipe (from his book *De re rustica*, a book not unlike yours): Reduce 12 pints of mustard to powder. Add 1 pound honey, 1 pound Spanish oil, a pint of strong vinegar. Blend thoroughly and use." Somebody else wrote and told me it's made with white wine.

DOUBLE CREAM—The cream skimmed from milk that has stood for 24 hours after milking. Substitute whipping cream. ("Single cream" was skimmed after only 12 hours.)

DOVER EGGBEATER—Old-time name for a rotary beater, to be distinguished from a whip, a whisk, a fork and other types of beaters.

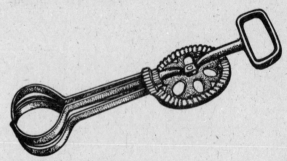

DRACHM—Sixty grains. A teaspoonful.

DRAM—One-eighth of a fluid ounce.

DRAWN—The feathers and innards have been removed and probably head and feet too, but the bird is not yet cut up into serving pieces.

DRAWN BUTTER—Clarified butter. Also, a sauce. Melt 2 tablespoons butter and stir in 2 tablespoons flour. Add gradually while stirring 1 cup boiling water. Season with ½ teaspoon salt and a dash *each* of pepper and paprika.

DREDGE—To sprinkle or coat with flour or crumbs.

DRESSED—The feathers have been removed, but the head, feet and entrails of the bird remain. That is what somebody told me, but to me it means innards out too. Doesn't make a lot of sense because what you really did is *undressed* the bird.

DRIPPINGS—Meat fats and juices which come out during drying or broiling.

DUCHESS CRUSTS—Croutons.

DUCKLING—A ten-week old duck, considered prime for frying.

DUTCH OVEN—A pan made of heavy cast iron from 8 to 16 inches across and 4 to 6 inches deep. It may have three short legs. The pot has a bail and a tight-fitting lid with a handle in the middle of the dome. Ones with legs are good for camping but awful in the kitchen.

E

ÉCLAIR—A chocolate covered elongated cream puff filled with whipped cream or custard.

EGG AND CRUMB—Dip food in egg, then coat with fine bread crumbs. Used for coating fish, cutlets, rissoles, croquettes and so on. Use fresh bread crumbs for raw food and browned crumbs for food that is already cooked.

EGG-O-SEE—Brand name of a dry cereal circa 1910.

EGGS BENEDICT—English muffin, ham and poached egg, with hollandaise sauce (thinned with cream).

EN BROCHETTE—Impaled on a skewer.

EN COQUILLE—Served in the shell, or in shells.

ENDIVE—A plant related to chicory used for salads. (See Vegetables chapter.)

ENTIRE WHEAT FLOUR—A grade of whole wheat flour considered better than "graham." It did not contain bran or coarse particles.

ENTREMETS—Hot side dishes which accompany or follow the soup and are before the main course.

ESCALOPED—See Scallop.

ESSENCE—Concentrated flavoring.

ESSENCE OF PEPSIN—Equivalent to liquid rennet or a junket tablet in its effect on milk. Used for making curds and whey.

EVAPORATED MILK—Canned milk from which a little more than half the water has been removed. Unsweetened.

EVERLASTING YEAST—Old fashioned homemade liquid yeast. (Recipe in Grains chapter.)

EXTRACT—A substance extracted by solution in water or alcohol.

F

FANCHONETTES—A variety of tart.

FARCI (Farcie)—Stuffed.

FARINA—1.) Coarsely ground wheat used as a cereal. 2.) A flour meal obtained from cereals, potatoes or corn.

FENUGREEK—The seed, whole or ground, from a plant of the pea family, an ingredient of imitation maple extract.

FERMENTED BREAD—Bread made with yeast.

FIELD PEAS—Black-eyed peas.

FILÉ—Sassafras leaves dried, powdered and used in gumbos as a seasoning and for their thickening properties.

FILLET—A long, thin piece of boneless meat or fish.

FINES HERBES—Mixture of chopped fresh or dried herbs, usually including parsley, chives, basil, and perhaps watercress and tarragon also, or basil or burnet and thyme.

FINOCCHIO—Fennel.

FIRELESS COOKERY—Preparing food in a heavily insulated container. Foods had to be thoroughly heated before placing in the well. The cooker was also used to chill foods by packing in ice and salt.

FLAME (to)—Warm a small amount of brandy, pour it over the food and light a portion of brandy in a spoon. Pour over to ignite the rest. Or ignite directly with a kitchen match. Spoon the burning brandy over the food until the flame dies down.

FLANGED LID—A lid turned up around the edges to hold hot coals (Dutch oven) or ice (See Ice Cave).

FLAN—A round cake containing cheese, milk, cream or fruit.

FLANK—The abdominal wall just "below" the ribs. In a pig this area furnishes the bacon.

FLAXSEED—The seed borne by common flax. Also called linseed.

FOIE GRAS—Goose liver pâté.

FOLD IN—Incorporate stiffly whipped egg whites into a bowl containing batter. With a metal spoon cut down to the bottom of the bowl and turn the batter mixture on top of the egg whites. Continue until the white is mixed in, but don't stir it around any extra, because the air held in the egg white is meant to be a leavening agent.

FONDANT—Sugar, cream of tartar and water cooked together, then stirred and creamed. A base for cream candies when combined with color, flavor, chocolate, fruits and/or nuts.

FOOD CHOPPER—Grinder.

FOOD MILL—A grinder or a sieve-bottomed vessel with a blade turned by a handle which forces food through the sieve.

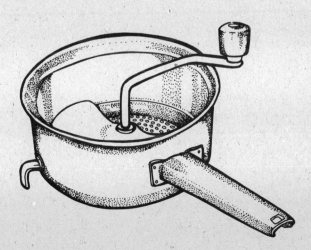

FOOL—A stewed fruit served with cream.

FORCEMEAT—Raw meat or fish, a panada, either butter, suet, or veal udder, eggs and seasoning combined. The meat or fish is chopped fine and pounded to a paste, then forced through a wire puree sieve with a wooden masher. For a simpler version, mince fine bits of cooked meat or bird, season well and bind with egg. Roll in crumbs. Make balls the size of an egg yolk and fry in lard. Victorian, of course.

FRAPPÉ—Semifrozen. Sweetened fruit juices frozen to a coarse mushy stage. ("Ices" were frozen to a firmer texture.)

FRENCH CHOPS—Lamb rib chops which have the bone cut short and scraped clean, nearly to the lean meat.

FRENCH ICE CREAM—Combination of a rich custard and cream. Supposed to be stirred while freezing.

FRICASSEE—In Victorian usage, to sauté and serve with a sauce. Tender meat is fricasseed without previous cooking. Less tender meat requires cooking in hot water first. (Often confused with "braise.") It now means to stew.

FRITTER—A piece of fruit enclosed in a batter, then fried in deep hot fat. Or chopped fruits or vegetables, stirred into the batter and then fried by spoonfuls. Or a bread fried in heated oil in a deep heavy kettle, using 1 tablespoon batter for each fritter, cooked 3 to 4 minutes, or until golden brown and turned once during cooking. Drain on absorbent material. (Recipes in Meat chapter.)

FROMAGE—Cheese.

FROST a glass (to)—Coat the rim of glass by dipping it in orange juice or other liquid, then into sugar.

FRUMENTY—Cooked unground wheat used as a cereal.

G

GALANTINE—Meat that has been boned, stuffed, rolled and poached. Always served cold.

GAMBREL—A stick or iron used by butchers and homesteaders to suspend slaughtered animals by passing it through between the Achilles tendon and the leg bone.

GAME—Any wild animal or fowl used for food.

GARNISH—"A garnish of pewter" was a favorite Colonial wedding gift and meant a full set of pewter platters, plates and dishes. Also, to decorate food with edible items.

GÂTEAU—Cake.

GELATIN—A transparent, tasteless substance obtained by boiling animal muscle, skin, cartilage, etc., in water.

GELÉE—Jelly. Or gelatin.

GEM IRONS—Iron muffin pans. Grease lightly and preheat in oven.

GERM—The portion of the seed in which new life is located and which will, under proper conditions, germinate.

GHERKIN—A small cucumber used for pickling.

GILL—Half a cup.

GLACÉ. Frozen. Or glazed.

GLACÉ SYRUP—A thin sugar syrup cooked to the crack stage. When used for pies and certain breads it may contain thickening and is not cooked to such a concentrated form as for fruits and nuts. Use 2 cups sugar, 1 cup water and ⅛ teaspoon cream of tartar. Place on stove. Do not stir. Keep side of kettle free from crystals by wiping with a damp cloth. Heat to 315°. Remove from stove. Put one piece of fruit or nut at a time on a fork and dip in the hot syrup. Then quickly remove and place on waxed paper or oiled marble. When the syrup becomes too thick reheat by placing over hot water.

GLACES. Ices. Or ice creams.

GLAZE (to)—Per 3 cups cooked item cover with a mixture of 2 tablespoons butter, ¼ cup brown sugar and 1 tablespoon of water in a heavy pan over low heat. Turn until coated.

GLAZE BREAD—Brush over the top with beaten egg or with water and sugar mixed before it is quite baked.

GLAZE PIE—Dot the upper crust with butter before baking or brush top with ice water or cream 10 minutes before pie is done.

GLUTEN FLOUR—An old-time whole wheat flour used by diabetics before they had insulin. Available now from Sioux Miller, 1609 Helmer Street, Sioux City, Iowa 51103.

GOLDEN SYRUP—A pale golden molasses with very little flavor.

GOSLING—A very young goose.

GRAHAM FLOUR—A former grade of whole wheat flour which contained bran and coarse particles.

GRANITE SUGAR—Loaf sugar crushed only to a particle size similar to that of coarse sand or gravel.

GRANITE WARE—A kind of ironware which was coated with an enamel suggestive of granite.

GRAPE LEAVES—Used in some old crock pickle recipes. The regular large, flat leaves of the climbing grape.

GRAPE SUGAR—A sugar made from cornstarch (Victorian).

GRATE—To finely divide food by rubbing it over a metal surface having sharp projections.

GREEN CORN—Green corn used to be a much more common item than it now is and was even canned and sold commercially during the early years of the canning industry. Seed is now available from some large seed companies.

GREEN TEA—Tea made from leaves consecutively withered, rolled and dried artificially or by sunshine.

GREENGAGE—A type of plum.

GREENS—Young tender beet tops, Swiss chard, dandelion greens, collards, kale, chicory, escarole, lettuce, spinach, turnip tops, mustard greens.

GRIDIRON—An iron grate used for broiling food over coals.

GRILL—To cook under broiler or over direct heat.

GRISTMILL—A small hand mill for grinding grain. The more times you put it through and the more you tightened the screw, the finer the flour. Also, a larger mill for grinding grain into meal or flour, usually set up by a short sharp fall of water for power.

GRITS—Ground hominy.

GRUEL—A very thin, watery cereal.

GUM ACACIA—The powdered dried gummy exudation of an African plant. Can be ordered through your druggist. Formerly used to make marshmallows.

GUM ARABIC—Another name for gum acacia.

GUM MASTIC—A gum made from paraffin.

GUM TRAGACANTH—A powdered white vegetable gum used in confectionery (gum paste formulas).

H

HAIR SIEVE—A sieve or strainer with a haircloth bottom. Haircloth was woven of camel or horsehair.

HARDTACK—A Swedish bread. Moisten whole wheat flour (or any freshly ground grain flour) with any liquid. Add a little salt. Roll out as for thin cookies. Cut in squares. Bake at 350°, then dry in slow oven until completely dry. Store dry and in an airtight container.

HARICOTS—A bean variety.

HASTY PUDDING—Boiled cereal of cornmeal and water. A misleading name since the cornmeal needs long boiling or baking.

HAUNCH—The hindquarters or "thigh." The haunch of pig is made into hams.

HAZELNUTS—Also known as "filberts."

HERB SPIRIT—An infusion of herbs bottled with brandy.

HOCK—Second joint above the hoof of the hind leg. (On front leg it's the "hoof" and "ankle" and the "knee.")

HOECAKES—Unleavened cornbread, a contribution of the Indian women to the pioneers.

HOG SCRAPER—A bell-shaped hand instrument for removing hair and dirt from the pig's skin after slaughter and scalding.

HOGSHEAD—A large cask. Or a liquid measure—63 wine gallons or 52½ Imperial gallons.

HOLLANDAISE SAUCE—Three egg yolks, beaten, 2 tablespoons lemon juice, ½ cup butter, melted, 2 tablespoons hot water, a few grains cayenne—all thickened for 5 minutes over low heat.

HOOCH—If you mix 1 cup flour, 1 cup water and 2 tablespoons molasses, then allow to complete natural fermentation, that deadly looking fluid on top would be "hooch," named in Alaskan sourdough days when it was the miners' liquor.

HORS D'OEUVRES—Small dainties served as the first course at lunch or dinner. They were meant to sharpen the appetite.

HOTCHPOT—A thick broth made of meat and many kinds of vegetables.

HUCKLEBERRY—A wild variety of blueberry with a rich, strong flavor.

HULLED CORN—Hominy.

HYPERION TEA—Raspberry leaves made into tea. (Revolutionary term.)

I

ICE—Combination of water, fruit juice and sugar—meant to be stirred while freezing.

ICE CAVE—Usually made of copper or tin, either round or square from 1 to 2 feet in diameter and about as deep. The tight-fitting lid was flanged so that ice could be put on the top. The cave was buried in an ice tub filled with pounded ice and salt in order to freeze its contents.

ICED—Frozen.

ICED CONFECTION—Ice cream.

INDIAN MEAL—Yellow cornmeal.

INDIAN PUDDING—A steamed pudding made of cornmeal, molasses and milk.

INDIGO—A plant product formerly used as a blue dye.

INFUSION—Made by pouring boiling water over dried leaves, flowers or other plant parts, and then straining. (Tea is one.)

INVERT SUGAR—Acid sugar. Made by combining 8 pounds of granulated sugar with 4 cups water and the juice of 4 lemons. Bring slowly to a boil, stirring, until the sugar is all dissolved. Then hold at a gentle boil for a half hour, stirring only occasionally. Cool and make up to exactly 1 gallon by adding boiled water. Used in making alcoholic beverages.

IRISH MOSS—A substance from which a gelatin-like dish can be made. Can be ordered through health food stores.

ISINGLASS—1.) A preparation of nearly pure gelatin which was made from the viscera of fish. 2.) Mica.

ITALIAN PASTE—The paste of wheat flour and water from which macaroni, spaghetti, vermicelli and the like are made.

J

JAM—Crushed or sliced fruit that has been cooked with sugar until it is thick and even-textured. Sugar is used in the proportion of about ¾ pound to 1 pound of fruit.

JAR CHEESE—Old term for commercially prepared soft cheese spreads such as Club House or McLaren's (antique brand names).

JARDINIÈRE—Mixed vegetables served in their own sauce.

JELLY—Flavored liquid plus gelatin. Or a pectin-jellied fruit juice, the product being clear and firm enough to hold its shape when removed from the container.

JELLY BAG—To make an old fashioned jelly bag, fold two opposite corners of a piece of cotton or flannel ¾ yard long. Sew up in the form of a cornucopia, round at the end. Make sure the seam is tightly sewed. It would be helpful if the jelly bag had two or three heavy loops at the top by which it could be hung. Through a jelly bag the material for jelly is strained. Jelly is made from the juice that drips through.

JOHNNYCAKE—Unleavened cornbread, a contribution of the Indian women to the pioneers.

JUJUBE—An edible fruit produced in the Mediterranean region. Also, a jelly made from jujubes and a lozenge flavored with them.

JULIENNE—A clear vegetable soup containing vegetables cut in matchlike strips (Victorian).

JULIENNE STRIPS—Food cut in pieces about the size and shape of wooden kitchen matches.

JUNKET—Contains rennet which curdles milk. Or a pudding made from milk set with junket.

K

KABOB—Something broiled on a skewer.

KEG—A small, strong barrel, usually of 5- to 10-gallon capacity.

KETTLE—The great pot of the colonist, of brass or copper, often holding 15 gallons. Iron ones sometimes weighed 40 pounds.

KICKSHAW—An unsubstantial, fancy, or unrecognizable dish of food.

KILLING TIME—For the cows and swine which had been fattened for slaughter—November.

KIPPER—To smoke at a relatively high temperature.

KNEADING—A stretching motion applied to dough when more flour is to be added than can be either stirred or beaten into the mixture. Kneading is also used to make a dough smooth and even in texture.

KORNLET—Green corn pulp. (Used to be on the market canned.)

KOUMISS—Originally a beverage of soured and fermented mare's milk. Later milk fermented with yeast. (See Dairy chapter.)

L

LAMB—Flesh of sheep from 6 weeks to 1 year old.

LARD—Pig fat rendered for kitchen use. Also, to insert strips of fat (lardoons) into or to place slices of fat on top of uncooked lean meat or fish to give flavor and prevent dryness. Fat salt pork was usually used.

LARDER—A room or place where meat and other articles of food were kept before they were cooked.

LARDING NEEDLE—Insert one end of lardoon into the hinged end of the needle. With pointed end take a stitch ⅓ inch deep and ¾ inch wide. Draw needle through.

LARDOONS—Strips of fat used to lard meat. To cut, remove rind from chilled pork and remove slices, cutting them to be ¼ inch thick, ¼ inch wide and 2½ inches long.

LAWN SIEVE—A sieve made from a fine thin linen cambric (lawn).

LEAF LARD—Made from the leaf-shaped pieces of solid fat which lie inside the pig's abdominal cavity.

LEAVEN—To lighten a mixture by adding yeast, baking powder or beaten eggs (to add air).

LEAVENING—A substance used to make foods light and porous.

LEMON BUTTER—Cream butter until very light and fluffy. Season with a few drops of lemon juice.

LEMON DRILL—A glass lemon squeezer. Press half a lemon or orange down over the "hill" and twist to get the juice.

LIBERTY TEA—Tea made from the four-leaved loosestrife. (Revolutionary term.)

LICORICE—The extract made from the dried root of the licorice plant.

LIME WATER—Dissolve 1 tablespoon calcium oxide in 2 quarts cold water. Or pour 2 quarts boiling water over a 1-inch cube unslaked lime. Stir thoroughly and let stand overnight. In the morning pour off the liquid that is clear and use. (Buy at drugstore.)

LINGONBERRIES—"Mountain cranberry." Small bright red berries that resemble miniature cranberries. Can be used in any recipe suitable for cranberries.

LIQUID YEAST—Potato water, sugar and a speck salt in which yeast plants are in an active condition. Or any homemade yeast.

LIQUOR—Liquid from shellfish or from food in which it has cooked.

LITTLE PIGS—Pigs 4 weeks old, killed, dressed and roasted whole.

LOAF SUGAR—Sugar purchased in loaves or cones averaging in weight about 9 to 10 pounds apiece. One cone would last thrifty people a year. The sugar cone was cut into lumps of equal size and regular shape by the mistress and daughters of the house to sweeten beverages. Various shaped "sugar shears" were used.

LOQUAT—Tree bearing a yellowish (or reddish), sweet, apple-shaped fruit. Does not bear unless it has a completely frost-free year. See also Medlar.

LOZENGE SUGAR—Confectioners' sugar. (Granulated sugar ground extremely fine.)

M

MACAROON—A one-time popular confection made of egg white, sugar and almond paste.

MACÉDOINE—1.) A mixture, usually vegetables, with or without meat. Sometimes applied to fruit mixtures. 2.) Vegetables cut in strips or fancy shapes.

MACÉDOINE, Jellied—Flavored liquid, plus gelatin, plus mixtures of fruit.

MAGNUM BONUM—A variety of large plum.

MAÎTRE D'HÔTEL BUTTER—Work some lemon juice and 1 teaspoon of minced parsley into ½ cup butter.

MAIZE—Corn.

MALT—A grain, generally barley, that has been softened by steeping in water and then allowed to sprout. At this stage it is called "green malt." The green malt is usually dried in a kiln and sometimes roasted like coffee. The sprouting develops the enzyme diastase, which is capable of sac-charifying the starch of the malt and also that of the raw grain mixed with it—hence, malt has been important in brewing. A simplified homemade malt can be prepared by cracking the green malt by going over it with a rolling pin and then toasting or roasting it to obtain the desired effect—pale, medium, dark, or very dark.

MALT EXTRACT—Extract of malt sold canned as a liquid in the form of syrups characterized as extra pale, light and dark.

MALTED MILK—Evaporated milk in combination with extracts of malted barley and wheat.

MANGELS—Beets. Now, stock beets.

MANGO—In Victorian usage, a young musk or nutmeg melon, pickled. (Cantaloupe or honeydew.)

MARASCHINO—A sweet liqueur distilled from the juice of bitter wild cherries.

MARCHPANE (Marchepane)—This name evolved to "marzipan." A paste of pounded almonds, sugar and egg white made into little molded confections.

MARINADE—A savory sauce in which a meat or vegetable is sometimes soaked before cooking or serving. Usually a blend of seasonings, oil and an acid.

MARINATE—Add salt, pepper, oil, vinegar and seasonings to a food item and let it soak until well seasoned.

MARRONS GLACÉS—Chestnuts preserved in a vanilla flavored syrup.

MARROW—A variety of summer squash.

MEAD—A fermented drink made from honey and water.

MEAL—A comparatively coarse-ground grain.

MEAT FORK—A three-tined fork.

MEDLAR—A tree fruit, which resembles a crab apple. Was much used for preserves in Victorian days. Also, the loquat.

MELON MOLD—See Bombe.

MERINGUE—Beat 2 egg whites. Gradually add 4 tablespoons sugar, then ½ teaspoon vanilla. Spread over desired pie or pudding and bake in oven at about 300° for approximately 20 minutes.

METHEGLIN—A drink made from honey, yeast, water and locustbeans.

MIDDLINGS—A combination of the coarser parts of wheat with the bran.

MINCE—To finely divide food with a sharp knife or scissors.

MINERAL WATERS—Alkaline beverages such as soda, seltzer, potash which are impregnated with carbon dioxide.

MOCK TURTLE SOUP—Soup made of a calf's head.

MOLD (Mould)—A dish in which to shape gelatin stiffened mixtures. Or a container in which to steam puddings.

MORTAR—A deep, heavy bowl in which spices, herbs and other things can be crushed and ground by hand with a pestle.

MOTHER (of Vinegar)—A gelatinous film which is developed on the surface of alcoholic liquids undergoing acetous fermentation. It is made of bacteria actively growing. When the bacteria reach a final stage the mother usually thickens and settles to the bottom. Mother is added to wine or cider to hasten the vinegar production.

MOUSSE—A combination of whipped cream, sugar and flavoring, frozen unstirred.

MULBERRY—An edible fruit. Can be made into jelly or the leaves fed to silkworms.

MULL—To gently heat a beverage such as cider or wine with sugar and spices.

MULLIGAN—Stew.

MUSKMELON—Cantaloupe.

MUTTON—Flesh of adult sheep.

N

NEAPOLITAN—Combination of two to four flavors of ice cream or ices frozen in layers and hardened in a mold.

NEWBURG SAUCE—A basic flour and butter paste diluted with cream and egg yolks and flavored with sherry.

NITRE—See Saltpeter.

NOCAKE (or nookick)—Corn parched (popped) in the hot ashes, the ashes then sifted from it. The popped corn was beaten to a powder and the powder put in a leather bag for a traveler's food. The nocake was mixed with snow in winter and water in summer. When the Pilgrims in famine time were allotted five kernels of corn apiece each day some say this is how they prepared it.

NOUGAT—A confection made usually of almonds or pistachio nuts stirred into a sugar paste.

NOYEAR—A liqueur.

NUTMEG—A honeydew melon or cantaloupe (Victorian).

O

OIL OF ANISE—Obtained from the seeds of the fennel plant.

OIL OF CASSIA—An imitation cinnamon flavoring.

OIL OF CLOVES—Obtained by distilling with water the buds and flower stalks of the clove tree.

OIL OF MYRBANE—An imitation bitter almond oil, now considered poisonous.

OIL OF NEROLI—The oil of orange flowers, once obtained either by distillation or enfleurage and used as the basis of perfumes and in liqueurs.

OILSTONE—A whetstone used with oil.

ORANGE WATER—An alcoholic beverage distilled from orange peels and sweetened, formerly a popular cordial.

ORRISROOT—Powdered from the root of the blue flag (iris). A fixative to hold fragrances.

OTTO OF ROSES—See Attar.

OX—Cow. To many people's surprise. Particularly when used in harness.

OYSTER PLANT—Salsify.

P

PANADA—A thick paste used for binding mixtures such as croquettes and quenelles and the basis of hot soufflés and choux pastry. 1.) In the proportion of half as much bread as liquid combine bread with cream, milk or stock. Cook until a smooth paste is formed. 2.) ½ cup meat or vegetable stock, 2 tablespoons drippings or butter, 4 heaping tablespoons flour, salt and pepper. Melt fat, stir in flour until smooth, cook 2 or 3 minutes. Gradually add stock, stirring constantly until smooth. Season to taste. Slowly boil for 2 or 3 minutes.

PARBOIL—To boil a few minutes until partially cooked, in preparation for next step of recipe.

PARCH—To brown by means of dry heat—applied to grains. With corn it means "to pop." Some people claim "parched corn" was an early term for popped corn. Another version is that shelled sweet corn kernels were dropped on a hot griddle without water or grease. They were then turned or stirred frequently enough to prevent burning, and done when brown and crunchy.

PARE—To cut off the skin of a vegetable or fruit.

PARFAIT—1.) A layered dessert such as whipped cream and pudding or alternate layers of ice and ice cream or of ice cream with fruit or syrup topped with whipped cream. 2.) A combination of egg white, water, sugar and whipped cream frozen unstirred.

PASTE—1.) Dough for crusts. 2.) Mixture of flour and liquid. 3.) Ground nuts and fruits or combinations of these with sugar.

PASTILLE—Drop candy made of clarified sugar syrup with a little water and flavoring.

PASTRY—Dough to be made into pie or tart shells. Basically a mixture of flour and fat. The size of the bits of fat varies, also the amount of water. For piecrusts—1½ cups flour sifted with ½ teaspoon salt. Use two forks or knives to work in ½ cup lard. When the fat has been worked in until it is more or less of uniform texture add 4 or 5 tablespoons cold water slowly until mixture becomes a stiff dough which will hold together in one ball. Roll out and cut into the shape you need.

PASTRY FLOUR—You can make your own by sifting 4 tablespoons cornstarch or potato flour into each 2 cups of plain flour (sifted before measuring).

PÂTÉ—1.) Paste. 2.) Patty. 3.) Seasoned liver paste.

PÂTE À CHOUX—Cream puffs.

PEACH KERNELS—The kernel is the seed inside the peach stone. It was sometimes mashed and added to peach ice cream for flavor.

PEARL BARLEY—Barley reduced to a round shotlike form by removing the outer coat of the grain.

PECTIN—A jellylike substance found in some fruits, especially in their "green" stage. You can make your own (recipe in Sweets chapter), or buy it, or use the right fruits at the right stage.

PENUCHE (Panocha)—1.) A Mexican brown sugar. 2.) A fudge usually made of brown sugar, butter, cream and nut meats.

PEPPERGRASS—Upland cress, not watercress. Used in salads.

PETTIJOHN—A partly precooked cereal of 1910.

PFARVEL (Farfel)—Combine 1 egg yolk with enough flour to make it too stiff to knead more. Grate on a coarse grater and spread the bits out to dry. Put in soup and boil 10 minutes before serving.

PHILADELPHIA ICE CREAM—Combination of cream, flavoring or fruits and sweetening. Stirred while freezing.

PICCALILLI (Pickle Lily)—A mixed relish.

PICKLE—To preserve in salt and water or in vinegar.

PIÈCE DE RÉSISTANCE—The main dish in a meal. Or the roast (especially if tough!).

PIEPLANT—Rhubarb.

PIGNOLIA—Imported pine nut. When the same thing is grown in the Southwest United States it is called pine, piñon or Indian nut.

PILAU (Pilaf)—An East Indian or Turkish dish of meat and seasoned rice.

PIMENTO—Skin of the large red pepper, preserved in oil or by freezing. Recipe in Vegetables chapter under Peppers.

PINCH—One-eighth teaspoon, more or less.

PIPS—Seeds.

PISTACHIO—A nut imported from the Middle East. Also now grown in inland California.

PIT (to)—To remove the stone from fruit.

PITH—White spongy substance between skin of orange and orange proper.

PLANK—Specially made planks could formerly be purchased for cooking. The problem was that if forgotten in the oven they burned. They were seasoned hickory or oak, about 1 inch thick. Fish and steak were favorite planked dishes. Oil the plank, especially where it will not be covered. Put meat on plank. For steak, brown quickly under the heat, then turn and crisp the other side. Then set plank further from flame and finish cooking more slowly. To season a new plank soak overnight in cold water. Brush with oil. Warm in 250° oven 1 hour. To clean a plank after using, scrape thoroughly and wipe with a paper towel but do not wash. Store in a cool spot.

PLANTAIN—A banana variety considered by Victorians suitable only for eating boiled, roasted or in preserves (not raw).

PLATE-WARMER—A three-legged metal stand meant to stand near or in the coals of a fireplace and hold the plates for warming.

PLUM PUDDING—A steamed bread with raisins or other fruit in it.

PLUMP—To enlarge and fill out fruit by letting it stand in a thin syrup before cooking to make jam or preserves. The fruit then plumps without being toughened by extra cooking. Or chickens, to let soak in water a few minutes before cleaning. I don't.

POACH—To cook in water, milk or stock just below the boiling temperature for a short time. Eggs and fish are often prepared this way.

POLENTA—A mush made of cornmeal or of ground chestnuts. (Italian name.)

POMACE—Ground apple for making cider. The pomace is pressed to extract the cider.

POMPION—Pumpkin (in Colonial recipes).

POPOVER—A quick muffin leavened only with the air bubbles introduced by hard beating just before baking.

PORCELAIN WARE—Iron lined with a hard, smooth enamel.

PORRIDGE—A very thick cereal.

PORRINGER—A child's dish in Colonial times. A pretty little shallow circular dish with a flat, pierced handle or a fishtail handle and varying in size from 2 to 9 inches across.

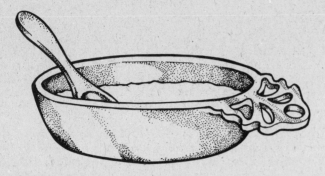

POT CHESSE—An old name for a commercially processed cheese spread sold in small "pots."

POTAGE—A family soup.

POTATO BOILER—A wrought-iron basket meant to hold potatoes or any vegetable in place within the huge general pot of Colonial days.

POTATO RICER—A utensil for squeezing potato or other soft material through a perforated plate.

POTATO WATER—The water in which potatoes were cooked.

POTHOOK—The iron hook or chain with a hook from which the pot could be swung over the fireplace. From such hooks pots could be hung at varying heights over the fire.

POTPOURRI—A highly seasoned stew of many ingredients. Or a fragrant concoction of flower petals meant to be smelled, not eaten! (See Herbs chapter.)

POTTED—Cooked, boned, chopped, seasoned, possibly jellied meat. (Usually packed in small crocks, hence "potted.")

POULT—A young turkey.

POULTRY—Chicken, turkey, duck, goose, squab, pheasant and guinea hen.

POUND CAKE—A cake containing a considerable quantity of butter, eggs, and sugar—"a pound" of each.

POWDER—A pulverized ingredient.

POWDERED SUGAR—A grade of sugar (2⅔ cups per pound) intermediate in fineness between our present granulated sugar (2 cups per pound) and confectioners' sugar (3½ cups per pound).

POWDERING TUB—A tub in which meat was salted and pickled.

PRAIRIE CHICKEN—Grouse.

PRAWLING (Variation of Praline)—A confection of nut kernels, usually of almonds, roasted in boiling sugar until brown and crisp. Sometimes any of various other confections, as a cake of brown sugar containing pecan meats.

PRESERVES—Whole fruits or pieces of fruit cooked in a heavy syrup until clear and tender. The fruit is actually preserved in a thick syrup of jellied juice.

PRESSURE COOKING—Cooking by steam under pressure. Steam under pressure increases the temperature and shortens the cooking period. Especially useful for canning nonacid vegetables.

PRUNELLES (Prunella)—A variety of fine dried plums.

PUDDING CLOTH—A bag in which to boil "pudding." See Grains chapter for details.

PUFF PASTE—Used for patty shells and small pastries: 4 cups flour, 1 teaspoon salt, 2 cups butter and ice water enough to mix into a dough.

PULSE FOODS—Dried peas, beans and lentils.

PUNCH—A water ice to which was added "spirit" and spice. Or mixed fruit juices.

PUREE—To rub cooked fruit, vegetables and the like through a sieve to remove skins, seeds and generally mash.

PUREE SOUP—The solid material is rubbed through a sieve and then reheated with the liquid and a little thickening agent is added.

PUT DOWN—To corn (beef) or cure (pork).

Q

QUENELLES—Portions of any kind of forcemeat, shaped into small balls and poached in boiling water or stock. They were served as a garnish to soups and other dishes or were served with a sauce as an entrée.

QUICK LIME—Unslaked lime.

QUICK OVEN—About 450°—a hot oven.

QUIDDANY (Quiddony)—Quince. A syrup or jelly, originally of quince.

QUINCE DRINK—Hot rum, sugar and quince marmalade or preserves. (Colonial.)

R

RACK—To draw or pour off from the lees (sediment), as of wine.

RAGOUT—A thick, highly seasoned stew.

RAILROAD YEAST—Homemade liquid yeast.

RAMEKIN (Ramequin)—A small individual baking dish.

RANGE—A wood and coal stove.

RASPINGS—Fine, browned bread crumbs.

RATAFIA LIQUEURS—Fine cordials made by mixing 3 pints filtered fruit juice, 1 quart cognac, 3 pounds sugar and a bit of vanilla, cinnamon and cloves. Then cork it and it will be ready for use after 6 to 12 months.

RAVIGOTE—Green mayonnaise. Boil and then force through a sieve watercress, spinach and/or parsley and add to mayonnaise.

RAW MILK—Milk just as it comes from the cow or goat.

RECHAUFFÉ—Reheated or warmed over. Fancy name for leftovers.

RECTIFIED SPIRIT—An alcoholic beverage "rectified" (concentrated) by redistillation (brandy).

RED WHEAT—Hard wheat varieties.

REFLECTOR—A curved metal plate put on the side away from the fire of a roast or other item to be cooked by the heat of an open fireplace fire.

REFRIGERATOR ICE CREAM—An ice cream or sherbet containing a stabilizer to retard development of ice crystals. It can be frozen in a refrigerator tray without stirring. The stabilizer is usually egg.

RELÈVE—A "course" of food items which replaces another (Victorian).

RELISH—Relishes include piccalilli, chutney, horseradish and corn relish. They are prepared from fruits and vegetables which are chopped, seasoned, then cooked to the desired consistency and pickled.

RENDER—To free fat from connective tissue by cooking or heating the meat until the fat liquefies and can be strained off.

RENNET—Was prepared from the fourth stomach of calves and used to curdle milk as in cheesemaking or to make junket. (See Dairy chapter for recipe.)

RICE (to)—To force cooked food through a ricer or sieve.

RICE FLOUR—Grind rice in your flour grinder or order through health food stores.

RISSOLES—Originally, meat was placed on a spit and allowed to revolve before an open fire, thick pieces always being used. Now the word also means to bake when applied to certain foods such as meats and chestnuts. The baking was usually done in an oven but occasionally in ashes, under coals, or on heated stones.

ROASTING KITCHEN—A boxlike metal structure, open on one side, which was kept turned to the fireplace. It stood on legs and in it birds or joints could be roasted or bread baked. (An early "reflector oven.")

ROCK CANDY—Used in making of rich brandy sauces for plum puddings and as a kind of marchpane ornamentation for desserts. It consisted of sugar in large crystals or crystalline masses obtained by slow evaporation.

ROE—Fish eggs.

ROLLICHE (Rollejee, rollichie)—A kind of sausage, made in a bag of tripe, sliced and fried, famous among the Dutch of New Amsterdam.

ROPY—Describes a liquid having a viscous or glutinous formation of unwanted bacteria. Boil the liquid to kill the organisms. Rope in bread appears sometimes after the bread is baked during hot, damp weather. The bread has a bad smell and is unusable. Sterilize all your bread making utensils and storage containers. Use 1 tablespoon of vinegar per 6 cups flour until that batch of flour is used up.

ROSETTE CASES—See Timbale.

ROTISSERIE—1.) A restaurant where patrons selected uncooked food and had it roasted and served to them. 2.) A store where food was roasted. 3.) Recently, a machine for cooking meat on a turning spit.

ROUNDED SPOONFUL—As much above the rim of the spoon as below.

ROUX (Pronounced "roo")—A paste of flour and melted butter or any other shortening used as a foundation for a sauce or gravy. Can be made ahead of time and stored in refrigerator.

ROYAL CUSTARD—A custard cut and served in consommé or chicken broth.

ROYALE—Garnished with custard dice.

RUB IN—A method of mixing flour and fat. Used in cakes and pastries. Chop the fat coarsely into the flour with a knife. Using only the tips of the fingers and thumbs, rub lightly until the contents of the bowl look like the bread crumbs. Have utensils and ingredients as cold as possible.

RUSK—Sliced bread baked until dry and crisp. Or the browned crumbs sprinkled into cold milk.

S

SACCHAROMETER—A syrup gauge to indicate the sweetness of a fluid, used in candymaking and in brewing. (Can be purchased from Herter's, Inc., Waseca, Minnesota 56093.)

SADDLE OF MUTTON—The loin removed whole before splitting the rest of the animal. It is made into a roast by removing some bones, rolling the flank ends and tieing the whole securely.

SAFFRON—A deep orange colored substance consisting of the dried stigmas of a species of crocus cultivated in southern Europe. It was used to color confectioneries, liquors and in cookery.

SAGO (Sago flour)—A dry granulated starch imported from the East Indies, formerly used in puddings, other foods, and for stiffening textiles. It was prepared chiefly from the trunk of the sago palm, but also from several other palms.

SALERATUS—Potassium or sodium bicarbonate for use in cookery; or baking soda, usually bicarbonate of soda—$NaHCO_3$. (An early coarse-grained baking soda.)

SALT PORK—It is made from the flesh on either side of the pig's backbone and heavily salted to preserve. (See Meat chapter.)

SALTPETER (Nitre)—Potassium nitrate, KNO_3, a strong oxidizer used to preserve color in cured meats.

SALTSPOON—One-eighth teaspoon.

SAMOVAR—A metal urn for making tea.

SAMP—Hulled corn (hominy) pounded or milled to a coarsely ground powder.

SAMP MILL—A simple hand mill for grinding corn.

SARATOGA CHIPS—Homemade potato chips. The potatoes are sliced thin and French fried.

SARMA—Seasoned minced meat and rice, stewed while wrapped in a scalded grape leaf.

SAUSAGE CASES—Originally, entrails cleaned and prepared to be stuffed with sausage—three sizes, mutton, pig or cow. Now also made of plastic.

SAUSAGE GUN (Sausage stuffer)—The sausage meat is forced out through the nozzle into a sausage casing.

SAUTÉ—To fry quickly in a small quantity of fat, first on one side and then on the other.

SAVORY (Summer savory)—An herb used for food flavoring. (Savories)—A tasty dish served either at the end of a meal, or as a luncheon or supper dish, or with cocktails. If served at a formal dinner it came after the sweet, but at an informal meal could easily replace it. Usually cheese dishes or canapés.

SCALLOP—To each cup of medium to thick white sauce, add 1 or 2 cups cooked vegetables, meat, fish, hard-cooked eggs, cooked macaroni or rice. Put into a baking dish, sprinkle with buttered crumbs and bake until brown on top.

SCANT—A little less than a full measure.

SCHMIERKASE (Schmier-Kaese)—Homemade cottage cheese.

SCORE—To cut across the surface of a food in several places.

SCRAG—The neck, as of venison or mutton. Also, anything lean and tough.

SCRUPLE—A unit of weight: 20 grains, 1/24 ounce, ⅓ dram, also a minute quantity.

SEA KALE—A perennial vegetable. The early spring leaf shoots are blanched and eaten like asparagus.

SEAR—To brown the surface of meat by a short application of intense heat (fry). Used to develop flavor, improve appearance and seal in juices, usually before roasting.

SELTZER WATER—Originally bottled water from mineral springs at Niederselters, Germany, which contains considerable carbon dioxide in solution.

SEMOLINA—Flour made from durum wheat, used in making pasta and for thickening. (Italian.)

SERVICE PLATE—Plate used with appetizer and soup, removed before the main course.

SET UP (to)—When candy hardens to the desired final consistency. Or gelatin "jells."

SHALLOTS—A mild variety of onion.

SHEEP'S OIL—Lanolin. Obtained from sheep wool.

SHELL BARK—The nut or fruit of a species of hickory.

SHERBET—1.) A combination of water, fruit juice, sugar and a small amount of gelatin or egg white for body (sometimes milk instead of water), stirred while freezing. 2.) A refreshing drink made of fruit juice, diluted, sweetened and flavored.

SHERBET POWDER—Was a preparation of bicarbonate of soda, tartaric acid and sugar variously flavored for making an effervescent drink.

SHIRR—To bake whole eggs with cream and crumbs in a small dish or muffin tin (usually 2 eggs per "hole") in the oven.

SHORTBREAD—A cookie made with flour, butter and a large amount of shortening, distinctive in texture, sandy and somewhat crumbly.

SHORTENING—Fat of any kind used in pastry, doughs, batters: butter (reduce salt in recipe), vegetable fats, oils, lard, drippings (not ham, bacon or sausage drippings though because of seasonings present).

SHORTS—The part of milled grain next finer than the bran. Sometimes the term meant middlings. Occasionally it meant reground bran, practically free from floury particles and sometimes containing mill sweepings. "Short oats" is a European variety of oats.

SHRED—To cut food into long thin strips with a scissors or sharp knife.

SHRUB—A beverage of sweetened fruit juice, sometimes intended to be diluted with water before drinking.

SIMMER—To cook slowly at a temperature just below boiling (about 185° at sea level). Bubbles form slowly and rise slowly to the surface.

SIMPLE SYRUP—Boil 2 cups sugar with 2 cups water for 5 minutes. Chill and store in a covered jar. This was used for flavoring old-time summer drinks because the sugar was already in solution and you didn't have trouble with sugar settling in the bottom of the glass.

SINGE—Remove hair and down by holding the bird over a flame and constantly changing its position until all surfaces have been exposed to the flame.

SINGLE CREAM—The cream that can be skimmed off after milk has stood 12 hours after milking.

SIRUP (Syrup)—Originally, a thick viscid liquid made from the juice of fruits, herbs and the like, boiled with sugar.

SKEWER—Skewers range from rapier-like "swords" to wooden pins. A heavy wire with a loop at one end for a handle would work. The skewer is used to hold skewered foods over an open fire to cook such things as hot dogs, marshmallows, shish kabobs.

SKILLET—Originally, a small kettle or pot with three or four legs and a handle. Or a shallow pan such as a saucepan. Now usually means a light frying pan.

SKIM—To clear a liquid from floating scum or substance. The cream is skimmed off the top of the milk.

SKIM MILK—Milk from which the cream has been removed.

SKIMMER—A utensil for skimming liquids, similar to a ladle.

SLAB—Means a marble slab for pouring candy mixes to cool.

SLACK LIME—Quick lime with water added ($Ca(OH)_2$). Powdered lime—purified calcium hydroxide—available at drugstores.

SLIPPERY ELM—The fragrant, mucilaginous inner bark of an American elm.

SLUMGULLION—A meat stew.

SMOKEHOUSE—Where beef, ham, bacon and the like are smoked.

SMOKING—Some foods after being salted are hung in a closed room or container for several hours or more, where hardwood is allowed to smother (smoke).

SMORGASBORD—A hearty buffet meal, originally a Scandinavian custom.

SNOW—Flavored liquid plus gelatin, whipped as it begins to set.

SNOW PEAS—Edible pod peas.

SOAPSTONE (of griddles)—A kind of soft stone with soapy feel (steatite).

SODA—"Baking soda," "cooking soda," "soda saleratus" mean sodium bicarbonate. "Washing soda," "sal soda," "soda crystals" mean sodium carbonate. "Caustic soda" means sodium hydroxide ($NaOH$). "Soda" also means soda water—fizzy water.

SODA WATER—Originally, a beverage consisting of a weak solution of sodium bicarbonate with some acid to cause effervescence. Later, a beverage consisting of water highly charged with carbon dioxide.

SORBET—A frozen punch (water ice where several kinds of fruit were used). Also, a sherbet.

SORGHUM—A variety of molasses made from a cereal grass, sorghum, cultivated in the warmer parts of the world.

SORREL—A salad green.

SOUFFLÉ—"Puffed up." A delicate baked custard which may contain fruit, cheese, flaked fish, minced poultry, meat or vegetables. Make a thick white sauce. Add ½ cup food to ¾ cup sauce. Add the well-beaten yolks of 3 eggs. Stir until blended. Gently fold in the 3 stiffly beaten egg whites and pour into a well-oiled baking dish. Bake in a moderate oven with the containing dish standing in hot water until an inserted knife comes out clean.

SOURDOUGH—A type of leavening for breads. Basically a fermenting starch and water mixture.

SPANISH CREAM—A custard set with gelatin.

SPERMACETI—A yellowish or white waxy solid which separated from the oil obtained from the sperm whale. It was used in making candles, ointments and cosmetics.

SPIDER—An iron pan with a long handle used in frying food. Originally it had long legs and was used to cook over coals on the hearth. Also, a trivet on tripod legs to support pans or pots over a fire.

SPIN—"Boiled until it will spin." Boiled to the thread stage when you hold up your spoon and one drop is attached to the next by a thread (of sugar solutions).

SPINACH GREEN—A green food coloring made by simply cooking and pureeing spinach.

SPIT—In barbecuing or roasting, a pointed metal rod on which poultry or roasts are fastened which can be rotated for cooking.

SPONGE (Method of Making Bread)—Add one-half of the flour to the liquid and yeast mixture and beat thoroughly. Set in a warm place. When the batter is light (usually several hours or more) add the remaining flour, or enough to make a dough of the desired stiffness. Knead, shape, let rise again and bake.

SPRING CHICKEN—A chicken which appeared in the market during January after development of artificial incubation. It weighed about 1½ pounds.

SQUAB—A pigeon just grown up—young, plump and tender.

STARTER YEAST—See Liquid Yeast.

STEAM—To cook food over or surrounded by steam, with or without pressure. The steam comes from boiling water.

STEELING THE KNIFE—Sharpening the blade on a smooth, high quality, 9- to 14-inch steel.

STEEP—To allow a substance to stand in liquid below the boiling point for the purpose of extracting flavor, color or other qualities.

STOCK—Liquid made from meat, vegetables, fish or poultry and used as a foundation for soups, sauces and stews.

STONE (to)—To remove the pit from a fruit.

STONE JAR—A crock.

SUCCOTASH—A corn and lima bean dish.

SUCKLING PIG—One from 3 to 6 weeks old, roasted.

SUET—The fatty tissues about the loins and kidneys of sheep and cows, used in cookery and for making tallow. Also the leaf lard from pigs. Sometimes generally applied to firm fat.

SUGAR SHEARS—An instrument for cutting loaf sugar into pieces of regular size and shape.

SULTANA—A variety of imported (Turkish) seedless raisins (Victorian).

SUPPAWN—A favorite dish of the New England settlers. It was a thick cornmeal and milk porridge.

SWEET PICKLE—Ripe cucumbers or melon rind pickled in a sweet, spiced vinegar solution.

SWEETBREADS—The thymus glands, made up of two parts—the heart sweetbread and the throat, or neck, sweetbread. They are white and soft and have a very delicate taste. Since the thymus gland disappears as the animal matures, sweetbreads are available only from veal and very young beef.

T

TALLOW—The suet or fat of a large animal which has firm fat such as goat, sheep or cow, as compared to the softer lard-fat of the pig.

TAMARIND—A fruit, formerly imported from India, now grown in the southern part of Florida and in Hawaii. The fruit has an outer shell with seeds inside embedded in a tasty flesh (resembles a date). The pulp can be substituted for lemon, being very tart, but sweet. Has been used in drinks, preserves and chutney.

TART—A miniature pie. Roll pastry ⅛ inch thick and cut pieces 3½ inches long by 3 inches wide. Put 2 teaspoons of filling on each piece. Moisten edge with cold water halfway round, fold over, press edges together with meat fork. First dipped in flour, then baked about 20 minutes in slow oven.

TARTLET—Small tart.

TEACUP—A half-cup quantity.

THREAD STAGE—Of candy making. It is reached when the boiling sugar begins to form a hair between drips as it drips from a spoon—200° by the thermometer.

TIE DOWN—To cover. Usually meant with a piece of paper which was tied around the "neck" of the container with a string to hold it on.

TIMBALE—An unsweetened custard, usually seasoned with fish, meat or vegetables baked in a timbale case.

TIMBALE CASE (Timbale rosette, rosette case mean same thing)—A small crust case of fried batter in which creamed mixtures and desserts were served. A timbale or rosette iron is needed to

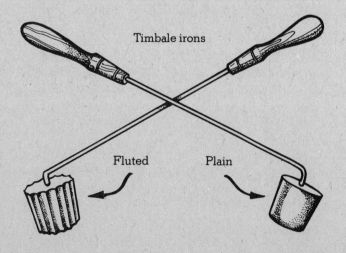

Timbale irons

Fluted   Plain

make them. (You can order from Maid of Scandinavia Company, 3246 Raleigh Avenue, Minneapolis, Minnesota 55416.) Make a batter of ½ cup flour, 1 egg, ½ teaspoon cooking oil, ½ cup milk, ½ teaspoon salt and 1 teaspoon sugar. Allow it to set 1 hour until free from bubbles. Heat the timbale iron by immersing in deep hot fat (360°). Dip heated iron into batter. Hold at an angle until the bottom is covered, then lower iron into batter until ½ inch from top. Hold iron straight and lower into hot fat. Cook until case is crisp and brown. Remove from fat. Slip case from iron. Drain case on absorbent material. If batter slips from iron back into bowl the iron is not hot enough. If case slips from iron back into fat the fat is too hot.

TINCTURE—An alcohol or a mixture of alcohol and water in which herbs have been soaked until desired property is dissolved out of them. Take the fresh or dried herb, chip and pound. To 1 ounce of the herb add 2 ounces of water and 2 ounces of alcohol (pure). Nowadays that means home distilled which I think is illegal. (You can't buy pure alcohol even to make vanilla extract unless you get a license, post a bond, pay a tax and buy a minimum of one barrel of the stuff.) Allow the mixture to stand in a bottle from 8 to 14 days in a cool place. Then bottle for use.

TINCTURE (to)—To flavor.

TOASTING FORKS—Long, wooden-handled forks to impale or clamp on a slice of bread or something else and hold it over an open fire without also cooking the holder.

TONGS—A device to turn broiling meat and the like without penetrating the meat as a fork would do. Also used for general purposes.

TONIC—Flavored with quinine.

TONKA BEANS—Once used to make a cheap imitation vanilla.

TORTE—A rich, often rather heavy, cake.

TREACLE (black or green)—1.) A dark strongly flavored molasses—English term. 2.) Sulfur and molasses. Enough powdered sulfur was stirred into dark molasses to make a thick paste.

TRENCHER—Made of wood, about 10 to 12 inches square and 3 to 4 inches deep, hollowed down into a sort of bowl in the middle. Used as a plate, usually shared by two people such as the man and his wife or two children—a Colonial term.

TRIPE—The plain or smooth lining from the first beef stomach, the honeycombed lining from the second stomach and the pocket-shaped part from the end of the second stomach—all from the cow. The pocket-shaped section is smooth on the outside and honeycombed inside.

TRIVETS—Three-legged stands, of varying heights, through which the pot could be raised to the exact desired proximity to the coals when cooking over an open fire.

TRUFFLE—A species of fungi, similar to mushrooms, growing in clusters some inches below the surface of the ground in France. Used for seasoning or a garnish.

TRUSS (a bird)—Draw the thighs and wings close against the body and fasten securely with skewers or tie with string. If the neck has been removed draw the skin of the neck to the back and fasten with a small skewer. This will hold the bird in shape during roasting. A suckling pig may also be trussed.

TRY OUT—To render.

TUB—A half barrel.

TUBERS—White potatoes. Also, Jerusalem artichokes.

TURBINADO SUGAR—Very coarse and dry cane sugar.

TURN IN (to)—To pour in.

TURNSPIT DOG—A dog trained to run in a revolving cylinder. The mechanism was devised to keep the roasting joint turning before the fire (Colonial usage).

TUTTI-FRUTTI—Fermented mixed fruits.

U

UNFERMENTED WINE—Grape juice.

V

VANILLA POD—A slender pod, 6 to 12 inches long, containing a number of small round vanilla beans.

VEAL—The meat obtained from a young calf killed when 6 to 8 weeks old.

VEGETABLE GELATIN—Pectin.

VEGETABLE MARROW—A variety of summer squash.

VEGETABLE OYSTER—Salsify.

VEGETABLE PRESS—Used as a potato and vegetable masher, a sauce and gravy strainer, a fruit press or any other purpose for which a colander or strainer is needed with pressure supplied to force the food through the holes.

VELOUTÉ SAUCE—A basic flour and butter sauce diluted with chicken stock and cream.

VENISON—Originally the term meant the meat of any animal or bird of the chase, then it meant the meat of antlered animals such as deer, elk, antelope, moose and reindeer. Now it usually means deer meat.

VERMICELLI—Made from flour moistened to a stiff dough with water and forced through small apertures in a plate by means of a press. Thinner in diameter than spaghetti.

VERMICELLIED—Rubbed through a coarse wire sieve to create a fine "spaghetti" effect.

VICHY WATER—Bottled water from mineral springs at Vichy, France, which contains a moderate amount of natural carbonation.

VIENNA COFFEE—Coffee served with whipped cream.

VOL-AU-VENT—A case of puff pastry, round or oval, which may be filled with either a meat or fruit filling. The pastry is baked in a mold.

W

WAFER—Cracker.

WASH OVER WITH EGG—Brush with egg whites.

WATERLESS COOKING—Cooking slowly in a tightly covered container. Most foods require the addition of a small quantity (¼ to ½ cup) of water.

WHEY—The watery liquid that remains after the white, thick curds have been removed from milk.

WHEY (to)—Of milk or custards, to separate into curds and whey.

WHIP—A dessert made of flavored liquid plus gelatin whipped as it begins to set.

WHITE SAUCE—One made from milk or white stock or part of each, thickened with plain flour or cornstarch.

WHITE SOUP STOCK—A soup stock made from chicken or veal with the addition of delicate seasonings.

WHITE WHEAT—Soft varieties (versus red hard wheat).

WHORTLEBERRY—A variety of blueberry. Sometimes used to mean huckleberry.

WILD CHERRY—Chokecherry. The bark was used to make homemade root beers. The cherries make wonderful pancake syrup or jelly. The leaves, however, contain poisonous amounts of prussic acid.

WINEGLASS—One-fourth cup (2 fluid ounces).

Y

YOUNGBERRY—A blackberry variety. The fruit is large, dark and sweet.

Z

ZEST—Citrus fruit peel, especially lemon and orange, used as a flavoring. Obtain oil by bending the skin sharply to squeeze it out. (The stuff that squirts into your eye and makes you cry.)

This Definitions and Measures chapter is the one I wrote first. There wasn't much writing to it. I had a big collection of definitions and I put them in alphabetical order. Same for the measures. I just sorted them out. I read about fifty antique recipe books before I started and that's where I got them. And that's where I started from to figure out the questions discussed in the introduction of this chapter. It was sleuthing and I really enjoyed it.

MEASURES

(and you always thought it was simple)

TEASPOON MEASURES

"a few grains"	less than ⅛ teaspoon
a dash	¼ to ⅓ teaspoon
a pinch	⅛ to ¼ teaspoon
1 saltspoon	⅛ teaspoon
1 fluid drachm	¾ teaspoon
60 drops	1 teaspoon
5 ccs.	1 teaspoon

TABLESPOON MEASURES

½ fluid ounce	1 tablespoon
3 teaspoons	1 tablespoon
15 ccs.	1 tablespoon
15 grams	1 tablespoon
1 wineglass	4 tablespoons
½ gill	4 tablespoons
1 gill	8 tablespoons
½ cup	8 tablespoons

CUP MEASURES

5⅓ tablespoons	⅓ cup
1 wineglass	¼ cup
4 tablespoons	¼ cup
8 tablespoons	½ cup
1 teacup	½ cup
1 gill	½ cup
10⅔ tablespoons	⅔ cup
12 tablespoons	¾ cup
4 wineglasses	1 cup
1 tumbler	1 cup
1 large coffee cup	1 cup
1 glassful	1 cup
8 fluid ounces	1 cup
2 gills	1 cup
1 pint	2 cups
1 quart	4 cups

A, B, C, & D—I've gone steadily downhill from the C at 17. Those were the Dagmar and Marilyn days when big bosoms were in style. Now I'm sort of flat and *that's* in style.

PINTS, PECKS, BUSHELS, KISSES MEASURES

1 gill	¼ pint
4 gills	1 pint
16 fluid ounces	1 pint
2 cups	1 pint
8 quarts	1 peck
4 pecks	1 bushel
1 quart	2 pints

GALLON GLUG MEASURES

4 quarts	1 gallon
1 (Great Britain) gallon Imperial	1.20 gal. U.S.
1 peck	2 gallons
½ bushel	4 gallons
1 bushel	8 gallons

APOTHECARIES' WEIGHTS

(If you're going to mix old-time prescriptions)

1 scruple	20 grains
1 dram	3 scruples
1 ounce	8 drams
1 pound	12 ounces

DISTANCE MEASURES

(For how far it is to town)

12 inches	1 foot
3 feet	1 yard
1,760 yards	1 mile
5,280 feet	1 mile
3 miles	1 league

SQUARE MEASURES

(To figure out how big your homestead is)

144 square inches	1 square foot
9 square feet	1 square yard
43,560 square feet	1 acre
4,840 square yards	1 acre
640 acres	1 square mile
36 square miles	1 township

FOOD EQUIVALENTS

ONE-BUSHEL PRODUCE EQUIVALENTS

Fruits		*Grains*	
Apples	44 lb.	Oats	32 lb.
Apricots	48 lb.	Rice (rough)	45 lb.
Pears	48 lb.	Barley	48 lb.
Peaches	48 lb.	Buckwheat	48 lb.
Plums	50 lb.	Shelled Corn	56 lb.
Cherries	56 lb.		

Vegetables		
Cucumbers	48 lb.	For one-peck equivalents,
Onions (dry)	50 lb.	divide by 4; for example,
Peas (in pods)	22 lb.	apples, 11 lb.
Potatoes	60 lb.	
Tomatoes	60 lb.	

ONE-POUND FOOD MEASURES

16 ounces (dry) per pound
4 ounces per ¼ pound
2½ cups shelled almonds
2½ cups dry beans
2 cups butter
2⅔ cups dried currants
2½ cups pitted dates
9-10 eggs, with shells
3¾ cups whole wheat flour
4 cups white flour
3¾ cups rye flour
2 cups lard
2 cups liquid
3 cups cornmeal
2 cups chopped meats
2 cups milk
4 cups shelled nuts (about)
2⅔ cups oatmeal
2 cups diced potatoes
2 good-sized whole potatoes
2⅔ cups seedless raisins
2½ cups long-grain rice
2 cups granulated sugar
2¼ cups brown sugar
3½ cups confectioners' sugar
3⅔ cups shelled walnuts
4 cups crumbs
3 cups chopped suet (beef fat)
3 cups candied fruit
5 cups coffee (ground)

In the old recipe books I read I would note down whenever an ingredient was described by the pound or ounce so I could be sure and have the cup equivalent in my Measures section of this book. There wasn't an ounce scale anywhere in town that I knew of except at the Post Office so we went down there with cans of mustard seed, peppercorns, and so on and found out how many tablespoons per ounce or per ½ ounce on the letter scale.

ONE-OUNCE FOOD MEASURES

2 tablespoons butter
1 square bitter chocolate
4 tablespoons flour
2½ cups dried hops
2 tablespoons of liquid
1 tablespoon salt
2 tablespoons soda
2 tablespoons sugar

ONE-HALF OUNCE FOOD MEASURES

(in teaspoons)

Allspice, ground	4¼
Allspice, whole	6
Caraway seed	5
Cinnamon, ground	5½
Cloves, whole	5
Cloves, ground	5
Coriander seed	6½
Cream of tartar	3¾
Ginger, ground	6
Gum arabic (acacia)	3½
Mace, ground	5½

Mustard seed	3
Nutmeg, ground	6
Peppercorns (black)	3½
Sarsaparilla	8
Sassafras	8

ON-THE-AVERAGE EQUIVALENTS

1 teaspoon	1/6 ounce
1 tablespoon	½ ounce
¼ cup	2 ounces
1 cup	8 ounces

CUP EQUIVALENTS OF CAN SIZES

#202 (baby food 4½ oz.)	½ cup
6 oz.	¾ cup
8 oz.	1 cup
#1 (11 oz.)	1⅓ cups
#303 (16 oz.)	2 cups
#2 (1 lb. 4 oz.)	2½ cups
#2½ (1 lb. 13 oz.)	3½ cups
#3 (2 lb. 1 oz.)	4 cups
#10 (6 lb. 10 oz.)	13 cups

EQUIVALENT INGREDIENTS

GRAINS

1 tablespoon flour	½ tablespoon cornstarch
1 cup cake flour	⅞ cup all-purpose flour
1 cup broken, uncooked macaroni	2⅔ cups, cooked
1 cup uncooked rice	4 cups, cooked
1 cup broken, uncooked spaghetti	2 cups, cooked

SUGARS

1½ cups corn syrup	1 cup sugar plus ½ cup water
1 cup honey	1 to 1¼ cups sugar plus ¼ cup liquid
1 cup sugar	½ to 1 cup honey (it's sweeter) less ¼ cup liquid
1 lump loaf sugar	1 cube sugar
Loaf sugar, "crushed"	substitute granulated sugar
Loaf sugar, ground in "mortar"	substitute powdered sugar

DAIRY PRODUCTS

1 cup butter	1 cup margarine
	⅞-1 cup hydrogenated fat plus ½ teaspoon salt
	⅞-1 cup lard plus ½ teaspoon salt
	⅞ cup rendered fat plus ½ teaspoon salt
1 cup sour milk	1 cup sweet milk plus 1 tablespoon vinegar or lemon juice
1 cup milk	½ cup of evaporated milk plus ½ cup water
1 cup coffee cream (20%)	3 tablespoons butter plus about ¾ cup milk
1 cup heavy cream (40%)	⅓ cup butter plus about ¾ cup milk

LEAVENING

1 teaspoon baking powder ..	1½ teaspoons phosphate baking powder
	2 teaspoons tartrate baking powder
	½ teaspoon soda plus acid of 1 tablespoon vinegar or lemon juice used with 1 cup sweet milk
	½ teaspoon soda plus acid of ½ to 1 cup molasses
	¼ teaspoon soda plus ½ teaspoon cream of tartar

CITRUS

Juice 1 lemon	about 2-3 tablespoons lemon juice
Juice 1 lime.	about 2 tablespoons lime juice
Juice 1 orange	about ⅓-½ cup orange juice

OTHER

1⅔ ounces semisweet chocolate	1 ounce unsweetened chocolate plus 4 teaspoons sugar
1 whole egg, for baking or thickening	2 egg yolks
1 ounce unsweetened chocolate	3 tablespoons cocoa plus 1 tablespoon fat

GENERAL OVEN CHART

Very Slow Oven	250°-300°
Slow Oven	300°-325°
Moderate Oven	325°-375°
Medium Hot Oven	375°-400°
Hot Oven	400°-450°
Very Hot Oven	450°-500°

BREADS

Baking Powder Biscuits	450° 12-15 min.
Muffins	400°-425° 20-25 min.
Quick Breads	350° 40-60 min.
Yeast Bread	375°-400° 45-60 min.
Yeast Rolls	400° 15-20 min.

CAKES

Butter Loaf Cakes	350° 45-60 min.
Butter Layer Cakes	350°-375° 25-35 min.
Cupcakes	375° 20-25 min.
Chiffon Cakes	325° 60 min.
Sponge Cakes	325° 60 min.
Angel Food Cakes	325° 60 min.

COOKIES

Bar Cookies	350° 25-30 min.
Drop Cookies	350°-375° 8-12 min.
Rolled and Refrigerator Cookies	350°-400° 8-12 min.

PASTRY

Meringues	350° 12-20 min.
Pie Shells	450° 12-15 min.
Filled Pies	450° 10 min.; lower to 350° 40 min.

ROASTS

Beef Roast	325° rare 18-20 min. per lb.; medium 22-25 min. per lb.; well-done 30 min. per lb.
Chicken	325° 30 min. per lb.
Duck	325° 25 min. per lb.
Fish Fillets	500° 15-20 min.
Goose	325°-350° 30 min. per lb.
Ham	350° 20-30 min. per lb.
Lamb	300° 35 min. per lb.
Meat Loaf	375° 60 min. for 2-lb. loaf
Pork Roast	350° 30 min. per lb.
Turkey	325°-350° 15-25 min. per lb.
Veal Roast	300° 30 min. per lb.
Venison	350° 20-25 min. per lb.

CANDY MAKING TEMPERATURES

		(in cold water)
Fudge, Fondant	234°-240°	. . . . . . Soft ball
Divinity, Caramels	244°-248°	. . . . . . Firm ball
Taffy	250°-266°	. . . . . Hard ball
Butterscotch	270°-290°	. . . . . . Soft crack
Brittle Candy.	300°-310°	. . . . . . Hard crack
Caramelized Sugar	310°-338°	. . . . . . Caramel stage

SAUCES

½ to 1 tablespoon flour per 1 cup liquid makes a *thin* sauce.

2 tablespoons flour per 1 cup liquid makes a *medium* sauce.

3 tablespoons flour per 1 cup liquid makes a *thick* sauce.

4 tablespoons flour per 1 cup liquid makes a *paste* when cold.

BREADS

1 measure liquid to 1 measure flour for *pour* batters.

1 measure liquid to about 2 measures flour for *drop* batters.

1 measure liquid to about 3 measures flour for *dough*.

(But what really matters is you add enough flour so the dough stops being sticky on your hands and quit adding before it gets so tough and hard you can't knead it.)

¼ teaspoon of salt to 2 cups flour
1 tablespoon or less sugar to 1 cup flour

NUTS

OUNCES PER CUP

Almonds, whole	5 1/5
Shredded coconut	2 7/9
Whole Brazil nuts	5 1/9
Whole filberts	4 8/9
Pecan halves	3 7/9
Roasted peanuts	5
Chopped black walnuts	4⅔
Halved English walnuts	3⅝

1 POUND IN THE SHELL WILL EQUAL ABOUT

Almonds	1 to 1½ cups shelled
Peanuts	2 cups shelled
Pecans	2¼ cups shelled
Walnuts	2 cups shelled

A 3½-pound chicken will yield about 1 pound meat. A snail needs 15 days to go 1 mile even when he's trying hard.

THE ORIGINAL EDITION OF THIS BOOK SET SEVERAL ENGLISH LANGUAGE RECORDS

1. More typographical errors, general horrors of composition, and inky fingerprints than any other book on record.
2. Where else have you seen ½ pages?
3. First author in history to have had three babies in the same four and one half years spent giving birth to a 5-pound book.
4. Biggest mimeographed book in general circulation (700 pages—more or less).
5. More copies sold than any self-printed book in history (50,000 as of this moment). That doesn't count the Bantam edition.
6. Other remarkable characteristics I'll let you note for yourself lest I be accused of all sorts of things.

CHRONOLOGY

December 25, 1969	Mother-in-law gave us back issues and a subscription to *Organic Gardening* magazine
February 12, 1970	Rebecca Neoma Emery was born.
Summer 1970	OLD FASHIONED RECIPE BOOK idea came to me.
September 1970	I wrote the Table of Contents. (Believed I could finish the book in two months.) Placed an ad to appear November and December of 1970.
November & December 1970	Received about 250 orders. Wrote all saying I'd send the book when done and promised the people it would only be a couple more months.
March 1971	First issue mailed to the "subscribers." It consisted of Herbs, Home Industries, except the candles part, and Definitions and Measures.
September 1, 1971	Luke Carl Emery was born (middle name after my father). Started dreaming of a School of Country Living.
December 17, 1971	Second issue mailed after advertising to get more subscribers raised the funds. About 200 more. It consisted of Beverages and half of Meats chapter. Then I was sick for a while. We traded our 3 acres and a house as a down payment on 115 acres and a house.
March 1972	I became a Christian. Between September and December with scarcely any help I printed and mailed the third issue which was Oddments (except all of Food Preparation) and half of the Dairy chapter. Also sent larger rings and replaced covers for all subscribers because their first rings were turning out too small to hold the book and some were dissatisfied with the flimsy blue paper covers I first printed.
May 17, 1973	Sara Ann Emery was born. Sold goats on neighbor's request. Bought Nelly the cow.
November 1973	I prayed and went back to work on the book.
January 1974	Dolly became very sick. Sara was also sick.
February 18, 1974	The book was finally finished. Dolly was better. Sara was well and I was happy!
March 1, 1974	1st and 2nd editions completely printed and in the mail to my customers thanks to Diann, Darlene and the good collaters.

April 10, 1974 .... 3rd edition finished. (As soon as I finished the first one I thought of all sorts of other things I wanted to say!)

May 15–September 15, 1974 .... The children and I started peddling copies of the books and passing out brochures at town fairs, art and craft fairs, county fairs.

May 24, 1974 .... Colored photos added and that became the 4th edition.

May 26, 1974 .... Index added and then we called it the 5th edition.

October 1–December 1, 1974 .... First trip to California. We got a press agent—Julaine—and some TV and radio interviews. A red and white van to sleep in when away from home . . . and a profit.

December 31, 1974 ..... We leave on a 4½-month trip in the van circling the entire United States to do radio and TV and newspaper interviews telling people about the book and School of Country Living.

January 1, 1975 .... We made down payment on 386 acres meant to become the School of Country Living. I've written the first "schedule of classes" and hope to open in May.

January 16, 1975 .... We added black and white photos to the book and rewritten and expanded chapters to become the 6th edition.

Spring 1975 .... A time of trials while on the road.

May 15, 1975 .... Home from our trip. Planning and Zoning Commissions of Nez Percé and Latah Counties (school property is partly in each) make it possible for us to proceed.

June 15, 1975 .... The School of Country Living opens for its first session.

August 30, 1975 .... And then it closed, deeply in debt, and beset with growing pains.

September 15, 1975 ..... The children and I are off again in the van on another tour to try to sell enough

books to pay off the debt and have another chance for the School.

December 1, 1975 ...... I collapse at a press club in Grand Rapids, Michigan, with irregular heartbeat.

December 4, 1975 ...... Another ambulance ride near Chicago, Illinois. Physical and emotional exhaustion. The children are flown home to Idaho and Grandma Emery. Mike flies out to be with me in the hospital.

December 1975 & January 1976 .... Still in the hospital, scarcely able to walk. The Mimeographer is going bankrupt. I can't seem to get well. I have told Julaine to auction paperback reprint rights to the book to raise enough money to get us out of debt.

January 10, 1976 .... Bantam is high bidder. I sign a contract. $115,000 cash advance from Bantam.

January 11, 1976 .... I get well.

January 13, 1976 .... I leave the hospital. Go back to work trying to make a School of Country Living happen.

April 28, 1976 .... We purchase the Kendrick Hotel to use for students to stay in.

May 2, 1976 .... I meet Cindy Davis, who subsequently agrees to illustrate the 7th edition.

June 1, 1976 .... The School of Country Living reopens.

July 15, 1976 .... The last of the Bantam money is spent, having built and equipped our wonderful School of Country Living.

August 2, 1976 .... After three days of terrible thunderstorms which inflict great crop loss in Latah County, flash floods down three different draws heavily damage the School of Country Living. Two buildings are completely destroyed.

August 8, 1976 .... The combination of crop loss, physical damage and accumulated debt from running the school is too much. The School of Country Living closes, it seems permanently.

August 15, 1976 .... The children and I (four months pregnant) leave on a 3½-month tour of the U.S. to help start schools of country living everywhere we can get people interested.

February 16, 1977 ...... Jacob Michael Emery was born.

WHAT HAPPENED THEN—1974

(Written December 20–January 15, 1975)

Tell us what happened, so many people said. How did you do it? I could write another book . . .

Here is the story of what happened then.

There was a collating bee. A simple enough thing. A librarian up at the Moscow Public Library organized it for me. (These bees all started from her idea.) And about six ladies came, most of whom I'd never met before, and they all worked very hard assembling the individual sheets into a complete book. We were doing 200 copies. That was the 2nd edition. The 1st edition came out in sections over a four-year period. I mailed them out and the people put them together themselves. I was hauling boxes full of envelopes holding the fourth issue in the back of my pickup from the work area, which was an empty apartment in Viola's place, to the post office. When I got back from one trip they had already finished about eight books and scarcely noticed me as I came in the door. Diann always introduces me, "This is our author" and everybody looks at me hard for a minute to see what authors look like and I say, "Hello," and "Thanks for coming to help," and that is sort of the end of it. So I walked in the door and having already been introduced they just kept going around the table putting books together. They had no way of knowing what was going on inside me. I had sort of thought I'd be the person to put the first whole book together. But no matter. I sort of elbowed my way into the line that was going around and around the table and picked up the first chapter. I couldn't say a word. I couldn't smile. I took a step, picked up the second chapter from its pile and laid it on top and so on around the table until the end, the back cover and I held it in my hand—a completed copy of the Recipe Book. The first one that I had ever held in my hand—a *miracle*. I stepped with it back out the door, so full of emotion I thought I'd burst from it. I found just up the hall an empty laundry room and there I knelt down and cried and talked to God and thanked Him.

Then there was more work to be done hauling boxes to the post office and things just took up again as if nothing spectacular had happened—only my heart knew better. Days went by and we had to look at some grim realities. It has cost more than $3.50 each to put out the many books for which I had accepted that payment. We had to sell books fast to earn enough to cover those expenses. Viola rented her extra apartment and the printing operation moved to Diann's living room. We started the 3rd edition. I did a lot of rewriting and racked my brain for a way to sell books. I had bought a classified ad in *Organic Gardening* for December and January at the horrendous sum of nearly $200 a month and in the two months it ran the ad brought in exactly one order. My neighbors weren't particularly interested in encouraging what they regarded as my insanity and the sooner I were mercifully discouraged the better. Cax-

ton, a quality book publisher in Southern Idaho, had once turned down the publication of my book so with that much of an introduction I wrote a desperate little letter and asked them would they please tell an amateur how they sold books?

Caxton wrote me back that they sold books by means of three books which I could purchase for about $115. I sent for them. One was a listing of names and addresses of all the libraries in the country. Another was a listing of bookstores in the United States and Canada and another was the *Literary Market Place*, which gives names and addresses of people like review editors. We started mailing ad brochures to Western bookstores and libraries advertising the book at $7.45, plus postage, wholesale. A lot of them griped because they wanted a full 40% markup to retail which was then $8 and soon became $9.95. But in not too long we had over 200 bookstore accounts. We offered 90 days for them to pay and full refund if they paid for the book and then wanted to return it. A few returned but most reported successful sales. We couldn't still seem to make ends meet financially though. We were making and selling more and more books, but the crisis for cash was never anything but desperate. We later learned a new way to figure up the money thing and discovered that we were spending more than $7.45 to produce each book and so had been losing money on every single book we sold to a bookstore. We raised the wholesale price to $9.95, plus postage, which promptly lost us all but 25 of our bookstore accounts, including those in my home area. The answer had to be in direct retail selling. The bookmaking outgrew Diann's living room and we had to find another place to do it.

We rented an empty restaurant on Main Street in Kendrick for $75 a month. We used the abandoned counters to collate on and with great care settled in the precious new $1,200 mimeograph machine that by the grace of God had been allowed to us on time payments of $45 a month. Diann and Darlene started keeping regular office hours at the store even though I owed each of them anywhere from $300 to $700, depending on which day or month you look at and the whole town was telling them they were fools. We painted huge brave red and white signs on the outside of our new home advertising the Recipe Book and did a little off the street business. Some college boys in Moscow visited me and urged me to take part in a craft fair there they were getting up on Main

Street. I never turn anybody down and as usual we were in a situation where if I didn't find $250 somewhere we wouldn't even be able to pay our paper bill and we'd be done forever the following Monday. I took a folding table and all the children and we set up out there in the sunshine. I passed out hundreds of brochures, signed up 60 collaters to come and work 7 hours for a book and sold $300 worth of books. It was a long day but great fun and I had the *money!*

I was told of a convention of booksellers from the northwestern United States in Seattle, Washington. I left all the children but my baby with Mike, scraped up the money for a bus ticket, took brochures and samples. I prayed all the way on that bus. I had a day extra. The next morning first thing in my hotel room I called every TV station, newspaper in the Seattle yellow pages. I said something like "Hello, my name is Carla Emery and I wrote a book. Could you use me?" I got a feature article in the big Seattle *Post Intelligencer* and a 10-minute part in a TV talk show in Tacoma. I had a brief encounter with the *PI* book reviewer, Archie Satterfield, and about 6 weeks later he did an enthusiastic book review on the Recipe Book in his very respectable and much-read column. That alone drew over 60 orders for me. I passed out brochures like mad at the booksellers' convention, talked to everybody I could buttonhole and made not one sale. Three of them ordered later. I figured it up after I got home. I'd missed the other children desperately. They had missed me, and I'd gone even more in the hole financially on the deal. How can you go in the hole even more week after week, month after month? I'm one person that can sure tell you how. It's by owing more all the time. You have to make bigger payments all the time and that's why those Monday mornings were always so desperate. Because that's when the checks that were out would hit the bank, and we had to have the money in there to cover them. Sometimes we didn't. We bounced more than a few checks, which is a good reason why I don't get in the least hysterical when somebody else's checks bounce in my account. I just send it back through. We always managed to cover our checks by at least the second time around.

The next week was Locust Blossom Festival in Kendrick. Every year on that date there's a parade, races in the park, and gymkhana, as well as a barbecue. They line up for a block waiting to get their coleslaw, beans and barbecued meat.

We were now in Main Street, too. We put out tables in front of the Mimeographer, and I passed out brochures all up and down the line of folks waiting to eat. We sold another $300 worth of books and everyone was ecstatic. We had made it through another Monday. I saw a poster on the front door of our town drugstore advertising a town day at a tiny town in western Washington called Kahlotus. I figured if Kendrick was that good why not Kahlotus. I loaded the kids up at about 4:00 A.M. that Saturday. We drove in the pickup because it was the only rig we had that would move. It was really crowded for all six of us in there, about half still asleep. The fellows in charge let me set up my folding tables right on Main Street and I stood there and passed out brochures and sold books until dark while the children wandered around looking at all the marvels of a small town in the full bloom of Its Day and the baby played on the top of a folding chair. I sold $300 worth of books again and we were all starting to relax in a sort of security. We got through Monday again. I asked some fellows with bright red shirts and a beautiful team of horses and old-time coach, who went to a lot of small town parades, where I could go the next weekend and do it again. They suggested Rosalia, Washington, that coming Saturday and said maybe I could get other names from the chambers of commerce. The next weekend I headed for Rosalia.

It was a disaster. The people in charge told me to set up in the grade school by a traveling concession of four kiddie rides. I sold four books. It was a one-day thing like all the others had been. But the previous three good days had me convinced and, besides, Monday was still there to be faced—I *had* to make some money. I drove back to Kendrick (about 80 miles). A few orders had come in the mail. I cashed those checks and started to drive down to southern Idaho, 300 miles, to a little town called Cambridge where a chamber of commerce had told me there would be a craft fair. I drove all night with the children sleeping in the car but with no time to sleep for myself except just a few moments off and on curled up in the frontseat at pull-off spots by the side of the road. We pulled into Cambridge early the next morning and learned that the whole thing was a big misunderstanding. The "craft fair" was paintings and selling. I was weary and discouraged. We had bought breakfast that morning. We had scarcely enough money left for even gas back. We visited a grocery store and I spent what I dared on milk for the baby's bottle, some cheese and nourishing bread for the other children. I did without food myself. I concentrated on driving. I was very tired. I don't remember too clearly the trip back except that going up White Bird Hill, which is a 1,200-foot climb out of Riggins Canyon up to Grangeville, the car overheated and sounded in a desperate way. We finished the climb slowly, praying every minute, and at the top I turned off the engine and rolled all the way down the mountain into Grangeville—maybe 10 miles. I had to because the car couldn't run without getting so desperately hot I was afraid I'd ruin the engine forever.

We got home with the gas gauge on E and down at the Mimeographer Diann, Darlene and I had to take stock of the situation. I had not only not come home with any money this time—I'd spent on my frantic travels what little had come in the mail that week. Monday was there and this time there was no deposit to be rushed off to the bank. We just gritted our teeth and bore it while checks bounced every which way. It looked like the end. I figured it would take $1,000 to bail us out and it had to be there within a week. On my best weekend yet I'd only done $300 and I appreciated now that I sure couldn't always count on that much.

I racked my brains for a way to get the money. Idea! I called a man in California who was our biggest single bookstore account. I offered his secretary a bargain and that California distributorship he had wanted if he would pay cash for $1,000 worth of books right away and she said she was sure he would agree. I set down the phone and bawled for pure joy and weariness while Diann and Darlene patted me on the back. Then the man himself called back and said that times were rough and he just couldn't do it right now. We heard of a craft fair at Bellevue, Washington. Thursday through Saturday I heard it was. A little money came in the mail. I said to Diann and Darlene I'll go just this one more time. I'll go clear to Seattle (maybe 500 miles—Bellevue is a suburb of Seattle) to this fair and if I don't make it this time I'll submit to the inevitable—we'll give it all up. The week's mail-order money was just enough to pay gas one way to Seattle and we took blankets with us and a bag of groceries bought on the good old charge account at Blewett's Market. We slept behind a shopping center and a policeman came and got very uptight about the whole idea of it. The next day we found out that I had the date wrong again and the fair existed but didn't start until Friday. I had Thursday to kill. I was very short of money. At the shopping center I hunted for a phone. In a real estate office a nice secretary let me use the phone. I called the "Seattle Today" TV show people to see if I could get on. Meanwhile my kids were kind of getting into things. The bosses at the real estate office came in. The "Seattle Today" people told me that they had a vacancy that very day and I should be there in one hour. The real estate people told me to please leave with my children and I did.

We headed for the KING studio, we'd never been there before. By a miracle found it in time. The children couldn't find half their shoes so I made them stay in the car in the parking lot looked after by the nice parking attendant. I rushed into the studio and there you had a study in contrasts. The hostess of the live show was in an evening gown, expertly done makeup, and lovely hairdo. I was in work clothes, tennis shoes, with bags under my eyes. And the show was a smashing success!

We headed back to the shopping center. The children had supper and I didn't and the next day bright and early we set up for our fair. I was afraid the lady in charge would turn me away because I

hadn't been able to get her on the phone to register properly. She didn't. We sold $300 worth that Friday. I met other people at the fair. People I was to become good friends with before the summer was over. People who make quickie trips to Mexico and buy up goods there to sell back at the fairs. People who spend long winter months working in their basement (or such where) craft shops painstakingly making beautiful things and then all summer long, weekend after weekend, they visit one craft fair after another trying to sell those things for enough money to keep them alive.

It's a very special way to make a living, and there's a real warm camaraderie among the folks who live that way. They took me in as a sister and began to teach me the things I so badly needed to know. When the big, good shows were. What you had to do to get into them. The fine points of just where to put your tables to catch the best crowd flow, how to hawk your wares, and how to get along with the management. They told me that although the fair there at Bellevue seemed so good that Friday there was going to be an even better one Saturday and Sunday up in the Fremont district of Seattle. They were all moving up there, some leaving a friend to tend their tables at Bellevue. I moved too, and Fremont was a whole new experience for me.

I thought I was plenty early Saturday morning at Fremont and WOW was I late. There were hundreds of craftsmen there—600 according to the brochure I saw later and mobile TV cameras and reporters out already getting film ready for the daily news program. All the good spots were already taken and I had to settle for a place way out on the edge of the fair. Nonetheless I did $500 worth of business that day. We slept in the car that night and nobody minded. The next day business was even better. I ran out of books although I had driven out with so many I thought the poor old car would scarcely make it over the mountain pass. Then I took orders. People didn't seem to mind. They gave me the money and their names and addresses and asked me to send them one or else ordered it C.O.D. People appeared from nowhere to help me because I was just overwhelmed.

They passed out brochures for me and helped sell books and take care of the children. They begged and insisted until finally I went off and bought myself a 7-Up in a little nearby restaurant and felt vacant in a sort of good way while they carried on the selling back at my table. I started to feel like a small sort of heroine. People would come up and say, "Everybody's talking about your book." I would walk down the street back from getting a hot dog or lemonade and see them gathered around one of my brochures talking. There was no problem eating now. Plenty of money only nothing at the fair to eat but hot dogs and lemonade. It didn't seem to matter at the time. I was grateful to eat.

That night the children and I slept in a motel and all had showers and reveled in our luxury. We bought a big bag of groceries—things like avocados and fruit juice to celebrate and Dolly and I sat up and totaled the money we had ready to take home, even after expenses, and could scarcely believe our eyes—it was over $1,000. It was the amount we had to have. No more but no less. I went home and deposited the money. We caught all our rubber checks the second time through and the business went on. For another week anyway.

Once I had numbly apologized to Darlene because I still had no money to pay her and I knew how much she needed it, she responded with words I'll never forget: "Oh, Carla, I just wish I had some money of my own so I could loan it to you." But now some bills were getting caught up with. Diann and Darlene got their much deserved and long-awaited wages.

Somewhere here it needs to be stopped and considered. God gave me so many miracles. Did I pray for each one? Maybe I should have done more praying, more talking to God. I know He was the one most important thing in my life. I trusted that in some undefined way I was leading the life He gave me to live and so struggling in a way for His sake even though not I nor anyone else could see very clearly the connection. The weeks that followed were a time of action. My constant prayer was my constant faithfulness to God wanting to be in the center of His will. I didn't have time to spend days or weeks in prayer. Do you understand what I'm trying to say? That it was like God and I were engaged in a titanic battle together. I knew what I had to do like an instinct, and He knew what I had to have without my telling Him because at the end of the day my lips were truly too weary to speak words to Him.

One week we sold books at the National Old-Time Fiddler's Festival in Weiser, Idaho, a 300-mile drive to the south again. We pulled up there in front of the Junior High School that campers were using as a headquarters. I got out the two folding tables I was using now and started passing out brochures. It was a marvelous weekend. There was music everywhere—jam sessions all over the big shaded lawns of the school. Water toilets and showers in the school. Grocery nearby. Business was wonderful. I sold about $500 worth of books that weekend. But I was getting really bothered with doubt. Was I in the Lord's will, I asked myself? Maybe I should be at home with Mike quietly tending my garden and my house. It had

bothered me all that week. It had bothered me that weekend. I thought maybe God was telling me to quit. If it had kept up, I would have stopped going out to sell books.

Most of the people there were what you'd call "hippies." I don't take much count of names. I've sold books in every kind of environment you can imagine and everywhere I met people and loved people and they loved me back. But I'm no believer in dope. A young man approached me and wanted to just talk. He had that weary, stressed, undernourished look I saw so often that weekend. His clothes weren't much. That didn't bother me. I'm not much for dressing up, either. But I sure do believe in eating. He had hitched from Oregon to Weiser. We got to talking. "I'm a Christian," he said. "I always pray over my joint before I smoke it." We talked back and forth about that. I tried to help him see that Jesus would never be wanting him to smoke a joint. That He would never bless *that* because Jesus wants the best for all of His children. That He is trying to lead us out of illusion into the pure and good reality that lies all around us just waiting to be lived in. We talked quietly. There were about two hundred other people in the same immediate area, talking, walking, sleeping on the grass, on the steps of the school, on the sidewalk. A pause. "I see what you mean," he said. A pause. "Will you pray with me about it right now?" I asked. "We'll ask God to help you get all this straightened out." He nodded. We knelt together on the grass in front of my table, holding hands. I prayed with all the heart and strength I could muster for this young man. That he should be right with his God again. That he should be given strength to do what he was supposed to do. That he should find a church congregation, a fellowship of Christians to help hold him up and share his burdens in the difficult times of a Christian's walk which all of us have to get through sooner or later. He was quiet as we prayed. When I finished he looked at me still on his knees and said softly, "God wants me to give you this." He pulled a bag out of his pocket and handed it toward me. I took it. "I came to Weiser to sell it," he said. "I've got just $10 made from one sale I already made. I want to buy one of your books." "I'm not going to take your only $10," I answered. "Give me your home address and I'll mail you one. That way you won't have to carry it." He walked away. I was happy and freed of the burden of my doubt whether I should be out selling or not beyond my ability to describe it to you. It was one of the best things that happened to me all summer and I simply walked on air for days thereafter. All doubt had left me. I was satisfied that God had given me a sign that I was indeed in His will. The children and I took that bag to the police station and left it on the counter and walked away. Then we went back to the school grounds, to our folding tables, and passed out more brochures and sold more books.

The next day that same young man came to my table again. The light in his face, the change in his whole expression and body—the way he carried himself—stunned me. I knew that in the difference between the man I had prayed with the day before and the man I was seeing now I was glimpsing the miracle of being born again. There was a strength, a purity, a glory radiating from him that in my memory is almost like a visible light around him. Today he did not have time to visit. He said, "I'm going home to my wife and baby." And walked away. I rejoiced. I could have jumped up and down and shouted praise to God. I was so full of joy for him. When I got home from Weiser we had $500. I sold out even before the Fiddler's Festival was over and I sent that young man a copy of the Recipe Book.

I can't remember clearly to tell you the details of the weeks that followed—or months. It was a time of tremendous spending of my inner strength and resources. I can tell you that from May 15 until November 15, I was only home one weekend and that was in August when I was just too sick and exhausted to go out. That at the beginning of the summer I was in a peak of physical health and stamina and by the end of it was chronically ill and had to get a great deal of rest at night just to meet a minimum schedule. But I never backed out but two weekends, that one in August and one in late November when also I was exhausted just back from 6 weeks on the road. All the first part of the summer, once I had learned that the good big fairs were out on the coast, I left on a

Wednesday or Thursday, the last minute to just give us time enough to drive out there. The old car would be loaded with boxes of books and brochures in the frontseat, backseat and the trunk, trying to spread out the weight a little bit (but I still ruined the springs). Blankets and pillows were on top and the children perched on top of that. I squeezed into the driver's seat with Sara sitting on my left leg, in my lap, where she always traveled. If we had to stop and sleep before we had a chance to sell off some of the books I'd stop some place like a truck stop where lots of trucks were parked or a rest area on the highway and unload enough boxes so I could make bed. Sara slept in a little pallet I had made on the floor by the frontseat. She was a year old at the time. Luke, 2, and Becca, 4, slept in the floor places at the back, plenty of blankets under and over them. Dolly and Danny got the car seat in back and I got the one in front. I found it all quite manageable except one time we accidentally ended up with a shortage of blankets which had to mean me being the one short and I pretty near froze or the time my pillow got stolen.

I'd leave just in time to get there and generally on the late side because I had so much I wanted to do at home—time with Mike, work in the garden, all the canning and freezing and general garden work, catching up with my milk cow that Mike tried to keep going while I was gone only she and Mike just couldn't seem to get along together. Then that pile of mail was always waiting for me, and there were calls to make and decisions to be made. So I generally didn't get any sleep the night going out because I'd be driving all night and I generally didn't get any sleep the night coming back because I was always so anxious to be home again that I'd just drive straight home. The upshot of all this, plus living on hot dogs and hamburgers at the fairs (because that was generally all you could get) was that I started having terribly sharp stomach pains. The first time they hit me it really scared me. I sort of wondered if I was going to die. I didn't but I got too scared to eat more than a little at a time. Well, Mike and I talked it over and we decided to submit to the necessities. I wouldn't try to come home every week like I'd been doing. Instead I would go out for a few weeks at a time. I did that and my cow went dry and the stock cows got into the garden about three different times and ate everything to the ground, what they didn't trample. We had to get rid of the extra animals because there wasn't anybody to be home with them and some of my young fruit trees died for lack of water. Sometimes I got home and felt like bawling because it all looked yellow with drought and deserted and rundown like nobody lived there. Here I was out telling everybody about the great country life raising your own food and there wasn't anything in my cellar but the green beans, turnips and peas that I had done that first part of the summer. But then I'd think about how they'd come up to me and tell me about the *first* garden they'd ever had or their new home in the country and what a miracle and a joy it was to them and how my book was a help to them in doing it all. I'd feel so good and tell myself that I'd have a milk cow and a garden again for sure *next* year.

Monday didn't stop being the day of reckoning. Not at all. Only the numbers involved steadily got bigger. We finally got a bookkeeper. Liliane (who is still with us and is a treasure) analyzed the figures and told us that from the beginning until November 1974, we steadily lost money. Not dramatically but steadily. And yet our volume kept growing and the way that we stayed in business is that our debt kept growing. We managed to pay off just enough of our debt just fast enough to keep our credit. The worst moment was when it looked like we couldn't get paper at all. Our regular supplier said he couldn't find any more. We made frantic phone calls and finally located the Zellerbach Paper Company in Portland who had some of what we needed. But they wanted $2,500 cash in advance. It seemed hopeless. We were still living from hand to mouth and getting that much cash in advance seemed impossible. How would we get the paper? It would take a big truck to haul it to Idaho, and to get it in time, we'd have to pick it up Monday. But we were determined to do it, anyway. We absolutely *had* to have that paper by the coming Tuesday to keep the mimeograph machine going. I knew of six different art and crafts fairs going on in Washington that weekend. We sent Zellerbach a check and told them to hold it until the Friday before the weekend then deposit and we would pick up the paper Monday. We mounted a regular battle campaign. Applications to all six fairs, recruiting helpers, getting the old one-ton truck Mike used to haul cows ready with tent, supplies, books, books, and more books and brochures. I have five children and Darlene has five children. In addition we took two other girls and a young man with us. Darlene and two of her children were going to work and my Dolly and Danny had sold many a book. We hoped that would give us the manpower to do all those fairs. We calculated that if we did well enough at all of them, we would have just enough money for me to get to the bank and cover that check.

So we were off to Seattle. Darlene in her station wagon loaded with children, tent, and the girls who were going to help us sell. I in the one-ton truck with the great big stock racks in the back, heavily loaded with cardboard boxes of books, brochures and more college kids and my children. Darlene was already out of sight as we started up the long climb over the Alpowa Grade, the first mountain pass out of Lewiston going to Seattle. About four-fifths of the way to the top I suddenly noticed the temperature gauge said the engine was running hot. A moment more and there

were flames and black smoke coming up through the crack all around where you lift up the hood and you could see the flames inside in the floorboard insulation around the brake pedal and gas pedal. I stopped as soon as I could get over to the side and got out. We got the hood up and there the engine was burning merrily away—I didn't know what to do next. I'm no great mechanic at all. I really depend on Mike for things like that. He buys old rigs and then endlessly revamps them or junks them in the field and then uses them for parts to keep the next old rigs going. But a Greyhound bus came along just then and saw us and stopped right in front of us. The driver got out and ran back with a fire extinguisher. It shot out some stuff that was a white powder all over the engine and the fire was out. We thanked him and he drove off in his big bus again. Then we realized the fire had got

going again especially down in the floorboard insulation. We had no liquid. We tried to put dirt on it but no good, the dirt couldn't get down into the places where the fire was smoldering. Now a farmer stopped by. He said he'd get us some water and left again and we kept moving dirt trying to hold down the flames until he could get back. He came back with water and we soaked the thing out good and final. He had a good strong pickup. We hooked up with a chain, and he pulled us up to the rest area at the top of Alpowa Grade. Then he took us to his home on a nearby farm where we made phone calls.

Mike and the wrecker came and towed us back to Lewiston. The truck's engine was a disaster. It wouldn't be going anywhere again for a long time. But I had to be in Seattle with those people and that load of books by the following morning. So Mike helped me rent a U-Haul trailer and we moved all that heavy load into it. This took a good bit of time and effort in that hot summer sun. We transferred the children and the blankets and the sleeping bags, bottles and diapers. Mike gave me his car to pull it all and called up a friend to get a ride home from work. Well, we took off again up Alpowa Grade in a cheerful frame of mind—and in the identical spot as before, about a mile short of the top, I suddenly realized the car was blowing its top. I quickly pulled over the side and got very, very sober. This seemed like just too much. We were so far behind schedule now we were going to have to drive all night to make it, anyway. And again Alpowa Grade had defeated us and we couldn't get over it. Alpowa started to loom in my mind like the headquarters of a sinister and determined enemy. We waited until the car had cooled down and then carefully drove to Lewiston once more.

A garage mechanic told us that the trouble was a broken radiator hose. I called Mike and said guess what. He was cheerful over the phone. It was only a radiator hose he said. Go ahead and try it again. We started off again and I was feeling grim. This time we not only drove slowly and carefully in the cooler air of night but we prayed and sang hymns every foot of the way up that Alpowa Grade and God brought us safely over the top. Then we drove all night. We got to our first fair in time to set up in a good place.

There was a good campsite about 5 miles away at Salt Water State Park. There we slept those nights and worked the fairs by day, every one of them. Day by day our pile of boxes of books and brochures dwindled and our pile of cash grew. Everybody got a real education in the fine art of passing out brochures and selling Recipe Books. It was a hard time, an easy time, an exciting time, a weary time. I had to lead Darlene to show her a fair site in Tacoma and we happened to get on the freeway at rush hour. I had already had my introduction to freeways and knew how different they were from our two-lane country roads here at home. But I had forgotten what a shock they were. I found out later that Darlene drove down that freeway in rush hour crying all the way. Monday we were done. My companion took my car back and I rented a U-Haul truck that would be big enough to get that load of paper and headed for Portland Zellerbach to pick it up. I was behind schedule as

usual. I got to the loading dock with a half hour to spare before 5:00 P.M.

I had promised to speak at a prayer breakfast in Lewiston Tuesday morning. It was a commitment I was determined not to fail. So I drove all night. It was a real adventure driving that huge heavily loaded truck. Once the baby did something, I didn't even know what, and suddenly the trouble lights were blinking like crazy making that whole big truck an enormous rolling Christmas tree going on and off, on and off in the trucker's SOS. I had no idea how to turn the things off. It was terribly embarrassing. We just had to drive down the highway like that for about half an hour until we finally came to a gas station that was still open and they showed me how to turn it off. I made a nice bed in the back of the truck for the bigger children and pallets in front for the little ones and we drove on down the road. Several times that night I awoke because of the sound of the tires hitting gravel instead of pavement just in time to get us back on the highway and save us from driving off some cliffside. We got home barely in time for me to change clothes, park the truck and drive back the 30 miles to Lewiston for the prayer meeting. On the way in our driveway with the truck I cut it too close to our gate and broke the sideview mirror. That was the only mishap of the whole trip.

At the prayer meeting I was weary but happy. It seemed like I was more ministered to than ministering. Though I managed a poor little speech, it didn't seem like much of an accomplishment to me and I seriously wondered if I had understood right the urgency of getting there. But the next day a man who had been there told me a strange story. Right after the prayer meeting he had been with friends in a public place and had told them the story of my all-night drive to make the appointment. He heard the sound of weeping and turned around. A man behind them had been overhearing the story, Before 15 minutes had passed that man had accepted Jesus. When I heard that story I knew why I had made that drive. It was all worthwhile! So many times God does that. You think He's got you doing something for one reason, and it turns out to be for something else entirely. But always for the victory!

The time came for my Spokane talk show. I was making it a first stop on a trip to Seattle to sell books. I had to load up the usual. Spokane is a 2½-hour drive from Kendrick. The show was to be at 12:00 noon. I left Kendrick at 9:30 A.M. I set some kind of speed record getting to Spokane and then set out to find the station. I asked three different people including a policeman, a garage man, and the secretary at a radio station, which I thought it was and it wasn't. I drove in a big circle around the TV station before I finally found it. I zoomed into the parking lot, left the older children in the car, grabbed my baby (I always have my baby) and ran into the station. The program MC was standing in the lobby looking worried. They had expected other guests besides me and the others never did show up at all. I was in my usual dreadful shape to go on TV. Only this time I wasn't tired. But I hadn't been able to find much in the way of clean clothes that morning so I had grabbed a brown vest that has pretty leather diamonds in the front and wore that for a blouse though the armholes were way too big and the neck too low. Sara was barefoot and wide awake. I was still gasping for air from my races to ask directions and back to the car and the whole thing was so ridiculous I never had a chance to get nervous. We were on the air, Zam, just like that and I had my time and the other guys', too. Sara was sitting in my lap and as the MC and I tried to talk first thing she did was get interested in my tiny little lapel mike. That's what they clip onto your blouse in those talk shows. It isn't very visible but it picks up what you say. It's a very, very sensitive little mike and Sara started playing with it and as she handled it the mike sent horrible screeching noises over the air. So the interviewer unhooked it from me and we finished the show with him unhooking his mike and holding it in front of my face when I talked and in front of his when he talked. Well the show was a smashing success and Sara was the hit of it! I had to take six calls before I could even get through the lobby and I guess the phone continued ringing for a while after that. That's how TV and radio shows measure the popularity of people they have on—if that switchboard lights up after their show. So bless the good people out

there because the talk show people saw me with whole new eyes. Because it doesn't matter how I looked to them—to all media people "the voice of the people is the voice of God," and bless those people in the Spokane audience they loved me. And so I got invited back to the talk show for a later date. And back home there were mail-orders coming in from people who had heard the show!

Did you take the children? my friends asked. Yes, of course. I always have the children. I couldn't bear to be away from them. Wasn't it hard on them? No. Children are almost infinitely adaptable. And they delight in a gypsy life. They played with each other as we rolled down the road. They shot out of the car like Mexican jumping beans at stops and I always made a lot of them. We read all the historical markers, stopped to admire all the scenic views. We toured the national parks that happened to be on our route and when I had time I would drive way out of my way to take them by some spot of historic or geographic significance. They learned names of states and cities. We rode on little ferries and on big ones. We went over mountains, across deserts to the ocean beaches, into big cities and slums, downtown and upper classes. We met wonderful people, friends I made and really hated to leave, that I'll always remember. Judy and Pat in Seattle living back of Roosevelt High School where they make beautiful enamel jewelry for sale; the lady in Eugene, Oregon, with the huge loom in her living room who was such a great cook (so was Judy—that beet soup!); the good lady in northern Washington who had 12 children, about half of them adopted, who saw me at the fair passing out brochures and asked me and all my five home, bathed us, and loved us.

I met another lady at that northern Washington fair. I offered her a brochure and she said angrily to me, "I don't want anything from anybody whose children look the way yours do." That was our first day at the fair and I was having a really hard time. I was just about broke. Nobody would buy a book though I passed out brochures as if my life and our next meal depended on it—which they did. The fair manager had been by and impatiently and angrily told me to clean up my site which the children and I earnestly tried to. But when you have five children, clothing, diapers, blankets, pillows, boxes of books and brochures, a bag of groceries, and a growing bag of garbage all perched on a site half dust and half grass which is about 20 x 10 feet and adjacent to a sidewalk with hundreds of people going up and down, it's hard to be an example of neatness. We tried though. I think most people didn't appreciate how hard we tried. We were across from the restrooms and it seemed like Dolly or I were forever crossing that road with one or another of the little ones washing faces, changing clothes, or britches. The hours were long—from nine in the morning until ten at night. It was a big five-day fair. The town was a conservative, pretty little country town called Lynden. So I was grateful when that lady asked us home though I've forgotten her name. She was, we soon discovered, a sister in Christ and in her I found a *friend* I won't forget.

What a difference between her and the other one—the one who criticized and walked on. That one made my burden heavier because to all my other struggles was added the anguish of her words to me. This lady made it lighter.

Toward the middle of the summer the county fairs began. I went to the first one (the Tri-City Fair, Pasco, Richland and Kennewick, Washington) because the fair manager was at Kahlotus, saw me there and said, "You have a good family item there. I want you to come to my fair." I got the idea from that and did many another fair. Eight straight weeks of them in August and September and some odd ones before and after. Mike and I were together at the Tri-City Fair and it was a beautiful time for us. I was weary from my summer of selling. It was the first time Mike had been out selling and I didn't know really how it would be. I needn't have worried. I hadn't seen him for weeks before that, but I knew he was close five minutes before he even walked into my sight. It was so good to see him again. We kept up our strength with great tall, real lemonades that had a half lemon floating in them and lots of ice, and eating buttered hot corn on the cob and sold books. Mike was a terrific salesman and it was a good thing he was there because that was the busiest spot we had all summer—even more than Fremont. The fair lasted five days. We passed out thousands of brochures. Each day the sales built until on Saturday we sold 50 books and on Sunday 55. I really enjoyed selling together with Mike and it was such a help having him there. We stayed in a motel and it was a regular honeymoon.

Marriage is a funny, wonderful, beautiful thing. You may have wondered in this tale of struggle where Mike was, why he wasn't right there helping me. I never asked him to. Most of the time I didn't tell him how tight it was and how worried I was. I didn't want him to have to worry, too, when there wasn't really anything he could do to help. But if Mike sees me really in need he's right there, and the proverbial wild horses couldn't keep him away.

In the meantime a curious correspondence had been going on between me and a lady in Hollywood named Millicent Braverman. Apparently she also had a connection with a bookstore that received my first mailing of the advertising brochure. She wrote me back that she was not interested in buying my book. I noticed the paper she wrote on carried the address of a public relations company. I knew almost nothing about the public relations business except that they set up dates for people in the news. But I'm willing to try anything, so I wrote her back and asked her if she would be willing to help me with publicity while I was in California (on one of my postcards). She wrote me back (on a postcard) that she didn't think anybody who mimeographed a book in their living room would be able to afford her services. I wrote her back (on a

OLD FASHIONED RECIPE BOOK

postcard) that it would be a whole lot more useful if she would tell me what she was good for and how much it would cost. By then I was off in Washington, Oregon and then to try my fortune in California and Mike carried on the negotiations with Millicent.

Mike had got my car ready and bought new tires—we figured I'd be out six weeks, the longest stretch away from home yet. He also bought me a little homemade trailer and we loaded it with over a ton of books and brochures, plus loading the car full of them too. The children had managed to get the month of September in school—the two that are big enough to go to school: Dolly and Danny, Dolly is a fifth grader and Danny is in the first. I visited their teachers and the principal before we left. "Well you know it's also educational to take a trip," Dolly's teacher said. I had books and workbooks for them. We did the Central Washington State Fair at Yakima then the Seattle Today show in Seattle again, then a weekend at the regular outdoor market at Eugene, which is a food and craft fair that goes on weekends year-round and has some of the best foods I've had the fortune to eat anywhere. Then over the border to California. Up to that point I'd been doing well.

Things got disastrous fast. Only I didn't realize it was going to be so rough. I sent my supply of cash home to pay bills only keeping the minimum as usual and traveled on down to San Francisco. I'd heard you could sell along Berkeley's Telegraph Avenue or downtown at Ghirardelli Square or Fisherman's Wharf. Only it wasn't so easy. It turned out there was a six-month waiting list for permission to sell at Telegraph Avenue. I couldn't sell downtown without a $100 deposit, which I didn't have, and without buying a license for more money and getting references and permission and going to the police station. I tried selling in bookstores and health food stores and there was just about no interest. I heard of a special craftsman market and tried to get into that, but the rules said I had to be present on a date a month in the future to be decided upon and there was no time. It was an ordeal driving in San Francisco traffic pulling that trailer. I could never find a parking space big enough. I got grumpy to the children and was ashamed of myself. I left without further trying. For the moment I detested the place. I left for Los Angeles.

I drove most of the night, pulled over and slept for a while in the churchyard of a small town, then pulled back onto the road about 6:00 A.M. when I woke up. The children woke up then. They were in high spirits. We had visited the beach both trips up and down, admired the oil wells, and done the zoo in Los Angeles until we were like old friends with the tram driver. Dolly and Becca were both naked and they were bouncing around the car like rubber balls. Sara woke up and I gave her a bottle with one hand as I drove on down the early morning quiet freeway. Luke was sitting tight by my right side and I was playing "if you don't hold it tight it pokes you" with my right hand with Dolly, Luke and Becca and driving with my left hand. Suddenly my sense of smell warned that there was a crisis in Sara's diaper, spotted a narrow dirt turnout just ahead, hit the brakes and trailer and

all stopped on it. I had just got the front side of Sara's diaper down and exposed that sure enough my nose was right and there was a major problem there needing immediate removal when a patrolman's face appeared at the window. Dolly, still naked, screamed and dived for cover under a blanket. Becca, also naked, continued to climb back and forth between the front and backseat. Danny, who wants to be a policeman when he grows up, regarded the whole event with studious fascination from the backseat. He, fortunately, had pants on. The policeman asked me for my driver's license and registration for the trailer. I got out my purse and embarked on what I knew was an almost impossible task. My purse was so full of miscellaneous papers it would scarcely close, vitamin pills, addresses, recipes, mail from the weeks of traveling previously. I found the driver's license but the trailer registration eluded me. Just then Sara, still lying on her back in the dirty diaper popped a pebble in her mouth which she'd had clutched in her little fist and obtained from I know not where and proceeded to choke on the thing. A little fierce struggle later she had managed to swallow the pebble and I went back to hunting for the trailer registration. Mike had given it to me before I left. He knows I'm unconscious of things like that and so he or somebody else always does it for me. I gave up. The policeman was stern with me. "I thought you were drunk," he said. "Never touch the stuff," I answered merrily. He looked at me disbelievingly. "You were all over the road," he said. "I thought you were going to tip the whole thing over." He looked us over a moment more. "You'd better

finish changing that diaper," he said. And went back to his patrol car with my driver's license. By the time he got back I had the diaper changed and Dolly and Becca into clothes. I found about five more pebbles of the sort Sara had swallowed and chucked them out the window. He gave me a ticket for failure to carry a trailer registration—to be suspended if I mailed him in the registration—and we thanked him and drove on.

We got to Los Angeles. I was trying to find a craft fair there that I'd heard about and was thoroughly lost. I had only $5 left and not much gas in the car. I drove by a craft fair—there it was set up on a lawn in a little Los Angeles suburb—just like the ones I knew so well in Washington. I stopped, found the manager and asked permission to join in. She said "Yes." I took it as a gift from God and happily the children and I unloaded and set up. Then the manager of the fair came back. She had seen my product. She said it was machine-made and mass-produced and so didn't qualify for a craft fair. She said she would help me pack up and go and she refunded the $5 I had given her for a deposit on my fair fee. I was crying. I insisted she take a copy of the book as a gift. She accepted. I repacked things. The children had a breakfast of hot dogs while I was packing and then we went to Church.

I was wrestling with my reaction to California. I was feeling almost an angry hatred for the place and the people. And I knew that wasn't what God wanted and that He couldn't give me any victories with that kind of stuff dominating my head. I was grateful that God hadn't given me opportunities to talk to people. Things were coming out of my mouth that I was ashamed of. The children and I talked about it as we drove away from the Church. "I'm going to love California," I told them. "I'm going to love the Californians. I'm not going to say a bad thing about them—'Judge not lest ye be judged.' Only good things. Now let's think of good things to say about California and Californians." And all the way back to town that's the game we played and it did us a lot of good. The best Californians of all are my mother and father-in-law who now live in Los Angeles. They loaned me money, rented us a motel, gave us a delicious supper every night. The kids and I went to Church again that night. We found a wonderful congregation right near where Grandma and Grandpa Emery live. I wasn't trying to sell books anymore. I was trying to get my head right with God and my fellow man. To become a Christian means you take responsibility for what you think as well as what you do. You think right and you live right, according to how you understand God would have you to do. A Christian is someone who wants so much to think right thoughts and do right acts that he is willing to suffer for the sake of it. Because sometimes it feels so much easier to react in the wrong way—the way you know Jesus doesn't want you to do. And that is when you must be willing to suffer in your own head, as you keep that internal house in order. Because in the end if you do succeed in keeping order in your head, according to God's laws, you'll have something worth more than any momentary ease of complaining—you'll have self-respect.

Going to Church really strengthened me. The children and I have been to a lot of different Churches along our travels. Yet every time I am in the House of the Lord it's a healing time in my heart and a time I learn things I really needed to know. No matter where. In the Sunday School class at Pisgah Temple in Los Angeles the children sang "Trust and obey, for it's the only way, to be happy in Jesus—just trust and obey." Dolly and Danny, Becca and little Luke and I have been singing that ever since. "Trust and obey!"

Back in Kendrick, Mike and Millicent, the PR lady, had moved from the exchange of postcards to a telephone conversation. When he talked with me he said for only $1,000 she'll give you three big days in Los Angeles. I could see he was already sold! OK, I said. There was nothing else to try.

Now things started to open up a little. An interview on the "Ralph Story AM Show" in Los Angeles. Somebody heard that and there was an opportunity to sell books wholesale to two different big stores. I paid back Grandma and had a supply of cash again. Millicent was in Israel and I never got to meet her then. A pretty young widow named Julaine (pronounced like "Elaine" except with a "Ju" in front) who had long experience booking authors into talk shows was working with my case. She always talked optimistically, but the "three big days" didn't happen just like that. She managed to get me a show here, an interview there. I spent an evening with the children at her house. She told me about the good old days working for Nash when she booked authors all over the country. Millicent only did PR in Los Angeles, she said. She got out her old date book from the previous job at Nash and we looked at names of shows in other towns. I wrote them down—all the talk shows in San Francisco, San Diego, Las Vegas, Salt Lake City. She had the producers' names and phone numbers. So then we started a two-pronged attack. Julaine worked to get me spots in Los Angeles, which is not all that simple when you're offering nobody from nowhere who mimeographed a recipe book, and I called the numbers in all those other cities. By mutual unspoken agreement we stopped talking about "three big days." I drove back up to San Francisco to do two radio talk shows I had managed to get booked on and attend an autograph party at a department store—my first.

I had exactly two days to get back down to Los Angeles. Julaine had landed me a preinterview with the Johnny Carson show—my big chance at network TV. But the car was making terrible clanking noises in the engine and generally signaling that it was good for about 25 more miles—maybe. I was pondering this problem, driving as gently as I could down the downtown freeway when we sighted over on the left a huge lot full of "recreation vehicles." There was an off ramp right there and we turned onto it. I had about $35 on me. But the children knew exactly what they wanted. We had spent many hours on the road studying all the recreation vehicles that went by, dreaming dreams about the one we would someday own—the day when we could afford to stop sleeping in the car once and for all. So we drove into the lot. The salesman tried to show us a camper or a pickup. No, we told him. We want one of the little vans with the high top because it will be easier to park when we're downtown and easier for Mama to drive on the freeways because she isn't a very good driver. And so he showed us our dream come true. Though it was only two feet longer than the car, inside there was the toilet and shower, a sink, hot-water heater and pump for pressure, a refrigerator, a thermostat controlled propane heater, propane stove with an oven, a couch that made into a big double bed, a table that could be removed when you wanted to make up the bed and a ceiling space that was convertible into another double bed! I had never had a new car before. The thought was almost embarrassing. But I believed I should buy it for the sake of the children. For myself I'm scarcely aware of discomfort if I'm doing something I care about, but I didn't want the children to suffer and they were all growing all the time—the fit into the car was tighter and the nights were getting colder. Inside we gave all kinds of credit information. We called Mike and I had the guy tell him about the engine and things that I have never understood and don't try to. Mike said, "OK, buy it." He wasn't very happy about it. The man wanted $1,000 down and they would have to mail it from Idaho for me. Idaho didn't have $1,000. I said, "Don't worry. Go ahead and send him the check. The money's going to be there." After overhearing a conversation like that you'd think the man would never go ahead but he did. He said come back tomorrow.

That last night we parked and slept by a park in a San Francisco suburb. A policeman came and tapped on the window in the middle of the night. I wearily rolled it down expecting to have to dig for that driver's license again. "That's all right," the policeman said. "I just wanted to make sure you were all right," and he went away again. I was grateful. I went back to the car company the next day and picked up our new van and we drove back to Los Angeles. I talked to Darlene later! $1,000 came in the mail the next day she said off those talk shows I did in San Francisco. We were setting new records in mail-order business. I didn't need to worry about selling at fairs if we could keep this up. And the check we had sent was going to be good. Of course.

Time for the Johnny Carson preinterview. I was parked in the lot outside the studio getting ready to change clothes. I didn't have but a few outfits. We spent a lot of time at laundromats. One newspaper described my "well-worn clothes and rumpled hairdo." Well, that's the way it was. But I did have one good outfit. Only Luke tipped over a bowl of cereal on it right then. So I wore my *really* well-worn clothes to the Johnny Carson preinterview. I never saw Johnny. Someone very brisk, very bright, very

Madison Avenue did the preinterview. Julaine had tried to sell me as a comedienne. Bless her heart. She started off with the premise that I could do anything but sing and dance and went from there. I tried to be funny. But he only laughed once. That's when I told him about the time I caused a traffic jam in Hollywood because I was beating my head against the steering wheel and never saw the green light. One of the problems with me as a comedienne is I just cannot tell a lie. So if the circumstances don't provide the comedy routine I haven't got one. But life itself gets so ridiculous that that generally isn't a problem.

Well, anyway, I flunked the interview. The report came to Julaine that I wasn't right for the Johnny Carson show. And I might have been down but there wasn't time to be down because Ralph Story of the "Today AM" show wanted me back again already, which was very unusal, and there was another TV show scheduled for the night after his, although of not nearly as much importance. Right before the show I asked Ralph what we were going to talk about. "Oh, what you've been doing since we last talked," he said vaguely. Then we got on the air and he introduced me again and added "Of the 5,000 guests we've had on this show I want you to meet the one who has drawn the biggest audience response." The people had spoken. God had spoken. Big blinding tears came to my eyes. The children were all up in the guests' waiting room with that very nice lady who ushers guests in and out, watching the show up there. I was the last guest of the morning. So we talked. I can scarcely remember what we said. But it was wonderful whatever happened. And those wonderful people out there redoubled their response. Darlene said that back in Idaho when the mail started to come in she couldn't believe it. Between 2,500 and 3,000 letters in one day. She never had time to count them. And $6,000 in one day to take to the bank. Liliane proudly announced that we were in the black at last and making money. I told her to use the money to pay off debts—pay off everybody. Some of them people we'd owed for years.

It was time for the next TV show. They had asked for a demonstration on the air. My first and I was feeling very uncertain. But Julaine had said—"Always, whatever they say, you just say OK." And she had said OK for me and then she'd said, "Don't worry, I'll get it all together for you." She picked a recipe out of my book that she thought would be interesting. Stirred up a batch for me. Brought her electric fry pan (I'd never used one before and she had to turn it on for me), fried me a couple samples to get me started and then went quietly to wait in the wings and let me be the star. But it turned out that the recipe she had chosen was one I had gotten out of a book because it sounded interesting to me, too, but I'd never tried it for myself. It was the one for Scottish oatcakes and what Julaine did was mix oatmeal with water until she got a sort of dough and then she patted out a sort of little pancake and fried it in oil in the pan. She'd brought along paper plates and plastic silverware and butter and honey to eat them with and the first two were a super new recipe, just right for city people and poor people starting with an idea from my book. Well I tried to talk and fry oatcakes at the same time and then the talk show co-host and hostess each ate one on camera and were surprised at how good they were. We had a fine show.

The next day was one radio show after another. Those "three big days" were happening after all. But it was time to go home. Back home Darlene said since the first day the mail hadn't stopped coming in. They were working frantically to keep up. I had my heart set on spending the last of November and all that precious month of December at home. So I said good-bye to Julaine and Millicent and to Grandpa and Grandma Emery and to Dan, Mike's little brother, drove down to San Diego for some shows there, then to Las Vegas, and to Salt Lake City, Blackfoot, and Boise in Idaho to meet the commitments I'd made over the phone from Julaine's list and some that Darlene had found for me. And home to Kendrick.

But that is only one of the stories. Like Chinese boxes, a box inside a box inside a box. And who's to say which is inside which. That was the story of "How did you do it?" Meaning sell all those books. And they did indeed sell. We to date have made 13,000 books. Suddenly the world started to notice. Publishers began to write. As of this moment there are offers from 21 different publishers in our file, one from England, several of them among the biggest names in publishing in this country. For a while I was besieged with phone calls and offers. But I didn't want to give up the book. I wanted to continue doing this thing—whatever it really is—wherever it is really meant to go. I want to find out where.

So I didn't have time in this story to tell you the love story of Mike and me, how we've loved and lived together, apart, together again but always married and loving through drastically changing circumstances. How what was once my dream and my calling has increasingly become Mike's, too. How Mike is now leaving his job, his career which has really been a very fine, useful and important one (he has a Ph.D. in clinical psychology from Columbia) to teach how to build fence, and split wood and irrigate and things like that at the School of Country Living.

And I haven't told the story of the School of Country Living and that's the biggest of all that's going on now. How Liliane announced that we had made a profit and we immediately decided to put down $25,000 on 386 acres that would be just perfect for the School. But we were still short and just then a fellow from California who had seen the Ralph Story show wrote and said he wanted to loan us money. His name was Herb Haas and he's moving up to Idaho to help make the school happen because he believes in it. We know that of ourselves we can't make this happen no matter how hard we try. But God can.

FROM THE SCHOOL OF COUNTRY LIVING

Here is an achievement CHECK LIST to help you measure your progress as a student of country living. If you are a vegetarian, skip the butchering items.

1. Grind a handful of grain on coarse for cereal ____ on fine ____
2. Mix, knead, rise, punch down, rise and bake a batch of bread by yourself ____
3. Do bee stuff ____
4. Make yogurt ____
5. All by yourself start with a batch of cream and take it through every step to be a salted ball of butter ____
6. Make cottage cheese all by yourself ____
7. Make a hard cheese by yourself ____
8. Milk a goat until you're good at it and comfortable. Take the goat in and out of the stanchion ____
9. Milk a cow until you're good at it and comfortable. Take the cow in and out of the stanchion ____
10. Feed the poultry and gather eggs ____
11. Catch, kill, scald, pick, singe, and cut up a chicken for frying all by yourself ____
12. Feed and water rabbits, clean out the hutch, understand how an ideal hutch is constructed and why ____
13. Plan a menu that is actually carried out in which the food is 100% farm grown except the spices and sugar-honey ingredient. Breakfast ____ Lunch ____ Supper ____
14. Dry a batch of something in the food dryer all by yourself ____
15. Take out the ashes. Build a fire in a wood stove, adjust the dampers ____
16. Freeze a batch of something ____
17. Make a batch of sourdough starter. Then cook everybody a breakfast of sourdough pancakes using your own starter ____
18. Make a batch of homemade noodles ____
19. Dry and save a batch of seeds. (You could get them out of any kind of melon or squash) ____
20. Separate milk, take apart, wash, dry and reassemble the separator ____
21. Make a batch of ice cream, every step of the way, all by yourself ____
22. Harness a team of horses all by yourself and hitch them up to an implement ____
23. Build something or repair something or help build something—carpentry kind of thing ____
24. Correctly identify 10 different herbs from sprigs laid out on a table. Make everybody a batch of herb tea from herbs you have picked yourself ____
25. Card a handful of wool ____

Here is a Sample Final Exam for you. Try yourself on it! These are some things that I think are really important. The answers are all in this book. After you do this test you could get more out of the book and take turns testing each other. But the best test of all is to really do it!

1. What is the basic bread recipe?
2. How can you start one beehive off another?
3. How do you make cottage cheese?
4. If you had no livestock feed store to buy goat ration at, what would you grow and how much of it would you feed your goat every day in winter? Rabbit? Cow? Chicken? Pig?
5. How do you make homemade noodles?
6. How do you make sourdough starter?
7. Why is it better to buy land direct from the owner than through a real estate agent?
8. What can you make a sort of homegrown coffee out of?
9. How could you preserve food if you had no electricity, gas, or any other "modern"-type energy source functioning for you?
10. How do you plant potatoes? What do you use for seed?
11. How do you keep onions over winter? Squash? Apples?
12. What is the correct weight and age to butcher a pig? A rabbit?
13. Compare the advantages and disadvantages of keeping a goat and keeping a cow.
14. What kinds of poultry can either graze or scavenge for themselves in summer so you don't have to feed them?
15. What aspect of soap making is very dangerous?
16. Can you cook whole wheat for breakfast cereal?
17. How do you make a homemade cheese press?
18. How do you catch a chicken?
19. What happens to a rabbit mama in a wire cage who doesn't have a nesting box provided for her before her babies are born? To the babies?
20. How do you make tea out of an herb?

OF GREEN LEAVES AND COURAGE AND FOOLISHNESS

In my front yard, outside my front door there's a foolish little almond tree. Perhaps it's appropriate—this foolish little almond tree living outside *my* door. Because this is the same winter, that so many people are calling me foolish. Again. This tree I bought down in Lewiston from Garden Square Nursery and it was maybe $6. And maybe it was a foolish thing that I bought it because almonds don't belong in cold climates, anyway, and though some people have managed to raise them down at Lewiston I'm maybe 500 or more feet higher yet. But I'm always trying to grow things that can't be grown—my nectarines are doing well, so, even though the fig I tried died (I'll try again next spring; I'm not convinced yet) I bought and set out two little almond trees. They are both practically alike—about four feet high with maybe eight little twig-type branches. We pruned them both when we set them out cutting off the tip of each branch. I kind of winced myself when we did that. I hate to hurt any-

thing but the nurseryman said it would help them—that there wouldn't be so much tree for the roots to support as they were just getting started. Well they both grew nice green leaves and made a fine start for themselves this summer and then I had to go away traveling and selling books and while I was gone fall came. And winter.

I'm back. I've been back six weeks. And here in my yard is this foolish almond tree. Right outside my front door. I don't know whether to laugh over it or weep. Time and again I jump up and run to the window to look at it—can it be real? Yet it is, all my visitors have seen it, too. Right this moment, in December, I am in my kitchen and my wood cook stove is burning with the hearty fire we need to keep warm. Outside it is snowing steadily and the snow is piling up on the ground where the two little almond trees are. And there is the one just the way it ought to be in a December snowstorm, its leaves long since shriveled, changed color, and fallen away, waiting patiently for spring to come for another season of growth like all sensible farmers and plants alike must do. And then there is that foolish tree.

I just got up and looked out the window in the front door again at it. There it is in the snow, in the snowstorm. Its branches aren't six inches long like those of the wise tree. They are over two feet, though there aren't quite so many of them. And there are 47 lovely springlike, green leaves on that foolish almond tree. I went out and counted them. I stood shivering without my coat in the storm and gently touched the smooth, green perfection of each one. Snow and ice were clinging to some so I gave the little tree a gentle shake. Then I looked down and saw three of those smooth, green perfect leaves lying on the snow. Had I done that by shaking it even so gently? It really gave me a pang. Yet even on the snow, separated from the tree they didn't seem in the least wounded, in the least dead. I've been watching that foolish tree ever since I got home from this trip waiting for it to give up and to cut off the life flowing sap to those green leaves like all the other deciduous trees I have but it doesn't do it. And I'm starting to cling to the thought of it in my heart as a symbol of Hope.

Has God given me a miracle? A promise? Or just a foolish almond tree? Is the tree going to make it all through the winter? Are 47 leaves enough if three fall each snowstorm? And I thought of how many times God has pruned me and I lost green leaves and I knew He was shaping me for better things. That little tree is mocking the annual death we all accept so calmly. Out there being summer in winter. Is it some genetic freak, not having the inner knowledge to accept a winter's hibernation, that will die completely after having made such a magnificent struggle not to sleep at all? Am I, too, foolish because I believe that life can be full of wonderful joyous miracles if we only stretch out our arms, our living branches, and let life flow through us unceasingly no matter what the weather report?

I'm the foolish one. Because I get weary. Discouraged. Because I consider just for a moment maybe it would be possible to agree with everyone else and say, "Yes it's too hard—it can't be done." It would be kind of a relief to agree with them. But God has set a foolish almond tree outside my front door. Sometimes I have wild thoughts of wrapping it in my big warm winter coat till spring. Or I go to the window thinking *now* finally it will have accepted the inevitable and dropped those leaves. No, there it stands. Green. I remember my pastor saying that he will die only at God's appointed hour for him to do so and no mere disease will change that fact. Oh, foolish tree. God's perfect thing. Reminding me that the valley of the shadow of death is just that, only the valley of the *shadow* of death.

My beloved, wonderful, foolish almond tree isn't a figment of literary imagination. Nothing in this book is. It's outside my front door and if you want to come and look at it you're welcome to. But be gentle with it.

Treat it like a miracle. The way you want to treat gently anyone's foolish faith kindly. I am often surrounded by the thoroughly sensible men of this world. They are atheists. They think it's ridiculous to believe in God. They don't believe in miracles. Even self-evident ones they will struggle and struggle to find one of their "reasonable" explanations. And then they drink another drink of their alcohol, or some other mind-deadening or deluding worldly sedation to help them try to escape the fact that they find their "reasonable" world cold and unbearable. God, let me live among miracles! Let me believe in them, trust in them, be a part of their happening, and declare them to the world! World, there's a miracle in my front yard and I'm declaring it to you. And you can come with your microscopes and your stethoscopes (but never, never your little axes) and it will declare itself to you. My almond tree. God has blessed it.

Brown Swiss cows, 293
  characteristics of, 363
Brussels sprouts
  growing of, 149
  preservation of, 150
Bubble blowing mixture, 451
Buckets, 133
Buckskin, 472, 475
  making of, 473
Buckwheat
  growing of, 76
  recipes with, 76–77
Budding, of fruit trees, 216
Bulb division, and onions, 176
Bulblets, and onions, 176–77
Bulbs, and growing onions, 178
Bulger, 90
Bull, definition of, 295
Bullets, and wild meat, 396
Bullfrogs, 402
Bulls
  and beef industry, 387
  and breeding, 295
  castrating of, 298
  and pedigreed breeding, 363
  and steers, 389
  See also Steers
Bum lambs, 395
Burnet, 427
Burns
  from lye, 466
  treatment for, 455
Butchering, 362, 368
  and cows, 390–93
  and sausage making, 403, 405
  of calves, 390
  of cows, 392–93
  of game animals, 397
  of kids, 396
  of pigs, 372–73, 379, 380
  of rabbits, 366
  of sheep, 395
  See also Slaughtering
Butchering meat, 370
Butter, 15
  egg, 245
  forms of, 331
  from fruit, 240–41
  from goat milk, 331
  from herbs, 424
  making of, 329–31
  mixed nut, 205
  parsley, 435
  peanut, 207–8
Butterhead lettuces, characteristics of, 165
Buttermilk
  rabbit, 367
  recipes for, 331–32
Buttermilk culture milk, making of, 317
Buttermilk rye bread, 87
Butternuts, 206
Buying
  and animal supplies, 297
  of animals, 9
  and artificial insemination, 390
  and auctions, 29–30
  and bees, 250, 251
  and bottling supplies, 444
  and butter-making supplies, 330
  and candlemaking supplies, 478
  and canning supplies, 45
  and cheese molds, 327
  and cheese supplies, 322
  and cider presses, 228
  and citrus fruits, 229
  of corkers, 445
  and crocks, 59
  and dairy supplies, 299
  and dairy thermometers, 468
  and dehydrators, 63
  and draft horses, 32
  and Dutch ovens, 29
  of farm animals, 17
  and freezers, 54
  and goats, 291
  and goslings, 352
  and grain, 72
  of grain seed, 69
  and grinders, 73
  and herbs, 422
  and honeycombs, 254
  of juicers, 203
  of land, 5–8
  and meat curing supplies, 384
  and pigs, 371
  and popsicle molds, 231–32
  and registered animals, 364
  and root beer extract, 446
  of rootstocks, 216
  and rototillers, 131
  and sausage grinders, 404
  and seeds, 124–27, 194
  and separators, 314
  and soybeans, 139
  and spices, 423
  and tanning supplies, 470
  of trees, 217
  tips on, 16–18
  and turkey poults, 355
  and veterinary supplies, 310
  of wood cook stove parts, 25–26
  and wooden barrels, 466

and wool supplies, 464
  at auction, 303
  homemade noodles, 117–18
  of beverage making supplies, 445
  See also Expenses

C

Cabbage
  growing of, 150
  mustard pickles, 270
  pickling of, 14
  preservation of, 152
  recipes for, 151
  See also Sauerkraut
Cactus, 427
Caffeine, 440, 445
Cake
  carrot ring, 153
  huckleberry, 224
  leavened with soda, 95
  popcorn, 84
  rhubarb, 226
  rose geranium, 437
  tutti-frutti fruit, 285
Cakes
  corn, 159
  flannel, 456
  potato, 187
  rye flour, 88
  sourdough applesauce, 112
  yeast, 110
  See also Fruitcakes
Calf, definition of, 295
Calf(ves) head soup, 418
Calf feeders, use of, 304
Calf's-foot jelly, making of, 413
Calves, 4, 295
  and beef industry, 387
  bull, 389
  butchering of, 390
  and calving, 297
  care of, 294, 303–4
  cost of, 289
  feeding pills to, 306
  rennet from 322–23
  vaccination of, 305–6
  weaning of, 297
  wintering of, 311–12
Calving, and calves, 297
Cambiotic
  and animal care, 308
  for animal care, 310
  and veterinary care, 305–6
Camomile
  shampoo, 450
  tea, 456
Camomile tea, 428
Cancer in animals, diagnosing of, 309
Candies, 257–60
  making of, 259–60
  and marshmallows, 259
  molded, 260
  recipes for, 259–60
  and taffy, 257–58
Candles
  from beeswax, 256
  making of, 477–80
  from wax, 479–80
Candling eggs, 340
Candy
  cactus, 427
  from citron, 428
  fruit paste, 236–37
  horehound, 431
Cane
  growing of, 246–48
  sorghum, 247–48
Canker sores, treatment for, 455–56
Canned pickles (cucumber)
  dill, 268
  making of, 266
  mustard, 267, 268
  recipes for, 267–269
  sweet, 267–68
  yellow, 269
Canning, 43–52, 57
  of apple cider, 228
  of apricots, 219
  and asparagus, 137
  of beans, 146
  of beets, 148
  of berries, 222
  and botulism, 58
  of broccoli, 149
  of Brussels sprouts, 150
  of cabbage, 152
  of carrots, 154
  of celery, 156
  of cheese, 324
  of cherries, 219
  of corn, 159
  of cucumber pickles, 266
  of fruit, 15
  of fruit batter, 240
  of fruit juice, 227
  of fruit sauces, 237
  grape juice, 230
  of grapes, 224

and green beans, 138
  of green peppers, 183
  of greens, 171
  and hot water bath, 57
  hot water bath method of, 49–51
  of jelly, 242
  of kohlrabi, 172
  of lard, 382
  of low acid foods, 48
  of meat, 52, 362
  of milk, 314
  of mincemeat, 415
  of mushrooms, 175
  of okra, 176
  of olives, 275
  and open kettle method, 48–49
  of peas, 182
  of peanut butter, 208
  of peaches, 220
  of pimentos, 183
  of potatoes, 189
  preparing food for, 45
  pressure cooker method of, 51–52
  procedure for, 46
  of pumpkins, 190
  of rhubarb, 226
  of soup stock, 418
  and storage, 46
  of strawberries, 225
  of summer squash, 194
  supplies for, 43, 44–45
  of sweet potatoes, 196–97
  timetables for, 47–48
  of tomato juice, 203
  of tomatoes, 200
  of wild meat, 400
Cans
  for indoor starting, 129
  steaming in, 97
  uses of, 44
Cantaloupe, sweet pickles, 284
Cantaloupes, 225, 226
Capers, pickled, 434
Carob, 441
Carp, recipe for, 403
Carrot
  juice, 203
  juice recipes, 203
  and nut loaf, 211
Carrot pudding, 97
Carrots
  freezing of, 55
  growing of, 152
  and radishes, 190–91
  recipes for, 153
Cara-coa, 441
Caramel
  making of, 259–60
  recipes for, 259–60
Caraway, 428
Carbon dioxide, in beverages, 445
Cardamom fruit yogurt, 318
Carding, of wool, 464, 465
Casing mushrooms, 174
Casings for sausage
  making of, 404–5
  stuffing of, 405–6
Casserole(s)
  eggplant, 163
  layered cabbage, 151
  millet, 85
  tofu, 142
"Castile soap," 468
Cast-iron cookware, use of, 27–28
Cast-iron frying pans, 13
Castrating
  of bull calves, 298
  of bulls, 389
  of farm animals, 290
  methods of, 298
Castration
  and farm animals, 295
  and pigs, 372
  of roosters, 343
Catalogs, seed, 124
Catching animals
  chickens, 347
  geese, 352–53
  pigs, 372
  rabbits, 366
Catnip, 428
Cats, and catnip, 428
Catsups, recipes for, 277–78
Cattail fibers, for stuffing, 462
Catworms, 129
Cauliflower
  cooking of, 155
  growing of, 154–55
Caustic, for dehorning, 298
Cayenne pepper, 435
Celeriac
  growing of, 155
  juice, 203
  preparation of, 155
Celery, 201
  as an herb, 428
  growing of, 155–56
  juice recipes, 203
  vinegar, 281
Cereal(s)
  barley, 75
  cracked wheat, 90

crackers, 116
  making of, 73–74
  millet, 85
  with oats, 86
  rye-wheat, 88
  See also Mush
Challah bread, 102, 103–4
Chapattis, 93
Chard, 156
  See also Swiss chard
Charged water, and beverage making, 445
Charolais cows, 387
Cheat grass, for animal feed, 8
Cheddar cheese
  making of, 326
Cheese, 15
  buttermilk, 331
  cottage, 317
  crackers, 116
  filling, 119
  record for, 324
  summer squash, 193
Cheese (hard)
  Blue, 327
  Cheddar cheese, 326
  Colby cheese, 325–26
  deep fat fried cheese, 326
  farm cheese, 325
  goat's milk cheese, 325
  grating cheese, 326
  Italian cheese, 327–28
  Monterey cheese, 326
  Roquefort, 326–27
  Swiss cheese, 324–25
  twenty-minute cheese, 328
Cheese (soft)
  and cheese spreads, 321
  cottage cheese, 319–21
  cream cheese, 318–19
  farmer cheese, 319–20
Cheese crackers, 116
Cheesemaking, 319–28, 354
Cheese a L'Obispo, making of, 328
Cheese spreads, recipes for, 321
Chemical preservatives, 43
Cherries, 219–20
  brandied, 285
  juice of, 229
  maraschino, 220
Cherry
  ice, 232
  sauce, 237
Chervil, 428
  vinegar, 281
Chestnuts, recipes for, 206
Chicken
  -foot jelly, 413
  for meat, 347–50
  in pot, 367
  in sandwich fillings, 418
Chickens, 14, 338
  body temperature of, 295
  breeds of, 344
  care of, 15
  cleaning of, 348–49
  diseases of, 349
  eggs of, 339–41
  feathers of, 463
  as feed, 370–71
  feed for, 311
  feeding of, 15, 343, 390
  as garden pests, 143
  housing of, 341, 342–43
  manure of, 157, 173
  and milk, 314
  and molting, 342
  and pest control, 4, 157, 198
  preparation of, 349
  recipes for, 350
  and roosters, 343–44
  and setting hens, 341–42
  care of, 338, 340–41, 342
  See also Chicks
Chicory, 428
  braising of, 169
  coffee from, 441
  cooking of, 169
  growing of, 169
Children
  bottling for, 444
  care of, 18–19, 449
  making toys for, 451
  tea for, 457
  toys for, 44
  See also Hazards
Chili, 143
  wild, 400
Chili pepper, 435
Chili sauce, 278
Chinese white geese, 17
Chitterlings, 405
Chives, 428
Choice beef. See Marbled beef
Chokecherry, 222, 428
  jelly, 242
  syrup, 244–45
Cholesterol, and beef, 388
Chopping, of parsley, 434
Chopping wood, methods of, 22
Chops, 370
  of pig, 379
  pork, 371
Christianity, of Carla Emery, 3, 4,

34, 194, 202, 238–40, 284, 362, 424, 510–11, 513, 516, 519–20
Christmas
  and tree ornaments, 452
  wrapping paper for, 452
Christmas dinner, 41
Christmas plum pudding, 98–99
Churning butter, 330
Cider
  ice, 232
  recipes for, 447
Cider vinegar, 280
  making of, 279
Citron, 428
  homemade, 415
  pickled, 283
  preserves, 283
Citronella, oil of, 467
Citrus fruits, juice of, 229
Clarifying
  of grease, 467
  of jelly, 413–14
Clary sage, 439
Clay, making of, 451
Cleaning, of rabbits, 366–67
Cleaning formulas, making of, 448–49
Cleansing creams, 450
Clipping, of goose wings, 352
Clothing
  making of, 19
  washing of, 20
  See also Tanning
Clove bloom vinegar, 428
Clove tea, 428
Clover, hay of, 312
Coal
  use of, 23
  for worming, 453
Coccidiosis, prevention of, 367
Coconut oil, 468
Coconuts, 206
Coffee
  from chicory root, 169
  dandelion root, 429
  jelly, 414
  as meat tenderizer, 363
  substitutes for, 440
Colby cheese, making of, 325–26
Cold pack canning
  and hot water bath, 49–50
  method for, 46
  See also Hot water bath canning
Cold frames, uses of, 129, 131
Coleman lanterns, 478
Coleslaw, 151
  buttermilk dressing for, 332
  recipe for, 152
Colitis, treatment of, 456
Collards, growing of, 168
Coloring
  for candles, 479
  for Easter eggs, 346–47
  of soap, 467
Coloring foods, 428
Colostrum milk, 303
  for auction calves, 303
Combiotic, and animal care, 309
Comfrey, 428–29
  for poultices, 456–57
  medicinal properties of, 422
  tea, 456
Commercial products, and wax candles, 479–80
Commercial tanning, 474–75
Compost, 131
  and cauliflower, 154
  and garden vegetables, 135, 147, 157, 161, 180, 201
  and mushroom growing, 173–74
Consommé, 418
Constipation, treatment for, 455
Containers
  for butchered meat, 377
  for dried foods, 65
  for freezing, 54, 228
  for freezing meat, 368–69
  for milk, 328
  for pickling, 265
  for sauerkraut, 271
  for storing, 44
  for storage, 59–60
Contracts, and buying land, 6, 8
Cookies
  mincemeat, 416
  mincemeat-oatmeal, 416
  potato and barley drop, 75
  sourdough spiced oatmeal, 112
Cooking
  by campfire, 15
  of frozen foods, 54, 56
  with home-ground flour, 73
  with honey, 256
  on open fire, 13
  of pigs, 376
  vegetarian, 209–12
Cookware, use of, 26
Coon
  cleaning of, 401
  recipe for, 401
Copper sulfate, for canker sores, 456
Coriander, 429
Corks, for bottling, 444–45